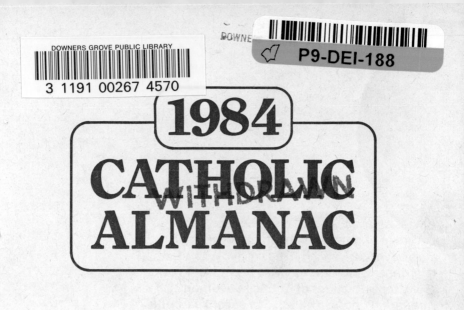

1984
CATHOLIC
ALMANAC

Felician A. Foy, O.F.M.
EDITOR

Rose M. Avato
ASSOCIATE EDITOR

Our Sunday Visitor, Inc.
HUNTINGTON • INDIANA

ACKNOWLEDGMENTS: NC News Service, for
coverage of news and documentary texts; *The
Documents of Vatican II*, ed. W. M. Abbott
(Herder and Herder, America Press: New York
1966), for quotations of Council documents;
Annuario Pontificio (1983); *Statistical Yearbook
of the Church* (1981); *The Official Catholic
Directory* (P. J. Kenedy & Sons, 1983); *The Papal
Encyclicals*, 5 vols., ed. C. Carlen (McGrath
Publishing: Wilmington, NC 1981); The United
States Catholic Mission Assoc. (1233 Lawrence
St. N.E., Washington, D.C. 20017), for U.S.
foreign-mission compilations and statistics;
*Catholic Press Directory (1983); CCCB 1983
Directory* (Canadian Conference of Catholic
Bishops: Ottawa, Ont. 1983), for Canadian
Catholic statistics; other sources as credited in
particular entries.

1984 Catholic Almanac

Copyright © Our Sunday Visitor, Inc., 1983
Published annually, with ecclesiastical
permission, by Our Sunday Visitor, Inc.,
200 Noll Plaza, Huntington, Indiana 46750.
Address inquiries to the Publisher.

ISBN 0-87973-254-7
Library of Congress Catalog Card No. 73-641001
International Standard Serial Number (ISSN) 0069-1208

TABLE OF CONTENTS

1983 ASSEMBLY OF THE SYNOD OF BISHOPS

See additional articles on the Synod of Bishops, Penance, General Absolution.

Several of the following articles were compiled from NC News releases.

"Reconciliation and Penance in the Mission of the Church" was the stated theme of the 1983 assembly of the Synod of Bishops which began Sept. 29 at the Vatican.

Bishops throughout the world contributed comments and suggestions for discussion at the assembly in a months-long period of preparation.

Actual delegates to the assembly were bishops chosen by and representative of national and regional episcopal conferences.

The U.S. delegates were: Cardinal Joseph L. Bernardin of Chicago; Archbishops John R. Roach, president of the National Conference of Catholic Bishops, and Patrick F. Flores of San Antonio; and Auxiliary Bishop Austin B. Vaughan of New York. Joining them were two papal appointees: Cardinal Timothy Manning of Los Angeles and Archbishop Edmund C. Szoka of Detroit.

Questions to be raised at the Synod were the sub-jects of comment by a number of U.S. bishops, as in the following articles.

THE SACRAMENT OF PENANCE IN DECLINE

Cardinal Joseph L. Bernardin addressed this subject in an article published in the Sept. 16 edition of "The Chicago Catholic."

The theme designated by Pope John Paul II for the 1983 Synod is "Penance and Reconciliation in the Mission of the Church." Although that is a very large subject and points to many questions which could profitably be explored, it is generally assumed that the discussion in Rome this fall will focus mainly on the sacrament of penance. If so, the Synod has its work cut out for it.

In the last 20 years reception of this sacrament has declined dramatically in the United States and many other countries. The postconciliar reform of the liturgy of penance has much to recommend it, but there is no evidence that it has stemmed the tide. To put it bluntly, people are staying away from the sacrament in droves.

It is not necessary to romanticize the past in order to be concerned about this present state of affairs. I have no trouble agreeing that many ideas and practices pertaining to penance in the past left a lot to be desired — that there was occasionally too much emphasis on sin and punishment and that "confession" itself was sometimes viewed in legalistic and even magical terms.

Abandonment of the Sacrament Not Good

But I do not believe anyone can argue convincingly that the virtual abandonment of the sacrament by many Catholics today is for the good. To be blunt again, it appears that not a few people have deluded themselves into thinking that they no longer need penance. That is a dangerous state of mind. The First Epistle of John pronounces the definitive word on this subject: "If we say, 'We are free of the guilt of sin,' we deceive ourselves; the truth is not to be found in us." (1 John 1:8)

There is, moreover, another and equally relevant aspect to our need for the sacrament of penance. The experience of sacramental reconciliation is a virtually indispensable element of spiritual growth for Catholics.

Positive Role of the Sacrament

Those who have formed the habit of frequent confession — I am fortunate enough to be one — universally attest to the important and enormously positive role that penance plays in their spiritual lives. People who do not take this opportunity to avail themselves of Christ's healing, strengthening grace short-change themselves spiritually.

Why, then, the painful decline in reception of the sacrament which has occurred in recent years? What can be done to change the situation for the better? What confused ideas about sin, guilt, and punishment does the current state of affairs reflect? What further steps may be needed in renewing the liturgy of penance? What new catechetical programs or other efforts are required to educate and motivate people concerning this beautiful sacrament?

These are among the questions the Synod will discuss. As an advisory body, it does not make decisions — it only provides information and recommendations to the Pope. But by the simple act of focusing attention on a difficult pastoral problem, the Synod can make a useful contribution to its solution.

I ask you, then, to keep me and the other participants in this important meeting in your prayers in the weeks ahead. May our deliberations help foster a renewed appreciation for the sacrament of penance among all Catholics in our times!

WHY THE FALL-OFF?

"Why has there been such a great fall-off in the sacrament of penance, and what does it represent? This is clearly one of the bigger questions the delegates will be considering" at the Synod of Bishops, said Auxiliary Bishop Austin B. Vaughan of New York, one of six U.S. delegates.

"The theme of this Synod is reconciliation, and it will weigh some very important questions, impor-

tant to individual Catholics," Bishop Vaughan said.

Few questions are likely to occupy more time than those concerning confession itself, he said.

Most U.S. bishops who responded to the Synod's working document expressed a concern over the decrease in Catholics who go to confession.

"My own opinion is that there's a great deal of confusion about the nature of sin," Bishop Vaughan said. "There's confusion about how much the sacrament of penance is necessary, and a certain amount of confusion on the role and purpose of the confession of venial sins."

Called "devotional confession" in the past, the value of the sacrament with respect to venial sin has been questioned.

"We were trained in the desirability of frequent confession" he said. "That hasn't happened in the last decade, and that's reflected in the substantial change in practice."

Bishop Vaughan said that some Catholics oppose the emphasis on private confession because they say it is "too negative an approach to God."

"I don't think that's ordinarily the case," he said. "In the sacrament, we acknowledge the need for redemption, we acknowledge the availability of God's mercy."

Penitential Services

Another question that should arise at the Synod, is whether the penitential services in parishes are satisfying the needs of Catholics.

"The communal penitential service has a value and a worth all its own," Bishop Vaughan said. "But it doesn't carry the same impact as private confession, where the penitent faces a personal discussion and a sense of responsibility for his own sins."

The revised rite of penance also has not succeeded in restoring frequent participation in private confession, Bishop Vaughan said. Many U.S. bishops said the rite has not had a noticeable effect because it has not been seriously tried, he said.

General Absolution, First Confession

Another question facing the bishops is that of general absolution.

"There was a sharply divided response from the bishops on this," he said. "Some feel the practice has many benefits, and some feel it's an abuse which has helped bring about the drop-off in penance in general."

The first-confession-before-first-Communion question will also be discussed at the Synod, Bishop Vaughan said.

"There can be no doubt that this is what the Church wants and intends. Some canonists oppose the practice on the grounds that no one has an obligation to confess unless a mortal sin has been committed, but I think that's a mistaken notion."

Bishop Vaughan also reaffirmed the value of confession. "The lack of the use of the sacrament of penance is especially harmful in our time, when so many people question their own worth; when they wonder, 'Do people care?' This sacrament is a constant reassurance. It's a sign that God cares about them."

GENERAL ABSOLUTION

General absolution might be the most controversial issue to surface at the Synod, according to interviews with some U.S. bishops.

Several American bishops who were in Rome shortly before the Synod predicted debate among the delegates on general absolution. While some said they would like to see greater opportunities for use of the sacrament in that form, most thought the Synod would ask for no change in the strict norms or maybe even for a clamping down on some current practices.

In Favor

Archbishop Francis Hurley of Anchorage said he thought the Church needs to expand the use of general absolution. He said the Church already allows use of general absolution if, in conjunction with other circumstances, the ratio of priests to penitents makes individual confession impossible. But he said that, beyond the numbers question, sometimes it it "psychologically impossible" for a person to make a private confession.

He cited, for instance, times when there is only one priest available to a penitent.

"It can be morally impossible to confess to this particular priest at this particular time," he said, "perhaps because the person is in a small town and easily would be recognizable to the confessor, or that in confessing he would implicate another person who could be recognizable."

"I have no problem with the theology of private confession," he added, "but it does raise real pastoral problems."

Archbishop Hurley said that general absolution could be a step toward individual confession of sins.

"Conversion is a long process," he said. "Some people are not ready personally to go to private confession because of fear, bad experiences in the past, or depression associated with sin. How can those people recapture the grace of God?"

Archbishop Hurley has allowed general absolution in the Archdiocese of Anchorage. He said it has had both positive and negative results.

"It's a positive factor in bringing people back to private confession, and back to better private confessions," when general absolution is given in the context of a well-planned and well-conducted penitential service, he said. "It's especially good for the large numbers of people who have no serious sins to confess," he added.

But —

There are also negative effects, he said, such as the confusion which people experience when they learn they still need to go to private confession even though they already have been absolved.

"Lack of private confession also means loss of an opportunity for personal counseling," he said.

He also noted a "tendency of some priests to see general absolution as a substitute for the time which should be devoted to being available for private confessions."

Archbishop Hurley theorized that the main fear of the Church when it discusses general absolution is that Catholics "will make a quantum leap to general absolution and forget about private confession and have the church lose what has historically been a powerful force for pastoral care in the Church."

While postconciliar church norms for the sacrament of reconciliation promote communal penance services with individual confession, they set strict conditions which must be met before general absolution can be given.

No Expansion Wanted

Archbishop John Whealon of Hartford, Conn., said he does not wish to promote expanded use of penance services with general absolution.

"I don't see that general absolution is the way to go for the future," he said. "General absolution does not talk about the problems of the individual and does not permit the required medicine, that is, articulation of sins and advice of the confessor, which the soul needs. it does not help with on-going conversion."

The synodal working document, reiterating church norms, points out that general absolution is allowed only "when there is imminent danger of death and the priest or priests do not have the time to hear the confession of each penitent," or "when sufficient confessors are not available to hear properly the individual confessions of a number of penitents within a suitable period of time, so that the penitents would, through no fault of their own, have to go without sacramental grace or holy Communion for a long period of time."

CARDINAL DEATHS

Cardinal Humberto S. Medeiros, 67, archbishop of Boston from 1970, died Sept. 17, 1983, in a Boston hospital, one day after he underwent triple-bypass surgery. (See his biography, page 170.)

His death and the death of Cardinal Joseph Schroeffer (see pages 174, 377) on Sept. 7 reduced the total number of cardinals to 132 and the number eligible to vote to 23.

PUBLICATION HISTORY

The *Catholic Almanac* originated remotely from *St. Anthony's Almanac,* a 64-page annual with calendar, feature and devotional contents, published by the Franciscans of Holy Name Province from 1904 to 1929.

Completely revised and enlarged, the publication was issued under the title, *The Franciscan Almanac,* by *The Franciscan Magazine* from 1931 to 1933, and by St. Anthony's Guild from 1936 to 1971. From 1940 to 1969, its title was *The National Catholic Almanac.* The present title was adopted in 1969. The 1959 to 1971 editions were produced jointly by St. Anthony's Guild and Doubleday & Co., Inc.

The *Catholic Almanac* was acquired in 1971 by Our Sunday Visitor, Inc., Huntington, Ind. 46750.

HOLY YEAR: 1950th ANNIVERSARY OF THE REDEMPTION

Excerpts in this article from "Aperite Portas Redemptori," the papal bull of proclamation of the Holy Year, are from the text circulated by the NC Documentary Service, Origins, Feb. 10, 1983 (Vol. 12, No. 35).

With three symbolic taps of a gold-and-ivory hammer, Pope John Paul II opened the Holy Door of St. Peter's Basilica late in the afternoon of Mar. 25, 1983, to begin an extraordinary 394-day Jubilee celebration of the 1950th anniversary of the redemptive death and resurrection of Jesus.

The ceremony was viewed by scores of thousands inside and outside the basilica, and was broadcast by television in 20 countries.

During Mass after the opening of the door, the Holy Father prayed in a homily:

"Grant, O Lord, that this Holy Year of your Redemption may also become an appeal to the modern world which sees justice and peace on the horizon of its desires — and yet yields ever more to sin and lives, day after day, in the midst of mounting tensions and threats, and seems to be traveling in a direction perilous for all!

"Help us to change the direction of the mounting threats and disasters in the modern world! Raise man up once more! Protect the nations and peoples! Do not permit the work of destruction that threatens humanity today!"

A Unique Holy Year

The Pope first mentioned his intention to proclaim the Holy Year at a meeting with the College of Cardinals Nov. 26, 1982. Nearly two months later, on Jan. 21, he published the bull of proclamation, *Aperite Portas Redemptori* ("Open the Doors to the Redeemer"). The opening came on the Solemnity of the Annunciation of the Lord, and the closing of the celebration was set for Easter Sunday, Apr. 22, 1984.

The bull of proclamation indicated that this Holy Year would be unique because it would be celebrated at the same time in Rome and throughout the world — not in Rome first for a year and then in the rest of the world.

Other distinctive features were the types of observances prescribed for gaining the plenary indulgence of the Jubilee.

The Jubilee indulgence was the same, however — full remission of temporal punishment due for sins already forgiven, to be gained by members of the faithful free of all attachment to sin and fulfilling the required conditions.

EXCERPTS

Following are excerpts from *Aperite Portas Redemptori,* sketching the nature, purposes, observances and spiritual benefits of the Jubilee Year of the Redemption.

This Jubilee will begin next March 25, 1983, the Solemnity of the Annunciation of the Lord, which recalls the providential moment when the eternal Word, becoming Man through the power of the

Holy Spirit in the womb of the Virgin Mary, became a sharer in our flesh, "that through death he might destroy him who has the power of death, that is, the devil, and deliver all those who through fear of death were subject to life-long bondage." It will end April 22, 1984, Easter Sunday, the day of the fullness of the joy obtained by the redeeming sacrifice of Christ, through which the Church is ever "wonderfully reborn and nourished."

Let this, therefore, be a year that is truly holy. Let it be a time of grace and salvation by being more intensely sanctified by the acceptance of the graces of the Redemption on the part of the people of our time, through a spiritual renewal of the whole people of God, which has for its head Christ, "who was put to death for our trespasses and raised for our justification."

Commitment to Reconciliation

Furthermore, it must be clear that this special time, when all Christians are called upon to realize more profoundly their vocation to reconciliation with their Father in the Son, will only reach its full achievement if it leads to a fresh commitment by each and every person to the service of reconciliation, not only among all the disciples of Christ but also among all men and women. It must also lead to a fresh commitment to the service of peace among all peoples. A faith and a life which are authentically Christian cannot fail to blossom in a love which constitutes truth and promotes justice.

The specific grace of the Year of the Redemption is therefore a renewed discovery of the love of God who gives himself, and a deeper realization of the inscrutable riches of the paschal mystery of Christ gained through the daily experience of Christian life in all its forms. The various practices of this Jubilee Year should be directed toward this grace, with a continual effort which presupposes and requires detachment from sin, from the mentality of the world which "lies in the power of the evil one," and from all that impedes or slows down the process of conversion.

In this perspective of grace is also situated the gift of the indulgence, proper to and characteristic of the Jubilee Year, which the Church, by virtue of the power conferred upon her by Christ, offers to all those who, with the proper dispositions, fulfill the appropriate prescriptions of the Jubilee. As my predecessor, Paul VI, emphasized in the Bull of Indiction of the Holy Year of 1975: "By means of the indulgence, the Church, making use of her power as the minister of the Redemption of Christ the Lord, communicates to the faithful a sharing in this fullness of Christ in the communion of saints, providing them with ample means of slavation."

A Call to Conversion

The celebration of this event is intended, above all, as a call to repentance and conversion as necessary dispositions for sharing the grace of the Redemption which he achieved, and thus for bringing about a spiritual renewal of individuals, families, parishes and dioceses, of religious communities and the other centers of Christian life and apostolate.

My principal wish is that fundamental importance be given to the two main conditions required for gaining a plenary indulgence, namely, individual and complete sacramental confession, wherein takes place the encounter between man's misery and God's mercy, and the worthy reception of Eucharistic Communion.

The Jubilee Indulgence

I decree that the Jubilee Indulgence may be gained by choosing one of the following ways, which will be at the same time an expression of and a renewed commitment to exemplary ecclesial living: by devoutly taking part in a community celebration organized on the diocesan level or, if in accordance with the regulations laid down by the bishop, also in individual parishes, for gaining the Jubilee. These celebrations must always include a prayer for my intentions, in particular that the event of the Redemption may be proclaimed to all peoples, and that in every nation those who believe in Christ the Redeemer may be able freely to profess their faith. It is to be hoped that the celebration will be accompanied, as far as possible, by a work of mercy in which the penitent will pursue and express his or her commitment to conversion.

Required Community Observance

The community act may consist, in a special way:

• In taking part in a Mass celebrated for the Jubilee.

• Or, in being present at a celebration of the word, which can be an adaptation or extension of the Office of Readings, or at Morning or Evening Prayer, as long as they are celebrated specifically for the Jubilee.

• Or, in taking part in a penitential service arranged for gaining of the Jubilee, concluding with the individual confession of the participants, according to the Rite of Penance.

• Or, in the solemn administration of baptism or of other sacraments.

• Or, in the pious exercise of the Stations of the Cross, organized for the gaining of the Jubilee.

• Diocesan bishops may also decree that the Jubilee Indulgence can be gained by taking part in a parish mission organized in connection with the Jubilee Year, or by taking part in days of spiritual retreat organized for groups or categories of persons.

• By visiting one of the churches or places indicated below and spending some time there in meditation, renewing one's faith by the recitation of the Creed and the Our Father, and praying for my intentions, as already indicated.

A) In Rome, a visit must be made to one of the four patriarchal basilicas (St. John Lateran, St. Peter's in the Vatican, St. Paul's Outside the Walls, St. Mary Major), or to one of the catacombs or to the Basilica of Santa Croce in Gerusalemme.

B) In the other dioceses of the world, the Jubilee may be gained by visiting one of the churches which the bishop will decide.

Persons in Special Circumstances

Those who, for reasons of health, cannot visit one of the churches indicated by the local bishop, can gain the Jubilee by a visit to their own parish church. For the sick prevented from making such a visit, it is enough that they join spiritually in the act for gaining the Jubilee made by members of their own family or by their parish, offering their prayers and sufferings to God. A similar concession is granted to the residents of old people's homes and to prisoners, all of whom shall be given special pastoral attention in the light of Christ, the Redeemer of all humanity.

Cloistered religious men and women can obtain the Jubilee in their own monastery or convent churches.

During the Jubilee Year, other indulgences granted remain in force. However, the norm that only one plenary indulgence can be gained each day will still hold. All indulgences can always be applied to the faithful departed.

BACKGROUND

Holy Year observances have biblical counterparts in the Years of Jubilee observed at 50-year intervals by the pre-exilic Israelites — when debts were pardoned and slaves freed (Lv. 25:25-54) — and in sabbatical years observed from the end of the Exile to 70 A.D. — in which debts to fellow Jews were remitted.

The practice of Christians from early times to go on pilgrimage to the Holy Land, the shrines of martyrs and the tombs of the Apostles in Rome influenced the institution of Holy Years. There was also a prevailing belief among the people that every 100th year was a year of "Great Pardon." Accordingly, even before Boniface VIII formally proclaimed the first Holy Year Feb. 22, 1300, scores of thousands of pilgrims were already on the way to or in Rome. One report said that two million pilgrims took part in the observance.

Holy Year Features

Medieval popes embodied in the observance of Holy Years the practice of good works 'reception of the sacraments of penance and the Eucharist, pilgrimages and/or visits to the tombs of the apostles, and related actions) and spiritual benefits (particularly, special indulgences for the souls in purgatory). These and related practices, with suitable changes for celebrations in local churches, remain staple features of Holy Year observances.

The first three Holy Years were observed in 1300, 1350 and 1390. Subsequent ones were celebrated at 25-year intervals except in 1800 and 1850 when, respectively, the French invasion of Italy and political turmoil made observance impossible. Pope Paul II (1464-1471) set the 25-year timetable. In 1500, Pope Alexander VI prescribed the start and finish ceremonies — the opening and closing of the Holy Doors in the major basilicas on successive Christmas Eves. All but a few of the earlier Holy Years were classified as ordinary. Several, like the one held in 1933 to commemorate the 19th centenary of the death and resurrection of Christ, were in the extraordinary category.

PASTORAL VISIT OF POPE JOHN PAUL TO SPAIN

Pope John Paul, on the 16th pastoral trip outside Italy since the beginning of his pontificate, became the first Bishop of Rome to visit Spain. He did so between Oct. 31 and Nov. 9, 1982.

Features of the tour included:

• visits during the 4,500-mile itinerary to 18 cities and towns as well as a number of shrines and sanctuaries dedicated to the honor of the Virgin Mary;

• special commemorations of Sts. Teresa of Avila, John of the Cross, Ignatius Loyola and Francis Xavier;

• the beatification of Sister Angela of the Cross;

• the ordination of 141 priests;

• nearly 50 addresses related to doctrinal, moral, pastoral, social, political and economic issues of topical and regional significance.

The trip was originally scheduled for 1981 but was twice postponed, once because of the attack on the Pope's life on May 13 of that year and again because of elections held in Spain a few days before the start of the tour.

Following are accounts of the major events of each day and coverage of a number of the Pope's homilies and addresses.

October 31

The Holy Father departed from Rome in midafternoon and arrived at about 5:00 p.m. at Madrid's Barajas Airport, where he was welcomed by King Carlos and Queen Sofia, along with members of the government and the hierarchy. In the capital city, he met first with municipal officials and later with the bishops of Spain at the headquarters of their national conference. Late in the evening, he attended a nocturnal adoration service at the Church of Our Lady of Guadalupe.

Purpose of the Visit: At brief ceremonies at the airport, he said his visit had an "exclusively religious-pastoral character which sets it above political or partisan purposes." His stated intention was to confirm his "brethren in the faith, so that the light of Christ might go on illuminating and inspiring each one's existence."

Function of Bishops: At an evening meeting with bishops, he said that "an important part of the episcopal function consists today in applying correctly the teachings of the last (Second Vatican) ecumenical council without deviations through defect or excess."

Christian Collaboration: Against the background of Spain's passage since 1975 from dictatorship to democracy, and in view of a socialist victory in elections Oct. 28, he said the nation was experiencing a "socio-cultural transition of grand proportions" in which Christians should "collaborate in the building of the temporal city. They must make their voice heard, consistent with the values in which they believe and respectful of the convictions of others."

November 1

At Avila in the morning, the Pope addressed about 3,000 contemplative nuns from all over Spain at the Convent of the Incarnation where St. Teresa entered the Carmelite Order in 1535; he also concelebrated Mass with the bishops of the country before a throng of 300,000 persons outside the walls of the city. At Alba de Tormes in the afternoon, he took part in a simple ceremony ending a worldwide, year-long commemoration of the 400th anniversary of the death there of St. Teresa. In the evening, he addressed a gathering of theologians at the Pontifical University of Salamanca.

Witness of Religious to Christian Values: This was the theme of the Pope's remarks to nuns at Avila. "Your cloistered life, lived in full fidelity," he said, "does not keep you apart from the Church nor distance you from an effective apostolate. The world needs, more than people sometimes believe, your presence and your witness. It is necessary to show the authentic and absolute values of the Gospel to a world which frequently exalts the relative values of life and which runs the risk of losing the sense of the divine, drowning in the excessive valuation of the material, of the transient, of that which ignores the joy of the spirit."

Tribute to Sts. Teresa and John of the Cross: "I would like to strengthen even more my bonds of devotion toward Teresa of Jesus (her name in the religious community) and John of the Cross. In them, not only do I venerate the spiritual teachers of my inner life but also two shining beacons of the Church in Spain that have enlightened ... my country, Poland."

Encouragement to Youths: The Pope urged several thousand young people at Alba de Tormes to "be faithful" to the message of St. Teresa and "to the virtues of the men and women of this land: honesty, industriousness, prudence, appreciation of man for what he is rather than for what he has." Noting the difficult times in which they were living, he called on them to "live (their) faith valiantly, trying to integrate the judgments and guidelines of the current society with Christian beliefs, morality and practices."

Theology in the Life of the Church: Addressing theologians at the Pontifical University of Salamanca, he stressed the fact that theology, which is necessary for "creative as well as faithful" renewal of the Church, must flow from faith because "doing theology is ... a task exclusively proper to the believer as believer; it is a task vitally aroused and sustained at every moment by faith."

"Christian faith is ecclesial," he added. "One cannot believe in Christ without believing in the Church, 'the body of Christ'; one cannot believe with Catholic faith within the Church without believing in her irrenounceable magisterium (teaching authority). So, fidelity to Christ implies fidelity to the Church, and fidelity to the Church entails fidelity to the magisterium in its turn. It is, consequently, necessary to bear in mind that it is with the same radical freedom of faith with which the Catholic theologian adheres to Christ that he adheres to the Church and the magisterium as well."

He called theology "ecclesial science at the service of the Church" and said it must be "dynamically integrated into the Church's mission. Thus, the theologian's task has the character of an ecclesial mission, as a participation in the Church's evangelizing mission and as outstanding service to the ecclesial community. This is where the theologian's grave responsibility rests."

November 2

The Pope celebrated Mass in the morning of All Souls' Day at Madrid's Almudena Cemetery before a gathering of 500,000 persons. At Zarzuela Palace, he met privately with the royal family and attended a reception with leaders of the government and military. He visited the headquarters of the World Tourism Organization, and met at the apostolic nunciature with diplomats and media personnel. He celebrated a second Mass late in the afternoon at a large plaza in the heart of the capital city before an enormous throng. In the evening, he met with men religious at the Church of Our Lady of Guadalupe.

Church-State Relations: These comprised the substance of papal remarks at a reception attended by government officials, including Prime Minister-elect Felipe Gonzalez, head of the socialist government due to go into office in December.

"Even though my trip to Spain is of an eminently religious nature," the Pope said, "through this courtesy visit I would like to pay my respects to the legitimate representatives of the Spanish people. In this way I would like to remove any doubts, if there were any, about my respect for the country's freely elected leaders."

At the same time: "The Church, rightly respecting the spheres that are not its own, marks out a moral course which coincides with and does not diverge from or contradict the demands of the dignity of the human person and the rights and freedoms inherent in it. This constitutes the platform of a healthy society."

"It is logical that, faithful to its duty and yet respecting the autonomy of the temporal order; the Church asks the same consideration toward its mission when it is a question of things having to do with God or the conscience of his sons and daughters."

Marriage and Family Subjects: Critical matters related to marriage and the family were treated by the Pope in a homily delivered during a Mass for Christian families; in attendance were about a million and half persons.

• "Matrimony," he said, "is an indissoluble communion of love. Therefore, any attack on conjugal indissolubility is at the same time against the original design of God and the dignity and truth of conjugal love." The obligation to live in permanent marital union exists "even in the presence of legal norms that may point in another direction" (a reference to the legalization of divorce in 1981).

• Turning to birth control, he quoted the key statement of Pope Paul VI on the subject: "Every conjugal act must remain open to the transmission of life."

• Of abortion (whose legalization appeared to be an objective of the incoming socialist government) he said: "I speak on the absolute respect for human life which no person or institution, private or public, can ignore. . . . Whoever denies defense to the most innocent and frailest human person, to the human person conceived but not yet born, commits a most grave violation of moral order. Nothing can legitimize the death of an innocent human being. What sense can there be in speaking of the dignity of man, of his fundamental rights, if one does not protect the innocent, if one goes so far even as to facilitate means and services, private or public, to destroy defenseless human lives?"

• He said of religious education (which the incoming socialist government seemed reluctant to support with funds): "The public authority . . . cannot substitute for the parents, since its duty is to help them in order that they may fulfill their right and duty to educate their children in accordance with their moral and religious convictions."

Example and Ministry of Men Religious: The Pope told a gathering of men religious in the evening that "the world needs to see" examples of "those who, giving up everything, have embraced as ideal the life according to Gospel counsels." While telling them not to "enter into the field of the laity," he stated: "This does not mean that your religious consecration and your eminently religious ministry do not have profound repercussions on the world and on the changing of structures."

November 3

In the morning, the Pope met with leaders of the Jewish community and various Christian churches, journalists and representatives of the academic world. He celebrated Mass late in the afternoon in a working-class section of Madrid and blessed cornerstones for 12 new churches to be built. He addressed 140,000 young people in the evening at Bernabeu Stadium.

Interfaith Relations: Addressing a group of Jewish leaders, he urged a continuation of "fraternal dialogue oriented toward better understanding and esteem between Jews and Catholics . . . even in the midst of inevitable difficulties."

He told Christian leaders: "Thank God that that situation (of past religious discrimination) has been overcome, giving way to progressive mutual drawing together, based on truth and love."

Responsibility of Intellectuals: "Men and women who represent science and culture, your moral power is enormous," declared the Pope before representatives of academic communities at the University of Madrid. While paying tribute to the cultural contributions of Spanish intellectuals of the past, he asked:

"Can you succeed in getting the scientific sector to serve the culture of man above all and to see that it is never perverted and used for destruction? It is a scandal of our times that many researchers are dedicated to perfecting new arms for war, which one day could prove fatal."

"Consciences must be awakened. Your responsibility and possibilities of influence on public opinion are immense. Make them serve the cause of peace and the real progress of man. What marvels could be realized in our world if the best talents and the best researchers took each other by the hand to explore the roads of development of all men and all regions of the earth."

The Church and Science: "Serious discords and misunderstandings occurred in the past between representatives of science and the Church. But those difficulties have now been practically overcome, thanks to the acknowledgment of errors of interpretation which had managed to disfigure relations between faith and science, thanks above all to better understanding of their respective fields of knowledge."

Challenge to Young People: The Pope called on 140,000 young people to keep themselves free of vice and "from the slavery of those who prefer to have more and not to be more." He said youths are "the hope of the Church and of society," and added:

"In the face of the manipulation of which he may feel himself the object by means of drugs, exaggerated sex and violence, the young Christian will not search for methods of action that will lead him to the spiral of terrorism. That would lead him to the same or worse evil than that which he criticizes and deprecates."

"He does not lapse into insecurity and demoralization, nor does he take refuge in empty paradises of escapism or indifference. Neither drugs, nor alcohol, nor sex, nor a resigned and uncritical passivity are a response to evil."

November 4

The Pope started the day at a Liturgy of the Word at the Sanctuary of Our Lady of Guadalupe in Madrid. He celebrated Mass at noon in an industrial park outside of Toledo, after which he visited the cathedral and lunched with more than 350 students at the Toledo seminary. Late in the afternoon, he took part in a second Liturgy of the Word at Segovia where the relics of St. John of the Cross have been preserved since 1593.

Policies Affecting Migrant Workers: Such policies, he said before 20,000 persons at the Marian sanctuary, "are not very often motivated by noble human aims, nor by the good of the national or international community" but, instead, by the law of supply and demand.

He suggested that governments should do more to promote equality and balance between the rich and the poor: "It would be more humane if the authorities responsible for economic affairs endeavored to have capital seek workers rather than vice versa." This would be a "challenge to the au-thorities of national and international affairs who must undertake programs for establishing a balance between regions of wealth and poverty."

Evangelical Responsibility of Christians: "No Christian is exempt from his evangelical responsibility," and "no one can be substituted for in the demands of the personal apostolate." So stated the Pope in a homily delivered during Mass in Toledo before a gathering of 200,000 persons.

Pointing to the apostolic roles of lay persons in the family, in the world of labor, in the defense of human rights and in fields of culture, he said: "Catholic lay persons are called to create a new and authentic culture of truth and goodness, beauty and progress, from the immense cultural wealth of the peoples of Spain."

"The Christian knows that, from the luminous teachings of the Church and without needing to follow a partisan political platform, he or she must contribute to the formation of a society more worthy and respectful of human rights, based on principles of justice and peace."

The content and application of the Gospel, he added, are not determined by "analyses of reality, or the use of social sciences, nor the keeping of statistics, nor the perfecting of organizing methods and techniques," but by Christ and his message.

Gratitude: Speaking at Segovia, the Holy Father said: "I thank Providence that I have been allowed to come to venerate the relics and to evoke the figure and doctrine of St. John of the Cross, to whom I owe much in my spiritual formation."

November 5

In the morning, the Pope flew to Seville where he beatified Sister Angela of the Cross (1846-1932), foundress of the Sisters of the Cross, and celebrated Mass at the fairgrounds outside the city before 500,000 persons. He visited the cathedral after Mass and prayed there before the statue of the Virgin of the Kings, patroness of Seville. Later, at Granada, he visited the Sanctuary of Our Lady of the Afflicted and addressed a throng of 250,000 people during a Liturgy of the Word.

Sister Angela of the Cross: He called her "a humble village girl (who), faithful to the example of the poverty of Christ, put her institute at the service of the poorest of the poor, the disinherited and the alienated."

Agrarian Problems: Speaking in the heavily agricultural Province of Seville, he said: "Public authorities must confront the urgent problems of the agrarian sector, readjusting properly the costs and prices of its yields; setting up subsidiary industries and transformations which free it from the anguishing plague of unemployment and the forced emigration which affects so many sons and daughters of this and other areas of Spain; rationing the sale of agrarian products; and obtaining for farm families, especially youths, conditions of life which stimulate them to consider themselves workers as worthy as those in industry."

He criticized "facile demagoguery which confuses the people without solving their problems," and said the nation's agricultural crisis should be confronted with "the same strength and love which animated Sister Angela of the Cross."

Religious Education: Addressing this subject for the second time during his trip, he said: "The transmission of the message of salvation through religious teaching in the schools, private and public, must be taken into account, especially in a country in which the great majority of parents ask for religious teaching for their children during school time.

"This teaching must be imparted with the proper discretion, in full respect for the correct freedom of conscience, but respecting at the same time the primordial right of parents, the primary educators of their children."

The task of educating people in the faith "is not limited to the priestly ministers or to the religious world, but must embrace the spheres of the laity, of the family, of the school. . . . Every Christian has to participate in the especially urgent task of Christian formation, which helps each Christian to maintain and develop his or her faith in the present situation of rapid social and cultural transformation which Spanish society is undergoing."

November 6

In Basque country for the day, the Pope celebrated Mass in Loyola and a Liturgy of the Word in Javier, the respective birthplaces of St. Ignatius, founder of the Society of Jesus, and St. Francis Xavier, whom he called "the prototype of missionaries in the line of the mission of the Church." He took part in a second Liturgy of the Word in Zaragoza, where he also met with an assembly of 5,000 sick persons and joined in a national act of homage to Mary at the Basilica of the Virgin of Pilar. He spent the night, the only one outside Madrid, at Zaragoza.

Jesuit Heritage: During a Mass at Loyola commemorating religious orders founded in Spain, he reminded Jesuits of their special heritage of obedience and loyalty to the Holy See.

He urged religious superiors "not to abdicate your duty to exercise authority" and to administer sanctions against members when necessary.

Principal Activity of Priests: He also said that the principal activity of priests and religious is not "in temporal reality, nor in that which is the field of laymen and must be left to them. . . . The ways of the religious world do not follow the calculations of men. They do not use as parameters the cults of power, riches or pleasure."

Violence: In the violence-prone region of Spain, the Pope addressed himself especially to young people in the throng of 150,000 at Mass: "I would like to tell you with affection and firmness — and my voice is that of one who has suffered personally from violence — to think about your path. Do not let your generosity and altruism be misused. Violence is never constructive."

"Once again, I repeat that Christianity understands and recognizes the noble and proper fight for justice at all levels, but prohibits seeking solutions in paths of hate and death."

Missionary Challenge: While presenting mission crosses to 52 lay persons in the small town of Javier, he urged young students and workers to regard the existence of the non-Christian world as a challenge to their faith and humanism, and to take up the missionary cross to carry the Gospel to its people. He contrasted this mission with "the temptation of the ideologies of hedonism, hatred and violence that menaces youth."

November 7

The Pope spent an hour and a half in the morning at Montserrat, the mountaintop site of a Benedictine abbey and a Marian sanctuary. He took part there in a Liturgy of the Word which had to be substituted for an outdoor Mass because of bad weather. In Barcelona, he addressed workers and businessmen in the afternoon, and afterwards celebrated Mass before a congregation of 100,000 people in the Camp Nou Soccer Stadium.

The Gospel of Work: "I come to announce the gospel of work to you," the Pope told attendants at the Universal Exposition in Barcelona. "During these four years of my pontificate, I have unceasingly proclaimed the centrality of man in my encyclicals and catechesis, insisting on his primacy over things and on the importance of the subjective dimension in work, based on the dignity of the human person."

Unemployment: "Through its social magisterium, the Church recalls that the ways to a just solution of this grave problem demand a revision of the economic order as a whole. Comprehensive planning of economic production, not simply planning by sectors, is needed. The correct and rational organization of work is necessary, not only on the national level but also on the international level. The solidarity of all working men is needed for this."

Responsibilities of Lay Persons: Repeating themes of earlier talks during his visit, the Pope said: "The Christian must be in the front lines as a witness to truth, honesty and justice." He focused special attention on the "crucial problems" of divorce, abortion, religious education and the battle against "social and economic injustice and discrimination." He called on the people to "follow the voice of the Church's teaching authority and to be faithful to the council of our times, Vatican II."

November 8

The Pope visited the Basilica of the Virgin of the Forsaken, patroness of Valencia, in the morning and met outside with 4,000 elderly persons. He ordained 141 men to the priesthood during an outdoor Mass attended by a million people. He visited flood victims of Alcira and met with 4,000 priests and seminarians at the Moncada Seminary. Back in Madrid, he addressed a gathering of women religious and secular institute members.

Elderly Persons: Referring to the "perspective of strong growth in the number of the elderly in relation to youth," the Pope said "society has to confront this problem with humanitarian and moral criteria, avoiding sorrowful and unjust alienation. . . . May the Most Blessed Virgin of the Forsaken protect all the persons of the third age in Spain, especially those who most need assistance, and inspire sentiments of solidarity and understanding in hearts in order that no elderly person may lack respect, affection and the help he or she needs."

Commitment of Priests: The Holy Father told candidates for the priesthood that the commitment as priests "absorbs you totally, dedicates you radically, makes you living instruments of the action of Christ in the world, an extension of his ministry for the glory of his Father."

Celibacy and Life-Style: Celibacy "is the expression of a full giving, of a special consecration, of an absolute availability. . . . The celibate does not renounce love. . . . The heart and faculties of the priest remain permeated with the love of Christ, in order to be the witness of a pastoral charity without boundaries among one's brothers."

"Being one of the crowd — in career, life-style, way of dressing, political commitment — does not help you fully realize your mission. It would defraud your faithful who want . . . liturgists, teachers, pastors, (as well as) like Christ, brothers and friends."

He expressed hope that "the celebration (of ordination) may bring to the entire Church in Spain a renewal of the inexhaustible grace of the Catholic priesthood (and) a considerable increase in priestly vocations among youths."

Message to Seminarians: In a document addressed to students for the priesthood, the Holy Father said: "The Church hopes to find in its priests spiritual persons; that is, those who with their life and behavior witness in a credible and convincing way to the presence of God and the values of the spirit in our society, which for the most part is characterized by theoretical and practical materialism but also by an insatiable thirst for God and spiritual values."

Community Life: This was one of the topics in the Pope's address in the evening to nuns and members of female secular institutes. He said: "You can be sure that your (nuns') life in community, lived in charity and selflessness, is the best assistance that you can give one another and the best antidote against the temptations which threaten your vocation. . . Your community life, your way of behaving and your way of dressing — which always distinguish you as religious women — are within the world a constant and intelligent preaching, without words, of the evangelical message."

November 9

Santiago de Compostela in the northwestern corner of Spain was the last stop on the Pope's itinerary. He spent 10 hours there, celebrating Mass at Labacolla Airport, meeting with fishermen, and taking part in a European Act in the cathedral dedicated to St. James the Apostle, patron of the country.

Impressions: Speaking to people at the airport, the Pope said in a homily: "I have passed through your homeland preaching of Christ crucified and resurrected, spreading his Gospel, acting as a witness of hope. And I have encountered on all sides openness, enthusiastic harmony, sincere affection, affable hospitality, creative capacity and labors of Christian renewal."

European Act: The Pope delivered a declaration to Europe in the course of a European Act held in the Cathedral of Santiago de Compostela and attended by 5,000 invited guests who included King Juan Carlos, leaders of the Common Market and presidents of the episcopal conferences of Europe. He said, in part:

"The history of the formation of the European nations runs parallel with their evangelization, to the point that the European frontiers coincided with those of the inroads of the Gospel. After twenty centuries of history, notwithstanding the bloody conflicts which have set the peoples of Europe in opposition to one another, and in spite of the spiritual crises which have marked the life of the continent — even to the point of raising serious questions in our own time about its future destiny — it can be said that the European identity is not understandable without Christianity, and that it is precisely in Christianity that are found those common roots by which the continent has seen its civilization mature: its culture, its dynamism, its activity, its capacity for constructive expansion in other continents as well; in a word, all that makes up its glory.

"And today still, the soul of Europe remains united because, beyond its common origin, it has similar Christian and human values.

"I . . . John Paul . . . Bishop of Rome and Shepherd of the Universal Church, from Santiago, utter to you, Europe of the ages, a cry full of love; *Find yourself again. Be yourself.* Discover your origins, revive your roots. Return to those authentic values which made your history a glorious one and your presence so beneficent in the other continents. Rebuild your spiritual unity in a climate of complete respect for other religions and other genuine liberties. Give to Caesar what belongs to Caesar, and to God what belongs to God. Do not become so proud of your achievements that you forget their possible negative effects. Do not become discouraged because of the quantitative loss of some of your greatness in the world or because of the social and cultural crises which affect you today. You can still be the guiding light of civilization and the stimulus of progress for the world. The other continents look to you and also hope to receive from you the same reply which James gave to Christ: 'I can do it.' "

PAPAL VISIT TO SICILY

Pope John Paul, on his 33rd pastoral visit in Italy, spent Nov. 20 and 21, 1982, in Sicily, the island which he said was "among the first regions of Italy to welcome the Apostles" (in the person of St. Paul who stopped there briefly on his way to Rome more than 1,900 years earlier).

The Holy Father was welcomed at the Palermo airport by an enthusiastic crowd headed by

Cardinal Salvatore Pappalardo, members of the hierarchy and government officials.

Plea for Help

Shortly after arriving, he was airborne again on a helicopter flight to Belice Valley. He celebrated Mass there on a hillside near Santa Ninfa before a gathering of 150,000, and appealed in a homily for greater efforts by government and other agencies to aid thousands of people still suffering from the effects of an earthquake which devastated the area several years earlier.

Back in Palermo, the Pope responded to greetings from the mayor of the city by praising Sicilians for their "orientation to family life; their exemplary capacity for self-giving and for solidarity toward others, especially the suffering; their innate respect for life, and their admirable sense of responsibility and of honor."

He also mentioned "incidents of barbarous violence which for too long have bloodied the streets of this splendid city."

Two groups addressed by the Pontiff were Eastern Catholic Albanians, whom he praised for their ecumenical contacts with members of the Orthodox Church, and dock workers, to whom he spoke about the dignity of work and their family life.

At a meeting with university faculty members in the afternoon of Nov. 20, the Pope called on them to use their influence to develop courageous young people capable of rejecting violence.

"You have a power," he said, "which springs from the strength of ideas and which is needed today more than ever as an antidote to profound evils, particularly those connected with the Mafia

phenomenon. . . . It is true that with repressive measures certain manifestations of violence can be halted. But the only way to overcome the evil completely is through the patient work of forming consciences."

Praise for the Christian traditions of Sicily was one of the themes of the Pope's homily at a Mass celebrated Nov. 21 in Palermo's hippodrome at the foot of Pilgrim Mountain. The Mass was attended by 200,000 persons.

Call for a New Society

The Holy Father delivered the last address of his visit before an assembly of 100,000 youths in Palermo's Piazza Politeama. He called on Sicilians to construct a society without violence or war, without unemployment or narcotics. He spoke about "a future and a new society in which would be isolated and destroyed the ramifications of the mafioso attitude of some," whom he called "operators of aberrant manifestations of criminality."

When speaking, the Pope did not mention an excommunication order in effect against Catholics involved in Mafia-like crimes of violence. In his written text, however, he said: "I share the bishops' pastoral anxiety and generous commitment" against Mafia violence, which "merits the open moral condemnation repeated just recently by your bishops" (Oct. 21, 1982, regarding excommunication orders dating from 1944 and 1952).

References to the Mafia in two of the 13 addresses delivered by the Pope were clear but muted out of deference to the sensibilities of the vast majority of the population of Sicily.

POPE JOHN PAUL IN CENTRAL AMERICA

Pope John Paul, on the 17th foreign pastoral trip of his pontificate, visited eight Central American nations Mar. 2 to 9, 1983.

• In Costa Rica (Mar. 2 and 3), he addressed the social implications of being Christian and called on young people to create a better world than that of their ancestors.

• In Nicaragua (Mar. 4), where he was harassed by the Marxist-oriented regime and its supporters, he called on the Church to remain independent of partisan political ideologies, stressed the need for unity in the Church, and reprimanded a priest (one of five) holding office in the government against the wishes of the bishops and the Vatican.

• In Panama (Mar. 5), he spoke about marital themes and appealed for the rights of *campesinos*.

• In El Salvador (Mar. 6), the locale of institutional violence and civil war with a toll of more than 30,000 deaths in three years, he called for efforts to overcome obstacles to dialogue and to promote reconciliation among all parties to conflict.

• In Guatemala (Mar. 7), he condemned discrimination and violence against Indians (the victims of several massacres) and the Church, and criticized the extremism of fundamentalist born-again Christians.

• In Honduras (Mar. 8), he prayed for peace

through the intercession of Mary at the shrine of Our Lady of Suyapa.

• In Belize (Mar. 9), small but with the largest percentage of non-Catholics in countries of the region, he spoke abut interfaith relations and the quest for Christian unity.

• In Haiti (Mar. 9), the last stop of the trip, he criticized social evils, declared that changes had to be made, and addressed the opening session of a plenary assembly of the Latin American Bishops' Council.

Following are accounts of each day's events and a number of the Holy Father's addresses and homilies.

March 2

Pope John Paul arrived late in the afternoon at the airport outside San Jose, Costa Rica, after a 6,400-mile flight from Rome via Lisbon. At the airport, he stated the purpose of his visit and stressed the need for change in Central America. He addressed the 66 bishops of the region in the evening at the central seminary in the capital city.

Purpose of the Visit: "I undertook this journey with my thoughts upon all, moved by the duty I feel to rekindle the light of the faith in peoples who already believe in Jesus Christ, so that this faith may enlighten and inspire their individual and community lives ever more effectively.

"But this pastoral stay of the successor of Peter among you has other purposes as well. The tortured cry which these lands raise . . . resounded with accents of urgency in my spirit. It implores reconciliation, which can banish divisions and hatred. It yearns for a justice which has been long, and until today vainly, awaited. It seeks to be a call to greater dignity, without renunciation of its Christian religious essence.

"This sorrowful cry is what I want to give voice to with my visit."

Change Is Possible and Necessary: "Change is possible: if we accept the voice of Christ, which calls us to respect and love each man as our brother; if we know how to renounce practices of blind egoism; if we learn to have more solidarity; if we apply with rigor the norms of social justice which the Church proclaims; if those responsible for the peoples open the door to an increasing sense of distributive justice in the burdens and duties of the various sectors of society; and if each people can confront its problems, in a climate of sincere dialogue, without foreign interference.

"Yes, these nations have the capacity progressively to reach goals of greater dignity for their sons and daughters. They must strive for this goal with ever more determined will and with the collaboration of the various sectors of the population.

"(They must do so) without having recourse to methods of violence or systems of collectivism which can end up no less oppressive to the dignity of man than a purely economic capitalism.

"The life of man, the humanism proclaimed by the Church in her social teaching, can lead to overcoming deplorable situations that await proper reforms.

"It is the pain of the peoples that I come to share, to try to understand more intimately, so as to leave them a word of encouragement and hope founded on a necessary change of attitudes."

Address to Bishops: Subjects of the Pope's talk included unity in the Church; evangelization and catechesis, with emphasis on the teaching of sound doctrine concerning Christ and the Church; the Eucharist; ecumenism, and unity in society.

Christology: In view of threats to authentic teaching about Christ, he said: "Authentic Christology may not leave aside the integral wholeness of the revelation in the New Testament, but it should duly profit by serious advances made by research; nor should it leave aside the indispensable reference to the magisterium. A Christology giving nourishment to our communities cannot exist if the theological labor does not have its roots deep in the faith of the Church and in a personal faith making an offering of one's own existence to the Lord."

March 3

In the morning of a full day in San Jose, the Pope met with a small group of Poles at the apostolic nunciature, visited the National Children's Hospital, met privately with President Luis Alberto Monge, and celebrated Mass at La Sabana Park before a gathering of a half-million people. In the afternoon, he met with religious at the cathedral

and addressed a large throng of young people in the National Stadium. In the evening, he addressed the judges of the Inter-American Court of Human Rights.

The Pope expressed "deepest sorrow" during the day at the execution of six men in Guatemala for whom he had initiated a plea for commutation of their death sentences to life imprisonment.

Christian Responsibility in the World: This was the theme of the Pope's homily during Mass at La Sabana. He said:

"This Church, with its teaching and example, that of its saints and teachers, exhorts us to concern ourselves not only with things of the spirit but also with the realities of this world and the human society of which we are a part. It exhorts us to undertake the elimination of injustice; to work for peace and the overcoming of hate and violence; to promote the dignity of man; to feel responsible for the poor, the sick, the alienated and oppressed, refugees, exiles and displaced persons, as well as so many others whom our solidarity must reach."

Social Implications of Being Christian: "It is indeed necessary and urgent in your countries for the Church, as she proclaims the good news of the Gospel to peoples who suffer intensely now and have done so for a long time, to go on effectively expounding all the social implications entailed in the condition of being Christian."

"All members of the Church must bear in mind that they may not have recourse to methods of violence repugnant to the Christian tradition, nor to ideologies inspired by reductive visions of man and his transcendental destiny. On the contrary, from the standpoint of the clear identity of the Gospel and an integral vision of the human being, they will seek with all their energies to eliminate oppression and injustice in their various forms and will try to make wider room for the dignifying of man."

"The Church's social teaching . . . rejects as inadequate and harmful both the materialist foundations and designs of purely economic capitalism and those of an equally materialistic collectivism — both of which are oppressors of mankind."

Mission of Women Religious: At a mixed congregation of priests, men and women religious, and others, the Pope addressed himself principally to the women. "You have," he said, "the capacity to make the Church present with a really maternal face, with sensibility and affection, with wisdom and balance."

"In order to accomplish this mission properly, remain firmly rooted in your faith, in love of Christ and in eccesial consciousness. You will thus avoid possible deviations or instrumentalization of the Gospel in that necessary, but not exclusive, preferential choice in favor of the poor. Be not deceived by party ideologies. Do not succumb to the temptation presented by options which might one day demand the price of your liberty. Trust in your pastors and be always in communion with them. In this communion with the Church, in identification with its directives, you will have the sure rule of action. Work together among yourselves to accomplish such discernment of reality in respect to what the light of the Gospel must fall on. Always, as if by supernatural instinct, guide the authenticity of your apostolic options with the compass needle of feeling with the Church, a sense made up of sincere communion with the magisterium, of unity with its shepherds.

"With this guarantee, embrace the cause of the poor: be present where Christ is suffering in needy brethren. Reach with your generosity to where a friendly presence is required. Be patient and generous in hopes of a better society, sowing the seed of a new humanity which will build and not destroy, which will transform the negative into the positive, as an announcement of the resurrection."

Break the Chain of Hatred and Violence: Thousands of young people attended a late afternoon Liturgy of the Word in the National Stadium at which the Holy Father said: "A great part of Central America is tasting the bitter fruits of the seed sown by injustice, by hatred and by violence."

"You have the grave responsibility to break the chain of hatred producing hatred and violence begetting violence. You have to create a world better than that of your ancestors. Unless you do so, the blood will continue flowing and tomorrow tears will attest to the pain of your own children."

He urged his listeners "to fight with all the energy of your youth against hatred and violence until love and peace are reestablished in your nations."

The profound motivation needed for this endeavor is provided by faith in Christ, which shows that "it is worthwhile making an effort to be better; that it is worth the trouble to work with a more just society . . . to defend the innocent, the oppressed and the poor . . . the trouble of suffering in order to relieve the sufferings of others . . . the trouble to dignify one's fellow man ever more and more."

Protection of Human Rights: In an address to judges of the Inter-American Court of Human Rights, the Pope called for stronger action against their violation in Central America. He said there must be "effective instruments of verification and, where necessary, appropriate sanctions for violations of rights. . . . I would give expression to a wish . . . that, in carrying out your functions, . . . you may cause respect to grow for the dignity and rights of man: that man whom you, reared in a Christian tradition, recognize as the image of God and, as having been redeemed by Christ, the most valuable being in creation."

March 4

In the morning, the Pope flew from San Jose to Managua, Nicaragua, and went from there to Leon where he conducted a Liturgy of the Word for lay people in the cathedral. Back in Managua for the afternoon, he met with members of the Nicaraguan government and celebrated Mass in the July 19 Plaza before a throng of 300,000 or more people. He returned to San Jose in the evening.

Messenger of Peace: At the airport, the Pope said: "I come as a messenger of peace, as a nourisher of hope, as a servant of the faith in order to strengthen the faithful with a word of love, that it may fill minds with sentiments of fraternity and reconciliation."

"I come also to launch an appeal for peace to those who, inside and outside this geographical area . . . favor tensions — ideological, economic or military — which impede the free development of these peoples who love peace, fraternity and true human progress — spiritual, social, civil and democratic."

Preceding the Pope's address was a speech by Daniel Ortega Saavedra in which the leader of the ruling junta charged the United States with aggressive actions against Nicaragua. Ortega also claimed: "Our experience shows that one may be a believer and at the same time a consistent revolutionary, and that there is no insurmountable contradiction between both things." The Pope took exception to this in a homily delivered later in the day at Mass in the July 19 Plaza.

Education: At the University of Leon, the Pope addressed himself "especially to the laity living their vocation to holiness and the apostolate in their profession as educators."

He continued: "The educational task is connatural to the laity because it is intimately linked with conjugal and family responsibilities. Laity actually share in the educational, evangelizing and sanctifying mission of the Church by virtue of their right and duty, which is primary and original, to educate their own children. . . . And there is not the slightest doubt that the school is the complement of the educational upbringing received in the bosom of the family. The Church recognizes this when she emphasizes the primacy of the family in education . . . in particular, the strict right of believing parents not to see their children subjected in the schools to programs inspired by atheism."

"If education is integral formation of the human person — and every education implicitly or explicitly presupposes a certain concept of man — the Catholic educator will inspire his activity with a Christian vision of man, whose supreme dignity is revealed in Jesus Christ, Son of God, model and goal of human growth in its fullness."

Unity of the Church: This unity, together with dangers threatening it, was the major theme of the Pope's homily during Mass in the July 19 Plaza in Managua. Backgrounding the remarks were several significant facts, among them: active participation in the government by several priests, against the will of the bishops and the Vatican; the reported existence and activities of a people's church — consisting of small Christian communities more in line with the government than the Church; and the Marxist character and/or trend of the regime.

"The unity of the Church is actually brought into question when before the powerful factors constituting and maintaining it — the faith itself, the revealed word, the sacraments, obedience to the bishops and the pope, the sense of a common vocation and responsibility in Christ's task in the world — are put earthly considerations, unacceptable ideological compromises and temporal options including conceptions of the Church which take the place of the true one."

Dangers to Unity: "When the Christian, whatever his condition may be, prefers any other doctrine or ideology to the teachings of the Apostles and the Church; when he makes these doctrines the criterion of our vocation; when he decides to reinterpret catechesis, religious teaching, preaching according to his own categories; when 'parallel magisteriums' are installed, as I said in my opening address to the Puebla Conference (Jan. 28, 1979): then is the Church's unity weakened and the exercise of her mission to be "the sacrament of unity" to all men made more difficult. The Church's unity signifies and demands from us a radical overcoming of all tendencies toward disassociation. It means and demands a revision of our scale of values. It means and demands that we submit our doctrinal conceptions and our pastoral projects to the magisterium of the Church, represented by the pope and the bishops. This applies in the field of the Church's social teaching as well, as developed by my predecessors and by myself.

"No Christian, especially those with titles signifying a special consecration in the Church, should become responsible for breaking this unity, acting outside of or against the will of the bishops 'whom the Holy Spirit has set to guide the Church of God' (Acts 20:28). This holds good in every situation and country; no process of development or social elevation which may be undertaken can legitimately compromise the identity and religious liberty of a people, the transcendent dimension of the human person and the sacred character of the Church and her ministers."

"A divided Church, as I said in my already mentioned letter to your bishops, will not be able to accomplish its mission 'of sacrament, that is to say, as sign and instrument of unity in the country.' I therefore alerted you then about how 'absurd and dangerous it is to imagine oneself alongside — not to say against — the Church built around the bishop, to imagine oneself thus as another church, conceived solely as 'charismatic' and not institutional, 'new' and not traditional, alternative and, as has been said lately, a people's church.' I want to reaffirm these words here before you. The Church must keep herself united in order to counter and arrest the various direct or indirect forms of materialism which her mission encounters in the world."

March 5

In Panama late in the morning, the Pope celebrated Mass at Albrook Field before a congregation of 250,000 people. In the afternoon, he recited the Rosary for worldwide broadcast by Vatican Radio, conducted a Liturgy of the Word for thousands of *campesinos* in Olympic City, and met privately with President Ricardo de la Espriella. Before returning to Costa Rica in the evening, he met at the Panama City cathedral with representatives of the country's priests, religious and seminarians.

Marital Themes: While reflecting on "the matrimonial alliance (as) a mystery of profound transcendence" during a homily at Mass, the Pope said:

"Dear husbands and wives: Renew your promise of mutual fidelity at this Eucharist. Take on the upbringing of your children as a specific service in the Church. Work with your bishops and priests in evangelization of the family. And always remember that the authentic Christian, even at the risk of converting himself into a 'sign of contradiction,' has to know how to choose well those practical options which stand in accord with his faith. He will therefore have to say no to unions not sanctified by holy matrimony and to divorce. He will say no to sterilization, most of all if it be imposed upon any person or ethnic group for fallacious reasons. He will say no to contraception, and he will say no to the crime of abortion which slays innocent beings.

"The Christian believes in life and love. So he will say yes to the indissoluble love of matrimony; . . . yes to the protection of life; yes to the stability and permanence of the family; yes to lawful living together which nourishes communion and favors the balanced upbringing of the children."

Campesinos: In an address to tens of thousands of farmers, the Pope said "the *campesino* population has frequently been abandoned to an ignoble level of life and has not rarely been tried and exploited harshly." Nevertheless, he urged his listeners: "In the search for greater justice and your elevation, you cannot let yourselves be dragged down by the temptation of violence . . . because this is not the route of Jesus Christ or of the Church or of your Christian faith."

He called on government officials to join with peasants and "the entire society" in "a joint effort . . . to create structures of true development, to bring to the fields new instruments and means to alleviate the fatigue of the peasant, to make his daily encounter with the land a more humane and happier situation, to increase productivity and to reward the efforts of his hands with just wages."

March 6

The Pope's flight from San Jose, Costa Rica, arrived shortly before 10:00 a.m. at Ilopango Air Base, El Salvador. He was greeted there by President Alvaro Magana and other leaders of Church and state. He visited the tomb of murdered Archbishop Oscar Arnulfo Romero in the San Salvador cathedral en route to the Metro Center where he celebrated Mass before a throng of 300,000. In the afternoon, he met again with President Magana and addressed a gathering of priests at the Marist high school in the capital city. He flew to Guatemala City in the evening.

Artisans of Peace: Throughout Central America, and not just in El Salvador, "each and every person — governors and the governed, city dwellers and rural people, businessmen and workers, teachers and students — all have the obligation to be artisans of peace," the Pope said in a homily at Mass. "That there may be peace among your nations, that the borders may not be zones of tensions but open arms of reconciliation, it is urgent to bury the violence which has cost so many victims in this and other nations."

Dialogue is the way to peace, he declared, and

added: "The dialogue asked for by the Church is not a tactical truce to fortify positions as part of a plan to continue the fighting. Instead, it is a sincere effort to answer, with the search for agreements, the anguish, the pain, the weariness, the fatigue of so many who long for peace."

Obstacles to dialogue which must be overcome include "ideologies which see in struggle the motor of history, in might the source of right, in the classification of enemies the ABC of politics."

"God's love," on the other hand, "does not reveal a dialectic of confrontation but one of love which renews everything."

The Priest, Man of Dialogue: This was the major point of the Pope's address directed principally to priests but heard also by seminarians and religious at the Marist high school.

"In recalling fidelity to Christ, our sole master and teacher, and his Gospel, I want to exhort you to keep the doctrine of the Church's faith alive and intense. It is worthwhile committing oneself even to the offering up of your life for that cause. It is worthless to give your life for an ideology, for a gospel that has been mutilated and instrumentalized for a partisan option. The priest to whom the Gospel and the wealth of the deposit of faith are entrusted must first identify himself with this doctrinal integrity in order to be a faithful transmitter at the same time of the Church's doctrine, in communion with the magisterium — a transmission of the faith which is not limited to one's own diocese or country, but which has to open itself up to the Church's missionary dimension."

"So, do not defraud the Lord's poor who ask you for the bread of the Gospel, the solid food of the secure and integral Catholic faith, so that they may know how to choose in the face of other preachings and ideologies which are not the message of Jesus Christ and of his Church. Your ecclesial task lies in this, your commitment of priority. Remember, my dear brothers, that — as I told the priests and religious of Mexico — 'You are not social directors, political leaders or officials of a temporal power' (Jan. 27, 1979)."

Accessibility: "The faithful in need of a word of counsel or consolation want to find the priest ready and easily identifiable, even through his manner of dress. All those who need the grace of forgiveness and reconciliation expect that it will be easy for them to find a priest exercising this indispensable ministry of salvation, where personal contact facilitates the growth and maturation of Christians.

"Today more than ever, in view of the shortage of priests and the great needs of the church community, the priest is called to an intelligent mission of promoting lay service, of inspiration of the community, of the faithful's taking responsibility for those ministries within their competence by reason of their baptism."

 Mediator: "The priest must be the man of dialogue. He must take on boldly the risky task of being a mediator and making himself a bridge between opposed tendencies, to nourish concord, to seek just solutions to difficult situations. The option of the Christian, and even more of the priest, becomes dramatic at times. Although he remains

firmly against error, he cannot be against anybody since we are all brothers or, at most, enemies who ought to love in accordance with the Gospel. The priest must embrace all, since all are God's children, and he has to give his life for all his brothers if necessary. It is here that the priest's drama is often rooted, for he is driven by opposing tendencies and harassed by partisan options."

"He is called to make a preferential option for the poor, but he cannot disregard the fact that there is radical poverty wherever God is not alive and in the hearts of people who are slaves to power, to pleasure, to money, to violence. He must extend his mission to these poor too.

"The priest is therefore the prisoner of God's mercy and not only a preacher of justice. He has to make the message of conversion resound for all, and he has to announce reconciliation in Christ Jesus who is our peace, and break down every wall of division among persons."

March 7

The Pope began the day in Guatemala City at meetings with a small group of Poles at the apostolic nunciature, 400 persons at the cathedral, and President Efrain Rios Montt at the presidential palace. He celebrated Mass after mid-morning at Mars Field before an assembly of about a million people. In the afternoon, he addressed about 500,000 Indians at Quezaltenango. Back in Guatemala City, he spoke to 1,500 priests, brothers and sisters at St. John Bosco College, and ended the day at a meeting with 100 persons of the academic community.

Love for the Church: This was one of the subjects of the Pope's homily during Mass at Mars Field.

"You ought to love this Church always," he said. "With the efforts of her best children, she did very much to help forge your personality and liberty. She has been present in the most glorious events of your history. She has been and still is by your side when fortune smiles or sorrow overcomes you. She has tried to dissipate ignorance by throwing the light of education on the minds and hearts of her children in her schools, colleges and universities. She has raised and continues to raise her voice to condemn injustices, to denounce outrages — above all, those against the poor and the humble — not in the name of ideologies, of whatever sort they be, but in the name of Jesus Christ, of his Gospel, of his message of love, peace, justice, truth and liberty.

"Love the Church, for she constantly calls upon you to do good and detest sin; to give up all vice and corruption; to live in holiness; to make Christ — the way, truth and life — the perfect model of your personal and social conduct; to follow paths of greater justice and respect for the rights of man; to live more as brothers than as adversaries."

Faith, Human Dignity and Rights: "Faith teaches us that man is the image and likeness of God (cf. Gn. 1:27). This means that man is endowed with immense dignity and that, when man is trampled, when his rights are violated, when flagrant injustices are committed against him, when he undergoes tortures, when he is violated by kidnapping or his right to life is violated: a crime and a very grave offense against God is committed. It is then that Christ goes back to walk again on the way of the cross and suffers the horrors of the crucifixion in the person who is destitute and oppressed."

"Beyond any social, political, ideological, racial and religious difference, the life of your brother, of each man, must always be assured above all.

"Let us remember . . . that one can make one's brother die little by little, day by day, when he is deprived of access to the goods which God created for the benefit of all, not just the profit of a few. This human promotion is an integral part of evangelization and the faith."

The Impulse of Faith: "I exhort you . . . to share your own faith clearly and boldly, so as to practice charity, especially with those most in need."

"I call upon those responsible for the peoples — above all, those feeling the interior call of the Christian faith — with affection I call upon them to commit themselves fully and decisively to effective and urgent means to bring the recourses of justice to the most unprotected sectors of society. Let those be the prime beneficiaries of appropriate legal safeguards."

"Faith in Christ obliges us to love God, and man as our brother. It teaches us to see man in all the depths of his transcendental value. The faith must, therefore, be a great impulse to work for the integral advancement of mankind, starting with the clear identity of one's own condition as a child of God and the Church, without ever letting this vision be darkened and without having recourse to ideological premises contrary to the faith."

"May this Christian faith, the glory of your nation, the soul of your people and of the Central American peoples, show itself in well defined acts — above all, toward the poorest, weakest and humblest of your brothers.

"This faith ought to lead to justice and peace. No more divorce between faith and life. If we accept Christ, let us do the works of Christ. Let us treat one another as brothers. And let us walk in the ways of the Gospel."

Rights of Indians: Addressing Indians at Quezaltenango, the Holy Father said: "The Church brings you the saving message of Christ in an attitude of profound respect and love."

"The Church not only respects and evangelizes peoples and cultures; she has also been the defender of the authentic cultural values of each ethnic group."

"The Church knows the marginalization which you suffer, the injustices which you have to contend with, the serious difficulties you meet in defending your lands and your rights, the frequent lack of respect for your customs and traditions.

"Therefore, as she carries on her evangelizing task, she seeks to be near you and raise her voice in condemnation when your dignity as human beings and children of God is violated. She wants to be together with you peacefully, as the Gospel demands, but with decision and energy, in obtaining acknowledgment and promotion of your dignity and your rights as persons."

Appeal for Protection: "For this reason, from this place and in solemn form, I call upon rulers, in the name of the Church, for ever more adequate legislation to shield you effectively from abuses and to assure you of the environment and means adequate for your normal development.

"I ask with insistence that the free practice of your Christian faith not be made difficult, that no one claim ever again to confuse authentic evangelization with subversion, and that ministers of religion may exercise their mission in security without hindrances. And do not let yourselves be made use of by ideologies inciting you to violence and death.

"I ask that your reservations be respected, above all that the sacred character of your life be safeguarded. Let no one on any account despise your existence, since God forbids us to kill and commands us to love each other as brothers."

"I exhort you to follow the ways of concrete solutions traced out by the Church in her social teaching so as to arrive in this way at necessary reforms while avoiding all recourse to violence."

The Pope invited Indians to cultivate their distinctive values of piety, hard work, love for their homes and families, and apostolic work — especially on the part of catechists and other lay ministers.

March 8

The Pope flew from Guatemala City to Tegucigalpa, Honduras, where he arrived at about 9:15 a.m. He celebrated Mass later in the morning outside the shrine of Our Lady of Suyapa, patroness of the country, before a gathering of about 200,000 people. He had a private meeting with President Roberto Suazo Cordova before leaving for San Pedro Sula where he addressed delegates of the word during a paraliturgical service. He returned to Guatemala City for the night.

Mary: During Mass at the shrine of Our Lady of Suyapa, the Holy Father prayed: "You who are the Mother of Peace, help so that the struggles cease, that hate end forever, that violent deaths are not repeated. You who are Mother, dry the tears of those who cry, those who have lost their loved ones, the exiled and those who are far from home. . . . Make the people preserve, as a most precious treasure, faith in Jesus Christ, love for you and fidelity to the Church."

He called Mary the model for the "new woman" who should "promote her dignity and active participate in society and the Church."

He also told the people: "You cannot invoke the Virgin as Mother while scorning and mistreating her children. . . . We must reject all that is contrary to the Gospel: hate, violence, injustices, lack of work, the imposition of ideologies which reduce the dignity of man and woman. And we must encourage all that follows the will of the Father in heaven: charity, mutual aid, education in the faith, culture, the promotion of the poorest, respect for all — especially the needy, those who suffer the most, the alienated."

Delegates of the Word: At the San Pedro Sula airport, the Pope praised the work of men and women who, because of the severe shortage of priests, conduct liturgies of the word and preach on Sundays and holy days. He urged them to continue their work, remaining "always faithful to the genuine doctrine of the Church." In view of the social implications of their work, he warned them against becoming instruments of radical political groups.

March 9

In the morning, the Pope flew from Guatemala City to Belize where he celebrated Mass at the airport before a gathering of about 30,000 people. A second Mass of the day, in the afternoon at Port-au-Prince, marked the end of a national Eucharistic Congress in Haiti. The Pontiff met with President Jean Claude Duvalier at about 6:00 p.m. The last event of the trip was an address to representatives of Latin American bishops attending the inaugural meeting of a plenary assembly of the Latin American Bishops' Council. He departed for Rome after the meeting.

Christian Unity: Speaking during Mass in Belize, the Pope appealed for "the unity to which the various churches and ecclesial communities are called." He was critical of the methods of some U.S.-based fundamentalist sects in the country, noting that they amounted to "an aggressive proselytism that disturbs and hurts — sometimes even with unworthy procedures — the degree of unity which an ecclesial community already possesses." He also warned against any "watering down" of doctrine for the sake of Christian unity.

Something Has To Change Here: This theme of the Haitian national Eucharistic Congress keynoted the homily delivered by the Pope at the Port-au-Prince airport.

In Haiti in particular and Central America in general, he said, Christians have "observed division, injustice, excessive inequality, degradation of the quality of life, poverty, hunger, fear in a great number of people. Christians have thought of the peasants unable to make a living from their land, of people crowded without work in the cities, of families broken up and displaced, of the victims of various other frustrations. And yet, they are convinced that solutions exist in solidarity. It is necessary for the 'poor' of all kinds to begin to hope again. The Church retains a prophetic mission in this field which is inseparable from her religious mission, and it calls for liberty to carry it through: not to accuse, not just to arouse consciousness of the evil, but to contribute positively to recovery by mustering all consciences, more particularly the consciences of all those with responsibility in the villages, in the cities and at the national level, to arouse them to act in conformity with the Gospel and the Church's social teaching."

Needs: "There is really a profound need of justice, of a better distribution of goods, of a more equitable organization of society, with more participation and a more disinterested concept of service to all on the part of those who have responsibilities. There is a rightful desire for free expression through the media and in politics, with re-

spect for the opinions of others and the common good; there is a need for more open and easier access to goods and services. These may not remain the privilege of a few. For example, there should be the possibility to eat one's fill; to satisfy one's hunger; to be well kept; to have housing, schooling, victory over illiteracy, honest and dignified work, social security, respect for family responsibilities and for the basic rights of man: in a few words, everything which ensures that men and women, children and the aged can live truly human lives.

"It is not a question of dreaming of riches or of the consumer society, but it is a question for all of a level of living worthy of the human person, the sons and daughters of God. And this is not impossible if all vital forces in the country unite in one, same effort and count also on that international solidarity which is always desirable. Christians wish to be people of hope, of love and of responsible action.

"Yes, the fact of being members of the body of Christ and of taking part in his Eucharistic Banquet commits you to promoting such change. . . . You will do this without violence, without murders, without fratricidal struggles, which often only engender further oppressions. You will do it in respect for love and liberty."

Task of a Latin American Bishop: The Holy Father delivered a wide-ranging pastoral address on this subject at the inaugural meeting of the 1983 plenary assembly of the Latin America Bishops' Council. Among other things, he said:

"Grave problems weigh upon this people from the religious and ecclesial point of view: the chronic and acute scarcity of priestly vocations and religious vocations and other pastoral workers, with the consequent result of religious ignorance, superstition and syncretism among the most lowly; an increasing indifference, if not atheism, because of contemporary secularism, especially in the big cities and among the more educated strata of the population; the bitterness of many who, because of an equivocal option for the poor, feel abandoned and neglected in their religious aspirations and needs; the advance of religious groups which are sometimes lacking in a true Gospel message and with their methods of action show little respect for true religious liberty and pose serious obstacles to the Catholic Church's mission and even to other Christian confessions."

Some Important Tasks: The Pope enumerated a few important tasks for the bishops:
• "calling numerous qualified young people and properly educating them for the priesthood or religious life;
• "giving the utmost attention to the laity in order to obtain their active insertion in the Church and their effective action in society;
• "catechesis, the sole instrument for educating future generations in the faith, a catechesis which orients them toward a social dynamism;
• "pastoral concern for the family."

Guidance in the Faith: "Be also masters and guides in the faith in this transcendental mission, propounding the Church's doctrine without ambiguities. Watch in goodness and with firmness over its integrity and purity, and correct doctrinal or moral deviations which create so much harm and confusion among the faithful. Be likewise sanctifiers of a people which, thanks to God, is open to the absolute of God and yearns for answers from the faith to questions which it asks about itself, about life, about suffering, death and the beyond."

"Being a bishop in Latin America today also means seeing onself as the pastor of a people which has certainly seen remarkable material progress in recent years and is beginning to offer the world the results of its efforts in many fields of civilization, but which still — and that is a radical contradiction — still has immense regions of poverty and misery, illiteracy, sickness and disease, marginalization. A sincere analysis of the situation shows how painful injustices are at the root of the matter, the exploitation of some people by others, and a grave lack of equity in the distribution of wealth and the goods of culture.

Temptation to Violence: "To this problem is added another of equal gravity. Recent history shows frequently that many young people yield to the temptation to combat injustice with violence, either through ill-directed idealism or ideological pressure or in the interests of a party of some system within the ambit of the hegemonies.

"Your pastoral sensitivity will suggest to you — and the orientations of Puebla confirm you in this — that amid the broad masses of the poor who form a great part of your churches, the poorest must have preference in your hearts as fathers and in your concern as pastors. But you know and proclaim that this option for them would be neither pastoral nor Christian if it were inspired by mere-

ly political or ideological criteria, if it were exclusive or excluding, or if it engendered feelings of hatred or struggle among brothers."

A New Evangelization: The Pope concluded his address with an appeal for commitment to a "new evangelization, new in ardor, methods and expression," to be accomplished through "numerous and well trained priests," through full engagement of lay persons in the Church and in society, and with adherence to guidelines of the Puebla document of 1979 in which the bishops' council plotted an overall pastoral pattern for Latin America.

The Puebla document, the Pontiff said, "is consecrated to this theme (of a new evangelization) inasmuch as it is impregnated with the teachings of the Second Vatican Council and is coherent with the Gospel. It is necessary in this sense for the wholeness and integrity of the Puebla message to be spread and eventually recovered, without deformed interpretations, without deforming reductions of it, and without applying some parts and eclipsing others."

AFTERTHOUGHT

Six days after his return to the Vatican, the Pope told a general audience Mar. 16 that the countries of Central America were in a state of "great internal tension." He also observed:

"The fundamental and central problem (in the region) is to insure the identity of the Church on doctrinal and pastoral levels in conformity with the teachings of the Second Vatican Council and the directives of the general conference of the Latin American episcopate at Puebla in 1979. In contradiction to this identity are many attempts to subordinate the evangelical contents to political categories and aims."

POLAND REVISITED

The Holy Father visited Poland for the second time in his pontificate June 16 to 23, 1983, for the purposes of celebrating the Jubilee of Our Lady of Czestochowa, confirming the Polish people in the faith and in the Catholic traditions of their country, supporting them in their struggle for rights withheld from them by an oppressive government, and calling on the regime to respect the rights of the people in religion, politics, labor relations and other areas of life.

The Pope celebrated Mass and delivered more than 20 homilies and addresses in key cities and Marian sanctuaries. He identified himself clearly with the people and was warmly received by them in great numbers. He was suspect to the government throughout the visit, and at its end found the regime, probably as expected beforehand, unmoved by his pleas for reconciliation with and justice for the people of Poland.

Some of the subjects in the Pope's addresses were rather similar to those in speeches delivered during his previous visit to Poland in 1979, but there were some differences.

Appearing below are portions of NC News reporting on some highlights of this 1983 visit and brief summaries of several of the Holy Father's talks.

Highlights

These are day-by-day highlights of the Pope's major actions and speeches on conditions in Poland during his second visit there.

• **June 16,** at Mass in the Warsaw cathedral: Poland's situation since the martial law crackdown of Dec. 13, 1981, is a "Calvary." "Together with all my compatriots . . . I stand beneath the cross of Christ."

• **June 17,** in a nationally televised address to government leaders in Warsaw: The 1980 social reforms achieved by the outlawed labor movement Solidarity and since suppressed under martial law are "indispensable" for Poland's recovery from its "internal crisis." Dialogue and social consensus are essential "to resolve social conflicts."

Meeting privately afterwards with Poland's Prime Minister, Gen. Wojciech Jaruzelski, the Pope extracted government permission to meet later with Solidarity leader Lech Walesa.

At an outdoor Mass in Warsaw: "The fullness of civic rights" is essential for social peace in Poland.

• **June 18,** to young people in Czestochowa: "We are fighting for the future form of our social life."

While achieving Polish freedom is difficult, "it is what costs that constiutes value."

To pilgrims from Szczecin, a Solidarity stronghold in the North: Events of the past year have caused "a wound in your heart . . . perhaps even anger."

• **June 19,** to Poland's bishops in Czestochowa: "The social doctrine of the Church and the true aspirations of workers do not pass alongside each other, but truly meet," and this requires of the Church "honest solidarity with workers."

At Vespers in Czestochowa: The Pope offered to Our Lady of Czestochowa, patroness of Poland, his sash torn by a bullet in the 1981 attempt on his life. He prayed to Mary to bring Poland back to "truth, liberty, justice, social solidarity" on the basis of the 1980 agreements.

• **June 20,** in rural Poznan: Defending private ownership of the land, he praised the efforts of Rural Solidarity to achieve "the fundamental rights of the human person" before the martial law crackdown.

To workers in Katowice: "Human work really is at the heart of all social life. Through it justice and social love are formed, if the whole working sector is governed by a just moral order. But, if this order is missing, injustice takes the place of justice and love is replaced by hatred." The 1980 strikes centered not just on wages but on "the moral order itself in relation to human work." The right to free unions "is a properly innate right . . . not given to us by the state."

• **June 21,** to workers in Wroclaw: "I bring my solidarity and that of the Church" to workers. Their hunger and thirst for justice "manifested in a particular way during these recent years . . . cannot be destroyed or suppressed. It cannot be ignored."

• **June 22,** at a Mass beatifying two Poles, Carmelite Father Jozef Kalinowski and lay Third Order Franciscan Brother Adam Chmielowski, in Cracow: "Greater love has no man than this, that a man lay down his life for his friends. . . . This giving of one's life for one's friends, for one's compatriots, was evidenced in 1963, through their (the two men's) participation in the insurrection (against Russia). . . . For Jozef Kalinowski and Adam Chmielowski, the January insurrection was a stage of the path to holiness, which is the heroism of the whole of one's life. . . . Their elevation to the altars in their homeland is the sign of that strength which is more powerful than any human weakness and more powerful than any situation, even the most difficult, not excluding the arrogant use of power."

At Cracow's Wawel Castel: The Pope met for the second time with Jaruzelski.

• **June 23,** at an undisclosed site south of Cracow: He met privately with Walesa and spent several hours relaxing in the Tatra Mountains. In his departure speech at Cracow's Belice airport, the Pope made a last plea for work in Poland to be "based on premises which guarantee the human being his rights and human dignity."

Tribute to Cardinal Wyszynski

On June 16, the day of his arrival in Poland, Pope John Paul delivered a homily in St. John's Cathedral in Warsaw, burial site of Cardinal Stefan Wyszynski, who died in May, 1981.

The cardinal was "a free man, and he taught us, his compatriots, true freedom. He was a tireless herald of the dignity of every person and of the good name of Poland among the nations," said the Pope. Wyszynski also was strong in his service, strong in faith.

The Pope spoke of Poland's suffering, saying: "Together with all my compatriots — especially with those who are most acutely tasting the bitterness of disappointment, humiliation, suffering, of being deprived of their freedom, of being wronged, of having their dignity trampled upon — I stand beneath the cross of Christ to celebrate on Polish soil the extraordinary Jubilee of the Year of the Redemption."

Hopes for Social Reform

The Pope told the highest authorities of Poland's communist government June 17 that he still hoped a social reform based on principles worked out in August, 1980, would gradually be put into effect in the nation. It was in August, 1980, that Solidarity, Poland's officially suppressed labor movement, was born.

The Pope's remarks during the meeting with state authorities at the Belvedere Palace in Warsaw were broadcast by state television, as were the remarks of Gen. Wojciech Jaruzelski, head of the government. The meeting was one of the few events of the visit that were carried live by national television.

In his remarks, the Pope recalled his Jan. 1, 1983, World Day of Peace message on the value of dialogue and the ways to conduct it. He quoted that document's observation that, when dialogue between government and people is absent, social peace also is threatened or absent; it is like a state of war.

He said he had come to Poland for the Jubilee of Our Lady of Czestochowa and in order "to be with my compatriots at a particularly difficult moment in the hisory of Poland." He said he would continue "to consider as my own every true good of my homeland as though I were still living in this land, and perhaps even more because of the distance."

The Moral Victory Needed

"Only a moral victory can draw society out of division and restore unity. Such an order can be both the victory of the governed as well as at the same time the victory of those who govern," Pope John Paul said in a homily June 17 during a Mass at the Dziesieciolecia Stadium in Warsaw. He said that "mutual dialogue and agreement" represent the way of achieving the needed moral vicotory.

He reminded the overflow crowd at the stadium of Poland's right to sovereignty. And he repeated the message of peace which he said "the Holy See constantly addresses to all nations and states, es-

‚ecially those upon which there rests the greatest responsibility for the cause of peace in the contemporary world."

In a homily that recounted numerous events from the history of Poland, the Pope said that "it is difficult to understand the history of our country, the 'yesterday' and 'today' of our history, without Christ." He referred to the "difficult period" that Poland has experienced in recent times, saying: "You yourselves, my dear compatriots, know this better than I, even if I too have lived deeply the whole eperience of these years since August, 1980."

Call to Polish Youth

Polish youth were addressed by Pope John Paul June 18 during his visit to Czestochowa where he celebrated the 600th anniversary of the arrival of the icon of Our Lady of Czestochowa in Poland.

The Virgin of Jasna Gora, he said, "knows your sufferings, your difficult youth, your sense of injustice and humiliation, the lack of prospects for the future that are so often felt, perhaps the temptations to flee to some other world."

He called Polish youth to a profound relationship with values, with truth. This, he explained, is the cost of true freedom. "We do not want a Poland which costs us nothing," he added.

He expressed thanks for all the proofs of solidarity given by the Polish people, including Polish young people, during recent and difficult times. Solidarity, in the sense of remaining open to others and their concerns, is part of the call of Our Lady of Jasna Gora, he said.

The call of Jasna Gora also is a call to responsibility "for this great common inheritance whose

name is Poland." Moreover, the call of Jasna Gora is a call to be a person with a conscience. This, he said, is a fundamental point which can never be minimized, especially in "circumstances which seem to favor our tolerance of evil and the fact that we easily excuse ourselves from this, especially if adults do so."

Jasna Gora, Place of Freedom

"Here we have always been free," Pope John Paul II said in a homily June 19 during a Mass at Czestochowa for the closing of the Jubilee of Our Lady of Czestochowa. He explained:

"It is difficult to express in a different way what the image of the Queen of Poland became for all Poles during the time when their homeland was wiped off the map of Europe as an independent state. Yes! Here at jasna Gora there also rested the hope of the nation and the persevering effort toward the recovery of independence."

The sovereignty of Poland was a theme of the Pope's homily.

In a remark widely interpreted as a veiled admonition to the Soviet Union, he said: "The nation is truly free when it can shape itself as a community determined by unity of culture, language and history. The state is firmly sovereign when it governs society and also serves the common good of society and allows the nation to realize its own subjectivity, its own identity."

At Jasna Gora, Pope John Paul said, the Polish people "learned the fundamental truth about the freedom of the nation: The nation perishes if it deforms its spirit; the nation grows when its spirit is ever more purified, and no external power is able to destroy it!"

POPE JOHN PAUL ON PILGRIMAGE AT LOURDES

The Holy Father, on his 19th trip abroad Aug. 14 and 15, 1983, visited the Marian sanctuary at Lourdes on a pilgrimage of devotion and commemoration of the 150th anniversary of the Virgin Mary's apparitions there and the 50th anniversary of the canonization of St. Bernadette Soubirous. He also took the occasion to suggest that, in lieu of a definite birthdate of Mary, the current Holy Year of the Redemption be a commemoration of the 2,000th anniversary of her birth.

Events

On Aug. 14, the Pope arrived at the Tarbes-Ossun airport at about mid-afternoon. He met for an hour with French President Francois Mitterand before proceeding to Lourdes 10 miles away. He addressed 100,000 people in the Grotto of Massabielle, where he called Lourdes a place of special grace. He took poart in the traditional candlelight procession in the evening, and after‑ wards addressed 200,0000 people in a plea for freedom for those laboring under various forms of persecution and oppression.

He met with priest-confessors and sisters in the morning of Aug. 15 before celebrating the Mass of the Solemnity of the Assumption of Mary in the shrine meadow before an assembly of 250,000 persons. Afterwards, he met with bishops and prayed

with and addressed young people in the shrine basilica. His last act of the visit was a stroll among sick and handicapped persons in the grotto; he shook hands and embraced many of them after speaking to them about the mystery of suffering.

The Pope left Lourdes shortly before 9:00 p.m. for the flight back to Rome.

The World's Need of Conversion

This was the theme of the Pope's address on arrival at the Grotto of Massabielle Aug. 14.

"It seems to me that there is a particular grace at Lourdes. The message is sober and clear, but fundamental." The world has a need of conversion.

"Today, the very sense of sin has partly disappeared because the sense of God is being lost. There has been an idea of constructing a humanism without God, and the faith is ceaselessly in danger of appearing to be the peculiarity of a few, without a necessary role for the salvation of all."

What Mary showed at Lourdes is that "awareness of sin is possible, along with awareness of the merciful love of God . . . who changes the heart of the sinner."

The effort at conversion and penance which is associated with Lourdes is especially in harmony with the current Holy Year of the Redemption: "Lourdes is a place where one undoubtedly understands (the) Redemption better than elsewhere, and where millions of pilgrims will live this Jubilee" of the Holy Year.

Subtle Forms of Persecution

Forms of persecution for the faith sometimes differ in modern times from those of earlier centuries, said the Pope in an address after the candlelight procession of Aug. 14.

"Today, to prisons, concentration camps, hard labor, expulsion from one's own country, have been added other forms of punishment, less remarked upon but more subtle: not a bloody death, but a sort of civil death; not only segregation in a prison or in a camp, but permanent restriction of personal freedom or social discrimination."

On every continent there are witnesses to the faith who put up with daily privations of the kind that are often ignored or forgotten by public opinion. Among them are "parents who are refused the possibility of securing for their children an education built on their faith."

(In the French context, some observers took this comment as a reference to the plan of the French socialist government to nationalize Catholic schools.)

The Pope also referred to others who are persecuted for their faith, including believers in various nations who are forced to meet secretly because their religious community is not authorized; dispersed religious forbidden to live in community and carry out their apostolic works; young persons impeded from entering a seminary or place of religious training; and others who, because of their faith, risk deprivations in their careers or studies.

POPE JOHN PAUL IN AUSTRIA

The Holy Father joined Austrians Sept. 10 to 13, 1983, for the celebration of their Katholikentag (Catholic Day), a celebration marking the close of a year-long program of study and prayer for the nation's Catholics. The visit, his 20th abroad since becoming Pope, also coincided with the observance of an historic anniversary.

Following is an NC round-up account of the visit.

Pope John Paul II pleaded for East-West unity, concord among religions and Catholic spiritual renewal during his Sept. 10 to 13, 1983, visit to Austria, a political and cultural crossroads between Eastern and Western Europe.

He also defended human rights and urged a more just international order, emphasizing that the Church's concern in those areas is based on the Gospel and not on partisan interests in international politics.

Greeting of Peace and Freedom

In his first major talk, at Vienna's Heroes Square shortly after his arrival Sept. 10, the Pope opened with a peace greeting to Austria and its seven neighboring nations of both Eastern and Western Europe.

To a crowd of some 100,000, including about 70 bishops from East and West, he emphasized Europe's unity in "the deep Christian roots and the human and cultural values which are sacred to all Europe."

While noting the continent's history of political and religious divisions, he urged fresh efforts "for peace and justice, for the rights of man and Christian solidarity among peoples." For the Christian, he said, "love is stronger than hatred or revenge."

Apparently referring to Soviet domination of Eastern Europe, Pope John Paul commented that "the Austria of today — sadly, not all of Europe — is free of foreign domination and military violence, free from immediate threat from the outside."

Historic Anniversary

One of the reasons for the papal trip to Austria was to mark the 300th anniversary of the breaking of the Turkish siege of Vienna by Polish Christian troops in 1683. Referring to that event, the Pope noted that atrocities were committed by both sides, to their "equal shame."

"We are aware that the language of weapons is not the language of Jesus Christ," he said.

"Armed conflict," he added, "is in every case an inevitable evil, from which Christians in tragic circumstances cannot escape. But here too the Christian commandment of love of one's enemy, of mercifulness, is binding."

He urged Austrians to make the tricentenary observances "not a celebration of victory in war but a celebration of the peace we now enjoy with grateful hearts."

He also urged religious toleration and understanding in contrast to the enmity of three centuries earlier. Many Moslems living in Austria today, he said, "may serve as a model for us in their devout worship of the one God."

The Holocaust of European Jews in World War II, he added, "admonishes us to seize every opportunity for promoting human and spiritual understanding so that we can stand before God together and serve humanity in his spirit."

Speaking to thousands of young people later that evening in Vienna's soccer stadium, the Pope praised their interest in human rights, peace and ecology, and urged them to work for an end to human and religious divisions.

Outdoor Mass

On Sept. 11, at an outdoor Mass for nearly a quarter of a million Austrian Catholics who had gathered in a drizzling rain to mark the closing of a year of spiritual renewal throughout the Church in Austria, Pope John Paul declared that technological progress has not made God "expendable."

He urged family prayer and reminded Catholics of "the Church's binding invitation to take part in the celebration of Holy Mass every Sunday."

Shortly before the mid-morning Mass, the Pope met with leaders of other Christian churches. Lamenting the religious discord, intolerance and persecution of past ages, he declared the Catholic Church's determination to pursue Christian unity.

After centuries of hostility, he said, "we have 'rediscovered' each other in the true sense of the word" in the ecumenical movement since the Second Vatican Council.

Mission of the Church

At a meeting that evening with Austrian governmental leaders, the Pope emphasized that the Church's mission is "religious and spiritual," not political, and that it "respects the responsibility of the state, without interfering with its political tasks."

"But it is for the sake of the Gospel entrusted to it that the Church also proclaims, as Vatican II emphasizes, 'the rights of man,' " he said.

The Church's spiritual mission leads it "to deal resolutely with the contemporary concerns of man; to advocate justice, peace and coexistence in human dignity; and to uphold morality both within the family and the society," he said.

Before his meeting with Austrian leaders, the Pope met with sick, handicapped and elderly persons, stopping to converse with many of them individually and recalling his own period of recovery from an assassination attempt in 1981.

The Pope warned that the world was moving from a "postwar" to a "new pre-war situation" as he met with diplomats stationed in Vienna following his meeting with government officials. Calling diplomacy "the art of peace," he urged the representatives of governments to work to ease tensions and create the conditions for international progress.

Need for Moral Progress

At a meeting Sept. 12 with scientists and artists, the Pope reiterated pleas for moral progress to accompany technological progress.

"It is not science and technology as such that threaten mankind, but their disengagement from moral values," he said.

He encouraged the growing concern of scientists for the moral implications of their work.

"Across the borders of countries and power blocs," he said, "a scientific world community is taking shape which, on ethical grounds, is no longer prepared to accept that the fate of man is threatened by genetic manipulation, biological experiments and the sophistication of chemical, bacteriological and nuclear weapons," he said.

In an evening speech to workers, the Pope criticized job discrimination against women, ethnic minorities, the elderly and the handicapped. He also supported the trade union movement and praised Austria for its integration of foreign workers into national life.

Visit to Marian Shrine

The Pope ended his four-day stay in Austria Sept. 13 with a visit to Mariazell, the country's main Marian shrine. At Mariazell, 60 miles from Vienna, he paid tribute to the 269 people killed when a Soviet jet shot down a South Korean passenger plane. He also prayed for victims of violence in other parts of the world.

"How could we forget today, above all, the dead whom the fratricidal war in Lebanon claims on both sides, as well as the victims of violence in Latin America and Africa, and finally also the dead from the recent tragic shooting down of the South Korean aircraft," he said. He departed from his prepared text to mention the shooting down of the airliner.

The Pope also visited the tomb of Hungarian Cardinal Jozsef Mindszenty, who is buried at the shrine site. Cardinal Mindszenty was a symbol of church opposition to communism in the 1950s when he was imprisoned by the communist government in Hungary.

THE MINISTER OF THE EUCHARIST

This is the text of a letter from the Congregation for the Doctrine of the Faith to bishops throughout the world concerning ordained priests as the only ones who can celebrate the Eucharist. The letter was made public Sept. 9, 1983.

The text was circulated by the NC Documentary Service, Origins, Sept. 15, 1983 (Vol. 13, No. 14)

I. INTRODUCTION

1. In teaching that the priestly or hierarchical ministry differs essentially and not only in degree from the common priesthood of the faithful, the Second Vatican Council expressed the certainty of faith that only bishops and priests can confect the Eucharistic Mystery. Although all the faithful indeed share in the one and the same priesthood of Christ and participate in the offering of the Eucharist, it is only the ministerial priest who, in virtue of the sacrament of holy orders, can confect the Eucharistic Sacrifice in the Person of Christ and offer it in the name of all Christian people.

2. In recent years, however, certain opinions have come to be promulgated and at times trans-

lated into practice which deny the above teaching and consequently cause harm to the innermost life of the Church. Such opinions, which are widespread in various forms and with different lines of argument, have begun to attract some of the faithful themselves, either because they claim to be based on a scholarly foundation or because they are presented as responding to the needs of the pastoral care and sacramental life of Christian communities.

3. That is why this Sacred Congregation, prompted by a desire to offer its particular services to the bishops in a true collegial spirit, wishes to restate here some of the essential points of the Church's doctrine on the minister of the Eucharist, transmitted by her living tradition and expressed in previous documents of the magisterium. The Congregation takes full account of the integral vision of the priestly ministry as presented by the Second Vatican Council, but in the present situation it considers it a matter of urgency to make clear the essential role of the priest.

II. ERRONEOUS OPINIONS

1. The promoters of these new opinions maintain

that every Christian community, from the very fact it is united in the name of Christ and thus enjoys his undivided presence (cf. Mt. 18:20), is endowed with all the powers which the Lord wished to give to his Church.

It is asserted, moreover, that the Church is apostolic in the sense that all those who have been washed in baptism and incorporated into her, having been made sharers in the priestly, prophetic and royal office of Christ, are also truly successors of the Apostles. From the fact that the whole Church was prefigured in the Apostles, it would then follow that the words of institution of the Eucharist addressed to them were intended for everyone.

2. As a consequence, although necessary for the good ordering of the Church, the ministry of bishops and priests would not differ from the common priesthood of the faithful with respect to the participation in the priesthood of Christ in the strict sense, but only insofar as its exercise is concerned. The so-called role of moderating the community — including also that of preaching and presiding at the Eucharist — would therefore be only a simple mandate conferred for the orderly functioning of the community itself, but it ought not to be "sacralized." The call to such a ministry would not amount to a new "priestly" capacity — strictly speaking — and for that reason the term "priesthood" is generally avoided — nor would it impart any character with ontological significance for the state of the ministers, but would simply give expression before the community that the original power conferred in the sacrament of baptism had become effective.

False Idea of Apostolicity

3. In virtue of the apostolicity of the single local communities, in which Christ would be no less present than in an episcopal structure, each community, no matter how small, in the event of its being deprived for some time of such a constituent element as the Eucharist, could "reappropriate" its original powers. Also, it would have the right of designating its own president and animator and conferring on him all the necessary faculties for leading the community itself, including that of presiding at and consecrating the Eucharist. It is moreover asserted that God himself would not refuse in such circumstances to grant, even without a sacramental rite, the power he normally gives through sacramental ordination.

Such is the conclusion also reached by the fact that the celebration of the Eucharist is often understood simply as the action of the local community, which is gathered together to commemorate in the breaking of bread the Last Supper of the Lord. It would therefore be more a fraternal celebration in which the community comes together and gives expression to its identity than the sacramental renewal of the sacrifice of Christ, whose saving power extends to everyone, be they present or absent, living or dead.

4. Ironically, erroneous opinions regarding the necessity of ordained ministers for the celebration of the Eucharist have even led some to place less and less value upon the sacraments of orders and the Eucharist in their catechesis.

III. THE DOCTRINE OF THE CHURCH

1. Although they may be expressed in various ways with different nuances, all these opinions lead to the same conclusion: that the power to confect the sacrament of the Eucharist is not necessarily connected with sacramental ordination. It is evident that such a conclusion is absolutely incompatible with the faith as it has been handed down, since not only does it deny the power conferred on priests, but it undermines the entire apostolic structure of the Church and distorts the sacramental economy of salvation itself.

2. According to the teaching of the Church, the word of the Lord and the divine life which he has given to us have been destined from the very beginning to be lived and shared in a single body, which the Lord builds up for himself throughout the ages. This body, which is the Church of Christ, is continually endowed with the gifts of ministries by him "from whom the whole body, nourished and knit together through its joints and sinews, grows with a growth that is from God" (Col. 2:19).

This structure of ministries finds clear expression in sacred tradition in the powers entrusted to the Apostles and their successors: to sanctify, to teach and to govern in the name of Christ. The apostolicity of the Church does not mean that all believers are Apostles, not even in a collective sense, and no community has the power to confer apostolic ministry, which is essentially bestowed by the Lord himself. Therefore, when the Church in her creeds calls herself apostolic, she expresses, besides the doctrinal identity of her teaching with that of the Apostles, the reality of the continuation of the work of the Apostles by means of the structure of succession in virtue of which the apostolic mission is to endure until the end of time.

This apostolic succession which constitutes the entire Church as apostolic is part of the living tradition which has been for the Church from the beginning, and continues to be, her particular form of life. And so, those who cite isolated texts of Scripture in opposition to this living tradition in trying to justify new structures have strayed from the truth.

3. The Catholic Church, which has developed through the ages and continues to grow by the life given to her by the Lord through the outpouring of the Holy Spirit, has always maintained her apostolic structure, faithful to the tradition of the Apostles which lives and endures in her.

When she imposes hands on those to be ordained and invokes upon them the Holy Spirit, she is conscious of handing on the power of the Lord, who makes the bishops, as successors of the Apostles, partakers in a special way of his threefold priestly, prophetic and royal mission. In turn, the bishops impart, in varying degrees, the office of their ministry to various persons in the Church.

And so, even though all the baptized enjoy the same dignity before God, in the Christian community, which was deliberately structured hierarchically by its divine Founder, there have existed from its earliest days specific apostolic powers deriving from the sacrament of holy orders.

Priest Acts in Persona Christi

4. Included among these powers which Christ entrusted exclusively to the Apostles and their successors is the power of confecting the Eucharist. To the bishops alone, and to the priests they have made sharers in their ministry which they themselves have received, is reserved the power of renewing in the Mystery of the Eucharist what Christ did at the Last Supper.

In order that they may be able to carry out their work, especially a work so important as confecting the Eucharistic Mystery, our Lord marks out in a spiritual manner those whom he calls to the episcopate and to the priesthood. He does this with a special sign through the sacrament of orders, a sign also called a "character" in solemn documents of the Church's magisterium. In this way he so configures them to himself that, when they pronounce the words of consecration, they do not act on a mandate from the community but " *'in persona Christi,'* which means more than just 'in the name of Christ' or 'in the place of Christ' since the celebrant, by reason of this special sacrament, identifies himself with the eternal High Priest, who is both author and principal agent of his own Sacrifice in which truly no one can take his place." Since it is of the very nature of the Church that the power to consecrate the Eucharist is imparted only to the bishops and priests who are constituted its ministers by the reception of holy orders, the Church holds that the Eucharistic Mystery cannot be celebrated in any community except by an ordained priest, as expressly taught by the Fourth Lateran Council.

Individual faithful or communities who, because of persecution or lack of priests, are deprived of the Holy Eucharist for either a short or longer period of time, do not thereby lack the grace of the Redeemer. If they are intimately animated by a desire for the sacrament and united in prayer with the whole Church, and call upon the Lord and raise their hearts to him, by virtue of the Holy Spirit, they live in communion with the whole Church, the living body of Christ, and with the Lord himself. Through their desire for the sacrament in union with the Church, no matter how distant they may be physically, they are intimately and really united to her and therefore receive the fruits of the sacrament; whereas those who would wrongly attempt to take upon themselves the right to confect the Eucharistic Mystery end up by having their community closed in on itself.

None of this derogates from the responsibility of bishops and priests and all members of the Church to pray that "the Lord of the harvest" will send workers according to the needs of the people and the times (cf. Mt. 9:37,ff), and to work with all their energy to make the Lord's call to the priestly ministry heard and welcomed, with humble and generous heart.

IV. CALL TO VIGILANCE

In recalling these points to the attention of the pastors of the Church, the Sacred Congregation for the Doctrine of the Faith desires to assist them in the ministry of feeding the flock of the Lord with the food of truth, of safeguarding the deposit of faith and of keeping intact the unity of the Church. It is necessary to be strong in faith and to resist error even when it masquerades as piety, so that by professing truth in love we may embrace in the love of the Lord those who have strayed (cf. Eph. 4:15).

Catholics who attempt to celebrate the Eucharist outside the sacred bond of apostolic succession established by the sacrament of orders exclude themselves from participating in the unity of the single body of the Lord. They neither nourish nor build up the community, they tear it apart.

Responsibility of Bishops

Therefore, it is the responsibility of the bishops to see to it that the erroneous opinions mentioned above do not continue to be spread either in catechetics or in the teaching of theology and, above all, to see to it that such theories are not put into practice. Whenever cases of this sort are discovered, it is their sacred responsibility to denounce them as completely foreign to the celebration of the Eucharistic Sacrifice and offensive to the community of the Church. If they should find that some catechists are even minimizing the central importance for the Church of the sacraments of holy orders and the Eucharist, they should likewise do all they can to correct so distorted a teaching. For in fact it is to us that these words were addressed: "Preach the word, be urgent in season and out of season, convince, rebuke and exhort, be unfailing in patience and in teaching . . . always be steady, endure suffering, do the work of an evangelist, fulfill your ministry" (2 Tm. 4:2-5).

In these circumstances, therefore, let this collegial concern find such a concrete application that the undivided Church, even in the variety of local churches working together, may keep safe what was entrusted to her by God through the Apostles. Fidelity to the will of Christ and the Christian dignity itself require that the faith handed down remain the same so that it may bring peace to all believers (cf. Rom. 15:13).

The Supreme Pontiff, John Paul II, in an audience granted to the undersigned Cardinal Prefect, gave his approval to this letter, drawn up in the ordinary session of this Sacred Congregation, and ordered its publication.

At Rome, from the offices of the Sacred Congregation for the Doctrine of the Faith, Aug. 6, 1983, Feast of the Transfiguration of Our Lord.

Cardinal Joseph Ratzinger, Prefect; Archbishop Jerome Hamer, O.P., Secretary.

COMMENT

Archbishop John R. Quinn, chairman of the Bishops' Committee on Doctrine, in a letter addressed Sept. 8 to people of the Archdiocese of San Francisco, commented on the foregoing letter from the Congregation for the Doctrine of the Faith. He said, in part:

"This document is a fresh occasion for all the

Church to deepen its faith and its gratitude to Christ for the great and treasured gifts of the Eucharist and the priesthood. It is an occasion also to renew and deepen our conviction about the central importance of the priesthood for the life, the vitality and the continuity of the Church. In the power of that conviction, the whole Church should be challenged to pray for priests that they may be holy and fruitful servants of Christ in the midst of his people. We should all be challenged as well to pray for vocations to the priesthood so that all the other ministries and charisms in the Church may be nourished and energized by the faithful preaching of the word of God and the celebration of the sacrifice and sacraments of salvation.

"The Church is not merely a human organization. Its origin is in the risen Christ who died on the cross and sent the Holy Spirit."

PROMULGATION OF THE REVISED CODE OF CANON LAW

Following are excerpts from the apostolic constitution "Sacrae Disciplinae Legis" ("Of the Sacred Discipline of Law") with which Pope John Paul II promulgated the revised Code of Canon Law Jan. 25, 1983.

The text was circulated by the N.C. Documentary Service, Origins, Feb. 10, 1983 (Vol. 12, No. 35).

Over the course of the centuries, the Catholic Church has regularly reformed and renewed the laws of canonical discipline so that, in constant fidelity to her divine Founder, these should adapt themselves well to the saving mission confided to her. Moved by this same purpose and finally bringing to fulfillment the expectation of the whole Catholic world, I today, Jan. 25, 1983, dispose publication of the (revised) Code of Canon Law.

Purpose and Nature of the Code

This Code has arisen from a single intention, that of restoring Christian living. All the work of the (Second Vatican) Council actually drew its norms and its orientation from such an intention.

A . . . question . . . arises about the very nature of the Code of Canon Law. In order to answer this question well, it is necessary to recall the distant heritage of law contained in the books of the Old and New Testaments, from which, as from its first spring, the whole juridical legislation of the Church derives.

Christ the Lord did not in fact will to destroy the very rich heritage of the law and the prophets which had been forming over the course of the history and experience of the people of God in the Old Testament. On the contrary, he gave fulfillment to it (cf. Mt. 5:17). Thus, in a new and more lofty way, it became part of the inheritance of the New Testament.

Therefore, although when expounding the paschal mystery, St. Paul teaches that justification is not obtained through the works of the law but through faith (cf. Rom. 3:28; Gal. 2:16), he does not thereby exclude the obligatory force of the Decalogue (cf. Rom. 13:28; Gal. 5:13-25 and 6:2), nor does he deny the importance of discipline in the Church of God (cf. 1 Cor. 5 and 6). The writings of the New Testament, therefore, allow us to understand the importance of discipline even better and to understand better how discipline is more closely connected with the salvific character of the Gospel message itself.

Church's Prime Legislative Document

Since this is so, it seems clear enough that the Code in no way has as its scope to substitute for faith, grace, the charisms, and especially charity in the life of the Church or the faithful. On the contrary, its end is rather to create such order in ecclesial society that, assigning primacy to love, grace and charisms, it at the same time renders more active their organic development in the life both of the ecclesial society and of the individuals belonging to it.

Inasmuch as it is the Church's prime legislative document, based on the juridical and legislative heritage of revelation and tradition, the Code must be regarded as the necessary instrument whereby due order is preserved in both individual and social life and in the Church's activity. Therefore, besides containing the fundamental elements of the hierarchical and organic structure of the Church, laid down by her divine Founder or founded on apostolic or at any rate most ancient tradition, and besides outstanding norms concerning the carrying out of the task mandated to the Church herself, the Code must also define a certain number of rules and norms of action.

Suits the Nature of the Church

The instrument the Code is fully suits the Church's nature, for the Church is presented, especially through the magisterium of the Second Vatican Council, in her universal scope, and especially through the Council's ecclesiological teaching. In a certain sense, indeed, this new Code may be considered as a great effort to transfer that same ecclesiological or conciliar doctrine into canonical language. And, if it is impossible for the image of the Church described by the Council's teaching to be perfectly converted into canonical language, the Code nonetheless must always be referred to that very image, as the primary pattern whose outline the Code ought to express as well as it can by its own nature.

From this derive a number of fundamental norms by which the whole of the new Code is ruled, of course within the limits proper to it as well as the limits of the very language befitting the material.

It may rather be rightly affirmed that from this comes that note whereby the Code is regarded as a complement to the magisterium expounded by the Second Vatican Council.

Key Elements

The following elements are most especially to be noted among those expressing a true and genuine image of the Church: the doctrine whereby the church is proposed as the people of God and the hierarchical authority is propounded as service. In addition, the doctrine which shows the Church to be a "communion" and from that lays down the mutual relationships which ought to exist between the particular and universal church and between collegiality and primacy. Likewise, the doctrine whereby all members of the people of God, each in the manner proper to him, share in Christ's three-fold office of priest, prophet and king. To this doctrine is also connected that regarding the duties and rights of the Christian faithful, particularly the laity. Then there is the effort which the Church has to make for ecumenism.

If, therefore, the Second Vatican Council brought out old and new from the treasury of tradition, and if its newness is also contained in these other forms, it is clear that the Code, too, contains that note of fidelity in newness and newness in fidelity, and that it conforms to this as regards its own material and its particular manner of expression.

Code Necessary for the Church

Indeed, the Code of Canon Law is extremely necessary for the Church. Since it is established for the sake of the manner of her social and visible framework, the Church needs it for her hierarchical and organic structure to be visible; so that exercise of the offices and tasks divinely entrusted to her, especially her sacred power and administration of the sacraments, should be rightly ordered; so that mutual relations of the Christian faithful may be carried out according to justice based on charity, with the rights of all being safeguarded and defined; so that we may then prepare and perform our common tasks, and that these, undertaken in order to live a Christian life more perfectly, may be fortified by means of the canonical laws.

Thus, canonical laws need to be observed because of their very nature. Hence it is of the greatest importance that the norms be carefully expounded on the basis of solid juridical, canonical and theological foundations.

In consideration of all these things, it is naturally to be hoped that this new canonical legislation will be an effective instrument which the Church herself may use to perfect herself in accordance with the Second Vatican Council, so that she may make herself ever more equal to her salvific task in this world.

Promulgation

Relying on divine grace, borne up by the authority of the blessed Apostles Peter and Paul, assenting to the certain knowledge and the prayers of the bishops of the whole world who collaborated with us in collegial affection, we, by the supreme authority we exert, and which is to hold good in the future by virtue of this our constitution, promulgate the present Code such as it has been digested and inspected; we command that it shall have force henceforth for the universal Latin Church and we give it to be guarded by the ward and vigilance of all those to whom it applies.

In order, however, that all may more accurately convey these prescripts rightly and may be able to get to know them clearly before they enter into effect, we decree and command that they shall be endowed with obligatory force from the first day of Advent of the year 1983 (Nov. 27), all ordinances, constitutions and privileges (even those worthy of special and individual mention), and customs notwithstanding.

We therefore exhort all our beloved children to observe the precepts laid down with sincere mind and ready will, borne up by hope that a fervent discipline may burgeon again in the Church and that thereby salvation of souls will be made always easier, under the protection of the most Blessed Virgin Mary, Mother of the Church.

Given at Rome, the 25th day of January of the year 1983, in the Vatican Palace, in the fifth year of our pontificate.

Joannes Paulus PP II.

REVISED CODE OF CANON LAW

Pope John Paul II promulgated a revised Code of Canon Law Jan. 25, 1983, with the apostolic constitution *Sacrae Disciplinae Legis* ("Of the Sacred Discipline of Law") and announced it would go into effect the following Nov. 27.

Promulgation of the Code marked the completion of the last major reform in the Church stemming from the Second Vatican Council.

Purpose

The revised Code was designed to replace the one which had been in effect since 1918. Framed in the context of pastoral concern, enactments of the Council, reforms introduced by Pope Paul VI and related developments, its 1,752 canons are grouped in seven books covering general norms, the people of God, the teaching office of the Church, the sanctifying office of the Church, temporal goods of the Church, sanctions and juridical procedures.

The principal purpose of the revision was not to break new ground in law but to incorporate into a new code of general law valid contents of the former Code along with developments that had been put in place in church law since 1918, especially since the Second Vatican Council.

Guiding Principles

When Pope John XXIII announced Jan. 25, 1959, that he was going to convoke the Second Vatican Council, he also called for a revision of the existing Code of Canon Law. His successor, Paul VI, appointed a commission for this purpose in 1963 and subsequently enlarged it. The commission, which began its work after the conclusion of the Council in 1965, was directed by the 1967 assembly of the Synod of Bishops to direct its efforts in line with 10 guiding principles. The bishops said the revised Code should:

• be juridical in character, not just a set of broad moral principles;

• be intended primarily for the external forum (regarding determinable fact, as opposed to the internal forum or private conscience);

• be clearly pastoral in spirit;

• incorporate most of the faculties bishops need in their ministry;
• provide for subsidiarity or decentralization;
• be sensitive to human rights;
• state clear procedures for administrative processes and tribunals;
• be based on the principle of territoriality;
• reduce the number of penalties for infractions of law;
• have a new structure.

The commission carried out its mandate with the collegial collaboration of bishops all over the world and in consultation and correspondence with individuals and bodies of experts in canon law, theology and related disciplines. The group finished its work in 1981 and turned its final draft over to Pope John Paul at its final plenary meeting in October of that year.

Features

The revised Code is shorter (1,752 canons) than the one it replaces (2,414 canons).

It is more pastoral and flexible, as well as more theologically oriented than the former Code.

And it gives greater emphasis than its predecessor to a number of significant facets and concepts in church life.

One of them, along with the hierarchical constitution of the Church, is the underlying notion of the *communio* or community of all members of the Church.

Another is the central significance of the sacraments and their far-reaching ramifications in the lives of the people of God.

The Code provides for greater participation by lay persons in the teaching, sanctifying and governing missions of the Church.

With respect to marriage, it stresses the covenant concept of the sacrament, emphasizes the pastoral responsibility of the Church to couples preparing for marriage and in marriage, and gives canonical expression to the already recognized annulling effect of personality deficiency in verifiable cases.

Changes in law regarding censures limit the penalty of automatic excommunication to seven crimes rather than more than 30 as in the Code of 1918.

Of general relevance and interest are the canons which deliniate the rights and obligations of all the faithful and of lay persons in particular.

(See other articles: Promulgation of the Revised Code of Canon Law, Contents of the Code, Rights and Obligations of All the Faithful, Rights and Obligations of Lay Persons, Liturgical Law and Canon Law, Essential Elements in Church Law on Religious Life.)

CONTENTS OF THE CODE

Following is a general index of the contents of the revised Code of Canon Law.

Book I, General Norms
(Canons 1-203)

Canons in this book cover: church laws in general, custom and law, general decrees and instructions, administrative acts, statutes, physical and juridical persons, juridical acts, the power of governing, ecclesiastical offices, prescription (rights having the force of law), the reckoning of time.

Book II, The People of God
(Canons 204-746)

Canons in Part I cover: the obligations and rights of all the faithful, the obligations and rights of lay persons, sacred ministers and clerics, personal prelatures and associations of the faithful.

Canons in Part II cover the hierarchic constitution of the Church under the headings: the supreme authority of the Church and the college of bishops, particular churches and the authority constituted in them, councils of particular churches and the internal order of particular churches.

Canons in Part III cover institutes of consecrated life and societies of apostolic life.

Book III, The Teaching Office of the Church
(Canons 747-833)

Canons under this heading cover: the ministry of the divine word, the missionary action of the Church, Catholic education, the instruments of social communication and books in particular, and the profession of faith.

Book IV, The Sanctifying Office of the Church
(Canons 834-1253)

Canons under this heading cover: each of the seven sacraments — baptism, confirmation, the Eucharist, penance, anointing of the sick, holy orders and matrimony; other acts of divine worship including sacramentals, the Liturgy of the Hours, ecclesiastical burial; the veneration of saints, sacred images and relics; vows and oaths.

Book V, Temporal Goods of the Church
(Canons 1254-1310)

Canons under this heading cover: the acquisition and administration of goods, contracts and the alienation of goods, wills and pious foundations.

Book VI, Sanctions in the Church
(Canons 1311-1399)

Canons in Part I cover crimes and penalties in general: the punishment of crimes in general, penal law and penal precept, persons subject to penal sanctions, penalties and other punishments, the application and cessation of penalties.

Canons in Part II cover penalties for particular crimes: crimes against religion and the unity of the Church; crimes against the authorities of the Church and the liberty of the Church; the usurpation of church offices and crimes in exercising office; false accusation of a confessor; crimes against special obligations; crimes against human life and liberty; a general norm regarding the punishment of external violations of divine and canon law not specifically covered in the Code.

Book VII, Procedures
(Canons 1400-1752)

Judicial proceedings are the principal subjects of canons under this heading: tribunals and their personnel, parties to proceedings, details regarding litigation and the manner in which it is conducted, special proceedings — with emphasis on matrimonial cases.

RIGHTS AND OBLIGATIONS OF ALL THE FAITHFUL

The following rights are listed in Canons 208-223 of the revised Code of Canon Law; additional rights are specified in other canons.

They are all equal in dignity because of their baptism and regeneration in Christ.

They are bound always to preserve communion with the Church.

According to their condition and circumstances, they should strive to lead a holy life and promote the growth and holiness of the Church.

They have the right and duty to work for the spread of the divine message of salvation to all peoples of all times and places.

They are bound to obey declarations and orders given by their pastors in their capacity as representatives of Christ, teachers of the faith and rectors of the Church.

They have the right to make known their needs, especially their spiritual needs, to pastors of the Church.

They have the right, and sometimes the duty, of making known to pastors and others of the faithful their opinions about things pertaining to the good of the Church.

They have the right to receive help from their pastors, from the spiritual goods of the Church and especially from the word of God and the sacraments.

They have the right to divine worship performed according to prescribed rules of their rite, and to follow their own form of spiritual life in line with the doctrine of the Church.

They have the right to freely establish and control associations for good and charitable purposes, to foster the Christian vocation in the world, and to hold meetings related to the accomplishment of these purposes.

They have the right to promote and support apostolic action but may not call it "Catholic" unless they have the consent of competent authority.

They have a right to a Christian education.

They have a right to freedom of inquiry in sacred studies, in accordance with the teaching authority of the Church.

They have a right to freedom in the choice of their state of life.

No one has the right to harm the good name of another person or to violate his or her right to maintain personal privacy.

They have the right to vindicate the rights they enjoy in the Church, and to defend themselves in a competent ecclesiastical forum.

They have the obligation to provide for the needs of the Church, with respect to things pertaining to divine worship, apostolic and charitable works, and the reasonable support of ministers of the Church.

They have the obligation to promote social justice and to help the poor from their own resources.

In exercising their rights, the faithful should have regard for the common good of the Church and for the rights and duties of others.

Church authority has the right to monitor the exercise of rights proper to the faithful, with the common good in view.

RIGHTS AND OBLIGATIONS OF LAY PERSONS

In addition to rights and obligations common to all the faithful and those stated in other canons, lay persons are bound by the obligations and enjoy the rights specified in these canons (224-231).

Lay persons, like all the faithful, are called by God to the apostolate in virtue of their baptism and confirmation. They have the obligation and right, individually or together in associations, to work for the spread and acceptance of the divine message of salvation among people everywhere; this obligation is more urgent in those circumstances in which people can hear the Gospel and get to know Christ only through them (lay persons).

They are bound to bring an evangelical spirit to bear on the order of temporal things and to give Christian witness in carrying out their secular pursuits.

Married couples are obliged to work for the building up of the people of God through their marital and family life.

Parents have the most serious obligation to provide for the Christian education of their children according to the doctrine handed down by the Church.

Lay persons have the same civil liberty as other citizens. In the use of this liberty, they should take care that their actions be imbued with an evangelical spirit. They should attend to the doctrine proposed by the magisterium of the Church but should take care that in, questions of opinion, they do not propose their own opinion as the doctrine of the Church.

Qualified lay persons are eligible to hold and perform the duties of ecclesiastical offices open to them in accord with the provisions of law.

Properly qualified lay persons can assist pastors of the Church as experts and counselors.

Lay persons have the obligation and enjoy the right to acquire knowledge of doctrine commensurate with their capacity and condition.

They have the right to pursue studies in the sacred sciences in pontifical universities or faculties and in institutes of religious sciences, and to obtain academic degrees.

If qualified, they are eligible to receive from ecclesiastical authority a mandate to teach sacred sciences.

Lay men can be invested by liturgical rite and in a stable manner in the ministries of lector and acolyte.

Lay persons, by temporary assignment, can fulfill the office of lector in liturgical actions; likewise, all lay persons can perform the duties of commentator or cantor.

In cases of necessity and in the absence of the usual ministers, lay persons — even if not lectors or acolytes — can exercise the ministry of the word, lead liturgical prayers, confer baptism and distribute Communion, according to the prescripts of law.

Lay persons who devote themselves permanently or temporarily to the service of the Church are obliged to acquire the formation necessary for carrying out their duties in a proper manner.

They have a right to a remuneration for their service which is just and adequate to provide for their own needs and those of their families; they also have a right to insurance, social security and health insurance.

ESSENTIAL ELEMENTS IN CHURCH TEACHING ON RELIGIOUS LIFE

Fundamental norms of religious life were the subject of the concluding portion of a document released June 22, 1983, by the Congregation for Religious and Secular Institutes. The document, entitled "Essential Elements in the Church's Teaching on Religious Life as Applied to Institutes Dedicated to Works of the Apostolate," was backgrounded by enactments of the Second Vatican Council and related documents issued by the Holy See since 1965. The following excerpt is, among other things, a digest of Canon Law on religious life. The cited Canons are from Book II, Part III, of the revised Code of Canon Law (effective Nov. 27, 1983), under the title, "Institutes of Consecrated Life and Societies of Apostolic Life."

This excerpt is from the text circulated by the N.C. Documentary Service, Origins, July 7, 1983 (Vol. 13, No. 8).

Some Fundamental Norms

The revised Code of Canon Law transcribes into canonical norms the rich conciliar and postconciliar teaching of the Church on religious life. Together with the documents of the Second Vatican Council and the pronouncements of successive popes in recent years, it gives the basis on which current church praxis regarding religious life is founded. The natural evolution necessary for ordinary living will always continue, but the period of special experimentation for religious institutes, as provided by the motu proprio *Ecclesiae Sanctae II*, ended with the celebration of the second ordinary general chapter (of each institute) after the special chapter of renewal.

Now the revised Code of Canon Law is the Church's juridical foundation for religious life, both in its evaluation of the experience of experimentation and its looking to the future. The following fundamental norms contain a comprehensive synthesis of the Church's provisions.

Call and Consecration

1. Religious life is a form of life to which some Christians, both clerical and lay, are freely called by God so that they may enjoy a special gift of grace in the life of the Church and may contribute each in his or her own way to the saving mission of the Church.

2. The gift of religious vocation is rooted in the gift of baptism but is not given to all the baptized.

It is freely given and unmerited, offered by God to those whom he chooses freely from among his people and for the sake of his people.

3. In accepting God's gift of vocation, religious respond to a divine call, dying to sin (cf. Rom. 6:11), renouncing the world and living for God alone. Their whole lives are dedicated to his service and they seek and love above all else "God who has first loved us" (cf. 1 Jn. 4:10). The focus of their lives is the closer following of Christ.

4. The dedication of the whole life of the religious to God's service constitutes a special consecration. It is a consecration of the whole person which manifests in the Church a marriage effected by God, a sign of the future life. This consecration is by public vows, perpetual or temporary, the latter renewable on expiration. By their vows, religious assume the observance of the three evangelical counsels; they are consecrated to God through the ministry of the Church (Can. 607 and 654); and they are incorporated into their institute with the rights and duties defined by law.

5. The conditions for validity of temporary profession, the length of this period and its possible extension, are determined in the constitutions of each institute, always in conformity with the common law of the Church (Can. 655-658).

6. Religious profession is made according to the formula of vows approved by the Holy See for each institute. The formula is common because all members undertake the same obligations and, when fully incorporated, have the same rights and duties. The individual religious may add an introduction and-or conclusion, if this is approved by competent authority.

7. Considering its character and the ends proper to it, every institute should define in its consititutions the way in which the evangelical counsels of chastity, poverty and obedience are to be observed in its own particular way of life (Can. 598, 1).

Community

8. Community life, which is one of the marks of a religious institute (Can. 607, 2), is proper to each religious family. It gathers all the members together in Christ and should be so defined that it becomes a source of mutual aid to all, while helping to fulfill the religious vocation of each (Can. 602). It should offer an example of reconciliation in Christ and of the communion that is rooted and founded in his love.

9. For religious, community life is lived in a

house lawfully erected under the authority of a superior designated by law (Can. 608). Such a house is erected with the written approval of the diocesan bishop (Can. 609) and should be able to provide suitably for the necessities of its members (Can. 610, 2), enabling community life to expand and develop with that understanding cordiality which nourishes hope.

10. The individual house should have at least an oratory in which the Eucharist may be celebrated and is reserved so that it is truly the center of the community (Can. 608).

11. In all religious houses, according to the character and mission of the institute and according to the specifications of its proper law, some part (cloister) should be reserved to the members alone (Can. 667, 1). This form of separation from the world, which is proper to the purpose of each institute, is part of the public witness which religious give to Christ and to the Church (cf. Can. 607, 3). It is also needed for the silence and recollection which foster prayer.

12. Religious should live in their own religious house, observing a common life. They should not live alone without serious reason, and should not do so if there is a community of their institute reasonably near. If, however, there is a question of prolonged absence, the major superior with the consent of his or her council may permit a religious to live outside the houses of the institute for a just cause, within the limits of common law (Can. 665, 1).

Identity

13. Religious should regard the following of Christ proposed in the Gospel and expressed in the constitutions of their institute as the supereme rule of life (Can. 662).

14. The nature, end, spirit and character of the institute, as established by the founder or foundress and approved by the Church, should be preserved by all, together with the institute's sound traditions (Can. 578).

15. To safeguard the proper vocation and identity of the individual institutes, the constitutions of each must provide fundamental norms concerning the government of the institute, the rule of life for its members, their incorporation and formation, and the proper object of the vows (Can. 587).

16. The constitutions are approved by competent ecclesiastical authority. For diocesan institutes, this is the local ordinary; for pontifical institutes, the Holy See. Subsequent modifications and authentic interpretations are also reserved to the same authority (Can. 576 and 587, 2).

17. By their religious profession, the members of an institute bind themselves to observe the constitutions faithfully and with love, for they recognize in them the way of life approved by the Church for the institute and the authentic expression of its spirit, tradition and law.

Chastity

18. The evangelical counsel of chastity embraced for the kingdom of heaven is a sign of the future life and a source of abundant fruitfulness in an un-

divided heart. It carries with it the obligation of perfect continence in celibacy (Can. 599).

19. Discretion should be used in all things that could be dangerous to the chastity of a consecrated person (Can. 666).

Poverty

20. The evangelical counsel of poverty in imitation of Christ calls for a life poor in fact and in spirit, subject to work and led in frugality and detachment from material possessions. Its profession by vow for the religious involves dependence and limitation in the use and disposition of temporalities according to the norms of the proper law of the institute (Can. 600).

21. By the vow of poverty, religious give up the free use and disposal of goods having material value. Before first profession, they cede the administration of their goods to whomsoever they wish and, unless the constitutions determine otherwise, they freely dispose of their use and usufruct (Can. 668). Whatever the religious acquires by personal industry, by gift or as a religious, is acquired for the institute; whatever is acquired by way of pension, subsidy or insurance is also acquired for the institute unless the proper law states otherwise (Can. 668, 3).

Obedience

22. The evangelical counsel of obedience, lived in faith, is a loving following of Christ who was obedient unto death.

23. By their vow of obedience, religious undertake to submit their will to legitimate superiors (Can. 601) according to the constitutions. The constitutions themselves state who may give a formal command of obedience and in what circumstances.

24. Religious institutes are subject to the supreme authority of the Church in a particular manner (Can. 590, 1). All religious are obliged to obey the Holy Father as their highest superior in virtue of the vow of obedience (Can. 590, 2).

25. Religious may not accept duties and offices outside their own institute without the permission of a lawful superior (Can. 671). Like clerics, they may not accept public offices which involve the exercise of civil power (Can. 285, 3; cf. also Can. 672 with the additional Canons to which it refers).

Prayer and Asceticism

26. The first and principal duty of religious is assiduous union with God in prayer. They participate in the Eucharistic Sacrifice daily insofar as possible and approach the sacrament of penance frequently. The reading of Sacred Scripture, time for mental prayer, the worthy celebration of the Liturgy of the Hours according to the prescriptions of proper law, devotion to the Blessed Virgin, and a special time for annual retreat are all part of the prayer of religious (Can. 663, 664 and 1174).

27. Prayer should be both individual and communitarian.

28. A generous asceticism is constantly needed for daily conversion to the Gospel. For this reason, religious communities must not only be prayerful

groups but also ascetical communities in the Church. In addition to being internal and personal, penance must also be external and communal.

Apostolate

29. The apostolate of all religious consists first in the witness of their consecrated life, which they are bound to foster by prayer and penance (Can. 673).

30. In institutes dedicated to works of the apostolate, apostolic action is of their very nature. The life of the members should be imbued with an apostolic spirit, and all apostolic activity should be imbued with the religious spirit (Can. 675, 1).

31. The essential mission of those religious undertaking apostolic works is the proclaiming of the word of God to those whom he places along their path, so as to lead them toward faith. Such a grace requires a profound union with the Lord, one which enables the religious to transmit the message of the Incarnate Word in terms which today's world is able to understand.

32. Apostolic action is carried out in communion with the Church, and in the name and by the mandate of the Church (Can. 675, 3).

33. Superiors and members should faithfully retain the mission and works proper to the institute. They should accommodate them with prudence to the needs of times and places (Can. 677, 1).

34. In apostolic relations with bishops, religious are bound by Canons 678-683. They have the special obligation of being attentive to the magisterium of the hierarchy and of facilitating for the bishops the exercise of the ministry of teaching and witnessing authentically to divine truth.

Witness

35. The witness of religious is public. This public witness to Christ and to the Church implies separation from the world according to the character and purpose of each institute (Can 607, 3).

36. Religious institutes should strive to render a quasi-collective witness of charity and poverty (Can. 640).

37. Religious should wear the religious garb of the institute, described in their proper law, as a sign of consecration and a witness of poverty (Can. 669, 1).

Formation

38. No one may be admitted to religious life without suitable preparation (Can. 597, 3).

39. Conditions for validity of admission, for validity of novitiate, and for temporary and perpetual profession are indicated in the common law of the Church and the proper law of each institute (Can. 641-658). So also are provisions for the place, time, program and guidance of the novitiate and the requirements for the director of novices.

40. The length of time of formation between first and perpetual vows is stated in the constitutions in accordance with common law (Can. 655).

41. Throughout their entire life, religious should continue their spiritual, doctrinal and practical formation, taking advantage of the opportunities and time provided by superiors for this (Can. 661).

Government

42. It belongs to the competent ecclesiastical authority to constitute stable forms of living by canonical approval (Can. 576). To this authority are also reserved aggregations (Can. 580) and the approval of constitutions (Can. 587, 2). Mergers, unions, federations, confederations, suppressions and the changing of anything already approved by the Holy See, are reserved to that See (Can. 582-584).

43. Authority to govern in religious institutes is invested in superiors who should exercise it according to the norms of common and proper law (Can. 617). This authority is received from God through the ministry of the Church (Can. 618). The authority of a superior at whatever level is personal and may not be taken over by a group. For a particular time and for a given purpose, it may be delegated to a designated person.

44. Superiors should fulfill their office generously, building with their brothers or sisters a community in Christ in which God is sought and loved before everything. In their role of service, superiors have the particular duty of governing in accordance with the constitutions of their institute and of promoting the holiness of its members. In their person, superiors should be examples of fidelity to the magisterium of the Church and to the law and tradition of their institute. They should also foster the consecrated lives of their religious by their care and correction, their support and their patience (cf. Can. 619).

45. Conditions for appointment or election, the length of term of office for the various superiors, and the mode of canonical election for the superior general are stated in the constitutions according to common law (Can. 623-625).

46. Superiors must each have their own council, which assists them in fulfilling their responsibility. In addition to cases prescribed in the common law, proper law determines those cases in which the superior must obtain the consent or the advice of the council for validity of action (Can. 627, 1 and 2).

47. The general chapter should be a true sign of the unity in charity of the institute. It represents the entire institute and, when in session, exercises supreme authority in accordance with common law and the norms of the constitutions (Can. 631). The general chapter is not a permanent body; its composition, frequency and functions are stated in the constitutions (Can. 631, 2). A general chapter may not modify its own composition but it may propose modifications for the composition of future chapters. Such modifications require the approval of the competent ecclesiastical authority. The general chapter may modify those elements of proper law which are not subject to the authority of the Church.

48. Chapters should not be convoked so frequently as to interfere with the good functioning of the ordinary authority of the major superior. The nature, authority, composition, mode of procedure and frequency of meeting of chapters and of similar assemblies of the institute are determined ex-

actly by proper law (Can. 632). In practice, the main elements of these should be in the constitutions.

49. Provision for temporal goods (Can. 634-640) and their administration, as well as norms concerning the separation of members from the institute by transfer, departure or dismissal (Can. 684-704), are also found in the common law of the Church and must be included, even if only in brief, in the constitutions.

Conclusion

These norms, based on traditional teaching, the revised Code of Canon Law and current praxis, do not exhaust the Church's provision for religious life. They indicate, however, her genuine concern that the life lived by institutes dedicated to works of the apostolate should develop ever more richly as a gift of God to the Church and to the human family. In drawing up this text, which the Holy Father has approved, the Sacred Congregation for Religious and for Secular Institutes wishes to help those institutes to assimilate the Church's revised provision for them and to put it in its doctrinal context. May they find in it a firm encouragement to the closer following of Christ in hope and joy in their consecrated lives.

From the Vatican, on the feast of the Visitation of the Blessed Virgin Mary, May 31, 1983.

THE CHALLENGE OF PEACE: GOD'S PROMISE AND OUR RESPONSE

This summary of the pastoral letter, "The Challenge of Peace: God's Promise and Our Response," copyright ©1983 by the United States Catholic Conference, Washington, D.C., is used with permission. All rights reserved. A copy of the complete text may be ordered from the Office of Publishing Services, USCC, 1312 Massachusetts Ave. N.W., Washington, D.C. 20005.

The letter was approved by a vote of 238 to 9 at a special meeting of U.S. bishops May 2 and 3, 1983, in Chicago.

The Second Vatican Council opened its evaluation of modern warfare with the statement: "The whole human race faces a moment of supreme crisis in its advance toward maturity." We agree with the Council's assessment; the crisis of the moment is embodied in the threat which nuclear weapons pose for the world and much that we hold dear in the world. We have seen and felt the effects of the crisis of the nuclear age in the lives of people we serve. Nuclear weaponry has drastically changed the nature of warfare, and the arms race poses a threat to human life and human civilization which is without precedent.

We write this letter from the perspective of Catholic faith. Faith does not insulate us from the daily challenges of life but intensifies our desire to address them precisely in light of the Gospel which has come to us in the person of the risen Christ. Through the resources of faith and reason we desire in this letter to provide hope for people in our day and direction toward a world freed of the nuclear threat.

Exercise of Teaching Ministry

As Catholic bishops we write this letter as an exercise of our teaching ministry. The Catholic tradition on war and peace is a long and complex one; it stretches from the Sermon on the Mount to the statements of Pope John Paul II. We wish to explore and explain the resources of the moral-religious teaching and to apply it to specific questions of our day. In doing this we realize, and we want readers of this letter to recognize, that not all statements in this letter have the same moral authority. At times we state universally binding moral principles found in the teaching of the Church; at other times the pastoral letter makes specific applications, observations and recommendations which allow for diversity of opinion on the part of those who assess the factual data of situations differently. However, we expect Catholics to give our moral judgments serious consideration when they are forming their own views on specific problems.

The experience of preparing this letter has manifested to us the range of strongly held opinion in the Catholic community on questions of fact and judgment concerning issues of war and peace. We urge mutual respect among individuals and groups in the Church as this letter is analyzed and discussed. Obviously, as bishops, we believe that such differences should be expressed within the framework of Catholic moral teaching. We need in the Church not only conviction and commitment but also civility and charity.

Contribution to Public Debate

While this letter is addressed principally to the Catholic community, we want it to make a contribution to the wider public debate in our country on the dangers and dilemmas of the nuclear age. Our contribution will not be primarily technical or political, but we are convinced that there is no satisfactory answer to the human problems of the nuclear age which fails to consider the moral and religious dimensions of the questions we face.

Although we speak in our own name, as Catholic bishops of the Church in the United States, we have been conscious in the preparation of this letter of the consequences our teaching will have not only for the United States but for other nations as well. One important expression of this awareness has been the consultation we have had, by correspondence and in an important meeting held at the Vatican (January 18-19, 1983), with representatives of European bishops' conferences. This consultation with bishops of other countries, and, of course, with the Holy See, has been very helpful to us.

Positive View of Peace

Catholic teaching has always understood peace in positive terms. In the words of Pope John Paul II: "Peace is not just the absence of war. . . . Like a cathedral, peace must be constructed patiently and with unshakable faith." (Coventry, England, 1982.) Peace is the fruit of order. Order in human society must be shaped on the basis of respect for the transcendence of God and the unique dignity of each person, understood in terms of freedom, justice, truth and love. To avoid war in our day we must be intent on building peace in an increasingly interdependent world. In Part III of this letter we set forth a positive vision of peace and the demands such a vision makes on diplomacy, national policy and personal choices.

While pursuing peace incessantly, it is also necessary to limit the use of force in a world comprised of nation states, faced with common problems but devoid of an adequate international political authority. Keeping the peace in the nuclear age is a moral and political imperative. In Parts I and II of this letter we set forth both the principles of Catholic teaching on war and a series of judgments, based on these principles, about concrete policies. In making these judgments we speak as moral teachers, not as technical experts.

I. SOME PRINCIPLES, NORMS AND PREMISES OF CATHOLIC TEACHING

A. On War

1. Catholic teaching begins in every case with a presumption against war and for peaceful settlement of disputes. In exceptional cases, determined by the moral principles of the just-war tradition, some uses of force are permitted.

2. Every nation has a right and duty to defend itself against unjust aggression.

3. Offensive war of any kind is not morally justifiable.

4. It is never permitted to direct nuclear or conventional weapons to "the indiscriminate destruction of whole cities or vast areas with their populations. . . ." (*Pastoral Constitution on the Church in the Modern World*, No. 80.) The intentional killing of innocent civilians or non-combatants is always wrong.

5. Even defensive response to unjust attack can cause destruction which violates the principle of proportionality, going far beyond the limits of legitimate defense. This judgment is particularly important when assessing planned use of nuclear weapons. No defensive strategy, nuclear or conventional, which exceeds the limits of proportionality is morally permissible.

B. On Deterrence

1. "In current conditions 'deterrence' based on balance, certainly not as an end in itself but as a step on the way toward a progressive disarmament, may still be judged morally acceptable. Nonetheless, in order to ensure peace, it is indispensable not to be satisfied with this minimum which is always susceptible to the real danger of explosion." (Pope John Paul II, Message to U.N. Special Session on Disarmament, No. 8, June, 1982.)

2. No *use* of nuclear weapons which would violate the principles of discrimination or proportionality may be *intended* in a strategy of deterrence. The moral demands of Catholic teaching require resolute willingness not to intend or to do moral evil even to save our own lives or the lives of those we love.

3. Deterrence is not an adequate strategy as a long-term basis for peace; it is a transitional strategy justifiable only in conjunction with resolute determination to pursue arms control and disarmament. We are convinced that "the fundamental principle on which our present peace depends must be replaced by another, which declares that the true and solid peace of nations consists not in equality of arms but in mutual trust alone." (Pope John XXIII, Encyclical *Peace on Earth*, No. 113.)

C. The Arms Race and Disarmament

1. The arms race is one of the greatest curses on the human race; it is to be condemned as a danger, an act of aggression against the poor, and a folly which does not provide the security it promises. (Cf. *Pastoral Constitution*, No. 81; Statement of the Holy See to the United Nations, 1976.)

2. Negotiations must be pursued in every reasonable form possible; they should be governed by the "demand that the arms race should cease; that the stockpiles which exist in various countries should be reduced equally and simultaneously by the parties concerned; that nuclear weapons should be banned; and that a general agreement should eventually be reached about progressive disarmament and an effective method of control." (Pope John XXIII, *Peace on Earth*, No. 112.)

D. On Personal Conscience

1. *Military Service:* "All those who enter the military service in loyalty to their country should look upon themselves as the custodians of the security and freedom of their fellow countrymen; and when they carry out their duty properly, they are contributing to the maintenance of peace." (*Pastoral Constitution*, No. 79.)

2. *Conscientious Objection:* "Moreover, it seems just that laws should make humane provision for the case of conscientious objectors who refuse to carry arms, provided they accept some other form of community service." (*Pastoral Constitution*, No. 79.)

3. *Non-violence:* "In this same spirit we cannot but express our admiration for all who forego the use of violence to vindicate their rights and resort to other means of defense which are available to weaker parties, provided it can be done without harm to the rights and duties of others and of the community." (*Pastoral Constitution*, No. 78.)

4. *Citizens and Conscience:* "Once again we deem it opportune to remind our children of their duty to take an active part in public life, and to contribute towards the attainment of the common good of the entire human family as well as to that of their own political community. . . . In other words, it is necessary that human beings, in the intimacy of their own consciences, should so live and act in their temporal lives as to create a synthesis between scientific, technical and professional elements on the one hand, and spiritual values on the other." (Pope John XXIII, *Peace on Earth*, Nos. 146, 150.)

II. MORAL PRINCIPLES AND POLICY CHOICES

As bishops in the United States, assessing the concrete circumstances of our society, we have made a number of observations and recommendations in the process of applying moral principles to specific policy choices.

A. On the Use of Nuclear Weapons

1. *Counter Population Use:* Under no circumstances may nuclear weapons or other instruments of mass slaughter be used for the purpose of destroying population centers or other predominantly civilian targets. Retaliatory action which would indiscriminately and disproportionately take many wholly innocent lives, lives of people who are in no way responsible for reckless actions of their government, must also be condemned.

2. *The Initiation of Nuclear War:* We do not perceive any situation in which the deliberate initiation of nuclear war, on however restricted a scale, can be morally justified. Non-nuclear attacks by another state must be resisted by other than nuclear means. Therefore, a serious moral obligation exists to develop non-nuclear defensive strategies as rapidly as possible. In this letter we urge NATO to move rapidly toward the adoption of a "no first use" policy, but we recognize this will take time to implement and will require the development of an adequate alternative defense posture.

3. *Limited Nuclear War:* Our examination of the various arguments on this question makes us highly skeptical about the real meaning of "limited." One of the criteria of the just-war teaching is that there must be a reasonable hope of success in bringing about justice and peace. We must ask whether such a reasonable hope can exist once nuclear weapons have been exchanged. The burden of proof remains on those who assert that meaningful limitation is possible. In our view the first imperative is to prevent any use of nuclear weapons and we hope that leaders will resist the notion that nuclear conflict can be limited, contained or won in any traditional sense.

B. On Deterrence

In concert with the evaluation provided by Pope John Paul II, we have arrived at a strictly conditional moral acceptance of deterrence. In this letter we have outlined criteria and recommendations which indicate the meaning of conditional acceptance of deterrence policy. We cannot consider such a policy adequate as a long-term basis for peace.

C. On Promoting Peace

1. We support immediate, bilateral, verifiable agreements to halt the testing, production and deployment of new nuclear weapons systems. This recommendation is not to be identified with any specific political initiative.

2. We support efforts to achieve deep cuts in the arsenals of both superpowers; efforts should concentrate first on systems which threaten the retaliatory forces of either major power.

3. We support early and successful conclusion of negotiations of a comprehensive test ban treaty.

4. We urge new efforts to prevent the spread of nuclear weapons in the world, and to control the conventional arms race, particularly the conventional arms trade.

5. We support, in an increasingly interdependent world, political and economic policies designed to protect human dignity and to promote the human rights of every person, especially the least among us. In this regard, we call for the establishment of some form of global authority adequate to the needs of the international common good.

This letter includes many judgments from the perspective of ethics, politics and strategy needed to speak concretely and correctly to the "moment of supreme crisis" identified by Vatican II. We stress again that readers should be aware, as we have been, of the distinction between our statement of moral principles and of official Church teaching and our application of these to concrete issues. We urge that special care be taken not to use passages out of context; neither should brief portions of this document be cited to support positions it does not intend to convey or which are not truly in accord with the spirit of its teaching.

Key Questions

In concluding this summary we respond to two key questions often asked about this pastoral letter:

Why do we address these matters fraught with such complexity, controversy and passion? We speak as pastors, not politicians. We are teachers, not technicians. We cannot avoid our responsibility to lift up the moral dimensions of the choices before our world and nation. The nuclear age is an era of moral as well as physical danger. We are the first generation since Genesis with the power to threaten the created order. We cannot remain silent in the face of such danger. Why do we address these issues? We are simply trying to live up to the call of Jesus to be peacemakers in our own time and situation.

What are we saying? Fundamentally, we are saying that the decisions about nuclear weapons are among the most pressing moral questions of our age. While these decisions have obvious military and political aspects, they involve fundamental moral choices. In simple terms, we are saying that good ends (defending one's country, protecting freedom, etc.) cannot justify immoral means (the use of weapons which kill indiscriminately and threaten whole societies). We fear that our world and nation are headed in the wrong direction. More weapons with greater destructive potential are produced every day. More and more nations are seeking to become nuclear powers. In our quest for more and more security we fear we are actually becoming less and less secure.

Called To Be Peacemakers

In the words of our Holy Father, we need a "moral about-face." The whole world must summon the moral courage and technical means to say no to nuclear conflict; no to weapons of mass destruction; no to an arms race which robs the poor and the vulnerable; and no to the moral danger of a nuclear age which places before humankind indefensible choices of constant terror or surrender. Peacemaking is not an optional commitment. It is a requirement of our faith. We are called to be peacemakers, not by some movement of the moment, but by our Lord Jesus. The content and context of our peacemaking is set not by some political agenda or ideological program, but by the teaching of his Church.

Ultimately, this letter is intended as an expression of Christian faith, affirming the confidence we have that the risen Lord remains with us precisely in moments of crisis. It is our belief in this presence and power among us which sustain us in confronting the awesome challenge of the nuclear age. We speak from faith to provide hope for all who recognize the challenge and are working to confront it with the resources of faith and reason.

To approach the nuclear issue in faith is to recognize our absolute need for prayer: we urge and invite all to unceasing prayer for peace with justice for all people. In a spirit of prayerful hope we present this message of peace.

BACKGROUND OF THE LETTER

The pastoral letter originated from a lengthy discussion of the moral and religious dimensions of the arms race and related topics at the annual meeting of U.S. bishops in November, 1980, during which several speakers cited the need for an updated statement on war and peace.

In January, 1981, Archbishop John R. Roach, president of the National Conference of Catholic Bishops and the U.S. Catholic Conference, appointed an ad hoc committee to prepare the letter. Its members were Cardinal Joseph L. Bernardin (then Archbishop), chairman, Bishops Daniel P. Reilly of Norwich and George A. Fulcher of Lafayette, Ind., and Auxiliary Bishops Thomas J. Gumbleton of Detroit and John J. O'Connor of the Military Vicariate.

Wide-ranging consultations with diverse groups of witnesses — peace advocates, proponents of nuclear strategy, government and civilian figures, bishops of Europe as well as of the United States — preceded and accompanied the composition of three drafts. The third draft of more than 40,000 words was approved by a vote of 238 to 9 at a special NCCB-USCC meeting May 2 and 3, 1983, in Chicago.

WOMEN IN THE CHURCH: 1983 REPORT

The ordination of women to the priesthood was one of the subjects in an address delivered by Pope John Paul Sept. 5, 1983, at a meeting with 23 U.S. bishops at Castel Gandolfo.

The Question of Ordination

The bishop's pastoral "zeal will be manifested in supporting the dignity of women and every legitimate freedom that is consonant with their human nature and their womanhood. The bishop is called upon to oppose any and all discrimination of women by reason of sex. In this regard, he must likewise endeavor to explain as cogently as he can that the Church's teaching on the exclusion of women from priestly ordination is extraneous to the issue of discrimination and that it is linked rather to Christ's own design for his priesthood. The bishop must give proof of his pastoral ability and leadership by withdrawing all support from individuals or groups who, in the name of progress, justice or compassion, or for any other alleged reason, promote the ordination of woman to the priesthood. In so doing, such individuals or groups are in effect damaging the very dignity of women that they profess to promote and advance. All efforts made against the truth are destined to produce not only failure but also acute personal frustration. Whatever the bishop can do to prevent this failure and frustration by explaining the truth, is an act not only of pastoral charity but of prophetic leadership."

The Pope's remarks about the dignity of women and their right to freedom from discrimination by reason of sex reflected key points in the revised Code of Canon Law (see separate entry) concerning the rights of women in the categories of the faithful and of lay persons.

Traditional Teaching

The remarks also reaffirmed the traditional teaching of the Church set forth in 1977 in a declaration by the Congregation for the Doctrine of the Faith. The declaration stated that the ministerial priesthood is not a "human right" but a "totally gratuitous vocation" which cannot be described in terms of justice and rights.

The Pope called the exclusion of women from the priesthood a matter of "Christ's own design for the priesthood," and said it is "extraneous to the issue of discrimination."

"The point of the Pope's remarks," commented Archbishop John Whealon of Hartford, "is that, to encourage any groups favoring women's ordination, would be unreal in terms of theology."

Bishop Daniel Reilly of Norwich said: "I thought that, if he addressed the issue, he'd speak in this way. It's what he has been saying all along."

Msgr. Daniel Hoye, general secretary of the National Conference of Catholic Bishops, said the Pope was telling the bishops "not to give encouragement to the idea that the ordination of women to the priesthood is an open question."

He also said that the conference "has not supported any organization" in any activity promoting the ordination of women.

Support for Dignity and Freedom

The bishops' Ad Hoc Committee on Women in Society and the Church began a dialogue with members of the Women's Ordination Conference in 1978. After its conclusion in 1981, Bishop Michael F. McAuliffe, chairman, recommended expanded dialogue with women's organizations and also study of the possibility of the ordination of women deacons. This study of a cloudy subject is under way. (See Deaconess entry in Glossary.)

The operative principle for the Church and society, according to the Pope, is to support "the dignity of women and every legitimate freedom that is consonant with their human nature and their womanhood."

ABORTION-RELATED COURT DECISIONS

Decision on Akron Ordinance

The U.S. Supreme Court struck down June 15, 1983, major provisions of an Akron, O., ordinance regulating the practice of abortion. In so doing, it reaffirmed its key decisions of Jan. 22, 1973, against any such restrictions.

The Court, in a 6-to-3 decision, struck requirements:

• that abortions after the first trimester be performed in hospitals;

• that women seeking abortions be informed by their physicians of the development of the fetus and complications that could result from an abortion;

• that there be a 24-hour waiting period before the performance of an abortion.

The Court also struck down a Missouri law requiring that abortions after 12 weeks of pregnancy be performed in hospitals.

At the same time, the Court upheld two Missouri laws: one requiring the presence of a second physician during abortions after viability, the other requiring a pathology report for each abortion performed.

In the main dissent in the Akron case, Justice Sandra Day O'Connor argued that the trimester, or "three-stage," approach the Court had used in its abortion decisions "cannot be supported as a legitimate or useful framework for accommodating the woman's right and the state's interests."

Since 1973

Following is a chronological list of abortion-related decisions handed down by the U.S. Supreme Court and other courts since Jan. 22, 1973.

• In Roe v. Wade, the Court ruled, 7 to 2, Jan. 22, 1973: (1) During the first three months of pregnancy a woman's right to privacy is paramount. Accordingly, she has an unrestricted right to abortion with the consent and cooperation of a physician. (2) In the second trimester, the principle controlling legislation on abortion is the health or welfare of the mother, understood in the widest possible sense. (3) In the "state subsequent to viability," the controlling principles are the State's "interest in the potentiality of human life" and "the preservation of the life or health of the mother." These rulings canonized the absolutely private right of a woman to have an abortion and denied to the unborn the right to life.

• In Dole v. Bolton, also decided Jan. 22, 1973, the Court ruled, 7 to 2, against restrictions on facilities that could be used in performing abortions.

• In Danforth v. Planned Parenthood, the Court ruled, 6 to 3, July 1, 1976, against the constitutionality of state laws requiring spousal (in the case of a married woman) or parental (in the case of a minor) consent for an abortion.

• (The first of three versions of the Hyde Amendment was adopted by Congress Sept. 30, 1976, in an appropriations measure for the Department of Labor and the Department of Health, Education and Welfare. The amendment provided for limiting federal funding of abortions under Medicaid to cases of danger to the life of a mother and to cases of rape or incest reported in a required manner. See below.)

• An injunction against the amendment was issued Oct. 22, 1976, by U.S. District Court Judge John F. Dooling Jr., in a suit originally filed by Cora McRae.

• In Maher v. Roe, the Court ruled, 6 to 3, June 20, 1977, that the Constitution does not require states to pay for non-therapeutic (elective) abortions and does not require public hospitals to provide them.

• The Court set aside June 19, 1977, Judge Dooling's injunction against the Hyde Amendment and ordered him to restudy his ruling of the previous October in the light of its decision in Maher v. Roe.

• Funding restrictions of the Hyde Amendment went into effect Aug. 4, 1977, and the McRae case went back to the Dooling courtroom.

• The Court ruled, 6 to 3, Jan. 9, 1979, in Colautti v. Franklin against the constitutionality of a 1974 Pennsylvania law because of its vagueness about the timing of fetal viability. The decision had the effect of meaning that a woman exercising a legal right to have an abortion had the right to a dead fetus and that the doctor performing the abortion could not be charged civilly or criminally for the death of the fetus.

• In Bellotti v. Baird, the Court ruled, 8 to 1, July 2, 1979, against the constitutionality of a Massachusetts law requiring a minor to consult with her parents before having an abortion. In the absence of parental consent (which the Court ruled in 1976 was not required) or parental consultation (not required either), a court could clear the way for the abortion of a minor judged to be mature enough to have one.

• Judge Dooling ruled Jan. 15, 1980, against the constitutionality of the Hyde Amendment but stayed enforcement of his decision to permit an appeal to the Supreme Court.

• The Court responded Feb. 19, 1980, to Judge Dooling's action with a one-sentence order requiring federal and state governments to provide Medicaid funding for abortions deemed "medically necessary." The Court also agreed to rule on the constitutionality of the Hyde Amendment, in connection with another case (Williams v. Zbaraz) that originated in Illinois.

Hyde Amendment Constitutional

• In Harris v. McRae, the Court, with a 5-to-4 decision June 30, 1980, upheld the constitutionality of the Hyde Amendment and its restrictions on Medicaid abortion funding. The decision overturned the Dooling ruling, of Jan. 15, 1980.

While deciding that neither the federal government nor state governments are required to provide funding for "medically necessary" abortions, the Court noted that "abortion is inherently different from other medical procedures because no other medical procedure involves the purposeful termination of a potential life."

The Hyde Amendment provided: "None of the funds provided for in this paragraph shall be used to perform abortions except where the life of the mother would be endangered if the fetus were carried to term; or except for such medical procedures necessary for the victims of rape or incest, where such rape or incest has been reported promptly to a law enforcement agency or public health service."

Medicaid payment for "medically necessary" abortions continued for about two and one-half months after the decision of June 30, pending a ruling by the Supreme Court on petitions for reconsideration. The decision not to reconsider was announced Sept. 17 and payment was discontinued thereafter.

About two-thirds of the states dropped elective abortion funding from their Medicaid programs after the 1977 decision of the Supreme Court.

1981 Decisions

The Supreme Court, by a 6-to-3 vote in H.L. v. Matheson, upheld Mar. 23 the constitutionality of a Utah law requiring physicians to notify the parents of an unmarried, immature minor daughter seeking an abortion. The decision said: "Although we have held that a state may not constitutionally legislate a blanket, unreviewable power of parents to veto their daughter's abortion, a statute setting out a 'mere requirement of parental notice' does not violate the constitutional rights of an immature, dependent minor."

With another 6-to-3 vote in Gary-Northwest Indiana Woman v. Orr, the Court ruled Apr. 27 that states may outlaw the performance of abortions outside of hospitals for women more than three months pregnant. The Court declared that states may seek to protect a mother's health during the second trimester and may move to protect fetal life only during the final trimester.

Pro and Anti Groups

Right-to-life supporters — of many different classes, income levels, religious faiths, political and philosophical persuasions — number in the millions. Some of their leading organizations and movements are the National Right-to-Life Committee, Americans United for Life, the Ad Hoc Committee in Defense of Life, the Right to Life Crusade, March for Life and Americans Concerned for Life.

Far out in front of the pro-abortion ranks are the National Abortion Rights Action League, the National Organization of Women and Planned Parenthood.

Statistics

Statistics on legal abortions performed in the U.S. each year from 1972 to 1979 provide reliable indices of the magnitude of the challenge facing right-to-life proponents. The rising numbers of abortions and years, as reported by the Center for Disease Control, U.S. Department of Health and Human Services, were: 586,760 (1972), 615,831 (1973), 763,476 (1974), 854,853 (1975), 988,267 (1976), 1,079,430 (1977), 1,157,776 (1978), 1,251,921 (1979).

The total number of abortions performed annually worldwide is estimated in the range of 30 to 35 million.

Charges Against the Church

The Catholic Church is the largest and strongest institutional opponent of abortion, because of its firm teaching and practice on the subject, and also because of the number of its members who are against it.

Because this is so in a cultural climate favoring abortion and moral liberalism, the Church has been accused and charged with:
- dominating the pro-life movement;
- trying to force its views on others who do not share its faith;
- violating a peculiar interpretation of the principle of separation of Church and state.

These accusations have been implicit and explicit in reporting of the abortion controversy ever since it began.

The Church insists, however, on its right to speak and act on moral issues on an equal basis with others who claim rights of conscience and freedom to influence others in a society which is subject not only to the laws of man but, above all, to universal moral law.

BIOETHICS

Bioethics "can be defined as the systematic study, in the light of moral values and principles, of human conduct in the area of the life sciences and health care," according to Warren T. Reich, editor of the *Encyclopedia of Bioethics* published by Macmillan and Free Press (New York, 1980).

Subjects of study include: reproductive technologies, prenatal diagnosis, abortion, human experimentation, genetic intervention, behavior control, psychosurgery, definition of death, prolongation of life, euthanasia, right to privacy, allocation of scarce health resources, dilemmas in the maintenance of environmental health.

Two subjects of current concern are treated below: several others are reported in News Events under October, November and December, 1982, May and June, 1983.

The Pope John XXIII Medical-Moral Research and Education Center is devoted specifically to examining the full range of emerging bioethical issues in the light of Catholic theology. Founded in 1973 by the Catholic Health Association and located in St. Louis, the center is supported by memberships, contributions and grants.

Similar research is the focus of the Institute for Theological Encounter with Science and Technology, located at St. Louis University and under the direction of Father Robert A. Brungs, S.J.

Research and Human Dignity

Modern biological research, particularly genetic engineering, offers new hope for treating disease and increasing world food production, Pope John Paul told participants in a study week on biological experimentation sponsored by the Pontifical Academy of Scientists.

"The new techniques of modification of the genetic code in particular cases of genetic or chromosomic diseases will be a motive of hope for the great number of people affected by those maladies," he said Oct. 23, 1982.

While the Pope praised the development of experimental techniques such as the use of artificial models, tissue cultures and animal embryos, he rejected human fetal experimentation.

"I condemn," he said, "in the most explicit and formal way, experimental manipulations of the human embryo, since the human being, from conception to death, cannot be exploited for any purpose whatsoever."

Biological research must be "subject to moral principles and values which respect and realize in its fullness the dignity of man."

The Pontiff urged scientists to help solve the problems of developing nations and to work toward developing new food supplies, "since one of the greatest challenges that humanity must face, together with the danger of nuclear holocaust, is the hunger of the poor of the world."

Definition-of-Death Legislation

In the spring of 1983, the Administrative Committee of the National Conference of Catholic Bishops stated its policy with respect to certain legislative proposals. The policy was formulated in 1977 by the Bishops' Committee for Pro-Life Activities.

The policy "firmly opposes all legalization of euthanasia, opposes so-called right-to-die and death-with-dignity laws because of the threat which they pose to the dignity and rights of dying persons, and discourages the adoption of definition-of-death statutes."

Regarding definition-of-death legislation, the policy resolution states:

" 'Legislative proposals that attempt to define when death occurs are unnecessary. We oppose them because there is no demonstrated need for such laws, nor any assurance that they would accomplish the intended purpose. In addition, they easily open the door to direct euthanasia legislation.' "

In 1981, a Uniform Determination of Death Act was proposed for adoption by the President's Commission for the Study of Ethical Problems in Medicine and Biomedical and Behavioral Research. The proposal had the support of the American Medical Association, the American Bar Association and the National Conference of Commissioners on Uniform State Laws.

The commission urged the states to adopt a uniform statute defining death as either "irreversible cessation of circulatory and respiratory functions" or "irreversible cessation of all functions of the entire brain, including the brain stem."

Father Edward Bryce of the Bishops' Committee for Pro-Life Activities said such laws are unnecessary, that the possibility of amendment by states makes a uniform definition of death unlikely, and that such laws could become a "stepping stone" to euthanasia.

As of May, 1983, more than half of the state legislatures had adopted some form of brain-death legislation.

WORLD COUNCIL OF CHURCHES: SIXTH GENERAL ASSEMBLY

Nine hundred delegates of 300 churches took part in the sixth general assembly of the World Council of Churches July 24 to Aug. 11, 1983, in Vancouver, British Columbia, Canada.

Assembly activities were related to a theme statement which declared: "We must confess our faith in Jesus Christ, the life of the world, and renew our commitment to him. This faith, this commitment must be the basis for our action on the issues of peace, justice and human liberation."

Key Document

The most important action of the assembly was the overwhelming Protestant-Anglican-Orthodox vote of approval for an agreed statement on "Baptism, Eucharist and Ministry." Drawn up by the Faith and Order Commission and completed in Lima, Peru, in January, 1982, the document was called an historic breakthrough and foundation for ecumenical progress. The assembly referred BEM, as the document was dubbed, to member churches for hoped-for adoption by the end of 1984.

BEM provided the inspiration for the liturgical high point of the assembly, a "Feast of Life" attended by 3,000 persons in the morning of July 31.

The eucharistic service, also called the "Lima Liturgy," was designed by Reformed Church theologian Max Thurian of the French ecumenical community of Taize.

Report

The assembly reviewed progress and problems in interchurch relations and the movement toward Christian unity since the last such gathering in 1975, in Nairobi, Kenya.

Delegates received the fifth report of the Joint Catholic Protestant Working Group, which took over some of the functions of the former Joint Commission on Society, Development and Peace that was phased out of operation in 1979. In its report, the group announced a common goal of "visible unity in one faith and in one eucharistic fellowship," and acknowledged that the Catholic Church and the World Council of Churches accepted "mutual responsibility and accountability before the world" as agents of reconciliation and common witness.

The Rev. Philip Potter, general secretary of the WCC, declared in an official report that the council should continue its involvement in political and social issues despite criticism and allegations that it had funded support for revolutionary movements in Third World countries. He said the council should continue its "bias" and related works for the poor, for justice and peace.

In resolutions passed by the assembly, member churches were urged to press governments to conduct effective negotiations toward arms reduction and to halt the deployment of nuclear weapons in Europe. Nuclear deterrence was called morally unacceptable.

Justice and peace were linked in resolutions concerning blacks in South Africa, Christians in South Korea and refugees from Central America. Delegates denounced U.S. policy in Central America, praised Nicaragua, endorsed economic sanctions against South Africa and favored a homeland for Palestinians.

Papal Message

Pope John Paul addressed delegates to the assembly in a message read by Archbishop James Carney of Vancouver July 25. He assured participants of his "deep pastoral interest and closeness in prayer," and asked them to bear witness to the ever increasing longing of Christians today for unity.

He said: "This urgent task, which still encounters many difficulties, is indeed challenging and multi-faceted. It requires obeisance to the will of God and cooperation with his grace. It demands persevering faith and steadfast hope. Above all, it impels us to constant prayer and continual conversion."

Of his contacts with leaders of other churches, the Pontiff said they had "advanced the cause of Christian unity," and he hoped "that the present gathering in Vancouver will bring about even further progress toward this goal for which we all long."

Catholic Presence

Eighteen "delegated observers" appointed by the Vatican Secretariat for Promoting Christian Unity attended the assembly. Among them were American Father John F. Hotchkin of the U.S. Bishops' Committee on Ecumenical and Interreligious Affairs, Sister Mary Motte and Paulist Father Thomas Stransky.

Twelve Catholic theologians had collaborated with members of the Faith and Order Commission in composing the document on "Baptism, Eucharist and Ministry."

Several times during the assembly, mention was made of the decision by the Vatican in 1975 not to join the World Council of Churches. This decision "by no means denies the special importance of the WCC," declared Cardinal Johannes Willebrands, head of the Unity Secretariat, in a message to the delegates.

The Rev. Philip Potter was on record to the effect that WCC-Vatican relations had been "far more intense" than those with many member churches.

THE VATICAN COLLECTIONS: THE PAPACY AND ART

The first major exhibition of art from the Vatican holdings ever sent abroad was viewed by 855,939 persons during its first U.S. presentation Feb. 26 to June 12, 1983, at The Metropolitan Museum of Art in New York City. Additional presentations were scheduled at the Art Institute of Chicago July 23 through Oct. 16 and at the M.H. de Young Memorial Museum of the Fine Arts Museums of San Francisco Nov. 19 to Feb. 19, 1984.

The 237 works of art in "The Vatican Collections: The Papacy and Art" were drawn from the vast holdings within the Vatican, not only from the Vatican Museums but also from the Apostolic Vatican Library, St. Peter's Basilica, its Grotte and Treasury, and the papal apartments. The works ranged in date from Egyptian and classical antiquity to the 20th century.

The works chosen for the exhibition exemplified the range and magnitude of the artistic resources housed in the Vatican. They also reflected the history of papal patronage and the manner in which the popes commissioned, collected and preserved works of art from the time of the foundation of old St. Peter's Basilica to the present day.

A Few of the Works of Art

The following were among the works in the exhibition.

• the front of a sarcophagus, a key monument of early Christian art dating from about 340, depicting Christ giving a scroll of the New Law to St. Peter;

• a tapestry of Raphael's composition, of the "Miraculous Draft of Fishes," woven about 1519 in Brussels;

• a marble Roman copy of the Apollo Belvedere, dating from 130-140 A.D., the first known piece of antique sculpture in the papal collections;

• the Belvedere Torso, a fragmentary marble sculpture dating from the mid-first century B.C., in the Belvedere courtyard (of the papal residence) since the 16th century;

• a cruciform silver casket for a reliquary of the True Cross, made for Pope Paschal I (817-824);

• a panel painting of St. Jerome, one of the last works of Leonardo da Vinci's Florentine period and his only work in the Vatican or in Rome;

• "The Rest on the Flight (of the Holy Family) into Egypt," one of the most cherished devotional paintings of the 16th century;

• the powerful "Deposition" of Christ from the Cross, by Caravaggio in 1604;

• a late third-century marble figure considered to be one of the earliest depictions of the parable of the Good Shepherd;

• a 16-feet tall collage of the "Tree of Life," the full-scale model for a stained-glass window designed by Henri Matisse, one of the most esteemed modern religious decorations.

Attendance at the New York showing of the exhibition was second only to that of the 1.2 million persons who viewed "The Treasures of Tutankhamun" in 1978-79.

Corporation Sponsorship and Support

The U.S. tour of the exhibition was sponsored by Philip Morris, Inc., through a $3-million grant to The Metropolitan Museum of Art as the show's organizing museum. This was the largest contribution ever made to an art exhibition by a corporation. Pan Am was designated by the Metropolitan Museum as the official carrier of the exhibition. An indemnity was granted by the Federal Council on the Arts and Humanities.

Local corporate support for the installation and presentation of the exhibition at the Metropolitan Museum came from Manufacturers Hanover Corporation; Merrill Lynch, Pierce, Fenner & Smith, Inc.; and the Robert Wood Johnson, Jr., Charitable Trust.

Support for the installation and presentation of the exhibition at The Art Institute of Chicago was provided by major funding from Continental Illinois National Bank with additional support from the City of Chicago; for the exhibition at The Fine Arts Museums of San Francisco, by a generous grant of $600,000 from Standard Oil Company of California and the Chevron Companies.

REPORT ON SEMINARIES

Changes

Institutions for the training of candidates for the priesthood have undergone change in recent years and now include not only traditional free-standing, residential seminaries with relatively self-sufficient faculties and resources, but also coalitions and consortiums of pooled faculties and non-academic houses and places of formation for students pursuing studies elsewhere in Catholic and/or secular colleges and universities. A number of seminarians reported membership in consortiums which included Protestant schools of theology. This "represented for Roman Catholicism a degree of contact strikingly different from pre-Vatican II seminary training," according to a 1982 report by the National Association of Diocesan Ecumenical Officers.

The composition of student bodies in some academic programs has changed considerably with the enrollment of lay persons, including women, for the study of theology and preparation for various kinds of ministry in the Church. Between 1975 and 1979, there was a 35 per cent increase in the enrollment of non-seminarians in theological degree programs, according to a September, 1981, report.

Bishops' Program, Special Study

The academic, spiritual and pastoral preparation of students for the priesthood (diocesan and members of religious institutes) is subject to norms of the U.S. Bishops' Program of Priestly Formation. Approval of this program for the third time by the Congregation for Catholic Education was reported early in January, 1982.

Archbishop John R. Roach, president of the National Conference of Catholic Bishops, notified bishops in a letter dated Sept. 18, 1981, that the Holy See had ordered a comprehensive study of theological and college-level seminaries in this country. The purpose of the study was to determine how well seminaries are meeting the goals of academic, pastoral, liturgical and spiritual formation of candidates for the priesthood.

The study was placed under the direction of Bishop John A. Marshall of Burlington, past chairman of the Bishops' Committee on Priestly Formation and former spiritual director of the North American College in Rome. The executive secretary for the project was Father Donald Wuerl, former staff member of the Congregation for the Clergy.

Study Plan

A 103-page study instrument, approved by the Vatican and made public Aug. 17, 1983, contained comprehensive norms for evaluating a seminary's effectiveness and set up two principal phases for the study of each of the nation's theological seminaries.

The first phase was to consist of a written report in response to an extensive questionnaire on a wide range of subjects, including administrative structures and personnel, finances, research facilities, faculty composition and qualifications, student data, spiritual and pastoral programs, and future planning.

The second phase, the heart of the study, was to be handled in three-day visits to each seminary by a five-member team of experts — two bishops, a religious superior and two priests from seminary faculties — for the purpose of interviewing seminary personnel and students in order to analyse in depth the quality of the seminary's spiritual, liturgical, pastoral and academic preparation of students for the priesthood.

It was planned that appropriate reports and recommendations would be circulated among all interested parties, including the Vatican Congregation for Catholic Education.

The study instrument was to be used for the evaluation of more than 50 theological seminaries. Variations of the instrument were in work during the summer of 1983, for intended use in evaluating 200 or more other institutions — houses of formation, theological unions and collegiate (pre-theology) seminaries.

Msgr. William Baumgaertner sketched several problems affecting seminaries at a July 17 to 30, 1983, meeting with bishops and theological seminary officials. One is the trend toward admitting students who are not candidates for the priesthood, raising the question: Will schools be able to sustain the "identity of the ordination program" as the percentage of priesthood candidates declines? Secondly, an increasing reliance on part-time faculty, while helping to cut costs, may harm academic programs. There was also a feeling that the quality of seminary programs might be in jeopardy because of limited resources.

OCTOBER 1982

VATICAN

Doctors and Patients — The Holy Father urged more than 4,000 physicians Oct. 3 to "humanize" their work and to make their patients partners in the healing process. Addressing participants in the 15th World Congress of the International Federation of Catholic Medical Associations, he said: "The patient to whom you dedicate your care and your studies is not an anonymous individual . . . but a responsible person who must be called on to participate in the improvement of his own health and the achievement of healing."

Concern for Ecology — "The future of humanity and of the planet earth is in danger because of the deterioration of the relationship between man and his environment, in addition to the relationships among men, classes and nations," declared the Pope in an address Oct. 3. He spoke before a throng of about 40,000 people, including participants in a just concluded "Mother Earth" conference which, among other things, marked the 800th anniversary of the birth of St. Francis of Assisi.

European Crises — Addressing 72 prelates attending the Fifth Symposium of European Bishops Oct. 5, the Holy Father said that "the crises of European man are the crises of the Christian man," and that "the crises of European culture are the crises of Christian culture." He said that Europe was "crisscrossed by currents, ideologies and ambitions extraneous to the faith" or "directly opposed to Christianity."

The Rosary — The Pope made a strong appeal for devotion to the Rosary at a general audience of 20,000 persons Oct. 6. "It is a devotion very dear to Mary," he said, "and a prayer very useful for growing in virtue and in the practice of the Christian life. . . . I wish to exhort you to love it and to make frequent use of it for nourishing your spirituality."

The Arafat Meeting — The meeting of Pope John Paul with Yasir Arafat, head of the Palestine Liberation Organization, Sept. 15 at the Vatican "cannot in any way be interpreted as hostile to Israel and the Jewish people." So stated Cardinal Johannes Willebrands Oct. 7 in a letter to Julius Berman, chairman of the Conference of Presidents of Major American Jewish Organizations. Writing in the name of the Pope, Cardinal Willebrands said that during the meeting the Pontiff expressed hope for lasting peace in the Middle East, explicitly rejected violence and terrorism, and voiced support not only for a Palestinian homeland but also for the right of Israel to "its own security."

Teresian Anniversary — Pope John Paul noted the 400th anniversary of the death of St. Teresa of Avila in a taped message for Spanish radio and television broadcast Oct. 15. He said of the first female Doctor of the Church: "The quality of her literary works, the subtlety of her style, her unique spiritual witness and even her popularity as a woman of powerful intelligence, exquisite sensitivity and realism, are a luminous example that fills us with consolation and stimulates us with a message fruitful and valid for our age."

Hunger in the World — This was the theme of remarks by the Pope to some 50,000 persons in St. Peter's Square the day after the Oct. 16 observance of World Food Day. He said the event "makes us think that in the richer countries many people egotistically consume more of the fruits of nature, which God has given to all, than they share with others. . . . Let us pray so that the cry of the poor and the hungry may be heard, that in a spirit of true fraternity and cooperation the problem of hunger in the world may be finally overcome."

Clerical Dress — Priests residing in the Diocese of Rome were directed by Cardinal Ugo Poletti to wear clerical garb as a sign of their distinctive identity and consecration to pastoral and sacramental service. The cardinal's directive was issued Oct. 18 at the urging of Pope John Paul who said in a letter dated Sept. 8: "Many times (I have pointed out) the value and significance of this distinctive sign (of clerical dress), not only because it contributes to the propriety of the priest in his external behavior or in the exercise of his ministry, but above all because it gives evidence within the ecclesiastical community of the public witness that each priest is held to give of his own identity and special belonging to God."

The directive said, in part:

• "From now on, the obligation of clerical or religious garb for both diocesan and religious priests resident in the Diocese of Rome is confirmed in all its force."

• "The cassock or religious habit is obligatory in liturgical celebrations, in the administration of the sacraments, in the exercise of preaching. It is heartily recommended in the ambit of one's pastoral ministry."

Union of Bishops with the Pope — "The union . . . of the bishops of a local church with the Pope, as Bishop of Rome, is the guarantee of the worldwide union of the Church of Christ; and it remains the essential condition for the necessary internal freedom and self-determination of every local church." So stated the Holy Father Oct. 28 in an address to six bishops from West Germany and communist-governed East Germany.

Doctrine and Pastoral Practice — The close connection of doctrine with pastoral ministry was the subject of papal remarks to a group of bishops of northern England Oct. 29. The Pope said: "Every genuine pastoral initiative needs a strong doctrinal basis precisely because there can be no dichotomy between God's word and man's true well-being and happiness. . . . If it is true — and it is — that our pastoral solicitude must embrace our people in all their needs, it is also true that our greatest contribution to them is the proclamation of God's word in all its fullness and power. . . . As we transmit the word of God with pastoral fidelity, the world will often rebel, and it may accuse us of intransigence or irrelevance. But our criterion remains fidelity to Christ's word which, in turn, is synonymous with the true welfare of our brothers and sisters."

The Pope Also:

• Called on the bishops of Hungary Oct. 7 to resolve as soon as possible problems created by "base communities" of Catholics which did not conform to teachings of the Church or which refused the guidance of local church authorities.

• Condemned the outlawing of the Solidarity labor movement by the Polish government, calling it a "violation of fundamental rights," Oct. 10.

• Prayed Oct. 11, the 20th anniversary of the start of the Second Vatican Council, that its works "might be constantly fulfilled."

• Said that young people should be "the first witnesses of beauty and strength" against "acts of violence and hate," at a general audience Oct. 13.

• Praised the writings of Jacques Maritain on the 100th anniversary of the philosopher's birth, in a letter made public Oct. 20.

• Made the 57th pastoral visit of his pontificate to a parish in a suburb of Rome on Oct. 24, World Mission Day.

• Praised Cardinal Giovanni Benelli, who died of a heart attack Oct. 26, as "a man who had a lively sense of duty and who never spared himself in carrying it out."

Vatican Brief:

• St. Teresa of Avila should be properly called St. Teresa of Jesus, according to Msgr. Pietro Galavotti, an official of the Congregation for the Causes of Saints. "She was canonized in 1622 as St. Teresa of Jesus, and that has never changed," he said.

Saints and Blessed

Pope John Paul canonized three saints during the month.

• Franciscan Conventual Father Maximilian Kolbe, Oct. 10, who died in place of another man Aug. 14, 1941, at the Auschwitz concentration camp. The man whose life he saved, 81-year-old Franciscek Gajowniczek, was present at the canonization. Father Kolbe was given the title of Martyr.

• Marguerite Bourgeoys (1620-1700), foundress of the Congregation of Notre Dame de Montreal.

• Jeanne Delanoue (1666-1736), foundress of the Sisters of St. Anne of Providence.

The Holy Father also advanced the causes of nine other Servants of God for canonization by giving the title of Blessed to Jeanne Jugan, foundress of the Little Sisters of the Poor, and Italian Franciscan Father Salvatore Lilli and his seven Armenian companions who were martyred for the faith in 1895 in Turkey.

NATIONAL

Amerasian Children — Bringing Amerasian children from Vietnam, where they were regarded as outcasts, to the United States was "the humanitarian thing to do," declared Don Hohl, associate director of Migration and Refugee Services, U.S. Catholic Conference. He made the remark in reference to the arrival Oct. 3 of 11 children in Los Angeles. Private agencies estimated that there were approximately 25,000 Amerasians in Vietnam and well over 80,000 in all of Southeast Asia.

Spirit of St. Francis — Humility, poverty, obedience and love are characteristics of the spirit of St. Francis, Cardinal John J. Krol told a congregation of more than 1,500 persons Oct. 3 in Philadelphia. He told Franciscans marking the 800th anniversary of the birth of St. Francis of Assisi that his spirit was quite different from that of some religious who emphasize personal growth instead of growth in Christ and optional placement instead of obedience in assignments to ministry.

Unemployment — Massive unemployment in the U.S. was called one of the most pressing moral issues of the day by Auxiliary Bishop Eugene A. Marino Oct. 8 at a rally for jobs in Washington. He said: "Our nation simply cannot afford to have more than 10 million workers unemployed. . . . We cannot afford the significant increases in crime, disease, child abuse, infant mortality and suicide that are associated with high unemployment. . . . What we can least afford is the assault on human dignity that occurs every time another person is left without adequate employment."

Concern for Hispanic Catholics — "We are people impelled to cry out for justice," declared Auxiliary Bishops Francisco Garmendia of New York and Rene Valero of Brooklyn in a pastoral letter issued on the occasion of the Day of Hispanic Unity, Oct. 12. "We are summoned," they said, "to make a clear choice for the poor and to put ourselves at their service in building here a civilization of love. We are challenged to proclaim by the way we live the true relationship we have in Christ and the bonds of faith and unity that draw us together."

Christianity Confronts Modernity — James Hitchcock, addressing participants in a conference focused on this theme, said that in every area of morality "Christians now learn to exalt their own consciences, however flawed or insensitive, into the only working moral absolute." Christians uncomfortable with the divinity of Christ, he said, reject a Jesus who threatens judgment and focus instead on an image that suits them, turning him into "a political agitator, a clown, a kindly elder brother, a kind of therapist, even, as the marriage feast of Cana is now often interpreted, as a kind of easy-going hedonist." Hitchcock, a professor of history at St. Louis University, spoke at a conference sponsored by the Center for Pastoral Renewal Oct. 21 to 23 at Ann Arbor, Mich.

Evangelization — More than 1,300 persons participated in the third event, a meeting Oct. 21 to 24 in Miami, of the Fourth Annual National Catholic Lay Celebration of Evangelization. The purpose of the meeting, as well as of others held earlier in Minneapolis and Los Angeles, was to "demonstrate the Church's broad-based commitment to the priority placed on evangelism," and to prepare people of the Church "to reach out in a spirit of friendship and concern to share the Lord Jesus with their family, friends and neighbors."

Anti-Pornography Effort — The Rev. Donald E. Wildmon, a Methodist clergyman, announced late in the month that about 70 Catholic bishops had joined Episcopal and Methodist prelates and other Protestant church leaders in his campaign to combat pornography. The religious leaders endorsed "Articles of Concern" in which they urged: President Reagan to enforce obscenity laws, corporations to stop advertising in sex-oriented magazines, retail stores to stop selling such publications, video outlets and theaters not to show or sell pornographic films, TV cable systems not to broadcast such films, and newspapers and other media not to advertise X-rated movies.

Abortion Ruling — A state law requiring physicians to notify the parents of dependent girls under age 18 seeking an abortion was upheld by a federal district court judge in New Albany, Ind. The law, in effect since Sept. 1, was challenged by Planned Parenthood, which indicated it would appeal the ruling of Judge Cale Holder. (The law was struck down Aug. 26, 1983.)

Meetings — The National Association of the Holy Name Society concluded a four-day convention Oct. 3 in Philadelphia after delegates committed themselves to a campaign for pledges of prayer for the canonization of Blessed John Vercelli, founder of the society in 1274.

• More than 800 persons attended the 68th annual convention of the National Conference of Catholic Charities Oct. 5 to 10 in Detroit. In response to the theme, "Retooling for the 1980s — Strategies for Justice," delegates passed a resolution sounding their "alarm over the continuing erosion of the economic and social well-being of Americans."

• "Alternatives to Violence" was the focus of the annual meeting of Pax Christi USA Oct. 8 to 10 in Rochester, Minn. The meeting was attended by about 700 persons.

• The Federation of Diocesan Liturgical Commissions, meeting Oct. 11 to 14 in Buffalo, resolved to conduct a nationwide survey of attitudes and practices regarding the rite of the sacrament of penance.

• Speakers at a symposium on St. Teresa of Avila hailed the Carmelite mystic and Doctor of the Church as a spiritual guide for all Christians. The symposium, attended Oct. 15 to 17 by more than 500 persons at the Catholic University of America, marked the 400th anniversary of the saint's death.

• Catholic and Lutheran bishops held their eighth annual meeting Oct. 27 and 28 in Washington, under the auspices of Lutheran World Ministries and the Committee for Ecumenical and Interreligious Affairs of the National Conference of Catholic Bishops.

National Briefs:
• The U.S. Supreme Court let stand Oct. 4 a decision of a federal appeals court allowing F.E.L. Publications, Ltd., of Los Angeles to continue a six-year-old suit against the Archdiocese of Chicago for alleged illegal copying of copyrighted hymns.

• Carole V. Norris, former public relations director of the National Office for Black Catholics, was named the first director of the Office of Black Ministry for the Diocese of Brooklyn.

• Singer Kate Smith, a convert to Catholicism in 1965, was awarded the Medal of Freedom, the highest U.S. civilian award, Oct. 26.

• John T. Muthig, former chief of the Rome Bureau of NC News Service, was ordained to the priesthood Oct. 30 in Trenton, N.J.

Anti-Catholic Bigotry

The Catholic League for Religious and Civil Rights complained to *The New York Times* after the newspaper's New Jersey section published an opinion piece calling the Mass an act of "ritual cannibalism." The article, in the edition of Sept. 19, was written by Betty McCollister of Haddonfield, N.J. The paragraph in question read:

"Religion, clearly, is an essential element of human nature. It goes back a long time . . . possibly to our forerunners, who 500,000 years ago cracked human bones, as some tribes do today, to ingest manna from their dead owners. (What, after all, is the Catholic Mass but a kind of ritual cannibalism in which worshippers ingest the body and blood of their god?)"

Father Peter Stravinskas, in a letter to the newspaper, called the statement "a blatant example of anti-Catholic bigotry" totally irrelevant to the article's main theme (opposition to prayer in public schools). He said the offensive statement could have been deleted by editors without affecting the sense of the article.

INTERNATIONAL

Anti-Nuclear Appeal — Four days before U.S. and Soviet representatives resumed arms reduction talks in Geneva, 59 scientists from 31 nations urged their governments Oct. 2 to "renew and increase efforts" to stop the arms race and eventually achieve complete nuclear disarmament. They said: "All disputes that we are concerned with today, . . . which are not to be undervalued, seem to lose their urgency when compared to the hazards of nuclear war." Their "Declaration on the Prevention of Nuclear War" was released at the Vatican following a meeting sponsored by the Pontifical Academy of Sciences.

Lourdes Cure — The Lourdes Foundation announced Oct. 4 that the Marian shrine's 16-member International Medical Committee had concluded that there was no medical explanation for the recovery of Delizia Cirolli from terminal bone cancer.

It was also reported that the Church had officially recognized as attributable to prayer at the shrine only 64 of thousands of cures considered miraculous in other circles.

Dignity of Men and Women — At an Oct. 2 to 5 meeting with Catholic women from five continents, West German Bishop Joseph Cordes, vice president of the Pontifical Council for the Laity, called for "a fundamental change in mentality in vast sectors within and outside the Church" leading to "full recognition of the dignity of men and women in theory and practice." He said there was "still much to be done in the Church and society before men and women reach an effective co-responsibility in all spheres and at all levels." The bishop's view was contained in a communique issued after a meeting sponsored by the council and the World Union of Catholic Women's Organizations.

Another Massacre — Guatemala's Peace and Justice Commission reported that about 300 Cakchiquel Indians were killed by security forces Oct. 5 after they and another 3,000 persons displaced by fighting had agreed to leave temporary shelters and go to camps provided by the army. The army's tactic of isolating villagers and clearing them from various areas was in line with efforts to eliminate actual or potential aid to guerrillas. A priest familiar with the situation said the government was "openly engaged in genocide and persecution of the Church."

Solidarity Outlawed — With legislation passed Oct. 8, the Polish Parliament dissolved all labor unions in existence before the declaration of martial law on Dec. 13, 1981, put tight controls on the formation of new unions and placed strict limits on the right to strike. The action was called: "a violation of fundamental rights," by Pope John Paul; "a great pain to many of our believers," by Archbishop Jozef Glemp, primate of Poland; a "backward step," by President Reagan. Solidarity members and thousands of their sympathizers protested against the legislation with demonstrations and limited strike action, but to no avail.

Argentine Documents — The bishops of Argentina published a book containing a series of previously private communiques to the military government on behalf of political prisoners and families of persons missing after being abducted. The book was released as the government faced increasing civilian pressure to account for the large number of persons missing since the military took control of the government in March, 1976. It was estimated that the number of missing persons ranged from 6,000 to 15,000.

Lefebvre Successor — Thirty-year-old West German Father Franz Schmidberger was elected vicar general of the Priestly Society of St. Pius X and eventual successor to Archbishop Marcel Lefebvre as head of the dissident society. The election, which took place Sept. 14, was reported Oct. 11. Archbishop Lefebvre was suspended from the exercise of orders by Pope Paul VI in 1976 for ordaining priests without appropriate authorization.

Defense of Pastoral Work among Guerrillas — Bishop Arturo Rivera Damas, apostolic administrator of the Archdiocese of San Salvador, defended priests in pastoral ministry among guerrillas in El Salvador. "Doing pastoral work among the armed forces does not mean a priest becomes a soldier; doing the same work among non-believers does not mean he becomes one. And, by engaging in pastoral work in conflict zones does not mean that the priest becomes a guerrilla. So stated the bishop in a homily Oct. 11, a few days after military officials accused a number of priests of aiding guerrillas.

Support for Priests in Philippines — Cardinal Jaime Sin of Manila spoke out in defense of priests

under attack by the Filipino government because of their pastoral and social-service ministry to the poor. "No layman is ready to speak out right now" against violations of human rights, he said in an interview carried by Reuters Oct. 19. "If you are a layman now, you will land in the stockade. So, the priest takes over. If nobody else releases the feelings of the people, there will be a revolution." The cardinal's remarks were prompted by a series of recent incidents involving security agents and priests (one killed, several arrested and one with a bounty on his head), religious (a nun arrested) and nine lay persons (arrested).

Democracy Threatened in Honduras — In a statement issued Oct. 28, members of the Honduran Bishops' Conference said that guerrilla activity and government reaction to it were exacerbating a climate of fear that "could finish our democracy." They said: "Violence, terrorism, disappearances, mysterious encounters, assaults, robberies, kidnappings, all have caused individual and collective insecurity and appear to have increased in these past two years. . . . It is certain that this violence is a consequence in great part of that in neighboring countries (Nicaragua and El Salvador). But some of it also has support and causes in our own country." ‾

Lithuanian Priests Criticized — Priests frighten parents into sending their children to Mass, according to the Lithuanian Communist Party newspaper, *Sovietskaya Litva.* The newspaper cited this as the reason for the high level of church attendance by young Lithuanians. It also said that Christian belief was being spread by the West as a way of subverting youths in the Soviet Union.

International Briefs:

• Mexican President Jose Lopez Portillo unveiled a monument honoring 16th-century Dominican Father Anton de Montestinos, whom he called a pioneer defender of human rights of Indians in the Americas. The ceremony took place Oct. 12 by the Bay of Santo Domingo.

• The 24 members of the Sicilian Bishops' Conference reaffirmed Oct. 21 a long-standing order of excommunication against any Catholic "guilty of kidnapping or unjust and voluntary homicide."

Limited Marxist Influence

Although Marxism has influence in some sectors of the Church in Latin America, its impact is limited and indirect, according to Archbishop Alfonso Lopez Trujillo, president of the Latin American Bishops' Council. "It is primarily a bibliographical phenomenon," he said in an interview in New York early in the month. "There are some theologians who use Marxist analysis, and their books are read," he said; "but I don't believe this has a strong impact. At the basic level, the Church instinctively rejects these opinions." he added that Marxist influence was "practically nonexistent" among Latin American bishops.

Regarding Nicaragua, Archbishop Trujillo said the church-state situation there was "very serious" because of the "open Marxism" of the Sandinista government.

NOVEMBER 1982

VATICAN

Pastoral Trips — The Holy Father completed two pastoral trips during the month: to Spain, Oct. 31 to Nov. 9, and to Sicily, Nov. 20 and 21. (See separate entries.)

Praise for U.S. Bishops — The Pope "profoundly appreciates your ecclesial union with him and your strong desire to manifest sensitivity to the complexity and urgency of pastoral issues, particularly justice and peace." So stated a letter addressed in the name of the Holy Father to the bishops of the United States who met in Washington Nov. 15 to 18.

Vatican Employees — Pope John Paul, in a letter dated Nov. 20, indicated his support for reasonable demands of the Vatican lay employees' association. He said: "The remuneration for lay workers of the Apostolic See ought to correspond to the tasks performed, taking into consideration at the same time the responsibility which they have to support their families. . . . In a spirit of lively solicitude and of justice, studies will have to be made concerning what are their objective material needs and those of their families, including those pertaining to the education of their children and to a fitting insurance for their old age." The association, formed in 1979, had a membership of about 1,600; their monthly salaries ranged from $650 to $1,000.

Marriage Is a Covenant of Love — Addressing a general audience of 6,500 persons Nov. 24, the Pope said the sacramental nature of marriage expressed in St. Paul's Letter to the Ephesians shows that God intended marriage to be "a communion of persons in which a man and a woman would be united in truth and love." Through the sacrament, he added, God "has made available to husbands and wives the grace and strength which flow from the redemption of the body. . . . Thus they are helped to overcome the attraction of sin and to build a covenant of love." He described marriage as "an effective sign of the saving action of God" and as "an exhortation for the man and woman to participate consciously in the redemption of the body . . . by struggling against concupiscence and sin."

Vatican Bank and Banco Ambrosiano — Cardinal Agostino Casaroli, Vatican secretary of state, told a plenary meeting of cardinals Nov. 26 that banking experts appointed by the Vatican in July, 1982, said in a provisional report that the Vatican had no financial liability for the collapse of Banco Ambrosiano. Letters of patronage alleged as a reason for liability, he said, were not issued until after Banco Ambrosiano had made loans which were not repaid. He also noted that letters of patronage are not instruments of guarantee.

Cardinal Casaroli said the banking experts did not regard their report to be absolutely conclusive and advised continuing cooperation with Italian banking officials in an attempt to set the record straight. The Pope said at the closing session of the plenary assembly that "the Holy See is prepared to take all the steps required for an agreement on the part of both sides so that the whole truth can come to light."

A principal figure in the Ambrosiano affair was the bank's president, Roberto Calvi, who was found dead, an apparent suicide, June 18 in London.

Another principal, Archbishop Paul C. Marcinkus, head of the Vatican Bank, was cleared of allegations of misconduct in the report issued by the three Roman bankers.

Financial Disclosure and Practice — Two days after the conclusion of the plenary assemby of cardinals, Pope John Paul told a group of Belgian journalists Nov. 28 that he recognized the need to publish a statement of Vatican finances. The Catholic people have a right to be "judiciously informed" about the Vatican's financial needs and also about the use made of their contributions, he said.

The Pope had declared earlier in the month that the Vatican, while a sovereign state, did not "possess all the ordinary characteristics of a political community." It must, therefore, avoid certain activities proper to ordinary states: "The Apostolic See does not develop, nor can it develop, the economic activity that is characteristic of a state; and the production of economic goods and the enrichment of its revenues are excluded from its institutional aims."

The Pope Also:

• Was among world leaders who expressed their sympathy to officials and the people of the Soviet Union on the death Nov. 10 of Leonid I Brezhnev, president of the Presidium of the Supreme Soviet Republic.

• Made his 58th pastoral visit to a parish of Rome, San Giustino, Nov. 14.

• Met privately Nov. 18 with West German Chancellor Helmut Kohl, a Christian Democrat.

Vatican Briefs:

• Catholic and Anglican representatives met Nov. 9 and 10 at the Vatican to plan activities of the reconstituted Anglican-Roman Catholic International Commission.

• European peace and security can be achieved only through full respect for human rights and the approval of a "precise and realistic" plan for disarmament, declared Msgr. Francesco Canalini, a Vatican representative at the Conference on European Security and Cooperation. The conference of 35 nations reconvened Nov. 9 in Madrid.

• An 80-page document released Nov. 16 stressed the need for effective programs to increase the number and quality of vocations to the religious life. The document embodied conclusions reached during the Second International Congress of Bishops and Others Responsible for Church Vocations, held in May, 1981.

• Two U.S. couples — Virgil and Ann Dechant, Dr. Richard and Barbara McBride — were among 37 members named Nov. 22 to the Pontifical Council for the Family.

• Maj. Roland Buchs was named commander of the Swiss Guards Nov. 25.

Meetings of Cardinals

The Pope convoked two meetings of cardinals during the month.

• A 15-member council met Nov. 19 to 22 for study and discussion of Vatican finances and re-organization of the Curia.

• A plenary meeting was attended by 97 members Nov. 23 to 26. Matters outlined for discussion by Cardinal Agostino Casaroli were: "(1) reform of the Curia, with projected revision of the apostolic constitution *Regimini Ecclesiae Universae* of Aug. 15, 1967; (2) present state of the revision of the Code of Canon Law; (3) questions concerning the economic balance of the Holy See; (4) relations between the Institute for the Works of Religion (Vatican Bank) and the Banco Ambrosiano." Reports were also presented regarding plans and activities of the Pontifical Council for Culture, the Pontifical Council for the Family and the Congregation for the Sacraments and Divine Worship.

At the conclusion of the plenary meeting, the Holy Father announced that a Holy Year of Jubilee would be held in 1983 to commemorate the 1950th anniversary of the redemptive death and resurrection of Jesus.

NATIONAL

Episcopal Clergymen Ordained Priests — Fathers Dennis Kuhn and Daniel Munn, married former Episcopal clergymen, were ordained Catholic priests Nov. 1 for the dioceses of Charlotte and Savannah, respectively. After Father James Parker, they were the second and third Episcopal clergymen so ordained under conditions approved by the Congregation for the Doctrine of the Faith in June, 1980.

Religious Education Programs — Archbishop Pio Laghi, addressing a symposium on catechetics Nov. 2 in Washington, said that the greatest challenge facing American religious educators is to devise programs that "are doctrinally sound and complete, and yet have a tone, language and method capable of touching the heart." The apostolic delegate observed: "There is reason for satisfaction that in many areas of Catholic teaching our students appear to be learning essential doctrines about the Trinity and the Incarnation. There is, however, reason for concern that their knowledge and attitudes in the areas of ecclesiology and morality are inadequate. Their response to issues of morality that affect married life and chastity are especially an area for your attention and for concern. We know that the secular atmosphere, the negative impact of the media and peer pressure can influence the moral judgments of our students. We, however, must redouble our efforts to see that they have the opportunity to be fully and thoroughly exposed to the importance, the beauty and the relevance of the Church's moral teaching. . . . To deprive a young person of a comprehensive and intellectually stimulating and challenging presentation of the word of God and of the Church's devel-opment of revelation in her doctrinal and moral teaching, is to deprive him or her of a precious inheritance of faith to which he or she is entitled by baptism."

Nuclear Freeze Resolutions — In the largest single-issue referendum in the nation's history, voters in eight states and several cities and counties called for U.S. participation in a worldwide freeze on nuclear arms. Resolutions, purely advisory in nature, were approved Nov. 2 by substantial margins in Massachusetts, Michigan, Montana, New Jersey, North Dakota, Oregon and Rhode Island, and by a narrow margin in California. Resolutions were defeated in Arizona and in two small counties in Arkansas and Colorado.

Marketing the Message — This was the theme of the 11th annual general assembly of Unda-USA, the association of Catholic broadcasters and allied communicators, held Nov. 2 to 5 in Chicago. One speaker, Msgr. John Egan, special assistant to the president of the University of Notre Dame, suggested that Catholic communicators "endeavor not to pull people from the world but call them through the Church to an even fuller engagement in the world." Recipients of Gabriel Awards for 1982 included: Robert Keeshan of TV's "Captain Kangaroo," TV journalist Bill Moyers, and CBS-TV's "Bill," an entertainment program by Alan Landsburg Productions.

Breviary Suit Settled — Costello Publishing Co. of Northport, N.Y., and the National Conference of Catholic Bishops reached an out-of-court settlement during the summer in a lawsuit over a set of imported breviaries the publisher tried to distribute in the United States. The publisher sued the NCCB in 1976 for allegedly violating antitrust laws by advising retailers not to stock *Morning and Evening Prayer* because it lacked approval of the conference for official liturgical use in their country. The breviaries had the approval of the bishops of Australia, England, Wales and Ireland. Terms of the settlement, reported during the annual meeting of U.S. bishops, were not revealed.

Abortion Cases before the Supreme Court — The U.S. Supreme Court heard arguments Nov. 3 on laws — in Missouri, Virginia and Akron, Ohio — requiring various restrictions on the manner and circumstances under which abortions may be performed. Rulings on the cases were expected in 1983.

NCC Resolutions — The governing board of the National Council of Churches adopted a resolution of protest Nov. 3 against U.S. "involvement in activities designed to destabilize the government in Nicaragua, including financing of opponents of the government."

In other actions during the Nov. 3 to 5 meeting, the board voted to:

• join the National Anti-Klan Network;

• oppose efforts to curtail the jurisdiction of federal courts over issues such as busing and school prayer;

• oppose an amendment to require a balanced federal budget or legislative measures that would mandate balancing the budget "without regard to human need";

• refer back to the appropriate committee a resolution to end U.S. aid to Israel.

The board also put off for a year decision on whether a denomination organized primarily for homosexuals is eligible for membership in the National Council of Churches.

Staging of Play Cancelled — Operators of the Gateway Hotel in St. Louis announced Nov. 17 that they would not permit the play, "Sister Mary Ignatius Explains It All for You," to be staged on its premises. The announcement was made after Archbishop John L. May had called the play "a vile diatribe against all things Catholic." Writing in the archdiocesan *St. Louis Review,* he said: "From beginning to end, this play (by Christopher Durand) caricatures and ridicules every doctrine in the catechism and every Catholic value." Frances Noonan, president of the St. Louis chapter of the Catholic League for Religious and Civil Rights, called the play a "vile and malicious" presentation of Catholic teachings.

Assessment of Genetic Research — Genetic research and intervention should be assessed "in terms of the basic values at stake," including "the sacredness of human life itself." So stated Father Richard A. McCormick, S.J., in testimony Nov. 17 before a subcommittee of the House Committee on Science and Technology. The Georgetown University professor of ethics said the values at stake also included: "the meaning of ourselves as social beings, the interconnection of life systems, the meaning of sexuality, the family and individual self-identity, the goals of genetic research and its environmental effects, and the priorities of our research effort, especially as supported by the federal and state governments."

Professional Boxing Is Immoral — "Professional boxing as it is today cannot pass moral scrutiny," declared Jesuit Father Richard A. McCormick, one of several moral theologians who commented on the morality of the sport after the death Nov. 17 of Duk Koo Kim. The South Korean boxer died four days after being knocked out by Ray Mancini in the 14th round of a title fight in Las Vegas, Nev. "The aim of the contestants" in professional boxing, Father McCormick said, "is to render each other incapable of continuing and to cause harm." Quoting views he expressed in an article in *Sports Illustrated* in November, 1962, he added: "Theologians believe that, when a man pounds another into helplessness, scars his face, smashes his nose, jars his brain and exposes it to lasting damage, or when he enters a contest where this could happen to him, he has surpassed the bounds of reasonable stewardship of the human person."

Creation Science Teaching Unconstitutional — Federal District Court Judge Adrian Duplantier struck down Nov. 22 a 1981 Louisiana law requiring public schools to teach creation science as well as the theory of evolution. The law was challenged on the grounds that creation science (biblical accounts of creation) is religion in disguise and that teaching it violates the No Establishment Clause of the First Amendment. A similar law had already been declared unconstitutional in Arkansas.

National Briefs:

• Father Stephen Hartdegen, O.F.M., director of the U.S. Center for the Catholic Biblical Apostolate, was chairman of the religious advisory council for National Bible Week, Nov. 14 to 21.

• Sister of Mercy Arlene Violet lost her bid to become attorney general of Rhode Island in the Nov. 2 election. Several months earlier, Bishop Louis E. Gelineau had said that her candidacy was not in line with provisions of church law.

• A university without a faith commitment is incomplete, declared Jesuit Father William J. Byron Nov. 18 at his inauguration as 12th president of the Catholic University of America. He said: "Just as a person who ignores his or her creator is a sad creation, living by choice or circumstance in a horizonless world, so a university without a conscious opening to the creator of all truth and beauty is an incomplete university."

NCCB and USCC Meeting

Nearly 300 bishops attended the annual meeting of the National Conference of Catholic Bishops and the U.S. Catholic Conference Nov. 15 to 18 in Washington.

Proceedings of the meeting were heavily weighted by discussion of the second draft of a proposed pastoral statement on peace and war, with emphasis on opposition to nuclear arms.

Among other subjects on the agenda were:

• approval of a $22.6 million NCCB-USCC budget for 1983;

• passage of a resolution critical of federal economic policies;

• agreement to prepare pastoral statements on ministry to Hispanics, campus ministry, prayer and worship;

• approval of several items related to the liturgy.

(See separate entry for complete coverage of the meeting.)

INTERNATIONAL

Need for Clergy in Sudan — The bishops of Sudan asked their counterparts in Kenya, Tanzania, Uganda, Malawi, Zambia and Ethiopia to send priests and religious to that country for the pastoral care of the faithful. Sudan, with a Catholic population of nearly one million, had only 46 diocesan priests, 99 missionary priests, 202 sisters and 40 brothers.

Israeli Pledge and Expulsions — Christian Brother Thomas Scanlon, vice president of Bethlehem University, said in a telephone interview Nov. 8 that the expulsion by Israeli authorities of a biology instructor was "the most serious attack that can be made on a university." The instructor, Mark Cheverton, a British citizen, was expelled from the West Bank because he refused to sign a pledge not to support the Palestine Liberation Organization. Twenty-two foreign teachers were reported ousted by Nov. 21 when Israel dropped the pledge requirement but retained its conditions in work permits for foreigners.

A Bishop for Latvia — For the first time in 10 years, a new bishop was named for Latvia, a formerly independent Baltic state annexed by the Soviet Union in the 1940s. The new prelate was Father Joannes Cakues, 56, appointed by Pope John Paul II Nov. 10 to be auxiliary bishop for the Archdiocese of Riga and the Diocese of Liepaja. Bishop Julijans Vaivods, 87, was the apostolic administrator of both dioceses, the only ones in the country.

Social Teachings — The bishops of England and Wales called on Catholics to bring the social teachings of the Church to bear on public life. Cardinal George Basil Hume, speaking for the hierarchy Nov. 13, said: "It is far too easy for an individual to divide religion from daily life. It is highly dangerous when social, political and industrial issues are regarded as exclusively secular without any reference to the Gospel. . . . It is the privilege and duty of every believer to bring the light and wisdom of Jesus Christ into every relationship, society and activity."

Pressure against Paper and Church — The five major English-language newspapers in the Caribbean area protested Nov. 16 against what they called discriminatory actions by the government against *The Catholic Standard,* weekly newspaper of the Diocese of Georgetown. Editors of the paper complained about the effects of government support for the *Guyana Chronicle* in allotting newsprint, placing ads and providing access to sources of news and revenue. Discrimination

Discrimination in Northern Ireland — Catholics were still the victims of real but "less formal" job discrimination, according to Bob Cooper, director of the Equal Opportunities Commission for Northern Ireland. His assessment was published in *The Southern Cross,* newspaper of the Diocese of San Diego. He said: "Many private employers have a reputation as 'Protestant' employers and many Catholics, given the present level of violence, would be reluctant to cross sectarian boundaries. There is not a great deal of direct, purposeful discrimination at this time in the private sector. . . . Religion does not appear on employment applications but, in 90 per cent of the cases, name, address, school, sports and references identify a person's religion."

Meeting of Walesa and Archbishop Glemp — Lech Walesa, head of the outlawed Solidarity labor union, and Archbishop Jozef Glemp met for two hours Nov. 20, several days after Walesa was released by the government from nearly 12 months of detention. It was the first meeting of the two men — representing Poland's chief institutions favoring less communist control of national life — since the imposition of martial law Dec. 13, 1981.

In a related development, Archbishop Glemp said Nov. 7 that the Church understood and sympathized with Solidarity's call for a general strike Nov. 10 but remained opposed to violence and in support of efforts toward a peaceful solution to conflict between workers and the military government. "No one can expect the Church to leave the way of peace," he said. "We will do everything to avoid bloodshed."

Missionaries, Bishop Freed — Six Consolata missionaries, two priests and four nuns, kidnapped by guerrillas in Mozambique during July and September were freed Nov. 26. Vatican Radio reported them to be "in good health" but gave no details about their detention.

The International Red Cross reported Nov. 17 the release of Archbishop Alexandre do Nascimento of Lubango who had been captured and held since Oct. 15 by UNITA, a guerrilla group in Angola.

Muggeridge and Wife Become Catholics — Malcolm Muggeridge and his wife were received into the Church Nov. 27 in London. The 79-year-old British journalist and television personality attributed his conversion in large part to the influence of Mother Teresa of Calcutta, foundress of the Missionaries of Charity. Writing in *The Times* of London, he said: "Words cannot convey how beholden I am to her. She has given me a whole new vision of what being a Christian means: of the amazing power of love and how, in one dedicated soul, it can burgeon to cover the whole world." He also spoke of the influence of St. Augustine, whose *Confessions,* he said, "show how worldliness and carnality can be transmuted into a life dedicated to the service of God," and who lived at a time in some ways like the present, when the Roman Empire was visibly collapsing and decadence, "what we call permissiveness," was everywhere apparent.

International Briefs:

• The Social Affairs Commission of the Canadian Conference of Catholic Bishops, calling attention to "critical moral issues at stake," asked the government "to refrain from allowing the testing of nuclear delivery systems such as the cruise missile over Canadian territory."

• Any attempt to have Protestant and Catholic children in Northern Ireland attend the same schools would "be resisted by both communities," said James Steinberg, assistant editor of San Diego's *The Southern Cross,* on returning from a tour fo the strife-torn country.

• Senator Robert Kasten of Wisconsin, addressing a session of the U.N. General Assembly's Social, Humanitarian and Cultural Committee, said Nov. 23 that the communist regime in the Soviet Union was "engaged in a struggle against God."

Violations of Rights in El Salvador

"Grave and massive" violations of human rights were continuing in El Salvador, according to a report submitted Nov. 29 to the Social Committee of the U.N. General Assembly by special representative Jose Antonio Pastor Ridruejo. He said violations stemmed mainly from a climate of violence and armed conflict resulting from a centuries-old denial of economic, social and cultural rights to people of the lower classes. His findings and analysis were paralleled to a large extent by those reported by church sources in the country.

Citing figures from the Office of the U.N. High Commissioner for Refugees, Pastor Ridruejo said that armed conflict had forced between 175,000 and 295,000 Salvadorans to take refuge in other countries, and that another 276,000 persons had been displaced within El Salvador.

DECEMBER 1982

VATICAN

Good Deeds in Advent — The Pope, at a general audience Dec. 1, urged young people during Advent "to meet with good deeds Christ who is coming." Observing that good works are a sign of "consistency between faith and daily life," he invited youths to show "generous charity toward our brothers, especially those who need our understanding and our aid."

The Holy Father spoke about an "interior Advent" at a pre-Christmas general audience Dec. 22, declaring: "For Christians, every day can and should be an advent, a coming of the Lord. For, when our souls are purified and when we make room for the love of God to come into our hearts, then Christ can come and be born in us."

Religous Freedom in India — At a private meeting with Thomas Abraham, India's new ambassador to Vatican City, the Pope said Dec. 3 that his country should maintain its tradition of religious freedom because freedom of belief and worship are essential to human development. Backgrounding the Pontiff's concern about religious freedom were legislative efforts toward passage of a national anti-conversion law which Catholic leaders described as "patently anti-Christian" because it would make it illegal in many cases for people to convert to Christianity. Some local governments had already passed such legislation.

Prenatal Diagnosis and Treatment — The Pope praised them both Dec. 4 but warned against their misuse as preludes to abortion. Addressing a special audience of about 700 physicians, he said: "The Church is very happy to encourage those who use their talents and intelligence in this very important sector of medical research, which concerns the first movements of existence of the human being. . . . I cannot but repeat (however) the severe condemnation, rooted in natural law itself, of every direct attempt on the life of the innocent, the human being that develops in the maternal womb. . . . Interuterine research that tends to spot defective embryos and fetuses very early in order to be able to eliminate them promptly by means of abortion . . . is morally inadmissible."

Role of Women — The role of women in contemporary society should be "more extensive and incisive," declared the Pope Dec. 7 during an audience attended by 350 delegates to a national convention of the Italian Feminine Center. At the same time, he told each delegate that her presence in society should be that of "a woman, with the contribution of the particular values of her femininity and without responding less to the responsibilities proper to her own conjugal and family vocation." He also said that equal male-female dignity is "undeniable and never sufficiently affirmed," but that it "would be poorly understood if it included an obscuring of the very originality of the mystery of femininity."

Devotion to Mary — The Holy Father paid tribute to Mary on Dec. 8, the Solemnity of the Immaculate Conception, at Mass in the Basilica of St. Mary Major and at the *Piazza di Spagna,* where he placed a wreath at the foot of a statue erected in 1856 to commemorate the proclamation of the dogma. Speaking of Marian devotion in a homily, he said: "This does not overshadow or diminish the absolute centrality of Jesus Christ in the order of salvation but illuminates and proclaims it with vigor, because Mary derives all her greatness from him. As the history of the Church teaches, the role of Mary is that of making her Son shine forth, of leading us to him and of helping us to welcome him." He also said that "love of Mary . . . is the simplest and easiest way of sanctifying ourselves."

Interdiocesan Seminaries — The Holy Father said such seminaries were necessary because of the difficulties faced by dioceses trying to maintain their own seminaries despite decreases in the number of priests and candidates for the priesthood. He told a group of French bishops Dec. 10 that "qualified, well equipped interdiocesan seminaries (as distinguished from those run by individual dioceses) . . . help to overcome narrowness, offer wider cultural horizons and open up missionary perspectives."

Support for Polish Union — The Pope told 8,000 persons Dec. 15 that he shared "the concerns for the Church and for the nation which the Polish bishops display in the communique from their recent conference." Quoting the bishops, he said: "In recent months some events have happened in our land which have struck grievously at entire social groups and numerous individuals. Among other things, all the unions were disbanded. . . . It is regrettable that different courses were not chosen. . . . The Church holds that the building of a lasting social peace requires respect for the just aspirations of society, organized in social groups, based on accords reached and agreements obtained as a result of dialogue."

God at Work in Priestly Ministry — The Pope told 34 U.S. priests in Rome for studies in theology that "the power of the cross and resurrection of Our Lord Jesus Christ is active in the Church today just as it has been in every age." He added: "In whatever you do and in whatever you are called to suffer, always have a deep confidence in the love of God at work in your heart and in the hearts of others as you reach out to them in faithful service."

Terrible Instruments — While speaking in praise of scientific research before 200 physicists attending an international symposium in Rome, the Pope called nuclear weapons "terrible instruments of death" and appealed Dec. 18 for a halt in the arms race. He said: "When one hears talk of nuclear and sub-nuclear energy, one cannot fail to think, alas, of the destructive effect of modern weapons. There is no doubt that they represent one of the most serious threats to humanity. My predecessors and I have repeatedly drawn the attention of politicians and scientists to this grave danger, above all if leaders of governments to not have the wisdom or the will to put the brakes on the production and accumulation of such terrible instruments of death."

The Elderly and the Young — At a mixed audience with 6,000 senior citizens of Rome and 3,000 teen-agers and young adults, the Holy Father said Dec. 20 that the elderly are an important link between the past and the present, and that young people can benefit from contact with their wisdom. "Contemporary society . . . denies to the elderly a sufficient role both in the context of the family . . . and in public projects . . . in the name of productive efficiency," he stated. Elderly persons, however, should be for younger people "a sure pole of orientation in times of uncertainty, an incitement to live the higher values of the spirit, which never grow old, and a precious link between past and present generations. . . . It is necessary that there be recognized and appreciated that rich treasure of experience and of wisdom of which the elderly person is the bearer."

The Pope Also:

• Praised the "nobility of spirit" and "Christian outlook" of the late Princess Grace of Monaco, Dec. 10.

• Named two priests as bishops for Czechs (Father Jaroslav Skarvada) and Slovaks (Father Domenico Krusovski) living in Western Europe, the Americas and Australia.

• Appointed Father Theodore M. Hesburgh, president of the University of Notre Dame, to membership in the Pontifical Council for Culture.

• Met with: Presiding Bishop David W. Preus of the American Lutheran Church, Dec. 10; U.S. Secretary of State George Shultz, Dec. 13.

Vatican Briefs:

• The Congregation for the Causes of Saints advanced the beatification causes of three nuns Dec. 17: Sister Maria Gabriella Sagghedu, by acknowledging a miracle attributed to her intercession, and Sisters Hedwig Borzecka and Maria Crocifissa di Gesu, by proclaiming "heroic" their practice of virtue.

• The Vatican and the Italian government announced Dec. 24 the formation of a joint commission of six lay banking and legal experts to study the relations between the bankrupt Banco Ambrosiano and the Vatican Bank.

Soviet Charge Rejected

The Vatican reacted promptly and vigorously to a personal attack on the Pope issued by Tass, the official Soviet news agency. Accusations that he and Vatican emissaries had carried out subversive activities in Poland and other countries, "need no comment or reply," said a communique released Dec. 30, a day after publication by Tass of an offensive article in the Soviet monthly *Political Self-Education.*

The Vatican communique said the article "contrasts with the reality of the facts and the situation that are well known to all, on which world public opinion has pronounced a judgment that can hardly be contradicted. It contradicts also the evaluations made by Soviet sources, including officials, which have recognized on various occasions the high skill

and untiring work of Pope John Paul for peace and a just solution of the grave problems that threaten humanity."

NATIONAL

"60 Minutes" at Fault — Treatment of the Church's marriage annulment process by Mike Wallace on "60 Minutes" Nov. 28 was called inadequate, biased and unbalanced by Ethel M. Gintoft, associate publisher of the *Catholic Herald* of Madison, Wis. Writing in the Dec. 2 edition of the newspaper, she said, in part, that Wallace: put words in the mouths of persons he interviewed; interviewed a few disgruntled people; made no effort to distinguish between civil-court annulments and pastoral decisions of church tribunals; did not give anyone a chance to point out why the Church is involved in the annulment process in the first place.

Organization of Evangelizers — A National Organization of Catholic Evangelization Directors was established Dec. 3 at a meeting in Washington of 43 persons representing various dioceses, religious communities and national organizations. Paulist Father Alvin Illig, director of the U.S. bishops' Committee on Evangelization, said in an interview Dec. 6 that the main purpose of the organization was "to broaden the leadership of Catholic evangelization . . . at diocesan and parochial levels."

Abortion and Family Planning Activities — The Department of Health and Human Services announced Dec. 6 that it had prepared new rules requiring federally subsidized family planning clinics to separate abortion activities completely from all family planning services. The new rules were in line with provisions of the Public Health Service Act, which authorized the government to fund family planning services but declared that none of the money may be used for "programs where abortion is a method of family planning." *The New York Times* reported Dec. 7; "Under Title X of the Public Health Service Act, the Government in 1981 distributed a total of $153 million to 5,200 family planning clinics, of which 74 performed abortions." Twenty-one of the clinics were affiliated with Planned Parenthood.

Appreciation for Catholics in Military Service — Cardinal Terence Cooke of New York, military vicar of the U.S., reassured Catholics in the armed services that the Church appreciated their service to the cause of peace. In an annual Christmas message dated Dec. 7, he said: "The Church continues to recognize and to appreciate the contributions to the cause of peace with justice made by you, the men and women in military service and your families. The bishops, in the efforts being made to help advance that same cause, do understand what you are doing. They and the vast majority of Catholics in the United States are grateful for the sacrifices you are making in your firm commitment in conscience to defend our nation and our allies against unjust aggression." Backgrounding the cardinal's letter were controversy, criticism and some confusion over the contents of the second draft of a proposed pastoral letter of the nation's bishops on peace and war, with emphasis on moral judgments on nuclear arms and warfare.

Cardinal Cody Cleared — Archbishop Joseph L. Bernardin of Chicago announced the end of an independent investigation into the financial dealings of his predecessor, Cardinal John Cody, declaring it had produced no evidence of wrongdoing. Before his death in April, the cardinal was the subject of allegations that he had unlawfully diverted tax-exempt church funds for the personal use of a relative. The charges were not substantiated by either a federal grand jury or the accounting firm of Peat, Marwick, Mitchell and Co.

Israeli Actions Criticized — Editorials and columns in 28 Catholic publications were "highly negative and often harshly critical" regarding Israeli actions in Lebanon, according to a report compiled by Alan M. Schwartz, assistant director of the research and evaluation department of the Anti-Defamation League of B'nai B'rith. He said his report, "while not exhaustive, reflects the fact that many Catholic press editorials and columns, using humanitarian, religious and political arguments, generally blamed Israel for the crisis in Lebanon." Three subjects at issue, he said, were civilian casualties in the conflict, the Palestinian problem, and the criticism that military action in general is rarely justified and that Israeli intervention in Lebanon was "unnecessary, unhelpful and even immoral."

Capital Punishment — Fifteen days after Texas carried out the first execution by lethal injection, of Charles Brooks, Jr., Massachusetts became the 38th state Dec. 22 to restore the death penalty and the sixth state to authorize execution by either electrocution or lethal injection. Bishops in each state were opposed to both developments.

Nuns Can Sue Bishop — The New Hampshire Supreme Court ruled Dec. 23 that four nuns had a right to sue Bishop Odore Gendron of Manchester for refusing to renew their teaching contracts at Sacred Heart Parochial School in Hampton. In reversing a lower court ruling, the high court said that religious entities "are not totally immune from responsibility under civil law. . . . In religious controversies involving property or contractual rights outside the doctrinal realm, a court may accept jurisdiction and render a decision without violating the First Amendment." The case was remanded to the superior court. The plaintiffs were Sisters Honora Reardon, Justine Colliton, Catherine Colliton and Mary Rita Furlong.

Catholics in the New Congress — Findings of a survey conducted by Americans United for Separation of Church and State indicated that a record number of 141 Catholics — 17 in the Senate and 124 in the House — would be in the 98th Congress. Among other religious affiliations of members were United Methodist (73), Episcopalian (61), Presbyterian (54), Baptist (46), Judaism (38) and Lutheran (25). States with the largest numbers of Catholic delegates were New York (15 of 36), Illinois (13 of 24), Pennsylvania (11 of 25), Massachusetts (nine of 13), New Jersey, (nine of 16), and California (nine of 47).

Anti-Semitic Charges Refuted — Allegations by Richard Cohen, a writer for *The Washington Post,* that recently canonized St. Maximilian Kolbe was anti-Semitic prompted refutations from several scholars. One of them, Eugene Fisher, executive secretary of the U.S. Bishops' Secretariat for Catholic-Jewish Relations, cited writings in which the saint repudiated anti-Semitism and noted also that between 1,500 and 2,000 Jewish refugees were harbored at the beginning of World War II in a monastery which he founded and directed. Two St. Louis University scholars, Daniel L. Schlafly, Jr., and Warren Green, called attention in a joint statement to the saint's "equitable treatment of Jewish and Polish refugees at the outbreak of World War II."

National Briefs:

• The National Conference of Catholic Bishops paid tribute to Arthur R. Kenedy, recently retired president of P.J. Kenedy and Sons and publisher of *The Official Catholic Directory,* for distinguished service to the Church in the United States.

• Gov. Edward J. King signed into law Dec. 23 a bill allowing retail stores in Massachusetts to open on Sundays, despite appeals for a veto by the four bishops in the state.

Leading News Stories of 1982

Fifty-three editors of U.S. and Canadian Catholic newspapers, in response to an NC News Service poll, rated the following as the leading news stories of 1982.

1. The U.S. bishops proposed pastoral letter on war and peace.

2. Church-state relations in Poland.

3. Papal trips to Africa, Portugal, Great Britain, Argentina, Switzerland, Spain and Sicily.

4. Vatican investigation of relations between the Vatican Bank and the bankrupt Banco Ambrosiano.

5. Persecution of church leaders in Central America.

6. Pope John Paul's meeting with Yasir Arafat, leader of the Palestine Liberation Organization.

7. The death of Cardinal John Cody of Chicago.

8. Religious tension in the Middle East.

9. Church efforts to help people suffering from economic hardship.

10. Pope John Paul's meeting with the College of Cardinals and his decision to publish a statement of Vatican finances.

INTERNATIONAL

Sentences of Missionaries Reduced — Brazil's Superior Military Court upheld Dec. 3 the convictions of two French missionaries accused of planning an ambush in which one person was killed, but reduced their prison sentences as a humanitarian gesture. Fathers Francois Gouriou and Aristides Camio were originally convicted June 22 of violating the National Security Law by inciting peasants to "collective disobedience to the law and to class struggle" in a land dispute with ranchers. Brazilian bishops had defended the priests, and the nation's cardinals contended they were not guilty as charged.

Church-State Relations in Hungary — "Without ties to the entire community and Hungary's socialist society, the work of the Church will take place in a vacuum, and its religious and moral education among the faithful cannot be truly judicious and creatively successful." So stated Bishop Jozsef Cserhati of Pecs in an article reflecting the views of the Hungarian Bishops' Conference. The Church, he said in the article published Oct. 31, should avoid "being dragged into particular social or political notions, objectives or desires going beyond the limits of (the Church's) moral influence." The target of the article was "a minority which, using unusual nuances and not infrequently erroneous interpretations of the faith and similarly strange, radical demands, wanted to see a more demanding and a more evangelical Christianity" which would create conflicts by acting in "a revolutionary and aggressive manner." The bishop added: "We must differentiate between well-intentioned, constructive interventions and interjections and provocations that are self-serving."

Lecturers Ordered Not To Teach — Three U.S. and two British lecturers at Bethlehem University in the West Bank were ordered by Israeli authorities to cease teaching by Dec. 6 because they refused to comply with a work-permit requirement that they sign a declaration of opposition to the Palestine Liberation Organization. This was the second action taken in a month by Israeli officials against faculty members at the university.

Patriotic Catholics Open Cathedral — The Canton daily *Yang-cheng Evening News* reported that about 300 Chinese and foreigners attended a Mass Dec. 12 in the Canton cathedral, which was reopened for use by the government-controlled and dissident Patriotic Association of Chinese Catholics. The celebrant of the Mass was illicitly ordained Bishop Ye Yin-Yun. The papally appointed head of the Canton Archdiocese was Archbishop Dominic Tang Yee-Ming, who was most recently denied admittance to China and was formerly a years-long prisoner of the communist government. The Canton newspaper reported that 120 Patriotic Chinese Catholic churches and 140 Protestant churches were open in China.

Opposition to Abortion Law in France — A group of French taxpayers launched a campaign to withhold a portion of their taxes in protest against a recently passed law, opposed by the Church, providing funding for 70 per cent of the cost of abortions. A statement published in two newspapers Dec. 28 said the use of state funds "makes unwilling accomplices of all who, rightly, disapprove of abortion."

South African Atrocities — The London-based Catholic Institute for International Relations, in a documentary booklet published Dec. 20, said that South Africa's Security Police practiced "systematic abuse of political prisoners" without fear of any civil or criminal penalties. The booklet, *Torture in South Africa: Recent Documents,* contained detailed allegations of physical and mental torture practiced on political detainees held indefinitely without charges under South Africa's Terrorism Act or Internal Security Act.

Appeal for Refugees — Cardinal Emmanuel Nsubuga of Kampala appealed in a Christmas sermon to the Uganda government to provide food and medical supplies for the relief of more than 4,000 Rwandan refugees in a crowded camp along the strife-ridden border with Rwanda.

Plan for Argentina — As 1982 drew to an end, the bishops of Argentina launched a reconciliation program aimed at diminishing antagonism between the military government and key sectors of civilian society. Among issues in conflict were a plan for returning the nation to civilian rule, responsibility for military defeat by Great Britain in the Falkland Islands adventure, information on persons seized for political reasons and missing since the military assumed power in 1976, and ways of ending the nation's triple-digit inflation and high unemployment.

Anti-Mafia March — Two bishops and two communist officials joined 10,000 persons in an opposition march against a Mafia organization involved in violence which resulted in the deaths of more than 200 people in and around Naples in 1982. One of the communist leaders, noting the unusual participation of himself and the two bishops in a single event like the march, said that, "beyond ideological differences, there are values for which we must all fight together."

Earlier in the month, Cardinal Salvatore Pappalardo of Palermo was honored Dec. 7 by the Merit Association of the Municipality and Province of Milan for his "courage in speaking out against Mafia criminality" in Sicily.

International Briefs:

• A spokesman for the Defense Ministry of the Philippines said Dec. 3 that two Dutch priests, Fathers Theo Bandsma and Herman Sanderink, faced subversion charges for alleged possession of communist literature. Their superior said they were innocent, declaring: "The truth of the matter is that these materials were planted."

• Chileans contributed $3.75 million during a Dec. 10 to 11 telethon for crippled children conducted by the TV station of the Catholic University in Santiago.

• Vatican Radio reported Dec. 13 that 98 inmates of a South Korean jail were baptized and received into the Catholic Church a month earlier. The bishop who baptized the prisoners credited their conversions to the Christian witness of an elderly woman who visited them over a long period of time.

Martial Law in Poland

Martial law, imposed Dec. 13, 1981, was suspended formally Dec. 31 but remained in effect implicitly in virtue of legislation approved by the Parliament Dec. 18.

The legislation was severely criticized by the bishops' conference in a letter issued over the signatures of Archbishop Jozef Glemp, president, and Auxiliary Bishop Bronislaw Dabrowski, secretary. The letter said the new legislation could undermine the "credibility of the authorities" and provided "imprecise" regulations as pretexts for "unjust and arbitrary decisions."

JANUARY 1983

VATICAN

Dialogue for Peace — "Dialogue for Peace, a Challenge for Our Times," was the theme chosen by Pope John Paul for the 16th annual observance Jan. 1 of the World Day of Prayer for Peace. In speaking about it in a homily on New Year's Day, he said: "Dialogue for peace ... requires all parties to work in common, to progress in common on the road of peace. It is ... difficult to imagine how the problem of peace in the world can be resolved in a unilateral manner, without the participation and the concerted commitment of all.

"In the search for peace the problem of disarmament occupies an important place, and the desire to see dialogue in this regard come to concrete results is more than legitimate. But, like dialogue, the request for progressive reduction of armaments, nuclear or conventional, must also be addressed at the same time to all the parties involved. The powers which confront one another must be able to go along the various steps of disarmament together and commit themselves to each step in equal measure. In our common prayer for peace, we ask today that dialogue may be undertaken in that spirit and lead to those concrete and practical decisions capable of assuring a real and lasting result."

End of Franciscan Celebration — The Pope visited two central Italian towns Jan. 2 for what he called a "Christmas pilgrimage" closing year-long celebrations of the 800th anniversary of the birth of St. Francis of Assisi. He delivered six addresses during his seven-hour visit to Rieti and nearby Greccio, where the saint set up the first known nativity scene at Christmas in 1223. The Pope said Greccio was "almost a second Bethlehem," and appealed for adoption of the "Christian radicalism" preached by St. Francis.

Cardinals Named — Pope John Paul announced Jan. 5 the names of 18 churchmen to be inducted into the College of Cardinals Feb. 2. Archbishop Joseph L. Bernardin of Chicago was among those named.

Desire To Visit Lebanon — The Pope reaffirmed his desire to visit Lebanon to encourage its citizens to work for national concord and independence. He did so Jan. 8 as he received the credentials of Nasri Salhab, the new Lebanese ambassador to the Vatican. Referring also to talks under way between Lebanon and Israel, he said: "I very much hope that these talks will bring progress toward the solution of the delicate problems under negotiation, without forgetting the fate of the Palestinian families who are also so tried."

Clemency Plea — "In its humanitarian concern, the Holy See is prompted to recommend clemency and mercy for those condemned to death, especially those who have been condemned for political reasons," said the Pope Jan. 15 in a traditional beginning-of-the-year message to diplomats. He also told the representatives of 105 nations that dialogue was "the only road to peace" in such trouble spots as Lebanon, Central America, Afghanistan, Northern Ireland, Iran and Iraq.

The Church and Culture — The Church's desire to be involved in cultural life derives from its mission to preach the Gospel and to defend human rights, declared the Pope Jan. 18 at the inaugural meeting of the Pontifical Council for Culture. He told participants in the meeting: "Your role is great because you have to help the Church become a creator of culture in the modern world. ... We would be ... unfaithful to the love which must animate us if we did not see how man is today threatened in his humanity and if we did not defend ... individual and collective man to save him from oppressions which enslave and humiliate him."

Holy Year Proclaimed — In a papal bull entitled *Aperite Portas Redemptori,* made public Jan. 21, the Holy Father formally announced that a special Holy Year of Redemption would be observed simultaneously in Rome and throughout the world between Mar. 25, 1983, and Apr. 22, 1984. (See separate entry.)

Directives to Dutch Bishops — "The general good (of the Church in The Netherlands) demands that the functions proper to the laity not be carried out by the clergy and that the ministerial role of the priest no longer be fulfilled by the laity," declared the Pope Jan. 22 at a meeting with Dutch bishops. He also called for an increase in vocations to the priesthood and religious life, reaffirmed the discipline of celibacy for priests, criticized liturgical practices unauthorized by the Church, and said that candidates for the priesthood must be educated in "true seminaries." The directives, like those issued in the wake of the Particular Synod of Dutch Bishops in January, 1980, were intended to curb serious irregularities in the Church in Holland.

Beatification of Nun Dedicated to Ecumenism — Pope John Paul closed the 1983 Week of Prayer for Christian Unity Jan. 25 by beatifying Sister Maria Gabriella Sagheddu (1914-1939). He called her "the first Blessed in history who comes from the ranks of the women's branch of Catholic Action, the first from the young people of Sardinia, the first from among Trappist monks and nuns, the first from among workers at the service of unity." The beatification ceremony was the first of its kind ever held in the Basilica of St. Paul outside the Walls.

Earlier in the month, the Pope attended ceremonies Jan. 13 at which the Congregation for the Causes of Saints promulgated decrees concerning the heroic practice of virtue by Pauline von Mallinckrodt (1817-1881), foundress of the Sisters of Christian Charity, and Karolina Gerhardinger (1796-1879), foundress of the School Sisters of Notre Dame. Decrees advancing the beatification causes of four other Servants of God were also issued Jan. 13.

Married Couples as Prophets — The Holy Father urged married couples Jan. 26 to be "true prophets" by giving witness to "spousal and procreative love." He said: "Through matrimony as a sacrament of the Church, the man and woman are in an explicit way called to give witness of spousal and procreative love, a witness worthy of true prophets. . . . They are responsible for choosing those actions which will continually deepen their love for one another, strengthen their fidelity to their marriage vows and keep them one in mind and heart until death. In doing this, they become an effective sign of Christ's love for his spouse, the Church."

The Pope Also:

• Held a meeting of reconciliation Jan. 4 with the Christian Association of Workers which had been without approval of the Church since 1971 because of its collaboration with Marxists.

• Ordained 14 bishops and archbishops from seven European and African countries, Jan. 6.

• Urged government leaders in Uganda Jan. 13 to assure to their citizens "greater stability and security," along with protection of their human rights.

Vatican Meeting of European and U.S. Bishops — Thirty-two European bishops met with U.S. Cardinal-elect Joseph L. Bernardin and Archbishop John R. Roach Jan. 18 and 19 for discussion about the contents of the second draft of the American bishops' proposed pastoral letter on peace and war, entitled "The Challenge of Peace: God's Promise and Our Response." The European prelates represented the hierarchies of Great Britain, France, Belgium, The Netherlands, West Germany and Italy.

Vatican Briefs:

• Press spokesman Father Romeo Panciroli rejected Jan. 23 charges by a Czechoslovakian communist newspaper that Pope John Paul's appointment of bishops for Czechs and Slovaks outside the country was an anti-socialist "provocation."

• The Congregation for the Sacraments and Divine Worship confirmed use in the U.S., beginning Nov. 27, of a new booklet entitled *Pastoral Care of the Sick: Rites of Anointing and Viaticum.*

Revised Code of Church Law

Pope John Paul promulgated a revised Code of Canon Law Jan. 25 with the publication of an apostolic constitution entitled *Sacrae Disciplinae Legis* ("Of the Sacred Discipline of Law"). The constitution stated that the revised code, replacing the one in force since 1918, would go into effect Nov. 27, 1983.

The revised code was framed in the context of pastoral concern, the teachings of the Second Vatican Council and subsequent developments. Its 1,752 canons are grouped in seven books dealing with general norms, the people of God, the teaching mission of the Church, the sanctifying mission of the Church, temporalities, penal law and procedural law.

(See separate entry.)

NATIONAL

E.R.A. — Two hundred and 21 members of the House of Representatives jointly introduced Jan. 3 an Equal Rights Amendment as the first bill of the 98th Congress. The introduction began another process toward ratification of the amendment which failed to gain the approval of 38 states by June 30, 1982. The amendment states: "Equality of rights under the law shall not be denied or abridged by the United States or by any state on account of sex."

Racism and Criminal Justice — These were the subjects of pastoral statements during the month.

• Several days after racial disturbances erupted in Miami, Archbishop Edward A. McCarthy said Jan. 4 that Catholics are obligated to undo racial injustices "lest we become bystanders tolerating and tacitly endorsing evil and thus share in the guilt." He added: "In no way may a Catholic be associated with organizations that promote racial injustice."

• The bishops of New York, in a call for reform of the criminal justice system Jan. 27, said: "We believe that response to crime must balance the protection of society with opportunities for healing, retribution and rehabilitation."

Military Aid to Guatemala — The Reagan administration announced a decision Jan. 7 to resume the sale of military equipment to Guatemala, declaring that there had been improvement in the human rights situation in the country since Gen. Efrain Rios Montt became head of the government in March, 1982. Improvement in respect for human rights, a condition for the resumption of aid, was questioned by Archbishop John R. Roach, president of the National Conference of Catholic Bishops. He said in November, 1982: "From a wide variety of independent sources, but especially from church sources within Guatemala, including American missionaries, we draw the inescapable conclusion that respect for human rights in Guatemala is at its nadir." Seventy-eight members of the House of Representatives were against the sale of equipment, saying that "minimum human rights standards" do not exist in Guatemala. President Reagan, after meeting with Rios Montt in December, said he was "totally dedicated to democracy" and was getting a "bum rap" from critics of the human rights situation.

1983 Stockholder Resolutions — Nuclear arms production, bank redlining, plant closings, equal opportunity employment policies, energy and environment, infant formula promotion, and activity by corporations in Latin America, South Africa and South Korea were among the subjects of 118 stockholder resolutions filed by religious groups with 85 companies in efforts to influence corporate policies. The compilation of resolutions was made by the Interfaith Center on Corporate Responsibility, which also reported that filing organizations included several communities of men and women religious and the Archdiocese of Milwaukee. Corporations addressed included some of the biggest, like American Telephone and Telegraph, DuPont, General Dynamics, General Electric, Rockwell and Monsanto.

Ukrainians Repudiate Puppet Regime — In a joint statement published Jan. 17, the four Ukrainian Catholic bishops in the U.S. repudiated Soviet rule in the Ukraine, calling it a "puppet regime" and "an instrument by which the Soviet Russian colonial government oppresses and persecutes the Ukrainian people." It was estimated that there were approximately four million loyal Catholics in the Ukraine despite the forced incorporation of the Ukrainian rite into the Russian Orthodox Church after World War II.

School Prayer Decisions — The U.S. Supreme Court left standing Jan. 17 a lower-court ruling that the policy of the Lubbock, Tex., school district concerning prayer in public schools was unconstitutional. The policy had permitted elementary and high school students who wanted to pray on school premises to "gather at school with supervision either before or after regular school hours on the same basis as other groups . . . so long as attendance at such meetings is voluntary."

Prayer for Unity — "Jesus Christ, Life of the World," was the theme of the Week of Prayer for Christian Unity, Jan. 18 to 25. The observance was marked at interfaith prayer services in Catholic and Protestant churches across the country.

Two days before the start of the week, the presiding bishop of the Episcopal Church and the leaders of three Lutheran denominations took part — for the first time ever — in an intercommunion service they called "an interim sharing of the Eucharist." The service was held in the Episcopal National Cathedral in Washington.

School Prayer, Tuition Tax Credits, Abortion — President Reagan, in the State of the Union address Jan. 25, reiterated his support for a constitutional amendment on school prayer and for tuition tax credits for parents with children in private and parochial schools. He repeated these stances Jan. 31 at the National Religious Broadcasters' convention, when he also condemned abortion. He said the anti-abortion effort is "a struggle to redress a great national wrong."

Anti-Catholic Play — "The attack upon the Catholic Church in the play, 'Sister Mary Ignatius Explains It All for You,' strikes at every one of us who respects the value of America's pluralistic culture," declared the Interfaith Clergy Council of Greater St. Louis in a statement issued Jan. 28. Twelve performances of the virulently anti-Catholic play were scheduled in St. Louis despite protests by Archbishop John L. May, the Anti-Defamation League of B'nai B'rith, the National Conference of Christians and Jews, and the Catholic League for Religious and Civil Rights.

Anti-Semitism — Anti-Semitic vandalism in the U.S., after more than doubling for three years in a row, declined by 14.9 per cent in 1982, according to an annual audit conducted by the Anti-Defamation League of B'nai B'rith. The survey found 829 reported incidents in 35 states and the District of Columbia, in comparison with 974 cases in 31 states and the District in 1981.

National Briefs:
• Bishop Raymond W. Lessard of Savannah named a commission to investigate the possible martyrdom of five Franciscans slain in the territory of the diocese late in the 16th century. The friars were Fathers Miguel de Anon, Pedro de Cor-

pa, Blas de Rodriguez, Francisco de Berascola and Brother Antonio de Badajoz.

• Mayor Dianne Feinstein of San Francisco refused to sign and put into effect a proclamation designating Jan. 22 as Women's Reproductive Freedom Day in the city. The apparent intent of the resolution, which had been approved on a 6-to-5 vote by the Board of Supervisors, was to canonize the right to abortion.

• Catholic Relief Services reported Jan. 31 a contribution of $25,000 for the relief of flood victims in Ecuador.

March for Life

Ten years and 15 million abortions after the U.S. Supreme Court legalized abortion on demand, well over 26,000 persons from all over the country took part in the 10th annual March for Life Jan. 22 in Washington. The purposes of the march were to protest the Roe v. Wade and Doe v. Bolton decisions, and to stimulate legislative action for their reversal. Similar purposes were the motives for other demonstrations and observances in various U.S. cities and dioceses.

In comment related to the decisions and the march, Archbishop John R. Roach of St. Paul and Minneapolis said: "Some called legalized abortion a way to enable physicians to practice 'good medicine' without the interference of the law and a solution to teen-age pregnancy, maternal mortality, child abuse and a host of other problems. But the predicted benefits have not materialized. Child abuse, teen pregnancy and even teen suicide have risen sharply; the rate of decrease in maternal mortality has remained unchanged; illegal abortions continue to cause women's deaths, while legal abortions take their own toll on women and children alike; and the law interferes with physicians' rights by punishing them for not advising women of the availability of abortion. Furthermore, we now find ourselves seriously discussing the pros and cons of such questions as infanticide, active euthanasia and the involvement of physicians in carrying out the death penalty. Those who would celebrate such a national disaster can only have blinded themselves to its consequences."

INTERNATIONAL

East German Militarism — The bishops of East Germany joined the chorus of Protestant and peace movement spokesmen in criticism of militarism in the communist-run country. They said in a letter published Jan. 2: "We observe with concern the growing incidence of thinking in militaristic categories in school and professional education. It is to be feared that this kind of education will encourage the solving of conflicts through force and therefore damage the next generation's attitude toward peace."

Call for Democracy in Chile — The bishops of Chile, according to a delayed report, appealed Dec. 17 to the military government in office since 1973 to return the country to civilian rule and to respect human rights. They said: "The disappearance of democratic structures has left the majority of Chileans with no real possibility of participation in government. . . . Provisions for the respect of human rights in the 1980 constitution are not observed. . . . Furthermore, laws leading to democratic rule are not implemented."

Nuclear Arms Condemned — "We believe that there is no cause that would morally justify the death and destruction caused by a nuclear conflagration." So stated 11 religious leaders and six eminent scientists in a joint statement issued at the end of a Jan. 13 to 15 meeting in Vienna. They said: "We join with the scientists (from 31 nations who met at the Vatican in October, 1982) in their call for urgent action to achieve verifiable disarmament agreements leading to the elimination of nuclear weapons. Nothing less is at stake than the future of humanity, with its rich and variegated cultures and religious traditions."

IRA Killers — At the funeral Mass for Catholic Judge William Doyle, who was killed by gunmen of the Irish Republican Army, Bishop Cahal B. Daly of Down and Connor said Jan. 18 that those who belong to the IRA "cut themselves away from the community of love which is the Christian church." He added: "May no Catholic harbor any illusions about the menace posed to our faith by such movements as those which plan, order and perpetrate deeds like this. Let no lies confuse them. Let no propaganda deceive them. The present and protracted campaign of violence is, I believe, the gravest danger which has been created for Belfast's Catholicism for half a century. It is a force for corruption from within far greater than any external danger."

Vocations to the Priesthod and Religious Life — In Poland between 1979 and 1982, the number of ordinations to the priesthood increased from 589 to 775, more than 30 per cent. The number of major seminarians also increased during the period, from 5,845 to 7,225, nearly 25 per cent.

• In Ireland between 1981 and 1982, vocations to the diocesan priesthood and to congregations of women religious increased by six per cent while the number of men entering religious orders declined.

Juan Diego — Petitions signed by 26,000 persons in the United States in support of the cause for the canonization of Juan Diego, the Aztec Indian to whom the Blessed Virgin Mary appeared as Our Lady of Guadalupe, were presented Jan. 22 to the official in charge of the cause in the Basilica of Our Lady of Guadalupe in Mexico City. In the decade following the appearance of Mary in 1531, eight million persons were baptized in Central America.

Anti-Mafia Protest — Thousands of shopowners and workers joined in a campaign backed by Cardinal Corrado Ursi of Naples to close down Italy's third largest city for 48 hours Jan. 26 and 27 as a sign of protest against the local Mafia organization. He said the organization derived from "ideologies which have expropriated the dignity of man, placing idols in place of values; the idols of riches, power and licentious passions." Addressing its members Jan. 26, he said: "The Church condemns you but awaits you with hope. You will always find the doors open if you are converted."

Charges against Lithuania Priest — The government news agency Tass reported Jan. 27 that criminal proceedings had been instituted against Father Alfonsas Svarinskas for alleged "illegal anti-constitutional and anti-state activities." The agency said he had "fabricated slanderous materials which were sent abroad through illegal channels for use by subversive centers with anti-Soviet aims," had held "anti-social assembles" encouraging disobedience to the government, and had "systematically instigated believers to go over to open struggle against the Soviet power." In New York, the Lithuanian Information Center issued a statement saying that Father Svarinskas, who had been "constantly persecuted by Soviet authorities," had been "the author of a number of courageous public statements criticizing the Soviet government's repression of human rights while demanding implementation of Soviet constitutional guarantees of religious freedom."

Disarmament — Two prominent churchmen in Great Britain called for nuclear disarmament initiatives by their country and a third announced he was withholding taxes in protest.

• Catholic Archbishop Derek Worlock of Liverpool said Jan. 30 that Great Britain should take unilateral initiatives to stimulate multilateral disarmament.

• Five days earlier, Anglican Archbishop Robert Runcie declared that "full-scale nuclear war cannot possibly qualify as a just war," and stressed the urgency of efforts toward disarmament.

• Anglican Canon Paul Oestreicher told the government in a letter published Jan. 26 that he was withholding part of his income tax "as an act of conscientious objection to the manufacture, possession and threatened use of nuclear weapons."

International Briefs:

• The bishops of Kenya issued a booklet, *Catholic Medical Ethics and Religious Care of the Sick,* in which they presented church teaching in opposition to abortion, contraception and euthanasia.

• CARA, the Center for Applied Research in the Apostolate, opened an affiliate in Ottawa to provide research and educational services for the Church in Canada.

Attack on Canadian Policies

The eight-member Social Affairs Commission of the Canadian Conference of Catholic Bishops stirred a national debate at the end of the old year and the beginning of 1983 with a statement attacking government and corporate economic policies as opposed to Gospel values, "Ethical Reflections on the Economic Crisis," reported in Canadian media Dec. 31, quickly prompted differing comments from people across the country.

Cardinal G. Emmett Carter of Toronto expressed serious reservations about the document and said at a press conference that it was produced by the commission, not by the whole conference. "There was no consultation of the collectivity of the bishops," he said. He called the commission's move "into the details of economic policy . . . risky."

FEBRUARY 1983

VATICAN

Joy in Suffering — Pope John Paul, at a Mass honoring Our Lady of Lourdes Feb. 12, spoke of joy before a congregation of 9,000 sick and handicapped persons in St. Peter's Basilica. This "may seem strange and contradictory," he said, but added: "Jesus . . . gave to all the treasure of true joy. It is an interior joy, mysterious, often even furrowed with tears, but is always living because it is born from the certainty of the love of God . . . even in the sorrowful and adverse circumstances of life, and from the meritorious and eternal value of the entire human existence, especially that which is tormented and without human satisfactions." He asked his listeners to offer their sufferings for the good of the Church.

Ukrainians Praised — The Pope praised Ukrainian-Rite Catholics for their consistent contribution to unity among bishops and to the communion of local bishops with the Pope. Speaking to Ukrainian prelates at the close of their two-week synod at the Vatican, he said Feb. 12 that "for this great cause (unity) your bishops have struggled unceasingly across the centuries, and not a few of them have even given their lives for it." He reminded the bishops of their responsibility "to develop the holiness of the clergy, the religious and the laity," and emphasized particularly "the care for priestly and religious vocations and the preparation of the faithful for the great missions of the apostolate of the laity."

Journalism, a Vocation — "The journalistic profession should be understood as a mission of information and of formation of public opinion, at the root of which is situated a strongly interior thrust which we can call a vocation," declared the Pope Feb. 14 at an audience for Italian Catholic journalists. He said: "The Church looks with great sympathy and friendship on the work of Catholic journalists. It has particularly at heart the specifically Catholic press — not on the basis of a precluding calculation or a monopolistic perspective, but in conformity with its own divine mission of facilitating the arrival of the Christian message at every level."

Lent — The Holy Father blessed and gave ashes to dozens of Roman parishioners on Ash Wednesday at the Basilica of Santa Sabina. He said in a homily: "The austere rite of the imposition of the holy ashes . . . calls all to reflect on the duty of conversion, recalling the inexorable transience and ephemeral fragility of human life, which is subject to death." Lent should be marked by a "spirit of penitence, not in its negative meaning of sadness and frustration, but in that of elevation of the spirit, liberation from evil, separation from sin and from all the conditioning that can hinder our path toward the fullness of life."

Campaign for Fraternity — The words, "yes to fraternity, no to violence," were pronounced three times in ringing tones by Pope John Paul during a six-minute radio address to the people of Brazil Feb. 16. His message coincided with the start of the bishops' Campaign for Fraternity, an educational and pastoral program planned for Lent. The pope invited "all without exception" to build their lives "on concord, peace and love."

Synod Document — The Vatican released Feb. 17 the working paper for the 1983 assembly of the Synod of Bishops, scheduled to convene Sept. 29 for discussion and action on the theme, "Reconciliation and Penance in the Life of the Church." The Pope said consideration of the document "can revive in peoples' consciences the sense of God and the sense of sin, the sense of the greatness of God's forgiveness, the sense of the importance of the sacrament of penance for human and Christian growth and, indeed, for the very renewal of society. . . . The sacrament of confession is the irreplaceable means of conversion and spiritual progress."

Foreigners Ousted from Nigeria — The Pope called Feb. 18 for a "just and effective solution" to the plight of foreigners forced to leave economically troubled Nigeria because they did not have authorization to work there. He said: "I express my heartfelt concern for those whose lives have been affected by this sad situation," resulting from an order issued by the government in late January. Affected by the situation were an estimated three million persons, mostly from Benin, Ghana and Togo.

Advice and Retreat — Before beginning a six-day retreat, the Holy Father made his 65th parish visit Feb. 20. He told parishioners of Santa Maria della Mercede and San Adriano: "If you do not want to yield to temptations, if you do not want to be led by them toward mistaken ways, be people of prayer. . . . Have faith in God and manifest it in prayer."

The papal retreat, from Feb. 20 to 26, was conducted by Cardinal Joseph Ratzinger, prefect of the Congregation for the Doctrine of the Faith.

Holy Year Celebrations — In a letter addressed to bishops throughout the world, the Holy Father asked them to mark the Holy Year beginning Mar. 25 with special celebrations and programs of spiritual enrichment in their respective dioceses. He said that current diocesan programs could take on a deeper meaning and be enlivened by a more intense spirituality during the year "by showing their connection with the mystery of redemption, by rediscovering their pastoral and formative power, and by adding to them a special dignity in the celebrations."

The Pope Also:

• Formally presented the revised Code of Canon Law to the entire Latin-Rite Church Feb. 3 at a ceremony attended by 57 cardinals, more than 100 archbishops and bishops, members of the Roman Curia, representatives of canon law societies, diplomats accredited to the Vatican, teachers and students of canon law at pontifical universities.

• Met privately Feb. 7 with U.S. Vice President George Bush.

• Approved Nov. 28, 1982, according to a delayed report, a decree for the start of an investigation into the cause for beatification of Padre Pio, an Italian Capuchin priest and reputed stigmatic (bearer of the wounds of the Christ).

Vatican Briefs:

• Masami Ota, Japanese ambassador to the Vatican, received the sacrament of baptism Feb. 5, the feast day of 27 Japanese martyrs who were crucified in 1597 in Nagasaki.

• Two new members were named to the Pontifical Academy of Sciences Feb. 12; Charles Townes of the University of California at Berkeley, a Nobel Prize laureate in physics for invention of the laser in 1958; Stanislao Lojasiewicz of the Jagellonian University in Cracow, Poland, a mathematician.

• Pope Pius XII wrote a four-page condemnation of the Nazis during World War II but burned it rather than publish it after hearing that some 40,000 persons in The Netherlands had been sent to concentration camps because of an anti-Nazi pastoral letter issued by the bishops there. The disclosure was made by Sister Pasqualina Lehnert, a member of the Pontiff's domestic staff for 40 years.

18 New Cardinals

Pope John Paul inducted an Eastern-Rite patriarch, 16 bishops and a priest into the College of Cardinals Feb. 2, raising its membership to 138. Archbishop Joseph L. Bernardin of Chicago was the only American among the new Princes of the Church. Father Henri de Lubac, an 86-year-old French theologian, was admitted to the college without being ordained a bishop. The Eastern-Rite patriarch was Antoine Pierre Khoraiche of the See of Antioch of the Maronites.

Ceremonies included:

• A secret consistory attended only by cardinals, old and new, at which the 18 were actually "created."

• A public consistory attended by 10,000 persons in the Paul VI Audience Hall, at which the scarlet skull cap (zucchetto) and biretta were conferred.

• A Mass in St. Peter's Basilica at which the Pope gave each of the new cardinals a gold ring shaped like a cross.

During the public consistory, the Holy Father told the new cardinals: "With the beginning of your membership today, the Sacred College has not only been enriched by men outstanding for learning and virtue; it has also become an ever clearer reflection of the unity and catholicity of the community of believers, and a reflection of the multiplicity of its ministries."

He said also that Catholics expect their leaders to be "secure points of reference" in the faith, and charged them "to be fearless" in upholding the faith, even to the point of death.

NATIONAL

School Prayer Stopped — U.S. Supreme Court Justice Lewis F. Powell ordered a halt Feb. 2 to prayer in public schools in Alabama, a practice that had begun after a lower federal court judge threw out a suit challenging prayer in public schools. At issue in the case were statutes allowing teachers to lead students in prayer and permitting silent prayer in classrooms. Justice Powell's decision was in line with a 1962 ruling of the Supreme Court against the constitutionality of voluntary prayer in public schools.

Parental Notification Enjoined — U.S. District Court Judge Henry F. Werker granted a preliminary injunction Feb. 14 in New York against a regulation that would require federally funded family planning clinics to notify parents within 10 days that they were providing prescription contraceptives to their daughters aged 17 years and younger. The regulation, pejoratively labeled the "squeal rule" as soon as it was published, had been scheduled to go into effect Feb. 25. Additional suits against the rule were pending in the District of Columbia and elsewhere.

Former Episcopal Clergyman Ordained — Father Raymond O. Ryland, a married former Episcopal clergyman and a Catholic for the previous 20 years, was ordained to the priesthood by Bishop Leo Maher Feb. 12 in St. Mary Magdalen Church, San Diego. He was the fourth former Episcopal clergyman ordained in about a year under conditions approved by the Vatican.

Jewish Marriage Contract — The New York State Court of Appeals ruled 4-to-3 Feb. 15 that the state can, without religious entanglement, enforce some contractual obligations undertaken in Conservative and Orthodox Jewish religious marriages. The court said that the *ketubah*, signed by Orthodox and Conservative Jews, is a binding civil contract as well as a religious covenant: "That the obligations undertaken by the parties to the *ketubah* are grounded in religious belief and practice does not preclude enforcement of its secular terms." At issue in the case was whether a woman could civilly force her husband to appear before a religious panel which had sole authority to grant religious divorces in Orthodox and Conservatve Judaism.

Lenten Pastoral Letters — In pastoral letters for Lent, bishops across the country called attention not only to the traditional penitential practices of prayer, fasting and almsgiving but also to a variety of subjects including concern for the unemployed and suffering, and efforts to promote peace and reconciliation in the Church and society in general.

Homosexuality — The Commission on Social Justice of the Archdiocese of San Francisco approved a resolution Feb. 17 stating that key views expressed in a 1982 report by its Task Force on Gay-Lesbian Issues were clearly incompatible with church teachings. The report, issued in September, said the Church does not have a viable sexual ethic on homosexuality, divorce and marriage, contraception and premarital sexual relations. It said the traditional distinction in moral theology between homosexual orientation, held to be morally neutral, and genital homosexual behavior, condemned as morally wrong, was "practically meaningless and pastorally useless."

The report was called "an attack on the Church" by Msgr. Peter G. Armstrong, chairman of the Social Justice Commission. The report used theology selectively in support of questionable points and disregarded natural law, in the judgment of two Sulpician Fathers of St. Patrick's Seminary, Menlo Park — Howard P. Bleichner, rector, and Gerald D. Coleman, associate professor of moral theology.

In another development, a controversial homosexual rights bill opposed by the archdiocese was defeated Feb. 23 in New York for the seventh time in 12 years.

Natural Family Planning — Results of a survey published in *Hospital Progress*, magazine of the Catholic Health Association, disclosed that 177 of 503 responding hospitals had started natural family planning programs and that 170 more had expressed interest in doing so. Msgr. James T. McHugh, director of the U.S. bishops' Diocesan Development Program, called the findings "a sign of the continuing growth in professionalism and acceptance of natural family planning in America." The fact that fewer than 200 couples a year were served in 142 of the institutions indicated a need for improved and systematic publicity as well as program accountability and development, he said.

Presbyterians To Unite — Voting was completed Feb. 22 on a plan to reunite two major churches separated from each other for 122 years because of differences about the slavery issue. The denominations were the southern-based Presbyterian Church in the United States and the United Presbyterian Church in the U.S.A. The reunion, resulting in one church with approximately 3.3 million members, was scheduled to take place officially in June.

Secretary of State Criticized — Sen. Patrick J. Leahy of Vermont, an opponent of U.S. policy toward El Salvador, accused Secretary of State George P. Shultz Feb. 28 of making a "gratuitous slam at the Catholic Church" after Shultz inferred that the Church was not concerned about Soviet influence in Central America. The accusation was made at a hearing in which Shultz criticized "churchmen who want to see Soviet influence in El Salvador improved." He made the remark after Leahy, in calling for a negotiated solution to civil war in El Salvador, read a series of quotations by Pope John Paul and Bishop Arturo Rivera Damas of San Salvador on the need to end bloodshed and to begin negotiations.

Religious Persecution Worldwide — A "phenomenal amount" of violations of rights to religious freedom was reported by John Healy, executive director of the U.S. section of Amnesty International. Among cases in point, he said: "In Russia, a nun can get five to 10 years (of imprisonment) for selling Bibles on the streets in Moscow. . . . In the Philippines, the Catholic clergy are being detained and executed by the government. . . . In Argentina, religious personnel disappear without a trace. The Baha'i have been killed in large numbers in Iran. In Namibia, Lutherans have been killed. In Lesotho, the ranks of Protestant leaders have been decimated."

National Briefs:

• Christian Brother Jeffrey Gros was named director of the Faith and Order Commission of the National Council of Churches Feb. 11.

• A number of Catholic newspapers reported publication of free job-wanted and job-available ads for the assistance of the unemployed.

• U.S. members of the Holy Childhood Association contributed $30,000 for the assistance of children and families returning to Ghana from economically distressed Nigeria.

• Honored: Cardinal Joseph L. Bernardin with the 1982 South Carolinian of the Year Award for "dedicated service to mankind and superior accomplishments in the Catholic Church," by WIS Television and Radio in Columbia.

• Observances: Catholic Press Month, with the theme, "Good News for the People of God"; Brotherhood-Sisterhood Week, Feb. 20 to 26, sponsored by the National Conference of Christians and Jews.

Nun vs. Archbishop and Church Law

Mercy Sisters Agnes Mary Mansour remained in office as head of Michigan's Department of Social Services despite the call of Detroit Archbishop Edmund C. Szoka for her resignation because she refused to oppose state funding of abortion.

Archbishop Szoka said in a statement Feb. 23 that he had spoken twice with Sister Mansour about the matter and had "waited patiently" for her "to declare her active opposition to Medicaid payments for abortion" ever since she was appointed to head the department in December, 1982. "This declaration," he said, "has not been made by Sister Mansour, and therefore I must now state, without any qualification, my objection and opposition to her appointment . . . I also call for her resignation from that office without delay. . . . It is now the responsibility of her religious superiors to require Sister Mansour's compliance with the law of the Church. Her acceptance and retention of public office, whether by election or appointment, require the approval of both her religious superiors and the local bishop. She does not have my approval."

Sister Mansour was on record to the effect that she was personally opposed to abortion but would not oppose state funding of abortiions.

Her refusal to comply with canon law and the archbishop's demand for her resignation was supported by her religious superiors and Groundwork, an organization including 15 communities of nuns and a number of social justice groups in Michigan.

INTERNATIONAL

Bethlehem University Protest — Christian Brother Robert Daszkiewicz, academic vice president of Vatican-sponsored Bethlehem University, issued a protest in the wake of a late-night entry Jan. 13 into the school's grounds and buildings by Israeli soldiers who confiscated posters, papers, photos, books and notebooks. He said in a statement: "We protest this infringement by the Israeli soldiers on Bethlehem University's and her students' rights to own property, to be free to hold opinions without interference and to seek, receive and impart information and ideas through any media and regardless of frontiers, and to be free to hold peaceful assemblies."

United Way Funds Turned Down — Archbishop James Carney of Vancouver announced that archdiocesan Catholic Charities and Catholic Community Services would not accept funds from United Way in 1983 because Planned Parenthood had been made a member of the campaign. The decision did not amount to formal withdrawal from United Way, but such a development, contingent on Planned Parenthood participation in the campaign, was not ruled out in the future.

Shared Blame in El Salvador — Bishop Arturo Rivera Damas said Feb. 6 in San Salvador that "indiscriminate bombing" by the Salvadoran Army was the cause of many civilian deaths during the just concluded battle for the town of Berlin. He also denounced right-wing death squads and had sharp words for rebels, wondering aloud whether their political and military aims justified "the suffering of thousands of persons" in Berlin.

No General Amnesty — A general amnesty for political prisoners in Poland would be an "exceptional act" that could not be considered under existing circumstances. So stated Jerzy Urban, a government spokesman, Feb. 8 in response to a request by authorities of the Church. The amnesty was sought as a gesture of good will before Pope John Paul's visit to the country in June.

Church of England Synod — Delegates to the General Synod of the Church of England Feb. 8 to 11 voted against unilateral disarmament (338 to 100), first use of nuclear weapons by Great Britain and other NATO nations (275 to 222), and a proposal to introduce a form of the sacrament of penance into Anglican practice.

Appeal for Freedom in Mozambique — At an unprecedented meeting with President Samora Moises Machel, Catholic, Protestant, Hindu and Moslem leaders appealed for equal treatment from the Marxist-oriented government and for greater respect for religious freedom. The All Africa Press Service reported Feb. 14 that Bishop Jaime Goncalves of Beira had presented a document to the president on behalf of the Church. In it, he asked for guarantees of freedom to train priests, to have religious instructors enter the country and to allow religious personnel to travel about more freely. He called for greater freedom for Catholics who wished to pursue a religious vocation, and said he wanted the government to open churches it had closed and to end its control over church property. He also demanded the opening of new churches, the guaranteeing of religious freedom for civil service workers and freedom for church members to raise their children in the Catholic faith.

Lithuanian Protest — The underground *Chronicle of the Catholic Church in Lithuania* reported in its February edition that by November, 1982, more than 460 priests had signed a letter addressed to former President Leonid Brezhnev of the Soviet Union. The letter protested against government regulations regarding religion in the country, charging that they were contrary to the Gospel, church law, the Soviet constitution and the Helsinki Accords of 1975.

Family Planning Courses — A law calling for family planning courses in high schools of the province was passed Feb. 17 by the Ontario Legislative Assembly. Included in the measure was a provision that would allow Catholic and other independent schools to set up their own programs with the approval of a regional medical health officer. Despite this provision, opponents of the law remained concerned because the health officers authorized to approve or disapprove of programs in Catholic schools would be government officials, some of whom were proponents of the pro-contraceptive and pro-abortion aims and objectives of Planned Parenthood.

Attacks on the Pope Condemned — At the end of a two-day meeting, the bishops of Poland condemned Feb. 24 recent attacks on the Holy Father, saying that articles accusing him of "subversive activity" in his native country were "obviously deprived of any foundation." The attacks "deeply offend the convictions and feelings of believers, for whom the Holy Father represents the supreme moral authority," they said. The articles referred to by the bishops appeared in January editions of journals published in Czechoslovakia and the Soviet Union.

International Briefs:

• The Spanish Bishops' Conference declared its opposition Feb. 5 to government proposals to legalize abortion in cases of rape, fetal malformation and danger to a mother's life.

• In a statement issued Feb. 7, leaders of the Catholic, United, Anglican, Presbyterian and Lutheran churches urged Canadians to "express your conviction that the moral and ethical costs associated with complicity in the arms race are too high."

• Brazilian Archbishop Helder Camara was named Feb. 14 the first winner of a peace prize awarded by a Japanese Buddhist organization, the Niwano Peace Foundation; the award included a grant of about $87,000.

• The International Committee of the Red Cross reported Feb. 24 that Angolan guerrillas had released 12 nuns, missionaries and Red Cross workers they had kidnapped in October, 1982.

Criticism and Tension in the Philippines

In a pastoral letter read in more than 3,000 churches throughout the Philippines Feb. 20, the nation's 102 bishops criticized the government of President Ferdinand Marcos and said it must use genuine means, not propaganda and repression, to overcome the country's ills. The letter said the government was responsible for growing poverty, social unrest, economic mismanagement, political corruption, favoritism to multinational corporations, and the stifling of legitimate dissent.

As expected, the letter intensified tension between the Church and the Marcos regime because of involvement in advocacy for the poor by priests and religious the government considered subversive.

MARCH 1983

VATICAN

Central American Trip — The Holy Father visited eight Central American nations Mar. 2 to 9 on probably the most challenging and gruelling of his 16 trips abroad since becoming Pope. (See separate article.)

Non-Aligned Nations and Peace — In a letter addressed to the Mar. 7 to 11 meeting of the Conference of Non-Aligned Nations in New Delhi, the Pope expressed hope that its work would "strengthen the commitment of the participating countries to an open and trusting dialogue of peace . . . in full respect for the sovereign rights of each people." The meeting was attended by 101 heads of state.

Injustice and Violence in Central America — Six days after concluding a pastoral visit to Central America, the Pope condemned Mar. 16 both "unjust structures" and foreign-aided violence in the region. He said Central Americans possessed "great sources of Christian devotion and faith," but added that "at this difficult moment in history I invite Christians throughout the world to offer heartfelt prayers for these brothers and sisters of ours whose faith is being tested." Predominant tensions in Central America, he said, "have their sources in old socio-economic structures, in unjust structures which permit the accumulation of the majority of goods in the hands of a numerically small elite, alongside the co-existing poverty and misery of an enormous majority of society. . . . This unjust system has to be changed." But the Pontiff rejected violence as the way to bring about change. He said violence in Central America had been conducted "in notable measure with the aid of foreign efforts and with arms furnished from the outside against the will of the vast majority of society, who instead desire peace and democracy."

Struggle against Unemployment — Pope John Paul asked people on all levels of society to join in efforts to reduce unemployment as he observed a three-year custom by visiting two factories on the feast of St. Joseph, the patron saint of workers. Speaking Mar. 19 in San Salvo, 160 miles from Rome, he said: "We have to ask ourselves sometimes if technological progress is a friend or an enemy of man, of workers." He hoped that a solution to problems of unemployment might come from the combined thrust of public officials and all social forces, "those who work in the industrial, social and economic fields, and all citizens."

Nationalization of Schools in France — Calling freedom "indivisible," the Pope criticized a proposal by the French government to nationalize Catholic schools. The nation's commitment to freedom required it to respect "the freedom of families to educate their children according to their own convictions," he said Mar. 21 as he received the credentials of Xavier Daufresne de la Chevalerie, the new French ambassador to the Holy See. Bishops and school groups had strongly denounced a proposal, outlined in December, 1982,

to nationalize 14,000 private schools with a total enrollment of approximately 2.3 million students. About 10,000 of such schools, with more than two million students, were run by the Church.

Relations with Sweden — Sweden and the Vatican formally reestablished diplomatic relations after a 456-year break which began during the Reformation. Marking the event was the acceptance by the Pope Mar. 24 of the credentials of Ambassador Gunnar Johan Ljungdahl.

In another church-state development, Ecuador and the Holy See formalized Mar. 26 an agreement on religious assistance to the armed forces and police of the South American nation. Details of the agreement, signed Aug. 3, 1978, in Quito, were not made public.

Shroud Willed to Pope — Father Romeo Panciroli, director of the Vatican Press Office, said Mar. 26 that news of the bequest of the Shroud of Turin to the Pope had been received "with pleasure and gratitude." The shroud, thought to be the burial cloth of Christ, was bequeathed to the Holy Father by Italy's deposed King Umberto who died Mar. 18. Umberto was head of the House of Savoy, owner of the shroud since the Middle Ages. (See Index: Shroud of Turin.)

Prayer for Holiness — During the first general audience of the year in St. Peter's Square, the Pope prayed Mar. 30 that the Holy Year of Redemption might lead people to "repentance for sins and aspiration to holiness." He said: "We ask the Redeemer, in the name of his cross, to grant his Church and all humanity the grace of the Holy Year, the gifts of conversion and holiness which we most need. . . . This is what the Holy Year wants, this is what Jesus asks us from the cross: a greater openness to his redemption with the repentance of sins and an aspiration to holiness." More than 20,000 persons attended the audience which was conducted as a Liturgy of the Word, with readings from the Bible, a penitential act and a profession of faith.

Renewal in the Priestly Vocation — In his annual Holy Thursday letter to priests, the Holy Father called on them to make the 1983 Holy Year "a year of renewal in the priestly vocation." He said: "The Jubilee Year is understood by the Church as a time for spiritual renewal for everyone. If we must be witnesses of this renewal for others . . . then we must be witnesses to it, and spokesmen for it, to ourselves: we must regard the Holy Year of the Redemption as a year of renewal in the priestly vocation."

He also said: "During the Jubilee Year, may you succeed in being in a special way the teachers of God's truth about forgiveness and remission of sins as this truth is constantly proclaimed by the Church."

The Pope Also:

• Said that the work of priests, brothers and sisters in the apostolate of the press "is more important than ever" in contemporary society, Mar. 21 at an audience for 400 members of the Societies of

St. Paul celebrating the centennial of the birth of their founder, Father Giacomo Alberione.

• While praising the memory of Archbishop Oscar Romero of San Salvador, who was murdered Mar. 24, 1980, prayed that his "sacrifice may not be exploited for partisan interests."

Agca Is Sorry — Mehmet Ali Agca, serving a sentence of life imprisonment for attempting to kill Pope John Paul May 13, 1981, said in a letter that he admired the Pontiff and was sorry for his crime. His letter was published Mar. 13 in *Hurriyet*, an Istanbul daily newspaper, as speculation and investigation continued about the alleged complicity of others in the attempt on the Pope's life.

Vatican Briefs:

• *L'Osservatore Romano* reported that delegates or observers representing the Holy See attended 253 international meetings in 1982. The newspaper prefaced a list of the meetings with the statement that "the dialogue which the Holy See seeks with international organizations is essentially designed for the service of men and of the common good of humanity."

• The recent installation of Stations of the Cross in the Vatican Grottoes where the tombs of dead popes are located made it possible, for the first time in history, for pilgrims to practice this form of devotion in St. Peter's Basilica.

Inauguration of Holy Year

Pope John Paul solemnly inaugurated the Holy Year of Redemption late in the afternoon of Mar. 25 by opening the Holy Door of St. Peter's Basilica. As he struck the door three times with a hammer, he said: "Open to me the doors of justice. This is the door of the Lord. I enter into your house, O Lord."

During Mass, the Holy Father reminded a congregation of 20,000 persons of the reality of sin and the need for repentance. He said: "We wish the Church to be particularly conscious of the fact that the redemption endures in her as a gift of her divine Spouse. . . . We wish her to be particularly sensitive to this gift, more deeply than usual, open and ready to accept this gift. . . . We wish her to be converted and to believe in the Gospel with greater joy than usual."

(See Index: Holy Year of Redemption.)

NATIONAL

Nuclear Survivability Curriculum — The Board of Education of the San Francisco Archdiocese rejected the nuclear disaster curriculum prepared by the Federal Emergency Management Agency for use in elementary and secondary schools. In a statement adopted in mid-February, the board said: "To teach children that nuclear war is a survivable disaster, is to teach them that nuclear war is an acceptable political or moral option."

Budget Cuts Protested — An official of the U.S. Catholic Conference urged Congress Mar. 10 not only to reject new social spending cuts in the federal budget but also to restore funding in several key programs benefitting the poor — food stamp and child nutrition programs, Aid to Families with Dependent Children, Medicaid, low-income hous-

ing, low-income energy assistance, and legal services. Msgr. Francis J. Lally told members of the House and Senate budget committees in a letter that "far too many people are going without the bare minimum required for basic human dignity."

In another development, Richard E. Duffy, also of the U.S. Catholic Conference, called "blatantly discriminatory" a provision of the National School Lunch Act which excluded from the program schools charging tuition of $1,500 or more a year. He said 164 Catholic secondary schools were disqualified in the 1982-83 school year, and that nearly 200 more schools would be disqualified in 1983-84.

Secularism, an Established Religion — The U.S. Supreme Court is making secularism "the established religion in the public school system." So stated Bishop Edward O'Rourke of Peoria Mar. 12 during the first Illinois First Amendment Congress in Springfield. For the previous 36 years, he said, the Court had "exaggerated the scope of the Establishment Clause, resulting in an impairment of the free exercise of religion." This impairment, he added, was particularly evident in the "severe restriction" regarding the cost of education of children in non-public schools.

Burial of Fetuses Stayed — A California state court of appeals granted a two-week stay, until Mar. 17, of a court order authorizing the burial of 16,433 fetuses. The stay was granted at the request of the Feminist Women's Center, an abortion clinic. Attorneys for the Catholic League for Religious and Civil Rights, which opposed the stay, said "the abortion clinic's contention is that, if the Supreme Court and other courts have denied the humanity of the unborn child, this prohibits private citizens from recognizing the fact" by treating them as human beings in the act of burial. It was expected that the clinic would appeal the decision authorizing the burial.

Mrs. Heckler in the Cabinet — Several weeks after defending her anti-abortion stance at a Senate confirmation hearing, Margaret Heckler, a Catholic, was confirmed as President Reagan's Secretary of the Department of Health and Human Services. In response to questioning by Sen. Packwood, an advocate of abortion on demand, she said: "When faced with a major question on the right-to-life issue, my own strong feelings will dominate my thinking. I can't imagine coming down on the other side."

Another Letter on War and Peace — A national group of Catholics, taking exception to portions of the U.S. bishops' proposed pastoral letter on war and peace, issued its own letter urging "moral clarity" in the debate over nuclear arms. The new letter, written by social commentator and author Michael Novak, defended several aspects of nuclear policy, particularly regarding "flexible response," questioned in the second draft of the pastoral letter. While the bishops called the first use of nuclear weapons morally indefensible, the Novak letter argued that a "no first use" pledge in Europe would be "divisive and destabilizing" since the NATO alliance did not have an adequate deterrent in conventional, non-nuclear, forces. "Moral Clarity in a Nuclear Age" was published in the March edition of *Catholicism in Crisis,* a lay-edited journal based at the University of Notre Dame.

Mission Congress — Cardinal Paulo Arns of Sao Paulo, Brazil, was one of the featured speakers at a national Mission Congress held Mar. 17 to 21 in Baltimore. He called on some 550 participants in the congress to set an agenda as "witnesses to the faith," as defenders of human rights, and as builders of base communities fostering openness and participation of people. He told missionaries to "continue to give witness and to do it in service of people and with people, not for people. Do it so people can participate in everything. Build a new communion — spiritual, social and cultural."

Tucson TV Station — Bishop Manuel D. Moreno announced Mar. 21 that his diocese had received permission from the Federal Communications Commission to operate a full-power TV station, Channel 18, in Tucson. He said the station, expected to begin broadcasting by the fall of 1984, would "be the first commercially licensed television station to be totally owned and operated by a diocese of the Catholic Church."

Amnesty and Sanctuary — Bishop John J. Fitzpatrick of Brownsville asked President Reagan to grant amnesty to Salvadoran and other Central American refugees seeking political asylum in the United States. In a letter dated Mar. 24, he noted that the U.N. Commission for Refugees had designated all Salvadorans outside their country as political refugees, and said: "We demand that the United States government recognize those Salvadorans among us as such and grant them political asylum and/or amnesty immediately. Not to do so is clearly in violation of their human rights and international law."

In St. Paul, despite opposition from Archbishop John R. Roach, the archdiocesan Urban Affairs Commission voted to endorse a Presbyterian church's offer of sanctuary to an illegal Salvadoran refugee.

Abbot Blessed in California — Father Claude Ehringer was blessed late in the month as the first abbot of the Prince of Peace Abbey, the first Benedictine abbey in California. Bishop Leo T. Maher, speaking at the ceremony in Oceanside, called the abbey "a spiritual center which will give witness to the things of God" and a "place which draws to itself for spiritual refreshment and encouragement those who have a different vocation."

National Briefs:
• The appointment of Sister Agnes Mary Mansour as head of Michigan's Department of Social Services was confirmed by the State Senate Mar. 9. (See related item in February News Events.)
• The Rev. Everett C. Parker, founder and director of the Office of Communication of the United Church of Christ, announced that he would retire from the post in August after 29 years of service.
• Honored: Benedictine Father Emmeran Bliemel, Confederate army chaplain, with the posthumous award Mar. 12 of the Confederate Medal of Honor by the Sons of Confederate Veter-

ans; Rosemary Radford Ruether, feminist theologian, with the 1983 award of *U.S. Catholic* magazine; Edmund A. Stephan, chairman emeritus of the Board of Trustees, University of Notre Dame, and his wife Evelyn, named to receive the Laetare Award of the university.

Permanent Injunction

U.S. District Judge Thomas A. Flannery issued a permanent injunction Mar. 2 in Washington against implementation by the government of a regulation requiring federally funded family planning clinics to notify parents of girls 17 and under when their children are given prescription contraceptives.

Twenty days after the injunction was issued, Father Edward Bryce, director of the U.S. bishops' Office for Pro-Life Activities, said: "Federally subsidized professionals now have virtually unlimited power over the services and counseling that teen-agers receive, with no accountability to the parents who are responsible for these children's health and welfare." He added that the number of teen-age pregnancies had increased largely because of "the isolation of children from the social and emotional context of the family unit, which alone can adequately provide for mature personal decision-making and self-discipline."

INTERNATIONAL

Explosion Possible in South Africa — Archbishop Denis Hurley of Durban said at a meeting in London Mar. 1 that South Africa faced a "final explosion" over apartheid unless the dim possibility of "peaceful revolution" was realized. Asked if anything but ruthless violence could end the system of strict racial separation, he said a peaceful solution did not seem possible under existing circumstances. He was particularly critical of two pending pieces of legislation by which the government could supply "the coping stone of the edifice of apartheid": one would reinforce efforts to relegate all black citizens to one of 10 black homelands; the other would close all gaps in existing laws restricting black people's opportunities with respect to place of residence, work and movement.

In another development, Sister Bernard Ncube, a member of an African community of black religious, was detained by police then released on bail and charged with possession of undesirable publications.

Government Urged To Step Down — In a statement issued Nov. 11, 1982, but not made available in the U.S. until Mar. 3, the bishops of Ghana called on the military government to step down for the sake of national salvation. The statement said the People's and Workers' Defense Committees ostensibly running the country had "no clear-cut guidelines for their operation," had usurped power and caused "chaos and subversion of duly constituted authority at work places." The bishops charged that in many instances the committees had become "instruments of terror, division and antagonism in our society," and a "haven of corruption, extortion and callousness."

Warning against Cults — In a joint pastoral letter read at Masses Mar. 6 in churches of the six dioceses of western Ireland, the bishops warned families against cults and sects active in the area. Young people, they said, were "not so much converted as taken over" into a state of dependency. "In their methods of recruitment and in the techniques by which they exercise power over young minds, they (the sects and cults) are often manipulating and taking advantage of them. The end can be a disturbed and disoriented mind." The bishops

Trial Put Off — A Salvadoran appeals court ruled during the month that more evidence was needed before a trial date could be set for five ex-members of the National Guard of El Salvador accused of murdering four U.S. Catholic women missionaries Dec. 2, 1980. Some observers speculate that there never would be a trial in the case for a variety of reasons, including implication in the killings of persons higher up than those accused.

New President of CELAM — Bishop Antonio Quarracino of Avellaneda, Argentina, was elected president of the Latin American Bishops' Council during the council's meeting Mar. 9 to 15 in Port-au-Prince, Haiti. After the election, he pledged that he would lead the council, the administrative agency for regional programs of 700 bishops, "with maximum fidelity to the Gospel and to the Church." The work, he said, "will not be easy and presents many difficulties" because "some churches on the continent have rather sad problems."

Tragedy of Religious Intolerance — Edoardo Rovida, representing the Holy See, told the United Nations Commission on Human Rights Mar. 11 in Geneva that religious intolerance is "one of the tragedies of our times, . . . an evil offense to human dignity and a disavowal of United Nations' principles." He said it was crucial to recall the consequences of the failure to respect these fundamental principles and to proceed toward further clarification of the concept of tolerance.

Missionaries Expelled — Three missionary priests — Franciscan Father Brendan Forde, Mill Hill Father Desmond McGillicuddy and Columban Father Brian McMahon — were expelled from Chile Mar. 16 and 19 after repeated but fruitless efforts by Vatican and local church officials to intercede with the government on their behalf. The priests were charged with participation in activities "contrary to public order" while running a soup kitchen in a poor section of Santiago. The Chilean Bishops' Conference said in comment on the expulsions: "These events provoke a grave deterioration in our relations (with the government) which will be difficult to restore."

Lefebvre Church in London — Dissident Archbishop Marcel Lefebvre formally opened a church in London Mar. 19, to be administered by priests belonging to his Priestly Fraternity of St. Pius X. Supporters of the archbishop, who was suspended from the exercise of orders in 1976 for ordaining priests in an irregular manner, said he had 3,000 followers and five priests in Great Britain.

Terror in Zimbabwe — The bishops of Zimbabwe, in a statement dated Mar. 30, charged the army with killing and maiming hundreds of innocent people in a "reign of terror" in the Province of Matabeleland in connection with the struggle between the government of Prime Minister Robert Mugabe and the opposition Zimbabwe African People's Union led by Joshua Nkomo. The government called the charges "utterly one-sided," but the bishops said: "Violent reaction against dissident activity has, to our certain knowledge, brought about the maiming and death of hundreds of innocent people who are neither dissidents nor collaborators."

International Briefs:
• Following several incidents of harassment, Israeli military authorities ordered the closing Mar. 10 of Bethlehem University in the West Bank.

• The World Health Organization reported that more than 100 nations had taken some kind of action to comply with an international code on infant formula marketing supported by some Catholic and other organizations.

• About 50,000 persons attended ceremonies Mar. 20 marking the formal start of first steps toward the possible beatification of Padre Pio; the ceremonies were held in San Giovanni Rotondo, Italy.

• Amnesty International reported Mar. 23 that it had detailed evidence of government-sponsored killings in 27 countries, including Afghanistan, Argentina, Bolivia, Chile, Colombia, El Salvador, Ethiopia, Equatorial Guinea, Guatemala, Iran, Libya, Mexico, Namibia and the Philippines.

• The Holy Year of Redemption was inaugurated in the Holy Land by Latin Rite Patriarch Giacomo Beltritti of Jerusalem Mar. 25 in ceremonies at the Basilica of the Annunciation, Nazareth.

• A major earthquake devastated the 350-year-old city of Popayan, Colombia, May 31 in a Holy Week of disaster.

Soviet Rituals

Efforts by the Soviet government to develop and popularize a series of social rites marking birth, marriage, entry into the work force and other significant life and death events, were the subjects of an article in the Mar. 15 edition of *The New York Times*. Scholars commented that the efforts had been going on for some time and had mixed results.

Cases in point were cited in connection with Palaces of Festive events in the Ukraine, where "women in long gowns and glittering chains of office are ready to perform the new rituals at altarlike tables flanked by a white bust of Lenin and accompanied by appropriate music from an organ or full choir."

The rites "are a deliberate attempt" to provide young persons and others with irreligious ceremonies comparable to those of religious significance in the liturgy of the Russian Orthodox Church. So stated Father John Meyendorf, professor of church history at St. Vladimir's Orthodox Theological Seminary, Crestwood, N.Y. He said he had the impression that some people laugh at the Soviet rites "because they're so clumsy."

APRIL 1983

VATICAN

Easter Message — "This year, more than ever, the Church wishes to be the witness to the resurrection; for it is the Holy Year of the Redemption, the special Jubilee." So stated the Holy Father in his Easter message "To the City and the World." He prayed: "O risen Christ, in your glorious wounds accept all the throbbing wounds of the men and women of today: the wounds which are so much talked about in the media, and also those wounds whose pain is silently endured in the hidden secret of human hearts. Let them be relieved in the mystery of the redemption. Let them be closed and healed through love, which is stronger than death." While conveying Easter greetings in 44 languages before a throng of 250,000 persons in St. Peter's Square, the Pope also said: "We are with all the suffering wounds of humanity today; and we are with all the expectations, hopes and joys of our brothers and sisters, to which the risen Christ gives meaning and value."

On Holy Thursday, the Pope concelebrated the Mass of Chrism with 1,200 priests and washed the feet of 12 homeless boys during the Mass of the Lord's Supper. He heard confessions in St. Peter's Basilica on Good Friday, when he also took part in the solemn celebration of the Lord's Passion and in the Stations of the Cross at the Colosseum in Rome. He presided at Easter Vigil ceremonies during which the sacraments of baptism, confirmation and the Eucharist were administered to 22 adults from 10 countries.

Holy Year Contrast — Addressing a general audience of 60,000 persons Apr. 6, the Pope said: "We want to celebrate (Christ's) victory of life and freedom because it gives the fullness of dimension to the mystery of the redemption and reveals the power of the cross. . . . Think of the contrast that this Holy Year presents between the celebration of the redemption, on one hand, and, on the other, offenses against God, crimes against man and defiances of Christ which at the same time continue to be committed."

Archbishop Excommunicated — The Pope, "by special mandate," ordered the excommunication of 85-year-old Archbishop Pierre Martin Ngo Dinh Thuc, former head of the Archdiocese of Hue, Vietnam. The principal reason for the censure, announced Apr. 7, was the archbishop's violation of church law by ordaining three bishops in an unauthorized manner in 1981.

Victims of Warsaw Uprising — The Pope rendered homage Apr. 13 to 65,000 Jews who were killed in the Warsaw Uprising of 1943. He called them "innocent victims" and said their action was "a desperate cry for the right to life, for freedom and for the salvation of the dignity of mankind."

Meeting with Armenian Prelate — The Pope and the head of the Armenian Orthodox Church discussed Apr. 16 conditions in Lebanon along with their hopes for greater Catholic-Orthodox cooperation. The Pope called the meeting with Katholikos Karekine II Sarkissian of Cilicia a "new step in the fraternal dialogue" between the two churches.

Bombing Condemned — Pope John Paul, addressing 50,000 people Apr. 20, condemned the bombing two days earlier of the U.S. embassy in Beirut, and called on the Lebanese to "keep alive the hope of a peaceful, just and lasting solution" to the nation's problems.

Meeting with Lithuanian Bishops — "The sorrows and joys" of the Church in Lithuania were subjects of the Pope's address Apr. 22 to four bishops of that country. He said: "How ardently I desire that this living faith of the people of God (in Lithuania) may find the necessary atmosphere to be able to manifest itself in all its richness, both in the lives of individuals, of families and of the Church itself, with full freedom of conscience and of religion, in all the individual and communitarian aspects which that liberty involves." Among the "sorrows" of the Church in Lithuania were a shortage of priests, the lack of facilities and freedom to train students for the priesthood, restrictions on the freedom of parents to "transmit the gift of faith to their children," and the erosion of the sanctity of marriage. The four bishops were the first ones permitted by the Soviet government to make *ad limina* visits in more than 40 years.

Prayer for Priestly and Religious Vocations — The Holy Father, marking the World Day of Prayer for Vocations Apr. 24, expressed pleasure at a reported increase in vocations to the priesthood and religious life between 1975 and 1980 (9.8 per cent in the number of candidates for the priesthood in major seminaries, 23 percent in the number of novices in religious institutes for women). He stressed the need of prayer for more priests, brothers and nuns: "It is necessary to intensify our prayers to invoke from the Lord a sufficient number of workers for his harvest, which is so abundant at the moment."

Family Ministry — The Pope told 18 bishops of Canada Apr. 28 at the Vatican about the responsibility to oppose divorce and artificial contraception "as long as the Lord gives us strength to preach." He said the Church's "ministry of love . . . toward the family . . . means constantly proclaiming the truth of God's plan for marriage." He added: "As bishops, we are not able to make the obstacles to Christian living disappear. We are not in a position to lift all the burdens that weigh upon our Christian families; and much less are we authorized to attempt to remove the cross from Christianity."

The African Contribution — At a meeting Apr. 30 with 15 bishops from Zaire, the Pope hailed the "fundamental values of an authentic African contribution" to the thinking of the Church. He reminded the prelates at the same time that all elements of African culture are not acceptable, noting that judgment had to be made "of the Christian authenticity" of ideas and experiences.

The Pope Also:
• Called Apr. 17 for the release of 64 Czecho-

slovakians kidnapped and held for more than a month in Angola by guerrillas opposed to the nation's Marxist government.

• Met Apr. 25 with a 30-member delegation from the Simon Wiesenthal Center of Los Angeles and expressed hope that the encounter would "deepen bonds of friendship and trust" among Christians and Jews.

• Told a group of British church leaders Apr. 29 that Christian witness to peace is "an extremely urgent problem" demanding ecumenical cooperation.

Vatican Briefs:

• Joseph Amichia, Ivory Coast's ambassador to the Holy See since 1971, became dean of the diplomatic corps accredited to the Vatican. He succeeded Guatemalan Ambassador Luis Valladares y Aycinena, who was removed from office by his government for allegedly failing to report a papal plea for clemency for six men who were executed during the Pope's trip to Central America. Ambassador Valladares denies the charge.

• The International Council for Catechesis reported progress in the development of a document on teaching doctrine, to be published eventually as a revision of the *General Catechetical Directory* issued in 1971.

• Vatican and Italian negotiators reported agreement on revisions to the concordat regulating church-state relations in Italy. Ratification of the revisions by Parliament was pending.

Ministry of Reconciliation

The "ministry of reconciliation in all its implications" was the theme of an Apr. 15 address by the Pope to the bishops of New York and the U.S. Military Ordinariate during their required five-year *ad limina* visits to the Vatican.

He said, in part:

This ministry "means reviving a sense of God, of his word, of his commandments — of the need for accepting his will as the real criterion for human action. Proclaiming reconciliation means reviving a sense of sin among our people; this in turn can lead us to recognize the roots of human responsibility in the varied fields of economic, social, historical, cultural and political ills."

"To proclaim reconciliation means in a particular way promoting the sacrament of penance. It means stressing the importance of the sacrament as it relates to conversion, to Christian growth, to the very renewal of society, which cannot be healed without the forgiveness of sins."

"I would ask once again for your zealous pastoral and collegial solicitude to help ensure that these norms (regarding general absolution), as well as the norms regulating the first confession of children, are understood and properly applied. The treasures of Christ's love in the sacrament of penance are so great that children too must be initiated into them. The patient effort of parents, teachers and priests needed to prepare children for this sacrament are of great value for the whole Church."

"In this Holy Year of Redemption I would ask that a whole pastoral program be developed around the sacrament of penance and be effected by practical means."

NATIONAL

NCEA Convention — Nearly 10,000 people attended sessions of the annual convention of the National Catholic Educational Association Apr. 4 to 7 in Washington. "Catholic Education: The Choices and the Challenges" was the theme of the meeting and the focus of addresses and discussions on a wide range of subjects. The maintenance and development of Catholic identity in schools of the Church were called the greatest challenges by Father Alfred A. McBride at the closing session. President Reagan, who addressed the convention earlier, pledged support for tuition tax credit legislation and for efforts to provide various forms of education-related assistance to the parents of disadvantaged children and college students.

Court Has False View — An official of the Catholic League for Religious and Civil Rights accused the U.S. Supreme Court of basing decisions on state aid to non-public schools on a false and unfair view of Catholic schools and their teachers. Father Peter M. J. Stravinskas, addressing the convention of the National Catholic Educational Association, said Apr. 7 that majority opinions in several decisions implied that teachers in Catholic schools could not be trusted to obey the law and that they would use secular subjects as vehicles for religious indoctrination.

Change of Direction — Auxiliary Bishop Moses Anderson of Detroit, speaking Apr. 10 in Brooklyn, said the Reagan administration was responsible for a "change of direction" in programs of special importance to black people: "It seems to be the national policy to dismantle or attempt to dismantle a tremendous amount of activity related to human rights and the entitlement programs that have given tremendous hope and meaning."

Unwarranted Raid — In a letter addressed to David N. Ilchert, director of the Immigration and Naturalization Service in the San Francisco district, Bishop Roger M. Mahony protested "the unwarranted raid by . . . Border Patrol Agents (Apr. 13) at St. Mary's Dining Hall here in Stockton." He stated: "I consider St. Mary's Dining Room to be fully within the definition of 'sanctuary,' since it is part of the Catholic parish's physical complex and spiritual ministry." The raid was a search operation for undocumented aliens. An INS official called the incident a misunderstanding.

It was also reported that hundreds of illegal aliens were being sheltered or otherwise aided by churches across the country. The granting of sanctuary was regarded as a borderline act of civil disobedience against the Refugee Act of 1980.

Another Anti-Catholic Play — The Minnesota chapter of the Catholic League for Religious and Civil Rights charged that "Haunted by the Holy Ghost," a play by Jan Magrane, was "blatantly anti-Catholic" and "a vicious attack on the Catholic Church." The league said the play, being performed at the Cedar Riverside People's Center in Minneapolis, "mocks Catholic rituals, mocks the Eucharist and the Mass, ridicules the doctrine of the Virgin Birth, desecrates the cross, depicts mothers and motherhood as stupid, (and) is profane and crude." The play belonged to the same anti-Catholic genre as "Sister Mary Ignatius Explains It All for You," which the Catholic league denounced two or three months earlier.

Euthanasia Threat — Dr. Richard Lamerton, a British physician active in the hospice movement, said Apr. 13 in Washington that persons involved in the anti-abortion movement should pay more attention to the battle over mercy killing. He felt that pro-lifers gave "inadequate attention" to the euthanasia issue, "while humanists have moved their principal thrust forward" to promote such acts as mercy killing or bringing about death through the withholding of food or medical care. People concerned with preserving respect for life, he added, would "still have to fight the euthanasia battle, even if all abortions stopped."

Reagan on Quality of Life — Denouncing those who "want to pick and choose" which members of the human race have qualities that bring them "up to snuff," President Reagan wrote that the United States "must choose between the sanctity of life ethic and the 'quality of life' ethic." His comments appeared in an article entitled "Abortion and the Conscience of the Nation," written for the spring edition of the *Human Life Review.* "Make no mistake, abortion on demand is not a right granted by the Constitution," he said, noting the 10th anniversary of the U.S. Supreme Court's decision in Roe v. Wade. "No serious scholar . . . has argued that the framers of the Constitution intended to create such a right."

Lay Persons Are Not Paraclerics — The main job of the laity is not to serve the Church as "paraclerics," declared Bishop James Hoffman of Toledo during an interview late in the month in New York. "We need to focus on their ministry in the world," he said. "That is where the big decisions are made on issues concerning justice and the kind of society we're going to have. I am not opposed to lay people becoming more involved in the ministries of the Church. But that is not their primary role." He noted that most efforts in lay formation since the Second Vatican Council seemed directed toward preparing lay persons for work in the Church, not in the world. He thought the Church appeared to be doing less than before Vatican II with respect to lay formation for ministry in the world.

Vain Plea for Clemency — Archbishop Oscar H. Lipscomb of Mobile, writing in the Apr. 29 edition of the *Catholic Week,* said he had appealed to Gov. George Wallace of Alabama for clemency for John E. Louis Evans II, who was executed Apr. 22 after being found guilty of robbery and murder committed in 1977. The bishop made the appeal 10 days before the execution.

Meetings — Meetings during the month included those of:
• The seventh National Workshop on Christian-Jewish Relations, attended by nearly 1,000 persons Apr. 24 to 28 in Boston.
• The National Federation of Priests' Councils,

attended by more than 100 delegates late in the month in Milwaukee.
National Briefs:
• A bronze *pieta,* a memorial to modern martyrs, was dedicated Apr. 16 in Miami.
• U.S. Catholics contributed more than $39.5 million to the worldwide general fund of the Society for the Propagation of the Faith in 1982, for the support of missionary work.
• Honored: Seventy-two-year-old Sister Madeline Chorman, named an Outstanding Peace Corp Volunteer for service in Ghana; Eileen Egan, a founding member of Pax Christi USA, named to the Hall of Fame of Hunter College, City University of New York.

Baby Doe Rule Struck Down

A rule on care for handicapped newborns published by the Reagan administration Mar. 7 was struck down Apr. 14 by U.S. District Judge Gerhard A. Gessell who declared it had been issued too hastily and was based on "inadequate consideration" of all relevant factors. The regulation would have required hospitals receiving federal funds to post notices that the denial of customary care to handicapped infants was a violation of federal law.

The ruling was handed down almost a year after the event which created controversy over the care of handicapped infants: the death of "Baby Doe" Apr. 15, 1982, in Bloomington, Ind., of Down's Syndrome, after being denied food and surgery that would have corrected his deformed esophagus.

A spokesman of the pro-life office of the National Conference of Catholic Bishops called the rejected rule a "long-overdue response" to abuses by physicians who allow handicapped newborns to die rather than receive life-saving treatment.

INTERNATIONAL

Sanctimonious Prelates — Prime Minister Robert Mugabe of Zimbabwe told a group of religious leaders Apr. 5 that those among them who charged that the army's anti-dissident campaign had led to atrocities were "sanctimonious prelates." He was especially critical of a Mar. 30 statement in which the Catholic bishops said "the army was killing and maiming hundreds of innocent people in a reign of terror" in Metabeleland. Some reports indicated the death toll exceeded 1,000 persons.

Brazilian Bishops Critical — The bishops of Brazil, meeting Apr. 6 to 15 in Rio de Janeiro, were critical of the military government's handling of the nation's economy, saying it had managed to increase industrial and agricultural production during 19 years in power but had "not eradicated hunger." It was reported that real wages and purchasing power were down, unemployment and inflation were high, and the nation had a foreign debt of approximately $90 billion.

Memorial Mass for Jews — Cardinal Jozef Glemp celebrated a memorial Mass Apr. 10 for the 65,000 Jews who were slaughtered during the June, 1943, three-week Warsaw uprising against German occupation troops. The Mass, attended by 3,000 people, was held in St. Augustine's Church, the only building in the Warsaw ghetto that escaped destruction during the uprising.

Shenouda Dethronement Upheld — An Egyptian appeals court upheld Apr. 12 the 1981 decision of the late President Anwar el-Sadat to depose and strictly limit the movement and activity of Pope Shenouda III, the 117th patriarch of the Coptic Orthodox Church. Sadat alleged that Shenouda had gone beyond the boundaries of his post by "fomenting sectarian conflicts in the country" and thus "threatening the institutions of the state." Sadat's action was symptomatic of the Egyptian government's antipathy toward Christians.

Murders Not Investigated — Archbishop Arturo Rivera Damas, commenting on the human rights situation in El Salvador, said April 17 that more than 30,000 Salvadoran noncombatants had been murdered in the previous four years and that few, if any, of their deaths had been the subject of investigation by the government. In contrast, some type of investigation had been made into circumstances surrounding the slaying of eight citizens of the United States.

Dissident Chinese Catholics — Members of the dissident Patriotic Association of Chinese Catholics marked the 25th anniversary of their 1958 decision to elect their own bishops, end "the colonial character of the Chinese church (and) direct its own religious affairs in an independent manner," free of any and all ties to the See of Rome. The anniversary was marked with a Mass celebrated Apr. 17 in the Peking cathedral by Bishop Bernard Dong Guangoing of Hankou, the first of about 60 patriotic bishops ordained without authorization of the Vatican since 1958.

Other reports from China noted:

• Four elderly Jesuit priests arrested in 1981 were sentenced to prison terms on charges of collusion with foreign countries and subversion.

• French-Chinese Catholic Raymond Ratillon left China for France Apr. 8 after being released from 27 years of detention for unspecified charges.

Peaceful Reform Needed — "The changes needed for a just social order must be achieved by a constant action, often gradual and progressive but always effective, along the road of peaceful reform." So stated Archbishop Miguel Obando Bravo in an article in the Apr. 25 edition of *The New York Times*. The article did not mention Nicaragua's Sandinist government, but its positions reflected increasing concern that Marxists in the governing coalition were gaining greater influence and were trying to install a communist regime in the country. The archbishop said: "Power must never serve to protect the interests of one group to the detriment of others. . . . The class struggle is no path to social order either, because it runs the risk of turning the underprivileged into the privileged and creating new situations of injustice for those previously better off. . . . The bold reforms needed should not exclusively aim at collectivising the means of production, especially if it means concentrating everything under the state, which then becomes the sole and truly capitalist force."

Jesuits Awaiting Trial — Vatican Radio reported

Apr. 27 that four Vietnamese Jesuits arrested more than two years earlier were being held in a Ho Chi Minhville prison for trial on charges of "counterrevolutionary crimes." The priests were Fathers Nguyen Cong Doan, Le Thanh Que, Hoang Si Qui and Dinh Van Trung.

Missing Persons in Argentina — Advocates of human rights in Argentina were critical of a government report justifying actions of security forces during anti-guerrilla campaigns of the late 1970s in which thousands of people disappeared without a trace. The report, released Apr. 28, said some errors were made that "might have trespassed the limits of respect for fundamental human rights." It implied that security forces should not be held responsible for disapperances and deaths because all military and police actions were "acts of service." The Mothers of *Plaza de Mayo,* a group of relatives of missing persons, wondered if "to kidnap, torture, assassinate and lie without shame are acts of service." The government report was issued in response to a steady stream of calls — by the bishops, political leaders and concerned relatives and citizens — for clarification of the fate of between 6,000 and 15,000 missing persons.

International Briefs:

• The Social Affairs Commission of the Canadian Conference of Catholic Bishops was circulating a set of suggestions encouraging parishes to join local labor groups and community organizations "to assist unemployed people in their struggles for justice." The number of unemployed was approximately 1.6 million.

• Father Vincent Kwabena Damuah, a former member of the Provisional National Defense Council of Ghana, announced he was leaving the Church in order to undertake "a completely new challenge to reform, update and organize the African traditional religion (Afrikania) so that it can take its rightful place among the major religions of the world."

• Cardinal Terence Cooke, head of the U.S. Military Ordinariate, was the principal celebrant of a Mass offered Apr. 20 at the North American College in Rome for victims of the bombing of the U.S. embassy in Beirut.

Franciscans Arrested in Czechoslovakia

Five of 20 Franciscans arrested during Holy Week remained in prison Apr. 6, according to the Justice and Peace Commission of the Order of Friars Minor in Rome. Three priests were held in a prison in Prague; two were jailed in Pizen. All were charged with "the unusual accusation of illegal religious activity," the communique said. The other 15 friars were released after interrogation.

The communique also said: "There is reason to believe that the new wave of oppression is connected with the recent Vatican document (of March, 1982) which forbids Czechoslovakian priests to belong to the government-based association, Pacem in Terris."

Church-state tensions in Czechoslovakia were the tightest in the communist bloc.

MAY 1983

VATICAN

Workers and Their Work — Addressing about 50,000 persons in St. Peter's Square May 1, the Holy Father said: "Our thoughts turn to St. Joseph the Worker and to all who, like him, work to reach their human fulfillment and their Christian dignity. . . . It is by means of labor that man procures for himself and for his loved ones the daily necessary sustenance and, at the same time, gives a personal and capable contribution to the scientific and technical progress of society and, above all, to the continual ethical elevation of all humanity."

Missing Persons — Missing persons in Argentina, the subject of a government report issued recently, were the focus of the Pope's address to a general audience May 4. He said: "In recent days, world public opinion has turned its attention with renewed and understandable sensitivity to the sorrowful drama of the *desaparecidos* in Argentina, expressing solidarity with the families tried by this anguishing situation. . . . The worrisome problem of the missing (estimated to number 60,000) has always been . . . in my heart, and I wish to renew for the families who have such a sharp thorn in their hearts for the fate of their dear ones my heartfelt participation in their suffering."

Individual Confession — The Pope told 35 American priests May 6 that the mercy of God is felt most keenly in individual confession: "Pastoral sensitivity teaches us that this experience of divine mercy reaches its highest intensity — and finds its most eloquent expression — at that moment when the individual penitent kneels before the minister of the sacrament of penance and asks Christ's forgiveness and absolution for his sins. . . . So much of our identity as men of God is associated in the minds of the faithful with our role as sacramental reconcilers. Much of the respect, the deference and the genuine affection our people show toward us is linked with our power to forgive sins in the name of Christ. We would be less than faithful to the essence of our priestly vocation by not seizing each possible opportunity to offer to our people the healing and reconciling power of Christ's mercy in the sacrament of penance."

The Galileo Affair — The Galileo affair has led the Church "to a more mature attitude and to a more accurate grasp" of its authority, declared the Pope May 9 at a meeting with 300 scientists marking the 350th anniversary of the publication of Galileo's *Dialogues on the Two Great World Systems*. Galileo was censured by the Church in 1633 for teaching that the sun is the center of the universe and that the earth revolves around it. His teaching, then a barely demonstrated scientific thesis, was thought by many in the Church to contradict a literal interpretation of Scripture that the sun moved around the earth and the theological belief in the centrality of man as redeemed by Christ. The Pope said that a team he set up several years earlier was still examining the Galileo question. He also noted: "Divine revelation, of which the Church is the guarantor and witness, does not

of itself involve any particular scientific theory, and the assistance of the Holy Spirit in no way lends itself to guaranteeing explanations that we would wish to profess concerning the physical constitution of reality."

Blessing with Orthodox Patriarch — Greek Orthodox Patriarch Ignatius IV Hazim of Antioch and all the East joined the Pope in blessing people attending Mass on Ascension Day in St. Peter's Basilica. The Pope noted the Patriarch's presence at the Mass and voiced hope that the current Holy Year would "contribute to hastening the time of the desired full union of all those who believe in Jesus Christ."

Missionaries to China Beatified — The Holy Father celebrated Mass in connection with ceremonies for the beatification May 15 of two Italian missionaries martyred in China in 1930, Bishop Luigi Versiglia and Father Callisto Caravario. He voiced hope in a homily for dialogue with the Chinese communist government.

A day earlier, the Pope attended ceremonies during which the Congregation for the Causes of Saints promulgated decrees acknowledging the practice of heroic virtue by five candidates for sainthood. One of the five was Jesuit Father Rupert Mayer, a vigorous opponent of the Nazi regime in Germany.

World Communications Day — In a message marking the 17th annual observance of World Communications Day May 15, Pope John Paul urged workers in the media to "re-think the fundamental principles and aims" of social communications and to become "workers for peace." He condemned mass media "manipulation of whatever kind, one-way information imposed arbitrarily from on high" or for advertising purposes, and the increasing concentration of monopoly ownership of media operations. "Not only are such things attacks upon the right order of social communication, but they also finish by injuring the rights to responsible information and by endangering peace," he said.

Confirmation — The Holy Father confirmed 298 persons from 13 countries May 29 during an evening Mass in St. Peter's Basilica. He told them that the sacrament "confirms and seals that which was mysteriously effected by baptism, which makes us fully adoptive sons of God and therefore included in the range of action of his love."

No Contraception — The Pope called on Catholics to be "totally faithful" to church teaching against artificial means of birth control. He did so May 30 in an address to 20 couples attending the first plenary assembly of the Pontifical Council for the Family. "It is absolutely necessary," he said, "that the pastoral action of the Christian community be totally faithful to what is taught by the encyclical *Humanae Vitae* and by the apostolic constitution *Familiaris Consortio*. . . . It would be a grave error to place pastoral needs and doctrinal teaching in opposition, since the first service that the Church must carry out in relation to man is to tell him the truth, of which it (the Church) is neither author nor arbitrator."

Charity — "Charity ought to be the distinctive sign of the disciples of Christ," Pope John Paul told 400 delegates to a meeting of Caritas Internationalis May 30. "Immediate assistance, response to emergencies, help to people in difficulty or to those victimized by calamities, maintain their importance," he said. "They are the ever-necessary expressions of a charity which does not wait to be asked for and which attaches a value to every person, as the Good Samaritan did."

A day earlier, Cardinal Alexandre do Nascimento of Lubango, Angola, was elected to a four-year term as president of the association of Catholic charitable agencies in 115 countries.

The Pope Also:

• Marked the 20th annual World Day of Prayer for Vocations May 1 with a special message.

• Made the 70th parish visit of his pontificate May 8, to St. Monica Parish in Ostia Lido.

• At a special Mass May 17, commemorated the 100th anniversary of the start of Mother Marianne Cope's work among the lepers of Hawaii.

• Attended a concert at La Scala opera house during a May 20 to 22 visit to Milan.

• Pledged that he would continue to speak out against nuclear arms, at a meeting May 31 with Mayor Takeshi Araki of Hiroshima.

Vatican Briefs:

• Twenty-seven recruits were inducted into the Swiss Guards May 6, the 456th anniversary of the sack of Rome during which 147 members of the corps gave their lives in defense of Pope Clement VII.

• Carlos Chagas, president of the Pontifical Academy of Sciences, praised the bishops of the United States for their pastoral letter, released early in the month, on war and peace.

Apostolic Spirituality Today

Pope John Paul delivered an address on this subject at an audience May 13 with 770 participants in a congress of the International Union of Superiors General.

He urged sisters to choose their apostolic works after "serious study" and "constant dialogue," making sure that the work chosen is "always in conformity with the most urgent demands and according to the character of (their) institute." He said this "will involve always carrying out such experiences in accord with the hierarchy."

He told them to "interpret in the light of the Gospel the option for the poor and for the victims of man's egoism without giving in to socio-political radicalism which, sooner or later, produces effects contrary to those desired and engenders new forms of oppression."

The Pontiff praised the "eminently apostolic role of cloistered nuns" and said: "The Pope and the Church need you. Christians count on your fidelity."

NATIONAL

Marriage Preparation Programs — Fifty to 60 per cent of the people married in the Catholic Church in 1980-81 in the U.S. participated in some kind of marriage preparation program, according to a study conducted by Catholic University's National Center for Family Studies. The study also indicated that 80 per cent of the dioceses in the U.S. had such programs.

Nun Separated from Sisters of Mercy — Agnes Mary Mansour was dispensed from vows and was canonically separated from the Sisters of Mercy May 9 after refusing to resign the office of director of Michigan's Department of Social Services. She had accepted the office without the permission of Archbishop Edmund C. Szoka of Detroit and had failed to publicly criticize state funding of abortions. Auxiliary Bishop Anthony Bevilacqua of Brooklyn, acting by authority of the Congregation for Religious and Secular Institutes, said of the affair that one relevant question was: "Does a religious have a right to determine the nature of his or her ministry and occupation in the face of a specific contrary determination by church authorities? The Church's answer has been and remains 'no.' "

Anti-Catholic Art Exhibit — Three days after the closing of an art exhibit at the University of Illinois at Chicago, the Catholic League for Religious and Civil Rights asked members of two state committees May 16 to see that the exhibit "not go unrebuked and that nothing like it will ever happen again." The league called 34 of 40 paintings by Douglas Van Dyke anti-Catholic; among them were depictions of Christ with the head of a pig on the cross, of the Eucharist in a toilet bowl, and of bishops and the pope as instruments of the devil. The exhibit was held in public facilities and was funded out of tax revenues.

Anti-Smut Action Sought — Nearly 100 bishops wrote to President Reagan recently to seek the appointment of an official authorized to coordinate the anti-obscenity activities of the Justice Department, the U.S. Customs Service, the Federal Bureau of Investigation and the U.S. Postal Service. Archbishop John R. Quinn of San Francisco said in his letter: "I firmly believe that the traffic in pornographic materials is a threat to the moral and spiritual well-being of our society, and I believe that the unfettered distribution of pornographic materials seriously erodes support for the values of family and human dignity."

Interfaith Proposals — United Methodist Bishop James Armstrong, speaking May 19 at the closing session of the 20th annual National Workshop on Christian Unity, cited four issues which churches should address: nuclear disarmament, racism, economic crisis and the family. In a keynote address delivered earlier, the Rev. Lois Wilson, former moderator of the United Church of Canada, mentioned seven "ecumenical convictions around which churches covenant in mission and evangelization": conversion; application of the Gospel to all areas of life; the church's unity in God's mission; mission in Christ's way; announcing the Good News to the poor; mission in and to other continents, and witness among people of living faith. The Louisville workshop was attended by about 500 Catholics, Protestants and Orthodox.

Bishop for Hungarians — Father Ladislaus A. Iranyi, former provincial of the American Province of the Piarist Fathers, was named by Pope John Paul May 20 to be the bishop for Hungarian Catholics living outside Hungary. He was the first bishop appointed for such specialized ministry. The 1980 Census revealed that this country had the largest concentration of Hungarians (1.5 million) living outside Hungary.

Bishop and Nuns in Agreement — The Diocese of Manchester announced May 20 that Bishop Odore Gendron and four Sisters of Mercy had reached an out-of-court settlement of a dispute that began in the spring of 1982 when the diocese made it known that it was not going to renew the nuns' teaching contracts. The reason for the refusal was the allegation by the diocese that the sisters — Honora Reardon, Mary Rita Furlong, Justine and Catherine Colliton — were not responsive to a parish community and school board. A joint statement by lawyers for the bishop and the nuns said the nuns, who would not continue to teach at Sacred Heart School, Hampton, could apply for teaching positions in other schools of the diocese and could continue to reside in their diocesan-maintained convent until July, 1984.

No Tax Exemption if Racial Discrimination — The U.S. Supreme Court ruled 8 to 1 May 24 that private schools — Bob Jones University and the Goldsboro Christian Schools — which discriminate on the basis of race can be denied tax-exempt status even when they base their practices on religious beliefs. The Court upheld the practice of the Internal Revenue Service in denying tax exemption to groups acting contrary to established public policy. The eradication of racial discrimination is such an important public policy, the Court declared, that "it would be wholly incompatible with the concepts underlying tax exemption to grant the benefit of tax-exempt status to racially discriminating educational entities." To the argument that the discriminatory practices at issue were protected by the constitutional guarantee of freedom of religion, the Court observed that sometimes governmental interests are "so compelling as to allow even regulations prohibiting religiously based conduct." General reaction to the decision was favorable, but there were observers who suggested the decision involved ominous implications regarding the role of government in determining acceptable religious beliefs and practices.

Catholic Relief Services — The U.S. overseas aid and development agency reported it had provided emergency financial aid valued at $123,000 since January to disaster victims in Ecuador, Bolivia, Peru and Colombia. Also reported May 11 was the signing of a $2.4 million grant agreement with the U.S. Agency for International Development to continue the reconstruction and rehabilitation of private health and educational facilities in Lebanon.

National Briefs:
• About 30,000 people in the San Diego area received some 400,000 pounds of food in a work-exchange program sponsored by the local St. Vincent de Paul Center.

• LaSalette Father John Toner was named chaplain for the Ringling Brothers and Barnum and Bailey Circus, to succeed the late Father David Hennessy.

• Honored: Sister Ann Jeanne Chisolm, with the 1983 Distinguished Administrator Award of the American College of Nursing Home Administrator.

War and Peace Pastoral Letter

The National Conference of Catholic Bishops, with a vote of 238 to 9 May 3, approved a 40,000-word pastoral letter on war and peace entitled "The Challenge of Peace: God's Promise and Our Response." The bishops called the letter "an invitation and a challenge to Catholics in the United States to join with others in shaping the conscious choices and deliberate policies required" to decisively influence the course of the nuclear age."
(See separate article.)

INTERNATIONAL

Catholic-Anglican Problem — Cardinal Joseph Ratzinger called the authority issue a "fundamental problem" in dialogue between the Catholic Church and the Anglican Communion. He said so in an article published in *Insight*, an Anglican journal, with reference to the final report of the Anglican-Roman Catholic International Commission. Writing in his personal capacity as a theologian, the prefect of the Congregation for the Doctrine of the Faith suggested that "too little attention has been paid to the actual functioning of authority" in the Anglican Communion. He said the report "left one completely in the dark as to the concrete structure of authority in the Anglican community." He also said that a first reading of the report might convey the (erroneous) impression that the only obstacles to complete interfaith agreement were the teaching of the First Vatican Council on papal primacy and dogmas concerning Mary.

No Amnesty in Poland — Pope John Paul's plea that all Polish political prisoners be granted amnesty before his June 16 to 22 visit to the country was rejected by the government. "There is no humanitarian basis for a legal act of amnesty, and at present the government is not proposing to adopt such a measure," said government spokesman Jerzy Urban May 3 at a news conference also attended by Adam Lopatka, minister of religious affairs. Urban added: "The release from prison of people who are not inclined to obey the law may be perceived as a bending of will, a weakening of our resolve to deal firmly with social unrest."

Lithuanian Priest Convicted — Father Alfonsas Svarinskas was convicted May 6 of "anti-constitutional and anti-state activity" and sentenced to seven years in jail, according to a report from the Soviet news agency Tass. He had been jailed since Jan. 26 on suspicion of distributing anti-Soviet material to the foreign press and of preaching against the government. A co-founder of the clandestine Catholic Committee for the Defense of the Rights of Believers, he was tried and found guilty in a two-day trial in Vilna.

Excommunication — A spokesman for Archbishop Mario Ismaele Castellano of Siena announced that a suspended priest and 300 parishioners of San Ansano Parish had incurred automatic excommunication for professing "heresy or schismatic causes" in support of Pierino Babbini, a former coalman calling himself "the Apostle Peter" and crediting himself with more than 3,000 miracles in 13 years. The errors for which the priest and people incurred excommunication included support for Babbini's authority over that of the pope and bishops, the belief that Babbini was the valid successor to St. Peter as the Vicar of Christ, and support for Babbini's interpretation of the Gospel over that of the Church.

Language and Religious Differences — Language and the different meanings Catholics and Presbyterians attach to the same words or phrases are important factors in differences between the two churches, said a Scottish dialogue commission May 17. "Key words and forms of expression, instinctive to one side but unfamiliar to the other, can render mutual understanding difficult, and even conceal areas of agreement in underlying meaning and intention," stated a report issued by the joint commission on doctrine of the (Presbyterian) Church of Scotland and the Catholic Church in Scotland.

Test-Tube-Baby Procedure — In testimony prepared for presentation to an official inquiry board, a bioethics committee representing the bishops of England, Wales and Scotland called for severe government restrictions on *in vitro* fertilization and expressed serious misgivings about the entire "test-tube-baby" procedure. The committee questioned the rationale of *in vitro* fertilization and artificial insemination because they separate procreation from sexual union in marriage. The committee also opposed surrogate motherhood, surrogate fatherhood and cloning.

Nuclear Morality — The influential Jesuit magazine, *Civilta Cattolica,* published May 21 an article on nuclear morality which closely resembled major aspects of the U.S. bishops' pastoral letter on the subject. The article stood for "an absolute 'no' to nuclear war," including first use of nuclear weapons and limited response to nuclear attack. Positions stated in the article were more like those in the American letter of May 3 than in the letter issued by the German hierarchy a week earlier. The German bishops, while aware of the cataclysmic horror of nuclear war, stopped short of the outright condemnation of first use, thus leaving open the possibility of a nuclear response for the purpose of halting an overwhelming attack with conventional weapons.

Blame for Criminal Actions in Nicaragua — The Nicaraguan Conference of Religious charged the United States with responsibility for the "criminal actions" of guerrillas fighting against the Sandinista government. The guerrillas were "terrorizing and killing innocent persons looking only to help their brothers in the fields of health, education and technology," said a letter written by the executive board of the conference. "It is incomprehensible to us," the letter added, "that the impulsor and patron of such criminal actions is precisely the government of a country, such as the United States, which has been and continues to be so generous in sending us priests and religious who are so sacrificing and giving in their service to the people." The letter was sent May 21 to religious working in the border areas where fighting was in progress.

Apartheid the Cause of Violence — Archbishop Denis Hurley of Durban, president of the South African Bishops' Conference, declared that the government's policy of strict racial segregation was responsible for escalating violence in the area. He did so in statements issued after the bombing May 20 of the South African Air Force headquarters and after the May 23 retaliation bombing by South African forces in neighboring Mozambique. "Essentially," the archbishop said, "'the escalation of violence is a response by desperate people to the built-in violence in an apartheid society."

International Briefs:

• Illicitly ordained Father Juan Fernandez was found guilty of attempting to kill Pope John Paul in May, 1982, at Fatima, Portugal, and was sentenced May 2 to six-and-a-half years in prison.

• Father John Vaughn, minister general of the Order of Friars Minor, called on more than 20,000 confreres to begin a worldwide campaign for the release of five Franciscan priests recently imprisoned in Czechoslovakia.

• Sixty-eight-year-old Jesuit Father Stefan Dzierzek was jailed by Polish authorities after appealing for donations to help persons imprisoned in the wake of anti-government demonstrations on May Day.

• The Lutheran-Roman Catholic Joint Commission issued a statement early in the month commemorating the 500th anniversary of the birth of Martin Luther.

• An International Youth Pro-Life Organization was established during the second International Congress of Youth for Life May 20 to 23 in Cologne.

Solzhenitsyn on Ills of the Century

"The failings of human consciousness, deprived of its divine dimension, have been a determining factor in all the major crimes of this century," declared Russian writer Alexander Solzhenitsyn May 10 in London as he received the 1983 Templeton Foundation Prize for Progress in Religion.

He said "the West yielded to the Satanic temptation of the 'nuclear umbrella' " after World War II, and added: "The pitifully helpless state to which the contemporary West has sunk is in large measure due to this fatal error: the belief that the only issue is that of nuclear weapons, whereas in reality the defense of peace reposes chiefly on stout hearts and steadfast men."

He also said: "All attempts to find a way out of the plight of today's world are fruitless without a repentant return of our consciousness to the Creator of all. ... No matter how formidably Communism bristles with tanks and rockets, no matter what successes it attains in seizing the planet, it is doomed never to vanquish Christianity."

JUNE 1983

VATICAN

Just Hearing Mass Is Not Enough — So stated the Holy Father June 1 before 35,000 people in St. Peter's Square: "It is not sufficient that they (Catholics) listen to the word of God or that they pray in community. It is necessary that they make their own the offering of Christ, offering with him and in him their pains, their difficulties, their trials and, even more, themselves, in order to make their gift ascend to the Father together with the gift which Christ makes of himself."

The Eucharist — Pope John Paul carried the Blessed Sacrament in a Corpus Christi procession in the evening of June 2 from the square outside the Basilica of St. John Lateran to the Basilica of St. Mary Major.

At a general audience of 35,000 people June 8, the Pope said the Eucharist provides "the spiritual strength necessary to confront all the obstacles and trials" of life. He added: "The Eucharist is not a luxury offered to those who want to live more intimately united to Christ. It is a demand of Christian life."

Anniversary of Pope John XXIII — Pope John Paul appeared at the window of his apartment in the evening of June 3 to join 30,000 persons in St. Peter's Square at the end of a two-hour vigil marking the 20th anniversary of the death of John XXIII. He called Pope John "that admirable servant of the Church, so loved and venerated," and added: "The universal dimensions that his magisterium has assumed in contemporary history calls us to keep alive his memory in our hearts and in our minds in order to understand ever more and ever better the authentic charism possessed by him and liberally diffused in the Church to the edification of the faithful and every man of good will."

Counsel to Senators — Addressing six U.S. Senators June 4, the Pope said: "You are men and women who exercise leadership in the United States and who influence the social, political and economic policies of America. . . . As you perform this important role, I would invite you to keep before your eyes a global vision of the events and happenings of our times. I would encourage you to reflect constantly on the moral implications and consequences of your actions and on your influence in the whole community. . . . Maintain a keen awareness of the dignity of the human person" and uphold "the inalienable rights which flow from that dignity. . . . In this way you will be serving not only your fellow citizens, but you will be protecting and strengthening the bonds that unite the entire human family."

Anointing of the Sick — The Pope concelebrated Mass with a handicapped archbishop and 11 handicapped priests June 5 in a special ceremony during which he administered the sacrament of anointing of the sick to them and more than 100 other persons. In a homily during the service, he said: "Whoever knows how to accept illness with faith and to endure it with love, in fact unites himself mystically with Christ, 'the Man of Sorrows,' and becomes a precious instrument for the redemption of his brothers." The anointing ceremony fulfilled part of the Holy Father's pledge to celebrate each of the seven sacraments in public ceremonies during the current Holy Year.

Praise for the Bishops of Haiti — The Pope praised statements published by the Haitian Bishops' Conference on the role of the Church in social and political affairs and in the promotion of human rights. He told the bishops at a meeting June 11: "In this way you wish to help all the Haitian people to respect the dignity of each one of their compatriots, to develop justice, true relations, participation and reconciliation, without a spirit of condemnation of anyone. . . . I encourage you in this route, and I am sure that such an attitude, if lived concretely, passing from words to deeds, with concern for unity and peace, will be a great progress for the entire Haitian nation."

Ordinations — Pope John Paul ordained 74 men from 20 countries to the priesthood June 12; ten of them were from the United States. He said in a homily: "You are the priests of the 1950th anniversary of the redemption. If this event means for all believers a pressing call to meditate on one's life and one's Christian vocation in light of the mystery of the redemption, then this call is addressed in a completely special way to those who are . . . ministers of Christ and administrators of the mysteries of God."

Appeal for Spreading the Gospel — In a message prepared for the observance of World Mission Day Oct. 23, the Holy Father said the current Holy Year "becomes a renewed appeal for the evangelization of those millions of persons who, after 1,950 years from the redemptive sacrifice of Calvary, are still not Christians and cannot, in suffering or in joy, invoke the name of the Savior because they still do not know it." Christ "calls each one of us not only to personal reconciliation but also to be instruments of redemption for those who are not yet redeemed. . . . There does not exist a service to man greater than the missionary service." Urging Christians to carry Christ to others, he suggested that they "unite their daily sufferings, even the most humble and hidden, to the great sacrifice of Christ, in order to make them precious and give them a redemptive value for our brothers." The Pope's message was released by the Vatican June 27.

Feast of Sts. Peter and Paul — The Holy Father highlighted Roman celebrations of the feast of Sts. Peter and Paul June 29 with an outdoor Mass in St. Peter's Square at which he conferred palliums on five recently appointed archbishops. The white woolen stoles with six black crosses are symbolic of a metropolitan archbishop's union with the Holy See and of his authority over dioceses within his province. In a homily during Mass, the Pope called Peter and Paul "the two foremost Apostles" and praised their "lives of generous and fruitful ministry."

Orthodox Visitors — The Pope gave thanks for

progress "toward full ecclesiastical communion" June 30 during an hour-long private meeting with an Orthodox delegation representing Greek Orthodox Patriarch Dimitrios I of Constantinople (Istanbul). Metropolitan Meliton, the Patriarch's chief representative for Catholic-Orthodox relations, headed the delegation, in Rome for the papal celebration a day earlier of the feast of Sts. Peter and Paul.

The Pope received a visit June 3 by Catholicos Mar Baselius Thoma Mathews I, head of the Syrian Orthodox Church in India. The Holy Father told his visitor: "I wish to assure Your Holiness, on the part of the Catholic Church, that no effort will be spared to give due attention to all that needs to be done" toward uniting the two churches. "May mutual respect and love grow, and let them be expressed in fraternal and constructive collaboration . . . above all, in the pastoral sphere, in order to testify before our neighbors that Jesus Christ is our God and our only Lord." Catholicos Mathews said: "What we hold in common is immensely greater than that which divides us. It is our task now to repent and to re-create history more in accordance with the will of the Lord."

The Pope Also:
• Appealed to priests, religious and lay persons to undertake missionary work in Chad.

• Called June 7 on representatives of 166 nations at the U.N. Conference on Trade and Development in Belgrade to renew North-South dialogue on a deeper and more sincere level, in a message highlighting the interdependence of nations as the key to the world's economic survival.

• Discussed restraints on church activity in Cuba at a meeting with its seven bishops June 30; he said the Church was willing to dialogue with the government in order to gain freedom for pastoral service to the people.

Vatican Briefs:
• The Sacred Roman Rota, the high marriage court of the Church, ruled in 1982 that neither latent homosexuality nor bisexuality in itself is a valid reason for a declaration of nullity of marriage.

• A protest was published by the Vatican Press Office June 30 against Malta's new Devolution of Certain Church Properties Act, 1983, which provided for the expropriation to the government of all church-owned real estate "as well as furnishings and all pertinent objects, not excluding sacred vestments and vessels, except buildings adapted to worship."

The Pope in Poland

The Holy Father, on the second visit of his pontificate to Poland June 16 to 23, celebrated Mass and delivered more than 20 homilies and addresses in key cities and Marian sanctuaries of his native land.

The visit was somber in many respects as well as tense, as the Pontiff challenged the government in speech after speech to end repression of all sectors of Polish society. He appealed for authentic patriotism, fidelity to Catholic tradition and Marian devotion, and called for personal and social reconciliation in the current Jubilee Year of the Redemption.

(See separate entry.)

NATIONAL

Moral Questions regarding War and Peace — The war-and-peace pastoral letter issued by the U.S. bishops in May raised moral questions for military personnel while reaffirming their work, said Cardinal Terence Cooke, head of the U.S. Military Ordinariate, in a letter sent to all Catholic military chaplains. The letter, released June 7, stressed the pastoral's affirmation of the right and duty of a country to defend itself and its positive affirmations of the role of the military in society — aspects that tended to get lost in media concern about more controversial issues treated in the letter. But the cardinal also said: "The pastoral letter raises many questions about certain longstanding attitudes on war and peace, and calls for a complete reappraisal of these issues. . . . It does question the morality of some strategies of defense, and requires us to examine our individual consciences and our 'national conscience' concerning some widely accepted attitudes and policies." On such issues, the pastoral letter "does not pretend to have the last word" but invites continuing reflection and dialogue, he said.

NCC vs. CBS — The National Council of Churches claimed vindication June 8 after CBS rejected its proposal for arbitrating a dispute over a "60 Minutes" feature that linked the council with communist causes. At issue was "The Gospel According to Whom?" aired Jan. 23. NCC attorney Thomas Shaw commented in a letter to CBS president Thomas Wyman: "The only possible inferences to be drawn from CBS's unconditional rejection of the NCC challenge to impartial arbitration are, in my opinion, that the '60 Minutes' segment about the NCC is indefensible and that CBS lacks the guts to subject its most lucrative enterprise — '60 Minutes' — to a prompt and inexpensive test of its fairness and accuracy." The council charged that the broadcast was "a gross and damaging distortion of the truth which violated professional journalism standards of accuracy and fairness, including CBS News' own self-proclaimed standards."

Weeping Statue — Bishop Roger Mahony of Stockton declared June 8 that evidence of mysterious events related to a "weeping statue" in Thornton, Calif., did not meet the criteria for an authenticated appearance of Mary. A statue of Our Lady of Fatima at the Meter Ecclesiae Mission Church had been reported to move from one place to another and to weep tears. Bishop Mahony, backed by investigative findings, said: "No report has ever been made of anyone actually observing the statue move from one location to another. Rather, it was reported that on a given day the statue happened to be in another location. . . . No one has ever reported actually seeing the 'tears' flow from the eyes of the statue."

Vatican Art Exhibition — More than 800,000 persons viewed "The Vatican Collections: The

Papacy and Art" between Feb. 26 and June 12, according to officials of the New York Metropolitan Museum of Art. Museum director Philippe de Montebello, noting the success of the exhibition of 237 works, said, "We remain thrilled with the experience." The collections were scheduled for viewing also in Chicago July 21 to Oct. 16, and in San Francisco Nov. 19 to Feb. 19, 1984.

Equality, Justice and Evangelism — Equality and justice were called two elements of evangelism essential to Hispanics, by Bishop Ricardo Ramirez of Las Cruces, N.M., at the national congress of PADRES in Denver. "Minority groups any place in the world," he said, "must be evangelized in this first element (equality). We must say, 'God loves you,' because society tells them otherwise. This simple idea of affirming people the way God made them is at the core of evangelization." Justice, he added, means that God loves his children equally. The theme of the biennial meeting was "Hand in Hand toward the Kingdom: The Development of Mutual Ministries."

Genetic Engineering Opposed — Twenty-one Catholic bishops were among religious leaders and scientists supporting a resolution opposing genetic engineering to improve the human species and calling on Congress to prohibit such engineering. They "resolved that efforts to engineer specific genetic traits into the germline of the human species should not be attempted. . . . Genetic engineering of the human germline cells represents a fundamental threat to the preservation of the human species as we know it and should be opposed with the same courage and conviction with which we now oppose nuclear extinction. . . . It is very likely that in attempting to 'perfect' the human species we will succeed in engineering our own extinction," because "eliminating so-called 'bad genes' will lead to a dangerous narrowing of diversity in the gene pool." The resolution was released June 8 by the Foundation on Economic Trends, directed by Jeremy Rifkin.

Religious Orders under Study — *L'Osservatore Romano* reported June 24 that Pope John Paul had appointed a commission of three bishops to study reasons behind the drastic decline in the numbers of men and women religious in the U.S. since the Second Vatican Council. The commission was also directed to develop ways in which bishops might support and collaborate with religious institutes for their internal good and the effectiveness of their apostolic work. On the commission were Archbishop John R. Quinn of San Francisco, chairman, Archbishop Thomas C. Kelly of Louisville, and Bishop Raymond W. Lessard of Savannah.

Tuition Tax Credit Constitutional — A 5-to-4 ruling by the U.S. Supreme Court June 29 upheld the constitutionality of a Minnesota tuition tax credit for parents of students attending parochial, other private and public schools. The majority opinion rejected arguments that the law benefitted religion in an unconstitutional manner, and said that the program did not involve excessive church-state entanglement. Msgr. John F. Meyers, president of the National Catholic Educational Association, said of the decision: "Contrary to its bigoted and/or uninformed opponents, the Minnesota tuition tax deduction is sound tax policy. Government customarily provides tax incentives to stimulate and encourage private initiatives which promote the common good. If the government believes it is appropriate to promote the symphony and ballet, why shouldn't it promote the education of American youth?" The decision was condemned by American Federation of Teachers president Albert Shanker, who vowed opposition to any program of tax relief for parents of private school students.

Meetings — Meetings during the month included those of the following organizations.

• Seventh national Conference on Lay Ministry, May 31 to June 3 in Kansas City.

• Catholic Health Assembly, June 5 to 8 in Denver, with 1,200 in attendance.

• National Council for Catholic Evangelization, June 12 to 14 in Chicago; first meeting of the newly formed council.

• Handicapped Encounter with Christ, in Wake Forest, N.C.; the first such workshop in the state.

• National Clergy Conference on Alcoholism and Related Drug Problems, June 19 to 24 in Indianapolis.

Abortion Restrictions Struck Down

The U.S. Supreme Court ruled 6-to-3 June 15 against an Akron, O., ordinance on requirements for the practice of abortion. Struck down were provisions that:

• abortions be performed in hospitals after the first trimester;

• women seeking abortions be informed by their physicians of the development of the fetus and about complications that could result from abortion;

• there be a 24-hour waiting period before an abortion.

In a related development, the U.S. Senate, after a two-day debate, defeated a proposed constitutional amendment that would have provided: "A right to abortion is not secured by this Constitution."

(See separate article.)

INTERNATIONAL

Biomedical Concerns — In testimony presented June 2 to a government board of inquiry, the Social Welfare Commission of the Catholic Bishops' Conference of England and Wales questioned the concept of artificial insemination by donor, saying it could cause more problems than it could solve. The bishops said artificial insemination by donor "gives the semblance of solving the problem but in fact leaves the real agony: 'not our child.' " They argued that it would be a mistake to think it would be possible to restrict artificial insemination by donor to marriage. The commission endorsed a call by the joint bioethics committee of the bishops of Scotland, England and Wales for strict controls over *in vitro* fertilization. It was also sharply critical of surrogate motherhood which, it said, "manifests an unscrupulous willingness to use a human being as a mere instrument, irrespective of her feelings."

Plea for British-Argentine Reconciliation — A plea for reconciliation between Great Britain and Argentina in the aftermath of their 1982 war over the Falkland Islands in the South Atlantic was signed by 36 church leaders in both countries. The plea was made public June 5 in London and Buenos Aires. The signatories pledged "to work to re-establish and strengthen those links of Christian fellowship which once joined our two nations. . . . Recalling the Christian traditions of our two countries, we . . . invite our Christian brothers and sisters and all people of good will in both nations to join with us, on this first anniversary of a tragic war, in a common effort to bring about mutual reconciliation."

Relief Workers Released — Ten foreign relief workers, including U.S. Christian Brother Gregory Flynn and two Italian nuns, were freed June 9, seven weeks after being kidnapped by Ethiopian guerrillas. Members of the Tigre Peoples' Liberation Front said the workers had not been captives but guests invited to view conditions in Tigre Province where fighting for independence was under way.

Dutch Bishops on Nuclear Weapons — The bishops of The Netherlands made public June 15 a pastoral letter virtually identical in spirit, thrust and major conclusions with the U.S. bishops' "The Challenge of Peace: God's Promise and Our Response." Like their U.S. counterparts, the Dutch bishops condemned virtually any use of nuclear weapons and accepted possession of such weapons for the sake of deterrence only as a temporary strategy within strict limits. Both hierarchies rejected unilateral disarmament.

Romanian Rights Violations — The U.S. Helsinki Watch Committee asked Congress to reject President Reagan's recommendation to renew Romania's "most-favored-nation" trade status because of that nation's "deplorable" human rights record in the areas of emigration procedures; imprisonment of political dissenters; limitations on free expression, freedom of religion and assembly; and discrimination against ethnic minorities. The non-governmental committee was established in 1979 to monitor compliance with human rights provisions of the Helsinki Final Act of 1975.

CRS Aid in Africa — Press coordinator Beth Griffin reported late in the month that Catholic Relief Services had increased emergency aid supplies to Ethiopia and Mauritania where severe droughts had created "emergency situations" affecting more than three million people. Aid to Ethiopia in May and June alone had an estimated value of $1 million.

Catholic-Native Rites — Liturgical reforms blending native customs into Catholic rituals were continuing in Zimbabwe with publication by the bishops of a Shona tribal rite for the dead transformed into a Catholic service. The rite was contained in a booklet entitled "To Purify the Spirit of the Dead," one of a series of publications on Shona rituals commissioned by the bishops.

No Agreement To Dump Walesa — A highly placed Vatican source denied "absolutely" June 30 that the Vatican had made any agreement with the Polish government which would provide for the withdrawal of Lech Walesa from reconstruction efforts in the country. "Absolutely not," said the source; "I can tell you that there was no such agreement."

On June 24, a day after the Pope met with the former head of the Solidarity labor union, Father Virgilio Levi suggested in an editorial in *L'Osservatore Romano* that, although Walesa had played an heroic role in the struggle for freedom in Poland, the time had come for him to leave the scene for the greater good of the people. The vice director's editorial fueled speculation that there had been a prior agreement by which the Pope would encourage Walesa's withdrawal from politics in return for the government's pledge to lift martial law. (Walesa told the press later that "neither the Pope nor anyone else ordered me to cease the struggle.") Father Levi submitted his resignation from *L'Osservatore Romano* the day after his editorial appeared. His departure, according to the Vatican source, indicated "a denial on the Vatican's part" of any prior agreement regarding Walesa. "If such an agreement had in fact been made, Father Levi would still be in his job."

International Briefs:

• Forty per cent of the respondents to a public opinion poll in France said the Pope was the most influential leader in the world.

• The International Catholic Charismatic Renewal announced plans for a retreat Oct. 5 to 7, 1984, in Rome for priests from all over the world.

Resignation of Archbishop Lefebvre

Dissident Archbishop Marcel Lefebvre announced his resignation as head of the Priestly Fraternity of St. Pius X June 9 during a Mass at Econe, Switzerland, at which he ordained 22 men to the priesthood.

He called the transfer of authority a "passage without shock," and said it was time "to consign the burden and the grace which accompanies it to younger forces. . . . The fraternity will be found in good hands. The work will continue with courage, the work of maintaining and carrying the Church forward. We have not wished to be schismatics or heretics, but Catholics."

The archbishop said he would continue to ordain priests. Doing so without appropriate authorization caused his suspension from the legitimate exercise of orders in 1976. Compounding his troubles with the Vatican was his opposition to actions of the Second Vatican Council, especially with respect to ecumenism, religious freedom and the liturgy.

His successor as head of the fraternity was 31-year-old West German Father Franz Schmidberger.

The movement originated by the archbishop had seminaries in Switzerland, West Germany, Italy, Argentina and the United States. Affiliated with it in various ways were more than 120 priests, 250 seminarians, 50 nuns and several thousand lay persons.

JULY 1983

VATICAN

Defense and Celebration of Life — The first commandment for health care workers is "that of defending and celebrating life from its first conception," said the Pope July 3 during a visit to San Camillo Hospital, Rome's largest. Addressing staff members of all of Rome's hospitals, he said: "Wherever there are victims of the fragility of the human condition, of calamities, of misfortunes, of every form of violence . . . the primary commandment of those responsible for health and those who work in the health field is that of defending and celebrating life from its first conception and not allowing it to be betrayed or broken off." He noted "the high significance of the choice of those who, called to the service of life, refuse out of consistency with their own consciences to lend themselves to suppressing it. . . . No man, believer or non-believer, can refuse to believe in life and not feel his responsibility to defend it and to preserve it, especially when it does not yet even have a voice to proclaim its own rights."

Significant Appointment in Holland — The Pope named July 8 a Dutch bishop identified as a moderate-conservative member of the nation's hierarchy as coadjutor archbishop with the right of succession to Cardinal Johannes Willebrands of Utrecht. In a letter to all churches in his archdiocese, the cardinal said he wanted to resign as archbishop of Utrecht because of the stress of combining that office with his presidency of the Vatican Secretariat for Christian Unity. The Church in The Netherlands remained fractured by so-called liberal-conservative conflicts despite efforts for reform stemming from a special synod of its bishops in 1980.

Blessed Fra Angelico — The Holy Father bypassed usual procedures and decreed in a document issued on his own initiative the beatification of Fra Angelico (1378-1455), a member of the Dominican Order and a Florentine painter of the early Renaissance. He set Feb. 18 as the date for limited liturgical commemoration of the friar.

Commitment to Ecumenism — The Pope reiterated the "irreversible" commitment of the Church to ecumenism July 24 and asked for prayers for the success of the General Assembly of the World Council of Churches being held in Vancouver, British Columbia. He called the assembly, whose theme was "Jesus Christ, Life of the World," a "sign of hope" for ecumenical efforts. He also said the Church was represented at the assembly by 20 Catholic observers.

Theme for Day of Peace — The Vatican announced July 26 the theme — "From a New Heart, Peace is Born" — for the World Day of Peace to be observed Jan. 1, 1984. The Pope chose the theme to stress his belief that conversion of hearts is "the basic path toward the attainment of peace." The communique noted "the grave threats to which peace is being subjected in many parts of the world at the present time," but added: "The undertakings promoted by governments, institutions and international organizations, as well as the mobilization of thousands of individuals, groups and churches in favor of peace, encourage one to have hope. This hope demands the generous action of all hearts, for the efforts of just a few are not enough."

Terrorism — The Pope mourned July 31 violent incidents in Lebanon, Sri Lanka, Sicily, France and Portugal. Addressing 7,000 people at Castel Gandolfo, he said: "We beg from the Lord mercy for the victims and consolation for the families struck and afflicted by grief and suffering. We pray that respect for the fundamental rights of man and the search for peaceful solutions may prevail everywhere, rejecting every form of terrorist or retaliatory attack."

Plea for Girl's Release — The Pope appealed seven times during the month for the release of Emanuela Orlandi who was abducted by unknown parties June 22 and held hostage to demands for the release from prison of Ali Mehmet Agca, the would-be assassin of the Holy Father. The 15-year-old girl was the daughter of a Vatican employee and a citizen of Vatican City. The Pope had no jurisdiction over Agca, who was in the custody of Italian authorities.

The Pope Also:

• At a meeting with Bishop John Marshall of Burlington, Vt., discussed the progress of a Vatican-requested study of major seminaries in the United States.

• Told participants in the 41st Serra International Congress July 4 to "never lose heart" in their work of promoting vocations to the priesthood and religious life.

• Thanked Our Lady of Czestochowa July 6 for her intercession in allowing him to fulfill "the desire of my heart and, at the same time, the wish of so many of my co-nationals" by his June 16 to 23 visit to his native Poland.

• Began a two-month stay at Castel Gandolfo July 10, to be interrupted by flights to Rome for general audiences on Wednesdays and trips to Lourdes August 14 and 15 and to Austria Sept. 10 to 13.

• Expressed his "deepest condolences" to the families of 188 victims of a plane crash in Ecuador.

Vatican Briefs:

• Gian Franco Svidercoschi was named by Pope John Paul July 2 to replace Father Virgilio Levi as assistant director of *L'Osservatore Romano*. Father Levi resigned the post June 25 after editorializing that Lech Walesa should withdraw from active participation in the struggle of Polish workers for union and other freedoms.

• Valerio Volpini, director of *L'Osservatore Romano*, warned in an editorial July 8 against "a strictly political interpretation of the actions of the Pope and the Church. He said papal actions sometimes seen as political have "a different origin, nature and quality."

• Archbishop Jean Jadot, president of the Vatican Secretariat for Non-Christians, extended greetings to Moslems throughout the world July 11 at the end of Ramadan, their sacred, month-long period of fasting.

Sunday Mass Attendance

At a meeting July 9 with 14 U.S. bishops at the Vatican for *ad limina* visits, the Holy Father urged them to lead Americans "to an ever greater conviction of the sacredness of the Lord's Day" and to "full and active participation" in Sunday Mass.

He called on the bishops "to strengthen the understanding of the faithful and their appreciation of their role in Eucharistic worship. . . . Participting in the Eucharist is only a small portion of the laity's week," he said, "but the total effectiveness of their lives and all Christian renewal depends on it: the primary and indispensable source of the true Christian spirit."

Various surveys in recent years indicated that about half of the adult Catholics in the U.S. attended Mass on a typical Sunday. There were also reports that Catholic churchgoing stopped declining in the mid-70s and had risen slightly since that time.

NATIONAL

Paid Chaplains — Opening sessions of state legislatures and Congress with prayers led by paid chaplains does not violate the constitutionally required separation of church and state, ruled the U.S. Supreme Court July 5. The Court voted 6 to 3 against an earlier decision by the U.S. District Court of Appeals for the 8th Circuit. Chief Justice Warren E. Burger wrote in the majority opinion: "There can be no doubt that the practice of opening legislative sessions with prayer has become part of the fabric of our society. . . . To invoke divine guidance on a public body entrusted with making laws is not, in these circumstances, an 'establishment' of religion nor a step toward establishment; it is simply a tolerable acknowledgment of beliefs widely held among the people of this country."

Textbook Aid Downed — The Kentucky Supreme Court ruled 5-to-2 against the constitutionality of a state law providing textbooks on loan to students of parochial and other non-public elementary and secondary schools. The decision, handed down July 6, reversed a 1982 ruling of the Franklin Circuit Court which had said the law did not violate either the state or federal constitution. The majority opinion noted that the U.S. Supreme Court had ruled 15 years earlier that a state may provide textbooks to students in parochial and other private schools without violating the U.S. Constitution. The opinion added, however, that Kentucky law was stricter than the federal law in this instance.

No Girl Mass Servers — Girls may not act as servers at Mass because church rules forbid it, but they should be involved as much as possible in the liturgy, said Cardinal Joseph L. Bernardin of Chicago in a letter on liturgical practices. "As regards the question of girls acting as altar servers," he wrote, "there are directives from li-turgical documents which exclude the practice. I would request that all our parishes follow these liturgical norms." He also said: "I am confident that, while remaining faithful to the norms and guidelines of the universal Church, they (priests) will enable each man and woman, each girl and boy, to have a better understanding of the various roles in the celebration of the liturgy." Despite the cardinal's letter, reports from some Chicago parishes indicated that girls were continuing to serve Mass.

Parental Notification Unlawful — The U.S. District Court of Appeals for the District of Columbia ruled unlawful a 1981 federal regulation requiring parental notification when minor, dependent teenagers receive contraceptives from federally funded family planning clinics. The regulation specifically required federally supported family planning clinics to notify a parent or guardian within 10 working days of initially prescribing contraceptives to a dependent minor. It also required clinics to comply with any state parental notification or consent laws, and to consider a teen-ager's financial eligibility for help on the basis of her parents' income, not her own finances. The court found early in the month that the regulation undermined the intent of Congress regarding Title X of the Public Health Service Act enacted in 1970 to make "comprehensive family planning services readily available to all persons desiring such services." The regulation had the support of the Pro-Life Activities Committee of the National Conference of Catholic Bishops. Approximately 5,000 clinics and many more thousands of teen-agers would be affected by the decision of the court.

Homosexual Task Force Disbanded — The San Francisco Archdiocesan Commission on Social Justice disbanded its Task Force on Gay and Lesbian Issues after members of the task force rejected an archdiocesan plan for ministry to homosexual men and women. The plan was based on church teaching that homosexual orientation is not sinful but homosexual acts are. The task force was apparently seeking a plan that would ratify the homosexual life-style.

El Salvador Certified for Aid — The Reagan administration, while conceding that the number of civilian deaths in El Salvador remained high, nevertheless certified July 20 that the U.S.-backed government was making enough progress in human rights to qualify for military aid. According to figures gathered by the monitoring agency of the Archdiocese of San Salvador, 2,527 civilians were killed in the first six months of 1983 compared with 2,340 during the previous six months. The U.S. embassy reported 1,054 civilians killed during the first six months of 1983 compared with 961 during the last half of 1982. Various U.S. church groups, including Catholic bishops, had serious objections to grants of aid to the government of El Salvador.

Visibility Wanted — U.S. representatives of four international lay spirituality movements — Charismatic Renewal, Worldwide Marriage Encounter, Focolare and the Cursillo — were urged to make their organizations more visible by Bishop Paul J.

Cordes, vice president of the Pontifical Council for the Laity. "Vatican II gives us this task, to be a public witness in society, not just in our own parishes," he said at the fourth Meeting of the Major Movements at St. Leo, Florida.

Voices for Justice — American Catholics were urged to apply the teachings of the Church on human rights, unemployment, labor unions and nuclear weapons at the first national Voices for Justice assembly July 21 to 23 at Notre Dame College of Maryland in Baltimore. Participants in a plenary panel session on "Common Traditions, Different Voices" included Harry Fagan of the National Pastoral Life Center, Msgr. George Higgins of the Catholic University of America, Michael Novak of the American Enterprise Institute, Sister Lora Quinonez of the Leadership Conference of Women Religious, and Melanne Verveer of the office of U.S. Rep. Marcy Kaptur of Ohio.

Loans To Help the Poor — Twenty-five religious orders in New York, New Jersey and Connecticut started a fund to make loans available at below-market rates of interest for projects to aid the poor. Mercy Sister Patricia Wolf, president of the Leviticus 25:23 Alternative Fund, said: "The fund is particularly interested in projects which encourage self-determination, meet basic needs — such as food, shelter, education, health or jobs — and which serve the victims of racism, ageism or sexism."

Missionary's Role — Heavy involvement in development work at the expense of evangelization may endanger a missionary's vocation, declared Father Nico de Bekker, a veteran of 30 years of ministry in Tanzania. "Call me a traditionalist or even a conservative," he said in an interview, but I still think that the primary task of a missionary is evangelization, teaching of the commandments and love of God. I'm for, not against development projects; but I believe that at least 80 percent of a missionary's work should be pastoral."

National Briefs:

• Franciscan Father Bruce Ritter opened Under 21 Houston, a multi-service center for runaway and homeless youths in the Texas city.

• Duquesne University was the recipient of a gift with an estimated value of $15 million from the late Noble J. Dick, founder and chairman of the board of a large construction company.

• Mercedarian Sister Antonia Brenner, noted for her work at La Mesa Penitentiary in Tijuana, Mexico, received the Golden Plate Award of the American Academy of Achievement during the Salute to Excellence weekend, July 7 to 9, in San Diego.

Natural Family Planning

One hundred and 20 persons from 70 U.S. dioceses attended the first National Meeting and Working Conference on Natural Family Planning July 17 to 21 in Washington, D.C. The agenda of the meeting was designed to explore themes from the theology of marriage and responsible parenthood and to provide a forum for diocesan natural family planning coordinators to meet and exchange strategies.

Cardinal Terence Cooke, chairman of the Pro-Life Activities Committee of the National Conference of Catholic Bishops, told those at the meeting: "In the contemporary world, especially in developed countries, sexuality is often trivialized, as is evidenced by the growing tide of pornography, in the promotion of sexual permissiveness, in the increase of out-of-wedlock pregnancy, in the efforts to legitimize homosexual and lesbian unions and place them on a par with the marriage union. In addition, the promotion of contraception — including sterilization and abortion — drives the wedge between the two purposes of conjugal love — that is, a deepening of conjugal intimacy and an openness to procreation. In effect, many people become victims of the contraceptive mentality and seek only the technologically most efficient and effective method of avoiding procreation."

Natural family planning, the focus of the meeting, he said, is "not simply another method of birth control. It involves a fundamental approach to human sexuality that places conjugal intimacy in the larger context of marital rights and responsibilities."

Three major provider-groups for natural family planning were the Couple-to-Couple League, Creighton University's Natural Family Planning Education and Research Center, and the Family of Americas Foundation.

INTERNATIONAL

Priests Jailed in Vietnam — Nhan Dan, the official daily newspaper of the Vietnamese Communist Party, reported July 3 that 12 religious and diocesan priests had been sentenced to jail terms ranging from five years to life. They were found guilty of "anti-state activities and anti-revolutionary propaganda" by the People's Court in Ho Chi Minh City.

Political Interpretations Scored — Cardinal Jozef Glemp assailed the international media July 10 for their "insistence on seeing everything in a political light" in Poland. "It seems that today's view of reality must include thinking about things that were never said or putting interpretations on events that were never meant to be there in the first place," he said in a homily during Mass in Rome.

No Capital Punishment in Great Britain — By a vote of 368 to 223, the House of Commons soundly rejected July 13 a return to the death penalty in Great Britain. The rejection came despite a solid 144-vote majority in the House held by Prime Minister Margaret Thatcher's Conservatives, the chief backers of the restoration of hanging for terrorists and certain murderers.

Five days before the vote, the Catholic bishops of England and Wales unanimously opposed reintroduction of death by hanging for certain crimes. "We believe that the reintroduction of capital punishment would be damaging and dehumanizing to the whole of our society," they said.

Expropriation in Malta — In a letter read July 17 in all Catholic churches, the two bishops of Malta condemned expropriation by the government of property given to the Church in exchange for the celebration of Masses. They called the action a "violation of a fundamental right of man." Sections of the Devolution of Certain Church Properties Act, which went into effect a day later, had to do with property willed or given to the Church in exchange for the celebration of Masses for the soul of the donor or another person named by the donor. Under terms of the law, any property obtained by the Church under such conditions 25 years earlier automatically becomes property of the government. Despite expropriation, the bishops promised that the priests of Malta would "fulfill the obligation of the foreseen celebration of Masses."

Troubled Nicaragua — Church leaders in Nicaragua were generally critical of the government four years after the overthrow of the 43-year-old Somoza dynasty by the Sandinista National Liberation Front. Reasons for criticism included the regime's hostility toward the Church, its attempts to use religion for revolutionary purposes, violations of human rights, restrictions on the media and political activity, continuing violence and civil war, and the disastrous condition of the economy. There were Catholics, however, with more favorable attitudes toward the Marxist-oriented government.

Martial Law in Poland — The Polish government announced the end of 19 months of martial law July 22, but the action was expected to make little difference in existing conditions because many of the controls in martial law had already been institutionalized in the legal code. Additional restrictive measures were also anticipated, despite efforts by church authorities to convince the government to ease curbs on civil liberties. Martial law had been imposed to break the independent Solidarity labor union.

Persecution in El Salvador — Persecution by government security forces was the biggest problem in church-associated refugee camps in El Salvador, according to Eileen Purcell who visited some of the camps July 18 to 25. The community organizer of Catholic Social Services of the San Francisco Archdiocese said death squads and security forces frequently entered the camps and abducted people suspected of being associated with guerrillas. She also said the Church was on a collision course in both El Salvador and the United States because it "plays a special role predicated on siding with the oppressed."

Priest and Catechists Killed in Chad — Capuchin Father Aurele Robidoux, a Canadian missionary, and five lay catechists were killed in an ambush June 26 in southern Chad, Vatican Radio reported June 5. No reason was given for the attack in an area not directly involved in the nation's civil war. Hostilities in other parts of the country were seriously crippling the work of the Church.

Cambodian Church Only in Hearts of the People — Almost all of the Church in Cambodia has been destroyed, said Bishop Yves-George Ramousse July 26 at an interview in Washington. Since 1970 he stated: "What could be destroyed, was; only the faith in the hearts of the people was not destroyed." Most of the nation's 55,000 Catholics were expelled in 1970. Former missionaries said that no bishops, priests or church structures remained there, and that no priests were allowed

to enter the country. Bishop Ramousse and two other priests were touring the United States to make contact with Cambodian refugees and immigrants and provide for their pastoral care.

Foreign Powers Asked To Get Out — Vatican Radio reported July 27 that 50 Latin American bishops had asked all "foreign powers" in Central America to get out and stay out. The bishops made their appeal in a document approved in Bogota during a preparatory session for a meeting of the Latin American Bishops' Council. They said: "Reconciliation among brothers and the reconstruction of the social fabric of these countries are indispensable for the achieving of a solid and lasting peace. . . . As do the majority of these peoples, we hope that the governments and opposition groups will abstain from asking for the intervention of foreign powers in these countries and, wherever such powers are already present, they will be withdrawn."

Deterrence Is Insane — Permanent reliance on a strategy of nuclear deterrence is "insane," said the Irish bishops July 28 in a joint statement on war and peace. They said a policy of deterrence can be morally acceptable under certain circumstances, but added tht the current stock of warheads "far exceeds any rational estimate of what deterrence requires."

International Briefs:

• Mother Teresa of Calcutta was released from Rome's Salvator Mundi Hospital July 4 after nearly a month of rest.

• Announcement was made July 5 of the election of Canadian Sister Katherine McDonald, superior of the Sisters of Our Lady of Zion, as president of the International Union of Superiors General.

• The Church of England marked the 150th anniversary of the Oxford Movement during the month.

• Auxiliary Bishop Gregorio Rosa Chavez of San Salvador said in a homily July 31 that the Salvadoran news media were keeping quiet about killings and abuses of human rights, and that their silence was forcing Catholic officials to publish weekly reports on political violence in the country.

Vatican-Czechoslovakian Relations Frozen

"Nothing is moving" in relations between the Vatican and Czechoslovakia, a Vatican source familiar with Eastern European affairs said July 5. The source said there had been no discussion of church-state matters since December, 1980, and added: "There have always been particular difficulties with Czechoslovakia." Among the difficulties were:

• government support for Vatican-banned clergy organizations — *Pacem in Terris* and the Priests' Movement for Peace;

• government opposition to 1982 appointments of bishops for Czech and Slovak emigrants;

• tension over the political situation in Poland;

• the lack of bishops in several dioceses;

• restrictions and controls in force in seminaries;

• hindrances to the religious formation of young people and families.

AUGUST 1983

VATICAN

Seek Freedom from Sin and Death — Pope John Paul dedicated his general audience Aug. 3 to the theme of redemption and asked Christians to free themselves from "the law of sin and death." He said: "St. Paul speaks of the law of the spirit which has freed us from the law of sin and death. . . . To live according to the law of the spirit means to carry out the will of God with the help of the Spirit who dwells within us. The Spirit of God enlightens our mind and moves our will so that we can turn away from sin and live the truth in love." The audience at Castel Gandolfo was attended by about 30,000 persons.

Resignation of Faith-Healing Archbishop — Pope John Paul accepted the resignation Aug. 6 of Archbishop Emmanuel Milingo from the Archdiocese of Lusaka, Zambia, who had been accused of faith-healing and exorcism practices inconsistent with church doctrine and practice. The Pope appointed him to serve as a special delegate to the Pontifical Commission for Pastoral Care for Migrants and Tourism.

Pope Paul VI Remembered — The teachings and example of Pope Paul were praised by Pope John Paul during the commemoration Aug. 6 and 7 of the fifth anniversary of his death. The Pontiff celebrated Mass Aug. 6 in memory of his predecessor at the parish church in Castel Gandolfo, and spoke about him later in the day and also on Aug. 7. Before 10,000 people on Aug. 7, the Pope said: "I wish to evoke the dear memory of that Pontiff who gave his entire life for service to the Church. (He) knew how to love the Church, exalt it, defend it and explain it with a patient and knowledgeable catechesis, showing its intimate nature, its visible reality and the invisible one." In the evening of Aug. 6, the Holy Father recalled: "Here in Castel Gandolfo, that Sunday, he left the earth for heaven. . . . He continued to pray until the great and solemn moment arrived for his meeting with Christ, whom he had always loved and served with tenderness and decisiveness. . . . Let us raise our prayer to the Blessed Virgin Mary, that her intercession may obtain for him eternal peace, and for us the strength to hear his message and follow his example."

Slavery of Misused Freedom — The freedom given to humanity by the redemption "is both a gift and duty," declared the Pope at a general audience of 40,000 persons Aug. 10 in St. Peter's Square. As a result of Christ's redemption of the world by his death and resurrection, said the Pope, every human person faces a decisive and dramatic alternative: the choice between a false freedom of self-affirmation, personal or collective, against God and against others, or a true freedom of self-giving to God and to others. "Whoever chooses self-affirmation remains under the slavery of the flesh, estranged from God. Whoever chooses self-giving is already living the eternal life."

A Right Conscience — Following one's conscience is not always enough, the Pope told 35,000 people at a general audience Aug. 17. What matters first, he said, is where the conscience gets its information for making moral judgments. "It is not enough to say that we must always follow our conscience. Each one of us must 'form' a right conscience, one that seeks to know the truth as revealed to us by God, according to his wise and loving plan." He called attention to "that inner moral sense, possessed by each one of us, which guides our steps on the path toward goodness in every situation in our lives," and said that the believer has the assistance of the Church in forming a "right conscience. . . . For it is the duty of the Church to give expression to that truth which is Christ himself, and to declare and confirm those principles of the moral order which have their origin in human nature itself."

Lack of Respect for Religious Liberty — Addressing 10,000 persons Aug. 21 at Castel Gandolfo, the Holy Father said: "It is necessary to defend human life which is threatened by war, and we ought to defend also the spiritual life of man which is threatened by sin and by the lack of respect for human rights regarding religious liberty and freedom of conscience. . . . We ought to pray that these liberties be respected and defended in the entire world." The Pope made these impromptu remarks after coming under attack by the Soviet news agency Tass for similar comments voiced during his visit to Lourdes Aug. 14 and 15. Tass criticized the "anti-socialist attacks" of the Pope, calling them part of "a strategy of the Vatican devoted to intensifying the line of ideological collision with the socialist countries."

For a Culture of Peace — In a message sent Aug. 22 on his behalf to 50 prominent scientists attending a seminar on nuclear war, the Pope asked them to become architects of a "culture of peace." He made a "strong appeal" to the scholars "that, as leaders of a generation marked by the persistent anxiety resulting from the threat of nuclear holocaust, they will direct all their scientific efforts toward a culture of peace."

Lead from Secularization to Faith — At a meeting Aug. 25 at Castel Gandolfo with more than 100 delegates to the general chapter of the Augustinian Order, the Holy Father called on them and their confreres to help lead the world "from the frightening phenomenon of secularization" to a mature and personalized faith.

The Pope Also:

• Linked the pro-life and peace movements during a general audience Aug. 24, saying: "The cause of peace is the cause of life; and everything that wounds, weakens or destroys life attacks peace and the destiny of humanity."

• Marked the feast of Our Lady of Czestochowa, patroness of Poland, Aug. 26 with a Mass attended by 350 of his Polish countrymen.

• Sent a message of condolence and comfort Aug. 29 to those who lost family members and homes in the worst floods in 30 years in the Basque region of northern Spain.

Vatican Briefs:

• *L'Osservatore Romano* praised Benigno Aquino, the Filipino opposition leader, as a fighter for human rights. Aquino was shot to death Aug. 21 at the Manila airport as he returned home after three years of exile in the United States.

• John Paul I, Pope for only 34 days in 1978, was called "the world's parish priest" in a front-page editorial in the Aug. 26 edition of *L'Osservatore Romano.*

Visit to Lourdes

The Holy Father, on the 19th foreign trip of his pontificate, flew to France for a 30-hour visit Aug. 14 and 15 to the Marian shrine at Lourdes.

While there, he took part in a traditional candlelight procession; celebrated Mass on the Solemnity of the Assumption of Mary before a throng of 250,000 people; met with priests, religious, young people and bishops; and mingled with 2,000 sick and handicapped persons in the Grotto of Massabielle before leaving for Rome in the evening of Aug. 15.

(See separate entry.)

NATIONAL

Ban on Incineration of Fetuses — Wichita's city manager and director of community health issued a ban Aug. 1 against the disposal of human fetuses in a city-owned incinerator after viewing photos of fetuses consigned for incineration. The photographs, supplied by a pro-life group, included one in which a "full-term baby is on the ground in front of the incinerator with flames going," said Michael Farmer, president of Wichita's Life, Inc. "The baby looked like it had been attacked by a pack of dogs, but probably had undergone an autopsy."

Family Dimension for Church Activities — Archbishop Edouard Gagnon, pro-president of the Pontifical Council for the Family, urged Knights of Columbus at their Aug. 2 to 4 convention in Columbus, O., not to set up any new family-oriented movements or organizations, but to give every church activity a family dimension. "The fundamental reason why the family should never cease to be at the center of our thoughts and activity is that it is 'the first and vital cell of society,' " he said.

Disagreement on Prayer in Public Schools — Representatives of several religious groups disagreed at a Senate committee hearing Aug. 3 over whether to support legislation giving prayer groups access to public school facilities. At issue were bills introduced by Sen. Jeremiah Denton and Sen. Mark D. Hatfield that would make it unlawful for public schools to deny students or faculty prayer groups access to public school facilities during non-instructional periods if the schools permit other groups to use the same facilities.

• A spokesman said the National Council of Churches, although opposed to school prayer amendments, supported voluntary student prayer meetings before and after school so long as the meetings were limited to those of high school students.

• Representatives of two Jewish organizations said permitting such meetings, even if voluntary, would lead to "majoritarian abuse" to the detriment of minority students.

The U.S. Catholic Conference, while taking no public stand on the bills, was on record to the effect that it would support a constitutional amendment on school prayer if it included permission for voluntary religious instruction on public school property.

No More Government-Sponsored Nativity Scenes — The nation's largest association of Protestant and Eastern Orthodox churches urged the U.S. Supreme Court not to permit local governments to sponsor nativity scenes at Christmas. The National Council of Churches, along with the American Jewish Committee, said in a friend-of-the-court brief that government sponsorship of such a "fundamentally religious symbol" is a violation of the separation-of-church-and-state principle. The brief was filed in mid-August in connection with a suit challenging the erection for the previous 40 years of a city-owned nativity scene in Pawtucket, R.I. The Court was expected to issue a ruling in its 1983-84 term.

Anti-Catholic Bigotry — Catholics were condemned by the World Congress of Fundamentalists headed by the Rev. Bob Jones, Jr., and the Rev. Ian Paisley of Northern Ireland. They, along with 2,000 others attending the July 29 to Aug. 7 assembly in Greenville, S.C., resolved that the Catholic Church is the "mother of harlots and abominations of the earth." A resolution also said: "The worldwide visits of the Pope, surrounded by the false charisma attributed to him by the corrupt media, are but a subtle window dressing behind which lies the unchanging hatred of that system for true biblical Protestant Christianity."

Bigoted Editorial in USA Today — *USA Today's* explanation of its July 5 editorial cartoon on tuition tax deductions made the situation even worse, declared Jesuit Father Virgil Blum, president of the Catholic League for Religious and Civil Rights. He said the statement by editorial director John Seigenthaler, that the cartoon was misinterpreted, implied that readers are "mentally incapable of grasping the meaning of a cartoon." The cartoon in question showed a Supreme Court Justice dipping into a chalice labeled "tax breaks" and placing a communion wafer embossed with a dollar sign on the tongue of a fat, fawning clergyman wearing a "church school" mortarboard and a clerical collar. Seigenthaler said the figure represented a Protestant as well as a Catholic clergyman. Father Blum, in addition to his earlier criticism of the cartoon, said: "The entire nation is deprecated when one of its leading newspapers . . . engages in religious bigotry and then goes to absurd lengths in a futile effort to explain away and justify that bigotry."

Fetus a Legal Person — The Missouri Supreme Court ruled during the month that under Missouri law a living fetus is legally a person. In an interpretation of the state's wrongful death law, the court said a husband and wife have the right to sue for damages on behalf of their stillborn baby because of alleged negligence in medical care for the pregnant woman and her fetus. "Parents clearly have an interest in being protected against or compensated for the loss of a child they wished to have," declared Special Judge James A. Pudlowski for the court. He added: "The fetus itself has an interest in being protected from injury before birth."

March on Washington — Several bishops and thousands of Catholics from across the country were among the 250,000 participants Aug. 27 in the 20th Anniversary March on Washington for Jobs, Peace and Freedom. Archbishop James A. Hickey of Washington said the themes of the march were the "unfinished agenda of America." The 20th anniversary was that of the 1963 march for civil rights in the nation's capital which sparked action for significant social legislation.

Meetings — Meetings during the month included those of the following organizations and movements.

• Catholic War Veterans, Aug. 2 to 7 in Philadelphia, attended by more than 300; voted acceptance of the bishops' pastoral letter, "The Challenge of Peace: God's Promise and Our Response," with reservations.

• Christian Family Movement, Aug. 4 to 7 at St. Mary's College, Notre Dame, Ind., attended by about 300 persons; resolved to develop "the most effective means through which members . . . can work to prevent nuclear war from ever occurring."

• Focolare, Aug. 8 to 14 at Fordham University, New York, attended by 900 and focused on a "Unity" theme; the last of four one-week programs known as Mariopolis held in the U.S. during the summer.

• Tekakwitha Conference, Aug. 10 to 14 at Collegeville, Minn., attended by more than 1,500 Indians from 100 tribes, along with bishops, priests, religious and lay persons engaged in related ministry.

• Worldwide Marriage Encounter, Aug. 12 to 14 in Philadelphia, St. Louis and Hayward, Calif., attended by 5,250 couples; the theme of the three simultaneous meetings was "That We May Be One."

National Briefs:

• The Archdiocese of New Orleans approved a final design for the Vatican Pavilion at the World's Fair scheduled to be held there May 12 to Nov. 11, 1984.

• Salvation Army Commissioner Andrew S. Miller was named the first non-Catholic recipient of the Father Paul Kaletta Award of the National Catholic Stewardship Council.

• New York responded with sadness, smypathy and prayers to the announcement Aug. 26 that Cardinal Terence Cooke was suffering from acute, terminal leukemia.

Jobs and Justice

Jobs, justice and the right to organize in current circumstances of high unemployment were among the subjects of Labor Day statements issued in advance of Sept. 5.

• Bishop Mark J. Hurley, chairman of the Committee on Social Development and World Peace:

"The fundamental assumption that underlies this approach — namely, that high rates of unemployment are a necessary element of our modern economy and that full employment is not a realistic goal — are deeply troubling. They raise important questions not only about the current economic policies that are being pursued but also about the long-term status of the American economy. The temptation to become resigned to high levels of unemployment must be vigorously resisted. For the very foundation of a just economy is the right to a job for all who are able and wish to work. An economic system which does not have full employment as a major goal is basically flawed."

• Cardinal Joseph L. Bernardin of Chicago: "Perhaps the most frightening aspect of high unemployment is that we seem to be getting used to it and seem to have concluded that there isn't much we can do about it. . . . Such thinking is totally unacceptable in the light of the Church's teaching on economic justice." He also called the feminization of poverty "one of the most serious" national problems.

• Msgr. George G. Higgins of the Catholic University of America: Americans must realize that "full employment is a compelling ethical imperative, that solving the problem of inflation by creating high levels of unemployment runs contrary to the dictates of social justice, and that voluntary agencies cannot be expected to pick up all the slack." He also said that the right of workers to organize was one of the "live issues" for this Labor Day.

INTERNATIONAL

Bishop Murdered in 1976 — Bishop Enrique Angelelli was murdered, probably by Argentinan security forces, in 1976, and did not die as officially reported in an automobile accident, according to a statement issued Aug. 4 by Bishop Jaime De Nevares of Neuquen. Bishop Angelelli, who had had numerous confrontations with military authorities, was killed while gathering evidence in the cases of two priests and a layman who were murdered in his diocese. Bishop De Nevares stated: "The official version of the facts is that Angelelli had a grave accident which cost his life. The other version, which is on the tongues of everyone in La Rioja because there were eyewitnesses to the events, is that the accident was provoked. These eyewitnesses were not moved to denounce it because they feared they also would lose their lives."

Two Priests Freed — Vatican Radio reported Aug. 5 that two Czechoslovakian Franciscan priests under prison sentences of six and eight months had been released from custody. Both priests had been sentenced July 13 for "illegal" membership in a religious order and for carrying out "illegal religious activity."

Hiroshima Anniversary — A rally in Hiroshima, Japan, together with demonstrations involving thousands of people in the United States and other countries, marked the 38th anniversary Aug. 6 of the first atomic attack in history which killed 120,000 persons immediately and left thousands of others affected by nuclear radiation.

Vatican Radio editorialized: "Since then, 38 years have passed and, while the world commemorates the innocent victims of that day, one cannot try to hide the fact that — thanks to an ever more exasperating technology addressed to destruction rather than to the good of humanity, thanks to an unrestrained arms race — the current atomic arsenals are capable of destroying not only just one city with all of its inhabitants but the entire earthly globe and all of humanity many times over."

Rios Montt Ousted — Gen. Efrain Rios Montt, a born-again Christian whose 16-month rule in Guatemala was marked by Indian massacres and numerous human rights conflicts with Catholic authorities, including Pope John Paul, was ousted from the presidency by the military Aug. 8. He was replaced by Oscar Humberto Mejia Victores, minister of defense. The coup was motivated because "a religious and fanatical group" was taking advantage of Rios Montt's position, said a military communique which also criticized the situation created by a "small group which for personal ambitions wants to perpetuate its powers." Rios Montt ordered the execution of six people condemned by military tribunals despite a papal plea for clemency. He was under attack by the bishops because of genocidal attacks on Indians which wreaked a toll of between 5,000 and 10,000 lives in the first 10 months of his presidency.

No Vatican Ties — Members of an interfaith delegation that visited mainland China in July said on returning to the United States that Chinese officials insisted on Catholics being independent of the Pope and Vatican, and being members of the de facto schismatic Patriotic Association of Chinese Catholics. Despite the attitude of the regime, there was an underground church in the country whose members retained allegiance to the Holy Father.

More Trouble in Malta — A dispute over ownership of the St. John Co-Cathedral in Valetta highlighted the worsening church-state clash in Malta over a government decision to expropriate church properties. Government authorities claimed the church belonged to the people; church authorities said it was the property of the Church, even though there was no legal deed to prove owenership.

In related developments, it was reported that the Vatican had severed diplomatic relations with Malta, and it was expected that the government would implement the entire new Devolution of Church Properties Act within the next six months.

Plea for Calm in the Philippines — Cardinal Jaime Sin of Manila, echoing fears expressed by political leaders, appealed for calm in the nation after Benigno Aquino, Jr., chief political rival of President Ferdinand Marcos, was assassinated Aug. 21 on his arrival at the Manila airport after three years of exile in the United States The cardinal cited Aquino's commitment to political reform without violence, saying: "If we allow his death to fan the flames of violence and division, then he will have died in vain." Aquino was buried in his home town after a week-long series of tributes and religious ceremonies.

Some Africans against Christian Names — A revolution of sorts against the adoption and use of foreign Christian names was in progress among some Africans following the organization of the Cultural Revolution Committee of Nigeria in March. The so-called revolution, against what some regarded as deculturization by Western influence, was viewed as a revival and recognition of the African personality and the promotion of African cultural values.

U.S. Military Intervention in Central America —It "would be a tragedy," according to Bishop Antonio Quarracino, president of the Latin American Bishops' Council. In an interview published Aug. 26 in the Rome daily, *Il Messaggero*, he said that, if Central American nations failed to reach agreement on issues in dispute, he feared "that Washington will intervene and this would be a tragedy because," he added, 'the Latin American countries in general do not like the United States, even if they understand that the United States cannot help but react before the prospect of the birth of another Soviet satellite."

International Briefs:

• Transportation difficulties because of civil war and truck shortages were the biggest obstacles to providing food to at least some of more than three million victims of famine in Ethiopia.

• American Father Aloysius Schwartz was named to receive the 1983 Magsaysay Award for International Understanding, for mobilizing and providing assistance to people of South Korea — more than 3,800 children in orphanages in Seoul and Pusan, 1,500 men in a home for the destitute and paients in two hospitals.

• Father Juan Antonio Ugarte Perez, a member of Opus Dei, was named auxiliary bishop of Abancay, Peru, by Pope John Paul Aug. 20.

• The Austrian Catholic news agency Kathpress reported Aug. 24 that Cardinal Frantisek Tomasek of Prague had asked the government of Czechoslovakia for "a more fruitful alternative to this old, continuous, superfluous (church-state) conflict."

Special Regulations in Poland

The bishops of Poland criticized Aug. 26 the tough "special regulations" enacted by the government in ending martial law, saying also that authorities had missed the chance for a "national accord" provided by Pope Paul's visit to the country in June.

In a communique issued after a one-day meeting at the national Marian shrine at Czestochowa, the bishops said: "Restrictive regulations passed by the Sejm (Parliament) in July . . . are a fresh cause for anxiety." The regulations, passed as part of the return from martial law to civilian government, incorporated into civilian law modified versions of major government powers that had been assumed as emergency measures under martial law.

The bishops called for a general amnesty for those imprisoned under martial law, the restoration of independent trade unions, rehiring of workers fired for their political views, and a government dialogue with workers and intellectuals "responding to their just aspirations."

SEPTEMBER 1983

VATICAN

No Support for Female Ordination Advocates

— In a strongly worded address to 23 U.S. bishops Sept. 5, Pope John Paul said: "The bishop must give proof of his pastoral ability and leadership by withdrawing all support from individuals or groups who, in the name of progress, justice or compassion, promote the ordination of women to the priesthood." The exclusion of women from the priesthood, he stated, is not a matter of sexist discrimination but "is linked to Christ's own design for the priesthood." At the same time, the Pope told bishops that they should work for "every legitimate freedom that is consonant with their human nature and their womenhood," and should "oppose any and all discrimination of women by reason of sex." (See Women in the Church: 1983 Report.)

The Pope also told the bishops to proclaim the Gospel "in all its purity and power, with all its demands," including the indissolubility of marriage, "the incompatibility of premarital sex and homosexual activity with God's plan for human love" and "the unpopular truth that artificial birth control is against God's law."

The Priesthood, a Full-Time Occupation

— In another forceful address to a group of U.S. bishops Sept. 9, the Pope said the primary role of priests is to celebrate Mass and administer the sacraments: "An understanding of the need for priests to perform, with full human commitment and deep compassion, those activities which only ordained priests can do, confirms the wisdom of the Bishops' Synod of 1971 in regard to the general exclusion of priests from secular and political activity."

Austrian Visit

— The Holy Father ended an Aug. 10 to 13 trip to Austria with a visit to the Marian shrine at Mariazell in the foothills of the Alps. (See separate entry for a summary account of the trip.)

The Pope Also:

• Sent a message of sympathy to the people of Korea in the wake of the Soviet attack Sept. 1 on a Korean Air Lines jet in which 269 passengers were killed.

• Met Sept. 2 with nuclear scientists attending an international symposium on nuclear weapons; he urged them to work for peace and the elimination of nuclear menace to the world.

• Pleaded again for peace in Lebanon and deplored the takeover of church property by the government of Malta.

Only Priests Can Consecrate the Eucharist

— "Since it is of the very nature of the Church that the power to consecrate the Eucharist is imparted only to the bishops and priests who are constituted its ministers by the reception of holy orders, the Church holds that the Eucharistic Mystery cannot be celebrated in any community except by an ordained priest." So stated the Congregation for the Doctrine of the Faith in a letter addressed to bishops throughout the world that was made public Sept. 8. (See separate entry, The Minister of the Eucharist.)

Marian Devotion

— The Pope called Mary "a sign of hope for the pilgrim people of God" and said Marian devotion since the Second Vatican Council has taken on a communal dimension that helps sustain the faithful. He underlined the strengthening of Marian devotion in a letter to the bishops of Malta on the occasion of the 16th International Mariological Congress being held there Sept. 16 to 18.

"The renewal desired by the Second Vatican Council," he said, "has also borne fruit in the field of Marian devotion, emphasizing its biblical, Christological, ecclesial and anthropological directions, so that it may become ever more a devotion that leads to our Lord Jesus Christ. . . . Today, the expressions of Marian devotion are often manifested more in a communal dimension, thus helping the faithful to renew together their fidelity to Christ, who is the only way to the Father."

He noted that the flourishing of Mariological studies was evidence of the "deep meaning Mary has in the dynamic growth of ecclesial life and activity."

One of the events of the congress was an observance marking the 100th anniversary of the Maltese shrine of Our Lady of Ta' Pinu where, according to a tradition, the Virgin Mary appeared to a young girl in 1883.

Synod Topics

— A decline in the practice of confession and the issue of general absolution were expected to be key subjects of discussion at the 1983 assembly of the Synod of Bishops due to start at the end of the month.

NATIONAL

Protest

— More than 150 persons protested publicly Sept. 3 against the use of St. James Cathedral in Seattle for the celebration of Mass in conjunction with a convention of Dignity, an international organization of homosexuals. Permission for use of the cathedral was granted by Archbishop Raymond G. Hunthausen. Protesters said it was a "sacrilege" and "profanation" for the cathedral to be used by an organization whose stated purpose was to influence a change in the Church's position on homosexuality.

Commission on Religious Optimistic

— The head of a papal commission named in June to help guide developments in religious life in the United States felt "even more positive" about the work of his commission after two weeks of meetings in Rome. "Both the Congregation for Religious and the Pope have been very open and understanding. They appreciate the work of religious in the United States, and we feel very positive about our task," said Archbishop John R. Quinn of San Francisco Sept. 9.

Some early observers theorized that the Pope had addressed the question of religious men and women only in the United States out of a feeling that there were more problems here which needed to be straightened out, but the commission members said they believed the Pope's motives were different.

"First," said Bishop Raymond Lessard, a member of the commission, "the history of religious life in the United States has been spectacular in terms of numbers. And second, the religious in the United States have wide influence because of their work throughout the world and because, through the impact of the American media, what they do is known elsewhere immediately." Archbishop Quinn added that "because of the large decline in the number of religious in the States, if the Vatican did not take note of it, it might be thought that the Vatican considered religious life trivial and unimportant."

INTERNATIONAL

Anglican-Catholic Commission — The second Anglican-Roman Catholic International Commission said it got "an encouraging start" with its first meeting, held Aug. 30 to Sept. 6 in Venice. The commission discussed justification, one of the chief points of division between the Church and the Reformers of the 16th century; the theology of the Church; how Roman Catholics and Anglicans can grow toward full communion; and the current state of relations between Anglicans and Roman Catholics around the world. In a communique, the commission said it planned to ask the help of national Anglican-Roman Catholic commissions in a number of countries in the discussion of "the theological implications of full communion and the way toward it." For its next meeting, to be held in about a year, the commission assigned further studies on the Church and salvation to be used as a basis for discussion.

Ban on Abortion in Ireland — Voters in the Irish Republic voted 2-to-1 Sept. 9 to amend the constitution with a ban on abortion guarding against any future effort to liberalize the existing law. Heavy support for the amendment came from conservative Catholics in rural areas of the West and South.

For Peace in the Philippines — Cardinal Jaime Sin of Manila wept openly at Mass Sept. 11 as he pleaded again for national reconciliation and called for the release of political prisoners in the wake of the slaying Aug. 21 of Benigno Aquino. The cardinal was criticized for celebrating the Mass in connection with the 66th birthday of President Ferdinand Marcos, head of the oppressive government and considered suspect by some of complicity in the Aquino murder. The cardinal said in response that the Church must seek reconciliation in "volatile and uncertain times. . . . Reconciliation is what I have been preaching. What kind of person am I if I do not practice what I preach? How can I call myself a man of God if, like a politician, I opt for the popular way?"

Jesuit Superior General — Father Peter-Hans Kolvenbach was chosen as the 29th superior general of the Jesuits Sept. 13 on the first ballot cast by 211 delegates to the general congregation of the Society of Jesus in Rome. The 54-year-old successor to Father Pedro Arrupe was born in The Netherlands; studied philosophy there and theology at the University of St. Joseph in Beirut, where he was ordained to the priesthood in 1961; completed graduate work in general and Eastern linguistics in The Hague and Paris; taught languages at Beirut University; served as provincial superior in Beirut from 1974 to 1981 and as rector of the Pontifical Oriental Institute in Rome since 1981. His election marked the end of the interim caretaker supervision of the Jesuits by Father Paolo Dezza, appointed for that purpose by Pope John Paul in October, 1981, because of the infirmity of Father Arrupe.

Legalized Abortion Is Radically Immoral — So said the Administrative Board of the Canadian Conference of Catholic Bishops in a statement released Sept. 7. The statement condemned abortion, upheld the sacredness of human life from conception, and called for laws and social structures that respect and welcome life. The bishops said: "As pressures mount to liberalize the law and to make abortion more easily accessible, we reaffirm all human rights and the specific right for a child to be born. . . . Human law cannot go against laws written by the Creator in the heart of every human being, even if social consensus contradicts them. A law which allows abortion is radically immoral."

Human beings are created in "the image of God," and abortion is an attack on life and an insult to God, the Creator." Referring to the influence of the mass media in forming public opinion, the bishops said: "The use of these means of communication demands that the information given respects the moral laws and the dignity of the human person."

Effects of Independence in Africa — "After 25 years of independence, most African countries find themselves in an economically more deplorable and socially more confused state than they were at the time they achieved self-government." So stated Father Joseph Osei, secretary general of the Bishops' Conferences of Africa and Madagascar, at the first all-Africa meeting of Catholic laity Aug. 15 to 20 in Nairobi, Kenya.

Traditional African kinship structures "have been buffeted from all sides," he said, according to a delayed report. "Modern formal education has enlarged people's knowledge of how others live, widened their horizons and increased their ambitions. This has brought about a lessening of social cohesion and the decline of respect and belief in the authority of the established institutions of traditional African society."

Modern education also has led to "social mobility and the consequent breakdown of the extended family. Community spirit has given way to a certain form of individualism and even anonymity."

Also affecting traditional family life has been "the advent of modern cash economy with the introduction of regular wages and their payment to individuals rather than to families."

Referring to another factor, Father Osei said the increase in technology in Africa "has been devastating in its social consequences."

Even the forms of government that started in African states when they gained independence "showed little consideration for the values and institutions which are native to Africa."

(See many related entries under John Paul II in the Index.)

Cardinal-Archbishop Karol Wojtyla of Cracow was elected Bishop of Rome Oct. 16, 1978, on the seventh or eighth ballot cast on the second day of voting at a conclave of 111 cardinals. He chose the name John Paul II and was invested with the pallium, the symbol of his papal office, Oct. 22 in ceremonies attended by more than 250,000 persons in St. Peter's Square.

The 263rd successor of St. Peter as Bishop of Rome and Supreme Pastor of the Universal Church, he is the first non-Italian Pope since Adrian VI (1522-23), the first Polish Pope in the history of the Church, and the youngest at the time of his election since Pius IX (1846-78).

Early Career

Karol Wojtyla was born May 18, 1920, in Wadowice, Poland.

He began higher studies at the age of 18, with major interests in poetry and theater arts. Forced to suspend university courses because of the outbreak of World War II, he went to work in a stone quarry and a chemical plant, thereby earning the later designation of himself as the "Worker Cardinal."

He started studies for the priesthood in 1942 in the underground seminary of Cracow, whose operations had been banned after the Nazi invasion of Poland.

Ordained to the priesthood Nov. 1, 1946, he was immediately sent to Rome for studies at the Angelicum University, where he earned a doctorate in ethics.

Back home in Poland, he worked as an assistant pastor in a village parish and as a chaplain to university students while continuing studies at the Catholic University of Lublin. He was awarded another doctorate there, in moral theology.

He began writing about this time, and eventually produced more than 100 articles and several books on ethical and other themes. Phenomenology was one of his fields of expertise.

University teaching came next, in 1953, with appointment in 1954 to the position of lecturer and later to the chair of ethics at the Catholic University of Lublin, the most prestigious institute of higher learning in Poland.

Bishop and Cardinal

He was ordained Auxiliary Bishop of Cracow Sept. 28, 1958, became vicar capitular in 1962 after the death of Apostolic Administrator Eugeniusz Baziak, and was appointed Archbishop Jan. 13, 1964. He was the first residential head of the see since the death of Cardinal Adam Sapieha in 1951. Between then and 1964 the archdiocese was run by administrators because the communist government refused to permit the appointment and ministry of a residential bishop.

Archbishop Wojtyla attended all sessions of the Second Vatican Council from 1962 to 1965, and was one of the writers of the *Pastoral Constitution on the Church in the Modern World*. He also contributed input to the *Declaration on Religious Freedom* and the *Decree on the Instruments of Social Communication*.

His efforts to put into effect the directives of the council induced him to write a book, *Foundations of Renewal*, in 1972 and to start that same year an archdiocesan synod he saw concluded as Pope during his visit to Poland in 1979.

He was inducted into the College of Cardinals June 26, 1967, as one of the younger members, and subsequently served actively in the Congregation for the Sacraments and Divine Worship, the Congregation for the Clergy, and the Congregation for Catholic Education.

He also served as a theological consultant to Pope Paul VI.

He attended assemblies of the Synod of Bishops as a representative of the Polish Bishops' Conference and was a member of the Synod's permanent council.

From the beginning of his priestly career, and especially during his episcopate, the Cardinal was vigorous in the defense of human and religious rights, the rights of workers, and rights to religious education.

Close to Cardinal Wyszynski and in company with his fellow bishops, he negotiated the tightrope of Catholic survival in a country under communist control. With them, and as their spokesman at times, he was stalwart in resisting efforts of the regime to impose atheism, materialism and secularism on the people and culture of Poland.

Active Pope

Since the beginning of his pontificate, John Paul has been active as Bishop of Rome, with frequent visits to parishes and institutions of the diocese for the celebration of Mass and participation in other events. During these visits, as well as others to places of pilgrimage and historic significance in Italy, he has had perhaps more personal contact with the faithful than any other Pope. The number of attendants at weekly general audiences at the Vatican and Castel Gandolfo has been unprecedented.

Unprecedented also has been the attention focused on him during and in connection with his 20 pastoral trips to 39 foreign countries between January, 1979, and mid-September, 1983.

Extensive Travels

Pastoral Pilgrimages: His first three, in 1979, were to the Dominican Republic and Mexico, Poland, Ireland and the United States.

He traveled to Turkey at the end of November, 1979, to meet with Orthodox Ecumenical Patriarch Dimitrios I. With him, he announced the establishment of a joint commission of theologians to begin formal dialogue in quest of the union of the Roman Catholic and Orthodox Churches.

He made four trips in 1980.

While touring six African nations in May, he spoke about Africanization of the Church, the cultural values of African peoples and the independence they should have from alien influences of other countries.

In France for an address before the United Nations Educational, Scientific and Cultural Organization also in May, he delineated with great clarity the stance of the Church on a wide variety of subjects, with special emphasis on its role in a secularized state, society and culture.

During a 13-city tour of Brazil in July, the Pope declared that the Church is on the side of the poor, appealed for across-the-board respect for human rights by governments and people of influence, called for measures of economic and social reform, and indicated his approval of non-violent social activism for the good of all peoples. He attended a plenary assembly of the bishops of the country and took part in opening ceremonies of a national Eucharistic congress.

His eighth and ninth pastoral pilgrimages were to West Germany, Nov. 15 to 19, 1980, and to the Philippines and Japan, Feb. 16 to 27, 1981. While in the Philippines, he beatified six 17th century martyrs of Japan.

Plans for additional trips in 1981 to Lourdes, for participation in the 42nd International Eucharistic Congress, and to Switzerland had to be cancelled because of the attack on the Pope's life in May.

The Pope made six trips outside of Italy by mid-September, 1982, to: the African nations of Nigeria, Benin, Gabon and Equatorial Guinea, Feb. 12 to 19; six cities of Portugal, May 12 to 15, as well as the shrine of Our Lady of Fatima where he consecrated the world to the Blessed Virgin Mary; nine major cities of Great Britain, May 28 to June 2; Argentina, June 11 and 12; Switzerland, June 15.

The 15th foreign trip of his pontificate was to the tiny Republic of San Marino, Aug. 29, when he also made his 28th pastoral visit to an Italian city other than Rome, Rimini.

The Holy Father visited Spain Oct. 31 to Nov. 9, 1982, to take part in celebrations marking the 400th anniversary of the death of St. Teresa of Avila, Carmelite mystic and reformer, and the first woman Doctor of the Church. He made a two-day trip to Sicily the following Nov. 20 and 21.

In 1983, the Pope visited eight nations of Central America — Costa Rica, Nicaragua, Panama, El Salvador, Guatemala, Honduras, Belize and Haiti — Mar. 2 to 9. He revisited Poland June 16 to 23 to take part in the observance of the 600th anniversary of the arrival in the country of the icon of Our Lady of Czestochowa. He made a devotional pilgrimage to the Marian shrine at Lourdes Aug. 14 and 15, and joined in the celebration of *Katholikentag* in Austria Sept. 10 to 13.

Key Writings

Encyclicals: The homilies and addresses delivered by the Pope on these trips were the equivalent of doctrinal, pastoral and social encyclical letters on a wide variety of subjects, all related to the key document of the first year of his pontificate. That was the formal encyclical, *Redemptor Hominis,* a treatise on Christian anthropology dealing with the divine and human aspects of redemption and the mission of the Church to carry on a dialogue of salvation with all peoples.

Two other encyclicals published within less than a year of each other were *Dives in Misericordia* ("Rich in Mercy"), issued Dec. 2, 1980, and *Laborem Exercens,* on work as a "way of sanctification," whose publication was announced Sept. 13, 1981.

Apostolic Exhortation: The Pope published a lenghty exhortation on the family, *Familiaris Consortio,* in December, 1981. It is an extensive synthesis of the theology of the family based not only on traditional doctrinal background but also on recommendations that emanated from the 1980 assembly of the Synod of Bishops.

Various Items

Doctrinal Concern: In December, 1980, the Pope directly confronted the controversial writings of Father Hans Kung by giving his approval to a declaration by the Congregation for the Doctrine of the Faith that he could not be regarded as a Catholic theologian.

On Aug. 6, 1983, he authorized release by the Doctrinal Congregation of a letter to bishops throughout the world in refutation of unorthodox views — especially those of Father Edward Schillebeeckx, O.P. — concerning "The Minister of the Eucharist."

These actions, along with various other statements and indications of attitude, mark John Paul as a pastor of decisive leadership for doctrinal orthodoxy and church discipline.

Canon Law: The Pope promulgated the revised Code of Canon Law Jan. 25 and set Nov. 27, 1983, as its effective date.

Synods: The Holy Father convoked three of them in 1980.

With the Dutch bishops at the Vatican for a particular synod in January, he called for measures to cope with differences among the prelates, polarization among the people and action to remedy doctrinal and disciplinary irregularities. Later reports indicated that results of the synod were less than satisfactory.

Meeting with Ukrainian bishops in March, he named a successor to Cardinal Josyf Slipyi as the ranking Ukrainian bishop and turned down demands of some Ukrainians for a patriarchate.

With more than 200 delegates from episcopal conferences around the world, he held the fifth ordinary assembly of the Synod of Bishops.

He designated "Reconciliation and Penance in the Mission of the Church" as the theme of the 1983 assembly of the Synod.

Holy Year: The Holy Father proclaimed a Jubilee celebration of the 1950th anniversary of the Redemption from the Solemnity of the Annunciation of the Lord Mar. 25, 1983, to Easter Sunday, Apr. 22, 1984.

Cardinals: In June, 1979, the Holy Father inducted 14 new cardinals into the Sacred College, raising its membership at that time to 135. A second group was inducted into the Sacred College

Feb. 3, 1983, at which time the total membership was 138.

Meetings with Bishops: In relations with the hierarchy since becoming Pope, John Paul has met with groups of bishops making required *ad limina* visits to the Vatican, for first-hand reports and admonitions regarding conditions in dioceses all over the world. He has also met with assemblies of bishops in the countries he has visited.

Ecumenism: He met with Anglican Archbishop Robert Runcie at the Canterbury Cathedral during his visit to Great Britain in May, 1982. The two prelates prayed together, renewed their baptismal promises and issued a joint statement in which they announced the formation of a new joint Catholic-Anglican theological commission for a second phase of interfaith dialogue.

Ever since the beginning of his pontificate, the Pope has maintained contact with Orthodox leaders and officials of other churches and religious bodies, and has encouraged interfaith relations at all levels.

Audiences and Addresses: The Pope has delivered hundreds of addresses at general and private audiences and on special occasions. All of them have characteristically been grounded in doctrinal essentials coupled with relevance to the people being addressed or the events being commemorated.

Subjects of more than passing concern in 1983 were: marriage and the family; celibacy and the dedication of priests and religious; the call to all Catholics to participate actively in the mission of the Church; pleas for peace, especially in the Middle East, El Salvador and Nicaragua; settlement of the Church-Solidarity-government crisis in Poland.

Near Tragedy: The Pope narrowly escaped death May 13, 1981, when he was fired upon at close range as he entered St. Peter's Square to address a general audience. Wounded more seriously than realized at first, he underwent emergency surgery and remained in Gemelli Polyclinic Hospital until June 3. On release, he stayed at the Vatican until June 20 when he was hospitalized a second time, until Aug. 14.

THE PLOT TO KILL THE POPE

Mehmet Ali Agca told reporters July 8, 1983, that the Bulgarian secret service and the KGB were involved in his attempt on the life of the Pope, but did not allege that the Soviets took direct part in the shooting.

His public admission was in agreement with the privately held opinion of Italian investigators that the Soviets and Bulgarians masterminded the attack in which the Pope was seriously wounded May 13, 1981.

Agca named several accomplices in the plot. Sergei Ivanov Antonov, a Bulgarian airlines official, was arrested in November, 1982, and was still in custody — and in poor condition, mentally and physically — in the fall of 1983. Two other Bulgarians, embassy officials Todor Ayvazov and Zhelyu Kolev, were at liberty.

Four Turks were suspected of complicity, one of them for allegedly supplying Agca with money and weapons, and the other, Bekir Celenk, for allegedly offering him more than $1.25 million to kill the Pope.

Circumstantial evidence seems to support theories that Agca did not act alone and that Bulgarian and Soviet agents were involved somehow in the action. Hard and convicting evidence is missing, however, despite a persistent, months-long investigation under the direction of Magistrate Ilario Martello.

NBC Report

NBC broadcast a televised report Sept. 21, 1982, which linked the Soviet Union, through Bulgaria, to the assassination attempt on the Pope. The report was similar to the findings of author Claire Sterling, an expert on international terrorism, who made substantially the same allegations in the September edition of *Reader's Digest.*

The NBC report, "The Man Who Shot the Pope: A Study in Terrorism," suggested that the Soviet Union was either behind the attempt to kill the Pope or was aware of the plot, and that the government feared the possible effects of the Pope's support for the independent Polish labor union, Solidarity.

Correspondent Marvin Kalb said that NBC News had "accumulated a great deal of evidence, some of it, to be sure, circumstantial. A Soviet connection is strongly suggested but it cannot be proved."

New York Times Report

The *New York Times* reported Mar. 23, 1983, that Iordan Mantarov, a Bulgarian defector, had told French authorities that the plot to kill the Pope was drawn up by the KGB and the Bulgarian secret service because they believed the Pope was the "keystone" of a U.S. effort to move the Polish government away from the communist bloc.

Mantarov was an attache at the Bulgarian embassy in Paris at the time of the shooting. He was also a friend of Dimiter Savov, an official in the counterintelligence division of the Bulgarian secret police.

According to *The Times,* Savov told Mantarov "about growing alarm in communist intelligence agencies that the Pope had been chosen as an instrument to help disrupt his native Poland." The KGB concluded that the election of a Polish Pope was "engineered" by Zbigniew Brzezinski, President Carter's national security advisor, who the KGB thought wanted to take advantage of unrest in Poland. After the election of John Paul, Soviet authorities conveyed to the Bulgarians the desire to "eliminate" the Pope, and the assignment was turned over to the Bulgarian security agency. Agca was the chosen assassin because he was known as a rightist with no links to any communist country.

Agca, found guilty in July, 1981, of shooting the Pope, was serving a life sentence of solitary confinement in the maximum security Marino Del Trono Prison in Ascoli Piceno.

FIRST CENTURY

Early 30's: First Christian Pentecost: gathering together of the Christian community, outpouring of the Holy Spirit, preaching of St. Peter to Jews in Jerusalem, baptism and aggregation of some 3,000 persons to the Christian community.

St. Stephen, deacon, was stoned to death at Jerusalem; he is venerated as the first Christian martyr.

34: St. Paul, formerly Saul the persecutor of Christians, was converted, baptized and joined to the college of Apostles. After three major missionary journeys, he was martyred in 64 or 67 at Rome.

39: The Gentile Cornelius and his family were baptized by St. Peter.

42: Persecution of Christians in Palestine broke out during the rule of Herod Agrippa; St. James the Greater, the first Apostle to die, was beheaded in 44; St. Peter was imprisoned for a short time; many Christians fled to Antioch and elsewhere.

At Antioch, the followers of Christ were first called Christians.

49: Christians at Rome, who were considered members of a Jewish sect, were adversely affected by a decree of Claudius which forbade Jewish worship there.

51: The Council of Jerusalem, in which all the Apostles participated under the presidency of St. Peter, decreed that circumcision, dietary regulations, and various other prescriptions of Mosaic Law were not obligatory for Gentile converts to the Christian community. The decree was issued in opposition to Judaizers who contended that observance of the Mosaic Law in its entirety was necessary for salvation.

64: Persecution under Nero. The emperor, accusing Christians of starting a fire which destroyed half of Rome, inaugurated the era of major Roman persecutions.

64 or 67: Martyrdom of St. Peter at Rome during the Neronian persecution. He established his see and spent his last years there after preaching in and around Jerusalem, establishing a see at Antioch, and presiding at the Council of Jerusalem.

70: Destruction of Jerusalem by Titus.

88-97: Pontificate of St. Clement I, third successor of St. Peter as bishop of Rome, one of the Apostolic Fathers. The *First Epistle of Clement to the Corinthians,* with which he has been identified, was addressed by the Church of Rome to the Church at Corinth, the scene of irregularities and divisions in the Christian community.

95: Domitian persecuted Christians, principally at Rome.

c. 100: Death of St. John, Apostle and Evangelist, marking the end of the Age of the Apostles and the first generation of the Church.

SECOND CENTURY

c. 107: St. Ignatius of Antioch was martyred at Rome. He was the first writer to use the expression, "the Catholic Church."

112: Emperor Trajan, in a rescript to Pliny the Younger, governor of Bithynia, instructed him not to search out Christians but to punish them if they were publicly denounced and refused to do homage to the Roman gods. This rescript set a pattern for Roman magistrates in dealing with Christians.

117-138: Persecution under Hadrian. Many *Acts of Martyrs* date from this period.

c. 125: Spread of Gnosticism.

c. 155: St. Polycarp, bishop of Smyrna and disciple of St. John the Evangelist, was martyred.

c. 156: Beginning of Montanism.

161-180: Reign of Marcus Aurelius. His persecution, launched in the wake of natural disasters, was more violent than those of his predecessors.

165: St. Justin, an important early Christian writer, was martyred at Rome.

c. 180: St. Irenaeus, bishop of Lyons and one of the great early theologians, wrote *Adversus Haereses.* He stated that the teaching and tradition of the Roman See was the standard for belief.

196: Easter Controversy.

The *Didache,* written in the second century, was an important record of Christian belief, practice and government in the first century.

Latin was introduced in the West as a liturgical language.

The Catechetical School of Alexandria, founded about the middle of the century, increased in importance.

THIRD CENTURY

202: Persecution under Septimius Severus, who wanted to establish one common religion in the Empire.

206: Tertullian, a convert since 197 and the first great ecclesiastical writer in Latin, joined the heretical Montanists. He died in 230.

215: Death of Clement of Alexandria, teacher of Origen and a founding father of the School of Alexandria.

217-235: St. Hippolytus, the first antipope. He was reconciled to the Church while in prison during persecution in 235.

232-254: Origen established the School of Caesarea after being deposed in 231 as head of the School of Alexandria; he died in 254. A scholar and voluminous writer, he was one of the founders of systematic theology and exerted wide influence for many years.

c. 242: Manichaeism originated in Persia.

249-251: Persecution under Decius. Many of those who denied the faith *(lapsi)* sought readmission to the Church at the end of the persecution in 251. Pope St. Cornelius had correspondence with St. Cyprian on the subject and ordered that *lapsi* were to be readmitted after suitable penance.

250-300: Neo-Platonism of Plotinus and Porphyry gained followers.

251: Novatian, an antipope, was condemned at Rome.

256: Pope St. Stephen I upheld the validity of

baptism administered by heretics, in the Rebaptism Controversy.

257: Persecution under Valerian, who attempted to destroy the Church as a social structure.

258: St. Cyprian, bishop of Carthage, was martyred.

c. 260: St. Lucian founded the exegetical School of Antioch.

Pope St. Dionysius condemned teachings of Sabellius and the Marcionites.

St. Paul of Thebes became a hermit.

261: Gallienus issued an edict of toleration which ended general persecution for nearly 40 years.

c. 266: Sabellianism was condemned and Paul of Samosata deposed.

c. 292: Diocletian divided the Roman Empire into East and West. The division emphasized political, cultural and other differences between the two parts of the Empire and influenced the Church in the East and West. The prestige of Rome began to decline.

FOURTH CENTURY

303: Persecution broke out under Diocletian. It ended in the West in 306 but continued for 10 years in the East; it was particularly violent in 304.

305: St. Anthony of Heracles established a foundation for hermits near the Red Sea in Egypt.

c. 306: The first local legislation on clerical celibacy was enacted by a council held at Elvira, Spain; bishops, priests, deacons and other ministers were forbidden to have wives.

310: St. Hilarion established a foundation for hermits in Palestine.

311: An edict of toleration issued by Galerius at the urging of Constantine and Licinius officially ended persecution in the West; some persecution continued in the East.

313: The *Edict of Milan* issued by Constantine and Licinius recognized Christianity as a lawful religion and the legal freedom of all religions in the Roman Empire.

314: The Council of Arles condemned Donatism in Africa and declared that baptism by heretics was valid.

318: St. Pachomius established the first foundation of the cenobitic (common) life, as compared with the solitary life of hermits in Upper Egypt.

325: The Ecumenical Council of Nicaea (I), first of its kind in the history of the Church, condemned Arianism; see separate entry.

326: Discovery of the True Cross on which Christ was crucified.

337: Baptism and death of Constantine.

c. 342: Beginning of a 40-year persecution in Persia.

343-344: A local Council of Sardica reaffirmed doctrine formulated by Nicaea I and declared that bishops had the right of appeal to the pope as the highest authority in the Church.

361-363: Julian the Apostate waged an unsuccessful campaign against the Church in an attempt to restore paganism as the religion of the Empire.

c. 365: Persecution under Valens in the East.

c. 376: Beginning of the barbarian invasion in the West.

379: Death of St. Basil, the Father of Monasticism in the East. His writings contributed greatly to the development of rules for the religious life.

381: The Ecumenical Council of Constantinople (I); see separate entry.

382: The *Decree of Pope St. Damasus* listed the Canon of Sacred Scripture.

382-c. 406: St. Jerome translated the Old and New Testaments into Latin. His work is called the Vulgate Version of the Bible.

396: St. Augustine became bishop of Hippo in North Africa.

397: A local Council of Carthage published the Canon of Sacred Scripture.

FIFTH CENTURY

410: Visigoths sacked Rome.

411: Donatism was condemned by a council at Carthage.

430: St. Augustine, bishop of Hippo for 35 years, died. He was a strong defender of orthodox doctrine against Manichaeism, Donatism and Pelagianism. The depth and range of his writings made him a dominant influence in Christian thought for many centuries.

431: The Ecumenical Council of Ephesus; see separate entry.

432: St. Patrick arrived in Ireland. By the time of his death in 461 most of the country had been converted, monasteries founded and the hierarchy established.

438: The *Theodosian Code,* a compilation of decrees for the Empire, was issued by Theodosius II. It had great influence on subsequent civil and ecclesiastical law.

449: The Robber Council of Ephesus, which did not have ecclesiastical sanction, declared itself in favor of the opinions of Eutyches who contended that Christ had only one nature.

451: The Ecumenical Council of Chalcedon; see separate entry.

452: Pope St. Leo the Great persuaded Attila the Hun to spare Rome.

455: Vandals sacked Rome. The decline of imperial Rome dates approximately from this time.

484: Patriarch Acacius of Constantinople was excommunicated for signing the *Henoticon,* a unity law published by Emperor Zeno in 482 to end the turmoil associated with the Monophysite heresy. The document capitulated to the heresy. The excommunication triggered a 35-year-long schism.

494: Pope St. Gelasius I declared in a letter to Emperor Anastasius that the pope had power and authority over the emperor in spiritual matters.

496: Clovis, King of the Franks, was converted and became the defender of Christianity in the West. The Franks became a Catholic people.

SIXTH CENTURY

520 and later: Irish monasteries flourished as centers for spiritual life, missionary training and scholarly activity.

529: The Second Council of Orange condemned Semi-Pelagianism.

c. 529: St. Benedict founded the Monte Cassino Abbey. Some years before his death in 543 he wrote a monastic rule which exercised tremendous influence on the form and style of religious life. He is called the Father of Monasticism in the West.

533: John II became the first pope to change his name. The practice did not become general until the time of Sergius IV (1009).

533-534: Emperor Justinian promulgated the *Corpus Juris Civilis* for the Roman world. Like the *Theodosian Code,* it influenced subsequent civil and ecclesiastical law.

c. 545: Death of Dionysius Exiguus who was the first to date history from the birth of Christ, a practice which resulted in use of the B.C. and A.D. abbreviations. His calculations were at least four years late.

553: The Ecumenical Council of Constantinople (II); see separate entry.

585: St. Columban founded an influential monastic school at Luxeuil. He died in 615.

589: The most important of several councils of Toledo was held. The Visigoths renounced Arianism, and St. Leander began the organization of the Church in Spain.

590-604: Pontificate of Pope St. Gregory I the Great. He set the form and style of the papacy which prevailed throughout the Middle Ages; exerted great influence on doctrine and liturgy; was strong in support of monastic discipline and clerical celibacy; authored writings on many subjects. Gregorian Chant is named in his honor.

596: Pope St. Gregory I the Great sent St. Augustine of Canterbury and 40 monks to do missionary work in England.

597: St. Columba died. He founded an important monastery at Iona, established schools and did notable missionary work in Scotland.

By the end of the century, monasteries of nuns were common; Western monasticism was flourishing; monasticism in the East, under the influence of Monophysitism and other factors, was losing its vigor.

SEVENTH CENTURY

613: St. Columban established the influential monastery of Bobbio in northern Italy.

622: The Hegira (flight) of Mohammed from Mecca to Medina signalled the beginning of Islam, which, by the end of the century, claimed almost all of the southern Mediterranean area.

629: Emperor Heraclius recovered the True Cross from the Persians.

649: A Lateran Council condemned two erroneous formulas *(Ecthesis* and *Type)* issued by emperors Heraclius and Constans II as means of reconciling Monophysites with the Church.

664: Actions of the Synod of Whitby advanced the adoption of Roman usages in England, especially regarding the date for the observance of Easter. (See Easter Controversy.)

680-681: The Ecumenical Council of Constantinople (III); see separate entry.

692: Trullan Synod. Eastern-Church discipline on clerical celibacy was settled, permitting marriage before ordination to the diaconate and continuation in marriage afterwards, but prohibiting marriage following the death of the wife thereafter. Anti-Roman canons contributed to East-West alienation.

During the century, the monastic influence of Ireland and England increased in Western Europe; schools and learning declined; regulations regarding clerical celibacy became more strict in the East.

EIGHTH CENTURY

711: Moslems began the conquest of Spain.

726: Emperor Leo III, the Isaurian, launched a campaign against the veneration of sacred images and relics; called Iconoclasm (image-breaking), it caused turmoil in the East until about 843.

731: Pope Gregory III and a synod at Rome condemned Iconoclasm, with a declaration that the veneration of sacred images was in accord with Catholic tradition.

Venerable Bede issued his *Ecclesiastical History of the English People.*

732: Charles Martel defeated the Moslems at Poitiers, halting advance by them in the West.

744: The Monastery of Fulda was established by St. Sturmi, a disciple of St. Boniface.

754: A council of more than 300 Byzantine bishops endorsed Iconoclast errors. This council and its actions were condemned by the Lateran Synod of 769.

Stephen II (III) crowned Pepin ruler of the Franks. Pepin twice invaded Italy, in 754 and 756, to defend the pope against the Lombards. His land grants to the papacy, called the Donation of Pepin, were later extended by Charlemagne (773) and formed part of the States of the Church.

c. 755: St. Boniface (Winfrid) was martyred. He was called the Apostle of Germany for his missionary work and organization of the hierarchy there.

781: Alcuin was chosen by Charlemagne to organize a Palace School, which became a center of intellectual leadership.

787: The Ecumenical Council of Nicaea (II); see separate entry.

792: A council at Ratisbon condemned Adoptionism.

The famous *Book of Kells* ("The Great Gospel of Columcille") dates from the early eighth or late seventh century.

NINTH CENTURY

800: Charlemagne was crowned Emperor by Pope Leo III on Christmas Day.

Egbert became king of West Saxons. He unified England and strengthened the See of Canterbury.

813: Emperor Leo V, the Armenian, revived Iconoclasm, which persisted until about 843.

814: Charlemagne died.

843: The Treaty of Verdun split the Frankish kingdom among Charlemagne's three grandsons.

844: A Eucharistic controversy involving the writings of St. Paschasius Radbertus, Ratramnus and Rabanus Maurus occasioned the development of terminology regarding the doctrine of the Real Presence.

846: The Moslems invaded Italy and attacked Rome.

847-852: Period of composition of the *False Decretals,* a collection of forged documents attributed to popes from St. Clement (88-97) to Gregory II (715-731). The *Decretals,* which strongly supported the autonomy and rights of bishops, were suspect for a long time before being repudiated entirely about 1628.

848: The Council of Mainz condemned Gottschalk for heretical teaching regarding predestination. He was also condemned by the Council of Quierzy in 853.

857: Photius displaced Ignatius as patriarch of Constantinople. This marked the beginning of the Photian Schism, a confused state of East-West relations which has not yet been cleared up by historical research. Photius, a man of exceptional ability, died in 891.

865: St. Ansgar, Apostle of Scandinavia, died.

869: St. Cyril died and his brother, St. Methodius (d. 885), was ordained a bishop. The Apostles of the Slavs devised an alphabet and translated the Gospels and liturgy into the Slavonic language.

869: The Ecumenical Council of Constantinople (IV); see separate entry.

871-c. 900: Reign of Alfred the Great, the only English king ever anointed by a pope at Rome.

TENTH CENTURY

910: William, Duke of Aquitaine, founded the Benedictine Abbey of Cluny, which became a center of monastic and ecclesiastical reform.

915: Pope John X played a leading role in the expulsion of Saracens from central and southern Italy.

955: St. Olga, of the Russian royal family, was baptized.

962: Otto I, the Great, crowned by Pope John XII, revived Charlemagne's kingdom, which became the Holy Roman Empire.

966: Mieszko, first of a royal line in Poland, was baptized; he brought Latin Christianity to Poland.

989: Vladimir, ruler of Russia, was baptized. Russia was subsequently Christianized by Greek missionaries.

993: John XV was the first pope to decree the official canonization of a saint (Ulrich) for the universal Church.

997: St. Stephen became ruler of Hungary. He assisted in organizing the hierarchy and establishing Latin Christianity in that country.

999-1003: Pontificate of Sylvester II (Gerbert of Aquitaine), a Benedictine monk and the first French pope.

ELEVENTH CENTURY

1009: Beginning of lasting East-West schism in the Church, marked by dropping of the name of Pope Sergius IV from the Byzantine diptychs (the listing of persons prayed for during the liturgy). The deletion was made by Patriarch Sergius II of Constantinople.

1012: St. Romuald founded the Camaldolese Hermits.

1025: The Council of Arras, and other councils later, condemned the Cathari (Neo-Manichaeans, Albigenses).

1027: The Council of Elne proclaimed the Truce of God as a means of stemming violence. The truce involved armistice periods of varying length, which were later extended.

1038: St. John Gualbert founded the Vallombrosians.

1043-1059: Constantinople patriarchate of Michael Cerularius, the key figure in a controversy concerning the primacy of the papacy. His and the Byzantine synod's refusal to acknowledge this primacy in 1054 widened and hardened the East-West schism in the Church.

1047: Pope Clement II died. He was the only pope ever buried in Germany.

1049-54: Pontificate of St. Leo IX, who inaugurated a movement of papal, diocesan, monastic and clerical reform.

1055: Condemnation of the Eucharistic doctrine of Berengarius.

1059: A Lateran Council issued new legislation regarding papal elections. Voting power was entrusted to the Roman cardinals.

1066: Death of St. Edward the Confessor, King of England from 1042 and restorer of Westminster Abbey.

Defeat, at Hastings, of Harold by William I, who subsequently exerted strong influence on the life style of the Church in England.

1073-1085: Pontificate of St. Gregory VII (Hildebrand). A strong pope, he carried forward programs of clerical and general ecclesiastical reform and struggled against Henry IV and other rulers to end the evils of lay investiture. He introduced the Latin liturgy in Spain and set definite dates for the observance of ember days.

1077: Henry IV, excommunicated and suspended from the exercise of imperial powers by Gregory VII, sought absolution from the Pope at Canossa. Henry later repudiated this action and in 1084 forced Gregory to leave Rome.

1079: The Council of Rome condemned Eucharistic errors of Berengarius, who retracted.

1004: St. Bruno founded the Carthusians.

1097-1099: The first of several Crusades undertaken between this time and 1265. Recovery of the Holy Places and gaining free access to them for Christians were the original purposes, but these were diverted to less worthy objectives in various ways. Results included: a Latin Kingdom of Jerusalem, 1099-1187; a military and political misadventure in the form of a Latin Empire of Constantino-ple, 1204-1261; acquisition, by treaties, of visiting rights for Christians in the Holy Land. East-West economic and cultural relationships increased during the period. In the religious sphere, actions of the Crusaders had the effect of increasing the alienation of the East from the West.

1098: St. Robert founded the Cistercians.

TWELFTH CENTURY

1108: Beginnings of the influential Abbey and School of St. Victor.

1115: St. Bernard established the Abbey of Clairvaux and inaugurated the Cistercian Reform.

1118: Christian forces captured Saragossa, Spain; the beginning of the Moslem decline in that country.

1121: St. Norbert established the original monastery of the Praemonstratensians near Laon, France.

1122: The Concordat of Worms (Pactum Callixtinum) was formulated and approved by Pope Callistus II and Emperor Henry V to settle controversy concerning the investiture of prelates. The concordat provided that the emperor could invest prelates with symbols of temporal authority but had no right to invest them with spiritual authority, which came from the Church alone, and that the emperor was not to interfere in papal elections. This was the first concordat in history.

1123: The Ecumenical Council of the Lateran (I), the first of its kind in the West; see separate entry.

1139: The Ecumenical Council of the Lateran (II); see separate entry.

1140: St. Bernard met Abelard in debate at the Council of Sens. Abelard, whose rationalism in theology was condemned for the first time in 1121, died in 1142 at Cluny.

1148: The Synod of Rheims enacted strict disciplinary decrees for communities of women religious.

1152: The Synod of Kells reorganized the Church in Ireland.

1160: Gratian, whose *Decretum* became a basic text of canon law, died.

Peter Lombard, compiler of the *Four Books of Sentences,* a standard theology text for nearly 200 years, died.

1170: St. Thomas Becket, archbishop of Canterbury, who clashed with Henry II over Church-state relations, was murdered in his cathedral.

1171: Pope Alexander III reserved the process of canonization of saints to the Holy See.

1179: The Ecumenical Council of the Lateran (III); see separate entry.

1184: Waldenses and other heretics were excommunicated by Pope Lucius III.

THIRTEENTH CENTURY

1198-1216: Pontificate of Innocent III, during which the papacy reached its medieval peak of authority, influence and prestige in the Church and in relations with civil rulers.

1208: Innocent III called for a crusade, the first in Christendom itself, against the Albigensians.

1209: Verbal approval was given by Innocent III to a rule of life for the Order of Friars Minor, started by St. Francis of Assisi.

1212: The Second Order of Franciscans, the Poor Clares, was founded.

1215: The Ecumenical Council of the Lateran (IV); see separate entry.

1216: Formal papal approval was given to a rule of life for the Order of Preachers, started by St. Dominic.

The Portiuncula Indulgence was granted by the Holy See at the request of St. Francis of Assisi.

1221: The Third Order of St. Francis for lay persons was founded.

1226: Death of St. Francis of Assisi.

1245: The Ecumenical Council of Lyons (I); see separate entry.

1247: Preliminary approval was given by the Holy See to a Carmelite rule of life.

1270: St. Louis IX, king of France, died.

Beginning of papal decline.

1274: The Ecumenical Council of Lyons (II); see separate entry.

Death of St. Thomas Aquinas, Doctor of the Church, of lasting influence; see separate entry.

1280: Pope Nicholas III, who made the *Breviary* the official prayer book for clergy of the Roman Church, died.

1281: The excommunication of Michael Palaeologus by Pope Martin IV ruptured the union effected with the Eastern Church in 1274.

FOURTEENTH CENTURY

1302: Pope Boniface VIII issued the bull *Unam Sanctam,* concerning the unity of the Church and the temporal power of princes, against the background of a struggle with Philip IV of France; it was the most famous medieval document on the subject.

1308-1378: For a period of approximately 70 years, seven popes resided at Avignon because of unsettled conditions in Rome and other reasons; see separate entry.

1311-1312: The Ecumenical Council of Vienne; see separate entry.

1321: Dante Alighieri died a year after completing the *Divine Comedy.*

1324: Marsilius of Padua completed *Defensor Pacis,* a work condemned by Pope John XXII as heretical because of its denial of papal primacy and the hierarchical structure of the Church, and for other reasons. It was a charter for conciliarism.

1337-1453: Period of the Hundred Years' War, a dynastic struggle between France and England.

1338: Four years after the death of Pope John XXII, who had opposed Louis IV of Bavaria in a years-long controversy, electoral princes declared at the Diet of Rhense that the emperor did not need papal confirmation of his title and right to rule. Charles IV later (1356) said the same thing in a *Golden Bull,* eliminating papal rights in the election of emperors.

1347-1350: The Black Death swept across Europe, killing perhaps one-fourth to one-third of the total population; an estimated 40 per cent of the clergy succumbed.

1374: Petrarch, poet and humanist, died.

1378: Return of the papacy from Avignon to Rome.

Beginning of the Western Schism; see separate entry.

FIFTEENTH CENTURY

1409: The Council of Pisa, without canonical authority, tried to end the Western Schism but succeeded only in complicating it by electing a third claimant to the papacy; see Western Schism.

1414-1418: The Ecumenical Council of Constance ended the Western Schism; see separate entry.

1431: St. Joan of Arc was burned at the stake.

1431-1449: The Council of Basle, which began with convocation by Pope Martin V in 1431, turned into an anti-papal forum of conciliarists seeking to subject the primacy and authority of the pope to the overriding authority of an assembly of bishops. It was not an ecumenical council.

1438: The Pragmatic Sanction of Bourges was enacted by Charles VIII and the French parliament to curtail papal authority over the Church in France, in the spirit of conciliarism. It found expression in Gallicanism and had effects lasting at least until the French Revolution.

1438-1443: The Ecumenical Council of Florence affirmed the primacy of the pope in opposition to conciliarism and effected a measure of union with separated Eastern Christians; see separate entry.

1453: The fall of Constantinople to the Turks.

c. 1456: Gutenberg issued the first edition of the Bible printed from movable type, at Mainz, Germany.

1476: Pope Sixtus IV ordered observance of the feast of the Immaculate Conception on Dec. 8 throughout the Church.

1492: Columbus discovered the Americas.

1493: Pope Alexander VI issued a *Bull of Demarcation* which determined spheres of influence for the Spanish and Portuguese in the Americas.

The Renaissance, a humanistic movement which originated in Italy in the 14th century, spread to France, Germany, the Low Countries and England. A transitional period between the medieval world and the modern secular world, it introduced profound changes which affected literature and the other arts, general culture, politics and religion.

SIXTEENTH CENTURY

1512-1517: The Ecumenical Council of the Lateran (V); see separate entry.

1517: Martin Luther signalled the beginning of the Reformation by posting 95 theses at Wittenberg. Subsequently, he broke completely from doctrinal orthodoxy in discourses and three published works (1519 and 1520); was excommunicated on more than 40 charges of heresy (1521); remained the dominant figure in the Reformation in Germany until his death in 1546.

1519: Zwingli triggered the Reformation in Zurich and became its leading proponent there until his death in combat in 1531.

1524: Luther's encouragement of German princes in putting down the two-year Peasants' Revolt gained political support for his cause.

1528: The Order of Friars Minor Capuchin was approved as an autonomous division of the Franciscan Order; like the Jesuits, the Capuchins became leaders in the Counter-Reformation.

1530: The *Augsburg Confession* of Lutheran faith was issued; it was later supplemented by the *Smalcald Articles* approved in 1537.

1533: Henry VIII divorced Catherine of Aragon, married Anne Boleyn, was excommunicated. In 1534 he decreed the Act of Supremacy, making the sovereign the head of the Church in England, under which Sts. John Fisher and Thomas More were executed in 1535. Despite his rejection of papal primacy and actions against monastic life in England, he generally maintained doctrinal orthodoxy until his death in 1547.

1536: John Calvin, leader of the Reformation in Switzerland until his death in 1564, issued the first edition of *Institutes of the Christian Religion*, which became the classical text of Reformed (non-Lutheran) theology.

1540: The constitutions of the Society of Jesus (Jesuits), founded by St. Ignatius of Loyola, were approved.

1541: Start of the 11-year career of St. Francis Xavier as a missionary to the East Indies and Japan.

1545-1563: The Ecumenical Council of Trent formulated statements of Catholic doctrine under attack by the Reformers and mobilized the Counter-Reformation; see separate entry.

1549: The first *Book of Common Prayer* was issued by Edward VI. Revised editions were published in 1552, 1559 and 1662 and later.

1553: Start of the five-year reign of Mary Tudor who tried to counteract actions of Henry VIII against the Roman Church.

1555: Enactment of the Peace of Augsburg, an arrangement of religious territorialism rather than toleration, which recognized the existence of Catholicism and Lutheranism in the German Empire and provided that citizens should adopt the religion of their respective rulers.

1558: Beginning of the reign of Elizabeth I, during which the Church of England took on its definitive form.

1559: Establishment of the hierarchy of the Church of England, with the consecration of Matthew Parker as archbishop of Canterbury.

1563: The first text of the *39 Articles* of the Church of England was issued. Also enacted were a new Act of Supremacy and Oath of Succession to the English throne.

1570: Elizabeth I was excommunicated. Penal measures against Catholics subsequently became more severe.

1571: Defeat of the Turkish armada at Lepanto staved off the invasion of Eastern Europe.

1577: The *Formula of Concord,* the classical statement of Lutheran faith, was issued; it was, generally, a Lutheran counterpart of the canons of the Council of Trent. In 1580, along with other formulas of doctrine, it was included in the *Book of Concord.*

1582: The Gregorian Calendar, named for Pope Gregory XIII, was put into effect and was eventually adopted in most countries: England delayed adoption until 1752.

SEVENTEENTH CENTURY

1605: The Gunpowder Plot, an attempt by Catholic fanatics to blow up James I of England and the houses of Parliament, resulted in an anti-Catholic

Oath of Allegiance; the Oath was condemned by Pope Paul V in 1606.

1610: Death of Matteo Ricci, outstanding Jesuit missionary to China, pioneer in cultural relations between China and Europe.

Founding of the first community of Visitation Nuns by Sts. Francis de Sales and Jane de Chantal.

1611: Founding of the Oratorians.

1613: Catholics were banned from Scandinavia.

1625: Founding of the Congregation of the Mission (Vincentians) by St. Vincent de Paul. He founded the Sisters of Charity in 1633.

1642: Death of Galileo, scientist, who was censured by the Congregation of the Holy Office for supporting the Copernican theory of the sun-centered planetary system.

Founding of the Sulpicians by Jacques Olier.

1643: Start of publication of the Bollandist *Acta Sanctorum,* a critical work on lives of the saints.

1648: Provisions in the Peace of Westphalia, ending the Thirty Years' War, extended terms of the Peace of Augsburg (1555) to Calvinists and gave equality to Catholics and Protestants in the 300 states of the Holy Roman Empire.

1649: Oliver Cromwell invaded Ireland and began a severe persecution of the Church there.

1653: Pope Innocent X condemned five propositions of Jansenism, a complex theory which distorted doctrine concerning the relations between divine grace and human freedom. Jansenism was also a rigoristic movement which seriously disturbed the Church in France, the Low Countries and Italy in this and the 18th century.

1673: The Test Act in England barred from public office Catholics who would not deny the doctrine of transubstantiation and receive Communion in the Church of England.

1678: Many English Catholics suffered death as a consequence of the Popish Plot, a false allegation by Titus Oates that Catholics planned to assassinate Charles I, land a French army in the country, burn London, and turn over the government to the Jesuits.

1682: The four articles of the *Gallican Declaration,* drawn up by Bossuet, asserted political and ecclesiastical immunities of France from papal control. The articles, which rejected the primacy of the pope, were condemned in 1690.

1689: The Toleration Act granted a measure of freedom of worship to other English dissenters but not to Catholics.

EIGHTEENTH CENTURY

1704: Chinese Rites — involving the Christian adaptation of elements of Confucianism, veneration of ancestors and Chinese terminology in religion — were condemned by Clement XI. An earlier ban was issued in 1645; a later one, in 172.

1720: The Passionists were founded by St. Paul of the Cross.

1724: Persecution in China.

1732: The Redemptorists were founded by St. Alphonsus Liguori.

1738: Freemasonry was condemned by Clement XII and Catholics were forbidden to join, under penalty of excommunication; the prohibition was repeated by Benedict XIV in 1751 and by later popes.

1760's: Josephinism, a theory and system of state control of the Church, was initiated in Austria; it remained in force until about 1850.

1764: Febronianism, an unorthodox theory and practice regarding the constitution of the Church and relations between Church and state, was condemned for the first of several times. Proposed by an auxiliary bishop of Trier using the pseudonym Justinus Febronius, it had the effects of minimizing the office of the pope and supporting national churches under state control.

1773: Clement XIV issued a brief of suppression against the Jesuits, following their expulsion from Portugal in 1759, from France in 1764 and from Spain in 1767. Political intrigue and unsubstantiated accusations were principal factors in these developments. The ban, which crippled the Society, contained no condemnation of the Jesuit constitutions, particular Jesuits or Jesuit teaching. The Society was restored in 1814.

1778: Catholics in England were relieved of some civil disabilities dating back to the time of Henry VIII, by an act which permitted them to acquire, own and inherit property. Additional liberties were restored by the Roman Catholic Relief Act of 1791 and subsequent enactments of Parliament.

1789: Religious freedom in the United States was guaranteed under the First Amendment to the Constitution.

Beginning of the French Revolution which resulted in: the secularization of church property and the Civil Constitution of the Clergy in 1790; the persecution of priests, religious and lay persons loyal to papal authority; invasion of the Papal States by Napoleon in 1796; renewal of persecution from 1797-1799; attempts to dechristianize France and establish a new religion; the occupation of Rome by French troops and the forced removal of Pius VI to France in 1798.

This century is called the age of Enlightenment or Reason because of the predominating rational and scientific approach of its leading philosophers, scientists and writers with respect to religion, ethics and natural law. This approach downgraded the fact and significance of revealed religion. Also characteristic of the Enlightenment were subjectivism, secularism and optimism regarding human perfectibility.

NINETEENTH CENTURY

1809: Pope Pius VII was made a captive by Napoleon and deported to France where he remained in exile until 1814. During this time he refused to cooperate with Napoleon who sought to bring the Church in France under his own control.

The turbulence in church-state relations in France at the beginning of the century recurred in connection with the Bourbon Restoration, the July Revolution, the second and third Republics, the Second Empire and the Dreyfus case.

1814: The Society of Jesus, suppressed since 1773, was restored.

1817: Reestablishment of the Congregation for the Propagation of the Faith (Propaganda) by Pius VII was an important factor in increasing missionary activity during the century.

1820: Years-long persecution, during which thousands died for the faith, ended in China. Thereafter, communication with the West remained cut off until about 1834. Vigorous missionary work got under way in 1842.

1822: The Pontifical Society for the Propagation of the Faith, inaugurated in France by Pauline Jaricot for the support of missionary activity, was established.

1829: The Catholic Emancipation Act relieved Catholics in England and Ireland of most of the civil disabilities to which they had been subject from the time of Henry VIII.

1832: Gregory XVI, in the encyclical *Mirari Vos,* condemned indifferentism, one of the many ideologies at odds with Christian doctrine which were proposed during the century.

1833: Start of the Oxford Movement which affected the Church of England and resulted in some notable conversions, including that of John Henry Newman in 1845, to the Catholic Church.

Frederick Ozanam founded the Society of St. Vincent de Paul in France. The society, whose objective was works of charity, became worldwide.

1848: The *Communist Manifesto,* a revolutionary document symptomatic of socio-economic crisis, was issued.

1850: The hierarchy was reestablished in England and Nicholas Wiseman made the first archbishop of Westminster. He was succeeded in 1865 by Henry Manning, an Oxford convert and proponent of the rights of labor.

1853: The Catholic hierarchy was reestablished in Holland.

1854: Pius IX proclaimed the dogma of the Immaculate Conception in the bull *Ineffabilis Deus.*

1858: The Blessed Virgin Mary appeared to St. Bernadette at Lourdes, France; see separate entry.

1864: Pius IX issued the encyclical *Quanta Cura* and the *Syllabus of Errors* in condemnation of some 80 propositions derived from the scientific mentality and rationalism of the century. The subjects in question had deep ramifications in many areas of thought and human endeavor; in religion, they explicitly and/or implicitly rejected divine revelation and the supernatural order.

1867: The first volume of *Das Kapital* was published. Together with the Communist First International, formed in the same year, it had great influence on the subsequent development of Communism and Socialism.

1869: The Anglican Church was disestablished in Ireland.

1869-1870: The First Vatican Council; see separate entry.

1870-1871: Victor Emmanuel II of Sardinia, crowned king of Italy after defeating Austrian and papal forces, marched into Rome in 1870 and expropriated the Papal States after a plebiscite in which Catholics, at the order of Pius IX, did not vote. In 1871, Pius IX refused to accept a Law of Guarantees. Confiscation of church property and hindrance of ecclesiastical administration by the regime followed.

1871: The German Empire, a confederation of 26 states, was formed. Government policy launched a Kulturkampf whose May Laws of 1873 were designed to annul papal jurisdiction in Prussia and other states and to place the Church under imperial control. Resistance to the enactments and the persecution they legalized forced the government to modify its anti-Church policy by 1887.

1878: Beginning of the pontificate of Leo XIII, who was pope until his death in 1903. Leo is best known for the encyclical *Rerum Novarum,* which greatly influenced the course of Christian social thought and the labor movement. His other accomplishments included promotion of a revival of Scholastic philosophy and the impetus he gave to scriptural studies.

1881: The first International Eucharistic Congress was held in Lille, France.

Alexander II of Russia died. His policies of Russification — as well as those of his two predecessors and a successor during the century — caused great suffering to Catholics, Jews and Protestants in Poland, Lithuania, the Ukraine and Bessarabia.

1882: Charles Darwin died. His theory of evolution by natural selection, one of several scientific highlights of the century, had extensive repercussions in the faith-and-science controversy.

1889: The Catholic University of America was founded in Washington, D.C.

1893: The U.S. apostolic delegation was set up in Washington, D.C.

TWENTIETH CENTURY

1901: Restrictive measures in France forced the Jesuits, Benedictines, Carmelites and other religious orders to leave the country. Subsequently, 14,000 schools were suppressed; religious orders and congregations were expelled; the concordat was renounced in 1905; church property was confiscated in 1906. For some years the Holy See, refusing to comply with government demands for the control of bishops' appointments, left some ecclesiastical offices vacant.

1903: Start of the 11-year pontificate of St. Pius X. He initiated the codification of canon law, 1904; removed the ban against participation by Catholics in Italian national elections, 1905; issued decrees calling upon the faithful to receive Holy Communion frequently and daily, and stating that children should begin receiving the Eucharist at the age of seven, 1905 and 1910, respectively; ordered the establishment of the Confraternity of Christian Doctrine in all parishes throughout the world, 1905; condemned Modernism in the decree *Lamentabili* and the encyclical *Pascendi,* 1907.

1908: The United States and England, long under the jurisdiction of the Congregation for the Propagation of the Faith as mission territories, were removed from its control and placed under the common law of the Church.

1910: Laws of separation were enacted in Portugal, marking a point of departure in church-state relations.

1911: The Catholic Foreign Mission Society of America — Maryknoll, the first U.S.-founded society of its type — was established.

1914: Start of World War I, which lasted until 1918.

Start of the eight-year pontificate of Benedict XV. Much of his pontificate was devoted to seeking ways and means of minimizing the material and spiritual havoc of World War I. In 1917 he offered his services as a mediator to the belligerent nations, but his pleas for settlement of the conflict went unheeded.

1917: The Blessed Virgin Mary appeared to three children at Fatima, Portugal; see separate entry.

A new constitution, embodying repressive laws against the Church, was enacted in Mexico. Its implementation resulted in persecution in the 1920's and 1930's.

Bolsheviks seized power in Russia and set up a communist dictatorship. The event marked the rise of Communism in Russian and world affairs. One of its immediate, and lasting, results was persecution of the Church, Jews and other segments of the population.

1918: The *Code of Canon Law,* in preparation for more than 10 years, went into effect in the Western Church.

1919: Benedict XV stimulated missionary work through the decree *Maximum Illud,* in which he urged the recruiting and training of native clergy in places where the Church was not firmly established.

1922: Beginning of the 17-year pontificate of Pius XI. He subscribed to the Lateran Treaty, 1929, which settled the Roman Question created by the confiscation of the Papal States in 1871; issued the encyclical *Casti Connubii,* 1930, an authoritative statement on Christian marriage; resisted the efforts of Benito Mussolini to control Catholic Action and the Church, in the encyclical *Non Abbiamo Bisogno,* 1931; opposed various Fascist policies; issued the encyclicals *Quadragesimo Anno,* 1931, developing the social doctrine of Leo XIII's *Rerum Novarum,* and *Divini Redemptoris,* 1937, calling for social justice and condemning atheistic Communism; condemned anti-Semitism, 1937.

Ireland was partitioned. All but two of the predominantly Catholic counties were included in the southern part of the country, which eventually attained the status of an independent republic in 1949.

1926: The Catholic Relief Act repealed virtually all legal disabilities of Catholics in England.

1931: Leftists proclaimed Spain a republic and proceeded to disestablish the Church, confiscate church property, deny salaries to the clergy, expel the Jesuits and ban teaching of the Catholic faith. These actions were preludes to the civil war of 1936-1939.

1933: Emergence of Adolf Hitler to power in Germany. By 1935 two of his aims were clear, the elimination of the Jews and control of a single national church. Persecution decimated the Jews over a period of years. The Church was subject to repressive measures, which Pius XI protested futilely in the encyclical *Mit Brennender Sorge* in 1937.

1936: A three-year civil war broke out in Spain between the leftist Loyalists and forces led by Francisco Franco. The Loyalists were defeated and one-man, one-party rule was established. A number of priests, religious and lay persons fell victims to Loyalist persecution.

1939: Start of World War II, which lasted until 1945.

Start of the 19-year pontificate of Pius XII; see separate entry.

1940: Start of a decade of communist conquest in more than 13 countries, resulting in conditions of persecution for a minimum of 60 million Catholics as well as members of other faiths; see various countries.

Persecution diminished in Mexico through non-enforcement of anti-religious laws still on record.

1950: Pius XII proclaimed the dogma of the Assumption of the Blessed Virgin Mary.

1954: St. Pius X was canonized.

1957: The communist regime of China attempted to start a national schismatic church.

1958: Beginning of the five-year pontificate of John XXIII; see separate entry.

1962: The Second Vatican Council began the first of four sessions; see separate entry.

1963: Beginning of 15-year pontificate of Paul VI; see separate entry.

1978: Thirty-four-day pontificate of John Paul I; see separate entry.

Beginning of pontificate of John Paul II; see separate entry.

1983: The revised *Code of Canon Law* was promulgated and placed in effect.

HERESIES

Heresy is the formal and obstinate denial or doubt by a baptized person, who remains a nominal Christian, of any truth which must be believed as a matter of divine and Catholic faith. Formal heresy involves deliberate resistance to the authority of God who communicates revelation through Scripture and tradition and the teaching authority of the Church. Obstinate refusal to accept the infallible teaching of the Church constitutes the canonical crime of heresy.

Formal heretics automatically incur the penalty of excommunication (Canon 1364 of the Code of Canon Law). Material heretics are those who, in good faith and without formal obstinacy, do not accept articles or matters of divine and Catholic faith.

Heresies have been significant not only as disruptions of unity of faith but also as occasions for the clarification and development of doctrine.

Heresies from the beginning of the Church to the 13th century are listed below.

Judaizers: Early converts from Judaism who claimed that members of the Church had to observe all the requirements of Mosaic Law as well as the obligations of Christian faith. This view was condemned by the Council of Jerusalem held in 51 under the presidency of St. Peter (Acts 15:28).

Gnosticism: A combination of elements of Platonic philosophy and Eastern mystery religions which claimed that its secret-knowledge principle gave its adherents a deeper insight into Christian doctrine than divine revelation and faith. One Gnostic thesis denied the divinity of Christ; others denied the reality of his humanity, calling it mere appearance **(Docetism, Phantasiasm).**

Modalism: A general term covering propositions **(Monarchianism, Patripassianism, Sabellianism)** that the Father, Son and Holy Spirit are not really distinct divine Persons but are only three different modes of being and self-manifestation of the one God. Various forms of Modalism, which appeared in the East in the second century and spread westward, were all condemned.

Marcionism: A Gnostic creation named for its author, who claimed there was total opposition and no connection at all between the Old Testament and the New Testament, between the God of the Jews and the God of the Christians; and that the canon of Scripture consisted only of portions of Luke's Gospel and 10 epistles of Paul. Marcion was excommunicated in 144 at Rome, and his tenets were condemned again by a Roman council about 260. The heresy was checked at Rome by 200 but persisted for several centuries in the East and had some adherents as late as the Middle Ages.

Montanism: A form of extremism preached about 170 by Montanus of Phrygia, Asia Minor. Its principal tenets were: an imminent second coming of Christ, denial of the divine nature of the Church and its power to forgive sin, excessively rigorous morality. The heresy was condemned by Pope St. Zephyrinus (199-217). Tertullian was one of its victims.

Novatianism: A heresy of excessive rigorism named for its author, a priest of Rome and antipope. Its principal tenet was that persons who fell away from the Church under persecution and or those guilty of serious sin after baptism could not be absolved and readmitted to communion with the Church. The heresy, condemned by a Roman synod in 251, slowly subsided in the West and died in the East by the end of the seventh century.

Subordinationism, Adoptionism: Christological errors and logical antecedents of Arianism. The key tenet was that Christ, while the most excellent of creatures, was subordinate to God whose Son he was by adoption rather than by nature. First proposed at Rome late in the second century, it was condemned by Pope St. Victor in 190 and again in the following century, in 785 by Pope Adrian I, in 794 by a council of Frankfurt, and in 1177 by Pope Alexander III.

Arianism: Denial of the divinity of Christ, the most devastating of the early heresies, authored by Arius of Alexandria, a priest, and condemned by the Council of Nicaea I in 325. Arians and several kinds of **Semi-Arians** propagandized their tenets widely, raised havoc in the Church for several centuries, and established their own hierarchies and churches.

Macedonianism: Denial of the divinity of the Holy Spirit, who was said to be a creature of the Son. Condemned by the Council of Constantinople I in 381. Macedonians were also called **Pneumatomachists,** enemies of the Spirit; and **Marathonians,** after the name of one of their leaders, a bishop of Nicomedia.

Nestorianism: Denial of the real unity of divine and human natures in the single divine Person of Christ, proposed by Nestorius, patriarch of Constantinople. He also held that Mary could not be called the Mother of God *(Theotokos);* that is, of the Second Person of the Trinity made Man. Condemned by the councils of Ephesus in 431 and Chalcedon in 451.

Monophysitism: Denial of Christ's human nature; also called **Eutychianism,** after the name of one of its leading advocates. The heresy was condemned by the Council of Chalcedon in 451.

Monothelitism: Denial of the human will of Christ. Severus of Antioch and Sergius, patriarch of Constantinople, were leading advocates of the heresy, which was condemned by the Council of Constantinople III in 681.

Priscillianism: A fourth century amalgamation of elements from various sources — Sabellianism, Arianism, Docetism, Pantheism, belief in the diabolical nature of marriage, corruption of Scripture. The heresy was condemned by a council of Braga in 563 on 17 different counts.

Donatism: A development of the error at the heart of the third century **Rebaptism Controversy** (baptism conferred by heretics is invalid because persons deprived of grace are incapable of being ministers of grace to others). Followers of Donatus the Great asserted throughout the fourth century that sacraments administered by sinners were invalid. Condemnation of the heresy is traced to Pope St. Stephen I (254-257) and the principle that sacraments have their efficacy from Christ, not from their human ministers.

Pelagianism: Denial of the supernatural order of things, proposed by Pelagius (360-420), a Breton monk. Proceeding from the assumption that Adam had a natural right to supernatural life, the theory held that man could attain salvation through the efforts of his own free will and natural powers. The theory involved errors concerning the nature of original sin, the meaning of grace and other matters. St. Augustine opposed the heresy, which was condemned by the Council of Ephesus in 431. **Semi-Pelagianism** was condemned by a council of Orange in 529.

Iconoclasm: An image-breaking campaign which resulted from an edict issued by Eastern Emperor Leo the Isaurian in 726, that the veneration of images, pictures and relics was idolatrous. The theoretical basis of the heresy was the Monophysite error which denied the humanity of Christ. It was denounced several times before its condemnation by the Council of Nicaea II in 787.

Berengarian Heresy: Denial of the Real Presence of Christ under the appearances of bread and wine, the first clear-cut Eucharistic heresy; proposed by Berengarius of Tours (c. 1000-1088). The heresy was condemned by various synods and finally by a council held at Rome in 1079.

Waldensianism: Claimed by Peter Waldo, a merchant of Lyons, to be a return to pure Christianity, the heresy rejected the hierarchical structure of the Church, the sacramental system and other doctrines. Its adherents were excommunicated in 1184 and their tenets were condemned several times thereafter.

Albigensianism, Catharism: Related errors based on the old **Manichaean** assumption that two supreme principles of good and evil were operative in creation and life, and that the supreme objective of human endeavor was liberation from evil (matter). The heresy denied the humanity of Christ, the sacramental system and the authority of the Church (and state), and endorsed a moral code which threatened seriously the fabric of social life in southern France and northern Italy in the 12th and 13th centuries. The heresy was condemned by councils of the Lateran III and Lateran IV in 1179 and 1215.

ECUMENICAL COUNCILS

An ecumenical council is an assembly of the college of bishops, with and under the presidency of the pope, which has supreme authority over the Church in matters pertaining to faith, morals, worship and discipline.

The Second Vatican Council stated: "The supreme authority with which this college (of bishops) is empowered over the whole Church is exercised in a solemn way through an ecumenical council. A council is never ecumenical unless it is confirmed or at least accepted as such by the successor of Peter. It is the prerogative of the Roman Pontiff to convoke these councils, to preside over them, and to confirm them" (*Dogmatic Constitution on the Church*, No. 22).

Pope Presides

The pope is the head of an ecumenical council; he presides over it either personally or through legates. Conciliar decrees and other actions have binding force only when confirmed and promulgated by him. If a pope dies during a council, it is suspended until reconvened by another pope. An ecumenical council is not superior to a pope; hence, there is no appeal from a pope to a council.

Collectively, the bishops with the pope represent the whole Church. They do this not as democratic representatives of the faithful in a kind of church parliament, but as the successors of the Apostles with divinely given authority, care and responsibility over the whole Church.

Council participants with a deliberative vote are: cardinals, including those who are retired; residential patriarchs, primates, archbishops and bishops, even if they are not yet consecrated; abbots and certain other prelates, an abbot primate, abbot superiors of monastic congregations and heads of exempt clerical religious; titular bishops, on invitation. Experts in theology and canon law may be given a consultative vote. Others, including lay persons, may address a council or observe its actions, but may not vote.

Basic legislation concerning ecumenical councils is contained in the Code of Canon Law. Basic doctrinal considerations were stated by the Second Vatican Council in the *Dogmatic Constitution on the Church.*

Background

Ecumenical councils had their prototype in the Council of Jerusalem in 51, at which the Apostles under the leadership of St. Peter decided that converts to the Christian faith were not obliged to observe all the prescriptions of Old Testament law (Acts 15). As early as the second century, bishops got together in regional meetings, synods or councils to take common action for the doctrinal and pastoral good of their communities of faithful. The expansion of such limited assemblies to ecumenical councils was a logical and historical evolution, given the nature and needs of the Church.

Emperors were active in summoning or convoking the first eight councils, especially the first five and the eighth. Among reasons for intervention of this kind were the facts that the emperors regarded themselves as guardians of the faith; that the settlement of religious controversies, which had repercussions in political and social turmoil, served the cause of peace in the state; and that the emperors had at their disposal ways and means of facilitating gatherings of bishops. Imperial actions, however, did not account for the formally ecumenical nature of the councils.

Some councils were attended by relatively few bishops, and the ecumenical character of several was open to question for a time. However, confirmation and de facto recognition of their actions by popes and subsequent councils established them as ecumenical.

Role in History

The councils have played a highly significant role in the history of the Church by witnessing to and defining truths of revelation, by shaping forms of worship and discipline, and by promoting measures for the ever-necessary reform and renewal of Catholic life. In general, they have represented attempts of the Church to mobilize itself in times of crisis for self-preservation, self-purification and growth.

The first eight ecumenical councils were held in the East; the other 13, in the West. The majority of separated Eastern Churches — e.g., the Orthodox — recognize the ecumenical character of the first seven councils, which formulated a great deal of basic doctrine. Nestorians, however, acknowledge only the first two councils; the Monophysite Armenians, Syrians, and Copts acknowledge the first three.

The 21 Councils

The 21 ecumenical councils in the history of the Church are listed below, with indication of their names or titles (taken from the names of the places where they were held); the dates; the reigning and/or approving popes; the emperors who were instrumental in convoking the eight councils in the East; the number of bishops who attended, when available; the number of sessions; the most significant actions.

1. Nicaea I, 325: St. Sylvester I (Emperor Constantine I); attended by approximately 300 bishops; sessions held between May 20 or June 19 to near the end of August. Condemned Arianism, which denied the divinity of Christ; contributed to formulation of the Nicene Creed; fixed the date of Easter; passed regulations concerning clerical discipline; adopted the civil division of the Empire as the model for the organization of the Church.

2. Constantinople I, 381: St. Damasus I (Emperor Theodosius I); attended by approximately 150 bishops; sessions held from May to July. Condemned various brands of Arianism, and Macedonianism which denied the divinity of the Holy Spirit; contributed to formulation of the Nicene Creed; approved a canon which made the bishop of Constantinople the ranking prelate in the East, with primacy next to that of the pope. Doubt about the ecumenical character of this council was resolved by the ratification of its acts by popes and the Council of Chalcedon.

3. Ephesus, 431: St. Celestine I (Emperor Theodosius II); attended by 150 to 200 bishops; five sessions held between June 22 and July 17. Condemned Nestorianism, which denied the real unity of the divine and human natures in the Person of Christ; defined *Theotokos* ("Bearer of God") as the title of Mary, Mother of the Son of God made Man; condemned Pelagianism, which reduced the supernatural to the natural order of things.

4. Chalcedon, 451: St. Leo I (Emperor Marcian); attended by approximately 600 bishops; 17 sessions held between Oct. 8 and Nov. 1. Condemned: Monophysitism, also called Eutychianism, which denied the humanity of Christ by holding that he had only one, the divine, nature; and the Monophysite Robber Synod of Ephesus, of 449.

5. Constantinople II, 553: Vigilius (Emperor Justinian I); attended by 165 bishops; eight sessions held between May 5 and June 2. Condemned the *Three Chapters,* Nestorian-tainted writings of Theodore of Mopsuestia, Theodoret of Cyprus and Ibas of Edessa.

6. Constantinople III, 680-681; St. Agatho, St. Leo II (Emperor Constantine IV); attended by approximately 170 bishops; 16 sessions held between Nov. 7, 680, and Sept. 16, 681. Condemned Monothelitism, which held that there was only one will, the divine, in Christ; censured Pope Honorius I for a letter to Sergius, bishop of Constantinople, in which he made an ambiguous but not infallible statement about the unity of will and/or operation in Christ. Constantinople III is also called the Trullan Council because its sessions were held in the domed hall, Trullos, of the imperial palace.

7. Nicaea II, 787: Adrian I (Empress Irene); attended by approximately 300 bishops; eight sessions held between Sept. 24 and Oct. 23. Condemned: Iconoclasm, which held that the use of images was idolatry; and Adoptionism, which claimed that Christ was not the Son of God by nature but only by adoption. This was the last council regarded as ecumenical by Orthodox Churches.

8. Constantinople IV, 869-870: Adrian II (Emperor Basil I); attended by 102 bishops; six sessions held between Oct. 5, 869, and Feb. 28, 870. Condemned Iconoclasm; condemned and deposed Photius as patriarch of Constantinople; restored Ignatius to the patriarchate. This was the last ecumenical council held in the East. It was first called ecumenical by canonists toward the end of the 11th century.

9. Lateran I, 1123: Callistus II; attended by approximately 300 bishops; sessions held between Mar. 18 and Apr. 6. Endorsed provisions of the Concordat of Worms concerning the investiture of prelates: approved reform measures in 25 canons.

10. Lateran II, 1139: Innocent II; attended by 900 to 1,000 bishops and abbots; three sessions held in April. Adopted measures against a schism organized by antipope Anacletus; approved 30 disciplinary measures and canons, one of which stated that holy orders is an invalidating impediment to marriage.

11. Lateran III, 1179: Alexander III; attended by at least 300 bishops; three sessions held between Mar. 5 and 19. Enacted measures against the Waldenses and Albigensians; approved reform decrees in 27 canons; provided that popes be elected by two-thirds vote of the cardinals.

12. Lateran IV, 1215: Innocent III; sessions held between Nov. 11 and 30. Ordered annual confession and Communion; defined and made first official use of the term "transubstantiation"; adopted measures to counteract the Cathari and Albigensians; approved 70 canons.

13. Lyons I, 1245: Innocent IV; attended by approximately 150 bishops; three sessions held between June 28 and July 17. Confirmed the deposition of Emperor Frederick II; approved 22 canons.

14. Lyons II, 1274: Gregory X; attended by approximately 500 bishops; six sessions held between May 7 and July 17. Accomplished a temporary reunion of separated Eastern Churches with the Roman Church; issued regulations concerning conclaves for papal elections; approved 31 canons.

15. Vienne, 1311-1312: Clement V; attended by 132 bishops; three sessions held between Oct. 16, 1311, and May 6, 1312. Suppressed the Knights Templar; enacted a number of reform decrees.

16. Constance, 1414-1418: Gregory XII, Martin V; attended by nearly 200 bishops, plus other prelates and many experts; 45 sessions held between Nov. 5, 1414, and Apr. 22, 1418. Took successful action to end the Western Schism; rejected the teachings of Wycliff; condemned Hus as a heretic. One decree, passed in the earlier stages of the council, asserted the superiority of an ecumenical council over the pope; this was later rejected.

17. Florence (also called Basel-Ferrara-Florence), 1438-1445: Eugene IV; attended by many Latin-Rite and Eastern-Rite bishops; preliminary sessions were held at Basel and Ferrara before definitive work was accomplished at Florence. Reaffirmed the primacy of the pope against the claims of Conciliarists that an ecumenical council is superior to the pope; formulated and approved decrees of union — with the Greeks, July 6, 1439; with the Armenians, Nov. 22, 1439; with the Jacobites, Feb. 4, 1442. These decrees failed to gain general or lasting acceptance in the East.

18. Lateran V, 1512-1517: Julius II, Leo X; 12 sessions held between May 3, 1512, and Mar. 16, 1517. Stated the relation and position of the pope with respect to an ecumenical council; acted to counteract the Pragmatic Sanction of Bourges and exaggerated claims of liberty by the French Church; condemned erroneous teachings concerning the nature of the human soul; stated doctrine concerning indulgences. The council reflected concern for abuses in the Church and the need for reforms but failed to take decisive action in the years immediately preceding the Reformation.

19. Trent, 1545-1563: Paul III, Julius III, Pius IV; 25 sessions held between Dec. 13, 1545, and Dec. 4, 1563. Issued a great number of decrees concerning doctrinal matters opposed by the Reformers, and mobilized the Counter-Reformation. Definitions covered the rule of faith, the nature of justification, grace, faith, original sin and its effects, the seven sacraments, the sacrificial nature of the Mass, the veneration of saints, use of sacred images, belief in purgatory, the doctrine of indulgences, the jurisdiction of the pope over the whole Church. Initiated many reforms for renewal in the liturgy and general discipline in the Church, the promotion of religious instruction, the education of the clergy through the foundation of seminaries, etc. Trent ranks with Vatican II as the greatest ecumenical council held in the West.

20. Vatican I, 1869-1870: Pius IX; attended by approximately 800 bishops and other prelates; four public sessions and 89 general meetings held between Dec. 8, 1869, and July 7, 1870. Defined papal primacy and infallibility in a dogmatic constitution on the Church; covered natural religion, revelation, faith, and the relations between faith and reason in a dogmatic constitution on the Catholic faith. The council suspended sessions Sept. 1 and was adjourned Oct. 20, 1870.

Vatican II

The Second Vatican Council, which was forecast by Pope John XXIII Jan. 25, 1959, was held in four sessions in St. Peter's Basilica.

Pope John convoked it and opened the first session, which ran from Oct. 11 to Dec. 8, 1962. Following John's death June 3, 1963, Pope Paul VI reconvened the council for the other three sessions which ran from Sept. 29 to Dec. 4, 1963; Sept. 14 to Nov. 21, 1964; Sept. 14 to Dec. 8, 1965.

A total of 2,860 Fathers participated in council proceedings, and attendance at meetings varied between 2,000 and 2,500. For various reasons, including the denial of exit from Communist-dominated countries, 274 Fathers could not attend.

The council formulated and promulgated 16 documents — two dogmatic and two pastoral constitutions, nine decrees and three declarations — all of which reflect its basic pastoral orientation toward renewal and reform in the Church. Given below are the Latin and English titles of the documents and their dates of promulgation.

• *Lumen Gentium* (Dogmatic Constitution on the Church), Nov. 21, 1964.

• *Dei Verbum* (Dogmatic Constitution on Divine Revelation), Nov. 18, 1965.

• *Sacrosanctum Concilium* (Constitution on the Sacred Liturgy), Dec. 4, 1963.

• *Gaudium et Spes* (Pastoral Constitution on the Church in the Modern World), Dec. 7, 1965.

• *Christus Dominus* (Decree on the Bishops' Pastoral Office in the Church), Oct. 28, 1965.

• *Ad Gentes* (Decree on the Church's Missionary Activity), Dec. 7, 1965.

• *Unitatis Redintegratio* (Decree on Ecumenism), Nov. 21, 1964.

• *Orientalium Ecclesiarum* (Decree on Eastern Catholic Churches), Nov. 21, 1964.

• *Presbyterorum Ordinis* (Decree on the Ministry and Life of Priests), Dec. 7, 1965.

• *Optatam Totius* (Decree on Priestly Formation), Oct. 28, 1965.

• *Perfectae Caritatis* (Decree on the Appropriate Renewal of the Religious Life), Oct. 28, 1965.

• *Apostolicam Actuositatem* (Decree on the Apostolate of the Laity), Nov. 18, 1965.

• *Inter Mirifica* (Decree on the Instruments of Social Communication), Dec. 4, 1963.

• *Dignitatis Humanae* (Declaration on Religious Freedom), Dec. 7, 1965.

• *Nostra Aetate* (Declaration on the Relationship of the Church to Non-Christian Religions), Oct. 28, 1965.

• *Gravissimum Educationis* (Declaration on Christian Education), Oct. 28, 1965.

The key documents were the four constitutions, which set the ideological basis for all the others. To date, the documents with the most visible effects are those on the liturgy, the Church, Church in the world, ecumenism, the renewal of religious life, the life and ministry of priests, the lay apostolate.

The main business of the council was to explore and make explicit dimensions of doctrine and Christian life requiring emphasis for the full development of the Church and the better accomplishment of its mission in the contemporary world.

REVISION OF RULES FOR CANONIZATION CAUSES

Changes in procedure for the conduct of causes for the canonization of saints were announced Feb. 26, 1983, by Msgr. Fabijan Veraja, undersecretary of the Congregation for the Causes of Saints.

Net results of the changes, it was reported, would be major responsibility on the part of local bishops to initiate proceedings, modification of the role of the promoter of faith (the devil's advocate), permission for lay persons to promote causes, and shortening of the time period between the death of a candidate and the start of a cause for canonization.

The changes, with the effect of law, were contained in an apostolic constitution entitled *Divinus Perfectionis Magister* ("Divine Teacher of Perfection") and two related documents.

The new norms stress the need for "maximum scientific and historic rigor" in investigating causes, and set up a College of Prelates Relators to assure the use of such methods on diocesan levels.

POPES

Information includes the name of the pope, in many cases his name before becoming pope, his birthplace or country of origin, the date of accession to the papacy, and the date of the end of reign which, in all but a few cases, was the date of death. Double dates indicate times of election and coronation.
Source: "Annuario Pontificio."

St. Peter (Simon Bar-Jona): Bethsaida in Galilee; d. c. 64 or 67.

St. Linus: Tuscany; 67-76.

St. Anacletus (Cletus): Rome; 76-88.

St. Clement: Rome; 88-97.

St. Evaristus: Greece; 97-105.

St. Alexander I: Rome; 105-115.

St. Sixtus I: Rome; 115-125.

St. Telesphorus: Greece; 125-136.

St. Hyginus: Greece; 136-140.

St. Pius I: Aquileia; 140-155.

St. Anicetus: Syria; 155-166.

St. Soter: Campania; 166-175.

St. Eleutherius: Nicopolis in Epirus; 175-189.

Up to the time of St. Eleutherius, the years indicated for the beginning and end of pontificates are not absolutely certain. Also, up to the middle of the 11th century, there are some doubts about the exact days and months given in chronological tables.

St. Victor I: Africa; 189-199.

St. Zephyrinus: Rome; 199-217.

St. Callistus I: Rome; 217-222.

St. Urban I: Rome; 222-230.

St. Pontian: Rome; July 21, 230, to Sept. 28, 235.

St. Anterus: Greece; Nov. 21, 235, to Jan. 3, 236.

St. Fabian: Rome; Jan. 10, 236, to Jan. 20, 250.

St. Cornelius: Rome; Mar., 251, to June, 253.

St. Lucius I: Rome; June 25, 253, to Mar. 5, 254.

St. Stephen I: Rome; May 12, 254, to Aug. 2, 257.

St. Sixtus II: Greece; Aug. 30, 257, to Aug. 6, 258.

St. Dionysius: July 22, 259, to Dec. 26, 268.

St. Felix I: Rome; Jan. 5, 269, to Dec. 30, 274.

St. Eutychian: Luni; Jan. 4, 275, to Dec. 7, 283.

St. Caius: Dalmatia; Dec. 17, 283, to Apr. 22, 296.

St. Marcellinus: Rome; June 30, 296, to Oct. 25, 304.

St. Marcellus I: Rome; May 27, 308, or June 26, 308, to Jan. 16, 309.

St. Eusebius: Greece; Apr. 18, 309 or 310, to Aug. 17, 309 or 310.

St. Melchiades (Miltiades): Africa; July 2, 311, to Jan. 11, 314.

St. Sylvester I: Rome; Jan. 31, 314, to Dec. 31, 335. (Most of the popes before St. Sylvester I were martyrs.)

St. Marcus: Rome; Jan. 18, 336, to Oct. 7, 336.

St. Julius I: Rome; Feb. 6, 337, to Apr. 12, 352.

Liberius: Rome; May 17, 352, to Sept. 24, 366.

St. Damasus I: Spain; Oct. 1, 366, to Dec. 11, 384.

St. Siricius: Rome; Dec. 15, or 22 or 29, 384, to Nov. 26, 399.

St. Anastasius I: Rome; Nov. 27, 399, to Dec. 19, 401.

St. Innocent I: Albano; Dec. 22, 401, to Mar. 12, 417.

St. Zosimus: Greece; Mar. 18, 417, to Dec. 26, 418.

St. Boniface I: Rome; Dec. 28 or 29, 418, to Sept. 4, 422.

St. Celestine I: Campania; Sept. 10, 422, to July 27, 432.

St. Sixtus III: Rome; July 31, 432, to Aug. 19, 440.

St. Leo I (the Great): Tuscany; Sept. 29, 440, to Nov. 10, 461.

St. Hilary: Sardinia; Nov. 19, 461, to Feb. 29, 468.

St. Simplicius: Tivoli; Mar. 3, 468, to Mar. 10, 483.

St. Felix III (II): Rome; Mar. 13, 483, to Mar. 1, 492.

He should be called Felix II, and his successors of the same name should be numbered accordingly. The discrepancy in the numerical designation of popes named Felix was caused by the erroneous insertion in some lists of the name of St. Felix of Rome, a martyr.

St. Gelasius I: Africa; Mar. 1, 492, to Nov. 21, 496.

Anastasius II: Rome; Nov. 24, 496, to Nov. 19, 498.

St. Symmachus: Sardinia; Nov. 22, 498, to July 19, 514.

St. Hormisdas: Frosinone; July 20, 514, to Aug. 6, 523.

St. John I, Martyr: Tuscany; Aug. 13, 523, to May 18, 526.

St. Felix IV (III): Samnium; July 12, 526, to Sept. 22, 530.

Boniface II: Rome; Sept. 22, 530, to Oct. 17, 532.

John II: Rome; Jan. 2, 533, to May 8, 535.

John II was the first pope to change his name. His given name was Mercury.

St. Agapitus I: Rome; May 13, 535, to Apr. 22, 536.

St. Silverius, Martyr: Campania; June 1 or 8, 536, to Nov. 11, 537 (d. Dec. 2, 537).

St. Silverius was violently deposed in March, 537, and abdicated Nov. 11, 537. His successor, Vigilius, was not recognized as pope by all the Roman clergy until his abdication.

Vigilius: Rome; Mar. 29, 537, to June 7, 555.

Pelagius I: Rome; Apr. 16, 556, to Mar. 4, 561.

John III: Rome; July 17, 561, to July 13, 574.

Benedict I: Rome; June 2, 575, to July 30, 579.

Pelagius II: Rome; Nov. 26, 579, to Feb. 7, 590.

St. Gregory I (the Great): Rome; Sept. 3, 590, to Mar. 12, 604.

Sabinian: Blera in Tuscany; Sept. 13, 604, to Feb. 22, 606.

Boniface III: Rome; Feb. 19, 607, to Nov. 12, 607.

St. Boniface IV: Abruzzi; Aug. 25, 608, to May 8, 615.

St. Deusdedit (Adeodatus I): Rome; Oct. 19, 615, to Nov. 8, 618.

Boniface V: Naples; Dec. 23, 619, to Oct. 25, 625.

Honorius I: Campania; Oct. 27, 625, to Oct. 12, 638.

Severinus: Rome; May 28, 640, to Aug. 2, 640.

John IV: Dalmatia; Dec. 24, 640, to Oct. 12, 642.

Theodore I: Greece; Nov. 24, 642, to May 14, 649.

St. Martin I, Martyr: Todi; July, 649, to Sept. 16, 655 (in exile from June 17, 653).

St. Eugene I: Rome; Aug. 10, 654, to June 2, 657.

St. Eugene I was elected during the exile of St. Martin I, who is believed to have endorsed him as pope.

St. Vitalian: Segni; July 30, 657, to Jan. 27, 672.

Adeodatus II: Rome; Apr. 11, 672, to June 17, 676.

Donus: Rome; Nov. 2, 676, to Apr. 11, 678.

St. Agatho: Sicily; June 27, 678, to Jan. 10, 681.

St. Leo II: Sicily; Aug. 17, 682, to July 3, 683.

St. Benedict II: Rome; June 26, 684, to May 8, 685.

John V: Syria; July 23, 685, to Aug. 2, 686.

Conon: birthplace unknown; Oct. 21, 686, to Sept. 21, 687.

St. Sergius I: Syria; Dec. 15, 687, to Sept. 8, 701.

John VI: Greece; Oct. 30, 701, to Jan. 11, 705.

John VII: Greece; Mar. 1, 705, to Oct. 18, 707.

Sisinnius: Syria; Jan. 15, 708, to Feb. 4, 708.

Constantine: Syria; Mar. 25, 708, to Apr. 9, 715.

St. Gregory II: Rome; May 19, 715, to Feb. 11, 731.

St. Gregory III: Syria; Mar. 18, 731, to Nov., 741.

St. Zachary: Greece; Dec. 10, 741, to Mar. 22, 752.

Stephen II (III): Rome; Mar. 26, 752, to Apr. 26, 757.

After the death of St. Zachary, a Roman priest named Stephen was elected but died (four days later) before his consecration as bishop of Rome, which would have marked the beginning of his pontificate. Another Stephen was elected to succeed Zachary as Stephen II. (The first pope with this name was St. Stephen I, 254-57.) The ordinal III appears in parentheses after the name of Stephen II because the name of the earlier elected but deceased priest was included in some lists. Other Stephens have double numbers.

St. Paul I: Rome; Apr. (May 29), 757, to June 28, 767.

Stephen III (IV): Sicily; Aug. 1 (7), 768, to Jan. 24, 772.

Adrian I: Rome; Feb. 1 (9), 772, to Dec. 25, 795.

St. Leo III: Rome; Dec. 26 (27), 795, to June 12, 816.

Stephen IV (V): Rome; June 22, 816, to Jan. 24, 817.

St. Paschal I: Rome; Jan. 25, 817, to Feb. 11, 824.

Eugene II: Rome; Feb. (May), 824, to Aug., 827.

Valentine: Rome; Aug. 827, to Sept., 827.

Gregory IV: Rome; 827, to Jan., 844.

Sergius II: Rome; Jan., 844 to Jan. 27, 847.

St. Leo IV: Rome; Jan. (Apr. 10), 847, to July 17, 855.

Benedict III: Rome; July (Sept. 29), 855, to Apr. 17, 858.

St. Nicholas I (the Great): Rome; Apr. 24, 858, to Nov. 13, 867.

Adrian II: Rome; Dec. 14, 867, to Dec. 14, 872.

John VIII: Rome; Dec. 14, 872, to Dec. 16, 882.

Marinus I: Gallese; Dec. 16, 882, to May 15, 884.

St. Adrian III: Rome; May 17, 884, to Sept., 885. Cult confirmed June 2, 1891.

Stephen V (VI): Rome; Sept., 885, to Sept. 14, 891.

Formosus: Portus; Oct. 6, 891, to Apr. 4, 896.

Boniface VI: Rome; Apr., 896, to Apr., 896.

Stephen VI (VII): Rome; May, 896, to Aug., 897.

Romanus: Gallese; Aug., 897, to Nov., 897.

Theodore II: Rome; Dec., 897, to Dec., 897.

John IX: Tivoli; Jan., 898, to Jan., 900.

Benedict IV: Rome; Jan. (Feb.), 900, to July, 903.

Leo V: Ardea; July, 903, to Sept., 903.

Sergius III: Rome; Jan. 29, 904, to Apr. 14, 911.

Anastasius III: Rome; Apr., 911, to June, 913.

Landus: Sabina; July, 913, to Feb., 914.

John X: Tossignano (Imola); Mar., 914, to May, 928.

Leo VI: Rome; May, 928, to Dec., 928.

Stephen VII (VIII): Rome; Dec., 928, to Feb., 931.

John XI: Rome; Feb. (Mar.), 931, to Dec., 935.

Leo VII: Rome; Jan. 3, 936, to July 13, 939.

Stephen VIII (IX): Rome; July 14, 939, to Oct., 942.

Marinus II: Rome; Oct. 30, 942, to May, 946.

Agapitus II: Rome; May 10, 946, to Dec., 955.

John XII (Octavius): Tusculum; Dec. 16, 955, to May 14, 964 (date of his death).

Leo VIII: Rome; Dec. 4 (6), 963, to Mar. 1, 965.

Benedict V: Rome; May 22, 964, to July 4, 966.

Confusion exists concerning the legitimacy of claims to the pontificate by Leo VIII and Benedict V. John XII was deposed Dec. 4, 963, by a Roman council. If this deposition was invalid, Leo was an antipope. If the deposition of John was valid, Leo was the legitimate pope and Benedict was an antipope.

John XIII: Rome; Oct. 1, 965, to Sept. 6, 972.

Benedict VI: Rome; Jan. 19, 973, to June, 974.

Benedict VII: Rome; Oct. 974, to July 10, 983.

John XIV (Peter Campenora): Pavia; Dec., 983, to Aug. 20, 984.

John XV: Rome; Aug., 985, to Mar., 996.

Gregory V (Bruno of Carinthia): Saxony; May 3, 996, to Feb. 18, 999.

Sylvester II (Gerbert): Auvergne; Apr. 2, 999, to May 12, 1003.

John XVII (Siccone): Rome; June, 1003, to Dec., 1003.

John XVIII (Phasianus): Rome; Jan., 1004, to July, 1009.

Sergius IV (Peter): Rome; July 31, 1009, to May 12, 1012.

The custom of changing one's name on election to the papacy is generally considered to date from the time of Sergius IV. Before his time, several popes had changed their names. After his time, this became a regular practice, with few exceptions; e.g., Adrian VI and Marcellus II.

Benedict VIII (Theophylactus): Tusculum; May 18, 1012, to Apr. 9, 1024.

John XIX (Romanus): Tusculum; Apr. (May), 1024, to 1032.

Benedict IX (Theophylactus): Tusculum; 1032, to 1044.

Sylvester III (John): Rome; Jan. 20, 1045, to Feb. 10, 1045.

Sylvester III was an antipope if the forcible removal of Benedict IX in 1044 was not legitimate.

Benedict IX (second time): Apr. 10, 1045, to May 1, 1045.

Gregory VI (John Gratian): Rome; May 5, 1045, to Dec. 20, 1046.

Clement II (Suitger, Lord of Morsleben and Hornburg): Saxony; Dec. 24 (25), 1046, to Oct. 9, 1047.

If the resignation of Benedict IX in 1045 and his removal at the December, 1046, synod were not legitimate, Gregory VI and Clement II were antipopes.

Benedict IX (third time): Nov. 8, 1047, to July 17, 1048 (d. c. 1055).

Damasus II (Poppo): Bavaria; July 17, 1048, to Aug. 9, 1048.

St. Leo IX (Bruno): Alsace; Feb. 12, 1049, to Apr. 19, 1054.

Victor II (Gebhard): Swabia; Apr. 16, 1055, to July 28, 1057.

Stephen IX (X) (Frederick): Lorraine; Aug. 3, 1057, to Mar. 29, 1058.

Nicholas II (Gerard): Burgundy; Jan. 24, 1059, to July 27, 1061.

Alexander II (Anselmo da Baggio): Milan; Oct. 1, 1061, to Apr. 21, 1073.

St. Gregory VII (Hildebrand): Tuscany; Apr. 22 (June 30), 1073, to May 25, 1085.

Bl. Victor III (Dauferius; Desiderius): Benevento; May 24, 1086, to Sept. 16, 1087. Cult confirmed July 23, 1887.

Bl. Urban II (Otto di Lagery): France; Mar. 12, 1088, to July 29, 1099. Cult confirmed July 14, 1881.

Paschal II (Raniero): Ravenna; Aug. 13 (14), 1099, to Jan. 21, 1118.

Gelasius II (Giovanni Caetani): Gaeta; Jan. 24 (Mar. 10), 1118, to Jan. 28, 1119.

Callistus II (Guido of Burgundy): Burgundy; Feb. 2 (9), 1119, to Dec. 13, 1124.

Honorius II (Lamberto): Fiagnano (Imola); Dec. 15 (21), 1124, to Feb. 13, 1130.

Innocent II (Gregorio Papareschi): Rome; Feb. 14 (23), 1130, to Sept. 24, 1143.

Celestine II (Guido): Citta di Castello; Sept. 26 (Oct. 3), 1143, to Mar. 8, 1144.

Lucius II (Gerardo Caccianemici): Bologna: Mar. 12, 1144, to Feb. 15, 1145.

Bl. Eugene III (Bernardo Paganelli di Montemagno): Pisa; Feb. 15 (18), 1145, to July 8, 1153. Cult confirmed Oct. 3, 1872.

Anastasius IV (Corrado): Rome; July 12, 1153, to Dec, 3, 1154.

Adrian IV (Nicholas Breakspear): England; Dec. 4 (5), 1154, to Sept. 1, 1159.

Alexander III (Rolando Bandinelli): Siena; Sept. 7 (20), 1159, to Aug. 30, 1181.

Lucius III (Ubaldo Allucingoli): Lucca; Sept. 1 (6), 1181, to Sept. 25, 1185.

Urban III (Uberto Crivelli): Milan; Nov. 25 (Dec. 1), 1185, to Oct. 20, 1187.

Gregory VIII (Alberto de Morra): Benevento; Oct. 21 (25), 1187, to Dec. 17, 1187.

Clement III (Paolo Scolari): Rome; Dec. 19 (20), 1187, to Mar., 1191.

Celestine III (Giacinto Bobone): Rome; Mar. 30 (Apr. 14), 1191, to Jan. 8, 1198.

Innocent III (Lotario dei Conti di Segni): Anagni; Jan. 8 (Feb. 22), 1198, to July 16, 1216.

Honorius III (Cencio Savelli): Rome; July 18 (24), 1216, to Mar. 18, 1227.

Gregory IX (Ugolino, Count of Segni): Anagni; Mar. 19 (21), 1227, to Aug. 22, 1241.

Celestine IV (Goffredo Castiglioni): Milan; Oct. 25 (28), 1241, to Nov. 10, 1241.

Innocent IV (Sinibaldo Fieschi): Genoa; June 25 (28), 1243, to Dec. 7, 1254.

Alexander IV (Rinaldo, Count of Segni): Anagni; Dec. 12 (20), 1254, to May 25, 1261.

Urban IV (Jacques Pantaléon): Troyes; Aug. 29 (Sept. 4), 1261, to Oct. 2, 1264.

Clement IV (Guy Foulques or Guido le Gros): France; Feb. 5 (15), 1265, to Nov. 29, 1268.

Bl. Gregory X (Teobaldo Visconti): Piacenza; Sept. 1, 1271 (Mar. 27, 1272), to Jan. 10, 1276. Cult confirmed Sept. 12, 1713.

Bl. Innocent V (Peter of Tarentaise): Savoy; Jan. 21 (Feb. 22), 1276, to June 22, 1276. Cult confirmed Mar. 13, 1898.

Adrian V (Ottobono Fieschi): Genoa: July 11, 1276, to Aug. 18, 1276.

John XXI (Petrus Juliani or Petrus Hispanus): Portugal; Sept. 8 (20), 1276, to May 20, 1277.

Elimination was made of the name of John XX in an effort to rectify the numerical designation of popes named John. The error dates back to the time of John XV.

Nicholas III (Giovanni Gaetano Orsini): Rome; Nov. 25 (Dec. 26), 1277, to Aug. 22, 1280.

Martin IV (Simon de Brie): France; Feb. 22 (Mar. 23), 1281, to Mar. 28, 1285.

The names of Marinus 1 (882-84) and Marinus II (942-46) were construed as Martin. In view of these two pontificates and the earlier reign of St. Martin I (649-55), this pope was called Martin IV.

Honorius IV (Giacomo Savelli): Rome; Apr. 2 (May 20), 1285, to Apr. 3, 1287.

Nicholas IV (Girolamo Masci): Ascoli; Feb. 22, 1288, to Apr. 4, 1292.

St. Celestine V (Pietro del Murrone): Isernia; July 5 (Aug. 29), 1294, to Dec. 13, 1294; d. 1296. Canonized May 5, 1313.

Boniface VIII (Benedetto Caetani): Anagni; Dec. 24, 1294 (Jan. 23, 1295), to Oct. 11, 1303.

Bl. Benedict XI (Niccolo Boccasini): Treviso; Oct. 22 (27), 1303, to July 7, 1304. Cult confirmed Apr. 24, 1736.

Clement V (Bertrand de Got): France; June 5 (Nov. 14), 1305, to Apr. 20, 1314. (First of Avignon popes.)

John XXII (Jacques d'Euse): Cahors; Aug. 7 (Sept. 5), 1316, to Dec. 4, 1334.

Benedict XII (Jacques Fournier): France; Dec. 20, 1334 (Jan. 8, 1335), to Apr. 25, 1342.

Clement VI (Pierre Roger): France; May 7 (19), 1342, to Dec. 6, 1352.

Innocent VI (Etienne Aubert): France; Dec. 18 (30), 1352, to Sept. 12, 1362.

Bl. Urban V (Guillaume de Grimoard): France; Sept. 28 (Nov. 6), 1362, to Dec. 19, 1370. Cult confirmed Mar. 10, 1870.

Gregory XI (Pierre Roger de Beaufort): France; Dec. 30, 1370 (Jan. 5, 1371), to Mar. 26, 1378. (Last of Avignon popes.)

Urban VI (Bartolomeo Prignano): Naples; Apr. 8 (18), 1378, to Oct. 15, 1389.

Boniface IX (Pietro Tomacelli): Naples; Nov. 2 (9), 1389, to Oct. 1, 1404.

Innocent VII (Cosma Migliorati): Sulmona; Oct. 17 (Nov. 11), 1404, to Nov. 6, 1406.

Gregory XII (Angelo Correr): Venice; Nov. 30 (Dec. 19), 1406, to July 4, 1415, when he voluntarily resigned from the papacy to permit the election of his successor. He died Oct. 18, 1417. (See The Western Schism.)

Martin V (Oddone Colonna): Rome; Nov. 11 (21), 1417, to Feb. 20, 1431.

Eugene IV (Gabriele Condulmer): Venice; Mar. 3 (11), 1431, to Feb. 23, 1447.

Nicholas V (Tommaso Parentucelli): Sarzana; Mar. 6 (19), 1447, to Mar. 24, 1455.

Callistus III (Alfonso Borgia): Jativa (Valencia); Apr. 8 (20), 1455, to Aug. 6, 1458.

Pius II (Enea Silvio Piccolomini): Siena; Aug. 19 (Sept. 3), 1458, to Aug. 15, 1464.

Paul II (Pietro Barbo): Venice; Aug. 30 (Sept. 16), 1464, to July 26, 1471.

Sixtus IV (Francesco della Rovere): Savona; Aug. 9 (25), 1471, to Aug. 12, 1484.

Innocent VIII (Giovanni Battista Cibo): Genoa; Aug. 29 (Sept. 12), 1484, to July 25, 1492.

Alexander VI (Rodrigo Borgia): Jativa (Valencia); Aug. 11 (26), 1492, to Aug. 18, 1503.

Pius III (Francesco Todeschini-Piccolomini): Siena; Sept. 22 (Oct. 1, 8), 1503, to Oct. 18, 1503.

Julius II (Giuliano della Rovere): Savona; Oct. 31 (Nov. 26), 1503, to Feb. 21, 1513.

Leo X (Giovanni de' Medici): Florence; Mar. 9 (19), 1513, to Dec. 1, 1521.

Adrian VI (Adrian Florensz): Utrecht; Jan. 9 (Aug. 31), 1522, to Sept. 14, 1523.

Clement VII (Giulio de' Medici): Florence; Nov. 19 (26), 1523, to Sept. 25, 1534.

Paul III (Alessandro Farnese): Rome; Oct. 13 (Nov. 3), 1534, to Nov. 10, 1549.

Julius III (Giovanni Maria Ciocchi del Monte): Rome; Feb. 7 (22), 1550, to Mar. 23, 1555.

Marcellus II (Marcello Cervini): Montepulciano; Apr. 9 (10), 1555, to May 1, 1555.

Paul IV (Gian Pietro Carafa): Naples; May 23 (26), 1555, to Aug. 18, 1559.

Pius IV (Giovan Angelo de' Medici): Milan; Dec. 25, 1559 (Jan. 6, 1560), to Dec. 9, 1565.

St. Pius V (Antonio-Michele Ghislieri): Bosco (Alexandria); Jan. 7 (17), 1566, to May 1, 1572. Canonized May 22, 1712.

Gregory XIII (Ugo Buoncompagni): Bologna; May 13 (25), 1572, to Apr. 10, 1585.

Sixtus V (Felice Peretti): Grottammare (Ripatransone); Apr. 24 (May 1), 1585, to Aug. 27, 1590.

Urban VII (Giovanni Battista Castagna): Rome; Sept. 15, 1590, to Sept. 27, 1590.

Gregory XIV (Niccolo Sfondrati): Cremona; Dec. 5 (8), 1590, to Oct. 16, 1591.

Innocent IX (Giovanni Antonio Facchinetti): Bologna; Oct. 29 (Nov. 3), 1591, to Dec. 30, 1591.

Clement VIII (Ippolito Aldobrandini): Florence; Jan. 30 (Feb. 9), 1592, to Mar. 3, 1605.

Leo XI (Alessandro de' Medici): Florence; Apr. 1 (10), 1605, to Apr. 27, 1605.

Paul V (Camillo Borghese): Rome; May 16 (29), 1605, to Jan. 28, 1621.

Gregory XV (Alessandro Ludovisi): Bologna; Feb. 9 (14), 1621, to July 8, 1623.

Urban VIII (Maffeo Barberini): Florence; Aug. 6 (Sept. 29), 1623, to July 29, 1644.

Innocent X (Giovanni Battista Pamfili): Rome; Sept. 15 (Oct. 4), 1644, to Jan. 7, 1655.

Alexander VII (Fabio Chigi): Siena; Apr. 7 (18), 1655, to May 22, 1667.

Clement IX (Giulio Rospigliosi): Pistoia; June 20 (26), 1667, to Dec. 9, 1669.

Clement X (Emilio Altieri): Rome; Apr. 29 (May 11), 1670, to July 22, 1676.

Bl. Innocent XI (Benedetto Odescalchi): Como; Sept. 21 (Oct. 4), 1676, to Aug. 12, 1689.

Alexander VIII (Pietro Ottoboni): Venice; Oct. 6 (16), 1689, to Feb. 1, 1691.

Innocent XII (Antonio Pignatelli): Spinazzola; July 12 (15), 1691, to Sept. 27, 1700.

Clement XI (Giovanni Francesco Albani): Urbino; Nov. 23, 30 (Dec. 8), 1700, to Mar. 19, 1721.

Innocent XIII (Michelangelo dei Conti): Rome; May 8 (18), 1721, to Mar. 7, 1724.

Benedict XIII (Pietro Francesco — Vincenzo Maria — Orsini): Gravina (Bari); May 29 (June 4), 1724, to Feb. 21, 1730.

Clement XII (Lorenzo Corsini): Florence; July 12 (16), 1730, to Feb. 6, 1740.

Benedict XIV (Prospero Lambertini): Bologna; Aug. 17 (22), 1740, to May 3, 1758.

Clement XIII (Carlo Rezzonico): Venice; July 6 (16), 1758, to Feb. 2, 1769.

Clement XIV (Giovanni Vincenzo Antonio — Lorenzo — Ganganelli): Rimini; May 19, 28 (June 4), 1769, to Sept. 22, 1774.

Pius VI (Giovanni Angelo Braschi): Cesena; Feb. 15 (22), 1775, to Aug. 29, 1799.

Pius VII (Barnaba — Gregorio — Chiaramonti): Cesena; Mar. 14 (21), 1800, to Aug. 20, 1823.

Leo XII (Annibale della Genga): Genga (Fabriano); Sept. 28 (Oct. 5), 1823, to Feb. 10, 1829.

Pius VIII (Francesco Saverio Castiglioni): Cingoli; Mar. 31 (Apr. 5), 1829, to Nov. 30, 1830.

Gregory XVI (Bartolomeo Alberto — Mauro — Cappellari): Belluno; Feb. 2 (6), 1831, to June 1, 1846.

Pius IX (Giovanni M. Mastai Ferretti): Senigallia; June 16 (21), 1846, to Feb. 7, 1878.

Leo XIII (Gioacchino Pecci): Carpineto (Anagni); Feb. 20 (Mar. 3), 1878, to July 20, 1903.

St. Pius X (Giuseppe Sarto): Riese (Treviso); Aug. 4 (9), 1903, to Aug. 20, 1914. Canonized May 29, 1954.

Benedict XV (Giacomo della Chiesa): Genoa; Sept. 3 (6), 1914, to Jan. 22, 1922.

Pius XI (Achille Ratti): Desio (Milan); Feb. 6 (12), 1922, to Feb. 10, 1939.

Pius XII (Eugenio Pacelli): Rome; Mar. 2 (12), 1939, to Oct. 9, 1958.

John XXIII (Angelo Giuseppe Roncalli): Sotto il Monte (Bergamo); Oct. 28 (Nov. 4). 1958, to June 3, 1963.

Paul VI (Giovanni Battista Montini): Concessio (Brescia); June 21 (June 30), 1963, to Aug. 6, 1978. (See separate entry.)

John Paul I (Albino Luciani): Forno di Canale (Belluno); Aug. 26 (Sept. 3), 1978, to Sept. 28, 1978. (See separate entry.)

John Paul II (Karol Wojtyla): Wadowice, Poland; Oct. 16 (22), 1978.

ANTIPOPES

This list of men who claimed or exercised the papal office in an uncanonical manner includes names, birthplaces and dates of alleged reigns.

Source: "Annuario Pontificio."

St. Hippolytus: Rome; 217-235; was reconciled before his death.

Novatian: Rome; 251.

Felix II: Rome; 355 to Nov. 22, 365.

Ursinus: 366-367.

Eulalius: Dec. 27 or 29, 418, to 419.

Lawrence: 498; 501-505.

Dioscorus: Alexandria; Sept. 22, 530, to Oct. 14, 530.

Theodore: ended alleged reign, 687.

Paschal: ended alleged reign, 687.

Constantine: Nepi; June 28 (July 5), 767, to 769.

Philip: July 31, 768; retired to his monastery on the same day.

John: ended alleged reign, Jan., 844.

Anastasius: Aug., 855, to Sept., 855; d. 880.

Christopher: Rome; July or Sept., 903, to Jan., 904.

Boniface VII: Rome; June, 974, to July, 974; Aug., 984, to July, 985.

John XVI: Rossano; Apr., 997, to Feb., 998.

Gregory: ended alleged reign, 1012.

Benedict X: Rome; Apr. 5, 1058, to Jan. 24, 1059.

Honorius II: Verona; Oct. 28, 1061, to 1072.

Clement III: Parma; June 25, 1080 (Mar. 24, 1084), to Sept. 8, 1100.

Theodoric: ended alleged reign, 1100; d. 1102.

Albert: ended alleged reign, 1102.

Sylvester IV: Rome; Nov. 18, 1105, to 1111.

Gregory VIII: France; Mar. 8, 1118, to 1121.

Celestine II: Rome; ended alleged reign, Dec., 1124.

Anacletus II: Rome; Feb. 14 (23), 1130, to Jan. 25, 1138.

Victor IV: Mar., 1138, to May 29, 1138; submitted to Pope Innocent II.

Victor IV: Montecelio; Sept. 7 (Oct. 4), 1159, to Apr. 20, 1164; he did not recognize his predecessor (Victor IV, above).

Paschal III: Apr. 22 (26), 1164, to Sept. 20, 1168.

Callistus III: Arezzo; Sept., 1168, to Aug. 29, 1178; submitted to Pope Alexander III.

Innocent III: Sezze; Sept. 29, 1179, to 1180.

Nicholas V: Corvaro (Rieti); May 12 (22), 1328, to Aug. 25, 1330; d. Oct. 16, 1333.

Four antipopes of the Western Schism:

Clement VII: Sept. 20 (Oct. 31), 1378, to Sept. 16, 1394.

Benedict XIII: Aragon; Sept. 28 (Oct. 11), 1394, to May 23, 1423.

Alexander V: Crete; June 26 (July 7), 1409, to May 3, 1410.

John XXIII: Naples; May 17 (25), 1410, to May 29, 1415.

Felix V: Savoy; Nov. 5, 1439 (July 24, 1440), to April 7, 1449; d. 1451.

AVIGNON PAPACY

Avignon was the residence of a series of French popes from Clement V to Gregory XI (1309-77). Prominent in the period were power struggles over the mixed interests of Church and state with the rulers of France (Philip IV, John II), Bavaria (Lewis IV), England (Edward III); factionalism of French and Italian churchmen; political as well as ecclesiastical turmoil in Italy, a factor of significance in prolonging the stay of popes in Avignon. Despite some positive achievements, the Avignon papacy was a prologue to the Western Schism which began in 1378.

WESTERN SCHISM

The Western Schism was a confused state of affairs which divided Christendom into two and then three papal obediences from 1378 to 1417.

It occurred some 50 years after Marsilius theorized that a general (not ecumenical) council of bishops and other persons was superior to a pope and nearly 30 years before the Council of Florence stated definitively that no kind of council had such authority.

It was a period of disaster preceding the even more disastrous period of the Reformation.

Urban VI, following transfer to Rome of the 70-year papal residence at Avignon, was elected pope Apr. 8, 1378, and reigned until his death in 1389. He was succeeded by Boniface IX (1389-1404), Innocent VII (1404-1406) and Gregory XII (1406-1415). These four are considered the legitimate popes of the period.

Some of the cardinals who chose Urban pope, dissatisfied with his conduct of the office, declared that his election was invalid. They proceeded to elect Clement VII, who claimed the papacy from 1378 to 1394. He was succeeded by Benedict XIII.

Prelates seeking to end the state of divided papal loyalties convoked the Council of Pisa which, without authority, found Gregory XII and Benedict XIII, in absentia, guilty on 30-odd charges of schism and heresy, deposed them, and elected a third claimant to the papacy, Alexander V (1409-1410). He was succeeded by John XXIII (1410-1415).

The schism was ended by the Council of Constance (1414-1418). This council, although originally called into session in an irregular manner, acquired authority after being convoked by Gregory XII in 1415. In its early irregular phase, it deposed John XXIII whose election to the papacy was uncanonical anyway. After being formally convoked, it accepted the abdication of Gregory in 1415 and dismissed the claims of Benedict XIII two years later, thus clearing the way for the election of Martin V on Nov. 11, 1417. The Council of Constance also rejected the theories of John Wycliff and condemned John Hus as a heretic.

CATHOLIC RIGHTS LEAGUE

The Catholic League for Religious and Civil Rights, founded in 1973, serves the Catholic community as an anti-defamation and civil-rights agency.

The league responds to defamation of Catholics and Catholicism in the media, and carries on educational activities in support of the religious and civil rights of Catholics in secular society.

It has a professional legal staff to defend in court the religious-freedom rights of Catholics and others. A research staff serves as a clearinghouse for information on public issues of concern to the Catholic community. Among the league's highest priorities are issues relating to the right to life and the right to freedom of choice in education.

The league, which has no official connection with the Church, is supported by contributions from its 30,000 members.

Father Virgil C. Blum, S.J., is president and founder of the league, which is headquartered at 1100 W. Wells St., Milwaukee, Wis. 53233. The league also has 15 local chapters across the country.

Speakers representing the league address groups which share its concern, interest and preoccupation with the defense and protection of civil and religious rights.

TWENTIETH CENTURY POPES

LEO XIII

Leo XIII (Gioacchino Vincenzo Pecci) was born May 2, 1810, in Carpineto, Italy. Although all but three years of his life and pontificate were of the 19th century, his influence extended well into the 20th century.

He was educated at the Jesuit college in Viterbo, the Roman College, the Academy of Noble Ecclesiastics, and the University of the Sapienza. He was ordained to the priesthood in 1837.

He served as an apostolic delegate to two States of the Church, Benevento from 1838 to 1841 and Perugia in 1841 and 1842. Ordained titular archbishop of Damietta, he was papal nuncio to Belgium from January, 1843, until May, 1846; in the post, he had controversial relations with the government over education issues and acquired his first significant experience of industrialized society.

He was archbishop of Perugia from 1846 to 1878. He became a cardinal in 1853 and chamberlain of the Roman Curia in 1877. He was elected to the papacy Feb. 20, 1878. He died July 20, 1903.

Canonizations: He canonized 18 saints and beatified a group of English martyrs.

Church Administration: He established 300 new dioceses and vicariates; restored the hierarchy in Scotland, set up an English, as contrasted with the Portuguese, hierarchy in India; approved the action of the Congregation for the Propagation of the Faith in reorganizing missions in China.

Encyclicals: He issued 86 encyclicals, on subjects ranging from devotional to social. In the former category were *Annum Sacrum,* on the Sacred Heart, in 1899, and 11 letters on Mary and the Rosary.

Interfaith Relations: He was unsuccessful in unity overtures made to Orthodox and Slavic Churches. He declared Anglican orders invalid in the apostolic bull *Apostolicae Curae* Sept. 13, 1896.

International Relations: Leo was frustrated in seeking solutions to the Roman Question arising from the seizure of church lands by the Kingdom of Italy in 1870. He also faced anticlerical situations in Belgium and France and in the Kulturkampf policies of Bismarck in Germany.

Social Questions: Much of Leo's influence stemmed from social doctrine stated in numerous encyclicals, concerning liberalism, liberty, the divine origin of authority; socialism, in *Quod Apostolici Muneris,* 1878; the Christian concept of the family, in *Arcanum,* 1880; socialism and economic liberalism, relations between capital and labor, in *Rerum Novarum,* 1891. Two of his social encyclicals were against the African slave trade.

Studies: In the encyclical *Aeterni Patris* of Aug. 4, 1879, he ordered a renewal of philosophical and theological studies in seminaries along scholastic, and especially Thomistic, lines, to counteract influential trends of liberalism and Modernism. He issued guidelines for biblical exegesis in *Providentissimus Deus* Nov. 18, 1893, and established the Pontifical Biblical Commission in 1902.

In other actions affecting scholarship and study, he opened the Vatican Archives to scholars in 1883 and established the Vatican Observatory.

United States: He authorized establishment of the apostolic delegation in Washington, D.C. Jan. 24, 1893. He refused to issue a condemnation of the Knights of Labor. With a document entitled *Testem Benevolentiae,* he eased resolution of questions concerning what was called an American heresy in 1899.

ST. PIUS X

St. Pius X (Giuseppe Melchiorre Sarto) was born in 1835 in Riese, Italy.

Educated at the college of Castelfranco and the seminary at Padua, he was ordained to the priesthood Sept. 18, 1858. He served as a curate in Trombolo for nine years before beginning an eight-year pastorate at Salzano. He was chancellor of the Treviso diocese from November, 1875, and bishop of Mantua from 1884 until 1893. He was cardinal-patriarch of Venice from that year until his election to the papacy by the conclave held from July 31 to Aug. 4, 1903.

Aims: Pius' principal objectives as pope were "to restore all things in Christ, in order that Christ may be all and in all," and "to teach (and defend) Christian truth and law."

Canonizations, Encyclicals: He canonized four saints and issued 16 encyclicals. One of the encyclicals was issued in commemoration of the 50th anniversary of the proclamation of the dogma of the Immaculate Conception of Mary.

Catechetics: He introduced a whole new era of religious instruction and formation with the encyclical *Acerbo Nimis* of Apr. 15, 1905, in which he called for vigor in establishing and conducting parochial programs of the Confraternity of Christian Doctrine.

Catholic Action: He outlined the role of official Catholic Action in two encyclicals in 1905 and 1906. Favoring organized action by Catholics themselves, he had serious reservations about interconfessional collaboration.

He stoutly maintained claims to papal rights in the anticlerical climate of Italy. He authorized bishops to relax prohibitions against participation by Catholics in some Italian elections.

Church Administration: With the motu proprio *Arduum Sane* of Mar. 19, 1904, he inaugurated the work which resulted in the Code of Canon Law; the code was completed in 1917 and went into effect in the following year. He reorganized and strengthened the Roman Curia with the apostolic constitution *Sapienti Consilio* of June 29, 1908. While promoting the expansion of missionary work, he removed from the jurisdiction of the Congregation for the Propagation of the Faith the Church in the United States, Canada, Newfoundland, England, Ireland, Holland and Luxembourg.

International Relations: He ended traditional

prerogatives of Catholic governments with respect to papal elections, in 1904. He opposed anti-Church and anticlerical actions in several countries: Bolivia in 1905, because of anti-religious legislation; France in 1906, for its 1901 action in annulling its concordat with the Holy See, and for the 1905 Law of Separation by which it decreed separation of Church and state, ordered the confiscation of church property, and blocked religious education and the activities of religious orders; Portugal in 1911, for the separation of Church and state and repressive measures which resulted in persecution later.

In 1912 he called on the bishops of Brazil to work for the improvement of conditions among Indians.

Liturgy: "The Pope of the Eucharist," he strongly recommended the frequent reception of Holy Communion in a decree dated Dec. 20, 1905; in another decree, *Quam Singulari,* of Aug. 8, 1910, he called for the early reception of the sacrament by children. He initiated measures for liturgical reform with new norms for sacred music and the start of work on revision of the *Breviary* for recitation of the Divine Office.

Modernism: Pius was a vigorous opponent of "the synthesis of all heresies," which threatened the integrity of doctrine through its influence in philosophy, theology and biblical exegesis. In opposition, he condemned 65 of its propositions as erroneous in the decree *Lamentabili* July 3, 1907; issued the encyclical *Pascendi* in the same vein Sept. 8, 1907; backed both of these with censures; and published the Oath against Modernism in September, 1910, to be taken by all the clergy. Ecclesiastical studies suffered to some extent from these actions, necessary as they were at the time.

Pius followed the lead of Leo XIII in promoting the study of scholastic philosophy. He established the Pontifical Biblical Institute May 7, 1909.

His death, Aug. 20, 1914, was hastened by the outbreak of World War I. He was beatified in 1951 and canonized May 29, 1954. His feast is observed Aug. 21.

BENEDICT XV

Benedict XV (Giacomo della Chiesa) was born Nov. 21, 1854, in Pegli, Italy.

He was educated at the Royal University of Genoa and Gregorian University in Rome. He was ordained to the priesthood Dec. 21, 1878.

He served in the papal diplomatic corps from 1882 to 1907; as secretary to the nuncio to Spain from 1882 to 1887, as secretary to the papal secretary of state from 1887, and as undersecretary from 1901.

He was ordained archbishop of Bologna Dec. 22, 1907, and spent four years completing a pastoral visitation there. He was made a cardinal just three months before being elected to the papacy Sept. 3, 1914. He died Jan. 22, 1922. Two key efforts of his pontificate were for peace and the relief of human suffering caused by World War I.

Canonizations: Benedict canonized three saints; one of them was Joan of Arc.

Canon Law: He published the Code of Canon Law, developed by the commission set up by St.

Pius X, June 28, 1917; it went into effect the following year.

Curia: He made great changes in the personnel of the Curia. He established the Congregation for the Oriental Churches May 1, 1917, and founded the Pontifical Oriental Institute in Rome later in the year.

Encyclicals: He issued 12 encyclicals. Peace was the theme of three of them. In another, published two years after the cessation of hostilities, he wrote about child victims of the war. He followed the lead of Leo XIII in *Spiritus Paraclitus,* Sept. 15, 1920, on biblical studies.

International Relations: He was largely frustrated on the international level because of the events and attitudes of the war period, but the number of diplomats accredited to the Vatican nearly doubled, from 14 to 26, between the time of his accession to the papacy and his death.

Peace Efforts: Benedict's stance in the war was one of absolute impartiality but not of uninterested neutrality. Because he would not take sides, he was suspected by both sides and the seven-point peace plan he offered to all belligerents Aug. 1, 1917, was turned down. The points of the plan were: recognition of the moral force of right; disarmament; acceptance of arbitration in cases of dispute; guarantee of freedom of the seas; renunciation of war indemnities; evacuation and restoration of occupied territories; examination of territorial claims in dispute.

Relief Efforts: Benedict assumed personal charge of Vatican relief efforts during the war. He set up an international missing persons bureau for contacts between prisoners and their families, but was forced to close it because of the suspicion of warring nations that it was a front for espionage operations. He persuaded the Swiss government to admit into the country military victims of tuberculosis.

Roman Question: Benedict arranged a meeting of Benito Mussolini and the papal secretary of state, which marked the first step toward final settlement of the question in 1929.

PIUS XI

Pius XI (Ambrogio Damiano Achille Ratti) was born May 31, 1857, in Desio, Italy.

Educated at seminaries in Seviso and Milan, and at the Lombard College, Gregorian University and Academy of St. Thomas in Rome, he was ordained to the priesthood in 1879.

He taught at the major seminary of Milan from 1882 to 1888. Appointed to the staff of the Ambrosian Library in 1888, he remained there until 1911, acquiring a reputation for publishing works on palaeography and serving as director from 1907 to 1911. He then moved to the Vatican Library, of which he was prefect from 1914 to 1918. In 1919, he was named apostolic visitor to Poland in April, nuncio in June, and was made titular archbishop of Lepanto Oct. 28. He was made archbishop of Milan and cardinal June 13, 1921, before being elected to the papacy Feb. 6, 1922. He died Feb. 10, 1939.

Aim: The objective of his pontificate, as stated in the encyclical *Ubi Arcano,* Dec. 23, 1922, was to establish the reign and peace of Christ in society.

Canonizations: He canonized 34 saints, including the Jesuit Martyrs of North America, and conferred the title of Doctor of the Church on Sts. Peter Canisius, John of the Cross, Robert Bellarmine and Albertus Magnus.

Eastern Churches: He called for better understanding of the Eastern Churches in the encyclical *Rerum Orientalium* of Sept. 8, 1928, and developed facilities for the training of Eastern-Rite priests. He inaugurated steps for the codification of Eastern-Church law in 1929. In 1935 he made Syrian Patriarch Tappouni a cardinal.

Encyclicals: His first encyclical, *Ubi Arcano,* in addition to stating the aims of his pontificate, blueprinted Catholic Action and called for its development throughout the Church. In *Quas Primas,* Dec. 11, 1925, he established the feast of Christ the King for universal observance. Subjects of some of his other encyclicals were: Christian education, in *Rappresentanti in Terra,* Dec. 31, 1929; Christian marriage, in *Casti Connubii,* Dec. 31, 1930; social conditions and pressure for social change in line with the teaching in *Rerum Novarum,* in *Quadragesimo Anno,* May 15, 1931; atheistic Communism, in *Divini Redemptoris,* Mar. 19, 1937; the priesthood, in *Ad Catholici Sacerdotii,* Dec. 20, 1935.

Missions: Following the lead of Benedict XV, Pius called for the training of native clergy in the pattern of their own respective cultures, and promoted missionary developments in various ways. He ordained six native bishops for China in 1926, one for Japan in 1927, and others for regions of Asia, China and India in 1933. He placed the first 40 mission dioceses under native bishops, saw the number of native priests increase from about 2,600 to more than 7,000 and the number of Catholics in missionary areas more than double from nine million.

In the apostolic constitution *Deus Scientiarum Dominus* of May 24, 1931, he ordered the introduction of missiology into theology courses.

Interfaith Relations: Pius was negative to the ecumenical movement among Protestants but approved the Malines Conversations, 1921 to 1926, between Anglicans and Catholics.

International Relations: Relations with the Mussolini government deteriorated from 1931 on, as indicated in the encyclical *Non Abbiamo Bisogno,* when the regime took steps to curb liberties and activities of the Church; they turned critical in 1938 with the emergence of racist policies. Relations deteriorated also in Germany from 1933 on, resulting finally in condemnation of the Nazis in the encyclical *Mit Brennender Sorge,* March, 1937. Pius sparked a revival of the Church in France by encouraging Catholics to work within the democratic framework of the Republic rather than foment trouble over restoration of a monarchy. Pius was powerless to influence developments related to the civil war which erupted in Spain in July, 1936, sporadic persecution and repression by the Calles regime in Mexico, and systematic persecution of the Church in the Soviet

Union. Many of the 10 concordats and two agreements reached with European countries after World War I became casualties of World War II.

Roman Question: Pius negotiated for two and one-half years with the Italian government to settle the Roman Question by means of the Lateran Agreement of 1929. The agreement provided independent status for the State of Vatican City; made Catholicism the official religion of Italy, with pastoral and educational freedom and state recognition of Catholic marriages, religious orders and societies; and provided a financial payment to the Vatican for expropriation of the former States of the Church.

PIUS XII

Pius XII (Eugenio Maria Giovanni Pacelli) was born Mar. 2, 1876, in Rome.

Educated at the Gregorian University and the Lateran University, in Rome, he was ordained to the priesthood Apr. 2, 1899.

He entered the Vatican diplomatic service in 1901, worked on the codification of canon law, and was appointed secretary of the Congregation for Ecclesiastical Affairs in 1914. Three years later he was ordained titular archbishop of Sardis and made apostolic nuncio to Bavaria. He was nuncio to Germany from 1920 to 1929, when he was made a cardinal, and took office as papal secretary of state in the following year. His diplomatic negotiations resulted in concordats between the Vatican and Bavaria (1924), Prussia (1929), Baden (1932), Austria and the German Republic (1933). He took part in negotiations which led to settlement of the Roman Question in 1929.

He was elected to the papacy Mar. 2, 1939. He died Oct. 9, 1958, at Castel Gandolfo after the 12th longest pontificate in history.

Canonizations: He canonized 34 saints, including Mother Frances X. Cabrini, the first U.S. citizen-Saint.

Cardinals: He raised 56 prelates to the rank of cardinal in two consistories held in 1946 and 1953. There were 57 cardinals at the time of his death.

Church Organization and Missions: He increased the number of dioceses from 1,696 to 2,048. He established native hierarchies in China (1946), Burma (1955) and parts of Africa, and extended the native structure of the Church in India. He ordained the first black bishop for Africa.

Communism: In addition to opposing and condemning Communism on numerous occasions, he decreed in 1949 the penalty of excommunication for all Catholics holding formal and willing allegiance to the Communist Party and its policies. During his reign the Church was persecuted in some 15 countries which fell under communist domination.

Doctrine and Liturgy: He proclaimed the dogma of the Assumption of the Blessed Virgin Mary Nov. 1, 1950 (apostolic constitution, *Munificentissimus Deus.*)

In various encyclicals and other enactments, he provided background for the *aggiornamento* introduced by his successor, John XXIII: by his formulations of doctrine and practice regarding the

Mystical Body of Christ, the liturgy, sacred music and biblical studies; by the revision of the Rites of Holy Week; by initiation of the work which led to the calendar-missal-breviary reform ordered into effect Jan. 1, 1961; by the first of several modifications of the Eucharistic fast; by extending the time of Mass to the evening. He instituted the feasts of Mary, Queen, and of St. Joseph the Worker, and clarified teaching concerning devotion to the Sacred Heart.

His 41 encyclicals and nearly 1,000 public addresses made Pius one of the greatest teaching popes. His concern in all his communications was to deal with specific points at issue and/or to bring Christian principles to bear on contemporary world problems.

Peace Efforts: Before the start of World War II, he tried unsuccessfully to get the contending nations — Germany and Poland, France and Italy — to settle their differences peaceably. During the war, he offered his services to mediate the widened conflict, spoke out against the horrors of war and the suffering it caused, mobilized relief work for its victims, proposed a five-point program for peace in Christmas messages from 1939 to 1942, and secured a generally open status for the city of Rcme. After the war, he endorsed the principles and intent of the United Nations and continued efforts for peace.

United States: Pius appointed more than 200 of the 265 American bishops resident in the U.S. and abroad in 1958, erected 27 dioceses in this country, and raised seven dioceses to archiepiscopal rank.

JOHN XXIII

John XXIII (Angelo Roncalli) was born Nov. 25, 1881, at Sotte il Monte, Italy.

He was educated at the seminary of the Bergamo diocese and the Pontifical Seminary in Rome, where he was ordained to the priesthood Aug. 10, 1904.

He spent the first nine or 10 years of his priesthood as secretary to the bishop of Bergamo and as an instructor in the seminary there. He served as a medic and chaplain in the Italian army during World War I. Afterwards, he resumed duties in his own diocese until he was called to Rome in 1921 for work with the Society for the Propagation of the Faith.

He began diplomatic service in 1925 as titular archbishop of Areópolis and apostolic visitor to Bulgaria. A succession of offices followed: apostolic delegate to Bulgaria (1931-1935); titular archbishop of Mesembria, apostolic delegate to Turkey and Greece, administrator of the Latin vicariate apostolic of Istanbul (1935-1944); apostolic nuncio to France (1944-1953). On these missions, he was engaged in delicate negotiations involving Roman, Eastern-Rite and Orthodox relations; the needs of people suffering from the consequences of World War II; and unsettling suspicions arising from wartime conditions.

He was made a cardinal Jan. 12, 1953, and three days later was appointed patriarch of Venice, the position he held until his election to the papacy

Oct. 28, 1958. He died of stomach cancer June 3, 1963.

John was a strong and vigorous pope whose influence far outmeasured both his age and the shortness of his time in the papacy.

Second Vatican Council: John announced Jan. 25, 1959, his intention of convoking the 21st ecumenical council in history to renew life in the Church, to reform its structures and institutions, and to explore ways and means of promoting unity among Christians. Through the council, which completed its work two and one-half years after his death, he ushered in a new era in the history of the Church.

Canon Law: He established a commission Mar. 28, 1963, for revision of the Code of Canon Law. The revised Code was promulgated in 1983.

Canonizations: He canonized 10 saints and beatified Mother Elizabeth Ann Seton, the first native of the U.S. ever so honored. He named St. Lawrence of Brindisi a Doctor of the Church.

Cardinals: He created 52 cardinals in five consistories, raising membership of the College of Cardinals above the traditional number of 70; at one time in 1962, the membership was 87. He made the college more international in representation than it had ever been, appointing the first cardinals from the Philippines, Japan and Africa. He ordered episcopal ordination for all cardinals. He relieved the suburban bishops of Rome of ordinary jurisdiction over their dioceses so they might devote all their time to business of the Roman Curia.

Eastern Rites: He made all Eastern-Rite patriarchs members of the Congregation for the Oriental Churches.

Ecumenism: He assigned to the Second Vatican Council the task of finding ways and means of promoting unity among Christians. He established the Vatican Secretariat for Promoting Christian Unity June 5, 1960. He showed his desire for more cordial relations with the Orthodox by sending personal representatives to visit Patriarch Athenagoras I June 27, 1961; approved a mission of five delegates to the General Assembly of the World Council of Churches which met in New Delhi, India, in November, 1961; removed a number of pejorative references to Jews in the Roman-Rite liturgy for Good Friday.

Encyclicals: Of the eight encyclicals he issued, the two outstanding ones were *Mater et Magistra* ("Christianity and Social Progress"), in which he recapitulated, updated and extended the social doctrine stated earlier by Leo XIII and Pius XI; and *Pacem in Terris* ("Peace on Earth"), the first encyclical ever addressed to all men of good will as well as to Catholics, on the natural-law principles of peace.

Liturgy: In forwarding liturgical reforms already begun by Pius XII, he ordered a calendar-missal-breviary reform into effect Jan. 1, 1961. He authorized the use of vernacular languages in the administration of the sacraments and approved giving Holy Communion to the sick in afternoon hours. He selected the liturgy as the first topic of major discussion by the Second Vatican Council.

Missions: He issued an encyclical on the missionary activity of the Church; established native hierarchies in Indonesia, Vietnam and Korea; and called on North American superiors of religious institutes to have one-tenth of their members assigned to work in Latin America by 1971.

Peace: John spoke and used his moral influence for peace in 1961 when tension developed over Berlin, in 1962 during the Algerian revolt from France, and later the same year in the Cuban missile crisis. His efforts were singled out for honor by the Balzan Peace Foundation. In 1963, he was posthumously awarded the U.S. Presidential Medal of Freedom.

PAUL VI

Paul VI (Giovanni Battista Montini) was born Sept. 26, 1897, at Concesio in northern Italy.

Educated at Brescia, he was ordained to the priesthood May 29, 1920. He pursued additional studies at the Pontifical Academy for Noble Ecclesiastics and the Pontifical Gregorian University. In 1924 he began 30 years of service in the Secretariat of State; as undersecretary from 1937 until 1954, he was closely associated with Pius XII and was heavily engaged in organizing informational and relief services during and after World War II.

He was ordained archbishop of Milan Dec. 12, 1954, and was inducted into the College of Cardinals Dec. 15, 1958. He was elected to the papacy June 21, 1963, two days after the conclave began. He died of a heart attack Aug. 6, 1978.

Second Vatican Council: He reconvened the Second Vatican Council after the death of John XXIII, presided over its second, third and fourth sessions, formally promulgated the 16 documents it produced, and devoted the whole of his pontificate to the task of putting them into effect throughout the Church. The main thrust of his pontificate — in a milieu of cultural and other changes in the Church and the world — was toward institutionalization and control of the authentic trends articulated and set in motion by the council.

Canonizations: He canonized more saints, 84, than any other pope. They included groups of 22 Ugandan martyrs and 40 martyrs of England and Wales, as well as two Americans — Elizabeth Ann Bayley Seton and John Nepomucene Neumann.

Cardinals: He created more cardinals, 137, than any other pope and gave the Sacred College a more international complexion than it ever had before. He limited participation in papal elections to 120 cardinals under the age of 80.

Collegiality: He established the Synod of Bishops in 1965 and called it into session five times. He stimulated the formation and operation of regional conferences of bishops, and of consultative bodies on other levels.

Creed and Holy Year: On June 30, 1968, he issued a Creed of the People of God in conjunction with the celebration of a Year of Faith. He proclaimed and led the observance of a Holy Year from Christmas Eve of 1974 to Christmas Eve of 1975.

Diplomacy: He met with many world leaders, including Soviet President Nikolai Podgorny in 1967, Marshal Tito of Yugoslavia in 1971 and President Nicólas Ceausescu of Rumania in 1973. He worked constantly to reduce tension between the Church and the intransigent regimes of Eastern European countries by means of a detente type of policy called Ostpolitik. He agreed to significant revisions of the Vatican's concordat with Spain and initiated efforts to revise the concordat with Italy. More then 40 countries established diplomatic relations with the Vatican during his pontificate.

Encyclicals: He issued seven encyclicals, three of which are the best known. In *Populorum Progressio* ("Development of Peoples") he appealed to wealthy countries to take "concrete action" to promote human development and to remedy imbalances between richer and poorer nations; this encyclical, coupled with other documents and related actions, launched the Church into a new depth of involvement as a public advocate for human rights and for humanizing social, political and economic policies. In *Sacerdotalis Caelibatus* ("Priestly Celibacy") he reaffirmed the strict observance of priestly celibacy throughout the Western Church. In *Humanae Vitae* ("Of Human Life") he condemned abortion, sterilization and artificial birth control, in line with traditional teaching and in "defense of life, the gift of God, the glory of the family, the strength of the people."

Interfaith Relations: He initiated formal consultation and informal dialogue on international and national levels between Catholics and non-Catholics — Orthodox, Anglicans, Protestants, Jews, Moslems, Buddhists, Hindus, and unbelievers. He and Greek Orthodox Patriarch Athenagoras I of Constantinople nullified in 1965 the mutual excommunications imposed by their respective churches in 1054.

Liturgy: He carried out the most extensive liturgical reform in history, involving a new Order of the Mass effective in 1969, a revised church calendar in 1970, revisions and translations into vernacular languages of all sacramental rites and other liturgical texts.

Ministries: He authorized the restoration of the permanent diaconate in the Roman Rite and the establishment of new ministries of lay persons.

Peace: In 1968, he instituted the annual observance of a World Day of Peace on New Year's Day as a means of addressing a message of peace to all the world's political leaders and the peoples of all nations. The most dramatic of his many appeals for peace and efforts to ease international tensions was his plea for "No more war!" before the United Nations Oct. 4, 1965.

Pilgrimages: A "Pilgrim Pope," he made pastoral visits to the Holy Land and India in 1964, the United Nations and New York City in 1965, Portugal and Turkey in 1967, Colombia in 1968, Switzerland and Uganda in 1969, and Asia, Pacific islands and Australia in 1970. While in Manila in 1970, he was stabbed by a Bolivian artist who made an attempt on his life.

Roman Curia: He reorganized the central administrative organs of the Church in line with provisions of the apostolic constitution, *Regimini Ecclesiae Universae*, streamlining procedures for more effective service and giving the agencies a more international perspective by drawing officials and consultors from all over the world. He also instituted a number of new commissions and other bodies. Coupled with curial reorganization was a simplification of papal ceremonies.

JOHN PAUL I

John Paul I (Albino Luciani) was born Oct. 17, 1912, in Forno di Canale (now Canale d'Agordo) in northern Italy.

Educated at the minor seminary in Feltre and the major seminary of the Diocese of Belluno, he was ordained to the priesthood July 7, 1935. He pursued further studies at the Pontifical Gregorian University in Rome and was awarded a doctorate in theology. From 1937 to 1947 he was vice rector of the Belluno seminary, where he taught dogmatic and moral theology, canon law and sacred art. He was appointed vicar general of his diocese in 1947 and served as director of catechetics.

Ordained bishop of Vittorio Veneto Dec. 27, 1958, he attended all sessions of the Second Vatican Council, participated in three assemblies of the Synod of Bishops (1971, 1974 and 1977), and was vice president of the Italian Bishops' Conference from 1972 to 1975.

He was appointed archbishop and patriarch of Venice Dec. 15, 1969, and was inducted into the College of Cardinals Mar. 5, 1973.

He was elected to the papacy Aug. 26, 1978, on the fourth ballot cast by the 111 cardinals participating in the largest and one of the shortest conclaves in history. The quickness of his election was matched by the brevity of his pontificate of 33 days, during which he delivered 19 addresses. He died of a heart attack Sept. 28, 1978.

JOHN PAUL II

See separate entry.

CANONIZATIONS BY LEO XIII AND HIS SUCCESSORS

Canonization is an infallible declaration by the pope that a person who suffered martyrdom and/or practiced Christian virtue to a heroic degree is in glory with God in heaven and is worthy of public honor by the universal Church and of imitation by the faithful.

(See Canonization entry in Glossary.)

Leo XIII
(1878-1903)

1881: Clare of Montefalco, virgin (d. 1308); John Baptist de Rossi, priest (1698-1764); Lawrence of Brindisi, doctor (d. 1619).

1883: Benedict J. Labre (1748-1783).

1888: Seven Holy Founders of the Servite Order; Peter Claver, priest (1581-1654); John Berchmans (1599-1621); Alphonsus Rodriguez, lay brother (1531-1617).

1897: Anthony M. Zaccaria, founder of Barnabites (1502-1539); Peter Fourier, co-founder of Augustinian Canonesses of Our Lady (1565-1640).

1900: John Baptist de La Salle, founder of Christian Brothers (1651-1719); Rita of Cascia (1381-1457).

St. Pius X
(1903-1914)

1904: Alexander Sauli, bishop (1534-1593); Gerard Majella, lay brother (1725-1755).

1909: Joseph Oriol, priest (1650-1702); Clement M. Hofbauer, priest (1751-1820).

Benedict XV
(1914-1922)

1920: Gabriel of the Sorrowful Mother (1838-1862); Margaret Mary Alacoque, virgin (1647-1690); Joan of Arc, virgin (1412-1431).

Pius XI
(1922-1939)

1925: Therese of Lisieux, virgin (1873-1897); Peter Canisius, doctor (1521-1597); Mary Magdalen Postel, foundress of Sisterhood of Christian Schools (1756-1846); Mary Magdalen Sophie Barat, foundress of Society of the Sacred Heart (1779-1865); John Eudes, founder of Eudist Fathers (1601-1680); John Baptist Vianney (Curé of Ars), priest (1786-1859).

1930: Lucy Filippini, virgin (1672-1732); Catherine Thomas, virgin (1533-1574); Jesuit North American Martyrs (see Index); Robert Bellarmine, bishop-doctor (1542-1621); Theophilus of Corte, priest (1676-1740).

1931: Albert the Great, bishop-doctor (1206-1280) (equivalent canonization).

1933: Andrew Fournet, priest (1752-1834); Bernadette Soubirous, virgin (1844-1879).

1934: Joan Antida Thouret, foundress of Sisters of Charity of St. Joan Antida (1765-1826); Mary Michaeli, foundress of Institute of Handmaids of the Blessed Sacrament (1809-1865); Louise de Marillac, foundress of Sisters of Charity (1591-1660); Joseph Benedict Cottolengo, priest (1786-1842); Pompilius M. Pirotti, priest (1710-1756); Teresa Margaret Redi, virgin (1747-1770); John Bosco, founder of Salesians (1815-1888); Conrad of Parzham, lay brother (1818-1894).

1935: John Fisher, bishop-martyr (1469-1535); Thomas More, martyr (1478-1535).

1938: Andrew Bobola, martyr (1592-1657); John Leonardi, founder of Clerics Regular of the Mother of God (c. 1550-1609); Salvatore of Horta, lay brother (1520-1567).

Pius XII
(1939-1958)

1940: Gemma Galgani, virgin (1878-1903); Mary Euphrasia Pelletier, foundress of Good Shepherd Sisters (1796-1868).

1943: Margaret of Hungary, virgin (d. 1270) (equivalent canonization).

1946: Frances Xavier Cabrini, foundress of Missionary Sisters of the Sacred Heart (1850-1917).

1947: Nicholas of Flue, hermit (1417-1487); John of Britto, martyr (1647-1693); Bernard Realini, priest (1530-1616); Joseph Cafasso, priest (1811-1860); Michael Garicoits, founder of Auxiliary Priests of the Sacred Heart (1797-1863); Jeanne Elizabeth des Ages, cofoundress of Daughters of the Cross (1773-1838); Louis Marie Grignon de Montfort, founder of Montfort Fathers (1673-1716); Catherine Laboure, virgin (1806-1876).

1949: Jeanne de Lestonnac, foundress of Religious of Notre Dame of Bordeaux (1556-1640); Maria Josepha Rossello, foundress of Daughters of Our Lady of Pity (1811-1880).

1950: Emily de Rodat, foundress of Congregation of the Holy Family of Villefranche (1787-1852); Anthony Mary Claret, bishop, founder of Claretians (1807-1870); Bartolomea Capitanio (1807-1833) and Vincenza Gerosa (1784-1847), foundresses of Sisters of Charity of Lovere; Jeanne de Valois, foundress of Annonciades of Bourges (1461-1504); Vincenzo M. Strambi, bishop (1745-1824); Maria Goretti, virgin-martyr (1890-1902); Mariana Paredes of Jesus, virgin (1618-1645).

1951: Maria Domenica Mazzarello, co-foundress of Daughters of Our Lady Help of Christians (1837-1881); Emilie de Vialar, foundress of Sisters of St. Joseph "of the Apparition" (1797-1856); Anthony M. Gianelli, bishop (1789-1846); Ignatius of Laconi, lay brother (1701-1781); Francis Xavier Bianchi, priest (1743-1815).

1954: Pius X, pope (1835-1914); Dominic Savio (1842-1857); Maria Crocifissa di Rosa, foundress of Handmaids of Charity of Brescia (1813-1855); Peter Chanel, priest-martyr (1803-1841); Gaspar del Bufalo, founder of Missioners of the Most Precious Blood (1786-1837); Joseph M. Pignatelli, priest (1737-1811).

1958: Herman Joseph, O. Praem., priest (1150-1241) (equivalent canonization).

John XXIII
(1958-1963)

1959: Joaquina de Vedruna de Mas, foundress of Carmelite Sisters of Charity (1783-1854); Charles of Sezze, lay brother (1613-1670).

1960: Gregory Barbarigo, bishop (1625-1697) (equivalent canonization); John de Ribera, bishop (1532-1611).

1961: Bertilla Boscardin, virgin (1888-1922).

1962: Martin de Porres, lay brother (1579-1639); Peter Julian Eymard, founder of Blessed Sacrament Fathers (1811-1868); Anthony Pucci, priest (1819-1892); Francis Mary of Camporosso, lay brother (1804-1866).

1963: Vincent Pallotti, founder of Pallottine Fathers (1795-1850).

Paul VI
(1963-1978)

1964: Charles Lwanga and Twenty-One Companions, Martyrs of Uganda.

1967: Benilde Romancon, lay brother (1805-1862).

1969: Julia Billiart, foundress of Sisters of Notre Dame de Namur (1751-1816).

1970: Maria Della Dolorato Torres Acosta, foundress of Servants Sisters of Mary (1826-1887);

Leonard Murialdo, priest, founder of Congregation of St. Joseph (1828-1900); Therese Couderc, foundress of Congregation of Our Lady of the Cenacle (1805-1885); John of Avila, preacher and spiritual director (1499-1569); Sts. Nicholas Tavelic, Deodatus of Aquitaine, Peter of Narbonne and Stephen of Cuneo, martyrs (d. 1391); Forty English and Welsh Martyrs (d. 16th cent.).

1974: Teresa of Jesus Jornet Ibars, foundress of Little Sisters of Abandoned Aged (1843-1897).

1975: Vicenta Maria Lopez y Vicuna, foundress of Institute of Daughters of Mary Immaculate (1847-1890); Elizabeth Bayley Seton, foundress of Sisters of Charity in the U.S. (1774-1821); John Masias, Dominican brother-missionary (1585-1645): Oliver Plunket, archbishop-martyr (1629-1681); Justin de Jacobis, missionary bishop (1800-1860); John Baptist of the Conception, priest, reformer of the Order of the Most Holy Trinity (1561-1613).

1976: Beatrice da Silva, foundress of Congregation of the Immaculate Conception of the BVM (1424 or 1426-1490); John Ogilvie, Scottish Jesuit martyr (1579-1615).

1977: Rafaela Maria Porras y Ayllon, foundress of Handmaids of the Sacred Heart (1850-1925); John Nepomucene Neumann, bishop (1811-1860); Sharbel Makhlouf, Maronite Rite monk (1828-1898).

John Paul II
(1978-   )

1982: Crispin of Viterbo, Capuchin brother (1668-1750); Maximilian Kolbe, Conventual Franciscan priest (1894-1941); Marguerite Bourgeoys, foundress of Congregation of Notre Dame (1620-1700); Jeanne Delanoue, foundress of Sisters of St. Anne of Providence of Saumur, France (1666-1736).

English and Welsh Martyrs

Forty Martyrs of England and Wales, victims of persecution from 1535 to 1671, were canonized by Pope Paul Oct. 25, 1970.

The martyrs were prosecuted and executed as traitors for refusal to comply with laws enacted by Henry VIII and Elizabeth I regarding supremacy (the sovereign was proclaimed the highest authority of the Church in England, acknowledgment of papal primacy was forbidden), succession and the prohibition of native-born to study for the priesthood abroad and return to England for practice of the ministry.

John Houghton, prior of the London Charterhouse, was the first of his group to die (1535) for opposing Henry's Acts of Supremacy and Succession. Cuthbert Mayne (d. 1577) was the protomartyr of the English seminary at Douay. Margaret Clitherow (d. 1586) and Swithun Wells (d. 1591) were executed for sheltering priests. Richard Gwyn (d. 1584), poet, was the protomartyr of Wales.

Others in the group were:

John Almond, Edmund Arrowsmith, Ambrose Barlow, John Boste, Alexander Briant, Edmund

Campion, Philip Evans, Thomas Garnet, Edmund Gennings;

Philip Howard, John Jones, John Kemble, Luke Kirby, Robert Lawrence, David Lewis, Ann Line, John Lloyd;

Henry Morse, Nicholas Owen, John Paine, Polydore Plasden, John Plessington, Richard Reynolds, John Rigby, John Roberts;

Alban Roe, Ralph Sherwin, Robert Southwell, John Southworth, John Stone, John Wall, Henry Walpole, Margaret Ward, Augustine Webster and Eustace White.

PAPAL ENCYCLICALS — BENEDICT XIV (1740) TO JOHN PAUL II

(Source: *The Papal Encyclicals* (5 vols.), Claudia Carlen, I.H.M.; a Consortium Book, © McGrath Publishing Co., Wilmington, N.C. Used with permission.)

An encyclical letter is a pastoral letter addressed by a pope to the whole Church. In general, it concerns matters of doctrine, morals or discipline. Its formal title consists of the first few words of the official text. A few encyclicals, notably *Pacem in Terris* by John XXIII and *Ecclesiam Suam* by Paul VI, have been addressed to "all men of good will" as well as to bishops and the faithful in communion with the Church.

An encyclical epistle, which is like an encyclical letter in many respects, is addressed to part of the Church, that is, to the bishops and faithful of a particular country or area. Its contents may concern other than doctrinal, moral or disciplinary matters of universal significance; for example, the commemoration of historical events, conditions in a certain country.

The authority of encyclicals was stated by Pius XII in the encyclical *Humani Generis* Aug. 12, 1950.

"Nor must it be thought that what is contained in encyclical letters does not of itself demand assent, on the pretext that the popes do not exercise in them the supreme power of their teaching authority. Rather, such teachings belong to the ordinary magisterium, of which it is true to say: 'He who hears you, hears me' (Lk. 10:16); for the most part, too, what is expounded and inculcated in encyclical letters already appertains to Catholic doctrine for other reasons. But if the supreme pontiffs in their official documents purposely pass judgment on a matter debated until then, it is obvious to all that the matter, according to the mind and will of the same pontiffs, cannot be considered any longer a question open for discussion among theologians."

The following list contains the titles and indicates the subject matter of encyclical letters and epistles. The latter are generally distinguishable by the limited scope of their titles or contents.

Benedict XIV
(1740-1758)

1740: *Ubi Primum* (On the duties of bishops), Dec. 3.

1741: *Quanta Cura* (Forbidding traffic in alms), June 30.

1743: *Nimian Licentiam* (To the bishops of Poland: on validity of marriages), May 18.

1745: *Vix Pervenit* (To the bishops of Italy: on usury and other dishonest profit), Nov. 1.

1748: *Magnae Nobis* To the bishops of Poland: on marriage impediments and dispensations), June 29.

1749: *Peregrinantes* (To all the faithful: proclaiming a Holy Year for 1750), May 5.

Apostolica Constitutio (On preparation for the Holy Year), June 26.

1751: *A Quo Primum* (To the bishops of Poland: on Jews and Christians living in the same place), June 14.

1754: *Cum Religiosi* (To the bishops of the States of the Church: on catechesis), June 26.

Quod Provinciale (To the bishops of Albania: on Christians using Mohammedan names), Aug. 1.

1755: *Allatae Sunt* (To missionaries of the Orient: on the observance of Oriental rites), July 26.

1756: *Ex Quo Primum* (To bishops of the Greek rite: on the Euchologion), Mar. 1.

Ex Omnibus (To the bishops of France: on the apostolic constitution, *Unigenitus*), Oct. 16.

Clement XIII
(1758-1769)

1758: *A Quo Die* (Unity among Christians), Sept. 13.

1759: *Cum Primum* (On observing canonical sanctions), Sept. 17.

Appetente Sacro (On the spiritual advantages of fasting), Dec. 20.

1761: *In Dominico Agro* (On instruction in the faith), June 14.

1766: *Christinae Reipublicae* (To bishops of Austria: on the dangers of anti Christian writings), Nov. 25.

1768: *Summa Quae* (To the bishops of Poland: on the Church in Poland), Jan. 6.

Clement XIV
(1769-1774)

1769: *Decet Quam Maxime* (To the bishops of Sardinia: on abuses in taxes and benefices), Sept. 21.

Inscrutabili Divinae Sapientiae (To all Christians: proclaiming a universal jubilee), Dec. 12.

Cum Summi (Proclaiming a universal jubilee), Dec. 12.

1774: *Salutis Nostrae* (To all Christians: proclaiming a universal jubilee), Apr. 30.

Pius VI
(1775-1799)

1775: *Inscrutabile* (On the problems of the pontificate), Dec. 25.

1791: *Charitas* (To the bishops of France: on the civil oath in France), Apr. 13.

Pius VII
(1800-1823)

1800: *Diu Satis* (To the bishops of France: on a return to Gospel principles), May 15.

Leo XII
(1823-1829)

1824: *Ubi Primum* To all bishops: on Leo XII's assuming the pontificate), May 5.

Quod Hoc Ineunte (Proclaiming a universal jubilee), May 24.

1825: *Charitate Christi* Extending jubilee to the entire church), Dec. 25.

Pius VIII
(1829-1830)

1829: *Traditi Humilitati* (On Pius VIII's program for the pontificate), May 24.

Gregory XVI
(1831-1846)

1832: *Summo Iugiter Studio* (To the bishops of Bavaria: on mixed marriages), May 27.

Cum Primum (To the bishops of Poland: on civil obedience), June 9.

Mirari Vos (On liberalism and religious indifferentism), Aug. 15.

1833: *Quo Graviora* (To the bishops of the Rhineland: on the "pragmatic Constitution"), Oct. 4.

1834: *Singulari Nos* (On the errors of Lammenais), June 25.

1835: *Commissum Divinitus* (To clergy of Switzerland: on Church and State), May 17.

1840: *Probe Nostis* (On the Propagation of the Faith), Sept. 18.

1841: *Quas Vestro* (To the bishops of Hungary: on mixed marriages), Apr. 30.

1844: *Inter Praecipuas* (On biblical societies), May 8.

Pius IX
(1846-1878)

1846: *Qui Pluribus* (On faith and religion), Nov. 9.

1847: *Praedecessores Nostros* (On aid for Ireland), Mar. 25.

Ubi Primum (To religious superiors: on discipline for religious), June 17.

1849: *Ubi Primum* (On the Immaculate Conception), Feb. 2.

Nostis et Nobiscum (To the bishops of Italy: on the Church in the Pontifical States), Dec. 8.

1851: *Exultavit Cor Nostrum* (On the effects of jubilee), Nov. 21.

1852: *Nemo Certe Ignorat* (To the bishops of Ireland: on the discipline for clergy), Mar. 25.

Probe Noscitis Venerabiles (To the bishops of Spain: on the discipline for clergy), May 17.

1853: *Inter Multiplices* (To the bishops of France: pleading for unity of spirit), Mar. 21.

1854: *Neminem Vestrum* (To clergy and faithful of Constantinople: on the persecution of Armenians), Feb. 2.

Optime Noscitis (To the bishops of Ireland: on the proposed Catholic university for Ireland), Mar. 20.

Apostolicae Nostrae Caritatis (Urging prayers for peace), Aug. 1.

1855: *Optime Noscitis* (To the bishops of Austria: on episcopal meetings), Nov. 5.

1856: *Singulari Quidem* (To the bishops of Austria: on the Church in Austria), Mar. 17.

1858: *Cum Nuper* (To the bishops of Sicily: on care for clerics), Jan. 20.

Amantissimi Redemptoris (On priests and the care of souls), May 3.

1859: *Cum Sancta Mater Ecclesia* (Pleading for public prayer), Apr. 27.

Qui Nuper (On Pontifical States), June 18.

1860: *Nullis Certe Verbis* (On the need for civil sovereignty), Jan. 19.

1862: *Amantissimus* (To bishops of the Oriental rite: on the care of the churches), Apr. 8.

1863: *Quanto Conficiamur Moerore* (To the bishops of Italy: on promotion of false doctrines), Aug. 10.

Incredibili (To the bishops of Bogota: on persecution in New Granada), Sept. 17.

1864: *Maximae Quidem* (To the bishops of Bavaria: on the Church in Bavaria), Aug. 18.

Quanta Cura (Condemning current errors), Dec. 8.

1865: *Meridionali Americae* (To the bishops of South America: on the seminary for native clergy), Sept. 30.

1867: *Levate* (On the afflictions of the Church), Oct. 27.

1870: *Respicientes* (Protesting the taking of the Pontifical States), Nov. 1.

1871: *Ubi Nos* (To all bishops: on Pontifical States), May 15.

Beneficia Dei (On the twenty-fifth anniversary of his pontificate), June 4.

Saepe Venerabiles Fratres (On thanksgiving for twenty-five years of pontificate), Aug. 5.

1872: *Quae in Patriarchatu* (To bishops and people of Chaldea: on the Church in Chaldea), Nov. 16.

1873: *Quartus Supra* (To bishops and people of the Armenian rite: on the Church in Armenia), Jan. 6.

Etsi Multa (On the Church in Italy, Germany and Switzerland), Nov. 21.

1874: *Vix Dum a Nobis* (To the bishops of Austria: on the Church in Austria), Mar. 7.

Omnem Sollicitudinem (To the bishops of the Ruthenian rite: on the Greek-Ruthenian rite), May 13.

Gravibus Ecclesiae (To all bishops and faithful: proclaiming a jubilee for 1875), Dec. 24.

1875: *Quod Nunquam* (To the bishops of Prussia: on the Church in Prussia), Feb. 5.

Graves ac Diuturnae (To the bishops of Switzerland: on the Church in Switzerland), Mar. 23.

Leo XIII
(1878-1903)

1878: *Inscrutabili Dei Consilio* (On the evils of society), Apr. 21.

Quod Apostolici Muneris (On socialism), Dec. 28.

1879: *Aeterni Patris* (On the restoration of Christian philosophy), Aug. 4.

1880: *Arcanum* (On Christian marriage), Feb. 10.

Grande Munus (On Sts. Cyril and Methodius), Sept. 30.

Sancta Dei Civitas (On mission societies), Dec. 3.

1881: *Diuturnum* (On the origin of civil power), June 29.

Licet Multa (To the bishops of Belgium: on Catholics in Belgium), Aug. 3.

1882: *Etsi Nos* (To the bishops of Italy: on conditions in Italy), Feb. 15.

Auspicato Concessum (On St. Francis of Assisi), Sept. 17.

Cum Multa (To the bishops of Spain: on conditions in Spain), Dec. 8.

1883: *Supremi Apostolatus Officio* (On devotion to the Rosary), Sept. 1.

1884: *Nobilissima Gallorum Gens* (To the bishops of France: on the religious question), Feb. 8.

Humanum Genus (On Freemasonry), Apr. 20.

Superiore Anno (On the recitation of the Rosary), Aug. 30.

1885: *Immortale Dei* (On the Christian constitution of states), Nov. 1.

Spectata Fides (To the bishops of England: on Christian education), Nov. 27.

Quod Auctoritate (Proclamation of extraordinary Jubilee), Dec. 22.

1886: *Iampridem* (To the bishops of Prussia: on Catholicism in Germany), Jan. 6.

Quod Multum (To the bishops of Hungary: on the liberty of the Church), Aug. 22.

Pergrata (To the bishops of Portugal: on the Church in Portugal), Sept. 14.

1887: *Vi e Ben Noto* (To the bishops of Italy: on the Rosary and public life), Sept. 20.

Officio Sanctissimo (To the bishops of Bavaria: on the Church in Bavaria), Dec. 22.

1888: *Quod Anniversarius* (On his sacerdotal jubilee), Apr. 1.

In Plurimis (To the bishops of Brazil: on the abolition of slavery), May 5.

Libertas (On the nature of human liberty), June 20.

Saepe Nos (To the bishops of Ireland: on boycotting in Ireland), June 24.

Paterna Caritas (To the Patriarch of Cilicia and the archbishops and bishops of the Armenian people: on reunion with Rome), July 25.

Quam Aerumnosa (To the bishops of America: on Italian immigrants), Dec. 10.

Etsi Cunctas (To the bishops of Ireland: on the Church in Ireland), Dec. 21.

Exeunte Iam Anno (On the right ordering of Christian life), Dec. 25.

1889: *Magni Nobis* (To the bishops of the United States: on the Catholic University of America), Mar. 7.

Quamquam Pluries (On devotion to St. Joseph), Aug. 15.

1890: *Sapientiae Christianae* (On Christians as citizens), Jan. 10.

Dall'Alto Dell'Apostolico Seggio (To the bishops and people of Italy: on Freemasonry in Italy), Oct. 15.

Catholicae Ecclesiae (On slavery in the missions), Nov. 20.

1891: *In Ipso* (To the bishops of Austria: on episcopal reunions in Austria), Mar. 3.

Rerum Novarum (On capital and labor), May 15.

Pastoralis (To the bishops of Portugal: on religious union), June 25.

Pastoralis Officii (To the bishops of Germany and Austria: on the morality of dueling), Sept. 12.

Octobri Mense (On the Rosary), Sept. 22.

1892: *Au Milieu des Sollicitudes* (To the bishops, clergy and faithful of France: on the Church and State in France), Feb. 16.

Quarto Abeunte Esaeculo (To the bishops of Spain, Italy, and the two Americas: on the Columbus quadricentennial), July 16.

Magnae Dei Matris (On the Rosary), Sept. 8.

Inimica Vis (To the bishops of Italy: on Freemasonry), Dec. 8.

Custodi di Quella Fede (To the Italian people: on Freemasonry), Dec. 8.

1893: *Ad Extremas* (On seminaries for native clergy), June 24.

Constanti Hungarorum (To the bishops of Hungary: on the Church in Hungary), Sept. 2.

Laetitiae Sanctae (Commending devotion to the Rosary), Sept. 8.

Non Mediocri (To the bishops of Spain: on the Spanish College in Rome), Oct. 25.

Providentissimus Deus (On the study of Holy Scripture), Nov. 18.

1894: *Caritatis* (To the bishops of Poland: on the Church in Poland), Mar. 19.

Inter Graves (To the bishops of Peru: on the Church in Peru), May 1.

Litterae a Vobis (To the bishops of Brazil: on the clergy in Brazil), July 2.

Iucunda Semper Expectatione (On the Rosary), Sept. 8.

Christi Nomen (On the propagation of the Faith and churches), Dec. 24.

1895: *Longinqua* (To the bishops of the United States: on Catholicism in the United States), Jan. 6.

Permoti Nos (To the bishops of Belgium: on social conditions in Belgium), July 10.

Adiutricem (On the Rosary), Sept. 5.

1896: *Insignes* (To the bishops of Hungary: on the Hungarian millennium), May 1.

Satis Cognitum (On the unity of the Church), June 29.

Fidentem Piumque Animum (On the Rosary), Sept. 20.

1897: *Divinum Illud Munus* (On the Holy Spirit), May 9.

Militantis Ecclesiae (To the bishops of Austria, Germany, and Switzerland: on St. Peter Canisius), Aug. 1.

Augustissimae Virginis Mariae (On the Confraternity of the Holy Rosary), Sept. 12.

Affari Vos (To the bishops of Canada: on the Manitoba school question), Dec. 8.

1898: *Caritatis Studium* (To the bishops of Scotland: on the Church in Scotland), July 25.

Spesse Volte (To the bishops, priests, and people of Italy: on the suppression of Catholic institutions), Aug. 5.

Quam Religiosa (To the bishops of Peru: on civil marriage law), Aug. 16.

Diuturni Temporis (On the Rosary), Sept. 5.

Quum Diuturnum (To the bishops of Latin America: on Latin American bishops' plenary council), Dec. 25.

1899: *Annum Sacrum* (On consecration to the Sacred Heart), May 25.

Depuis le Jour (To the archbishops, bishops, and clergy of France: on the education of the clergy), Sept. 8.

Paternae (To the bishops of Brazil: on the education of the clergy), Sept. 18.

1900: *Omnibus Compertum* (To the Patriarch and bishops of the Greek-Melkite rite: on unity among the Greek Melkites), July 21.

Tametsi Futura Prospicientibus (On Jesus Christ the Redeemer), Nov. 1.

1901: *Graves de Communi Re* (On Christian democracy), Jan. 18.

Gravissimas (To the bishops of Portugal: on religious orders in Portugal), May 16.

Reputantibus (To the bishops of Bohemia and Moravia: on the language question in Bohemia), Aug. 20.

Urbanitatis Veteris (To the bishops of the Latin church in Greece: on the foundation of a seminary in Athens), Nov. 20.

1902: *In Amplissimo* (To the bishops of the United States: on the Church in the United States), Apr. 15.

Quod Votis (To the bishops of Austria: on the proposed Catholic University), Apr. 30.

Mirae Caritatis (On the Holy Eucharist), May 28.

Quae ad Nos (To the bishops of Bohemia and Moravia: on the Church in Bohemia and Moravia), Nov. 22

Fin dal Principio (To the bishops of Italy: on the education of the clergy), Dec. 8.

Dum Multa (To the bishops of Ecuador: on marriage legislation), Dec. 24.

Saint Pius X
(1903-1914)

1903: *E Supremi* (On the restoration of all things in Christ), Oct. 4.

1904: *Ad Diem Illum Laetissimum* (On the Immaculate Conception), Feb. 2.

Iucunda Sane (On Pope Gregory the Great), Mar. 12.

1905: *Acerbo Nimis* (On teaching Christian doctrine), Apr. 15.

Il Fermo Proposito (To the bishops of Italy: on Catholic Action in Italy), June 11.

1906: *Vehementer Nos* (To the bishops, clergy, and people of France: on the French Law of Separation), Feb. 11.

Tribus Circiter (On the Mariavites or Mystic Priests of Poland), Apr. 5.

Pieni l'Animo (To the bishops of Italy: on the clergy in Italy), July 28.

Gravissimo Officio Munere (To the bishops of France: on French associations of worship), Aug. 10.

1907: *Une Fois Encore* (To the bishops, clergy, and people of France: on the separation of Church and State), Jan. 6.

Pascendi Dominici Gregis (On the doctrines of the Modernists), Sept. 8.

1909: *Communium Rerum* (On St. Anselm of Aosta), Apr. 21.

1910: *Editae Saepe* (On St. Charles Borromeo), May 26.

1911: *Iamdudum* (On the Law of Separation in Portugal), May 24.

1912: *Lacrimabili Statu* (To the bishops of Latin America: on the Indians of South America), June 7.

Singulari Quadam (To the bishops of Germany: on labor organizations), Sept. 24.

Benedict XV
(1914-1922)

1914: *Ad Beatissimi Apostolorum* (Appeal for peace), Nov. 1.

1917: *Humani Generis Redemptionem* (On preaching the Word of God), June 15.

1918: *Quod Iam Diu* (On the future peace conference), Dec. 1.

1919: *In Hac Tanta* (To the bishops of Germany: on St. Boniface), May 14.

Paterno Iam Diu (On children of central Europe), Nov. 24.

1920: *Pacem, Dei Munus Pulcherrimum* (On peace and Christian reconciliation), May 23.

Spiritus Paraclitus (On St. Jerome), Sept. 15.

Principi Apostolorum Petro (On St. Ephrem the Syrian), Oct. 5.

Annus Iam Plenus (On children of central Europe), Dec. 1.

1921: *Sacra Propediem* (On the Third Order of St. Francis), Jan. 6.

In Praeclara Summorum (To professors and students of fine arts in Catholic institutions of learning: on Dante), Apr. 30.

Fausto Appetente Die (On St. Dominic), June 29.

Pius XI
(1922-1939)

1922: *Ubi Arcano Dei Consilio* (On the peace of Christ in the Kingdom of Christ), Dec. 23.

1923: *Rerum Omnium Perturbationem* (On St. Francis de Sales), Jan. 26.

Studiorum Ducem (On St. Thomas Aquinas), June 29.

Ecclesiam Dei (On St. Josaphat), Nov. 12.

1924: *Maximam Gravissimamque* (To the bishops, clergy, and people of France: on French diocesan associations), Jan. 18.

1925: *Quas Primas* (On the feast of Christ the King), Dec. 11.

1926: *Rerum Ecclesiae* (On Catholic missions), Feb. 28.

Rite Expiatis (On St. Francis of Assisi), Apr. 30.

Iniquis Afflictisque (On the persecution of the Church in Mexico), Nov. 18.

1928: *Mortalium Animos* (On religious unity), Jan. 6.

Miserentissimus Redemptor (On reparation to the Sacred Heart), May 8.

Rerum Orientalium (On the promotion of Oriental studies), Sept. 8.

1929: *Mens Nostra* (On the promotion of Spiritual Exercises), Dec. 20.

Quinquagesimo Ante (On his sacerdotal jubilee), Dec. 23.

Rappresentanti in Terra (On Christian education), Dec. 31.

1930: *Ad Salutem* (On St. Augustine), Apr. 20.

Casti Connubii (On Christian marriage), Dec. 31.

1931: *Quadragesimo Anno* (Commemorating the fortieth anniversary of Leo XIII's *Rerum novarum:* on reconstruction of the social order), May 15.

Non Abbiamo Bisogno (On Catholic Action in Italy), June 29.

Nova Impendet (On the economic crisis), Oct. 2.

Lux Veritatis (On the Council of Ephesus), Dec. 25.

1932: *Caritate Christi Compulsi* (On the Sacred Heart), May 3.

Acerba Animi (To the bishops of Mexico: on persecution of the Church in Mexico), Sept. 29.

1933: *Dilectissima Nobis* (To the bishops, clergy, and people of Spain: on oppression of the Church in Spain), June 3.

1935: *Ad Catholici Sacerdotii* (On the Catholic priesthood), Dec. 20.

1936: *Vigilanti Cura* (To the bishops of the United States: on motion pictures), June 29.

1937: *Mit Brennender Sorge* (To the bishops of Germany: on the Church and the German Reich), Mar. 14.

Divini Redemptoris (On atheistic communism), Mar. 19.

Nos Es Muy Conocida (To the bishops of Mexico: on the religious situation in Mexico), Mar. 28.

Ingravescentibus Malis (On the Rosary) Sept. 29.

Pius XII
(1939-1958)

1939: *Summi Pontificatus* (On the unity of human society), Oct. 20.

Sertum Laetitiae (To the bishops of the United States: on the 150th anniversary of the establishment of the hierarchy in the United States), Nov. 1.

1940: *Saeculo Exeunte Octavo* (To the bishops of Portugal and its colonies: on the eighth centenary of the independence of Portugal), June 13.

1943: *Mystici Corporis Christi* (On the Mystical Body of Christ), June 29.

Divino Afflante Spiritu (On promoting biblical studies, commemorating the fiftieth anniversary of *Providentissimus Deus*), Sept. 30.

1944: *Orientalis Ecclesiae* (On St. Cyril, Patriarch of Alexandria), Apr. 9.

1945: *Communium Interpretes Dolorum* (To the bishops of the world: appealing for prayers for peace during May), Apr. 15.

Orientales Omnes Ecclesias (On the 350th anniversary of the reunion of the Ruthenian Church with the Apostolic See), Dec. 23.

1946: *Quemadmodum* (Pleading for the care of the world's destitute children), Jan. 6.

Deiparae Virginis Mariae (To all bishops: on the possibility of defining the Assumption of the Blessed Virgin Mary as a dogma of faith), May 1.

1947: *Fulgens Radiatur* (On St. Benedict), Mar. 21.

Mediator Dei (On the sacred liturgy), Nov. 20.

Optatissima Pax (Prescribing public prayers for social and world peace), Dec. 18.

1948: *Auspicia Quaedam* (On public prayers for world peace and solution of the problem of Palestine), May 1.

In Multiplicibus Curis (On prayers for peace in Palestine), Oct. 24.

1949: *Redemptoris Nostri Cruciatus* (On the holy places in Palestine), Apr. 15.

1950: *Anni Sacri* (On the program for combatting atheistic propaganda throughout the world), Mar. 12.

Summi Maeroris (On public prayers for peace), July 19.

Humani Generis (Concerning some false opinions threatening to undermine the foundations of Catholic doctrine), Aug. 12.

Mirabile Illud (On the crusade of prayers for peace), Dec. 6.

1951: *Evangelii Praecones* (On the promotion of Catholic missions), June 2.

Sempiternus Rex Christus (On the Council of Chalcedon), Sept. 8.

Ingruentium Malorum (On reciting the Rosary), Sept. 15.

1952: *Orientales Ecclesias* (On the persecuted Eastern Church), Dec. 15.

1953: *Doctor Mellifluus* (On St. Bernard of Clairvaux, the last of the fathers), May 24.

Fulgens Corona (Proclaiming a Marian Year to commemorate the centenary of the definition of the dogma of the Immaculate Conception), Sept. 8.

1954: *Sacra Virginitas* (On consecrated virginity), Mar. 25.

Ecclesiae Fastos (To the bishops of Great Britain, Germany, Austria, France, Belgium, and Holland: on St. Boniface), June 5.

Ad Sinarum Gentem (To the bishops, clergy, and people of China: on the supranationality of the Church), Oct. 7.

Ad Caeli Reginam (Proclaiming the Queenship of Mary), Oct. 11.

1955: *Musicae Sacrae* (On sacred music), Dec. 25.

1956: *Haurietis Aquas* (On devotion to the Sacred Heart), May 15.

Luctuosissimi Eventus (Urging public prayers for peace and freedom for the people of Hungary), Oct. 28.

Laetamur Admodum (Renewing exhortation for prayers for peace for Poland, Hungary, and especially for the Middle East), Nov. 1.

Datis Nuperrime (Lamenting the sorrowful events in Hungary and condemning the ruthless use of force), Nov. 5.

1957: *Fidei Donum* (On the present condition of the Catholic missions, especially in Africa), Apr. 21.

Invicti Athletae (On St. Andrew Bobola), May 16.

Le Pelerinage de Lourdes (Warning against materialism on the centenary of the apparitions at Lourdes), July 2.

Miranda Prorsus (On the communications field: motion picture, radio, television), Sept. 8.

1958: *Ad Apostolorum Principis* (To the bishops of China; on Communism and the Church in China), June 29.

Meminisse Juvat (On prayers for persecuted Church), July 14.

John XXIII
(1958-1963)

1959: *Ad Petri Cathedram* (On truth, unity, and peace, in a spirit of charity), June 29.

Sacerdotii Nostri Primordia (On St. John Vianney), Aug. 1.

Grata Recordatio (On the Rosary: prayer for the Church, missions, international and social problems), Sept. 26.

Princeps Pastorum (On the missions, native clergy, lay participation), Nov. 28.

1961: *Mater et Magistra* (On Christianity and social progress), May 15.

Aeterna Dei Sapientia (On fifteenth centenary of the death of Pope St. Leo I: the see of Peter as the center of Christian unity), Nov. 11.

1962: *Paenitentiam Agere* (On the need for the practice of interior and exterior penance), July 1.

1963: *Pacem in Terris* (On establishing universal peace in truth, justice, charity, and liberty), Apr. 11.

Paul VI
(1963-1978)

1964: *Ecclesiam Suam* (On the Church), Aug. 6.

1965: *Mense Maio* (On prayers during May for the preservation of peace), Apr. 29.

Mysterium Fidei (On the Holy Eucharist), Sept. 3.

1966: *Christi Matri* (On prayers for peace during October), Sept. 15.

1967: *Populorum Progressio* (On the development of peoples), Mar. 26.

Sacerdotalis Caelibatus (On the celibacy of the priest), June 24.

1968: *Humanae Vitae* (On the regulation of birth), July 25.

John Paul II
(1978-)

1979: *Redemptor Hominis* (On redemption and the dignity of the human race), Mar. 4.

1980: *Dives in Misericordia* (On the mercy of God), Nov. 30.

1981: *Laborem Exercens* (On human work), Sept. 14.

EUCHARISTIC MINISTERS

The designation of lay men and women to serve as special ministers of the Eucharist was authorized by Pope Paul in an "Instruction on Facilitating Communion in Particular Circumstances" *(Immensae Caritatis),* dated Jan. 29, 1973, and published by the Congregation for Divine Worship the following Mar. 29.

Qualified lay persons may serve as special ministers for specific occasions or extended periods in the absence of a sufficient number of priests and deacons to provide reasonable and appropriate pastoral service in the distribution of Holy Communion, during Mass and outside of Mass (to the sick and shut-ins).

Appointments of special ministers are made by priests with the approval of the appropriate bishop.

BIRTHRIGHT

Birthright is a nondenominational guidance and referral service organization offering pregnant women alternatives to abortion, in line with the motto, "It is the right of every pregnant woman to give birth and the right of every child to be born."

Started by Mrs. Louise Summerhill of Toronto, Canada, in 1968, it has chapters in Canada, the United States, the United Kingdom, Ireland, New Zealand, Australia and South Africa.

The executive director of Birthright, U.S.A., is Mrs. D. Cocciolone, 686 N. Broad St., Woodbury, N.J. 08096.

Birthright, although it has Catholics among its volunteers and draws some support from Catholic sources, is independent and nondenominational. Birthright telephone numbers are listed in many local directories.

APPALACHIA COMMITTEE

The 600-member Catholic Committee of Appalachia consists of bishops, priests, religious and lay persons engaged in pastoral and social justice ministry in the 13-state region. Appalachia has been defined by Congress as including all of West Virginia and parts of Alabama, Georgia, Kentucky, Maryland, Mississippi, New York, North Carolina, Ohio, Pennsylvania, South Carolina, Tennessee and Virginia. The committee is the Catholic Caucus of the Commission on Religion in Appalachia, an interfaith group.

Michelle Farabaugh is the executive coordinator. Address: P.O. Box 953, Whiteburg, Ky 41858.

ORGANIZATION AND GOVERNMENT

As a structured society, the Catholic Church is organized and governed along lines corresponding mainly to the jurisdictions of the pope and bishops.

The pope is the supreme head of the Church. He has primacy of jurisdiction as well as honor over the entire Church.

Bishops, in union with and in subordination to the pope, are the successors of the Apostles for care of the Church and for the continuation of Christ's mission in the world. They serve the people of their own dioceses, or local churches, with ordinary authority and jurisdiction. They also share, with the pope and each other, in common concern and effort for the general welfare of the whole Church.

Bishops of exceptional status are Eastern Rite patriarchs who, subject only to the pope, are heads of the faithful belonging to their rites throughout the world.

Subject to the Holy Father and directly responsible to him for the exercise of their ministry of service to people in various jurisdictions or divisions of the Church throughout the world are: resident archbishops and metropolitans (heads of archdioceses), resident bishops (heads of dioceses), vicars and prefects apostolic (heads of vicariates apostolic and prefectures apostolic), certain abbots and prelates, apostolic administrators. Each of these, within his respective territory and according to the provisions of canon law, has ordinary jurisdiction over pastors (who are responsible for the administration of parishes), priests, religious and lay persons.

Also subject to the Holy Father are titular archbishops and bishops (who have delegated jurisdiction), religious orders and congregations of pontifical right, pontifical institutes and faculties, papal nuncios and apostolic delegates.

Assisting the pope and acting in his name in the central government and administration of the Church are cardinals and other officials of the Roman Curia.

THE HIERARCHY

The ministerial hierarchy is the orderly arrangement of the ranks and orders of the clergy to provide for the spiritual care of the faithful, the government of the Church, and the accomplishment of the Church's total mission in the world. Persons belong to this hierarchy by virtue of ordination and canonical mission.

The term hierarchy is also used to designate an entire body or group of bishops; for example, the hierarchy of the Church, the hierarchy of the United States.

Hierarchy of Order: Consists of the pope, bishops, priests and deacons, by divine law. Their purpose, for which they are ordained to holy orders, is to carry out the sacramental and pastoral ministry of the Church.

Hierarchy of Jurisdiction: Consists of the pope and bishops by divine law, and other church officials by ecclesiastical institution and mandate, who have authority to govern and direct the faithful for spiritual ends.

Prelates: Clerics with the authority of public office in the Church — i.e., the authority of jurisdiction in the external forum. They are: the pope, patriarchs, residential archbishops and bishops, certain abbots and prelates, vicars and prefects apostolic, vicars general, certain superiors in clerical exempt religious communities. Titular archbishops and bishops without ordinary jurisdiction are not prelates in the strict sense of the term; neither are pastors, who have very limited jurisdiction in the external forum.

The Pope

His Holiness the Pope is the Bishop of Rome, the Vicar of Jesus Christ, the successor of St. Peter, Prince of the Apostles, the Supreme Pontiff who has the primacy of jurisdiction and not merely of honor over the universal Church, the Patriarch of the West, the Primate of Italy, the Archbishop and Metropolitan of the Roman Province, the Sovereign of the State of Vatican City, Servant of the Servants of God.

Cardinals

(See Index)

Patriarchs

Patriarch, a term which had its origin in the Eastern Church, is the title of a bishop who, second only to the pope, has the highest rank in the hierarchy of jurisdiction. He is the incumbent of one of the sees listed below. Subject only to the pope, an Eastern-Rite patriarch is the head of the faithful belonging to his rite throughout the world. The patriarchal sees are so called because of their special status and dignity in the history of the Church.

The Council of Nicaea (325) recognized three patriarchs — the bishops of Alexandria and Antioch in the East, and of Rome in the West. The First Council of Constantinople (381) added the bishop of Constantinople to the list of patriarchs and gave him rank second only to that of the pope, the bishop of Rome and patriarch of the West; this action was seconded by the Council of Chalcedon (451) and was given full recognition by the Fourth Lateran Council (1215). The Council of Chalcedon also acknowledged patriarchal rights of the bishop of Jerusalem.

Eastern Rite patriarchs are as follows: one of Alexandria, for the Copts; three of Antioch, one each for the Syrians, Maronites and Greek Melkites (the latter also has the personal title of Greek Melkite patriarch of Alexandria and of Jerusalem). The patriarch of Babylonia, for the Chaldeans, and the patriarch of Sis, or Cilicia, for the Armenians, should be called, more properly, *Katholikos* — that is, a prelate delegated for a universality of causes. These patriarchs are elected by bishops of their rites: they receive approval and the pallium, symbolic of their office, from the pope.

Latin Rite patriarchates were established for Antioch, Jerusalem, Alexandria and Constantinople during the Crusades; afterwards, they became patriarchates in name only. Jerusalem, however, was reconstituted as a patriarchate by Pius IX, in virtue of the bull *Nulla Celebrior* of July 23, 1847. In 1964, the Latin titular patriarchates of Constantinople, Alexandria and Antioch, long a bone of contention in relations with Eastern Rites, were abolished.

As of July 1, 1983, the patriarchs in the Church were:

The Pope, Bishop of Rome, Patriarch of the West; Cardinal Stephanos I Sidarouss, C.M., of Alexandria, for the Copts; Ignace Antoine II Hayek, of Antioch, for the Syrians; Maximos V Hakim, of Antioch, for the Greek Melkites (he also has the titles of Alexandria and Jerusalem for the Greek Melkites); Cardinal Antoine Khoraiche, of Antioch, for the Maronites; Giacomo Beltritti, of Jerusalem, for the Latin Rite; Paul II Cheikho, of Babylon, for the Chaldeans; Jean Pierre XVIII Kasparian, of Cilicia, for the Armenians.

The titular patriarchs (in name only) of the Latin Rite were: Cardinal Antonio Ribeiro, of Lisbon; Cardinal Marco Cé of Venice and Archbishop Raul Nicolau Goncalves of the East Indies (Archbishop of Goa and Daman, India). The patriarchate of the West Indies has been vacant since 1963.

Archbishops, Metropolitans

Archbishop: A bishop with the title of an archdiocese.

Metropolitan Archbishop: Head of the principal see, an archdiocese, in an ecclesiastical province consisting of several dioceses. He has the full powers of bishop in his own archdiocese and limited supervisory jurisdiction and influence over the other (suffragan) dioceses in the province.

Titular Archbishop: Has the title of an archdiocese which formerly existed in fact but now exists in title only. He does not have ordinary jurisdiction over an archdiocese.

Archbishop ad personam: A title of personal honor and distinction granted to some bishops. They do not have ordinary jurisdiction over an archdiocese.

Primate: A title given to the ranking prelate of some countries or regions.

Bishops

Residential Bishop: A bishop in charge of a diocese.

Titular Bishops: Have the titles of dioceses which formerly existed in fact but now exist in title only. They have delegated authority of jurisdiction, by grant in line with their assignments, rather than the ordinary jurisdiction of office which belongs to a residential bishop. An auxiliary bishop (titular) is an assistant to a residential bishop. A coadjutor bishop (titular) is an assistant bishop of higher status; some coadjutors have the right of succession to residential sees.

Episcopal Vicar: An assistant, who may or may not be a bishop, appointed by a residential bishop as his deputy for a certain part of a diocese, a determined type of apostolic work, or the faithful of a certain rite.

Eparch, Exarch: Titles of bishops of Eastern-Rite churches.

Nomination of Bishops: Nominees for episcopal ordination are selected in several ways. Final appointment and/or approval in all cases is subject to decision by the pope.

In the U.S., bishops periodically submit the names of candidates to the archbishop of their province. The names are then considered at a meeting of the bishops of the province, and those receiving a favorable vote are forwarded to the apostolic delegate for transmission to the Holy See. Bishops are free to seek the counsel of priests, religious and lay persons with respect to nominees.

Eastern-Rite churches have their own procedures and synodal regulations for nominating and making final selection of candidates for episcopal ordination. Such selection is subject to approval by the pope.

The revised Code of Canon Law in effect since late 1983 concedes no future rights and privileges to civil authorities with respect to the election, nomination, presentation or designation of candidates for the episcopate.

Ad Limina Visit: Residential bishops and military vicars are obliged to make a periodic *ad limina* visit ("to the threshold" of the Apostles) to the tombs of Sts. Peter and Paul, have audience with the Holy Father, consult with appropriate Vatican officials and present a written report on conditions in their jurisdictions. The most recent regulations concerning the formalities and scheduling of visits by bishops from various countries, generally every five years, were issued by the Congregation for Bishops in a decree dated Nov. 27, 1975.

Other Prelates

Some bishop-prelates and abbots, with jurisdiction like that of diocesan bishops, are pastors of the people of God in territories (prelatures, abbacies *nullius*) not under the jurisdiction of diocesan bishops.

Vicar Apostolic: Usually a titular bishop who has ordinary jurisdiction over a mission territory. A vicar apostolic could also serve as the administrator of a vacant diocese or a diocese whose bishop is impeded from the exercise of his office.

Prefect Apostolic: A prelate with ordinary jurisdiction over a mission territory.

Apostolic Administrator: Usually a bishop appointed to administer an ecclesiastical jurisdiction temporarily. Administrators of lesser rank are also appointed for special and more restricted supervisory duties.

Vicar General: A bishop's deputy for the administration of a diocese. Such a vicar does not have to be a bishop.

Honorary prelates belonging to the Pontifical Household are: Apostolic Prothonotaries, Honorary Prelates of His Holiness, and Chaplains of His Holiness. Their title is Reverend Monsignor.

SYNOD OF BISHOPS

The Synod of Bishops was chartered by Pope Paul VI Sept. 15, 1965, in a document he issued on his own initiative under the title, *Apostolica Sollicitudo*. Provisions of this *motu proprio* are contained in Canons 342 to 348 of the revised Code of Canon Law, effective Nov. 27, 1983. According to major provisions of the Synod charter:

• The purposes of the Synod are: "to encourage close union and valued assistance between the Sovereign Pontiff and the bishops of the entire world; to insure that direct and real information is provided on questions and situations touching upon the internal action of the Church and its necessary activity in the world of today; to facilitate agreement on essential points of doctrine and on methods of procedure in the life of the Church."

• The Synod is a central ecclesiastical institution, permanent by nature.

• The Synod is directly and immediately subject to the Pope, who has authority to assign its agenda, to call it into session, and to give its members deliberative as well as advisory authority.

• In addition to a limited number of ex officio members and a few heads of male religious institutes, the majority of the members are elective by and representative of national or regional episcopal conferences. The Pope reserved the right to appoint the general secretary, special secretaries and no more than 15 per cent of the total membership. The numbers of members of ordinary assemblies of the Synod have varied between 197 and 210.

The Pope is president of the Synod.

The secretary general is Archbishop Jozef Tomko of Czechoslovakia.

FIRST MEETING, 1967

The Synod met for the first time from Sept. 29 to Oct. 29, 1967, in Vatican City. Its objectives, as stated by Pope Paul, were "the preservation and strengthening of the Catholic faith, its integrity, its force, its development, its doctrinal and historical coherence."

One result of synodal deliberations was a recommendation to the Pope to establish an international commission of theologians to assist the Congregation for the Doctrine of the Faith and to broaden approaches to theological research. The commission was subsequently set up by Pope Paul in 1969.

In other actions, the Synod called for the formulation of a Code of Canon Law more pastoral than the one in force since 1918 and more in touch with the mentality, aspirations and needs of people in contemporary circumstances; favored the view that episcopal conferences should have major control over seminaries in their respective areas; suggested some changes in pastoral procedures with respect to mixed marriages, which were authorized in 1970; gave general approval to the New Order of the Mass which was promulgated and put into effect in 1969.

EXTRAORDINARY SESSION

The second Synod of Bishops, meeting in extraordinary session Oct. 11 to 28, 1969, opened the door to wider participation by the bishops with the Pope and each other in the government of the Church.

The business assigned to the meeting by Pope Paul was to seek and examine ways and means of putting into practice the principle of collegiality which figured largely in declarations of the Second Vatican Council on the Church and the pastoral office of bishops.

Accordingly, proceedings were oriented to three main points: (1) the nature and implications of collegiality; (2) the relationships of bishops and their conferences to the Pope; (3) the relationships of bishops and their conferences to each other. The end results were three proposals approved by the bishops and the Pope, and five times that number approved and placed under advisement by the Pope. All proposals pointed in the direction of more cooperative action by all the bishops with the Pope in the conduct of church affairs.

The three proposals which were approved and moved for action provided for regular meetings of the Synod at two-year intervals (later extended to three years), staff organization and operations of the general secretariat in the interim between meetings, and openness of the synodal agenda to suggestions by bishops.

Between the second and third meetings of the Synod, an advisory council of 15 members (12 elected, three appointed by the Pope) was formed to provide the secretariat with adequate staff for carrying on liaison with episcopal conferences and for drawing up the agenda of synodal meetings. The council, at its first meeting May 12 to 15, 1970, followed the lead of the second assembly by opening the agenda of the 1971 meeting to the suggestions of bishops from all over the world.

SYNOD '71

The ministerial priesthood and justice in the world were the principal topics of discussion at the third and longest meeting, the Second General Assembly of the Synod, Sept. 30 to Nov. 6, 1971.

Advisory reports on these subjects, compiled from views expressed by the bishops before and during the synodal sessions, were presented to Pope Paul at the end of the meeting. He authorized publication of the reports and said, in a letter made public Dec. 9, that he accepted conclusions reached by the bishops which "conform to the current norms" of church teaching.

The Priesthood

In its report on the priesthood, the Synod described difficulties experienced by priests, stated traditional doctrinal principles on the priesthood, and drew from these principles a set of guidelines for priestly life and ministry in the mission of Christ and the Church, and in the communion of the Church.

The report emphasized the primary and permanent dedication of priests in the Church to the ministry of word, sacrament and pastoral service as a full-time occupation.

The synodal Fathers — with 168 votes in favor without reservations, 21 votes in favor with reservations, and 10 votes against — supported the existing discipline of clerical celibacy. They favored leaving to the discretion of the Pope decisions regarding the ordination of already married men in special circumstances. They did not consider the question of permitting already ordained priests to marry. The majority voted against permitting priests who had left the ministry to resume priestly duties, although they said such priests could serve the Church in other ways and should be treated in a just and fraternal manner.

Justice in the World

In connection with "The Mission of the People of God To Further Justice in the World," a synodal report reviewed a wide range of existing injustices; cited the social-justice imperatives of the Gospel; called for the practice of justice throughout the Church and for greater efforts in education and ecumenical collaboration for justice; and outlined an eight-point program for international action.

Behind the Synod's recommendations were the convictions:

• "The Church . . . has a proper and specific responsibility which is identified with her mission of giving witness before the world of the need for love and justice contained in the Gospel message, a witness to be carried out in church institutions themselves and in the lives of Christians."

• "Action on behalf of justice and participation in the transformation of the world fully appear to us as a constitutive dimension of the preaching of the Gospel; or, in other words, of the Church's mission for the redemption of the human race and its liberation from every oppressive situation."

• "The present situation of the world, seen in the light of faith, calls us back to the very essence of the Christian message, creating in us a deep awareness of its true meaning and of its urgent demands. The mission of preaching the Gospel dictates at the present time that we should dedicate ourselves to the liberation of man even in his present existence in this world. For, unless the Christian message of love and justice shows its effectiveness through action in the cause of justice in the world, it will only with difficulty gain credibility with the men of our times."

FOURTH ASSEMBLY

"Evangelization of the Modern World" was the theme of the fourth assembly of the Synod, Sept. 27 to Oct. 26, 1974. Its major product was a general statement on the subject, covering the need for it and its relationship to efforts for total human liberation from personal and social evil.

The statement reconfirmed "that the mandate to evangelize all men constitutes the essential mission of the Church," that "the duty to proclaim the Gospel belongs to the whole people of God," and that "this work demands incessant interior conversion on the part of individual Christians and continual renewal of our communities and institutions."

The bishops noted that evangelization is impeded by atheism, secularism, and the repression of religious liberty in a number of countries.

Communication of the Gospel was called "a dynamic process" which "takes place through word, work and life," and which needs "translation," expression and indigenization in terms of the religious and cultural patterns of people in different places.

The statement cited the need and intention for ecumenical collaboration with other Christians for the purpose of rendering "to the world a much broader common witness to Christ, while at the same time working to obtain full union in the Lord."

Liberation

Regarding the relationship between evangelization and human liberation, the bishops said:

"Faithful to her evangelizing mission, the Church, as a truly poor, praying and fraternal community, can do much to bring about the integral salvation or the full liberation of men. She can draw from the Gospel the most profound reasons and ever new incentives to promote generous dedication to the service of all men — the poor especially, the weak and the oppressed — and to eliminate the social consequences of sin which are translated into unjust social and political structures.

"The Church does not remain within merely political, social and economic limits (elements which she must certainly take into account) but leads towards freedom under all its forms — liberation from sin, from individual or collective selfishness — and to full communion with God and with men who are like brothers. In this way the Church, in her evangelical way, promotes the true and complete liberation of all men, groups and peoples."

SYNOD '77

"Catechetics in Our Time, with Special Reference to Children and Young People," was the theme of the fifth assembly, Sept. 30 to Oct. 29, 1977. Its major products were a "Message to the People of God," the first synodal statement issued since inception of the body, and two documents presented to Pope Paul — a set of 34 propositions and some 900 suggestions regarding the substance of the propositions and the message on catechetics.

The propositions covered six general subjects in considerable detail: the importance of catechetical renewal, the theme of authentic catechesis, the mode of authentic catechizing, the necessity of catechesis for all Christians, the community as the context and milieu of catechesis, attitudes and other factors affecting catechesis.

The "Message to the People of God" consisted of three parts, dealing with: the world, young people and catechesis; the manifestation of salvation in Christ; catechesis as the task of all people in the Church.

SIXTH ASSEMBLY, 1980

"The Role of the Christian Family in the Modern World" was the theme of the sixth assembly, Sept. 26 to Oct. 25, 1980. Its major products were "A Message to Christian Families in the Modern World" and a proposal for a "Charter of Family Rights."

In the message to families, the bishops said: "Today the family is sometimes obliged to choose a way of life that goes contrary to modern culture in such matters as sexuality, individual autonomy and material wealth. In the face of sin and failure, it gives witness to an authentically Christian spirit."

The message criticized unjust structures which increase poverty in the world, the "spiritual emptiness" of materialistic cultures, and disregard for the rights of families by some governments and international agencies.

It reaffirmed the indissolubility of marriage and the contents of the Encyclical *Humanae Vitae* (see separate entry), and urged those who find it hard to live up to "the difficult but loving demands" of Christ not to be discouraged.

The document called for the family to be a "domestic church," a "community of faith living in hope and love," which promotes the Christian formation of its members and others.

The bishops said the Christian family must not live closed in on itself but must be open to the community around it and, moved by a sense of justice and concern for others, must "foster social justice and relief of the poor and oppressed."

Family Rights

In addition to its message to families, the assembly drafted a proposal for a "Charter of Family Rights" consisting of two fundamental principles and 14 specific points. The proposal was forwarded to the Pope with the request that he develop and publish a similar charter.

The basic principles of the proposed charter were:

1. "The family is the basic cell of society, a subject of rights and duties, with priority over the state and any other community."

2. "The state by its laws and institutions must recognize and protect the family with respect to its liberty and assist it, not replacing it."

The draft stated that the family has rights:

• to exist and progress as a family; every person, especially of the poor, has the right to form a family and sustain it with appropriate assistance;

• to exercise its role in transmitting life right from its conception and to educate children;

• to intimacy of both conjugal and family life;

• to stability of the bond and institution of marriage;

• to believe and profess one's own faith and propagate it;

• to educate one's children according to one's own traditions and religious and cultural values, with the necessary instruments, means and institutions;

• to obtain physical, social, political and economic security, especially for the poor and weak;

• to habitation fit for leading a family life properly;

• to expression and representation before public authorities, economic, social and cultural, and those subject to them, either by oneself or through associates;

• to create associations with other families and institutions so that one may fulfill one's role fittingly and effectively;

• to protection for minors, with the help of adequate institutions and laws, against harmful drugs, pornography and alcoholism;

• to fruitful leisure which may foster family values;

• to dignified life and dignified death;

• to emigrate as a family to seek a better life.

Pope John Paul acknowledged the work of the 1980 assembly and gave it appropriate expression in *Familiaris Consortio,* his apostolic exhortation on the family, dated Nov. 22, 1981 (see separate entry). In the introduction to the exhortation he wrote:

"At the close of their assembly, the Synod Fathers presented me with a long list of proposals in which they had gathered the fruits of their reflections, which had matured over intense days of work, and they asked me unanimously to be a spokesman before humanity of the Church's lively care for the family and to give suitable indications for renewed pastoral effort in this fundamental sector of the life of man and of the Church.

"As I fulfill that mission with this exhortation, thus actuating in a particular matter the apostolic ministry with which I am entrusted, I wish to thank all the members of the Synod for the very valuable contribution of teaching and experience that they made."

1983 ASSEMBLY

"Reconciliation and Penance in the Mission of the Church" was the theme of the 1983 assembly, scheduled to convene Sept. 29 for deliberations lasting about a month.

Preparations for the assembly included a wide sampling of views from bishops' conferences, individual bishops, Catholic organizations, several congregations of the Roman Curia and the Union of Superiors General of Religious. Provisional guidelines for reflection and comment were circulated Jan. 28, 1982. Responses to these *lineamenta* provided the substance of a working paper made public Feb. 17, 1983.

Indications were that individual confession and absolution would be high priority items on the Synod agenda.

(See separate article.)

ROMAN CURIA

The Roman Curia consists of the Secretariat of State, the Sacred Council for the Public Affairs of the Church, nine congregations, three tribunals, three secretariats, and a complex of commissions, councils and offices which administer church affairs at the highest level.

Background

The Curia evolved gradually from advisory assemblies or synods of the Roman clergy with whose assistance the popes directed church affairs during the first 11 centuries. Its original office was the Apostolic Chancery, dating from the fourth century. The antecedents of its permanently functioning agencies and offices were special commissions of cardinals and prelates. Its establishment in a form resembling what it is now dates from the second half of the 16th century.

Pope Paul VI gave the following short account of the background of the Curia in the apostolic constitution *Regimini Ecclesiae Universae* ("For the Government of the Universal Church"), dated Aug. 15, 1967.

"The Roman Pontiffs, successors to Blessed Peter, have striven to provide for the government of the Universal Church by making use of experts to advise and assist them.

"In this connection, we should remember both the Presbyterium of the City of Rome and the College of Cardinals of the Holy Roman Church which in the course of centuries evolved from it. Then, little by little, as we know, out of that office (Apostolic Chancery) which was set up in the fourth century to transmit papal documents, many offices developed; to these was added the Auditorium, which was a well-developed tribunal in the 13th century and which was more thoroughly organized by John XXII (1316-1334).

"With an increase in the volume of things to be dealt with, bodies or commissions of cardinals selected to treat of specific questions began to be more efficiently organized in the 16th century, from which eventually arose the congregations of the Roman Curia. It is to the credit of our predecessor Sixtus V that, in the constitution *Immensa Aeterni Dei* of Jan. 22, 1588, he arranged the sacred councils in an orderly manner and wisely described the structure of the Roman Curia.

"With the progress of time, however, it happened that some of them became obsolete, others had to be added, and others had to be restructured. This is the work our predecessor St. Pius X set out to do with the constitution *Sapienti Consilio* of June 29, 1908. Its provisions, a lasting testimony to that wise and ingenious pastor of the Church, were with a few changes incorporated into the Code of Canon Law."

Reorganization

Pope Paul initiated a four-year reorganization study in 1963 which resulted in the constitution *Regimini Ecclesiae Universae*. The document was published Aug. 18, 1967, and went into full effect in March, 1968.

While the study was under way, the Pope took preliminary steps toward curial reorganization by reorienting and changing the title of the Sacred Congregation of the Holy Office (to the Sacred Congregation for the Doctrine of the Faith) and by appointing a number of non-Italians to key curial positions.

The stated purposes of the reorganization were to increase the efficiency of the Curia and to make it more responsive to the needs and concerns of the Universal Church. The pursuit of these objectives involved various modifications.

Curial Departments

• The Office of the Pope, including the Papal Secretariat or Secretariat of State and the Council for the Public Affairs of the Church.

• Nine congregations, instead of twelve as formerly. The functions of the Sacred Congregation of Ceremonies were transferred to the Prefecture of the Pontifical Household; the duties of the Sacred Congregation for Extraordinary Ecclesiastical Affairs were taken over by the Sacred Council for the Public Affairs of the Church; the Sacred Congregation of the Basilica of St. Peter was reduced in rank. In 1969, the Sacred Congregation of Rites was phased out of existence and its functions were assigned to the Sacred Congregation for the Causes of Saints and the Sacred Congregation for Divine Worship.

In 1975 the Congregation for the Sacraments and Divine Worship was established to replace the Congregation for the Discipline of the Sacraments and the Congregation for Divine Worship.

• Three secretariats, the Council of the Laity and the Pontifical Commission on Justice and Peace.

• Three tribunals.

• Six offices, including the former Apostolic Chancery (abolished in 1973) and Apostolic Chamber, and the newly constituted Prefecture of Economic Affairs, Prefecture of the Pontifical Household, Administration of the Patrimony of the Apostolic See, and Central Statistics Office. Functions of the former Apostolic Datary and the Secretariats of State, of Briefs to Princes, and of Latin Letters were transferred to the Secretariat of State.

Operational Procedures

• The papal secretary or secretary of state has authority to take initiative in coordinating and expediting business through meetings and other cooperative procedures.

• Officials of departments have five-year terms of office, which may be renewed. Terms end automatically on the death of a pope. The five-year terms of consultors are renewable.

• Diocesan bishops as well as full-time curial personnel have membership in curial departments, in accordance with provisions of the decree *Pro Comperto Sane* of Aug. 6, 1967. Seven diocesan bishops hold five-year membership in each congregation, with full rights to participation in the more important plenary assemblies scheduled once a year. They are also entitled to take part in routine meetings whenever they are in Rome. Three general superiors of male religious institutes hold similar membership in the Sacred Congregation for Religious and Secular Institutes.

• Lay persons are eligible to serve as consultors to curial departments.

• Close liaison with episcopal conferences is required. They should be given prior notice of forthcoming curial decrees affecting them in any special way.

• In line with customary procedure, matters in which the competence of two or more departments is involved are handled on a cooperative basis, with mutual consultation and decision.

• Although Latin remains the official language of the Curia, communication in any of the widely known modern languages is acceptable.

• Informational and financial services are centralized in the Central Statistics Office and the Prefecture of Economic Affairs, respectively.

• Heads of curial departments are required to notify the pope before conducting any serious or extraordinary business.

• Authority to act and decide on many matters belongs to departmental officials in virtue of delegation from the pope. Some matters, however, have to be referred to the pope for final decision.

Internationalization

As of July 1, 1983, principal officials of the Roman Curia (cardinals unless indicated otherwise) were from the following countries: Italy (Baggio, Caprio, Casaroli, Oddi, Palazzini, Paupini, Opilio Rossi, Casoria, Sabattani); Poland (Rubin, Abp. Deskur); Germany (Ratzinger, Bp. Cordes); United States (Baum, Abp. Marcinkus); Argentina (Pironio); Belgium (Abp. Jadot); Benin (Gantin); Brazil (Agnelo Rossi); France (Abp. Poupard); India (Abp. Lourdusamy); Netherlands (Willebrands); Ukraine (Abp. Marusyn); Venezuela (Abp. Castillo Lara).

DEPARTMENTS

Secretariat of State: Provides the pope with the closest possible assistance in the care of the Universal Church and in dealings with all departments of the Curia.

The cardinal secretary is the key coordinator of curial operations. He has authority to call meetings of the prefects of all departments for expediting the conduct of business, for consultation and intercommunication. He handles: any and all matters entrusted to him by the pope, and ordinary matters which are not within the competence of other departments; some relations with bishops; relations with representatives of the Holy See, civil governments and their representatives, without prejudice to the competence of the Council for the Public Affairs of the Church.

The cardinal secretary has been likened to a prime minister or head of government because of the significant role he plays in coordinating curial operations at the highest level.

The secretariat has two offices for preparing and writing letters for the pope (functions formerly performed by the Secretariat of Briefs to Princes and the Secretariat of Latin Letters), and a Central Statistics Office.

It also handles work formerly done by the Apostolic Datary (the dating and countersigning of papal documents, and the management of church benefices), and the Apostolic Chancery, abolished in 1973 (care of the pope's leaden seal and the Fisherman's Ring).

It has supervisory duties over the Commission for the Instruments of Social Communication, two Vatican publications, *Acta Apostolicae Sedis* and *Annuario Pontificio,* and the Vatican Personnel Office.

The Prefecture of Vatican City is answerable to the secretary of state.

OFFICIALS: Cardinal Agostino Casaroli, secretary of state; Most Rev. Eduardo Martinez Somalo, undersecretary and secretary of the Cifra.

Council for the Public Affairs of the Church: Handles diplomatic and other relations with civil governments. With the Secretariat of State, it supervises matters concerning nunciatures and apostolic delegations. It also has supervision of the Pontifical Commission for Russia.

OFFICIALS: Cardinal Agostino Casaroli, prefect, secretary of state; Most Rev. Achille Silvestrini, secretary.

BACKGROUND: Originated by Pius VI in 1793 as the Congregation for Extraordinary Affairs from the Kingdom of the Gauls; given wider scope by Pius VII, July 19, 1814, formerly called the Sacred Congregation for Extraordinary Ecclesiastical Affairs.

CONGREGATIONS

Sacred Congregation for the Doctrine of the Faith: Has responsibility to safeguard the doctrine of faith and morals.

Accordingly, it examines doctrinal questions; promotes studies thereon; evaluates theological opinions and, when necessary and after prior consultation with concerned bishops, reproves those regarded as opposed to principles of the faith; examines books on doctrinal matters and can reprove such works, if the contents so warrant, after giving authors the opportunity to defend themselves.

It examines matters pertaining to the Privilege of Faith (Petrine Privilege) in marriage cases, and safeguards the dignity of the sacrament of penance.

It has working relations with the Pontifical Biblical Commission (see separate entry).

In 1969, Pope Paul set up a Theological Commission (see separate entry) as an adjunct to the congregation, to provide it with the advisory services of additional experts in theology and allied disciplines.

OFFICIALS: Cardinal Joseph Ratzinger, prefect; Most Rev. Jean Jerome Hamer, O.P., secretary.

BACKGROUND: At the beginning of the 13th century, legates of Innocent III were commissioned as the Holy Office of the Inquisition to combat heresy; the same task was entrusted to the Dominican Order by Gregory IX in 1231 and to the Friars Minor by Innocent IV from 1243 to 1254. On July 21, 1542 (apostolic constitution *Licet*), Paul III instituted a permanent congregation of cardinals with supreme and universal competence over matters concerning heretics and those suspected of heresy. Pius IV, St. Pius V and Sixtus V further defined the work of the congregation. St. Pius X changed its name to the Congregation of the Holy Office.

Paul VI, in virtue of the motu proprio *Integrae Servandae* of Dec. 7, 1965, began reorganization of the Curia with this body, to which he gave the new title, Sacred Congregation for the Doctrine of the Faith. Its orientation is not merely negative, in the condemnation of error, but positive, in the promotion of orthodox doctrine. The right of appeal, judicial representation, and the consultation of their proper regional conference of bishops, are assured to persons accused of unorthodox doctrine. The office for the censorship of books and the Roman Index of Prohibited Books were abolished.

Sacred Congregation for the Oriental Churches: Has competence in matters concerning the persons and discipline of Eastern Rite Churches. It has jurisdiction over territories in which the majority of Christians belong to Oriental Rites (i.e., Egypt, the Sinai Peninsula, Eritrea, Northern Ethiopia, Southern Albania, Bulgaria, Cyprus, Greece, Iran, Iraq, Lebanon, Palestine, Syria, Jordan, Turkey, Afghanistan, the part of Thrace subject to Turkey); also, over minority communities of Orientals no matter where they live.

To assure adequate and equal representation, it has as many offices as there are rites of Oriental Churches in communion with the Holy See.

It is under mandate to consult with the Secretariat for Promoting Christian Unity on questions concerning separated Oriental Churches, and with the Secretariat for Non-Christians, especially in relations with Moslems.

It has a special commission on the liturgy and an Oriental Church Information Service.

OFFICIALS: Cardinal Wladyslaw Rubin, prefect; Most Rev. Miroslav Stefan Marusyn, secretary.

Members include all Eastern Rite patriarchs and the president of the Secretariat for Promoting Christian Unity. Consultors include the secretary of the same secretariat.

BACKGROUND: Special congregations for the affairs of the Greek and other Oriental Churches were founded long before this body was created by Pius IX Jan. 6, 1862 (apostolic constitution *Romani Pontifices*), and united with the Sacred Congregation for the Propagation of the Faith. The congregation was made autonomous by Benedict XV May 1, 1917 (motu proprio *Dei Providentis*), and given wider authority by Pius XI Mar. 25, 1938 (motu proprio *Sancta Dei Ecclesia*). John XXIII appointed six patriarchs, five of Eastern Rites and one of the Roman Rite, to the congregation and

gave them the same rights as cardinals belonging to the body, in March, 1963. Paul VI named representatives of all Eastern-Rite bodies to serve as consultors of the congregation, in November, 1963.

Sacred Congregation for Bishops, formerly called the Sacred Consistorial Congregation: Has functions related in one way or another to bishops and the jurisdictions in which they serve.

Its concerns are: the establishment and changing of dioceses, provinces, military vicariates and other jurisdictions; providing for the naming of bishops and other prelates; studying things concerning the persons, work and pastoral activity of bishops; providing for the care of bishops when they leave office; receiving and studying reports on the conditions of dioceses; general supervision of the holding and recognition of particular councils and conferences of bishops; publishing and circulating pastoral norms and guidelines through conferences of bishops.

It supervises the Pontifical Commission for Latin America and the Pontifical Commission for Migration and Tourism.

OFFICIALS: Cardinal Sebastiano Baggio, prefect; Most Rev. Lucas Moreira Neves, O.P., secretary.

Ex officio members are the prefects of the Council for the Public Affairs of the Church, and of the Congregations for the Doctrine of the Faith, for the Clergy, and for Catholic Education. The substitute secretaries and undersecretaries of these curial departments are ex officio consultors.

BACKGROUND: Established by Sixtus V Jan. 22, 1588 (apostolic constitution *Immensa*); given an extension of powers by St. Pius X June 20, 1908, and Pius XII Aug. 1, 1952 (apostolic constitution *Exsul Familia*).

Sacred Congregation for the Sacraments and Divine Worship: Established in 1975 to replace the Congregation for the Discipline of the Sacraments and the Congregation for Divine Worship.

The congregation consists of two sections — for the sacraments and for divine worship. The former supervises the discipline of the sacraments without prejudice to the competencies of the Sacred Congregation for the Doctrine of the Faith and other curial departments. The latter has general competence over the ritual and pastoral aspects of divine worship in the Roman and other Latin Rites.

OFFICIALS: Cardinal Giuseppe Casoria, prefect; Most Rev. Luigi Dadaglio, secretary (Sacraments section); Most Rev. Virgilio Noe, secretary (Divine Worship section).

BACKGROUND: The congregation was established by Paul VI Aug. 1, 1975 (apostolic constitution, *Constans novis studium*, dated July 11, 1975). Formerly its duties were carried out by the Congregation for the Discipline of the Sacraments (instituted by St. Pius X June 29, 1908) and the Congregation for Divine Worship (established by Paul VI, May 8, 1969, to replace the Congregation of Rites instituted by Sixtus V in 1588).

Sacred Congregation for the Causes of Saints: Handles all matters connected with beatification and canonization procedures, and the preservation of relics. These affairs were formerly under the supervision of the Congregation of Rites.

The congregation carries on its work through three sections or offices.

One section is a juridical office with supervisory responsibility over procedures and examinations conducted to determine the holiness of prospective saints. It includes a medical commission for the study of miracles attributed to the intercession of candidates for sainthood.

A second section, headed by the promoter general of the faith, who is popularly called the "Devil's Advocate," serves the purpose of establishing beyond reasonable doubt the evidence of holiness advanced in support of beatification and canonization causes.

Research and evaluation of documentary evidence figuring in canonization causes are the functions of the historic-hagiographical section.

OFFICIALS: Cardinal Pietro Palazzini, prefect; Most Rev. Traian Crisan, secretary.

BACKGROUND: The functions and title of this congregation were determined by Paul VI May 8, 1969 (apostolic constitution Sacra Rituum Congregatio). Formerly, its duties were carried out by the Congregation of Rites, which was established by Sixtus V in 1588 and affected by legislation of Pius XI in 1930.

Sacred Congregation for the Clergy, formerly called the Sacred Congregation of the Council: Handles matters concerning the persons, work and pastoral ministry of clerics who exercise their apostolate in a diocese. Such clerics are diocesan deacons and priests, and religious who are engaged in ordinary parochial ministry in a diocese.

It carries on its work through three offices.

One office promotes the spiritual growth and formation as well as the professional competence of priests by encouraging the establishment and operation of pastoral institutes and other study opportunities; oversees the general discipline of the clergy, the establishment and conduct of pastoral councils and senates of priests, and resolves controversies among clerics; has a mandate to draw up a set of general principles to direct a better distribution of priests for pastoral service.

A second office, in view of its primary concern for preaching of the word of God, encourages effective apostolic programs and methods, with special emphasis on catechetical and other forms of religious training and formation for the faithful.

A third office has supervisory responsibility over church property and the temporalities of priestly life; among its functions are efforts to provide for the support of the clergy through suitable salary scales, pensions, security and health insurance programs, and other measures.

OFFICIALS: Cardinal Silvio Oddi, prefect; Most Rev. Maximino Romero de Lema, secretary.

BACKGROUND: Established by Pius IV Aug. 2, 1564 (apostolic constitution Alias Nos), under the title, Sacred Congregation of the Cardinals Interpreters of the Council of Trent; affected by legislation of Gregory XIII and Sixtus V.

Sacred Congregation for Religious and Secular Institutes, formerly known as the Sacred Congregation of Religious or for the Affairs of Religious: Has dual competence over institutes of religious, together with societies of the common life without vows, and secular institutes.

One section deals with the affairs of all religious institutes and societies of the common life, and their members. It has authority in matters related to the establishment, general direction and suppression of institutes; general discipline in line with their rules and constitutions; the movement toward renewal and adaptation of institutes in contemporary circumstances; the setting up and encouragement of councils and conferences of major religious superiors for intercommunication and other purposes.

A second section has the same competence over the affairs and members of secular institutes as the first has over religious.

OFFICIALS: Cardinal Eduardo Pironio, prefect; Most. Rev. Augustin Mayer, O.S.B., secretary.

BACKGROUND: Founded by Sixtus V May 27, 1586, with the title, Sacred Congregation for Consultations of Regulars (apostolic constitution Romanus Pontifex); confirmed by the apostolic constitution Immensa Jan. 22, 1588; made part of the Congregation for Consultations of Bishops and other Prelates in 1601; made autonomous by St. Pius X in 1908.

Sacred Congregation for Catholic Education, formerly known as the Sacred Congregation of Seminaries and Universities: Has supervisory competence over institutions and works of Catholic education.

It carries on its work through three offices.

One office handles matters connected with the direction, discipline and temporal administration of seminaries, and with the education of diocesan clergy, religious and members of secular institutes.

A second office oversees Catholic universities, faculties of study and other institutions of higher learning inasmuch as they depend on the authority of the Church; encourages cooperation and mutual assistance among Catholic institutions, and the establishment of Catholic hospices and centers on campuses of non-Catholic institutions.

A third office is concerned in various ways with all Catholic schools below the college-university level, with general questions concerning education and studies, and with the cooperation of conferences of bishops and civil authorities in educational matters.

The congregation supervises Pontifical Works for Priestly Vocations.

OFFICIALS: Cardinal William Wakefield Baum, prefect; Most Rev. Antonio M. Javierre Ortas, S.D.B., secretary.

BACKGROUND: The title and functions of the congregation were defined by Benedict XV Nov. 4, 1915; Pius XI, in 1931 and 1932, and Pius XII, in 1941 and 1949, extended its functions. Its work had previously been carried on by two other congregations erected by Sixtus V in 1588 and Leo XII in 1824.

Sacred Congregation for the Evangelization of Peoples

(for the Propagation of the Faith): Directs and coordinates missionary work throughout the world.

Accordingly, it has competence over those matters which concern all the missions established for the spread of Christ's kingdom. These include: fostering missionary vocations; providing for the training of missionaries in seminaries; assigning missionaries to fields of work; establishing ecclesiastical jurisdictions and proposing candidates to serve them as bishops and in other capacities; encouraging the recruitment and development of indigenous clergy; mobilizing spiritual and financial support for missionary activity.

In general, the varied competence of the congregation extends to most persons and affairs of the Church in areas classified as mission territories.

To promote missionary cooperation, the congregation has a Supreme Council for the Direction of Pontifical Missionary Works. Subject to this council are the general councils of the Missionary Union of the Clergy, the Society for the Propagation of the Faith, the Society of St. Peter the Apostle for Native Clergy, the Society of the Holy Childhood, the International Center of Missionary Animation and the *Fides* news agency.

OFFICIALS: Cardinal Agnelo Rossi, prefect; Most Rev. D. Simon Lourdusamy, secretary.

The heads of the Secretariats for Promoting Christian Unity, for Non-Christians, and for Non-Believers are ex officio members of the congregation.

BACKGROUND: Originated as a commission of cardinals by Gregory XIII and modified by Clement VIII to promote the reconciliation of separated Eastern Christians; erected as a stable congregation by Gregory XV June 22, 1622 (apostolic constitution *Inscrutabili*).

TRIBUNALS

Sacred Apostolic Penitentiary: Has jurisdiction for the internal forum only (sacramental and non-sacramental). It issues decisions on questions of conscience; grants absolutions, dispensations, commutations, sanations and condonations; has charge of non-doctrinal matters pertaining to indulgences.

OFFICIALS: Cardinal Giuseppe Paupini, major penitentiary; Msgr. Luigi de Magistris, regent.

BACKGROUND: Origin dates back to the 12th century; affected by the legislation of many popes; radically reorganized by St. Pius V in 1569; jurisdiction limited to the internal forum by St. Pius X; Benedict XV annexed the Office of Indulgences to it Mar. 25, 1917.

Apostolic Signatura: The principal concerns of this supreme court of the Church are to resolve questions concerning juridical procedure and to supervise the observance of laws and rights at the highest level. It decides the jurisdictional competence of lower courts and has jurisdiction in cases involving personnel and decisions of the Rota. It is the supreme court of the State of Vatican City.

OFFICIAL: Cardinal Aurelio Sabattani, prefect; Msgr. Zenon Grocholewski, secretary.

BACKGROUND: A permanent office of the Signatura has existed since the time of Eugene IV in the 15th century; affected by the legislation of many popes; reorganized by St. Pius X in 1908 and made the supreme tribunal of the Church.

Sacred Roman Rota: The ordinary court of appeal for cases appealed to the Holy See. It is best known for its competence and decisions in cases concerning the validity of marriage.

OFFICIAL: Msgr. Arturo De Jorio, dean.

BACKGROUND: Originated in the Apostolic Chancery; affected by the legislation of many popes; reorganized by St. Pius X in 1908 and further revised by Pius XI in 1934.

SECRETARIATS

Secretariat for Promoting Christian Unity: Handles relations with members of other Christian ecclesial communities; deals with the correct interpretation and execution of the principles of ecumenism; initiates or promotes Catholic ecumenical groups and coordinates on national and international levels the efforts of those promoting Christian unity; undertakes dialogue regarding ecumenical questions and activities with churches and ecclesial communities separated from the Apostolic See; sends Catholic observer-representatives to Christian gatherings, and invites to Catholic gatherings observers of other churches; orders into execution conciliar decrees dealing with ecumenical affairs.

The Commission for Catholic-Jewish Relations is attached to the secretariat.

It has two offices, for the West and for the East. Each office is under the immediate direction of a delegate.

The prefects of the Congregation for the Oriental Churches and of the Congregation for the Evangelization of Peoples are ex officio members of the secretariat. Consultors include the secretaries of these two departments.

OFFICIAL: Cardinal Johannes Willebrands, president.

BACKGROUND: Established by John XXIII June 5, 1960, as a preparatory secretariat of the Second Vatican Council; raised to commission status during the first session of the council in the fall of 1962; this status confirmed Jan. 3, 1966.

Secretariat for Non-Christians: Is concerned with persons who are not Christians but profess some kind of religious faith. Its function is to promote studies and dialogue for the purpose of increasing mutual understanding and respect between Christians and non-Christians.

The Commission for Catholic-Moslem Relations is attached to the secretariat.

The prefect of the Congregation for the Evangelization of Peoples is an ex officio member of the secretariat.

OFFICIALS: Most Rev. Jean Jadot, pro-

president; Msgr. Pietro Rossano, secretary.

BACKGROUND: Established by Paul VI May 19, 1964.

Secretariat for Non-Believers: Studies the background and philosophy of atheism, and initiates and carries on dialogue with non-believers. *OFFICIAL: Most Rev. Paul Poupard, propresident.*

BACKGROUND: Established by Paul VI Apr. 9, 1965.

COUNCILS, COMMISSIONS

Laity, Pontifical Council for: Instituted on an experimental basis by Paul VI Jan. 6, 1967; given permanent status Dec. 10, 1976 (motu proprio *Apostolatus Peragendi*); its competence covers the apostolate of the laity in the Church and the discipline of the laity as such. Members are mostly lay people from different parts of the world and involved in different apostolates. The council is headed by a cardinal. The Council for the Family is attached to the Council while retaining its own identity. Cardinal Opilio Rossi, president.

Justice and Peace, Pontifical Commission: Instituted by Paul VI Jan. 6, 1967, on an experimental basis; reconstituted and made a permanent body Dec. 10, 1976 (motu proprio *Iustitiam et Pacem*). Holy See's organization for examining and studying (from the point of view of doctrine, pastoral practice and the apostolate) problems connected with justice and peace and awakening the sensitivity of the people of God to their responsibility in these areas. Cardinal Bernardin Gantin, president.

Revision of the Code of Oriental Canon Law: Reconstituted by Paul VI in 1972 to replace a former commission dating from July 17, 1935, "to prepare . . . the reform of the Code of Oriental Canon Law, both in the sections already published by . . . four motu proprios" (1,950 canons concerning marriage; processes, religious, church property and terminology; Eastern Rites and persons), "and in the remaining sections which have been completed but not published" (the balance of a total of 2,666 canons); Cardinal Joseph Parecattil, president.

Interpretation of the Decrees of the Second Vatican Council, Commission: Most Rev. Mariano De Nicolo, registrar

Social Communications: Instituted on an experimental basis by Pius XII in 1948; reorganized three times in the 1950's; made permanent commission by John XXIII Feb. 22, 1959; name changed to presgt title Apr. 11, 1964; authorized to implement the *Decree on the Instruments of Social Communication* promulgated by the Second Vatican Council; under supervision of the Secretariat of State and the Council for the Public Affairs of the Church; Most Rev. Andrzej-Maria Deskur, president; Most Rev. Martin J. O'Connor, president emeritus.

Latin America, Commission: Instituted by Pius XII Apr. 19, 1958; placed under supervision of the Congregation for Bishops July, 1969; Cardinal Sebastiano Baggio, president.

Migration and Tourism, Commission: Instituted by Paul VI Mar. 19, 1970, for pastoral assistance to migrants, nomads, tourists, sea and air travelers; placed under the general supervision and direction of the Congregation for Bishops; Cardinal Sebastiano Baggio, president.

Cor Unum, Council: Instituted by Paul VI July 15, 1971, to provide informational and coordinating services for Catholic aid and human development organizations and projects on a worldwide scale; Cardinal Bernardin Gantin, president.

Family, Pontifical Council: Instituted by John Paul II May 9, 1981, replacing the Committee for the Family established Jan. 11, 1973, for "promoting the pastoral care of the family . . . by putting into effect the teachings and directives of the ecclesiastical magisterium, so that Christian families may carry out the educative, evangelizing and apostolic mission to which they have been called"; has special relations with the Pontifical Council for the Laity.

Theological Commission: Instituted by Paul VI Apr. 11, 1969, as an advisory adjunct of no more than 30 theologians to the Congregation for the Doctrine of the Faith; Cardinal Joseph Ratzinger, president. (See separate entry.)

Biblical Commission: Instituted by Leo XIII Oct. 30, 1902; completely restructured by Paul VI June 27, 1971; Cardinal Joseph Ratzinger, president. (See separate entry.)

Abbey of St. Jerome for the Revision and Emendation of the Vulgate: Instituted by Pius XI June 15, 1933, to replace an earlier commission established by St. Pius X; Rev. Vincent Truijen, O.S.B., superior.

Sacred Archeology, Commission: Instituted by Pius IX Jan. 6, 1852; Most Rev. Gennaro Verolino, president.

Historical Sciences, Committee: Instituted by Pius XII Apr. 7, 1954, as a continuation of a commission dating from 1883; Msgr. Michele Maccarrone, president.

Ecclesiastical Archives of Italy, Commission: Instituted by Pius XII Apr. 5, 1955; Msgr. Martino Giusti, president.

Sacred Art in Italy, Commission: Instituted by Pius XI Sept. 1, 1924; Most Rev. Giovanni Fallani, president.

Sanctuaries of Pompei, Loreto and Bari, Commission: Originated by Leo XIII for Sanctuary of Pompei, Loreto placed under commission in 1965, St. Nicholas of Bari, 1980; under supervision of the Congregation for the Clergy; Cardinal Umberto Mozzoni, president.

Russia, Commission: Instituted by Pius XI Apr. 6, 1930, to handle all ecclesiastical affairs of the country; placed under supervision of the Congregation for Extraordinary Ecclesiastical Affairs (now the Council for the Public Affairs of the Church) in 1934, with jurisdiction limited to clergy and faithful of the Roman Rite; under supervision of the Council for the Public Affairs of the Church; Most Rev. Achille Silvestrini, president.

Catholic-Jewish Relations, Commission: Instituted by Paul VI, Oct. 22, 1974, to promote and foster relations of a religious nature between Jews and Christians; attached to the Secretariat for

Christian Unity; Cardinal Johannes Willebrands, president.

Catholic-Moslem Relations, Commission: Instituted by Paul VI, Oct. 22, 1974, to promote, regulate and interpret relations between Catholics and Moslems; attached to the Secretariat for Non-Christians; Most Rev. Jean Jadot, pro-president.

State of Vatican City, Commission: Cardinal Agostino Casaroli, president; Most Rev. Paul Marcinkus pro-president.

Protection of the Historical and Artistic Monuments of the Holy See, Commission: Instituted by Pius XI in 1923, reorganized by Paul VI in 1963; Most Rev. Giovanni Fallani, president.

Preservation of the Faith, Erection of New Churches in Rome: Instituted by Pius XI Aug. 5, 1930, to replace a commission dating from 1902; Cardinal Ugo Poletti, president.

Roman Curia, Commission for Discipline: Most Rev. Rosalio Jose Castillo Lara, president.

Works of Religion, Commission: Instituted by Pius XII June 27, 1942, to bank and administer funds for works of religion; replaced an earlier administration established by Leo XIII in 1887; Most Rev. Paul C. Marcinkus, president.

Study of Organizational and Economic Problems of the Holy See: Council established in 1981 by Pope John Paul II; composed of 15 cardinals — residential archbishops — from countries outside of Italy.

Culture, Pontifical Council: Established in 1982 by Pope John Paul II to facilitate contacts between the saving message of the Gospel and the plurality of cultures. Cardinal Gabriel-Marie Garrone, head of presidential committee; Most Rev. Paul Poupard, president of executive committee.

OFFICES

Prefecture of the Economic Affairs of the Holy See: A financial office which coordinates and supervises administration of the temporalities of the Holy See.

OFFICIALS: Cardinal Giuseppe Caprio, president; Msgr. Giovanni Angelo Abbo, secretary.

BACKGROUND: Established by Paul VI Aug. 15, 1967.

Apostolic Chamber: Administers the temporal goods and rights of the Holy See between the death of one pope and the election of another, in accordance with special laws.

OFFICIALS: Cardinal Paolo Bertoli, chamberlain of the Holy Roman Church; Most Rev. Ettore Cunial, vice-chamberlain.

BACKGROUND: Originated in the 11th century; reorganized by Pius XI in 1934.

Administration of the Patrimony of the Apostolic See: Handles the estate of the Apostolic See under the direction of papal delegates acting with ordinary or extraordinary authorization.

OFFICIALS: Cardinal Agostino Casaroli, president; Most Rev. Lorenzo Antonetti, secretary.

BACKGROUND: Some of its functions date back to 1878; established by Paul VI Aug. 15, 1967.

Prefecture of the Pontifical Household: Oversees the papal chapel — which is at the service of the pope in his capacity as spiritual head of the Church — and the pontifical family — which is at the service of the pope as a sovereign. It arranges papal audiences, has charge of preparing non-liturgical elements of papal ceremonies, makes all necessary arrangements for papal visits and trips outside the Vatican, and settles questions of protocol connected with papal audiences and other formalities.

OFFICIALS: Most Rev. Jacques Martin, prefect; Msgr. Dino Monduzzi, regent.

BACKGROUND: Established by Paul VI Aug. 15, 1967, under the title, Prefecture of the Apostolic Palace; it supplanted the Sacred Congregation for Ceremonies founded by Sixtus V Jan. 22, 1588. The office was updated and reorganized under the present title by Paul VI, Mar. 28, 1968.

Central Statistics Office: Compiles. systematizes and analyzes information on the status and condition of the Church and the needs of its pastoral ministry, from parish to top levels.

The office is one of the organs of the Secretariat of State.

BACKGROUND: Established by Paul VI Aug. 15, 1967.

Aid Office: Distributes alms and aid to the aged, sick, handicapped and other persons in need.

OFFICIAL: Most Rev. Antonio M. Travia, director.

BACKGROUND: The office originated as a charitable office in the time of Bl. Gregory X (1271-1276).

Vatican II Archives: Preserves the acts and other documents of the Second Vatican Council.

Personnel: Set up by Paul VI May 9, 1971, to handle personnel relations in the offices and other agencies of the Vatican.

OFFICIAL: Msgr. Michele Buro.

THEOLOGICAL COMMISSION

Establishment with experimental status of a Theological Commission as an adjunct to the Congregation for the Doctrine of the Faith was announced by Pope Paul VI Apr. 28, 1969. The move had been recommended by the Second Vatican Council and was proposed by the Synod of Bishops in 1967. The commission was removed from experimental status in virtue of a *motu proprio* of John Paul II dated Aug. 6, 1982, and effective the following Oct. 1.

The purpose of the commission is to provide the Doctrinal Congregation with the consultative and advisory services of theologians and scriptural and liturgical experts representative of various schools of thought. The international membership is restricted to 30, and the ordinary term of membership is five years (renewable).

Membership

The commission is headed by Cardinal Joseph Ratzinger, prefect of the Doctrinal Congregation. Msgr. Philippe Delhaye of Belgium is secretary. Members appointed to five-year terms in 1980 and listed in the 1983 edition of *Annuario Pontificio* were as follows.

Barnabas Ahern, C.P. (U.S.); Juan Alfaro, S.J. (Spain); Catalino Arevalo (Philippines); Hans Urs von Balthasar (Switzerland); Carlo Caffara (Italy); Giuseppe Colombo (Italy); Ives Congar, O.P. (France); Wilhelm Ernst (West Germany); Pierre Eyt (France); Ivan Fucek (Yugoslavia); Ferenc Gal (Hungary); Edouard Hamel, S.J. (Canada); Walter Kasper (West Germany); Hachem Elie Khalife, O.L.M. (Lebanon); Bishop Bonaventure Kloppenburg, O.F.M. (Brazil); Michael Ledwith (Ireland); Karl Lehmann (West Germany); Jorge Medina Estevez (Chile); Bp. John Onaiyekan (Nigeria); Carl Peter (U.S.); Candido Pozo, S.J. (Spain); Walter Principe, C.S.B. (Canada); Ignacy Rozycki (Poland); Heinz Schurmann (West Germany); Bernard Sesboue, S.J. (France); John Thornhill, S.M. (Australia); Cipriano Vagaggini, O.S.B. (Italy); Christophe von Schonborn, O.P. (Switzerland); Jan Walgrave, O.P. (Belgium).

Meetings

The commission met for the first time Oct. 6 to 8, 1969, for organizational purposes and the assignment of subcommissions to studies on the priesthood, the theology of hope, unity of faith and pluralism in theology, the criteria of moral knowledge, and collegiality.

Week-long general assemblies, for discussion and decision on subjects of individual and group research have been held annually, except in 1978, since 1969.

Twenty-six members attending the second meeting, Oct. 5 to 10, 1970, discussed reports on the priestly ministry and collegiality. Views were exchanged about the question of ordaining married men, but marriage was ruled out for already ordained priests wanting to continue in the ministry. With respect to collegiality, no doubt was raised about the pope's authority to act independently in the Church; the consensus, however, was that he would be prudent to engage in wide consultation before acting.

By early 1971, the commission prepared the basis of a feasible working paper on the priesthood for the Synod of Bishops, which met for the third time in the fall. The ordination of women was one of the subjects covered, but it did not figure significantly in discussion by the commission because the issue was not considered urgent. Agreement was reported on two points: tradition militated against ordination but permitted a form of diaconal ordination with a rite and purpose distinctive and proper to women.

Various Studies

Pluralism in theology — concerning different ways of treating, presenting and expressing in practice the unity of faith — was the main subject under consideration at the fourth general assembly Oct. 5 to 11, 1972. The topic had been under study since the first meeting of the commission in 1969.

The October, 1973, meeting, attended by 21 members, completed work on a statement concerning apostolic succession and ordination to holy orders. The necessary sacramental sign of both, the statement said, is the imposition of hands by successors of the Apostles acting in accord with the intention of the Church.

The results of research on Christian morality were discussed at the 1974 meeting, and several articles on the subject were published in 1975.

The majority of members attending the Sept. 25 to Oct. 1, 1975, meeting approved a number of conclusions concerning the relationship between "the mandate given to the ecclesiastical magisterium (the teaching authority of the Church) to protect divine revelation and the task given to theologians to investigate and explain the doctrine of the faith." These conclusions were published by the U.S. Catholic Conference in April, 1977.

Christian salvation and human progress, centering on the nature of and relationship between evangelization and human liberation, was the subject of the meeting held Oct. 4 to 9, 1976. The subject was connected with earlier consideration of the matter by the Synod of Bishops, and also with the contents and tenor of the *Pastoral Constitution on the Church in the Modern World* issued by the Second Vatican Council.

The meeting of Dec. 1 to 6, 1977, focused attention on pastoral aspects of Christian marriage and agreed on a summary of conclusions which: (1) reaffirmed the indissolubility of marriage and the stance of the Church against divorce; (2) declared that the Church should not witness the marriage of Catholics who have rejected the faith and the sacramental nature of marriage.

Various aspects of Christology were under consideration from 1979 to 1981.

The 1982 meeting was devoted entirely to the preparation of material related to the Sacrament of Reconciliation, the theme of the 1983 assembly of the Synod of Bishops. The theology of reconciliation was the main concern of the commission, whose findings were made available to the Permanent Secretariat of the Synod.

BIBLICAL COMMISSION

The Pontifical Biblical Commission, which has been instrumental in directing the course of Catholic biblical scholarship, was established by Leo XIII Oct. 30, 1902, with the apostolic letter *Vigilantiae Studiique,* at a time when biblical studies were open to great promise as well as to the serious threat of Modernism.

The commission was ordered to promote biblical studies; to safeguard the correct interpretation of Scripture, in the pattern of the rule of faith and against the background of sound scholarship; to state positions which had to be held by Catholics on biblical questions; to indicate questions requiring further study and/or those which were open to the judgment of competent scholars. The commission was also authorized — by St. Pius X in 1904, Pius XI in 1924 and 1931, and Pius X II in 1942 — to set up standards for biblical studies and to grant degrees in Sacred Scripture.

The commission issued 23 decrees or decisions between 1905 and 1953; letters on the scientific study of the Bible (1941) and the Pentateuch

(1948); instructions on teaching Scripture in seminaries (1950), biblical associations (1955), and the historical truth of the Gospels (1964).

Authority of Decisions

Pope St. Pius X stated the authority of decisions of the commission in the letter *Illibatae,* which he issued June 29, 1910, on his own initiative:

"All are bound in conscience to submit to the decisions of the Pontifical Biblical Commission pertaining to doctrine, whether already issued or to be issued in the future, in the same way as to the decrees of the Sacred Congregations (of the Roman Curia) approved by the Pontiff; nor can they avoid the stigma both of disobedience and temerity or be free from grave sin who by any spoken or written words impugn these decisions."

Decisions of the commission regarding points of doctrine are not infallible of themselves. They require religious assent, however, so long as there is no positive evidence that they are wrong. They do not close the door to continuing investigation and study.

New Norms

The commission was reorganized June 27, 1971, in line with directives issued by Paul VI on his own initiative under the title *Sedula Cura.*

Fifteen new norms changed its structure from a virtually independent office of cardinals aided by lifetime consultors into a group consisting ordinarily of 20 biblical scholars with five-year terms (renewable) linked with the Congregation for the Doctrine of the Faith. Functionally, however, it remains the same.

The commission:
• receives questions and studies topics referred to it by a variety of sources, from the pope to Catholic universities and biblical associations;

• is required to meet in plenary session at least once a year and to submit conclusions reached in such meetings to the pope and the Congregation for the Doctrine of the Faith;

• is under directive to promote relationships with non-Catholic as well as Catholic institutes of biblical studies;

• is to be consulted before any new norms on biblical matters are issued;

• retains its authorization to confer academic degrees in biblical studies.

Membership

Cardinal Joseph Ratzinger, prefect of the Congregation for the Doctrine of the Faith, is president of the commission. The other members, as reported in the 1983 edition of *Annuario Pontificio,* are as follows.

Jose Alonso-Diaz, S.J.; Jean-Dominique Barthelemy, O.P.; Pierre Benoit, O.P.; Henri Cazelles, P.S.S.; Guy Couturier, C.S.C.; Msgr. Alfons Deissler; Ignace de la Potterie, S.J.; Jacques Dupont, O.S.B.; Joachim Gnilka; John Greehy; Pierre Grelot; Augustine Jankowski, O.S.B.; Cardinal. Carlo M. Martini, S.J.; Antonio Moreno Casamitjana; Laurent Nare; Msgr. Jerome D. Quinn (U.S.); Matthew Vellanickal; Benjamin Wambacq, O.Praem.

Recent Studies

Since its plenary assembly of April, 1980, the commission has focused attention on the hermeneutic problem in Christology, i.e., the interpretation of what Scripture says about the nature and mission of Jesus.

At its 1979 meeting, the commission initiated a study of acculturation in the Old and New Testaments. The purpose of the study, as stated by Pope John Paul, was "to establish the distinction" between what is culturally conditioned (language, manner of expression, historical circumstances) "and what must always retain its value" (truth relating to salvation) in the words and events used to communicate divine revelation in the Bible.

COLLEGE OF CARDINALS

Cardinals are chosen by the pope to serve as his principal assistants and advisers in the central administration of church affairs. Collectively, they form the Sacred College of Cardinals. Provisions regarding their selection, rank, roles and prerogatives are detailed in Canons 349 to 359 of the revised Code of Canon Law, effective Nov. 27, 1983.

The college evolved gradually from synods of Roman clergy with whose assistance popes directed church affairs in the first 11 centuries. The first cardinals, in about the sixth century, were priests of the leading churches of Rome who were assigned liturgical, advisory and administrative duties with the Holy See, and the regional deacons of Rome.

History of the College

For all cardinals except Eastern patriarchs, membership in the college involves aggregation to the clergy of Rome. This aggregation is signified by the assignment to each cardinal, except the patriarchs, of a special or titular church in Rome.

The Sacred College of Cardinals was constituted in its present form and categories of membership in the 12th century. Before that time the pope had a body of advisers selected from among the bishops of dioceses neighboring Rome, priests and deacons of Rome. The college was given definite form in 1150, and in 1179 the selection of cardinals was reserved exclusively to the pope. Sixtus V fixed the number at 70, in 1586. John XXIII set aside this rule when he increased membership at the 1959 and subsequent consistories. The number of cardinals reached an all-time high of 145 under Paul VI in 1973. The number of cardinals entitled to participate in papal elections was limited to 120.

In 1567 the title of cardinal was reserved to members of the college; previously it had been used by priests attached to parish churches of Rome and by the leading clergy of other notable churches. The Code of Canon Law promulgated in 1918 decreed that all cardinals must be priests. Previously there had been lay cardinals (e.g., Cardinal Giacomo Antonelli, d. 1876, Secretary of

State to Pius IX). John XXIII provided in the motu proprio *Cum Gravissima* Apr. 15, 1962, that cardinals would henceforth be bishops; this provision is included in the revised Code of Canon Law.

Pope Paul VI placed age limits on the functions of cardinals in the apostolic letter *Ingravescentem Aetatem*, dated Nov. 21, 1970, and effective as of Jan. 1, 1971. At 80, they cease to be members of curial departments and offices, and become ineligible to take part in papal elections. They retain membership in the College of Cardinals, however, with relevant rights and privileges.

Three Categories

The three categories of members of the college are cardinal bishops, cardinal priests and cardinal deacons.

Cardinal bishops include the six titular bishops of the suburban sees of Rome and Eastern patriarchs.

First in rank are the titular bishops of the suburban sees, neighboring Rome: Ostia, Palestrina, Porto and Santa Rufina, Albano, Velletri, Frascati, Sabina and Poggio Mirteto. The dean of the college holds the title of the See of Ostia as well as his other suburban see. These cardinal bishops are engaged in full-time service in the central administration of church affairs in departments of the Roman Curia.

Full recognition is given in the revised Code of Canon Law to the position of Eastern patriarchs as the heads of ancient liturgies and of sees of apostolic origin. Because of their patriarchal dignity and titles, which antedate the dignity and titles of cardinals, they are not aggregated to the Roman clergy and are not, like other cardinals, given title to Roman churches. The patriarchs are assigned rank among the cardinals in order of seniority, following the suburban titleholders.

Cardinal priests, who were formerly in charge of leading churches in Rome, are bishops whose dioceses are outside Rome.

Cardinal deacons, who were formerly chosen according to regional divisions of Rome, are titular bishops assigned to full-time service in the Roman Curia.

The officers of the college are the dean and sub-dean, a chamberlain and a secretary. Pope Paul decreed Feb. 26, 1965, that the dean and sub-dean were to be elected by the cardinal bishops. He set this ruling aside in December, 1977, however, when he appointed Cardinals Carlo Confalonieri and Paolo Marella, respectively, as dean and sub-dean.

Selection and Duties

Cardinals are selected by the pope and are inducted into the college in a three-step process. Their nomination is announced and approved at a meeting (secret consistory) attended only by the pope and cardinals who are already members of the college; word of their election and confirmation is then communicated to the cardinals designate by means of a document called a *biglietto*. In successive and more public ceremonies, they receive the cardinalatial red biretta and ring, and concelebrate Mass with the pope and their fellow cardinals.

Cardinals under the age of 80: elect the pope when the Holy See becomes vacant (see Papal Election), and are major administrators of church affairs, serving in one or more departments of the Roman Curia. Cardinals in charge of agencies of the Roman Curia and Vatican City are asked to submit their resignation from office to the Pope on reaching the age of 75. All cardinals enjoy a number of special rights and privileges. Their title, while symbolic of high honor, does not signify any extension of the powers of holy orders. They are called princes of the Church.

A **cardinal in pectore** is one whose selection has been made by the pope but whose name has not been disclosed; he has no title, rights or duties until such disclosure is made, at which time he takes precedence from the time of the secret selection.

BIOGRAPHIES OF CARDINALS

Biographies of the cardinals, as of July 10, 1983, are given below in alphabetical order. For historical notes, order of seniority and geographical distribution of cardinals, see separate entries.

An asterisk indicates cardinals ineligible to take part in papal elections.

Alfrink,* Bernard Jan: b. July 5, 1900, Nijkerk, Netherlands; ord. priest Aug. 15, 1924; professor of Sacred Scripture at Utrecht major seminary, 1933; consultor to Pontifical Biblical Commission, Rome, 1944; professor at Catholic University of Nijmegen, 1945; ord. titular archbishop of Tiana and coadjutor archbishop of Utrecht, July 17, 1951; archbishop of Utrecht, 1955-75; cardinal Mar. 28, 1960; titular church, St. Joachim. Former archbishop of Utrecht.

Antonelli,* Ferdinando Giuseppe, O.F.M.: b. July 14, 1896, Subbiano, Italy; solemnly professed in Order of Friars Minor, Apr. 7, 1914; ord. priest July 25, 1922; taught church history, 1928-32, and Christian archeology, 1932-65, at Antonianum; rector magnificus of Antonianum, 1937-43, 1953-59; definitor general of Friars Minor, 1939-45; held various offices in Roman Curia; secretary of Congregation of Rites, 1965-69, and Congregation for Causes of Saints, 1969-73; ord. titular archbishop of Idicra, Mar. 19, 1966; cardinal Mar. 5, 1973; titular church, San Sebastian (on the Palatine).

Aponte Martinez, Luis: b. Aug. 4, 1922, Lajas, Puerto Rico; ord. priest Apr. 10, 1950; parish priest at Ponce; ord. titular bishop of Lares and auxiliary of Ponce, Oct. 12, 1960; bishop of Ponce, 1963-64; archbishop of San Juan, Nov. 4, 1964; cardinal Mar. 5, 1973; titular church, St. Mary Mother of Providence (in Monteverde). Archbishop of San Juan, president of Puerto Rican Episcopal Conference, member of:

Congregation: Causes of Saints.

Aramburu, Juan Carlos: b. Feb. 11, 1912, Reduccion, Argentina; ord. priest in Rome, Oct. 28, 1934; ord. titular bishop of Plataea and auxiliary of Tucuman, Argentina, Dec. 15, 1946; bishop, 1953, and first archbishop, 1957, of Tucuman; titular archbishop of Torri di Bizacena and coadjutor archbishop of Buenos Aires, June 14, 1967; archbishop of Buenos Aires, Apr. 22, 1975; cardinal May 24, 1976; titular church, St. John Baptist of the Florentines. Archbishop of Buenos Aires, ordinary for Eastern Rite Catholics in Brazil without ordinaries of their own rites, member of:

Congregations: Oriental Churches, Catholic Education.

Office: Prefecture of Economic Affairs.

Arns, Paulo Evaristo, O.F.M.: b. Sept. 14, 1921, Forquilhinha, Brazil; ord. priest Nov. 30, 1945; held various teaching posts; director of *Sponsa Christi*, monthly review for religious, and of the Franciscan publication center in Brazil; ord. titular bishop of Respetta and auxiliary of Sao Paulo, July 3, 1966; archbishop of Sao Paulo, Oct. 22, 1970; cardinal Mar. 5, 1973; titular church, St. Anthony of Padua (in Via Tuscolana). Archbishop of Sao Paulo, member of:

Congregation: Sacraments and Divine Worship;

Secretariat: Non-Believers.

Bafile,* Corrado: b. July 4, 1903, L'Aquila, Italy; practiced law in Rome for six years before beginning studies for priesthood; ord. priest Apr. 11, 1936; served in Vatican secretariat of state, 1939-59; ord. titular archbishop of Antiochia in Pisidia, Mar. 19, 1960; apostolic nuncio to Germany, 1960-75; pro-prefect of Congregation for Causes of Saints, July 18, 1975; cardinal May 24, 1976; deacon, S. Maria (in Portico); prefect of Congregation for Causes of Saints, 1976-80. Member of:

Congregation: Clergy;

Tribunal: Apostolic Signatura.

Baggio, Sebastiano: b. May 16, 1913, Rosa, Italy; ord. priest Dec. 21, 1935; ord. titular archbishop of Ephesus, July 26, 1953; served in Vatican diplomatic corps, 1953-69; nuncio to Chile, apostolic delegate to Canada, nuncio to Brazil; cardinal Apr. 28, 1969; archbishop of Cagliari, 1969-73; entered order of cardinal bishops as titular bishop of Velletri, Dec. 12, 1974. Prefect of Congregation for Bishops, 1973, member of:

Council for Public Affairs of Church;

Congregations: Doctrine of the Faith, Religious and Secular Institutes, Catholic Education, Evangelization of Peoples;

Commissions: Latin America (President), Migration and Tourism (President), Sanctuaries of Pompei, Loreto, and Bari, Interpretation of Decrees of Vatican II;

Office: Patrimony of Holy See.

Ballestrero, Anastasio Alberto, O.C.D.: b. Oct. 3, 1913, Genoa, Italy; professed in Order of Discalced Carmelites, 1929; ord. priest June 6, 1936; provincial, 1942-48, and superior general, 1955-67, of Carmelites; author of many books on Christian life; ord. archbishop of Bari, Feb. 2, 1974; archbishop of Turin, Aug. 1, 1977; cardinal June 30, 1979; titular church, S. Maria (sopra Minerva). Archbishop of Turin, president of the Italian Episcopal Conference, 1979, member of:

Congregation: Religious and Secular Institutes.

Baum, William Wakefield: b. Nov. 21, 1926, Dallas, Tex.; moved to Kansas City, Mo., at an early age; ord. priest May 12, 1951; executive director of U.S. bishops commission for ecumenical and interreligious affairs, 1964-69; attended Second Vatican Council as *peritus* (expert adviser); ord. bishop of Springfield-Cape Girardeau, Mo., Apr. 6, 1970; archbishop of Washington, D.C., 1973-80; cardinal May 24, 1976; titular church, Holy Cross (on the Via Flaminia). Prefect of Congregation for Catholic Education, 1980, grand chancellor of Pontifical Gregorian University, and member of:

Council for Public Affairs of the Church;

Congregations: Doctrine of the Faith, Bishops, Evangelization of Peoples;

Secretariat: Non-Believers;

Office: Administration of Patrimony of Holy See;

Commission: Council for Laity.

Beras Rojas, Octavio Antonio: b. Nov. 16, 1906, Seibo, Dominican Republic; ord. priest Aug. 13, 1933; founded national Catholic youth movement; ord. titular archbishop of Euchaitae and coadjutor archbishop of Santo Domingo, Aug. 12, 1945; archbishop of Santo Domingo, 1961-81; cardinal May 24, 1976; titular church, San Sisto. Former archbishop of Santo Domingo, member of:

Congregation: Bishops.

Bernardin, Joseph L.: b. Apr. 2, 1928, Columbia, S.C.; ord. priest Apr. 26, 1952; ord. titular bishop of Lugura and auxiliary bishop of Atlanta, Ga., Apr. 26, 1966; general secretary, 1968-72, and president, 1974-77, of NCCB/USCC; archbishop of Cincinnati, 1972-82; archbishop of Chicago, July 10, 1982, installed Aug. 25, 1982; cardinal Feb. 2, 1983; titular church, Jesus the Divine Worker. Archbishop of Chicago, member of:

Congregation: Sacraments and Divine Worship.

Bertoli, Paolo: b. Feb. 1, 1908, Poggio Garfagnana, Italy; ord. priest Aug. 15, 1930; entered diplomatic service of the Holy See, serving in nunciatures in Yugoslavia, France, Haiti and Switzerland; ord. titular archbishop of Nicomedia, May 11, 1952; apostolic delegate to Turkey (1952-53), nuncio to Colombia (1953-59), Lebanon (1959-60), France (1960-69); cardinal Apr. 28, 1969; prefect of Congregation for Causes of Saints, 1969-73; entered order of cardinal bishops as titular bishop of Frascati, June 30, 1979. Chamberlain (Camerlengo) of Holy Roman Church, 1979, member of:

Council for Public Affairs of Church:

Congregations: Doctrine of the Faith, Bishops, Oriental Churches, Evangelization of Peoples;

Secretariat: Non-Believers;

Tribunal; Apostolic Signatura;

Commission: Latin America, State of Vatican City.

Brandao Vilela, Avelar: b. June 13, 1912, Vicosa, Brazil; ord. priest Oct. 27, 1935; professor and spiritual director at diocesan seminary at Aracaju; ord. bishop of Petrolina, Oct. 27, 1946; archbishop of Teresina, Nov. 5, 1955; established 20 social centers and a radio station; introduced agrarian reform of church properties; erected the Institute of Catechetics: archbishop of Sao Salvador da Bahia, Mar. 25, 1971; president of CELAM, 1967-72; co-president of Medellin Conference, 1968; cardinal Mar. 5, 1973; titular church, Sts. Boniface and Alexius. Archbishop of Sao Salvador da Bahia, member of:

Congregations: Clergy, Causes of Saints, Catholic Education:

Commission: Latin America.

Bueno y Monreal, Jose Maria: b. Sept. 11, 1904, Zaragoza, Spain; ord. priest Mar. 19, 1927; ord. bishop of Jaca, Mar. 19, 1946; bishop of Vitoria, May 13, 1950; titular archbishop of Antioch in Pisidia and coadjutor archbishop of Seville, Oct. 27, 1954; archbishop of Seville, 1957-82; cardinal Dec. 15, 1958; titular church, Sts. Vitus, Modestus and Crescentia. Former archbishop of Seville.

Caprio, Giuseppe: b. Nov. 15, 1914, Lapio, Italy; ord. priest Dec. 17, 1938; served in diplomatic missions in China (1947-51, when Vatican diplomats were expelled by communists), Belgium (1951-54), and South Vietnam (1954-56); internuncio in China with residence at Taiwan, 1959-67; ord. titular archbishop of Apollonia, Dec. 17, 1961; pro-nuncio in India, 1967-69; secretary, 1969-77, and president, 1979-81, of Administration of Patrimony of Holy See; substitute secretary of state, 1977-79; cardinal June 30, 1979; deacon, St. Mary Auxiliatrix in Via Tuscolana. President of Prefecture of Economic Affairs of the Holy See, 1981, member of:

Council for Public Affairs of Church;

Congregations: Bishops, Causes of Saints, Evangelization of Peoples.

Carberry, John J.: b July 31, 1904, Brooklyn, N.Y.; ord. priest July 28, 1929; ord. titular bishop of Elis and coadjutor bishop of Lafayette, Ind., July 25, 1956; bishop of Lafayette, Nov. 20, 1957; bishop of Columbus, Ohio, Jan. 16, 1965; archbishop of St. Louis, Mo., 1968-79; cardinal Apr. 28, 1969; titular church, St. John Baptist de Rossi (Via Latina). Former archbishop of St. Louis, member of:

Congregation: Evangelization of Peoples.

Carpino, Francesco: b. May 18, 1905, Palazzolo Acreide, Italy; ord. priest Aug. 14, 1927; ord. titular archbishop of Nicomedia and coadjutor archbishop of Monreale, Apr. 8, 1951; archbishop of Monreale, 1951-61; titular archbishop of Sardica, Jan. 19, 1961; assessor of Consistorial Congregation, 1961; pro-prefect of Congregation of the Council, Apr. 7, 1967; cardinal June 26, 1967; archbishop of Palermo, 1967-70; entered order of cardinal bishops as titular bishop of Albano, Jan. 27, 1978. Referendary of the Congregation of Bishops, 1970, and member of:

Council for Public Affairs of the Church;

Congregation: Causes of Saints;

Tribunal: Apostolic Signatura.

Carter, Gerald Emmett: b. Mar. 1, 1912, Montreal, Canada; ord. priest May 22, 1937; engaged in pastoral and teaching ministry in Montreal; founder and president of St. Joseph Teachers' College and co-founder and director of Thomas More Institute for adult education; ord. titular bishop of Altiburo and auxiliary bishop of London, Ont., Feb. 2, 1962; bishop of London, 1964-78; vice president,

1971-73, and president, 1975-77, of Canadian Conference of Catholic Bishops; archbishop of Toronto, Apr. 27, 1978; cardinal June 30, 1979; titular church, St. Mary (in Traspontina). Archbishop of Toronto, member of:

Secretariats: Christian Unity, Non-Christians.

Casaroli, Agostino: b. Nov. 24, 1914, Castel San Giovanni, Italy; ord. priest May 27, 1937; entered service of Vatican secretariat of state, 1940; undersecretary, 1961-67, of the Congregation for Extraordinary Ecclesiastical Affairs, and secretary, 1967-79, of its successor the Council for Public Affairs of the Church; ord. titular archbishop of Cartagina, July 16, 1967; chief negotiator for the Vatican with East European communist governments; missions included visits to Hungary, Yugoslavia, Poland, Czechoslovakia, Bulgaria; headed Vatican delegations to several UN conferences and the Helsinki Conference (1975); Pro-Secretary of State and Pro-Prefect of Council for Public Affairs of the Church, Apr. 28, 1979; cardinal June 30, 1979; titular church, the Twelve Apostles. Secretary of State and prefect of Council for Public Affairs of the Church, July 1, 1979, president of Administration of Patrimony of Holy See, 1981, and of Pontifical Commission for Vatican City and member of:

Congregations: Doctrine of the Faith, Bishops;

Secretariat: Non-Believers;

Commission: Institute for Works of Religion.

Casoria, Giuseppe: b. Oct. 1, 1908, Acerra, Italy; ord. priest Dec. 21, 1930; jurist; Roman Curia official from 1937; under-secretary, 1959-69, and secretary, 1969-73, of Congregation for Sacraments and Divine Worship; secretary of Congregation for Causes of Saints, 1973-81; ord. titular archbishop of Vescovia, Feb. 13, 1972; pro-prefect of Congregation for Sacraments and Divine Worship, 1981-83; cardinal Feb. 2, 1983; deacon, St. Joseph on Via Trionfale. Prefect of Congregation for Sacraments and Divine Worship, 1983, member of:

Congregations: Doctrine of the Faith, Causes of Saints.

Cé, Marco: b. July 8, 1925, Izano, Italy; ord. priest Mar. 27, 1948; taught sacred scripture and dogmatic theology at seminary in his home diocese of Crema; rector of seminary, 1957; presided over diocesan liturgical commission, preached youth retreats; ord. titular bishop of Vulturia, May 17, 1970; auxiliary bishop of Bologna, 1970-76; general ecclesiastical assistant of Italian Catholic Action, 1976-78; patriarch of Venice, Dec. 7, 1978; cardinal June 30, 1979; titular church, St. Mark. Patriarch of Venice, member of:

Congregations: Clergy, Catholic Education.

Ciappi, Mario Luigi, O.P.: b. Oct. 6, 1909, Florence, Italy; ord. priest Mar. 26, 1932; papal theologian from 1955, serving Pius XII, John XXIII and Paul VI; ord. titular bishop of Misenum June 18, 1977; cardinal June 27, 1977; deacon, Our Lady of the Sacred Heart (in Piazza Navona). Pro-theologian of pontifical household, member of:

Congregation: Causes of Saints.

Civardi, Ernesto: b. Oct. 21, 1906, Fossarmato, Italy; ord. priest June 29, 1930; assistant rector of Pontifical Lombard Seminary in Rome; held vari-

ous curial offices; undersecretary, 1953-67, and secretary, 1967-79, of the Congregation for Bishops (known as the Consistorial Congregation until 1967); ord. titular archbishop of Sardica, July 16, 1967; secretary of College of Cardinals, 1967-79; filled office of secretary at 1978 conclaves which elected Popes John Paul I and John Paul II; cardinal June 30, 1979; deacon, St. Theodore. Member of:
Congregations: Causes of Saints, Evangelization of Peoples;
Tribunal: Apostolic Signatura.

Colombo,* Giovanni: b. Dec. 6, 1902, Caronno, Italy; ord. priest May 29, 1926; rector of Milan Seminary, 1953; ord. titular bishop of Filippopoli and auxiliary bishop of Milan, Dec. 7, 1960; archbishop of Milan, 1963-79; cardinal Feb. 22, 1965; titular church, Sts. Sylvester and Martin (in Montibus). Former archbishop of Milan.

Confalonieri,* Carlo: b. July 25, 1893, Seveso, Italy; ord. priest Mar. 18, 1916; private secretary to Pius XI for 17 years, to Pius XII for two years; ord. archbishop of L'Aquila, May 4, 1941; transferred to titular archbishopric of Nicopoli al Nesto, Feb. 22, 1950; cardinal Dec. 15, 1958; titular bishop of suburban see of Palestrina, Mar. 14, 1972, when he entered order of cardinal bishops, and Ostia, Dec. 12, 1977, when he was named dean of College of Cardinals; prefect of Congregation for Bishops, 1967-73; sub-dean of college of cardinals, 1974-77. Archpriest of Patriarchal Liberian Basilica, dean of College of Cardinals, Dec. 12, 1977.

Cooke, Terence J.: b. Mar. 1, 1921, New York, N.Y.; ord. priest Dec. 1, 1945; ord. titular bishop of Summa and auxiliary bishop of New York, Dec. 13, 1965; archbishop of New York, Mar. 2, 1968; military vicar for the U.S.; cardinal Apr. 28, 1969; titular church, Sts. John and Paul. Archbishop of New York, military vicar of U.S., member of:
Congregations: Bishops, Oriental Churches, Evangelization of Peoples;
Commission: Migration and Tourism.

Cooray,* Thomas B., O.M.I.: b. Dec. 28, 1901, Periyamulla Negombo, Ceylon (now Sri Lanka); ord. priest June 23, 1929; ord. titular archbishop of Preslavo, Mar. 7, 1946; coadjutor archbishop of Colombo, Sri Lanka, 1946-47; succeeded as archbishop of Colombo, July 26, 1947 (retired 1976); cardinal Feb. 22, 1965; titular church, Sts. Nereus and Achilleus. Former archbishop of Colombo, Sri Lanka.

Cordeiro, Joseph: b. Jan. 19, 1918, Bombay, India; ord. priest Aug. 24, 1946; served in educational and other diocesan posts at Karachi, Pakistan; ord. archbishop of Karachi, Aug. 24, 1958, the first native-born prelate in that see; cardinal Mar. 5, 1973; titular church, St. Andrew Apostle ("de Hortis"). Archbishop of Karachi, member of:
Congregation: Religious and Secular Institutes;
Secretariat: Non-Christians;
Commission: Pontifical Council Cor Unum.

Corripio Ahumada, Ernesto: b. June 29, 1919, Tampico, Mexico; ord. priest Oct. 25, 1942, in Rome, where he remained until almost the end of World War II; taught and held various positions in local seminary of Tampico, 1945-50; ord. titular

bishop of Zapara and auxiliary bishop of Tampico, Mar. 19, 1953; bishop of Tampico, 1956-67; archbishop of Antequera, 1967-76; archbishop of Puebla de los Angeles, 1976-77; archbishop of Mexico City and primate of Mexico, July 19, 1977; cardinal June 30, 1979; titular church, Mary Immaculate al Tiburtino. Archbishop of Mexico City, member of:
Congregation: Sacraments and Divine Worship;
Commission: Latin America.

Danneels, Godfried: b. June 4, 1933, Kanegem, Belgium; ord. priest Aug. 17, 1957; professor of liturgy and sacramental theology at Catholic University of Louvain, 1969-77; ord. bishop of Antwerp Dec. 18, 1977; app. archbishop of Mechelen-Brussel, Dec. 21, 1979; installed Jan. 4, 1980; elected member of general secretariat of Synod of Bishops, 1981; cardinal Feb. 2, 1983; titular church, St. Anastasia. Archbishop of Mechelen-Brussel, military vicar of Belgium, president of Belgian Episcopal Conference, member of:
Congregation: Catholic Education.

Darmojuwono, Justin: b. Nov. 2, 1914, Godean, Indonesia; ord. priest May 25, 1947; ord. archbishop of Semarang, Apr. 6, 1964 (resigned July 3, 1981, for health reasons); cardinal June 26, 1967; titular church, Most Holy Names of Jesus and Mary. Former archbishop of Semarang, military vicar of Indonesia, member of:
Congregation: Sacraments and Divine Worship.

De Araujo Sales, Eugenio: b. Nov. 8, 1920, Acari, Brazil; ord. priest Nov. 21, 1943; ord. titular bishop of Tibica and auxiliary bishop of Natal, Aug. 15, 1954; archbishop of Sao Salvador, 1968-71; cardinal Apr. 28, 1969; titular church, St. Gregory VII. Archbishop of Rio de Janeiro (1971), ordinary for Eastern Rite Catholics in Brazil without ordinaries of their own rites, member of:
Congregations: Bishops, Clergy, Evangelization of Peoples;
Commissions: Social Communications, Council for Culture.

Dearden, John Francis.: b. Oct. 15, 1907, Valley Falls, R. I.; ord. priest Dec. 8, 1932; ord. titular bishop of Sarepta and coadjutor bishop of Pittsburgh, May 18, 1948; bishop of Pittsburgh, Dec. 22, 1950; archbishop of Detroit, 1958-80; first president of the National Conference of Catholic Bishops and the United States Catholic Conference, 1966-71; cardinal Apr. 28, 1969; titular church, St. Pius X (alla Balduina). Former archbishop of Detroit, member of:
Congregation: Sacraments and Divine Worship.

De Furstenberg, Maximilien: b. Oct. 23, 1904, Heerlen, Netherlands; ord. priest Aug. 9, 1931; ord. titular archbishop of Palto and apostolic delegate to Japan, Apr. 25, 1949; internuncio, 1952, when Japan established diplomatic relations with the Vatican; apostolic delegate to Australia, New Zealand and Oceania, Feb. 11, 1960; nuncio to Portugal, 1962-67; cardinal June 26, 1967; titular church, Most Sacred Heart of Jesus (a Castro Pretorio); prefect of the Congregation for the Oriental Churches, 1969-73. Grand Master of Equestrian Order of Holy Sepulchre of Jerusalem, Chamberlain of the Sacred College of Cardinals, 1983, member of:

Council for Public Affairs of Church; Congregations: Bishops, Causes of Saints, Evangelization of Peoples; Commissions: State of Vatican City, Institute for Works of Religion.

De Lubac,* Hanri, S.J.: b. Feb. 20, 1896, Cambrai, France; entered Society of Jesus, October, 1913; ord. priest August, 1917; taught fundamental theology and history of religions at the Theology Faculty of Lyons from 1929 to the early 50s when he was dismissed because of misunderstanding of his book *The Supernatural,* intended to re-emphasize the doctrine on supernatural destiny; reinstated to his teaching post by Pope John XXIII; chief consultor of preparatory theological commission for Vatican II and *peritus* for Council itself; appointed member of International Theological Commission by Paul VI; cardinal Feb. 2, 1983, with permission to decline episcopal ordination; deacon, St. Mary in Domnica.

do Nascimento, Alexandre: b. Mar. 1, 1925, Malanje, Angola; ord. priest Dec. 20, 1952, in Rome; professor of dogmatic theology in major seminary of Luanda, Angola; editor of *O Apostolada,* Catholic newspaper; forced into exile in Lisbon, Portugal, 1961-71; returned to Angola, 1971; active with student and refugee groups; professor at Pius XII Institute of Social Sciences; ord. bishop of Malanje, Aug. 13, 1975; archbishop of Lubango and apostolic administrator of Onjiva, Feb. 3, 1977; held hostage by Angolan guerrillas, Oct. 15 to Nov. 16, 1982; cardinal Feb. 2, 1983; titular see, St. Mark in Agro Laurentino. Archbishop of Lubango, apostolic administrator of Onjiva, member of: Congregation: Evangelization of Peoples.

Duval, Leon-Etiennei b. Nov. 9, 1903, Chenex, France; ord. priest Dec. 18, 1926; ord. bishop of Constantine, Algeria, Feb. 11, 1947; archbishop of Algiers, Feb. 3, 1954; cardinal Feb. 22, 1965; titular church, St. Balbina. Archbishop of Algiers, member of: Congregation: Evangelization of Peoples.

Ekandem, Dominic Ignatius: b. 1917, Ibiono, Nigeria; ord. priest Dec. 7, 1947; ord. titular bishop of Gerapoli di Isauri and auxiliary bishop of Calabar, Feb. 7, 1954, the first Nigerian to become a bishop; first bishop of Ikot Ekpene, Mar. 1, 1963; cardinal May 24, 1976; titular church, San Marcello. Bishop of Ikot Ekpene, member of: Secretariat: Non-Christians.

Enrique y Tarancon, Vicente: b. May 14, 1907, Burriana, Spain; ord. priest Nov. 1, 1929; ord. bishop of Solsona, Mar. 24, 1946; bishop of Oviedo, Apr. 12, 1964; archbishop of Toledo, 1969-71; cardinal Apr. 28, 1969; titular church, St. John Chrysostom; archbishop of Madrid, 1971-83. Former archbishop of Madrid, member of: Congregation: Bishops.

Etchegaray, Roger: b. Sept. 25, 1922, Espelette, France; ord. priest July 13, 1947; deputy director, 1961-66, and secretary general, 1966-70, of French Episcopal Conference; ord. titular bishop of Gemelle di Numidia and auxiliary bishop of Paris, May 27, 1969; archbishop of Marseilles, Dec. 22, 1970; prelate of Mission de France, 1975-82; presi-

dent of French Episcopal Conference, 1979-81; cardinal June 30, 1979; titular church, St. Leo I. Archbishop of Marseilles, member of: Congregation: Catholic Education; Secretariat: Christian Unity; Commission: Social Communications.

Flahiff, George B., C.S.B.: b. Oct. 26, 1905, Paris, Ont., Canada; ord. priest Aug. 17, 1930; professor of medieval history at the University of Toronto and Pontifical Institute of Medieval Studies in Toronto, 1934-54; superior general of Basilian Fathers, 1954; ord. archbishop of Winnipeg, May 31, 1961 (retired 1982); president of Canadian Conference of Bishops, 1963-65; cardinal Apr. 28, 1969; titular church, St. Mary della Salute (Primavalle). Former archbishop of Winnipeg, member of: Congregation: Religious and Secular Institutes.

Florit,* Ermenegildo: b. July 5, 1901, Fagagna, Italy; ord. priest Apr. 11, 1925; taught Sacred Scripture at Lateran University from 1929; prorector of Lateran University and Institute of Civil and Canon Law, 1951-54; ord. titular archbishop of Hieropolis and coadjutor archbishop of Florence, Sept. 12, 1954; archbishop of Florence, 1962-77; cardinal Feb. 22, 1965; titular church, Queen of the Apostles. Former archbishop of Florence.

Freeman, James Darcy: b. Nov. 19, 1907, Sydney, Australia; ord. priest July 13, 1930; ord. titular bishop of Ermopoli minore and auxiliary of Sydney, Jan. 24, 1957; bishop of Armidale, 1968-71; archbishop of Sydney, 1971-83; cardinal Mar. 5, 1973; titular church, St. Mary Queen of Peace. (in Ostia Mare). Former archbishop of Sydney, member of; Congregation: Catholic Education.

Gantin, Bernardin: b. May 8, 1922, Toffo, Dahomey (now Benin): ord. priest Jan. 14, 1951; ord. titular bishop of Tipasa di Mauritania and auxiliary bishop of Cotonou, Feb. 3, 1957; archbishop of Cotonou, 1960-71; associate secretary (1971-73) and secretary (1973-75) of Congregation for Evangelization of Peoples; vice-president (1975) and president (1976) of Pontifical Commission for Justice and Peace; cardinal June 27, 1977; deacon, Sacred Heart of Christ the King. President of Pontifical Commission for Justice and Peace and the Pontifical Council *Cor Unum,* member of: Council for Public Affairs of the Church; Congregations: Doctrine of the Faith, Bishops, Causes of Saints, Evangelization of Peoples, Oriental Churches, Religious and Secular Institutes, Catholic Education; Secretariats: Non-Believers, Non-Christians; Tribunal: Apostolic Signatura; Commissions: Social Communications, Institute for Works of Religion.

Garrone,* Gabriel-Marie: b. Oct. 12, 1901, Aix-les-Bains, France; ord. priest Apr. 11, 1925; captain during World War II, cited for bravery, taken prisoner; rector of major seminary of Chambery, 1947; ord. titular archbishop of Lemno and coadjutor of Toulouse, June 24, 1947; archbishop of Toulouse, 1956-66; titular archbishop of Torri di Numidia and pro-prefect of Congregation of Seminaries and Universities, Mar. 24, 1966; cardinal

June 26, 1967; titular church, St. Sabina; prefect of Congregation for Catholic Education, 1968-80. Former prefect of Congregation for Catholic Education, head of presidential committee of Pontifical Council for Culture.

Glemp. Jozef: b. Dec. 18, 1928, Inowroclaw, Poland; assigned to forced labor on German farm in Rycerzow during Nazi occupation; ord. priest May 25, 1956; studied in Rome, 1958-64, receiving degree in Roman and canon law from Pontifical Lateran University; secretary of primatial major seminary at Gniezno on his return to Poland, 1964; spokesman for secretariat of primate of Poland and chaplain of primate for archdiocese of Gniezno, 1967; ord. bishop of Warmia, Apr. 21, 1979; archbishop of Gniezno, July 7, 1981, with title of archbishop of Warsaw and primate of Poland; cardinal Feb. 2, 1983; titular church, St. Mary in Trastevere. Archbishop of Gniezno and Warsaw, primate of Poland, member of:
Congregation: Oriental Churches.

Gonzalez Martin, Marcelo: b. Jan. 16, 1918, Villanubla, Spain; ord. priest June 29, 1941; taught theology and sociology at Valladolid diocesan seminary; founded organization for construction of houses for poor; ord. bishop of Astorga, Mar. 5, 1961; titular archbishop of Case Mediane and coadjutor of Barcelona, Feb. 21, 1966; archbishop of Barcelona, 1967-71; archbishop of Toledo, Dec. 3, 1971; cardinal Mar. 5, 1973; titular church, St. Augustine. Archbishop of Toledo, member of:
Congregation: Evangelization of Peoples.

Gouyon, Paul: b. Oct. 24, 1910, Bordeaux, France; ord. priest Mar. 13, 1937; ord. bishop of Bayonne, Oct. 7, 1957; titular archbishop of Pessinonte and coadjutor archbishop of Rennes, Sept. 6, 1963; archbishop of Rennes, Sept. 4, 1964; cardinal Apr. 28, 1969; titular church, Nativity of Our Lord Jesus Christ. (Via Gallia). Archbishop of Rennes, member of:
Secretariat: Non-Believers.

Gray, Gordon Joseph: b. Aug. 10, 1910, Edinburgh, Scotland; ord. priest June 15, 1935; ord. archbishop of Saint Andrews and Edinburgh, Sept. 21, 1951; chairman of International Committee for English in the Liturgy; cardinal Apr. 28, 1969; titular church, St. Clare. Archbishop of Saint Andrews and Edinburgh, member of:
Congregations: Evangelization of Peoples, Sacraments and Divine Worship;
Commission: Social Communications.

Guerri, Sergio: b. Dec. 25, 1905, Tarquinia, Italy; ord. priest Mar. 30, 1929; ord. titular archbishop of Trevi, Apr. 27, 1969; cardinal Apr. 28, 1969; titular church, Most Holy Name of Mary; pro-president of Pontifical Commission for State of Vatican City, 1968-81. Member of:
Congregations: Oriental Churches, Causes of Saints, Evangelization of Peoples;
Commission: Patrimony of Holy See.

Guyot, Jean: b. July 7, 1905, Bordeaux, France; ord. priest June 29, 1932; held various offices in Bordeaux diocese; ord. titular bishop of Helenopolis and coadjutor of Constance, May 4, 1949; bishop of Constance, 1950-66; archbishop of Toulouse, 1966-78; invested with Legion of Honor

by French government; cardinal Mar. 5, 1973; titular church, Saint Agnes Outside the Walls. Former archbishop of Toulouse, member of:
Congregation: Catholic Education.

Hoeffner, Joseph: b. Dec. 24, 1906, Horhausen, Germany; ord. priest Oct. 30, 1932; ord. bishop of Munster, Sept. 14, 1962; titular archbishop of Aquileia and coadjutor archbishop of Cologne, Jan. 6, 1969; archbishop of Cologne, Feb. 23, 1969; cardinal Apr. 28, 1969; titular church, St. Andrew of the Valley. Archbishop of Cologne, member of:
Congregations: Oriental Churches, Religious and Secular Institutes, Evangelization of Peoples, Catholic Education;
Secretariat: Non-Believers;
Office: Prefecture of Economic Affairs.

Hume, George Basil, O.S.B.: b. Mar. 2, 1923, Newcastle-upon-Tyne, England; began monastic studies at Benedictine Abbey of St. Laurence at Ampleforth, 1941; made solemn perpetual vows as Benedictine, 1945; ord. priest July 23, 1950; abbot of Ampleforth, 1963-76; ord archbishop of Westminster, Mar. 25, 1976; cardinal May 24, 1976; titular church, S. Silvestro (in Capite). Archbishop of Westminster, member of:
Congregation: Religious and Secular Institutes;
Secretariat: Christian Unity.

Jubany Arnau, Narciso: b. Aug. 12, 1913, Santa Coloma de Farnes, Spain; ord. priest July 30, 1939; professor of law at Barcelona seminary; served on ecclesiastical tribunal; ord. titular bishop of Ortosia and auxiliary of Barcelona, Jan. 22, 1956; bishop of Gerona, 1964-71; archbishop of Barcelona, Dec. 3, 1971; cardinal Mar. 5, 1973; titular church, San Lorenzo (in Damaso). Archbishop of Barcelona, member of:
Congregations: Sacraments and Divine Worship, Religious and Secular Institutes.

Khoraiche, Antoine Pierre: b. Sept. 20, 1907, Ain-Ebel, Lebanon; ord. priest Apr. 12, 1930; ord. titular bishop of Tarsus and auxiliary bishop of Sidon of the Maronites, Oct. 15, 1950; bishop of Sidon, Nov. 25, 1957; elected patriarch of Antioch for Maronites, Feb. 3, 1975, granted ecclesial communion by Paul VI, Feb. 15, 1975; advocate of reconciliation among various Lebanese ethnic and religious groups and withdrawal of foreign troops from country; cardinal Feb. 2, 1983. Patriarch of Antioch for Maronites (residence in Beirut), member of:
Congregation: Oriental Churches;
Commission: Revision of Code of Oriental Canon Law.

Kim, Stephan Sou Hwan: b. May 8, 1922, Tae Gu, Korea; ord. priest Sept. 15, 1951; ord. bishop of Masan, May 31, 1966; archbishop of Seoul, Apr. 9, 1968; cardinal Apr. 28, 1969; titular church, St. Felix of Cantalice (Centocelle). Archbishop of Seoul, apostolic administrator of Pyeong Yang, president of Korean Episcopal Conference (1981), member of:
Congregation: Evangelization of Peoples;
Secretariat: Non-Christians.

Kitbunchu, Michael Michai: b. Jan. 25, 1929, Samphran, Thailand; ord. priest Dec. 20, 1959, in Rome; rector of metropolitan seminary in Bang-

Cardinals   169

kok, 1965-72; ord. archbishop of Bangkok, June 3,
1973; cardinal Feb. 2, 1983, the first from Thailand; titular church, St. Laurence in Panisperna.
Archbishop of Bangkok, member of:
Congregation: Evangelization of Peoples.
Koenig, Franz: b. Aug. 3, 1905, Rabenstein, Lower Austria; ord. priest Oct. 28, 1933; ord. titular
bishop of Livias and coadjutor bishop of Sankt
Poelten, Aug. 31, 1952; archbishop of Vienna, May
10, 1956; cardinal Dec. 15, 1958; titular church, St.
Eusebius; president of Secretariat for Non-Believers, 1965-80. Archbishop of Vienna, ordinary for
faithful of Byzantine Rite living in Austria, member of:
Congregation: Bishops.
Krol, John Joseph: b. Oct. 26, 1910, Cleveland,
Ohio; ord. priest Feb. 20, 1937; ord. titular bishop
of Cadi and auxiliary bishop of Cleveland, Sept. 2,
1953; archbishop of Philadelphia, Feb. 11, 1961, installed Mar. 22, 1961; cardinal June 26, 1967;
titular church, St. Mary (della Merced) and St.
Adrian Martyr; vice-president, 1966-72, and president, 1972-74, of NCCB/USCC. Archbishop of Philadelphia, member of:
Congregation: Oriental Churches;
Office: Prefecture of Economic Affairs.
Kuharic, Franjo: b. Apr. 15, 1919, Pribic, Yugoslavia; ord. priest July 15, 1945; ord. titular bishop
of Meta and auxiliary bishop of Zagreb, May 3,
1964; apostolic administrator of archdiocese of
Zagreb, 1968-70; archbishop of Zagreb, June 16,
1970; cardinal Feb. 2, 1983; titular church, St.
Jerome of the Schiavoni. Archbishop of Zagreb,
president of Yugoslav Bishops Conference, 1970-,
member of:
Council for Public Affairs of the Church;
Congregations: Bishops, Clergy.
Landazuri Ricketts, Juan, O.F.M: b. Dec. 19,
1913, Arequipa, Peru; entered Franciscans, 1933;
ord. priest Apr. 16, 1939; ord. titular archbishop of
Rulna and coadjutor archbishop of Lima, Aug. 24,
1952; archbishop of Lima, May 2, 1955; cardinal
Mar. 19, 1962; titular church, St. Mary (in
Aracoeli). Archbishop of Lima, member of:
Congregations: Clergy, Religious and Secular
Institutes, Catholic Education.
Lebrun Moratinos, Jose Ali: b. Mar. 19, 1919,
Puerto Cabello, Venezuela; ord. priest Dec. 19,
1943; ord. titular bishop of Arado and auxiliary
bishop of Maracaibo, Sept. 2, 1956; first bishop of
Maracay, 1958-62; bishop of Valencia, 1962-72;
titular archbishop of Voncaria and coadjutor archbishop of Caracas, Sept. 21, 1972; archbishop of Caracas, May 24, 1980; cardinal Feb. 2, 1983; titular
church, St. Pancratius. Archbishop of Caracas,
vice-president of Venezuelan Bishops Conference,
member of:
Congregation: Catholic Education.
Leger, Paul Emile, S.S.: b. Apr. 26, 1904, Valleyfield, Quebec, Canada; ord. priest May 25, 1929;
rector Canadian College, Rome, 1947; ord. archbishop of Montreal, Apr. 26, 1950; cardinal Jan. 12,
1953; titular church, St. Mary (of the Angels); resigned as archbishop of Montreal (Apr. 20, 1968) to
become missionary to lepers, retired 1979. Former
archbishop of Montreal, member of:

Congregation: Evangelization of Peoples.
Lekai, Laszlo: b. Mar. 12, 1910, Zalalovo, Hungary; ord. priest Oct. 28, 1934; professor of philosophy and dogmatic theology at major seminary at
Veszprem; arrested and imprisoned by Nazis during World War II; engaged in pastoral work and
held diocesan offices after the war; ord. titular
bishop of Girus Tirasii and apostolic administrator
of Esztergom, Mar. 16, 1972; archbishop of
Esztergom and primate of Hungary, Feb. 12, 1976;
cardinal May 24, 1976; titular church, S. Teresa
(on the Corso d'Italia). Archbishop of Esztergom,
member of:
Congregation: Catholic Education.
Lopez Trujillo, Alfonso: b. Nov. 8, 1935, Vil-
lahermosa, Colombia; ord. priest Nov. 13, 1960, in
Rome; returned to Colombia, 1963; taught at major seminary; was pastoral coordinator for 1968 International Eucharistic Congress in Bogota; vicar
general of Bogota, 1970-72; ord. titular bishop of
Boseta (with personal title of archbishop), Mar.
25, 1971; auxiliary bishop of Bogota, 1971-72; secre-
tary-general of CELAM, 1972-78; helped organize
1979 Puebla Conference in which Pope John Paul II
participated; app. coadjutor archbishop of Medellin, 1978; archbishop of Medellin, Jan. 2, 1979;
president of CELAM, 1979-83; cardinal Feb. 2,
1983; titular church, St. Prisca. Archbishop of
Medellin, member of:
Commissions: Social Communications, Latin
America.
Lorscheider, Aloisio, O.F.M.: b. Oct. 8, 1924,
Linha Geraldo, Brazil; received in Franciscan Order, Feb. 1, 1942; ord. priest Aug. 22, 1948; professor of theology at the Antonianum, Rome, and
director of Franciscan international house of studies; ord. bishop of Santo Angelo, Brazil, May 20,
1962; archbishop of Fortaleza, Mar. 26, 1973; president of CELAM, 1975-79; cardinal May 24, 1976;
titular church, S. Pietro (in Montorio). Archbishop
of Fortaleza, member of:
Congregations: Religious and Secular Institutes,
Clergy;
Secretariat: Non-Christians.
Lustiger, Jean-Marie: b. Sept. 16, 1926, Paris,
France, of Polish Jewish parents who emigrated
to France after World War I; taken in by Catholic
family in Orleans when his parents were deported
during Nazi occupation (his mother died in 1943 at
Auschwitz); convert to Catholicism, baptized Aug.
25, 1940; active in Young Christian Students during
university days; ord. priest Apr. 17, 1954; ord.
bishop of Orleans, Dec. 8, 1979; archbishop of Par-
is, Jan. 31, 1981; cardinal Feb. 2, 1983; titular
church, Sts. Marcellinus and Peter. Archbishop of
Paris, ordinary for Eastern-Rite faithful without
ordinaries of their own, member of:
Council for Public Affairs of Church;
Congregations: Sacraments and Divine Worship,
Bishops.
McCann, Owen: b. June 29, 1907, Woodstock,
South Africa; ord. priest Dec. 21, 1935; ord. titular
bishop of Stettorio and vicar apostolic of Cape
Town, May 18, 1950; first archbishop of Cape
Town, Jan. 11, 1951; opponent of apartheid policy;
cardinal Feb. 22, 1965; titular church, St. Prax-

edes. Archbishop of Cape Town, member of:
Congregation: Evangelization of Peoples.

Macharski, Franciszek: b. May 20, 1927, Cracow, Poland; ord. priest Apr. 2, 1950; engaged in pastoral work, 1950-56; continued theological studies in Fribourg, Switzerland, 1956-60; taught pastoral theology at the Faculty of Theology in Cracow; app. rector of archdiocesan seminary at Cracow, 1970; ord. archbishop of Cracow, Jan. 6, 1979, by Pope John Paul II; cardinal June 30, 1979; titular church, St. John at the Latin Gate. Archbishop of Cracow, member of:
Congregations: Clergy, Catholic Education; Secretariat: Non-Believers.

Malula, Joseph: b. Dec. 17, 1917, Kinshasa, Zaire; ord. priest June 9, 1946; ord. titular bishop of Attanaso and auxiliary bishop of Kinshasa, Sept. 20, 1959; archbishop of Kinshasa. July 7, 1964; cardinal Apr. 28, 1969; titular church, Ss. Protomartyrs (Via Aurelia Antica). Archbishop of Kinshasa, member of:
Congregation: Evangelization of Peoples.

Manning, Timothy: b. Nov. 15, 1909, Ballingeary, Ireland; completed studies for the priesthood at St. Patrick's Seminary, Menlo Park, Calif.; ord. priest June 16, 1934; became American citizen, Jan. 14, 1944; ord. titular bishop of Lesvi and auxiliary of Los Angeles, Oct. 15, 1946; first bishop of Fresno, 1967-69; titular archbishop of Capri and coadjutor of Los Angeles, May 26, 1969; archbishop of Los Angeles, Jan. 21, 1970; cardinal Mar. 5, 1973; titular church, Santa Lucia. Archbishop of Los Angeles, member of:
Congregations: Evangelization of Peoples, Religious and Secular Institutes.

Marella,* Paolo: b. Jan. 25, 1895, Rome, Italy; ord. priest Feb. 23, 1918; aide in Congregation for Propagation of the Faith; on staff of apostolic delegation, Washington, D.C., 1923-33; ord. titular archbishop of Doclea, Oct. 29, 1933; apostolic delegate to Japan, 1933-48, to Australia, New Zealand and Oceania, 1948-53; nuncio to France, 1953-59; cardinal Dec. 14, 1959; entered order of cardinal bishops as titular bishop of Porto and Santa Rufina, Mar. 14, 1972; president of Secretariat for Non-Christians, 1967-73. Archpriest emeritus of St. Peter's Basilica, sub-dean of College of Cardinals, 1977.

Martini, Carlo Maria, S.J.: b. Feb. 15, 1927, Turin, Italy; entered Jesuits Sept. 25, 1944; ord. priest July 13, 1952, at the age of 25; biblical scholar; seminary professor, Chieti, Italy, 1958-61; professor and later rector, 1969-78, of Pontifical Biblical Institute; rector of Pontifical Gregorian University, 1978-79; author of theological, biblical and spiritual works; ord. archbishop of Milan, Jan. 6, 1980, by Pope John Paul II; cardinal Feb. 2, 1983; titular church, St. Cecilia. Archbishop of Milan, member of:
Council for Public Affairs of the Church;
Congregations: Doctrine of the Faith, Bishops, Catholic Education.

Marty, Francois: b. May 18, 1904, Pachins, France; ord. priest June 28, 1930; ord. bishop of Saint-Flour, May 1, 1952; titular archbishop of Emesa and coadjutor archbishop of Rheims, Dec.

14, 1959; archbishop of Rheims, May 9, 1960; archbishop of Paris, 1968-81; cardinal Apr. 28, 1969; titular church, St. Louis of France. Former archbishop of Paris, member of:
Congregations: Oriental Churches, Clergy, Sacraments and Divine Worship.

Maurer,* Jose Clemente, C.SS.R.: b. Mar. 13, 1900, Puttlingen, Germany; ord. priest Sept. 19, 1925; assigned to Bolivian missions, 1926; became a Bolivian citizen; ord. titular bishop of Cea and auxiliary bishop of La Paz, Apr. 16, 1950; archbishop of Sucre, Oct. 27, 1951; cardinal June 26, 1967; titular church, Most Holy Redeemer and St. Alphonsus. Archbishop of Sucre.

Medeiros, Humberto S.: b. Oct. 6, 1915, Arrifes, S. Miguel, Azores; came to U.S. at age of 15; became American citizen, 1940; ord. priest June 15, 1946; ord. bishop of Brownsville, Tex., June 9, 1966; archbishop of Boston, Sept. 8, 1970; cardinal Mar. 5, 1973; titular church, Santa Susanna. Archbishop of Boston, member of:
Congregations: Bishops, Catholic Education.

Meisner, Joachim: b. Dec. 25, 1933, Breslau, Silesia, Germany (present-day Wroclaw, Poland); ord. priest Dec. 22, 1962; regional director of Caritas; ord. titular bishop of Vina and auxiliary of apostolic administration of Erfurt-Meiningen, E. Germany, May 17, 1975; app. bishop of Berlin, Apr. 22, 1980, installed May 17, 1980 (resides in East Berlin); cardinal Feb. 2, 1983; titular church, St. Prudenziana. Bishop of Berlin, president of Bishops' Conference of Berlin (1982), member of:
Congregation: Catholic Education.

Miranda y Gomez,* Miguel Dario: b. Dec. 19, 1895, Leon, Mexico; ord. priest Oct. 28, 1918; ord. bishop of Tulancingo, Dec. 8, 1937; titular archbishop of Selimbra and coadjutor archbishop of Mexico City, Dec. 20, 1955; archbishop of Mexico City, 1956-77; served as president of the Latin American Bishops' Council (CELAM); cardinal Apr. 28, 1969; titular church, St. Mary of Guadalupe (Montemario). Former archbishop of Mexico City.

Mozzoni, Umberto: b. June 29, 1904, Buenos Aires, Argentina; holds Italian citizenship; ord. priest Aug. 14, 1927; professor of theology and canon law at Macerata seminary, Italy; served on Vatican diplomatic staff in Canada, England and Portugal; ord. titular archbishop of Side, Dec. 5, 1954; nuncio to Bolivia, 1954-58, Argentina, 1958-69, Brazil, 1969-73; cardinal Mar. 5, 1973; titular church, St. Eugene. Member of:
Congregations: Oriental Churches, Clergy, Religious and Secular Institutes, Evangelization of Peoples, Causes of Saints;
Tribunal: Apostolic Signatura;
Commissions: Sanctuaries of Pompei, Loreto and Bari (President), Institute for Works of Religion.

Munoz Duque, Anibal: b. Oct. 3, 1908, Santa Rosa de Osos, Colombia; ord. priest Nov. 19, 1933; ord. bishop of Soccoro y San Gil, May 27, 1951; bishop of Bucaramango, 1952-59; archbishop of Nueva Pamplona, 1959-68; titular archbishop of Cariana and coadjutor archbishop of Bogota, 1968; archbishop of Bogota, July 29, 1972; cardinal Mar.

5, 1973; titular church, St. Bartholomew. Archbishop of Bogota, military vicar, member of:

Congregation: Sacraments and Divine Worship.

Munoz Vega,* Pablo, S. J.: b. May 23, 1903, Mira, Ecuador; ord. priest July 25, 1933; ord. titular bishop of Ceramo and auxiliary bishop of Quito, Mar. 19, 1964; archbishop of Quito, June 23, 1967; cardinal Apr. 28, 1969; titular church, St. Robert Bellarmine. Archbishop of Quito, member of:

Congregation: Religious and Secular Institutes.

Nasalli Rocca di Corneliano,* Mario: b. Aug. 12, 1903, Piacenza, Italy; ord. priest Apr. 9, 1927; ord. titular archbishop of Anzio, Apr. 20, 1969; cardinal Apr. 28, 1969; titular church, St. John the Baptist. Member of:

Congregations: Sacraments and Divine Worship, Causes of Saints;

Secretariat: Non-Believers.

Nsubuga, Emmanuel: b. Nov. 5, 1914, Kisule, Uganda; ord. priest Dec. 15, 1946; ord. bishop of Kampala, Oct. 30, 1966; cardinal May 24, 1976; titular church, S. Maria Nuova. Archbishop of Kampala, member of:

Congregation: Evangelization of Peoples.

O'Boyle,* Patrick A.: b. July 18, 1896, Scranton, Pa.; ord. priest May 21, 1921; executive director of War Relief Services, NCWC, 1943; ord. archbishop of Washington, Jan. 14, 1948 (retired, 1973); cardinal June 26, 1967; titular church, St. Nicholas (in Carcere). Former archbishop of Washington.

Oddi, Silvio: b. Nov. 14, 1910, Morfasso, Italy; ord. priest May 21, 1933; ord. titular archbishop of Mesembria, Sept. 27, 1953; served in Vatican diplomatic corps, 1953-69; apostolic delegate to Jerusalem, Palestine, Jordan and Cyprus, internuncio to the United Arab Republic, and nuncio to Belgium and Luxembourg; cardinal Apr. 28, 1969; titular church, St. Agatha of the Goths. Pontifical legate for Patriarchal Basilica of St. Francis of Assisi, prefect of Sacred Congregation for the Clergy, 1979, member of:

Council for Public Affairs of Church;

Congregations: Bishops, Oriental Churches, Causes of Saints, Evangelization of Peoples;

Tribunal: Apostolic Signatura;

Commissions: State of Vatican City, Sanctuaries of Pompei, Loreto and Bari.

O'Fiaich, Tomas: b. Nov. 3, 1923; Crossmaglen, Ireland; ord. priest July 6, 1948; lecturer, 1953, and professor, 1959, of modern history at Maynooth College; vice president, 1970, and president, 1974, of Maynooth; prolific author of scholarly works; recognized authority on early Irish Christianity; ord. archbishop of Armagh and primate of All Ireland, Oct. 2, 1977; pledged to work for the cause of peace in Northern Ireland; outspoken in his condemnation of violence; president of Irish Episcopal Conference; cardinal June 30, 1979; titular church, St. Patrick. Archbishop of Armagh, primate of All Ireland, member of:

Congregations: Clergy, Catholic Education;

Secretariat: Christian Unity.

Otunga, Maurice: b. January, 1923, Chebukwa, Kenya; son of pagan tribal chief; baptized 1935, at age of 12; ord. priest Oct. 3, 1950, at Rome; taught at Kisumu major seminary for three years; attaché in apostolic delegation at Mombasa, 1953-56; ord. titular bishop of Tacape and auxiliary of Kisumu, Feb. 25, 1957; bishop of Kisii, 1960-69; titular archbishop of Bomarzo and coadjutor of Nairobi, Nov. 15, 1969; archbishop of Nairobi, Oct. 24, 1971; cardinal Mar. 5, 1973; titular church, St. Gregory Barbarigo. Archbishop of Nairobi, military vicar of Kenya, 1981, member of:

Congregations: Sacraments and Divine Worship, Religious and Secular Institutes.

Palazzini, Pietro: b. May 19, 1912, Piobbico, Pesaro, Italy; ord. priest Dec. 6, 1934; assistant vice-rector of Pontifical Major Roman Seminary and vice-rector and bursar of Pontifical Roman Seminary for Juridical Studies; professor of moral theology at Lateran University; held various offices in Roman Curia; secretary of Congregation of Council (now Clergy), 1958-73; ord. titular archbishop of Caesarea in Cappadocia, Sept. 21, 1962; author of numerous works on moral theology and law; cardinal Mar. 5, 1973; titular church, St. Jerome. Prefect of Congregation for Causes of Saints, 1980, member of:

Congregations: Oriental Churches, Sacraments and Divine Worship, Clergy;

Tribunal: Apostolic Signatura;

Commission: Interpretation of Decrees of Vatican II.

Pappalardo, Salvatore: b. Sept. 23, 1918, Villafranca Sicula, Sicily; ord. priest Apr. 12, 1941; entered diplomatic service of secretariat of state, 1947; ord. titular archbishop of Miletus, Jan. 16, 1966; pro-nuncio in Indonesia, 1966-69; president of Pontifical Ecclesiastical Academy, 1969-70; archbishop of Palermo, Oct. 17, 1970; cardinal Mar. 5, 1973; titular church, St. Mary Odigitria of the Sicilians. Archbishop of Palermo, member of:

Congregations: Oriental Churches, Clergy.

Parecattil, Joseph: b. Apr. 1, 1912, Kidangoor, India; ord. priest Aug. 24, 1939; ord. titular bishop of Aretusa for Syrians and auxiliary bishop of Ernakulam, Nov. 30, 1953; archbishop of Ernakulam (Chaldean-Malabar Rite), July 20, 1956; appointed one of seven members of Pope Paul VI's advisory council for Eastern Rite churches, 1968; cardinal Apr. 28, 1969; titular church, Our Lady Queen of Peace (Monte Verde). Archbishop of Ernakulam of the Chaldean-Malabar Rite, member of:

Congregation: Oriental Churches;

Secretariat: Non-Christians;

Commission: Revision of Oriental Code of Canon Law (President).

Parente,* Pietro: b. Feb. 16, 1891, Casalnuovo, Monterotaro, Italy; ord. priest Mar. 18, 1916; director of Archiepiscopal Seminary at Naples, 1916-26; rector of Pontifical Urban College of Propagation of the Faith, 1934-38; Consultor of the Congregations of the Holy Office, Council, Propagation of the Faith, and Seminaries and Universities; ord. archbishop of Perugia, Oct. 23, 1955; titular archbishop of Tolemaide di Tebaide, Oct. 23, 1959; assessor (1959-65) and secretary (1965-67) of Congregation of Holy Office (now Doctrinal

Congregation); cardinal June 26, 1967; titular church, St. Lawrence (in Lucina).

Paupini, Giuseppe: b. Feb. 25, 1907, Mondavio, Italy; ord. priest Mar. 19, 1930; ord. titular archbishop of Sebastopolis in Abasgia, Feb. 26, 1956; served in Vatican diplomatic corps, 1956-69; internuncio to Iran, 1956-57; nuncio to Guatemala and El Salvador, 1957-58, nuncio to Colombia, 1959-69; cardinal Apr. 28, 1969; titular church, All Saints Church. Major penitentiary 1973, member of:
Congregation: Causes of Saints;
Commission: State of Vatican City.

Pellegrino,* Michele: b. Apr. 25, 1903, Centallo, Italy; ord. priest Sept. 19, 1925; ord. archbishop of Turin, Oct. 17, 1965 (resigned 1977); cardinal June 26, 1967; titular church, Most Holy Name of Jesus. Former archbishop of Turin, member of:
Congregation: Catholic Education.

Philippe, Pierre Paul, O.P.: b. Apr. 16, 1905, Paris, France; entered Dominican Order, 1926; ord. priest July 6, 1932; professor at Angelicum, Rome, from 1935; founded Institute of Spirituality for masters of novices at Angelicum, 1950, and school for mistresses of novices, 1953; apostolic visitor of various religious institutes, 1951-56; commissary of the Holy Office, 1955; consultor of various pontifical commissions and congregations from 1958; secretary of Congregation for Religious, 1959; ord. titular archbishop of Heracleopolis Magna, Sept. 21, 1962; secretary of Congregation for Doctrine of Faith, 1967-73; cardinal Mar. 5, 1973; titular church, St. Pius V; prefect of Congregation for Oriental Churches, 1973-80. Member of:
Congregations: Religious and Secular Institutes, Causes of Saints, Evangelization of Peoples;

Picachy, Lawrence Trevor, S.J.: b. Aug. 7, 1916, Lebong, India; ord. priest Nov. 21, 1947; dean, 1950-54, and then rector, 1954-60, of St. Francis Xavier University College, Calcutta; ord. bishop of Jamshedpur, Sept. 9, 1962; archbishop of Calcutta, May 29, 1969; cardinal May 24, 1976; titular church, Sacred Heart of Mary. Archbishop of Calcutta, member of:
Congregation: Evangelization of People.

Pironio, Eduardo: b. Dec. 3, 1920, Nueve de Julio, Argentina; ord. priest Dec. 5, 1943; taught theology at Pius XII Seminary of Mercedes diocese, 1944-59; vicar general of diocese 1958-60; attended Second Vatican Council as *peritus*; ord. titular bishop of Ceciri, May 31, 1964; apostolic administrator of diocese of Avellaneda, 1967-72; secretary general 1967-72, and president, 1973-75, of CELAM; bishop of Mar del Plata, 1972-75; titular archbishop of Thiges and pro-prefect of Sacred Congregation for Religious and Secular Institutes, Sept. 20, 1975; cardinal May 24, 1976; deacon, Sts. Cosmas and Damian. Prefect of the Sacred Congregation for Religious and Secular Institutes, 1976, member of:
Council for Public Affairs of the Church.
Congregations: Bishops, Sacraments and Divine Worship, Catholic Education, Oriental Churches;
Commissions: Council for the Laity, Latin America, Interpretation of Decrees of Vatican II.

. **Poletti, Ugo:** b. Apr. 19, 1914, Omegna, Italy;

ord. priest June 29, 1938; served in various diocesan offices at Novara; ord. titular bishop of Medeli and auxiliary of Novaro, Sept. 14, 1958; president of Pontifical Mission Aid Society for Italy, 1964-67; archbishop of Spoleto, 1967-69; titular archbishop of Cittanova, 1969; served as second viceregent of Rome, 1969-72; pro-vicar general of Rome, 1972, following the sudden death of Cardinal Dell'Acqua; cardinal Mar. 5, 1973; titular church, Sts. Ambrose and Charles. Vicar general of Rome, 1973, archpriest of Patriarchal Lateran Archbasilica, 1973, grand chancellor of Lateran University, member of:
Congregations: Clergy, Sacraments and Divine Worship, Oriental Churches, Religious and Secular Institutes;
Commission: Council for the Laity.

Poma, Antonio: b. June 12, 1910, Villanterio, Italy; ord. priest Apr. 15, 1933; ord. titular bishop of Tagaste and auxiliary bishop of Mantova, Dec. 9, 1951; bishop of Mantova, Sept. 8, 1954; titular archbishop of Gerpiniano and coadjutor archbishop of Bologna, July 16, 1967; archbishop of Bologna, Feb. 12, 1968 (resigned Feb. 11, 1983); cardinal Apr. 28, 1969; titular church, St. Luke (a Via Prenestina). Former archbishop of Bologna, member of:
Congregations: Clergy, Catholic Education.

Primatesta, Raul Francisco: b. Apr. 14, 1919, Capilla del Senor, Argentina; ord. priest Oct. 25, 1942, at Rome; taught at minor and major seminaries of La Plata; contributed to several theology reviews; ord. titular bishop of Tanais and auxiliary of La Plata, Aug. 15, 1957; bishop of San Rafael, 1961-65; archbishop of Cordoba, Feb. 16, 1965; cardinal Mar. 5, 1973; titular church, St. Mary Sorrowful Virgin. Archbishop of Cordoba, Argentina, member of:
Congregations: Bishops, Religious and Secular Institutes, Sacraments and Divine Worship;

Quintero,* Jose Humberto: b. Sept. 22, 1902, Mucuchies, Venezuela; ord. priest Aug. 22, 1926; ord. titular archbishop of Acrida and coadjutor archbishop of Merida, Dec. 6, 1953; archbishop of Caracas 1960-80; cardinal Jan. 16, 1961; titular church, Sts. Andrew and Gregory (al Monte Celio). Former archbishop of Caracas.

Ratzinger, Joseph: b. Apr. 16, 1927, Marktl am Inn, Germany; ord. priest June 29, 1951; professor of dogmatic theology at University of Regensburg, 1969-77; member of International Theological Commission, 1969-80; ord. archbishop of Munich-Freising, May 28, 1977 (resigned Feb. 15, 1982); cardinal June 27, 1977; titular church, St. Mary of Consolation (in Tiburtina). Prefect of Congregation for Doctrine of the Faith, 1981, member of:
Council for Public Affairs of the Church;
Congregations: Bishops, Sacraments and Divine Worship, Catholic Education;
Secretariat: Christian Unity;
Commissions: Biblical (President), Theological (President).

Razafimahatratra, Victor, S.J.: b. Sept. 8, 1921, Ambanitsilena-Ranomasina, Madagascar; entered Society of Jesus, 1945; ord. priest July 28, 1956; rector of Fianarantsoa Minor Seminary, 1960-63;

Cardinals 173

superior of Jesuit residence at Ambositra, 1963-69; rector of Tananarive Major Seminary, 1969-71; ord. bishop of Farafangana, Apr. 18, 1971; archbishop of Tananarive, Apr. 10, 1976; cardinal May 24, 1976; titular church, Holy Cross in Jerusalem. Archbishop of Tananarive, president of Madagascar Episcopal Conference, member of: Congregation: Evangelization of Peoples.

Renard, Alexandre Charles: b. June 7, 1906, Avelin, France; ord. priest July 12, 1931; ord. bishop of Versailles, Oct. 19, 1953; archbishop of Lyons, 1967-81; cardinal June 26, 1967; titular church, Most Holy Trinity (at Monte Pincio). Former archbishop of Lyons, member of: Congregations: Religious and Secular Institutes, Evangelization of Peoples.

Ribeiro, Antonio: b. May 21, 1928, Gandarela di Basto, Portugal; ord. priest July 5, 1953; professor of fundamental theology at major seminary at Braga; ord. titular bishop of Tigillava and auxiliary of Braga, Sept. 17, 1967; patriarch of Lisbon, May 10, 1971; cardinal Mar. 5, 1973; titular church, St. Anthony of Padua (in Rome). Patriarch of Lisbon, military vicar, member of: Congregation: Catholic Education; Commission: Social Communications.

Righi-Lambertini, Egano: b. Feb. 22, 1906, Casalecchio di Reno, Italy; ord. priest May 25, 1929; entered service of secretariat of state, 1939; served in diplomatic missions in France (1949-54), Costa Rica (1955), England (1955-57); first apostolic delegate to Korea, 1957-60; ord. titular archbishop of Doclea, Oct. 28, 1960; apostolic nuncio in Lebanon, 1960-63, Chile, 1963-67, Italy, 1967-69; France, 1969-79; while nuncio in France he also served as special envoy at the Council of Europe, 1974-79; cardinal June 30, 1979; deacon, St. John Bosco in Via Tuscolana. Member of: Council for Public Affairs of the Church; Congregations: Bishops, Causes of Saints; Secretariat: Non-Christians; Commission: Sacred Art in Italy (Honorary President).

Rossi, Agnelo: b. May 4, 1913, Joaquim Egidio, Brazil; ord. priest Mar. 27, 1937; ord. bishop of Barra do Pirai, Apr. 15, 1956; archbishop of Ribeirao Preto, 1962-64; archbishop of Sao Paulo, 1964-70; cardinal Feb. 22, 1965; titular church, Mother of God. Prefect of Congregation for Evangelization of Peoples, 1970, grand chancellor of Pontifical Urban University, member of: Council for Public Affairs of Church; Congregations: Clergy, Doctrine of Faith, Bishops, Oriental Churches, Causes of Saints, Religious and Secular Institutes, Catholic Education; Secretariats: Christian Unity, Non-Christians; Commissions: Revision of Oriental Code of Canon Law, Institute for Works of Religion.

Rossi, Opilio: b. May 14, 1910, New York, N.Y.; holds Italian citizenship; ord. priest for diocese of Piacenza, Italy, Mar. 11, 1933; served in nunciatures in Belgium, The Netherlands and Germany, 1938-53; ord. titular archbishop of Ancyra, Dec. 27, 1953; nuncio in Ecuador, 1953-59, Chile, 1959-61, Austria, 1961-76; cardinal May 24, 1976; deacon, S.

Maria Liberatrice (on the Monte Testaccio). Member of: Council for Public Affairs of the Church; Congregations: Bishops, Oriental Churches, Sacraments and Divine Worship, Religious and Secular Institutes, Evangelization of Peoples; Commission: Council for Laity (President).

Roy, Maurice: b. Jan. 25, 1905, Quebec, Canada; ord. priest June 12, 1927; chief of chaplains of Canadian Armed Forces during World War II; ord. bishop of Trois Rivieres, May 1, 1946; military vicar, 1946-81; archbishop of Quebec, 1947-81; primate of Canada, Jan. 25, 1956; cardinal Feb. 22, 1965; titular church, Our Lady of the Most Holy Sacrament and the Holy Canadian Martyrs; president of Council for the Laity and the Pontifical Commission for Justice and Peace (1967-76). Former archbishop of Quebec, member of: Congregations: Clergy, Catholic Education.

Rubin, Wladyslaw: b. Sept. 20, 1917, Toki, Poland; seminary studies interrupted during World War II when he was arrested and deported to labor camp; completed studies at St. Joseph's University in Beirut; ord. priest in Beirut June 30, 1946, and served Polish community there; sent to Rome for further studies, 1949; chaplain for Polish refugees in Italy, 1953-58; rector of Polish College in Rome, 1959-64; ord. titular bishop of Serta, primate of Poland's delegate for emigration and auxiliary of Gniezno, Nov. 29, 1964; established contact with Polish emigrants throughout the world; secretary general of Synod of Bishops, 1967-79; cardinal June 30, 1979; deacon, St. Mary in Via Lata. Prefect of Congregation for Oriental Churches, 1980, member of: Congregations: Doctrine of the Faith, Causes of Saints; Tribunal: Apostolic Signatura; Secretariat: Christian Unity; Commissions: Interpretation of Decrees of Vatican II.

Rugambwa, Laurean: b. July 12, 1912, Bukongo, Tanzania; ord. priest Dec. 12, 1943; ord. titular bishop of Febiano and vicar apostolic of Lower Kagera, Feb. 10, 1952; bishop of Rutabo, Mar. 25, 1953; cardinal Mar. 28, 1960; titular church, St. Francis of Assisi (a Ripa); bishop of Bukoba, 1960-68. Archbishop of Dar-es-Salaam, 1968, member of: Congregation: Causes of Saints.

Sabattani, Aurelio: b. Oct. 18, 1912, Casal Fiumanese, Italy; ord. priest July 26, 1935; jurist; served in various assignments in his native diocese of Imola and as judge and later an official of the regional ecclesiastical tribunal of Bologna; called to Rome in 1955 as prelate auditor of the Roman Rota; ord. titular archbishop of Justinian Prima, July 25, 1965; prelate of Loreto, 1965-71; secretary of Supreme Tribunal of Apostolic Signatura and consultor of Secretariat of State, 1971; pro-prefect of Apostolic Signatura, 1982-83; cardinal Feb. 2, 1983; deacon, St. Apollinaris. Prefect of Apostolic Signatura, 1983, archpriest of St. Peter's Basilica, 1983, member of: Council for Public Affairs of the Church; Congregation: Bishops.

Salazar Lopez, Jose: b. Jan. 12, 1910, Ameca, Mexico; ord. priest May 26, 1934, in Rome; instrumental in building of new seminary at Guadalajara, the largest in Mexico; vice-rector and later rector of seminary; ord. titular bishop of Prusiade and coadjutor bishop of Zamora, Aug. 20, 1961; bishop of Zamora, 1967-70; archbishop of Guadalajara, Feb. 21, 1970; cardinal Mar. 5, 1973; titular church, Santa Emerentia. Archbishop of Guadalajara, member of:
Congregations: Sacraments and Divine Worship, Clergy.

Satowaki, Joseph Asajiro: b. Feb. 1, 1904, Shittsu, Japan; ord. priest Dec. 17, 1932; served in various pastoral capacities in Nagasaki archdiocese after his ordination; apostolic administrator of Taiwan (then a Japanese possession), 1941-45; director of Nagasaki minor seminary, 1945-57; vicar general of Nagasaki, 1945; ord. first bishop of Kagoshima, May 3, 1955; archbishop of Nagasaki, Dec. 19, 1968; president of Japanese Episcopal Conference, 1979-   ; cardinal June 30, 1979; titular church, St. Mary of Peace. Archbishop of Nagasaki, member of:
Congregation: Evangelization of Peoples;
Secretariat: Non-Christians.

Scherer,* Alfred Vicente: b. Feb. 5, 1903, Bom Principio, Brazil; ord. priest Apr. 3, 1926; ord. archbishop of Porto Alegre, Feb. 23, 1947 (retired Aug. 29, 1981); cardinal Apr. 28, 1969; titular church, Our Lady of La Salette. Former archbishop of Porto Alegre, Brazil.

Schroeffer,* Joseph: b. Feb. 20, 1903, Ingolstadt, Germany; ord. priest Oct. 28, 1928; studied at the Gregorian University, Rome, 1922-31; returned to Germany 1931; professor at Higher Institute for Philosophical and Theological Studies at Eichstatt; vicar general of diocese of Eichstatt, 1941-48; ord. bishop of Eichstatt, Sept. 21, 1948; app. titular archbishop of Volturnum and secretary of Congregation for Catholic Education, 1968; cardinal May 24, 1976; deacon, San Saba. Member of:
Council for Public Affairs of the Church;
Congregations: Doctrine of the Faith, Bishops;
Tribunal: Apostolic Signatura;
Commission: Council for Laity;
Office: Administration of Patrimony of Holy See.

Sensi, Giuseppe Maria: b. May 27, 1907, Cosenza, Italy; ord. priest Dec. 21, 1929; entered Vatican diplomatic service; served in nunciatures in Hungary, Switzerland, Belgium and Czechoslovakia, 1934-49; ord. titular archbishop of Sardes, July 24, 1955; apostolic nuncio to Costa Rica, 1955; apostolic delegate to Jerusalem, 1956-62; nuncio to Ireland, 1962-67, and Portugal, 1967-76; cardinal May 24, 1976; deacon, SS. Biagio e Carlo (ai Catinari). Member of:
Congregations: Oriental Churches, Causes of Saints, Evangelization of Peoples;
Commission: State of Vatican City.

Shehan,* Lawrence J.: b. Mar. 18, 1898, Baltimore, Md.; ord. priest Dec. 23, 1922; ord. titular bishop of Lidda and auxiliary bishop of Baltimore and Washington, Dec. 12, 1945; bishop of

Bridgeport, 1953-61; titular archbishop of Nicopolis ad Nestum and coadjutor archbishop of Baltimore, July 10, 1961; archbishop of Baltimore, 1961-74; cardinal Feb. 22, 1965; titular church, St. Clement. Former archbishop of Baltimore.

Sidarouss, Stephanos I, C.M.: b. Feb. 22, 1904, Cairo, Egypt; ord. priest July 2, 1939; ord. titular bishop of Sais, Jan. 25, 1948; auxiliary to the patriarch of Alexandria for the Copts, 1948-58; patriarch of Alexandria, May 10, 1958; cardinal Feb. 22, 1965. Patriarch of Alexandria for the Copts, member of:
Congregation: Oriental Churches;
Secretariat: Christian Unity;
Commission: Revision of Code of Oriental Canon Law.

Silva Henriquez, Raul, S.D.B.: b. Sept. 27, 1907, Talca, Chile; ord. priest July 3, 1938; ord. bishop of Valparaiso, Nov. 29, 1959; archbishop of Santiago de Chile, 1961-83; cardinal Mar. 19, 1962; titular church, St. Bernard (alle Terme). Former archbishop of Santiago de Chile.

Sin, Jaime L.: b. Aug. 31, 1928, New Washington, Philippines; ord. priest Apr. 3, 1954; diocesan missionary in Capiz, 1954-57; app. first rector of the St. Pius X Seminary, Roxas City, 1957; ord. titular bishop of Obba and auxiliary bishop of Jaro, Mar. 18, 1967; apostolic administrator of archdiocese of Jaro, June 20, 1970; titular archbishop of Massa Lubrense and coadjutor archbishop of Jaro, Jan. 15, 1972; archbishop of Jaro, Oct. 8, 1972; archbishop of Manila, Jan. 21, 1974; cardinal May 24, 1976; titular church, S. Maria (ai Monti). Archbishop of Manila, member of:
Congregations: Evangelization of Peoples, Catholic Education;
Secretariat: Non-Christians;
Commission: Social Communications;
Office: Prefecture of Economic Affairs.

Siri, Giuseppe: b. May 20, 1906, Genoa, Italy; ord. priest Sept. 22, 1928; ord. titular bishop of Liviade and auxiliary bishop of Genoa, May 7, 1944; archbishop of Genoa, May 14, 1946; cardinal Jan. 12, 1953; titular church, St. Mary (della Vittoria). Archbishop of Genoa, apostolic administrator of Bobbio, member of:
Congregations: Clergy, Catholic Education.

Slipyi or Slipyj,* Josyf (Kobernyckyj-Dyckowskyj): b. Feb. 17, 1892, Zazdrist in the Ukraine; ord. priest Sept. 30, 1917; ord. titular archbishop of Serre, Dec. 22, 1939; coadjutor archbishop of Lwow for the Ukrainians, 1939-44; archbishop of Lwow, Nov. 1, 1944; imprisoned 1945-63 for unspecified crimes; released by Soviets and allowed to go to Rome in February, 1963; named major archbishop by Paul VI, 1963; cardinal Feb. 22, 1965; titular church, St. Athanasius. Major Archbishop of Lwow of the Ukrainians (not permitted to exercise his office; he resides in Vatican City).

Suenens, Leo Josef: b. July 16, 1904, Brussels, Belgium; ord. priest Sept. 4, 1927; ord. titular bishop of Isinda, Dec. 16, 1945; auxiliary bishop of Mechelen, 1945-61; archbishop of Mechelen-Brussels, 1961-79; cardinal Mar. 19, 1962; titular church, St. Peter in Chains. Former archbishop of Mechelen-Brussels, member of:

Congregations: Evangelization of Peoples, Causes of Saints;
Commission: Revision of Canon Law.

Taofinu'u, Pio, S.M.: b. Dec. 9, 1923, Falealupo, W. Samoa; ord. priest Dec. 8, 1954; joined Society of Mary, 1955; ord. bishop of Apia (Samoa and Tokelau), May 29, 1968, the first Polynesian bishop; cardinal Mar. 5, 1973; titular church, St. Humphrey (on the Janiculum). Archbishop of Samoa-Apia and Tokelau (Oct 10, 1982), member of:
Congregation: Causes of Saints.

Thiandoum, Hyacinthe: b. Feb. 2, 1921, Poponguine, Senegal; ord. priest Apr. 18, 1949; studied at Gregorian University, Rome, 1951-53; returned to Senegal, 1953; ord. archbishop of Dakar, May 20, 1962; cardinal May 24, 1976; titular church, S. Maria (del Popolo). Archbishop of Dakar, president of Senegal-Mauretania Episcopal Conference, member of:
Congregation: Religious and Secular Institutes;
Commission: Social Communications.

Tomasek,* Frantisek: b. June 30, 1899, Studenka, Moravia, Czechoslovakia; ord. priest July 5, 1922; professor of pedagogy and catechetics at the theology faculty of Olomouc, 1934-39; resumed academic activity after liberation in 1945; author, *Catechism of the Catholic Religion;* ord. titular bishop of Butus and auxiliary of Olomouc, Oct. 13, 1949; only Czech bishop to attend Second Vatican Council; apostolic administrator of Prague, Feb. 18, 1965; cardinal May 24, 1976 (*in pectore*); solemnly proclaimed at June 27, 1977, consistory; titular church, Sts. Vitalis, Valeria, Gervase and Protase. Archbishop of Prague, 1978, member of:
Congregation: Clergy.

Trinh van-Can, Joseph-Marie: b. Mar. 19, 1921, Trac But, Vietnam; ord. priest Dec. 3, 1949; held various offices in Hanoi archdiocese; ord. titular bishop of Ela (with personal title of archbishop) and coadjutor archbishop of Hanoi, June 2, 1963; archbishop of Hanoi, Nov. 27, 1978; cardinal June 30, 1979; titular church, St. Mary in Via. Archbishop of Hanoi, member of:
Congregation: Evangelization of Peoples.

Ursi, Corrado: b. July 26, 1908, Andria, Italy; ord. priest July 25, 1931; vice-rector and later rector of the Pontifical Regional Seminary of Molfetta, 1931-51; ord. bishop of Nardo, Sept. 30, 1951; archbishop of Acerenza, Nov. 30, 1961; archbishop of Naples, May 23, 1966; cardinal June 26, 1967; titular church, St. Callistus. Archbishop of Naples, member of:
Congregation: Catholic Education.

Vaivods,* Julijans: b. Aug. 18, 1895, Vorkova, Latvia; ord. priest Apr. 7, 1918; chaplain of various schools, 1918-23; wrote and published catechetical books and theatrical works for youth; vicar general of Liepaja, 1944; apostolic activity curtailed by political situation, he resumed writing; publications denounced as hostile to regime, he was tried and sentenced to two years' exile, 1958-60; released early but not permitted to exercise his priestly ministry for a time; vicar general of Riga, 1962; attended Vatican II, 1964; ord. titular bishop of Macriana Maior and apostolic administrator of archdiocese of Riga and diocese of Liepaja, Nov. 18, 1964, in Rome; cardinal Feb. 2, 1983; titular church, SS. Quattro Coronati. Apostolic administrator of Riga and Liepaja.

Volk, Hermann: b. Dec. 27, 1903, Steinheim, Germany; ord. priest Apr. 2, 1927; professor of dogmatic theology at University of Muenster; ord. bishop of Mainz, June 5, 1962 (retired Dec. 27, 1982); cardinal Mar. 5, 1973; titular church, Saints Fabian and Venanzio (at Villa Fiorelli). Former bishop of Mainz, member of:
Secretariat: Christian Unity.

Willebrands, Johannes: b. Sept. 4, 1909, Bovenkarspel, The Netherlands; ord. priest May 26, 1934; ord. titular bishop of Mauriana, June 28, 1964; secretary of Secretariat for Christian Unity, 1960-69; cardinal Apr. 28, 1969; titular church, St. Sebastian (alle Catacombe). President of Secretariat for Christian Unity, 1969, Archbishop of Utrecht, 1975, member of:
Congregations: Doctrine of Faith, Sacraments and Divine Worship, Oriental Churches, Catholic Education, Evangelization of Peoples;
Commission: Revision of Oriental Code of Canon Law.

Williams, Thomas Stafford: b. Mar. 20, 1930, Wellington, New Zealand; ord. priest Dec. 20, 1959, in Rome; studied in Ireland after ordination, receiving degree in social sciences; served in various pastoral assignments on his return to New Zealand; missionary in Western Samoa to 1976; ord. archbishop of Wellington, New Zealand, Dec. 20, 1979; cardinal Feb. 2, 1983; titular church, Jesus the Divine Teacher at Pineda Sacchetti. Archbishop of Wellington, president of New Zealand Bishops' Conference, member of:
Secretariat: Non-Christians.

Yago, Bernard: b. July, 1916, Pass, Ivory Coast; ord. priest May 1, 1947; ord. archbishop of Abidjan, May 8, 1960, by Pope John XXIII in St. Peter's Basilica, becoming the first native member of the hierarchy of Ivory Coast; cardinal Feb. 2, 1983; titular church, St. Chrysogonus. Archbishop of Abidjan, president of Ivory Coast Episcopal Conference, member of:
Secretariat: Christian Unity.

Zoungrana, Paul, P.A.: b. Sept. 3, 1917, Ouagadougou, Upper Volta; ord. priest May 2, 1942, in the Missionaries of Africa; ord. archbishop of Ouagadougou at St. Peter's Basilica by John XXIII, May 8, 1960; cardinal Feb. 22, 1965; titular church, St. Camillus de Lellis. Archbishop of Ouagadougou, member of:
Congregation: Evangelization of Peoples.

U.S. BISHOPS OVERSEAS

Cardinal William W. Baum, prefect of the Sacred Congregation for Catholic Education; Archbishop Raymond P. Etteldorf, consultor to several Curial bodies; Bishop Anthony L. Deksnys, pastoral work among Lithuanians in Western Europe; Bishop Ladislaus Iranyi, Sch. P., pastoral care of Hungarian Catholics living outside of Hungary; Archbishop Paul C. Marcinkus, president of Institute for Works of Religion (Vatican Bank) and pro-president of Pontifical Commission for the State of Vatian City.

CATEGORIES OF CARDINALS

(As of Aug. 15, 1983.)

Information below includes categories of cardinals and dates of consistories at which they were created. Seniority or precedence usually depends on order of elevation, except in the case of cardinal bishops whose seniority depends on date of appointment to suburban see.

Two of these cardinals were named by Pius XII (consistory of Jan. 12, 1953); 10 by John XXIII (consistories of Dec. 15, 1958, Dec. 14, 1959, Mar. 28, 1960, Jan. 16, 1961, and Mar. 19, 1962); 90 by Paul VI (consistories of Feb. 22, 1965, June 26, 1967, Apr. 28, 1969, Mar. 5, 1973, May 24, 1976, and June 27, 1977); 32 by John Paul II (consistories of June 30, 1979, and Feb. 2, 1983).

Order of Bishops

Titular Bishops of Suburban Sees: Carlo Confalonieri, Dean (Dec. 15, 1958); Paolo Marella (Dec. 14, 1959); Sebastiano Baggio (Apr. 28, 1969); Francesco Carpino (June 26, 1967); Paolo Bertoli (Apr. 28, 1969).

Eastern Rite Patriarchs: Stephanos I Sidarouss, C.M. (Feb. 22, 1965); Antoine Pierre Khoraiche (Feb. 2, 1983).

Order of Priests

1953 (Jan. 12): Giuseppe Siri, Paul Emile Leger, S.S.

1958 (Dec. 15): Jose M. Bueno y Monreal, Franz Koenig.

1960 (Mar. 28): Bernard Jan Alfrink, Laurean Rugambwa.

1961 (Jan. 16): Jose Humberto Quintero.

1962 (Mar. 19): Juan Landazuri Ricketts, O.F.M., Raul Silva Henriquez, S.D.B., Leo Josef Suenens.

1965 (Feb. 22): Josyf Slipyi, Thomas B. Cooray, Maurice Roy, Owen McCann, Leon-Etienne Duval, Ermenegildo Florit, Paul Zoungrana, Lawrence J. Shehan, Agnelo Rossi, Giovanni Colombo.

1967 (June 26): Gabriel Garrone, Patrick O'Boyle, Maximilien de Furstenberg, Jose Clemente Maurer, C.SS.R., Pietro Parente, John J. Krol, Corrado Ursi, Justin Darmojuwono, Michele Pellegrino, Alexandre Renard.

1969 (Apr. 28): Alfredo Vicente Scherer, Gordon J. Gray, Silvio Oddi, Miguel Dario Miranda y Gomez, Giuseppe Paupini, Joseph Parecattil, John F. Dearden, Francois Marty;

George Flahiff, Paul Gouyon, Vicente Enrique y Tarancon, Joseph Malula, Pablo Muñoz Vega, S.J., Antonio Poma;

John J. Carberry, Terence J. Cooke, Stephan Sou Hwan Kim, Eugenio de Araujo Sales, Joseph Hoeffner, Johannes Willebrands, Mario Nasalli Rocca di Corneliano, Sergio Guerri.

1973 (Mar. 5): Antonio Ribeiro, Umberto Mozzoni, Avelar Brandao Vilela, Joseph Cordeiro, Anibal Muñoz Duque, Pierre Paul Phillippe, Pietro Palazzini, Luis Aponte Martinez, Raul Francisco Primatesta, Salvatore Pappalardo, Ferdinando Giuseppe Antonelli, Marcelo Gonzalez Martin, Louis Jean Guyot, Ugo Poletti, Timothy

Manning, Maurice Otunga, Jose Salazar Lopez, Humberto S. Medeiros, Paulo Evaristo Arns, James Darcy Freeman, Narciso Jubany Arnau, Hermann Volk, Pio Taofinu'u.

1976 (May 24): Octavio Beras Rojas, Juan Carlos Aramburu, Hyacinthe Thiandoum, Emmanuel Nsubuga, Lawrence Trevor Picachy, Jaime L. Sin, William W. Baum, Aloisio Lorscheider, Laszlo Lekai, George Basil Hume, O.S.B., Victor Razafimahatratra, Frantisek Tomasek, Dominic Ekandem.

1977 (June 27): Joseph Ratzinger.

1979 (June 30): Agostino Casaroli, Marco Ce, Joseph-Marie Trinh van-Can, Ernesto Corripio Ahumada, Joseph Asajiro Satowaki, Roger Etchegaray, Anastasio Alberto Ballestrero, O.C.D., Tomas O'Fiaich, Gerald Emmett Carter, Franciszek Macharski.

1983 (Feb. 2): Bernard Yago, Franjo Kuharic, Jose Ali Lebrun Moratinos, Joseph L. Bernardin, Michael Michai Kitbunchu, Alexandre do Nascimento, Alfonso Lopez Trujillo, Godfried Danneels, Thomas Stafford Williams, Carlo Maria Martini, Jean-Marie Lustiger, Jozef Glemp, Julijans Vaivods, Joachim Meisner.

Order of Deacons

1976 (May 24): Opilio Rossi, Giuseppe Maria Sensi, Corrado Bafile, Joseph Schroeffer, Eduardo Pironio.

1977 (June 27): Bernardin Gantin, Luigi Ciappi.

1979 (June 30): Giuseppe Caprio, Egano Righi-Lambertini, Ernesto Civardi, Wladyslaw Rubin.

1983 (Feb. 2): Aurelio Sabattani, Giuseppe Casoria, Henri de Lubac.

Ineligible To Vote

As of Aug. 15, 1983, 24 of the 134 cardinals were ineligible to take part in a papal election in line with the apostolic letter *Ingravescentem Aetatem* effective Jan. 1, 1971, which limited the functions of cardinals after completion of their 80th year.

Cardinals affected were: Alfrink, Antonelli, Bafile, Colombo, Confalonieri, Cooray, de Lubac, Florit, Garrone, Marella, Maurer, Miranda y Gomez, Munoz Vega, Nasalli Rocca di Corneliano, O'Boyle, Parente, Pellegrino, Quintero, Scherer, Schroeffer, Shehan, Slipyi, Tomasek, Vaivods.

Two more cardinals were due to become ineligible to vote by the end of 1983: Leon-Etienne Duval, after Nov. 9; Hermann Volk, after Dec. 27.

Cardinals completing their 80th year in 1984: Joseph Asajiro Satowaki, Feb. 1; Patriarch Stephanos I Sidarouss, Feb. 22; Paul Emile Leger, Apr. 26; Francois Marty, May 18; Umberto Mozzoni, June 29; Leo Josef Suenens, July 16; John J. Carberry, July 31; Jose Maria Bueno y Monreal, Sept. 11; Maximilien de Furstenberg, Oct. 23.

Archbishop John R. Whealon of Hartford announced Aug. 12, 1983: fewer Sunday Masses, beginning Jan. 1, 1984; no more than one Saturday-night-for-Sunday Mass per parish; dropping Masses with only half-full churches; Masses 90 minutes apart; no Masses after 12:30 p.m. on Sunday.

DISTRIBUTION OF CARDINALS

As of Aug. 15, 1983, there were 134 cardinals from more than 50 countries or areas. Listed below are areas, countries, number and last names.

Europe — 70

Italy (34): Antonelli, Bafile, Baggio, Ballestrero, Bertoli, Caprio, Carpino, Casaroli, Casoria, Cé, Ciappi, Civardi, Colombo, Confalonieri, Florit, Guerri, Marella, Martini, Mozzoni, Nasalli Rocca di Corneliano, Oddi, Palazzini, Pappalardo, Parente, Paupini, Pellegrino, Poletti, Poma, Righi-Lambertini, Rossi, Sabattani, Sensi, Siri, Ursi.

France (9): De Lubac, Etchegaray, Garrone, Gouyon, Guyot, Lustiger, Marty, Philippe, Renard.

Germany (5): Hoeffner, Meisner, Ratzinger, Schroeffer, Volk.

Spain (4): Bueno y Monreal, Enrique y Tarancon, Gonzalez Martin, Jubany Arnau.

Netherlands (3): Alfrink, De Furstenberg, Willebrands.

Poland (3): Glemp, Macharski, Rubin.

Belgium (2): Danneels, Suenens.

One from each of the following countries: Austria, Koenig; Czechoslovakia, Tomasek; England, Hume; Hungary, Lekai; Ireland, O'Fiaich; Latvia (USSR), Vaivods; Portugal, Ribeiro; Scotland, Gray; Ukraine (now in USSR), Slipyi; Yugoslavia, Kuharic.

Asia — 11

India (2): Parecattil, Picachy.

One from each of the following countries: Indonesia, Darmojuwono; Japan, Satowaki; Korea, Kim; Lebanon, Khoraiche; Pakistan, Cordeiro; Philippines, Sin; Sri Lanka, Cooray; Thailand, Kitbunchu, Vietnam, Trinh van-Can.

Oceania — 3

Australia, Freeman; New Zealand, Williams; Pacific Islands (Samoa), Taofinu'u.

Africa — 14

One from each of the following countries: Algeria, Duval; Angola, do Nascimento; Benin, Gantin; Egypt, Sidarouss; Ivory Coast, Yago; Kenya, Otunga; Madagascar, Razafimahatratra; Nigeria, Ekandem; Senegal, Thiandoum; South Africa, McCann; Tanzania, Rugambwa; Uganda, Nsubuga; Upper Volta, Zoungrana; Zaire, Malula.

North America — 18

United States (10): Baum, Bernardin, Carberry, Cooke, Dearden, Krol, Manning, Medeiros, O'Boyle, Shehan.

Canada (4): Carter, Flahiff, Leger, Roy.

Mexico (3): Corripio Ahumada, Miranda y Gomez, Salazar Lopez.

Puerto Rico (1): Aponte Martinez.

Central and South America — 18

Brazil (6): Arns, Brandao Vilela, De Araujo Sales, Lorscheider, Rossi, Scherer.

Argentina (3): Aramburu, Pironio, Primatesta.

Colombia (2): Lopez Trujillo, Munoz Duque.

Venezuela (2): Lebrun Moratinos, Quintero.

One from each of the following countries: Bolivia, Maurer; Chile, Silva Henriquez; Dominican Republic, Beras Rojas; Ecuador, Munoz Vega, S.J.; Peru, Landazuri Ricketts.

Cardinals of U.S.

As of July 10, 1983, U.S. cardinals, years of elevation and sees.

Lawrence J. Shehan, 1965, Baltimore (retired 1974); Patrick A. O'Boyle, 1967, Washington (retired 1973); John J. Krol, 1967, Philadelphia; John F. Dearden, 1969, Detroit (retired 1980); John J. Carberry, 1969, St. Louis (retired 1979); Terence J. Cooke, 1969, New York; Timothy Manning, 1973, Los Angeles; Humberto S. Medeiros, 1973, Boston; William W. Baum, 1976, Washington, D.C. (1973-80); prefect of Congregation for Catholic Education, 1980; Joseph L. Bernardin, 1983, Chicago.

Deceased cardinals of the United States,. Data: years of elevation, sees, years of birth and death.

John McCloskey, 1875, New York, 1810-1885; James Gibbons, 1886, Baltimore, 1834-1921; John Farley, 1911, New York, 1842-1918; William O'Connell, 1911, Boston, 1859-1944; Dennis Dougherty, 1921, Philadelphia, 1865-1951; Patrick Hayes, 1924, New York, 1867-1938; George Mundelein, 1924, Chicago, 1872-1939; John Glennon, 1946, St. Louis, 1862-1946; Edward Mooney, 1946, Detroit, 1882-1958;

Francis Spellman, 1946, New York, 1889-1967; Samuel Stritch, 1946, Chicago, 1887-1958; James F. McIntyre, 1953, Los Angeles, 1886-1979; John O'Hara, C.S.C., 1958, Philadelphia, 1888-1960; Richard Cushing, 1958, Boston, 1895-1970; Albert Meyer, 1959, Chicago, 1903-1965; Aloysius Muench, 1959, Fargo (and papal nuncio), 1889-1962; Joseph Ritter, 1961, St. Louis, 1892-1967; Francis Brennan, 1967, official of Roman Curia, 1894-1968; John P. Cody, 1967, Chicago 1907-1982; John J. Wright, 1969, prefect of Congregation for Clergy, 1909-1979.

AMERICAN COLLEGE, LOUVAIN

The American College was founded by the bishops of the United States in 1857 as a residence and house of formation for U.S. seminarians and graduate students pursuing courses in theology and related subjects at the Catholic Universities of Leuven and Louvain-la-Neuve (dating from 1425) in Belgium.

The college is administered by an American rector and staff, and operates under the auspices of a special committee of the National Conference of Catholic Bishops. Archbishop Peter L. Gerety of Newark is chairman of the committee. The present rector, the 11th, is Father John J. Costanzo of Pueblo, Colo.

The address is: The American College, University of Louvain, Naamsestraat 100, B-3000 Leuven, Belgium.

The current enrollment of The American College includes students from more than 49 dioceses in the U.S., Canada, Europe and the Third World countries.

REPRESENTATIVES OF THE HOLY SEE

Papal representatives and their functions were the subject of a document entitled *Sollicitudo Omnium Ecclesiarum* which Pope Paul VI issued on his own initiative under the date of June 24, 1969.

Delegates and Nuncios

Papal representatives "receive from the Roman Pontiff the charge of representing him in a fixed way in the various nations or regions of the world.

"When their legation is only to local churches, they are known as apostolic delegates. When to this legation, of a religious and ecclesial nature, there is added diplomatic legation to states and governments, they receive the title of nuncio, pronuncio, and internuncio."

[An apostolic nuncio has the diplomatic rank of ambassador extraordinary and plenipotentiary. Traditionally, because the Vatican diplomatic service has the longest uninterrupted history in the world, a nuncio has precedence among diplomats in the country to which he is accredited and serves as dean of the diplomatic corps on state occasions. Since 1965 pro-nuncios, also of ambassadorial rank, have been assigned to countries in which this prerogative is not recognized.]

(Other representatives, who are covered in the Almanac article, Vatican Representatives to International Organizations, are clerics and lay persons "who form . . . part of a pontifical mission attached to international organizations or take part in conferences and congresses." They are variously called delegates or observers.)

"The primary and specific purpose of the mission of a papal representative is to render ever closer and more operative the ties that bind the Apostolic See and the local churches.

"The ordinary function of a pontifical representative is to keep the Holy See regularly and objectively informed about the conditions of the ecclesial community to which he has been sent, and about what may affect the life of the Church and the good of souls.

"On the one hand, he makes known to the Holy See the thinking of the bishops, clergy, religious and faithful of the territory where he carries out his mandate, and forwards to Rome their proposals and their requests; on the other hand, he makes himself the interpreter, with those concerned, of the acts, documents, information and instructions emanating from the Holy See."

Service and Liaison

Representatives, while carrying out their general and special duties, are bound to respect the autonomy of local churches and bishops. Their service and liaison responsibilities include the following:

• **Nomination of Bishops:** To play a key role in compiling, with the advice of ecclesiastics and lay persons, and submitting lists of names of likely candidates to the Holy See with their own recommendations.

• **Bishops:** To aid and counsel local bishops with-out interfering in the affairs of their jurisdictions.

• **Episcopal Conferences:** To maintain close relations with them and to assist them in every possible way. (Papal representatives do not belong to these conferences.)

• **Religious Communities of Pontifical Rank:** To advise and assist major superiors for the purpose of promoting and consolidating conferences of men and women religious and to coordinate their apostolic activities.

• **Church-State Relations:** The thrust in this area is toward the development of sound relations with civil governments and collaboration in work for peace and the total good of the whole human family.

The mission of a papal representative begins with appointment and assignment by the pope and continues until termination of his mandate. He acts "under the guidance and according to the instructions of the cardinal secretary of state and prefect of the Council for the Public Affairs of the Church, to whom he is directly responsible for the execution of the mandate entrusted to him by the Supreme Pontiff." Normally, representatives are required to retire at the age of 75.

NUNCIOS AND DELEGATES

(Sources: *Annuario Pontificio, L'Osservatore Romano, Acta Apostolicae Sedis,* NC News Service.)

Data, as of July 1, 1983, country, rank of legation (corresponding to rank of legate unless otherwise noted), name of legate (archbishop unless otherwise noted) as available.

Delegate for Papal Representatives: Archbishop Giovanni Coppa. The post was established in 1973 to coordinate papal diplomatic efforts throughout the world. The office entails responsibility for "following more closely through timely visits the activities of papal representatives . . . and encouraging their rapport with the central offices" of the Secretariat of State and the Council for the Public Affairs of the Church.

Africa, Southern (Botswana, South Africa, Namibia, Swaziland): Pretoria, South Africa, Apostolic Delegation; Edward Cassidy (also Pro-Nuncio to Lesotho).

Algeria: Algiers, Nunciature; Gabriel Montalvo, Pro-Nuncio (He is also Pro-Nuncio to Tunisia and Apostolic Delegate to Libya.)

Angola: Luanda, Apostolic Delegation; Fortunato Baldelli (also Apostolic Delegate to Sao Tome and Principe).

Antilles: Apostolic Delegation; Paul Fouad Tabat (resides in Port of Spain, Trinidad).

Argentina: Buenos Aires, Nunciature; Ubaldo Calabresi.

Australia: Canberra, Nunciature; Luigi Barbarito, Pro-Nuncio.

Austria: Vienna, Nunciature; Mario Cagna.

Bahamas: Nunciature; Paul Fouad Tabat, Pro-Nuncio (resides in Port of Spain, Trinidad).

Bangladesh: Dacca, Nunciature; Luigi Accogli,

Pro-Nuncio (also serves as Apostolic Delegate to Burma.)

Barbados: Nunciature; Paul Fouad Tabat, Pro-Nuncio (resides in Port of Spain, Trinidad).

Belgium: Brussels, Nunciature; Angelo Pedroni (also Nuncio to Luxembourg and European Community).

Belize: Diplomatic relations established in 1983.

Benin (formerly Dahomey): Nunciature; Ivan Dias, Pro-Nuncio (resides in Accra, Ghana).

Bolivia: La Paz, Nunciature; Alfio Rapisarda.

Botswana: See Africa, Southern.

Brazil: Brasilia, Nunciature; Carlo Furno.

Burma: See Bangladesh.

Burundi: Bujumbura, Nunciature; Bernard Jacqueline, Pro-Nuncio.

Cameroon: Yaounde, Nunciature; Donato Squicciarino, Pro-Nuncio (also Pro-Nuncio to Gabon Republic and Equatorial Guinea).

Canada: Ottawa, Nunciature; Angelo Palmas, Pro-Nuncio.

Cape Verde, Republic of: Nunciature; Luigi Dossena, Pro-Nuncio (resides in Dakar, Senegal).

Central African Republic: Bangui, Nunciature; Giovanni Bulaitis, Pro-Nuncio (also Pro-Nuncio to Congo and Apostolic Delegate to Chad).

Chad: Apostolic Delegation; Giovanni Bulaitis (resides in Bangui, Central African Republic).

Chile: Santiago, Nunciature; Angelo Sodano.

China: Taipei (Taiwan), Nunciature.

Colombia: Bogota, Nunciature; Angelo Acerbi.

Congo Republic: Brazzaville, Nunciature; Giovanni Bulaitis, Pro-Nuncio (resides in Bangui, Central African Republic).

Costa Rica: San Jose, Nunciature; Lajos Kada (also Nuncio to El Salvador).

Cuba: Havana, Nunciature; Giulio Einaudi, Pro-Nuncio.

Cyprus: Nicosia, Nunciature; William A. Carew, Pro-Nuncio (also Apostolic Delegate to Jerusalem).

Denmark: Copenhagen, Nunciature; Luigi Bellotti, Pro-Nuncio (also Pro-Nuncio to Finland, Iceland, Norway and Sweden).

Djibouti: See Red Sea Region.

Dominica: Nunciature: Paul Fouad Tabet, Pro-Nuncio (resides in Port-of-Spain, Trinidad).

Dominican Republic: Santo Domingo, Nunciature; Blasco Francisco Collaco (also Apostolic Delegate to Puerto Rico).

Ecuador: Quito, Nunciature; Vincenzo Farano.

Egypt: Cairo, Nunciature; Achille Glorieux, Pro-Nuncio.

El Salvador: San Salvador, Nunciature; Lajos Kada (also Nuncio to Costa Rica).

Equatorial Guinea: Santa Isabel, Nunciature; Donato Squicciarino, Pro-Nuncio (resides in Yaounde, Cameroon).

Ethiopia: Addis Ababa, Nunciature; Thomas White, Pro-Nuncio.

Fiji: Nunciature; Antonio Magnoni, Pro-Nuncio (resides in New Zealand).

Finland: Helsinki, Nunciature; Luigi Bellotti, Pro-Nuncio (resides in Denmark).

France: Paris, Nunciature; Angelo Felici.

Gabon: Libreville, Nunciature; Donato Squicciarino, Pro-Nuncio (resides in Yaounde, Cameroon).

Gambia: Nunciature; Pro-Nuncio (resides in Monrovia, Liberia).

Germany: Bonn, Nunciature; Guido Del Mestri.

Ghana: Accra, Nunciature; Ivan Dias, Pro-Nuncio (also Pro-Nuncio to Benin and Togo).

Great Britain: London, Nunciature; Bruno Heim, Pro-Nuncio (also papal representative to Gibraltar).

Greece: Athens, Nunciature; Giovanni Mariani, Pro-Nuncio.

Grenada: Nunciature.

Guatemala: Guatemala City, Nunciature; Oriano Quilici.

Guinea: Conakry, Apostolic Delegation (resides in Monrovia, Liberia).

Guinea-Bissau: Apostolic Delegation; Luigi Dossena (resides at Dakar, Senegal).

Haiti: Port-au-Prince, Nunciature; Luigi Conti.

Honduras: Tegucigalpa, Nunciature; Andrea Cordero Lanza di Montezemolo. (also Nuncio to Nicaragua).

Iceland: Nunciature; Luigi Bellotti, Pro-Nuncio (resides in Denmark).

India: New Delhi, Nunciature; Agostino Caccavillan, Pro-Nuncio.

Indonesia: Jakarta, Nunciature; Pablo Puente, Pro-Nuncio.

Iran: Teheran, Nunciature; Giovanni De Andrea, Pro-Nuncio.

Iraq: Baghdad, Nunciature; Pro-Nuncio (also Pro-Nuncio to Kuwait).

Ireland: Dublin, Nunciature; Gaetano Alibrandi.

Italy: Rome, Nunciature; Romolo Carboni.

Ivory Coast: Abidjan, Nunciature; Justo Mullor Garcia (also Pro-Nuncio to Niger and Upper Volta).

Jamaica: Nunciature; Paul Fouad Tabat, Pro-Nuncio (resides in Port of Spain, Trinidad).

Japan: Tokyo, Nunciature; Mario Pio Gaspari, Pro-Nuncio.

Jerusalem, Palestine, Jordan, Israel: Jerusalem, Apostolic Delegation; William A. Carew (also Pro-Nuncio to Cyprus).

Kenya: Nairobi, Nunciature; Clemente Faccani, Pro-Nuncio (also Apostolic Delegate to Seychelles Is.).

Korea: Seoul, Nunciature; Francesco Monterisi, Pro-Nuncio.

Kuwait: Al Kuwait, Nunciature; Pro-Nuncio (resides in Baghdad, Iraq).

Laos and Malaysia: Apostolic Delegation; Renato Raffaele Martino (resides in Bangkok, Thailand).

Lebanon: Beirut, Nunciature; Luciano Angeloni.

Lesotho: Maseru, Nunciature; Edward Cassidy, Pro-Nuncio (resides in Pretoria, S. Africa).

Liberia: Monrovia, Nunciature; Pro-Nuncio (also Pro-Nuncio to Gambia and Apostolic Delegate to Guinea and Sierra Leone).

Libya: Apostolic Delegation; Gabriel Montalvo (resides in Algiers, Algeria).

Luxembourg: Nunciature; Angelo Pedroni (resides in Brussels, Belgium).

Madagascar: Tananarive, Nunciature; Sergio Sebastiani, Pro-Nuncio (also Pro-Nuncio to Mauritius and Apostolic Delegate to Reunion).

Malawi: Lilongwe, Nunciature; Georg Zur, Pro-Nuncio (resides in Zambia).

Mali: Nunciature; Luigi Dossena, Pro-Nuncio (resides in Dakar, Senegal).

Malta: La Valletta, Nunciature.

Mauritania: Nouakchott, Apostolic Delegation; Luigi Dossena (resides in Dakar, Senegal).

Mauritius: Port Louis, Nunciature; Sergio Sebastiani, Pro-Nuncio (resides in Tananarive, Madagascar).

Mexico: Mexico City, Apostolic Delegation; Girolamo Prigione.

Morocco: Rabat, Nunciature; Pro-Nuncio.

Mozambique: Maputo, Apostolic Delegation; Francesco Colasuonna (also Pro-Nuncio to Zimbabwe).

Namibia: See Africa, Southern.

Netherlands: The Hague, Nunciature; Bruno Wustenberg, Pro-Nuncio.

New Zealand: Wellington, Nunciature; Antonio Magnoni, Pro-Nuncio. (He is also Pro-Nuncio to Fiji and Apostolic Delegate to Pacific Islands).

Nicaragua: Managua, Nunciature; Andrea Cordero Lanza di Montezemolo (also Nuncio to Honduras).

Niger: Niamey, Nunciature; Justo Mullor Garcia, Pro-Nuncio (resides in Abidjan, Ivory Coast).

Nigeria: Lagos, Nunciature; Carlo Curis, Pro-Nuncio.

Norway: Nunciature; Luigi Bellotti, Pro-Nuncio (resides in Denmark).

Pacific Islands: See New Zealand.

Pakistan: Islamabad, Nunciature; Emmanuele Gerada, Pro-Nuncio.

Panama: Panama, Nunciature; Jose Sebastian Laboa.

Papua New Guinea: Port Moresby; Nunciature; Francesco De Nittis, Pro-Nuncio. (He is also Apostolic Delegate to western and southern Solomon Islands.)

Paraguay: Asuncion, Nunciature; Joseph Mees.

Peru: Lima, Nunciature; Mario Tagliaferri.

Philippines: Manila, Nunciature; Bruno Torpigliani.

Portugal: Lisbon, Nunciature; Sante Portalupi.

Puerto Rico: See Dominican Republic.

Red Sea Region (Somalia, Djibouti, part of Arabian Peninsula): Apostolic Delegation; Giovanni Moretti (resides in Khartoum, Sudan).

Reunion: See Madagascar.

Rhodesia: See Zimbabwe.

Rwanda: Kigali, Nunciature.

Sao Tome and Principe: See Angola.

Senegal: Dakar, Nunciature; Luigi Dossena, Pro-Nuncio (also Pro-Nuncio to Cape Verde and Mali; Apostolic Delegate to Guinea-Bissau, and Mauritania.)

Seychelles Islands: See Kenya.

Sierra Leone: Apostolic Delegation (resides in Monrovia, Liberia).

Singapore: Nunciature; Renato Raffaele

Martino, Pro-Nuncio (resides in Bangkok, Thailand).

Solomon Islands: Apostolic Delegation; Francesco De Nittis (resides in Port Moresby, Papua New Guinea).

Somalia: See Red Sea Region.

South Africa: See Africa, Southern.

Spain: Madrid, Nunciature; Antonio Innocenti.

Sri Lanka: Colombo, Nunciature; Nicola Rotunno, Pro-Nuncio.

Sudan: Khartoum, Nunciature; Giovanni Moretti, Pro-Nuncio (also Apostolic Delegate to Red Sea Region).

Swaziland: See Africa, Southern.

Sweden: Nunciature; Luigi Bellotti, Pro-Nuncio (resides in Denmark).

Switzerland: Bern, Nunciature; Ambrogio Marchioni.

Syria (Syrian Arab Republic): Damascus, Nunciature; Pro-Nuncio.

Tanzania: Dar-es-Salaam, Nunciature; Gian Vincenzo Moreni, Pro-Nuncio.

Thailand: Bangkok, Nunciature; Renato Raffaelo Martino, Pro-Nuncio (also Pro-Nuncio to Singapore and Apostolic Delegate to Laos and Malaysia).

Togo: Lome, Nunciature; Ivan Dias, Pro-Nuncio (resides in Accra, Ghana).

Trinidad and Tobago: Port of Spain, Trinidad, Nunciature; Paul Fouad Tabat, Pro-Nuncio (also Pro-Nuncio to Bahamas, Barbados, Dominica, Jamaica and Apostolic Delegate to Antilles).

Tunisia: Tunis, Nunciature; Gabriel Montalvo, Pro-Nuncio (resides in Algiers, Algeria).

Turkey: Ankara, Nunciature; Salvatore Asta, Pro-Nuncio.

Uganda: Kampala, Nunciature; Karl Joseph Rauber, Pro-Nuncio.

United States of America: Washington, D.C., Apostolic Delegation; Pio Laghi.

Upper Volta: Ouagadougou, Nunciature; Justo Mullor Garcia, Pro-Nuncio (resides in Abidjan, Ivory Coast).

Uruguay: Montevideo, Nunciature; Franco Brambilla.

Venezuela: Caracas, Nunciature; Luciano Storero.

Vietnam and Cambodia: Apostolic Delegation.

Yugoslavia: Belgrade, Nunciature; Michele Cecchini, Pro-Nuncio.

Zaire: Kinshasa-Gombe, Nunciature; Giuseppe Uhac, Pro-Nuncio.

Zambia: Lusaka, Nunciature; Georg Zur, Pro-Nuncio (also Pro-Nuncio to Malawi).

Zimbabwe: Nunciature; Francesco Colasuonno, Pro-Nuncio (is also Apostolic Delegate to Mozambique).

European Community: Brussels, Belgium, Nunciature; Angelo Pedroni, Nuncio.

Apostolic Delegate to U.S.

The representative of the Pope to the Church in the United States is Archbishop Pio Laghi, apostolic delegate. Archbishop Laghi was born May 21, 1922, in Castiglione, Italy. Ordained to the priesthood Apr. 20, 1946, he entered the Vatican diplomatic service in 1952. He served in Nicaragua, the U.S. (as secretary of the apostolic delegation, 1954-61) and India. He was recalled to Rome and served on the Council for the Public Affairs of the Church. He was appointed to the titular see of Mauriana and received episcopal ordination June 22, 1969. He was apostolic delegate to Jerusalem and Palestine, 1969-74, and apostolic nuncio to Argentina, 1974-80. On Dec. 10, 1980, he was appointed apostolic delegate to the United States and permanent observer to the Organization of American States.

The U.S. Apostolic Delegation was established Jan. 21, 1893. It is located at 3339 Massachusetts Ave. N.W., Washington, D.C. 20008.

Archbishop Laghi's predecessors were Archbishops: Francesco Satolli (1893-1896), Sebastiano Martinelli, O.S.A. (1896-1902), Diomede Falconio, O.F.M. (1902-1911), Giovanni Bonzano (1911-1922), Pietro Fumasoni-Biondi (1922-1933), Amleto Cicognani (1933-1958), Egidio Vagnozzi (1958-1967); Luigi Raimondi (1967-1973); Jean Jadot (1973-1980).

DIPLOMATS AT VATICAN

(Sources: *Annuario Pontificio, L'Osservatore Romano, Acta Apostolicae Sedis*, NC News Service. As of July 1, 1983.)

The dean of the diplomatic corps at the Vatican is Ambassador Joseph Amichia of Ivory Coast (from 1971) who succeeded to the post in 1983.

Algeria: Abdelmalek Benhalyles, Ambassador.
Argentina: Jose Maria Alvarez de Toledo, Ambassador.
Australia: Lloyd Thomson, Ambassador.
Austria: Johannes Proksch, Ambassador.
Bahamas: Ambassador.
Bangladesh: Ambassador.
Barbados: Algernon Washington Symmonds, Ambassador.
Belgium: Eugene Rittweger de Moor, Ambassador.
Belize: Diplomatic relations established in 1983.
Benin (formerly Dahomey): Douwa David Ghaguidi, Ambassador.
Bolivia: Ernesto Ruiz Rada, Ambassador.
Brazil: Antonio Correa do Lago, Ambassador.
Burundi: Ambassador.
Cameroon: Enoch Kwayeb, Ambassador.
Canada: Yvon Beaulne, Ambassador.
Cape Verde, Republic of: Ambassador.
Central African Republic: Albert Sato, Ambassador.
Chile: Hector Riesle Contreras, Ambassador.
China (Taiwan): Chow Shu-Kai, Ambassador.
Colombia: Jose Manuel Rivas Sacconi, Ambassador.
Congo Republic: Jean-Pierre Nonault, Ambassador.
Costa Rica: Ambassador.
Cuba: Manuel Estevez Perez, Ambassador.
Cyprus: Polys Modinos, Ambassador.
Denmark: Hans Erik Thrane, Ambassador.

Dominica: Ambassador (relations established in 1981).
Dominican Republic: Victor Gomez Berges, Ambassador.
Ecuador: Manuel De Guzman Polanco, Ambassador.
Egypt: Mostafa Kamal El-Diwani, Ambassador.
El Salvador: Prudencio Llach Schonenberg, Ambassador.
Equatorial Guinea: Ambassador (relations established 1981).
Ethiopia: Ambassador.
Fiji: Ambassador.
Finland: Bjorn-Olof Alholm, Ambassador.
France: Xavier Daufresne de la Chavalier, Ambassador.
Gabon: Ambassador.
Gambia, The: Abdullah M.K. Boygang, Ambassador.
Germany: Walter Gehlhoff, Ambassador.
Ghana: Joseph Quao Cleland, Ambassador.
Great Britain: Mark Evelyn Heath, Ambassador.
Greece: Stephanos Stathatos, Ambassador.
Grenada: Ambassador.
Guatemala: Ambassador.
Haiti: Jean-Claude Andre, Ambassador.
Honduras: Alejandro Banegas, Ambassador.
Iceland: Niels P. Sigurdsson, Ambassador.
India: Thomas Abraham, Ambassador.
Indonesia: Raymond Toto Prawira Supradja, Ambassador.
Iran: Seyed Hadi Khosrovshahian, Ambassador.
Iraq: Anwar Sabri Abdul Razzak, Ambassador.
Ireland: Francis A. Coffey, Ambassador.
Italy: Claudio Chelli, Ambassador.
Ivory Coast: Joseph Amichia, Ambassador.
Jamaica: Keith Johnson, Ambassador.
Japan: Teruhiko Nakamuro, Ambassador.
Kenya: John Kamau Kimani, Ambassador.
Korea: Joa Soo Kim, Ambassador.
Kuwait: Essa Ahmad Al-Hamad, Ambassador.
Lebanon: Nasri Salhab, Ambassador.
Lesotho: Ambassador.
Liberia: Harry Fumba Moniba, Ambassador.
Lithuania: Stasys Lozoraitis, Jr., first secretary.
Luxembourg: Jean Wagner, Ambassador.
Madagascar: Salomon Rahatoka, Ambassador.
Malawi: Ambassador.
Mali: Yaya Diarra, Ambassador.
Malta: Paolo Farrugia, Ambassador.
Mauritius: Ambassador.
Monaco: Cesar Charles Solamito, Ambassador.
Morocco: Youssef Ben Abbes, Ambassador.
Netherlands: Johan Anthony Beelaerts Van Blokland, Ambassador.
New Zealand: John Vivian Scott, Ambassador.
Nicaragua: Ricardo Agustin Peter Silva, Ambassador.
Niger: Alzouma Tiecoura, Ambassador.
Nigeria: Isaac Jemide Sagay, Ambassador.
Norway: Torbjorn Kristoffer Christiansen, Ambassador.
Order of Malta: Christophe de Kallay, Ambassador.
Pakistan: Fazli Raziq, Ambassador.
Panama: Jaime Ingram Jaen, Ambassador.

Papua New Guinea: Peter Ipu Paipul, Ambassador.

Paraguay: Juan Livieres Argana, Ambassador.

Peru: Jorge Nicholson Sologuren, Ambassador.

Philippines: Bienvenido R. Tantoco, Sr., Ambassador.

Portugal: Goncalo Caldeiro Coelho, Ambassador.

Rwanda: Callixte Hatungimana, Ambassador.

San Marino: Dr. Giovanni Galassi, Minister.

Senegal: Paul Ndiaye, Ambassador.

Singapore: Chiang Hai Ding, Ambassador.

Spain: Nuno Guirre de Carcer y Lopez de Sagredo, Ambassador.

Sri Lanka: Nadaraja Balasubramaniam, Ambassador.

Sudan: Bashir Bakri, Ambassador.

Sweden: Gunnar Johan Ljungdahl, Ambassador.

Syria (Arab Republic): Adib Daoudy, Ambassador.

Tanzania: Nicholas J. Merinyo Maro, Ambassador.

Thailand: Varachit Nitibhon, Ambassador.

Togo: Vigniko A. Amedegnato, Ambassador.

Trinidad and Tobago: Ambassador.

Tunisia: Hedi Baccouche, Ambassador.

Turkey: Sulhi Dislioglu, Ambassador.

Uganda: James Nagai Obua-Otoa, Ambassador.

Upper Volta: Ambassador.

Uruguay: Carlos Maria Romero, Ambassador.

Venezuela: Luciano Joguera Mora, Ambassador.

Yugoslavia: Zvonimir Stenek, Ambassador.

Zaire: Tshimbalanga Shala-Dibwe, Ambassador.

Zambia: Peter Dingiswayo Zuze, Ambassador.

Zimbabwe: Ambassador.

U.S. — VATICAN RELATIONS

Official relations for trade and diplomatic purposes were maintained by the United States and the Papal States while the latter had the character of and acted like other sovereign powers in the international community.

Consular Relations

Consular relations developed in the wake of an announcement, made by the papal nuncio in Paris to the American mission there Dec. 15, 1784, that the Papal States had agreed to open several Mediterranean ports to U.S. shipping.

U.S. consular representation in the Papal States began with the appointment of John B. Sartori, a native of Rome, in June, 1797. Sartori's successors as consuls were: Felix Cicognani, also a Roman, and Americans George W. Greene, Nicholas Browne, William C. Sanders, Daniel LeRoy, Horatio V. Glentworth, W.J. Stillman, Edwin C. Cushman, David M. Armstrong.

Consular officials of the Papal States who served in the U.S. were: Count Ferdinand Lucchesi, 1826 to 1829, who resided in Washington; John B. Sartori, 1829 to 1841, who resided in Trenton, N.J.; Daniel J. Desmond, 1841 to 1850, who resided in Philadelphia; Louis B. Binsse, 1850 to 1895, who resided in New York.

U.S. recognition of the consul of the Papal States did not cease when the states were absorbed into the Kingdom of Italy in 1871, despite pressure from

Baron Blanc, the Italian minister. Binsse held the title until his death Mar. 28, 1895. No one was appointed to succeed him.

Diplomatic Relations

The U.S. Senate approved a recommendation, made by President James K. Polk in December, 1847, for the establishment of a diplomatic post in the Papal States. Jacob L. Martin, the first charge d'affaires, arrived in Rome Aug. 2, 1848, and presented his credentials to Pius IX Aug. 19. Martin, who died within a month, was succeeded by Lewis Cass, Jr. Cass became minister resident in 1854 and served in that capacity until his retirement in 1858.

John P. Stockton, who later became a U.S. Senator from New Jersey, was minister resident from 1858 to 1861. Rufus King was named to succeed him but, instead, accepted a commission as a brigadier general in the Army. Alexander W. Randall of Wisconsin took the appointment. He was succeeded in August, 1862, by Richard M. Blatchford who served until the following year. King was again nominated minister resident and served in that capacity until 1867 when the ministry was ended because of objections from some quarters in the U.S. and failure to appropriate funds for its continuation. J. C. Hooker, a secretary, remained in the Papal States until the end of March, 1868, closing the ministry and performing functions of courtesy.

Personal Envoys

Myron C. Taylor was appointed by President Franklin D. Roosevelt in 1939 to serve as his personal representative to Pope Pius XII and continued serving in that capacity during the presidency of Harry S. Truman until 1951. Henry Cabot Lodge was named to the post by President Richard M. Nixon in 1970, served also during the presidency of Gerald Ford, and represented President Carter at the canonization of St. John Neumann in 1977. Neither Taylor nor Lodge had diplomatic status.

Miami attorney David Walters, a Catholic, served as the personal envoy of President Jimmy Carter to the Pope from July, 1977, until his resignation Aug. 16, 1978. He was succeeded by Robert F. Wagner, also a Catholic and former mayor of New York, who served from October, 1978, to the end of the Carter presidency in January, 1981. William A. Wilson, a California businessman and Catholic, was appointed by President Ronald Reagan in February, 1981, to serve as his personal envoy to the Pope.

None of the personal envoys had diplomatic status.

President Harry S. Truman nominated Gen. Mark Clark to be ambassador to the Vatican in 1951, but withdrew the nomination at Clark's request because of controversy over the appointment.

None of Truman's three successors — Dwight D. Eisenhower, John F. Kennedy or Lyndon B. Johnson — had a personal representative to the Pope.

At the time of Walters' designation for the nondiplomatic post, the House of Representatives had under consideration an amendment, already passed by the Senate, that would have lifted an 1867 prohibition against funding for diplomatic relations with the Vatican.

Any initiative for the establishment of formal diplomatic relations would have to be undertaken by the U.S. government.

VATICAN CITY

The State of Vatican City (Stato della Citta del Vaticano) is the territorial seat of the papacy. The smallest sovereign state in the world, it is situated within the city of Rome, embraces an area of 108.7 acres, and includes within its limits the Vatican Palace, museums, art galleries, gardens, libraries, radio station, post office, bank, astronomical observatory, offices, apartments, service facilities, St. Peter's Basilica, and neighboring buildings between the Basilica and Viale Vaticano.

The extraterritorial rights of Vatican City extend to more than 10 buildings in Rome, including the major basilicas and office buildings of various congregations of the Roman Curia, and to the **Villa of Castel Gandolfo** 15 miles southeast of the City of Rome. Castel Gandolfo is the summer residence of the Holy Father.

The government of Vatican City is in the hands of the reigning pope, who has full executive, legislative and judicial power. The administration of affairs, however, is handled by the Pontifical Commission for the State of Vatican City. The legal system is based on Canon Law; in cases where this code does not obtain, the laws of the City of Rome apply. The City is an absolutely neutral state and enjoys all the rights and privileges of a sovereign power. The Secretariat of State (Papal Secretariat) maintains diplomatic relations with other nations. The citizens of Vatican City, and they alone, owe allegiance to the pope as a temporal head of state.

Cardinals of the Roman Curia residing outside Vatican City enjoy the privileges of extraterritoriality.

The normal population is approximately 1,000. While the greater percentage is made up of priests and religious, there are several hundred lay persons living in Vatican City. They are housed in their own apartments in the City and are engaged in secretarial, domestic, trade and service occupations. About 4,000 persons are employed by the Vatican.

Services of honor and order are performed by the Swiss Guards, who have been charged with responsibility for the personal safety of popes since 1506. Additional police and ceremonial functions are under the supervision of a special office. These functions were formerly handled by the Papal Gendarmes, the Palatine Guard of Honor, and the Guard of Honor of the Pope (Pontifical Noble Guard) which Pope Paul disbanded Sept. 14, 1970.

The **Basilica of St. Peter,** built between 1506 and 1626, is the largest church in Christendom and the site of most papal ceremonies. The pope's own patriarchal basilica, however, is **St. John Lateran,** whose origins date back to 324.

St. Ann's is the parish church of Vatican City.

The vicar general of the pope for Vatican City, which is part of the diocese of Rome, is Most Rev. Peter Canisius Van Lierde, O.S.A., titular bishop of Porfireone.

The **Vatican Library,** one of five in the City, has among its holdings 70,000 manuscripts, 770,000 printed books, and 7,500 incunabula.

The independent temporal power of the pope, which is limited to the confines of Vatican City and small areas outside, was for many centuries more extensive than it is now. As late as the nineteenth century, the pope ruled 16,000 square miles of Papal States across the middle of Italy, with a population of over 3,000,000. In 1870 forces of the Kingdom of Italy occupied these lands which, with the exception of the small areas surrounding the Vatican and Lateran in Rome and the Villa of Castel Gandolfo, became part of the Kingdom by the Italian law of May 13, 1871.

The **Roman Question,** occasioned by this seizure and the voluntary confinement of the pope to the limited papal lands, was finally settled with ratification of the Lateran Agreement on June 7, 1929, by the Italian government and Vatican City and provided a financial indemnity for the former Papal States, which became recognized as part of Italy. The Lateran Agreement became Article 7 of the Italian Constitution on Mar. 26, 1947.

Papal Flag

The papal flag consists of two equal vertical stripes of yellow and white, charged with the insignia of the papacy on the white stripe — a triple crown or tiara over two crossed keys, one of gold and one of silver, tied with a red cord and two tassels. The divisions of the crown represent the teaching, sanctifying and ruling offices of the pope. The keys symbolize his jurisdictional authority.

The papal flag is a national flag inasmuch as it is the standard of the Supreme Pontiff as the sovereign of the state of Vatican City. It is also universally accepted by the faithful as a symbol of the supreme spiritual authority of the Holy Father.

In a Catholic church, the papal flag is displayed on a staff on the left side of the sanctuary (facing the congregation), and the American flag is displayed on the right.

Vatican Radio

The declared purpose of Vatican Radio Station HVJ is "that the voice of the Supreme Pastor may be heard throughout the world by means of the ether waves, for the glory of Christ and the salvation of souls." Designed by Guglielmo Marconi, the inventor of radio, and supervised by him until his death, the station was inaugurated by Pope Pius XI in 1931. The original purpose has been extended to a wide variety of programming.

Vatican Radio operates on international wave lengths, transmits programs in 35 languages, and serves as a channel of communication between the Vatican, church officials and listeners in general in many parts of the world. The station broadcasts about 240 hours a week throughout the world.

The staff of 350 broadcasters and technicians in-
cludes 40 Jesuits and is directed by Father Robert
Tucci, S.J. Headquarters are located in Vatican
City. Studios and offices are at Palazzo Pio, Piazza
Pia, 3. The transmitters are situated at Santa
Maria di Galeria, a short distance north of Rome.

1983 Vatican Stamps

The Vatican Philatelic Office scheduled the following issues of stamps and postal stationery for
1983. (Issue date is given where available.)

• Series commemorating 1983-1984 Extraordinary Holy Year. Issued Mar. 10, 1983, in four values (300, 350, 400 and 2,000 lire) featuring four subjects.

• Series commemorating Vatican Art Collections in the United States, in three issues during
the year. First issue, Mar. 10, 1983, in six values
(100, 200, 250, 300, 350 and 400 lire) featuring six
subjects. Second issue, June 14, 1983, in six values
(100, 200, 300, 400, 500 and 1,000 lire) featuring six
subjects. Third issue, late 1983.

• Series commemorating the fifth centenary of
the birth of the painter Raphael Sanzio. Issued
June 14, 1983, in four values (50, 400, 500, and 1,200
lire) featuring four subjects.

• Series commemorating World Year of Communications.

• Aerogramme. Issued June 14, 1983.

• Illustrated stamped postcards.

Vatican Coins

The Vatican Numismatics Office issued a series
of coins Apr. 26, 1974, for the fourth year of the
pontificate of Pope John Paul II. The set consisted
of seven coins (10, 20, 50, 100, 200, 500 and 1,000
lire).

Papal Audiences

General audiences are scheduled weekly, on
Wednesday.

In Vatican City, they are held in the Audience
Hall on the south side of St. Peter's Basilica or,
weather permitting, in St. Peter's Square. The
hall, which was opened in 1971, has a seating capacity of 6,800 and a total capacity of 12,000.

Audiences are also held during the summer at
Castel Gandolfo when the pope is there on a working vacation.

General audiences last from about 60 to 90 minutes, during which the pope gives a talk and his
blessing. A résumé of the talk, which is usually in
Italian, is given in several languages.

Arrangements for papal audiences are handled
by an office of the Prefecture of the Apostolic
Household.

American visitors can obtain passes for general
audiences by applying to the Bishops' Office for
United States Visitors to the Vatican, Casa Santa
Maria, Via dell'Umilita, 30, 00187 Rome.

Private and group audiences are reserved for
dignitaries of various categories and for special
occasions.

Publications

Acta Apostolicae Sedis: The only "official commentary" of the Holy See, was established in 1908
for the publication of activities of the Holy See,
laws, decrees and acts of congregations and tribunals of the Roman Curia. The first edition was published in January, 1909.

St. Pius X made *AAS* an official organ in 1908.
Laws promulgated for the Church ordinarily take
effect three months after the date of their publication in this commentary.

The publication, mostly in Latin and Italian, is
printed by the Vatican Polyglot Press.

The immediate predecessor of this organ was
Acta Sanctae Sedis, founded in 1865 and given official status by the Congregation for the Propagation of the Faith in 1904.

Annuario Pontificio: The yearbook of the Holy
See. It is edited by the Central Statistics Office of
the Church and is printed in Italian, with some portions in other languages, by the Vatican Polyglot
Press. It covers the worldwide organization of the
Church, lists members of the hierarchy, and includes a wide range of statistical information.

The publication of a statistical yearbook of the
Holy See dates back to 1716, when a volume called
Notizie appeared. Publication under the present
title began in 1860, was suspended in 1870, and resumed again in 1872 under the title *Catholic Hierarchy.* This volume was printed privately at first,
but has been issued by the Vatican Press since
1885. The title *Annuario Pontificio* was restored
in 1912, and the yearbook was called an "official
publication" until 1924.

L'Osservatore Romano: The daily newspaper of
the Holy See. It began publication July 1, 1861, as
an independent enterprise under the ownership
and direction of four Catholic laymen headed by
Marcantonio Pacelli, vice minister of the interior
under Pope Pius IX and a grandfather of the late
Pius XII. Leo XIII bought the publication in 1890,
making it the "pope's" own newspaper.

The only official material in *L'Osservatore
Romano* is that which appears under the heading,
"Nostre Informazioni." This includes notices of
appointments by the Holy See, the texts of papal
encyclicals and addresses by the Holy Father and
others, various types of documents, accounts of
decisions and rulings of administrative bodies, and
similar items. Additional material includes news
and comment on developments in the Church and
the world. Italian is the language most used.

The editorial board is directed by Valerio Volpini. A staff of about 15 reporters covers Rome
news sources. A corps of correspondents provides
foreign coverage.

A weekly roundup edition in English was inaugurated in 1968. Other weekly editions are printed in French, Spanish, Portuguese and German.
Publication of a monthly Polish edition was begun
in February, 1980.

Vatican Press Office: The establishment of a
single Vatican Press Office was announced Feb.
29, 1968, to replace service agencies formerly operated by *L'Osservatore Romano* and an office
created for press coverage of the Second Vatican
Council. Rev. Romeo Panciroli is the director.

Vatican Polyglot Press: The official printing
plant of the Vatican.

The Vatican press was conceived by Marcellus II and Pius IV but was actually founded by Sixtus V on Apr. 27, 1587, to print the Vulgate and the writings of the Fathers of the Church and other authors. A Polyglot Press was established in 1626 by the Congregation for the Propagation of the Faith to serve the needs of the Oriental Church. St. Pius X merged both presses under this title.

The plant has facilities for the printing of a wide variety of material in about 30 languages.

Activities of the Holy See: An annual documentary volume covering the activities of the pope — his daily work, general and special audiences, discourses and messages on special occasions, visits outside the Vatican, missionary and charitable endeavors, meetings with diplomats, heads of state and others — and activities of the congregations, commissions, tribunals and offices of the Roman Curia.

Statistical Yearbook of the Church: Issued by the Central Statistics Office of the Church, it contains principal data concerning the presence and work of the Church in the world. The first issue was published in 1972 under the title *Collection of Statistical Tables, 1969.* It is printed in corresponding columns of Italian and Latin. Some of the introductory material is printed in other languages.

VATICAN REPRESENTATIVES

(Sources: *Annuario Pontificio;* NC News Service.)

The Vatican has representatives to a number of quasi-governmental and international organizations.

Governmental Organizations: United Nations (Abp. Giovanni Cheli, permanent observer); UN Office in Geneva and Specialized Institutes (Abp. Edoardo Rovida, permanent observer); International Atomic Energy Agency (Msgr. Giovanni Ceirano, permanent representative); UN Organization for Industrial Development (Msgr. Giovanni Ceirano, permanent observer); UN Food and Agriculture Organization (Bp. Agostino Ferrari-Toniolo, permanent observer); UN Educational, Scientific and Cultural Organization (Msgr. Renzo Frana, permanent observer);

Council of Europe (Msgr. Luigi Bressan, special envoy with function of permanent observer); Council for Cultural Cooperation of the Council of Europe (Msgr. Luigi Bressan, delegate); Organization of American States (Abp. Pio Laghi, permanent observer); International Institute for the Unification of Private Law (Prof. Pio Ciprotti, delegate); International Committee of Military Medicine and Pharmacy (Adolphe Vander Perre, delegate); World Organization of Tourism (Rev. Giovanni Arrighi, O.P., permanent observer).

Universal Postal Union; International Telecommunications Union; International Council on Grain; World Organization of Intellectual Property; International Union for the Protection of Literary and Artistic Works; International Union for the Protection of Industrial Property; International Organization of Telecommunication via Satellite (Intelsat); European Conference of Postal and Telecommunication Administration (CEPT).

Non-Governmental Organizations: International Committee of Historical Sciences (Msgr. Michele Maccarrone); International Committee of Paleography (Msgr. Jose Ruysschaert, delegate); International Committee of the History of Art (Prof. Carlo Pietrangeli, delegate); International Committee of Anthropological and Ethnological Sciences;

International Committee for the Neutrality of Medicine (Rev. Michel Riquet, S.J., permanent observer); International Center of Study for the Preservation and Restoration of Cultural Goods (Prof. Carlo Pietrangeli, permanent observer); International Council of Monuments and Sites (Prof. Carlo Pietrangeli, delegate); International Alliance on Tourism; International Astronomical Union; International Institute of Administrative Sciences; International Technical Committee for Prevention and Extinction of Fires; World Medical Association.

AMERICAN CHURCH

The Church of Santa Susanna was established as the national church for Americans in Rome Feb. 28, 1922, and entrusted to the Paulist Fathers who have served there continuously since then except for several years during World War II.

NORTH AMERICAN COLLEGE

The North American College was founded by the bishops of the United States in 1859 as a residence and house of formation for U.S. seminarians and graduate students in Rome. The first ordination of an alumnus took place June 14, 1862. Pontifical status was granted the college by Leo XIII Oct. 25, 1884.

Students living at the college study theology and related subjects in the various pontifical universities and institutes in Rome, principally at the Pontifical Gregorian University.

The college is directed by an American rector and staff, and operates under the auspices of a U.S. bishops' committee which was set up in 1924.

JOHN XXIII CENTER

The John XXIII Ecumenical Center was established in 1951 (as the Russian Center) by Father Feodor Wilcock, S.J., in cooperation with Fordham University. It is sponsored by the Jesuit Conference of the United States as a center for study as well as for apostolic and ecumenical activity with Eastern Christians, Catholics and Orthodox, in America. It publishes the periodical *Diakonia,* conducts special seminars and conferences, and sponsors the John XXIII Summer Institute which offers an academic degree for studies in the Eastern traditions of Christianity. It also maintains an Icon and Book Service which provides materials and information about the various Eastern churches.

Father John F. Long, S.J., is superior and director of the center, located at 2502 Belmont Ave., Bronx, N.Y 10458.

Following are excerpts from the first two chapters of the "Dogmatic Constitution on the Church" promulgated by the Second Vatican Council. They describe the relation of the Catholic Church to the Kingdom of God, the nature and foundation of the Church, the People of God, the necessity of membership and participation in the Church for salvation.

Additional subjects in the constitution are treated in other Almanac entries.

I. MYSTERY OF THE CHURCH

By her relationship with Christ, the Church is a kind of sacrament or sign of intimate union with God, and of the unity of all mankind (No. 1).

He (the eternal Father) planned to assemble in the holy Church all those who would believe in Christ. Already from the beginning of the world the foreshadowing of the Church took place. She was prepared for in a remarkable way throughout the history of the people of Israel and by means of the Old Covenant. Established in the present era of time, the Church was made manifest by the outpouring of the Spirit. At the end of time she will achieve her glorious fulfillment. Then . . . all just men from the time of Adam, "from Abel, the just one, to the last of the elect," will be gathered together with the Father in the universal Church (No. 2).

When the work which the Father had given the Son to do on earth (cf. Jn. 17:4) was accomplished, the Holy Spirit was sent on the day of Pentecost in order that he might forever sanctify the Church, and thus all believers would have access to the Father through Christ in the one Spirit (cf. Eph. 2:18).

The Spirit dwells in the Church and in the hearts of the faithful as in a temple (cf. 1 Cor. 3:16; 6:19). . . . The Spirit guides the Church into the fullness of truth (cf. Jn. 16:13) and gives her a unity of fellowship and service. He furnishes and directs her with various gifts, both hierarchical and charismatic, and adorns her with the fruits of His grace (cf. Eph. 4:11-12; 1 Cor. 12:4; Gal. 5:22). By the power of the Gospel he makes the Church grow, perpetually renews her, and leads her to perfect union with her Spouse (No. 4).

Foundation of the Church

The mystery of the holy Church is manifest in her very foundation, for the Lord Jesus inaugurated her by preaching the Good News, that is, the coming of God's Kingdom, which, for centuries, had been promised in the Scriptures. . . . In Christ's word, in his works, and in his presence this Kingdom reveals itself to men.

The miracles of Jesus also confirm that the Kingdom has already arrived on earth.

Before all things, however, the Kingdom is clearly visible in the very Person of Christ, Son of God and Son of Man.

When Jesus rose up again after suffering death on the cross for mankind, he manifested that he had been appointed Lord, Messiah, and Priest forever (cf. Acts 2:36; Heb. 5:6; 7:17-21), and he poured out on his disciples the Spirit promised by the Father (cf. Acts 2:33). The Church, consequently, equipped with the gifts of her Founder and faithfully guarding his precepts . . . receives the mission to proclaim and to establish among all peoples the Kingdom of Christ and of God. She becomes on earth the initial budding forth of that Kingdom. While she slowly grows, the Church strains toward the consummation of the Kingdom and, with all her strength, hopes and desires to be united in glory with her King (No. 5).

Figures of the Church

In the Old Testament the revelation of the Kingdom had often been conveyed by figures of speech. In the same way the inner nature of the Church was now to be made known to us through various images.

The Church is a sheepfold . . . a flock . . . a tract of land to be cultivated, the field of God . . . his choice vineyard . . . the true vine is Christ . . . the edifice of God . . . the house of God . . . the holy temple (whose members are) . . . living stones . . . this holy city . . . a bride . . . our Mother . . . the spotless spouse of the spotless Lamb . . . an exile (No. 6).

In the human nature which he united to himself, the Son of God redeemed man and transformed him into a new creation (cf. Gal. 6:15; 2 Cor. 5:17) by overcoming death through his own death and resurrection. By communicating his Spirit to his brothers, called together from all peoples, Christ made them mystically into his own body.

In that body, the life of Christ is poured into the believers, who, through the sacraments, are united in a hidden and real way to Christ who suffered and was glorified. Through baptism we are formed in the likeness of Christ.

Truly partaking of the body of the Lord in the breaking of the eucharistic bread, we are taken up into communion with him and with one another (No. 7).

One Body in Christ

As all the members of the human body, though they are many, form one body, so also are the faithful in Christ (cf. 1 Cor. 12:12). Also, in the building up of Christ's body there is a flourishing variety of members and functions. There is only one Spirit who . . . distributes his different gifts for the welfare of the Church (cf. 1 Cor. 12:1-11). Among these gifts stands out the grace given to the apostles. To their authority, the Spirit himself subjected even those who were endowed with charisms (cf. 1 Cor. 14).

The head of this body is Christ (No. 7).

Mystical Body of Christ

Christ, the one Mediator, established and ceaselessly sustains here on earth his holy Church, the community of faith, hope, and charity, as a visible structure. Through her he communicates truth and grace to all. But the society furnished with hierarchical agencies and the Mystical Body of Christ are not to be considered as two realities, nor are the visible assembly and the spiritual community, nor the earthly Church and the Church enriched with heavenly things. Rather they form one interlocked reality which is comprised of a divine and a human element. For this reason . . . this reality is compared to the mystery of the incarnate Word. Just as the assumed nature inseparably united to the divine Word serves him as a living instrument of salvation, so, in a similar way, does the communal structure of the Church serve Christ's Spirit, who vivifies it by way of building up the body (cf. Eph. 4:16).

This is the unique Church of Christ which in the Creed we avow as one, holy, catholic, and apostolic. After his Resurrection our Savior handed her over to Peter to be shepherded (Jn. 21:17), commissioning him and the other apostles to propagate and govern her (cf. Mt. 28:18, ff.). Her he erected for all ages as "the pillar and mainstay of the truth" (1 Tm. 3:15). This Church, constituted and organized in the world as a society, subsists in the Catholic Church, which is governed by the successor of Peter and by the bishops in union with that successor, although many elements of sanctification and of truth can be found outside of her visible structure. These elements, however, as gifts properly belonging to the Church of Christ, possess an inner dynamism toward Catholic unity.

The Church, embracing sinners in her bosom, is at the same time holy and always in need of being purified, and incessantly pursues the path of penance and renewal.

The Church, "like a pilgrim in a foreign land, presses forward . . ." announcing the cross and death of the Lord until he comes (cf. 1 Cor. 11:26) (No. 8).

II. THE PEOPLE OF GOD

At all times and among every people, God has given welcome to whosoever fears him and does what is right (cf. Acts 10:35). It has pleased God, however, to make men holy and save them not merely as individuals without any mutual bonds, but by making them into a single people, a people which acknowledges him in truth and serves him in holiness. He therefore chose the race of Israel as a people unto himself. With it he set up a covenant. Step by step he taught this people by manifesting in its history both himself and the decree of his will, and by making it holy unto himself. All these things, however, were done by way of preparation and as a figure of that new and perfect covenant which was to be ratified in Christ.

Christ instituted this New Covenant, that is to say, the New Testament, in his blood (cf. 1 Cor. 11:25), by calling together a people made up of Jew and Gentile, making them one, not according to the flesh but in the Spirit.

This was to be the new People of God . . . reborn . . . through the Word of the living God (cf. 1 Pt. 1:23) . . . from water and the Holy Spirit (cf. Jn. 3:5-6) . . . "a chosen race, a royal priesthood, a holy nation, a purchased people. . . . You who in times past were not a people, but are now the People of God" (1 Pt. 2:9-10).

That messianic people has for its head Christ. . . . Its law is the new commandment to love as Christ loved us (cf. Jn. 13:34). Its goal is the Kingdom of God, which has been begun by God himself on earth, and which is to be further extended until it is brought to perfection by him at the end of time.

This messianic people, although it does not actually include all men, and may more than once look like a small flock, is nonetheless a lasting and sure seed of unity, hope, and salvation for the whole human race. Established by Christ as a fellowship of life, charity, and truth, it is also used by him as an instrument for the redemption of all, and is sent forth into the whole world as the light of the world and the salt of the earth (cf. Mt. 5:13-16).

Israel according to the flesh . . . was already called the Church of God (Neh. 13:1; cf. Nm. 20:4; Dt. 23:1, ff.). Likewise the new Israel . . . is also called the Church of Christ (cf. Mt. 16:18). For he has bought it for himself with his blood (cf. Acts 20:28), has filled it with his Spirit, and provided it with those means which befit it as a visible and social unity. God has gathered together as one all those who in faith look upon Jesus as the author of salvation and the source of unity and peace, and has established them as the Church, that for each and all she may be the visible sacrament of this saving unity (No. 9).

Priesthood

The baptized, by regeneration and the anointing of the Holy Spirit, are consecrated into . . . a holy priesthood.

[All members of the Church participate in the priesthood of Christ, through the common priesthood of the faithful. See Priesthood of the Laity.]

Though they differ from one another in essence and not only in degree, the common priesthood of the faithful and the ministerial or hierarchical priesthood are nonetheless interrelated. Each of them in its own special way is a participation in the one priesthood of Christ (No. 10).

It is through the sacraments and the exercise of the virtues that the sacred nature and organic structure of the priestly community is brought into operation (No. 11). (See Role of the Sacraments.)

Prophetic Office

The holy People of God shares also in Christ's prophetic office. It spreads abroad a living witness to him, especially by means of a life of faith and charity and by offering to God a sacrifice of praise. . . . The body of the faithful as a whole, anointed as they are by the Holy One (cf. Jn. 2:20, 27), cannot err in matters of belief. Thanks to a supernatural sense of faith which characterizes the People as a whole, it manifests this unerring quality when, "from the bishops down to the last member of the laity," it shows universal agreement in matters of faith and morals.

God's People accepts not the word of men but the very Word of God (cf. 1 Thes. 2:13). It clings

188

The Church

without fail to the faith once delivered to the saints (cf. Jude 3), penetrates it more deeply by accurate insights, and applies it more thoroughly to life. All this it does under the lead of a sacred teaching authority to which it loyally defers.

It is not only through the sacraments and Church ministries that the same Holy Spirit sanctifies and leads the People of God. . . . He distributes special graces among the faithful of every rank. By these gifts he makes them fit and ready to undertake the various tasks or offices advantageous for the renewal and upbuilding of the Church. . . . These charismatic gifts . . . are to be received with thanksgiving and consolation, for they are exceedingly suitable and useful for the needs of the Church.

Judgment as to their genuineness and proper use belongs to those who preside over the Church, and to whose special competence it belongs . . . to test all things and hold fast to that which is good (cf. 1 Thes. 5:12; 19-21) (No. 12).

All Are Called

All men are called to belong to the new People of God. Wherefore this People, while remaining one and unique, is to be spread throughout the whole world and must exist in all ages, so that the purpose of God's will may be fulfilled. In the beginning God made human nature one. After his children were scattered, he decreed that they should at length be united again (cf. Jn. 11:52). It was for this reason that God sent his Son . . . that he might be Teacher, King, and Priest of all, the Head of the new and universal People of the sons of God. For this God finally sent his Son's Spirit as Lord and Lifegiver. He it is who, on behalf of the whole Church and each and every one of those who believe, is the principle of their coming together and remaining together in the teaching of the apostles and in fellowship, in the breaking of bread and in prayers (cf. Acts 2:42) (No. 13).

One People of God

It follows that among all the nations of earth there is but one People of God, which takes its citizens from every race, making them citizens of a Kingdom which is of a heavenly and not an earthly nature. For all the faithful scattered throughout the world are in communion with each other in the Holy Spirit. . . . the Church or People of God . . . foster(s) and take(s) to herself, insofar as they are good, the ability, resources and customs of each people. Taking them to herself, she purifies, strengthens, and ennobles them . . . This characteristic of universality which adorns the People of God is a gift from the Lord himself. By reason of it, the Catholic Church strives energetically and constantly to bring all humanity with all its riches back to Christ its Head in the unity of his Spirit.

In virtue of this catholicity each individual part of the Church contributes through its special gifts to the good of the other parts and of the whole Church. Thus through the common sharing of gifts . . . the whole and each of the parts receive increase.

All men are called to be part of this catholic unity of the People of God. . . . And there belong to it or are related to it in various ways, the Catholic faithful as well as all who believe in Christ, and indeed the whole of mankind. For all men are called to salvation by the grace of God (No. 13).

The Catholic Church

This sacred Synod turns its attention first to the Catholic faithful. Basing itself upon sacred Scripture and tradition, it teaches that the Church . . . is necessary for salvation. For Christ, made present to us in his Body, which is the Church, is the one Mediator and the unique Way of salvation. In explicit terms he himself affirmed the necessity of faith and baptism (cf. Mk. 16:16; Jn. 3:5) and thereby affirmed also the necessity of the Church, for through baptism as through a door men enter the Church. Whosoever, therefore, knowing that the Catholic Church was made necessary by God through Jesus Christ, would refuse to enter her or to remain in her could not be saved.

They are fully incorporated into the society Church who, possessing the Spirit of Christ, accept her entire system and all the means of salvation given to her, and through union with her visible structure are joined to Christ, who rules her through the Supreme Pontiff and the bishops. This joining is effected by the bonds of professed faith, of the sacraments, of ecclesiastical government, and of communion. He is not saved, however, who, though he is part of the body of the Church, does not persevere in charity. He remains indeed in the bosom of the Church, but . . . only in a "bodily" manner and not "in his heart."

Catechumens who, moved by the Holy Spirit, seek with explicit intention to be incorporated into the Church, are by that very intention joined to her. . . . Mother Church already embraces them as her own (No. 14).

Other Christians, The Unbaptized

The Church recognizes that in many ways she is linked with those who, being baptized, are honored with the name of Christian, though they do not profess the faith in its entirety or do not preserve unity of communion with the successor of Peter.

We can say that in some real way they are joined with us in the Holy Spirit, for to them also he gives his gifts and graces, and is thereby operative among them with his sanctifying power (No. 15).

Finally, those who have not yet received the Gospel are related in various ways to the People of God. In the first place there is the people to whom the covenants and the promises were given and from whom Christ was born according to the flesh (cf. Rom. 9:4-5). On account of their fathers, this people remains most dear to God, for God does not repent of the gifts he makes nor of the calls he issues (cf. Rom. 11:28-29).

But the plan of salvation also includes those who acknowledge the Creator. In the first place among these are the Moslems. . . . Nor is God himself far distant from those who in shadows and images seek the unknown God.

Those also can attain to everlasting salvation

who through no fault of their own do not know the Gospel of Christ or his Church, yet sincerely seek God and, moved by grace, strive by their deeds to do his will as it is known to them through the dictates of conscience. Nor does divine Providence deny the help necessary for salvation to those who, without blame on their part, have not yet arrived

at an explicit knowledge of God, but who strive to live a good life, thanks to his grace. Whatever goodness or truth is found among them is looked upon by the Church as a preparation for the Gospel. She regards such qualities as given by him who enlightens all men so that they may finally have life (No. 16).

THE POPE, TEACHING AUTHORITY, COLLEGIALITY

The Roman Pontiff — the successor of St. Peter as the Vicar of Christ and head of the Church on earth — has full and supreme authority over the universal Church in matters pertaining to faith and morals (teaching authority), discipline and government (jurisdictional authority).

The primacy of the pope is real and supreme power. It is not merely a prerogative of honor — that is, of his being regarded as the first among equals. Neither does primacy imply that the pope is just the presiding officer of the collective body of bishops. The pope is the head of the Church.

Catholic belief in the primacy of the pope was stated in detail in the dogmatic constitution on the Church, *Pastor Aeternus,* approved in 1870 by the fourth session of the First Vatican Council. Some elaboration of the doctrine was made in the *Dogmatic Constitution on the Church* which was approved and promulgated by the Second Vatican Council Nov. 21, 1964. The entire body of teaching on the subject is based on Scripture and tradition and the centuries-long experience of the Church.

Infallibility

The essential points of doctrine concerning infallibility in the Church and the infallibility of the pope were stated by the Second Vatican Council in the *Dogmatic Constitution on the Church,* as follows:

"This infallibility with which the divine Redeemer willed his Church to be endowed in defining a doctrine of faith and morals extends as far as extends the deposit of divine revelation, which must be religiously guarded and faithfully expounded. This is the infallibility which the Roman Pontiff, the head of the college of bishops, enjoys in virtue of his office, when, as the supreme shepherd and teacher of all the faithful who confirms his brethren in their faith (cf. Lk. 22:32), he proclaims by a definitive act some doctrine of faith or morals. Therefore his definitions, of themselves, and not from the consent of the Church, are justly styled irreformable, for they are pronounced with the assistance of the Holy Spirit, an assistance promised to him in blessed Peter. Therefore they need no approval of others, nor do they allow an appeal to any other judgment. For then the Roman Pontiff is not pronouncing judgment as a private person. Rather, as the supreme teacher of the universal Church, as one in whom the charism of the infallibility of the Church herself is individually present, he is expounding or defending a doctrine of Catholic faith.

"The infallibility promised to the Church resides also in the body of bishops when that body exercises supreme teaching authority with the suc-

cessor of Peter. To the resultant definitions the assent of the Church can never be wanting, on account of the activity of that same Holy Spirit, whereby the whole flock of Christ is preserved and progresses in unity of faith.

"But when either the Roman Pontiff or the body of bishops together with him defines a judgment, they pronounce it in accord with revelation itself. All are obliged to maintain and be ruled by this revelation, which, as written or preserved by tradition, is transmitted in its entirety through the legitimate succession of bishops and especially through the care of the Roman Pontiff himself.

"Under the guiding light of the Spirit of truth, revelation is thus religiously preserved and faithfully expounded in the Church. The Roman Pontiff and the bishops, in view of their office and of the importance of the matter, strive painstakingly and by appropriate means to inquire properly into that revelation and to give apt expression to its contents. But they do not allow that there could be any new public revelation pertaining to the divine deposit of faith" (No. 25).

Authentic Teaching

The pope rarely speaks *ex cathedra* — that is, "from the chair" of St. Peter, for the purpose of making an infallible pronouncement. More often and in various ways he states authentic teaching in line with Scripture, tradition, the living experience of the Church, and the whole analogy of faith. Of such teaching, the Second Vatican Council said in its *Dogmatic Constitution on the Church* (No. 25):

"Religious submission of will and of mind must be shown in a special way to the authentic teaching authority of the Roman Pontiff, even when he is not speaking *ex cathedra.* That is, it must be shown in such a way that his supreme magisterium is acknowledged with reverence, the judgments made by him are sincerely adhered to, according to his manifest mind and will. His mind and will in the matter may be known chiefly either from the character of the documents, from his frequent repetition of the same doctrine, or from his manner of speaking."

With respect to bishops, the constitution states: "They are authentic teachers, that is, teachers endowed with the authority of Christ, who preach to the people committed to them the faith they must believe and put into practice. By the light of the Holy Spirit, they make that faith clear, bringing forth from the treasury of revelation new things and old (cf. Mt. 13:52), making faith bear fruit and vigilantly warding off any errors which threaten their flock (cf. 2 Tm. 4:1-4).

"Bishops, teaching in communion with the Roman Pontiff, are to be respected by all as witnesses to divine and Catholic truth. In matters of faith and morals, the bishops speak in the name of Christ and the faithful are to accept their teaching and adhere to jt with a religious assent of soul."

Magisterium—Teaching Authority

Responsibility for teaching doctrine and judging orthodoxy belongs to the official teaching authority of the Church.

This authority is personalized in the pope, the successor of St. Peter as head of the Church, and in the bishops together and in union with the pope, as it was originally committed to Peter and to the whole college of apostles under his leadership. They are the official teachers of the Church.

Others have auxiliary relationships with the magisterium: theologians, in the study and clarification of doctrine; teachers — priests, religious, lay persons — who cooperate with the pope and bishops in spreading knowledge of religious truth; the faithful, who by their sense of faith and personal witness contribute to the development of doctrine and the establishment of its relevance to life in the Church and the world.

The magisterium, Pope Paul VI noted in an address at a general audience Jan. 11, 1967, "is a subordinate and faithful echo and secure interpreter of the divine word." It does not reveal new truths, "nor is it superior to sacred Scripture." Its competence extends to the limits of divine revelation manifested in Scripture and tradition and the living experience of the Church, with respect to matters of faith and morals and related subjects.

Official teaching in these areas is infallible when it is formally defined, for belief and acceptance by all members of the Church, by the pope, acting in the capacity of supreme shepherd of the flock of Christ; also, when doctrine is proposed and taught with moral unanimity of bishops with the pope in a solemn collegial manner, as in an ecumenical council, and/or in the ordinary course of events. Even when not infallibly defined, official teaching in the areas of faith and morals is authoritative and requires religious assent.

The teachings of the magisterium have been documented in creeds, formulas of faith, decrees and enactments of ecumenical and particular councils, various kinds of doctrinal statements, encyclical letters and other teaching instruments. They have also been incorporated into the liturgy, with the result that the law of prayer is said to be a law of belief.

Collegiality

The bishops of the Church, in union with the pope, have supreme teaching and pastoral authority over the whole Church in addition to the authority of office they have for their own dioceses.

This collegial authority is exercised in a solemn manner in an ecumenical council and can be exercised in other ways as well, "provided that the head of the college calls them to collegiate action, or at least so approves or freely accepts the united action of the dispersed bishops that it is made a true collegiate act."

This doctrine is grounded on the fact that: "Just as, by the Lord's will, St. Peter and the other apostles constituted one apostolic college, so in a similar way the Roman Pontiff as the successor of Peter, and the bishops as the successors of the apostles are joined together."

Doctrine on collegiality was stated by the Second Vatican Council in the *Dogmatic Constitution on the Church* (Nos. 22 and 23).

REVELATION

Following are excerpts from the "Constitution on Revelation" promulgated by the Second Vatican Council. They describe the nature and process of divine revelation, inspiration and interpretation of Scripture, the Old and New Testaments, and the role of Scripture in the life of the Church.

I. REVELATION ITSELF

God chose to reveal himself and to make known to us the hidden purpose of his will (cf. Eph. 1:9) by which through Christ, the Word made flesh, man has access to the Father in the Holy Spirit and comes to share in the divine nature (cf. Eph. 2:18; 2 Pt. 1:4). Through this revelation, therefore, the invisible God (cf. Col. 1:15; 1 Tm. 1:17) . . . speaks to men as friends (cf. Ex. 33:11; Jn. 15:14-15) and lives among them (cf. Bar. 3:38) so that he may invite and take them into fellowship with himself. This plan of revelation is realized by deeds and words having an inner unity: the deeds wrought by God in the history of salvation manifest and confirm the teaching and realities signified by the words, while the words proclaim the deeds and clarify the mystery contained in them. By this revelation then, the deepest truth about God and the salvation of man is made clear to us in Christ, who is the Mediator and at the same time the fullness of all revelation (No. 2).

God . . . from the start manifested himself to our first parents. Then after their fall his promise of redemption aroused in them the hope of being saved (cf. Gn. 3:15), and from that time on he ceaselessly kept the human race in his care, in order to give eternal life to those who perseveringly do good in search of salvation (cf. Rom. 2:6-7). . . . He called Abraham in order to make of him a great nation (cf. Gn. 12:2). Through the patriarchs, and after them through Moses and the prophets, he taught this nation to acknowledge himself as the one living and true God . . . and to wait for the Savior promised by him. In this manner he prepared the way for the Gospel down through the centuries (No. 3).

Revelation in Christ

Then, after speaking in many places and varied ways through the prophets, God "last of all in these days has spoken to us by his Son" (Heb. 1:1-2). . . . Jesus perfected revelation by fulfilling it through his whole work of making himself present and manifesting himself: through his words and deeds, his signs and wonders, but especially through his death and glorious resurrection from the dead and final sending of the Spirit of truth. Moreover, he confirmed with divine testimony what revelation proclaimed: that God is with us to free us from the darkness of sin and death, and to raise us up to life eternal.

The Christian dispensation, therefore, as the new and definitive covenant, will never pass away, and we now await no further new public revelation before the glorious manifestation of our Lord Jesus Christ (cf. 1 Tm. 6:14; Ti. 2:13) (No. 4).

II. TRANSMISSION OF REVELATION

God has seen to it that what he had revealed for the salvation of all nations would abide perpetually in its full integrity and be handed on to all generations. Therefore Christ the Lord, in whom the full revelation of the supreme God is brought to completion (cf. 2 Cor. 1:20; 3:16; 4:6), commissioned the apostles to preach to all men that Gospel which is the source of all saving truth and moral teaching, and thus to impart to them divine gifts. This Gospel had been promised in former times through the prophets, and Christ himself fulfilled it and promulgated it with his own lips. This commission was faithfully fulfilled by the apostles who, by their oral preaching, by example, and by ordinances, handed on what they had received from . . . Christ . . . or what they had learned through the prompting of the Holy Spirit. The commission was fulfilled, too, by those apostles and apostolic men who under the inspiration of the same Holy Spirit committed the message of salvation to writing (No. 7).

Tradition

But in order to keep the Gospel forever whole and alive within the Church, the apostles left bishops as their successors, "handing over their own teaching role" to them. This sacred tradition, therefore, and sacred Scripture of both the Old and the New Testament are like a mirror in which the pilgrim Church on earth looks at God (No. 7).

The apostolic preaching, which is expressed in a special way in the inspired books, was to be preserved by a continuous succession of preachers until the end of time. Therefore the apostles, handing on what they themselves had received, warn the faithful to hold fast to the traditions which they have learned. . . . Now what was handed on by the apostles includes everything which contributes to the holiness of life, and the increase in faith of the People of God; and so the Church, in her teaching, life, and worship, perpetuates and hands on to all generations all that she herself is, all that she believes (No. 8).

Development of Doctrine

This tradition which comes from the apostles develops in the Church with the help of the Holy Spirit. For there is a growth in the understanding of the realities and the words which have been handed down. This happens through the contemplation and study made by believers . . . through the intimate understanding of spiritual things they experience, and through the preaching of those who have received through episcopal succession the sure gift of truth. For, as the centuries succeed one another, the Church constantly moves forward toward the fullness of divine truth until the words of God reach their complete fulfillment in her.

The words of the holy Fathers witness to the living presence of this tradition, whose wealth is poured into the practice and life of the believing and praying Church. Through the same tradition the Church's full canon of the sacred books is known, and the sacred writings themselves are more profoundly understood and unceasingly made active in her; . . . and the Holy Spirit, through whom the living voice of the Gospel resounds in the Church, and through her, in the world, leads unto all truth those who believe and makes the word of Christ dwell abundantly in them (cf. Col. 3:16) (No. 8).

Tradition and Scripture

Hence there exist a close connection and communication between sacred tradition and sacred Scripture. For both of them, flowing from the same divine wellspring, in a certain way merge into a unity and tend toward the same end. For sacred Scripture is the word of God inasmuch as it is consigned to writing under the inspiration of the divine Spirit. To the successors of the apostles, sacred tradition hands on in its full purity God's word, which was entrusted to the apostles by Christ the Lord and the Holy Spirit. Thus, led by the light of the Spirit of truth, these successors can in their preaching preserve this word of God faithfully, explain it, and make it more widely known. Consequently, it is not from sacred Scripture alone that the Church draws her certainty about everything which has been revealed. Therefore both sacred tradition and sacred Scripture are to be accepted and venerated with the same sense of devotion and reverence (No. 9).

Sacred tradition and sacred Scripture form one sacred deposit of the word of God, which is committed to the Church (No. 10).

Teaching Authority of Church

The task of authentically interpreting the word of God, whether written or handed on, has been entrusted exclusively to the living teaching office of the Church, whose authority is exercised in the name of Jesus Christ. This teaching office is not above the word of God, but serves it, teaching only what has been handed on . . . it draws from this one deposit of faith everything which it presents for belief as divinely revealed.

It is clear, therefore, that sacred tradition, sacred Scripture, and the teaching authority of the Church . . . are so linked and joined together that one cannot stand without the others, and that all together and each in its own way under the action of the one Holy Spirit contribute effectively to the salvation of souls (No. 10).

III. INSPIRATION, INTERPRETATION

Those . . . revealed realities . . . contained and presented in sacred Scripture have been committed to writing under the inspiration of the Holy

Spirit. Holy Mother Church, relying on the belief of the apostles, holds that the books of both the Old and New Testament in their entirety, with all their parts, are sacred and canonical because, having been written under the inspiration of the Holy Spirit (cf. Jn. 20:31; 2 Tm. 3:16; 2 Pt. 1:19-21; 3:15-16) they have God as their author and have been handed on as such to the Church herself. In composing the sacred books, God chose men and, while employed by him, they made use of their powers and abilities, so that, with him acting in them and through them, they, as true authors, consigned to writing everything and only those things which he wanted (No. 11).

Inerrancy

Therefore, since everything asserted by the inspired authors or sacred writers must be held to be asserted by the Holy Spirit, it follows that the books of Scripture must be acknowledged as teaching firmly, faithfully, and without error that truth which God wanted put into the sacred writings for the sake of our salvation. Therefore "all Scripture is inspired by God and useful for teaching, for reproving, for correcting, for instruction in justice; that the man of God may be perfect, equipped for every good work" (2 Tm. 3:16-17) (No. 11).

Literary Forms

However, since God speaks in sacred Scripture through men in human fashion, the interpreter of sacred Scripture, in order to see clearly what God wanted to communicate to us, should carefully investigate what meaning the sacred writers really intended, and what God wanted to mainfest by means of their words.

The interpreter must investigate what meaning the sacred writer intended to express and actually expressed in particular circumstances as he used contemporary literary forms in accordance with the situation of his own time and culture. For the correct understanding of what the sacred author wanted to assert, due attention must be paid to the customary and characteristic styles of perceiving, speaking, and narrating which prevailed at the time of the sacred writer, and to the customs men normally followed at that period in their everyday dealings with one another (No. 12).

Analogy of Faith

No less serious attention must be given to the content and unity of the whole of Scripture, if the meaning of the sacred texts is to be correctly brought to light. The living tradition of the whole Church must be taken into account along with the harmony which exists between elements of the faith. . . . All of what has been said about the way of interpreting Scripture is subject finally to the judgment of the Church, which carries out the divine commission and ministry of guarding and interpreting the word of God (No. 12).

IV. THE OLD TESTAMENT

In carefully planning and preparing the salvation of the whole human race, the God of supreme love,

by a special dispensation, chose for himself a people to whom he might entrust his promises. First he entered into a covenant with Abraham (cf. Gn. 15:18) and, through Moses, with the people of Israel (cf. Ex. 24:8). To this people which he had acquired for himself, he so manifested himself through words and deeds as the one true and living God that Israel came to know by experience the ways of God with men. . . . The plan of salvation, foretold by the sacred authors, recounted and explained by them, is found as the true word of God in the books of the Old Testament: these books, therefore, written under divine inspiration, remain permanently valuable (No. 14).

Principal Purpose

The principal purpose to which the plan of the Old Covenant was directed was to prepare for the coming both of Christ, the universal Redeemer, and of the messianic Kingdom. . . . Now the books of the Old Testament, in accordance with the state of mankind before the time of salvation established by Christ, reveal to all men the knowledge of God and of man and the ways in which God . . . deals with men. These books . . . show us true divine pedagogy (No. 15).

The books of the Old Testament with all their parts, caught up into the proclamation of the Gospel, acquire and show forth their full meaning in the New Testament (cf. Mt. 5:17; Lk. 24:27; Rom. 16:25-26; 2 Cor. 3:14-16) and in turn shed light on it and explain it (No. 16).

V. THE NEW TESTAMENT

The word of God . . . is set forth and shows its power in a most excellent way in the writings of the New Testament. For when the fullness of time arrived (cf. Gal. 4:4), the Word was made flesh and dwelt among us in the fullness of grace and truth (cf. Jn. 1:14). Christ established the Kingdom of God on earth, manifested his Father and himself by deeds and words, and completed his work by his death, resurrection, and glorious ascension and by the sending of the Holy Spirit. Having been lifted up from the earth, he draws all men to himself (cf. Jn. 12:32). . . . This mystery had not been manifested to other generations as it was now revealed to his holy apostles and prophets in the Holy Spirit (cf. Eph. 3:4-6), so that they might preach the Gospel, stir up faith in Jesus, Christ and Lord, and gather the Church together. To these realities, the writings of the New Testament stand as a perpetual and divine witness (No. 17).

The Gospels and Other Writings

The Gospels have a special preeminence . . . for they are the principal witness of the life and teaching of the incarnate Word, our Savior.

The Church has always and everywhere held and continues to hold that the four Gospels are of apostolic origin. For what the apostles preached . . . afterwards they themselves and apostolic men, under the inspiration of the divine Spirit, handed on to us in writing: the foundation of faith, namely, the fourfold Gospel, according to Matthew, Mark, Luke, and John (No. 18).

The four Gospels, . . . whose historical character the Church unhesitatingly asserts, faithfully hand on what Jesus Christ, while living among men, really did and taught for their eternal salvation until the day he was taken up into heaven (see Acts 1:1-2). Indeed, after the ascension of the Lord the apostles handed on to their hearers what he had said and done. . . . The sacred authors wrote the four Gospels, selecting some things from the many which had been handed on by word of mouth or in writing, reducing some of them to a synthesis, explicating some things in view of the situation of their churches, and preserving the form of proclamation but always in such fashion that they told us the honest truth about Jesus. For their intention in writing was that . . . we might know "the truth" concerning those matters about which we have been instructed (cf. Lk. 1:2-4) (No. 19).

Besides the four Gospels, the canon of the New Testament also contains the Epistles of St. Paul and other apostolic writings, composed under the inspiration of the Holy Spirit. In these writings . . . those matters which concern Christ the Lord are confirmed, his true teaching is more and more fully stated, the saving power of the divine work of Christ is preached, the story is told of the beginnings of the Church and her marvelous growth, and her glorious fulfillment is foretold (No. 20).

VI. SCRIPTURE IN CHURCH LIFE

The Church has always venerated the divine Scriptures just as she venerates the body of the Lord. . . . She has always regarded the Scriptures together with sacred tradition as the supreme rule of faith, and will ever do so. For, inspired by God

and committed once and for all to writing, they impart the word of God himself without change, and make the voice of the Holy Spirit resound in the words of the prophets and apostles. Therefore, like the Christian religion itself, all the preaching of the Church must be nourished and ruled by sacred Scripture (No. 21).

Easy access to sacred Scripture should be provided for all the Christian faithful. That is why the Church from the very beginning accepted as her own that very ancient Greek translation of the Old Testament which is named after seventy men (the Septuagint); and she has always given a place of honor to other translations, Eastern and Latin, especially the one known as the Vulgate. But since the word of God should be available at all times, the Church with maternal concern sees to it that suitable and correct translations are made into different languages, especially from the original texts of the sacred books. And if, given the opportunity and the approval of Church authority, these translations are produced in cooperation with the separated brethren as well, all Christians will be able to use them (No. 22).

Biblical Studies, Theology

The constitution encouraged the development and progress of biblical studies "under the watchful care of the sacred teaching office of the Church."

It noted also: "Sacred theology rests on the written word of God, together with sacred tradition, as its primary and perpetual foundation," and that "the study of the sacred page is, as it were, the soul of sacred theology" (Nos. 23, 24).

THE BIBLE

The Canon of the Bible is the Church's official list of sacred writings. These works, written by men under the inspiration of the Holy Spirit, contain divine revelation and, in conjunction with the tradition and teaching authority of the Church, constitute the rule of Catholic faith. The Canon was fixed and determined by the tradition and teaching authority of the Church.

The Catholic Canon

The Old Testament Canon of 45 books is as follows.

• **The Pentateuch,** the first five books: Genesis (Gn.), Exodus (Ex.), Leviticus (Lv.), Numbers (Nm.), Deuteronomy (Dt.).

• **Historical Books:** Joshua (Jos.), Judges (Jgs.), Ruth (Ru.) 1 and 2 Samuel (Sm.), 1 and 2 Kings (Kgs.), 1 and 2 Chronicles (Chr.), Ezra (Ezr.), Nehemiah (Neh.), Tobit (Tb.), Judith (Jdt.), Esther (Est.), 1 and 2 Maccabees (Mc.).

• **Wisdom Books:** Job (Jb.), Psalms (Ps.), Proverbs (Prv.), Ecclesiastes (Eccl.), Song of Songs (Song), Wisdom (Wis.), Sirach (Sir.).

• **The Prophets:** Isaiah (Is.), Jeremiah (Jer.), Lamentations (Lam.), Baruch (Bar.), Ezechiel (Ez.), Daniel (Dn.), Hosea (Hos.), Joel (Jl.), Amos (Am.), Obadiah (Ob.), Jonah (Jon.), Micah (Mi.), Nahum (Na.), Habakkuk (Hb.), Zephaniah

(Zep.), Haggai (Hg.), Zechariah (Zec.) Malachi (Mal.).

The New Testament Canon of 27 books is as follows.

• **The Gospels** of Matthew (Mt.), Mark (Mk.), Luke (Lk.), John (Jn.)

• **The Acts of the Apostles** (Acts).

• **The Pauline Letters** — Romans (Rom.), 1 and 2 Corinthians (Cor.), Galatians (Gal.), Ephesians (Eph.), Philippians (Phil.), Colossians (Col.), 1 and 2 Thessalonians (Thes.) 1 and 2 Timothy (Tm.), Titus (Ti.), Philemon (Phlm.), Hebrews (Heb.).

• **The Catholic Letters** — James (Jas.), 1 and 2 Peter (Pt.), 1, 2 and 3 John (Jn.), Jude (Jude).

• **Revelation** (Rv.).

Developments

The Canon of the Old Testament was firm by the fifth century despite some questioning by scholars. It was stated by a council held at Rome in 382, by African councils held in Hippo in 393 and in Carthage in 397 and 419, and by Innocent I in 405.

All of the New Testament books were generally known and most of them were acknowledged as inspired by the end of the second century. The Muratorian Fragment, dating from about 200, listed most of the books recognized as canonical in later decrees. Prior to the end of the fourth cen-

tury, however, there was controversy over the inspired character of several works — the Letter to
the Hebrews, James, Jude, 2 Peter, 2 and 3 John
and Revelation. Controversy ended in the fourth
century and these books, along with those about
which there was no dispute, were enumerated in
the canon stated by the councils of Hippo and
Carthage and affirmed by Innocent I in 405.

The Canon of the Bible was solemnly defined by
the Council of Trent in the dogmatic decree *De
Canonicis Scripturis,* Apr. 8, 1546.

Hebrew and Other Canons

The Hebrew Canon of sacred writings was fixed
by tradition and the consensus of rabbis, probably
by about 100 A.D. by the Synod or Council of Jam-
nia and certainly by the end of the second or early
in the third century. It consists of the following
works in three categories.

• **The Law (Torah),** the five books of Moses:
Genesis, Exodus, Leviticus, Numbers, Deuteronomy.

• **The Prophets:** former prophets — Joshua,
Judges, 1 and 2 Samuel, 1 and 2 Kings; latter
prophets — Isaiah, Jeremiah, Ezekiel, and 12 mi-
nor prophets (Hosea, Joel, Amos, Obadiah, Jonah,
Micah, Nahum, Habakkuk, Zephaniah, Haggai,
Zechariah, Malachi).

• **The Writings:** 1 and 2 Chronicles, Ezra,
Nehemiah, Job, Psalms, Proverbs, Ecclesiastes,
Song of Songs, Ruth, Esther, Daniel.

This Canon, embodying the tradition and practice of the Palestine community, did not include a
number of works contained in the Alexandrian version of sacred writings translated into Greek between 250 and 100 B.C. and in use by Greek-speaking Jews of the Dispersion (outside Palestine).
The rejected works, called apocrypha and not regarded as sacred, are: Tobit, Judith, Wisdom,
Sirach, Baruch, 1 and 2 Maccabees, the last six
chapters of Esther and three passages of Daniel
(3:24-90; 13; 14). These books have also been rejected from the Protestant Canon, although they
are included in bibles under the heading,
Apocrypha.

The aforementioned books are held to be inspired and sacred by the Catholic Church. In Catholic usage, they are called deuterocanonical because they were under discussion for some time
before questions about their canonicity were settled. Books regarded as canonical with little or no
debate were called protocanonical. The status of
both categories of books is the same in the Catholic
Bible.

The Protestant Canon of the Old Testament is
the same as the Hebrew.

The Old Testament Canon of some separated
Eastern churches differs from the Catholic Canon.

Christians are in agreement on the Canon of the
New Testament.

Languages

Hebrew, Aramaic and Greek were the original
languages of the Bible. Most of the Old Testament
books were written in Hebrew. Portions of Daniel,
Ezra, Jeremiah, Esther, and probably the books of

Tobit and Judith were written in Aramaic. The
Book of Wisdom, 2 Maccabees and all the books of
the New Testament were written in Greek.

Manuscripts and Versions

The original writings of the inspired authors
have been lost. The Bible has been transmitted
through ancient copies called manuscripts and
through translations or versions.

Authoritative Greek manuscripts include the Si-
naitic and Vatican manuscripts of the fourth century and the Alexandrine of the fifth century A.D.

The Septuagint and Vulgate translations are in a
class by themselves.

The Septuagint version, a Greek translation of
the Old Testament for Greek-speaking Jews, was
begun about 250 and completed about 100 B.C. The
work of several Jewish translators at Alexandria,
it differed from the Hebrew Bible in the arrangement of books and included several, later called
deuterocanonical, which were not acknowledged
as sacred by the community in Palestine.

The Vulgate was a Latin version of the Old and
New Testaments produced from the original languages by St. Jerome from about 383 to 404. It became the most widely used Latin text for centuries
and was regarded as basic long before the Council
of Trent designated it as authentic and suitable for
use in public reading, controversy, preaching and
teaching. Because of its authoritative character, it
became the basis for many translations into other
languages. A critical revision was completed by a
pontifical commission in 1977.

Hebrew and Aramaic manuscripts of great antiquity and value have figured more significantly
than before in recent scriptural work by Catholic
scholars, especially since their use was strongly
encouraged, if not mandated, in 1943 by Pius XII in
the encyclical *Divino Afflante Spiritu.*

The English translation of the Bible in general
use among Catholics until well into the 20th century was the *Douay-Rheims,* so called because
of the places where it was prepared and published,
the New Testament at Rheims in 1582 and the Old
Testament at Douay in 1609. The translation was
made from the Vulgate text. As revised and issued
by Bishop Richard Challoner in 1749 and 1750, it became the standard Catholic English version for
about 200 years.

A revision of the Challoner New Testament,
made on the basis of the Vulgate text by scholars
of the Catholic Biblical Association of America,
was published in 1941 in the United States under
the sponsorship of the Episcopal Committee of the
Confraternity of Christian Doctrine.

New American Bible

A new translation of the entire Bible, the first
ever made directly into English from the original
languages under Catholic auspices, was projected
in 1944 and completed in the fall of 1970 with publication of the *New American Bible.* The Episcopal Committee of the Confraternity of Christian
Doctrine sponsored the NAB. The translators were
members of the Catholic Biblical Association of
America and several fellow scholars of other

faiths. The typical edition was produced by St. Anthony Guild Press, Paterson, N.J.

Old Testament portions of the NAB were published in separate volumes before undergoing final revision and being bound in one cover. Genesis and Psalms were issued in 1948 and 1950; Genesis to Ruth, in 1952; Job to Sirach, in 1955; the Prophets, in 1961; Samuel to the Maccabees, in 1969. The new translation of the New Testament was issued for the first time in 1970.

The *Jerusalem Bible* is an English translation of a French version based on the original languages. It was published by Doubleday & Co., Inc., which is also working toward completion of the *Anchor Bible.*

The Protestant counterpart of the *Douay-Rheims Bible* was the *King James Bible,* called the *Authorized Version* in England. Originally published in 1611, it was in general use for more than three centuries. Its modern revisions include the *English Revised Version,* published between 1881 and 1885; the *American Revised Version,* 1901, and revisions of the New Testament (1946) and the Old Testament (1952) published in 1957 in the United States as the *Revised Standard Version.* The latest revision, a translation in the language of the present day made from Greek and Hebrew sources, is the *New English Bible,* published Mar. 16, 1970. Its New Testament portion was originally published in 1961.

Biblical Federation

In November, 1966, Pope Paul commissioned the Secretariat for Promoting Christian Unity to start work for the widest possible distribution of the Bible and to coordinate endeavors toward the production of Catholic-Protestant Bibles in all languages.

The World Catholic Federation for the Biblical Apostolate, established in 1969, sponsors a program designed to create greater awareness among Catholics of the Bible and its use in everyday life.

The U. S. Center for the Catholic Biblical Apostolate, under the direction of Father Stephen Hartdegen, O.F.M., is related to the Department of Education, U.S. Catholic Conference. Address: 1312 Massachusetts Ave. N.W., Washington, D.C. 20005.

APOCRYPHA

In Catholic usage, Apocrypha are books which have some resemblance to the canonical books in subject matter and title but which have not been recognized as canonical by the Church. They are characterized by a false claim to divine authority; extravagant accounts of events and miracles alleged to be supplemental revelation; material favoring heresy (especially in "New Testament" apocrypha); minimal, if any, historical value.

Among examples of this type of literature itemized by J. McKenzie, S.J., in *Dictionary of the Bible* are: *the Books of Adam and Eve, Martyrdom of Isaiah, Testament of the Patriarchs, Assumption of Moses, Sibylline Oracles; Gospel of James, Gospel of Thomas, Arabic Gospel of the Infancy, History of Joseph the Carpenter; Acts of John, Acts of Paul, Acts of Peter, Acts of Andrew,* and numerous epistles.

Books of this type are called pseudepigrapha by Protestants.

In Protestant usage, some books of the Catholic Bible (deuterocanonical) are called apocrypha because their inspired character is rejected.

DEAD SEA SCROLLS

The Qumran Scrolls, popularly called the Dead Sea Scrolls, are a collection of manuscripts, all but one of them in Hebrew, found since 1947 in caves in the Desert of Juda west of the Dead Sea.

Among the findings were a complete text of Isaiah dating from the second century, B.C., more or less extensive fragments of other Old Testament texts (including the deuterocanonical Tobit), and a commentary on Habakkuk. Until the discovery of these materials, the oldest known Hebrew manuscripts were from the 10th century, A.D.

Also found were messianic and apocalyptic texts, and other writings describing the beliefs and practices of the Essenes, a rigoristic Jewish sect

The scrolls, dating from about the first century before and after Christ, are important sources of information about Hebrew literature, Jewish history during the period between the Old and New Testaments, and the history of Old Testament texts. They established the fact that the Hebrew text of the Old Testament was fixed before the beginning of the Christian era and have had definite effects in recent critical studies and translations of the Old Testament. Together with other scrolls found at Masada, they are still the subject of intensive study.

BOOKS OF THE BIBLE

OLD TESTAMENT
(Dates are before Christ.)

Pentateuch

The Pentateuch is the collective title of the first five books of the Bible. Substantially, they identify the Israelites as Yahweh's Chosen People, cover their history from Egypt to the threshold of the Promised Land, contain the Mosaic Law and Covenant, and disclose the promise of salvation to come. Principal themes concern the divine promise of salvation, Yahweh's fidelity and the Covenant. Work on the composition of the Pentateuch was completed in the sixth century.

Genesis: The book of origins, according to its title in the Septuagint. In two parts, covers: religious prehistory, including accounts of the origin of the world and man, the original state of innocence and the fall, the promise of salvation, patriarchs before and after the Deluge, the Tower of Babel narrative, genealogies (first 11 chapters);

the Covenant with Abraham and patriarchal history from Abraham to Joseph (balance of the 50 chapters). Significant are the themes of Yahweh's universal sovereignty and mercy.

Exodus: Named with the Greek word for departure, is a religious epic which describes the oppression of the 12 tribes in Egypt and their departure, liberation or passover therefrom under the leadership of Moses; Yahweh's establishment of the Covenant with them, making them his Chosen People, through the mediation of Moses at Mt. Sinai; instructions concerning the tabernacle, the sanctuary and Ark of the Covenant; the institution of the priesthood. The book is significant because of its theology of liberation and redemption. In Christian interpretation, the Exodus is a figure of baptism.

Leviticus: Mainly legislative in theme and purpose, contains laws regarding sacrifices, ceremonies of ordination and the priesthood of Aaron, legal purity, the holiness code, atonement, the redemption of offerings and other subjects. Summarily, Levitical laws provided directives for all aspects of religious observance and for the manner in which the Israelites were to conduct themselves with respect to Yahweh and each other. Leviticus was the liturgical handbook of the priesthood.

Numbers: Taking its name from censuses recounted at the beginning and near the end, is a continuation of Exodus. It combines narrative of the Israelites' desert pilgrimage from Sinai to the border of Canaan with laws related to and expansive of those in Leviticus.

Deuteronomy: The concluding book of the Pentateuch, recapitulates, in the form of a testament of Moses, the Law and much of the desert history of the Israelites; enjoins fidelity to the Law as the key to good or bad fortune for the people; gives an account of the commissioning of Joshua as the successor of Moses. Notable themes concern the election of Israel by Yahweh, observance of the Law, prohibitions against the worship of foreign gods, worship of and confidence in Yahweh, the power of Yahweh in nature. The Deuteronomic Code or motif, embodying all of these elements, was the norm for interpreting Israelite history.

Joshua, Judges, Ruth

Joshua: Records the fulfillment of Yahweh's promise to the Israelites in their conquest, occupation and division of Canaan under the leadership of Joshua. It also contains an account of the return of Transjordanian Israelites and of a renewal of the Covenant. It was redacted in final form probably in the sixth century or later.

Judges: Records the actions of charismatic leaders, called judges, of the tribes of Israel between the death of Joshua and the time of Samuel, and a crisis of idolatry among the people. The basic themes are sin and punishment, repentance and deliverance; its purpose was in line with the Deuteronomic motif, that the fortunes of the Israelites were related to their observance or nonobservance of the Law and the Covenant. It was redacted in final form probably in the sixth century.

Ruth: Named for the Gentile (Moabite) woman who, through marriage with Boaz, became an Israelite and an ancestress of David (her son, Obed, became his grandfather). Themes are filial piety, faith and trust in Yahweh, the universality of messianic salvation. Dates ranging from c. 950 to the seventh century have been assigned to the origin of the book, whose author is unknown.

Historical Books

These books, while they contain a great deal of factual material, are unique in their preoccupation with presenting and interpreting it, in the Deuteronomic manner, in primary relation to the Covenant on which the nation of Israel was founded and in accordance with which community and personal life were judged.

The books are: Samuel 1 and 2, from the end of Judges (c. 1020) to the end of David's reign (c. 961); Kings 1 and 2, from the last days of David to the start of the Babylonian Exile and the destruction of the Temple (587); Chronicles 1 and 2, from the reign of Saul (c. 1020-1000) to the return of the people from the Exile (538); Ezra and Nehemiah, covering the reorganization of the Jewish community after the Exile (458-397); Maccabees 1 and 2, recounting the struggle against attempted suppression of Judaism (168-142).

Three of the books listed below — Tobit, Judith and Esther — are categorized as religious novels.

Samuel 1 and 2: A single work in concept and contents, containing episodic history of the last two Judges, Eli and Samuel, the establishment and rule of the monarchy under Saul and David, and the political consequences of David's rule. The royal messianic dynasty of David was the subject of Nathan's oracle in 2 Sm. 7. The books were edited in final form probably late in the seventh century or during the Exile.

Kings 1 and 2: Cover the last days of David and the career of Solomon, including the building of the Temple and the history of the kingdom during his reign; stories of the prophets Elijah and Elisha; the history of the divided kingdom to the fall of Israel in the North (721) and the fall of Judah in the South (587), the destruction of Jerusalem and the Temple. They reflect the Deuteronomic motif in attributing the downfall of the people to corruption of belief and practice in public and private life. They were completed probably in the sixth century.

Chronicles 1 and 2: A collection of historical traditions interpreted in such a way as to present an ideal picture of one people governed by divine law and united in one Temple worship of the one true God. Contents include genealogical tables from Adam to David, the careers of David and Solomon, coverage of the kingdom of Judah to the Exile, and the decree of Cyrus permitting the return of the people and rebuilding of Jerusalem. Both are related to and were written about 400 by the same author, the Chronicler, who composed Ezra and Nehemiah.

Ezra and Nehemiah: A running account of the return of the people to their homeland after the Exile and of practical efforts, under the leadership of Ezra and Nehemiah, to restore and reorganize the religious and political community on the basis of Israelite traditions, divine worship and observance of the Law. Events of great significance were the building of the second Temple, the building of a wall around Jerusalem and the proclamation of the Law by Ezra. This restored community was the start of Judaism. Both are related to and were written about 400 by the same author, the Chronicler, who composed Chronicles 1 and 2.

Tobit: Written in the literary form of a novel and having greater resemblance to wisdom than to historical literature, narrates the personal history of Tobit, a devout and charitable Jew in exile, and persons connected with him, viz., his son Tobiah, his kinsman Raguel and Raguel's daughter Sarah. Its purpose was to teach people how to be good Jews. One of its principal themes is patience under trial, with trust in divine Providence which is symbolized by the presence and action of the angel Raphael. It was written about 200.

Judith: Recounts, in the literary form of a historical novel or romance, the preservation of the Israelites from conquest and ruin through the action of Judith. The essential themes are trust in God for deliverance from danger and emphasis on observance of the Law. It was written probably during the Maccabean period.

Esther: Relates, in the literary form of a historical novel or romance, the manner in which Jews in Persia were saved from annihilation through the central role played by Esther, the Jewish wife of Ahasuerus; a fact commemorated by the Jewish feast of Purim. Like Judith, it has trust in divine Providence as its theme and indicates that God's saving will is sometimes realized by persons acting in unlikely ways. Its origin and date are uncertain; it may have been written about 200 near the beginning of the period of strong Hellenistic influence on the Jews.

Maccabees 1 and 2: While related to some extent because of common subject matter, are quite different from each other.

The first book recounts the background and events of the 40-year (175-135) struggle for religious and political freedom led by Judas Maccabaeus and his brothers against the Hellenist Seleucid kings and some Hellenophiles among the Jews. Victory was symbolized by the rededication of the Temple. Against the background of opposition between Jews and Gentiles, the author equated the survival of belief in the one true God with survival of the Jewish people, thus identifying religion with patriotism. It was written probably by a Palestinian Jew after 104.

The second book supplements the first to some extent, covering and giving a theological interpretation to events from 180 to 162. It explains the feast of the Dedication of the Temple, a key event in the survival of Judaism which is commemorated in the feast of Hanukkah; stresses the primacy of God's action in the struggle for survival; and indicates belief in an afterlife and the resurrection of the body. It was written probably by a Jew of Alexandria after 120.

Wisdom Books

With the exceptions of Psalms and the Song of Songs, the titles listed under this heading are called wisdom books because their purpose was to formulate the fruits of human experience in the context of meditation on sacred Scripture and to present them as an aid toward understanding the problems of life. Hebrew wisdom literature was distinctive from pagan literature of the same type, but it had limitations; these were overcome in the New Testament, which added the dimensions of the New Covenant to those of the Old. Solomon was regarded as the archtype of the wise man.

Job: A dramatic, didactic poem consisting mainly of several dialogues between Job and his friends concerning the mystery involved in the coexistence of the just God, evil and the suffering of the just. It describes an innocent man's experience of suffering and conveys the truth that faith in and submission to God rather than complete understanding, which is impossible, make the experience bearable; also, that the justice of God cannot be defended by affirming that it is realized in this world. Of uncertain authorship, it was written probably between the fifth and third centuries.

Psalms: A collection of 150 religious songs or lyrics reflecting Israelite belief and piety dating from the time of the monarchy to the post-Exilic period, a span of well over 500 years. The psalms, which are a compendium of Old Testament theology, were used in the temple liturgy and were of several types suitable for the king, hymns, lamentations, expressions of confidence and thanksgiving, prophecy, historical meditation and reflection, and the statement of wisdom. About one-half of them are attributed to David; many, by unknown authors, date from the early post-Exilic period.

Proverbs: The oldest book of the wisdom type in the Bible, consisting of collections of sayings attributed to Solomon and other persons regarding a wide variety of subjects including wisdom and its nature, rules of conduct, duties with respect to one's neighbor, the conduct of daily affairs. It reveals many details of Jewish life. Its nucleus dates from the period before the Exile, but no definite date can be assigned for its final compilation.

Ecclesiastes: A treatise about many subjects whose unifying theme is the vanity of strictly human efforts and accomplishments with respect to the achievement of lasting happiness; the only things which are not vain are fear of the Lord and observance of his commandments. The pessimistic tone of the book is due to the absence of a concept of afterlife. It was written by an unknown author about 250.

Song of Songs: A collection of erotic lyrics reflecting various themes, including the celebration of fidelity and love between man and woman. According to one interpretation, the book is a parable of the love of Yahweh for Israel. It was written by an unknown author after the Exile.

Wisdom: Deals with many subjects including the reward of justice; praise of wisdom, a gift of Yahweh proceeding from belief in him and the practice of his Law; the part played by him in the history of his people, especially in their liberation from Egypt; the folly and shame of idolatry. Its contents are taken from the whole sacred literature of the Jews and represent a distillation of its wisdom based on the law, beliefs and traditions of Israel. The last book of the Old Testament to be written, it was probably composed about 100 years before Christ by an unknown author to confirm the faith of the Jewish community at Alexandria.

Sirach: Resembling Proverbs, is a collection of sayings handed on by a grandfather to his grandson. It contains a variety of moral instruction and eulogies of patriarchs and other figures in Israelite history. Its moral maxims apply to individuals, the family and community, relations with God, friendship, education, wealth, the Law, divine worship. Its theme is that true wisdom consists in the Law. (It was formerly called Ecclesiasticus, the Church Book, because of its extensive use by the Church for moral instruction.) It was written in Hebrew between 200 and 175, during a period of strong Hellenistic influence, and was translated into Greek after 132.

The Prophets

These books and the prophecies they contain "express judgments of the people's moral conduct, on the basis of the Mosaic alliance between God and Israel. They teach sublime truths and lofty morals. They contain exhortations, threats, announcements of punishment, promises of deliverance. . . . In the affairs of men, their prime concern is the interests of God, especially in what pertains to the Chosen People through whom the Messiah is to come; hence their denunciations of idolatry and of that externalism in worship which exclude the interior spirit of religion. They are concerned also with the universal nature of the moral law, with personal responsibility, with the person and office of the Messiah, and with the conduct of foreign nations" (*The Holy Bible,* Prophetic Books, CCD Edition, 1961; Preface). There are four major (Isaiah, Jeremiah, Ezekiel, Daniel) and 12 minor prophets (distinguished by the length of books), Lamentations and Baruch. Earlier prophets, mentioned in historical books, include Samuel, Gad, Nathan, Elijah and Elisha.

Before the Exile, prophets were the intermediaries through whom God communicated revelation to the people. Afterwards, prophecy lapsed and the written word of the Law served this purpose.

Isaiah: Named for the greatest of the prophets whose career spanned the reigns of three Hebrew kings from 742 to the beginning of the seventh century, in a period of moral breakdown in Judah and threats of invasion by foreign enemies. It is an anthology of poems and oracles credited to him and a number of followers deeply influenced by him. Of special importance are the prophecies concerning Immanuel (6 to 12), including the prophecy of the virgin birth (7:14). Chapters 40 to 55, called Deutero-Isaiah, are attributed to an anonymous poet toward the end of the Exile; this portion contains the Songs of the Servant. The concluding part of the book (56-66) contains oracles by later disciples.

One of many themes in Isaiah concerned the saving mission of the remnant of Israel in the divine plan of salvation. It was edited in its present form by 180.

Jeremiah: Combines history, biography and prophecy in a setting of crisis caused by internal and external factors, viz., idolatry and general infidelity to the Law among the Israelites and external threats from the Assyrians, Egyptians and Babylonians. Jeremiah prophesied the promise of a new covenant as well as the destruction of Jerusalem and the Temple. His career began in 626 and ended some years after the beginning of the Exile. The book, the longest in the Bible, was edited in final form after the Exile.

Lamentations: A collection of five laments or elegies over the fall of Jerusalem and the fate of the people in Exile, written by an unknown eyewitness not long after 587. They convey the message that Yahweh struck the people because of their sins and reflect confidence in his love and power to restore his converted people.

Baruch: Against the background of the already begun Exile, it consists of an introduction and several parts: an exile's prayer of confession and petition for forgiveness and the restoration of Israel; a poem praising wisdom and the Law of Moses; a lament in which Jerusalem, personified, bewails the fate of her people and consoles them with the hope of blessings to come; and a polemic against idolatry. Although ascribed to Baruch, Jeremiah's secretary, it was written by several authors probably in the second century.

Ezekiel: Named for the priest-prophet who prophesied in Babylon from 593 to 571, during the first phase of the Exile. To prepare his fellow early exiles for the impending fall of Jerusalem, he reproached the Israelites for past sins and predicted woes to come upon them. After the destruction of the city, the burden of his message was hope and promise of restoration. Ezekiel had great influence on the religion of Israel after the Exile. The book, which contains the substance of his teaching, had a number of authors and editors.

Daniel: The protagonist is a fictional young Jew, taken early to Babylon where he lived until 537, who figured in a series of edifying stories. The stories, which originated from Israelite tradition, recount the trials and triumphs of Daniel and his three companions, and other episodes including those concerning Susannah, Bel, and the Dragon. The book is more apocalyptic than prophetic: it envisions Israel in glory to come and conveys the message that men of faith can resist temptation and overcome adversity. It states the prophetic themes of right conduct, divine control of men and events, and the final triumph of the kingdom. It was written by an unknown author in the 160's to give moral support to Jews during the persecutions of the Maccabean period.

Hosea: Consists of a prophetic parallel between Hosea's marriage and Yahweh's relations with his people. As the prophet was married to a faithless wife whom he would not give up, Yahweh was bound in Covenant with an idolatrous and unjust Israel whom he would not desert but would chastise for purification. Hosea belonged to the Northern Kingdom of Israel and began his career about the middle of the eighth century. He inaugurated the tradition of describing Yahweh's relation to Israel in terms of marriage.

Joel: Is apocalyptic and eschatological regarding divine judgment, the Day of the Lord, which is symbolized by a ravaging invasion of locusts, the judgment of the nations in the Valley of Josaphat and the outpouring of the Spirit in the messianic era to come. Its message is that God will vindicate and save Israel, in view of the prayer and repentance of the people, and will punish their enemies. It was composed after the period of Nehemiah.

Amos: Consists of an indictment against foreign enemies of Israel; a strong denunciation of the people of Israel, whose infidelity, idolatry and injustice made them subject to divine judgment and punishment; and a messianic oracle regarding Israel's restoration. Amos prophesied in the Northern Kingdom of Israel, at Bethel, in the first half of the eighth century; chronologically, he was the first of the canonical prophets.

Obadiah: A 21-verse prophecy, the shortest and one of the sternest in the Bible, against the Edomites, invaders of southern Judah and enemies of those returning from the Exile to their homeland. It was redacted in final form no later than the end of the fourth century.

Jonah: A parable of divine mercy with the theme that Yahweh wills the salvation of all, not just a few, men who respond to his call. Its protagonist is a disobedient prophet; forced by circumstances beyond his control to preach penance among Gentiles, he is highly successful in his mission but baffled by the divine concern for those who do not belong to the Chosen People. It was written after the Exile.

Micah: Attacks the injustice and corruption of priests, false prophets, officials and people; announces judgment and punishment to come; foretells the restoration of Israel; refers to the saving remnant of Israel. Micah was a contemporary of Isaiah.

Nahum: Dating from about 613, concerns the destruction of Nineveh in 612 and the overthrow of the Assyrian Empire by the Babylonians.

Habakkuk: Dating from about 605-597, concerns sufferings to be inflicted by oppressors on the people of Judah because of their infidelity to the Lord. It also sounds a note of confidence in the Lord, the Savior, and declares that the just will not perish.

Zephaniah: Exercising his ministry in the second half of the seventh century, during a time of widespread idolatry, superstition and religious degradation, he prophesied impending judgment and punishment for Jerusalem and its people. He prophesied too that a holy remnant of the people (*anawim,* mentioned also by Amos) would be spared. Zephaniah was a forerunner of Jeremiah.

Haggai: One of the first prophets after the Exile, Haggai in 520 encouraged the returning exiles to reestablish their community and to complete the second Temple (dedicated in 515), for which he envisioned greater glory, in a messianic sense, than that enjoyed by the original Temple of Solomon.

Zechariah: A contemporary of Haggai, he prophesied in the same vein. A second part of the book, called Deutero-Zechariah and composed by one or more unknown authors, relates a vision of the coming of the Prince of Peace, the Messiah of the Poor.

Malachi: Written by an anonymous author, presents a picture of life in the post-Exilic community between 516 and the initiation of reforms by Ezra and Nehemiah about 432. Blame for the troubles of the community is placed mainly on priests for failure to carry out ritual worship and to instruct the people in the proper manner; other factors were religious indifference and the influence of doubters who were scandalized at the prosperity of the wicked. The vision of a universal sacrifice to be offered to Yahweh (1:11) is interpreted in Catholic theology as a prophecy of the sacrifice of the Mass. Malachi was the last of the minor prophets.

OLD TESTAMENT DATES

c. 1800 — c. 1600: Period of the patriarchs (Abraham, Isaac, Jacob).

c. 1600: Israelites in Egypt.

c. 1250: Exodus of Israelites from Egypt.

c. 1210: Entrance of Israelites into Canaan.

c. 1210 — c. 1020: Period of the Judges.

c. 1020 — c. 1000: Reign of Saul, first king.

c. 1000 — c. 961: Reign of David.

c. 961 — 922: Reign of Solomon. Temple built during his reign.

922: Division of the Kingdom into Israel (North) and Judah (South).

721: Conquest of Israel by Assyrians.

587-538: Conquest of Judah by Babylonians. Babylonian Captivity and Exile. Destruction of Jerusalem and the Temple, 587. Captivity ended with the return of exiles, following the decree of Cyrus permitting the rebuilding of Jerusalem.

515: Dedication of the Second Temple.

458-397: Restoration and reform of the Jewish religious and political community; building of the Jerusalem wall, 439. Leaders in the movement were Ezra and Nehemiah.

168-142: Period of the Maccabees; war against Syrians.

142: Independence granted to Jews by Demetrius II of Syria.

135-37: Period of the Hasmonean dynasty.

63: Beginning of Roman rule.

37-4: Period of Herod the Great.

FOCOLARE

Focolare is not a secular institute by statute, but vows are professed by its totally dedicated core membership of 4,000 who live in small communities called Focolare (Italian word for "hearth") centers. There are 15 resident centers in the U.S. and two in Canada. GEN (New Generation) is the youth organization of the movement. An estimated 70,000 are affiliated with the movement in the U.S. and Canada; 3 million worldwide. Publications include *Living City,* monthly; *GEN II* and *GEN III* for young people and children. Five week-long summer conventions, called "Mariapolis" ("City of Mary"), are held annually.

NEW TESTAMENT BOOKS

Gospels

The term Gospel is derived from the Anglo-Saxon god-spell and the Greek euangelion, meaning good news, good tidings. In Christian use, it means the good news of salvation proclaimed by Christ and the Church, and handed on in written form in the Gospels of Matthew, Mark, Luke and John.

The initial proclamation of the coming of the kingdom of God was made by Jesus in and through his Person, teachings and actions, and especially through his Passion, death and resurrection. This proclamation became the center of Christian faith and the core of the oral Gospel tradition with which the Church spread the good news by apostolic preaching for some 30 years before it was committed to writing by the Evangelists.

Nature of the Gospels

The historical truth of the Gospels was the subject of an instruction issued by the Pontifical Commission for Biblical Studies Apr. 21, 1964.

• The sacred writers selected from the material at their disposal (the oral Gospel tradition, some written collections of sayings and deeds of Jesus, eyewitness accounts) those things which were particularly suitable to the various conditions (liturgical, catechetical, missionary) of the faithful and the aims they had in mind, and they narrated these things in such a way as to correspond with those circumstances and their aims.

• The life and teaching of Jesus were not simply reported in a biographical manner for the purpose of preserving their memory but were "preached" so as to offer the Church the basis of doctrine concerning faith and morals.

• In their works, the Evangelists presented the true sayings of Jesus and the events of his life in the light of the better understanding they had following their enlightenment by the Holy Spirit. They did not transform Christ into a "mythical" Person, nor did they distort his teaching.

Passion narratives are the core of all the Gospels, covering the suffering, death and resurrection of Jesus as central events in bringing about and establishing the New Covenant. Leading up to them are accounts of the mission of John the Baptizer and the ministry of Jesus, especially in Galilee and finally in Jerusalem before the Passion. The infancy of Jesus is covered by Luke and Matthew with narratives inspired in part by appropriate Old Testament citations.

Matthew, Mark and Luke, while different in various respects, have so many similarities that they are called Synoptic; their relationships are the subject of the Synoptic Problem.

Matthew: Written in the 70's or 80's for Jewish Christians, with clear reference to Jewish background and identification of Jesus as the divine Messiah, the fulfillment of the Old Testament. Distinctive are the use of Old Testament citations regarding the Person, activity and teaching of Jesus, and the presentation of doctrine in sermons and discourses. The canonical Matthew was written in Greek, with dependence on Mark.

Mark: The first of the Gospels, dating from about 65. Written for Gentile Christians, it is noted for the realism and wealth of concrete details with which it reveals Jesus as Son of God and Savior more by his actions and miracles than by his discourses. Theologically, it is less refined than the other Gospels.

Luke: Written in the 70's or 80's for Gentile Christians. It is noted for the universality of its address, the insight it provides into the Christian way of life, the place it gives to women, the manner in which it emphasizes Jesus' friendship with sinners and compassion for the suffering.

John: Written sometime in the 90's, is the most sublime and theological of the Gospels, and is different from the Synoptics in plan and treatment. Combining accounts of signs with longer discourses and reflections, it progressively reveals the Person and mission of Jesus — as Word, Way, Truth, Life, Light — in line with the purpose, "to help you believe that Jesus is the Messiah, the Son of God, so that through this faith you may have life in his name" (Jn. 20:31). There are questions about the authorship but no doubt about the Johannine tradition behind the Gospel.

Acts of the Apostles

Acts of the Apostles: Written by Luke in the 70's or 80's as a supplement to his Gospel. It describes the origin and spread of Christian communities through the action of the Holy Spirit from the resurrection of Christ to the time when Paul was placed in custody in Rome in the early 60's.

Letters (Epistles)

These letters, many of which antedated the Gospels, were written in response to existential needs of the early Christian communities for doctrinal and moral instruction, disciplinary action, practical advice, and exhortation to true Christian living.

Pauline Letters

These letters, which comprise approximately one-fourth of the New Testament, are primary and monumental sources of the development of Christian theology. Several of them may not have had Paul as their actual author, but evidence of the Pauline tradition behind them is strong. The letters to the Colossians, Philippians, Ephesians and Philemon have been called the "Captivity Letters" because of a tradition that they were written while Paul was under house arrest in Rome from 61 to 63.

Romans: Written in the late 50's from Corinth on the central significance of Christ and faith in him for salvation, and the relationship of Christianity to Judaism; the condition of mankind without Christ; justification and the Christian life; duties of Christians.

Corinthians 1: Written near the beginning of 57 from Ephesus to counteract factionalism and disorders, it covers community dissensions, moral irregularities, marriage and celibacy, conduct at religious gatherings, the Eucharist, spiritual gifts (charisms) and their function in the Church, charity, the resurrection of the body.

Corinthians 2: Written later in the same year as 1 Cor., concerning Paul's defense of his apostolic life and ministry, and an appeal for a collection to aid poor Christians in Jerusalem.

Galatians: Written probably between 54 and 57 (perhaps earlier, according to some scholars) to counteract Judaizing opinions and efforts to undermine his authority, it asserts the divine origin of Paul's authority and doctrine, states that justification is not through Mosaic Law but through faith in Christ, insists on the practice of evangelical virtues, especially charity.

Ephesians: Written probably between 61 and 63, or perhaps in the 70's, mainly on the Church as the Mystical Body of Christ.

Philippians: Written between 61 and 63 primarily to thank the Philippians for their kindness to him while he was under house arrest in Rome.

Colossians: Written while he was under house arrest in Rome from 61 to 63 to counteract the influence of self-appointed teachers who were watering down doctrine concerning Christ. It includes two highly important Christological passages, a warning against false teachers, and an instruction on the ideal Christian life.

Thessalonians 1 and 2: Written within a short time of each other probably in 51 from Corinth, mainly on doctrine concerning the Parousia, the second coming of Christ.

Timothy 1 and 2, Titus: Written between 65 and 67, or perhaps in the 70's, giving pastoral counsels to Timothy and Titus who were in charge of churches in Ephesus and Crete, respectively. 1 Tm. emphasizes pastoral responsibility for preserving unity of doctrine; 2 Tm. describes Paul's imprisonment in Rome.

Philemon: A private letter written between 61 and 63 to a wealthy Colossian concerning a slave, Onesimus, who had escaped from him; Paul appealed for kind treatment of the man.

Hebrews: Dating from sometime between the mid 60's and the 80's, a complex theological treatise on Christology, the priesthood and sacrifice of Christ, the New Covenant, and the pattern for Christian living. Critical opinion is divided as to whether it was addressed to Judaeo or Gentile Christians.

Catholic Letters, Revelation

These seven letters have been called "catholic" because it was thought for some time, not altogether correctly, that they were not addressed to particular communities.

James: Written sometime between the mid-60's

and the 80's (although datable before 62 according to some scholars) in the spirit of Hebrew wisdom literature and the moralism of Tobit. An exhortation to practical Christian living, it is also noteworthy for the doctrine it states on good works and its citation regarding anointing of the sick.

Peter 1 and 2: The first letter may have been written in the mid-60's; the second dates from 100 to 125. Addressed to Christians in Asia Minor, both are exhortations to perseverance in the life of faith despite trials and difficulties arising from pagan influences, isolation from other Christians and false teaching.

John 1: Written sometime in the 90's and addressed to Asian churches, its message is that God is made known to us in the Son and that fellowship with the Father is attained by living in the light, justice and love of the Son.

John 2: Written sometime in the 90's and addressed to a church in Asia, it commends the people for standing firm in the faith and urges them to perseverance.

John 3: Written sometime in the 90's, it appears to represent an effort to settle a jurisdictional dispute in one of the churches.

Jude: Written sometime between the 70's and 90's, it is a brief treatise against erroneous teachings and practices opposed to law, authority and true Christian freedom.

Revelation: Written in the 90's along the lines of Johannine thought, it is a symbolic and apocalyptic treatment of things to come and of the struggle between the Church and evil combined with warning but hope and assurance to the Church regarding the coming of the Lord in glory.

BIBLICAL AUTHORSHIP

Some books of the Bible were not written by the authors whose names they bear; New Testament examples are the Gospels of Matthew and John, Hebrews, 1 and 2 Timothy, Titus, James, Jude.

This fact, which has never been the subject of dogmatic definition by the Church, does not militate against the canonicity of the books, since canonicity concerns the theological matter of inspiration rather than the historical question of human authorship.

Questions concerning authorship are explained in various ways: (1) according to an old custom whereby literary works of importance were sometimes attibuted to famous persons so they would get a reading; (2) authorship, by a disciple or school of disciples, of works derived from the doctrine of a master; (3) authorship by persons writing in the spirit and tradition of a master.

INTERPRETATION OF THE BIBLE

According to the *Constitution on Revelation* issued by the Second Vatican Council, "the interpreter of Sacred Scripture, in order to see clearly what God wanted to communicate to us, should carefully investigate what meaning the sacred writers really intended, and what God wanted to manifest by means of their words" (No. 12).

Hermeneutics, Exegesis

This careful investigation proceeds in accordance with the rules of hermeneutics, the normative science of biblical interpretation and explanation. Hermeneutics in practice is called exegesis.

The principles of hermeneutics are derived from

various disciplines and many factors which have to be considered in explaining the Bible and its parts. These include: the original languages and languages of translation of the sacred texts, through philology and linguistics; the quality of texts, through textual criticism; literary forms and genres, through literary and form criticism; cultural, historical, geographical and other conditions which influenced the writers, through related studies; facts and truths of salvation history; the truths and analogy of faith.

Distinctive to biblical hermeneutics, which differs in important respects from literary interpretation in general, is the premise that the Bible, though written by human authors, is the work of divine inspiration in which God reveals his plan for the salvation of men through historical events and persons, and especially through the Person and mission of Christ.

Textual, Form Criticism

Textual criticism is the study of biblical texts, which have been transmitted in copies several times removed from the original manuscripts, for the purpose of establishing the real state of the original texts. This purpose is served by comparison of existing copies; by application to the texts of the disciplines of philology and linguistics; by examination of related works of antiquity; by study of biblical citations in works of the Fathers of the Church and other authors; and by other means of literary study.

Since about 1920, the sayings of Christ have been a particular object of New Testament study, the purpose being to analyze the forms of expression used by the Evangelists in order to ascertain the words actually spoken by him.

Literary Criticism

Literary criticism aims to determine the origin and kinds of literary composition, called forms or genres, employed by the inspired authors. Such determinations are necessary for decision regarding the nature and purpose and, consequently, the meaning of biblical passages. Underlying these studies is the principle that the manner of writing was conditioned by the intention of the authors, the meaning they wanted to convey, and the then-contemporary literary style, mode or medium best adapted to carry their message — e.g., true history, quasi-historical narrative, poems, prayers, hymns, psalms, aphorisms, allegories, discourses. Understanding these media is necessary for the valid interpretation of their message.

Literal Sense

The key to all valid interpretation is the literal sense of biblical passages. Regarding this matter and the relevance to it of the studies and procedures described above, Pius XII wrote the following in the encyclical *Divino Afflante Spiritu.*

"What the literal sense of a passage is, is not always as obvious as in the speeches and writings of ancient authors of the East as it is in the works of our own time. For what they wished to express is not to be determined by the rules of grammar and philology alone nor solely by the context; the interpreter must, as it were, go back wholly in spirit to those remote centuries of the East and with the aid of history, archeology, ethnology, and other sciences accurately determine what modes of writing, so to speak, the authors of that ancient period would be likely to use and in fact did use. . . . In explaining the Sacred Scripture and in demonstrating and proving its immunity from all error (the Catholic interpreter) should make a prudent use of this means, determine to what extent the manner of expression or literary mode adopted by the sacred writer may lead to a correct and genuine interpretation; and let him be convinced that this part of his office cannot be neglected without serious detriment to Catholic exegesis."

The literal sense of the Bible is the meaning in the mind of and intended by the inspired writer of a book or passage of the Bible. This is determined by the application to texts of the rules of hermeneutics. It is not to be confused with word-for-word literalism.

Typical Sense

The typical sense is the meaning which a passage has not only in itself but also in reference to something else of which it is a type or foreshadowing. A clear example is the account of the Exodus of the Israelites: in its literal sense, it narrates the liberation of the Israelites from death and oppression in Egypt; in its typical sense, it foreshadowed the liberation of men from sin through the redemptive death and resurrection of Christ. The typical sense of this and other passages emerged in the working out of God's plan of salvation history. It did not have to be in the mind of the author of the original passage.

Accommodated Senses

Accommodated, allegorical and consequent senses are figurative and adaptive meanings given to books and passages of the Bible for moral and other purposes. Such interpretations involve the danger of stretching the literal sense beyond proper proportions. Hermeneutical principles require that interpretations like these respect the integrity of the literal sense of the passages in question.

In the Catholic view, the final word on questions of biblical interpretation belongs to the teaching authority of the Church. In other views, generally derived from basic principles stated by Martin Luther, John Calvin and other reformers, the primacy belongs to individual judgment acting in response to the inner testimony of the Holy Spirit, the edifying nature of biblical subject matter, the sublimity and simplicity of the message of salvation, the intensity with which Christ is proclaimed.

Biblical Studies

The first center for biblical studies, in some strict sense of the term, was the School of Alexandria, founded in the latter half of the second century. It was noted for allegorical exegesis. Literal interpretation was a hallmark of the School of Antioch.

St. Jerome, who produced the Vulgate, and St.

Augustine, author of numerous commentaries, were the most important figures in biblical studies during the patristic period. By the time of the latter's death, the Old and New Testament canons had been stabilized. For some centuries afterwards, there was little or no progress in scriptural studies, although commentaries were written, collections were made of scriptural excerpts from the writings of the Fathers of the Church, and the systematic reading of Scripture became established as a feature of monastic life.

Advances were made in the 12th and 13th centuries with the introduction of new principles and methods of scriptural analysis stemming from renewed interest in Hebraic studies and the application of dialectics.

By the time of the Reformation, the Bible had become the first book set in movable type, and more than 100 vernacular editions were in use throughout Europe.

The Council of Trent

In the wake of the Reformation, the Council of Trent formally defined the Canon of the Bible; it also reasserted the authoritative role of tradition and the teaching authority of the Church as well as Scripture with respect to the rule of faith. In the heated atmosphere of the 16th and 17th centuries, the Bible was turned into a polemical weapon; Protestants used it to defend their doctrines, and Catholics countered with citations in support of the dogmas of the Church. One result of this state of affairs was a lack of substantial progress in biblical studies during the period.

Rationalists from the 18th century on and later Modernists denied the reality of the supernatural and doctrine concerning inspiration of the Bible, which they generally regarded as a strictly human production expressive of the religious sense and experience of mankind. In their hands, the tools of positive critical research became weapons for biblical subversion. The defensive Catholic reaction to their work had the temporary effect of alienating scholars of the Church from solid advances in archeology, philology, history, textual and literary criticism.

Catholic Developments

Major influences in bringing about a change in Catholic attitude toward use of these disciplines in biblical studies were two papal encyclicals and two institutes of special study, the Ecole Biblique, founded in Jerusalem in 1890, and the Pontifical Biblical Institute established in Rome in 1909. The encyclical *Providentissimus Deus,* issued by Leo XIII in 1893, marked an important breakthrough; in addition to defending the concept of divine inspiration and the formal inspiration of the Scriptures, it encouraged the study of allied and ancillary sciences and techniques for a more fruitful understanding of the sacred writings. The encyclical *Divino Afflante Spiritu,* 50 years later, gave encouragement for the use of various forms of criticism as tools of biblical research. The documents encouraged the work of scholars and stimulated wide communication of the fruits of their study.

Great changes in the climate and direction of biblical studies have occurred in recent years. One of them has been an increase in cooperative effort among Catholic, Protestant, Orthodox and Jewish scholars. Their common investigation of the Dead Sea Scrolls is well known. Also productive has been the collaboration of Catholics and Protestants in turning out various editions of the Bible.

The development and results of biblical studies in this century have directly and significantly affected all phases of the contemporary renewal movement in the Church. Their influence on theology, liturgy, catechetics, and preaching indicate the importance of their function in the life of the Church.

APOSTLES AND EVANGELISTS

The Apostles were the men selected, trained and commissioned by Christ to preach the Gospel, to baptize, to establish, direct and care for his Church as servants of God and stewards of his mysteries. They were the first bishops of the Church.

St. Matthew's Gospel lists the Apostles in this order: Peter, Andrew, James the Greater, John, Philip, Bartholomew, Thomas, Matthew, James the Less, Jude, Simon and Judas Iscariot. Matthias was elected to fill the place of Judas. Paul became an Apostle by a special call from Christ. Barnabas was called an Apostle.

Two of the Evangelists, John and Matthew, were Apostles. The other two, Luke and Mark, were closely associated with the apostolic college.

Andrew: Born in Bethsaida, brother of Peter, disciple of John the Baptist, a fisherman, the first Apostle called; according to legend, preached the Gospel in northern Greece, Epirus and Scythia, and was martyred at Patras about 70; in art, is represented with an x-shaped cross, called St. Andrew's Cross; feast, Nov. 30; is honored as the patron of Russia and Scotland.

Barnabas: Originally called Joseph but named Barnabas by the Apostles, among whom he is ranked because of his collaboration with Paul; a Jew of the Diaspora, born in Cyprus; a cousin of Mark and member of the Christian community at Jerusalem, influenced the Apostles to accept Paul, with whom he became a pioneer missionary outside Palestine and Syria, to Antioch, Cyprus and southern Asia Minor; legend says he was martyred in Cyprus during the Neronian persecution; feast, June 11.

Bartholomew (Nathaniel): A friend of Philip; according to various traditions, preached the Gospel in Ethiopia, India, Persia and Armenia, where he was martyred by being flayed and beheaded; in art, is depicted holding a knife, an instrument of his death; feast, Aug. 24 in the Roman Rite, Aug. 25 in the Byzantine Rite.

James the Greater: A Galilean, son of Zebedee, brother of John (with whom he was called a "Son of Thunder"), a fisherman; with Peter and John, witnessed the raising of Jairus' daughter to life, the transfiguration, the agony of Jesus in the Garden of Gethsemani; first of the Apostles to die, by the sword in 44 during the rule of Herod Agrippa; there is doubt about a journey legend says he made to Spain and also about the authenticity of relics said to be his at Santiago de Compostela; in art, is depicted carrying a pilgrim's bell; feast, July 25 in the Roman Rite, Apr. 30 in the Byzantine Rite.

James the Less: Son of Alphaeus, called "Less" because he was younger in age or shorter in stature than James the Greater; one of the Catholic Epistles bears his name; was stoned to death in 62 or thrown from the top of the temple in Jerusalem and clubbed to death in 66; in art, is depicted with a club or heavy staff; feast, May 3 in the Roman Rite, Oct. 9 in the Byzantine Rite.

John: A Galilean, son of Zebedee, brother of James the Greater (with whom he was called a "Son of Thunder"), a fisherman, probably a disciple of John the Baptist, one of the Evangelists, called the "Beloved Disciple"; with Peter and James the Greater, witnessed the raising of Jairus' daughter to life, the transfiguration, the agony of Jesus in the Garden of Gethsemani; Mary was commended to his special care by Christ; the fourth Gospel, three Catholic Epistles and Revelation bear his name; according to various accounts, lived at Ephesus in Asia Minor for some time and died a natural death about 100; in art, is represented by an eagle, symbolic of the sublimity of the contents of his Gospel; feast, Dec. 27 in the Roman Rite, May 8 in the Byzantine Rite.

Jude Thaddeus: One of the Catholic Epistles, the shortest, bears his name; various traditions say he preached the Gospel in Mesopotamia, Persia and elsewhere, and was martyred; in art, is depicted with a halberd, the instrument of his death; feast, Oct. 28 in the Roman Rite, June 19 in the Byzantine Rite.

Luke: A Greek convert to the Christian community, called "our most dear physician" by Paul, of whom he was a missionary companion; author of the third Gospel and Acts of the Apostles; the place — Achaia, Bithynia, Egypt — and circumstances of his death are not certain; in art, is depicted as a man, a writer, or an ox (because his Gospel starts at the scene of temple sacrifice); feast, Oct. 18.

Mark: A cousin of Barnabas and member of the first Christian community at Jerusalem; a missionary companion of Paul and Barnabas, then of Peter; author of the Gospel which bears his name; according to legend, founded the Church at Alexandria, was bishop there and was martyred in the streets of the city; in art, is depicted with his Gospel and a winged lion, symbolic of the voice of John the Baptist crying in the wilderness, at the beginning of his Gospel; feast, Apr. 25.

Matthew: A Galilean, called Levi by Luke and John and the son of Alphaeus by Mark, a tax collector, one of the Evangelists; according to various accounts, preached the Gospel in Judea, Ethiopia, Persia and Parthia, and was martyred; in art, is depicted with a spear, the instrument of his death, and as a winged man in his role as Evangelist; feast, Sept. 21 in the Roman Rite, Nov. 16 in the Byzantine Rite.

Matthias: A disciple of Jesus whom the faithful 11 Apostles chose to replace Judas before the Resurrection; uncertain traditions report that he preached the Gospel in Palestine, Cappadocia or Ethiopia; in art, is represented with a cross and a halberd, the instruments of his death as a martyr; feast, May 14 in the Roman Rite, Aug. 9 in the Byzantine Rite.

Paul: Born at Tarsus, of the tribe of Benjamin, a Roman citizen; participated in the persecution of Christians until the time of his miraculous conversion on the way to Damascus; called by Christ, who revealed himself to him in a special way; became the Apostle of the Gentiles, among whom he did most of his preaching in the course of three major missionary journeys through areas north of Palestine, Cyprus, Asia Minor and Greece; 14 epistles bear his name; two years of imprisonment at Rome, following initial arrest in Jerusalem and confinement at Caesarea, ended with martyrdom, by beheading, outside the walls of the city in 64 or 67 during the Neronian persecution; in art, is depicted in various ways with St. Peter, with a sword, in the scene of his conversion; feasts, June 29, Jan. 25 (Roman Rite).

Peter: Simon, son of Jona, born in Bethsaida, brother of Andrew, a fisherman; called Cephas or Peter by Christ who made him the chief of the Apostles and head of the Church as his vicar; named first in the listings of Apostles in the Synoptic Gospels and the Acts of the Apostles; with James the Greater and John, witnessed the raising of Jairus' daughter to life, the transfiguration, the agony of Jesus in the Garden of Gethsemani; was the first to preach the Gospel in and around Jerusalem and was the leader of the first Christian community there; established a local church in Antioch; presided over the Council of Jerusalem in 51; wrote two Catholic Epistles to the Christians in Asia Minor; established his see in Rome where he spent his last years and was martyred by crucifixion in 64 or 65 during the Neronian persecution; in art, is depicted carrying two keys, symbolic of his primacy in the Church; feasts, June 29, Feb. 22 (Roman Rite).

Philip: Born in Bethsaida; according to legend, preached the Gospel in Phrygia where he suffered martyrdom by crucifixion; feast, May 3 in the Roman Rite, Nov. 14 in the Byzantine Rite.

Simon: Called the Cananean or the Zealot; according to legend, preached in various places in the Middle East and suffered martyrdom by being sawed in two; in art, is depicted with a saw, the instrument of his death, or a book, symbolic of his zeal for the Law; feast, Oct. 28 in the Roman Rite, May 10 in the Byzantine Rite.

Thomas (Didymus): Notable for his initial incredulity regarding the Resurrection and his subsequent forthright confession of the divinity of Christ risen from the dead; according to legend, preached the Gospel in places from the Caspian Sea to the Persian Gulf and eventually reached India where he was martyred near Madras; Thomas Christians trace their origin to him; in art, is depicted kneeling before the risen Christ, or with a carpenter's rule and square; feast, July 3 in the Roman Rite, Oct. 6 in the Byzantine Rite.

Judas

The Gospels record only a few facts about Judas, the Apostle who betrayed Christ.

The only non-Galilean among the Apostles, he was from Carioth, a town in southern Judah. He was keeper of the purse in the apostolic band. He was called a petty thief by John. He voiced dismay at the waste of money, which he said might have been spent for the poor, in connection with the anointing incident at Bethany. He took the in-

itiative in arranging the betrayal of Christ. Afterwards, he confessed that he had betrayed an innocent man and cast into the Temple the money he had received for that action. Of his death, Matthew says that he hanged himself; the Acts of the Apostles states that he swelled up and burst open; both reports deal more with the meaning than the manner of his death — the misery of the death of a sinner.

The consensus of speculation over the reason why Judas acted as he did in betraying Christ focuses on disillusionment and unwillingness to accept the concept of a suffering Messiah and personal suffering of his own as an Apostle.

APOSTOLIC FATHERS, FATHERS, DOCTORS OF THE CHURCH

The writers listed below were outstanding and authoritative witnesses to authentic Christian belief and practice, and played significant roles in giving them expression.

Apostolic Fathers

The Apostolic Fathers were Christian writers of the first and second centuries whose writings echo genuine apostolic teaching.

Chief in importance are: St. Clement (d.c. 97), bishop of Rome and third successor of St. Peter in the papacy; St. Ignatius (50-c. 107), bishop of Antioch and second successor of St. Peter in that see, reputed to be a disciple of St. John; St. Polycarp (69-155), bishop of Smyrna and a disciple of St. John. The authors of the *Didache* and the *Epistle of Barnabas* are also numbered among the Apostolic Fathers.

Other early ecclesiastical writers included: St. Justin, martyr (100 165), of Asia Minor and Rome, a layman and apologist; St. Irenaeus (130-202), bishop of Lyons, who opposed Gnosticism; and St. Cyprian (210-258), bishop of Carthage, who opposed Novatianism.

Fathers and Doctors

The Fathers of the Church were theologians and writers of the first eight centuries who were outstanding for sanctity and learning. They were such authoritative witnesses to the belief and teaching of the Church that their unanimous acceptance of doctrines as divinely revealed has been regarded as evidence that such doctrines were so received by the Church in line with apostolic tradition and Sacred Scripture. Their unanimous rejection of doctrines branded them as heretical. Their writings, however, were not necessarily free of error in all respects.

The greatest of these Fathers were: Sts. Ambrose, Augustine, Jerome and Gregory the Great in the West; Sts. John Chrysostom, Basil the Great, Gregory of Nazianzen and Athanasius in the East.

The Doctors of the Church were ecclesiastical writers of eminent learning and sanctity who have been given this title because of the great advantage the Church has derived from their work. Their writings, however, were not necessarily free of error in all respects.

Albert the Great, St. (c. 1200-1280): Born in Swabia, Germany; Dominican; bishop of Regensburg (1260-1262); wrote extensively on logic, natural sciences, ethics, metaphysics, Scripture, systematic theology; contributed to development of Scholasticism; teacher of St. Thomas Aquinas; canonized and proclaimed doctor, 1931; named patron of natural scientists, 1941; called Doctor Universalis, Doctor Expertus; feast, Nov. 15.

Alphonsus Liguori, St. (1696-1787): Born near Naples, Italy; bishop of Saint Agatha of the Goths (1762-1775); founder of the Redemptorists; in addition to his principal work, *Theologiae Moralis*, wrote on prayer, the spiritual life and doctrinal subjects in response to controversy; canonized, 1839; proclaimed doctor, 1871; named patron of confessors and moralists, 1950; feast, Aug. 1.

Ambrose, St. (c. 340-397): Born in Trier, Germany; bishop of Milan (374-397); one of the strongest opponents of Arianism in the West; his homilies and other writings — on faith, the Holy Spirit, the Incarnation, the sacraments and other subjects — were pastoral and practical; influenced the development of a liturgy at Milan which was named for him; Father and Doctor of the Church; feast, Dec. 7.

Anselm, St. (1033-1109): Born in Aosta, Piedmont, Italy; Benedictine; archbishop of Canterbury (1093-1109); in addition to his principal work, *Cur Deus Homo*, on the atonement and reconciliation of man with God through Christ, wrote about the existence and attributes of God and defended the *Filioque* explanation of the procession of the Holy Spirit from the Father and the Son; proclaimed doctor, 1720; called Father of Scholasticism; feast, Apr. 21.

Anthony of Padua, St. (1195-1231): Born in Lisbon, Portugal; first theologian of the Franciscan Order; preacher; canonized, 1232; proclaimed doctor, 1946; called Evangelical Doctor; feast, June 13.

Athanasius, St. (c. 297-373): Born in Alexandria, Egypt; bishop of Alexandria (328-373); participant in the Council of Nicaea I while still a deacon; dominant opponent of Arians whose errors regarding Christ he refuted in *Apology against the Arians, Discourses against the Arians* and other works; Father and Doctor of the Church; called Father of Orthodoxy; feast, May 2.

Augustine, St. (354-430): Born in Tagaste, North Africa; bishop of Hippo (395-430) after conversion from Manichaeism; works include the auto-biographical and mystical *Confessions, City of God,* treatises on the Trinity, grace, passages of the Bible and doctrines called into question and denied by Manichaeans, Pelagians and Donatists; had strong and lasting influence on Christian theology and philosophy; Father and Doctor of the Church; called Doctor of Grace; feast, Aug. 28.

Basil the Great, St. (c. 329-379): Born in Caesarea, Cappadocia, Asia Minor; bishop of Caesarea (370-379); wrote three books *Contra Eunomium* in refutation of Arian errors, a treatise on the Holy Spirit, many homilies and several rules for monastic life, on which he had lasting influence; Father and Doctor of the Church; called Father of Monasticism in the East; feast, Jan. 2.

Bede the Venerable, St. (c. 673-735): Born in Northumberland, England; Benedictine; in addition to his principal work, *Ecclesiastical History of the English Nation* (covering the period 597-731), wrote scriptural commentaries; regarded as probably the most learned man in Western Europe of his time; called Father of English History; feast, May 25.

Bernard of Clairvaux, St. (c. 1090-1153): Born near Dijon, France; abbot; monastic reformer, called the second founder of the Cistercian Order; mystical theologian with great influence on devotional life; opponent of the rationalism brought forward by Abelard and others; canonized, 1174; proclaimed doctor, 1830; called Mellifluous Doctor because of his eloquence; feast, Aug. 20.

Bonaventure, St. (c. 1217-1274): Born near Viterbo, Italy; Franciscan; bishop of Albano (1273-1274); cardinal; wrote *Itinerarium Mentis in Deum, De Reductione Artium ad Theologiam, Breviloquium,* scriptural commentaries, additional mystical works affecting devotional life and a life of St. Francis of Assisi; canonized, 1482; proclaimed doctor, 1588; called Seraphic Doctor; feast, July 15.

Catherine of Siena, St. (c. 1347-1380): Born in Siena, Italy; member of the Third Order of St. Dominic; mystic; authored a long series of letters, mainly concerning spiritual instruction and encouragement, to associates, and *Dialogue,* a spiritual testament in four treatises; was active in support of a crusade against the Turks and efforts to end war between papal forces and the Florentine allies; had great influence in inducing Gregory XI to return himself and the Curia to Rome in 1376, to end the Avignon period of the papacy; canonized, 1461; proclaimed the second women doctor, Oct. 4, 1970; feast, Apr. 29.

Cyril of Alexandria, St. (c. 376-444): Born in Egypt; bishop of Alexandria (412-444); wrote treatises on the Trinity, the Incarnation and other subjects, mostly in refutation of Nestorian errors; made key contributions to the development of Christology; presided at the Council of Ephesus, 431; proclaimed doctor, 1882; feast, June 27.

Cyril of Jerusalem, St. (c. 315-387): Bishop of Jerusalem (350-387); vigorous opponent of Arianism; principal work, *Catecheses,* a pre-baptismal explanation of the creed of Jerusalem; proclaimed doctor, 1882; feast, Mar. 18.

Ephraem, St. (c. 306-373): Born in Nisibis, Mesopotamia; counteracted the spread of Gnostic and Arian errors with poems and hymns of his own composition; wrote also on the Eucharist and Mary; proclaimed doctor, 1920; called Deacon of Edessa and Harp of the Holy Spirit; feast, June 9.

Francis de Sales, St. (1567-1622): Born in Savoy; bishop of Geneva (1602-1622); spiritual writer with strong influence on devotional life through treatises such as *Introduction to a Devout Life,* and *The Love of God;* canonized, 1665; proclaimed doctor, 1877; patron of Catholic writers and the Catholic press; feast, Jan. 24.

Gregory Nazianzen, St. (c. 330-c. 390): Born in Arianzus, Cappadocia, Asia Minor; bishop of Constantinople (381-390); vigorous opponent of Arianism; in addition to five theological discourses on the Nicene Creed and the Trinity for which he is best known, wrote letters and poetry; Father and Doctor of the Church; called the Christian Demosthenes because of his eloquence and, in the Eastern Church, The Theologian; feast, Jan. 2.

Gregory I, the Great, St. (c. 540-604): Born in Rome; pope (590-604); wrote many scriptural commentaries, a compendium of theology in the *Book of Morals* based on Job, *Dialogues* concerning the lives of saints, the immortality of the soul, death, purgatory, heaven and hell, and 14 books of letters; enforced papal supremacy and established the position of the pope vis-a-vis the emperor; worked for clerical and monastic reform and the observance of clerical celibacy; Father and Doctor of the Church; feast, Sept. 3.

Hilary of Poitiers, St. (c. 315-368): Born in Poitiers, France; bishop of Poitiers (c. 353-368); wrote *De Synodis,* with the Arian controversy in mind, and *De Trinitate,* the first lengthy study of the doctrine in Latin; introduced Eastern theology to the West; contributed to the development of hymnology; proclaimed doctor, 1851; called the Athanasius of the West because of his vigorous defense of the divinity of Christ against Arians; feast, Jan. 13.

Isidore of Seville, St. (c. 560-636): Born in Cartagena, Spain; bishop of Seville (c. 600-636); in addition to his principal work, *Etymologiae,* an encyclopedia of the knowledge of his day, wrote on theological and historical subjects; regarded as the most learned man of his time; proclaimed doctor, 1722; feast, Apr. 4.

Jerome, St. (c. 343-420): Born in Stridon, Dalmatia; translated the Old Testament from Hebrew into Latin and revised the existing Latin translation of the New Testament to produce the Vulgate version of the Bible; wrote scriptural commentaries and treatises on matters of controversy; regarded as Father and Doctor of the Church from the eighth century; called Father of Biblical Science; feast, Sept. 30.

John Chrysostom, St. (c. 347-407): Born in Antioch, Asia Minor; archbishop of Constantinople (398-407); wrote homilies, scriptural commentaries and letters of wide influence in addition to a classical treatise on the priesthood; proclaimed doctor by the Council of Chalcedon, 451; called the greatest of the Greek Fathers; named patron of preachers, 1909; called Golden-Mouthed because of his eloquence; feast, Sept. 13.

John Damascene, St. (c. 675-c. 749): Born in Damascus, Syria; monk; wrote *Fountain of Wisdom*, a three-part work including a history of heresies and an exposition of the Christian faith, three *Discourses against the Iconoclasts*, homilies on Mary, biblical commentaries and treatises on moral subjects; proclaimed doctor, 1890; called Golden Speaker because of his eloquence; feast, Dec. 4.

John of the Cross, St. (1542-1591): Born in Old Castile, Spain; Carmelite; founder of Discalced Carmelites; one of the greatest mystical theologians, wrote *The Ascent of Mt. Carmel — The Dark Night, The Spiritual Canticle, The Living Flame of Love;* canonized, 1726; proclaimed doctor, 1926; called Doctor of Mystical Theology; feast, Dec. 14.

Lawrence of Brindisi, St. (1559-1619): Born in Brindisi, Italy; Franciscan (Capuchin); vigorous preacher of strong influence in the post-Reformation period; 15 tomes of collected works include scriptural commentaries, sermons, homilies and doctrinal writings; canonized, 1881; proclaimed doctor, 1959; feast, July 21.

Leo I, the Great, St. (c. 400-461): Born in Tuscany, Italy; pope (440-461); wrote the *Tome of Leo*, to explain doctrine concerning the two natures and one Person of Christ, against the background of the Nestorian and Monophysite heresies; other works included sermons, letters and writings against the errors of Manichaeism and Pelagianism; was instrumental in dissuading Attila from sacking Rome in 452; proclaimed doctor, 1574; feast, Nov. 10.

Peter Canisius, St. (1521-1597): Born in Nijmegen, Holland; Jesuit; wrote popular expositions of the Catholic faith in several catechisms which were widely circulated in 20 editions in his lifetime alone; was one of the moving figures in the Counter-Reformation period, especially in southern and western Germany; canonized and proclaimed doctor, 1925; feast, Dec. 21.

Peter Chrysologus, St. (c. 400-450): Born in Imola, Italy; served as archbishop of Ravenna (c. 433-450); his sermons and writings, many of which were designed to counteract Monophysitism, were pastoral and practical; proclaimed doctor, 1729; feast, July 30.

Peter Damian, St. (1007-1072): Born in Ravenna, Italy; Benedictine; cardinal; his writings and sermons, many of which concerned ecclesiastical and clerical reform, were pastoral and practical; proclaimed doctor, 1828; feast, Feb. 21.

Robert Bellarmine, St. (1542-1621): Born in Tuscany, Italy; Jesuit; archbishop of Capua (1602-1605); wrote *Controversies*, a three-volume exposition of doctrine under attack during and after the Reformation, two catechisms and the spiritual work, *The Art of Dying Well;* was an authority on ecclesiology and Church-state relations; canonized, 1930; proclaimed doctor, 1931; feast, Sept. 17.

Teresa of Avila, St. (1515-1582): Born in Avila, Spain; entered the Carmelite Order, 1535; in the early 1560's, initiated a primitive Carmelite, discalced-Alcantarine reform which greatly influenced men and women religious, especially in Spain; wrote extensively on spiritual and mystical subjects; principal works included her *Autobiography, Way of Perfection, The Interior Castle, Meditations on the Canticle, The Foundations, Visitation of the Discalced Nuns;* canonized, 1614; proclaimed first woman doctor, Sept. 27, 1970; feast, Oct. 15.

Thomas Aquinas, St. (1225-1274): Born near Naples, Italy; Dominican; teacher and writer on virtually the whole range of philosophy and theology; principal works were *Summa contra Gentiles*, a manual and systematic defense of Christian doctrine, and *Summa Theologiae*, a new (at that time) exposition of theology on philosophical principles; canonized, 1323; proclaimed doctor, 1567; called Doctor Communis, Doctor Angelicus, the Great Synthesizer because of the way in which he related faith and reason, theology and philosophy (especially that of Aristotle), and systematized the presentation of Christian doctrine; named patron of Catholic schools and education, 1880; feast, Jan. 28.

CREEDS

Creeds are formal and official statements of Christian doctrine. As summaries of the principal truths of faith, they are standards of orthodoxy and are useful for instructional purposes, for actual profession of the faith and for expression of the faith in the liturgy.

The classical creeds are the Apostles' Creed and the Creed of Nicaea-Constantinople. Two others are the Athanasian Creed and the Creed of Pius IV.

Apostles' Creed

Text: I believe in God, the Father almighty, Creator of heaven and earth.

And in Jesus Christ, his only Son, our Lord; who was conceived by the Holy Spirit, born of the Virgin Mary, suffered under Pontius Pilate, was crucified, died, and was buried. He descended into hell; the third day he arose again from the dead; he ascended into heaven, sits at the right hand of God, the Father almighty; from thence he shall come to judge the living and the dead.

I believe in the Holy Spirit, the holy Catholic Church, the communion of saints, the forgiveness of sins, the resurrection of the body, and life everlasting. Amen.

Background: The Apostles' Creed reflects the teaching of the Apostles but is not of apostolic origin. It probably originated in the second century as a rudimentary formula of faith professed by catechumens before the reception of baptism. Baptismal creeds in fourth-century use at Rome and elsewhere in the West closely resembled the present text, which was quoted in a handbook of Christian doctrine written between 710 and 724. This text was in wide use throughout the West by the ninth century. The Apostles' Creed is common to all Christian confessional churches in the West, but is not used in Eastern Churches.

Nicene Creed

The following translation of the Latin text of the creed was prepared by the International Committee on English in the Liturgy.

Text: We believe in one God, the Father, the Almighty, maker of heaven and earth, of all that is seen and unseen.

We believe in one Lord, Jesus Christ, the only Son of God, eternally begotten of the Father, God from God, Light from Light, true God from true God, begotten, not made, one in Being with the Father. Through him all things were made. For us men and for our salvation he came down from heaven: by the power of the Holy Spirit he was born of the Virgin Mary, and became man. For our sake he was crucified under Pontius Pilate; he suffered, died, and was buried. On the third day he rose again in fulfillment of the Scriptures; he ascended into heaven and is seated at the right hand of the Father. He will come again in glory to judge the living and the dead, and his kingdom will have no end.

We believe in the Holy Spirit, the Lord, the giver of life, who proceeds from the Father and the Son. With the Father and the Son he is worshiped and glorified. He has spoken through the prophets.

We believe in one holy catholic and apostolic Church. We acknowledge one baptism for the forgiveness of sins. We look for the resurrection of the dead, and the life of the world to come. Amen.

Background: The Nicene Creed (Creed of Nicaea-Constantinople) consists of elements of doctrine contained in an early baptismal creed of Jerusalem and enactments of the Council of Nicaea (325) and the Council of Constantinople (381). Its strong trinitarian content reflects the doctrinal errors, especially of Arianism, it served to counteract. Theologically, it is much more sophisticated than the Apostles' Creed. Since late in the fifth century, the Nicene Creed has been the only creed in liturgical use in the Eastern Churches. The Western Church adopted it for liturgical use by the end of the eighth century.

The Athanasian Creed

The Athanasian Creed, which has a unique structure, is a two-part summary of doctrine concerning the Trinity and the Incarnation-Redemption bracketed at the beginning and end with the statement that belief in the cited truths is necessary for salvation; it also contains a number of anathemas or condemnatory clauses regarding doctrinal errors. Although attributed to St. Athanasius, it was probably written after his death, between 381 and 428, and may have been authored by St. Ambrose. It is not accepted in the East; in the West, it has place in the liturgy of some other Christian churches as well as in the Roman-Rite Liturgy of the Hours and for the Solemnity of the Holy Trinity.

Creed of Pius IV

The Creed of Pius IV, also called the Profession of Faith of the Council of Trent, was promulgated in the bull *Injunctum Nobis*, Nov. 13, 1564. It is a summary of doctrine defined by the council concerning: Scripture and tradition, original sin and justification, the Mass and sacraments, veneration of the saints, indulgences, the primacy of the See of Rome. It was slightly modified in 1887 to include doctrinal formulations of the First Vatican Council.

Redditio of the Creed

The "giving back," by profession, of a baptismal creed by candidates for baptism to a bishop or his representative was one of the immediate preliminaries to reception of the sacrament at the conclusion of the catechumenate in the early Church.

The interrogation concerning truths of faith in the present baptismal rite is reminiscent of this ancient practice.

MORAL OBLIGATIONS

The basic norm of Christian morality is life in Christ. This involves, among other things, the observance of the Ten Commandments, their fulfillment in the twofold law of love of God and neighbor, the implications of the Sermon on the Mount and the whole New Testament, and membership in the Church established by Christ.

The Ten Commandments

The Ten Commandments, the Decalogue, were given by God through Moses to his Chosen People for the guidance of their moral conduct in accord with the demands of the Covenant he established with them as a divine gift.

In the traditional Catholic enumeration and according to Dt. 5:6-21, the Commandments are:

1. "I, the Lord, am your God . . . You shall not have other gods besides me. You shall not carve idols. . . ."
2. "You shall not take the name of the Lord, your God, in vain. . . ."
3. "Take care to keep holy the Sabbath day. . . ."
4. "Honor your father and your mother. . . ."
5. "You shall not kill."
6. "You shall not commit adultery."
7. "You shall not steal."
8. "You shall not bear dishonest witness against your neighbor."
9. "You shall not covet your neighbor's wife."
10. "You shall not desire your neighbor's house or field, nor his male or female slave, nor his ox or ass, nor anything that belongs to him" (summarily, his goods).

Another version of the Commandments, substantially the same, is given in Ex. 20:1-17.

The traditional enumeration of the Commandments in Protestant usage differs from the above. Thus: two commandments are made of the first, as above; the third and fourth are equivalent to the second and third, as above, and so on; and the 10th includes the ninth and 10th, as above.

Love of God and Neighbor

The first three of the commandments deal directly with man's relations with God, viz.: acknowledgment of one true God and the rejection of false gods and idols; honor due to God and his name; observance of the Sabbath as the Lord's day.

The rest cover interpersonal relationships, viz.: the obedience due to parents and, logically, to other persons in authority, and the obligations of parents to children and of persons in authority to those under their care; respect for life and physical integrity; fidelity in marriage, and chastity; justice and rights; truth; internal respect for faithfulness in marriage, chastity, and the goods of others.

Perfection in Christian Life

The moral obligations of the Ten Commandments are complemented by others flowing from the twofold law of love, the whole substance and pattern of Christ's teaching, and everything implied in full and active membership and participation in the community of salvation formed by Christ in his Church. Some of these matters are covered in other sections of the Almanac under appropriate headings.

Precepts of the Church

These are moral precepts binding Roman Catho-

lics in conscience. They originated in the Middle Ages; five of them were mentioned in the writings of St. Peter Canisius and St. Robert Bellarmine in the second half of the 16th century.

1. Assist at Mass on Sundays and holy days of obligation. (Also, to desist from unnecessary servile work on these days.)

2. Fast and abstain on the days appointed. (The fasting obligation binds persons from the 21st until the 59th birthday; the days of fast are Ash Wednesday and Good Friday. The abstinence obligation binds from the 14th birthday on these days, and is obligatory for all Fridays in Lent in the U.S.) These regulations, which have been modified in recent years, are penitential in purpose but do not exhaust the obligations of penance. Other ways of doing penance are left to personal option.

3. Confess their sins at least once a year.

4. Receive Holy Communion during the Easter time. (In the U.S., the Easter time extends from the First Sunday of Lent to Trinity Sunday.)

5. Contribute to the support of the Church.

6. Observe the laws of the Church concerning marriage.

SOCIAL DOCTRINE

Since the end of the last century, Catholic social doctrine has been formulated in a progressive manner in a number of authoritative documents. Outstanding examples are the encyclicals: *Rerum Novarum*, issued by Leo XIII in 1891; *Quadragesimo Anno*, by Pius XI in 1931; *Mater et Magistra* ("Christianity and Social Progress") and *Pacem in Terris* ("Peace on Earth"), by John XXIII in 1961 and 1963, respectively; *Populorum Progressio* ("Development of Peoples"), by Paul VI in 1967; and *Laborem Exercens* ("On Human Work"), by John Paul II in 1981. Pius XII, among other accomplishments of ideological importance in the social field, made a distinctive contribution with his formulation of a plan for world peace and order in Christmas messages from 1939 to 1941, and in other documents.

These documents represent the most serious attempts in modern times to systematize the social implications of the Gospel and the rest of divine revelation as well as the socially relevant writings of the Fathers and Doctors of the Church. Their contents are theological penetrations into social life, with particular reference to human rights, the needs of the poor and those in underdeveloped countries, and humane conditions of life, freedom, justice and peace. In some respects, they read like juridical documents; underneath, however, they are Gospel-oriented and pastoral in intention.

Nature of the Doctrine

Pope John XXIII, writing in *Christianity and Social Progress,* made the following statement about the nature and scope of the doctrine stated in the encyclicals in particular and related writings in general.

"What the Catholic Church teaches and declares regarding the social life and relationships of men is beyond question for all time valid.

"The cardinal point of this teaching is that individual men are necessarily the foundation, cause, and end of all social institutions . . . insofar as they are social by nature, and raised to an order of existence that transcends and subdues nature.

"Beginning with this very basic principle whereby the dignity of the human person is affirmed and defended, Holy Church — especially during the last century and with the assistance of learned priests and laymen, specialists in the field — has arrived at clear social teachings whereby the mutual relationships of men are ordered. Taking general norms into account, these principles are in accord with the nature of things and the changed conditions of man's social life, or with the special genius of our day. Moreover, these norms can be approved by all."

The Church in the World

Even more Gospel-oriented and pastoral in a distinctive way is the *Pastoral Constitution on the Church in the Modern World* promulgated by the Second Vatican Council in 1965.

Its purpose is to search out the signs of God's presence and meaning in and through the events of this time in human history. Accordingly, it deals with the situation of men in present circumstances of profound change, challenge and crisis on all levels of life.

The first part of the constitution develops the theme of the Church and man's calling, and focuses attention on the dignity of the human person, the problem of atheism, the community of mankind, man's activity throughout the world, and the serving and saving role of the Church in the world. This portion of the document, it has been said, represents the first presentation by the Church in an official text of an organized Christian view of man and society.

The second part of the document considers several problems of special urgency: fostering the nobility of marriage and the family (see Marriage Doctrine), the proper development of culture, socio-economic life, the life of the political community, the fostering of peace (see Peace and War), and the promotion of a community of nations.

In conclusion, the constitution calls for action to implement doctrine regarding the role and work of the Church for the total good of mankind.

Excerpts

Following are a number of key excerpts from the ideological heart of the constitution.

One Human Family and Community: God, who has fatherly concern for everyone, has willed that all men should constitute one family and treat one another in a spirit of brotherhood.

For this reason, love for God and neighbor is the first and greatest commandment. Sacred Scripture . . . teaches us that the love of God cannot be separated from love of neighbor. . . . To men growing daily more dependent on one another, and to a world becoming more unified every day, this truth proves to be of paramount importance (No. 24).

Human Person Is Central: Man's social nature makes it evident that the progress of the human person and the advance of society itself hinge on each other. For the beginning, the subject and the goal of all social institutions is and must be the human person, which for its part and by its very nature stands completely in need of social life. This social life is not something added on to man. Hence, through his dealings with others, through reciprocal duties and through fraternal dialogue, he develops all his gifts and is able to rise to his destiny.

Influence of Social Circumstances: But if by this social life the human person is greatly aided in responding to his destiny, even in its religious dimensions, it cannot be denied that men are often diverted from doing good and spurred toward evil by the social circumstances in which they live and are immersed from their birth. To be sure, the disturbances which so frequently occur in the social order result in part from the natural tensions of economic, political and social forms. But at a deeper level they flow from man's pride and selfishness, which contaminate even the social sphere. When the structure of affairs is flawed by the consequences of sin, man, already born with a bent toward evil, finds there new inducements to sin which cannot be overcome without strenuous efforts and the assistance of grace (No. 25).

Human Necessities: Every social group must take account of the needs and legitimate aspirations of other groups, and even of the general welfare of the entire human family.

At the same time, however, there is a growing awareness of the exalted dignity proper to the human person, since he stands above all things and his rights and duties are universal and inviolable. Therefore, there must be made available to all men everything necessary for leading a life truly human, such as food, clothing, and shelter; the right to choose a state of life freely and to found a family; the right to education, to employment, to a good reputation, to respect, to appropriate information, to activity in accord with the upright norm of one's own conscience, to protection of privacy and to rightful freedom in matters religious too.

Hence, the social order and its development must unceasingly work to the benefit of the human person if the disposition of affairs is to be subordinate to the personal realm and not contrariwise, as the Lord indicated when he said that the Sabbath was made for man, and not man for the Sabbath.

Improvement of Social Order: This social order requires constant improvement. It must be founded on truth, built on justice and animated by love; in freedom it should grow every day toward a more humane balance. An improvement in attitudes and widespread changes in society will have to take place if these objectives are to be gained.

God's Spirit, who with a marvelous providence directs the unfolding of time and renews the face of the earth, is not absent from this development. The ferment of the Gospel, too, has aroused and continues to arouse in man's heart the irresistible requirements of his dignity (No. 26).

Regard for Neighbor as Another Self: Coming down to practical and particularly urgent consequences, this Council lays stress on reverence for man; everyone must consider his every neighbor without exception as another self, taking into account first of all his life and the means necessary to living it with dignity.

In our times a special obligation binds us to make ourselves the neighbor of absolutely every person and to actively help him when he comes across our path.

Inhuman Evils: . . . Whatever is opposed to life itself, such as any type of murder, genocide, abortion, euthanasia, or willful self-destruction; whatever violates the integrity of the human person, such as mutilation, torments inflicted on body or mind, attempts to coerce the will itself; whatever insults human dignity, such as subhuman living conditions, arbitrary imprisonment, deportation, slavery, prostitution, the selling of women and children; as well as disgraceful working conditions, where men are treated as mere tools for profit rather than as free and responsible persons: all these things and others of their like are infamies indeed. They poison human society, but they do more harm to those who practice them than those who suffer from the injury. Moreover, they are a supreme dishonor to the Creator (No. 27).

Respect for Those Who Are Different: Respect and love ought to be extended also to those who think or act differently than we do in social, political and religious matters. In fact, the more deeply we come to understand their ways of thinking through such courtesy and love, the more easily will we be able to enter into dialogue with them.

Distinction between Error and Persons in Error: This love and good will, to be sure, must in no way render us indifferent to truth and goodness. Indeed, love itself impels the disciples of Christ to speak the saving truth to all men. But it is necessary to distinguish between error, which always merits repudiation, and the person in error, who never loses the dignity of being a person, even when he is flawed by false or inadequate religious notions. God alone is the judge and searcher of hearts; for that reason he forbids us to make judgments about the internal guilt of anyone.

The teaching of Christ even requires that we forgive injuries, and extends the law of love to include every enemy (No. 28).

Men Are Equal but Different: Since all men possess a rational soul and are created in God's likeness; since they have the same nature and origin, have been redeemed by Christ, and enjoy the same divine calling and destiny: the basic equality of all must receive increasingly greater recognition.

True, all men are not alike from the point of view of varying physical power and the diversity of intellectual and moral resources. Nevertheless, with respect to the fundamental rights of the person, every type of discrimination, whether social or cultural, whether based on sex, race, color, social condition, language or religion, is to be overcome and eradicated as contrary to God's intent.

Humane Conditions for All: Although rightful differences exist between men, the equal dignity of persons demands that a more humane and just condition of life be brought about. For excessive economic and social differences between the members of the one human family . . . cause scandal and militate against social justice, equity and the dignity of the human person as well as social and international peace.

Human institutions, both private and public, must labor to minister to the dignity and purpose of man. At the same time, let them put up a stubborn fight against any kind of slavery, whether social or political, and safeguard the basic rights of man under every political system. Indeed, human institutions themselves must be accommodated by degrees to the highest of all realities, spiritual ones, even though, meanwhile, a long enough time will be required before they arrive at the desired goal (No. 29).

Profound and rapid changes make it particularly urgent that no one, ignoring the trend of events or drugged by laziness, content himself with a merely individualistic morality. It grows increasingly true that the obligations of justice and love are fulfilled only if each person, contributing to the common good according to his own abilities and the needs of others, also promotes and assists the public and private institutions dedicated to bettering the conditions of human life.

Social Necessities Are Prime Duties: Let everyone consider it his sacred obligation to count social necessities among the primary duties of modern man and to pay heed to them. For the more unified the world becomes, the more plainly do the offices of men extend beyond particular groups and spread by degrees to the whole world. But this challenge cannot be met unless individual men and their associations cultivate in themselves the moral and social virtues and promote them in society.

Thus, with the needed help of divine grace, men who are truly new and artisans of a new humanity can be forthcoming (No. 30).

In order for individual men to discharge with greater exactness the obligations of their conscience toward themselves and the various groups to which they belong, they must be carefully educated to a higher degree of culture through the use of the immense resources available today to the human race.

Living Conditions and Freedom: A man can scarcely arrive at the needed sense of responsibility unless his living conditions allow him to become conscious of his dignity and to rise to his destiny by spending himself for God and for others. But human freedom is often crippled when a man falls into extreme poverty, just as it withers when he indulges in too many of life's comforts and imprisons himself in a kind of splendid isolation. Freedom acquires new strength, by contrast, when a man consents to the unavoidable requirements of social life, takes on the manifold demands of human partnership and commits himself to the service of the human community.

Hence, the will to play one's role in common endeavors should be everywhere encouraged (No. 31).

Communitarian Character of Life: God did not create man for life in isolation but for the formation of social unity. So also "it has pleased God to make men holy and save them not merely as individuals, without any mutual bonds, but by making them into a single people, a people which acknowledges him in truth and serves him in holiness" (*Dogmatic Constitution on the Church,* No. 9). So from the beginning of salvation history he has chosen men not just as individuals but as members of a certain community. Revealing his mind to them, God called these chosen ones "his people" (Ex. 3:7-12) and, furthermore, made a covenant with them on Sinai.

This communitarian character is developed and consummated in the work of Jesus Christ. For the very Word made flesh willed to share in the human fellowship. He was present at the wedding of Cana, visited the house of Zacchaeus, ate with publicans and sinners. He revealed the love of the Father and the sublime vocation of man in terms of the most common of social realities and by making use of the speech and the imagery of plain everyday life. Willingly obeying the laws of his country, he sanctified those human ties, especially family ones, from which social relationships arise. He chose to lead the life proper to an artisan of his time and place.

In his preaching he clearly taught the sons of God to treat one another as brothers. In his prayers he pleaded that all his disciples might be "one." Indeed, as the Redeemer of all, he offered himself for all even to the point of death. He commanded his Apostles to preach to all peoples the Gospel message so that the human race might become the Family of God, in which the fullness of the Law would be love.

The Community Founded by Christ: As the first-born of many brethren and through the gift of his Spirit, he founded after his death and resurrection a new brotherly community composed of all those who receive him in faith and in love. This he did through his Body, which is the Church. There everyone, as members one of the other, would render mutual service according to the different gifts bestowed on each.

This solidarity must be constantly increased until that day on which it is brought to perfection. Then, saved by grace, men will offer flawless glory to God as a family beloved of God and of Christ their Brother (No. 32).

WORK

The nature of work, its relation to social issues and its significance, along with prayer, as the "way of sanctification," are among key subjects treated in Pope John Paul's third encyclical letter, *Laborem Exercens.* Following are several paragraphs from the encyclical delineating a definition of work together with capsule coverge of a number of salient points in the letter.

Definition

"Through work man must earn his daily bread and contribute to the continual advance of science and technology and, above all, to elevating unceasingly the cultural and moral level of the society within which he lives in community with those who belong to the same family.

"And work means any activity by man, whether manual or intellectual, whatever its nature or circumstances; it means any human activity that can and must be recognized as work, in the midst of all the many activities of which man is capable and to which he is predisposed by his very nature, by virtue of humanity itself.

"Man is made to be in the visible universe an image and likeness of God himself, and he is placed in it in order to subdue the earth. From the beginning, therefore, he is called to work.

"Work is one of the characteristics that distinguish man from the rest of creatures, whose activity for sustaining their lives cannot be called work. Only man is capable of work and only man works, at the same time by work occupying his existence on earth. Thus, work bears a particular mark of man and of humanity, the mark of a person operating within a community of persons. And this mark decides its interior characteristics; in a sense, it constitutes its very nature."

Salient Points

Fundamental Criterion of Economics: "Respect for the objective rights of the worker . . . must constitute the adequate and fundamental criterion for shaping the whole economy, both on the level of the individual society and state and within the whole of the world economic policy as well as the systems of international relationships that derive from it."

Work and Family: "Work constitutes a foundation of the formation of family life" by providing the economic means necessary to maintain a family.

Just Wage: "A just wage is the concrete means

of verifying the justice of the whole socio-economic system and, in any case, of checking that it is functioning justly."

Family Wage: A "family wage" is needed, "a single salary given to the head of the family for his work, sufficient for the needs of the family without the other spouse having to take up gainful employment outside the home," or without the need of recourse to other social provisions for aid.

Women: Women who work "should be able to fulfill their tasks in accordance with their own nature without being discriminated against and without being excluded from jobs for which they are capable." Respect is due "for their family aspirations and for their specific role in contributing, together with men, to the good of society."

Mothers: Provisions should be made for "measures such as family allowances or grants to mothers devoting themselves exclusively to their families."

Unions: Workers have the right to form a union to protect their vital interests and to be "a mouthpiece for the struggle for social justice."

"Union activity undoubtedly enters the field of politics, understood as prudent concern for the common good." But unions should not engage in partisan politics; otherwise, "they become an instrument used for other purposes."

Strike: Workers should be assured the right to strike without being subject to personal sanctions, but have the responsibility of not striking if a strike "is contrary to requirements of the common good."

Unemployment Benefits: "The obligation to provide unemployment benefits . . . is a duty springing from the fundamental principle of the common use of goods or, to put it in another way, the right to life and subsistence."

Disabled Persons: Society should provide work for disabled persons in keeping with their physical disabilities. Failure to do so means "a serious form of discrimination, that of the strong and healthy against the weak and sick."

Health Care: "The expenses involved in health care, especially in the case of accidents at work, demand that medical assistance should be easily available for workers."

Technology: It is meant to be the worker's ally but can become his enemy when mechanization supplants him or takes away "all personal satisfaction and the incentive to creativity and responsibility," thus reducing "man to the status of slave."

Haves and Have-Nots: "A disconcerting fact of immense proportions" occurs on the world scene. "While conspicuous natural resources remain unused, there are huge numbers of people who are unemployed or underemployed, and countless multitudes of people suffering from hunger." This means that there is "something wrong with the organization of work and employment" on national and international levels.

Foreign Workers: People have a right to emigrate in search of work. "The person working away from his native land, whether as a permanent emigrant or as a seasonal worker, should not be placed at a disadvantage in comparison with the workers in that society in the matter of working rights. Emigration in search of work must in no way become an opportunity for financial or social exploitation."

Marxism: Catholic social teaching "diverges radically from the program of collectivism proclaimed by Marxism and put into practice in various countries."

Private Property and Capitalism: "Christian tradition has never upheld" the right to private property "as absolute and untouchable. On the contrary, it has always understood this right common to all to use the goods of the whole creation."

"Deeply desired reforms" of capitalism "cannot be achieved by an *a priori* elimination of private ownership of the means of production." This is not sufficient to insure "satisfactory socialization" because new managers form another special group "from the fact of exercising power in society. This group . . . may carry out this task badly by claiming for itself a monopoly of the administration and disposal of the means of production and not refraining even from offending basic human rights."

Exploitation by Multinationals: "The highly industrialized countries, and even more so the businesses that direct on a large scale the means of industrial production, fix the highest possible prices for their products while trying at the same time to fix the lowest possible prices for raw materials or semi-manufactured goods."

PEACE AND WAR

The following excerpts, stating principles and objectives of social doctrine concerning peace and war, are from the "Pastoral Constitution on the Church in the Modern World" (Nos. 77 to 82) promulgated by the Second Vatican Council.

(See also: "The Challenge of Peace: God's Promise and Our Purpose.")

Call to Peace: This Council fervently desires to summon Christians to cooperate with all men in making secure among themselves a peace based on justice and love, and in setting up agencies of peace. This Christians should do with the help of Christ, the Author of peace (No. 77).

Conditions for Peace: Peace is not merely the absence of war. Nor can it be reduced solely to the maintenance of a balance of power between enemies. Nor is it brought about by dictatorship. Instead, it is rightly and appropriately called "an enterprise of justice" (Is. 32:7). Peace results from that harmony built into human society by its divine Founder and actualized by men as they thirst after ever greater justice.

The common good of men is in its basic sense determined by the eternal law. Still the concrete demands of this common good are constantly changing as time goes on. Hence peace is never attained once and for all, but must be built up ceaselessly. Moreover, since the human will is unsteady and wounded by sin, the achievement of peace requires that everyone constantly master his passions and that lawful authority keep vigilant.

But such is not enough. This peace cannot be obtained on earth unless personal values are safeguarded and men freely and trustingly share with one another the riches of their inner spirits and their talents. A firm determination to respect other men and peoples and their dignity, as well as the studied practice of brotherhood, are absolutely necessary for the establishment of peace. Hence peace is likewise the fruit of love, which goes beyond what justice can provide.

Renunciation of Violence: We cannot fail to praise those who renounce the use of violence in the vindication of their rights and who resort to methods of defense which are otherwise available to weaker parties too, provided that this can be done without injury to the rights and duties of others or of the community itself (No. 78).

Mass Extermination: The Council wishes to recall first of all the permanent binding force of universal natural law and its all-embracing principles. Man's conscience itself gives ever more emphatic voice to these principles. Therefore, actions which deliberately conflict with these same principles, as well as orders commanding such actions, are criminal. Blind obedience cannot excuse those who yield to them. Among such must first be counted those actions designed for the methodical extermination of an entire people, nation, or ethnic minority. These actions must be vehemently condemned as horrendous crimes. The courage of those who openly and fearlessly resist men who issue such commands merits supreme commendation.

International Agreements: On the subject of war, quite a large number of nations have subscribed to various international agreements aimed at making military activity and its consequences less inhuman. Such are conventions concerning the handling of wounded or captured soldiers, and various similar agreements. Agreements of this sort must be honored. They should be improved upon.

Conscientious Objectors: It seems right that laws make humane provisions for the case of those who for reasons of conscience refuse to bear arms, provided, however, that they accept some other form of service to the human community.

Legitimate Defense: Certainly, war has not been rooted out of human affairs. As long as the danger of war remains and there is no competent and sufficiently powerful authority at the international level, governments cannot be denied the right to legitimate defense once every means of peaceful settlement has been exhausted. Therefore, government authorities and others who share public responsibility have the duty to protect the welfare of the people entrusted to their care and to conduct such grave matters soberly.

But it is one thing to undertake military action for the just defense of the people, and something else again to seek the subjugation of other nations. Nor does the possession of war potential make every military or political use of it lawful. Neither does the mere fact that war has unhappily begun mean that all is fair between the warring parties.

Nature of Military Service: Those who are pledged to the service of their country as members of its armed forces should regard themselves as agents of security and freedom on behalf of their people. As long as they fulfill this role properly, they are making a genuine contribution to the establishment of peace (No. 79).

Total War Condemned: This most holy Synod makes its own the condemnations of total war already pronounced by recent popes, and issues the following declaration:

Any act of war aimed indiscriminately at the destruction of entire cities or of extensive areas along with their population is a crime against God and man himself. It merits unequivocal and unhesitating condemnation.

The unique hazard of modern warfare consists in this: it provides those who possess modern scientific weapons with a kind of occasion for perpetrating just such abominations. Moreover, through a certain inexorable chain of events, it can urge men on to the most atrocious decisions. That such in fact may never happen in the future, the bishops of the whole world, in unity assembled, beg all men, especially government officials and military leaders, to give unremitting thought to the awesome responsibility which is theirs before God and the entire human race (No. 80).

Retaliation and Deterrence: Scientific weapons, to be sure, are not amassed solely for use in war. The defensive strength of any nation is considered to be dependent upon its capacity for immediate retaliation against an adversary. Hence this accumulation of arms, which increases each year, also serves, in a way heretofore unknown, as a deterrent to possible enemy attack. Many regard this state of affairs as the most effective way by which peace of a sort can be maintained between nations at the present time.

Arms Race: Whatever be the case with this method of deterrence, men should be convinced that the arms race in which so many countries are engaged is not a safe way to preserve a steady peace. Nor is the so-called balance resulting from this race a sure and authentic peace. Rather than being eliminated thereby, the causes of war threaten to grow gradually stronger.

While extravagant sums are being spent for the furnishing of ever new weapons, an adequate remedy cannot be provided for the multiple miseries afflicting the whole modern world. Disagreements between nations are not really and radically healed. On the contrary, other parts of the world are infected with them. New approaches initiated by reformed attitudes must be adopted to remove this trap and to restore genuine peace by emancipating the world from its crushing anxiety.

Therefore, it must be said again: the arms race is an utterly treacherous trap for humanity, and one which injures the poor to an intolerable degree. It is much to be feared that, if this race persists, it will eventually spawn all the lethal ruin whose path it is now making ready (No. 81).

Outlaw War: It is our clear duty, then, to strain every muscle as we work for the time when all war can be completely outlawed by international consent. This goal undoubtedly requires the establishment of some universal public authority acknowledged as such by all, and endowed with effective power to safeguard, on behalf of all, security, regard for justice, and respect for rights.

Multilateral and Controlled Disarmament: But before this hoped-for authority can be set up, the highest existing international centers must devote themselves vigorously to the pursuit of better means for obtaining common security. Peace must be born of mutual trust between nations rather than imposed on them through fear of one another's weapons. Hence everyone must labor to put an end at last to the arms race, and to make a true beginning of disarmament, not indeed a unilateral disarmament, but one proceeding at an equal pace according to agreement, and backed up by authentic and workable safeguards.

In the meantime, efforts which have already been made and are still under way to eliminate the danger of war are not to be underrated. On the contrary, support should be given to the good will of the very many leaders who work hard to do away with war, which they abominate.

Public Opinion: Men should take heed not to entrust themselves only to the efforts of others, while remaining careless about their own attitudes. For government officials, who must simultaneously guarantee the good of their own people and promote the universal good, depend on public opinion and feeling to the greatest possible extent. It does them no good to work at building peace so long as feelings of hostility, contempt, and distrust, as well as racial hatred and unbending ideologies, continue to divide men and place them in opposing camps.

Hence arises a surpassing need for renewed education of attitudes and for new inspiration in the area of public opinion. Those who are dedicated to the work of education . . . should regard as their most weighty task the effort to instruct all in fresh sentiments of peace (No. 82).

INTEREST IN PASTORAL LETTER

The U.S. bishop's pastoral letter, "The Challenge of Peace: God's Promise and Our Response," was reported in August, 1983, to be generating a variety of follow-up activities which appeared to be making it one of the most well-studied documents in recent church history.

Father Brian McCullough, in charge of monitoring the follow-up for the bishops, said interest in the letter was higher than in anything published by the Church except the documents of the Second Vatican Council.

The interest extended beyond the Church in the U.S. Overseas, the letter was already being translated into several languages, while in this country it was getting what some observers termed unprecedented support and endorsement from Protestant and Jewish groups and leaders.

More than one million copies of the letter had been circulated through the Catholic press by the middle of August. A month earlier, the Office of Publishing Services, U.S. Catholic Conference, reported 50,000 copies on order.

Efforts for dissemination of the letter were under the direction of a three-bishop committee headed by Bishop George A. Fulcher of Lafayette, Ind.

The nature and purpose of the liturgy, along with norms for its revision, were the subject matter of the "Constitution on the Sacred Liturgy" promulgated by the Second Vatican Council. The principles and guidelines stated in this document, the first issued by the Council, are summarized here and/or are incorporated in other Almanac entries on liturgical subjects.

Nature and Purpose of Liturgy

The paragraphs under this and the following subhead are quoted directly from the "Constitution on the Sacred Liturgy."

"It is through the liturgy, especially the divine Eucharistic Sacrifice, that 'the work of our redemption is exercised.' The liturgy is thus the outstanding means by which the faithful can express in their lives, and manifest to others, the mystery of Christ and the real nature of the true Church . . ." (No. 2).

"The liturgy is considered as an exercise of the priestly office of Jesus Christ. In the liturgy the sanctification of man is manifested by signs perceptible to the senses, and is effected in a way which is proper to each of these signs; in the liturgy full public worship is performed by the Mystical Body of Jesus Christ, that is, by the Head and his members.

"From this it follows that every liturgical celebration, because it is an action of Christ the priest and of his Body the Church, is a sacred action surpassing all others. No other action of the Church can match its claim to efficacy, nor equal the degree of it" (No. 7).

"The liturgy is the summit toward which the activity of the Church is directed; at the same time it is the fountain from which all her power flows. For the goal of apostolic works is that all who are made sons of God by faith and baptism should come together to praise God in the midst of his Church, to take part in her sacrifice, and to eat the Lord's Supper.

". . . From the liturgy, therefore, and especially from the Eucharist, as from a fountain, grace is channeled into us; and the sanctification of men in Christ and the glorification of God, to which all other activities of the Church are directed as toward their goal, are most powerfully achieved" (No. 10).

Full Participation

"Mother Church earnestly desires that all the faithful be led to that full, conscious, and active participation in liturgical celebrations which is demanded by the very nature of the liturgy. Such participation by the Christian people as 'a chosen race, a royal priesthood, a holy nation, a purchased people' (1 Pt. 2:9; cf. 2:4-5), is their right and duty by reason of their baptism.

"In the restoration and promotion of the sacred liturgy, this full and active participation by all the people is the aim to be considered before all else; for it is the primary and indispensable source from which the faithful are to derive the true Christian spirit . . ." (No. 14).

"In order that the Christian people may more securely derive an abundance of graces from the sacred liturgy, holy Mother Church desires to undertake with great care a general restoration of the liturgy itself. For the liturgy is made up of unchangeable elements divinely instituted, and elements subject to change. The latter not only may but ought to be changed with the passing of time if features have by chance crept in which are less harmonious with the intimate nature of the liturgy, or if existing elements have grown less functional.

"In this restoration, both texts and rites should be drawn up so that they express more clearly the holy things which they signify. Christian people, as far as possible, should be able to understand them with ease and to take part in them fully, actively, and as befits a community . . ." (No. 21).

Norms

Norms regarding the reforms concern the greater use of Scripture; emphasis on the importance of the sermon or homily on biblical and liturgical subjects; use of vernacular languages for prayers of the Mass and for administration of the sacraments; provision for adaptation of rites to cultural patterns.

Approval for reforms of various kinds — in liturgical texts, rites, etc. — depends on the Holy See, regional conferences of bishops and individual bishops, according to provisions of law. No priest has authority to initiate reforms on his own. Reforms may not be introduced just for the sake of innovation, and any that are introduced in the light of present-day circumstances should embody sound tradition.

To assure the desired effect of liturgical reforms, training and instruction are necessary for the clergy, religious and the laity. The functions of diocesan and regional commissions for liturgy, music and art are to set standards and provide leadership for instruction and practical programs in their respective fields.

Most of the constitution's provisions regarding liturgical reforms have to do with the Roman Rite. The document clearly respects the equal dignity of all rites, leaving to the Eastern Churches control over their ancient liturgies.

(For coverage of the Mystery of the Eucharist, see The Mass; Other Sacraments, see separate entries.)

Sacramentals

Sacramentals, instituted by the Church, "are sacred signs which bear a resemblance to the sacraments: they signify effects, particularly of a spiritual kind, which are obtained through the Church's intercession. By them men are disposed to receive the chief effect of the sacraments, and various occasions in life are rendered holy" (No. 60).

"Thus, for well-disposed members of the faithful, the liturgy of the sacraments and sacramentals sanctifies almost every event in their lives; they are given access to the stream of divine grace which flows from the paschal mystery of the passion, death, and resurrection of Christ, the fountain from which all sacraments and sacramentals draw their power. There is hardly any proper use of material things which cannot thus be directed toward the sanctification of men and the praise of God" (No. 61).

Some common sacramentals are priestly blessings, blessed palm, candles, holy water, medals, scapulars, prayers and ceremonies of the Roman Ritual.

Liturgy of the Hours

The Liturgy of the Hours (Divine Office) is the public prayer of the Church for praising God and sanctifying the day. Its daily celebration is required as a sacred obligation by men in holy orders and by men and women religious who have professed solemn vows. Its celebration by others is highly commended and is to be encouraged in the community of the faithful.

"By tradition going back to early Christian times, the Divine Office is arranged so that the whole course of the day and night is made holy by the praises of God. Therefore, when this wonderful song of praise is worthily rendered by priests and others who are deputed for this purpose by Church ordinance, or by the faithful praying together with the priest in an approved form, then it is truly the voice of the bride addressing her bridegroom; it is the very prayer which Christ himself, together with his Body, addresses to the Father" (No. 84).

"Hence all who perform this service are not only fulfilling a duty of the Church, but also are sharing in the greatest honor accorded to Christ's spouse, for by offering these praises to God they are standing before God's throne in the name of the Church their Mother" (No. 85).

The Liturgy of the Hours, revised since 1965, was the subject of Pope Paul VI's apostolic constitution *Laudis Canticum,* dated Nov. 1, 1970. The master Latin text was published in 1971; its first volumes have been published in authorized English translation since May, 1975.

One-volume, partial editions of the Liturgy of the Hours containing Morning and Evening Prayer and other elements, have been published in approved English translation.

The revised Liturgy of the Hours consists of:

• Office of Readings, for reflection on the word of God. The principal parts are three psalms, biblical and non-biblical readings.

• Morning and Evening Prayer, called the "hinges" of the Liturgy of the Hours. The principal parts are a hymn, two psalms, an Old or New Testament canticle, a brief biblical reading, Zechariah's canticle (the *Benedictus,* morning) or Mary's canticle (the *Magnificat,* evening), responsories, intercessions and a concluding prayer.

• Daytime Prayer. The principal parts are a hymn, three psalms, a brief biblical reading and one of three concluding prayers corresponding to the time at which the prayer is offered (midmorning, midday, midafternoon).

• Night Prayer: The principal parts are one or two psalms, a brief biblical reading, Simeon's canticle *(Nunc Dimittis),* a concluding prayer and an antiphon in honor of Mary.

In the revised Liturgy of the Hours, the hours are shorter than they had been, with greater textual variety, meditation aids, and provision for intervals of silence and meditation. The psalms are distributed over a four-week period instead of a week; some psalms, entirely or in part, are not included. Additional canticles from the Old and New Testaments are assigned for Morning and Evening Prayer. Additional scriptural texts have been added and variously arranged for greater internal unity, correspondence to readings at Mass, and relevance to events and themes of salvation history. Readings include some of the best material from the Fathers of the Church and other authors, and improved selections on the lives of saints.

The book used for recitation of the Office is the **Breviary.**

For coverage of the **Liturgical Year,** see Church Calendar.

Sacred Music

"The musical tradition of the universal Church is a treasure of immeasurable value, greater even than that of any other art. The main reason for this pre-eminence is that, as sacred melody united to words, it forms a necessary or integral part of the solemn liturgy.

". . . Sacred music increases in holiness to the degree that it is intimately linked with liturgical action, winningly expresses prayerfulness, promotes solidarity, and enriches sacred rites with heightened solemnity. The Church indeed approves of all forms of true art, and admits them into divine worship when they show appropriate qualities" (No. 112).

The constitution decreed:

• Vernacular languages for the people's parts of the liturgy, as well as Latin, may be used.

• Participation in sacred song by the whole body of the faithful, and not just by choirs, is to be encouraged and brought about.

• Provisions should be made for proper musical training for clergy, religious and lay persons.

• While Gregorian Chant has a unique dignity and relationship to the Latin liturgy, other kinds of music are acceptable.

• Native musical traditions should be used, especially in mission areas.

• Various instruments compatible with the dignity of worship may be used.

Gregorian Chant: A form and style of chant called Gregorian was the basis and most highly regarded standard of liturgical music for centuries. It originated probably during the formative period of the Roman liturgy and developed in conjunction with Gallican and other forms of chant. Gregory the Great's connection with it is not clear, although it is known that he had great concern for and interest in church music. The earliest extant written versions of Gregorian Chant date from the ninth century. A thousand years later, the Benedictines of Solesmes, France, initiated a revival of chant which gave impetus to the modern liturgical movement.

Sacred Art and Furnishings

"Very rightly the fine arts are considered to rank among the noblest expressions of human genius. This judgment applies especially to religious art and to its highest achievement, which is sacred art. By their very nature both of the latter are related to God's boundless beauty, for this is the reality which these human efforts are trying to express in some way. To the extent that these works aim exclusively at turning men's thoughts to God persuasively and devoutly, they are dedicated to God and to the cause of his greater honor and glory" (No. 122).

The objective of sacred art is "that all things set apart for use in divine worship should be truly worthy, becoming, and beautiful, signs and symbols of heavenly realities. . . . The Church has . . . always reserved to herself the right to pass judgment upon the arts, deciding which of the works of artists are in accordance with faith, piety, and cherished traditional laws, and thereby suited to sacred purposes.

". . . Sacred furnishings should worthily and beautifully serve the dignity of worship . . ." (No. 122).

According to the constitution:

• Contemporary art, as well as that of the past, shall "be given free scope in the Church, provided that it adorns the sacred buildings and holy rites with due honor and reverence . . ." (No. 123).

• Noble beauty, not sumptuous display, should be sought in art, sacred vestments and ornaments.

• "Let bishops carefully exclude from the house of God and from other sacred places those works of artists which are repugnant to faith, morals, and Christian piety, and which offend true religious sense either by their distortion of forms or by lack of artistic worth, by mediocrity or by pretense.

• "When churches are to be built, let great care be taken that they be suitable for the celebration of liturgical services and for the active participation of the faithful" (No. 124).

• "The practice of placing sacred images in churches so that they may be venerated by the faithful is to be firmly maintained. Nevertheless, their number should be moderate and their relative location should reflect right order. Otherwise they may create confusion among the Christian people and promote a faulty sense of devotion" (No. 125).

• Artists should be trained and inspired in the spirit and for the purposes of the liturgy.

• The norms of sacred art should be revised. "These laws refer especially to the worthy and well-planned construction of sacred buildings, the shape and construction of altars, the nobility, location, and security of the Eucharistic tabernacle, the suitability and dignity of the baptistery, the proper use of sacred images, embellishments, and vestments . . ." (No. 128).

RITES

A rite is the manner in which liturgical worship is carried out. It includes the forms and ceremonial observances of liturgical worship.

Different rites have evolved in the course of church history, giving to liturgical worship forms and usages peculiar and proper to the nature of worship itself and to the culture of the faithful in various circumstances of time and place. Thus, there has been development since apostolic times in prayers and ceremonies of the Mass, the administration of the sacraments, requirements for celebration of the Liturgy of the Hours (Divine Office). Practices within the patriarchates of Antioch, Rome, Alexandria and Constantinople were the principal sources of the rites in present use.

Eastern Rites, described elsewhere in the Almanac, are proper to Eastern Catholic Churches.

The **Roman** or **Latin Rite,** described in this section, prevails in the Western Church. It was derived from Roman practices and the use of Latin as an official language from the third century onward. Other rites in limited use in the Western Church have been the Ambrosian (Milan archdiocese), the Mozarabic (Toledo, Spain, archdiocese), the Lyonnais, the Braga, and rites peculiar to some religious orders like the Dominicans, Carmelites and Carthusians.

The revision of rites in progress since the Second Vatican Council is meant to renew them, not to eliminate the rites of particular churches or to reduce all rites to uniformity.

MASS, EUCHARISTIC SACRIFICE AND BANQUET

Declarations of Vatican II

The Second Vatican Council made the following declarations, among others, with respect to the Mass.

"At the Last Supper, on the night when he was betrayed, our Savior instituted the Eucharistic Sacrifice of his Body and Blood. He did this in order to perpetuate the Sacrifice of the Cross throughout the centuries until he should come again, and so to entrust to his beloved spouse, the Church, a memorial of his death and resurrection: a sacrament of love, a sign of unity, a bond of charity, a paschal banquet in which Christ is consumed, the mind is filled with grace, and a pledge of future glory is given to us" (*Constitution on the Sacred Liturgy,* No. 47).

". . . As often as the Sacrifice of the Cross in which 'Christ, our Passover, has been sacrificed' (1 Cor. 5:7) is celebrated on an altar, the work of our redemption is carried on. At the same time, in the sacrament of the Eucharistic bread the unity of all believers who form one body in Christ (cf. 1 Cor. 10:17) is both expressed and brought about. All men are called to this union with Christ . . ." (*Dogmatic Constitution on the Church.* No. 3).

". . . The ministerial priest, by the sacred power

he enjoys, molds and rules the priestly people. Acting in the person of Christ, he brings about the Eucharistic Sacrifice, and offers it to God in the name of all the people. For their part, the faithful join in the offering of the Eucharist by virtue of their royal priesthood . . ." (*Ibid.*, No. 10).

Declarations of Trent

Among its decrees on the Holy Eucharist, the Council of Trent stated the following points of doctrine on the Mass.

1. There is in the Catholic Church a true Sacrifice, the Mass instituted by Jesus Christ. It is the Sacrifice of his Body and Blood, Soul and Divinity, himself, under the appearances of bread and wine.

2. This Sacrifice is identical with the Sacrifice of the Cross, inasmuch as Christ is the Priest and Victim in both. A difference lies in the manner of offering, which was bloody upon the Cross and is bloodless on the altar.

3. The Mass is a propitiatory Sacrifice, atoning for sins of the living and dead for whom it is offered.

4. The efficacy of the Mass is derived from the Sacrifice of the Cross, whose superabundant merits it applies to men.

5. Although the Mass is offered to God alone, it may be celebrated in honor and memory of the saints.

6. Christ instituted the Mass at the Last Supper.

7. Christ ordained the Apostles priests, giving them power and the command to consecrate his Body and Blood to perpetuate and renew the Sacrifice.

ORDER OF MASS

The Mass consists of two principal divisions called the **Liturgy of the Word**, which features the proclamation of the Word of God, and the **Eucharistic Liturgy**, which focuses on the central act of sacrifice in the Consecration and on the Eucharistic Banquet in Holy Communion. (Formerly, these divisions were called, respectively, the **Mass of the Catechumens** and the **Mass of the Faithful**.) In addition to these principal divisions, there are ancillary introductory and concluding rites.

The following description covers the Mass as celebrated with participation by the people. This Order of the Mass was approved by Pope Paul VI in the apostolic constitution *Missale Romanum* dated Apr. 3, 1969, and promulgated in a decree issued Apr. 6, 1969, by the Congregation for Divine Worship. The assigned effective date was Nov. 30, 1969.

Introductory Rites

Entrance: The introductory rites begin with the singing or recitation of an entrance song consisting of one or more scriptural verses stating the theme of the mystery, season or feast commemorated in the Mass.

Greeting: The priest and people make the Sign of the Cross together. The priest then greets them in one of several alternative ways and they reply in a corresponding manner.

Introductory Remarks: At this point, the priest or another of the ministers may introduce the theme of the Mass.

Penitential Rite: The priest and people together acknowledge their sins as a preliminary step toward worthy celebration of the sacred mysteries. This rite includes a brief examination of conscience, a general confession of sin and plea for divine mercy in one of several ways, and a prayer for forgiveness by the priest.

Glory to God: A doxology, a hymn of praise to God, sung or said on festive occasions.

Opening Prayer: A prayer of petition offered by the priest on behalf of the worshipping community.

I. Liturgy of the Word

Readings: The featured elements of this liturgy are several readings of passages from the Bible. If three readings are in order, the first is usually from the Old Testament, the second from the New Testament (Epistles, Acts, Revelation), and the third from one of the Gospels; the final reading is always a selection from a Gospel. The first reading(s) is concluded with the formula, "This is the Word of the Lord," to which the people respond, "Thanks be to God." The Gospel reading is concluded with the formula, "This is the Gospel of the Lord," to which the people respond, "Praise to you, Lord Jesus Christ," Between the readings, psalm verses and a Gospel acclamation are sung or said.

Homily: Sermon on a scriptural or liturgical subject; ideally, it should be related to the liturgical service in progress.

Creed: The Nicene profession of faith, by priest and people, on certain occasions.

Prayer of the Faithful: Litany-type prayers of petition, with participation by the people. Called general intercessions, they concern needs of the Church, the salvation of the world, public authorities, persons in need, the local community.

II. Eucharistic Liturgy

Offertory Song: Scriptural verses related to the theme of the Mass, or a suitable hymn, may be sung or said while things are prepared at the altar for the Eucharistic Liturgy and while the offerings of bread and wine are brought to the altar.

Offertory Procession: Presentation to the priest of the gifts of bread and wine, principally, by participating members of the congregation.

Offering of and Prayer over the Gifts: Consists of the prayers and ceremonies with which the priest offers bread and wine as the elements of the sacrifice to take place during the Eucharistic Prayer and of the Lord's Supper to be shared in Holy Communion.

Washing of Hands: After offering the bread and wine, the priest cleanses his fingers with water in a brief ceremony of purification.

Pray, Brethren: Prayer that the sacrifice to take place will be acceptable to God. The first part of the prayer is said by the priest; the second, by the people.

Prayer over the Gifts: A prayer of petition offered by the priest on behalf of the worshipping community.

Eucharistic Prayer

Preface: A hymn of praise, introducing the Eucharistic Prayer or Canon, sung or said by the priest following responses by the people. The Order of the Mass contains a variety of prefaces, for use on different occasions.

Holy, Holy, Holy; Blessed Is He: Divine praises sung or said by the priest and people.

Canon: The Eucharistic Prayer of the Mass whose central portion is the Consecration, when the essential act of sacrificial offering takes place with the changing of bread and wine into the Body and Blood of Christ. The prayers of the Canon, which are said by the celebrant only, commemorate principal mysteries of salvation history and include petitions for the Church, the living and dead, and remembrances of saints. There are four Eucharistic Prayers, for use on various occasions and at the option of the priest. (Additional Canons for Masses with children and for reconciliation were approved in 1975.)

Doxology: A formula of divine praise sung or said by the priest while he holds aloft the chalice containing the consecrated wine in one hand and the paten containing the consecrated host in the other.

Communion Rite

Lord's Prayer: Sung or said by the priest and people.

Prayer for Deliverance from evil: Called an **embolism** because it is a development of the final petition of the Lord's Prayer; said by the priest. It concludes with a memorial of the return of the Lord to which the people respond, "For the kingdom, the power, and the glory are yours, now and forever."

Prayer for Peace: Said by the priest, with corresponding responses by the people. The priest can, in accord with local custom, bid the people to exchange a greeting of peace with each other.

Lamb of God: A prayer for divine mercy sung or said while the priest breaks the consecrated host and places a piece of it into the consecrated wine in the chalice.

Communion: The priest, after saying a preparatory prayer, administers Holy Communion to himself and then to the people, thus completing the sacrifice-banquet of the Mass. (This completion is realized even if the celebrant alone receives the Eucharist.) On giving the Eucharist to the people, the priest says, "The Body of Christ," to each recipient; the customary response is "Amen." If the Eucharist is administered under the forms of bread and wine, the priest says, "The Body and Blood of Christ."

Communion Song: Scriptural verses or a suitable hymn sung or said during the distribution of Holy Communion. After Holy Communion is received, some moments may be spent in silent meditation or in the chanting of a psalm or hymn of praise.

Prayer after Communion: A prayer of petition offered by the priest on behalf of the worshipping community.

Concluding Rite

Announcements: Brief announcements to the people are in order at this time.

Dismissal: Consists of a final greeting by the priest, a blessing, and a formula of dismissal. This rite is omitted if another liturgical action immediately follows the Mass; e.g., a procession, the blessing of the body during a funeral rite.

Some parts of the Mass are changeable with the liturgical season or feast, and are called the **proper** of the Mass. Other parts are said to be **common** because they always remain the same.

Additional Mass Notes

Catholics are seriously obliged to attend Mass in a worthy manner on Sundays and holy days of obligation. Failure to do so without a proportionately serious reason is gravely wrong.

It is the custom for priests to celebrate Mass daily whenever possible. To satisfy the needs of the faithful on Sundays and holy days of obligation, they are authorized to say Mass twice (**bination**) or even three times (**trination**). Bination is also permissible on weekdays. On Christmas and All Souls' Day every priest may say three Masses. Mass may be celebrated at any time.

The **fruits of the Mass**, which in itself is of infinite value, are: **general**, for all the faithful; **special (ministerial)**, for the intentions or persons specifically intended by the celebrant; **most special (personal)**, for the celebrant himself. On Sundays and certain other days pastors are obliged to offer Mass for their parishioners. If a priest accepts a stipend or offering for a Mass, he is obliged in justice to apply the Mass for the designated intention. Mass may be applied for the living and the dead, or for any good intention.

Mass can be celebrated in several ways: e.g., with people present, without their presence (privately), with two or more priests as co-celebrants (concelebration), with greater or less solemnity.

Some of the various types of Masses are: **for the dead** (Funeral Mass or Mass of Christian Burial, Mass for the Dead — formerly called Requiem Mass); **nuptial**, for married couples, with or after the wedding ceremony; **votive**, to honor a Person of the Trinity, a saint, or for some special intention. A **red Mass** is a Votive Mass of the Holy Spirit, celebrated for members of the legal profession that they might exercise prudence and equity in their official capacities. **Gregorian Masses** are a series of 30 Masses celebrated on 30 consecutive days for a deceased person.

Mass is not celebrated on Good Friday. In its place, there is a Celebration of the Lord's Passion consisting of a Liturgy of the Word, Veneration of the Cross and Holy Communion.

Places, Altars for Mass

The ordinary place for celebrating the Eucharist is a church or other sacred place, at a fixed or movable altar.

The altar is a table at which the Eucharistic Sacrifice is celebrated.

A *fixed altar* is attached to the floor of the church. It should be of stone, preferably, and should be consecrated. The revised Code of Canon Law urges observance of the custom of placing in or under a fixed altar relics of martyrs or other saints.

A *movable altar* can be made of any solid and suitable material, and should be blessed or consecrated.

Outside of a sacred place, Mass may be celebrated in an appropriate place at a suitable table covered with a linen cloth and corporal. An **altar stone** containing the relics of saints, which was formerly prescribed, is not required by regulations in effect since the promulgation Apr. 6, 1969, of *Institutio Generalis Missalis Romani*.

LITURGICAL VESTMENTS

In the early years of the Church, vestments worn by the ministers at liturgical functions were the same as the garments in ordinary popular use. They became distinctive when their form was not altered to correspond with later variations in popular style. Liturgical vestments are symbolic of the sacred ministry and add appropriate decorum to divine worship.

Mass Vestments

Alb: A body-length tunic of white fabric; a vestment common to all ministers of divine worship.

Amice: A rectangular piece of white cloth worn about the neck, tucked into the collar and falling over the shoulders; prescribed for use when the alb does not completely cover the ordinary clothing at the neck.

Chasuble: Originally, a large mantle or cloak covering the body, it is the outer vestment of a priest celebrating Mass or carrying out other sacred actions connected with the Mass.

Cincture: A cord which serves the purpose of a belt, holding the alb close to the body.

Dalmatic: The outer vestment worn by a deacon in place of a chasuble.

Stole: A long, band-like vestment worn about the neck and falling to about the knees. (A stole is used for other functions also.)

The material, form and ornamentation of the aforementioned and other vestments are subject to variation and adaptation, according to norms and decisions of the Holy See and concerned conferences of bishops. The overriding norm is that they should be appropriate for use in divine worship. The customary ornamented vestments are the chasuble, dalmatic and stole.

The minimal vestments required for a priest celebrating Mass are the alb, stole and chasuble.

Chasuble-Alb: A vestment combining the features of the chasuble and alb; for use with a stole by concelebrants and, by way of exception, by celebrants in certain circumstances.

Liturgical Colors

The colors of outer vestments vary with liturgical seasons, feasts and other circumstances. The colors and their use are:

Green: For the season of the year; symbolic of hope and the vitality of the life of faith.

Purple: For Advent and Lent; may also be used in Masses for the dead; symbolic of penance.

Red: For the Sunday of the Passion, Good Friday, Pentecost; feasts of the Passion of Our Lord, the Apostles and Evangelists, martyrs; symbolic of the supreme sacrifice of life for the love of God.

Rose: May be used in place of purple on the Third Sunday of Advent (Gaudete Sunday) and the Fourth Sunday of Lent (Laetare Sunday); symbolic of anticipatory joy during a time of penance.

White: For the seasons of Christmas and Easter; feasts and commemorations of Our Lord, except those of the Passion; feasts and commemorations of the Blessed Virgin Mary, angels, saints who are not martyrs, All Saints (Nov. 1), St. John the Baptist (June 24), St. John the Evangelist (Dec. 27), the Chair of St. Peter (Feb. 22), the Conversion of St. Paul (Jan. 25). White, symbolic of purity and integrity of the life of faith, may generally be substituted for other colors, and can be used for funeral and other Masses for the dead.

Options are provided regarding the color of vestments used in offices and Masses for the dead. The newsletter of the U.S. Bishops' Committee on the Liturgy, in line with No. 308 of the "General Instruction of the Roman Missal," announced in July, 1970: "In the dioceses of the United States, white vestments may be used, in addition to violet (purple) and black, in offices and Masses for the dead."

On more solemn occasions, better than ordinary vestments may be used, even though their color (e.g., gold) does not match the requirements of the day.

Considerable freedom is permitted in the choice of colors of vestments worn for votive Masses.

Other Vestments

Cappa Magna: Flowing vestment with a train, worn by bishops and cardinals.

Cassock: A non-liturgical, full-length, close-fitting robe for use by priests and other clerics under liturgical vestments and in ordinary use; usually black for priests, purple for bishops and other prelates, red for cardinals, white for the pope. In place of a cassock, priests belonging to religious institutes wear the habit proper to their institute.

Cope: A mantle-like vestment open in front and fastened across the chest; worn by sacred ministers in processions and other ceremonies, as prescribed by appropriate directives.

Gremial: A rectangular veil of silk or linen placed over the knees of a bishop when he is seated during various episcopal ceremonies.

Habit: The ordinary (non-liturgical) garb of members of religious institutes, analogous to the cassock of diocesan priests; the form of habits varies from institute to institute.

Humeral Veil: A rectangular vestment worn about the shoulders by a deacon. or priest in Eucharistic processions and for other prescribed liturgical ceremonies.

Mitre: A headdress worn at some liturgical

functions by bishops, abbots and, in certain cases, other ecclesiastics.

Pallium: A circular band of white wool about two inches wide, with front and back pendants, marked with six crosses, worn about the neck. It is a symbol of the fullness of the episcopal office. Pope Paul VI, in a document issued July 20, 1978, on his own initiative and entitled *Inter Eximia Episcopalis,* restricted its use to the pope and archbishops of metropolitan sees. The pallium is made from the wool of lambs blessed by the pope on the feast of St. Agnes (Jan. 21).

Rochet: A knee-length, white linen-lace garment of prelates worn under outer vestments.

Surplice: A loose, flowing vestment of white fabric with wide sleeves. For some functions, it is interchangeable with an alb.

Zucchetto: A skullcap worn by bishops and other prelates.

SACRED VESSELS, LINENS

Vessels

Chalice and Paten: The principal sacred vessels required for the celebration of Mass are the chalice (cup) and paten (plate) in which wine and bread, respectively, are offered, consecrated and consumed. Both should be made of solid and noble material which is not easily breakable or corruptible. Gold coating is required of the interior parts of sacred vessels subject to rust. The cup of a chalice should be made of non-absorbent material.

Vessels for containing consecrated hosts (see below) can be made of material other than solid and noble metal — e.g., ivory, more durable woods — provided the substitute material is locally regarded as noble or rather precious and is suitable for sacred use.

Sacred vessels should be blessed or consecrated, according to prescribed requirements.

Vessels, in addition to the paten, for containing consecrated hosts are:

Ciborium: Used to hold hosts for distribution to the faithful and for reservation in the tabernacle.

Luna, Lunula, Lunette: A small receptacle which holds the sacred host in an upright position in the monstrance.

Monstrance, Ostensorium: A portable receptacle so made that the sacred host, when enclosed therein, may be clearly seen, as at Benediction or during extended exposition of the Blessed Sacrament.

Pyx: A watch-shaped vessel used in carrying the Eucharist to the sick.

Linens

Altar Cloth: A white cloth, usually of linen, covering the table of an altar. One cloth is sufficient. Three were used according to former requirements.

Burse: A square, stiff flat case, open at one end, in which the folded corporal can be placed; the outside is covered with material of the same kind and color as the outer vestments of the celebrant.

Corporal: A square piece of white linen spread on the altar cloth, on which rest the vessels holding the Sacred Species — the consecrated host(s) and wine — during the Eucharistic Liturgy. The corporal is similarly used whenever the Blessed Sacrament is removed from the tabernacle; e.g., during Benediction the vessel containing the Blessed Sacrament rests on a corporal.

Finger Towel: A white rectangular napkin used by the priest to dry his fingers after cleansing them following the offering of gifts at Mass.

Pall: A square piece of stiff material, usually covered with linen, which can be used to cover the chalice at Mass.

Purificator: A white rectangular napkin used for cleansing sacred vessels after the reception of Communion at Mass.

Veil: The chalice intended for use at Mass can be covered with a veil made of the same material as the outer vestments of the celebrant.

THE CHURCH BUILDING

A church is a building set aside and dedicated for purposes of divine worship, the place of assembly for a worshiping community.

A Catholic church is the ordinary place in which the faithful assemble for participation in the Eucharistic Liturgy and other forms of divine worship.

In the early years of Christianity, the first places of assembly for the Eucharistic Liturgy were private homes (Acts 2:46; Rom. 16:5; 1 Cor. 16:5; Col. 4:15) and, sometimes, catacombs. Church building began in the latter half of the second century during lulls in persecution and became widespread after enactment of the Edict of Milan in 313, when it finally became possible for the Church to emerge completely from the underground. The oldest and basic norms regarding church buildings date from about that time.

The essential principle underlying all norms for church building was reformulated by the Second Vatican Council, as follows: "When churches are to be built, let great care be taken that they be suitable for the celebration of liturgical services and for the active participation of the faithful" (*Constitution on the Sacred Liturgy,* No. 124).

This principle was subsequently elaborated in detail by the Congregation for Divine Worship in a document entitled *Institutio Generalis Missalis Romani,* which was approved by Paul VI Apr. 3 and promulgated by a decree of the congregation dated Apr. 6, 1969. Coverage of the following items reflects the norms stated in Chapter V of this document.

Main Features

Sanctuary: The part of the church where the altar of sacrifice is located, the place where the ministers of the liturgy lead the people in prayer, proclaim the word of God and celebrate the Eucharist. It is set off from the body of the church by a distinctive structural feature — e.g., elevation above the main floor — or by ornamentation. (The traditional **communion rail,** which has been removed in recent years in many churches, served this purpose of demarcation.) The customary location of the sanctuary is at the front of the church; it may, however, be centrally located.

Altar: The main altar of sacrifice and table of the Lord is the focal feature of the sanctuary and entire church. It stands by itself, so that the ministers can move about it freely, and is so situated that they face the people during the liturgical action. In addition to this main altar, there may also be others; in new churches, these are ideally situated in side chapels or alcoves removed to some degree from the body of the church.

Adornment of the Altar: The altar table is covered with a suitable linen cloth. Required candelabra and a cross are placed upon or near the altar in plain sight of the people and are so arranged that they do not obscure their view of the liturgical action.

Seats of the Ministers: The seat of the celebrant, corresponding with his role as the presiding minister of the assembly, is best located behind the altar and facing the people; it is raised a bit above the level of the altar but must not have the appearance of a throne. The seats of other ministers are also located in the sanctuary.

Ambo, Pulpit, Lectern: The stand at which scriptural lessons and psalm responses are read, the word of God preached, and the prayer of the faithful offered. It is so placed that the ministers can be easily seen and heard by the people.

Places for the People: Seats and kneeling benches (pews) and other accommodations for the people are so arranged that they can participate in the most appropriate way in the liturgical action and have freedom of movement for the reception of Holy Communion. Reserved seats are out of order.

Place for the Choir: Where it is located depends on the most suitable arrangement for maintaining the unity of the choir with the congregation and for providing its members maximum opportunity for carrying out their proper function and participating fully in the Mass.

Tabernacle: The best place for reserving the Blessed Sacrament is in a chapel suitable for the private devotion of the people. If this is not possible, reservation should be at a side altar or other appropriately adorned place. In either case, the Blessed Sacrament should be kept in a tabernacle, i.e., a safe-like, secure receptacle.

Statues: Images of the Lord, the Blessed Virgin Mary and the saints are legitimately proposed for the veneration of the faithful in churches. Their number and arrangement, however, should be or-

dered in such a way that they do not distract the people from the central celebration of the Eucharistic Liturgy. There should be only one statue of one and the same saint in a church.

General Adornment and Arrangement of Churches: Churches should be so adorned and fitted out that they serve the direct requirements of divine worship and the needs and reasonable convenience of the people.

Other Items

Ambry: A box containing the holy oils, attached to the wall of the sanctuary in some churches.

Baptistery: The place for administering baptism. Some churches have baptisteries adjoining or near the entrance, a position symbolizing the fact that persons are initiated in the Church and incorporated in Christ through this sacrament. Contemporary liturgical practice favors placement of the baptistery near the sanctuary and altar, or the use of a portable font in the same position, to emphasize the relationship of baptism to the Eucharist, the celebration in sacrifice and banquet of the death and resurrection of Christ.

Candles: Used more for symbolical than illuminative purposes, they represent Christ, the light and life of grace, at liturgical functions. They are made of beeswax. (See Index: Paschal Candle.)

Confessional: A booth-like structure for the hearing of confessions, with separate compartments for the priest and penitents and a grating or screen between them. The use of confessionals became general in the Roman Rite after the Council of Trent. Since the Second Vatican Council, there has been a trend in the U.S. to replace or supplement confessionals with small reconciliation rooms so arranged that priest and penitent can converse face-to-face.

Crucifix: A cross bearing the figure of the body of Christ, representative of the Sacrifice of the Cross.

Cruets: Vessels containing the wine and water used at Mass. They are placed on a credence table in the sanctuary.

Holy Water Fonts: Receptacles containing holy water, usually at church entrances, for the use of the faithful.

Sanctuary Lamp: A lamp which is kept burning continuously before a tabernacle in which the Blessed Sacrament is reserved, as a sign of the Real Presence of Christ.

LITURGICAL DEVELOPMENTS

The principal developments covered in this article are enactments of the Holy See and actions related to their implementation in the United States.

Modern Movement

Origins of the modern movement for renewal in the liturgy date back to the 19th century. The key contributing factor was a revival of liturgical and scriptural studies. Of special significance was the work of the Benedictine monks of Solesmes,

France, who aroused great interest in the liturgy through the restoration of Gregorian Chant. St. Pius X approved their work in a motu proprio of 1903 and gave additional encouragement to liturgical study and development.

St. Pius X did more than any other single pope to promote early first Communion and the practice of frequent Communion, started the research behind a revised breviary, and appointed a group to investigate possible revisions in the Mass.

The movement attracted some attention in the 1920's and 30's but made little progress.

Significant pioneering developments in the U.S. during the 20's, however, were the establishment of the Liturgical Press, the beginning of publication of *Orate Fratres* (now *Worship*), and the inauguration of the League of the Divine Office by the Benedictines at St. John's Abbey, Collegeville, Minn. Later events of influence were the establishment of the Pius X School of Liturgical Music at Manhattanville College of the Sacred Heart and the organization of a summer school of liturgical music at Mary Manse College by the Gregorian Institute of America. The turning point toward real renewal was reached during and after World War II.

Pius XII gave it impetus and direction, principally through the background teaching in his encyclicals on the *Mystical Body* (1943), *Sacred Liturgy* (1947), and the *Discipline of Sacred Music* (1955), and by means of specific measures affecting the liturgy itself. His work was continued during the pontificates of John XXIII and Paul VI. The Second Vatican Council, in virtue of its *Constitution on the Sacred Liturgy,* inaugurated changes of the greatest significance.

Before and After Vatican II

The most significant liturgical changes made in the years immediately preceding the Second Vatican Council were the following:

(1) Revision of the Rites of Holy Week, for universal observance from 1956.

(2) Modification of the Eucharistic fast and permission for afternoon and evening Mass, in effect from 1953 and extended in 1957.

(3) The Dialogue Mass, introduced in 1958.

(4) Use of popular languages in administration of the sacraments.

(5) Calendar missal breviary reform, in effect from Jan. 1, 1961.

(6) Seven-step administration of baptism for adults, approved in 1962.

The *Constitution on the Sacred Liturgy* approved (2,174 to 4) and promulgated by the Second Vatican Council Dec. 4, 1963, marked the beginning of a profound renewal in the Church's corporate worship. Implementation of some of its measures was ordered by Paul VI Jan. 25, 1964, in the motu proprio *Sacram Liturgiam.* On Feb. 29, a special commission, the Consilium for Implementing the Constitution on the Sacred Liturgy, was formed to supervise the execution of the entire program of liturgical reform. Implementation of the program on local and regional levels was left to bishops acting through their own liturgical commissions and in concert with their fellow bishops in national conferences.

Liturgical reform in the United States has been carried out under the direction of the Liturgy Committee, National Conference of Catholic Bishops. Its secretariat, established early in 1965, is located at 1312 Massachusetts Ave. N.W., Washington, D.C. 20005.

Liturgical development after the Second Vatican Council proceeded in several stages. It started with the formulation of guidelines and directives, and with the translation into vernacular languages of virtually unchanged Latin ritual texts. Then came structural changes in the Mass, the sacraments, the calendar, the Divine Office and other phases of the liturgy. These revisions were just about completed with the publication of a new order for the sacrament of penance in February, 1974. A continuing phase of development, in progress from the beginning, involves efforts to deepen the liturgical sense of the faithful, to increase their participation in worship and to relate it to full Christian life.

Texts and Translations

The master texts of all documents on liturgical reform were in Latin. Effective dates of their implementation depended on the completion and approval of appropriate translations into vernacular languages. English translations were made by the International Committee for English in the Liturgy.

The principal features of liturgical changes and the effective dates of their introduction in the United States are covered below under topical headings. (For expanded coverage of various items, especially the sacraments, see additional entries.)

The Mass

A new Order of the Mass, supplanting the one authorized by the Council of Trent in the 16th century, was introduced in the U.S. Mar. 22, 1970. It had been approved by Paul VI in the apostolic constitution *Missale Romanum,* dated Apr. 3, 1969.

Preliminary and related to it were the following developments.

Mass in English: Introduced Nov. 29, 1964. In the same year, Psalm 42 was eliminated from the prayers at the foot of the altar.

Incidental Changes: The last Gospel (prologue of John) and vernacular prayers following Mass were eliminated Mar. 7, 1965. At the same time, provision was made for the celebrant to say aloud some prayers formerly said silently.

Rubrics: An instruction entitled *Tres Abhinc Annos,* dated May 4 and effective June 29, 1967, simplified directives for the celebration of Mass, approved the practice of saying the canon aloud, altered the Communion and dismissal rites, permitted purple instead of black vestments in Masses for the dead, discontinued wearing of the maniple, and approved in principle the use of vernacular languages for the canon, ordination rites, and lessons of the Divine Office when read in choir.

Canons or Eucharistic Prayers: Three additional Eucharistic prayers authorized May 23, 1968, were approved for use in vernacular translation the following Aug. 15. They have the same basic structure as the traditional Roman Canon, whose use in English was introduced Oct. 22, 1967.

The customary Roman Canon, which dates at least from the beginning of the fifth century and has remained substantially unchanged since the seventh century, is the first in the order of listing of the Eucharistic prayers. It can be used at any time, but is the one of choice for most Sundays, some special feasts like Easter and Pentecost, and for feasts of the Apostles and other saints who are commemorated in the canon. Any preface can be used with it.

The second Eucharistic prayer, the shortest and simplest of all, is best suited for use on weekdays and various special circumstances. It has a preface of its own, but others may be used with it. This canon bears a close resemblance to the one framed by St. Hippolytus about 215.

The third Eucharistic prayer is suitable for use on Sundays and feasts as an alternative to the Roman Canon. It can be used with any preface and has a special formula for remembrance of the dead.

The fourth Eucharistic prayer, the most sophisticated of them all, presents a broad synthesis of salvation history. Based on the Eastern tradition of Antioch, it is best suited for use at Masses attended by persons versed in Sacred Scripture. It has an unchangeable preface.

Five additional Eucharistic prayers — three for Masses with children and two for Masses of reconciliation — were approved in 1974 and 1975, respectively, by the Congregation for the Sacraments and Divine Worship. The original approval for a limited period of experimentation was extended indefinitely, until further notice, according to a letter issued by the congregation Dec. 15, 1980.

Lectionary: A new compilation of scriptural readings and psalm responsories for Mass was published in 1969. The *Lectionary* contains a three-year cycle of readings for Sundays and solemn feasts, a two-year weekday cycle, and a one-year cycle for the feasts of saints, in addition to readings for a great variety of Masses, ritual Masses and Masses for various needs. There are also responsorial psalms to follow the first readings, and gospel or alleluia versicles to follow the second readings.

A second edition of the *Lectionary*, substantially the same as the first, was published in 1981. New features included an expanded introduction, extensive scriptural references and additional readings for a number of solemnities and feasts.

Sacramentary (Missal): The Vatican Polyglot Press began distribution in June, 1970, of the Latin text of a new *Roman Missal,* the first revision published in 400 years. The English translation was authorized for optional use beginning July 1, 1974; the mandatory date for use was Dec. 1, 1974.

The missal is the celebrant's book of prayers and sacramental formulas and does not include the readings of the Mass, such as the Gospel and the Epistle. It contains the texts of entrance songs, prefaces and other prayers of the Mass. The number of prefaces is four times greater than it had been. There are 10 commons (or sets of Mass prayers) of martyrs, two of doctors of the Church, and a dozen for saints or groups of saints of various kinds, such as religious, educators and mothers of families. There are Masses during which certain sacraments are administered and others for religious profession, the Church, the pope, priests,

Christian unity, the evangelization of nations, persecuted Christians, and other intentions.

Mass for Special Groups: Reasons and norms for the celebration of Mass at special gatherings of the faithful were the subject of an instruction issued May 15, 1969. Two years earlier, the U.S. Bishops' Liturgy Committee went on record in support of the celebration of Mass in private homes.

Sunday Mass on Saturday: The Congregation for the Clergy, under date of Jan. 10, 1970, granted the request that the faithful, where bishops consider it pastorally necessary or useful, may satisfy the precept of participating in Mass in the late afternoon or evening hours of Saturdays and the days before holy days of obligation.

This permission was subsequently renewed for five-year periods Dec. 14, 1974, and June 13, 1979.

Trination: The Congregation for the Sacraments, under date of Jan. 20, 1970, granted to all U.S. bishops the authority to permit priests to celebrate Mass three times on Saturdays and days preceding holy days of obligation, on condition that the first and second Masses are celebrated for weddings and/or funerals and the third Mass is celebrated in the evening so that the precept (of participating in Mass) will be satisfied by the faithful.

Mass in Latin: According to notices issued by the Congregation for Divine Worship June 1, 1971, and Oct. 28, 1974: (1) Bishops may permit the celebration of Mass in Latin for mixed-language groups. (2) Bishops may permit the celebration of one or two Masses in Latin on weekdays or Sundays in any church, irrespective of mixed-language groups involved (1971). (3) Priests may celebrate Mass in Latin when people are not present. (4) The approved revised Order of the Mass is to be used in Latin as well as vernacular languages . (5) By way of exception, bishops may permit older and handicapped priests to use the Council of Trent's Order of the Mass in private celebration of the holy Sacrifice.

Inter-Ritual Concelebration: The Apostolic Delegation in Washington, D.C., announced in June, 1971, that it had received authorization to permit priests of Roman and Eastern rites to celebrate Mass together in the rite of the host church. It was understood that the inter-ritual concelebrations would always be "a manifestation of the unity of the Church and of communion among particular churches."

Ordo of the Sung Mass: In a decree dated June 24 and made public Aug. 24, 1972, the Congregation for Divine Worship issued a new *Ordo of the Sung Mass* — containing Gregorian chants in Latin — to replace the *Graduale Romanum.*

Mass for Children: Late in 1973, the Congregation for Divine Worship issued special guidelines for children's Masses, providing accommodations to the mentality and spiritual growth of pre-adolescents while retaining the principal parts and structures of the Mass. The *Directory for Masses with Children* was approved by Paul VI Oct. 22 and was dated Nov. 1, 1973. Three Eucharistic prayers for Masses with children were approved by the congregation in 1974; English versions were approved June 5, 1975. Their use, authorized originally for a limited period of experimentation, was extended indefinitely Dec. 15, 1980.

Sacraments

The general use of English in administration of the sacraments was approved for the U.S. Sept. 14, 1964. Structural changes of the rites were subsequently made and introduced in the U.S. as follows.

Anointing of the Sick: Revised rites, covering also administration of the Eucharist to sick persons, were approved Nov. 30,. 1972, and published Jan. 18, 1973. The effective date for use of the provisional English prayer formula was Dec. 1, 1974.

Baptism: New rites for the baptism of infants, approved Mar. 19, 1969, were introduced June 1, 1970.

Christian Initiation of Adults: Revised rites were issued Jan. 6, 1972, for the Christian initiation of adults — affecting preparation for and reception of baptism, the Eucharist and confirmation; also, the reception of already baptized adults into the Church. These rites, which were introduced in the U.S. on the completion of English translation, nullified a seven-step baptismal process approved in 1962.

Confirmation: Revised rites, issued Aug. 15, 1971, became mandatory in the U.S. Jan. 1, 1973.

Eucharist: Several enactments concerning the Eucharist have been issued since 1966 when permission was given for the superiors of convents to administer Holy Communion in the absence of priests. Paul VI issued an instruction on *Worship of the Eucharistic Mystery* May 25, 1967, and another on the manner of administering Holy Communion May 20, 1969. Limited permission for lay persons to serve as special ministers of the Eucharist was given in 1971 and extended in 1972. Also in 1972, instructions were issued regarding administration of the Eucharist to other Christians, and in particular circumstances.

Holy Orders: Revised ordination rites for deacons, priests and bishops, validated by prior experimental use, were approved in 1970. The sacrament of holy orders underwent further revision in 1972 with the elimination of the Church-instituted orders of porter, reader, exorcist, acolyte and subdeacon, and of the tonsure ceremony symbolic of entrance into the clerical state. The former minor orders of reader and acolyte were changed from orders to ministries.

Matrimony: New rites, issued Mar. 19, 1969, were introduced June 1, 1970. Minor revisions had been made in 1964 in conjunction with a directive for imparting the nuptial blessing at all weddings.

Penance: Ritual revision of the sacraments was completed with the approval by Paul VI Dec. 2, 1973, of new directives for the sacrament of penance or reconciliation. The U.S. Bishops' Committee on the Liturgy set Feb. 27, 1977, as the mandatory date for use of the new rite. The committee also declared that it could be used from Mar. 7, 1976, after adequate preparation of priests and people. Earlier, authorization was given by the Holy See in 1968 for the omission of any reference to excommunication or other censures in the formula of absolution unless there was some indication that a censure had actually been incurred by a penitent.

Additional Developments

Calendar: A revised liturgical calendar, approved by Paul VI Feb. 14 and made public May 9, 1969, went into effect in the U.S. in 1972.

Funeral Rites: Revised rites oriented to the resurrection theme went into effect Nov. 1, 1971.

Holy Week: The English version of revised Holy Week rites went into effect in 1971. They introduced concelebration of Mass, placed new emphasis on commemorating the institution of the priesthood on Holy Thursday, and modified Good Friday prayers for other Christians, Jews and other non-Christians.

Liturgy of the Hours: The background, contents, scope and purposes of the revised Divine Office, called the Liturgy of the Hours, were described by Paul VI in the apostolic constitution *Laudis Canticum,* dated Nov. 1, 1970. A provisional English version, incorporating basic features of the master Latin text, was published in 1971. The four complete volumes of the Hours in English have been published since May, 1975. One-volume, partial editions, intended for use by religious and lay persons not bound to pray the Liturgy of the Hours, have also been published in approved form. Nov. 27, 1977, was set by the Congregation for Divine Worship and the National Conference of Catholic Bishops as the effective date for exclusive use in liturgical worship of the translation of the Latin text of the Office approved by the International Committee on English in the Liturgy.

Music: An *Instruction on Music in the Liturgy,* dated Mar. 5 and effective May 14, 1967, encouraged congregational singing during liturgical celebrations and attempted to clarify the role of choirs and trained singers. More significantly, the instruction indicated that a major development under way in the liturgy was a gradual erasure of the distinctive lines traditionally drawn between the sung liturgy and the spoken liturgy, between what had been called the high Mass and the low Mass.

In the same year, the U.S. Bishops' Liturgy Committee approved the use of contemporary music, as well as guitars and other suitable instruments, in the liturgy. The Holy See authorized in 1968 the use of musical instruments other than the organ in liturgical services, "provided they are played in a manner suitable to worship."

Oils: The Congregation for Divine Worship issued a directive in 1971 permitting the use of other oils — from plants, seeds or coconuts — instead of the traditional olive oil in administering some of the sacraments. The directive also provided that oils could be blessed at other times than at the usual Mass of Chrism on Holy Thursday, and authorized bishops' conferences to permit priests to bless oils in cases of necessity.

Environment and Art in Catholic Worship: A booklet with this title was issued by the U.S. Bishops' Committee on the Liturgy in March, 1978.

Eucharistic Ministers: Approval by the Congregation for Divine Worship was reported in August, 1978, of a provisional translation of a "Rite of Commissioning Special Ministers of Holy Communion." Note was made of the fact that such ministers should be called "special" instead of "extraordinary."

Doxology: The bishops' committee called attention in August, 1978, to the directive that the Doxology concluding the Eucharistic Prayer is said or sung by the celebrant (concelebrants) alone, to which the people respond, "Amen."

Churches, Altars, Chalices: The *Newsletter* of the U.S. Bishops' Committee on the Liturgy reported in November, 1978, that the Congregation for Divine Worship had given provisional approval of a new English translation for the rite of dedicating churches and altars, and of a new form for the blessing of chalices.

Study of the Mass: The Bishops' Committee on the Liturgy, following approval of the project by the National Conference of Catholic Bishops in May, 1979, began a study of the function and position of some elements of the Mass, including the Gloria, the sign of peace, the penitential rite and the readings. Completion of the first phase of the study was reported in July, 1980; its product was a 175-page study document. The second phase of the project got under way in the spring of 1981 with publication of a work book entitled *The Mystery of Faith: A Study of the Structural Elements of the Order of Mass.*

Eucharistic Hosts: Father Thomas Krosnicki, a staff member of the Bishops' Committee on the Liturgy, reported in July, 1979, that the committee was preparing new guidelines on the preparation of hosts, in compliance with a request from the Congregation for the Doctrine of the Faith. He said the congregation had "questioned the contents of some of the recipes" used in this country. Cardinal Franjo Seper, prefect of the congregation, stressed the importance of carefully observing traditional theological principles relating to the making of hosts — which should be of wheat, unleavened, with the appearance of food, and capable of being broken and distributed to communicants. In 1980, the congregation ruled definitely against changes in the preparation of hosts, and so informed the bishops' committee. The same prohibition was stated in the "Instruction on Certain Norms concerning Worship of the Eucharistic Mystery" approved by the Pope Apr. 17, and released May 23, 1980.

Eucharistic Worship: This was the subject of two documents issued in 1980. *Dominicae Coenae* was a letter addressed by Pope John Paul to bishops throughout the world in connection with the celebration of Holy Thursday; it was dated Feb. 24 and released Mar. 18. It was more doctrinal in content than the "Instruction on Certain Norms concerning Worship of the Eucharistic Mystery" (*Inaestimabile Donum,* "The Priceless Gift"), which was approved by the Pope Apr. 17 and published by the Congregation for the Sacraments and Divine Worship May 23. Its stated purpose was to reaffirm and clarify teaching on liturgical renewal contained in enactments of the Second Vatican Council and in several related implementing documents.

Marian Statues: A new rite (order) for the coronation of statues of the Blessed Virgin Mary was approved and published in 1981 by the Congregation for the Sacraments and Divine Worship.

Sunday Communion

More than two-thirds of the U.S. bishops voted (187 to 82) during the general meeting of their national conference in November, 1978, or afterwards for allowing the reception of Holy Communion under the forms of bread and wine on Sundays and holy days — subject to the options of bishops of dioceses, priests celebrating Mass and persons receiving the Eucharist. (Reception of Communion in this manner on certain occasions was already provided for in directives of the Congregation for Divine Worship, but Sundays and holy days were not mentioned.)

In 1980 or earlier, the Congregation for the Sacraments and Divine Worship said unofficially that the National Conference of Catholic Bishops acted improperly in 1978 when it authorized U.S. bishops to allow distribution of Holy Communion under the forms of bread and wine at certain parish Masses on Sundays and holy days. The conference had authority to do by law, said Father Ronald Krisman, associate director of the Bishops' Committee on the Liturgy, in July, 1983.

Report on Liturgical Books, Rites

The Bishops' Committee on the Liturgy published in August, 1981, a compendium of information on the status of liturgical books and rites revised since 1965.

The *BCL Report: Ritual Revisions — A Status Report,* covered *The Roman Ritual, The Roman Pontifical, The Roman Missal* and *The Liturgy of the Hours.* The contents also included a chronological review of the revisions of rites initiated by the Second Vatican Council, from decrees of promulgation through publication in Latin, translations into English and adaptations authorized for use in the U.S.

Dancing and Worship

Dancing and worship was the subject of an essay which appeared in a 1975 edition of Notitiae (11, pp. 202-205), the official journal of the Congregation for the Sacraments and Divine Worship. The article was called a "qualified and authoritative sketch," and should be considered "an authoritative point of reference for every discussion of the matter."

The principal points of the essay were:

● "The dance has never been made an integral part of the official worship of the Latin Church."

● "If the proposal of the religious dance in the West is really to be made welcome, care will have to be taken that in its regard a place be found outside of the liturgy, in assembly areas which are not strictly liturgical. Moreover, the priests must always be excluded from the dance."

CANON LAW AND LITURGICAL LAW

Canon 2 states that, for the most part, the revised Code of Canon Law, effective Nov. 27, 1983, does not regulate liturgical rites and ceremonies, and that existing liturgical norms retain the force of law unless they are contrary to legislation in the code.

The *Newsletter* of the Bishops' Committee on the Liturgy (May, 1983) observed in comment:

"The norms in the (approved) liturgical books and in the decrees of the Roman Pontiff, the Roman Congregations and, in matters where they have a right to legislate, the National Conference of Catholic Bishops, are truly liturgical law and not just suggestions. This should be kept in mind, especially since the new Code contains only a minimum of liturgical law. Highlights from that law contained in the code follow."

Right to Correct Celebration

"All the Christian faithful (the laity, religious and those ordained) have a right to the spiritual goods of the Church, especially the Word of God and the sacraments. They also have a right to divine worship according to the prescriptions of the proper rite, which is approved by the legitimate pastors of the Church. (They have a right not only to the liturgy but to correctly celebrated liturgy.) (Canons 213 and 214)

"Liturgical actions are not private actions but are celebrations of the Church itself. . . . Individual members of the faithful are related to the liturgical actions in different ways, depending on the variety of orders, duties and actual participation. (Canon 837)

"The regulation of the liturgy depends solely on the authority of the Church, and this rests with the Holy See and, according to the norms of law, with the conference of bishops or the individual diocesan bishop. (Canon 838)

"Under certain limited circumstances non-Catholic Christians may receive the sacraments of penance, Holy Eucharist and the anointing of the sick. (Canon 844)"

No Additions, Deletions, Changes

"In celebrating the sacraments the liturgical books approved by the competent authority must be faithfully followed. No one may add, delete or change anything on one's own initiative. (Canon 846)

"Lay men can assume the instituted ministry of lector and acolyte. By temporary deputation all the laity can perform in liturgical ceremonies the duties of lector, commentator, cantor, and other ministries permitted by the law. And where proper ministers are lacking and necessity urges it, the laity (even if they are not lectors or acolytes) may fulfill other offices, namely, exercising the ministry of the word, presiding over liturgical prayer, conferring baptism and distributing Holy Communion, according to the prescripts of the law. (Canon 230)"

The June/July, 1983, edition of the *Newsletter* cited the following canons of the revised code.

"If, in certain circumstances, necessity requires it or usefulness urges it, lay persons may be permitted to preach in churches or oratories, following the norms laid down by the episcopal conference. However, they may not preach a *homily*. The homily is reserved to the priest and deacon. It is to be preached at all Masses with a congregation on Sundays and holy days of obligation, and it cannot be omitted except for grave reason. A homily is recommended as well for other celebrations with a congregation, especially at weekday celebrations in Advent and Lent. (Canons 766 and 767)

"The ordinary minister of baptism is the bishop, priest and deacon. However, a catechist or another lay person may licitly administer baptism if the ordinary minister is absent or impeded. (Canon 861)

"The baptism of adults, at least of those who have reached the age of fourteen, is to be deferred to the diocesan bishop so that, if he judges it to be advantageous, he may administer the sacrament. (Canon 863)"

Baptism and Confirmation Sponsors

"The godparent for one who is to be baptized or confirmed should:

"1. be designated by the one being baptized or by his/her parents or the person standing in for the parents or, if these are lacking, by the pastor or minister of the sacrament; such a godparent should have the aptitude and intention of carrying on this function;

"2. be at least sixteen years old, unless another age shall have been established by the diocesan bishop or, by reason of a just cause, an exception appears to the pastor or minister to be allowed;

"3. be a fully initiated Catholic (baptism, confirmation, Eucharist) who leads a life of faith consistent with the function being assumed; (Note: a "Christian witness," that is, a baptized non-Catholic in good standing, is still permitted at baptism as long as he or she witnesses the baptism along with a godparent who fulfills the requirements noted above.)

"4. be under no canonical penalty, either legitimately imposed or declared;

"5. not be the father or mother of the one to be baptized. (Canon 874)"

"Deacons and lay persons are not to say the prayers, especially the Eucharistic Prayer, or perform actions which are proper to the priest who is presiding at the Eucharist. (Canon 907)

"Catholic priests are prohibited from concelebrating the Eucharist with ministers of other churches or ecclesial communities who do not have full communion with the Catholic Church. (Canon 908)

"The ordinary minister of Holy Communion is the bishop, priest and deacon. The special (*extraordinarius*) minister of holy communion is the instituted acolyte and also any other member of the faithful who has been properly designated according to Canon 230. (Canon 910)"

NORMS ON GENERAL ABSOLUTION

A document entitled "Pastoral Norms concerning the Administration of General Sacramental Absolution" was approved by Paul VI June 16, 1972, and published the following July 13 by the Congregation for the Doctrine of the Faith.

Following are excerpts from a commentary on the norms issued by the Doctrinal Congregation Feb. 8, 1977.

1) The pastoral norms for general absolution were developed to assist pastors in confronting those existing situations in the life of the Church which are attended by extraordinary circumstances. They are not intended to provide a basis for convoking large gatherings of faithful for the purpose of imparting general absolution, in the absence of such extraordinary circumstances.

Conditions: 2) For the licit use of general absolution all the conditions specified in Norm III of the above-mentioned pastoral norms must be simultaneously verified. This means that the large number of penitents for whom there are insufficient confessors would be deprived of the sacramental grace of Holy Communion for a long time and without any fault of their own. In ordinary circumstances, the faithful would be able to provide for their proper reception of the sacrament of penance in the normal way if not during, then before or after, the large gatherings mentioned.

3) The examples explicitly mentioned in Norm III as inappropriate situations for the use of general absolution — the large crowds foreseen on the occasions of festivals and pilgrimages, when arrangements for confessions can prudently be provided for — would *a fortiori* implicitly exclude the convocation of a large crowd for the primary purpose of giving general absolution.

Confession Afterwards: 4) Norm VI explicitly requires the diligent reminder that the penitent's sincere intention to bring his serious sins to individual confession within a reasonable time is a condition necessary for validity.

(Norm VII in the 1972 document deals with confession after the reception of general absolution, stating: "Those who have serious sins forgiven by general absolution should make an auricular confession before receiving absolution in this collective form another time, unless a just cause prevents them. They are strictly obliged, unless prevented by moral impossibility, to go to confession within a year. They too are affected by the precept that obliges every Christian to confess privately to a priest once a year at least all his serious sins that he has not yet specifically confessed.")

5) Norm X clearly indicates that communal celebrations of the sacrament of penance must be distinct from the celebration of Mass.

Removal of Scandal: 6) Norm XI explicitly calls for the penitent to have a serious intention to remove scandal, where that may be present, before receiving general sacramental absolution. Moreover, the norm also clearly states that, before one receives Holy Communion in this case, such scandal must have been removed in accord with the personal judgment of one's individual confessor. This norm will certainly find some application in the case of divorced Catholics who have remarried outside the Church.

The granting of general sacramental absolution without observing the norms given above is to be considered a serious abuse. Let all pastors carefully prevent such abuses out of awareness of the moral duty enjoined upon them for the welfare of souls and for the protection of the dignity of the sacrament of penance.

COMMUNION IN HAND

(Source: *Notitiae,* the official bulletin of the Congregation for Divine Worship.)

The Holy See has approved in recent years the practice of in-hand reception of Holy Communion in regions and countries where it had the approval of the appropriate bishops' conferences. Areas with this practice and the dates of approval are as follows.

Europe

Belgium (May, 1969), France and Germany (June, 1969), The Netherlands (September, 1969), Luxembourg, Scandinavia and Monaco (October, 1969), Austria (February, 1970), Yugoslavia (January, 1971), Portugal (July, 1975), Spain (February, 1976), England and Wales (March, 1976), Ireland (September, 1976), Scotland (July, 1977), Gibraltar (August, 1977).

Africa

Chad (September, 1969), North Africa (October, 1969), South Africa (February, 1970), Djibouti (March, 1970), Upper Volta and Niger (February, 1971), Zimbabwe (October, 1971), Madagascar (May, 1972), Mozambique (October, 1972), Angola (September, 1973), Zambia (March, 1974), Mali (July, 1974), Zaire (July, 1979).

Asia and Oceania

Japan (June, 1970), Indonesia (March, 1971), Korea (January, 1974), New Zealand (April, 1974), Australia (September, 1975), Pacific Episcopal Conference area: New Caledonia, New Hebrides (now Vanuatu), Gilbert Islands (now Kiribati), Wallis and Futuna, Cook Islands and Fiji (December, 1975), Papua New Guinea (April, 1976), Pakistan (October, 1976), Malaysia-Singapore (October, 1977), Turkey (September, 1978).

Central and South America

Bolivia and Uruguay (October, 1969), Jamaica (March, 1970), Paraguay (September, 1971), Panama (May, 1973), Chile (June, 1973), Costa Rica (September, 1973), Peru and Brazil (March, 1975), Cuba (March, 1978).

North America

Canada (February, 1970), Mexico (September, 1976), United States (June, 1977).

Father John Catoir, director of The Christophers and co-host of "Christopher Closeup," was elected president of the association of Catholic Television and Radio Syndicators in July, 1983.

SACRAMENTS

The sacraments are actions of Christ and his Church (itself a kind of sacrament) which signify grace, cause it in the act of signifying it, and confer it upon persons properly disposed to receive it. They perpetuate the redemptive activity of Christ, making it present and effective. They infallibly communicate the fruit of that activity — namely grace — to responsive persons with faith. Sacramental actions consist of the union of sensible signs (matter of the sacraments) with the words of the minister (form of the sacraments).

Christ himself instituted the seven sacraments of the New Law by determining their essence and the efficacy of their signs to produce the grace they signify.

Christ is the principal priest or minister of every sacrament; human agents — an ordained priest, baptized persons contracting marriage with each other, any person conferring emergency baptism in a proper manner — are secondary ministers. Sacraments have efficacy from Christ, not from the personal dispositions of their human ministers.

Each sacrament confers sanctifying grace for the special purpose of the sacrament; this is, accordingly, called sacramental grace. It involves a right to actual graces corresponding to the purposes of the respective sacraments.

While sacraments infallibly produce the grace they signify, recipients benefit from them in proportion to their personal dispositions. One of these is the intention to receive sacraments as sacred signs of God's saving and grace-giving action. The state of grace is also necessary for fruitful reception of the Holy Eucharist, confirmation, matrimony, holy orders and anointing of the sick. Baptism is the sacrament in which grace is given in the first instance and original sin is remitted. Penance is the secondary sacrament of reconciliation, in which persons guilty of serious sin after baptism are reconciled with God and the Church, and in which persons already in the state of grace are strengthened in that state.

Role of Sacraments

The Second Vatican Council prefaced a description of the role of the sacraments with the following statement concerning participation by all the faithful in the priesthood of Christ and the exercise of that priesthood by receiving the sacraments (*Dogmatic Constitution on the Church*, Nos. 10 and 11).

"The baptized by regeneration and the anointing of the Holy Spirit are consecrated into a spiritual house and a holy priesthood. Thus through all those works befitting Christian men they can offer spiritual sacrifice and proclaim the power of him who has called them out of darkness into his marvelous light (cf. 1 Pt. 2:4-10)."

"Though they differ from one another in essence and not only in degree, the common priesthood of the faithful and the ministerial or hierarchical priesthood (of those ordained to holy orders) are nonetheless interrelated. Each of them in its own special way is a participation in the one priesthood of Christ. The ministerial priest, by the sacred power he enjoys, molds and rules the priestly people. Acting in the Person of Christ, he brings about the Eucharistic Sacrifice, and offers it to God in the name of all the people. For their part, the faithful join in the offering of the Eucharist by virtue of their royal priesthood. They likewise exercise that priesthood by receiving the sacraments, by prayer and thanksgiving, by the witness of a holy life, and by self-denial and active charity."

"It is through the sacraments and the exercise of the virtues that the sacred nature and organic structure of the priestly community is brought into operation."

Baptism: "Incorporated into the Church through baptism, the faithful are consecrated by the baptismal character to the exercise of the cult of the Christian religion. Reborn as sons of God, they must confess before men the faith which they have received from God through the Church."

Confirmation: "Bound more intimately to the Church by the sacrament of confirmation, they are endowed by the Holy Spirit with special strength. Hence they are more strictly obliged to spread and defend the faith both by word and by deed as true witnesses of Christ."

Eucharist: "Taking part in the Eucharistic Sacrifice, which is the fount and apex of the whole Christian life, they offer the divine Victim to God, and offer themselves along with It. Thus, both by the act of oblation and through holy Communion, all perform their proper part in this liturgical service, not, indeed, all in the same way but each in that way which is appropriate to himself. Strengthened anew at the holy table by the Body of Christ, they manifest in a practical way that unity of God's People which is suitably signified and won drously brought about by this most awesome sacrament."

Penance: "Those who approach the sacrament of penance obtain pardon from the mercy of God for offenses committed against him. They are at the same time reconciled with the Church, which they have wounded by their sins, and which by charity, example, and prayer seeks their conversion."

Anointing of the Sick: "By the sacred anointing of the sick and the prayer of her priests, the whole Church commends those who are ill to the suffering and glorified Lord, asking that he may lighten their suffering and save them (cf. Jas. 5:14-16). She exhorts them, moreover, to contribute to the welfare of the whole People of God by associating themselves freely with the passion and death of Christ (cf. Rom. 8:17; Col. 1:24; 2 Tm. 2:11-12; 1 Pt. 4:13)."

Holy Orders: "Those of the faithful who are consecrated by holy orders are appointed to feed the Church in Christ's name with the Word and the grace of God."

Matrimony: "Christian spouses, in virtue of the sacrament of matrimony, signify and partake of the mystery of that unity and fruitful love which

229

exists between Christ and his Church (cf. Eph. 5:32). The spouses thereby help each other to attain to holiness in their married life and by the rearing and education of their children. And so, in their state and way of life, they have their own special gift among the People of God (cf. 1 Cor. 7:7).

"For from the wedlock of Christians there comes the family, in which new citizens of human society are born. By the grace of the Holy Spirit received in baptism these are made children of God, thus perpetuating the People of God through the centuries. The family is, so to speak, the domestic Church. In it parents should, by their word and example, be the first preachers of the faith to their children. They should encourage them in the vocation which is proper to each of them, fostering with special care any religious vocation."

"Fortified by so many and such powerful means of salvation, all the faithful, whatever their condition or state, are called by the Lord, each in his own way, to that perfect holiness whereby the Father himself is perfect."

Baptism

Baptism is the sacrament of spiritual regeneration by which a person is incorporated in Christ and made a member of his Mystical Body, given grace, and cleansed of original sin. Actual sins and the punishment due for them are remitted also if the person baptized was guilty of such sins (e.g., in the case of a person baptized after reaching the age of reason). The theological virtues of faith, hope and charity are given with grace. The sacrament confers a character on the soul and can be received only once.

The matter is the pouring of water. The form is: "I baptize you in the name of the Father and of the Son and of the Holy Spirit."

The minister of solemn baptism is a priest or deacon, but in case of emergency anyone, including a non-Catholic, can validly baptize. The minister pours water on the forehead of the person being baptized and says the words of the form while the water is flowing. The water used in solemn baptism is blessed during the rite.

Baptism is conferred in the Roman Rite by immersion or infusion (pouring of water), depending on the directive of the appropriate conference of bishops, according to the revised Code of Canon Law. The Church recognizes as valid baptisms properly performed by non-Catholic ministers. The baptism of infants has always been considered valid and the general practice of infant baptism was well established by the fifth century. Baptism is conferred conditionally when there is doubt about the validity of a previous baptism or the dispositions of the person.

Baptism is necessary for salvation. If a person cannot receive the baptism of water described above, this can be supplied by baptism of blood (martyrdom suffered for the Catholic faith or some Christian virtue) or by baptism of desire (perfect contrition joined with at least the implicit intention of doing whatever God wills that men should do for salvation).

A sponsor is required for the person being baptized. (See Godparents, below).

A person must be validly baptized before he can receive any of the other sacraments.

Christian Initiation of Infants: Infants should be solemnly baptized as soon after birth as conveniently possible. In danger of death, anyone may baptize an infant. If the child survives, the ceremonies of solemn baptism should be supplied.

The sacrament is ordinarily conferred by a priest or deacon of the parents' parish.

Catholics 16 years of age and over who have received the sacraments of confirmation and the Eucharist and are practicing their faith are eligible to be sponsors or godparents. Only one is required. Two, one of each sex, are permitted. A non-Catholic Christian cannot be a godparent for a Catholic child, but may serve as a witness to the baptism. A Catholic may not be a godparent for a child baptized in a non-Catholic religion, but may be a witness.

The role of godparents in baptismal ceremonies is secondary to the role of the parents. They serve as representatives of the community of faith and with the parents request baptism for the child and perform other ritual functions. Their function after baptism is to serve as proxies for the parents if the parents should be unable or fail to provide for the religious training of the child.

At baptism every child should be given a name with Christian significance, usually the name of a saint, to symbolize newness of life in Christ.

Christian Initiation of Adults: According to the *Ordo Initiationis Christianae Adultorum* ("Rite of the Christian Initiation of Adults") issued by the Congregation for Divine Worship under date of Jan. 6, 1972, adults are prepared for baptism and reception into the Church in several stages:

• An initial period of inquiry, instruction and evangelization.

• The catechumenate, a period of formal instruction and progressive formation in and familiarity with Christian life. It starts with a statement of purpose and includes a rite in which the catechumen is signed with the cross, blessings, exorcisms, and introduction into church for celebration of the word of God.

• Immediate preparation, called a period of purification and enlightenment, from the beginning of Lent to reception of the sacraments of initiation — baptism, confirmation, Holy Eucharist — at Easter. The period is marked by scrutinies, formal giving of the creed and the Lord's Prayer, the choice of a Christian name, and a final statement of intention.

• A final phase whose objective is greater familiarity with Christian life in the Church through observances of the Easter season and association with the community of the faithful.

The priest who baptizes a catechumen can also administer the sacrament of confirmation.

A sponsor is required for the person being baptized.

The *Ordo* also provides a simple rite of initiation for adults in danger of death and for cases in which all stages of the initiation process are not necessary, and guidelines for: (1) the preparation of adults for the sacraments of confirmation and Holy Eucharist in cases where they have been baptized but have not received further formation in the Christian life; (2) for the formation and initiation of children of catechetical age.

The Church recognizes the right of anyone over the age of seven to request baptism and to receive the sacrament after completing a course of instruction and giving evidence of good will. Practically, in the case of minors in a non-Catholic family or environment, the Church accepts them when other circumstances favor their ability to practice the faith — e.g., well-disposed family situation, the presence of another or several Catholics in the family. Those who are not in such favorable circumstances are prudently advised to defer reception of the sacrament until they attain the maturity necessary for independent practice of the faith.

Reception of Baptized Christians: Procedure for the reception of already baptized Christians into full communion with the Catholic Church is distinguished from the catechumenate, since they have received some Christian formation. Instruction and formation are provided as necessary, however; and conditional baptism is administered if there is reasonable doubt about the validity of the person's previous baptism.

In the rite of reception, the person is invited to join the community of the Church in professing the Nicene Creed and is asked to state: "I believe and profess all that the holy Catholic Church believes, teaches, and proclaims as revealed by God." The priest places his hand on the head of the person, states the formula of admission to full communion, confirms (in the absence of a bishop), gives a sign of peace, and administers Holy Communion during a Eucharistic Liturgy.

Confirmation

Confirmation is the sacrament by which a baptized person, through anointing with chrism and the imposition of hands, is endowed with the gifts and special strength of the Holy Spirit for mature Christian living. The sacrament, which completes the Christian initiation begun with baptism, confers a character on the soul and can be received only once.

According to the apostolic constitution *Divinae Consortium Naturae* dated Aug. 15, 1971, in conjunction with the *Ordo Confirmationis* ("Rite of Confirmation"): "The sacrament of confirmation is conferred through the anointing with chrism on the forehead, which is done by the imposition of the hand (matter of the sacrament), and through the words: 'N . . . . , receive the seal of the Holy Spirit, the Gift of the Father' " (form of the sacrament). On May 5, 1975, bishops' conferences in English-speaking countries were informed by the Congregation for Divine Worship that Pope Paul had approved this English version of the form of the sacrament: "Be sealed with the gift of the Holy Spirit."

The ordinary minister of confirmation in the Roman Rite is a bishop. Priests may be delegated for the purpose. A pastor can confirm a parishioner in danger of death, and a priest can confirm in ceremonies of Christian initiation and at the reception of a baptized Christian into union with the Church.

Ideally, the sacrament is conferred during the Eucharistic Liturgy. Elements of the rite include renewal of the promises of baptism, which confirmation ratifies and completes, and the laying on of hands — by symbolic elevation over the heads of those being confirmed — by the confirming bishop and priests participating in the ceremony.

"The entire rite," according to the *Ordo;* "has a twofold meaning. The laying of hands upon the candidates, done by the bishop and the concelebrating priests, expresses the biblical gesture by which the gift of the Holy Spirit is invoked. . . . The anointing with chrism and the accompanying words clearly signify the effect of the Holy Spirit. Signed with the perfumed oil by the bishop's hand, the baptized person receives the indelible character, the seal of the Lord, together with the Spirit who is given and who conforms the person more perfectly to Christ and gives him the grace of spreading the Lord's presence among men."

A sponsor is required for the person being confirmed. Eligible is any Catholic 16 years of age or older who has received the sacraments of confirmation and the Eucharist and is practicing the faith. The baptismal sponsor, preferably, can also be the sponsor for confirmation.

In the Roman Rite, it has been customary for children to receive confirmation within a reasonable time after first Communion and confession. There is a developing trend, however, to defer confirmation until later when its significance for mature Christian living becomes more evident. In the Eastern Rites, confirmation is administered at the same time as baptism.

Eucharist

The Holy Eucharist is a sacrifice (see The Mass) and the sacrament in which Christ is present and is received under the appearances of bread and wine.

The matter is bread of wheat, unleavened in the Roman Rite and leavened in the Eastern Rites, and wine of grape. The form consists of the words of consecration said by the priest at Mass: "This is my body. . . . This is the cup of my blood" (according to the traditional usage of the Roman Rite).

Only a priest can consecrate bread and wine so they become the body and blood of Christ. After consecration, however, the Eucharist can be administered by deacons and, for various reasons, by religious and lay persons.

Priests celebrating Mass receive the Eucharist under the appearances of bread and wine. In the Roman Rite, others receive under the appearances of bread only, i.e., the consecrated host, or in some circumstances they may receive under the appearances of both bread and wine. In Eastern-Rite practice, the faithful generally receive a piece of consecrated leavened bread which has been dipped into consecrated wine (i.e., by intinction).

Conditions for receiving the Eucharist, commonly called Holy Communion, are the state of grace, the right intention and observance of the Eucharistic fast.

The faithful of Roman Rite are required by a precept of the Church to receive the Eucharist at least once a year, during the Easter time (in the U.S., from the First Sunday of Lent to Trinity Sunday, inclusive).

(See Eucharistic Fast, Mass, Transubstantiation, Viaticum.)

First Communion and Confession: Children are to be prepared for and given opportunity for receiving both sacraments (Eucharist and reconciliation, or penance) on reaching the age of discretion, at which time they become subject to general norms concerning confession and Communion. This, together with a stated preference for first confession before first Communion, was the central theme of a document entitled *Sanctus Pontifex* and published May 24, 1973, by the Congregation for the Discipline of the Sacraments and the Congregation for the Clergy, with the approval of Pope Paul VI.

What the document prescribed was the observance of practices ordered by St. Pius X in the decree *Quam Singulari* of Aug. 8, 1910. Its purpose was to counteract pastoral and catechetical experiments virtually denying children the opportunity of receiving both sacraments at the same time. Termination of such experiments was ordered by the end of the 1972-73 school year.

At the time the document was issued, two- or three-year experiments of this kind — routinely deferring reception of the sacrament of penance until after the first reception of Holy Communion — were in effect in more than half of the dioceses of the U.S. They have remained in effect in many places, despite the advisory from the Vatican.

One reason stated in support of such experiments is the view that children are not capable of serious sin at the age of seven or eight, when Communion is generally received for the first time, and therefore prior reception of the sacrament of penance is not necessary. Another reason is the purpose of making the distinctive nature of the two sacraments clearer to children.

The Vatican view reflected convictions that the principle and practice of devotional reception of penance are as valid for children as they are for adults, and that sound catechetical programs can avoid misconceptions about the two sacraments.

A second letter on the same subject and in the same vein was released May 19, 1977, by the aforementioned congregations. It was issued in response to the question:

" 'Whether it is allowed after the declaration of May 24, 1973, to continue to have, as a general rule, the reception of first Communion precede the reception of the sacrament of penance in those parishes in which this practice developed in the past few years.'

"The Sacred Congregations for the Sacraments and Divine Worship and for the Clergy, with the approval of the Supreme Pontiff, reply: Negative, and according to the mind of the declaration.

"The mind of the declaration is that one year after the promulgation of the same declaration, all experiments of receiving first Communion without the sacrament of penance should cease so that the discipline of the Church might be restored, in the spirit of the decree, *Quam Singulari.*"

The two letters from the Vatican congregations have not produced uniformity of practice in this country. Simultaneous preparation for both sacraments is provided in some dioceses where a child has the option of receiving either sacrament first, with the counsel of parents, priests and teachers. Programs in other dioceses are geared first to reception of Communion and later to reception of the sacrament of reconciliation.

Commentators on the letters note that: they are disciplinary rather than doctrinal in content; they are subject to pastoral interpretation by bishops; they cannot be interpreted to mean that a person who is not guilty of serious sin must be required to receive the sacrament of penance before (even first) Communion.

Holy Communion under the Forms of Bread and Wine (by separate taking of the consecrated bread and wine or by intinction, the reception of the host dipped in the wine): Such reception is permitted under conditions stated in instructions issued by the Congregation for Divine Worship (May 25, 1967; June 29, 1970), the *General Instruction on the Roman Missal* (No. 242), and directives of bishops' conferences and individual bishops.

Accordingly, Communion can be administered in this way to: persons being baptized, received into communion with the Church, confirmed, receiving anointing of the sick; couples at their wedding or jubilee; religious at profession or renewal of profession; lay persons receiving an ecclesiastical assignment (e.g., lay missionaries); participants at concelebrated Masses, retreats, pastoral commission meetings, daily Masses and on other occasions.

Holy Communion Twice a Day: The reception of Holy Communion at Mass a second time on the same day is permitted in accord with provisions of the "Instruction on Facilitating Communion in Particular Circumstances" (*Immensae Caritatis*) approved by Pope Paul VI Jan. 20 and published by the Congregation for Divine Worship Mar. 29, 1973.

The occasions are: Sunday Mass on Saturday evening or a holy day Mass the previous evening; a second Mass on Christmas or Easter, following reception at midnight Mass or the Mass of the Easter Vigil; the evening Mass of Holy Thursday, following reception at the earlier Mass of Chrism; Masses in which baptism, confirmation, holy orders, matrimony, anointing of the sick, first Communion, Viaticum are administered; some Masses for the dead (e.g., of Christian burial, first anniversary); special occasions — consecration of a church or altar, religious profession, conferring an ecclesiastical assignment (e.g., to lay missionaries), feast of Corpus Christi, parochial visitation, canonical visitation or special meetings of religious, Eucharistic and other congresses, pilgrimages, preaching missions; other occasions designated by the local bishop.

Holy Communion and Eucharistic Devotion

outside of Mass: These were the subjects of an instruction *(De Sacra Communione et de Cultu Mysterii Eucharistici extra Missam)* dated June 21 and made public Oct. 18, 1973, by the Congregation for Divine Worship.

Holy Communion can be given outside of Mass to persons unable for a reasonable cause to receive it during Mass on a given day. The ceremonial rite is modeled on the structure of the Mass, consisting of a penitential act, a scriptural reading, the Lord's Prayer, a sign or gesture of peace, giving of the Eucharist, prayer and final blessing. Viaticum and Communion to the sick can be given by extraordinary ministers (authorized lay persons) with appropriate rites.

Forms of devotion outside of Mass are exposition of the Blessed Sacrament (by men or women religious, especially, or lay persons in the absence of a priest; but only a priest can give the blessing), processions and congresses with appropriate rites.

Intercommunion: Church policy on intercommunion was stated in an "Instruction on the Admission of Other Christians to the Eucharist," dated June 1 and made public July 8, 1972, against the background of the *Decree on Ecumenism* approved by the Second Vatican Council, and the *Directory on Ecumenism* issued by the Secretariat for Promoting Christian Unity in 1967.

Basic principles related to intercommunion are:

• "There is an indissoluble link between the mystery of the Church and the mystery of the Eucharist, or between ecclesial and Eucharistic communion; the celebration of the Eucharist of itself signifies the fullness of profession of faith and ecclesial communion" (1972 Instruction).

• "Eucharistic communion practiced by those who are not in full ecclesial communion with each other cannot be the expression of that full unity which the Eucharist of its nature signifies and which in this case does not exist; for this reason such communion cannot be regarded as a means to be used to lead to full ecclesial communion" (1972 Instruction).

• The question of reciprocity "arises only with those churches which have preserved the substance of the Eucharist, the sacrament of orders and apostolic succession" (1967 Directory).

• "A Catholic cannot ask for the Eucharist except from a minister who has been validly ordained" (1967 Directory).

The policy distinguishes between separated Eastern Christians and other Christians.

With Separated Eastern Christians (e.g., Orthodox): These may be given the Eucharist (as well as penance and anointing of the sick) at their request. Catholics may receive these same sacraments from priests of separated Eastern churches if they experience genuine spiritual necessity, seek spiritual benefit, and access to a Catholic priest is morally or physically impossible. This policy (of reciprocity) derives from the facts that the separated Eastern churches have apostolic succession through their bishops, valid priests, and sacramental beliefs and practices in accord with those of the Catholic Church .

With Other Christians (e.g., members of Reformation-related churches, others): Admission to the Eucharist in the Catholic Church, according to the *Directory on Ecumenism,* "is confined to particular cases of those Christians who have a faith in the sacrament in conformity with that of the Church, who experience a serious spiritual need for the Eucharistic sustenance, who for a prolonged period are unable to have recourse to a minister of their own community and who ask for the sacrament of their own accord; all this provided that they have proper dispositions and lead lives worthy of a Christian." The spiritual need is defined as "a need for an increase in spiritual life and a need for a deeper involvement in the mystery of the Church and of its unity."

Circumstances under which Communion may be given to other properly disposed Christians are danger of death, imprisonment, persecution, grave spiritual necessity coupled with no chance of recourse to a minister of their own community. Judgment regarding these and other special circumstances rests with the local bishop.

Catholics cannot ask for the Eucharist from ministers of other Christian churches who have not been validly ordained to the priesthood.

Penance

Penance is the sacrament by which sins committed after baptism are forgiven and a person is reconciled with God and the Church.

A revised ritual for the sacrament — *Ordo Paenitentiae,* published by the Congregation of Divine Worship Feb. 7, 1974, and made mandatory in the U.S. from the first Sunday of Lent, 1977 — reiterates standard doctrine concerning the sacrament; emphasizes the social (communal and ecclesial) aspects of sin and conversion, with due regard for personal aspects and individual reception of the sacrament; prescribes three forms for celebration of the sacrament; and presents models for community penitential services.

The basic elements of the sacrament are sorrow for sin because of a supernatural motive, confession (of previously unconfessed mortal or grave sins, required; of venial sins also, but not of necessity), and reparation (by means of prayer or other act enjoined by the confessor), all of which comprise the matter of the sacrament; and absolution, which is the form of the sacrament.

The traditional words of absolution — "I absolve you from your sins in the name of the Father, and of the Son, and of the Holy Spirit" — remain unchanged at the conclusion of a petition in the new rite that God may grant pardon and peace through the ministry of the Church.

The minister of the sacrament is an authorized priest — i.e., one who, besides having the power of orders to forgive sins, also has faculties of jurisdiction granted by an ecclesiastical superior and/or by canon law.

The sacrament can be celebrated in three ways.

• For individuals: The traditional manner remains acceptable but is enriched with additional elements including: reception of the penitent and making of the Sign of the Cross; an exhortation by the confessor to trust in God; a possible reading from Scripture; confession of sins; manifestation of repentance; petition for God's forgiveness through the ministry of the Church and the absolution of the priest; praise of God's mercy, and dismissal in peace. Some of these elements are optional.

• For several penitents, in the course of a community celebration including a liturgy of the Word of God and prayers, individual confession and absolution, and an act of thanksgiving.

• For several penitents, in the course of a community celebration, with general confession and general absolution. This method is reserved for extraordinary circumstances in which it is morally or physically impossible — for an extended period of time and through no fault of their own — for persons to confess and be absolved individually, and in view of their need for reconciliation and reception of the Eucharist. Penitents are required to confess at their next individual confession any grave sins absolved in such a general celebration of the sacrament. Judgment regarding circumstances that warrant general confession and absolution belongs principally to the bishop of the place. (See: Norms on General Absolution.)

Communal celebrations of the sacrament are not held in connection with Mass.

The place of individual confession, as determined by episcopal conferences in accordance with given norms, can be the traditional confessional or another appropriate setting.

The sacrament is necessary, by the institution of Christ, for the reconciliation of persons guilty of grave sins committed after baptism.

A precept of the Church obliges the faithful guilty of grave sin to confess at least once a year.

The Church favors more frequent reception of the sacrament not only for the reconciliation of persons guilty of serious sins but also for reasons of devotion. Devotional confession — in which venial sins or previously forgiven sins are confessed — serves the purpose of confirming persons in penance and conversion.

Penitential Celebrations: Communal penitential celebrations are designed to emphasize the social dimensions of Christian life — the community aspects and significance of penance and reconciliation.

Elements of such celebrations are community prayer, hymns and songs, scriptural and other readings, examination of conscience, general confession and expression of sorrow for sin, acts of penance and reconciliation, and a form of non-sacramental absolution resembling the one in the penitential rite of the Mass.

If the sacrament is celebrated during the service, there must be individual confession and absolution of sin.

(See Absolution, Confession, Confessional, Confessor, Contrition, Faculties, Forgiveness of Sin, Power of the Keys, Seal of Confession, Sin.)

Anointing of the Sick

This sacrament, promulgated by St. James the Apostle (Jas. 5:13-15), is administered to persons who are dangerously ill. By the anointing with blessed oil and the prayer of a priest, the sacrament confers on the person comforting grace; the remission of venial sins and inculpably unconfessed mortal sins, together with at least some of the temporal punishment due for sins; and, sometimes, results in an improved state of health.

The matter of this sacrament is the anointing with blessed oil (of the sick — olive oil, or vegetable oil if necessary) of the forehead and hands; in cases of necessity, a single anointing of another portion of the body suffices. The form is: "Through this holy anointing and his most loving mercy, may the Lord assist you by the grace of the Holy Spirit so that, when you have been freed from your sins, he may save you and in his goodness raise you up."

Anointing of the sick, formerly called extreme unction, may be received more than once, e.g., in new or continuing stages of serious illness. Ideally, the sacrament should be administered while the recipient is conscious and in conjunction with the sacraments of penance and the Eucharist. It may be administered conditionally even after apparent death.

The sacrament can be administered during a communal celebration in some circumstances, as in a home for the aged.

Pope Paul VI authorized a revision of the rite for administration of the sacrament in the apostolic constitution *Sacram Unctionem Infirmorum* ("Sacred Anointing of the Sick") which was approved Nov. 30, 1972, and made public Jan. 18, 1973.

Matrimony

Coverage of the sacrament of matrimony is given in the articles, Marriage Doctrine, *Humanae Vitae*, Marriage Laws, Pastoral Ministry for Divorced and Remarried.

Holy Orders

Holy orders is the sacrament by which spiritual power and grace are given to enable an ordained minister to consecrate the Eucharist, forgive sins, perform other pastoral and ecclesiastical functions, and form the community of the People of God. Holy orders confers a character on the soul and can be received only once. The minister of the sacrament is a bishop.

Holy orders, like matrimony but in a different way, is a social sacrament. As the Second Vatican Council declared in the *Dogmatic Constitution on the Church:*

'For the nurturing and constant growth of the People of God, Christ the Lord instituted in his Church a variety of ministries, which work for the good of the whole body. For those ministers who are endowed with sacred power are servants of their brethren, so that all who are of the People of God, and therefore enjoy a true Christian dignity, can work toward a common goal freely and in an orderly way, and arrive at salvation' (No. 18).

Bishop: The fullness of the priesthood belongs to those who have received the order of bishop. Bishops, in hierarchical union with the pope and their fellow bishops, are the successors of the apostles as pastors of the Church: they have individual responsibility for the care of the local churches they serve and collegial responsibility for the care of the universal Church (see Collegiality). In the ordination or consecration of bishops, the essential form is the imposition of hands by the consecrator(s) and the assigned prayer in the preface of the rite of ordination.

"With their helpers, the priests and deacons, bishops have . . . taken up the service of the community presiding in place of God over the flock whose shepherds they are, as teachers of doctrine, priests of sacred worship, and officers of good order" (No. 20).

Priests: A priest is an ordained minister with the power to celebrate Mass, administer the sacraments, preach and teach the word of God, impart blessings, and perform additional pastoral functions, according to the mandate of his ecclesiastical superior.

Concerning priests, the Second Vatican Council stated in the *Dogmatic Constitution on the Church* (No. 28):

"The divinely established ecclesiastical ministry is exercised on different levels by those who from antiquity have been called bishops, priests, and deacons. Although priests do not possess the highest degree of the priesthood, and although they are dependent on the bishops in the exercise of their power, they are nevertheless united with the bishops in sacerdotal dignity. By the power of the sacrament of orders, and in the image of Christ the eternal High Priest (Hb. 5:1-10; 7:24; 9:11-28), they are consecrated to preach the Gospel, shepherd the faithful, and celebrate divine worship as true priests of the New Testament. . . .

"Priests, prudent cooperators with the episcopal order as well as its aides and instruments, are called to serve the People of God. They constitute one priesthood with their bishop, although that priesthood is comprised of different functions."

In the ordination of a priest of Roman Rite, the essential matter is the imposition of hands on the heads of those being ordained by the ordaining bishop. The essential form is the accompanying prayer in the preface of the ordination ceremony. Other elements in the rite are the presentation of the implements of sacrifice — the chalice containing wine and the paten containing a host — with accompanying prayers.

Deacon: There are two kinds of deacons: those who receive the order and remain in it permanently, and those who receive the order while advancing to ordination to the priesthood. The following quotation — from Vatican II's *Dogmatic Constitution on the Church* (No. 29) — describes the nature and role of the diaconate, with emphasis on the permanent diaconate.

"At a lower level of the hierarchy are deacons, upon whom hands are imposed 'not unto the priesthood, but unto a ministry of service.' For strengthened by sacramental grace, in communion with the bishop and his group of priests, they serve the People of God in the ministry of the liturgy, of the word, and of charity. It is the duty of the deacon, to the extent that he has been authorized by competent authority, to administer baptism solemnly, to be custodian and dispenser of the Eucharist, to assist at and bless marriages in the name of the Church, to bring Viaticum to the dying, to read the sacred Scripture to the faithful, to instruct and exhort the people, to preside at the worship and prayer of the faithful, to administer sacramentals, and to officiate at funeral and burial services. (Deacons are) dedicated to duties of charity and administration."

"The diaconate can in the future be restored as a proper and permanent rank of the hierarchy. It pertains to the competent territorial bodies of bishops, of one kind or another, to decide, with the approval of the Supreme Pontiff, whether and where it is opportune for such deacons to be appointed for the care of souls. With the consent of the Roman Pontiff, this diaconate will be able to be conferred upon men of more mature age, even upon those living in the married state. It may also be conferred upon suitable young men. For them, however, the law of celibacy must remain intact" (No. 29).

The Apostles ordained the first seven deacons (Acts 6:1-6): Stephen, Philip, Prochorus, Nicanor, Timon, Parmenas, Nicholas.

Other Ministries: The Church later assigned ministerial duties to men in several other orders, as:

Subdeacon, with specific duties in liturgical worship, especially at Mass. The order, whose first extant mention dates from about the middle of the third century, was regarded as minor until the 13th century; afterwards, it was called a major order in the West but not in the East.

Acolyte, to serve in minor capacities in liturgical worship; a function now performed by Mass servers.

Exorcist, to perform services of exorcism for expelling evil spirits; a function which came to be reserved to specially delegated priests.

Lector, to read scriptural and other passages during liturgical worship; a function now generally performed by lay persons.

Porter, to guard the entrance to an assembly of Christians and to ward off undesirables who tried to gain admittance; an order of early origin and utility but of present insignificance.

Long after it became evident that these positions and functions had fallen into general disuse or did not require clerical ordination, the Holy See started a revision of the orders in 1971. By an indult of Oct. 5, the bishops of the United States were permitted to omit ordaining porters and exorcists. Another indult, dated three days later, permitted the use of revised rites for ordaining acolytes and lectors, and authorized the use of a service celebrating admission to the clerical state in place of the ceremony of tonsure which had previously served this purpose.

To complete the revision, Pope Paul VI abolished Sept. 14, 1972, the orders of porter, exorcist and subdeacon; decreed that laymen, as well as candidates for the diaconate and priesthood, can be installed (rather than ordained) in the ministries (rather than orders) of acolyte and lector; reconfirmed the suppression of tonsure and its replacement with a service of dedication to God and the Church; and stated that a man enters the clerical state on ordination to the diaconate.

PERMANENT DIACONATE

Authorization for restoration of the permanent diaconate in the Roman Rite — making it possible for men to become deacons permanently, without going on to the priesthood — was promulgated by Pope Paul VI June 18, 1967, in a document entitled *Sacrum Diaconatus Ordinem* ("Sacred Order of the Diaconate").

The Pope's action implemented the desire expressed by the Second Vatican Council for reestablishment of the diaconate as an independent order in its own right not only to supply ministers for carrying on the work of the Church but also to complete the hierarchical structure of the Church of Roman Rite.

Permanent deacons have been traditional in the Eastern Church. The Western Church, however, since the fourth or fifth century, generally followed the practice of conferring the diaconate only as a sacred order preliminary to the priesthood, and of restricting the ministry of deacons to liturgical functions.

The Pope's document, issued on his own initiative, provided:

• Qualified unmarried men 25 years of age or older may be ordained permanent deacons. They cannot marry after ordination.

• Qualified married men 35 years of age or older may be ordained permanent deacons. The consent of the wife of a prospective deacon is required. A married deacon cannot remarry after the death of his wife.

• Preparation for the diaconate includes a course of study and formation over a period of at least three years.

• Candidates who are not religious must be affiliated with a diocese. Reestablishment of the permanent diaconate among religious is reserved to the Holy See.

• Deacons will practice their ministry under the direction of a bishop and with the priests with whom they will be associated. (For functions, see the description of deacon, under Holy Orders.)

Restoration of the permanent diaconate in the United States was approved by the Holy See in October, 1968. Shortly afterwards the U.S. bishops established a committee of the same name, which is chaired by Bishop John J. Snyder of St. Augustine. The committee operates through a secretariat, of which Msgr. Ernest J. Fiedler is executive director. Its offices are located at 1312 Massachusetts Ave. N. W., Washington, D.C. 20005.

Present Status

The bishops' secretariat reported in October, 1982, that 5,886 permanent deacons had been ordained in the U.S.; that 142 dioceses either had approved programs of formation or were in the process of preparing formation programs; that a total of 2,349 candidates were in training.

Deacons have various functions, depending on the nature of their assignments. Liturgically, they can officiate at baptisms, weddings, wake services and funerals, can preach and distribute Holy Communion. Some are engaged in religious education work. All are intended to carry out works of charity and pastoral service of one kind or another.

The majority of permanent deacons, 94 per cent of whom are married, continue in their secular work. Their ministry of service is developing in three dimensions: of liturgy, of the word, and of charity. Depending on the individual deacon's abilities and preference, he is assigned by his bishop to either a parochial ministry or to one particular field of service. The latter is the most challenging ministry to develop. Deacons are now active in a variety of ministries including those to prison inmates and their families, the sick in hospitals, nursing homes and homes for the aged, alienated youth, the elderly and the poor, and in various areas of legal service to the indigent, of education and campus ministry. Thirty deacons have been assigned as administrators of parishes. The unlimited possibilities for diaconal ministry are under realistic assessment, diocese by diocese.

Training Programs

There were 138 training centers for deacons as of October, 1982. The first four were established in 1969. One center may serve two or more dioceses in the formation of diaconal candidates.

Continuing efforts are made to recruit Spanish-speaking, black and other minority candidates in training programs. Of the permanent deacons ordained up to October, 1982, four per cent were black, and 13 per cent were Hispanic.

Training programs of spiritual, doctrinal and pastoral formation are generally based on *Permanent Deacons in the United States: Guidelines on Their Formation and Ministry*, published by the Bishops' Committee on the Permanent Diaconate in September, 1971.

National Association of Permanent Diaconate Directors: Membership organization of directors, vicars and other staff personnel of permanent diaconate programs. Established in 1977 to promote effective communication and facilitate the exchange of information and resources of members; to develop professional expertise and promote research, training and self evaluation; to foster accountability and seek ways to promote means of implementing solutions to problems. NAPDD is governed by an executive board of elected officers. President for the 1983-84 term: Rev. Thomas Axe, 100 E. 8th St., Cincinnati, O. 45202.

"The Explosive Impact of Diaconal Ministry" was the theme of the meeting of the National Association of Permanent Diaconate Directors in May, 1983, in San Francisco. The Philbin Award was presented to Father Lawrence Gorman of Chicago.

At a meeting of deacons in Newark, N.J., in August, Auxiliary Bishop Joseph A. Francis said: "Ordained ministry benefits from the sensitivity a deacon can bring from his natural intimacy with the situation of the majority of the faithful.

MARRIAGE DOCTRINE

The following excerpts, stating key points of doctrine on marriage, are from the "Pastoral Constitution on the Church in the Modern World" (Nos. 48 to 51) promulgated by the Second Vatican Council.

Conjugal Covenant

The intimate partnership of married life and love has been established by the Creator and qualified by his laws. It is rooted in the conjugal covenant of irrevocable personal consent.

God himself is the author of matrimony, endowed as it is with various benefits and purposes. All of these have a very decisive bearing on the continuation of the human race, on the personal development and eternal destiny of the individual members of a family, and on the dignity, stability, peace, and prosperity of the family itself and of human society as a whole. By their very nature, the institution of matrimony itself and conjugal love are ordained for the procreation and education of children, and find in them their ultimate crown.

Thus a man and a woman . . . render mutual help and service to each other through an intimate union of their persons and of their actions. Through this union they experience the meaning of their oneness and attain to it with growing perfection day by day. As a mutual gift of two persons, this intimate union, as well as the good of the children, imposes total fidelity on the spouses and argues for an unbreakable oneness between them (No. 48).

Sacrament of Matrimony

Christ the Lord abundantly blessed this many-faceted love. . . . The Savior of men and the Spouse of the Church comes into the lives of married Christians through the sacrament of matrimony. He abides with them thereafter so that, just as he loved the Church and handed himself over on her behalf, the spouses may love each other with perpetual fidelity through mutual self-bestowal.

Graced with the dignity and office of fatherhood and motherhood, parents will energetically acquit themselves of a duty which devolves primarily on them; namely, education, and especially religious education.

The Christian family, which springs from marriage as a reflection of the loving covenant uniting Christ with the Church, and as a participation in that covenant, will manifest to all men the Savior's living presence in the world, and the genuine nature of the Church (No. 48).

Conjugal Love

The biblical Word of God several times urges the betrothed and the married to nourish and develop their wedlock by pure conjugal love and undivided affection.

This love is an eminently human one since it is directed from one person to another through an affection of the will. It involves the good of the whole person. Therefore it can enrich the expressions of body and mind with a unique dignity, ennobling these expressions as special ingredients and signs of the friendship distinctive of marriage. This love the Lord has judged worthy of special gifts, healing, perfecting, and exalting gifts of grace and of charity.

Such love, merging the human with the divine, leads the spouses to a free and mutual gift of themselves, a gift proving itself by gentle affection and by deed. Such love pervades the whole of their lives. Indeed, by its generous activity it grows better and grows greater. Therefore it far excels mere erotic inclination, which, selfishly pursued, soon enough fades wretchedly away.

This love is uniquely expressed and perfected through the marital act. The actions within marriage by which the couple are united intimately and chastely are noble and worthy ones. Expressed in a manner which is truly human, these actions signify and promote that mutual self-giving by which spouses enrich each other with a joyful and a thankful will.

Sealed by mutual faithfulness and hallowed above all by Christ's sacrament, this love remains steadfastly true in body and in mind, in bright days or dark. It will never be profaned by adultery or divorce. Firmly established by the Lord, the unity of marriage will radiate from the equal personal dignity of wife and husband, a dignity acknowledged by mutual and total love.

The steady fulfillment of the duties of this Christian vocation demands notable virtue. For this reason, strengthened by grace for holiness of life, the couple will painstakingly cultivate and pray for constancy of love, largeheartedness, and the spirit of sacrifice (No. 49).

Fruitfulness of Marriage

Marriage and conjugal love are by their nature ordained toward the begetting and educating of children. Children are really the supreme gift of marriage and contribute very substantially to the welfare of their parents. . . . God himself . . . wished to share with man a certain special participation in his own creative work. Thus he blessed male and female, saying: "Increase and multiply" (Gn. 1:28).

Hence, while not making the other purposes of matrimony of less account, the true practice of conjugal love, and the whole meaning of the family life which results from it, have this aim: that the couple be ready with stout hearts to cooperate with the love of the Creator and the Savior, who through them will enlarge and enrich his own family day by day.

Parents should regard as their proper mission the task of transmitting human life and educating those to whom it has been transmitted. They should realize that they are thereby cooperators with the love of God the Creator, and are, so to speak, the interpreters of that love. Thus they will fulfill their task with human and Christian responsibility (No. 50).

Norms of Judgment

They will thoughtfully take into account both their own welfare and that of their children, those already born and those who may be foreseen. For this accounting 'they will reckon with both the material and the spiritual conditions of the times as well as of their state in life. Finally, they will consult the interests of the family group, of temporal society, and of the Church herself.

The parents themselves should ultimately make this judgment in the sight of God. But in their manner of acting, spouses should be aware that they cannot proceed arbitrarily. They must always be governed according to a conscience dutifully conformed to the divine law itself, and should be submissive toward the Church's teaching office, which authentically interprets that law in the light of the Gospel. That divine law reveals and protects the integral meaning of conjugal love, and impels it toward a truly human fulfillment.

Marriage, to be sure, is not instituted solely for procreation. Rather, its very nature as an unbreakable compact between persons, and the welfare of the children, both demand that the mutual love of the spouses, too, be embodied in a rightly ordered manner, that it grow and ripen. Therefore, marriage persists as a whole manner and communion of life, and maintains its value and indissolubility, even when offspring are lacking — despite, rather often, the very intense desire of the couple (No. 50).

Love and Life

This Council realizes that certain modern conditions often keep couples from arranging their married lives harmoniously, and that they find themselves in circumstances where at least temporarily the size of their families should not be increased. As a result, the faithful exercise of love and the full intimacy of their lives are hard to maintain. But where the intimacy of married life is broken off, it is not rare for its faithfulness to be imperiled and its quality of fruitfulness ruined. For then the upbringing of the children and the courage to accept new ones are both endangered.

To these problems there are those who presume to offer dishonorable solutions. Indeed, they do not recoil from the taking of life. But the Church issues the reminder that a true contradiction cannot exist between the divine laws pertaining to the transmission of life and those pertaining to the fostering of authentic conjugal love.

For God, the Lord of Life, has conferred on men the surpassing ministry of safeguarding life — a ministry which must be fulfilled in a manner which is worthy of men. Therefore from the moment of its conception life must be guarded with the greatest care, while abortion and infanticide are unspeakable crimes. The sexual characteristics of man and the human faculty of reproduction wonderfully exceed the dispositions of lower forms of life. Hence the acts themselves which are proper to conjugal love and which are exercised in accord with genuine human dignity must be honored with great reverence (No. 51).

Church Teaching

Therefore when there is question of harmonizing conjugal love with the responsible transmission of life, the moral aspect of any procedure does not depend solely on the sincere intentions or on an evaluation of motives. It must be determined by objective standards. These, based on the nature of the human person and his acts, preserve the full sense of mutual self-giving and human procreation in the context of true love. Such a goal cannot be achieved unless the virtue of conjugal chastity is sincerely practiced. Relying on these principles, sons of the Church may not undertake methods of regulating procreation which are found blameworthy by the teaching authority of the Church in its unfolding of the divine law.

Everyone should be persuaded that human life and the task of transmitting it are not realities bound up with this world alone. Hence they cannot be measured or perceived only in terms of it, but always have a bearing on the eternal destiny of men (No. 51).

HUMANAE VITAE

Marriage doctrine and morality were the subjects of the encyclical "Humanae Vitae" ("Of Human Life") issued by Pope Paul, July 29, 1968. Following are a number of key excerpts from the document, which was framed in the pattern of traditional teaching and statements by the Second Vatican Council.

Each and every marriage act ("quilibet matrimonii usus") must remain open to the transmission of life (No. 11).

Indeed, by its intimate structure, the conjugal act, while most closely uniting husband and wife, capacitates them for the generation of new lives, according to laws inscribed in the very being of man and of woman. By safeguarding both these essential aspects, the unitive and the procreative, the conjugal act preserves in its fullness the sense of true mutual love and its ordination toward man's most high calling to parenthood (No. 12).

It is, in fact, justly observed that a conjugal act imposed upon one's partner without regard for his or her condition and lawful desires is not a true act of love, and therefore denies an exigency of right moral order in the relationships between husband and wife. Hence, one who reflects well must also recognize that a reciprocal act of love which jeopardizes the responsibility to transmit life — which God the Creator, according to particular laws, inserted therein — is in contradiction with the design constitutive of marriage and with the will of the Author of life. To use this divine gift, destroying, even if only partially, its meaning and its purpose, is to contradict the nature both of man and of woman and of their most intimate relationship, and therefore it is to contradict also the plan of God and his will (No. 13).

Forbidden Actions

The direct interruption of the generative process already begun, and, above all, directly willed and procured abortion, even if for therapeutic reasons, are to be absolutely excluded as licit means of regulating birth.

Equally to be excluded . . . is direct sterilization, whether perpetual or temporary, whether of the man or of the woman. Similarly excluded is every action which, either in anticipation of the conjugal act, or in its accomplishment, or in the development of its natural consequences, proposes, whether as an end or as a means, to render procreation impossible.

Inadmissible Principles

To justify conjugal acts made intentionally infecund, one cannot invoke as valid reasons the lesser evil, or the fact that such acts would constitute a whole together with the fecund acts already performed or to follow later and hence would share in one and the same moral goodness. In truth, if it is sometimes licit to tolerate a lesser evil in order to avoid a greater evil or to promote a greater good, it is not licit, even for the gravest reasons, to do evil so that good may follow therefrom; that is, to make into the object of a positive act of the will something which is intrinsically disorder, and hence unworthy of the human person, even when the intention is to safeguard or promote individual, family or social well-being.

Consequently, it is an error to think that a conjugal act which is deliberately made infecund, and so is intrinsically dishonest, could be made honest and right by the ensemble of a fecund conjugal life (No. 14).

Family Planning

If, then, there are serious motives to space out births, which derive from the physical or psychological conditions of husband and wife, or from external conditions, the Church teaches that it is then licit to take into account the natural rhythms immanent in the generative functions, for the use of marriage in the infecund periods only, and in this way to regulate birth without offending earlier stated principles (No. 16).

Authoritative Teaching

(Pope Paul called the foregoing teaching authoritative, although not infallible. He left it open for further study. As a practical norm to be followed, however, he said it involved the binding force of religious assent.)

We do not at all intend to hide the sometimes serious difficulties inherent in the life of Christian married persons; for them, as for everyone else, "the gate is narrow and the way is hard that leads to life." But the hope of that life must illuminate their way, as with courage they strive to live with wisdom, justice and piety in this present time, knowing that the figure of this world passes away.

Let married couples, then, face up to the efforts needed, supported by the faith and hope which "do not disappoint . . . because God's love has been poured into our hearts through the Holy Spirit, who has been given to us." Let them implore divine assistance by persevering prayer; above all, let them draw from the source of grace and charity in the Eucharist. And, if sin should still keep its hold over them, let them not be discouraged but rather have recourse with humble perseverance to the mercy of God, which is poured forth in the sacrament of penance (No. 25).

MARRIAGE LAWS

The Catholic Church claims jurisdiction over its members in matters pertaining to marriage, which is a sacrament. Church legislation on the subject is stated principally in 111 canons of the Revised Code of Canon Law, effective Nov. 27, 1983.

Marriage laws of the Church provide juridical norms in support of the marriage covenant. In 10 chapters, the revised Code covers: pastoral directives for preparing men and women for marriage; impediments in general and in particular; matrimonial consent; form for the celebration of marriage; mixed marriages; secret celebration of marriage; effects of marriage; separation of spouses, and convalidation of marriage.

Catholics are bound by all marriage laws of the Church. Non-Catholics, whether baptized or not, are not considered bound by these ecclesiastical laws except in cases of marriage with a Catholic. Certain natural laws, in the Catholic view, bind all men and women, irrespective of their religious beliefs; accordingly, marriage is prohibited before the time of puberty, without knowledge and free mutual consent, in the case of an already existing valid marriage bond, in the case of antecedent and perpetual impotence.

Formalities

These include, in addition to arrangements for the time and place of the marriage ceremony, doctrinal and moral instruction concerning marriage and the recording of data which verifies in documentary form the eligibility and freedom of the persons to marry. Records of this kind, which are confidential, are preserved in the archives of the church where the marriage takes place.

Premarital instructions are the subject matter of Pre-Cana Conferences.

Banns

The banns are public announcements made in their parish churches, usually on three successive Sundays, of the names of persons who intend to marry. Persons who know of reasons in church law why a proposed marriage should not take place, are obliged to make them known to the pastor.

Marital Consent

The exchange of consent to the marriage covenant, which is essential for valid marriage, must be rational, free, true and mutual.

Matrimonial consent can be invalidated by an essential defect, substantial error, the strong influence of force and fear, the presence of a condition or intention against the nature of marriage.

Form of Marriage

A Catholic is required, for validity and lawfulness, to contract marriage — with another

Catholic or with a non-Catholic — in the presence of a competent priest or deacon and two witnesses.

There are two exceptions to this law. A Roman Rite Catholic (since Mar. 25, 1967) or an Eastern Rite Catholic (since Nov. 21, 1964) can contract marriage validly in the presence of a priest of a separated Eastern Rite Church, provided other requirements of law are complied with. With permission of the competent Roman-Rite or Eastern-Rite bishop, this form of marriage is lawful, as well as valid. (See Eastern Rite Laws, below.)

With these two exceptions, and aside from cases covered by special permission, the Church does not regard as valid any marriages involving Catholics which take place before non-Catholic ministers of religion or civil officials.

An excommunication formerly in force against Catholics who celebrated marriage before a non-Catholic minister was abrogated in a decree issued by the Sacred Congregation for the Doctrine of the Faith on Mar. 18, 1966.

The ordinary place of marriage is the parish of the bride, of the Catholic party in case of a mixed marriage, or of an Eastern Rite groom.

Church law regarding the form of marriage does not affect non-Catholics in marriages among themselves. The Church recognizes as valid the marriages of non-Catholics before ministers of religion and civil officials, unless they are rendered null and void on other grounds.

Impediments

Impediments to marriage are factors which render a marriage unlawful or invalid.

Prohibitory Impediments, which make a marriage unlawful but do not affect validity:

• simple vows of virginity, perpetual chastity, celibacy, to enter a religious order or to receive sacred orders;

• difference of religion, which obtains when one party is a Catholic and the other is a baptized non-Catholic.

Diriment Impediments, which make a marriage invalid as well as unlawful:

• age, which obtains before completion of the 14th year for a woman and the 16th year for a man;

• impotency, if it is antecedent to the marriage and permanent (this differs from sterility, which is not an impediment);

• the bond of an existing valid marriage;

• disparity of worship, which obtains when one party is a Catholic and the other party is unbaptized;

• sacred orders;

• religious profession of the perpetual vow of chastity;

• abduction, which impedes the freedom of the person abducted;

• crime, variously involving elements of adultery, promise or attempt to marry, conspiracy to murder a husband or wife;

• blood relationship in the direct line (father-daughter, mother-son, etc.) and to the fourth degree inclusive of the collateral line (brother-sister, first, second and third cousins);

• affinity, or relationship resulting from a valid marriage, in any degree of the direct line;

• public honesty, arising from an invalid marriage or from public or notorious concubinage; it renders either party incapable of marrying blood relatives of the other in the first degree of the direct line.

• legal relationship arising from adoption; it renders either party incapable of marrying relatives of the other in the direct line or in the second degree of the collateral line.

Dispensations from Impediments: Persons hindered by impediments either may not or cannot marry unless they are dispensed therefrom in view of reasons recognized in canon law. Local bishops can dispense from the impediments most often encountered (e.g., difference of religion, disparity of worship) as well as others.

Decision regarding some dispensations is reserved to the Holy See.

Separation

A valid and consummated marriage of baptized persons cannot be dissolved by any human authority or any cause other than the death of one of the persons.

In other circumstances:

• 1. A valid but unconsummated marriage of baptized persons, or of a baptized and an unbaptized person, can be dissolved:

a. by the solemn religious profession of one of the persons, made with permission of the pope. In such a case, the bond is dissolved at the time of profession, and the other person is free to marry again;

b. by dispensation from the pope, requested for a grave reason by one or both of the persons. If the dispensation is granted, both persons are free to marry again.

Dispensations in these cases are granted for reasons connected with the spiritual welfare of the concerned persons.

• 2. A legitimate marriage, even consummated, of unbaptized persons can be dissolved in favor of one of them who subsequently receives the sacrament of baptism. This is the Pauline Privilege, so called because it was promulgated by St. Paul (1 Cor. 7:12-15) as a means of protecting the faith of converts. Requisites for granting the privilege are:

a. marriage prior to the baptism of either person;

b. reception of baptism by one person;

c. refusal of the unbaptized person to live in peace with the baptized person and without interfering with his or her freedom to practice the Christian faith. The privilege does not apply if the unbaptized person agrees to these conditions.

• 3. A legitimate and consummated marriage of a baptized and an unbaptized person can be dissolved by the pope in virtue of the Privilege of Faith, also called the Petrine Privilege.

Because of the unity and the indissolubility of marriage, the Church denies that civil divorce can break the bond of a valid marriage, whether the marriage involves two Catholics, a Catholic and a non-Catholic, or non-Catholics with each other.

In view of serious circumstances of marital distress, the Church permits an innocent and aggrieved party, whether wife or husband, to seek and obtain a civil divorce for the purpose of acquiring title and right to the civil effects of divorce, such as separate habitation and maintenance, and the custody of children. Permission for this kind of action should be obtained from proper church authority. The divorce, if obtained, does not break the bond of a valid marriage.

Under other circumstances — as would obtain if a marriage was invalid (see Decree of Nullity, below) — civil divorce is permitted for civil effects and as a civil ratification of the fact that the marriage bond really does not exist.

Decree of Nullity

This is a decision by a competent church authority — e.g., a bishop, a diocesan marriage tribunal, the Sacred Roman Rota — that an apparently valid marriage was actually invalid from the beginning because of the unknown or concealed existence, from the beginning, of a diriment impediment, an essential defect in consent, radical incapability for marriage, or a condition placed by one or both of the parties against the very nature of marriage.

Eastern Rite Laws

Marriage laws of the Eastern Church differ in several respects from the legislation of the Roman Rite. The regulations in effect since May 2, 1949, were contained in the motu proprio *Crebre Allatae* issued by Pius XII the previous February.

According to both the Roman Code of Canon Law and the Oriental Code, marriages between Roman Rite Catholics and Eastern Rite Catholics ordinarily take place in the rite of the groom and have canonical effects in that rite.

Regarding the form for the celebration of marriages between Eastern Catholics and baptized Eastern non-Catholics, the Second Vatican Council declared:

"By way of preventing invalid marriages between Eastern Catholics and baptized Eastern non-Catholics, and in the interests of the permanence and sanctity of marriage and of domestic harmony, this sacred Synod decrees that the canonical 'form' for the celebration of such marriages obliges only for lawfulness. For their validity, the presence of a sacred minister suffices, as long as the other requirements of law are honored" (*Decree on Eastern Catholic Churches,* No. 18).

Marriages taking place in this manner are lawful, as well as valid, with permission of a competent Eastern Rite bishop.

The Rota

The Sacred Roman Rota is the ordinary court of appeal for marriage, and some other cases, which are appealed to the Holy See from lower church courts. Appeals are made to the Rota if decisions by diocesan and archdiocesan courts fail to settle the matter in dispute.

MIXED MARRIAGES

"Mixed Marriages" (*Matrimonia Mixta*) was the subject of: (1) a letter issued under this title by Pope Paul VI Mar. 31, 1970, and (2) a statement, *Implementation of the Apostolic Letter on Mixed Marriages,* approved by the National Conference of Catholic Bishops Nov. 16, 1970.

One of the key points in the bishops' statement referred to the need for mutual pastoral care by ministers of different faiths for the sacredness of marriage and for appropriate preparation and continuing support of parties to a mixed marriage.

Pastoral experience, which the Catholic Church shares with other religious bodies, confirms the fact that marriages of persons of different beliefs involve special problems related to the continuing religious practice of the concerned persons and to the religious education and formation of their children.

Pastoral measures to minimize these problems include instruction of a non-Catholic party in essentials of the Catholic faith for purposes of understanding. Desirably, some instruction should also be given the Catholic party regarding his or her partner's beliefs.

Requirements

The Catholic party to a mixed marriage is required to declare his (her) intention of continuing practice of the Catholic faith and to promise to do all in his (her) power to share his (her) faith with children born of the marriage by having them baptized and raised as Catholics. No declarations or promises are required of the non-Catholic party, but he (she) must be informed of the declaration and promise made by the Catholic.

Notice of the Catholic's declaration and promise is an essential part of the application made to a bishop for dispensation from the impediment of mixed religion or disparity of worship.

A mixed marriage can take place with a Nuptial Mass. (The bishops' statement added this caution: "To the extent that Eucharistic sharing is not permitted by the general discipline of the Church, this is to be considered when plans are being made to have the mixed marriage at Mass or not.")

The ordinary minister at a mixed marriage is an authorized priest, and the ordinary place is the parish church of the Catholic party. A non-Catholic minister may not only attend the marriage ceremony but may also address, pray with and bless the couple.

For appropriate pastoral reasons, a bishop can grant a dispensation from the Catholic form of marriage and can permit the marriage to take place in a non-Catholic Church with a non-Catholic minister as the officiating minister. A priest may not only attend such a ceremony but may also address, pray with and bless the couple.

"It is not permitted," however, the bishops' statement declared, "to have two religious services or to have a single service in which both the Catholic marriage ritual and a non-Catholic marriage ritual are celebrated jointly or successively."

PASTORAL MINISTRY FOR DIVORCED AND REMARRIED

Ministry to divorced and remarried Catholics is a difficult field of pastoral endeavor, situated as it is in circumstances tantamount to the horns of a dilemma.

At Issue

On the one side is firm church teaching on the permanence of marriage and norms against reception of the Eucharist and full participation in the life of the Church by Catholics in irregular unions.

On the other side are men and women with broken unions followed by second and perhaps happier attempts at marriage which the Church does not recognize as valid and which may not be capable of being validated because of the existence of an earlier marriage bond.

The forces at work in these circumstances are those of the Church, upholding its doctrine and practice regarding the permanence of marriage, and those of many men and women in irregular second marriages who desire full participation in the life of the Church.

Sacramental participation is not possible for those whose first marriage was valid, although there is no bar to their attendance at Mass, to sharing in other activities of the Church, or to their efforts to have children baptized and raised in the Catholic faith.

An exception to this rule is the condition of a divorced and remarried couple living in a brother-sister relationship.

There is no ban against sacramental participation by separated or divorced persons who have not attempted a second marriage.

Unverified estimates of the number of U.S. Catholics who are divorced and remarried vary between three and five million.

Tribunal Action

What can the Church do for them and with them in pastoral ministry, is an old question charged with new urgency because of the rising number of divorced and remarried Catholics.

One way to help is through the agency of marriage tribunals charged with responsibility for investigating and settling questions concerning the validity or invalidity of a prior marriage. There are reasons in canon law justifying the Church in declaring a particular marriage null and void from the beginning, despite the short- or long-term existence of an apparently valid union.

Decrees of nullity are not new in the history of the Church. If such a decree is issued, a man or woman is free to validate a second marriage and live in complete union with the Church.

Canonist L. Mason Knox, writing in the Oct. 16, 1976, edition of *America*, reported that 442 formal decisions, of which 338 were declarations of nullity, were issued by U.S. tribunals in 1968. Following adoption of the American Procedural Norms in 1970, the number of formal decisions rose in 1974 to 9,293, of which about 80 to 90 per cent were declarations of nullity. Similar decisions were rendered the same year in other canonical processes on grounds of: defect of form (15,722), papal dispensation for non-consummation (120), Pauline Privilege (691), Privilege of Faith (1,761), summary procedure (1,331).

U.S. tribunals handed down approximately 43,000 decisions in 1978; more have been issued since that time.

The increase in the number of declarations of nullity is a result not just of new procedures but also, and more significantly, of tribunal judgments regarding the radical incapability of persons to contract valid marriage in the first place.

(The American Procedural Norms have been superseded by provisions of the revised Code of Canon Law, effective Nov. 27, 1983. One change requires automatic review of first decisions regarding the nullity of marriage.)

Reasons behind Decrees

Pastoral experience reveals that some married persons, a short or long time after contracting an apparently valid marriage, exhibit signs that point back to the existence, at the time of marriage, of latent and serious personal deficiencies which made them incapable of valid consent and sacramental commitment.

Such deficiencies might include gross immaturity and those affecting in a serious way the capacity to love, to have a true interpersonal and conjugal relationship, to fulfill marital obligations, to accept the faith aspect of marriage.

Psychological and behavioral factors like these have been given greater attention by tribunals in recent years and have provided grounds for numerous decrees of nullity.

Decisions of this type do not indicate any softening of the Church's attitude regarding the permanence of marriage. They affirm, rather, that some persons who have married were really not capable of doing so.

Serious deficiencies in the capacity for real interpersonal relationship in marriage were the reasons behind a landmark decree of nullity issued in 1973 by the Roman Rota, the Vatican high court of appeals in marriage cases.

Decree Not Always Possible

The tribunal way to a decree of nullity regarding a previous marriage is not open to many persons in second marriages — because grounds are either lacking or, if present, cannot be verified in tribunal process.

Many men and women in this second category are aligned and in sympathy with aims of the North American Conference of Separated and Divorced Catholics, which has several hundred support groups in various parts of the United States and Canada. Formed early in 1972, the conference seeks a special pastoral ministry for divorced Catholics in second irregular unions.

This purpose is shared by the Judeans (founded in 1952) and by official ministries in many U.S. dioceses, by other church agencies and by hosts of priests.

The principal problem involved in such ministry is the degree of sacramental participation open to persons in irregular unions.

Unacceptable Solution

One solution of the problem, called "good conscience procedure," involves administration of the sacraments of penance and the Eucharist to divorced and remarried Catholics unable to obtain a decree of nullity for a first marriage who are living in a subsequent marriage "in good faith."

This procedure, despite the fact that it has no standing or recognition in church law, is being advocated and practiced by some priests and remarried Catholics.

MARRIAGE ENCOUNTER

Marriage Encounter originated in Spain through the efforts of Father Gabriel Calvo who worked out its principal features between the early 1950s and 1962 with the collaboration of Diego and Fina Bartoneo and other parties interested in ministry to married couples. Along with Charismatic Renewal, it has been called one of the fastest growing contemporary movements in the Church, with an estimated participation of one and one-half to two million couples in more than 35 countries.

The first encounter was held with 28 couples in 1962 in Barcelona. Five years later the first encounter in the U.S. was conducted in conjunction with a convention of the Christian Family Movement at Notre Dame University. Marriage Encounter caught on from this beginning and went nationwide in 1969.

The Encounter

Marriage Encounter brings couples together for a weekend program of events directed by a team of several couples and a priest, for the purpose of developing their abilities to communicate with each other in their life together as husband and wife. This purpose is served by direction in techniques given by the team and by private dialogue of each couple. Subjects of the dialogue extend to the whole range of personal and marital concerns. The anticipated result is the enrichment and revitalization of all personal-marital relationships.

This communication and sharing by husband and wife, spurred by the encounter and open to development by subsequent daily dialogue between them, is the positive substance of the movement.

The composition of Marriage Encounter groups for the encounter varies; some of them are exclusively Catholic while others have participants of different religious, professional or other special-interest affiliations.

Commentators insist that Marriage Encounter is not for troubled marriages and is not an exercise in group dynamics. Neither is it a retreat, although it has potential for spiritual development.

National

National Marriage Encounter of the U.S. follows the program initiated by Father Calvo. Deeply rooted in Roman Catholic tradition, it is open to members of other faiths in accordance with teachings of the Second Vatican Council. Its stated purpose is continuing development and growth in marital and family relationships in the context of God's activity as perceived by married partners.

An executive team (Noel and Jo McCracken, 7241 N. Whippoorwill, Peoria, Ill. 61614, and Father Robert White, O.F.M., St. Bonaventure, N.Y. 14778), elected to a three-year term in August, 1981, serves approximately 150 groups in the U.S. The national office is maintained at the aforementioned address in Peoria.

The identifying logo or emblem of National Marriage Encounter consists of two wedding bands intertwined with the Greek letters Chi-Rho.

Worldwide

Worldwide Marriage Encounter is a weekend experience for married couples, priests and religious. Its stated purpose is to change the world. Catholic participants seek to accomplish this through renewal of the Church by renewal of the sacraments of matrimony and holy orders.

The movement was developed by Father Charles Gallagher and several couples after they experienced a weekend of events conducted under the leadership of Father Calvo at a conference of the Christian Family Movement at the University of Notre Dame in the late 1960s. Since then, the movement has struck roots in 57 countries. In addition to the Catholic expression of the movement, there are 13 other faith expressions of the weekend experience and follow-up programs.

The U.S. national executive team consists of Father Dick Reis of the Youngstown Diocese and Frank and Barbara Jelinek. The national office is located at 1025 W. 3rd Ave., Columbus, O. 43212. Communication is maintained by the national office with other faith expressions of the movement in the U.S. and other countries.

The identifying logo or emblem of Worldwide Marriage Encounter consists of wedding bands intertwined with a cross and surmounted by a red heart.

ENGAGED ENCOUNTER

Catholic Engaged Encounter is designed to prepare couples for marriage by focusing attention on its sacramental aspects and by increasing their potential for communication with each other. With appropriate modifications, it follows the pattern of the Marriage Encounter weekend and subsequent practice of dialogue.

Since 1975, Catholic Engaged Encounter has given new direction to marriage preparation programs in many dioceses of the United States. In 1977, it was incorporated as a national organization in the State of New Jersey.

The director of the movement is Father Robert Harrington, located at 1 Summer Ave., Newark, N.J. 07104. Serving with him on the national executive team are William and Shelly Meehan (elected to serve Aug. 1, 1982, to 1984), 20 Cranberry Lane, South Easton, Mass. 02375.

In 1983, almost 80 per cent of U.S. dioceses had special preparation-for-marriage programs.

THE CHURCH CALENDAR

The calendar of the Roman Church consists of an arrangement throughout the year of a series of liturgical seasons, commemorations of divine mysteries and commemorations of saints for purposes of worship.

The purposes of this calendar were outlined in the "Constitution on the Sacred Liturgy" (Nos. 102-105) promulgated by the Second Vatican Council.

Within the cycle of a year . . . (the Church) unfolds the whole mystery of Christ, not only from his incarnation and birth until his ascension, but also as reflected in the day of Pentecost, and the expectation of a blessed, hoped-for return of the Lord.

Recalling thus the mysteries of redemption, the Church opens to the faithful the riches of her Lord's powers and merits, so that these are in some way made present at all times, and the faithful are enabled to lay hold of them and become filled with saving grace (No. 102).

In celebrating this annual cycle of Christ's mysteries, holy Church honors with special love the Blessed Mary, Mother of God (No. 103).

The Church has also included in the annual cycle days devoted to the memory of the martyrs and the other saints. . . . (who) sing God's perfect praise in heaven and offer prayers for us. By celebrating the passage of these saints from earth to heaven the Church proclaims the paschl mystery as achieved in the saints who have suffered and been glorified with Christ; she proposes them to the faithful as examples who draw all to the Father through Christ, and through their merits she pleads for God's favors (No. 104).

In the various seasons of the year and according to her traditional discipline, the Church completes the formation of the faithful by means of pious practices for soul and body, by instruction, prayer, and works of penance and mercy (No. 105).

THE ROMAN CALENDAR

Norms for a revised calendar for the Western Church as decreed by the Second Vatican Council were approved by Paul VI in the motu proprio Mysterii Paschalis dated Feb. 14, 1969. The revised calendar was promulgated a month later by a decree of the Congregation for Divine Worship and went into effect Jan. 1, 1970, with provisional modifications. Full implementation of all its parts was delayed in 1970 and 1971, pending the completion of work on related liturgical texts. The U.S. bishops ordered the calendar into effect for 1972.

The Seasons

Advent: The liturgical year begins with the first Sunday of Advent, which introduces a season of four weeks or slightly less duration with the theme of expectation of the coming of Christ. During the first two weeks, the final coming of Christ as Lord and Judge at the end of the world is the focus of attention. From Dec. 17 to 24, the emphasis shifts to anticipation of the celebration of his Nativity on the Solemnity of Christmas.

Advent has four Sundays. Since the 10th century, the first Sunday has marked the beginning of the liturgical year in the Western Church. In the Middle Ages, a kind of pre-Christmas fast was in vogue during the season.

Christmas Season: The Christmas season begins with the vigil of Christmas and lasts until the Sunday after January 6, inclusive.

The period between the end of Christmastide and the beginning of Lent belongs to the Ordinary Time of the year. Of variable length, the pre-Lenten phase of this season includes what were formerly called the Sundays after Epiphany and the suppressed Sundays of Septuagesima, Sexagesima and Quinquagesima.

Lent: The penitential season of Lent begins on Ash Wednesday, which occurs between Feb. 4 and Mar. 11, depending on the date of Easter, and lasts until the Mass of the Lord's Supper (Holy Thursday). It has six Sundays. The sixth Sunday marks the beginning of Holy Week and is known as Passion (Palm) Sunday.

The origin of Lenten observances dates back to the fourth century or earlier.

Easter Triduum: The Easter Triduum begins with evening Mass of the Lord's Supper and ends with Evening Prayer on Easter Sunday.

Easter Season: The Easter season whose theme is resurrection from sin to the life of grace, lasts for 50 days, from Easter to Pentecost. Easter, the first Sunday following the vernal equinox, occurs between Mar. 22 and Apr. 25. The terminal phase of Eastertide, between the Solemnities of the Ascension of the Lord and Pentecost, stresses anticipation of the coming and action of the Holy Spirit.

Ordinary Time: The season of Ordinary Time begins on the Monday after the Sunday following January 6 and continues until the day before Ash Wednesday, inclusive. It begins again on the Monday after Pentecost and ends on the Saturday before the first Sunday of Advent. It consists of 33 or 34 weeks. The last Sunday is celebrated as the Solemnity of Christ the King. The overall purpose of the season is to elaborate the themes of salvation history.

The various liturgical seasons are characterized in part by the scriptural readings and Mass prayers assigned to each of them. During Advent, for example, the readings are messianic; during Eastertide, from the Acts of the Apostles, chronicling the Resurrection and the original proclamation of Christ by the Apostles, and from the Gospel of John; during Lent, baptismal and penitential passages. Mass prayers reflect the meaning and purpose of the various seasons.

Commemorations of Saints

The commemorations of saints are celebrated concurrently with the liturgical seasons and feasts of our Lord. Their purpose is to illustrate the paschal mysteries as reflected in the lives of saints, to honor them as heroes of holiness, and to appeal for their intercession.

In line with revised regulations, some former

feasts were either abolished or relegated to observance in particular places by local option for one of two reasons: (1) lack of sufficient historical evidence for observance of the feasts; (2) lack of universal significance.

The commemoration of a saint, as a general rule, is observed on the day of death (*dies natalis*, day of birth to glory with God in heaven). Exceptions to this rule include the feasts of St. John the Baptist, who is honored on the day of his birth; Sts. Basil the Great and Gregory Nazianzen, and the brother Saints, Cyril and Methodius, who are commemorated in joint feasts.

Application of this general rule in the revised calendar resulted in date changes of some observances.

Sundays and Feast Days

Sunday is the original Christian feast day because of the unusually significant events of salvation history which took place and are commemorated on the first day of the week — viz., the Resurrection of Christ, the key event of his life and the fundamental fact of Christianity; and the descent of the Holy Spirit upon the Apostles on Pentecost, the birthday of the Church. The transfer of observance of the Lord's Day from the Sabbath to Sunday was made in apostolic times. The Mass and Liturgy of the Hours (Divine Office) of each Sunday reflect the themes and set the tones of the various liturgical seasons.

Categories of observances according to dignity and manner of observance are: solemnity (highest, corresponding to former first-class feasts); feast (corresponding to former second-class feasts); memorial (corresponding to former third-class feasts); optional memorial (observable by choice). Observances of the first three categories are universal in the Roman Rite.

Fixed observances are those which are regularly celebrated on the same calendar day each year.

Movable observances are those which are not observed on the same calendar day each year. Examples of these are Easter (the first Sunday after the first full moon following the vernal equinox), Ascension (40 days after Easter), Pentecost (50 days after Easter), Trinity Sunday (first after Pentecost), Christ the King (last Sunday of the liturgical year).

Holy Days of Obligation

Holy days of obligation are special occasions on which Catholics who have reached the age of reason are seriously obliged, as on Sundays, to assist at Mass and to avoid unnecessary servile work. Serious reasons excuse from the observance of either or both of these obligations.

By enactment of the Third Plenary Council of Baltimore in 1884, and with the approval of the Holy See, the holy days of obligation observed in the United States are: Christmas, the Nativity of Jesus, Dec. 25; Solemnity of Mary the Mother of God, Jan. 1; Ascension of the Lord; Assumption of Blessed Mary the Virgin, Aug. 15; All Saints' Day, Nov. 1; Immaculate Conception of Blessed Mary the Virgin, Dec. 8.

In addition to these, there are four other holy days of obligation prescribed in the general law of the Church which are not so observed in the U.S.: Epiphany, Jan. 6; St. Joseph, Mar. 19; Corpus Christi; Sts. Peter and Paul, June 29. The solemnities of Epiphany and Corpus Christi are transferred to a Sunday in countries where they are not observed as holy days of obligation.

Weekdays, Days of Prayer

Weekdays are those on which no proper feast or vigil is celebrated in the Mass or Liturgy of the Hours (Divine Office). On such days, the Mass may be that of the preceding Sunday, which expresses the liturgical spirit of the season, an optional memorial, a votive Mass, or a Mass for the dead. Weekdays of Advent and Lent are in a special category of their own.

Days of Prayer: Dioceses, at times to be designated by local bishops, should observe "days or periods of prayer for the fruits of the earth, prayer for human rights and equality, prayer for world justice and peace, and penitential observance outside of Lent." So stated the *Instruction on Particular Calendars* (No. 331) issued by the Congregation for the Sacraments and Divine Worship June 24, 1970.

These days are contemporary equivalents of what were formerly called ember and rogation days.

Ember days originated at Rome about the fifth century, probably as Christian replacements for seasonal festivals of agrarian cults. They were observances of penance, thanksgiving, and petition for divine blessing on the various seasons; they also were occasions of special prayer for clergy to be ordained. These days were observed four times a year.

Rogation days originated in France about the fifth century. They were penitential in character and also occasions of prayer for a bountiful harvest and protection against evil.

Days of Abstinence and Fast

The apostolic constitution *Paenitemini*, in effect since Feb. 23, 1966, authorized the substitution of other works of penance for the customary and common observances of abstinence and fast on various days of the year.

In this country, in line with provisions of the constitution and a 1974 decision of the National Conference of Catholic Bishops, Ash Wednesday and Good Friday are days of fast and abstinence, and all Fridays of Lent are days of abstinence. Fasting is recommended on Holy Saturday until the Easter Vigil.

The obligation to abstain from meat binds Catholics 14 years of age and older. The obligation to fast, limiting oneself to one full meal and two lighter meals in the course of a day, binds Catholics from the ages of 21 to 59.

Almsgiving, the giving of goods or services to persons in need, can be a penitential act along with prayer, fasting and abstinence.

JANUARY 1984

1—Sun. Solemnity of Mary, Mother of God. (Nm. 6:22-27; Gal. 4:4-7; Lk. 2:16-21.)

2—Mon. Sts. Basil the Great and Gregory Nazianzen, bishops-doctors; memorial.

3—Tues. Weekday.

4—Wed. St. Elizabeth Ann Seton; memorial (in U.S.).

5—Thurs. St. John Neumann, bishop; memorial (in U.S.).

6—Fri. Weekday. Bl. Andre Bessette religious; optional memorial (in U.S.). Epiphany is celebrated on a Sunday between Jan. 2 and Jan. 8 in the U.S.

7—Sat. Weekday. St. Raymond of Peñafort, priest; optional memorial.

8—Sun. Epiphany of the Lord (in U.S.); solemnity. (Is. 60:1-6; Eph. 3:2-3a, 5-6; Mt. 2:1-12.)

9—Mon. Baptism of the Lord; feast.

10—Tues. Weekday. (First Week of the Year.)

11—Wed. Weekday.

12—Thurs. Weekday.

13—Fri. Weekday. St. Hilary, bishop-doctor; optional memorial.

14—Sat. Weekday.

15—Second Sunday of the Year (Is. 49:3, 5-6; 1 Cor. 1:1-3; Jn. 1:29-34.)

16—Mon. Weekday.

17—Tues. St. Anthony, abbot; memorial.

18—Wed. Weekday.

19—Thurs. Weekday.

20—Fri. Weekday. St. Fabian, pope-martyr, or St. Sebastian, martyr; optional memorials.

21—Sat. St. Agnes, virgin-martyr; memorial.

22—Third Sunday of the Year. (Is. 8:23b to 9:3; 1 Cor. 1:10-13, 17; Mt. 4:12-23.) [St. Vincent, deacon-martyr; optional memorial.]

23—Mon. Weekday.

24—Tues. St. Francis de Sales, bishop-doctor; memorial.

25—Wed. Conversion of St. Paul, apostle; feast.

26—Thurs. Sts. Timothy and Titus, bishops; memorial.

27—Fri. Weekday. St. Angela Merici, virgin; optional memorial.

28—Sat. St. Thomas Aquinas, priest-doctor; memorial.

29—Fourth Sunday of the Year. (Zep. 2:3, 3:12-13; 1 Cor. 1:26-31; Mt. 5:1-12a.)

30—Mon. Weekday.

31—Tues. St. John Bosco, priest; memorial.

GENERAL PRAYER INTENTION: Implementation of the Second Vatican Council's *Decree on Ecumenism.* Nearly 20 years have passed since the promulgation of *Unitatis Redintegratio.* Reflection on it and application of its norms are in order during the Week of Prayer for Christian Unity, Jan. 18 to 25.

MISSION PRAYER INTENTION: A World View on the Part of Everyone. With the growth of nationalism, people are running the risk of closing in upon themselves. The Church teaches all to seek the good of their country without becoming alienated from the rest of mankind.

FEBRUARY 1984

1—Wed. Weekday.

2—Thurs. Presentation of the Lord; feast.

3—Fri. Weekday. St. Blase, bishop-martyr, or St. Ansgar, bishop; optional memorials.

4—Sat. Weekday.

5—Fifth Sunday of the Year. (Is. 58:7-10; 1 Cor. 2:1-5; Mt. 5:13-16.) [St. Agatha, virgin-martyr; memorial.]

6—Mon. Sts. Paul Miki and Companions, martyrs; memorial.

7—Tues. Weekday.

8—Wed. Weekday. St. Jerome Emiliani; optional memorial.

9—Thurs. Weekday.

10—Fri. St. Scholastica, virgin; memorial.

11—Sat. Weekday. Our Lady of Lourdes; optional memorial.

12—Sixth Sunday of the Year. (Sir. 15:15-20; 1 Cor. 2:6-10; Mt. 5:17-37.)

13—Mon. Weekday.

14—Tues. Sts. Cyril, monk, and Methodius, bishop; memorial.

15—Wed. Weekday.

16—Thurs. Weekday.

17—Fri. Weekday. Seven Holy Founders of the Servite Order; optional memorial.

18—Sat. Weekday.

19—Seventh Sunday of the Year. (Lv. 19:1-2, 17-18; 1 Cor. 3:16-23; Mt. 5:38-48.)

20—Mon. Weekday.

21—Tues. Weekday. St. Peter Damien, bishop-doctor; optional memorial.

22—Wed. Chair of Peter, apostle; feast.

23—Thurs. St. Polycarp, bishop-martyr; memorial.

24—Fri. Weekday.

25—Sat. Weekday.

26—Eighth Sunday of the Year. (Is. 49:14-15; 1 Cor. 4:1-5; Mt. 6:24-34.)

27—Mon. Weekday.

28—Tues. Weekday.

29—Wed. Weekday.

GENERAL PRAYER INTENTION: The Youth of China. The future of the country depends on its young people. It is hoped that they may be instructed in true human values in harmony with those promulgated by the Christian faith. The young people of China have been subjected to many influences opposed to values fostered by their ancestral traditions and also by the teachings and practices of Christian faith, especially since the end of World War II and by the effects of the Cultural Revolution of the late 1960s.

MISSION PRAYER INTENTION: Insertion of the Gospel into the Culture of Every Race. The Holy Father has frequently referred to the question of inculturation. He has also established a Pontifical Commission for Culture, whose primary objective is to promote efforts to fuse elements of Catholic practice with the usages of native cultures without sacrificing the integrity of either.

MARCH 1984

1—Thurs. Weekday.
2—Fri. Weekday.
3—Sat. Weekday.
4—**Ninth Sunday of the Year.** (Dt. 11:18, 26-28; Rom. 3:21-25a, 28; Mt. 7:21-27.) [St. Casimir; optional memorial.]
5—Mon. Weekday.
6—Tues. Weekday.
7—Ash Wednesday. Beginning of Lent. *Fast and abstinence.* Ashes are blessed on this day and imposed on the forehead of the faithful to remind them of their obligation to do penance for sin and to seek spiritual renewal by means of prayer, fasting, good works, and by bearing with patience and for God's purposes the trials and difficulties of everyday life. [Sts. Perpetua and Felicity, martyrs; memorial.]
8—Thurs. Weekday of Lent. [St. John of God, religious; optional memorial.]
9—Fri. Weekday of Lent. *Abstinence.* [St. Frances of Rome, religious; optional memorial.]
10—Sat. Weekday of Lent.
11—**First Sunday of Lent.** (Gn. 2:7-9 and 3:1-7; Rom. 5:12-19; Mt. 4:1-11.)
12—Mon. Weekday of Lent.
13—Tues. Weekday of Lent.
14—Wed. Weekday of Lent.
15—Thurs. Weekday of Lent.
16—Fri. Weekday of Lent. *Abstinence.*
17—Sat. Weekday of Lent. [St. Patrick, bishop; optional memorial.]
18—**Second Sunday of Lent.** (Gn. 12:1-4a; 2 Tm. 1:8b-10; Mt. 17:1-9.) [St. Cyril of Jerusalem, bishop-doctor; optional memorial.]
19—Mon. St. Joseph; solemnity. Weekday of Lent.
20—Tues. Weekday of Lent.
21—Wed. Weekday of Lent.
22—Thurs. Weekday of Lent.
23—Fri. Weekday of Lent. *Abstinence.* [St. Turibius, bishop; optional memorial.]
24—Sat. Annunciation of the Lord; solemnity (transferred from Mar. 25). Weekday of Lent.
25—**Third Sunday of Lent.** (Ex. 17:3-7; Rom. 5:1-2, 5-8; Jn. 4:5-42.)
26—Mon. Weekday of Lent.
27—Tues. Weekday of Lent.
28—Wed. Weekday of Lent.
29—Thurs. Weekday of Lent.
30—Fri. Weekday of Lent. *Abstinence.*
31—Sat. Weekday of Lent.

GENERAL PRAYER INTENTION: The Fruits of the Holy Year of Our Redemption. The extraordinary observance proclaimed by the Pope requires prayer so that the fruits expected from it may be gained. The year marks the 1950th anniversary of the redemptive death and resurrection of Jesus.

MISSION PRAYER INTENTION: Justice and Evangelization in Africa. The general meeting of the episcopal conferences of Africa and Madagascar in 1981 pointed to the importance of these and related issues to the continent and the life-styles of its people.

APRIL 1984

1—**Fourth Sunday of Lent.** (1 Sm. 16:1b, 6-7, 10-13a; Eph. 5:8-14; Jn. 9:1-41.)
2—Mon. Weekday of Lent. [St. Francis of Paola, hermit; optional memorial.]
3—Tues. Weekday of Lent.
4—Wed. Weekday of Lent. [St. Isidore of Seville, bishop-doctor; optional memorial.]
5—Thurs. Weekday of Lent. [St. Vincent Ferrer, priest; optional memorial.]
6—Fri. Weekday of Lent. *Abstinence.*
7—Sat. Weekday of Lent. [St. John Baptist de la Salle, priest; memorial.]
8—**Fifth Sunday of Lent.** (Ez. 37:12-14; Rom. 8:8-11; Jn. 11:1-45.)
9—Mon. Weekday of Lent.
10—Tues. Weekday of Lent.
11—Wed. Weekday of Lent. [St. Stanislaus, bishop-martyr; memorial.]
12—Thurs. Weekday of Lent.
13—Fri. Weekday of Lent. *Abstinence.* [St. Martin I, pope-martyr; optional memorial.]
14—Sat. Weekday of Lent.
15—**Sunday of the Passion (Palm Sunday).** (Procession — Mt. 21:1-11. Mass — Is. 50:4-7; Phil. 2:6-11; Mt. 26:14 to 27:66.)
16—Monday of Holy Week.
17—Tuesday of Holy Week.
18—Wednesday of Holy Week.
19—Thursday of Holy Week. Holy Thursday. The Paschal Triduum begins with the evening Mass of the Supper of the Lord.
20—Friday of the Passion of the Lord. Good Friday. *Fast and abstinence.*
21—Holy Saturday. The Easter Vigil. [St. Anselm, bishop-doctor; optional memorial.]
22—**Easter Sunday; solemnity.** (Acts 10:34a, 37-43; 2 Col. 3:1-4 or 1 Cor. 5:6b-8; Jn. 20:1-9 or Mt. 28:1-10, or (Evening) Lk. 24:13-35.)
23—Monday of Easter Octave. [St. George, martyr; optional memorial.]
24—Tuesday of Easter Octave. [St. Fidelis of Sigmaringen, priest-martyr; optional memorial.]
25—Wednesday of Easter Octave. [St. Mark, evangelist; feast.]
26—Thursday of Easter Octave.
27—Friday of Easter Octave.
28—Saturday of Easter Octave. [St. Peter Chanel, priest-martyr; optional memorial.]
29—**Second Sunday of Easter.** (Acts. 2:42-47; 1 Pt. 1:3-9; Jn. 20:19-31.) [St. Catherine of Siena, virgin-doctor; memorial.]
30—Mon. Weekday. [St. Pius V, pope; optional memorial.]

GENERAL PRAYER INTENTION: Increase of Vocations to a Consecrated Life. The people of God must become aware of their responsibility to foster such vocations.

MISSION PRAYER INTENTION: The Contemplative Life in Mission Countries. On visits to various countries, the Pope has stressed the importance of the presence of contemplatives as witness and prayerful support to the life and work of the Church.

MAY 1984

1—Tues. Weekday. St. Joseph the Worker; optional memorial.

2—Wed. St. Athanasius, bishop-doctor; memorial.

3—Thurs. Sts. Philip and James, apostles; feast.

4—Fri. Weekday.

5—Sat. Weekday.

6—**Third Sunday of Easter.** (Acts 2:14, 22-28; 1 Pt. 1:17-21; Lk. 24:13-35.)

7—Mon. Weekday.

8—Tues. Weekday.

9—Wed. Weekday.

10—Thurs. Weekday.

11—Fri. Weekday.

12—Sat. Weekday. Sts. Nereus and Achilleus, martyrs, or St. Pancras, martyr; optional memorials.

13—**Fourth Sunday of Easter.** (Acts 2:14a, 36-41; 1 Pt. 2:20b-25; Jn. 10:1-10.)

14—Mon. St. Matthias, apostle; feast.

15—Tues. Weekday.

16—Wed. Weekday.

17—Thurs. Weekday.

18—Fri. Weekday. St. John I, pope-martyr; optional memorial.

19—Sat. Weekday.

20—**Fifth Sunday of Easter.** (Acts 6:1-7; 1 Pt. 2:4-9; Jn. 14:1-12.) [St. Bernardine of Siena, priest; optional memorial.[

21—Mon. Weekday.

22—Tues. Weekday.

23—Wed. Weekday.

24—Thurs. Weekday.

25—Fri. Weekday. St. Bede the Venerable, priest-doctor, or St. Gregory VII, pope, or St. Mary Magdalene de Pazzi, virgin; optional memorials.

26—Sat. St. Philip Neri, priest; memorial.

27—**Sixth Sunday of Easter.** (Acts 8:5-8, 14-17; 1 Pt. 3:15-18; Jn. 14:15-21.) [St. Augustine of Canterbury, bishop; optional memorial.]

28—Mon. Weekday.

29—Tues. Weekday.

30—Wed. Weekday.

31—**Thurs. Ascension of the Lord; solemnity. Holy day of obligation.** (Acts 1:1-11; Eph. 1:17-23; Mt. 28:16-20.) [Visitation of Blessed Mary the Virgin; feast.]

GENERAL PRAYER INTENTION: Witness to the Faith by Lay Persons in Our Schools. A document on the ministry of teaching, issued by the Congregation for Catholic Education in October, 1982, should be more widely publicized and put into greater practice by administrators and teachers.

MISSION PRAYER INTENTION: The Second Centenary of the Church in Korea. The Church in Korea, founded by a few laymen from China, is experiencing an extraordinary period of grace, and is preparing for a visit by the Holy Father. The Church, as a champion of human rights in the country, has on occasion been singled out for adverse attention by the government.

JUNE 1984

1—Fri. St. Justin, martyr; memorial.

2—Sat. Weekday. Sts. Marcellinus and Peter, martyrs; optional memorial.

3—**Seventh Sunday of Easter.** (Acts 1:12-14; 1 Pt. 4:13-16; Jn. 17:1-11a.) [Sts. Charles Lwanga and Companions, martyrs; memorial.]

4—Mon. Weekday.

5—Tues. St. Boniface, bishop-martyr; memorial.

6—Wed. Weekday. St. Norbert, bishop; optional memorial.

7—Thurs. Weekday.

8—Fri. Weekday.

9—Sat. Weekday. St. Ephraem, deacon-doctor; optional memorial.

10—**Sun. Pentecost; solemnity.** (Acts 2:1-11; 1 Cor. 12:3b-7, 12-13; Jn. 20:19-23.)

11—Mon. St. Barnabas, apostle; memorial. (Tenth Week of the Year.)

12—Tues. Weekday.

13—Wed. St. Anthony of Padua, priest-doctor; memorial.

14—Thurs. Weekday.

15—Fri. Weekday.

16—Sat. Weekday.

17—**Trinity Sunday; solemnity.** (Ex. 34:4b-6, 8-9; 2 Cor. 13:11-13; Jn. 3:16-18.)

18—Mon. Weekday. (Eleventh Week of the Year.)

19—Tues. Weekday. St. Romuald, abbot; optional memorial.

20—Wed. Weekday.

21—Thurs. St. Aloysius Gonzaga, religious; memorial.

22—Fri. Weekday. St. Paulinus of Nola, bishop, or Sts. John Fisher, bishop-martyr, and Thomas More, martyr; optional memorials.

23—Sat. Weekday.

24—**Sun. Corpus Christi (in U.S.); solemnity.** (Dt. 8:2-3, 14b-16a; 1 Cor. 10:16-17; Jn. 6:51-58.)

25—Mon. Birth of St. John the Baptist; solemnity (transferred from June 24). (Twelfth Week of the Year.)

26—Tues. Weekday.

27—Wed. Weekday. St. Cyril of Alexandria, bishop-doctor; optional memorial.

28—Thurs. St. Irenaeus, bishop-martyr; memorial.

29—Fri. Sacred Heart of Jesus; solemnity.

30—Sat. Sts. Peter and Paul, apostles; solemnity (transferred from June 29). [First Martyrs of the Roman Church; optional memorial. Immaculate Heart of Mary; optional memorial.]

GENERAL PRAYER INTENTION: The Consecration of Families to the Sacred Heart of Jesus and the Immaculate Heart of Mary. The apostolic exhortation, *Familiaris Consortio*, called the Catholic family a "Domestic Church." It should be nourished by practices of piety like this dual consecration and common family prayer.

MISSION PRAYER INTENTION: Interfaith Dialogue in India. Almost all the great religions of antiquity are found there, but there is no easy dialogue among either their leaders or ordinary members.

JULY 1984

1—Thirteenth Sunday of the Year. (2 Kgs. 4:8-11, 14-16a; Rom. 6:3-4, 8-11; Mt. 10:37-42.)
2—Mon. Weekday.
3—Tues. St. Thomas, apostle; feast.
4—Wed. Weekday. St. Elizabeth of Portugal; optional memorial. Independence Day Votive Mass (permitted in U.S.).
5—Thurs. Weekday. St. Anthony Zaccaria, priest; optional memorial.
6—Fri. Weekday. St. Maria Goretti, virgin-martyr; optional memorial.
7—Sat. Weekday.
8—Fourteenth Sunday of the Year. (Zec. 9:9-10; Rom. 8:9, 11-13; Mt. 11:25-30.)
9—Mon. Weekday.
10—Tues. Weekday.
11—Wed. St. Benedict, abbot; memorial.
12—Thurs. Weekday.
13—Fri. Weekday. St. Henry; optional memorial.
14—Sat. Bl. Kateri Tekakwitha, virgin; memorial (in U.S.). Weekday. St. Camillus de Lellis, priest; optional memorial.
15—Fifteenth Sunday of the Year. (Is. 55:10-11; Rom. 8:18-23; Mt. 13:1-23.) [St. Bonaventure, bishop-doctor; memorial.]
16—Mon. Weekday. Our Lady of Mt. Carmel; optional memorial.
17—Tues. Weekday.
18—Wed. Weekday.
19—Thurs. Weekday.
20—Fri. Weekday.
21—Sat. Weekday. St. Lawrence of Brindisi, priest-doctor; optional memorial.
22—Sixteenth Sunday of the Year. (Wis. 12:13, 16-19; Rom. 8:26-27, Mt. 13.24-43.) [St. Mary Magdalene; memorial.]
23—Mon. Weekday. St. Bridget, religious; optional memorial.
24—Tues. Weekday.
25—Wed. St. James, apostle; feast.
26—Thurs. Sts. Joachim and Anne, parents of Blessed Mary the Virgin; memorial.
27—Fri. Weekday.
28—Sat. Weekday.
29—Seventeenth Sunday of the Year. (1 Kgs. 3:5, 7-12; Rom. 8:28-30; Mt. 13:44-52.) [St. Martha; memorial.]
30—Mon. Weekday. St. Peter Chrysologus, bishop-doctor; optional memorial.
31—Tues. St. Ignatius of Loyola, priest; memorial.

GENERAL PRAYER INTENTION: Inclusion of the Teaching of Justice in Our Evangelization. From the first moments of evangelization, the demands of justice should be presented as an inseparable part of responsible Christian conduct as well as of the social doctrine of the Church. The 1971 Synod of Bishops stressed this point.

MISSION PRAYER INTENTION: Victory over Famine in the World. The scourge of famine is particularly prevalent among peoples of the Third World. Coupled with this critical problem are others related to justice, solidarity and the exigencies of the Gospel.

AUGUST 1984

1—Wed. St. Alphonsus Liguori, bishop-doctor; memorial.
2—Thurs. Weekday. St. Eusebius of Vercelli, bishop; optional memorial.
3—Fri. Weekday.
4—Sat. St. John Vianney, priest; memorial.
5—Eighteenth Sunday of the Year. (Is. 55:1-3; Rom. 8:35, 37-39; Mt. 14:13-21.) [Dedication of St. Mary Major Basilica; optional memorial]
6—Mon. Transfiguration of the Lord; feast.
7—Tues. Weekday. Sts. Sixtus II, pope, and Companions, martyrs; or St. Cajetan, priest; optional memorials.
8—Wed. St. Dominic, priest; memorial.
9—Thurs. Weekday.
10—Fri. St. Lawrence, deacon-martyr; feast.
11—Sat. St. Clare, virgin; memorial.
12—Nineteenth Sunday of the Year. (1 Kgs. 19:9a, 11-13a; Rom. 9:1-5; Mt. 14:22-33.)
13—Mon. Weekday. Sts. Pontian, pope, and Hippolytus, priest; martyrs; optional memorial.
14—Tues. St. Maximilian Kolbe, martyr; memorial.
15—Wed. Assumption of Blessed Mary the Virgin; solemnity. Holy day of obligation. (Rv. 11:19a and 12:1-6a, 10ab; 1 Cor. 15:20-26; Lk. 1:39-56.)
16—Thurs. Weekday. St. Stephen of Hungary; optional memorial.
17—Fri. Weekday.
18—Sat. Weekday.
19—Twentieth Sunday of the Year. (Is. 56: 1, 6-7; Rom. 11:13-15, 29-32; Mt. 15:21-28.) [St. John Eudes, priest; optional memorial.]
20—Mon. St. Bernard of Clairvaux, abbot-doctor; memorial.
21—Tues. St. Pius X, pope; memorial.
22—Wed. Queenship of Mary; memorial.
23—Thurs. Weekday. St. Rose of Lima; optional memorial.
24—Fri. St. Bartholomew, apostle; feast.
25—Sat. Weekday. St. Louis, or St. Joseph Calasanz, priest; optional memorials.
26—Twenty-First Sunday of the Year. (Is. 22:19-23; Rom. 11:33-36; Mt. 16:13-20.)
27—Mon. St. Monica, memorial.
28—Tues. St. Augustine, bishop-doctor; memorial.
29—Wed. Beheading of St. John the Baptist; memorial.
30—Thurs. Weekday.
31—Fri. Weekday.

GENERAL PRAYER INTENTION: Reverence for the Eucharist by Families. The occasion for this intention is to be found in the International Eucharistic Congress to be held in 1985 in Kenya.

MISSION PRAYER INTENTION: Vocations in Mozambique. Not only is there a scarcity of native and foreign priests in the country, but young men experience great difficulty in entering seminaries. There has been a gradual reduction of tension between the Church and the Marxist-oriented government in power since 1975.

SEPTEMBER 1984

1—Sat. Weekday.
2—**Twenty-Second Sunday of the Year.** (Jer. 20:7-9; Rom. 12:1-2; Mt. 16:21-27.)
3—Mon. Labor Day Votive Mass (prescribed in U.S.). [St. Gregory the Great, pope-doctor; memorial.]
4—Tues. Weekday.
5—Wed. Weekday.
6—Thurs. Weekday.
7—Fri. Weekday.
8—Sat. Birth of Mary; feast.
9—**Twenty-Third Sunday of the Year.** (Ez. 33:7-9; Rom. 13:8-10; Mt. 18:15-20.) [St. Peter Claver, priest; memorial (in U.S.).]
10—Mon. Weekday.
11—Tues. Weekday.
12—Wed. Weekday.
13—Thurs. St. John Chrysostom, bishop-doctor; memorial.
14—Fri. Triumph of the Cross; feast.
15—Sat. Our Lady of Sorrows; memorial.
16—**Twenty-Fourth Sunday of the Year.** (Sir. 27:30 to 28:7; Rom. 14:7-8; Mt. 18:21-35.) [Sts. Cornelius, pope, and Cyprian, bishop, martyrs; memorial.]
17—Mon. Weekday. St. Robert Bellarmine, bishop-doctor; optional memorial.
18—Tues. Weekday.
19—Wed. Weekday. St. Januarius, bishop-martyr; optional memorial.
20—Thurs. Weekday.
21—Fri. St. Matthew, apostle-evangelist; feast.
22—Sat. Weekday.
23—**Twenty-Fifth Sunday of the Year.** (Is. 55:6-9; Phil 1:20c-24, 27a; Mt. 20: 1-16a.)
24—Mon. Weekday.
25—Tues. Weekday.
26—Wed. Weekday. Sts. Cosmas and Damian, martyrs; optional memorial.
27—Thurs. St. Vincent de Paul, priest; memorial.
28—Fri. Weekday. St. Wenceslaus, martyr; optional memorial.
29—Sat. Sts. Michael, Gabriel and Raphael, archangels; feast.
30—**Twenty-Sixth Sunday of the Year.** (Ez. 18:25-28; Phil 2:1-11; Mt. 21:28-32.) [St. Jerome, priest-doctor; memorial.]

GENERAL PRAYER INTENTION: The Revitalization of European Civilization. The civilization of both Eastern and Western Europe is basically Christian. This fact should be recognized and its consequences developed, as the Holy Father observed in an address at Compostela, Spain, Nov. 9, 1982. Hopes and appeals for European unity have been expressed by popes for years. One step toward it is the existing and operating European Common Market.

MISSION PRAYER INTENTION: Mutual understanding between Christians and Moslems. Christians and Moslems should be strongly urged to forget problems of the past and to strive for mutual understanding and cooperation in work for social justice.

OCTOBER 1984

1—Mon. St. Therese of the Child Jesus, virgin; memorial.
2—Tues. Guardian Angels; memorial.
3—Wed. Weekday.
4—Thurs. St. Francis of Assisi; memorial.
5—Fri. Weekday.
6—Sat. Weekday. Bl. Marie-Rose Durocher, virgin; optional memorial (in U.S.). St. Bruno, priest; optional memorial.
7—**Twenty-Seventh Sunday of the Year.** (Is. 5:1-7; Phil. 4:6-9; Mt. 21:33-43.) [Our Lady of the Rosary; memorial.]
8—Mon. Weekday.
9—Tues. Weekday. Sts. Denis, bishop, and Companions, martyrs; or St. John Leonard, priest; optional memorials.
10—Wed. Weekday.
11—Thurs. Weekday.
12—Fri. Weekday.
13—Sat. Weekday.
14—**Twenty-Eighth Sunday of the Year.** (Is. 25:6-10a; Phil. 4:12-14, 19-20; Mt. 22:1-14.) [St. Callistus I, pope-martyr; optional memorial.]
15—Mon. St. Teresa of Avila, virgin-doctor; memorial.
16—Tues. Weekday. St. Hedwig, religious, or St. Margaret Mary Alacoque, virgin; optional memorials.
17—Wed. St. Ignatius of Antioch, bishop-martyr; memorial.
18—Thurs. St. Luke, evangelist; feast.
19—Fri. Sts. Isaac Jogues, John de Brebeuf, priests, and Companions, martyrs; memorial (in U.S.). Weekday. St. Paul of the Cross; optional memorial.
20—Sat. Weekday.
21—**Twenty-Ninth Sunday of the Year.** (Is. 45:1, 4-6; 1 Thes. 1:1-5b; Mt. 22:15-21.)
22—Mon. Weekday.
23—Tues. Weekday. St. John of Capistrano, priest; optional memorial.
24—Wed. Weekday. St. Anthony Mary Claret, bishop; optional memorial.
25—Thurs. Weekday.
26—Fri. Weekday.
27—Sat. Weekday.
28—**Thirtieth Sunday of the Year.** (Ex. 22:20-26; 1 Thes. 1:5c-10; Mt. 22:34-40.) [Sts. Simon and Jude, apostles; feast.]
29—Mon. Weekday.
30—Tues. Weekday.
31—Wed. Weekday.

GENERAL PRAYER INTENTION: Increase in Pastoral Work among University Students. These students, the future leaders of society, should be provided with suitable assistance as they mature in faith.

MISSION PRAYER INTENTION: The Catholic Church in Vietnam. Prayer should be offered for the Church in Vietnam so that it might remain firm in the faith and in allegiance to the Universal Church, and thus be able to overcome the serious difficulties it is experiencing.

NOVEMBER 1984

1—Thurs. All Saints; solemnity. Holy day of obligation. (Rv. 7:2-4, 9-14; 1 Jn. 3:1-3; Mt. 5:1-12a.)

2—Fri. Commemoration of All the Faithful Departed. (All Souls' Day). Three Masses proper.

3—Sat. Weekday. St. Martin de Porres, religious; optional memorial.

4—Thirty-First Sunday of the Year. (Mal. 1:14b to 2:2b, 8-10; 1 Thes. 2:7b-9, 13; Mt. 23:1-12.) [St. Charles Borromeo, bishop; memorial.]

5—Mon. Weekday.

6—Tues. Weekday.

7—Wed. Weekday.

8—Thurs. Weekday.

9—Fri. Dedication of St. John Lateran (Archbasilica of Most Holy Savior); feast.

10—Sat. St. Leo the Great, pope-doctor; memorial.

11—Thirty-Second Sunday of the Year. (Wis. 6:12-16; 1 Thes. 4:13-18; Mt. 25:1-13.) [St. Martin of Tours, bishop; memorial.]

12—Mon. St. Josaphat, bishop-martyr; memorial.

13—Tues. St. Frances Xavier Cabrini, virgin; memorial (in U.S.).

14—Wed. Weekday.

15—Thurs. Weekday. St. Albert the Great, bishop-doctor; optional memorial.

16—Fri. Weekday. St. Margaret of Scotland, or St. Gertrude, virgin; optional memorials.

17—Sat. St. Elizabeth of Hungary, religious; memorial.

18—Thirty-Third Sunday of the Year. (Prv. 31:10-13, 19-20, 30-31; 1 Thes. 5.1-6; Mt. 25:14-30.) [Dedication of Basilicas of Sts. Peter and Paul, apostles; optional memorial.]

19—Mon. Weekday.

20—Tues. Weekday.

21—Wed. Presentation of Blessed Mary the Virgin; memorial.

22—Thurs. St. Cecilia, virgin-martyr; memorial. Thanksgiving Day Votive Mass (permitted in U.S.).

23—Fri. Weekday. St. Clement I, pope-martyr, or St. Columban, abbot; optional memorials.

24—Sat. Weekday.

25—Sun. Christ the King; solemnity. (Ez. 34:11-12, 15-17; 1 Cor. 15:20-26, 28; Mt. 25.31-46.)

26—Mon. Weekday. (Thirty-Fourth [Last] Week of the Year.)

27—Tues. Weekday.

28—Wed. Weekday.

29—Thurs. Weekday.

30—Fri. St. Andrew, apostle; feast.

GENERAL PRAYER INTENTION: The Increase of "Basic Communities" in the Church. Their increase, especially in certain countries, is a source of hope for the Church even though they can be the cause of some problems.

MISSION PRAYER INTENTION: That the Church in Africa Might Become More "African." The Pope did not hesitate to use these words when, speaking to African bishops Nov. 14, 1982, he referred to the ever-present problem of inculturation.

DECEMBER 1984

1—Sat. Weekday.

2—First Sunday of Advent. (Is. 63:16-17, 19b and 64:2b-7; 1 Cor. 1:3-9; Mk. 13:33-37.)

3—Mon. St. Francis Xavier, priest; memorial.

4—Tues. Weekday of Advent. St. John Damascene, priest-doctor; optional memorial.

5—Wed. Weekday of Advent.

6—Thurs. Weekday of Advent. St. Nicholas, bishop; optional memorial.

7—Fri. St. Ambrose, bishop-doctor; memorial.

8—Sat. Immaculate Conception of Blessed Mary the Virgin; solemnity. Holy day of obligation. (Gn. 3:9-15, 20; Eph. 1:3-6, 11-12; Lk. 1:26-38.)

9—Second Sunday of Advent. (Is. 40:1-5, 9-11; 2 Pt. 3:8-14; Mk. 1:1-8.)

10—Mon. Weekday of Advent.

11—Tues. Weekday of Advent. St. Damasus I, pope; optional memorial.

12—Wed. Our Lady of Guadalupe; memorial (in U.S.). Weekday of Advent. St. Jane Frances de Chantal, religious; optional memorial.

13—Thurs. St. Lucy, virgin-martyr; memorial.

14—Fri. St. John of the Cross, priest-doctor; memorial.

15—Sat. Weekday of Advent.

16—Third Sunday of Advent. (Is. 61:1-2a, 10-11; 1 Thes. 5:16-24; Jn. 1:6-8, 19-28.)

17—Mon. Weekday of Advent.

18—Tues. Weekday of Advent.

19—Wed. Weekday of Advent.

20—Thurs. Weekday of Advent.

21—Fri. Weekday of Advent. [St. Peter Canisius, priest-doctor; optional memorial.]

22—Sat. Weekday of Advent.

23—Fourth Sunday of Advent. (2 Sm. 7:1-5, 8b-11, 16; Rom. 16:25-27; Lk. 1:26-38.) [St. John of Kanty, priest; optional memorial.]

24—Mon. Weekday of Advent.

25—Tues. Christmas. Birth of the Lord; solemnity. (Midnight—Is. 9:1-6; Ti. 2:11-14; Lk. 2:1-14. Dawn—Is. 62:11-12; Ti. 3:4-7; Lk. 2:15-20. During the Day—Is. 52:7-10; Heb. 1:1-6; Jn. 1:1-18.)

26—Wed. St. Stephen, first martyr; feast.

27—Thurs. St. John, apostle-evangelist; feast.

28—Fri. Holy Innocents, martyrs; feast.

29—Sat. Fifth Day of Christmas Octave. St. Thomas Becket, bishop-martyr; optional memorial.

30—Sun. Holy Family; feast. (Sir. 3:2-6, 12-14; Col. 3:12-21; Lk. 2:22-40.)

31—Mon. Seventh Day of Christmas Octave. St. Sylvester I, pope; optional memorial.

GENERAL PRAYER INTENTION: The Church, Sacrament of Unity among Peoples. This intention should lead us to pray for peace. St. Augustine's definition of peace is the tranquillity of God's order in our lives.

MISSION PRAYER INTENTION: Reconciliation of All the Nations of the World. This intention is related to the appropriate response of people to themes of the 1983 assembly of the Synod of Bishops, the Jubilee Year of Redemption and the celebration of the annual World Day of Peace Jan. 1, 1985.

TABLE OF MOVABLE FEASTS

Year	Ash Wednesday	Easter	Ascension	Pentecost	Weeks of Ordinary Time				
					Before Lent		After Pent.		
					Week	Ends	Week	Begins	
1984	Mar. 7	Apr. 22	May 31	June 10	9	Mar. 6	10	June 11	Dec. 2
1985	Feb. 20	Apr. 7	May 16	May 26	6	Feb. 19	8	May 27	Dec. 1
1986	Feb. 12	Mar. 30	May 8	May 18	5	Feb. 11	7	May 19	Nov. 30
1987	Mar. 4	Apr. 19	May 28	June 7	9	Mar. 3	10	June 8	Nov. 29
1988	Feb. 17	Apr. 3	May 12	May 22	6	Feb. 16	8	May 23	Nov. 27
1989	Feb. 8	Mar. 26	May 4	May 14	5	Feb. 7	6	May 15	Dec. 3
1990	Feb. 28	Apr. 15	May 24	June 3	8	Feb. 27	9	June 4	Dec. 2
1991	Feb. 13	Mar. 31	May 9	May 19	5	Feb. 12	7	May 20	Dec. 1
1992	Mar. 4	Apr. 19	May 28	June 7	9	Mar. 3	10	June 8	Nov. 29
1993	Feb. 24	Apr. 11	May 20	May 30	7	Feb. 23	9	May 31	Nov. 28
1994	Feb. 16	Apr. 3	May 12	May 22	6	Feb. 15	8	May 23	Nov. 27
1995	Mar. 1	Apr. 16	May 25	June 4	8	Feb. 28	9	June 5	Dec. 3
1996	Feb. 21	Apr. 7	May 16	May 26	7	Feb. 20	8	May 27	Dec. 1
1997	Feb. 12	Mar. 30	May 8	May 18	5	Feb. 11	7	May 19	Nov. 30
1998	Feb. 25	Apr. 12	May 21	May 31	7	Feb. 24	9	June 1	Nov. 29
1999	Feb. 17	Apr. 4	May 13	May 23	6	Feb. 16	8	May 24	Nov. 28
2000	Mar. 8	Apr. 23	June 1	June 11	9	Mar. 7	10	June 12	Dec. 3
2001	Feb. 28	Apr. 15	May 24	June 3	8	Feb. 27	9	June 4	Dec. 2
2002	Feb. 13	Mar. 31	May 9	May 19	5	Feb. 12	7	May 20	Dec. 1
2003	Mar. 5	Apr. 20	May 29	June 8	8	Mar. 4	10	June 9	Nov. 30
2004	Feb. 25	Apr. 11	May 20	May 30	7	Feb. 24	9	May 31	Nov. 28
2005	Feb. 9	Mar. 27	May 5	May 15	5	Feb. 8	7	May 16	Nov. 27
2006	Mar. 1	Apr. 16	May 25	June 4	8	Feb. 28	9	June 5	Dec. 3
2007	Feb. 21	Apr. 8	May 17	May 27	7	Feb. 20	8	May 28	Dec. 2

Season of Ordinary Time

Weeks between the end of the Christmas season and the beginning of Lent, and from the day after Pentecost to the last Sunday of the liturgical year, belong to the season of Ordinary Time. The table indicates the number and terminal date of the week ending the first part, and the number and starting date of the week beginning the second part, of this season. In some years, a week of this season is eliminated because of calendar conditions.

Holiday Masses

Liturgical experiments in recent years have led to the development of votive Masses for national holidays, like those introduced in the U.S. for Thanksgiving Day in 1969 and July 4 in 1972. This development is in line with a custom whereby "from the earliest times the Church has crowned many non-Christian feasts with Christian fulfillment by instituting its own liturgical festivals" to coincide with them.

Readings at Mass

The texts of scriptural readings for Mass on Sundays, holy days and some other days are indicated under the respective dates. The first (A) cycle of readings in the Lectionary is prescribed for the 1984 liturgical year (Nov. 27, 1983, to Dec. 1, 1984); the second (B) cycle is prescribed for the 1985 liturgical year which begins with the first Sunday of Advent, Dec. 2, 1984.

Weekday cycles of readings are the second and first, respectively, for liturgical years 1984 and 1985.

Monthly Prayer Intentions

General and mission intentions chosen and recommended by Pope John Paul II to the prayers of the Apostles of Prayer are given under each month of the 1983 calendar. He has expressed his desire that all Catholics make these intentions their own "in the certainty of being united with the Holy Father and praying according to his intentions and desires."

HOLY DAYS AND OTHER FEASTS

The following list includes the six holy days of obligation observed in the United States and additional observances of devotional and historical significance. The dignity or rank of observances is indicated by the terms: **solemnity** (highest in rank); **feast**; **memorial** (for universal observance); **optional memorial** (for celebration by choice).

All Saints, Nov. 1, holy day of obligation, solemnity. Commemorates all the blessed in heaven, and is intended particularly to honor the blessed who have no special feasts. The background of the feast dates to the fourth century when groups of martyrs, and later other saints, were honored on a common day in various places. In 609 or 610, the Pantheon, a pagan temple at Rome, was consecrated as a Christian church for the honor of Our Lady and the martyrs (later all saints). In 835, Gregory IV fixed Nov. 1 as the date of observance.

All Souls, Commemoration of the Faithful Departed, Nov. 2. The dead were prayed for from the earliest days of Christianity. By the sixth century it was customary in Benedictine monasteries to hold a commemoration of deceased members of the order at Pentecost. A common commemoration of all the faithful departed on the day after All Saints was instituted in 998 by St. Odilo, of the Abbey of Cluny, and an observance of this kind was accepted in Rome in the 14th century. In 1915, Benedict XV granted priests throughout the world permission to celebrate three Masses for this commemoration. He also granted a special indulgence for the occasion.

Annunciation of the Lord (formerly, Annunciation of the Blessed Virgin Mary), Mar. 25, solemnity. A feast of the Incarnation which commemorates the announcement by the Archangel Gabriel to the Virgin Mary that she was to become the Mother of Christ (Lk. 1:26 38), and the miraculous conception of Christ by her. The feast was instituted about 430 in the East. The Roman observance dates from the seventh century, when celebration was said to be universal.

Ascension of the Lord, movable observance held 40 days after Easter, holy day of obligation, solemnity. Commemorates the Ascension of Christ into heaven 40 days after his Resurrection from the dead (Mk. 16:19; Lk. 24:51; Acts 1:2). The feast recalls the completion of Christ's mission on earth for the salvation of all people and his entry into heaven with glorified human nature. The Ascension is a pledge of the final glorification of all who achieve salvation. Documentary evidence of the feast dates from early in the fifth century, but it was observed long before that time in connection with Pentecost and Easter.

Ash Wednesday, movable observance, six and one-half weeks before Easter. It was set as the first day of Lent by Pope St. Gregory the Great (590-604) with the extension of an earlier and shorter penitential season to a total period including 40 weekdays of fasting before Easter. It is a day of fast and abstinence. Ashes, symbolic of penance, are blessed and distributed among the faithful during the day. They are used to mark the forehead with the Sign of the Cross, with the reminder: "Remember, man, that you are dust, and unto dust you shall return," or: "Repent, and believe the Good News."

Assumption Aug. 15, holy day of obligation, solemnity. Commemorates the taking into heaven of Mary, soul and body, at the end of her life on earth, a truth of faith that was proclaimed a dogma by Pius XII on Nov. 1, 1950. One of the oldest and most solemn feasts of Mary, it has a history dating back to at least the seventh century when its celebration was already established at Jerusalem and Rome.

Baptism of the Lord, movable, usually celebrated on the Sunday after Epiphany, feast. Recalls the baptism of Christ by John the Baptist (Mk. 1:9-11), an event associated with the liturgy of the Epiphany. This baptism was the occasion for Christ's manifestation of himself at the beginning of his public life.

Birth of Mary, Sept. 8, feast. This is a very old feast which originated in the East and found place in the Roman liturgy in the seventh century.

Candlemas Day, Feb. 2. See Presentation of the Lord.

Chair of Peter, Feb. 22, feast. Commemorates establishment of the see of Antioch by Peter. The feast, which has been in the Roman calendar since 336, is a liturgical expression of belief in the episcopacy and hierarchy of the Church.

Christmas, Birth of Our Lord Jesus Christ, Dec. 25, holy day of obligation, solemnity. Commemorates the birth of Christ (Lk. 2:1-20). This event was originally commemorated in the East on the feast of Epiphany or Theophany. The Christmas feast itself originated in the West; by 354 it was certainly kept on Dec. 25. This date may have been set for the observance to offset pagan ceremonies held at about the same time to commemorate the birth of the sun at the winter solstice. Priests may celebrate three Masses on Christmas Day.

Christ the King, movable, celebrated on the last Sunday of the liturgical year, solemnity. Commemorates the royal prerogatives of Christ and is equivalent to a declaration of his rights to the homage, service and fidelity of men in all phases of individual and social life. Pius XI instituted the feast Dec. 11, 1925.

Conversion of St. Paul, Jan. 25, feast. An observance mentioned in some calendars from the 8th and 9th centuries. Pope Innocent III (1198-1216) ordered its observance with great solemnity.

Corpus Christi, movable, celebrated on the Thursday (or Sunday, as in the U.S.) following Trinity Sunday, solemnity. Commemorates the institution of the Holy Eucharist (Mt. 26:26-28). The feast originated at Liege in 1246 and was extended throughout the Church in the West by Urban IV in 1264. St. Thomas Aquinas composed the Liturgy of the Hours for the feast.

Dedication of St. John Lateran, Nov. 9, feast. Commemorates the first public consecration of a church; that of the Basilica of the Most Holy Savior by Pope St. Sylvester Nov. 9, 324. The church, as well as the Lateran Palace, was the gift of Emperor Constantine. Since the 12th century it has been known as St. John Lateran, in honor of John the Baptist after whom the adjoining baptistery was named. It was rebuilt by Innocent X (1644-55), reconsecrated by Benedict XIII in 1726, and enlarged by Leo XIII (1878-1903). This basilica is regarded as the church of highest dignity in Rome and throughout the Roman Rite.

Dedication of St. Mary Major, Aug. 5, optional memorial. Commemorates the rebuilding and dedication by Pope Sixtus III (432-40) of a church in honor of Blessed Mary the Virgin. This is the Basilica of St. Mary Major on the Esquiline Hill in Rome. An earlier building was erected during the pontificate of Liberius (352-66); according to legend, it was located on a site covered by a miraculous fall of snow seen by a nobleman favored with a vision of Mary.

Easter, movable celebration held on the first Sunday after the full moon following the vernal equinox (between Mar. 22 and Apr. 25), solemnity with an octave. Commemorates the Resurrection of Christ from the dead (Mk. 16:1-7). The observance of this mystery, kept since the first days of the Church, extends throughout the Easter season which lasts until the feast of Pentecost, a period of 50 days. Every Sunday in the year is regarded as a "little" Easter. The date of Easter determines the dates of movable feasts, such as Ascension and Pentecost, and the number of weeks before Lent and after Pentecost.

Easter Vigil, called by St. Augustine the "Mother of All Vigils," the night before Easter. Ceremonies are all related to the Resurrection and renewal-in-grace theme of Easter: blessing of the new fire and Paschal Candle, reading of prophecies, blessing of water and the baptismal font, the baptism of converts and renewal of baptismal vows by the faithful, the Litany of the Saints, and the celebration of the Mass of the Resurrection. The vigil ceremonies are held after sundown, preferably at a time that makes possible the celebration of Mass at midnight.

Epiphany of Our Lord, Jan. 6 or (in the U.S.) a Sunday between Jan. 2 and 8, solemnity. Commemorates the manifestations of the divinity of Christ. It is one of the oldest Christian feasts, with an Eastern origin traceable to the beginning of the third century and antedating the Western feast of Christmas. Originally, it commemorated the manifestations of Christ's divinity — or Theophany — in his birth, the homage of the Magi, and baptism by John the Baptist. Later, the first two of these commemorations were transferred to Christmas when the Eastern Church adopted that feast between 380 and 430. The central feature of the Eastern observance now is the manifestation or declaration of Christ's divinity in his baptism and at the beginning of his public life. The Epiphany was adopted by the Western Church during the same period in which the Eastern Church accepted Christmas. In the Roman Rite, commemoration is made in the Mass of the homage of the wise men from the East (Mt. 2:1-12).

Good Friday, the Friday before Easter, the second day of the Easter Triduum. Liturgical elements of the observance are commemoration of the Passion and Death of Christ in the reading of the Passion (according to John), special prayers for the Church and people of all ranks, the veneration of the Cross, and a Communion service. The celebration takes place in the afternoon, preferably at 3:00 p.m.

Guardian Angels, Oct. 2, memorial. Commemorates the angels who protect people from spiritual and physical dangers and assist them in doing good. A feast in their honor celebrated in Spain in the 16th century was extended to the whole Church by Paul V in 1608. In 1670, Clement X set Oct. 2 as the date of observance. Earlier, guardian angels were honored liturgically in conjunction with the feast of St. Michael.

Holy Family, movable observance on the Sunday after Christmas, feast. Commemorates the Holy Family of Jesus, Mary and Joseph as the model of domestic society, holiness and virtue. The devotional background of the feast was very strong in the 17th century. In the 18th century, in prayers composed for a special Mass, a Canadian bishop likened the Christian family to the Holy Family. Leo XIII consecrated families to the Holy Family. In 1921, Benedict XV extended the Divine Office and Mass of the feast to the whole Church.

Holy Innocents, Dec. 28, feast. Commemorates the infants who suffered death at the hands of Herod's soldiers seeking to kill the child Jesus (Mt. 2:13-18). A feast in their honor has been observed since the fifth century.

Holy Saturday, the day before Easter. The Sacrifice of the Mass is not celebrated, and Holy Communion may be given only as Viaticum. If possible the Easter fast should be observed until the Easter Vigil.

Holy Thursday, the Thursday before Easter. Commemorates the institution of the sacraments of the Eucharist and holy orders, and the washing of the feet of the Apostles by Jesus at the Last Supper. The Mass of the Lord's Supper in the evening marks the beginning of the Easter Triduum. Following the Mass, there is a procession of the Blessed Sacrament to a place of reposition for adoration by the faithful. At an earlier Mass of Chrism, bishops bless oils (of catechumens, chrism, the sick) for use during the year. (For pastoral reasons, diocesan bishops may permit additional Masses, but these should not overshadow the principal Mass of the Lord's Supper.)

Holy Saturday, the day before Easter. The Sacrifice of the Mass is not celebrated, and Holy Communion may be given only as Viaticum. If possible the Easter fast should be observed until the Easter Vigil.

Immaculate Conception, Dec. 8, holy day of obligation, solemnity. Commemorates the fact that Mary, in view of her calling to be the Mother of Christ and in virtue of his merits, was preserved from the first moment of her conception from original sin and was filled with grace from the very beginning of her life. She was the only person so preserved from original sin. The present form of the feast dates from Dec. 8, 1854, when Pius IX defined the dogma of the Immaculate Conception. An earlier feast of the Conception, which testified to long-existing belief in this truth, was observed in the East by the eighth century, in Ireland in the ninth, and subsequently in European countries. In 1846, Mary was proclaimed patroness of the U.S. under this title.

Immaculate Heart of Mary, Saturday following the second Sunday after Pentecost, optional memorial. On May 4, 1944, Pius XII ordered this feast observed throughout the Church in order to obtain Mary's intercession for "peace among nations, freedom for the Church, the conversion of sinners, the love of purity and the practice of virtue." Two years earlier, he consecrated the entire human race to Mary under this title. Devotion to Mary under the title of her Most Pure Heart originated during the Middle Ages. It was given great impetus in the 17th century by the preaching of St. John Eudes, who was the first to celebrate a Mass and Divine Office of Mary under this title. A feast, celebrated in various places and on different dates, was authorized in 1799.

Joachim and Ann, July 26, memorial. Commemorates the parents of Mary. A joint feast, celebrated Sept. 9, originated in the East near the end of the sixth century. Devotion to Ann, introduced in the eighth century at Rome, became widespread in Europe in the 14th century; her feast was extended throughout the Latin Church in 1584. A feast of Joachim was introduced in the West in the 15th century.

John the Baptist, Birth, June 24, solemnity. The precursor of Christ, whose cousin he was, was commemorated universally in the liturgy by the fourth century. He is the only saint, except the Blessed Virgin Mary, whose birthday is observed as a feast. Another feast, on Aug. 29, commemorates his passion and death at the order of Herod (Mk. 6:14-29).

Joseph, Mar. 19, solemnity. Joseph is honored as the husband of the Blessed Virgin Mary, the patron and protector of the universal Church and workman. Devotion to him already existed in the eighth century in the East, and in the 11th in the West. Various feasts were celebrated before the 15th century when Mar. 19 was fixed for his commemoration; this feast was extended to the whole Church in 1621 by Gregory XV. In 1955, Pius XII instituted the feast of St. Joseph the Workman for observance May 1; this feast, which may be celebrated by local option, supplanted the Solemnity or Patronage of St. Joseph formerly observed on the third Wednesday after Easter. St. Joseph was proclaimed protector and patron of the universal Church in 1870 by Pius IX.

Michael, Gabriel and Raphael, Archangels, Sept. 29, feast. A feast bearing the title of Dedication of St. Michael the Archangel formerly commemorated on this date the consecration in 530 of a church near Rome in honor of Michael, the first angel given a liturgical feast. For a while, this feast was combined with a commemoration of the Guardian Angels. The separate feasts of Gabriel (Mar. 24) and Raphael (Oct. 24) were suppressed by the calendar reform of 1969 and this joint feast of the three archangels was instituted.

Octave of Christmas, Jan. 1. See Solemnity of Mary, Mother of God.

Our Lady of Sorrows, Sept. 15, memorial. Recalls the sorrows experienced by Mary in her association with Christ: the prophecy of Simeon (Lk. 2:34-35), the flight into Egypt (Mt. 2:13-21), the three-day separation from Jesus (Lk. 2:41-50), and four incidents connected with the Passion: her meeting with Christ on the way to Calvary, the crucifixion, the removal of Christ's body from the cross, and his burial (Mt. 27:31-61; Mk. 15:20-47; Lk. 23:26-56; Jn. 19:17-42). A Mass and Divine Office of the feast were celebrated by the Servites, especially, in the 17th century, and in 1817 Pius VII extended the observance to the whole Church.

Our Lady of the Rosary, Oct. 7, memorial. Commemorates the Virgin Mary through recall of the mysteries of the Rosary which recapitulate events in her life and the life of Christ. The feast was instituted to commemorate a Christian victory over invading Mohammedan forces at Lepanto on Oct. 7, 1571, and was extended throughout the Church by Clement XI in 1716.

Passion (Palm) Sunday, the Sunday before Easter. Marks the start of Holy Week by recalling the triumphal entry of Christ into Jerusalem at the beginning of the last week of his life (Mt. 21:1-9). A procession and other ceremonies commemorating this event were held in Jerusalem from very early Christian times and were adopted in Rome by the ninth century, when the blessing of palm for the occasion was introduced. Full liturgical observance includes the blessing of palm and a procession before the principal Mass of the day. The Passion, by Matthew, Mark or Luke, is read during the Mass.

Pentecost, also called **Whitsunday,** movable celebration held 50 days after Easter, solemnity. Commemorates the descent of the Holy Spirit upon the Apostles, the preaching of Peter and the other Apostles to Jews in Jerusalem, the baptism and aggregation of some 3,000 persons to the Christian community (Acts 2:1-41). It is regarded as the birthday of the Catholic Church. The original observance of the feast antedated the earliest extant documentary evidence from the third century.

Peter and Paul, Sts., June 29, solemnity. Commemorates the martyrdoms of Peter by crucifixion and Paul by beheading during the Neronian persecution. This joint commemoration of the two greatest Apostles dates at least from 258 at Rome.

Presentation of the Lord (formerly called Purification of the Blessed Virgin Mary, also Candlemas), Feb. 2, feast. Commemorates the presentation of Jesus in the Temple — according to prescriptions of Mosaic Law (Lv. 12:2-8; Ex. 13:2; Lk. 2:22-32) — and the purification of Mary 40 days after his birth. In the East, where the feast antedated fourth century testimony regarding its existence, it was observed primarily as a feast of Our Lord; in the West, where it was adopted later, it was regarded more as a feast of Mary until the calendar reform of 1969. Its date was set for Feb. 2 after the celebration of Christmas was fixed for

256 Holy Days and Feasts — Saints

Dec. 25, late in the fourth century. The blessing of candles, probably in commemoration of Christ who was the Light to enlighten the Gentiles, became common about the 11th century and gave the feast the secondary name of Candlemas.

Queenship of Mary, Aug. 22, memorial. Commemorates the high dignity of Mary as Queen of heaven, angels and men. Universal observance of the memorial was ordered by Pius XII in the encyclical *Ad Caeli Reginam,* Oct. 11, 1954, near the close of a Marian Year observed in connection with the centenary of the proclamation of the dogma of the Immaculate Conception and four years after the proclamation of the dogma of the Assumption. The original date of the memorial was May 31.

Resurrection. See Easter.

Sacred Heart of Jesus, movable observance held on the Friday after the second Sunday after Pentecost (Corpus Christi, in the U.S.), solemnity. The object of the devotion is the divine Person of Christ, whose heart is the symbol of his love for men — for whom he accomplished the work of Redemption. The Mass and Office now used on the feast were prescribed by Pius XI in 1929. Devotion to the Sacred Heart was introduced into the liturgy in the 17th century through the efforts of St. John Eudes who composed an Office and Mass for the feast. It was furthered as the result of the revelations of St. Margaret Mary Alacoque after 1675 and by the work of Claude de la Colombiere, S.J. In 1765, Clement XIII approved a Mass and Office for the feast, and in 1856 Pius IX extended the observance throughout the Roman Rite.

Solemnity of Mary, Mother of God, Jan. 1, holy day of obligation, solemnity. The calendar reform of 1969, in accord with Eastern tradition, reinstated the Marian character of this commemoration on the octave day of Christmas. The former feast of the Circumcision, dating at least from the first half of the sixth century, marked the initiation of Jesus (Lk. 2:21) in Judaism and by analogy focused attention on the initiation of persons in the Christian religion and their incorporation in Christ through baptism. The feast of the Solemnity sup-

plants the former feast of the Maternity of Mary observed on Oct. 11.

Transfiguration of the Lord, Aug. 6, feast. Commemorates the revelation of his divinity by Christ to Peter, James and John on Mt. Tabor (Mt. 17:1-9). The feast, which is very old, was extended throughout the universal Church in 1457 by Callistus III.

Trinity, Most Holy, movable observance held on the Sunday after Pentecost, solemnity. Commemorates the most sublime mystery of the Christian faith, i.e., that there are Three Divine Persons — Father, Son and Holy Spirit — in one God (Mt. 28:18-20). A votive Mass of the Most Holy Trinity dates from the seventh century; an Office was composed in the 10th century; in 1334, John XXII extended the feast to the universal Church.

Triumph of the Cross, Sept. 14, feast. Commemorates the finding of the cross on which Christ was crucified, in 326 through the efforts of St. Helena, mother of Constantine; the consecration of the Basilica of the Holy Sepulchre nearly 10 years later: and the recovery in 628 or 629 by Emperor Heraclius of a major portion of the cross which had been removed by the Persians from its place of veneration at Jerusalem. The feast originated in Jerusalem and spread through the East before being adopted in the West. General adoption followed the building at Rome of the Basilica of the Holy Cross "in Jerusalem," so called because it was the place of enshrinement of a major portion of the cross of crucifixion.

Visitation, May 31, feast. Commemorates Mary's visit to her cousin Elizabeth after the Annunciation and before the birth of John the Baptist, the precursor of Christ (Lk. 1:39-47). The feast had a medieval origin and was observed in the Franciscan Order before being extended throughout the Church by Urban VI in 1389. It is one of the feasts of the Incarnation and is notable for its recall of the Magnificat, one of the few New Testament canticles, which acknowledges the unique gifts of God to Mary because of her role in the redemptive work of Christ. The canticle is recited at Evening Prayer in the Liturgy of the Hours.

SAINTS

Biographical sketches of additional saints are under other Almanac titles. See Index.

An asterisk with a feast date indicates that a memorial or feast is observed according to the general Roman-Rite calendars.

Adjutor, St. (d. 1131): Norman knight; fought in First Crusade; monk-recluse after his return; legendary accounts of incidents on journey to Crusade probably account for his patronage of yachtsmen; Apr. 30.

Agatha, St. (d. c. 250): Sicilian virgin-martyr; her intercession credited in Sicily with stopping eruptions of Mt. Etna; patron of nurses; Feb. 5*.

Agnes, St. (d. c. 304): Roman virgin-martyr; martyred at age of 10 or 12; patron of young girls; Jan. 21*.

Aloysius Gonzaga, St. (1568-1591): Italian Jesuit; died while nursing plague-stricken; canonized 1726; patron of youth; June 21*.

Amand, St. (d. c. 676): Apostle of Belgium; b. France; established monasteries throughout Belgium; Feb. 6.

Andre Bessette, Bl. (Bro. Andre) (1845-1937): Canadian Holy Cross Brother; prime mover in building of St. Joseph's Oratory, Montreal; beatified May 23, 1982; Jan. 6* (U.S.).

Andre Grasset de Saint Sauveur, Bl. (1758-1792): Canadian priest; martyred in France, Sept. 2, 1792, during the Revolution; one of a group called the Martyrs of Paris who were beatified in 1926; Sept. 2.

Andrew Corsini, St. (1302-1373): Italian Carmelite; bishop of Fiesoli; mediator between quarrelsome Italian states; canonized 1629; Feb. 4.

Andrew Fournet, St. (1752-1834): French priest; co-founder with St. Jeanne Elizabeth des Anges of the Congregation of Daughters of the Cross; canonized 1933; May 13.

Angela Merici, St. (1474-1540): Italian nun; foundress of Institute of St. Ursula, 1535, the first teaching order of nuns in the Church; canonized 1807; Jan. 27*.

Anne Mary Javouhey, Bl. (1779-1851): French virgin; foundress of Institute of St. Joseph of Cluny, 1812; beatified 1950; July 15.

Ansgar, St. (801-865): Bishop, Benedictine monk; b. near Amiens; missionary in Denmark, Sweden, Norway and Northern Germany; apostle of Denmark; Feb. 3*.

Anthony Abbot, St. (c. 251-c. 354): Egyptian hermit; patriarch of all monks; established communities for hermits which became models for monastic life, especially in the East; friend and supporter of St. Athanasius in the latter's struggle with the Arians; Jan. 17*.

Anthony Mary Claret, St. (1807-1870): Spanish priest; founder of Missionary Sons of the Immaculate Heart of Mary (Claretians), 1849; archbishop of Santiago, Cuba, 1851-57; canonized 1950; Oct. 24*.

Anthony Mary Zaccaria, St. (1502-1539): Italian priest; founder of Barnabites (Clerks Regular of St. Paul), 1530; canonized 1897; July 5*.

Apollonia, St. (d. 249): Deaconess of Alexandria; martyred during persecution of Decius; her patronage of dentists probably rests on tradition that her teeth were broken by pincers by her persecutors; Feb. 9.

Augustine of Canterbury, St. (d. 604 or 605): Italian missionary; apostle of the English; sent by Pope Gregory I with 40 monks to evangelize England; arrived there 597; first archbishop of Canterbury; May 27*.

Benedict of Nursia, St. (c. 480-547): Abbot; founder of monasticism in Western Europe; established monastery at Monte Cassino; proclaimed patron of Europe by Paul VI in 1964; July 11*.

Benedict the Black (il Moro), St. (1526-1589): Sicilian Franciscan; born a slave; joined Franciscans as lay brother; appointed guardian and novice master; canonized 1807; Apr. 4.

Bernadette Soubirous, St. (1844-1879): French peasant girl favored with series of visions of Blessed Virgin Mary at Lourdes (see Lourdes Apparitions); joined Institute of Sisters of Notre Dame at Nevers, 1866; canonized 1933; Apr. 16.

Bernard of Menthon, St. (d. 1081): Italian priest; founded Alpine hospices near the two passes named for him; patron of mountaineers; May 28.

Bernardine of Feltre, Bl. (1439-1494): Italian Franciscan preacher; a founder of montes pietatis; Sept. 28.

Bernardine of Siena, St. (1380-1444): Italian Franciscan; noted preacher and missioner; spread of devotion to Holy Name is attributed to him; represented in art holding to his breast the monogram IHS; canonized 1450; May 20*.

Blase, St. (d. c. 316): Armenian bishop; martyr; the blessing of throats on his feast day derives from tradition that he miraculously saved the life of a boy who had half-swallowed a fish bone; Feb. 3*.

Boniface (Winfrid), St. (d. 754): English Benedictine; bishop, martyr; apostle of Germany; established monastery at Fulda which became center of German missionary work; archbishop of Mainz; martyred near Dukkum in Holland; June 5*.

Brendan, St. (c. 489-583): Irish abbot; founded monasteries; his patronage of sailors probably rests on tradition that he made a seven-year voyage in search of a fabled paradise; called Brendan the Navigator; May 16.

Bridget (Brigid), St. (c. 450-525): Irish nun; founded nunnery at Kildare, the first erected on Irish soil; patron, with Sts. Patrick and Columba, of Ireland; Feb. 1.

Bridget (Birgitta), St. (c. 1303-1373): Swedish mystic; widow; foundress of Order of Our Savior (Brigittines); canonized 1391; wrote *Revelationes*, accounts of her visions; patroness of Sweden; July 23*.

Bruno, St. (1030-1101): German monk; founded Carthusians, 1084, in France; Oct. 6*.

Cabrini, Mother: See Index.

Cajetan of Thiene, St. (1480-1547): Italian lawyer; religious reformer; a founder of Oratory of Divine Love, forerunner of the Theatines; canonized 1671; Aug. 7*.

Callistus I, St. (d. 222): Pope, 217-222; martyr; condemned Sabellianism and other heresies; advocated a policy of mercy toward repentant sinners; Oct. 14*.

Camillus de Lellis, St. (1550-1614): Italian priest; founder of Camillians (Ministers of the Sick); canonized 1746; patron of the sick and of nurses; July 14*.

Casimir, St. (1458-1484): Polish prince; grand duke of Lithuania; noted for his piety; buried at cathedral in Vilna, Lithuania; canonized 1521, patron of Poland and Lithuania; Mar. 4*.

Cassian, St. (d. 298): Roman martyr; an official court stenographer who declared himself a Christian; patron of stenographers; Dec. 3.

Catherine Laboure, St. (1806-1876): French nun; favored with series of visions; first Miraculous Medal (see Index) struck as the result of one of the visions; canonized 1947; Dec. 31.

Catherine of Bologna, St. (1413-1463): Italian Poor Clare; mystic, writer, artist; canonized 1712; patron of artists; Mar. 9.

Cecilia, St. (2nd-3rd century): Roman virgin-martyr; traditional patron of musicians; Nov. 22*.

Charles Borromeo, St. (1538-1584): Italian cardinal; nephew of Pope Pius IV; cardinal bishop of Milan; influential figure in Church reform in Italy; promoted education of clergy; canonized 1610; Nov. 4*.

Charles Lwanga and Companions, Sts. (d. 1886 and 1887): Martyrs of Uganda; pages of King Mwanga of Uganda; Charles Lwanga and 12 companions were martyred near Rubaga, June 3, 1886; the other nine were martyred between May 26, 1886, and Jan. 27, 1887; canonized 1964; first martyrs of black Africa; June 3*.

Christopher, St. (3rd cent.): Early Christian

martyr inscribed in Roman calendar about 1550; feast relegated to particular calendars because of legendary nature of accounts of his life; traditional patron of travelers; July 25.

Clare, St. (1194-1253): Foundress of Poor Clares; b. at Assisi; later joined in religious life her sisters Agnes and Beatrice, and her mother Ortolana; canonized 1255; patroness of television; Aug. 11*.

Clement I, St. (d. c. 100): Pope, 88-97; third successor of St. Peter; wrote important letter to Church in Corinth settling disputes there; venerated as a martyr; Nov. 23*.

Columba, St. (521-597): Irish monk; founded monasteries in Ireland; missionary in Scotland; established monastery at Iona which became the center for conversion of Picts, Scots, and Northern English; Scotland's most famous saint; June 9.

Columban, St. (545-615): Irish monk; scholar; founded monasteries in England and Brittany (famous abbey of Luxeuil), forced into exile because of his criticism of Frankish court; spent last years in northern Italy where he founded abbey at Bobbio; Nov. 23*.

Contardo Ferrini, Bl. (1859-1902): Italian secular Franciscan; model of the Catholic professor; beatified 1947; patron of universities; Oct. 17.

Cornelius, St. (d. 253): Pope, 251-253; promoted a policy of mercy with respect to readmission of repentant Christians who had fallen away during the persecution of Decius (*lapsi*); banished from Rome during persecution of Gallus; regarded as a martyr; Sept. 16 (with Cyprian)*.

Cosmas and Damian, Sts. (d. c. 303): Arabian twin brothers; physicians who were martyred during Diocletian persecution; patrons of physicians; Sept. 26*.

Crispin and Crispinian, Sts. (3rd cent.): Early Christian martyrs; said to have met their deaths in Gaul; patrons of shoemakers, a trade they pursued; Oct. 25.

Crispin of Viterbo, St. (1668-1750); Capuchin brother; beatified 1806; canonized June 20, 1982; May 21.

Cyprian, St. (d. 258): Early ecclesiastical writer; b. Africa; bishop of Carthage, 249-258; supported Pope St. Cornelius concerning the readmission of Christians who had apostasized in time of persecution; erred in his teaching that baptism administered by heretics and schismatics was invalid; wrote *De Unitate;* Sept. 16 (with St. Cornelius)*.

Cyril and Methodius, Sts.: Greek missionaries; brothers venerated as apostles of the Slavs; Cyril (d. 869) and Methodius (d. 885) began their missionary work in Moravia in 863; developed a Slavonic alphabet; eventually their use of the vernacular in the liturgy was approved; declared patrons of Europe with St. Benedict, Dec. 31, 1980; Feb. 14*.

Damasus I, St. (d. 384): Pope, 366-384; opposed Arians and Apollinarians; commissioned St. Jerome to work on Bible translation; developed Roman liturgy; Dec. 11*.

Damian, St.: See Cosmas and Damian, Sts.

David, St. (5th-6th cent.): Welsh monk; founded monastery at Menevia; patron saint of Wales; Mar. 1.

Denis and Companions, Sts. (d. 3rd cent.): Denis, bishop of Paris, and two companions identified by early writers as Rusticus, a priest, and Eleutherius, a deacon; martyred near Paris; Denis is popularly regarded as apostle of France; Oct. 9*.

Dismas, St. (1st cent.): Name given to repentant thief (Good Thief) to whom Jesus promised salvation; regarded as patron of prisoners; Mar. 25.

Dominic, St. (Dominic de Guzman) (1170-1221): Spanish priest; founder of Dominican Order (Friars Preachers), 1215; preached against the Albigensian heresy; a contemporary of St. Francis of Assisi; canonized 1234; Aug. 8*.

Dominic Savio, St. (1842-1857): Italian youth; pupil of St. John Bosco; died before his 15th birthday; canonized 1954; patron of choir boys; Mar. 9.

Dunstan, St. (c. 910-988): English monk; archbishop of Canterbury; initiated reforms in religious life; royal counselor to several kings; considered one of greatest Anglo-Saxon saints; patron of armorers, goldsmiths, locksmiths, jewelers; May 17.

Durocher, Marie-Rose, Bl. (1811-1849): Canadian religious; foundress of Sisters of Holy Names of Jesus and Mary; beatified May 23, 1982; Oct. 6* (in U.S.).

Dymphna, St. (dates uncertain): Nothing certain known of her life; presumably she was an Irish maiden whose relics were discovered at Gheel near Antwerp, Belgium, in the 13th century; since that time many cases of mental illness and epilepsy have been cured at her shrine; patron of those suffering from mental illness; May 15.

Edmund Campion, St. (1540-1581): English Jesuit; convert 1573; martyred at Tyburn; canonized 1970, one of the Forty English and Welsh Martyrs; Dec. 1.

Elizabeth Bayley Seton, St. (1774-1821): American foundress; convert, 1905; founded Sisters of Charity in the U.S.; beatified 1963; canonized Sept. 14, 1975; the first American-born saint; Jan. 4 (U.S.)*.

Elizabeth of Hungary, St. (1207-1231): Queen; became secular Franciscan after death of her husband in 1227; devoted life to poor and destitute; a patron of the Secular Franciscan Order; Nov. 17*.

Elizabeth of Portugal, St. (1271-1336): Queen of Portugal; b. Spain; retired to Poor Clare convent as a secular Franciscan after the death of her husband; July 4*.

Erasmus, St. (d. 303): Life surrounded by legend; martyred during Diocletian persecution; patron of sailors; June 2.

Ethelbert, St. (552-676): King of Kent; baptized by St. Augustine 597; issued legal code; furthered spread of Christianity; Feb. 24.

Euphrasia Pelletier, St. (1796-1868): French nun; founded Sisters of the Good Shepherd at Angers, 1829; canonized 1940; Apr. 24.

Eusebius of Vercelli, St. (283-370): Italian bishop; exiled from his see for a time because of his opposition to Arianism; considered a martyr because of sufferings he endured; Aug. 2*.

Fabian, St. (d. 250): Pope, 236-250; martyred under Decius; Jan. 20*.

Felicity, St.: See Perpetua and Felicity, Sts.

Ferdinand III, St. (1198-1252): King of Castile and Leon; waged successful crusade against Mohammedans in Spain; founded university at Salamanca; canonized 1671; May 30.

Fiacre, St. (d. c. 670): Irish hermit; patron of gardeners; Aug. 30.

Fidelis of Sigmaringen, St. (Mark Rey) (1577-1622): German Capuchin; lawyer before he joined the Capuchins; missionary to Swiss Protestants; stabbed to death by peasants who were told he was agent of Austrian emperor; Apr. 24*.

Frances of Rome, St. (1384-1440): Italian model for housewives and widows; happily married for 40 years; after death of her husband in 1436 joined community of Benedictine Oblates she had founded; canonized 1608; patron of motorists; Mar. 9*.

Frances Xavier Cabrini, St. (Mother Cabrini) (1850-1917): American foundress; b. Italy; foundress of Missionary Sisters of the Sacred Heart, 1877; settled in the U.S. 1889; became an American citizen at Seattle 1909; worked among Italian immigrants; canonized 1946, the first American citizen so honored; Nov. 13 (U.S.)*.

Francis Borgia, St. (1510-1572): Spanish Jesuit; joined Jesuits after death of his wife in 1546; became general of the Order, 1565; Oct. 10.

Francis of Assisi, St. (Giovanni di Bernardone) (1182-1226): Founder of the Franciscans, 1209; received stigmata 1224; canonized 1228; one of best known and best loved saints; patron of Italy, Catholic Action and ecologists; Oct. 4*.

Francis of Paola, St. (1416-1507): Italian hermit; founder of Minim Friars; Apr. 2*.

Francis Xavier, St. (1506-1552): Spanish Jesuit; missionary to Far East; canonized 1602; patron of foreign missions; considered one of greatest Christian missionaries; Dec. 3*.

Gabriel of the Sorrowful Mother, St. (Francis Possenti) (1838-1862): Italian Passionist; died while a scholastic; canonized 1920; Feb. 27.

Genesius, St. (d. c. 300): Roman actor; according to legend, was converted while performing a burlesque of Christian baptism and was subsequently martyred; patron of actors.

Genevieve, St. (422-500): French nun; a patroness and protectress of Paris; events of her life not authenticated; Jan. 3.

George, St. (d. c. 300): Martyr, probably during Diocletian persecution in Palestine; all other incidents of his life, including story of the dragon, are legendary; patron of England; Apr. 23*.

Gerard Majella, St. (1725-1755): Italian Redemptorist lay brother; noted for supernatural occurrences in his life including bilocation and reading of consciences; canonized 1904; patron of mothers; Oct. 16.

Gertrude, St. (1256-1302): German mystic; writer; helped spread devotion to the Sacred Heart; Nov. 16*.

Gregory VII (Hildebrand), St. (1020?-1085): Pope, 1075-1085; Benedictine monk; adviser to several popes; as pope, strengthened interior life of Church and fought against lay investiture; driven from Rome by Henry IV; died in exile; May 25*.

Gregory the Illuminator, St. (257-332): Martyr; bishop; apostle and patron saint of Armenia; helped free Armenia from the Persians; Sept. 30.

Hedwig, St. (1174-1243): Moravian noblewoman; married duke of Silesia, head of Polish royal family; fostered religious life in country; canonized 1266; Oct. 16.

Helena, St. (250-330): Empress; mother of Constantine the Great; associated with discovery of the True Cross; Aug. 18.

Henry, St. (972-1024): Bavarian emperor; cooperated with Benedictine abbeys in restoration of ecclesiastical and social discipline; canonized 1146; July 13*.

Hippolytus, St. (d. c. 236): Roman priest; opposed Pope St. Callistus I in his teaching about the readmission of Christians who had apostasized during time of persecution; elected antipope; reconciled before his martyrdom; important ecclesiastical writer; Aug. 13*.

Hubert, St. (d. 727): Bishop; his patronage of hunters is based on legend that he was converted while hunting; Nov. 3.

Hugh of Cluny (the Great), St. (1024-1109): Abbot of Benedictine foundation at Cluny; supported popes in efforts to reform ecclesiastical abuses; canonized 1120; Apr. 29.

Ignatius of Antioch, St. (d. c. 107): Early ecclesiastical writer; martyr; bishop of Antioch in Syria for 40 years; Oct. 17*.

Ignatius of Loyola, St. (1491-1556): Spanish soldier; renounced military career after recovering from wounds received at siege of Pampeluna (Pamplona) in 1521; founded Society of Jesus (Jesuits), 1534, at Paris; canonized 1622; author *The Book of Spiritual Exercises;* July 31*.

Irenaeus of Lyons, St. (130-202): Early ecclesiastical writer; opposed Gnosticism; bishop of Lyons; traditionally regarded as a martyr; June 28*.

Isidore the Farmer, St. (d. 1170): Spanish layman; farmer; canonized 1622; patron of farmers; May 15 (U.S.).*

Jane Frances de Chantal, St. (1572-1641): French widow; foundress, under guidance of St. Francis de Sales, of Order of the Visitation; canonized 1767; Dec. 12*.

Januarius (Gennaro), St. (d. 304): Bishop of Benevento; martyred during Diocletian persecution; fame rests on liquefication of some of his blood preserved in a phial at Naples, an unexplained phenomenon which has occurred regularly several times each year for over 400 years; declared patron of Campania region around Naples, 1980; Sept. 19*.

Jerome Emiliani, St. (1481-1537): Venetian priest; founded Somascan Fathers, 1532, for care of orphans; canonized 1767; patron of orphans and abandoned children; Feb. 8*.

Joan of Arc, St. (1412-1431): French heroine, called The Maid of Orleans, La Pucelle; led French army against English invaders; captured by Burgundians, turned over to ecclesiastical court on charge of heresy, found guilty and burned at the stake; her innocence was declared in 1456; canonized 1920; patroness of France; May 30.

John I, St. (d. 526): Pope, 523-526; martyr; May 18*.

John Baptist de la Salle, St. (1651-1719): French priest; founder of Brothers of the Christian Schools, 1680; canonized 1900; Apr. 7*.

John Berchmans, St. (1599-1621): Belgian Jesuit scholastic; patron of Mass servers; canonized 1888; Aug. 13.

John Bosco, St. (1815-1888): Italian priest; founded Salesians, 1859, for education of boys and cofounded the Daughters of Mary Help of Christians for education of girls; canonized 1934; Jan. 31*.

John Capistran, St. (1386-1456): Italian Franciscan; preacher; papal diplomat; canonized 1690; Oct. 23*.

John Eudes, St. (1601-1680): French priest; founder of Sisters of Our Lady of Charity of Refuge, 1642, and Congregation of Jesus-Mary (Eudists), 1643; canonized 1925; Aug. 19*.

John Fisher, St. (1469-1535): English prelate; theologian; martyr; bishop of Rochester, cardinal; refused to recognize validity of Henry VIII's marriage to Anne Boleyn; upheld supremacy of the pope; beheaded for refusing to acknowledge Henry as head of the Church; canonized 1935; June 22 (with St. Thomas More)*.

John Kanty (Cantius), St. (1395-1473): Polish theologian; canonized 1767; Dec. 23*.

John Leonardi, St. (1550-1609): Italian priest; worked among prisoners and the sick; founded Clerics Regular of the Mother of God; canonized 1938; Oct. 9*.

John Nepomucene, St. (1345-1393): Bohemian priest; regarded as a martyr; canonized 1729; patron of Czechoslovakia; May 16.

John Nepomucene Neumann, St. (1811-1860): American prelate; b. Bohemia; ordained in New York 1836; missionary among Germans near Niagara Falls before joining Redemptorists, 1840; bishop of Philadelphia, 1852; first bishop in U.S. to prescribe Forty Hours devotion in his diocese; beatified 1963; canonized June 19, 1977; Jan. 5 (U.S.)*.

John of God, St. (1495-1550): Portuguese founder; his work among the sick poor led to foundation of Brothers Hospitallers of St. John of God, 1540, in Spain; canonized 1690; patron of sick, hospitals, nurses; Mar. 8*.

John Vianney (Cure of Ars), St. (1786-1859): French parish priest; noted confessor, spent 16 to 18 hours a day in confessional; canonized 1925; patron of parish priests; Aug. 4*.

Josaphat Kuncevyc, St. (1584-1623): Basilian monk; b. Poland; archbishop of Polotsk, Lithuania; worked for reunion of separated Easterners; martyred by mob of schismatics; canonized 1867; Nov. 12*.

Joseph Benedict Cottolengo, St. (1786-1842): Italian priest; established Little Houses of Divine Providence (Piccolo Casa) for care of orphans and the sick; canonized 1934; Apr. 30.

Joseph Cafasso, St. (1811-1860): Italian priest;

renowned confessor; promoted devotion to Blessed Sacrament; canonized 1947; June 22.

Joseph Calasanz, St. (1556-1648): Spanish priest; founder of Piarists (Order of Pious Schools); canonized 1767; Aug. 25*.

Joseph of Cupertino, St. (1603-1663): Italian Franciscan; noted for remarkable incidents of levitation; canonized 1767; Sept. 18.

Jugan, Jeanne Bl. (1792-1879): French religious; foundress of Little Sisters of the Poor; beatified Oct. 5, 1982; Aug. 29.

Justin Martyr, St. (100-165): Early ecclesiastical writer; *Apologies for the Christian Religion, Dialog with the Jew Tryphon;* martyred at Rome; June 1*.

Kateri Tekakwitha, Bl. (1656-1680): "Lily of the Mohawks." Indian maiden born at Ossernenon (Auriesville), N.Y.; baptized Christian, Easter, 1676, by Jesuit missionary Father Jacques de Lambertville; lived life devoted to prayer, penitential practices and care of sick and aged in Christian village near Montreal; buried at Caughnawaga, Ont.; beatified June 22, 1980; July 14* (in U.S.).

Ladislaus, Saint (1040-1095): King of Hungary; supported Pope Gregory VII against Henry IV; canonized 1192; June 27.

Lawrence, St. (d. 258): Widely venerated martyr who suffered death, according to a long-standing but unverifiable legend, by being roasted alive on a gridiron; Aug. 10*.

Leonard of Port Maurice, St. (1676-1751): Italian Franciscan; ascetical writer; preached missions throughout Italy; canonized 1867; patron of parish missions; Nov. 26.

Louis IX, St. (1215-1270): King of France, 1226-1270; participated in Sixth Crusade; patron of Secular Franciscan Order; canonized 1297; Aug. 25*.

Louis de Montfort, St. (1673-1716): French priest; founder of Sisters of Divine Wisdom, 1703, and Missionaries of Company of Mary, 1715; wrote *True Devotion to the Blessed Virgin;* canonized 1947; Apr. 28.

Louise de Marillac, St. (1591-1660): French foundress, with St. Vincent de Paul, of the Sisters of Charity; canonized 1934; Mar. 15.

Lucy, St. (d. 304): Sicilian maiden; martyred during Diocletian persecution; one of most widely venerated early virgin-martyrs; patron of Syracuse, Sicily; invoked by those suffering from eye diseases (based on legend that she offered her eyes to a suitor who admired them); Dec. 13*.

Marcellinus and Peter, Sts. (d.c. 304): Early Roman martyrs; June 2*.

Margaret Clitherow, St. (1556-1586): English martyr; convert shortly after her marriage; one of Forty Martyrs of England and Wales; canonized 1970; Mar. 25.

Margaret Mary Alacoque, St. (1647-1690): French nun; spread devotion to Sacred Heart in accordance with revelations made to her in 1675 (see Sacred Heart); canonized 1920; Oct. 16*.

Margaret of Scotland, St. (1050-1093): Queen of Scotland; noted for solicitude for the poor and promotion of justice; canonized 1251; Nov. 16*.

Saints   261

Maria Goretti, St. (1890-1902): Italian virgin-martyr; a model of purity; canonized 1950; July 6*.

Mariana Paredes of Jesus, St. (1618-1645): South American recluse; Lily of Quito; canonized, 1950; May 26.

Martha, St. (1st cent.): Sister of Lazarus and Mary of Bethany; Gospel accounts record her concern for homely details; patron of cooks; July 29*.

Martin I, St. (d. 655): Pope, 649; banished from Rome by emperor because of his condemnation of Monothelites; considered a martyr; Apr. 13*.

Martin of Tours, St. (316-397): Bishop of Tours; opposed Arianism and Priscillianism; pioneer of Western monasticism, before St. Benedict; Nov. 11*.

Mary Magdalene, St. (1st cent.): Gospels record her as devoted follower of Christ to whom he appeared after the Resurrection; her identification with Mary of Bethany (sister of Martha and Lazarus) and the woman sinner (Lk 7:36-50) has been questioned; July 22*.

Mary Magdalene de Pazzi, St. (1566-1607): Italian Carmelite nun; recipient of mystical experiences; canonized 1669; May 25*.

Maximilian Kolbe, St. (1894-1941): Polish Conventual Franciscan; prisoner at Auschwitz who heroically offered his life in place of a fellow prisoner; beatified 1971, canonized 1982; Aug. 14.

Methodius, St.: See Index.

Monica, St. (332-387): Mother of St. Augustine; model of a patient mother; her feast is observed in the Roman calendar the day before her son's; Aug. 27*.

Nereus and Achilleus, Sts. (d. c. 100): Early Christian martyrs; soldiers who, according to legend, were baptized by St. Peter; May 12*.

Nicholas of Myra, St. (4th cent.): Bishop of Myra in Asia Minor; one of most popular saints in both East and West; most of the incidents of his life are based on legend; patron of Russia; Dec. 6*.

Nicholas of Tolentino, St. (1245-1365): Italian hermit; famed preacher; canonized 1446; Sept. 10.

Norbert, St. (1080-1134): German bishop; founder of Norbertines or Premonstratensians, 1120; promoted reform of the clergy, devotion to Blessed Sacrament; canonized 1582; June 6*.

Odilia, St. (d. c. 720): Benedictine abbess; according to legend she was born blind, abandoned by her family and adopted by a convent where her sight was miraculously restored; patron of blind; Dec. 13.

Oliver Plunket, St. (1629-1681): Irish martyr; theologian; archbishop of Armagh and primate of Ireland; beatified 1920; canonized, 1975; July 1.

Pancras, St. (d. c. 304): Roman martyr; May 12*.

Paschal Baylon, St. (1540-1592): Spanish Franciscan lay brother; spent life as door-keeper in various Franciscan friaries; defended doctrine of Real Presence in Blessed Sacrament; canonized 1690; patron of all Eucharistic confraternities and congresses, 1897; May 17.

Patrick, St. (389-461): Famous missionary of Ireland; began missionary work in Ireland about 432; organized the Church there and established it on a lasting foundation; patron of Ireland, with Sts. Bridget and Columba; Mar. 17*.

Paul Miki and Companions, Sts. (d. 1597): Martyrs of Japan; Paul Miki, Jesuit, and twenty-five other priests and laymen were martyred at Nagasaki; canonized 1862, the first canonized martyrs of the Far East; Feb. 6*.

Paul of the Cross, St. (1694-1775): Italian religious; founder of the Passionists; canonized 1867; Oct. 19*.

Paulinus of Nola, St. (d. 451): Bishop of Nola (Spain); writer; June 22*.

Peregrine, St. (1260-1347): Italian Servite; invoked against cancer (he was miraculously cured of cancer of the foot after a vision); canonized 1726; May 1.

Perpetua and Felicity, Sts. (d. 203): Martyrs; Mar. 7*.

Peter Chanel, St. (1803-1841): French Marist; missionary to Oceania, where he was martyred; canonized 1954; Apr. 28*.

Peter Gonzalez, St. (1190-1246): Spanish Dominican; worked among sailors; court chaplain and confessor of King St. Ferdinand of Castile; patron of sailors; Apr. 14.

Peter of Alcantara, St. (1499-1562): Spanish Franciscan; mystic; initiated Franciscan reform; confessor of St. Teresa of Avila; canonized 1669; Oct. 19.

Philip Neri, St. (1515-1595): Italian religious; founded Congregation of the Oratory; considered a second apostle of Rome because of his mission activities there; canonized 1622; May 26*.

Philip of Jesus, St. (1571-1597): Mexican Franciscan; martyred at Nagasaki, Japan; canonized 1862; patron of Mexico City; Feb. 6*.

Pius V, St. (1504-1572): Pope, 1566-1572; enforced decrees of Council of Trent; organized expedition against Turks resulting in victory at Lepanto; canonized 1712; Apr. 30*.

Polycarp, St. (2nd cent.): Bishop of Smyrna; ecclesiastical writer; martyr; Feb. 23*.

Pontian, St. (d. c. 235): Pope, 230-235; exiled to Sardinia by the emperor; regarded as a martyr; Aug. 13 (with Hippolytus)*.

Raymond Nonnatus, St. (d. 1240): Spanish Mercedarian; cardinal; devoted his life to ransoming captives from the Moors; Aug. 31.

Raymond of Penyafort, St. (1175-1275): Spanish Dominican; confessor of Gregory IX; systematized and codified canon law, in effect until 1917; master general of Dominicans, 1238; canonized 1601; Jan. 7*.

Rita of Cascia, St. (1381-1457): Widow; cloistered Augustinian religious of Umbria; invoked in impossible and desperate cases; May 22.

Robert Southwell, St. (1561-1595): English Jesuit; poet; martyred at Tyburn; canonized 1970, one of the Forty English and Welsh Martyrs; Feb. 21.

Roch, St. (1350-1379): French layman; pilgrim; devoted life to care of plague-stricken; widely venerated; invoked against pestilence; Aug. 17.

Romuald, St. (951-1027): Italian monk; founded Camaldolese Benedictines; June 19*.

Rose of Lima, St. (1586-1617): Peruvian Dominican tertiary; first native-born saint of the New World; canonized 1671; Aug. 23*.

Scholastica, St. (d. c. 559): Sister of St. Benedict; regarded as first nun of the Benedictine Order; Feb. 10*.

Sebastian, St. (3rd cent.): Roman martyr; traditionally pictured as a handsome youth with arrows; martyred; patron of athletes, archers; Jan. 20*.

Seven Holy Founders of the Servants of Mary (Buonfiglio Monaldo, Alexis Falconieri, Benedict dell'Antello, Bartholomew Amidei, Ricovero Uguccione, Gerardino Sostegni, John Buonagiunta Monetti): Florentine youths who founded Servites, 1233, in obedience to a vision; canonized 1888; Feb. 17*.

Sixtus II and Companions, Sts. (d. 258): Sixtus, pope 257-258, and four deacons, martyrs; Aug. 7*.

Stanislaus, St. (1030-1079): Polish bishop; martyr; canonized 1253; Apr. 11*.

Stephen, St. (d. c. 33): First Christian martyr; chosen by the Apostles as the first of the seven deacons; stoned to death; Dec. 26*.

Stephen, St. (975-1038): King; apostle of Hungary; welded Magyars into national unity; canonized 1087; Aug. 16*.

Sylvester I, St. (d. 335): Pope 314-335; first ecumenical council held at Nicaea during his pontificate; Dec. 31*.

Tarcisius, St. (d. 3rd cent.): Early martyr; according to tradition, was martyred while carrying the Blessed Sacrament to some Christians in prison; patron of first communicants; Aug. 15.

Therese Couderc, St. (1805-1885): French religious; foundress of the Religious of Our Lady of the Retreat in the Cenacle, 1827; canonized 1970; Sept. 26.

Therese of Lisieux, St. (1873-1897): French Carmelite nun; b. Therese Martin; allowed to enter Carmel at 15, died nine years later of tuberculosis; her "little way" of spiritual perfection became widely known through her spiritual autobiography; despite her obscure life, became one of the most popular saints; canonized 1925; patron of foreign missions; Oct. 1*.

Thomas Becket, St. (1118-1170): English martyr; archbishop of Canterbury; chancellor under Henry II; murdered for upholding rights of the Church; canonized 1173; Dec. 29*.

Thomas More, St. (1478-1535): English martyr; statesman, chancellor under Henry VIII; author of *Utopia;* opposed Henry's divorce, refused to renounce authority of the papacy; beheaded; canonized 1935; June 22 (with St. John Fisher)*.

Timothy, St. (d. c. 97): Bishop of Ephesus; disciple and companion of St. Paul; martyr; Jan. 26*.

Titus, St. (d. c. 96): Bishop; companion of St. Paul; recipient of one of Paul's epistles; Jan. 26*.

Valentine, St. (d. 269): Priest, physician; martyred at Rome; legendary patron of lovers; Feb. 14.

Vincent, St. (d. 304): Spanish deacon; martyr; Jan. 22*.

Vincent de Paul, St. (1581?-1660): French priest; founder of Congregation of the Mission (Vincentians, Lazarists) and co-founder of Sisters of Charity; declared patron of all charitable organizations and works by Leo XIII; canonized 1737; Sept. 27*.

Vincent Ferrer, St. (1350-1418): Spanish Dominican; famed preacher; Apr. 5*.

Wenceslaus, St. (d. 935): Duke of Bohemia; martyr; patron of Bohemia; Sept. 28*.

Zita, St. (1218-1278): Italian maid; noted for charity to poor; patron of domestics.

SAINTS—PATRONS AND INTERCESSORS

A patron is a saint who is venerated as a special intercessor before God. Most patrons have been so designated as the result of popular devotion and long-standing custom. In many cases, the fact of existing patronal devotion is clear despite historical obscurity regarding its origin. The Church has made official designation of relatively few patrons; in such cases, the dates of designation are given in the list below. The theological background of the patronage of saints includes the dogmas of the Mystical Body of Christ and the Communion of Saints.

Listed below are patron saints of occupations and professions, and saints whose intercession is sought for special needs.

Accountants: Matthew.
Actors: Genesius.
Advertisers: Bernardine of Siena (May 20, 1960).
Alpinists: Bernard of Menthon (Aug. 20, 1923).
Altar boys: John Berchmans.
Anesthetists: Rene Goupil.
Angina: Swithbert.
Archers: Sebastian.
Architects: Thomas, Apostle.
Armorers: Dunstan.

Art: Catherine of Bologna.
Artists: Luke, Catherine of Bologna.
Astronomers: Dominic.
Athletes: Sebastian.
Authors: Francis de Sales.
Aviators: Our Lady of Loreto (1920), Therese of Lisieux, Joseph of Cupertino.
Bakers: Elizabeth of Hungary, Nicholas.
Bankers: Matthew.
Barbers: Cosmas and Damian, Louis.
Barren women: Anthony of Padua, Felicity.
Basket-makers: Anthony, Abbot.
Blacksmiths: Dunstan.
Blind: Odilia, Raphael.
Blood banks: Januarius.
Bodily ills: Our Lady of Lourdes.
Bookbinders: Peter Celestine.
Bookkeepers: Matthew.
Booksellers: John of God.
Boy Scouts: George.
Brewers: Augustine of Hippo, Luke, Nicholas of Myra.
Bricklayers: Stephen.
Brides: Nicholas of Myra.
Brush makers: Anthony, Abbot.
Builders: Vincent Ferrer.

Butchers: Anthony (Abbot), Luke.
Cab drivers: Fiacre.
Cabinetmakers: Anne.
Cancer patients: Peregrine.
Canonists: Raymond of Peñafort.
Carpenters: Joseph.
Catechists: Viator, Charles Borromeo, Robert Bellarmine.
Catholic Action: Francis of Assisi (1916).
Chandlers: Ambrose, Bernard of Clairvaux.
Charitable societies: Vincent de Paul (May 12, 1885).
Children: Nicholas of Myra.
Children of Mary: Agnes, Maria Goretti.
Choir boys: Dominic Savio (June 8, 1956), Holy Innocents.
Church: Joseph (Dec. 8, 1870).
Clerics: Gabriel of the Sorrowful Mother.
Comedians: Vitus.
Communications personnel: Bernardine.
Confessors: Alphonsus Liguori (Apr. 26, 1950), John Nepomucene.
Convulsive children: Scholastica.
Cooks: Lawrence, Martha.
Coopers: Nicholas of Myra.
Coppersmiths: Maurus.
Dairy workers: Brigid.
Deaf: Francis de Sales.
Dentists: Apollonia.
Desperate situations: Gregory of Neocaesarea, Jude Thaddeus, Rita of Cascia.
Dietitians (in hospitals): Martha.
Dyers: Sts. Maurice and Lydia.
Dying: Joseph.
Ecologists: Francis of Assisi (Nov. 29, 1979).
Editors: John Bosco.
Emigrants: Frances Xavier Cabrini (Sept. 8, 1950).
Epilepsy: Vitus.
Engineers: Ferdinand III.
Eucharistic congresses and societies: Paschal Baylon (Nov. 28, 1897).
Expectant mothers: Raymund Nonnatus, Gerard Majella.
Eye diseases: Lucy.
Falsely accused: Raymund Nonnatus.
Farmers: George, Isidore.
Farriers: John the Baptist.
Firemen: Florian.
Fire prevention: Catherine of Siena.
First communicants: Tarcisius.
Fishermen: Andrew.
Florists: Therese of Lisieux.
Forest workers: John Gualbert.
Foundlings: Holy Innocents.
Fullers: Anastasius the Fuller, James the Less.
Funeral directors: Joseph of Arimathea, Dismas.
Gardeners: Adelard, Tryphon, Fiacre, Phocas.
Glassworkers: Luke.
Goldsmiths: Dunstan, Anastasius.
Gravediggers: Anthony, Abbot.
Greetings: Valentine.
Grocers: Michael.
Hairdressers: Martin de Porres.
Happy meetings: Raphael.
Hatters: Severus of Ravenna, James the Less.

Haymakers: Gervase and Protase.
Headache sufferers: Teresa of Avila.
Heart patients: John of God.
Hospital administrators: Basil the Great, Frances X. Cabrini.
Hospitals: Camillus de Lellis and John of God (June 22, 1886), Jude Thaddeus.
Housewives: Anne.
Hunters: Hubert, Eustachius.
Infantrymen: Maurice.
Innkeepers: Amand, Martha.
Invalids: Roch.
Jewelers: Eligius, Dunstan.
Journalists: Francis de Sales (Apr. 26, 1923).
Jurists: John Capistran.
Laborers: Isidore, James, John Bosco.
Lawyers: Ivo, Genesius, Thomas More.
Learning: Ambrose.
Librarians: Jerome.
Lighthouse keepers: Venerius.
Locksmiths: Dunstan.
Maids: Zita.
Marble workers: Clement I.
Mariners: Michael, Nicholas of Tolentino.
Medical record librarians: Raymond of Peñafort.
Medical social workers: John Regis.
Medical technicians: Albert the Great.
Mentally ill: Dymphna.
Merchants: Francis of Assisi, Nicholas of Myra.
Messengers: Gabriel.
Metal workers: Eligius.
Millers: Arnulph, Victor.
Missions, Foreign: Francis Xavier (Mar. 25, 1904), Therese of Lisieux (Dec. 14, 1927).
Missions, Black: Peter Claver (1896, Leo XIII), Benedict the Black.
Missions, Parish: Leonard of Port Maurice (Mar. 17, 1923).
Mothers: Monica.
Motoroyolisto: Our Lady of Grace.
Motorists: Christopher, Frances of Rome.
Mountaineers: Bernard of Menthon.
Musicians: Gregory the Great, Cecilia, Dunstan.
Nail makers: Cloud.
Notaries: Luke, Mark.
Nurses: Camillus de Lellis and John of God (1930, Pius XI), Agatha, Raphael.
Nursing and nursing service: Elizabeth of Hungary, Catherine of Siena.
Orators: John Chrysostom (July 8, 1908).
Organ builders: Cecilia.
Orphans: Jerome Emiliani.
Painters: Luke.
Paratroopers: Michael.
Pawnbrokers: Nicholas.
Pharmacists: Cosmas and Damian, James the Greater.
Pharmacists (in hospitals): Gemma Galgani.
Philosophers: Justin.
Physicians: Pantaleon, Cosmas and Damian, Luke, Raphael.
Pilgrims: James the Greater.
Plasterers: Bartholomew.
Poets: David, Cecilia.
Poison sufferers: Benedict.
Policemen: Michael.

Poor: Lawrence, Anthony of Padua.
Poor souls: Nicholas of Tolentino.
Porters: Christopher.
Possessed: Bruno, Denis.
Postal employees: Gabriel.
Priests: Jean-Baptiste Vianney (Apr. 23, 1929).
Printers: John of God, Augustine of Hippo, Genesius.
Prisoners: Dismas, Joseph Cafasso.
Protector of crops: Ansovinus.
Public relations: Bernardine of Siena (May 20, 1960).
Public relations (of hospitals): Paul, Apostle.
Radiologists: Michael (Jan. 15, 1941).
Radio workers: Gabriel.
Retreats: Ignatius Loyola (July 25, 1922).
Rheumatism: James the Greater.
Saddlers: Crispin and Crispinian.
Sailors: Cuthbert, Brendan, Eulalia, Christopher, Peter Gonzales, Erasmus, Nicholas.
Scholars: Brigid.
Schools, Catholic: Thomas Aquinas (Aug. 4, 1880), Joseph Calasanz (Aug. 13, 1948).
Scientists: Albert (Aug. 13, 1948).
Sculptors: Claude.
Seamen: Francis of Paola.
Searchers for lost articles: Anthony of Padua.
Secretaries: Genesius.
Seminarians: Charles Borromeo.
Servants: Martha, Zita.
Shoemakers: Crispin and Crispinian.
Sick: Michael, John of God and Camillus de Lellis (June 22, 1886).
Silversmiths: Andronicus.
Singers: Gregory, Cecilia.
Skaters: Lidwina.
Skiers: Bernard.
Social workers: Louise de Marillac (Feb. 12, 1960).
Soldiers: Hadrian, George, Ignatius, Sebastian, Martin of Tours, Joan of Arc.
Speleologists: Benedict.
Stenographers: Genesius, Cassian.
Stonecutters: Clement.
Stonemasons: Stephen.
Students: Thomas Aquinas.
Surgeons: Cosmas and Damian, Luke.
Swordsmiths: Maurice.
Tailors: Homobonus.
Tanners: Crispin and Crispinian, Simon.
Tax collectors: Matthew.
Teachers: Gregory the Great, John Baptist de la Salle (May 15, 1950).
Telecommunications workers: Gabriel (Jan. 12, 1951).
Telegraph/telephone workers: Gabriel.
Television: Clare of Assisi (Feb. 14, 1958).
Television workers: Gabriel.
Tertiaries (Franciscan): Louis of France, Elizabeth of Hungary.
Theologians: Augustine, Alphonsus Liguori.
Throat sufferers: Blase.
Travelers: Anthony of Padua, Nicholas of Myra, Christopher, Raphael.
Travel hostesses: Bona (Mar. 2, 1962).
Universities: Blessed Contardo Ferrini.
Vocations: Alphonsus.

Watchmen: Peter of Alcantara.
Weavers: Paul the Hermit, Anastasius the Fuller, Anastasia.
Wine merchants: Amand.
Women in labor: Anne.
Women's Army Corps: Genevieve.
Workingmen: Joseph.
Writers: Francis de Sales (Apr. 26, 1923), Lucy.
Yachtsmen: Adjutor.
Young girls: Agnes.
Youth: Aloysius Gonzaga (1729, Benedict XIII; 1926, Pius XI), John Berchmans, Gabriel of the Sorrowful Mother.

Patron Saints of Places

Alsace: Odilia.
Americas: Our Lady of Guadalupe, Rose of Lima.
Argentina: Our Lady of Lujan.
Armenia: Gregory Illuminator.
Asia Minor: John, Evangelist.
Australia: Our Lady Help of Christians.
Belgium: Joseph.
Bohemia: Wenceslaus, Ludmilla.
Borneo: Francis Xavier.
Brazil: Nossa Senhora de Aparecida, Immaculate Conception, Peter of Alcantara.
Canada: Joseph, Anne.
Chile: James, Our Lady of Mt. Carmel.
Cina: Joseph.
Colombia: Peter Claver, Louis Bertran.
Corsica: Immaculate Conception.
Czechoslovakia: Wenceslaus, John Nepomucene, Procopius.
Denmark: Ansgar, Canute.
Dominican Republic: Our Lady of High Grace, Dominic.
East Indies: Thomas, Apostle.
Ecuador: Sacred Heart.
England: George.
Europe: Benedict (1964), Cyril and Methodius, co-patrons (Dec. 31, 1980).
Finland: Henry.
France: Our Lady of the Assumption, Joan of Arc, Therese.
Germany: Boniface, Michael.
Gibraltar: Blessed Virgin Mary under title, "Our Lady of Europe" (May 31, 1979).
Greece: Nicholas, Andrew.
Holland: Willibrord.
Hungary: Blessed Virgin, "Great Lady of Hungary," Stephen, King.
India: Our Lady of Assumption.
Ireland: Patrick, Brigid and Columba.
Italy: Francis of Assisi, Catherine of Siena.
Japan: Peter Baptist.
Lesotho: Immaculate Heart of Mary.
Lithuania: Casimir, Bl. Cunegunda.
Malta: Paul, Our Lady of the Assumption.
Mexico: Our Lady of Guadalupe.
Monaco: Devota.
Moravia: Cyril and Methodius.
New Zealand: Our Lady Help of Christians.
Norway: Olaf.
Papua New Guinea (including northern Solomon Islands): Michael the Archangel (May 31, 1979).
Paraguay: Our Lady of Assumption.

Peru: Joseph.

Philippines: Sacred Heart of Mary.

Poland: Casimini, Bl. Cunegunda, Stanislaus of Cracow, Our Lady of Czestochowa.

Portugal: Immaculate Conception, Francis Borgia, Anthony of Padua, Vincent, George.

Russia: Andrew, Nicholas of Myra, Therese of Lisieux.

Scandinavia: Ansgar.

Scotland: Andrew, Columba.

Silesia: Hedwig.

Slovakia: Our Lady of Sorrows.

South Africa: Our Lady of Assumption.

South America: Rose of Lima.

Spain: James the Greater, Teresa.

Sri Lanka (Ceylon): Lawrence.

Sweden: Bridget, Eric.

United States: Immaculate Conception.

Uruguay: Our Lady of Lujan.

Wales: David.

West Indies: Gertrude.

Emblems, Portrayals of Saints

Agatha: Tongs, veil.

Agnes: Lamb.

Ambrose: Bees, dove, ox, pen.

Andrew: Transverse cross.

Anne, Mother of the Blessed Virgin: Door.

Anthony, Abbot: Bell, hog.

Anthony of Padua: Infant Jesus, bread, book, lily.

Augustine of Hippo: Dove, child, shell, pen.

Barnabas: Stones, ax, lance.

Bartholomew: Knife, flayed and holding his skin.

Benedict: Broken cup, raven, bell, crosier, bush.

Bernard of Clairvaux: Pen, bees, instruments of the Passion

Bernardine of Siena: Tablet or sun inscribed with IHS.

Blase: Wax, taper, iron comb.

Bonaventure: Communion, ciborium, cardinal's hat.

Boniface: Oak, ax, book, fox, scourge, fountain, raven, sword.

Bridget of Sweden: Book, pilgrim's staff.

Bridget of Kildare: Cross, flame over her head, candle.

Catherine of Ricci: Ring, crown, crucifix.

Catherine of Siena: Stigmata, cross, ring, lily.

Cecilia: Organ.

Charles Borromeo: Communion, coat of arms with word *Humilitas*.

Christopher: Giant, torrent, tree, Child Jesus on his shoulders.

Clare of Assisi: Monstrance.

Cosmas and Damian: A phial, box of ointment.

Cyril of Alexandria: Blessed Virgin holding the Child Jesus, pen.

Cyril of Jerusalem: Purse, book.

Dominic: Rosary, star.

Edmund the Martyr: Arrow, sword.

Elizabeth of Hungary: Alms, flowers, bread, the poor, a pitcher.

Francis of Assisi: Deer, wolf, birds, fish, skull, the Stigmata.

Francis Xavier: Crucifix, bell, vessel, Negro.

Genevieve: Bread, keys, herd, candle.

George: Dragon.

Gertrude: Crown, taper, lily.

Sts. Gervase and Protase: Scourge, club, sword.

Gregory I (the Great): Tiara, crosier, dove.

Helena: Cross.

Hilary: Stick, pen, child.

Ignatius Loyola: Communion, chasuble, book, apparition of Our Lord.

Isidore: Bees, pen.

James the Greater: Pilgrim's staff, shell, key, sword.

James the Less: Square rule, halberd, club.

Jerome: Lion.

John Berchmans: Rule of St. Ignatius, cross, rosary.

John Chrysostom: Bees, dove, pen.

John of God: Alms, a heart, crown of thorns.

John the Baptist: Lamb, head cut off on platter, skin of an animal.

John the Evangelist: Eagle, chalice, kettle, armor.

Josaphat Kuncevyc: Chalice, crown, winged deacon.

Joseph, Spouse of the Blessed Virgin: Infant Jesus, lily, rod, plane, carpenter's square.

Jude: Sword, square rule, club.

Justin Martyr: Ax, sword.

Lawrence: Cross, book of the Gospels, gridiron.

Leander of Seville: A pen.

Liborius: Pebbles, peacock.

Longinus: In arms at foot of the cross.

Louis IX of France: Crown of thorns, nails.

Lucy: Cord, eyes.

Luke: Ox, book, brush, palette.

Mark: Lion, book.

Martha: Holy water sprinkler, dragon.

Mary Magdalene: Alabaster box of ointment.

Matilda: Purse, alms.

Matthew: Winged man, purse, lance.

Matthias: Lance.

Maurus: Scales, spade, crutch.

Meinrad: Two ravens.

Michael: Scales, banner, sword, dragon.

Monica: Girdle, tears.

Nicholas: Three purses or balls, anchor or boat, child.

Patrick: Cross, harp, serpent, baptismal font, demons, shamrock.

Paul: Sword, book or scroll.

Peter: Keys, boat, cock.

Philip, Apostle: Column.

Philip Neri: Altar, chasuble, vial.

Rita of Cascia: Rose, crucifix, thorn.

Roch: Angel, dog, bread.

Rose of Lima: Crown of thorns, anchor, city.

Sebastian: Arrows, crown.

Simon Stock: Scapular.

Teresa of Avila: Heart, arrow, book.

Therese of Lisieux: Roses entwining a crucifix.

Thomas, Apostle: Lance, ax.

Thomas Aquinas: Chalice, monstrance, dove, ox, person trampled under foot.

Vincent: Gridiron, boat.

Vincent de Paul: Children.

Vincent Ferrer: Pulpit, cardinal's hat, trumpet, captives.

THE MOTHER OF JESUS IN CATHOLIC UNDERSTANDING

This article was written by the Rev. Eamon R. Carroll, O. Carm., professor in the Department of Theology, School of Religious Studies, Catholic University of America; author of "Understanding the Mother of Jesus" (published by M. Glazier, Wilmington, Del.; 1979).

Documents of the Second Vatican Council have provided the charter for current Catholic understanding of the Virgin Mary, Mother of Jesus. This conciliar teaching was expanded and applied in the pastoral letter, "Behold Your Mother: Woman of Faith," issued by the U.S. bishops Nov. 21, 1973. Pope Paul VI added guidelines for devotion, in the revised liturgy and with respect to the Rosary, in the letter *Marialis Cultus* ("To Honor Mary"), dated Feb. 2, 1974.

Conciliar Documents

The first conciliar document, the *Constitution on the Sacred Liturgy*, linked Mary with the life, death and exaltation of Jesus, stating: "In celebrating this annual cycle of Christ's mysteries, holy Church honors with special love blessed Mary, Mother of God, who is joined by an inseparable bond to the saving work of her Son. In her the Church holds up and admires the most excellent fruit of the redemption, and joyfully contemplates, as in a faultless manner, that which she herself wholly desires and hopes to be" (No. 103).

The eighth and final chapter of the *Dogmatic Constitution on the Church* is entitled "The Blessed Virgin Mary, Mother of God, in the Mystery of Christ and the Church." The seventh chapter deals with the communion of saints, the bond between the pilgrim Church on earth and the blessed joined to the risen Christ — what John de-Satgé, an English Anglican, describes as the "mutual sharing and caring in Christ for one another." At the Eucharist, above all, "in union with the whole Church we honor Mary, the ever-Virgin Mother of Jesus Christ our Lord and God" (First Eucharistic Prayer; cf. *Constitution on the Church*, No. 50).

What Catholics believe about the Mother of Jesus is the basis for her place in their prayer life, both in the liturgy and particularly the Eucharist, and in other forms of piety, especially the Rosary. The Church's growth in insight about the Blessed Virgin comes about as Christians ponder the meaning of Mary in prayer as well as in study. The Church has come to know Mary's role by experience and by contemplation of her hidden holiness (*Constitution on the Church*, No. 64). The tradition about Mary has been transmitted by doctrinal teaching and also by life and worship, even as in her own life Mary treasured in her heart God's words and deeds (*Dogmatic Constitution on Divine Revelation*, No. 8).

Mary in the Bible

The possibility of consensus on the Virgin Mary in the Bible was the theme of a book published in 1978, entitled *Mary in the New Testament* (edited by R. E. Brown, J. A. Fitzmyer, J. Reumann and K. P. Donfried). Limiting their study to the New Testament and using critical techniques of interpretation, a team of 12 authors — Catholics, Lutherans, Anglicans and others — agreed on a biblical portrait of Mary the Virgin as the great gospel model of faith commitment.

One valuable insight centers on the "true kinsmen" incident (Mk. 3:31-35; Mt. 12:46-50; Lk. 8:19-21). One day while Jesus was preaching, word was sent to him that his "mother and brethren" wished to see him. In St. Mark, the oldest account, there is a sharp distinction between the circle of the hearers of Jesus, who were "inside" and counted as his "true family," and the relatives "outside," who failed to understand him. St. Mark does not clearly place Mary among the outsiders, but neither does he carefully distinguish her from the other relatives who did not esteem Jesus. St. Luke shifts the focus completely, placing the relatives, especially the Mother of Jesus, among the true followers, as he does also in the Acts of the Apostles by mentioning them in the Upper Room before Pentecost.

St. Luke is fond of speaking of the "word of God." At the Annunciation, Mary consented with the statement, "Be it done to me according to your word" (Lk. 1:26-38), and "the Word was made flesh" (Jn. 1:14). Jesus said in reply to the message about his visitors, "My mother and my brothers are those who hear the word of God and do it" (Lk. 8:21). St. Luke relates this event just after the parables of the sower and the seed and the lamp on the lampstand. Consistent with his high praise of the Virgin Mary in the infancy chapters, he regards Mary as the rich soil — she heard the word and brought forth fruit in abundance, the Holy One who is the Son of God. She is the pure light, rekindled by the coming of the Redeemer; she is the "woman clothed with the sun" (Rv. 12:1), for Jesus is the "sun of justice."

St. Luke alone saved one other mention of Mary during the public ministry of Jesus, in the story of the "enthusiastic woman" (Lk. 11:27-28). One day while Jesus was preaching, a woman cried out, "Blessed is the womb that bore you and the breasts that nursed you." He replied, "Still more blessed are those who hear the word of God and keep it." The obedient Mary, handmaid of the Lord, brought together opposed beatitudes — the anonymous woman's praise of her motherhood and Jesus' tribute to her faith.

In the opening chapter of St. Luke, Elizabeth did the same when, filled with the Holy Spirit, she returned Mary's greeting with the loud cry, "Of all women you are the most blessed, and blessed is the fruit of your womb." Continuing in praise of her young cousin's faith, she added: "Yes, blessed is she who has believed, for the things promised her by the Lord will be fulfilled" (Lk. 1:39-45).

Mary the Virgin

Both St. Luke and St. Matthew, whose infancy narratives differ so much otherwise, agree that

Mary conceived Jesus virginally, that her Son had no human father. The Creed affirms that Jesus was "conceived of the Virgin Mary by the power of the Holy Spirit."

St. Luke writes of the virginal conception of Jesus from the standpoint of Mary. To her question, "How can this be since I know not man?" the angel replied by appealing to God's power.

St. Matthew's viewpoint is that of Joseph, who was informed in a dream-vision that Mary's child was of no human father. God accomplishes his saving purposes without dependence on the will of the flesh and the will of man (Jn. 1:13). God shows his favor where he chooses — whether for the barren Sara, wife of Abraham, or aged Elizabeth, the wife of Zechariah, or the Virgin Mary. In the words of the promise to Abraham, repeated by Gabriel to Mary, "Nothing is impossible to God" (Lk. 1:37; Gn. 18:14).

Mary and Joseph accepted as God's will the virginal conception, an unprecedented event, the sign of God sending his Son to be the Savior. Their lives were henceforth totally dedicated to the service of Jesus.

As various forms of Christian witness developed in the Church, the conviction that Mary remains always a virgin came to be held as Catholic doctrine. The Gospels leave undecided the identity of the "brethren" of Jesus. From lived experience, by the fourth century the Church had come to see Mary's life-long virginity as part of her commitment to her Son and his mission. Such "development of doctrine" remains a point of difference between Catholics and Protestants, although the great Reformers — Luther, Calvin and later John Wesley — all held that Mary was ever-Virgin.

St. Luke and St. John on Mary

Along with the role of Mary in the childhood of Jesus, St. Luke sees her as part of the fulfillment of messianic prophecy. The Second Vatican Council spoke of "the exalted daughter of Zion in whom the times are fulfilled after the long waiting for the promise, and the new economy inaugurated when the Son of God takes on human nature from her in order to free men from sin by the mysteries of his flesh." The expectations of Israel for the Messiah reach their peak in Mary of Nazareth: "She stands out among the Lord's lowly and poor who confidently look for salvation from him" (*Constitution on the Church*, No. 55).

The Gospel of St. John introduces Mary at the opening and closing of her Son's ministry, which began with the first of his signs at Cana (Jn. 2:1-11) and ended on Calvary (Jn. 19). Both scenes deal with a "third day," both turn on the "hour," not yet come at Cana but achieved in the decisive event of Calvary. In both, Jesus addresses his Mother with the unaccustomed title, "Woman." The request of Mary at Cana is for more than wine to save the wedding feast. She stands for Israel of old, symbolized by the water pots required for religious purifications; Mary stands also for the new Israel, the Church, the bride of Christ, symbolized by the abundant choice wine of the messianic banquet. The marriage feast looks forward to the hour

when Christ, the bridegroom, will lay down his life in love for his bride, the Church.

When Jesus spoke from the cross to his Mother and the beloved disciple, "Woman, behold your son," and "Behold your Mother," more was meant than that the disciple should provide for Mary's care (Jn. 19:26-27). In his farewell discourse at the Last Supper, Jesus spoke of the woman in agony because her hour had come. "But when she has borne her child, she no longer remembers her pain for joy that a man has been born into the world" (Jn. 16:21). The longing of Israel for the coming of the Messiah was sometimes compared to labor pains. The "daughter of Zion" had been promised she would become the mother of all races and all nations. The words of Jesus on Calvary announced the fulfillment of that promise; Mary stands for the "woman" who is mother Church, new Israel, new People of God.

In St. John's Gospel, it is only after his words to his Mother and the disciple that Jesus, knowing "that everything was now finished," said, "I am thirsty," and then, "Now it is finished." "Then he bowed his head and delivered over his spirit" (Jn. 19:28-29).

The giving up of the spirit means both the expiring of Jesus and the giving of the Holy Spirit to the Church. The wine Mary requested at Cana was the wine of the Spirit, to be poured out at the messianic banquet. The prayer for the wine of the Spirit is answered through the self-surrender of Jesus on the cross. The triumphant Christ "gives up his spirit," and the Church comes into being. The Acts of the Apostles describes the effects of the outpouring of the Spirit at Pentecost and afterwards. What Mary requested at Cana, what she prayed for in agony at the cross of Jesus, what she sought before Pentecost in union with the Apostles and relatives and the women — all "with one accord devoted to prayer" — is the gift of the Spirit. At Nazareth Mary conceived her Son, and God became man by the power of the Holy Spirit; in the Upper Room she prayed for the Spirit that Jesus be born again in the members of his Church (*Constitution on the Church*, No. 59).

The New Eve

To the titles of Mary already familiar from the Gospels — "the Virgin," "Favored One," "Mother of Jesus," "Mother of my Lord" (Elizabeth's greeting, meaning "Mother of the Messianic King") — the early Church added other descriptions. By the mid-second century Mary was being compared to Eve. Eve was deceived by the word of the evil angel and by disobedience brought death; Mary, the obedient Virgin, heeded the message of the good angel and by her consent brought Life to the world. The title of "New Eve" became common for Mary. By the time of St. Jerome (d. 419), it was proverbial to say, "Death through Eve, life through Mary."

Immaculate Conception

Reflecting on the Blessed Virgin, Christians pondered various aspects of her holiness. The question arose of her freedom from original sin, God's gift of grace that came to be called her Immaculate Conception (not to be confused with the virginal conception of Jesus, for Mary was the child of the father and mother recalled as Joachim and Anne). It took centuries of development before the Immaculate Conception was held to be revealed by God and defined as dogma by Pius IX in 1854. The absence of clear scriptural evidence was one delaying factor; another was lack of clarity about the meaning of original sin; and most cogent was the requirement that Mary be beneficiary of the saving work of Christ. As the English Anglican John deSatgé expresses it, "Mary, who rejoiced in her Savior, was the last person to have no need of one." The Franciscan John Duns Scotus (d. 1308) suggested that Mary was kept free of original sin by a "preservative redemption" — in anticipation of the foreseen merits of Jesus Christ — the explanation eventually recognized as revealed truth.

The Assumption

The final facet of Mary's holiness is the Assumption, her union body and soul with the risen Christ in the glory of heaven, defined as dogma by Pope Pius XII in 1950. By the sixth century the feast of the Assumption was being celebrated in the East, a development from a still earlier August 15 feast that had been known as the Memory of Mary (like the birthdays into heaven of the martyrs), as the Passing of Mary, and as the Dormition or Falling Asleep of the Mother of God. There is no compelling biblical testimony; the appeal is to the concordant faith of the Church, convinced that the promise of the resurrection of the flesh in union with the risen Savior has already been fulfilled for the Mother of the Lord, who gave him human birth in her pure body and was his loyal disciple unto the end.

Model of the Church

All beliefs about the Blessed Virgin lead to Christ. God kept her free from original sin for the sake of Jesus, that she might give herself wholeheartedly to his life and work (*Constitution on the Church*, No. 56), and in consideration of his redemptive mission. Mary's Assumption is her reunion with her Son in the power of his resurrection. The Marian privileges of the Immaculate Conception and the Assumption enrich also the self-understanding of the Church, for she is the "most excellent fruit of the redemption, the spotless model of the Church," the one in whom Christians admire God's plan for his Church. "In the most holy Virgin the Church has already reached that perfection whereby she exists without spot or wrinkle (Eph. 5:27)" (*Constitution on the Church*, No. 65).

Mary Immaculate is a sign of the love of Christ for his bride, the Church; the bridegroom purifies her by his blood to make her all-holy. The preface for the Solemnity of the Immaculate Conception (December 8) addresses the Father: "You allowed no stain of sin to touch the Virgin Mary. Full of grace, she was to be a worthy Mother of your Son, your sign of favor to the Church at its beginning, and the promise of its perfection as the bride of Christ, radiantly beautiful."

Faithful to his promise, Christ has prepared a place for his bride, the Church. In Mary, daughter of the Church, now joined to Christ body and soul in glory, the pilgrim Church sees the successful completion of its own journey. The resurrection of Jesus is the central truth; the Assumption of Mary is the living sign of the Church's call to glory, to loving union with the victorious Redeemer. The preface at Mass for August 15 reads: "Today the Virgin Mother of God was taken up into heaven to be the beginning and the pattern of the Church in its perfection, and a sign of sure hope and comfort for your pilgrim people. You would not allow decay to touch her body, for she had given birth in the glory of the Incarnation to your Son, the Lord of all life." (Cf. also *Constitution on the Church*, No. 68.)

Mother of God

In 325 the first ecumenical council, at Nicaea, proclaimed that Jesus is truly Son of God. Defenders of the faith there were the first to call Mary "Mother of God." At the third ecumenical council, Ephesus, in 431, it was solemnly established that the Virgin Mary is indeed "Mother of God," for the Son to whom she gave birth is the pre-existent Second Person of the Blessed Trinity. "Mother of God" had already been used as a popular title in some parts of the Church, and after Ephesus it was adopted in the prayers of the Mass, as is still the practice in the Catholic Church and all Eastern Churches. For example, the current third Eucharistic Prayer reads: "May he (the Holy Spirit) make us an everlasting gift to you (the Father) and enable us to share in the inheritance of your saints, with Mary, the Virgin Mother of God."

Mother of the Church

When the Church began to celebrate the Assumption of Mary, it did so in the conviction Mary did not leave the members of the Church orphans when her days on earth were ended. She continues her interest for them in union with her Son, the supreme intercessor. By the time of the Council of Ephesus in 431, authors of both the East and West — like St. Ephrem of Syria (d. 373) and St. Ambrose of Italy (d. 397) — proposed Mary as the model of Christian life, and the practice of asking her to pray for her clients on earth began to appear. The feasts of the Nativity of Mary (September 8), the Annunciation (March 25) and the Presentation of Jesus (February 2, also known as the Purification of Mary or Candlemas) have been kept from the sixth and seventh centuries.

When the words of Gabriel and Elizabeth from St. Luke's infancy narrative became part of prayer, the first part of the Hail Mary, their use led to deeper awareness of Mary's holiness as well as to counting on her heavenly help — well expressed in the second part of the Hail Mary — "Holy Mary, Mother of God, pray for us sinners now and at the hour of our death," which reached its fixed form only in the fifteenth century. Mary's place in liturgical prayer and in private prayer reflected and strengthened the sense of her continuing role as loving friend in heaven of the Church on earth. People asked Mary's prayers on their behalf, recalling Mary's own "pilgrimage of faith" and trusting in her abiding maternal care.

Greek homilists like St. John of Damascus (d. ca. 749), St. Andrew of Crete (d. 740) and St. Germanus of Constantinople (d. ca. 733) sang Mary's praises and urged confidence in her loving intercession with Christ. In the West, after the upsurge of the Carolingian times (about 800), remembered for the origin of the Saturday observance in honor of Mary, came the flowering of medieval piety, as evidenced in the writings of St. Anselm (d. 1109), St. Bernard (d. 1153) and his fellow Cistercians, and the great scholastic doctors like St. Thomas Aquinas (d. 1274) and St. Bonaventure (d. 1274). The medieval authors described Mary as Mediatrix of grace, Dispensatrix of grace, spiritual Mother. Blessed Guerric, the Cistercian abbot of Igny (France, d. 1157), emphasized the maternal role of Mary in the formation of Christ in the faithful: "Like the Church of which she is a figure, Mary is Mother of all who are born to life."

Christian Unity and Mary

At the Reformation, in reaction to abuses, the invocation of the saints was rejected as harmful to confidence in Christ, the unique Mediator. Since the sixteenth century Western Christians have been sharply divided in their understanding of the communion of saints and the legitimacy of "praying to Mary." Recent events, however, hold out hope for a meeting of minds and hearts even in this sensitive area. The Second Vatican Council offered a biblical portrait of Mary without neglecting later developments in doctrine and devotion. The council described the place of Mary in words designed to meet Protestant difficulties; e.g., the much misunderstood word, Mediatrix, was used once only and was explained as com-

pletely dependent on the unique mediatorship of Christ (*Constitution on the Church,* Nos. 67, 69).

The conciliar *Decree on Ecumenism,* issued Nov. 21, 1964, spoke of the "order" or "hierarchy of truths" among Catholic doctrines, which differ in their relationship to the foundation of the faith (No. 11). The foundation is Jesus Christ, and here all Christians share a common profession of faith. The document mentioned realistically some differences that still divide Catholics and other Christians, in this "order of truths': the meaning of the Incarnation and Redemption, the mystery and ministry of the Church, and the role of Mary in the work of salvation (No. 20). The decree also said in this context: "We rejoice to see our separated brethren looking to Christ as the source and center of ecclesiastical communion. Inspired by longing for union with Christ, they feel compelled to search for unity ever more ardently, and to bear witness to their faith among all the peoples of the earth."

The formation of the Ecumenical Society of the Blessed Virgin Mary in England in 1967, and of the American branch in 1976, is an encouraging sign. The American bishops' pastoral, *"Behold Your Mother,"* appealed to the "basic reverence" of all Christians for Mary, "a veneration deeper than doctrinal differences and theological disputes" (Nos. 101-112). Pope Paul VI's major document, *Marialis Cultus,* contains an appeal to other Christians (Nos. 32 and 33). With Christians of the East, said Pope Paul, Catholics honor the Mother of God as "hope of Christians." Catholics join with Anglicans and Protestants in common praise of God, using the Virgin's own words (Lk. 1:46-55).

It may well be that the growing interest in the bonds between the Blessed Virgin and the Holy Spirit will help Christians together. The Spirit of unity inspired Mary's prophecy: "All generations will call me blessed, because he who is mighty has done great things for me" (Lk. 1:48-49).

APPARITIONS OF THE BLESSED VIRGIN MARY

Only seven of the best known apparitions of the Blessed Virgin Mary are described briefly below.

The sites of the following apparitions have become shrines and centers of pilgrimage. Miracles of the moral and physical orders have been reported as occurring at these places and/or in connection with related practices of prayer and penance.

Banneux, near Liege, Belgium: Mary appeared eight times between Jan. 15 and Mar. 2, 1933, to an 11-year-old peasant girl, Mariette Beco, in a garden behind the family cottage in Banneux, near Liege. She called herself the Virgin of the Poor, and has since been venerated as Our Lady of the Poor, the Sick, and the Indifferent. A small chapel was built by a spring near the site of the apparitions and was blessed Aug. 15, 1933. Approval of devotion to Our Lady of Banneux was given in 1949 by Bishop Louis J. Kerkhofs of Liege, and a statue of that title was solemnly crowned in 1956.

Over 100 sanctuaries throughout the world are dedicated to the honor of Our Lady of Banneux.

The International Union of Prayer, for devotion to the Virgin of the Poor, has approximately two million members.

Beauraing, Belgium: Mary appeared 33 times between Nov. 29, 1932, and Jan. 3, 1933, to five children in the garden of a convent school in Beauraing. A chapel, which became a pilgrimage center, was erected on the spot. Reserved approval of devotion to Our Lady of Beauraing was given Feb. 2, 1943, and final approbation July 2, 1949, by Bishop Charue of Namur.

The Marian Union of Beauraing, a prayer association for the conversion of sinners, has thousands of members throughout the world (see Pro Maria Committee).

Fatima, Portugal: Mary appeared six times between May 13 and Oct. 13, 1917, to three children in a field called Cova da Iria near Fatima, north of Lisbon. She recommended frequent recitation of the Rosary; urged works of mortification for the conversion of sinners; called for devotion to herself under the title of her Immaculate Heart; asked that the people of Russia be consecrated to her under this title, and that the faithful make a Communion of reparation on the first Saturday of each month.

The apparitions were declared worthy of belief in October, 1930, after a seven-year canonical investigation, and devotion to Our Lady of Fatima was authorized under the title of Our Lady of the Rosary. In October, 1942, Pius XII consecrated the world to Mary under the title of her Immaculate Heart. Ten years later, in the first apostolic letter addressed directly to the peoples of Russia, he consecrated them in a special manner to Mary.

Fatima, with its sanctuary and basilica, ranks with Lourdes as the greatest of modern Marian shrines.

(See First Saturday Devotion.)

Guadalupe, Mexico: Mary appeared four times in 1531 to an Indian, Juan Diego, on Tepeyac hill outside of Mexico City, and instructed him to tell Bishop Zumarraga of her wish that a church be built there. The bishop complied with the request about two years later after being convinced of the genuineness of the apparition by the evidence of a miraculously painted life-size figure of the Virgin on the mantle of the Indian. The mantle bearing the picture has been preserved and is enshrined i· the Basilica of Our Lady of Guadalupe, which has a long history as a center of devotion and pilgrimage in Mexico. The shrine church, originally dedicated in 1709 and subsequently enlarged, has the title of basilica.

Benedict XIV, in a decree issued in 1754, authorized a Mass and Office under the title of Our Lady of Guadalupe for celebration on Dec. 12, and named Mary the patroness of New Spain. Our Lady of Guadalupe was designated patroness of Latin America by St. Pius X in 1910 and patroness of the Americas by Pius XII in 1945.

La Salette, France: Mary appeared as a sorrowing and weeping figure Sept. 19, 1846, to two peasant children, Melanie Matthieu, 15, and Maximin Giraud, 11, at La Salette in southern France. The message she confided to them, regarding the necessity of penance, was communicated to Pius IX in 1851 and has since been known at the "secret" of La Salette. Bishop de Bruillard of Grenoble declared in 1851 that the apparition was credible, and devotion to Mary under the title of Our Lady of La Salette was authorized. The devotion has been confirmed by popes since the time of Pius IX, and a Mass and Office with this title were authorized in 1942. The shrine church was given the title of minor basilica in 1879.

Lourdes, France: Mary, identifying herself as the Immaculate Conception, appeared 18 times between Feb. 11 and July 16, 1858, to 14-year-old Bernadette Soubirous at the grotto of Massabielle near Lourdes in southern France. Her message concerned the necessity of prayer and penance for the conversion of peoples. Mary's request that a chapel be built at the grotto and spring was fulfilled in 1862 after four years of rigid examination established the credibility of the apparitions.

Devotion under the title of Our Lady of Lourdes was authorized later, and a Feb. 11 feast commemorating the apparitions was instituted by Leo XIII. St. Pius X extended this feast throughout the Church in 1907.

The Church of Notre Dame was made a basilica in 1870, and the Church of the Rosary was built later. The underground Church of St. Pius X, consecrated Mar. 25, 1958, is the second largest church in the world, with a capacity of 20,000 persons.

Our Lady of the Miraculous Medal, France: Mary appeared three times in 1830 to Catherine Laboure in the chapel of the motherhouse of the Daughters of Charity of St. Vincent de Paul, Rue de Bac, Paris. She commissioned Catherine to have made the medal of the Immaculate Conception, now known as the Miraculous Medal, and to spread devotion to her under this title. In 1832, the medal was struck according to the model revealed to Catherine.

Secret of Fatima

Sister Lucy, a Carmelite nun and one of the trio of shepherd children to whom Mary appeared, wrote a three-part account of an apparition which occurred July 13, 1917. The first part concerned a vision of hell. The second dealt with the conversion of the peoples of Russia through devotion to Mary under the title of her Immaculate Heart. The third part was the so-called "secret" which, it was said, was not to be opened until 1960 or the death of Sister Lucy, whichever came first. Presumably, the "secret" was a prophecy of dire events. To date, it has not been disclosed. Church officials have decried morbid concern about it.

NATIONAL SHRINE

The National Shrine of the Immaculate Conception is dedicated to the honor of the Blessed Virgin Mary, who was declared patroness of the United States in 1846.

The shrine project was launched in 1914; the site and foundation stone were blessed in 1920; the crypt, an underground church, was completed in 1926; the main church and superstructure were dedicated Nov. 20, 1959; more than 56 chapels and additional interior furnishings have been installed since the dedication. The shrine has a distinctive bell tower housing a 56-bell carillon.

The shrine is the seventh largest religious building in the world and the largest Catholic church in the Western Hemisphere, with normal seating and standing accommodations for 6,000 persons. The shrine contains some of the largest mosaics in the world.

Approximately one million persons visit the shrine each year. Open daily, it is located adjacent to the Catholic University of America, Michigan Ave. and Fourth St. N.E., Washington, D.C., 20017. The shrine director is Msgr. Eugene G. Bilski.

The Second Vatican Council, in its "Decree on Eastern Catholic Churches", stated the following points. regarding Eastern heritage, patriarchs, sacraments and worship.

The Catholic Church holds in high esteem the institutions of the Eastern Churches, their liturgical rites, ecclesiastical traditions, and Christian way of life. For, distinguished as they are by their venerable antiquity, they are bright with that tradition which was handed down from the Apostles through the Fathers, and which forms part of the divinely revealed and undivided heritage of the universal Church (No. 1).

That Church, Holy and Catholic, which is the Mystical Body of Christ, is made up of the faithful who are organically united in the Holy Spirit through the same faith, the same sacraments, and the same government and who, combining into various groups held together by a hierarchy, form separate Churches or rites. . . . It is the mind of the Catholic Church that each individual Church or rite retain its traditions whole and entire, while adjusting its way of life to the various needs of time and place (No. 2).

Such individual Churches, whether of the East or of the West, although they differ somewhat among themselves in what are called rites (that is, in liturgy, ecclesiastical discipline, and spiritual heritage) are, nevertheless, equally entrusted to the pastoral guidance of the Roman Pontiff, the divinely appointed successor of St. Peter in supreme government over the universal Church. They are consequently of equal dignity, so that none of them is superior to the others by reason of rite (No. 3),

Eastern Heritage: Each and every Catholic, as also the baptized . . . of every non-Catholic Church or community who enters into the fullness of Catholic communion, should everywhere retain his proper rite, cherish it, and observe it to the best of his ability (No. 4).

The Churches of the East, as much as those of the West, fully enjoy the right, and are in duty bound, to rule themselves. Each should do so according to its proper and individual procedures (No. 5).

All Eastern rite members should know and be convinced that they can and should always preserve their lawful liturgical rites and their established way of life, and that these should not be altered except by way of an appropriate and organic development (No. 6)

Patriarchs: The institution of the patriarchate has existed in the Church from the earliest times and was recognized by the first ecumenical Synods.

By the name Eastern Patriarch is meant the bishop who has jurisdiction over all bishops (including metropolitans), clergy, and people of his own territory or rite, in accordance with the norms of law and without prejudice to the primacy of the Roman Pontiff (No. 7).

Though some of the patriarchates of the Eastern Churches are of later origin than others, all are equal in patriarchal dignity. Still the honorary and lawfully established order of precedence among them is to be preserved (No. 8).

In keeping with the most ancient tradition of the Church, the Patriarchs of the Eastern Churches are to be accorded exceptional respect, since each presides over his patriarchate as father and head.

This sacred Synod, therefore, decrees that their rights and privileges should be re-established in accord with the ancient traditions of each Church and the decrees of the ecumenical Synods.

The rights and privileges in question are those which flourished when East and West were in union, though they should be somewhat adapted to modern conditions.

The Patriarchs with their synods constitute the superior authority for all affairs of the patriarchate, including the right to establish new eparchies and to nominate bishops of their rite within the territorial bounds of the patriarchate, without prejudice to the inalienable right of the Roman Pontiff to intervene in individual cases (No. 9).

What has been said of Patriarchs applies as well, under the norm of law, to major archbishops, who preside over the whole of some individual Church or rite (No. 10).

Sacraments: This sacred Ecumenical Synod endorses and lauds the ancient discipline of the sacraments existing in the Eastern Churches, as also the practices connected with their celebration and administration (No. 12).

With respect to the minister of holy chrism (confirmation), let that practice be fully restored which existed among Easterners in most ancient times. Priests, therefore, can validly confer this sacrament, provided they use chrism blessed by a Patriarch or bishop (No. 13).

In conjunction with baptism or otherwise, all Eastern-Rite priests can confer this sacrament validly on all the faithful of any rite, including the Latin; licitly, however, only if the regulations of both common and particular law are observed. Priests of the Latin rite, to the extent of the faculties they enjoy for administering this sacrament, can confer it also on the faithful of Eastern Churches, without prejudice to rite. They do so licitly if the regulations of both common and particular law are observed (No. 14).

The faithful are bound on Sundays and feast days to attend the divine liturgy or, according to the regulations or custom of their own rite, the celebration of the Divine Praises. That the faithful may be able to satisfy their obligation more easily, it is decreed that this obligation can be fulfilled from the Vespers of the vigil to the end of the Sunday or the feast day (No. 15).

Because of the everyday intermingling of the communicants of diverse Eastern Churches in the same Eastern region or territory, the faculty for hearing confession, duly and unrestrictedly granted by his proper bishop to a priest of any rite, is applicable to the entire territory of the grantor, also to the places and the faithful belonging to any other rite in the same territory, unless an Ordinary of the place explicitly decides otherwise with respect to the places pertaining to his rite (No. 16).

This sacred Synod ardently desires that where it has fallen into disuse the office of the permanent diaconate be restored. The legislative authority of each individual church should decide about the subdiaconate and the minor orders (No. 17).

By way of preventing invalid marriages between Eastern Catholics and baptized Eastern non-Catholics, and in the interests of the permanence and sanctity of marriage and of domestic harmony, this sacred Synod decrees that the canonical 'form' for the celebration of such marriages obliges only for lawfulness. For their validity, the presence of a sacred minister suffices, as long as the other requirements of law are honored (No. 18).

Worship: Henceforth, it will be the exclusive right of an ecumenical Synod or the Apostolic See to establish, transfer, or suppress feast days common to all the Eastern Churches. To establish, transfer, or suppress feast days for any of the individual Churches is within the competence not only of the Apostolic See but also of a patriarchal or archiepiscopal synod, provided due consideration is given to the entire region and to other individual Churches (No. 19).

Until such time as all Christians desirably concur on a fixed day for the celebration of Easter, and with a view meantime to promoting unity among the Christians of a given area or nation, it is left to the Patriarchs or supreme authorities of a place to reach a unanimous agreement, after ascertaining the views of all concerned, on a single Sunday for the observance of Easter (No. 20).

With respect to rules concerning sacred seasons, individual faithful dwelling outside the area or territory of their own rite may conform completely to the established custom of the place where they live. When members of a family belong to different rites, they are all permitted to observe sacred seasons according to the rules of any one of these rites (No. 21).

From ancient times the Divine Praises have been held in high esteem among all Eastern Churches. Eastern clerics and religious should celebrate these Praises as the laws and customs of their own traditions require. To the extent they can, the faithful too should follow the example of their forebears by assisting devoutly at the Divine Praises (No. 22).

Origin

The Church had its beginnings in Palestine, whence it spread to other regions of the world. As it spread, certain cities or jurisdictions became key centers of Christian life and missionary endeavor — notably, Jerusalem, Alexandria, Antioch and Constantinople in the East, and Rome in the West — with the result that their practices became diffused throughout their spheres of influence. Various rites originated from these practices which, although rooted in the essentials of Christian faith, were different in significant respects because of their relationships to particular cultural patterns.

Patriarchal Jurisdictions

The main lines of Eastern Church organization and liturgy were drawn before the Roman Empire was separated into Eastern and Western divisions in 292. It was originally co-extensive with the boundaries of the Eastern Empire. Its jurisdictions were those of the patriarchates of Alexandria and Antioch (recognized as such by the Council of Nicaea in 325), and of Jerusalem and Constantinople (given similar recognition by the Council of Chalcedon in 451). These were the major parent bodies of the Eastern Rite Churches which for centuries were identifiable only with limited numbers of nationality and language groups in Eastern Europe, the Middle East and parts of Asia and Africa. Their members are now scattered throughout the world.

RITES AND FAITHFUL OF EASTERN CHURCHES

(Principal source of statistics: *Annuario Pontificio*. The statistics are for Eastern-Rite jurisdictions only, and do not include Eastern-Rite Catholics under the jurisdiction of Roman-Rite bishops. Some of the figures reported are only approximate. Some of the jurisdictions listed may be inactive because of government suppression.)

The Byzantine, Alexandrian, Antiochene, Armenian and Chaldean are the five principal rites used in their entirety or in modified form by the various Eastern churches. The number of Eastern Catholics throughout the world is more than 12 million.

Alexandrian Rite

Called the Liturgy of St. Mark, the Alexandrian Rite was modified by the Copts and Melkites, and contains elements of the Byzantine Rite of St. Basil and the liturgies of Sts. Mark, Cyril and Gregory of Nazianzen. The liturgy is substantially that of the Coptic Church, which is divided into two branches — the Coptic or Egyptian, and the Ethiopian or Abyssinian.

The faithful of this rite are:

COPTS: Returned to Catholic unity about 1741; situated in Egypt, the Near East; liturgical languages are Coptic, Arabic. Jurisdictions (located in Egypt): patriarchate of Alexandria, five dioceses; 133,760.

ETHIOPIANS: Returned to Catholic unity in 1846: situated in Ethiopia, Eritrea, Jerusalem, Somalia; liturgical language is Geez. Jurisdictions (located in Ethiopia): one archdiocese, two dioceses; 76,810.

Antiochene Rite

This is the source of more derived rites than any of the other parent rites. Its origin can be traced to the Eighth Book of the *Apostolic Constitutions* and to the Liturgy of St. James of Jerusalem, which ultimately spread throughout the whole patriarchate and displaced older forms based on the *Apostolic Constitutions.*

The faithful of this rite are:

MALANKARESE: Returned to Catholic unity in 1930; situated in India; liturgical languages are Syriac, Malayalam. Jurisdictions (located in India): one archdiocese, two dioceses; 251,632.

MARONITES: United to the Holy See since the time of their founder, St. Maron; have no counterparts among the separated Eastern Christians: situated throughout the world: liturgical languages are Syriac, Arabic. Jurisdictions (located in Lebanon, Cyprus, Egypt, Syria, U.S., Brazil, Australia, Canada): patriarchate of Antioch, 17 archdioceses and dioceses, one patriarchal vicariate; 1,661,200. Where no special jurisdictions exist, they are under jurisdiction of local Roman-Rite bishops.

SYRIANS: Returned to Catholic unity in 1781; situated in Asia, Africa, the Americas, Australia; liturgical languages are Syriac, Arabic. Jurisdictions (located in Lebanon, Iraq, Egypt, Syria and Turkey): patriarchate of Antioch, seven archdioceses and dioceses, three patriarchal vicariates; 88,864.

Armenian Rite

Substantially, although using a different language, this is the Greek Liturgy of St. Basil; it is considered an older form of the Byzantine Rite, and incorporates some modifications from the Antiochene Rite.

The faithful of this rite are:

ARMENIANS, exclusively: Returned to Catholic unity during the time of the Crusades; situated in the Near East, Europe, Africa, the Americas, Australasia: liturgical language is Classical Armenian. Jurisdictions (located in Lebanon, Iran, Iraq, Egypt, Syria, Turkey, Poland, France, Greece, Rumania, Argentina (for Latin America including Mexico), and the United States (for Canada and the U.S.): patriarchate of Cilicia, eight archdioceses and dioceses, two patriarchal vicariates, three exarchates, two ordinariates; 131,949.

Byzantine Rite

Based on the Rite of St. James of Jerusalem and the churches of Antioch, and reformed by Sts. Basil and John Chrysostom, the Byzantine Rite is proper to the Church of Constantinople. (The city was called Byzantium before Constantine changed its name; the modern name is Istanbul.) It is now used by the majority of Eastern Catholics and by the Eastern Orthodox Church (which is not in union with Rome). It is, after the Roman, the most widely used rite.

The faithful of this rite are:

ALBANIANS: Returned to Catholic unity about 1628; situated in Albania; liturgical language is Albanian. Jurisdiction (located in Albania): one apostolic administration.

BULGARIANS: Returned to Catholic unity about 1861; situated in Bulgaria; liturgical language is Old Slavonic. Jurisdiction (located in Bulgaria): one apostolic exarchate.

BYELORUSSIANS, also known as WHITE RUS-SIANS: Returned to Catholic unity in the 17th century; situated in Europe, the Americas, Australia; liturgical language is Old Slavonic. They have an apostolic visitator.

GEORGIANS: Returned to Catholic unity in 1861; situated in Georgia (Southern Russia), France; liturgical language is Georgian. They have an apostolic administrator.

GREEKS: Returned to Catholic unity in 1829; situated in Greece, Asia Minor, Europe; liturgical language is Greek. Jurisdictions (located in Greece and Turkey): two exarchates; 2,560.

HUNGARIANS: Descendants of Ruthenians who returned to Catholic unity in 1646; situated in Hungary, the rest of Europe, the Americas; liturgical languages are Greek, Hungarian, English. Jurisdictions (located in Hungary): one diocese and one exarchate: 322,800.

ITALO-ALBANIANS: Have never been separated from Rome; situated in Italy, Sicily, the Americas; liturgical languages are Greek, Italo-Albanian. Jurisdictions (located in Italy): two dioceses, one abbacy; 70,829.

MELKITES (GREEK CATHOLICS-MELKITES): Returned to Catholic unity during the time of the Crusades, but definitive reunion did not take place until early in the 18th century; situated in the Middle East, Asia, Africa, Europe, the Americas, Australia; liturgical languages are Greek, Arabic, English, Portuguese, Spanish. Jurisdictions (located in Syria, Lebanon, Jordan, Israel, U.S., Brazil, Canada): patriarchate of Antioch (with patriarchal vicariates in Egypt, Sudan, Jerusalem, Iraq and Kuwait), 16 archdioceses and dioceses and one exarchate; 611,022, (*Annuario Pontificio* figures. Some sources estimate 1,000,000).

ROMANIANS: Returned to Catholic unity in 1697; situated in Romania, the rest of Europe, the Americas; liturgical language is Modern Romanian. Jurisdictions (located in Romania and U.S.): one archdiocese, four dioceses, one exarchate. There were 1.5 million members in 1948 when they were forcibly incorporated into the Romanian Orthodox Church. They have an apostolic exarchate in the U.S. where they number approximately 5,000.

RUSSIANS: Returned to Catholic unity about 1905; situated in Europe, the Americas, Australia, China; liturgical language is Old Slavonic. Jurisdictions (located in Russia and China): two exarchates.

RUTHENIANS, or CARPATHO-RUSSIANS (Rusins): Returned to Catholic unity in the Union of Brest-Litovek, 1596, and the Union of Uzhorod, Apr. 24, 1646; situated in Hungary, Czechoslovakia, elsewhere in Europe, the Americas, Australia; liturgical languages are Old Slavonic, English. Jurisdictions (located in Russia and the U.S.): one archdiocese, four dioceses.

SLOVAKS: Jurisdictions (located in Czechoslovakia and Canada): two dioceses.

UKRAINIANS, or GALICIAN RUTHENIANS: Returned to Catholic unity about 1595; situated in Europe, the Americas, Australasia; liturgical languages are Old Slavonic and Ukrainian. Jurisdictions (located in Russian Galicia, Poland, the U.S., Canada, England, Australia, Germany, France, Brazil, Argentina): three archdioceses, 11 dioceses, four apostolic exarchates: 4,390,111. This total includes the 1943 figure of 3.5 million Ukrainian Catholics in jurisdictions subsequently forced into the Russian Orthodox Church.

YUGOSLAVS, SERBS and CROATIANS: Returned to Catholic unity in 1611; situated in Yugoslavia, the Americas; liturgical language is Old Slavonic. Jurisdiction (located in Yugoslavia): one diocese (which also has jurisdiction over all Byzantine-Rite faithful in Yugoslavia); 48,655. They are under the jurisdiction of Ruthenian bishops elsewhere.

Chaldean Rite

This rite, listed as separate and distinct by the Sacred Congregation for the Oriental Churches, was derived from the Antiochene Rite.

The faithful of this rite are:

CHALDEANS: Descendants of the Nestorians, returned to Catholic unity in 1692; situated throughout the Middle East, in Europe, Africa, the Americas; liturgical languages are Syriac, Arabic. Jurisdictions (located in Egypt, Iraq, Iran, Lebanon, Syria, Turkey, U.S.); patriarchate of Babylonia, 20 archdioceses and dioceses, one apostolic exarchate; 368,798. There are patriarchal vicars for Jordan and Egypt.

SYRO-MALABARESE: Descended from the St. Thomas Christians of India; situated mostly in the Malabar region of India; they use a Westernized and Latinized form of the Chaldean Rite in Syriac and Malayalam. Jurisdictions (located in India): two archdioceses, 16 dioceses; 2,444,107.

EASTERN JURISDICTIONS

For centuries Eastern-Rite Catholics were identifiable with a limited number of nationality and language groups in certain countries of the Middle East, Eastern Europe, Asia and Africa. The persecution of religion in the Soviet Union since 1917 and in communist-controlled countries since World War II, however — in addition to decimating and destroying the Church in those places — has resulted in the emigration of many Eastern-Rite Catholics from their homelands. This forced emigration, together with voluntary emigration, has led to the spread of Eastern Rites and their faithful to many other countries.

Europe

(Bishop Vasile Cristea, A.A., is apostolic visitor for Romanian Byzantine Rite Catholics in Europe.)

ALBANIA: Byzantine Rite, apostolic administration.

AUSTRIA: Byzantine Rite, ordinariate.

BULGARIA: Byzantine Rite (Bulgarians), apostolic exarchate.

CZECHOSLOVAKIA: Byzantine Rite (Slovakians and other Byzantine-Rite Catholics), eparchy.

FRANCE: Byzantine Rite (Ukrainians), apostolic exarchate.

Armenian Rite, apostolic exarchate.

Ordinariate for all other Eastern-Rite Catholics.

GERMANY: Byzantine Rite (Ukrainians), apostolic exarchate.

GREAT BRITAIN: Byzantine Rite (Ukrainians), apostolic exarchate.

GREECE: Byzantine Rite, apostolic exarchate. Armenian Rite, ordinariate.

HUNGARY: Byzantine Rite (Hungarians), eparchy, apostolic exarchate.

ITALY: Byzantine Rite (Italo-Albanians), two eparchies, one abbacy.

POLAND: Byzantine Rite (Ukrainian), apostolic exarchate.

Armenian Rite, archeparchy.

RUMANIA: Byzantine Rite (Romanians), metropolitan, four eparchies.

Armenian Rite, ordinariate.

RUSSIA: Byzantine Rite (Russians), apostolic exarchate; (Ruthenians), eparchy; (Ukrainians), major archeparchy, two eparchies.

YUGOSLAVIA: Byzantine Rite (Yugoslav and other Byzantine-Rite Catholics), eparchy.

Asia

CHINA: Byzantine Rite (Russians), apostolic exarchate.

CYPRUS: Antiochene Rite (Maronites), archeparchy.

INDIA: Antiochene Rite (Malankarese), metropolitan see, two eparchies.

Chaldean Rite (Syro-Malabarese), two metropolitan sees, 16 eparchies.

IRAN: Chaldean Rite (Chaldeans), two metropolitan sees, one archeparchy, one eparchy.

Armenian Rite, eparchy.

IRAQ: Antiochene Rite (Syrians), two archeparchies.

Byzantine Rite (Greek-Melkites), patriarchal vicariate.

Chaldean Rite (Chaldeans), patriarchate, two metropolitan sees, eight archeparchies and eparchies.

Armenian Rite, archeparchy.

ISRAEL (includes Jerusalem): Antiochene Rite (Syrians), patriarchal vicariate; (Maronites), patriarchal vicariate.

Byzantine Rite (Greek-Melkites), archeparchy, patriarchal vicariate.

Chaldean Rite (Chaldeans), patriarchal vicariate.

Armenian Rite, patriarchal vicariate.

JORDAN: Byzantine Rite (Greek-Melkites), archeparchy.

KUWAIT: Byzantine Rite (Greek-Melkites), patriarchal vicariate.

LEBANON: Antiochene Rite (Maronites), patriarchate, eight archeparchies and eparchies; (Syrians), patriarchate.

Byzantine Rite (Greek-Melkites), seven metropolitan and archeparchal sees.

Chaldean Rite (Chaldeans), eparchy.

Armenian Rite, patriarchate, eparchy.

SYRIAN ARAB REPUBLIC: Antiochene Rite (Maronites), two archeparchies, one eparchy; (Syrians), four archeparchies.

Byzantine Rite (Greek-Melkites), patriarchate, four metropolitan sees, one archeparchy.

Chaldean Rite (Chaldeans), eparchy.

Armenian Rite, archeparchy, eparchy, patriarchal vicariate.

TURKEY (Europe and Asia): Antiochene Rite (Syrians), patriarchal vicariate.

Byzantine Rite (Greeks), apostolic exarchate.

Chaldean Rite (Chaldeans), one archeparchy, two eparchies.

Armenian Rite, archeparchy.

Oceania

AUSTRALIA: Byzantine Rite (Ukrainians), eparchy.

Antiochene Rite (Maronites), eparchy.

Africa

EGYPT, ARAB REPUBLIC OF: Alexandrian Rite (Copts), patriarchate, five eparchies.

Antiochene Rite (Maronites), eparchy; (Syrians), eparchy.

Byzantine Rite (Greek-Melkites), patriarchal vicariate.

Chaldean Rite (Chaldeans), eparchy.

Armenian Rite, eparchy.

ETHIOPIA: Alexandrian Rite (Ethiopians), metropolitan see, two eparchies.

SUDAN: Byzantine Rite (Greek-Melkites), patriarchal vicariate.

North America

CANADA: Byzantine Rite (Ukrainians), one metropolitan, four eparchies; (Slovaks), eparchy; (Greek-Melkites), apostolic exarchate.

Armenian Rite, apostolic exarchate for Canada and the U.S. (New York is see city).

Antiochene Rite (Maronites), eparchy.

UNITED STATES: Antiochene Rite (Maronites), eparchy.

Byzantine Rite (Ukrainians), one metropolitan see, two eparchies; (Ruthenians), one metropolitan see, three eparchies; (Greek-Melkites), eparchy; (Romanians), apostolic exarchate; (Byelorussians), apostolic visitator.

Armenian Rite, apostolic exarchate for Canada and U.S. (New York is see city).

Chaldean Rite, apostolic exarchate.

Other Eastern-Rite Catholics are under the jurisdiction of local Roman-Rite bishops. (See Eastern-Rite Catholics in the United States.)

South America

Armenian-Rite Catholics in Latin America (including Mexico) are under the jurisdiction of an apostolic exarchate (see city, Buenos Aires, Argentina).

ARGENTINA: Byzantine Rite (Ukrainians), eparchy.

Armenian Rite, apostolic exarchate (for Latin America)

Ordinariate for all other Eastern-Rite Catholics.

BRAZIL: Antiochene Rite (Maronites), eparchy.

Byzantine Rite (Greek-Melkites), eparchy; (Ukrainians), eparchy.

Ordinariate for all other Eastern-Rite Catholics.

SYNODS, ASSEMBLIES

These assemblies are collegial bodies which have pastoral authority over members of the Eastern Rite Churches.

Patriarchal Synods: Maronites: Cardinal Antoine Khoraiche, patriarch of Antioch of the Maronites.

Melkites: Maximos V Hakim, patriarch of Antioch of the Greek Catholics-Melkites.

Chaldeans: Paul II Cheikho, patriarch of Babylonia of the Chaldeans.

Copts: Cardinal Stephanos I Sidarouss, C.M., patriarch of Alexandria of the Copts.

Syrians: Ignace Antoine II Hayek, patriarch of Antioch of the Syrians.

Armenians: Jean Pierre XVIII Kasparian, patriarch of Cilicia of the Armenians.

Non-Patriarchal Synod: The Synod of the Ukrainian Catholic Hierarchy is an extraterritorial synod convoked with the assent of the Pope. Cardinal Josyf Slipyi, major archbishop of Lwow of the Ukrainians, is president.

Assemblies: Assembly of Ordinaries of the Arab Republic of Egypt: Cardinal Stephanos I Sidarouss, C.M., patriarch of Alexandria of the Copts, president.

Assembly of Catholic Patriarchs and Bishops of Lebanon: Cardinal Antoine Khoraiche, patriarch of Antioch of the Maronites, president.

Assembly of Ordinaries of the Syrian Arab Republic: Maximos V Hakim, patriarch of Antioch of the Greek Catholics-Melkites, president.

Interritual Union of the Bishops of Iraq: Paul II Cheikho, patriarch of Babylonia of the Chaldeans, president.

Malabarese Episcopal Conference (June 4, 1970): Cardinal Joseph Parecattil, Ernakulam, president.

Iranian Episcopal Conference (Aug. 11, 1977): Most Rev. Youhannan Semaan Issayi, metropolitan of Teheran of the Chaldeans, president.

Of the collegial bodies listed above, the patriarchal synods have the most authority. In addition to other prerogatives, they have the right to elect bishops and regulate discipline for their respective rites.

EASTERN RITES IN U.S.

(Statistics, from the *Official Catholic Directory,* are membership figures reported by Eastern-Rite jurisdictions. Additional Eastern-Rite Catholics are included in statistics for Roman-Rite dioceses.)

Byzantine Rite

Ukrainians: There are 232,733 in three jurisdictions in the U.S.: the metropolitan see of Philadelphia (1924, metropolitan 1958) and the suffragan sees of Stamford, Conn. (1956), and St. Nicholas of Chicago (1961).

Ruthenians: There are 278,616 in four jurisdictions in the U.S.: the metropolitan see of Pittsburgh (est. 1924 at Pittsburgh; metropolitan and transferred to Munhall, 1969; transferred to Pittsburgh, 1977) and the suffragan sees of Passaic,

N.J. (1963), Parma, Ohio (1969) and Van Nuys, Calif. (1981). Hungarian and Croatian Byzantine Catholics in the U.S. are also under the jurisdiction of Ruthenian-Rite bishops.

Melkites (Greek Catholics-Melkites): In 1983, 22,907 (of approximately 55,000) were reported under the jurisdiction of the Melkite eparchy of Newton, Mass. (established as an exarchate, 1965; eparchy, 1976).

Romanians: There are approximately 5,000 in 16 Romanian Catholic Byzantine Rite parishes in the U.S., under the jurisdiction of an apostolic exarchate established in 1982 (see city, Canton, Ohio).

Byelorussians: Have one parish in the U.S. — Christ the Redeemer, Chicago, Ill. Archimandrite Vladimir Tarasevitch, O.S.B., pastor, was ordained titular bishop of Mariamme, Sept. 8, 1983, and named apostolic visitator of Byelorussian Catholics living outside Byelorussia.

Russians: Have parishes in California (St. Andrew, El Segundo, and Our Lady of Fatima Center, San Francisco); Massachusetts (Our Lady of Kazan, Boston); New York (St. Michael's Chapel of St. Patrick's Old Cathedral, Pope John XXIII Ecumenical Center). They are under the jurisdiction of local Roman-Rite bishops.

Antiochene Rite

In 1983, 30,588 (of approximately 153,000) Maronites were reported under the jurisdiction of the eparchy of St. Maron, Brooklyn (established at Detroit as an exarchate, 1966; eparchy, 1972; transferred to Brooklyn, 1977).

Armenian Rite

An apostolic exarchate for Canada and the United States (see city, New York) was established July 3, 1981. The *1983 Annuario Pontificio* reported 38,000 Armenian-Rite Catholics in both countries.

Chaldean Rite

An apostolic exarchate for the United States (see city, Detroit) was established Jan. 26, 1982.

BYZANTINE DIVINE LITURGY

The Divine Liturgy in all rites is based on the consecration of bread and wine by the narration-reactualization of the actions of Christ at the Last Supper. Aside from this fundamental usage, there are differences between the Roman (Latin) Rite and Eastern Rites, and among the Eastern Rites themselves. Following is a general description of the Byzantine Divine Liturgy which is in widest use in the Eastern-Rite Churches.

In the Byzantine, as in all Eastern Rites, the bread and wine are prepared at the start of the Liturgy. The priest does this in a little niche or at a table in the sanctuary. Taking a round loaf of leavened bread stamped with religious symbols, he cuts out a square host and other particles while reciting verses expressing the symbolism of the action. When the bread and wine are ready, he says a prayer of offering and incenses the oblations, the altar, the icons and the people.

Liturgy of the Catechumens: At the altar a litany for all classes of people is sung by the priest. The congregation answers, "Lord, have mercy."

The Little Entrance comes next. In procession, the priest leaves the sanctuary carrying the Book of the Gospels, and then returns. He sings prayers especially selected for the day and the feast. These are followed by the solemn singing of the prayer, "Holy God, Holy Mighty One, Holy Immortal One."

The Epistle follows. The Gospel is sung or read by the priest facing the people at the middle door of the sanctuary.

An interruption after the Liturgy of the Catechumens, formerly an instructional period for those learning the faith, is clearly marked. Catechumens, if present, are dismissed with a prayer. Following this are a prayer and litany for the faithful.

Great Entrance: The Great Entrance or solemn Offertory Procession then takes place. The priest first says a long silent prayer for himself, in preparation for the great act to come. Again he incenses the oblations, the altar, the icons and people. He goes to the table on the gospel side for the veil-covered paten and chalice. When he arrives back at the sanctuary door, he announces the intention of the Mass in the prayer: "May the Lord God remember all of you in his kingdom, now and forever."

After another litany, the congregation recites the Nicene Creed.

Consecration: The most solemn portion of the sacrifice is introduced by the preface, which is very much like the preface of the Roman Rite. At the beginning of the last phrase, the priest raises his voice to introduce the singing of the Sanctus. During the singing he reads the introduction to the words of consecration.

The words of consecration are sung aloud, and the people sing "Amen" to both consecrations. As the priest raises the Sacred Species in solemn offering, he sings: "Thine of Thine Own we offer unto Thee in behalf of all and for all."

A prayer to the Holy Spirit is followed by the commemorations, in which special mention is made of the all-holy, most blessed and glorious Lady, the Mother of God and ever-Virgin Mary. The dead are remembered and then the living.

Holy Communion: A final litany for spiritual gifts precedes the Our Father. The Sacred Body and Blood are elevated with the words, "Holy Things for the Holy." The Host is then broken and commingled with the Precious Blood. The priest recites preparatory prayers for Holy Communion, consumes the Sacred Species, and distributes Holy Communion to the people under the forms of both bread and wine. During this time a communion verse is sung by the choir or congregation.

The Liturgy closes quickly after this. The consecrated Species of bread and wine are removed to the side table to be consumed later by the priest. A prayer of thanksgiving is recited, a prayer for all the people is said in front of the icon of Christ, a blessing is invoked upon all, and the people are dismissed.

BYZANTINE CALENDAR

The Byzantine-Rite calendar has many distinctive features of its own, although it shares common elements with the Roman-Rite calendar — e.g., general purpose, commemoration of the mysteries of faith and of the saints, identical dates for some feasts. Among the distinctive things are the following.

The liturgical year begins on Sept. 1, the **Day of Indiction**, in contrast with the Latin or Roman start on the First Sunday of Advent late in November or early in December. The Advent season begins on Dec. 10.

Cycles of the Year

As in the Roman usage, the dating of feasts follows the Gregorian Calendar. Formerly, until well into this century, the Julian Calendar was used. (The Julian Calendar, which is now about 13 days late, is still used by some Eastern-Rite Churches.)

The year has several cycles, which include proper seasons, the feasts of saints, and series of New Testament readings. All of these elements of worship are contained in liturgical books of the rite.

The ecclesiastical calendar, called the **Menologion,** explains the nature of feasts, other observances and matters pertaining to the liturgy for each day of the year. In some cases, its contents include the lives of saints and the history and meaning of feasts.

The Divine Liturgy (Mass) and Divine Office for the proper of the saints, fixed feasts, and the Christmas season are contained in the **Menaion.** The **Triodion** covers the pre-Lenten season of preparation for Easter; Lent begins two days before the Ash Wednesday observance of the Roman Rite. The **Pentecostarion** contains the liturgical services from Easter to the Sunday of All Saints, the first after Pentecost. The **Evangelion** and **Apostolos** are books in which the Gospels, and Acts of the Apostles and the Epistles, respectively, are arranged according to the order of their reading in the Divine Liturgy and Divine Office throughout the year.

The cyclic progression of liturgical music throughout the year, in successive and repetitive periods of eight weeks, is governed by the **Oktoechos,** the Book of Eight Tones.

Sunday Names

Many Sundays are named after the subject of the Gospel read in the Mass of the day or after the name of a feast falling on the day — e.g., Sunday of the Publican and Pharisee, of the Prodigal Son, of the Samaritan Woman, of St. Thomas the Apostle, of the Fore-Fathers (Old Testament Patriarchs). Other Sundays are named in the same manner as in the Roman calendar — e.g., numbered Sundays of Lent and after Pentecost.

Holy Days

The calendar lists about 28 holy days. Many of the major holy days coincide with those of the Roman calendar, but the feast of the Immaculate Conception is observed on Dec. 9 instead of Dec. 8, and the feast of All Saints falls on the Sunday after Pentecost rather than on Nov. 1. Instead of a single All Souls' Day, there are five All Souls' Saturdays.

According to regulations in effect in the Byzantine-Rite (Ruthenian) Archeparchy of Pittsburgh and its suffragan sees of Passaic, Parma and Van Nuys, holy days are obligatory, solemn and simple, and attendance at the Divine Liturgy is required on five obligatory days — the feasts of the Epiphany, the Ascension, Sts. Peter and Paul, the Assumption of the Blessed Virgin Mary, and Christmas. Although attendance at the liturgy is not obligatory on 15 solemn and seven simple holy days, it is recommended.

In the Byzantine-Rite (Ukrainian) Archeparchy of Philadelphia and its suffragan sees of St. Nicholas (Chicago) and Stamford, the obligatory feasts are the Circumcision, Epiphany, Annunciation, Easter, Ascension, Pentecost, Dormition (Assumption of Mary), Immaculate Conception and Christmas.

Lent

The first day of Lent — the Monday before Ash Wednesday of the Roman Rite — and Good Friday are days of strict abstinence for persons between the ages of 21 and 59. No meat, eggs, or dairy products may be eaten on these days.

All persons over the age of 14 must abstain from meat on Fridays during Lent, Holy Saturday, and the vigils of the feasts of Christmas and Epiphany; abstinence is urged, but is not obligatory, on Wednesdays of Lent. The abstinence obligation is not in force on certain "free" or "privileged" Fridays.

Synaxis

An observance without a counterpart in the Roman calendar is the synaxis. This is a commemoration, on the day following a feast, of persons involved with the occasion for the feast — e.g., Sept. 9, the day following the feast of the Nativity of the Blessed Virgin Mary, is the Synaxis of Joachim and Anna, her parents.

Holy Week

In the Byzantine Rite, Lent is liturgically concluded with the Saturday of Lazarus, the day before Palm Sunday, which commemorates the raising of Lazarus from the dead.

On the following Monday, Tuesday and Wednesday, the Liturgy of the Presanctified is prescribed.

On Holy Thursday, the Liturgy of St. Basil the Great is celebrated together with Vespers.

The Divine Liturgy is not celebrated on Good Friday.

On Holy Saturday, the Liturgy of St. Basil the Great is celebrated along with Vespers.

In July, 1983, Msgr. Leo E. McFadden, pastor of Our Lady of Snows Church, Reno, Nev., and Air National Guard assistant to the Air Force chief of chaplains, was appointed brigadier general.

BYZANTINE FEATURES

Art: Named for the empire in which it developed, Byzantine art is a unique blend of imperial Roman and classic Hellenic culture with Christian inspiration. The art of the Greek Middle Ages, it reached a peak of development in the 10th or 11th century. Characteristic of its products, particularly in mosaic and painting, are majesty, dignity, refinement and grace. Its sacred paintings, called icons, are reverenced highly in all Eastern Rites.

Church Building: The classical model of Byzantine church architecture is the Church of the Holy Wisdom (Hagia Sophia), built in Constantinople in the first half of the sixth century and still standing. The square structure, extended in some cases in the form of a cross, is topped by a distinctive onion-shaped dome and surmounted by a triple-bar cross. The altar is at the eastern end of building, where the wall bellies out to form an apse. The altar and sanctuary are separated from the body of the church by a fixed or movable screen, the iconostas, to which icons or sacred pictures are attached (see below).

Clergy: The Byzantine Rite has married as well as celibate priests. In places other than the US, where married candidates have not been accepted for ordination since about 1929, men already married can be ordained to the diaconate and priesthood and can continue in marriage after ordination. Celibate deacons and priests cannot marry after ordination; neither can a married priest remarry after the death of his wife. Bishops must be unmarried.

Iconostas: A large screen decorated with sacred pictures or icons which separates the sanctuary from the nave of a church; its equivalent in the Roman Rite, for thus separating the sanctuary from the nave, is an altar rail.

An iconostas has three doors through which the sacred ministers enter the sanctuary during the Divine Liturgy: smaller (north and south) Deacons' Doors and a large central Royal Door.

The Deacons' Doors usually feature the icons of Sts. Gabriel and Michael; the Royal Door, the icons of the Evangelists — Matthew, Mark, Luke and John. To the right and left of the Royal Door are the icons of Christ the Teacher and of the Blessed Virgin Mary with the Infant Jesus. To the extreme right and left are the icons of the patron of the church and St. John the Baptist (or St. Nicholas of Myra).

Immediately above the Royal Door is a picture of the Last Supper. To the right are six icons depicting the major feasts of Christ, and to the left are six icons portraying the major feasts of the Blessed Virgin Mary. Above the picture of the Last Supper is a large icon of Christ the King.

Some icon screens also have pictures of the 12 Apostles and the major Old Testament prophets surmounted by a crucifixion scene.

Liturgical Language: In line with Eastern tradition, Byzantine practice has favored the use of the language of the people in the liturgy. Two great advocates of the practice were Sts. Cyril and Methodius, apostles of the Slavs, who devised the Cyrillic alphabet and pioneered the adoption of Slavonic in the liturgy.

Sacraments: Baptism is administered by immersion, and confirmation is conferred at the same time. The Eucharist is administered by intinction, i.e., by giving the communicant a piece of consecrated leavened bread which has been dipped into the consecrated wine. When giving absolution in the sacrament of penance, the priest holds his stole over the head of the penitent. Distinctive marriage ceremonies include the crowning of the bride and groom. Ceremonies for anointing the sick closely resemble those of the Roman Rite. Holy orders are conferred by a bishop.

Sign of the Cross: Eastern-Rite Catholics have a distinctive way of making it (see entry in the Glossary). The sign of the cross in conjunction with a deep bow, instead of a genuflection, expresses reverence for the presence of Christ in the Blessed Sacrament.

VESTMENTS, APPURTENANCES

Sticharion: A long white garment of linen or silk with wide sleeves and decorated with embroidery; formerly the vestment for clerics in minor orders, acolytes, lectors, chanters, and subdeacons; symbolic of purity.

Epitrachelion: A stole with ends sewn together, having a loop through which the head is passed; its several crosses symbolize priestly duties.

Zone: A narrow clasped belt made of the same material as the epitrachelion; symbolic of the wisdom of the priest, his strength against enemies of the Church and his willingness to perform holy duties.

Epimanikia: Ornamental cuffs; the right cuff symbolizing strength, the left, patience and good will.

Phelonion: An ample cape, long in the back and sides and cut away in front; symbolic of the higher gifts of the Holy Spirit.

Antimension: A silk or linen cloth laid on the altar for the Liturgy; it may be decorated with a picture of the burial of Christ and the instruments of his passion; the relics of martyrs are sewn into the front border.

Eileton: A linen cloth which corresponds to the Roman-Rite corporal.

Poterion: A chalice or cup which holds the wine and Precious Blood.

Diskos: A shallow plate, which may be elevated on a small stand, corresponding to the Roman-Rite paten.

Asteriskos: Made of two curved bands of gold or silver which cross each other to form a double arch; a star depends from the junction, which forms a cross; it is placed over the diskos holding the consecrated bread and is covered with a veil.

Veils: Three are used, one to cover the poterion, the second to cover the diskos, and the third to cover both.

Spoon: Used in administering Holy Communion by intinction; consecrated leavened bread is dipped into consecrated wine and spooned onto the tongue of the communicant.

SEPARATED EASTERN CHURCHES

Orthodox

Orthodox Churches, the largest and most widespread of the separated Eastern Churches, have much in common with their Eastern Catholic counterparts, including many matters of faith and morals, general discipline, valid orders and sacraments, and liturgy. One important difference is their acceptance of only the first seven ecumenical councils. Another is their rejection of any single supreme head of the Church. They do not acknowledge and hold communion with the pope.

Like their Catholic counterparts, Orthodox Churches are organized in jurisdictions under patriarchs. The patriarchs are the heads of approximately 15 autocephalic and several other autonomous jurisdictions organized along lines of nationality and/or language.

The Ecumenical Patriarch of Constantinople, Dimitrios I, has the primacy of honor among his equal patriarchs but his actual jurisdiction is limited to his own patriarchate. As the spiritual head of worldwide Orthodoxy, he keeps the book of the Holy Canons of the Autocephalous Churches, in which recognized Orthodox Churches are registered, and has the right to call Pan-Orthodox assemblies.

The definitive Orthodox break with Rome dates from 1054.

Top-level relations between the Churches have improved in recent years through the efforts of former Ecumenical Patriarch Athenagoras I, John XXIII, Paul VI and Patriarch Dimitrios I. Pope Paul met with Athenagoras three times before the latter's death in 1972. The most significant action of both spiritual leaders was their mutual nullification of excommunications imposed by the two Churches on each other in 1054.

The largest Orthodox body in the western hemisphere is the Greek Orthodox Archdiocese of North and South America consisting of the Archdiocese of New York, nine dioceses in the U.S., and one diocese each in Canada and South America; it is headed by Archbishop Iakovos and has an estimated membership of 1.9 million. The second largest is the Orthodox Church in America, with approximately one million members; it was given independent status by the Patriarchate of Moscow May 18, 1970, against the will of Athenagoras I who refused to register it in the book of the Holy Canons of Autocephalous Churches. An additional 650,000 or more Orthodox belong to smaller national and language jurisdictions.

Heads of Orthodox jurisdictions in this hemisphere hold membership in the Standing Conference of Canonical Orthodox Bishops in the Americas.

Jurisdictions

The principal jurisdictions of the Greek, Russian and other Orthodox Churches are as follows.

Greek: Patriarchate of Constantinople, with jurisdiction in Turkey, Crete, the Dodecanese, Western Europe, the Americas, Australia; Dimitrios I is Ecumenical Patriarch.

Patriarchate of Alexandria, with jurisdiction in Egypt and the rest of Africa; there is also a native African Orthodox Church in Kenya and Uganda.

Patriarchate of Antioch (Melkites or Syrian Orthodox), with jurisdiction in Syria, Lebanon, Iraq, Australasia, the Americas; Syrian or Arabic, in place of Greek, is the liturgical language.

Patriarchate of Jerusalem, with jurisdiction in Israel and Jordan.

Churches of Greece, Cyprus and Sinai are autocephalic but maintain relations with their fellow Orthodox.

Russian: Patriarchate of Moscow with jurisdiction centered in the Soviet Union.

Other: Patriarchate of Serbia, with jurisdiction in Yugoslavia, Western Europe, the Americas, Australasia.

Patriarchates of Rumania and Bulgaria.

Katholikate of Georgia, the Soviet Union.

Byelorussians and Ukrainian Byzantines.

Churches of Albania, China, Czechoslovakia, Estonia, Finland, Hungary, Japan, Latvia, Lithuania, Poland.

Other minor communities in various places; e.g., Korea, the US, Carpatho-Russia.

The Division of Archives and Statistics of the Eastern Orthodox World Foundation reported a 1970 estimate of more than 200 million Orthodox Church members throughout the world. Other sources estimate the total to be approximately 125 million.

Nestorians, Monophysites

Unlike the majority of Eastern Christian Churches, several bodies do not acknowledge all of the first seven ecumenical councils. Nestorians acknowledge only the first two councils; they do not accept the doctrinal definition of the Council of Ephesus concerning Mary as the Mother of God. Monophysite Armenians, Syrians, Copts, Ethiopians and Jacobites acknowledge only the first three councils; they do not accept the doctrinal definition of the Council of Chalcedon concerning the two natures in Christ.

The Armenian Church has communicants in the Soviet Union, the Middle and Far East, the Americas.

The Coptic Church has communicants in Egypt and elsewhere.

The Ethiopian or Abyssinian Church has communicants in Africa, the Middle East, the Americas, India.

The Jacobite Church (West Syrians) has communicants in the Middle East, the Americas, India.

Nestorians (Assyrians) are scattered throughout the world.

It is estimated that there are approximately 10 million or more members of these other Eastern Churches throughout the world. For various reasons, a more accurate determination is not possible.

Conference of Orthodox Bishops

The Standing Conference of Canonical Orthodox Bishops in the Americas was established in 1960 to achieve cooperation among the various ethnic churches Office: 8-10 East 79th St., New York, N.Y. 10021.

Member churches of the conference are the: Albanian Orthodox Diocese of America (Ecumenical Patriarchate), American Carpatho-Russian Orthodox Greek Catholic Diocese in the U.S.A., Antiochian Orthodox Christian Archdiocese of North America, Bulgarian Eastern Orthodox Church, Greek Orthodox Archdiocese of North and South America, Orthodox Church in America, Romanian Orthodox Missionary Archdiocese in America and Canada, Serbian Orthodox Church in the United States of America and Canada, Ukrainian Orthodox Church in America (Ecumenical Patriarchate).

EASTERN ECUMENISM

The Second Vatican Council, in the "Decree on Eastern Catholic Churches," pointed out the special role they have to play "in promoting the unity of all Christians, particularly Easterners." The document also stated in part as follows.

The Eastern Churches in communion with the Apostolic See of Rome have a special role to play in promoting the unity of all Christians, particularly Easterners, according to the principles of this sacred Synod's *Decree on Ecumenism* first of all by prayer, then by the example of their lives, by religious fidelity to ancient Eastern traditions, by greater mutual knowledge, by collaboration, and by a brotherly regard for objects and attitudes (No. 24).

If any separated Eastern Christian should, under the guidance of grace of the Holy Spirit, join himself to Catholic unity, no more should be required of him than what a simple profession of the Catholic faith demands. A valid priesthood is preserved among Eastern clerics. Hence, upon joining themselves to the unity of the Catholic Church, Eastern clerics are permitted to exercise the orders they possess, in accordance with the regulations established by the competent authority (No. 25).

Divine Law forbids any common worship (*communicatio in sacris*) which would damage the unity of the Church, or involve formal acceptance of falsehood or the danger of deviation in the faith, of scandal, or of indifferentism. At the same time, pastoral experience clearly shows that with respect to our Eastern brethren there should and can be taken into consideration various circumstances affecting individuals, wherein the unity of the Church is not jeopardized nor are intolerable risks involved, but in which salvation itself and the spiritual profit of souls are urgently at issue.

Hence, in view of special circumstances of time, place, and personage, the Catholic Church has often adopted and now adopts a milder policy, offering to all the means of salvation and an example of charity among Christians through participation in the sacraments and in other sacred functions and objects. With these considerations in mind, and "lest because of the harshness of our judgment we prove an obstacle to those seeking salvation," and in order to promote closer union with the Eastern Churches separated from us, this sacred Synod lays down the following policy:

In view of the principles recalled above, Eastern Christians who are separated in good faith from the Catholic Church, if they ask of their own accord and have the right dispositions, may be granted the sacraments of penance, the Eucharist, and the anointing of the sick. Furthermore, Catholics may ask for these same sacraments from those non-Catholic ministers whose Churches possess valid sacraments, as often as necessity or a genuine spiritual benefit recommends such a course of action, and when access to a Catholic priest is physically or morally impossible (Nos. 26, 27).

Again, in view of these very same principles, Catholics may for a just cause join with their separated Eastern brethren in sacred functions, things, and places (No. 28).

This more lenient policy with regard to common worship involving Catholics and their brethren of the separated Eastern Churches is entrusted to the care and execution of the local Ordinaries so that, by taking counsel among themselves and, if circumstances warrant, after consultation also with the Ordinaries of the separated Churches, they may govern relations between Christians by timely and effective rules and regulations (No. 29).

EASTERN ECUMENICAL BRIEFS
Statement on the Church

Catholic and Orthodox theologians, meeting for their 10th consultation since 1966, issued an "Agreed Statement on the Church" Dec. 10, 1974. One of the central points in the statement was the difference of views regarding the position and status of the Pope and the Patriarch of Constantinople in the hierarchy of their churches.

The statement said:

"The Catholic Church recognizes that the position of Peter in the college of the Apostles finds visible expression in the Bishop of Rome who exercises those prerogatives defined by Vatican Council I within the whole church of Christ in virtue of this primacy.

"The Orthodox Church finds this teaching at variance with its understanding of primacy within the whole church. It appears to destroy the tension between independence and collegiality (in the universal and particular churches). For independence, a basic condition for collegiality, appears to be removed as a consequence of the jurisdictional teaching role attributed to the Patriarch of the West by Vatican Council I. The Orthodox believe that a necessary primacy in the church depends on the consent of the church and is at present exercised by the Patriarch of Constantinople.

"Our two traditions are not easily harmonized. Yet we believe that the Spirit is ever active to show us the way by which we can live together as one and many. We have the hope that we will be open to his promptings wherever they may lead."

The theological consultation was under the joint

sponsorship of the U.S. Bishops' Committee for Ecumenical and Interreligious Affairs and the Standing Conference of Canonical Orthodox Bishops in America.

Orthodox Guidelines

A 66-page document entitled "Guidelines for Orthodox Churches in Ecumenical Relations" was published in February, 1974, by the Standing Conference of Canonical Orthodox Bishops in the Americas. Among the subjects of guidelines were:

• Marriage: Normally marriage in the Orthodox Church "takes place only between members of that Church." There are, however, occasions in which an Orthodox priest may perform a "mixed marriage," under certain conditions. Clergy of other churches may give a blessing or exhort a couple, but do not actually "assist" or "participate" in the marriage service.

• Baptism: Orthodox Churches accept baptism in the name of the Trinity in another church if "proof of the fact of baptism" can be authenticated.

• Eucharist: "Holy Communion will not be sought by Orthodox Christians outside the Church, nor will it be offered to those who do not confess the Orthodox Church as their mother."

• Reciprocity: The "principle of reciprocity" governs preaching in ecumenical situations, meaning that Orthodox priests may preach in non-Orthodox churches and non-Orthodox may speak in Orthodox churches.

Bishops and Presbyters

A document published in July, 1976, by the Orthodox-Roman Catholic Consultation in the U.S. Signatories indicated the following points of common understanding: (1) Ordination in apostolic succession is required for pastoral office in the Church. (2) Presiding at the Eucharistic celebration is a task belonging to those ordained to pastoral service. (3) The offices of bishop and presbyter are different realizations of the sacrament of order. (4) Those ordained are claimed permanently for the service of the Church. The statement noted that questions requiring serious study were the possible ordination of women, clerical celibacy, and the compatibility of certain occupations with pastoral office.

Principle of Economy

A statement issued by the same body at the same time, concerning God's plan and activity in human history for salvation. The concept of "economy" was not completely defined. It appeared that Orthodox understanding precludes recognition of the validity of the sacraments of other Christian churches.

Ministry

Ministry, especially that of bishop, was the principal subject under discussion at a meeting of an international group of Catholic and Orthodox theologians held in December, 1977, in Chambesy, Switzerland. In the context of a joint statement on the relationship between the incarnational and spiritual aspects of church life, they said: "There is no church of Christ without ministries of the Spirit, but there are no ministries without the church; hence, (there are) no ministries apart from or above the community" of the church.

Marriage

A statement entitled "The Sanctity of Marriage," issued in December, 1978, by the Eastern Orthodox-Roman Catholic Consultation in the U.S., acknowledged agreement about the sacramental nature and permanence of marriage while noting Orthodox positions regarding divorce (permitted in some circumstances) and validity (the marriage of Orthodox communicants must be blessed by an Orthodox priest).

Another statement related to marriage, regarding the religious faith and training of children of Catholic-Orthodox parents, was approved at a meeting of the consultation Oct. 10 and 11, 1980.

Russian Orthodox Dialogue

Catholic and Orthodox delegates met for the fifth time, Mar. 13 to 17, 1980, in Odessa for discussions related to the theme, "The Local Church and the Universal Church." In a communique issued at the end of the meeting, they said they "found themselves fully in accord on the following points:

• "The local church, in the ambit of the diocese, represents the people of God united around the bishop, legitimately ordained in the uninterrupted apostolic succession. The bishop, with whom the other members of the clergy collaborate and to whom they are subordinate, is the teacher of the faith, the minister of the sacraments — first of all, of the Eucharist — and the one in charge of the Christian life of this flock."

• "The concept of catholicity, understood as organic wholeness of the Church, as the fullness of the possession of the truth revealed by God and of the means of grace given for men's salvation, was deepened. The presence of the episcopate in the local churches guarantees the fullness of their Eucharistic life in grace."

• Despite their state of separation, the Catholic and Orthodox churches recognize one another as sister churches."

Catholic-Orthodox Commission

The Coordinating Committee of the Joint Commission for Dialogue between the Roman Catholic Church and the Orthodox Church reported signs of progress at a meeting May 25 to 30, 1981, in Venice. Reviewed at the meeting were Catholic and Orthodox views of the relationship between the mysteries of the Church, the Eucharist and the Holy Trinity.

The 60-member commission, meeting for the second time June 30 to July 6, 1982, in Vienna, focused discussion and study on the central significance of the Eucharist for an understanding of unity within the local church and unity among local churches and the universal Church. A press re-

The commission, the highest ranking and largest of its kind, was established after the meeting of Pope John Paul and Ecumenical Orthodox Patriarch Dimitrios I Nov. 29 and 30, 1979, in Istanbul.

MEN, DOCTRINES, CHURCHES OF THE REFORMATION

Some of the leading figures, doctrines and churches of the Reformation are covered below. A companion article covers Major Protestant Churches in the United States.

John Wycliff (c. 1320-1384): English priest and scholar who advanced one of the leading Reformation ideas nearly 200 years before Martin Luther — that the Bible alone is the sufficient rule of faith — but had only an indirect influence on the 16th century Reformers. Supporting belief in an inward and practical religion, he denied the divinely commissioned authority of the pope and bishops of the Church; he also denied the Real Presence of Christ in the Holy Eucharist, and wrote against the sacrament of penance and the doctrine of indulgences. Nearly 20 of his propositions were condemned by Gregory XI in 1377; his writings were proscribed more extensively by the Council of Constance in 1415. His influence was strongest in Bohemia and Central Europe.

John Hus (c. 1369-1415): A Bohemian priest and preacher of reform who authored 30 propositions condemned by the Council of Constance. Excommunicated in 1411 or 1412, he was burned at the stake in 1415. His principal errors concerned the nature of the Church and the origin of papal authority. He spread some of the ideas of Wycliff but did not subscribe to his views regarding faith alone as the condition for justification and salvation, the sole sufficiency of Scripture as the rule of faith, the Real Presence of Christ in the Eucharist, and the sacramental system. In 1457 some of his followers founded the Church of the Brotherhood which later became known as the United Brethren or Moravian Church and is considered the earliest independent Protestant body.

Martin Luther (1483-1546): An Augustinian friar, the key figure in the Reformation. In 1517, as a special indulgence was being preached in Germany, and in view of needed reforms within the Church, he published at Wittenberg 95 theses concerning matters of Catholic belief and practice. Leo X condemned 41 statements from Luther's writings in 1520. Luther, refusing to recant, was excommunicated the following year. His teachings strongly influenced subsequent Lutheran theology; its statements of faith are found in the Book of Concord (1580).

Luther's doctrine included the following:

The sin of Adam, which corrupted human nature radically (but not substantially), has affected every aspect of man's being. Justification, understood as the forgiveness of sins and the state of righteousness, is by grace for Christ's sake through faith. Faith involves not merely intellectual assent but an act of confidence by the will. Good works are indispensably necessary concomitants of faith, but do not merit salvation. Of the sacraments, Luther retained baptism, penance and the Holy Communion as effective vehicles of the grace of the Holy Spirit; he held that in the Holy Communion the consecrated bread and wine are the Body and Blood of Christ. The rule of faith is the divine revelation in the Sacred Scriptures. He rejected purgatory, indulgences and the invocation of the saints, and held that prayers for the dead have no efficacy.

Lutheran tenets not in agreement with Catholic doctrine were condemned by the Council of Trent.

Anabaptism: Originated in Saxony in the first quarter of the 16th century and spread rapidly through southern Germany. Its doctrine included several key Lutheran tenets but was not regarded with favor by Luther, Calvin or Zwingli. Anabaptists believed that baptism is for adults only and that infant baptism is invalid. Their doctrine of the Inner Light, concerning the direct influence of the Holy Spirit on the believer, implied rejection of Catholic doctrine concerning the sacraments and the nature of the Church. Eighteen articles of faith were formulated in 1632 in Holland. Mennonites are Anabaptists.

Ulrich Zwingli (1484-1531): A priest who triggered the Reformation in Switzerland with a series of New Testament lectures in 1519, later disputations and by other actions. He held the Gospel to be the only basis of truth; rejected the Mass (which he suppressed in 1525 at Zurich), penance and other sacraments; denied papal primacy and doctrine concerning purgatory and the invocation of saints; rejected celibacy, monasticism and many traditional practices of piety. His symbolic view of the Eucharist, which was at odds with Catholic doctrine, caused an irreconcilable controversy with Luther and his followers. Zwingli was killed in a battle between the forces of Protestant and Catholic cantons in Switzerland.

John Calvin (1509-1564): French leader of the Reformation in Switzerland, whose key tenet was absolute predestination of some persons to heaven and others to hell. He rejected Catholic doctrine in 1533 after becoming convinced of a personal mission to reform the Church. In 1536 he published the first edition of *Institutes of the Christian Religion*, a systematic exposition of his doctrine which became the classic textbook of Reformed — as distinguished from Lutheran — theology. To Luther's principal theses — regarding Scripture as the sole rule of faith, the radical corruption of human nature, and justification by faith alone — he added absolute predestination, certitude of salvation for the elect, and the incapability of the elect to lose grace. His Eucharistic theory, which failed to mediate the Zwingli-Luther controversy, was at odds with Catholic doctrine. From 1555 until his death Calvin was the virtual dictator of Geneva, the capital of the non-Lutheran Reformation in Europe.

Arminianism: A modification of the rigid predestinationism of Calvin, set forth by Jacob Arminius (1560-1609) and formally stated in the *Remonstrance* of 1610. Arminianism influenced some Calvinist bodies.

Unitarianism: A 16th century doctrine which rejected the Trinity and the divinity of Christ in favor of a uni-personal God. It claimed scriptural support for a long time but became generally rationalistic with respect to "revealed" doctrine as well as in ethics and its world-view. One of its principal early proponents was Faustus Socinus (1539-1604), a leader of the Polish Brethren.

A variety of communions developed in England in the Reformation and post-Reformation periods.

Anglican Communion: This communion, which regards itself as the same apostolic Church as that which was established by early Christians in England, derived not from Reformation influences but from the renunciation of papal jurisdiction by Henry VIII (1491-1547). His Act of Supremacy in 1534 called Christ's Church an assembly of local churches subject to the prince, who was vested with fullness of authority and jurisdiction. In spite of Henry's denial of papal authority, this Act did not reject substantially other principal articles of faith. Notable changes, proposed and adopted for the reformation of the church, took place in the subsequent reigns of James VI and Elizabeth, with respect to such matters as Scripture as the rule of faith, the sacraments, the nature of the Mass, and the constitution of the hierarchy.

The Anglican Communion is called Episcopal because its prelates have the title and function of bishops. (See Anglican Orders.)

Puritans: Extremists who sought church reform along Calvinist lines in severe simplicity. (Use of the term was generally discontinued after 1660.)

Presbyterians: Basically Calvinistic, called Presbyterian because church polity centers around assemblies of presbyters or elders. John Knox (c. 1513-1572) established the church in Scotland.

Congregationalists: Evangelical in spirit and seeking a return to forms of the primitive church, they uphold individual freedom in religious matters, do not require the acceptance of a creed as a condition for communion, and regard each congregation as autonomous. Robert Browne influenced the beginnings of Congregationalism.

Quakers: Their key belief is in internal divine illumination, the inner light of the living Christ, as the only source of truth and inspiration. George Fox (1624-1691) was one of their leaders in England. Called the Society of Friends, the Quakers are noted for their pacificism.

Baptists: So called because of their doctrine concerning baptism. They reject infant baptism and consider only baptism by immersion as valid. Leaders in the formation of the church were John Smyth (d. 1612) in England and Roger Williams (d. 1683) in America.

Methodists: A group who broke away from the Anglican Communion under the leadership of John Wesley (1703-1791), although some Anglican beliefs were retained. Doctrines include the witness of the Spirit to the individual and personal assurance of salvation. Wesleyan Methodists do not subscribe to some of the more rigid Calvinistic tenets held by other Methodists.

Universalism: A product of 18th-century liberal Protestantism in England. The doctrine is not Trinitarian and includes a tenet that all men will ultimately be saved.

MAJOR PROTESTANT CHURCHES IN THE UNITED STATES

There are more than 250 Protestant church bodies in the United States.

The majority of U.S. Protestants belong to the following denominations: Baptist, Methodist, Lutheran, Presbyterian, Protestant Episcopal, the United Church of Christ, the Christian Church (Disciples of Christ), Holiness Sects.

See Ecumenical Dialogues, Briefs and related entries for coverage of relations between the Catholic Church and other Christian churches.

Baptist Churches

(Courtesy of the Division of Communication, American Baptist Churches in the U.S.A.)

Baptist churches, comprising the largest of all American Protestant denominations, were first established by John Smyth near the beginning of the 17th century in England. The first Baptist church in America was founded at Providence by Roger Williams in 1639.

Largest of the nearly 30 Baptist bodies in the U.S. are:

The Southern Baptist Convention, 460 James Robertson Parkway, Nashville, Tenn. 37219, with 13.6 million members;

The National Baptist Convention, U.S.A., Inc., 915 Spain St., Baton Rouge, La. 70802, with 6.5 million members;

The National Baptist Convention of America, 954 Kings Rd., Jacksonville, Fla. 32204, with 2.6 million members.

The American Baptist Churches in the U.S.A., P.O. Box 851, Valley Forge, Pa. 19482, with 1.5 million members.

The total number of U.S. Baptists is more than 29 million. The world total is 33 million.

Proper to Baptists is their doctrine on baptism. Called an "ordinance" rather than a sacrament, baptism by immersion is a sign that one has experienced and decided in favor of the salvation offered by Christ. It is administered only to persons who are able to make a responsible decision. It is the sole criterion of salvation and involves the obligation to a life of virtue. Baptism is not administered to infants.

Baptists do not have a formal creed but generally subscribe to two professions of faith formulated in 1689 and 1832 and are in general agreement with classical Protestant theology regarding Scripture as the sole rule of faith, original sin, justification through faith in Christ, and the nature of the Church. Their local churches are autonomous.

Worship services differ in form from one congregation to another. Usual elements are the reading of Scripture, a sermon, hymns, vocal and silent prayer. The Lord's Supper, called an "ordinance," is celebrated at various intervals.

Methodist Churches

(Courtesy of Joe Hale, General Secretary of the World Methodist Council.)

John Wesley (1703-1791), an Anglican clergyman, was the founder of Methodism. In 1738, following a period of missionary work in America and strongly influenced by the Moravians, he experienced a new conversion to Christ and shortly thereafter became a leader in a religious awakening in England. By the end of the 18th century, Methodism was strongly rooted also in America.

The United Methodist Church, formed in 1968 by a merger of the Methodist Church and the Evangelical United Brethren Church, is the second largest Protestant denomination in the U.S., with nine million members; its principal agencies are located in New York, Evanston, Ill., Nashville, Tenn., Washington, D.C., Dayton, O., and Lake Junaluska, N.C. (World Methodist Council, P.O. Box 518. 28745). The second largest body, with more than two million communicants, is the African Methodist Episcopal Church. Four other major churches in the U.S. are the African Methodist Episcopal Zion, Christian Methodist Episcopal, Free Methodist Church and the Wesleyan Church. The total Methodist membership in the U.S. is about 14 million.

Worldwide, there are more than 63 autonomous Methodist/Wesleyan churches in 90 countries, with a membership of more than 21 million. All of them participate in the World Methodist Council, which gives global unity to the witness of Methodist communicants.

Methodism, although it has a base in Calvinistic theology, rejects absolute predestination and maintains that Christ offers grace freely to all men, not just to a select elite. Wesley's distinctive doctrine was the "witness of the Spirit" to the individual soul and personal assurance of salvation. He also emphasized the central themes of conversion and holiness. Methodists are in general agreement with classical Protestant theology regarding Scripture as the sole rule of faith, original sin, justification through faith in Christ, the nature of the Church, and the sacraments of baptism and the Lord's Supper. Church polity is structured along episcopal lines in America, with ministers being appointed to local churches by a bishop; churches stemming from British Methodism do not have bishops but vest appointive powers within an appropriate conference. Congregations are free to choose various forms of worship services; typical elements are readings from Scripture, sermons, hymns and prayers.

Lutheran Churches

(Courtesy of Thomas Hartley Dorris, editor of Ecumenical Press Service, Box 66, CH-1211 Geneva 20, Switzerland.)

The origin of Lutheranism is generally traced to Oct. 31, 1517, when Martin Luther tacked "95 Theses" to the door of the castle church in Wittenberg, Germany. This call to debate on the subject of indulgences and related concerns has come to symbolize the beginning of the Reformation. Luther and his supporters intended to reform the Church they knew. Though Lutheranism has come to be visible in separate denominations and national churches, at its heart it professes itself to be a confessional movement within the one, holy, catholic and apostolic Church.

The world's 70 million Lutherans form the third largest grouping of Christians, following Roman Catholics and Eastern Orthodox. About 54 million belong to churches which make up the Lutheran World Federation, headquartered in Geneva; its president, Josiah Kibira, is bishop of the Northwest Diocese of the Evangelical Lutheran Church in Tanzania. Nine countries count more than one million Lutherans each: West Germany (20.9 million), United States (8.5 million), Sweden (7.7 million), East Germany (6.5 million), Denmark (4.8 million), Finland (4.6 million), Norway (3.9 million), Indonesia (2.2 million), India (1 million).

Numbering about 9 million, Lutherans are the fourth largest grouping of North American Christians, exceeded by Roman Catholics, Baptists and Methodists. About 95 per cent of them belong to one of three denominations: Lutheran Church in America, three million members, 231 Madison Avenue, New York, N.Y. 10016; Lutheran Church-Missouri Synod, 2.6 million, 500 N. Broadway, St. Louis, Mo. 63102; American Lutheran Church, 2.3 million, 422 S. Fifth St., Minneapolis, Minn. 55415.

In addition, there are about a dozen other smaller Lutheran denominations in North America. The three largest are: Wisconsin Evangelical Lutheran Synod, 400,000 members, 3512 W. North Ave., Milwaukee, Wis. 53208; the Association of Evangelical Lutheran Churches, 110,000, 12015 Manchester Rd., St. Louis, Mo. 63131; Evangelical Lutheran Church of Canada, 82,000, 247 First Ave. North, Saskatoon, Saskatchewan S7K 4H5. (This is the only independent Canadian denomination; most other Canadian Lutherans belong to the Lutheran Church in America or the Missouri Synod.)

A union of the American Lutheran Church, the Lutheran Church in America and the Association of Evangelical Lutheran Churches is projected for 1988. Their Canadian counterparts are moving toward a merger in 1985. The new denominations would account for about two-thirds of the Lutherans in each country.

The three large bodies, the Association of Evangelical Lutheran Churches and the Latvian Evangelical Church in America form the Lutheran Council in the U.S.A., a cooperative agency for work in theological studies; communication; research and planning; institutional, military and campus ministry; governmental affairs; higher education; immigration and refugee services; youth agency relations; American Indian concerns; domestic disaster relief and other social ministries. The council's main offices are at 360 Park Ave. South, New York, N.Y. 10010. A similar organization, the Lutheran Council in Canada, is headquartered at 500-365 Hargrave St., Winnipeg, Manitoba R3B 2K3.

The Lutheran Church in America, the American Lutheran Church and the Association of Evangelical Lutheran Churches also form Lutheran World

Ministries, the U.S. agency of the Lutheran World Federation, headquartered at 360 Park Ave. South, New York, N.Y. 10010. Its Canadian counterpart is the Canadian National Committee of the Lutheran World Federation, headquartered at 500-365 Hargrave St., Winnipeg, Manitoba R3B 2K3.

The statements of faith which have shaped the confessional life of Lutheranism are found in the *Book of Concord.* This 1580 collection includes the three ancient ecumenical creeds (Apostles', Nicene and Athanasian), Luther's *Large and Small Catechisms* (1529), the *Augsburg Confession* (1530) and the *Apology* in defense of it (1531), the *Smalcald Articles* (including the "Treatise on the Power and Primacy of the Pope") (1537), and the *Formula of Concord* (1577).

The central Lutheran doctrinal proposition is that Christians "receive forgiveness of sins and become righteous before God by grace, for Christ's sake."

Baptism and the Lord's Supper (Holy Communion, the eucharist) are universally celebrated among Lutherans as sacramental means of grace in which the Word and promise of God are made visible by being bound to earthly elements — water, bread and wine. In baptism, a person is reborn and by God's gracious action is made a member of the Church catholic. Likewise, the eucharist celebrates and re-presents God's gracious action. With the body and blood of Christ — "in, with, and under" the bread and wine — come the gifts of life, salvation, forgiveness.

Lutherans also treasure the Word proclaimed in the reading of the Scriptures, preaching from the pulpit, and pronouncement of absolution. The Word read and preached is always part of the celebration of the sacrament of the altar. Absolution is usually imparted generally, but it may also be given individually in connection with private confession.

Although it was not the wish of the early Lutherans to deny the bishop's place as the ordinary minister of ordination, the general unwillingness of 16th century bishops to ordain Lutheran pastors led to the usual Lutheran system of presbyteral rather than episcopal ordination. Lutherans are concerned to preserve apostolic succession in life and doctrine, and generally concede the value, though not the necessity, of ordination by bishops.

Marriage and confirmation continue among Lutherans. Confirmation has been generally connected with first communion, though recent years have seen a tendency to separate the two. In the U.S., the tendency is to have first communion around grade-five age, though infant communion is not unknown. Confirmation, sometimes called affirmation of the baptismal covenant, generally occurs during the junior high school years, slightly younger than in European practice.

Lutheran jurisdictions corresponding to dioceses are called districts or synods in North America. There are more than 100 of them on the continent. Because they relate to different national denominations, more than one of these jurisdictions includes the same geographic area. The head of a district or synod, chosen by lay and clergy delegates to a convention, is known as a bishop or a president, depending on the denomination and jurisdiction. The terms "diocese" and "bishop" are common among European Lutherans and Asian, African and Latin American Lutherans whose roots derive from European missionary efforts.

A visitor to a North American Lutheran parish would generally find adornments, vestments, church calendars and an order of service similar to that of many Episcopal or Roman Catholic congregations. Though the Reformers continued to celebrate the eucharist every Sunday and on other special days, Lutherans strayed from their confessional norm under various historical and philosophic influences. The North American practice has until recent years been monthly celebration. Weekly celebration is increasingly common and is generally stressed as the desired practice by Lutheran liturgical and sacramental theologians. Lutherans generally like to sing in worship, and successive generations have built up a rich tradition of church music and hymnody. A new North American *Lutheran Book of Worship* was introduced in 1978. The Missouri Synod issued its own revision of the book in 1982.

Presbyterian Churches

(Courtesy of Gerald W. Gillette, United Presbyterian Church in the U.S.A.; and Office of the General Assembly, Presbyterian Church in the United States.)

Presbyterians are so called because of their tradition of governing the church through a system of representative bodies composed of elders (presbyters).

Presbyterianism is a part of the Reformed Family of Churches that grew out of the theological work of John Calvin following the Lutheran Reformation, to which it is heavily indebted. Countries in which it acquired early strength and influence were Switzerland, France, Holland, Scotland and England.

Presbyterianism spread widely in this country in the latter part of the 18th century and afterwards. Presently, it has approximately 4.5 million communicants in nine bodies.

The two largest Presbyterian bodies in the country — the United Presbyterian Church in the U.S.A. and the Presbyterian Church in the United States — were reunited in June, 1983, to form the Presbyterian Church (U.S.A.), with a membership of 3.3 million.

The United Presbyterian Church in the U.S.A., with a membership of 2.5 million, was headquartered at 475 Riverside Drive, New York, N.Y. 10027. It was formed May 28, 1958, by a merger of the Presbyterian Church in the U.S.A. and the United Presbyterian Church of North America.

The Presbyterian Church in the United States, with 815,000 members, had headquarters at 341 Ponce de Leon Avenue N.E., Atlanta, Ga. 30308.

These churches, now merged, are closely allied with the Reformed Church in America, the United Church of Christ, the Cumberland Presbyterian

Churches and the Associate Reformed Presbyterian Church.

In Presbyterian doctrine, baptism and the Lord's Supper, viewed as seals of the covenant of grace, are regarded as sacraments. Baptism, which is not necessary for salvation, is conferred on infants and adults The Lord's Supper is celebrated as a covenant of the Sacrifice of Christ. In both sacraments, a doctrine of the real presence of Christ is considered the central theological principle.

The Church is twofold, being invisible and also visible; it consists of all of the elect and all those Christians who are united in Christ as their immediate head.

Presbyterians are in general agreement with classical Protestant theology regarding Scripture as the sole rule of faith and practice, salvation by grace, and justification through faith in Christ.

Presbyterian congregations are governed by a session composed of elders (presbyters) elected by the communicant membership. On higher levels there are presbyteries, synods and a general assembly with various degrees of authority over local bodies; all such representative bodies are composed of elected elders and ministers in approximately equal numbers.

Worship services, simple and dignified, include sermons, prayer, reading of the Scriptures and hymns. The Lord's Supper is celebrated at intervals.

Doctrinal developments of the past several years included approval in May, 1967, by the General Assembly of the United Presbyterian Church of a contemporary confession of faith to supplement the historic Westminster Confession. The new confession emphasizes the commitment of the Church and its members to reconciliatory and apostolic works in society. A statement entitled "The Declaration of Faith" was approved in 1977 by the Presbyterian Church in the U.S. for teaching and liturgical use.

Episcopal Church

The Episcopal Church in the U.S.A. regards itself as the same apostolic church as that which was established by early Christians in England. It was established in this country during the Revolutionary period. Its constitution and Prayer Book were adopted at a general convention held in 1789. It has approximately 3 million members.

Offices of the U.S. executive council are located at 815 Second Ave., New York, N.Y. 10017.

This church, which belongs to the Anglican Communion, subscribes to the branch theory of the Church of Christ, holding that it consists of the Church of Rome, the Eastern Orthodox Church, and the Anglican Communion. It accepts the pope as the "first among equals."

Worldwide, the Anglican Communion has 65 million members in 41 provinces. The chief prelate is the Archbishop of Canterbury.

There is considerable variety in Episcopalian beliefs and practices. Official statements of belief and practice are found in the Apostles' Creed, the Nicene Creed and the Book of Common Prayer,

but interpretation is not uniform. Scripture has primary importance with respect to the rule of faith, and some authority is attached to tradition.

All seven sacraments, veneration of the saints, and a great many other Catholic teachings are accepted by Episcopalians but are not used by all.

An episcopal system of church government prevails, but clergymen of lower rank and lay persons also have an active voice in ecclesiastical affairs. The levels of government are the general convention, the executive council, territorial provinces and dioceses, and local parishes. At the parish level, the congregation has the right to select its own rector or pastor, with the consent of the bishop.

Liturgical worship is according to the Book of Common Prayer as adopted in 1979, but ceremonial practices correspond with the doctrinal positions of the various congregations and range from a ceremony similar to the Roman Mass to services of a less elaborate character.

United Church of Christ

(Courtesy of Joseph H. Evans, secretary of the United Church of Christ.)

The 1,726,535-member United Church of Christ was formed in 1957 by a union of the Congregational Christian and the Evangelical and Reformed Churches. The former was originally established by the Pilgrims and the Puritans of the Massachusetts Bay Colony, while the latter was founded in Pennsylvania in the early 1700's by settlers from Central Europe. The denomination has 6,443 congregations throughout the United States.

It considers itself "a united and uniting church" and keeps itself open to all ecumenical options.

Its headquarters are located at 105 Madison Ave., New York, N.Y. 10016.

Its statement of faith recognizes Jesus Christ as "our crucified and risen Lord (who) shared our common lot, conquering sin and death and reconciling the world to himself." It believes in the life after death, and the fact that God "judges men and nations by his righteous will declared through prophets and apostles."

The United Church further believes that Christ calls its members to share in his baptism "and eat at his table, to join him in his passion and victory." Ideally, according to its Lord's Day Service, Communion is to be celebrated weekly. Like other Calvinistic bodies, it believes that Christ is spiritually present in the sacrament.

The United Church is governed along congregational lines, and each local church is autonomous. However, the actions of its biennial General Synod are taken with great seriousness by congregations. Between synods, a 43-member executive council oversees the work of the church.

Christian Church (Disciples of Christ)

(Courtesy of Robert L. Friedly, Vice President for Communication.)

The Christian Church (Disciples of Christ) originated early in the 1800's from two movements against rigid denominationalism led by Presbyterians Thomas and Alexander Campbell in western Pennsylvania and Barton W. Stone in Kentucky. The two movements developed separately for about 25 years before being merged in 1832.

The church, which identifies itself with the Protestant mainstream, now has approximately 1.2 million members in the U.S. and Canada. The greatest concentration of members in the U.S. is located roughly along the old frontier line, in an arc sweeping from Ohio and Kentucky through the Midwest and down into Oklahoma and Texas.

The general offices of the church are located at 222 South Downey Ave., Box 1986, Indianapolis, Ind. 46206.

The church's persistent concern for Christian unity is based on a conviction expressed in a basic document, *Declaration and Address,* dating from its founding. The document states: "The church of Christ up on earth is essentially, intentionally and constitutionally one."

The Disciples have no official doctrine or dogma. Their worship practices vary widely from more common informal services to what could almost be described as "high church" services. Membership is granted after a simple statement of belief in Jesus Christ and baptism by immersion; most congregations admit un-immersed transfers from other denominations. The Lord's Supper, generally called Communion, is always open to Christians of all persuasions. Lay men and women routinely preside over the Lord's Supper, which is celebrated each Sunday; they often preach and perform other pastoral functions as well. Distinction between ordained and non-ordained members is blurred somewhat because of the Disciples' emphasis on all members of the church as ministers.

The Christian Church is oriented to congregational government, and has a unique structure in which three levels of polity (general, regional and congregational) operate as equals rather than in a pyramid of authority. At the national or international level, it is governed by a general assembly which has voting representation direct from congregations and regions as well as all ordained clergy.

Evangelicalism

Evangelicalism, dating from 1735 in England (the Evangelical Revival) and after 1740 in the United States (the Great Awakening), has had and continues to have widespread influence in Protestant churches. It has been estimated that at least 50 per cent of American Protestants — communicants of both large denominations and small bodies — are evangelicals.

The Bible is their rule of faith and religious practice. Being born again in a life-changing experience through faith in Christ is the promise of salvation. Missionary work for the spread of the Gospel is a normal and necessary activity. Additional matters of belief and practice are generally of a conservative character.

Fundamentalists comprise an extreme rightwing subculture of evangelicalism.They are distinguished mainly by militant biblicism, belief in the absolute inerrancy of the Bible and emphasis on the Second Coming of Christ. Fundamentalism developed in the first third of the 20th century in reaction against liberal theology and secularizing trends in mainstream and other Protestant denominations.

The Holiness or Perfectionist wing of evangelicalism evolved from Methodist efforts to preserve, against a contrary trend, the personal-piety and inner-religion concepts of John Wesley. There are at least 30 Holiness bodies in the U.S.

Pentecostals, probably the most demonstrative of evangelicals, are noted for speaking in tongues and the stress they place on healing, prophecy and personal testimony to the practice and power of evangelical faith.

HUMAN DEVELOPMENT

The Campaign for Human Development was inaugurated by the U.S. Catholic Conference in November, 1969, to combat injustice, oppression, alienation and poverty in this country in three significant ways:

• by making people in this country, especially Catholics, aware of the poverty, oppression and/or injustice afflicting some 35 million persons, through programs of education and public awareness;

• by funding self-help programs begun and carried out by the poor or by the poor and non-poor working together;

• by seeking a re-evaluation of the priorities of individuals, families, the Church and the civic community with respect to the stewardship of God-given goods.

The campaign got under way with a collection taken up in all parishes throughout the country on Nov. 22, 1970. Seventy-five per cent of the money contributed in this and subsequent annual collections was placed in a national fund principally for funding self-help projects and also for educational purposes; 25 per cent remained in the dioceses where it was collected, for similar use on the local levels.

More than $55 million in grants have been allocated by the national office since 1970; grants to 160 projects in 1982 totaled a bit more than $6½ million. Diocesan allocations since 1970 have amounted to approximately $20 million.

Aid requests are reviewed by a broadly representative committee of 40 members which passes its recommendations for funding on to the 13-member Bishops' Committee for the Campaign for Human Development. Requests for aid from the national office are about 10 times greater than the some 200 programs funded each year. Local-level requests and funding are handled by diocesan offices for the Campaign for Human Development.

More than $10 million was contributed to the campaign in 1982.

Father Marvin Mottet is executive director of the campaign; Timothy Collins is assistant director. Bishop William B. Friend of Alexandria-Shreveport, La., is chairman of the bishops' committee.

The national office is located at 1312 Massachusetts Ave. N.W., Washington, D.C. 20005.

The modern ecumenical movement, which started about 1910 among Protestants and led to formation of the World Council of Churches in 1948, developed outside the mainstream of Catholic interest for many years. It has now become for Catholics as well one of the great religious facts of our time.

The magna charta of ecumenism for Catholics is a complex of several documents which include, in the first place, the *Decree on Ecumenism* promulgated by the Second Vatican Council Nov. 21, 1964. Other enactments underlying and expanding this decree are the *Dogmatic Constitution on the Church*, the *Decree on Eastern Catholic Churches,* and the *Pastoral Constitution on the Church in the Modern World*.

VATICAN II DECREE

The following excerpts from the "Decree on Ecumenism" cover the broad theological background and principles and indicate the thrust of the Church's commitment to ecumenism, under the subheads: Elements Common to Christians, Unity Lacking, What the Movement Involves, Primary Duty of Catholics.

Men who believe in Christ and have been properly baptized are brought into a certain, though imperfect, communion with the Catholic Church. Undoubtedly, the differences that exist in varying degrees between them and the Catholic Church — whether in doctrine and sometimes in discipline, or concerning the structure of the Church — do indeed create many and sometimes serious obstacles to full ecclesiastical communion. These the ecumenical movement is striving to overcome (No. 3).

Elements Common to Christians

Moreover some, even very many, of the most significant elements or endowments which together go to build up and give life to the Church herself can exist outside the visible boundaries of the Catholic Church: the written word of God; the life of grace; faith, hope, and charity, along with other interior gifts of the Holy Spirit and visible elements. All of these, which come from Christ and lead back to Him, belong by right to the one Church of Christ (No. 3).

[In a later passage, the decree singled out a number of elements which the Catholic Church and other churches have in common but not in complete agreement: confession of Christ as Lord and God and as mediator between God and man; belief in the Trinity; reverence for Scripture as the revealed word of God; baptism and the Lord's Supper; Christian life and worship; faith in action; concern with moral questions.]

The brethren divided from us also carry out many of the sacred actions of the Christian religion. Undoubtedly, in ways that vary according to the condition of each church or community, these actions can truly engender a life of grace, and can be rightly described as capable of providing access to the community of salvation.

It follows that these separated Churches and Communities, though we believe they suffer from defects already mentioned, have by no means been deprived of significance and importance in the mystery of salvation. For the Spirit of Christ has not refrained from using them as means of salvation which derive their efficacy from the very fullness of grace and truth entrusted to the Catholic Church (No. 3).

Unity Lacking

Nevertheless, our separated brethren, whether considered as individuals or as Communities and Churches, are not blessed with that unity which Jesus Christ wished to bestow on all those whom he has regenerated and vivified into one body and newness of life — that unity which the holy Scriptures and the revered tradition of the Church proclaim. For it is through Christ's Catholic Church alone, which is the all-embracing means of salvation, that the fullness of the means of salvation can be obtained. It was to the apostolic college alone, of which Peter is the head, that we believe our Lord entrusted all the blessings of the New Covenant, in order to establish on earth the one Body of Christ into which all those should be fully incorporated who already belong in any way to God's People (No. 3).

What the Movement Involves

Today, in many parts of the world, under the inspiring grace of the Holy Spirit, multiple efforts are being expended through prayer, word, and action to attain that fullness of unity which Jesus Christ desires. This sacred Synod, therefore, exhorts all the Catholic faithful to recognize the signs of the times and to participate skillfully in the work of ecumenism.

The "ecumenical movement" means those activities and enterprises which, according to various needs of the Church and opportune occasions, are started and organized for the fostering of unity among Christians. These are:

• First, every effort to eliminate words, judgments, and actions which do not respond to the condition of separated brethren with truth and fairness and so make mutual relations between them more difficult.

• Then, "dialogue" between competent experts from different Churches and Communities [scholarly ecumenism].

• In addition, these Communions cooperate more closely in whatever projects a Christian conscience demands for the common good [social ecumenism].

• They also come together for common prayer, where this is permitted [spiritual ecumenism].

• Finally, all are led to examine their own faithfulness to Christ's will for the Church and, wherever necessary, undertake with vigor the task of renewal and reform.

It is evident that the work of preparing and reconciling those individuals who wish for full Catholic communion is of its nature distinct from ecumenical action. But there is no opposition between the two, since both proceed from the wondrous providence of God (No. 4).

Primary Duty of Catholics

In ecumenical work, Catholics must assuredly be concerned for their separated brethren, praying for them, keeping them informed about the Church, making the first approaches toward them. But their primary duty is to make an honest and careful appraisal of whatever needs to be renewed and achieved in the Catholic household itself, in order that its life may bear witness more loyally and luminously to the teachings and ordinances which have been handed down from Christ through the Apostles.

Every Catholic must . . . aim at Christian perfection (cf. Jas. 1:4; Rom. 12:1-2) and, each according to his station, play his part so that the Church . . . may daily be more purified and renewed, against the day when Christ will present her to himself in all her glory, without spot or wrinkle (cf. Eph. 5:27).

Catholics must joyfully acknowledge and esteem the truly Christian endowments from our common heritage which are to be found among our separated brethren.

Nor should we forget that whatever is wrought by the grace of the Holy Spirit in the hearts of our separated brethren can contribute to our own edification. Whatever is truly Christian never conflicts with the genuine interests of the faith; indeed, it can always result in a more ample realization of the very mystery of Christ and the Church (No. 4).

Participation in Worship

Norms concerning participation by Catholics in the worship of other Christian Churches were sketched in this conciliar decree and elaborated in a number of other documents such as: the *Decree on Eastern Catholic Churches*, promulgated by the Second Vatican Council in 1964; *Interim Guidelines for Prayer in Common*, issued June 18, 1965, by the U.S. Bishops' Committee for Ecumenical and Inter-Religious Affairs; a *Directory on Ecumenism*, published in 1967 by the Vatican Secretariat for Promoting Christian Unity; additional communications from the U.S. Bishops' Committee, and numerous sets of guidelines issued locally by and for dioceses throughout the U.S.

The norms encourage common prayer services for Christian unity and other intentions. Beyond that, they draw a distinction between separated churches of the Reformation tradition and separated Eastern churches, in view of doctrine and practice the Catholic Church has in common with the latter concerning the apostolic succession of bishops, holy orders, liturgy, and other credal matters.

Full participation by Catholics in official Protestant liturgies is prohibited, because it implies profession of the faith expressed in the liturgy. Intercommunion by Catholics at Protestant liturgies is prohibited. Under certain conditions, Protestants may be given Holy Communion in the Catholic Church (see Intercommunion). A Catholic may stand as a witness, but not as a sponsor, in baptism, and as a witness in the marriage of separated Christians. Similarly, a Protestant may stand as a witness, but not as a sponsor, in a Catholic baptism, and as a witness in the marriage of Catholics.

Separated Eastern Churches

The principal norms regarding liturgical participation with separated Eastern Christians are included under Eastern Ecumenism.

ECUMENICAL AGENCIES

Vatican Secretariat

The top-level agency for Catholic ecumenical efforts is the Vatican Secretariat for Promoting Christian Unity, which originated in 1960 as a preparatory commission for the Second Vatican Council. Its purposes are to provide guidance and, where necessary, coordination for ecumenical endeavor by Catholics, and to establish and maintain relations with representatives of other Christian Churches for ecumenical dialogue and action.

The secretariat, first under the direction of Cardinal Augustin Bea, S. J., and now of Cardinal Johannes Willebrands, has established firm working relations with representative agencies of other churches and the World Council of Churches. It has joined in dialogue with Orthodox Churches, the Anglican Communion, the Lutheran World Federation, the World Alliance of Reformed Churches, the World Methodist Council and other religious bodies. In the past several years, staff members and representatives of the secretariat have been involved in one way or another in nearly every significant ecumenical enterprise and meeting held throughout the world, including the Fifth General Assembly of the World Council of Churches.

While the secretariat and its counterparts in other churches have focused primary attention on theological and other related problems of Christian unity, they have also begun, and in increasing measure, to emphasize the responsibilities of the churches for greater unity of witness and effort in areas of humanitarian need.

Bishops' Committee

The U.S. Bishops' Committee for Ecumenical and Interreligious Affairs was established by the American hierarchy in 1964. Its purposes are to maintain relationships with other Christian churches and other religious communities at the national level, to advise and assist dioceses in developing and applying ecumenical policies, and to maintain liaison with corresponding Vatican offices — the Secretariats for Christian Unity and Non-Christian Religions.

This standing committee of the National Conference of Catholic Bishops is chaired by Archbishop John F. Whealon of Hartford. Operationally, the committee is assisted by the Rev. John F. Hotchkin, director; the Rev. Joseph W. Witmer, associate director; Dr. Eugene J. Fisher, executive secretary of the Secretariat for Catholic-Jewish Relations.

The committee co-sponsors several national consultations with other churches and confessional families. These bring together on a regular basis Catholic representatives and their counterparts from the Episcopal Church, the Lutheran World Federation (U.S. Committee), the United Methodist Church, the Orthodox Churches, the Oriental Orthodox Churches, the Alliance of Reformed Churches (North American area), the Interfaith Witness Department of the Home Mission Board of the Southern Baptist Convention. Reports of consultations conducted under committee auspices are published periodically and are available through the Publications Office of the U.S. Catholic Conference. (See Ecumenical Dialogues.)

The committee relates with the National Council of Churches of Christ, through membership in the Faith and Order Commission and through observer relationship with the Commission on Regional and Local Ecumenism, and has sponsored a joint study committee investigating the possibility of Roman Catholic membership in that body.

Advisory and other services are provided by the committee to ecumenical commissions and agencies in dioceses throughout the country.

Through the Secretariat for Catholic-Jewish Relations, the committee is in contact with several national Jewish agencies and bodies. Issues of mutual interest and shared concern are reviewed for the purpose of furthering deeper understanding between the Catholic and Jewish communities.

Through the Secretariat for Non-Christians, the committee promotes activity in wider areas of dialogue. The Rev. John F. Hotchkin serves as executive secretary for this secretariat.

Offices of the committee are located at 1312 Massachusetts Ave. N.W., Washington, D.C. 20005.

World Council

The World Council of Churches is a fellowship of churches which acknowledge "Jesus Christ as Lord and Savior." It is a permanent organization providing constituent members — 301 churches with some 450 million communicants in 100 countries — with opportunities for meeting, consultation and cooperative action with respect to doctrine, worship, practice, social mission, evangelism and missionary work, and other matters of mutual concern.

The WCC was formally established Aug. 23, 1948, in Amsterdam with ratification of a constitution by 147 communions. This action merged two previously existing movements — Life and Work (social mission), Faith and Order (doctrine) — which had initiated practical steps toward founding a fellowship of Christian churches at meetings held in Oxford, Edinburgh and Utrecht in 1937 and 1938. A third movement for cooperative missionary work, which originated about 1910 and, remotely, led to formation of the WCC, was incorporated into the council in 1971 under the title of the International Missionary Council (World Mission and Evangelism).

Additional general assemblies of the council have been held since the charter meeting of 1948: in Evanston, Ill. (1954), New Delhi, India (1961), Uppsala, Sweden (1968), Nairobi, Kenya (1975) and Vancouver, British Columbia, Canada (1983).

Between assemblies, the council operates through a central committee which meets every 12 or 18 months, and an executive committee which meets every six months.

The council continues the work of the International Missionary Council, the Commission on Faith and Order, and the Commission on Church and Society. The structure of the council has three program units: Faith and Witness, Justice and Service, Education and Communication.

Liaison between the council and the Vatican has been maintained since 1966 through a joint working group. Roman Catholic membership in the WCC is a question officially on the agenda of this body. The Joint Commission on Society, Development and Peace (SODEPAX) was an agency of the council and the Pontifical Commission for Justice and Peace from 1968 to Dec. 31, 1980, after which another working group was formed. Roman Catholics serve individually as full members of the Commission on Faith and Order and in various capacities on other program committees of the council.

WCC headquarters are located in Geneva, Switzerland. The United States Conference for the World Council of Churches at 475 Riverside Drive, New York, N.Y. 10115, provides liaison between the U.S. churches and Geneva. The WCC also maintains fraternal relations with regional, national and local councils of churches throughout the world.

The Rev. Philip A. Potter, a Methodist from the Island of Dominica, West Indies, was elected secretary general of the WCC in August, 1972.

WCC presidents are: Ms. Annie Jiagge, Ghana; the Rev. J. Miguez-Bonino, Argentina; General T. B. Simatupang, Indonesia; Archbishop O. Sundby, Sweden; Dr. Cynthia Wedel, U.S.A.; His Holiness Ilia, patriarch of the Gregorian Orthodox Church, S.S.R.

National Council

The National Council of the Churches of Christ in the U.S.A., the largest ecumenical body in the United States, is a cooperative organization of 32 Protestant, Orthodox and Anglican church bodies having about 40 million members.

The NCCC, established by the churches in 1950, was structured through the merger of 12 separate cooperative agencies. Presently, through three main program divisions and five commissions, the NCCC carries on work in behalf of member churches in home and overseas missions, Christian education, communications, disaster relief and rehabilitation, family life, stewardship, regional and local ecumenism, and other areas.

Policies of the NCCC are determined by a governing board of approximately 250 members appointed by the constituent churches. The governing board meets twice a year.

The NCCC's annual budget approximates $34 million, about 80 per cent of which is devoted to compassionate ministries of aid and relief to victims of disasters and endemic poverty in lands overseas.

The president and general secretary, respectively, are Bishop James Armstrong and Dr. Claire Randall.

NCCC headquarters are located at 475 Riverside Drive, New York, N.Y. 10115.

Consultation on Church Union

The Consultation on Church Union, officially begun in 1962, is a venture of American churches seeking a united church "truly catholic, truly evangelical, and truly reformed." The churches engaged in this process, representing 25 million Christians, are the African Methodist Episcopal Church, the African Methodist Episcopal Zion Church, the Christian Church (Disciples of Christ), the Christian Methodist Episcopal Church, the Episcopal Church, the Presbyterian Church in the United States, the United Church of Christ, the United Methodist Church, and the United Presbyterian Church in the U.S.A. The National Council of Community Churches is also a member of COCU.

From 1970 to 1973 the member churches studied the first draft of a plan of union for the proposed Church of Christ Uniting. The responses to this plan, on the one hand, gave evidence of an historic consensus on faith, worship, and ministry; on the other hand, they revealed the need for mature involvement in order to discover the structures of a united church. The 11th plenary at Memphis, April, 1973, called for a future agenda involving the congregations more intimately, explored divisive factors such as racism, and affirmed the doctrinal and liturgical rapprochement already achieved. An affirmation of mutual recognition of mem-

bership was accepted and sent to the churches at the 12th plenary held at Cincinnati Nov. 4 to 8, 1974. At the 1976 plenary meeting, six chapters of "an emerging consensus" as a "theological basis for union" were approved for study by COCU members.

A series of Eucharistic texts was published in 1978. The 1979 plenary accepted a series of questions to be posed to each church arising out of the mutual recognition of members, and moved ahead on a draft agreement on the ordained ministry. The 1980 plenary accepted a seventh chapter on ministry.

The 1982 plenary celebrated the 20th anniversary of the Consultation. During the meeting, two commissions — Interim Eucharistic Fellowship and Generating Communities, and the Task Force of Persons with Disabilities — made their final reports and were discharged. The 10 denominations were called upon to "covenant" together until the Uniting Church becomes a reality.

COCU publications include: three experimental liturgies — "An Order of Worship for the Proclamation of the Word of God and the Celebration of the Lord's Supper with Commentary" (1968), "An Order for Holy Baptism" (1973), "The Sacrament of the Lord's Supper: a New Text" (1982); an ecumenical lectionary; "An Order for and Affirmation of the Baptismal Covenant" (1980); "An Order of Thanksgiving for the Birth or Adoption of a Child" (1980); "God's Power and Our Weakness" (1982); "Oneness in Christ: The Quest and the Questions" (1981), by Gerald F. Moede, general secretary of the Consultation.

Bishop Arthur Marshall, Jr., of the A.M.E. Zion Church, was elected COCU president in March, 1981. Dr. William D. Watley was appointed associate general secretary in 1982.

Offices are located at 228 Alexander St., Princeton, N.J. 08540.

ECUMENICAL DIALOGUES

(Source: Bishops' Committee for Ecumenical and Interreligious Affairs, National Conference of Catholic Bishops.)

Following is a list of principal consultations, from Mar. 16, 1965, involving representatives of the U.S. Catholic Bishops' Committee for Ecumenical and Interreligious Affairs and representatives of other Christian Churches, with names of the churches, places and dates of meetings, and the subject matter of discussions.

Baptist Convention, American (Division of Cooperative Christianity): (1) De Witt, Mich., Apr. 3, 1967 — American Baptist and Roman Catholic dialogue; a Baptist view of areas of theological agreement. (2) Green Lake, Wis., Apr. 29, 1968 — Baptism and confirmation; Christian freedom and ecclesiastical authority. (3) Schiller Park, Ill., Apr. 28, 1969 — Nature and communication of grace; Christian freedom and ecclesiastical authority; baptism and confirmation.

(4) Atchison, Kan., Apr. 17, 1970 — Role of the Church, resume of years past and the future; Roman Catholic-American Baptist dialogues; ob-

servations concerning bilateral ecumenical conversations and the future course of American Baptist-Roman Catholic conversations.

(5) Detroit, Mich., Apr. 23 to 24, 1971 — Theological perspective on clergy and lay issues and relations; theology of the local church; growth in understanding. (6) Liberty, Mo., Apr. 14 to 15, 1972 — Relationships between Church and State.

Baptists, Southern (Ecumenical Institute, Wake Forest University): (1) Winston-Salem, N.C., May 8, 1969 — Impact of biblical criticism on Roman Catholicism and contemporary Christianity in general; holy use of the world; creeds and the Faith; liturgy and spontaneity in worship; retreat, revival and monasticism; world view of ecumenism.

(2) St. Benedict, La., Feb. 4, 1970 — Liturgy and spontaneity in worship; perspectives on Baptist views on Scripture and tradition; the priesthood of all Christians; authority of the Old Testament; Baptist concepts of the Church; retreat, revival and monasticism. (3) Louisville, Ky., May 13, 1970 — The priesthood of all Christians; the ecumenical tide — a pastoral perspective; the enduring mean-

ing of the Old Testament; retreat, revival and monasticism.

(4) Daytona Beach, Fla., Feb. 1 to 3, 1971 — Issues and answers, prepared by the Interfaith Witness Department of the Home Mission Board, Southern Baptist Convention. (5) Houston, Tex., Oct. 16 to 18, 1972 — Second regional conference planned in conjunction with the Interfaith Witness Department. (6) Marriottsville, Md., Feb. 4 to 6, 1974 — Third regional conference, planned in conjunction with the Interfaith and Witness Department, concerning different types of reform and their appropriateness at different levels of church life. (7) Menlo Park, Calif., Oct. 27 to 29, 1975 — Fourth regional conference. The theme: "Conversion to Christ and Life-Long Growth in the Spirit." (8) Winston-Salem, N.C., Nov. 10-12, 1975 — Fraternal dialogue, planned in conjunction with the Ecumenical Institute of Wake Forest University and Belmont Abbey College, on the abortion issue in Christian perspective, with publication of a statement and proceedings. (9) Winston-Salem, N.C., Nov. 3-5, 1976 — Dialogue, planned as above, on Church-state issues, with publication of a statement and proceedings. (10) Kansas City, Mo., Nov. 28 to 30, 1977 — Fifth regional conference on the theme, "The Theology and Experience of Worship." (11) Cincinnati, O., Apr. 28 to 30, 1978 — Inauguration of a scholars' dialogue, with presentation of papers on the Church in the New Testament and the experience of God in the Church. (12) Cincinnati, O., Nov. 3 to 5, 1978 — Roman Catholicism in the U.S.A., an historical perspective; Southern Baptist experience in America; overviews of each tradition by the other; the local congregation or church. (13) St. Louis, Mo., Apr. 20 to 22, 1979 — Salvation as understood and taught in both traditions. (14) Cincinnati, O., Nov. 9 to 11, 1979 — The authority of Scripture from Southern Baptist and Roman Catholic viewpoints. (15) Conyers, Ga., Apr. 11 to 13, 1980 — Spirituality as understood in each tradition, including sacraments, saints and social justice; Roman Catholic teaching on ministry from the Scriptures and the Fathers of the Church. (16) Kerrville, Tex., Nov. 21 to 23, 1980 — Mission and social action in Southern Baptist life; eschatology; review of previous papers toward publication. (17) Cincinnati, O., Apr. 16 to 18, 1982 — Initial meeting of second round of dialogue, on the theme, "The Life of Grace within Us." (18) Atlanta, Ga., Nov. 12 to 14, 1982 — "The Life of Grace within Us," continued. (19) Browns, Summit, N.C., Apr. 22 to 24, 1983 — "The Life of Grace within Us," continued. (2) Belmont, N.C., Nov. 18 to 20, 1983 — "The Life of Grace within Us," continued.

Christian Church, Disciples of Christ (Council on Christian Unity): (1) Indianapolis, Ind., Mar. 16, 1967 — A look at Disciples for Catholics. (2) Kansas City, Mo., Sept. 25, 1967 — Roman Catholic view of the nature of unity being sought; opportunities in the contemporary ecumenical movement.

(3) St. Louis, Mo., Apr. 29, 1968 — Eucharistic sharing. (4) Washington, D.C., Oct. 16, 1968 — Disciple of Christ inquiry regarding the sacramentality of marriage; pastoral reflections on mixed marriage. (5) New York, N.Y., Apr. 25, 1969 — Recognition and reconciliation of ministries; theological presuppositions concerning ministry among the Disciples; role of the priest in the Catholic community. (6) Columbus, O., Nov. 3 to 5, 1970 — The parish concept in a plan of union (Consultation on Church Union); directions emerging in Catholic parish life. (7) New York, N.Y., June 8 to 10, 1971 — Disciples' theology of baptism; meaning of baptism as liberation, incorporation, empowerment. (8) Indianapolis, Ind., Mar. 8 to 10, 1972 — Ministry of healing and reconciliation as practiced in the two communities. (9) Madison, Wis., June 26 to 28, 1972 — Review and summary of five years of dialogue; planning for future themes. (10) Pleasant Hill, Shaker Town, Ky., May 22 to 24, 1973 — The Church in the New Testament. (11) Indianapolis, Ind., Jan. 5-6, 1977 — Planning session, with the Council on Christian Unity of the Christian Church and the International Disciples Ecumenical Consultative Council, for a five-year consultation on the topic, "Apostolicity and Catholicity in the Visible Unity of the Church." (12) Indianapolis, Ind., Sept. 22 to 27, 1977 — First session of a new and international consultation on the nature of the Church and elements of unity relating to it from New Testament and historical perspectives. (13) Rome, Italy, Dec. 9 to 14, 1978 — Baptism, gift and call in the search for unity; study of various modes of baptism. (14) Annapolis, Md., Sept. 7 to 12, 1979 — The faith of the individual and the faith of the Church; tradition and the faith of the Church; an agreed account on both subjects. (15) New Orleans, La., Dec. 5 to 10, 1980 — Unity as gift and call; dynamics of division of the church. (16) Ardfert, Kerry, Ireland, Sept. 10 to 17, 1981 — Completion of final report of this round, "Apostolicity and Catholicity in the Visible Unity of the Church," published June 1, 1982.

Episcopal (The Anglican-Roman Catholic Consultation, Joint Commission on Ecumenical Relations): (1) Washington, D.C., June 22, 1965 — Preliminary discussions. (2) Kansas City, Mo., Feb. 2, 1966 — Eucharist as source or expression of community; Eucharist as sign and cause of unity, and the Church as a Eucharistic fellowship. (3) Providence, R.I., Oct. 10, 1966 — Function of the minister in Eucharistic celebration; minister of the Eucharist. (4) Milwaukee, Wis., May 2, 1967 — Eucharist. (5) Jackson, Miss., Jan. 5, 1968 — Various aspects of the ministerial priesthood and the priesthood of the faithful in Eucharistic celebration; the priest's place and function in the Church's mission of service; the laity in Episcopal Church government. (6) Liberty, Mo., Dec. 2, 1968 — Directions of the ecumenical movement; episcopal symbol of unity in the Christian community; collegiality; Citizens for Educational Freedom; a layman's view of jurisdictional and cultural factors in division; Church and society in contemporary America.

(7) Boynton Beach, Fla., Dec. 8, 1969 — All in each place; toward the reconciliation of the Roman Catholic Church and Churches of the Anglican Communion; an approach to designing a Roman Catholic-Episcopal parish; preparation of joint statement on the meeting. (8) Green Bay, Wis., June 17, 1970 — Is the (COCU — Consultation on Church Union) plan of union truly Catholic, with special reference to the priest and the episcopacy?; Anglican-Roman Catholic dialogue — achievement and prognostication.

(9) St. Benedict, La., Jan. 26 to 29, 1971 — The primacy of jurisdiction of the Roman Pontiff according to the First Vatican Council; the teaching of the Second Vatican Council concerning the hierarchy of truths; analysis of the ground of "Church Elements: An Ecclesiological Investigation."

(10) Liberty, Mo., June 20 to 23, 1971 — Gift of infallibility; sharing in the teaching authority of the Church; official view of episcopacy in the Episcopal Church in the USA; symposium on Hans Kung's *Infallibility? An Inquiry*; dogma as an ecumenical problem; Revelation and statement in Anglicanism; revised working paper on theological truth, propositions and Christian unity; reflections on the teaching ministry of the Church.

(11) New York, N.Y., Jan 20 to 24, 1972 — Theological truth, propositions and Christian unity; the Protestant Episcopal Church's view of authority, tradition and the Bible; a comment on the Windsor "Statement of Eucharistic Agreement" issued by the International Anglican-Roman Catholic Consultation.

(12) Cincinnati, O., June 12 to 15, 1972 — The notion of *typos* and *typoi* as applied to the forms of the Christian Church; correspondences and differences in the Anglican and Roman Catholic understanding and exercise of teaching authority.

(13) Cincinnati, O., Mar. 18 to 22, 1973 — Formulation of a preliminary draft on the purpose of the Church. (14) Vicksburg, Miss., Jan. 6 to 10, 1974 — Formulation of a response to the "Canterbury Statement" of the International Anglican-Roman Catholic Consultation on ministry and ordination; discussion and amendment of a draft on the purpose of the Church; other subjects in a continuing dialogue on the mission of the Church.

(15) Cincinnati, O., Nov. 10 to 13, 1974 — Discussion on the nature of authority in Anglicanism and Roman Catholicism. Report prepared on the purpose of the Church. (16) Cincinnati, O., June 22 to 25, 1975 — Special ad hoc consultation on women and orders.

(17) Erlanger, Ky., Oct. 21-24, 1975 — Continuation of discussion on women and orders, with release of joint statement on the ordination of women. (18) Overland Park, Kan., Mar. 10-13, 1976 — Continuation of discussion on authority in the Church.

(19) New Orleans, La., Jan. 19-22, 1977 — Presentation and discussion of a paper entitled "Some Implications of a 'Communio Ecclesiology' for the Authority Question"; formulation of an initial response to the "Venice Statement" (see separate entry); near completion of a 12-year report on the consultation.

(20) Cincinnati, O., Aug. 9 to 12, 1977 — Preparation of a second response to the Venice Statement, "Authority in the Church," and of a 12-year report, "Where We are: A Challenge for the Future" (planned for publication). (21) Savannah, Ga., Mar. 7 to 10, 1978 — Christian anthropology and discussion of issues raised by the topic of the 12-year report in dialogue.

(22) Cincinnati, O., Jan. 3 to 6, 1979 — Christian anthropology in the patristic period and documents of the Second Vatican Council on the subject; New Testament arguments for and against the ordination of women.

(23) Cincinnati, O., Oct. 29 to Nov. 1, 1979 — Christian anthropology from the viewpoints of biotechnology/bodiliness, and Mariology. (24) Cincinnati, O., June 17 to 20, 1980 — Maleness and femaleness in Christian anthropology.

(25) Cincinnati, O., Mar. 10 to 13, 1981 — Human sexuality in relation to Christology; ordination of women; homosexuality.

(26) Cincinnati, O., Dec. 8 to 11, 1981 — Work on the first draft of a document on Christian anthropology. (27) Savannah, Ga., June 7 to 10, 1982 — additional work on the aforementioned document. (28) Columbus, O., Feb. 22 to 25, 1983 — Completion of final report, "Images of God: Reflections on Christian Anthropology."

Lutheran, U.S.A. (National Committee of the Lutheran World Federation): (1) Baltimore, Md., Mar. 16, 1965 — Exploratory discussion. (2) Baltimore, Md., July 6, 1965 — Nicene Creed as dogma of the Church. (3) Chicago, Ill., Feb. 10, 1966 — Baptism, in the context of the New Testament; Lutheran understanding; teaching of the Council of Trent.

(4) Washington, D.C., Sept. 22, 1966 — Eucharist as sacrifice, in traditional and contemporary Catholic and Lutheran contexts. (5) New York, N.Y., Apr 7, 1967 — Propitiation and five presentations on various aspects of the Eucharist. (6) St. Louis, Mo., Sept. 29, 1967 — Eucharist. (7) New York, Mar. 8, 1968 — Intercommunion, with respect to Catholic discipline, Lutheran practice, and theological reflections.

(8) Williamsburg, Va., Sept. 27, 1968 — Ministry; the competent minister of the Eucharist; scriptural foundations of diakonia (ministry of service). (9) San Francisco, Calif., Feb. 21, 1969 — Apostolic succession in the patristic era and in a contemporary view; Lutheran view of the validity of Lutheran orders; Christian priesthood in the light of documents of the Second Vatican Council.

(10) Baltimore, Md., Sept. 26, 1969 — The minister of the Eucharist, according to the Council of Trent; the use of "Church" as applied to Protestant denominations in the documents of Vatican II; Lutheran doctrine of the ministry — Catholic and Reformed; the ordained minister and layman in Lutheranism. (11) St. George, Bermuda, Feb.

19, 1970 — Preparation of joint statement on the ministry.
(12) New York, N.Y., May, 1970. (13) Chicago, Ill., Oct. 30 to Nov. 1, 1970. (14) Miami, Fla., Feb. 19 to 22, 1971 — Peter and the New Testament; the papacy in the late patristic era, Middle Ages, Renaissance; text of the *Dogmatic Constitution on the Church* (Vatican II) with respect to the papacy and infallibility.
(15) Seabury, Conn., Sept. 24 to 27, 1971 — An investigation of the concept of divine right *(jus divinum)*; teaching of the First Vatican Council on primacy and infallibility; a Lutheran understanding of what papal primacy in the Church might mean.
(16) New Orleans, La., Feb. 18 to 21, 1972 — Further discussion of the concept of divine right; ecumenical projections concerning the Petrine office; teaching authority in the Lutheran Church.
(17) Minneapolis, Minn., Sept. 22 to 25, 1972 — Further investigation of the Petrine function; councils and conciliarism.
(18) San Antonio, Tex., Feb. 16 to 19, 1973 — Discussion of work and papers of the Petrine panel concerning ministry and the Church universal, Catholic and Lutheran interpretive statements; work on papal primacy papers. (19) Allentown, Pa., Sept. 21 to 24, 1973 — Work on a joint statement concerning ministry and the Church universal, the concluding session on this topic; selection of infallibility as the next topic for consideration.
(20) Marriottsville, Md., Feb. 15 to 17, 1974 — Start of discussion on infallibility; commissioning of 16 future research papers.
(21) Princeton, N.J., Sept. 19 to 22, 1974 — Scriptural studies re infallibility, inquiries into the teachings of early Lutheranism. (22) St. Louis, Mo., Jan. 30 to Feb. 2, 1975 — Historical and systematic studies of the teaching of infallibility. (23) Washington, D.C., Apr. 2 to 3, 1975 — Special meeting of several Lutheran presidents and Catholic bishops to review the work of the scholars' consultation and propose future directions. Press report issued.
(24) Washington, D.C. Sept. 17 to 21, 1975 — Further historical and case studies re infallibility: ecumenical councils and marian definitions. (25) Scottsdale, Ariz., Feb. 19 to 22, 1976 — Infallibility discussion continued.
(26) Washington, D.C., Apr. 2-3, 1975 — Meeting of Lutheran presidents and Catholic bishops to evaluate the direction and progress of Lutheran-Catholic dialogue in the U.S., with release of a joint statement. (27) Washington, D.C., Feb. 4-5, 1976 — Continuation of discussion concerning the direction and progress of dialogue.
(28) Gettysburg, Pa., Sept. 15-18, 1976 — Presentation of papers entitled: "Draft I — Authority and Doctrine," "The Roman View of the Petrine Office in the Church 366-461," "The Status of the Nicene Creed as Dogma in the Church," "Ecumenical Methodology — Report of Task Force."
(29) Washington, D.C., Feb. 16-20, 1977 — Discussion of the second draft of a common statement; presentation of a "Note on the Papacy as an Object of Faith."

(30) Columbia, S.C., Sept. 14 to 18, 1977 — Continued discussion of the common statement, "Infallibility and Teaching Authority in the Church."
(31) Lantana, Fla., Feb. 15 to 19, 1978 — Discussion on the fourth draft of a comon statement reporting the findings of dialogue on infallibility.
(32) Minneapolis, Minn., Sept. 13 to 17, 1978 — Statement on infallibility produced. (33) Cincinnati, O., Feb. 14 to 18, 1979 — Beginning of study of justification. (34) Princeton, N.J., Sept. 13 to 16, 1979 — Further study of justification.
(35) Atlanta, Ga., Mar. 5 to 9, 1980 — Justification by faith, in the Bible and the teaching of the Council of Trent.
(36) Gettysburg, Pa., Sept. 18 to 21, 1980 — Justification by faith, patristic and medieval views.
(37) Cincinnati, O., Feb. 19 to 22, 1981 — Merit and reward language; additional biblical material on justification by faith.
(38) Paoli, Pa., Sept. 23 to 27, 1981 — Drafting session on document on justification by faith. (39) Biloxi, Miss., Feb. 18 to 21, 1982 — Drafting session. (40) New York, N.Y., Sept. 23 to 26, 1982 — Drafting session. (41) Belmont, N.C., Feb. 17 to 20, 1983 — Drafting session. (42) Milwaukee, Wis., Sept. 15 to 18, 1983 — Final report, "Justification by Faith."

Methodist (United Methodist Church): (1) Chicago, Ill., June 28, 1966 — Methodists and Roman Catholics: comments for Catholic-Methodist conversation. (2) Chicago, Ill., Dec. 18, 1966 — Salvation, faith and good works; Catholic Church and faith. (3) Lake Junaluska, N.C., June 28, 1967 — Roman Catholic position regarding the Spirit in the Church; mission of the Holy Spirit, in the light of the Second Vatican Council's *Dogmatic Constitution on the Church* and the writings of John Wesley.
(4) New York, N.Y., Dec. 17, 1967 — Three generations of Church-State argumentation. (5) San Antonio, Tex., Sept. 30, 1968 — Shared convictions about education. (6) Delaware, O., Oct. 9, 1969 — Major Methodist ecumenical documents; an appraisal of some documents of Vatican II; racial confrontation in Roman Catholicism, Methodism and the National Council of Churches. (7) Chicago, Ill., Jan. 30, 1970 — Review and planning.
(8) Washington, D.C., Dec. 16, 1970 — Completion of a statement of shared convictions about education. Task force meetings during 1971. (9) Cincinnati, O., Feb. 25 to 26, 1972 — Ministry in the United Methodist Church and the spirituality of the ordained ministry; problems of ministry. (10) Dayton, O., Oct. 13 to 14, 1972 — Dialogue on the holiness of the Church and Christian holiness.
(11) Washington, D.C., Mar. 9 to 10, 1973 — Spirituality of the ministry. (12) Washington, D.C., Nov. 1 to 2, 1973 — Start of preparatory work on a consensus statement on spirituality of the ministry.
(13) Washington, D.C., Jan. 30 to Feb. 2, 1975 — Report prepared on Catholic and United Methodist understandings of holiness and spirituality in the ordained ministry; statement on holiness and spir-

ituality of the ordained ministry released in January, 1976.

(14) Washington, D.C., May 16, 1977 — Planning session for the next round of dialogue.

(15) Washington, D.C., Dec. 4 to 6, 1977 — New phase of dialogue on the Eucharist in both traditions. (16) Marriottsville, Md., Apr. 16 to 18, 1978 — Continuing research on Eucharistic theology as developed in the two churches.

(17) Washington, D.C., Oct. 12 to 14, 1978 — Eucharistic practice in both traditions. (18) Marriottsville, Md., May 17 to 19, 1979 — The Eucharist; contemporary eucharistic devotional practices of both traditions.

(19) Washington, D.C., Nov. 4 to 6, 1979 — The presence of Christ in the word, related to Eucharistic presence; the notion of sacrifice in the Eucharist. (20) Washington, D.C., May 4 to 6, 1980 — Comparison of liturgical texts of Methodists and Catholics; further exploration of the relationship of word and sacrament.

(21) Erlanger, Ky., Dec. 6 to 8, 1981 — Completion of statement, "Eucharistic Celebration: Converging Theology — Divergent Practice."

Orthodox (Standing Conference of Canonical Orthodox Bishops of America): Sept. 9, 1965 — Preliminary discussions. (1) New York, N.Y., Sept. 29, 1966 — Consultation led to appointment of task forces to investigate differences in theological methods, questions of sacramental sharing, possible cooperation in theological education and the formation of seminarians. (2) Worcester, Mass., May 5, 1967 — Theological diversity and unity; intercommunion; common witness in theological education. (3) Maryknoll, N.Y., Dec. 7, 1968 — Eucharist and Church; indissolubility of marriage; cooperation in theological education.

(4) Worcester, Mass., Dec. 12, 1969 — Orthodox and Catholic views of the Eucharist and membership in the Church; an agreed statement on the Eucharist. (5) New York, N.Y., May 19, 1970 — New Order of the Mass; membership of schismatics and heretics in the ancient Church; current legislation of the Catholic Church and current practices of the Greek Orthodox Church concerning common worship; current legislation of the Catholic Church concerning mixed marriages; Orthodox view of mixed marriages; an agreed statement on mixed marriages.

(6) Brookline, Mass., Dec. 4, 1970 — Ministers, doctrine and practice of matrimony in Eastern and Western traditions. (7) Barlin Acres, Mass., Nov. 3 to 4, 1971 — Ethical issues relating to marriage; revision of an agreed statement on mixed marriages; the primacy of Rome as seen by the Eastern Church.

(8) New York, N.Y., Dec. 6, 1973 — Study of a draft statement on the sanctity of marriage. (9) Washington, D.C., May 23 to 24, 1974 — Dialogical process; witness of the Church on the American scene; approval of an agreed statement on respect for life; Orthodox and Catholic views of contemporary Orthodoxy and Catholicism.

(10) New York, N.Y., Dec. 9 to 10, 1974 — Prepared and issued an agreed statement on the Church. (11) Washington, D.C., May 19 to 20, 1975 — Dialogue on the local church and on the theology of priesthood. (12) New York, N.Y., Jan. 23 to 24, 1976 — Further dialogue on the theology of priesthood, et al.

(13) Washington, D.C., May 18-19, 1976 — Additional discussion of theology of the priesthood, and ecumenical councils; release of joint statements entitled "The Principle of Economy" and "The Pastoral Office."

(14) Brookline, Mass., Jan. 13-14, 1977 — Presentations on "Orthodox/Roman Catholic Marriages Revisited" and of two reports on the first pre-synodal Pan-Orthodox Conference in preparation for the coming Great and Holy Council.

(15) Washington, D.C., Sept. 28 to 29, 1977 — Presentation and discussion of papers concerning the agenda of the forthcoming Great and Holy Council of the Orthodox Church, the theology of marriage and Orthodox-Roman Catholic marriages.

(16) New York, N.Y., Jan. 24 to 25, 1978 — Preparation of a common statement on the sanctity of marriage, authorization for writing a history of the Orthodox-Roman Catholic Consultation.

(17) Washington, D.C., May 15 to 16, 1978 — Additional work on a common statement on the sanctity of marriage, and initial discussion concerning the religious upbringing of children in Orthodox-Catholic marriages.

(18) New York, N.Y., Dec. 7 to 8, 1978 — Study of the religious formation of children of marriages between Eastern Orthodox and Roman Catholics; release of "An Agreed Statement on the Sanctity of Marriage."

(19) Washington, D.C., Mar. 15 to 16, 1979 — Continued study of a draft entitled "Joint Recommendations on the Spiritual Formation of Children of Marriages between Orthodox and Roman Catholics."

(20) Pittsburgh, Pa., Nov. 2 to 3, 1979 — Additional work on a document, "Spiritual Formation of Children"; study of early Christian commissioning rites.

(21) New York, N.Y., Oct. 10 to 11, 1980 — Study of the theology of ordained ministry; approval of "Joint Recommendations on the Spiritual Formation of Children of Marriages between Orthodox and Roman Catholics."

(22) New York, N.Y., Oct. 1 to 3, 1981 — Papers on "The Priest as Icon of Christ" and "The Sacramental Life of the Church in Light of Trinitarian Ecclesiology." (23) Milwaukee, Wis., May 27 to 29, 1982 — Papers on "Aspects of the Theme: Spirit and Sacrament," and "The Theological and Canonical Traditions of Marriage in the Orthodox and Roman Catholic Traditions."

(24) Pittsburgh, Pa., Nov. 18 to 20, 1982 — "Pneumatology and Sacramentology: A View of Systematic Theology"; an analysis of the most recent statement issued by the Anglican-Roman Catholic International Commission.

(25) New York, N.Y., May 23 to 25, 1983 — Beginning of a theological statement on the relationship of the Holy Spirit to Christ, especially in the Eucharist; preparation of an official reaction to

"The Mystery of the Church and of the Eucharist in Light of the Mystery of the Holy Trinity," a statement issued by the Joint International Commission for Theological Dialogue between the Roman Catholic Church and the Orthodox Church. (26) Milwakee, Wis., Oct. 27 to 29, 1983 — Sacraments of initiation.

Orthodox, Oriental (Armenian, Coptic, Ethiopian, Indian Malabar and Syrian Orthodox Churches): (1) New York N.Y., Jan. 27, 1978 — Start of a new consultation, with initial consideration of a historical study of Oriental Orthodoxy. (2) New York, N.Y., May 26 to 27, 1978 — Purpose and method of dialogue; histories of Oriental Orthodox Churches. (3) Washington, D.C., Dec. 1 to 2, 1978 — Presentation of papers on the Council of Chalcedon, Christology and the Church today, concluding that ancient controversy over Christology does not seem to apply at the present time. (4) New York, N.Y., May 25 to 26, 1979 — Roman Catholic Christology; Eucharistic Liturgy of the Syrian Orthodox Church. (5) New York, N.Y., Dec. 27 to 28, 1979 — Paper on Byzantine liturgical commentary; reflection on joint statements of Paul VI with Vasken I, Ignatius Jacoub III and Amba Shenouda III. (6) New York, N.Y., Apr. 18 to 19, 1980 — Paper on Coptic Orthodox Divine Liturgy followed by that Eucharistic Liturgy. (7) Jamaica, N.Y., Nov. 14 to 15, 1980 — Adoption of a statement on the purpose, scope and method of the dialogue between the Oriental Orthodox and Roman Catholic Churches, and a paper on celebration of the Eucharistic liturgy of the Roman Catholic Church. (8) New York, N.Y., Dec. 3 and 4, 1981 — Papers on the role of Christ and the Spirit in the Divine Liturgies of each tradition, and on the development of the Public Office in the Armenian Church. (9) New York, N.Y., Sept. 9 to 11, 1982 — Draft of "An Agreed Statement on the Church Crises in Egypt and Lebanon." (10) New York, N.Y., June 8 to 10, 1983 — Official release of the aforementioned agreed statement and also of an "Agreed Statement on the Eucharist"; discussion of history of the churches' views on mixed marriages, and of the Armenian liturgy. (11) Plymouth, Mich., Jan. 12 to 14, 1984 — Discussion of pastoral practice concerning mixed marriages; theological reflection on the Eucharist as Sacrifice.

Presbyterian and Reformed (The Roman Catholic-Presbyterian Consultation Group, North American Council of the World Alliance of Reformed Churches): (1) Washington, D.C., July 27, 1965 — Exploratory discussions. (2) Philadelphia, Pa., Nov. 26, 1965 — Role of the Holy Spirit in renewal and reform of the Church. (3) New York, May 12, 1966 — Roman Catholic view of Scripture and tradition; apostolic and ecclesiastical tradition. (4) Chicago, Ill., Oct. 27, 1966 — Development of doctrine; dialogue, a program of peace, prayer and study for Roman Catholics and Protestants.

(5) Collegeville, Minn., Apr. 26, 1967 — Order and ministry in the Reformed tradition; validity of orders; changes in mixed marriage. (6) Lancaster, Pa., Oct. 26, 1967 — Work was begun on a joint statement on ministry. (7) Bristow, Va., May 9, 1968 — Structures and ministries. (8) Allen Park, Mich., Oct. 24, 1968 — Marriage. (9) Charleston, S.C., May 21, 1969 — Validation of ministries and ministry; theological view of marriage. (10) Macatawa, Mich., Oct. 30, 1969 — Apostles and apostolic succession in the patristic era; report concerning office; divorce and remarriage as understood in the United Presbyterian Church in the USA; the Church and second marriage; recommendations for changes regarding inter-Christian marriages. (11) Morristown, N.J., May 13, 1970 — Joint statements on ministry in the Church and women in Church and society. (12) Princeton, N.J., Oct. 29 to 30, 1970 — Episcopal presbyteral polity; episcopacy. (13) Columbus, O., May 13 to 15, 1971 — Ministry in the Church; man-woman relationships; the future of the Church. (14) Richmond, Va., Oct. 28 to 30, 1971 — Reports finalized on women in the Church and ministry in the Church. (15) Oct. 26 to 29, 1972 — The shape of the unity we seek. (16) Columbus, O., May 30 to June 2, 1973 — Theological and sociological views of the shape of unity we seek. (17) Columbus, O., Oct. 24 to 27, 1973 — Renewed discussion of the previous topic. (18) Columbus, O., May 8 to 11, 1974 — Further discussion of the previous topic in the light of Scripture, tradition, theology and reflection on the total Christian experience; worship and belief; discussion of plans for publication of a book on progress of the dialogue.

(17) Cincinnati, O., Oct. 24 to 26, 1974 — Dialogue on the unity we seek in worship and in structures. (18) Washington, D.C., May 22 to 24, 1975 — Report prepared on the mission and nature of the one Church of Christ, with attention to the unity sought in worship, in structure and in common faith. (19) Princeton, N.J., Oct. 20-23, 1976 — Presentation of: an overview of the history of the consultation; a paper covering a Roman Catholic summary of the diversity and unity of current Christian responses to moral issues facing the Church; a paper on ethics and ethos in the Reformed/Presbyterian tradition. (20) Washington, D.C., May 25 to 27, 1977 — Human rights, distributive justice and the abortion issue as faced by the churches. (21) Princeton, N.J., Oct. 6 to 7, 1977 — Discussion of racism in South Africa and continuation of a study on human rights. (22) Washington, D.C., May 30 to June 1, 1978 — Study of the problem of unwanted pregnancies; preparation of statements on abortion and human rights. (23) Washington, D.C., Mar. 4 to 6, 1979 — Re-drafting of proposed statements on abortion and human rights. (24) Washington, D.C., Sept. 27 to 29, 1979 — Statements on abortion and human rights approved along with commentaries, and an interpretative report. (25) Princeton, N.J., May 19 to 21, 1982 — Beginning of the fourth round of dia-

logue, on the theme, "Church, Society and Kingdom of God," related to the theme of international bilateral dialogue.

(26) Washington, D.C., Nov. 17 to 19, 1982 — Papers on "Church, Society and Kingdom in the Roman Catholic and Reformed Traditions."

(27) Princeton, N.J., Mar. 24 to 26, 1983 — Paper on the Church and society from a political-science point of view; case-study analysis of respective statements on nuclear arms.

(28) Washington, D.C., Oct. 20 to 22, 1983 — Papers on Church-State issues; discussion of initial drafts of statements on "Church, State, Kingdom," and "Convergences and Divergences in Approaches to Nuclear Arms."

INTERFAITH STATEMENTS

The ecumenical statements listed below, and others like them, reflect the views of participants in the dialogues which produced them. They have not been formally accepted by the respective churches as formulations of doctrine or points of departure for practical changes in discipline.

• The "Windsor Statement" on Eucharistic doctrine, published Dec. 31, 1971, by the Anglican-Roman Catholic International Commission of theologians. (For text, see pages 132-33 of the 1973 *Catholic Almanac*.)

• The "Canterbury Statement" on ministry and ordination, published Dec. 13, 1973, by the same commission (For excerpts, see pages 127-30 of the 1975 *Catholic Almanac*.)

• "Papal Primacy / Converging Viewpoints," published Mar. 4, 1974, by the dialogue group sanctioned by the U.S.A. National Convention of the World Lutheran Federation and the U.S. Bishops' Committee for Ecumenical and Interreligious Affairs. (For excerpts, see pages 130-31 of the 1975 *Catholic Almanac*.)

• An "Agreed Statement on the Purpose of the Church," published Oct. 31, 1975, by the Anglican-Roman Catholic Consultation in the U.S., in which the signatories agreed on the purpose and mission of the Church "insofar as it faithfully preaches the Gospel of salvation and manifests the love of God in service." It noted that "Roman Catholics and Episcopalians believe that there is but one Church of Christ," and endorsed social action for human liberation.

• "Christian Unity and Women's Ordination," published Nov. 7, 1975, by the same consultation, in which it was said that the ordination of women (approved in principle by the Anglican Communion but not by the Catholic Church) would "introduce a new element" in dialogue but would not mean the end of consultation nor the abandonment of its declared goal of full communion and organic unity. (A similar view was expressed in an exchange of letters between Pope Paul and Anglican Archbishop Donald Coggan of Canterbury, between July 8, 1975, and Mar. 23, 1976.)

• "Holiness and Spirituality of the Ordained Ministry," issued early in 1976 by theologians of the Catholic Church and the United Methodist Church; the first statement resulting from dialogue begun in 1966.

• "Mixed Marriages," published in the spring of 1976 by the Anglican-Roman Catholic Consultation in the U.S. It was similar in some respects to the statement, "Implementation of the Apostolic Letter on Mixed Marriages," approved by the National Conference of Catholic Bishops Nov. 16, 1970. It differed in softening the statement of a Catholic party's responsibility to do everything possible to raise children in the Catholic faith and favored greater freedom for having the marriage ceremony according to the rite of another Christian church.

• "Bishops and Presbyters," see under Eastern Ecumenical Briefs.

• "The Principle of Economy," see under Eastern Ecumenical Briefs.

• "Venice Statement" on authority in the Church, published Jan. 20, 1977, by the Anglican-Roman Catholic International Commission of theologians. Its major headings were Christian authority, authority of the ordained ministry and of the community, authority in the community of churches, the primacy of the bishop of Rome, authority in matters of faith, conciliar and primatial authority. Differences were cited in Catholic and Anglican views with respect to scriptural passages related to claims of the Roman See to primacy of authority, the divine right of the successors of St. Peter, papal infallibility and universal jurisdiction over the Church. (For text, see pages 145-50 of the 1978 *Catholic Almanac*.)

• "Response to the Venice Statement," issued Jan. 4, 1978, by the Anglican-Roman Catholic Consultation in the U.S.A., citing additional questions regarding the sharing of authority in the Church, the nature of the primacy of Rome, and the relation of indefectibility to infallibility.

• "The Presence of Christ in Church and World," published early in 1978 by representatives of the Vatican Secretariat for Promoting Christian Unity and the World Alliance of Reformed Churches. The wide-ranging statement noted considerable degrees of mutual understanding and some agreement, along with substantial differences of view on several subjects — especially papal infallibility.

• "An Ecumenical Approach to Marriage," published in January, 1978, in the form of a report on five or more years of dialogue among representatives of the Catholic Church, the Lutheran World Federation and the World Alliance of Reformed Churches. Significant agreement was reported on doctrinal and pastoral aspects of marriage. Objections continued from the Lutheran and Reformed sides, however, with respect to the sacramental nature of marriage, and to Catholic requirements in cases of mixed marriages: (1) that the marriage normally take place with a priest as the officiating minister, and (2) that the Catholic party promise to do everything possible to raise children in the Catholic faith.

• "Teaching Authority and Infallibility in the Church," released in October, 1978, by the Catholic-Lutheran dialogue group in the U.S., noting similarities and differences between Lutheran understanding of the indefectibility of the Church and the Catholic doctrine of papal infallibility.

• "The Eucharist," reported early in 1979, in which the Roman Catholic-Lutheran Commission indicated developing convergence of views concerning the nature and sacrificial aspect of the Mass, and the significance of believing, active participation in the Eucharist.

• "The Holy Spirit," issued Feb. 12, 1979, by the International Catholic-Methodist Commission, citing points of common faith in the Holy Spirit.

• A statement on "Ministry in the Church," approved in draft form in February, 1980, and published in March, 1981, by the International Roman Catholic-Lutheran Joint Commission, regarding possible mutual recognition of ministries.

• The Final Report of the Anglican-Roman Catholic International Commission, released late in March, 1982, on the results of 12 years of dialogue. (See following article.)

• A report released June 9, 1982, by the Catholic Church-Disciples of Christ international commission concluded after five years of dialogue that the two churches already have a "unity of grace" which is "bearing fruit and which is disposing us for visible unity and urging us to move ahead to it." The report noted, however, that the two churches differ in their views of the relationship between the New Testament and later Catholic treaching embodied in liturgical texts, creeds and conciliar and papal statements.

ANGLICAN-CATHOLIC FINAL REPORT

The report which is the subject of this article is significant because it was one of the first, if not the first, of its kind to elicit critical comment from the Congregation for the Doctrine of the Faith.

The Anglican-Roman Catholic International Commission of theologians officially published Mar. 31, 1982, a Final Report on 12 years of dialogue concerning subjects of belief and practice which have divided the two churches for more than 400 years.

The report included "Authority in the Church II," a new agreed statement, as well as earlier documents:

• the "Windsor Statement" on Eucharistic doctrine, published Dec. 31, 1971;

• the "Canterbury Statement" on ministry and ordination, published Dec. 13, 1973;

• the "Venice Statement" on authority in the Church, agreed to in 1976 and published Jan. 20, 1977;

• elucidations of these documents issued in 1979 and 1981;

• additional documentary material on the commission and related developments.

Key Issues

"Controversy between our two communions," the report said, "has centered on the Eucharist, on the meaning and function of ordained ministry, and on the nature and exercise of authority in the Church. Although we are not yet in full communion, what the commission has done has convinced us that substantial agreement on these divisive issues is now possible."

The "divisive issues," subsequently called "four difficulties," were "the interpretation of the Petrine texts, the meaning of the language of 'divine right,' the affirmation of papal infallibility, and the nature of the jurisdiction ascribed to the Bishop of Rome as Universal Primate."

Bishop Raymond W. Lessard of Savannah, chairman of the Anglican-Roman Catholic Consultation in the United States, said in a statement for publication:

"The Final Report maintains that, despite differences of vocabulary and theological emphasis, the Anglican Communion and the Roman Catholic Church are in fundamental agreement in the three areas on which, since the 16th century, Anglicans and Roman Catholics have maintained they differ from one another so sharply that in conscience their Christian communities would have to remain officially separated from each other."

Catholic Critique

The claim to fundamental agreement made in the Final Report was questioned by Cardinal Joseph Ratzinger, prefect of the Congregation for the Doctrine of the Faith, in a letter addressed to Bishop Alan C. Clark of East Anglia, England, co-president of the Anglican-Roman Catholic International Commission.

The claim was also questioned by the Congregation for the Doctrine of the Faith in the conclusion of a set of observations, dated Mar. 29, 1982, concerning the Final Report.

"At the conclusion of its doctrinal examination, the congregation thinks that the Final Report, which represents a notable ecumenical endeavor and a useful basis for further steps on the road to reconciliation between the Catholic Church and the Anglican Communion, does not yet constitute a substantial and explicit agreement on some essential elements of Catholic faith:

• "a) because the report explicitly recognizes that one or another Catholic dogma is not accepted by our Anglican brethren (for example, Eucharistic adoration, infallibility, the Marian dogmas);

• "b) because one or another Catholic doctrine is accepted only in part by our Anglican brethren (for example, the primacy of the Bishop of Rome);

• "c) because certain formulations in the report are not explicit enough to ensure that they exclude interpretations not in harmony with the Catholic faith (for example, that which concerns the Eucharist as sacrifice, the Real Presence, the nature of the priesthood);

• "d) because certain affirmations in the report are inexact and not acceptable as Catholic doctrine (for example, the relationship between the primacy and the structure of the Church, the doctrine of 'reception' — regarding the validation of doctrine by the acceptance of the people);

• "e) finally, because some important aspects of the teaching of the Catholic Church have either not been dealt with or have been only in an indirect way (for example, apostolic succession, the rule of faith, moral teaching)."

Recommendation

Regarding next steps to be taken, the congregation said "the results of its examination would recommend:

• "a) that the dialogue be continued, since there are sufficient grounds for thinking its continuation will be fruitful;

• "b) that it be deepened in regard to the points already addressed where the results are not satisfactory;

• "c) that it be extended to new themes, particularly those which are necessary with a view to the restoration of full church unity between the two communions."

ECUMENICAL BRIEFS, 1983

• Christian Brother Jeffrey Gros was elected director of the Faith and Order Commission of the National Council of Churches at a meeting of the NCC executive committee Feb. 11, 1983. He was the first Catholic chosen to serve as a chief staff executive of a major unit of the council.

• The Graymoor Ecumenical Institute announced in July, 1983, that it was moving its main office from Garrison, N.Y., to the Interchurch Center, 475 Riverside Drive, New York, N.Y. 10115. The directors of the institute were Father Charles LaFontaine, S.A., editor of *Ecumenical Trends,* and Brother William Martyn, S.A., editor of *At-one-ment,* a monthly newsletter.

• A covenant relationship between the Archdiocese of Milwaukee and the Episcopal Diocese of Milwaukee was signed at a prayer and worship service late in July in All Saints Episcopal Cathedral. A document co-signed by Archbishop Rembert G. Weakland and Episcopal Bishop Charles T. Gaskell said the covenant was intended to promote active cooperation not only between the dioceses but also between individual Catholic and Episcopal parishes for the purpose of removing "any existing obstacles to union while supporting and preserving the traditions of each other."

• The Catholic-Episcopal members of the Church of the Holy Apostles, founded in 1977 in Norfolk, Va., reported participation in shared prayer before and after the separate celebration of their respective liturgies.

• The second Anglican-Roman Catholic International Commission for theological dialogue was scheduled to hold its first meeting Aug. 3 to Sept. 6, 1983, in Venice. On the agenda were such subjects as justification, ecclesiology and moral questions, along with extended study of: "all that hinders the mutual recognition of the ministries of our two communions," doctrinal differences and practical steps necessary for progress toward the restoration of full communion of the churches.

The establishment of ARCIC II was announced jointly by Pope John Paul and Anglican Archbishop Robert Runcie May 29, 1982, at Canterbury Cathedral. It was chartered to continue the work of ARCIC I which issued in March, 1982, a final report on its 12 years of dialogue (see separate entry).

• Additional 1983 ecumenical developments reported elsewhere in the Almanac were the authorization of intercommunion by members of the Episcopal Church and three Lutheran denominations, and the merger of two major Presbyterian denominations.

Anglican Identity Parish

The "Anglican identity personal parish" of Our Lady of Atonement in San Antonio was established by Archbishop Patrick Flores Aug. 15, 1983. Its members were Episcopalians who had become Catholics and would be permitted to retain and practice elements of their Anglican tradition compatible with Catholic doctrine and liturgy. Their pastor was Father Christopher Phillips, a married former Episcopal clergyman who was ordained to the Catholic priesthood on the day the parish was established.

The creation of the Anglican identity parish stemmed from Vatican approval in 1980 of a proposal by the U.S. bishops to develop terms under which Episcopal clergymen and other members of the Episcopal Church could be admitted to the Catholic Church and still retain some elements of their former tradition.

It was also reported that a second Anglican identity parish, St. Mary the Virgin in Las Vegas, Nev., had been approved by the Vatican but had not yet been formally established.

CATHOLIC-JEWISH RELATIONS

The Second Vatican Council, in addition to the "Decree on Ecumenism" concerning the movement for unity among Christians, stated the mind of the Church on a similar matter in a "Declaration on the Relationship of the Church to Non-Christian Religions." This document, as the following excerpts indicate, backgrounds the reasons and directions of the Church's regard for the Jews. (Other portions of the document, not cited here, refer to Hindus, Buddhists and Moslems.)

Spiritual Bond

As this sacred Synod searches into the mystery of the Church, it recalls the spiritual bond linking the people of the New Covenant with Abraham's stock.

For the Church of Christ acknowledges that, according to the mystery of God's saving design, the beginnings of her faith and her election are already found among the patriarchs, Moses, and the prophets. She professes that all who believe in Christ, Abraham's sons according to faith (cf. Gal. 3:7), are included in the same patriarch's call, and likewise that the salvation of the Church was mystically foreshadowed by the Chosen People's exodus from the land of bondage.

The Church, therefore, cannot forget that she received the revelation of the Old Testament through the people with whom God in his inexpressible mercy deigned to establish the Ancient Covenant. Nor can she forget that she draws sustenance from the root of that good olive tree onto which have been grafted the wild olive branches of the Gentiles (cf. Rom.11:17-24). Indeed, the Church believes that by his cross Christ, our Peace, reconciled Jew and Gentile, making them both one in himself (cf. Eph. 2:14-16).

The Jews still remain most dear to God because of their fathers, for he does not repent of the gifts he makes nor of the calls he issues (cf. Rom. 11:28-29). In company with the prophets and the same Apostle (Paul), the Church awaits that day, known to God alone, on which all peoples will address the Lord in a single voice and "serve him with one accord" (Zeph. 3:9; Cf. Is. 66:23; Ps. 65:4; Rom. 11:11-32).

Since the spiritual patrimony common to Christians and Jews is thus so great, this sacred Synod wishes to foster and recommend that mutual understanding and respect which is the fruit above all of biblical and theological studies, and of brotherly dialogues.

No Anti-Semitism

True, authorities of the Jews and those who followed their lead pressed for the death of Christ (cf. Jn. 19:6); still, what happened in his passion cannot be blamed upon all the Jews then living, without distinction, nor upon the Jews of today. Although the Church is the new People of God, the Jews should not be presented as repudiated or cursed by God, as if such views followed from the holy Scriptures. All should take pains, then, lest in catechetical instruction and in the preaching of God's Word they teach anything out of harmony with the truth of the Gospel and the spirit of Christ.

The Church repudiates all persecutions against any man. Moreover, mindful of her common patrimony with the Jews, and motivated by the Gospel's spiritual love and by no political considerations, she deplores the hatred, persecutions, and displays of anti-Semitism directed against the Jews at any time and from any source. (No. 4).

The Church rejects, as foreign to the mind of Christ, any discrimination against men or harassment of them because of their race, color, condition of life, or religion. (No. 5).

Bishops' Secretariat

The American hierarchy's first move toward implementation of the Vatican II *Declaration on the Relationship of the Church to Non-Christian Religions* was to establish, in 1965, a Subcommission for Catholic-Jewish Relations in the framework of its Commission for Ecumenical and Interreligious Affairs. This subcommission was reconstituted and given the title of secretariat in September, 1967. Its moderator is Bishop Francis J. Mugavero of Brooklyn. The Secretariat for Catholic-Jewish Relations is located at 1312 Massachusetts Ave. N.W., Washington, D.C. 20005. The executive director is Dr. Eugene J. Fisher.

According to the key norm of a set of guidelines issued by the secretariat Mar. 16, 1967: "The general aim of all Catholic-Jewish meetings (and relations) is to increase our understanding both of Judaism and the Catholic faith, to eliminate sources of tension and misunderstanding, to initiate dialogue or conversations on different levels, to multiply intergroup meetings between Catholics and Jews, and to promote cooperative social action."

Vatican Guidelines

In a document issued Jan. 3, 1975, the Vatican Commission for Religious Relations with the Jews offered a number of suggestions and guidelines for implementing the Christian-Jewish portion of the Second Vatican Council's *Declaration on Relations with Non-Christian Religions*.

Among "suggestions from experience" were those concerning dialogue, liturgical links between Christian and Jewish worship, the interpretation of biblical texts, teaching and education for the purpose of increasing mutual understanding, and joint social action.

The document concluded with the statement: "On Oct. 22, 1974, the Holy Father instituted for the universal Church this Commission for Religious Relations with the Jews, joined to the Secretariat for Promoting Christian Unity. This special commission, created to encourage and foster religious relations between Jews and Catholics — and to do so in collaboration with other Christians — will be, within the limits of its competence, at the service of all interested organizations, providing information for them and helping them to pursue their task in conformity with the instructions of the Holy See.

"The commission wishes to develop this collaboration in order to implement, correctly and effectively, the express intentions of the (Second Vatican) Council."

NCCB Statement

In a statement issued Nov. 20, 1975, in commemoration of the 10th anniversary of the Second Vatican Council's declaration on non-Christian religions, the National Conference of Catholic Bishops welcomed the Vatican guidelines and hailed the "new era in Catholic-Jewish affairs" which "ended a centuries-long silence between Church and Synagogue."

Lamenting the "de-Judaizing process" that set in early in the Church's history — and which "dulled our awareness of our Jewish beginnings," the bishops affirmed that "most essential concepts in the Christian creed grew at first in Judaic soil. Uprooted from that soil, these basic concepts cannot be perfectly understood."

The bishops called on theologians to reconsider the "long-neglected passages" of the Letter to the Romans (Chapters 9 to 11) as a base for "exploring the continuing relationship of the Jewish people with God and their spiritual bonds with the New Covenant" in a positive manner.

Noting also that "an overwhelming majority of Jews see themselves bound in one way or another to the land of Israel," the bishops stated that, "whatever difficulties Christians may experience in sharing this view, they should strive to understand this link between land and people which Jews have expressed in their writings and worship throughout two millennia as a longing for the homeland, holy Zion.''

Papal Statements

(Courtesy of Dr. Eugene Fisher, Executive Director of the Secretariat for Catholic-Jewish Relations, National Conference of Catholic Bishops, and Consultor, since April, 1981, to the Vatican Commission for Religious Relations with the Jews.)

Pope John Paul, in a remarkable series of addresses beginning in 1979, has sought to promote and give shape to the development of dialogue between Catholics and Jews.

In a homily delivered June 7, 1979, at Auschwitz, which he called the "Golgotha of the Modern World," he prayed movingly for "the memory of the people whose sons and daughters were intended for total extermination."

In a key address delivered Nov. 17, 1980, to the Jewish community in Mainz during his visit to West Germany, the Pope articulated his vision of the three "dimensions" of the dialogue. The first — "that is, the meeting between the people of God of the Old Covenant never retracted by God (Rm. 11:29) on the one hand and the people of the New Covenant on the other" — he said, "is at the same time a dialogue within our own Church, so to speak, a dialogue between the first and second part of its Bible." The second dimension is the encounter of "mutual esteem" between today's Christian churches and today's people of the Covenant concluded with Moses." The third is the "holy duty" of witnessing to the one God in the world and "jointly to work for peace and justice."

In addressing representatives of episcopal conferences gathered in Rome by the Vatican Commission from around the world, the Pope again stressed Mar. 6, 1982, the continuing validity of God's covenant with the Jewish people, noting that "our two religious communities are linked at the very level of their identities," forging links between the two that "are grounded in the design of the God of the Covenant." In his 1982 address, the Pope called especially for a renewal of catechesis that "will not only present Jews and Judaism in an honest and objective manner, but will also do so with a lively awareness" of "our common spiritual heritage . . . taking into account the faith and religious life of the Jewish people as professed and lived now as well." The delegates to the meeting began the process of considering the biblical, theological, and contemporary dynamics of such a catechesis.

International Liaison Committee

The International Catholic-Jewish Liaison Committee, meeting for the ninth time in March, 1981, in London, held discussions on "The Challenge of Secularism to Our Religious Commitments." Speakers warned against "pernicious revisions of the history of the Holocaust," referring pointedly to recent pseudo-scholarly attempts to deny the reality of the Nazi genocide policy against the Jews.

"The Sanctity and Meaning of Human Life in the Present Situation of Violence" was the topic of the 10th meeting, held in September, 1982, in Milan.

Previous meetings discussed such topics as mission and witness (Venice, 1977), religious education (Madrid, 1978), and religious liberty and pluralism (Regensburg, 1979).

U.S. Dialogue

National Workshops on Christian-Jewish Relations, an increasingly important forum for dialogue, have been held since 1975 in several U.S. cities.

A continuing dialogue on religious tradition and social policy — sponsored by the Synagogue Council of America and the NCCB Secretariat for Catholic-Jewish Relations — has been held annually since 1979.

Ongoing relationships are also maintained by the NCCB Secretariat with other Jewish agencies, such as the American Jewish Committee and the Anti-Defamation League of B'nai B'rith.

JUDAISM

Judaism is the religion of the Old Testament and of contemporary Jews. Divinely revealed and with a patriarchal background (Abraham, Isaac, Jacob), it originated with the Mosaic Covenant, was identified with the Israelites, and achieved distinctive form and character as the religion of The Law from this Covenant and reforms initiated by Ezra and Nehemiah after the Babylonian Exile.

Judaism does not have a formal creed but its principal points of belief are clear. Basic is belief in one transcendent God who reveals himself through The Law, the prophets, the life of his people and events of history. The fatherhood of God involves the brotherhood of men. Religious faith and practice are equated with just living according to The Law. Moral conviction and practice are regarded as more important than precise doctrinal formulation and profession. Formal worship, whose principal act was sacrifice from Canaanite times to 70 A.D., is by prayer, reading and meditating upon the sacred writings, and observance of the Sabbath and festivals.

Judaism has messianic expectations of the complete fulfillment of the Covenant, the coming of God's kingdom, the ingathering of his people, final judgment and retribution for all men. Views differ regarding the manner in which these expectations will be realized — through a person, the community of God's people, an evolution of historical events, an eschatological act of God himself. Individual salvation expectations also differ, depending on views about the nature of immortality, punishment and reward, and related matters.

Sacred Books

The sacred books are the 24 books of the Masoretic Hebrew Text of The Law, the Prophets and the Writings (see The Bible). Together, they contain the basic instruction or norms for just living. In some contexts, the term Law or Torah refers only to the Pentateuch (Genesis, Exodus,

Leviticus, Numbers, Deuteronomy); in others, it denotes all the sacred books and/or the whole complex of written and oral tradition.

Also of great authority are two Talmuds which were composed in Palestine and Babylon in the fourth and fifth centuries A.D., respectively. They consist of the Mishna, a compilation of oral laws, and the Gemara, a collection of rabbinical commentary on the Mishna. Midrash are collections of scriptural comments and moral counsels.

Priests were the principal official ministers during the period of sacrificial and temple worship. Rabbis were, and continue to be, teachers and leaders of prayer. The synagogue is the place of community worship. The family and home are focal points of many aspects of Jewish worship and practice.

Of the various categories of Jews, Orthodox are the most conservative in adherence to strict religious traditions. Others — Reformed, Conservative, Reconstructionist — are liberal in comparison with the Orthodox. They favor greater or less modification of religious practices in accommodation to contemporary culture and living conditions.

Principal events in Jewish life include the circumcision of males, according to prescriptions of the Covenant; the bar mitzvah which marks the coming-of-age of boys in Judaism at the age of 13; marriage; and observance of the Sabbath and festivals.

Sabbath and Festivals

Observances of the Sabbath and festivals begin at sundown of the previous calendar day and continue until the following sundown.

Sabbath: Saturday, the weekly day of rest prescribed in the Decalogue.

Booths (Tabernacles): A seven-to-nine-day festival in the month of Tishri (Sept.-Oct.), marked by some Jews with Covenant-renewal and reading of The Law. It originated as an agricultural feast at the end of the harvest and got its name from the temporary shelters used by workers in the fields.

Hanukkah (The Festival of Lights, the Feast of Consecration and of the Maccabees): Commemorates the dedication of the new altar in the Temple at Jerusalem by Judas Maccabeus in 165 B.C. The eight-day festival, during which candles in an eight-branch candelabra are lighted in succession, one each day, occurs near the winter solstice, close to Christmas time.

Passover: A seven-day festival commemorating the liberation of the Israelites from Egypt. The narrative of the Exodus, the Haggadah, is read at ceremonial Seder meals on the first and second days of the festival, which begins on the 14th day of Nisan (Mar.-Apr.).

Pentecost (Feast of Weeks): Observed 50 days after Passover. Some Jews regard it as commemorative of the anniversary of the revelation of The Law to Moses.

Purim: A joyous festival observed on the 14th day of Adar (Feb.-Mar.), commemorating the rescue of the Israelites from massacre by the Persians through the intervention of Esther. The festival is preceded by a day of fasting. A gift- and alms-giving custom became associated with it in medieval times.

Rosh Hashana (Feast of the Trumpets, New Year): Observed on the first day of Tishri (Sept.-Oct.), the festival focuses attention on the day of judgment and is marked with meditation on the ways of life and the ways of death. It is second in importance only to the most solemn observance of Yom Kippur, which is celebrated 10 days later.

Yom Kippur (Day of Atonement): The highest holy day, observed with strict fasting. It occurs 10 days after Rosh Hashana.

ISLAM

Islam is the religion of Mohammed and his followers, called Moslems, or Muslims. Islam, meaning submission to God, originated with Mohammed (570-632), an Arabian, who taught that he had received divine revelation and was the last and greatest of the prophets.

Moslems believe in one God. There were six great prophets—Adam, Noah, Abraham, Moses, Jesus and Mohammed—and Mohammed was the greatest. The creed states: "There is no God but Allah and Mohammed is the prophet of Allah."

The principal duties of Moslems are to: profess the faith by daily recitation of the creed; pray five times a day facing in the direction of the holy city of Mecca; give alms; fast daily from dawn to dusk during the month of Ramadan; make a pilgrimage to Mecca once if possible.

Moslems believe in a final judgment, heaven and hell. Polygamy is practiced. Some dietary regulations are in effect. The weekly day of worship is Friday, and the principal service is at noon in a mosque. Moslems do not have an ordained ministry. The general themes of their prayer are adoration and thanksgiving.

The basis of Islamic belief is the Koran, the created word of God revealed to Mohammed by the angel Gabriel over a period of 20 years. The contents of this sacred book are complemented by the Sunna, a collection of sacred traditions, and reinforced by Ijma, the consensus of Moslems which guarantees them against error in matters of belief and practice.

There are several sects of Moslems.

Conciliar Statement

The attitude of the Church toward Islam was stated as follows in the Second Vatican Council's *Declaration on the Relationship of the Church to Non-Christian Religions* (No. 3).

"Upon the Moslems, too, the Church looks with esteem. They adore one God, living and enduring, merciful and all-powerful, Maker of heaven and earth and Speaker to men. They strive to submit wholeheartedly even to his inscrutable decrees, just as did Abraham, with whom the Islamic faith is pleased to associate itself. Though they do not acknowledge Jesus as God, they revere him as a prophet. They also honor Mary, his virgin mother; at times they call on her, too, with devotion. In addition they await the day of judgment when God will give each man his due after raising him up. Consequently, they prize the moral life, and give worship to God especially through prayer, almsgiving and fasting.

"Although in the course of the centuries many quarrels and hostilities have arisen between Christians and Moslems, this most sacred Synod urges all to forget the past and to strive sincerely for mutual understanding. On behalf of all mankind, let them make common cause of safeguarding and fostering social justice, moral values, peace and freedom."

NON-REVEALED RELIGIONS

Hinduism

Hinduism is the traditional religion of India with origins dating to about 5,000 B.C. Its history is complex, including original Vedic Hinduism, with a sacred literature (Veda) of hymns, incantations and other elements, and with numerous nature gods; Brahmanism, with emphasis on ceremonialism and its power over the gods; philosophical speculation, reflected in the Upanishads, with development of ideas concerning Karma, reincarnation, Brahman, and the manner of achieving salvation; the cults of Vishnu, Shiva and other deities; reforms in Hinduism and in relation to Islam and Christianity.

The principal tenets of Hinduism are open to various interpretations. Karma is the law of the deed, of sowing and reaping, of retribution. It determines the progress of a person toward liberation from the cycle of rebirths necessary for salvation. Liberation is accomplished in stages, through successive reincarnations which indicate the previous as well as the existing state of a person. The means of liberation are the practice of ceremonialism and asceticism; faith in, devotion to and worship of the gods Vishnu and Shiva in their several incarnations; and/or knowledge attained through disciplined meditation called Yoga. Salvation, according to philosophical Hinduism, consists in absorption in Brahman, the neuter world-soul. Vishnu, the sun-god, and Shiva, the destroyer or generative force of the universe, are the principal popular deities. Ancient belief in nature gods (pantheism) is reflected in sacred respect for some animals. The concept of reincarnation underlies the caste system in Indian society.

There are many sects in Hinduism, which does not have a definite creed. It lends itself easily to syncretism or amalgamation with other beliefs, as evidenced in the 15th century Sikh movement which adopted the monotheism and militancy of Islam. Hindu rituals are various and elaborate, with respect to foods, festivals, pilgrimages, marriage and other life-events.

Buddhism

Buddhism originated in the sixth century B.C. in reaction to formalism, pantheism and other trends in Hinduism. The Buddha, the Enlightened One, was Sidartha Gautama, an Indian prince, who sought to explain human suffering and evil and to find a middle way between the extremes of austerity and sensuality.

The four noble truths of Buddhism are: (1) existence involves suffering or pain; (2) suffering comes from craving: (3) craving can be overcome; (4) the way to overcome craving is to follow the "noble eightfold path" of right views, right intention, right speech, right action, right livelihood, right effort, right mindfulness and right concentration.

Karma, the deed-principle of judgment and retribution, and reincarnation are elements of Buddhism. The ultimate objective of life is Nirvana — the absorption of a person in the absolute — which ends the cycles of rebirth.

Buddhism is essentially atheistic and more of a moral philosophy and ethical system than a religion. It has a cultic element in veneration for Buddha. Monasteries, temples and shrines are places of contemplation and ritualistic observance. There are several categories of Buddhist monks and nuns.

Buddhism has many sects. Mahayana Buddhism, with an elaborate ideology, is strong in China, Korea and Japan. Hinayana Buddhism is common in Southeast Asia. Zen Buddhism is highly contemplative. Lamaism in Tibet is a combination of Buddhism and local demonolatry.

Confucianism

Confucianism is an ethical system based on the teachings of Confucius (c. 551-479 B.C.). It is oriented toward the moral perfection of individuals and society, the attainment of the harmony of individual and social life with the harmony of the universe, through conduct governed by the relationships of humanity, justice, ritual and courtesy, wisdom, and fidelity. Originally and basically humanistic, Confucianism was eventually mingled with elements of Chinese religion.

Taoism

Taoism originated in China several centuries before the Christian era and became a fully developed religious system by the fifth century A.D. As a religion of mystery, it developed extreme polytheism, with the Jade Emperor as the highest deity; sought blessings and long life by means of alchemy; fostered superstition and witchcraft; took on organizational and other aspects of Buddhism, with several categories of priests and nuns; exerted strong ethical influence on the lower classes; split into many sects; adopted features from other religions; became the starting point of many secret societies.

Shinto

Shinto is the way of the gods, the sum total of the cultic beliefs and practices of the ancestral religion of Japan which originated from nature and ancestor worship. Shinto is pantheistic and has many objects of devotion, the highest being the Ruler of Heaven; is practiced with detailed rituals in public shrines, which are cultic centers; has strong social influence. Sectarian Shinto has about 13 recognized sects and many offshoots. Shinto, with principal concern for this-worldly blessing, has been affected by Buddhist and Confucian influences.

A

Abbess: The female superior of a monastic community of nuns; e.g., Benedictines, Poor Clares, some others. Elected by members of the community, an abbess has general authority over her community but no sacramental jurisdiction. Earliest evidence of the use of the title, a feminine derivative of the Aramaic *abba* (father), dates from early in the sixth century.

Abbey: See Abbot, Monastery.

Abbot: The male superior of a monastic community of men religious; e.g., Benedictines, Cistercians, some others. Elected by members of the community, an abbot has ordinary jurisdiction and general authority over his community. He has some episcopal privileges. The title derives from the Aramaic *abba* (father); first given to the spiritual fathers and guides of hermits in Egypt in the fourth century, it was appropriated in the Rule of St. Benedict to the heads of abbeys and monasteries. Eastern-Rite equivalents of an abbot are a *hegumen* and an *archimandrite.*

A regular abbot is the head of an abbey or monastery. An abbot general or archabbot is the head of a congregation consisting of several monasteries. An abbot primate is the head of the modern Benedictine Confederation.

A few regular abbots have had jurisdiction, similar in some respects to that of a bishop in his diocese, over the residents and institutions of districts (*abbacies nullius*) not belonging to a diocese. Pope Paul VI stated in a document issued on his own initiative in 1976 that no more such abbacies would be established, except in cases of extraordinary necessity; also, that such abbacies, with the possible exception of ones of historical significance (like Monte Cassino, the cradle of the Benedictine Order) would be phased out of existence. The only *abbacy nullius* ever in the U.S. was Belmont Abbey, N.C.

Abjuration: Renunciation of apostasy, heresy or schism by a solemn oath.

Ablution: A term derived from Latin, meaning washing or cleansing, and referring to the cleansing of the hands of a priest celebrating Mass, after the offering of gifts; and to the cleansing of the chalice with water and wine after Communion.

Abortion: The expulsion of a nonviable human fetus from the womb of the mother, with moral implications stemming from the humanity of the fetus from the moment of conception and its consequent right to life.

Accidental expulsion, as in cases of miscarriage, is without moral fault.

Direct abortion, in which a fetus is intentionally removed from the womb, constitutes a direct attack on an innocent human being, a violation of the Fifth Commandment. It is punished in church law by the penalty of excommunication, which is automatically incurred by the consenting mother and necessary physical and/or moral cooperators. Direct abortion is not justifiable for any reason, e.g.: therapeutic, for the physical and/or psycho-logical welfare of the mother; preventive, to avoid the birth of a defective or unwanted child; social, in the interests of family and/or community.

Indirect abortion, which occurs when a fetus is expelled during medical or other treatment of the mother for a reason other than procuring expulsion, is permissible under the principle of double effect for a proportionately serious reason; e.g., when a medical or surgical procedure is necessary to save the life of the mother.

Absolution: The act by which an authorized priest, acting as the agent of Christ and minister of the Church, grants forgiveness of sins in the sacrament of penance. The essential formula of absolution is: "I absolve you from your sins; in the name of the Father, and of the Son, and of the Holy Spirit. Amen."

Priests receive the power to absolve in virtue of their ordination and the right to exercise this power in virtue of faculties of jurisdiction given them by their bishop, their religious superior, or by canon law. The faculties of jurisdiction can be limited or restricted regarding certain sins and penalties or censures.

In cases of necessity, and also in cases of the absence of their own confessors, Eastern- and Roman-Rite Catholics may ask for and receive sacramental absolution from a priest of a separated Eastern Church. Separated Eastern Christians may similarly ask for and receive sacramental absolution from an Eastern- or Roman-Rite priest.

Any priest can absolve a person in danger of death; in the absence of a priest with the usual faculties, this includes a laicized priest or a priest under censure.

(See additional entry under Sacraments.)

Absolution, General: A blessing of the Church to which a plenary indulgence is attached, given at the hour of death, and at stated times to members of religious institutes and third orders.

(See also under Penance, Sacrament; Norms on General Absolution.)

Accessory to Another's Sin: One who culpably assists another in the performance of an evil action. This may be done by counsel, command, provocation, consent, praise, flattery, concealment, participation, silence, defense of the evil done.

Adoration: The highest act and purpose of religious worship, which is directed in love and reverence to God alone in acknowledgment of his infinite perfection and goodness, and of his total dominion over creatures. Adoration, which is also called *latria,* consists of internal and external elements, private and social prayer, liturgical acts and ceremonies, and especially sacrifice.

Adultery: (1) Sexual intercourse between a married person and another to whom one is not married; a violation of the obligations of chastity and justice. The Sixth Commandment prohibition against adultery also prohibits all external sins of a sexual nature.

(2) Any sin of impurity (thought, desire, word,

action) involving a married person who is not one's husband or wife has the nature of adultery.

Adventists: Members of several Christian sects whose doctrines are dominated by belief in a more or less imminent second advent or coming of Christ upon earth for a glorious 1,000-year reign of righteousness. This reign, following victory by the forces of good over evil in a final Battle of Armageddon, will begin with the resurrection of the chosen and will end with the resurrection of all others and the annihilation of the wicked. Thereafter, the just will live forever in a renewed heaven and earth. A sleep of the soul takes place between the time of death and the day of judgment. There is no hell. The Bible, in fundamentalist interpretation, is regarded as the only rule of faith and practice.

About six sects have developed in the course of the Adventist movement which originated with William Miller (1782-1849) in the United States. Miller, on the basis of calculations made from the Book of Daniel, predicted that the second advent of Christ would occur between 1843 and 1844. After the prophecy went unfulfilled, divisions occurred in the movement and the Seventh Day Adventists, whose actual formation dates from 1860, emerged as the largest single body. The observance of Saturday instead of Sunday as the Lord's Day dates from 1844.

Advent Wreath: A wreath of laurel, spruce, or similar foliage with four candles which are lighted successively in the weeks of Advent to symbolize the approaching celebration of the birth of Christ, the Light of the World, at Christmas. The wreath originated among German Protestants.

Agape: A Greek word, meaning love, love feast, designating the meal of fellowship eaten at some gatherings of early Christians. Although held in some places in connection with the Mass, the agape was not part of the Mass, nor was it of universal institution and observance. It was infrequently observed by the fifth century and disappeared altogether between the sixth and eighth centuries.

Age of Reason: (1) The time of life when one begins to distinguish between right and wrong, to understand an obligation and take on moral responsibility; seven years of age is the presumption in church law.

(2) Historically, the 18th century period of Enlightenment in England and France, the age of the Encyclopedists and Deists. According to a basic thesis of the Enlightenment, human experience and reason are the only sources of certain knowledge of truth; consequently, faith and revelation are discounted as valid sources of knowledge, and the reality of supernatural truth is called into doubt and/or denied.

Aggiornamento: An Italian word having the general meaning of bringing up to date, renewal, revitalization, descriptive of the processes of spiritual renewal and institutional reform and change in the Church; fostered by the Second Vatican Council.

Agnosticism: A theory which holds that a person cannot have certain knowledge of immaterial reality, especially the existence of God and things pertaining to him. Immanuel Kant, one of the philosophical fathers of agnosticism, stood for the position that God, as well as the human soul, is unknowable on speculative grounds; nevertheless, he found practical imperatives for acknowledging God's existence, a view shared by many agnostics. The First Vatican Council declared that the existence of God and some of his attributes can be known with certainty by human reason, even without divine revelation. The word agnosticism was first used, in the sense given here, by T. H. Huxley in 1869.

Agnus Dei: A Latin phrase, meaning Lamb of God.

(1) A title given to Christ, the Lamb (victim) of the Sacrifice of the New Law (on Calvary and in Mass).

(2) A prayer said at Mass before the reception of Holy Communion.

(3) A sacramental. It is a round paschal-candle fragment blessed by the pope. On one side it bears the impression of a lamb, symbolic of Christ. On the reverse side, there may be any one of a number of impressions; e.g., the figure of a saint, the name and coat of arms of the reigning pope. The *agnus dei* may have originated at Rome in the fifth century. The first definite mention of it dates from about 820.

Alleluia: An exclamation of joy derived from Hebrew, All hail to him who is, praise God, with various use in the liturgy and other expressions of worship.

Allocution: A formal type of papal address, as distinguished from an ordinary sermon or statement of views.

Alms: An act, gift or service of compassion, motivated by love of God and neighbor, for the help of persons in need; an obligation of charity, which is measurable by the ability of one person to give assistance and by the degree of another's need. Almsgiving, along with prayer and fasting, is regarded as a work of penance as well as an exercise of charity. (See Corporal and Spiritual Works of Mercy.)

Alpha and Omega: The first and last letters of the Greek alphabet, used to symbolize the eternity of God (Rv. 1:8) and the divinity and eternity of Christ, the beginning and end of all things (Rv. 21:6; 22:13). Use of the letters as a monogram of Christ originated in the fourth century or earlier.

Amen: A Hebrew word meaning truly, it is true. In the Gospels, Christ used the word to add a note of authority to his statements. In other New Testament writings, as in Hebrew usage, it was the concluding word to doxologies. As the concluding word of prayers, it expresses assent to and acceptance of God's will.

Anathema: A Greek word with the root meaning of cursed or separated and the adapted meaning of excommunication, used in church documents, especially the canons of ecumenical councils, for the condemnation of heretical doctrines and of practices opposed to proper discipline.

Anchorite: A kind of hermit living in complete isolation and devoting himself exclusively to exercises of religion and severe penance according to a rule and way of life of his own devising. In early Christian times, anchorites were the forerunners of the monastic life. The closest contemporary approach to the life of an anchorite is that of Carthusian and Camaldolese hermits.

Angels: Purely spiritual beings with intelligence and free will, whose name indicates their mission as ministers of God and ministering spirits to men. They were created before the creation of the visible universe; the devil and bad angels, who were created good, fell from glory through their own fault. In addition to these essentials of defined doctrine, it is held that angels are personal beings; they can intercede for persons; fallen angels were banished from God's glory in heaven to hell; bad angels can tempt persons to commit sin. The doctrine of guardian angels, although not explicitly defined as a matter of faith, is rooted in long-standing tradition. No authoritative declaration has ever been issued regarding choirs or various categories of angels: according to theorists, there are nine choirs, consisting of seraphim, cherubim, thrones, dominations, principalities, powers, virtues, archangels and angels. In line with scriptural usage, only three angels can be named—Michael, Raphael and Gabriel.

Angelus: A devotion which commemorates the Incarnation of Christ. It consists of three versicles, three Hail Marys and a special prayer, and recalls the announcement to Mary by the Archangel Gabriel that she was chosen to be the Mother of Christ, her acceptance of the divine will, and the Incarnation (Lk. 1:26-38). The Angelus is recited at 6 a.m., noon and 6 p.m. The practice of reciting the Hail Mary in honor of the Incarnation was introduced by the Franciscans in 1263. The *Regina Caeli,* commemorating the joy of Mary at Christ's Resurrection, replaces the Angelus during the Easter season.

Anger: Passionate displeasure arising from some kind of offense suffered at the hands of another person, frustration or other cause, combined with a tendency to strike back at the cause of the displeasure; a violation of the Fifth Commandment and one of the capital sins if the displeasure is out of proportion to the cause and or if the retaliation is unjust.

Anglican Orders: Holy orders conferred according to the rite of the Anglican Church, which Leo XIII declared null and void in the bull *Apostolicae Curae,* Sept. 13, 1896. The orders were declared null because they were conferred according to a rite that was substantially defective in form and intent, and because of a break in apostolic succession that occurred when Matthew Parker became head of the Anglican hierarchy in 1559.

In making his declaration, Pope Leo cited earlier arguments against validity made by Julius III in 1553 and 1554 and by Paul IV in 1555. He also noted related directives requiring absolute ordination, according to the Catholic ritual, of convert ministers who had been ordained according to the Anglican Ordinal.

Antichrist: The man of sin, the lawless and wicked antagonist of Christ and the work of God; a mysterious figure of prophecy mentioned in the New Testament. Supported by Satan, submitting to no moral restraints, and armed with tremendous power, Antichrist will set himself up in opposition to God, work false miracles, persecute the People of God, and employ unimaginable means to lead people into error and evil during a period of widespread defection from the Christian faith before the end of time; he will be overcome by Christ. Catholic thinkers have regarded Antichrist as a person, a caricature of Christ, who will lead a final violent struggle against God and his people; they have also applied the title to personal and impersonal forces in history hostile to God and the Church. Official teaching has said little about Antichrist. In 1318, it labeled as partly heretical, senseless, and fanciful the assertions made by the Fraticelli about his coming; in 1415, the Council of Constance condemned the Wycliff thesis that excommunications made by the pope and other prelates were the actions of Antichrist.

Antiphon: (1) A short verse or text, generally from Scripture, recited in the Liturgy of the Hours before and after psalms and canticles.

(2) Any verse sung or recited by one part of a choir or congregation in response to the other part, as in antiphonal or alternate chanting.

Apologetics: The science and art of developing and presenting the case for the reasonableness of the Christian faith, by a wide variety of means including facts of experience, history, science, philosophy. The constant objective of apologetics, as well as of the total process of pre-evangelization, is preparation for response to God in faith; its ways and means, however, are subject to change in accordance with the various needs of people and different sets of circumstances.

Apostasy: (1) The total and obstinate rejection or abandonment of the Christian faith by a baptized person who continues to call himself a Christian. External manifestation of this rejection constitutes the crime of apostasy, and the person, called an *apostate,* automatically incurs a penalty of excommunication.

(2) Apostasy from orders is the unlawful withdrawal from or rejection of the obligations of the clerical state by a man who has received major orders. An apostate from orders is subject to a canonical penalty.

(3) Apostasy from the religious life occurs when a religious with perpetual vows unlawfully leaves the community with the intention of not returning, or actually remains outside the community without permission. An apostate from religious life is subject to a canonical penalty.

Apostolate: The ministry or work of an apostle. In Catholic usage, the word is an umbrella-like term covering all kinds and areas of work and endeavor for the service of God and the Church and the good of people. Thus, the apostolate of bishops is to carry on the mission of the Apostles as pastors of the People of God: of priests, to preach the word of God and to carry out the sacramental and pastoral ministry for which they are ordained; of religious, to follow and do the work of Christ in conformity with the evangelical counsels and their rule of life; of lay persons, as individuals and/or in groups, to give witness to Christ and build up the kingdom of God through practice of their faith, professional competence and the performance of good works in the concrete circumstances of daily life. Apostolic works are not limited to those done within the Church or by specifically Catholic groups, although some apostolates are officially assigned to certain persons or groups and are under the direction of church authorities. Apostolate derives from the commitment and obligation of baptism, confirmation, holy orders, matrimony, the duties of one's state in life, etc.

Apostolic Succession: Bishops of the Church, who form a collective body or college, are successors to the Apostles by ordination and divine right; as such they carry on the mission entrusted by Christ to the Apostles as guardians and teachers of the deposit of faith, principal pastors and spiritual authorities of the faithful. The doctrine of apostolic succession is based on New Testament evidence and the constant teaching of the Church, reflected as early as the end of the first century in a letter of Pope St. Clement to the Corinthians. A significant facet of the doctrine is the role of the pope as the successor of St. Peter, the vicar of Christ and head of the college of bishops. The doctrine of apostolic succession means more than continuity of apostolic faith and doctrine; its basic requisite is ordination by the laying on of hands in apostolic succession.

Archangel: An angel who carries out special missions for God in his dealings with persons. Three of them are named in the Bible: Michael, leader of the angelic host and protector of the synagogue; Raphael, guide of Tobiah and healer of his father, who is regarded as the patron of travelers; Gabriel, called the angel of the Incarnation because of his announcement to Mary that she was to be the Mother of Christ.

Archdiocese: An ecclesiastical jurisdiction headed by an archbishop. An archdiocese is usually a metropolitan see, i.e., the principal one of a group of dioceses comprising a province; the other dioceses in the province are suffragan sees.

Archives: Documentary records, and the place where they are kept, of the spiritual and temporal government and affairs of the Church, a diocese, church agencies like the departments of the Roman Curia, bodies like religious institutes, and individual parishes. The collection, cataloguing, preserving, and use of these records are governed by norms stated in canon law and particular regulations. The strictest secrecy is always in effect for confidential records concerning matters of conscience, and documents of this kind are destroyed as soon as circumstances permit.

Archpriest: For some time, before and during the Middle Ages, a priest who took the place of a bishop at liturgical worship. In Europe, the term is sometimes used as an honorary title. It is also an honorary title in Eastern-Rite Churches.

Ark of the Covenant: The sacred chest of the Israelites in which were placed and carried the tablets of stone inscribed with the Ten Commandments, the basic moral precepts of the Old Cove-

nant (Ex. 25: 10-22; 37:1-9). The Ark was also a symbol of God's presence. The Ark was probably destroyed with the Temple in 587 B.C.

Asceticism: The practice of self-discipline. In the spiritual life, asceticism — by personal prayer, meditation, self-denial, works of mortification, and outgoing interpersonal works — is motivated by love of God and contributes to growth in holiness.

Ashes: Religious significance has been associated with their use as symbolic of penance since Old Testament times. Thus, ashes of palm blessed on the previous Sunday of the Passion are placed on the foreheads of the faithful on Ash Wednesday to remind them to do works of penance, especially during the season of Lent, and that they are dust and unto dust will return. Ashes are a sacramental.

Aspergillum: A vessel or device used for sprinkling holy water. The ordinary type is a metallic rod with a bulbous tip which absorbs the water and discharges it at the motion of the user's hand.

Aspersory: A portable metallic vessel, similar to a pail, for carrying holy water.

Aspiration: Short exclamatory prayer; e.g., My Jesus, mercy.

Atheism: Denial of the existence of God, finding expression in a system of thought (speculative atheism) or a manner of acting (practical atheism) as though there were no God.

The Second Vatican Council, in its *Pastoral Constitution on the Church in the Modern World* (Nos. 19 to 21), noted that a profession of atheism may represent an explicit denial of God, the rejection of a wrong notion of God, an affirmation of man rather than of God, an extreme protest against evil. It said that such a profession might result from acceptance of such propositions as: there is no absolute truth; man can assert nothing, absolutely nothing, about God; everything can be explained by scientific reasoning alone; the whole question of God is devoid of meaning.

The constitution also cited two opinions of influence in atheistic thought. One of them regards recognition of dependence on God as incompatible with human freedom and independence. The other views belief in God and religion as a kind of opiate which sedates man on earth, reconciling him to the acceptance of suffering, injustice, shortcomings, etc., because of hope for greater things after death, and thereby hindering him from seeking and working for improvement and change for the better here and now.

All of these views, in one way or another, have been involved in the No-God and Death-of-God schools of thought in recent and remote history.

Atonement: The redemptive activity of Christ, who reconciled man with God through his Incarnation and entire life, and especially by his suffering and Resurrection. The word also applies to prayer and good works by which persons join themselves with and take part in Christ's work of reconciliation and reparation for sin.

Attributes of God: Perfections of God. God possesses — and is — all the perfections of being, without limitation. Because he is infinite, all of these perfections are one, perfectly united in him. Man, however, because of the limited power of understanding, views these perfections separately, as distinct characteristics — even though they are not actually distinct in God. God is: almighty, eternal, holy, immortal, immense, immutable, incomprehensible, ineffable, infinite, invisible, just, loving, merciful, most high, most wise, omnipotent, omniscient, omnipresent, patient, perfect, provident, supreme, true.

Avarice (Covetousness): A disorderly and unreasonable attachment to and desire for material things; called a capital sin because it involves preoccupation with material things to the neglect of spiritual goods and obligations of justice and charity.

Ave Maria: See Hail Mary.

B

Baldachino: A canopy over an altar.

Beatification: A preliminary step toward canonization of a saint. It begins with an investigation of the candidate's life, writings and heroic practice of virtue, and the certification of at least two miracles worked by God through his intercession. If the findings of the investigation so indicate, the pope decrees that the Servant of God may be called *Blessed* and may be honored locally or in a limited way in the liturgy. Additional procedures lead to canonization (see separate entry).

Beatific Vision: The intuitive, immediate and direct vision and experience of God enjoyed in the light of glory by all the blessed in heaven. The vision is a supernatural mystery.

Beatitude: A literary form of the Old and New Testaments in which blessings are promised to persons for various reasons. Beatitudes are mentioned 26 times in the Psalms, and in other books of the Old Testament. The best known beatitudes — identifying blessedness with participation in the kingdom of God and his righteousness, and descriptive of the qualities of Christian perfection — are those recounted in Mt. 5:3-11 and Lk. 6:20-22.

In Matthew's account, the beatitudes are:

"How blest are the poor in spirit: the reign of God is theirs.

"Blest too are the sorrowing; they shall be consoled.

"(Blest are the lowly; they shall inherit the land.)

"Blest are they who hunger and thirst for holiness; they shall have their fill.

"Blest are they who show mercy; mercy shall be theirs.

"Blest are the single-hearted for they shall see God.

"Blest too are the peacemakers; they shall be called sons of God.

"Blest are those persecuted for holiness' sake; the reign of God is theirs.

"Blest are you when they insult you and persecute you and utter every kind of slander against you because of me."

In Luke's account, the beatitudes are:

"Blest are you poor; the reign of God is yours.

"Blest are you who hunger; you shall be filled.

"Blest are you who are weeping; you shall laugh.

"Blest shall you be when men hate you, when they ostracize you and insult you and proscribe your name as evil because of the Son of Man."

Benediction of the Blessed Sacrament: A short exposition of the Eucharist for adoration by and blessing of the faithful. Devotional practices include the singing of Eucharistic and other hymns, and recitation of the Divine Praises. Benediction, in its present form, dates from about the 15th century and is a form of liturgical worship.

Benedictus: The canticle or hymn of Zechariah at the circumcision of St. John the Baptist (Lk. 1:68-79). It is an expression of praise and thanks to God for sending John as a precursor of the Messiah. The *Benedictus* is recited in the Liturgy of the Hours as part of the Morning Prayer.

Bible Service: A devotion consisting essentially of common prayer of a biblical or liturgical character, several readings from Scripture, and a homily on the texts.

Biglietto: A papal document of notification of appointment to the cardinalate.

Biretta: A stiff, square hat with three ridges on top worn by clerics in church and on other occasions.

Blasphemy: Any expression of insult or contempt with respect to God, principally, and to holy persons and things, secondarily; a violation of the honor due to God in the context of the First and Second Commandments.

Blasphemy of the Spirit: Deliberate resistance to the Holy Spirit, called the unforgivable sin (Mt. 12:31) because it makes his saving action impossible. Thus, the only unforgivable sin is the one for which a person will not seek pardon from God.

Blessing: Invocation of God's favor, by official ministers of the Church or by private individuals. Blessings are recounted in the Old and New Testaments, and are common in the Christian tradition. The Church, through its ordained ministers (bishops and priests, especially), invokes divine favor in liturgical blessings; e.g., of the people at Mass, of the gifts to be consecrated at Mass, of persons and things on various occasions. Sacramentals — such as crucifixes, crosses, rosaries, scapulars, medals — are blessed by ministers of the Church for the invocation of God's favor on those who use them in the proper manner. Many types of blessings are listed in the *Roman Ritual*. Private blessings, as well as those of an official kind, are efficacious. Blessings are imparted with the Sign of the Cross and appropriate prayer.

Boat: A small vessel used to hold incense which is to be placed in the censer.

Brief, Apostolic: A papal letter, less formal than a bull, signed for the pope by a secretary and impressed with the seal of the Fisherman's Ring. Simple apostolic letters of this kind are issued for beatifications and with respect to other matters.

Bull, Apostolic: The most solemn form of papal document, beginning with the name and title of the pope (e.g., John Paul II, Servant of the Servants of God), dealing with an important subject, and having attached to it either a leaden seal called a *bulla* or a red ink imprint of the device on the seal.

Bulls are known as apostolic letters with the seal. The seal, on one side, has representations of the heads of Sts. Peter and Paul; on the other side, the name of the reigning pope. Bulls are issued to confer the titles of bishops and cardinals, to promulgate canonizations, and for other purposes. A collection of bulls is called a *bullarium*.

Burial, Ecclesiastical: Interment with church rites and in consecrated ground. Catechumens as well as baptized Catholics have a right to ecclesiastical burial. A non-Catholic partner in a mixed marriage may be buried in a Catholic cemetery with the Catholic partner.

C

Calumny: Harming the name and good reputation of a person by lies; a violation of obligations of justice and truth. Restitution is due for calumny.

Calvary: A knoll about 15 feet high just outside the western wall of Jerusalem where Christ was crucified, so called from the Latin *calvaria* (skull) which described its shape.

Canon: A Greek word meaning rule, norm, standard, measure.

(1) The word designates the Canon of Sacred Scripture, which is the list of books recognized by the Church as inspired by the Holy Spirit.

(2) In the sense of regulating norms, the word designates the Code of Canon Law enacted and promulgated by ecclesiastical authority for the orderly administration and government of the Church. A revised code, effective Nov. 27, 1983, consists of 1,752 canons in seven books under the titles of general norms, the people of God, the teaching mission of the Church, the sanctifying mission of the Church, temporal goods of the Church, penal law and procedural law. The antecedent of this code was promulgated in 1917 and became effective in 1918; it consisted of 2,414 canons in five books covering general rules, ecclesiastical persons, sacred things, trials, crimes and punishments. Eastern-Rite Churches have their own canon law.

(3) The term also designates the four canons, (Eucharistic prayers, anaphoras) of the Mass, the core of the liturgy.

(4) Certain dignitaries of the Church have the title of Canon, and some religious are known as Canons.

Canonization: An infallible declaration by the pope that a person, who died as a martyr and/or practiced Christian virtue to a heroic degree, is now in heaven and is worthy of honor and imitation by all the faithful. Such a declaration is preceded by the process of beatification and another detailed investigation concerning the person's reputation for holiness, writings, and (except in the case of martyrs) miracles ascribed to his or her intercession after death. Miracles are not required for martyrs. The pope can dispense from some of the formalities ordinarily required in canonization procedures (equivalent canonization), as Pope John XXIII did in the canonization of St. Gregory Barbarigo on May 26, 1960. A saint is worthy of honor in liturgical worship throughout the universal Church.

From its earliest years the Church has venerated saints. Public official honor always required the approval of the bishop of the place. Martyrs were the first to be honored. St. Martin of Tours, who died in 397, was an early non-martyr venerated as a saint. The first official canonization by a pope for the universal Church was that of St. Ulrich by John XV in 993. Alexander III reserved the process of canonization to the Holy See in 1171. In 1588 Sixtus V established the Sacred Congregation of Rites for the principal purpose of handling causes for beatification and canonization: this function is now the work of the Congregation for the Causes of Saints.

The essential portion of a canonization decree states:

"For the honor of the holy and undivided Trinity; for the exaltation of the Catholic faith and the increase of Christian life; with the authority of our Lord Jesus Christ, of the blessed Apostles Peter and Paul, and with our own authority; after mature deliberation and with the divine assistance, often implored; with the counsel of many of our brothers.

"We decree and define that (name) is a saint and we inscribe him (her) in the Catalogue of Saints, stating that he (she) shall be venerated in the universal Church with pious devotion.

"In the name of the Father and of the Son and of the Holy Spirit. Amen."

The official listing of saints and blessed is contained in the *Roman Martyrology* and related decrees issued after its last publication. Butler's unofficial *Lives of the Saints* (1956) contains 2,565 entries.

The Church regards all persons in heaven as saints, not just those who have been officially canonized.

(See Beatification, Saints, Canonizations by Leo XIII and His Successors.)

Canticle: A scriptural chant or prayer differing from the psalms. Three of the canticles prescribed for use in the Liturgy of the Hours are: the *Magnificat* (Lk. 1:46-55), the *Benedictus* (Lk. 1:68-79), and the *Nunc Dimittis* (Lk. 2:29-32).

Capital Punishment: Punishment for crime by means of the death penalty. The political community, which has authority to provide for the common good, has the right to defend itself and its members against unjust aggression and may in extreme cases punish with the death penalty persons found guilty before the law of serious crimes against individuals and a just social order. Such punishment is essentially vindictive. Its value as a crime deterrent is a matter of perennial debate. The prudential judgment as to whether or not there should be capital punishment belongs to the civic community. The U.S. Supreme Court, in a series of decisions dating from June 29, 1972, ruled against the constitutionality of statutes on capital punishment except in specific cases and with appropriate consideration, with respect to sentence, of mitigating circumstances of the crime.

Capital punishment was the subject of a statement issued Mar. 1, 1978, by the Committee on Social Development and World Peace, U.S. Catholic

Conference. The statement said, in part: "The use of the death penalty involves deep moral and religious questions as well as political and legal issues. In 1974, out of a commitment to the value and dignity of human life, the Catholic bishops of the United States declared their opposition to capital punishment. We continue to support this position, in the belief that a return to the use of the death penalty can only lead to the further erosion of respect for life in our society. Violent crime in our society is a serious matter which should not be ignored. We do not challenge society's right to punish the serious and violent offender, nor do we wish to debate the merits of the arguments concerning this right. Past history, however, shows that the death penalty in its present application has been discriminatory with respect to the disadvantaged, the indigent and the socially impoverished. Furthermore, recent data from correction sources definitely question the effectiveness of the death penalty as a deterrent to crime."

Additional statements against capital punishment have been issued by Pope John Paul II, numerous bishops and other sources.

Capital Sins: Moral faults which, if habitual, give rise to many more sins. They are pride, covetousness, lust, anger, gluttony, envy, sloth.

The opposite virtues are: humility, liberality, chastity, meekness, temperance, brotherly love, diligence.

Cardinal Virtues: The four principal moral virtues are prudence, justice, temperance and fortitude.

Catacombs: Underground Christian cemeteries in various cities of the Roman Empire and Italy, especially in the vicinity of Rome; the burial sites of many martyrs and other Christians. Developed from aboveground cemeteries, their passageways, burial niches and assembly rooms were dug out of tuffa, a soft clay which hardened into rock-like consistency on drying. The earliest ones date from the third century; in the fourth, they became the scene of memorial services as the veneration of martyrs increased in popularity; in the seventh and eighth centuries, they were plundered by the Lombards and other invaders. The relics of many martyrs were removed to safer places in the ninth century; afterwards, the catacombs fell into neglect and oblivion until interest in them revived in the 16th century. The catacombs have been excavated extensively, yielding considerable information about early Christian symbolism and art, dating from the third century on, and other aspects of Christian life and practice.

Catechesis: Religious instruction and formation not only for persons preparing for baptism but also for the faithful in various stages of their spiritual development.

Catechism: A summary of Christian doctrine in question and answer form, used for purposes of instruction.

Catechumen: A person preparing in a program of instruction and spiritual formation for baptism and reception into the Church. The Church has a special relationship with catechumens. It invites them to lead the life of the Gospel, introduces them to the celebration of the sacred rites, and grants them various prerogatives that are proper to the faithful (one of which is the right to ecclesiastical burial).

Cathedra: A Greek word for chair, designating the chair or seat of a bishop in the principal church of his diocese, which is therefore called a cathedral (see separate entry).

Cathedraticum: The tax paid to a bishop by all churches and benefices subject to him for the support of episcopal administration and for works of charity.

Catholic: A Greek word, meaning universal, first used in the title Catholic Church in a letter written by St. Ignatius of Antioch about 107 to the Christians of Smyrna.

Celebret: A Latin word, meaning Let him celebrate, the name of a document issued by a bishop or other superior stating that a priest is in good standing and therefore eligible to celebrate Mass or perform other priestly functions.

Celibacy: The unmarried state of life, required in the Roman Church of candidates for holy orders and of men already ordained to holy orders, for the practice of perfect chastity and total dedication to the service of people in the ministry of the Church. Celibacy is enjoined as a condition for ordination by church discipline and law, not by dogmatic necessity.

In the Roman Church, a consensus in favor of celibacy developed in the early centuries while the clergy included both celibates and men who had been married once. The first local legislation on the subject was enacted by a local council held in Elvira, Spain, about 306; it forbade bishops, priests, deacons and other ministers to have wives. Similar enactments were passed by other local councils from that time on, and by the 12th century particular laws regarded marriage by clerics in major orders to be not only unlawful but also null and void. The latter view was translated by the Second Lateran Council in 1139 into what seems to be the first written universal law making holy orders an invalidating impediment to marriage. In 1563 the Council of Trent ruled definitely on the matter and established the discipline in force in the Roman Church.

Some exceptions to this discipline have been made in recent years. Several married Protestant and Episcopalian (Anglican) clergymen who became converts and were subsequently ordained to the priesthood have been permitted to continue in marriage. Married men over the age of 35 can be ordained to the permanent diaconate.

Eastern Church discipline on celibacy differs from that of the Roman Church. In line with legislation enacted by the Synod of Trullo in 692 and still in force, candidates for holy orders may marry before becoming deacons and may continue in marriage thereafter, but marriage after ordination is forbidden. Eastern-Rite bishops in the U.S., however, do not ordain married candidates for the priesthood. Eastern-Rite bishops are unmarried.

Cenacle: The upper room in Jerusalem where Christ ate the Last Supper with his Apostles.

Censer: A metal vessel with a perforated cover

and suspended by chains, in which incense is burned. It is used at some Masses, Benediction of the Blessed Sacrament and other liturgical functions.

Censorship of Books: An exercise of vigilance by the Church for safeguarding authentic religious teaching.

Pertinent legislation in a decree issued by the Congregation for the Doctrine of the Faith Apr. 9, 1975, is embodied in the revised Code of Canon Law, effective Nov. 27, 1983 (Book III, Title IV).

(1) Pre-publication clearance is required for: editions of Sacred Scripture, liturgical texts and books of private devotion, catechisms and other writings relating to catechetical instruction. Books dealing with Scripture, theology, canon law, church history and religious or moral disciplines may not be used as basic texts in educational institutions (from elementary to university levels) unless they have been published with the approval of competent church authority.

(2) Pre-publication clearance is recommended for all books on the aforementioned subjects, even though they are not used as basic texts in teaching.

(3) Books or other writings dealing with religion or morals may not be displayed, sold or given out in churches or oratories unless published with the approval of competent ecclesiastical authority.

(4) Except for a just and reasonable cause, Catholics should not write for newspapers, magazines or periodicals which regularly and openly prove to be inimical to the Catholic religion and good morals. The approval of the local bishop is required before clerics or members of religious institutes (who also need the approval of their superior) may write for such publications.

Permission to publish works of a religious character, together with the apparatus of reviewing them beforehand, falls under the authority of the bishop of the place where the writer lives or where the works are published.

Clearance for publication is usually indicated by the terms *Nihil obstat* (Nothing stands in the way) issued by the censor and *Imprimatur* (Let it be printed) authorized by the bishop; an equivalent statement is, Published with ecclesiastical permission. The clearing of works for publication does not necessarily imply approval of an author's viewpoint or his manner of handling a subject.

Censures: Spiritual penalties inflicted by the Church on baptized persons for committing certain serious sins, which are classified as crimes in canon law, and for being or remaining obstinate therein. Excommunication, suspension and interdict have been the censures in force since the time of Innocent III (1214). Their intended purposes are to deter persons from committing sins which, more seriously and openly than others, threaten the common good of the Church and its members; to punish and correct offenders; and to provide for the making of reparation for harm done to the community of the Church. Censures may be incurred automatically (*ipso facto*) on the commission of certain offenses for which fixed penalties have been laid down in church law (*latae*

sententiae); or they may be inflicted by sentence of a judge (*ferendae sententiae*). Obstinacy in crime — also called contumacy, disregard of a penalty, defiance of church authority — is presumed by law in the commission of crimes for which automatic censures are decreed. The presence and degree of contumacy in other cases, for which judicial sentence is required, is subject to determination by a judge. Absolution can be obtained from any censure, provided the person repents and desists from obstinacy. Absolution may be reserved to the pope, the bishop of a place, or the major superior of an exempt clerical religious institute. In danger of death, any priest can absolve from all censures; in other cases, faculties to absolve from reserved censures can be exercised by competent authorities or given to other priests.

The penal law of the Church is contained in Book VI of the revised Code of Canon Law, effective Nov. 27, 1983.

Ceremonies, Master of: One who directs the proceedings of a rite or ceremony during the function.

Chamberlain: (1) The Chamberlain of the Holy Roman Church is a cardinal who administers the property and revenues of the Holy See. On the death of the pope he becomes head of the College of Cardinals and summons and directs the conclave until a new pope is elected.

(2) The Chamberlain of the Sacred College of Cardinals has charge of the property and revenues of the College and keeps the record of business transacted in consistories.

(3) The Chamberlain of the Roman Clergy is the president of the secular clergy of Rome.

Chancellor: Notary of a diocese, who draws up written documents in the government of the diocese; takes care of, arranges and indexes diocesan archives, records of dispensations and ecclesiastical trials.

Chancery (1) A branch of church administration that handles written documents used in the government of a diocese.

(2) The administrative office of a diocese, a bishop's office.

Chapel: A building or part of another building used for divine worship; a portion of a church set aside for the celebration of Mass or for some special devotion.

Chaplain: A priest appointed for the pastoral service of any division of the armed forces, religious communities, institutions, various groups of the faithful.

Chaplet: A term, meaning little crown, applied to a rosary or, more commonly, to a small string of beads used for devotional purposes; e.g., the Infant of Prague chaplet.

Chapter: A general meeting of delegates of religious orders for elections and the handling of other important affairs of their communities.

Charisms: Gifts or graces given by God to persons for the good of others and the Church. Examples are special gifts for apostolic work, prophecy, healing, discernment of spirits, the life of evangelical poverty, here-and-now witness to faith in various circumstances of life.

The Second Vatican Council made the following statement about charisms in the *Dogmatic Constitution on the Church* (No. 12):

"It is not only through the sacraments and Church ministries that the same Holy Spirit sanctifies and leads the People of God and enriches it with virtues. Allotting his gifts 'to everyone according as he will' (1 Cor. 12:11), he distributes special graces among the faithful of every rank. By these gifts he makes them fit and ready to undertake the various tasks or offices advantageous for the renewal and upbuilding of the Church, according to the words of the Apostle: 'The manifestation of the Spirit is given to everyone for profit' (1 Cor. 12:7). These charismatic gifts, whether they be the most outstanding or the more simple and widely diffused, are to be received with thanksgiving and consolation, for they are exceedingly suitable and useful for the needs of the Church.

"Still, extraordinary gifts are not to be rashly sought after, nor are the fruits of apostolic labor to be presumptuously expected from them. In any case, judgment as to their genuineness and proper use belongs to those who preside over the Church, and to whose special competence it belongs, not indeed to extinguish the Spirit, but to test all things and hold fast to that which is good" (cf. 1 Thes. 5:12; 19-21).

Charity: Love of God above all things for his own sake, and love of one's neighbor as oneself because and as an expression of one's love for God; the greatest of the three theological virtues. The term is sometimes also used to designate sanctifying grace.

Chastity: Properly ordered behavior with respect to sex. In marriage, the exercise of the procreative power is integrated with the norms and purposes of marriage. Outside of marriage, the rule is self-denial of the voluntary exercise and enjoyment of the procreative faculty in thought, word or action.

The vow of chastity, which reinforces the virtue of chastity with the virtue of religion, is an evangelical counsel and one of the three vows professed by religious.

Chirograph or Autograph Letter: A letter written by a pope himself, in his own handwriting.

Christ: The title of Jesus, derived from the Greek translation *Christos* of the Hebrew term *Messiah*, meaning the Anointed of God, the Savior and Deliverer of his people. Christian use of the title is a confession of belief that Jesus is the Savior.

Christianity: The sum total of things related to belief in Christ — the Christian religion, Christian churches, Christians themselves, society based on and expressive of Christian beliefs, culture reflecting Christian values.

Christians: The name first applied about the year 43 to followers of Christ at Antioch, the capital of Syria. It was used by the pagans as a contemptuous term. The word applies to persons who profess belief in the divinity and teachings of Christ and who give witness to him in life.

Christian Science: A religious doctrine consisting of Mary Baker Eddy's interpretation and formulation of the actions and teachings of Christ. Its basic tenets reflect Mrs. Eddy's ideas regarding the reality of spirit and its control and domination of what is not spirit. The basic statement of the doctrine is contained in *Science and Health, with Key to the Scriptures,* which she first published in 1875, nine years after being saved from death and healed on reading the New Testament.

Mary Baker Eddy (1821-1910) established the church in 1879, and in 1892 founded at Boston the First Church of Christ, Scientist, of which all other Christian Science churches are branches. The individual churches are self-governing and self-supporting under the general supervision of a board of directors. Services consist of readings of portions of Scripture and *Science and Health.* One of the church's publications, *The Christian Science Monitor,* has a worldwide reputation as a journal of news and opinion.

Church: (1) See several entries under Church, Catholic. The universal Church is the Church spread throughout the world. The local Church is the Church in a particular locality; e.g., a diocese. Inasmuch as the members of the Church are on earth, in purgatory, or in glory in heaven, the Church is called militant, suffering, or triumphant.

(2) In general, any religious body.

(3) Place of divine worship.

Churching: A rite of thanksgiving in which a blessing is given to women after childbirth. The rite is reminiscent of the Old Testament ceremony of purification (Lv. 12:2-8).

Circumcision: A ceremonial practice symbolic of initiation and participation in the covenant between God and Abraham.

Circumincession: The indwelling of each divine Person of the Holy Trinity in the others.

Clergy: Men ordained to holy orders and assigned to pastoral and other ministries for the service of the people and the Church.

(1) Diocesan or secular clergy are committed to pastoral ministry in parishes and in other capacities in a local church (diocese) under the direction of their bishop, to whom they are bound by a promise of obedience.

(2) Regular clergy belong to religious institutes (orders, congregations, societies — institutes of consecrated life) and are so called because they observe the rule (*regula,* in Latin) of their respective institutes. They are committed to the ways of life and apostolates of their institutes. In ordinary pastoral ministry, they are under the direction of local bishops as well as their own superiors.

Clericalism: A term generally used in a derogatory sense to mean action, influence and interference by the Church and the clergy in matters with which they allegedly should not be concerned. Anticlericalism is a reaction of antipathy, hostility, distrust and opposition to the Church and clergy arising from real and/or alleged faults of the clergy, overextension of the role of the laity, or for other reasons.

Cloister: Part of a monastery, convent or other house of religious reserved for use by members of the institute. Contemplative monasteries have a strict cloister. Monasteries of totally contemplative nuns have papal cloister.

Code: A digest of rules or regulations, such as the Code of Canon Law.

Collegiality: The bishops of the Church, in union with and subordinate to the pope — who has full, supreme and universal power over the Church which he can always exercise independently — have supreme teaching and pastoral authority over the whole Church. In addition to their proper authority of office for the good of the faithful in their respective dioceses or other jurisdictions, the bishops have authority to act for the good of the universal Church. This collegial authority is exercised in a solemn manner in an ecumenical council and can also be exercised in other ways sanctioned by the pope. Doctrine on collegiality was set forth by the Second Vatican Council in the *Dogmatic Constitution on the Church.* (See separate entry.)

By extension, the concept of collegiality is applied to other forms of participation and co-responsibility by members of a community.

Commissariat of the Holy Land: A special jurisdiction within the Order of Friars Minor, whose main purposes are the collecting of alms for support of the Holy Places in Palestine and staffing of the Holy Places and missions in the Middle East with priests and brothers. There are 69 such commissariats in 33 countries. One of them has headquarters at Mt. St. Sepulchre, Washington, D.C. Franciscans have had custody of the Holy Places since 1342.

Communion of Faithful, Saints: The communion of all the People of God — on earth, in heavenly glory, in purgatory — with Christ and each other in faith, grace, prayer and good works.

Concelebration: The liturgical act in which several priests, led by one member of the group, offer Mass together, all consecrating the bread and wine. Concelebration has always been common in churches of Eastern Rite. In the Roman Rite, it was long restricted, taking place only at the ordination of bishops and the ordination of priests. The *Constitution on the Sacred Liturgy* issued by the Second Vatican Council set new norms for concelebration, which is now relatively common in the Roman Rite.

Concordance, Biblical: An alphabetical verbal index enabling a user knowing one or more words of a scriptural passage to locate the entire text.

Concordat: A Church-state treaty with the force of law concerning matters of mutual concern — e.g., rights of the Church, appointment of bishops, arrangement of ecclesiastical jurisdictions, marriage laws, education. Approximately 150 agreements of this kind have been negotiated since the Concordat of Worms in 1122.

Concupiscence: Any tendency of the sensitive appetite. The term is most frequently used in reference to desires and tendencies for sinful sense pleasure.

Confession: Sacramental confession is the act by which a person tells or confesses his sins to a priest who is authorized to give absolution in the sacrament of penance.

Confessor: A priest who administers the sacrament of penance.

The title of confessor, formerly given to a category of male saints, was suppressed with publication of the calendar reform of 1969.

Confraternity: An association whose members practice a particular form of religious devotion and/or are engaged in some kind of apostolic work.

Conscience: Practical judgment concerning the moral goodness or sinfulness of an action. In the Catholic view, this judgment is made by reference of the action, its attendant circumstances and the intentions of the person to the requirements of moral law as expressed in the Ten Commandments, the summary law of love for God and neighbor, the life and teaching of Christ, and the authoritative teaching and practice of the Church with respect to the total demands of divine Revelation.

A person is obliged: (1) to obey a certain and correct conscience; (2) to obey a certain conscience even if it is inculpably erroneous; (3) not to obey, but to correct, a conscience known to be erroneous or lax; (4) to rectify a scrupulous conscience by following the advice of a confessor and by other measures; (5) to resolve doubts of conscience before acting.

It is legitimate to act for solid and probable reasons when a question of moral responsibility admits of argument (see Probabilism). It is also legitimate to resolve doubts in difficult cases by having recourse to a reflex principle (e.g., by following the manner of acting of a well-informed and well-intentioned group of persons in similar circumstances).

Conscience, Examination of: Self-examination to determine one's spiritual state before God, especially regarding one's sins and faults. It is recommended as a regular practice and is practically necessary in preparing for the sacrament of penance. The *particular examen* is a regular examination to assist in overcoming specific faults and imperfections.

Consecration of a Church: See Dedication of a Church.

Consistory: An assembly of cardinals presided over by the pope. Consistories are secret (pope and cardinals only), semi-public (plus other prelates), and public (plus other attendants).

Constitution: (1) An apostolic or papal constitution is a document in which a pope enacts and promulgates law.

(2) A formal and solemn document issued by an ecumenical council on a doctrinal or pastoral subject, with binding force in the whole Church; e.g., the four constitutions issued by the Second Vatican Council on the Church, liturgy, Revelation, and the Church in the modern world.

(3) The constitutions of institutes of consecrated life and societies of apostolic life spell out details of and norms drawn from the various rules for the guidance and direction of the life and work of their members.

Consubstantiation: A theory which holds that

the Body and Blood of Christ coexist with the substance of bread and wine in the Holy Eucharist. This theory, also called *impanation,* is incompatible with the doctrine of transubstantiation.

Contraception: Anything done by positive interference to prevent sexual intercourse from resulting in conception. Direct contraception is against the order of nature. Indirect contraception — as a secondary effect of medical treatment or other action having a necessary, good, non-contraceptive purpose — is permissible under the principle of the double effect. The practice of periodic continence is not contraception because it does not involve positive interference with the order of nature.

Contrition: Sorrow for sin coupled with a purpose of amendment. Contrition arising from a supernatural motive is necessary for the forgiveness of sin.

(1) Perfect contrition is total sorrow for and renunciation of attachment to sin, arising from the motive of pure love of God. Perfect contrition, which implies the intention of doing all God wants done for the forgiveness of sin (including confession in a reasonable period of time), is sufficient for the forgiveness of serious sin and the remission of all temporal punishment due for sin. (The intention to receive the sacrament of penance is implicit — even if unrealized, as in the case of some persons — in perfect contrition.)

(2) Imperfect contrition or attrition is sorrow arising from a quasi-selfish supernatural motive; e.g., the fear of losing heaven, suffering the pains of hell, etc. Imperfect contrition is sufficient for the forgiveness of serious sin when joined with absolution in confession, and sufficient for the forgiveness of venial sin even outside of confession.

Contumely: Personal insult, reviling a person in his presence by accusation of moral faults, by refusal of recognition or due respect; a violation of obligations of justice and charity.

Corporal Works of Mercy: Feeding the hungry, giving drink to the thirsty, clothing the naked, visiting the imprisoned, sheltering the homeless, visiting the sick, burying the dead.

Councils: Bodies representative of various categories of members of the Church which participate with bishops and other church authorities in making decisions and carrying out action programs for the good of the Church and the accomplishment of its mission to its own members and society in general. Examples are priests' senates or councils, councils of religious and lay persons, parish councils, diocesan pastoral councils.

Councils, Plenary: National councils or councils of the bishops of several ecclesiastical provinces, can be convoked to take action related to the life and mission of the Church in the area under their jurisdiction. The membership of such councils is fixed by canon law; their decrees, when approved by the Holy See, are binding in the territory (see Index, Plenary Councils of Baltimore).

Councils, Provincial: Meetings of the bishops of a province. The metropolitan, or ranking archbishop, of an ecclesiastical province convenes and presides over such councils in a manner prescribed by canon law to take action related to the life and mission of the Church in the province. Acts and decrees must be approved by the Holy See before being promulgated. Provincial councils should be held at least once every 20 years.

Counsels, Evangelical: Gospel counsels of perfection, especially voluntary poverty, perfect chastity and obedience, which were recommended by Christ to those who would devote themselves exclusively and completely to the immediate service of God. Religious (members of institutes of consecrated life) bind themselves by public vows to observe these counsels in a life of total consecration to God and service to people through various kinds of apostolic works.

Counter-Reformation: The period of approximately 100 years following the Council of Trent, which witnessed a reform within the Church to stimulate genuine Catholic life and to counteract effects of the Reformation.

Covenant: A bond of relationship between parties pledged to each other. God-initiated covenants in the Old Testament included those with Abraham, Noah, Moses, Levi, David. The Mosaic (Sinai) covenant made Israel God's Chosen People on terms of fidelity to true faith, true worship, and righteous conduct according to the Decalogue. The New Testament covenant, prefigured in the Old Testament, is the bond persons have with God through Christ. All persons are called to be parties to this perfect and everlasting covenant, which was mediated and ratified by Christ. The marriage covenant seals the closest possible relationship between a man and a woman.

Creation: The production by God of something out of nothing. The biblical account of creation is contained in the first two chapters of Genesis.

Creator: God, the supreme, self-existing Being, the absolute and infinite First Cause of all things.

Creature: Everything in the realm of being is a creature, except God.

Cremation: The reduction of a human corpse to ashes by means of fire. Cremation is not in line with Catholic tradition and practice, even though it is not opposed to any article of faith.

The Congregation for the Doctrine of the Faith, under date of May 8, 1963, circulated among bishops an instruction which upheld the traditional practices of Christian burial but modified anticremation legislation. Cremation may be permitted for serious reasons, of a private as well as public nature, provided it does not involve any contempt of the Church or of religion, or any attempt to deny, question, or belittle the doctrine of the resurrection of the body. The person may receive the last rites and be given ecclesiastical burial. A priest may say prayers for the deceased at the crematorium, but full liturgical ceremonies may not take place there.

The principal reason behind an earlier prohibition against cremation was the fact that, historically, the practice had represented an attempt to deny the doctrine of the resurrection of the body. It also appeared to be a form of violence against the body which, as the temple of the Holy Spirit during life, should be treated with reverence.

Crib: A devotional representation of the birth of Jesus. The custom of erecting cribs is generally attributed to St. Francis of Assisi who in 1223 obtained from Pope Honorius III permission to use a crib and figures of the Christ Child, Mary, St. Joseph, and others, to represent the mystery of the Nativity.

Crosier: The bishop's staff, symbolic of his pastoral office, responsibility and authority.

Crypt: An underground or partly underground chamber; e.g., the lower part of a church used for worship and/or burial.

Cura Animarum: A Latin phrase, meaning care of souls, designating the pastoral ministry and responsibility of bishops and priests.

Curia: The personnel and offices through which (1) the pope administers the affairs of the universal Church, the *Roman Curia* (see separate entry), or (2) a bishop the affairs of a diocese, *diocesan curia*. The principal officials of a diocesan curia are the vicar general of the diocese, the chancellor, officials of the diocesan tribunal or court, examiners, consultors, auditors, notaries.

Custos: A religious superior who presides over a number of convents collectively called a custody. In some institutes of consecrated life a custos may be the deputy of a higher superior.

D

Deaconess — A woman officially appointed and charged by the Church to carry out service-like functions. Phoebe apparently was one (Rom. 16:1-2); a second probable reference to the office is in Tm. 3:11.

The office — for assistance at the baptism of women, for pastoral service to women and for works of charity — had considerable development in the third and also in the fourth century when the actual term came into use (in place of such designations as *diacona, vidua, virgo canonica*). Its importance declined subsequently with the substitution of infusion in place of immersion as the common method of baptism in the West, and with the increase of the practice of infant baptism. There is no record of the ministry of deaconess in the West after the beginning of the 11th century. The office continued, however, for a longer time in the East.

The Vatican's Theological Commission, in a paper prepared in 1971, noted that there had been in the past a form of diaconal ordination for women. With a rite and purpose distinctive to women, it differed essentially from the ordination of deacons, which had sacramental effects.

Several Christian churches have had revivals of the office of deaconess since the 1830s. There is a contemporary movement in support of such a revival among some Catholics.

Dean: (1) A priest with supervisory responsibility over a section of a diocese known as a deanery. The post-Vatican II counterpart of a dean is an episcopal vicar.

(2) The senior or ranking member of a group.

Dean of the Sacred College: The president of the College of Cardinals (the ranking cardinal bishop).

Decision: A judgment or pronouncement on a cause or suit, given by a church tribunal or official with judicial authority. A decision has the force of law for concerned parties.

Declaration: (1) An ecclesiastical document which presents an interpretation of an existing law.

(2) A position paper on a specific subject; e.g., the three declarations issued by the Second Vatican Council on religious freedom, non-Christian religions, and Christian education.

Decree: An edict or ordinance issued by a pope and/or by an ecumenical council, with binding force in the whole Church; by a department of the Roman Curia, with binding force for concerned parties; by a territorial body of bishops, with binding force for persons in the area; by individual bishops, with binding force for concerned parties until revocation or the death of the bishop.

The nine decrees issued by the Second Vatican Council were combinations of doctrinal and pastoral statements with executive orders for action and movement toward renewal and reform in the Church.

Dedication of a Church: The ceremony whereby a church is solemnly set apart for the worship of God. The custom of dedicating churches had an antecedent in Old Testament ceremonies for the dedication of the Temple, as in the times of Solomon and the Maccabees. The earliest extant record of the dedication of a Christian church dates from early in the fourth century, when it was done simply by the celebration of Mass. Other ceremonies developed later. A church can be dedicated by a simple blessing or a solemn consecration. The rite of consecration is generally performed by a bishop.

Definitors: Members of the governing council of a religious order, each one having a decisive vote equal to the vote of the general or provincial superior.

Deism: A system of natural religion which acknowledges the existence of God but regards him as so transcendent and remote from man and the universe that divine revelation and the supernatural order of things are irrelevant and unacceptable. It developed from rationalistic principles in England in the 17th and 18th centuries, and had Voltaire, Rousseau and the Encyclopedists among its advocates in France.

Despair: Abandonment of hope for salvation arising from the conviction that God will not provide the necessary means for attaining it, that following God's way of life for salvation is impossible, or that one's sins are unforgivable; a serious sin against the Holy Spirit and the theological virtues of hope and faith, involving distrust in the mercy and goodness of God and a denial of the truths that God wills the salvation of all persons and provides sufficient grace for it. Real despair is distinguished from unreasonable fear with respect to the difficulties of attaining salvation, from morbid anxiety over the demands of divine justice, and from feelings of despair.

Detachment: Control of affection for creatures by two principles: (1) supreme love and devotion belong to God; (2) love and service of creatures should be an expression of love for God.

Detraction: Revelation of true but hidden faults of a person without sufficient and justifying reason; a violation of requirements of justice and charity, involving the obligation to make restitution when this is possible without doing more harm to the good name of the offended party. In some cases, e.g., to prevent evil, secret faults may and should be disclosed.

Devil: (1) Lucifer, Satan, chief of the fallen angels who sinned and were banished from heaven. Still possessing angelic powers, he can cause such diabolical phenomena as possession and obsession, and can tempt men to sin.

(2) Any fallen angel.

Devil's Advocate: See Promoter of the Faith.

Devotion: (1) Religious fervor, piety; dedication.

(2) The consolation experienced at times during prayer; a reverent manner of praying.

Devotions: Pious practices of members of the Church include not only participation in various acts of the liturgy but also in other acts of worship generally called popular or private devotions. Concerning these, the Second Vatican Council said in the *Constitution on the Sacred Liturgy* (No. 13): "Popular devotions of the Christian people are warmly commended, provided they accord with the laws and norms of the Church. Such is especially the case with devotions called for by the Apostolic See. Devotions proper to the individual churches also have a special dignity. . . . These devotions should be so drawn up that they harmonize with the liturgical seasons, accord with the sacred liturgy, are in some fashion derived from it, and lead the people to it, since the liturgy by its very nature far surpasses any of them."

Devotions of a liturgical type are Benediction of the Blessed Sacrament, recitation of the Little Office of the Blessed Virgin Mary or of Evening Prayer and Night Prayer of the Liturgy of the Hours. Examples of paraliturgical devotion are a Bible Service or Vigil, and the Angelus, Rosary and Stations of the Cross, which have a strong scriptural basis.

Dies Irae: The opening Latin words, Day of Wrath, of a hymn for requiem Masses, written in the 13th century by the Franciscan Thomas of Celano.

Diocese: A fully organized ecclesiastical jurisdiction under the pastoral direction of a bishop as local ordinary.

Discalced: Of Latin derivation and meaning without shoes, the word is applied to religious orders or congregations whose members go barefoot or wear sandals.

Disciple: A term used sometimes in reference to the Apostles but more often to a larger number of followers (70 or 72) of Christ mentioned in Lk. 10:1.

Disciplina Arcani: A Latin phrase, meaning discipline of the secret and referring to a practice of the early Church, especially during the Roman persecutions, to: (1) conceal Christian truths from those who, it was feared, would misinterpret, ridicule and profane the teachings, and persecute Christians for believing them; (2) instruct catechumens in a gradual manner, withholding the teaching of certain doctrines until the catechumens proved themselves of good faith and sufficient understanding.

Dispensation: The relaxation of a law in a particular case. Laws made for the common good sometimes work undue hardship in particular cases. In such cases, where sufficient reasons are present, dispensations may be granted by proper authorities. Bishops, religious superiors and others may dispense from certain laws; the pope can dispense from all ecclesiastical laws. No one has authority to dispense from obligations of the divine law.

Divination: Attempting to foretell future or hidden things by means of things like dreams, necromancy, spiritism, examination of entrails, astrology, augury, omens, palmistry, drawing straws, dice, cards, etc. Practices like these attribute to creatural things a power which belongs to God alone and are violations of the First Commandment.

Divine Praises: Fourteen praises recited or sung at Benediction of the Blessed Sacrament in reparation for sins of sacrilege, blasphemy and profanity. Some of these praises date from the end of the 18th century.

Blessed be God. / Blessed be his holy Name. / Blessed be Jesus Christ, true God and true Man. / Blessed be the Name of Jesus. / Blessed be his most Sacred Heart. / Blessed be his most Precious Blood. / Blessed be Jesus in the most holy Sacrament of the Altar. / Blessed be the Holy Spirit, the Paraclete. / Blessed be the great Mother of God, Mary most holy. / Blessed be her holy and Immaculate Conception. / Blessed be her glorious Assumption. / Blessed be the name of Mary, Virgin and Mother. / Blessed be St. Joseph, her most chaste Spouse. / Blessed be God in his Angels and in his Saints.

Double Effect Principle: Actions sometimes have two effects closely related to each other, one good and the other bad, and a difficult moral question can arise: Is it permissible to place an action from which two such results follow? It is permissible to place the action, if: the action is good in itself and is directly productive of the good effect; the circumstances are good; the intention of the person is good; the reason for placing the action is proportionately serious to the seriousness of the indirect bad effect. For example: Is it morally permissible for a pregnant woman to undergo medical or surgical treatment for a pathological condition if the indirect and secondary effect of the treatment will be the loss of the child? The reply is affirmative, for these reasons: The action, i.e., the treatment, is good in itself, cannot be deferred until a later time without very serious consequences, and is ordered directly to the cure of critically grave pathology. By means of the treatment, the woman intends to save her life, which she has a right to do. The loss of the child is not directly sought as a means for the cure of the mother but results indirectly and in a secondary manner from the placing of the action, i.e., the treatment, which is good in itself.

The double effect principle does not support the principle that the end justifies the means.

Doxology: (1) The lesser doxology, or ascription of glory to the Trinity, is the Glory be to the Father. The first part dates back to the third or fourth century, and came from the form of baptism. The concluding words, As it was in the beginning, etc., are of later origin.

(2) The greater doxology, Glory to God in the highest, begins with the words of angelic praise at the birth of Christ recounted in the Infancy Narrative (Lk. 2:14). It is often recited at Mass. Of early Eastern origin, it is found in the *Apostolic Constitutions* in a form much like the present.

Dulia: A Greek term meaning the veneration or homage, different in nature and degree from that given to God, paid to the saints. It includes honoring the saints and seeking their intercession with God.

Duty: A moral obligation deriving from the binding force of law, the exigencies of one's state in life, and other sources.

E

Easter Controversy: A three-phase controversy over the time for the celebration of Easter.

Some early Christians in the Near East, called Quartodecimans, favored the observance of Easter on the 14th day of Nisan, the spring month of the Hebrew calendar, whenever it occurred. Against this practice, Pope St. Victor I, about 190, ordered a Sunday observance of the feast.

The Council of Nicaea, in line with usages of the Church at Rome and Alexandria, decreed in 325 that Easter should be observed on the first Sunday following the first full moon of spring.

Uniformity of practice in the West was not achieved until several centuries later, when the British Isles, in delayed compliance with measures enacted by the Synod of Whitby in 664, accepted the Roman date of observance.

Unrelated to the controversy is the fact that some Eastern Christians, in accordance with traditional calendar practices, celebrate Easter at a different time than the Roman and Eastern-Rite churches.

Easter Duty: The serious obligation binding Catholics of Roman Rite, by a precept of the Church, to receive Holy Communion during the Easter time; in the U.S., from the first Sunday of Lent to Trinity Sunday.

Easter Water: Holy water blessed with special ceremonies and distributed on the Easter Vigil; used during Easter Week for blessing the faithful and homes.

Ecclesiology: Study of the nature, constitution, members, mission, functions, etc., of the Church.

Ecstasy: An extraordinary state of mystical experience in which a person is so absorbed in God that the activity of the exterior senses is suspended.

Ecumenism: The movement of Christians and their churches toward the unity willed by Christ. The Second Vatican Council called the movement "those activities and enterprises which, according to various needs of the Church and opportune occasions, are started and organized for the fostering of unity among Christians" (*Decree on Ecumenism,* No. 4). Spiritual ecumenism, i.e., mutual prayer for unity, is the heart of the movement. The movement also involves scholarly and pew-level efforts for the development of mutual understanding and better interfaith relations in general, and collaboration by the churches and their members in the social area.

Elevation: The raising of the host after consecration at Mass for adoration by the faithful. The custom was introduced in the Diocese of Paris about the close of the 12th century to offset an erroneous teaching of the time which held that transubstantiation of the bread did not take place until after the consecration of the wine in the chalice. The elevation of the chalice following the consecration of the wine was introduced in the 15th century.

End Justifies the Means: An unacceptable ethical principle which states that evil means may be used to produce good effects.

Envy: Sadness over another's good fortune because it is considered a loss to oneself or a detraction from one's own excellence; one of the seven capital sins, a violation of the obligations of charity.

Epikeia: A Greek word meaning reasonableness and designating a moral theory and practice, a mild interpretation of the mind of a legislator who is prudently considered not to wish positive law to bind in certain circumstances. Use of the principle is justified in practice when the lawgiver himself cannot be appealed to and when it can be prudently assumed that in particular cases, e.g., because of special hardship, he would not wish the law to be applied in a strict manner. Epikeia may not be applied with respect to acts that are intrinsically wrong or those covered by laws which automatically make them invalid.

Episcopate: (1) The office, dignity and sacramental powers bestowed upon a bishop at his ordination.

(2) The body of bishops collectively.

Equivocation: (1) The use of words, phrases, or gestures having more than one meaning in order to conceal information which a questioner has no strict right to know. It is permissible to equivocate (have a broad mental reservation) in some circumstances.

(2) A lie, i.e., a statement of untruth. Lying is intrinsically wrong. A lie told in joking, evident as such, is not wrong.

Eschatology: Doctrine concerning the last things: death, judgment, heaven and hell, and the final state of perfection of the people and kingdom of God at the end of time.

Eternity: The interminable, perfect possession of life in its totality without beginning or end; an attribute of God, who has no past or future but always is. Man's existence has a beginning but no end and is, accordingly, called immortal.

Ethics: Moral philosophy, the science of the morality of human acts deriving from natural law, the natural end of man, and the powers of human reason. It includes all the spheres of human activity — personal, social, economic, political, etc. Ethics is distinct from but can be related to moral theology, whose primary principles are drawn from divine revelation.

Eucharistic Congresses: Public demonstrations of faith in the Holy Eucharist. Combining liturgical services, other public ceremonies, subsidiary meetings, different kinds of instructional and inspirational elements, they are unified by central themes and serve to increase understanding of and devotion to Christ in the Eucharist, and to relate this liturgy of worship and witness to life.

The first international congress developed from a proposal by Marie Marthe Tamisier of Touraine, organizing efforts of Msgr. Louis Gaston de Segur, and backing by industrialist Philibert Vrau. It was held with the approval of Pope Leo XIII at the University of Lille, France, and was attended by some 800 persons from France, Belgium, Holland, England, Spain and Switzerland.

International congresses are planned and held under the auspices of a permanent committee for international Eucharistic congresses. Participants include clergy, religious and lay persons from many countries, and representatives of national and international Catholic organizations. Popes have usually been represented by legates, but Paul VI attended two congresses personally, the 38th at Bombay and the 39th at Bogota.

Forty-two international congresses were held from 1881 to 1981:

Lille (1881), Avignon (1882), Liege (1883), Freiburg (1885), Toulouse (1886), Paris (1888), Antwerp (1890), Jerusalem (1893), Rheims (1894), Paray-le-Monial (1897), Brussels (1898), Lourdes (1899), Angers (1901), Namur (1902), Angouleme (1904), Rome (1905), Tournai (1906), Metz (1907), London (1908), Cologne (1909), Montreal (1910), Madrid (1911), Vienna (1912), Malta (1913), Lourdes (1914), Rome (1922), Amsterdam (1924), Chicago (1926), Sydney (1928), Carthage (1930), Dublin (1932), Buenos Aires (1934), Manila (1937), Budapest (1938), Barcelona (1952), Rio de Janeiro (1955), Munich, Germany (1960), Bombay, India (1964), Bogota, Colombia (1968), Melbourne, Australia (1973), Philadelphia (1976), Lourdes (1981).

The 43rd international congress will be held in 1985 in Nairobi, Kenya.

Eugenics: The science of heredity and environment for the physical and mental improvement of offspring. Extreme eugenics is untenable in practice because it advocates immoral means, such as compulsory breeding of the select, sterilization of persons said to be unfit, abortion, and unacceptable methods of birth regulation.

Euthanasia: Mercy killing, the direct causing of death for the purpose of ending human suffering. Euthanasia is murder and is totally illicit, for the natural law forbids the direct taking of one's own life or that of an innocent person.

The use of drugs to relieve suffering in serious cases, even when this results in a shortening of life as an indirect and secondary effect, is permissible under conditions of the double effect principle. It is also permissible for a seriously ill person to refuse to follow — or for other responsible persons to refuse to permit — extraordinary medical procedures even though the refusal might entail shortening of life.

Evolution: Scientific theory concerning the development of the physical universe from unorganized matter (inorganic evolution) and, especially, the development of existing forms of vegetable, animal and human life from earlier and more primitive organisms (organic evolution). Various ideas about evolution were advanced for some centuries before scientific evidence in support of the main-line theory of organic evolution, which has several formulations, was discovered and verified in the second half of the 19th century and afterwards. This evidence — from the findings of comparative anatomy and other sciences — confirmed evolution within species and cleared the way to further investigation of questions regarding the processes of its accomplishment. While a number of such questions remain open with respect to human evolution, a point of doctrine not open to question is the immediate creation of the human soul by God.

For some time, theologians regarded the theory with hostility, considering it to be in opposition to the account of creation in the early chapters of Genesis and subversive of belief in such doctrines as creation, the early state of man in grace, and the fall of man from grace. This state of affairs and the tension it generated led to considerable controversy regarding an alleged conflict between religion and science. Gradually, however, the tension was diminished with the development of biblical studies from the latter part of the 19th century onwards, with clarification of the distinctive features of religious truth and scientific truth, and with the refinement of evolutionary concepts.

So far as the Genesis account of creation is concerned, the Catholic view is that the writer(s) did not write as a scientist but as the communicator of religious truth in a manner adapted to the understanding of the people of his time. He used anthropomorphic language, the figure of days and other literary devices to state the salvation truths of creation, the fall of man from grace, and the promise of redemption. It was beyond the competency and purpose of the writer(s) to describe creation and related events in a scientific manner.

Excommunication: A penalty or censure by which a baptized person is excluded from the communion of the faithful, for committing and remaining obstinate in certain sins specified in canon law and technically called crimes. As by baptism a person is made a member of the Church in which there is a communication of spiritual goods, so by excommunication he is deprived of the same spiritual goods until he repents and receives absolution. Even though excommunicated, a person is still responsible for fulfillment of the normal obligations of a Catholic.

Existentialism: A philosophy with radical concern for the problems of individual existence and identity viewed in particular here-and-now patterns of thought which presuppose irrationality and absurdity in human life and the whole universe. It is preoccupied with questions about freedom, moral decision and responsibility against a background of denial of objective truth and universal norms of conduct; is characterized by prevailing anguish, dread, fear, pessimism, despair; is generally atheistic, although its modern originator, Soren Kierkegaard (d. 1855), and Gabriel Marcel (d. 1973) attempted to give it a Christian orientation. Pius XII called it "the new erroneous philosophy which, opposing itself to idealism, immanentism and pragmatism, has assumed the name of existentialism, since it concerns itself only with the existence of individual things and neglects all consideration of their immutable essences" (Encyclical *Humani Generis*, Aug. 12, 1950).

Exorcism: (1) Driving out evil spirits; a rite in which evil spirits are charged and commanded on the authority of God and with the prayer of the Church to depart from a person or to cease causing harm to a person suffering from diabolical possession or obsession. The sacramental is officially administered by a priest delegated for the purpose by the bishop of the place. Elements of the rite include the Litany of Saints; recitation of the Our Father, one or more creeds, and other prayers; specific prayers of exorcism; the reading of Gospel passages and use of the Sign of the Cross. Private exorcism for the liberation of a person from the strong influence of evil spirits, through prayer and the use of sacramentals like holy water, can be done by anyone.

(2) Exorcisms which do not imply the conditions of either diabolical possession or obsession form part of the ceremony of baptism, and are also included in formulas for various blessings; e.g., of water.

F

Faculties: Grants of jurisdiction or authority by the law of the Church or superiors (pope, bishop, religious superior) for exercise of the powers of holy orders; e.g., priests are given faculties to hear confessions, officiate at weddings; bishops are given faculties to grant dispensations, etc.

Faith: In religion, faith has several aspects. Catholic doctrine calls faith the assent of the mind to truths revealed by God, the assent being made with the help of grace and by command of the will on account of the authority and trustworthiness of God revealing. The term faith also refers to the truths that are believed (content of faith) and to the way in which a person, in response to Christ, gives witness to and expresses belief in daily life (living faith).

All of these elements, and more, are included in the following statement:

" 'The obedience of faith' (Rom. 16:26; 1:5; 2 Cor. 10:5-6) must be given to God who reveals, an obedience by which man entrusts his whole self freely to God, offering 'the full submission of intellect and will to God who reveals' (First Vatican Council, *Dogmatic Constitution on the Catholic Faith*, Chap. 3), and freely assenting to the truth revealed by him. If this faith is to be shown, the grace of God and the interior help of the Holy Spirit must precede and assist, moving the heart and turning it to God, opening the eyes of the mind, and giving 'joy and ease to everyone in assenting to the truth and believing it' " (Second Council of Orange, Canon 7) (Second Vatican Council, *Constitution on Revelation*, No. 5). Faith is necessary for salvation.

Faith, Rule of: The norm or standard of religious belief. The Catholic doctrine is that belief must be professed in the divinely revealed truths in the Bible and tradition as interpreted and proposed by the infallible teaching authority of the Church.

Fast, Eucharistic: According to Canon 919 of the revised Code of Canon Law, effective Nov. 27, 1983: Abstinence from food and drink, except water and medicine, is required for one hour before the reception of the Eucharist. Persons who are advanced in age or suffer from infirmity or illness, together with those who care for them, can receive Holy Communion even if they have not abstained from food and drink for an hour.

A priest celebrating two or three Masses on the same day can eat and drink before the second or third Mass without regard for the hour limit.

Father: A title of priests, who are regarded as spiritual fathers because they are the ordinary ministers of baptism, by which persons are born to supernatural life, and because of their pastoral service to people.

Fear: A mental state caused by the apprehension of present or future danger. Grave fear does not necessarily remove moral responsibility for an act, but may lessen it.

First Friday: A devotion consisting of the reception of Holy Communion on the first Friday of nine consecutive months in honor of the Sacred Heart of Jesus and in reparation for sin. (See Sacred Heart, Promises.)

First Saturday: A devotion tracing its origin to the apparitions of the Blessed Virgin Mary at Fatima in 1917. Those practicing the devotion go to confession and, on the first Saturday of five consecutive months, receive Holy Communion, recite five decades of the Rosary, and meditate on the mysteries for 15 minutes.

Fisherman's Ring: A signet ring engraved with the image of St. Peter fishing from a boat, and encircled with the name of the reigning pope. It is not worn by the pope. It is used to seal briefs, and is destroyed after each pope's death.

Forgiveness of Sin: Catholics believe that sins are forgiven by God through the mediation of Christ in view of the repentance of the sinner and by means of the sacrament of penance. (See Penance, Contrition).

Fortitude: Courage to face dangers or hardships for the sake of what is good; one of the four cardinal virtues and one of the seven gifts of the Holy Spirit.

Fortune Telling: Attempting to predict the future or the occult by means of cards, palm reading, etc.; a form of divination, prohibited by the First Commandment.

Forty Hours Devotion: A Eucharistic observance consisting of solemn exposition of the Blessed Sacrament coupled with special Masses and forms of prayer, for the purposes of making reparation for sin and praying for God's blessings of grace and peace. The devotion was instituted in 1534 in Milan. St. John Neumann of Philadelphia was the first bishop in the U.S. to prescribe its observance in his diocese. For many years in this country, the observance was held annually on a rotating basis in all parishes of a diocese. Simplified and abbreviated Eucharistic observances have taken the place of the devotion in some places.

Forum: The sphere in which ecclesiastical authority or jurisdiction is exercised.

(1) External: Authority is exercised in the external forum to deal with matters affecting the public welfare of the Church and its members. Those who have such authority because of their office (e.g., diocesan bishops) are called ordinaries.

(2) Internal: Authority is exercised in the internal forum to deal with matters affecting the private spiritual good of individuals. The sacramental forum is the sphere in which the sacrament of penance is administered; other exercises of jurisdiction in the internal forum take place in the non-sacramental forum.

Franciscan Crown: A seven-decade rosary used to commemorate the seven Joys of the Blessed Virgin: the Annunciation, the Visitation, the Nativity of Our Lord, the Adoration of the Magi, the Finding of the Child Jesus in the Temple, the Apparition of the Risen Christ to his Mother, the Assumption and Coronation of the Blessed Virgin. Introduced in 1422, the Crown originally consisted only of seven Our Fathers and 70 Hail Marys. Two Hail Marys were added to complete the number 72 (thought to be the number of years of Mary's life), and one Our Father, Hail Mary and Glory be to the Father are said for the intention of the pope.

Freedom, Religious: The Second Vatican Council declared that the right to religious freedom in civil society "means that all men are to be immune from coercion on the part of individuals or of social groups and of any human power, in such wise that in matters religious no one is to be forced to act in a manner contrary to his own beliefs. Nor is anyone to be restrained from acting in accordance with his own beliefs, whether privately or publicly, whether alone or in association with others, within due limits" of requirements for the common good. The foundation of this right in civil society is the "very dignity of the human person" (_Declaration on Religious Freedom,_ No. 2).

The conciliar statement did not deal with the subject of freedom within the Church. It noted the responsibility of the faithful "carefully to attend to the sacred and certain doctrine of the Church" (No. 14).

Freemasons: A fraternal order which originated in London in 1717 with the formation of the first Grand Lodge of Freemasons. From England, the order spread to Europe and elsewhere. Its original deistic and nondenominational ideology was transformed in Latin countries into a compound of atheism, anticlericalism and irreligion. Since 1877, Grand Orient Freemasonry has been denied recognition by the Scottish and York Rites because of its failure to require belief in God and the immortality of the soul as a condition of membership. In some places, Freemasonry has been regarded as subversive of the state; in Catholic quarters, it has been considered hostile to the Church and its doctrine. In the United States, Freemasonry is generally known as a fraternal and philanthropic order.

Catholics have been forbidden to join the Freemasons, under penalty of excommunication, for serious pastoral reasons. Eight different popes in 17 different pronouncements, and at least six different local councils, condemned Freemasonry. The first condemnation was made by Clement XII in 1738. Eastern Orthodox and many Protestant bodies have also opposed the order.

The existing prohibition against membership in the Freemasons by Catholics was modified by the contents of a letter written in 1974 by Cardinal Franjo Seper, prefect of the Congregation for the Doctrine of the Faith. The letter said that Catholic laymen may join Masonic lodges which are not anti-Catholic. The letter also said: "Clerics, religious and members of secular institutes are still forbidden in every case to join any Masonic association."

Free Will: The faculty or capability of making a reasonable choice among several alternatives. Freedom of will underlies the possibility and fact of moral responsibility.

Friar: Term applied to members of mendicant orders to distinguish them from members of monastic orders. (See Mendicants.)

Fruits of the Holy Spirit: Charity, joy, peace, patience, benignity, goodness, long-animity, mildness, faith, modesty, continence, chastity.

G

Gambling: The backing of an issue with a sum of money or other valuables, which is permissible if the object is honest, if the two parties have the free disposal of their stakes without prejudice to the rights of others, if the terms are thoroughly understood by both parties, and if the outcome is not known beforehand. Gambling often falls into disrepute and may be forbidden by civil law, as well as by divine law, because of cheating, fraud and other accompanying evils.

Gehenna: Greek form of a Jewish name, _Gehinnom,_ for a valley near Jerusalem, the site of Moloch worship; used as a synonym for hell.

Genuflection: Bending of the knee, a natural sign of adoration or reverence, as when persons genuflect with the right knee in passing before the tabernacle to acknowledge the Eucharistic presence of Christ.

Gethsemani: A Hebrew word meaning oil press, designating the place on the Mount of Olives where Christ prayed and suffered in agony the night before he died.

Gifts of the Holy Spirit: Supernatural habits disposing a person to respond promptly to the inspiration of grace; promised by Christ and communicated through the Holy Spirit, especially in the sacrament of confirmation. They are: wisdom, understanding, counsel, fortitude, knowledge, piety, fear of the Lord.

Gluttony: An unreasonable appetite for food and drink; one of the seven capital sins.

God: The infinitely perfect Supreme Being, uncaused and absolutely self-sufficient, eternal, the Creator and final end of all things. The one God subsists in three equal Persons, the Father and the Son and the Holy Spirit. God, although transcendent and distinct from the universe, is present and active in the world in realization of his plan for the salvation of men, principally through Revelation, the operations of the Holy Spirit, the life and ministry of Christ, and the continuation of Christ's ministry in the Church.

The existence of God is an article of faith, clearly communicated in divine Revelation. Even without this Revelation, however, the Church teaches, in a declaration by the First Vatican Council, that men can acquire certain knowledge of the existence of God and some of his attributes. This can be done on the bases of principles of reason and reflection on human experience.

Non-revealed arguments or demonstrations for the existence of God have been developed from the principle of causality; the contingency of man and the universe; the existence of design, change and movement in the universe; human awareness of moral responsibility; widespread human testimony to the existence of God.

Grace: A free gift of God to men (and angels), grace is a created sharing or participation in the life of God. It is given to men through the merits of Christ and is communicated by the Holy Spirit. It is necessary for salvation. The principal means of grace are the sacraments (especially the Eucharist), prayer and good works.

Sanctifying or habitual grace makes men holy and pleasing to God, adopted children of God, members of Christ, temples of the Holy Spirit, heirs of heaven capable of supernaturally meritorious acts. With grace, God gives men the supernatural virtues and gifts of the Holy Spirit. The sacraments of baptism and penance were instituted to give grace to those who do not have it; the other sacraments, to increase it in those already in the state of grace. The means for growth in holiness, or the increase of grace, are prayer, the sacraments, and good works. Sanctifying grace is lost by the commission of serious sin.

Each sacrament confers sanctifying grace for the special purpose of the sacrament; in this context, grace is called sacramental grace.

Actual grace is a supernatural help of God which enlightens and strengthens a person to do good and to avoid evil. It is not a permanent quality, like sanctifying grace. It is necessary for the performance of supernatural acts. It can be resisted and refused. Persons in the state of serious sin are given actual grace to lead them to repentance.

Grace at Meals: Prayers said before meals, asking a blessing of God, and after meals, giving thanks to God. In addition to traditional prayers for these purposes, many variations suitable for different occasions are possible, at personal option.

H

Habit: (1) A disposition to do things easily, given with grace (and therefore supernatural) and/or acquired by repetition of similar acts.

(2) The garb worn by religious.

Hagiography: Writings or documents about saints and other holy persons.

Hail Mary: A prayer addressed to the Blessed Virgin Mary; also called the *Ave Maria* (Latin equivalent of Hail Mary) and the Angelic Salutation. In three parts, it consists of the words addressed to Mary by the Archangel Gabriel on the occasion of the Annunciation, in the Infancy Narrative (Hail full of grace, the Lord is with you, blessed are you among women.); the words addressed to Mary by her cousin Elizabeth on the occasion of the Visitation (Blessed is the fruit of your womb.); a concluding petition (Holy Mary, Mother of God, pray for us sinners now and at the hour of our death. Amen.). The first two salutations were joined in Eastern Rite formulas by the sixth century, and were similarly used at Rome in the seventh century. Insertion of the name of Jesus at the conclusion of the salutations was probably made by Urban IV about 1262. The present form of the petition was incorporated into the breviary in 1514.

Heaven: The state of those who, having achieved salvation, are in glory with God and enjoy the beatific vision.

The phrase, kingdom of heaven, refers to the order or kingdom of God, grace, salvation.

Hell: The state of punishment of the damned — i.e., those who die in mortal sin, in a condition of self-alienation from God and of opposition to the divine plan of salvation. The punishment of hell begins immediately after death and lasts forever.

Hermit: See Anchorite.

Heroic Act of Charity: The completely unselfish offering to God of one's good works and merits for the benefit of the souls in purgatory rather than for oneself. Thus a person may offer to God for the souls in purgatory all the good works he performs during life, all the indulgences he gains, and all the prayers and indulgences that will be offered for him after his death. The act is revocable at will, and is not a vow. Its actual ratification depends on the will of God.

Heterodoxy: False doctrine, teaching or belief; a departure from truth.

Holy See: (1) The diocese of the pope, Rome.

(2) The pope himself and/or the various officials and bodies of the Church's central administration at Vatican City — the Roman Curia — which act in the name and by authority of the pope.

Holy Spirit: God the Holy Spirit, third Person of the Holy Trinity, who proceeds from the Father and the Son and with whom he is equal in every respect; inspirer of the prophets and writers of sacred Scripture; promised by Christ to the Apostles as their advocate and strengthener; appeared in the form of a dove at the baptism of Christ and as tongues of fire at his descent upon the Apostles; soul of the Church and guarantor, by his abiding presence and action, of truth in doctrine; communicator of grace to men, for which reason he is called the sanctifier.

Holy Water: Water blessed by the Church and used as a sacramental, a practice which originated in apostolic times.

Holy Year: A year during which the pope grants the plenary Jubilee Indulgence to the faithful who fulfill certain conditions. For those who make a pilgrimage to Rome during the year, the conditions are reception of the sacraments of penance and the Eucharist, visits and prayer for the intention of the pope in the basilicas of St. Peter, St. John Lateran, St. Paul and St. Mary Major. For those who do not make a pilgrimage to Rome, the conditions are reception of the sacraments and prayer for the pope during a visit or community celebration in a church designated by the bishop of the locality.

Holy Year observances have biblical counterparts in the Years of Jubilee observed at 50-year intervals by the pre-exilic Israelites — when debts were pardoned and slaves freed (Lv. 25:25-54) — and in sabbatical years observed from the end of the Exile to 70 A.D. — in which debts to fellow Jews were remitted.

The practice of Christians from early times to go on pilgrimage to the Holy Land, the shrines of martyrs and the tombs of the Apostles in Rome influenced the institution of Holy Years. There was also a prevailing belief among the people that every 100th year was a year of "Great Pardon." Accordingly, even before Boniface VIII formally proclaimed the first Holy Year Feb. 22, 1300, scores of thousands of pilgrims were already on the way to or in Rome.

Medieval popes embodied in the observance of Holy Years the practice of good works (reception of the sacraments of penance and the Eucharist, pilgrimages and/or visits to the tombs of the Apostles, and related actions) and spiritual benefits (particularly, special indulgences for the souls in purgatory). These and related practices, with suitable changes for celebrations in local churches, remain staple features of Holy Year observances.

The first three Holy Years were observed in 1300, 1350 and 1390. Subsequent ones were celebrated at 25-year intervals except in 1800 and 1850 when, respectively, the French invasion of Italy and political turmoil made observance impossible. Pope Paul II (1464-1471) set the 25-year timetable. In 1500, Pope Alexander VI prescribed the start and finish ceremonies — the opening and closing of the Holy Doors in the major basilicas on successive Christmas Eves. All but a few of the earlier Holy Years were classified as ordinary. Several — like those of 1933 and 1983-84 to commemorate the 1900th and 1950th anniversaries of the death and resurrection of Christ — were in the extraordinary category.

Holy Year 1975 coincided with the 10th anniversary of the closing of the Second Vatican Council. Its themes also coincided with the renewal emphasis which dominated the council, and were related to the main topic — the evangeliza-

tion of the modern world — on the 1974 agenda of the Synod of Bishops.

Homosexuality: The condition of a person whose sexual orientation is toward persons of the same rather than the opposi—e sex. Some psychologists regard it as an arrested state of emotional development. The condition, usually discovered during adolescence rather than deliberately caused, is not normal but is not sinful in itself. Homosexual acts against nature are objectively wrong; subjective responsibility for such acts, however, may be conditioned and diminished by compulsion and related factors.

Hope: One of the three theological virtues, by which one firmly trusts that God wills his salvation and will give him the means to attain it.

Hosanna: A Hebrew word, meaning O Lord, save, we pray.

Host, The Sacred: The bread under whose appearances Christ is and remains present in a unique manner after the consecration which takes place during Mass. (See Transubstantiation.)

Humility: A virtue which induces a person to evaluate himself at his true worth, to recognize his dependence on God, and to give glory to God for the good he has and can do.

Hyperdulia: The special veneration accorded the Blessed Virgin Mary because of her unique role in the mystery of Redemption, her exceptional gifts of grace from God, and her preeminence among the saints. Hyperdulia is not adoration; only God is adored.

Hypnosis: A mental state resembling sleep, induced by suggestion, in which the subject does the bidding of the hypnotist. Hypnotism is permissible under certain conditions: the existence of a serious reason, e.g., for anesthetic or therapeutic purposes, and the competence and integrity of the hypnotist. Hypnotism may not be practiced for the sake of amusement. Experiments indicate that, contrary to popular opinion, hypnotized subjects may be induced to perform immoral acts which, normally, they would not do.

Hypostatic Union: The union of the human and divine natures in the one divine Person of Christ.

I

Icons: Byzantine-style paintings or representations of Christ, the Blessed Virgin and other saints, venerated in the Eastern Churches where they take the place of statues.

Idolatry: Worship of any but the true God; a violation of the First Commandment.

IHS: In Greek, the first three letters of the name of Jesus — Iota, Eta, Sigma.

Immortality: The survival and continuing existence of the human soul after death.

Immunity of the Clergy: Exemption of clerics from military duty and civil service.

Impurity: Unlawful indulgence in sexual pleasure. (See Chastity.)

Incardination: The affiliation of a priest to his diocese. Every secular priest must belong to a certain diocese. Similarly, every priest of a religious community must belong to some jurisdiction of his community; this affiliation, however, is not called incardination.

Incarnation: (1) The coming-into-flesh or taking of human nature by the Second Person of the Trinity. He became human as the Son of Mary, being miraculously conceived by the power of the Holy Spirit, without ceasing to be divine. His divine Person hypostatically unites his divine and human natures.

(2) The supernatural mystery coextensive with Christ from the moment of his human conception and continuing through his life on earth; his sufferings and death; his resurrection from the dead and ascension to glory with the Father; his sending, with the Father, of the Holy Spirit upon the Apostles and the Church; and his unending mediation with the Father for the salvation of men.

Incense: A granulated substance which, when burnt, emits an aromatic smoke. It symbolizes the zeal with which the faithful should be consumed, the good odor of Christian virtue, the ascent of prayer to God.

Incest: Sexual intercourse with relatives by blood or marriage; a sin of impurity and also a grave violation of the natural reverence due to relatives. Other sins of impurity (desire, etc.) concerning relatives have the nature of incest.

Inculturation: This was one of the subjects of an address delivered by Pope John Paul II Feb. 15, 1982, at a meeting in Lagos with the bishops of Nigeria.

"An important aspect of your own evangelizing role is the whole dimension of the inculturation of the Gospel into the lives of your people."

"The Church truly respects the culture of each people. In offering the Gospel message, the Church does not intend to destroy or to abolish what is good and beautiful. In fact, she recognizes many cultural values and, through the power of the Gospel, purifies and takes into Christian worship certain elements of a people's customs. The Church comes to bring Christ; she does not come to bring the culture of another race. Evangelization aims at penetrating and elevating culture by the power of the Gospel."

"It is through the Providence of God that the divine message is made incarnate and is communicated through the culture of each people. It is forever true that the path of culture is the path of man, and it is on this path that man encounters the one who embodies the values of all cultures and fully reveals the man of each culture to himself. The Gospel of Christ, the Incarnate Word, finds its home along the path of culture, and from this path it continues to offer its message of salvation and eternal life."

Index of Prohibited Books: A list of books which Catholics were formerly forbidden to read, possess or sell, under penalty of excommunication. The books were banned by the Holy See after publication because their treatment of matters of faith and morals and related subjects were judged to be erroneous or serious occasions of doctrinal error. Some books were listed in the Index by name; others were covered under general norms. The Congregation for the Doctrine of the Faith declared June 14, 1966, that the Index and its related penalties of excommunication no longer had the force of law in the Church. Persons are still obliged, however, to take normal precautions against occasions of doctrinal error.

Indifferentism: A theory that any one religion is as true and good — or false — as any other religion, and that it makes no difference, objectively, what religion one professes, if any. The theory is completely subjective, finding its justification entirely in personal choice without reference to or respect for objective validity. It is also self-contradictory, since it regards as equally acceptable — or unacceptable — the beliefs of all religions, which in fact are not only not all the same but are in some cases opposed to each other.

Indulgence: According to *The Doctrine and Practice of Indulgences,* an apostolic constitution issued by Paul VI Jan. 1, 1967, an indulgence is the remission before God of the temporal punishment due for sins already forgiven as far as their guilt is concerned, which a follower of Christ — with the proper dispositions and under certain determined conditions — acquires through the intervention of the Church. The Church grants indulgences in accordance with doctrine concerning the superabundant merits of Christ and the saints, the Power of the Keys, and the sharing of spiritual goods in the Communion of Saints.

An indulgence is partial or plenary, depending on whether it does away with either part or all of the temporal punishment due for sin. Both types of indulgences can always be applied to the dead by way of suffrage; the actual disposition of indulgences applied to the dead rests with God.

(1) Partial indulgence: Properly disposed faithful who perform an action to which a partial indulgence is attached obtain, in addition to the remission of temporal punishment acquired by the action itself, an equal remission of punishment through the intervention of the Church. (This grant was formerly designated in terms of days and years.) The proper dispositions for gaining a partial indulgence are sorrow for sin and freedom from serious sin, performance of the required good work, and the intention (which can be general or immediate) to gain the indulgence.

In addition to customary prayers and other good works to which partial indulgences are attached, the *Enchiridion Indulgentiarum* published in 1968 included general grants of partial indulgences to the faithful who: (a) with some kind of prayer, raise their minds to God with humble confidence while carrying out their duties and bearing the difficulties of everyday life; (b) motivated by the spirit of faith and compassion, give of themselves or their goods for the service of persons in need; (c) in a spirit of penance, spontaneously refrain from the enjoyment of things which are lawful and pleasing to them.

2) Plenary indulgence: To gain a plenary indulgence, it is necessary for a person to be free of all attachment to sin, to perform the work to which the indulgence is attached, and to fulfill the three conditions of sacramental confession, Eucharistic Communion, and prayer for the intention of the

pope. The three conditions may be fulfilled several days before or after the performance of the prescribed work, but it is fitting that Communion be received and prayers for the intentions of the pope be offered on the same day the work is performed. The condition of praying for the pope's intention is fully satisfied by praying one Our Father and one Hail Mary, and sometimes the Creed, but persons are free to choose other prayers.

Four of the several devotional practices for which a plenary indulgence is granted are: (a) adoration of the Blessed Sacrament for at least one-half hour; (b) devout reading of sacred Scripture for at least one-half hour; (c) the Way of the Cross; (d) recitation of the Marian Rosary in a church or public oratory or in a family group, a religious community or pious association. Only one plenary indulgence can be gained in a single day.

Indult: A favor or privilege granted by competent ecclesiastical authority, giving permission to do something not allowed by the common law of the Church.

Infant Jesus of Prague: An 18-inch-high wooden statue of the Child Jesus which has figured in a form of devotion to the Holy Childhood and Kingship of Christ since the 17th century. Of uncertain origin, the statue was presented by Princess Polixena to the Carmelites of Our Lady of Victory Church, Prague, in 1628.

Infused Virtues: The theological virtues of faith, hope, and charity; principles or capabilities of supernatural action, they are given with sanctifying grace by God rather than acquired by repeated acts of a person. They can be increased by practice; they are lost by contrary acts. Natural-acquired moral virtues, like the cardinal virtues of prudence, justice, temperance, and fortitude, can be considered infused in a person whose state of grace gives them supernatural orientation.

Inquisition: A tribunal for dealing with heretics, authorized by Gregory IX in 1231 to search them out, hear and judge them, sentence them to various forms of punishment, and in some cases to hand them over to civil authorities for punishment. The Inquisition was a creature of its time when crimes against faith, which threatened the good of the Christian community, were regarded also as crimes against the state, and when heretical doctrines of such extremists as the Cathari and Albigensians threatened the very fabric of society. The institution, which was responsible for many excesses, was most active in the second half of the 13th century.

Inquisition, Spanish: An institution peculiar to Spain and the colonies in Spanish America. In 1478, at the urging of King Ferdinand, Pope Sixtus IV approved the establishment of the Inquisition for trying charges of heresy brought against Jewish (Marranos) and Moorish (Moriscos) converts. It acquired jurisdiction over other cases as well, however, and fell into disrepute because of irregularities in its functions, cruelty in its sentences, and the manner in which it served the interests of the Spanish crown more than the accused persons and the good of the Church. Protests by the Holy See failed to curb excesses of the Inquisition, which lingered in Spanish history until early in the 19th century.

I N R I: The first letters of words in the Latin inscription atop the cross on which Christ was crucified: (I)esus (N)azaraenus, (R)ex (J)udaeorum — Jesus of Nazareth, King of the Jews.

Insemination, Artificial: The implanting of human semen by some means other than consummation of natural marital intercourse. In view of the principle that procreation should result only from marital intercourse, donor insemination is not permissible. The use of legitimate artificial means to further the fruitfulness of marital intercourse is permissible.

In Sin: The condition of a person called spiritually dead because he does not possess sanctifying grace, the principle of supernatural life, action and merit. Such grace can be regained through repentance.

Instruction: A document containing doctrinal explanations, directive norms, rules, recommendations, admonitions, issued by the pope, a department of the Roman Curia or other competent authority in the Church. To the extent that they so prescribe, instructions have the force of law.

Intercommunion: The common celebration and reception of the Eucharist by members of different Christian churches; a pivotal issue in ecumenical theory and practice. Catholic participation and intercommunion in the Eucharistic liturgy of another church without a valid priesthood and with a variant Eucharistic belief is out of order. Under certain conditions, other Christians may receive the Eucharist in the Catholic Church (see additional Intercommunion entry). Intercommunion is acceptable to some Protestant churches and unacceptable to others.

Interdict: An ecclesiastical penalty imposed on persons and places for certain violations of church law. If the interdict is personal, the interdicted persons may not take part in certain liturgical services, administer or receive certain sacraments. If the interdict is local, persons may not take part in certain liturgical services, administer or receive certain sacraments in the interdicted places.

Interdict is different from excommunication, and does not involve exclusion of a person from the community of the faithful.

Interregnum: The period of time between the death of a pope and the election of his successor. Another term applied to the period is *Sede vacante,* meaning the See (of Rome) being vacant.

The main concerns during an interregnum are matters connected with the death and burial of the pope, the election of his successor, and the maintenance of ordinary routine for the proper functioning of the Roman Curia and the Diocese of Rome.

Interregnum procedures follow norms contained in the apostolic constitution *Romano Pontifici Eligendo* (concerning the vacancy of the Apostolic See and the election of the Roman Pontiff) issued by Paul VI Oct. 1, 1975. This constitution superseded two others previously in force: *Vacantis*

Apostolicae Sedis, issued by Pius XII Dec. 8, 1945, and *Summi Pontificis Electione,* issued by John XXIII Sept. 5, 1962.

"During the vacancy of the Apostolic See," the constitution states, "the government of the Church is entrusted to the Sacred College of Cardinals for the sole dispatch of ordinary business and of matters which cannot be postponed, and for the preparation of everything necessary for the election of the new pope."

The general congregation of the whole college, presided over by the dean, sub-dean or senior cardinal, has responsibility for major decisions during an interregnum. Other decisions of a routine nature are left to a particular congregation consisting of the chamberlain of the Holy Roman Church and three assistant cardinals.

The chamberlain of the Holy Roman Church and the dean of the college are the key officials, with directive responsibilities before and during the electoral conclave. The chamberlain is in general charge of ordinary administration. He — or the dean prior to a chamberlain's election by the cardinals — certifies the death of the pope; orders the destruction of the Fisherman's Ring and personal seals of the pope; and sets in motion procedures, carried out in collaboration with the dean, for informing the world about the pope's death, for funeral preparations, and for summoning and supervising the conclave for the election of a new pope.

Cardinals in charge of departments of the Roman Curia relinquish their offices at the death of the pope. Remaining in office, however, are the vicar of Rome, for ordinary jurisdiction over the diocese, and the major penitentiary. The substitute secretary of state or papal secretariat maintains the secretariat in a status quo. Papal representatives, such as nuncios and apostolic delegates, remain in office.

The congregations, offices and tribunals of the Curia retain ordinary jurisdiction for routine affairs but may not initiate new business during an interregnum.

If the pope should die during sessions of an ecumenical council or the Synod of Bishops, they would automatically be suspended.

The deceased pope is buried in St. Peter's Basilica, following prescribed ceremonies and traditional customs during a mourning period of nine days.

The conclave for the election of a new pope begins no sooner than 15 and no later than 20 days after the death of his predecessor. On the election of the new pope, the interregnum comes to an end. (See Papal Election.)

Intinction: A method of administering Holy Communion under the dual appearances of bread and wine, in which the consecrated host is dipped in the consecrated wine before being given to the communicant. The administering of Holy Communion in this manner, which has been traditional in Eastern-Rite liturgies, was authorized in the Roman Rite for various occasions by the *Constitution on the Sacred Liturgy* promulgated by the Second Vatican Council.

Irenicism: Peace-seeking, conciliation, as opposed to polemics; an important element in ecumenism, provided it furthers pursuit of the Christian unity willed by Christ without degenerating into a peace-at-any-price disregard for religious truth.

Irregularity: An impediment to the lawful reception or exercise of holy orders. The Church instituted irregularities — which include apostasy, heresy, homicide, attempted suicide — out of reverence for the dignity of the sacraments.

Itinerarium: Prayers for a spiritually profitable journey.

J

Jansenism: Opinions developed and proposed by Cornelius Jansenius (1585-1638). He held that: human nature was radically and intrinsically corrupted by original sin; some men are predestined to heaven and others to hell; Christ died only for those predestined to heaven; for those who are predestined, the operations of grace are irresistible. Jansenism also advocated an extremely rigorous code of morals and asceticism. The errors were proscribed by Urban VIII in 1642, by Innocent X in 1653, by Clement XI in 1713, and by other popes. Despite these condemnations, the rigoristic spirit of Jansenism lingered for a long time afterwards, particularly in France.

Jehovah's Witnesses: The Witnesses, together with the Watchtower and Bible Tract Society, trace their beginnings to a Bible class organized by Charles Taze Russell in 1872 at Allegheny, Pa. They take their name from a passage in Isaiah (43:12): " 'You are my witnesses,' says Jehovah." They are generally fundamentalist and revivalist with respect to the Bible, and believe that Christ is God's Son but is inferior to God. They place great emphasis on the Battle of Armageddon (as a decisive confrontation of good and evil) that is depicted vividly in Revelation, believing that God will then destroy the existing system of things and that, with the establishment of Jehovah's Kingdom, a small band of 144,000 spiritual sons of God will go to heaven, rule with Christ, and share in some way their happiness with some others.

Each Witness is considered by the society to be an ordained minister charged with the duty of spreading the message of Jehovah, which is accomplished through publications, house-to-house visitations, and other methods. The Witnesses refuse to salute the flag of any nation, regarding this as a form of idolatry, or to sanction blood transfusions even for the saving of life. There are approximately one million Witnesses in more than 22,000 congregations in some 80 countries. The freedom and activities of Witnesses are restricted in some places.

Jesus: The name of Jesus, meaning Savior in Christian usage, derived from the Aramaic and Hebrew *Yeshua* and *Joshua,* meaning *Yahweh* is salvation.

Jesus Prayer: A form of prayer dating back to the fifth century, "Lord Jesus Christ, Son of God, have mercy on me (a sinner)."

Judgment: (1) Last or final judgment: Final

judgment by Christ, at the end of the world and the general resurrection.

(2) Particular judgment: The judgment that takes place immediately after a person's death, followed by entrance into heaven, hell or purgatory.

Jurisdiction: Right, power, authority to rule. Jurisdiction in the Church is of divine institution; has pastoral service for its purpose; includes legislative, judicial and executive authority; can be exercised only by persons with the power of orders.

(1) Ordinary jurisdiction is attached to ecclesiastical offices by law; the officeholders, called ordinaries, have authority over those who are subject to them.

(2) Delegated jurisdiction is that which is granted to persons rather than attached to offices. Its extent depends on the terms of the delegation.

Justice: One of the four cardinal virtues by which a person gives to others what is due to them as a matter of right. (See Cardinal Virtues.)

Justification: The act by which God makes a person just, and the consequent change in the spiritual status of a person, from sin to grace; the remission of sin and the infusion of sanctifying grace through the merits of Christ and the action of the Holy Spirit.

K

Kerygma: Proclaiming the word of God, in the manner of the Apostles, as here and now effective for salvation. This method of preaching or instruction, centered on Christ and geared to the facts and themes of salvation history, is designed to dispose people to faith in Christ and or to intensify the experience and practice of that faith in those who have it.

Keys, Power of the: Spiritual authority and jurisdiction in the Church, symbolized by the keys of the kingdom of heaven. Christ promised the keys to St. Peter, as head-to-be of the Church (Mt. 16:19), and commissioned him with full pastoral responsibility to feed his lambs and sheep (Jn. 21:15-17), The pope, as the successor of St. Peter, has this power in a primary and supreme manner. The bishops of the Church also have the power, in union with and subordinate to the pope. Priests share in it through holy orders and the delegation of authority.

Examples of the application of the Power of the Keys are the exercise of teaching and pastoral authority by the pope and bishops, the absolving of sins in the sacrament of penance, the granting of indulgences, the imposing of spiritual penalties on persons who commit certain serious sins.

L

Laicization: The process by which a man ordained to holy orders is relieved of the obligations of orders and the ministry and is returned to the status of a lay person. Applications by diocesan clergy are filed with their bishop and forwarded for processing to the congregation of the Roman Curia authorized to grant the indult of laicization.

Languages of the Church: The first language in church use, for divine worship and the conduct of ecclesiastical affairs, was Aramaic, the language of the first Christians in and around Jerusalem. As the Church spread westward, Greek was adopted and prevailed until the third century when it was supplanted by Latin for official use in the West.

According to traditions established very early in churches of the Eastern Rites, many different languages were adopted for use in divine worship and for the conduct of ecclesiastical affairs. The practice was, and still is, to use the vernacular or a language closely related to the common tongue of the people.

In the Western Church, Latin prevailed as the general official language until the promulgation on Dec. 4, 1963, of the *Constitution on the Sacred Liturgy* by the second session of the Second Vatican Council. Since that time, vernacular languages have come into use in the Mass, administration of the sacraments, and the Liturgy of the Hours. The change was introduced in order to make the prayers and ceremonies of divine worship more informative and meaningful to all. Latin, however, remains the official language for documents of the Holy See, administrative and procedural matters.

Law: An ordinance or rule governing the activity of things.

(1) Natural law: Moral norms corresponding to man's nature by which he orders his conduct toward God, neighbor, society and himself. This law, which is rooted in human nature, is of divine origin, can be known by the use of reason, and binds all men having the use of reason. The Ten Commandments are declarations and amplifications of natural law. The primary precepts of natural law, to do good and to avoid evil, are universally recognized, despite differences with respect to understanding and application resulting from different philosophies of good and evil.

(2) Divine positive law: That which has been revealed by God. Among its essentials are the twin precepts of love of God and love of neighbor, and the Ten Commandments.

(3) Ecclesiastical law: That which is established by the Church for the spiritual welfare of the faithful and the orderly conduct of ecclesiastical affairs. (See Canon Law.)

(4) Civil law: That which is established by a socio-political community for the common good.

Liberalism: A multiphased trend of thought and movement favoring liberty, independence and progress in moral, intellectual, religious, social, economic and political life. Traceable to the Renaissance, it developed through the Enlightenment, the rationalism of the 19th century, and modernist- and existentialist-related theories of the 20th century. Evaluations of various kinds of liberalism depend on the validity of their underlying principles. Extremist positions — regarding subjectivism, libertarianism, naturalist denials of the supernatural, and the alienation of individuals and society from God and the Church were condemned by Gregory XVI in the 1830's, Pius IX in 1864, Leo XIII in 1899, and St. Pius X in 1907. There is, however, nothing objectionable about forms of liberalism patterned according to sound principles of Christian doctrine.

Life in Outer Space: Whether rational life exists on other bodies in the universe besides earth, is a question for scientific investigation to settle. The possibility can be granted, without prejudice to the body of revealed truth.

Limbo: The limbo of the fathers was the state of rest and natural happiness after death enjoyed by the just of pre-Christian times until they were admitted to heaven following the Ascension of Christ. Belief in this matter is stated in the Apostles' Creed. The existence of a limbo for unbaptized persons of infant status — a state of rest and natural happiness — has never been formally defined.

Litany: A prayer in the form of responsive petition; e.g., St. Joseph, pray for us, etc. Examples are the litanies of Loreto (Litany of the Blessed Mother), the Holy Name, All Saints, the Sacred Heart, the Precious Blood, St. Joseph, Litany for the Dying.

Little Office of the Blessed Virgin Mary: A shortened version of a Liturgy of the Hours honoring the Blessed Virgin. It dates from about the middle of the eighth century.

Loreto, House of: A Marian shrine in Loreto, Italy, consisting of the home of the Holy Family which, according to an old tradition, was transported in a miraculous manner from Nazareth to Dalmatia and finally to Loreto between 1291 and 1294. Investigations conducted shortly after the appearance of the structure in Loreto revealed that its dimensions matched those of the house of the Holy Family missing from its place of enshrinement in a basilica at Nazareth. Among the many popes who regarded it with high honor was John XXIII, who went there on pilgrimage Oct. 4, 1962. The house of the Holy Family is enshrined in the Basilica of Our Lady.

Lust: A disorderly desire for sexual pleasure; one of the seven capital sins.

M

Magi: In the Infancy Narrative of St. Matthew's Gospel (2:1-12), three wise men from the East whose visit and homage to the Child Jesus at Bethlehem indicated Christ's manifestation of himself to non-Jewish people. The narrative teaches the universality of salvation. The traditional names of the Magi are Caspar, Melchior and Balthasar.

Magnificat: The canticle or hymn of the Virgin Mary on the occasion of her visitation to her cousin Elizabeth (Lk. 1:46-55). It is an expression of praise, thanksgiving and acknowledgment of the great blessings given by God to Mary, the Mother of the Second Person of the Blessed Trinity made Man. The Magnificat is recited in the Liturgy of the Hours as part of the Evening Prayer.

Martyr: A Greek word, meaning witness, denoting one who voluntarily suffered death for the faith or some Christian virtue.

Martyrology: A catalogue of martyrs and other saints, arranged according to the calendar. The *Roman Martyrology* contains the official list of saints venerated by the Church. Additions to the list are made in beatification and canonization

decrees of the Congregation for the Causes of Saints.

Mass for the People: On Sundays and certain feasts throughout the year pastors are required to offer Mass for the faithful committed to their care. If they cannot offer the Mass on these days, they must do so at a later date or provide that another priest offer the Mass.

Master of Novices: The person in charge of the training and formation of candidates for an institute of consecrated life during novitiate.

Materialism: Theory which holds that matter is the only reality, and everything in existence is merely a manifestation of matter; there is no such thing as spirit, and the supernatural does not exist. Materialism is incompatible with Christian doctrine.

Meditation: Mental, as distinguished from vocal, prayer, in which thought, affections, and resolutions of the will predominate. There is a meditative element to all forms of prayer, which always involves the raising of the heart and mind to God.

Mendicants: A term derived from Latin and meaning beggars, applied to members of religious orders without property rights; the members, accordingly, worked or begged for their support. The original mendicants were Franciscans and Dominicans in the early 13th century; later, the Carmelites, Augustinians, Servites and others were given the mendicant title and privileges, with respect to exemption from episcopal jurisdiction and wide faculties for preaching and administering the sacrament of penance. The practice of begging is limited at the present time, although it is still allowed with the permission of competent superiors and bishops. Mendicants are supported by free will offerings and income received for spiritual services and other work.

Mercy, Divine: The love and goodness of God, manifested particularly in a time of need.

Merit: In religion, the right to a supernatural reward for good works freely done for a supernatural motive by a person in the state of and with the assistance of grace. The right to such reward is from God, who binds himself to give it. Accordingly, good works, as described above, are meritorious for salvation.

Metempsychosis: Theory of the passage or migration of the human soul after death from one body to another for the purpose of purification from guilt. The theory denies the unity of the soul and human personality, and the doctrine of individual moral responsibility.

Millennium: A thousand-year reign of Christ and the just upon earth before the end of the world. This belief of the Millenarians, Chiliasts, and some sects of modern times is based on an erroneous interpretation of Rv. 20.

Miracles: Observable events or effects in the physical or moral order of things, with reference to salvation, which cannot be explained by the ordinary operation of laws of nature and which, therefore, are attributed to the direct action of God. They make known, in an unusual way, the concern and intervention of God in human affairs for the salvation of men. The most striking examples are the miracles worked by Christ. Numbering about 35, they included his own Resurrection; the raising of three persons to life (Lazarus, the daughter of Jairus, the son of the widow of Naim); the healing of blind, leprous and other persons; nature miracles; and prophecies, or miracles of the intellectual order.

The foregoing notion of miracles, which is based on the concept of a fixed order of nature, was not known by the writers of Sacred Scripture. In the Old Testament, particularly, they called some things miraculous which, according to the definition in contemporary use, may or may not have been miracles. Essentially, however, the occurrences so designated were regarded as exceptional manifestations of God's care and concern for the salvation of his people. The miracles of Christ were miracles in the full sense of the term.

The Church believes it is reasonable to accept miracles as manifestations of divine power for purposes of salvation. God, who created the laws of nature, is their master; hence, without disturbing the ordinary course of things, he can — and has in the course of history before and after Christ — occasionally set aside these laws and has also produced effects beyond their power of operation. The Church does not call miraculous anything which does not admit of easy explanation; on the contrary, miracles are admitted only when the events have a bearing on the order of grace and every possible natural explanation has been tried and found wanting.

(The transubstantiation — i.e., the conversion of the whole substance of bread and wine, their sensible appearances alone remaining, into the Body and Blood of Christ in the act of Consecration at Mass — is not an observable event. Traditionally, however, it has been called a miracle.)

Missal: A liturgical book of Roman Rite also called the *Sacramentary,* containing the celebrant's prayers of the Mass, along with general instructions and ceremonial directives. The Latin text of the new *Roman Missal,* replacing the one authorized by the Council of Trent in the 16th century, was published by the Vatican Polyglot Press in 1970. Its use in English was made mandatory in the U.S. from Dec. 1, 1974. Readings and scriptural responsories formerly in the missal are contained in the *Lectionary.*

Missiology: Study of the missionary nature, constitution and activity of the Church in all aspects: theological reasons for missionary activity, laws and instructions of the Holy See, history of the missions, social and cultural background, methods, norms for carrying on missionary work.

Mission: (1) Strictly, it means being sent to perform a certain work, such as the mission of Christ to redeem mankind, the mission of the Apostles and the Church and its members to perpetuate the prophetic, priestly and royal mission of Christ.

(2) A place where: the Gospel has not been proclaimed; the Church has not been firmly established; the Church, although established, is weak.

(3) An ecclesiastical territory with the simplest kind of canonical organization, under the jurisdiction of the Congregation for the Evangelization of Peoples.

(4) A church or chapel without a resident priest.

(5) A special course of sermons and spiritual exercises conducted in parishes for the purpose of renewing and deepening the spiritual life of the faithful and for the conversion of lapsed Catholics.

Modernism: The "synthesis of all heresies," which appeared near the beginning of the 20th century. It undermines the objective validity of religious beliefs and practices which, it contends, are products of the subconscious developed by mankind under the stimulus of a religious sense. It holds that the existence of a personal God cannot be demonstrated, the Bible is not inspired, Christ is not divine, nor did he establish the Church or institute the sacraments. A special danger lies in modernism, which is still influential, because it uses Catholic terms with perverted meanings. St. Pius X condemned 65 propositions of modernism in 1907 in the decree *Lamentabili* and issued the encyclical *Pascendi* to explain and analyze its errors.

Monastery: The dwelling place, as well as the community thereof, of monks belonging to the Benedictine and Benedictine-related orders like the Cistercians and Carthusians; also, the Augustinians and Canons Regular. Distinctive of monasteries are: their separation from the world; the enclosure or cloister; the permanence or stability of attachment characteristic of their members; autonomous government in accordance with a monastic rule, like that of St. Benedict in the West or of St. Basil in the East; the special dedication of its members to the community celebration of the liturgy as well as to work that is suitable to the surrounding area and the needs of its people. Monastic superiors of men have such titles as abbot and prior; of women, abbess and prioress. In most essentials, an abbey is the same as a monastery.

Monk: A member of a monastic order — e.g., the Benedictines, the Benedictine-related Cistercians and Carthusians, and the Basilians, who bind themselves by religious profession to stable attachment to a monastery, the contemplative life and the work of their community. In popular use, the title is wrongly applied to many men religious who really are not monks.

Monotheism: Belief in and worship of one God.

Morality: Conformity or difformity of behavior to standards of right conduct. (See Moral Obligations, Commandments of God, Precepts of the Church, Conscience, Law.)

Mormons: Members of the Church of Jesus Christ of Latter-Day Saints. The church was established by Joseph Smith (1805-1844) at Fayette, N.Y., three years after he said he had received from an angel golden tablets containing the *Book of the Prophet Mormon.* This book, the Bible, *Doctrine and Covenants,* and *The Pearl of Great Price,* are the basic doctrinal texts of the church. Characteristic of the Mormons are strong belief in the revelations of their leaders, among whom was Brigham Young; a strong community of religious-secular concern; a dual secular and spiritual priesthood, and vigorous missionary activity. The headquarters of the church are located at Salt Lake City, Utah, where the Mormons first settled in 1847.

Mortification: Acts of self-discipline, including prayer, hardship, austerities and penances undertaken for the sake of progress in virtue.

Motu Proprio: A Latin phrase designating a document issued by a pope on his own initiative. Documents of this kind often concern administrative matters.

Mysteries of Faith: Supernatural truths whose existence cannot be known without revelation by God and whose intrinsic truth, while not contrary to reason, can never be wholly understood even after revelation. These mysteries are above reason, not against reason. Among them are the divine mysteries of the Trinity, Incarnation and Eucharist.

Some mysteries — e.g., concerning God's attributes — can be known by reason without revelation, although they cannot be fully understood.

N

Necromancy: Supposed communication with the dead; a form of divination.

Non-Expedit: A Latin expression. It is not expedient (fitting, proper), used to state a prohibition or refusal of permission.

Novena: A term designating public or private devotional practices over a period of nine consecutive days; or, by extension, over a period of nine weeks, in which one day a week is set aside for the devotions.

Novice: A man or woman preparing, in a formal period of trial and formation called a novitiate, for membership in an institute of consecrated life. The novitiate lasts a minimum of 12 and a maximum of 24 months; at its conclusion, the novice professes temporary vows of poverty, chastity and obedience. Norms require that certain periods of time be spent in the house of novitiate: the first three months, one solid period of six months, the final month before the profession of temporary commitment. Periods of apostolic work are also required, to acquaint the novice with the apostolate(s) of the institute. A novice is not bound by the obligations of the professed members of the institute, is free to leave at any time, and may be discharged at the discretion of competent superiors. The immediate superior of a novice is a master or mistress of novices.

Nun (1) Strictly, a member of a religious order of women with solemn vows (moniales).

(2) In general, all women religious, even those in simple vows who are more properly called sisters.

Nunc Dimittis: The canticle or hymn of Simeon at the sight of Jesus at the Temple on the occasion of his presentation (Lk. 2:29-32). It is an expression of joy and thanksgiving for the blessing of having lived to see the Messiah. It is prescribed for use in the Night Prayer of the Liturgy of the Hours.

O

Oath: Calling upon God to witness the truth of a statement. Violating an oath, e.g., by perjury in court, or taking an oath without sufficient reason, is a violation of the honor due to God.

Obedience: Submission to one in authority. General obligations of obedience fall under the Fourth Commandment. The vow of obedience professed by religious is one of the evangelical counsels.

Obsession, Diabolical: The extraordinary state of one who is seriously molested by evil spirits in an external manner. Obsession is more than just temptation.

Occultism: Practices involving ceremonies, rituals, chants, incantations, other cult-related activities intended to affect the course of nature, the lives of practitioners and others, through esoteric powers of magic, diabolical or other forces; one of many forms of superstition.

Octave: A period of eight days given over to the celebration of a major feast such as Easter.

Oils, Holy: The oils consecrated by bishops on Holy Thursday or another suitable day, and by priests under certain conditions for use in certain sacraments and consecrations.

(1) The oil of catechumens (olive or vegetable oil), used at baptism; also, poured with chrism into the baptismal water blessed in Easter Vigil ceremonies.

(2) Chrism (olive or vegetable oil mixed with balm), used at baptism, in confirmation, at the ordination of a priest and bishop, in the dedication of churches and altars.

(3) Oil of the sick (olive or vegetable oil) used in anointing the sick.

Old Catholics — Several sects, including: (1) the Church of Utrecht, which severed relations with Rome in 1724; (2) the National Polish Church in the U.S., which had its origin near the end of the 19th century; (3) German, Austrian and Swiss Old Catholics, who broke away from union with Rome following the First Vatican Council in 1870 because they objected to the dogma of papal infallibility.

The formation of the Old Catholic communion of Germans, Austrians and Swiss began in 1870 at a public meeting held in Nuremberg under the leadership of A. Dollinger. Four years later episcopal succession was established with the ordination of an Old Catholic German bishop by a prelate of the Church of Utrecht. In line with the "Declaration of Utrecht" of 1889, they accept the first seven ecumenical councils and doctrine formulated before 1054, but reject communion with the pope and a number of other Catholic doctrines and practices. They have a valid priesthood and valid sacraments. *The Oxford Dictionary of the Christian Church* notes that they have recognized Anglican ordinations since 1925, that they have had full communion with the Church of England since 1932, and that their bishops, using their own formula, have taken part in the ordination of Anglican bishops.

This communion does not recognize the "Old Catholic" status of several smaller sects calling themselves such. In turn, connection with it is disavowed by the Old Roman Catholic Church headquartered in Chicago, which contends that it has abandoned the traditions of the Church of Utrecht.

The United States is the only English-speaking country with Old Catholic communities.

Oratory: A chapel.

Ordinariate: An ecclesiastical jurisdiction for special purposes and people. Examples are the military ordinariate of the U.S., for service personnel, and Eastern-Rite ordinariates in places where Eastern-Rite dioceses do not exist.

Ordinary: One who has the jurisdiction of an office: the pope, diocesan bishops, vicars general, prelates of missionary territories, vicars apostolic, prefects apostolic, vicars capitular during the vacancy of a see, superiors general, abbots primate and other major superiors of men religious.

Ordination: The consecration of sacred ministers for divine worship and the service of people in things pertaining to God. The power of ordination comes from Christ and the Church, and must be conferred by a minister capable of communicating it.

Organ Transplants: The transplanting of organs from one person to another is permissible provided it is done with the consent of the concerned parties and does not result in the death or essential mutilation of the donor. Advances in methods and technology have increased the range of transplant possibilities in recent years.

Original Sin: The sin of Adam (Gn. 2:8—3:24), personal to him and passed on to all persons as a state of privation of grace. Despite this privation and the related wounding of human nature and weakening of natural powers, original sin leaves unchanged all that man himself is by nature. The scriptural basis of the doctrine was stated especially by St. Paul in 1 Cor. 15:21, ff., and Romans 5:12-21. Original sin is remitted by baptism and incorporation in Christ, through whom grace is given to persons.

O Salutaris Hostia: The first three Latin words, O Saving Victim, of a Benediction hymn.

Ostpolitik: Policy adopted by Pope Paul VI in an attempt to improve the situation of Eastern European Catholics through diplomatic negotiations with their governments.

Oxford Movement: A movement in the Church of England from 1833 to about 1845 which had for its objective a threefold defense of the church as a divine institution, the apostolic succession of its bishops, and the Book of Common Prayer as the rule of faith. The movement took its name from Oxford University and involved a number of intellectuals who authored a series of influential *Tracts for Our Times*. Some of its leading figures — e.g., F. W. Faber, John Henry Newman and Henry Edward Manning — became converts to the Catholic Church. In the Church of England, the movement affected the liturgy, historical and theological scholarship, the status of the ministry, and other areas of ecclesiastical life.

P

Paganism: A term referring to non-revealed religions, i.e., religions other than Christianity, Judaism and Mohammedanism.

Palms: Blessed palms are a sacramental. They are blessed and distributed on the Sunday of the Passion in commemoration of the triumphant entrance of Christ into Jerusalem. Ashes of the burnt palms are used on Ash Wednesday.

Pange Lingua: First Latin words, Sing, my tongue, of a hymn in honor of the Holy Eucharist, used particularly on Holy Thursday and in Eucharistic processions.

Pantheism: Theory that all things are part of God, divine, in the sense that God realizes himself as the ultimate reality of matter or spirit through being and/or becoming all things that have been, are, and will be. The theory leads to hopeless confusion of the Creator and the created realm of being, identifies evil with good, and involves many inherent contradictions.

Papal Election: The pope is elected by members of the College of Cardinals in a secret conclave or meeting convened ordinarily in secluded quarters of the Vatican Palace between 15 and 20 days after the death of his predecessor. Cardinals under the age of 80, totaling no more than 120, are eligible to participate in a papal election.

Following are some of the principal regulations decreed by Paul VI Oct. 1, 1975, in the apostolic constitution *Romano Pontifici Eligendo* (concerning the vacancy of the Apostolic See and the election of the Roman Pontiff).

The ordinary manner of election is by scrutiny, with two votes each morning and afternoon in the Sistine Chapel until one of the candidates receives a two-thirds plus one vote majority.

Alternative methods, which can be adopted by unanimous agreement of the cardinals in difficult cases, are provided for: (1) by delegation, in which the cardinals designate a limited number (nine to 15) to make the choice; (2) by changing the majority rule from two-thirds plus one vote to an absolute majority plus one; (3) by limiting final choice, if the procedure in force becomes protracted, to one between the two candidates who received the largest numbers of votes, but not a required majority, in the most recent balloting.

An unusual manner of election is by acclamation or inspiration — that is, by spontaneous, unanimous choice without any need for normal voting procedure.

The elected candidate is asked by the dean of the college if he accepts the election. If he does so and is already a bishop, he immediately becomes the bishop of Rome and pope, and signifies the name by which he will be called. The cardinals then pledge their obedience to him before the senior cardinal deacon proclaims his election to the world from the main balcony of the Vatican and the new pope imparts his blessing *Urbi et Orbi* (to the City and the World). If the candidate is not a bishop, he is so ordained before receiving the pledge of obedience and being proclaimed pope. The subsequent coronation of the pope is a ceremonial recognition of the fact of his election.

The pope is elected for life. If one should resign, a new pope would be elected in accordance with the foregoing regulations.

Rigid rules govern the conclave — its personnel, freedom from internal and external influence and interference, absolute secrecy (with a ban on recording devices and a prohibition against any disclosures).

Ordinarily, the first indication that a new pope has been elected is a plume of white smoke rising from the Vatican on burning of the last ballots.

(See College of Cardinals, Interregnum.)

Early methods of electing a pope — with various degrees of participation by the clergy and people of Rome and others — were set aside by Pope Nicholas II, who decreed in 1059 that cardinal bishops would be the electors. Further modification of the process was decreed by the Lateran Council in 1179 (that election would take place by a two-thirds majority vote of the cardinals) and by Pope Gregory X in 1274 (regarding a secluded conclave arrangement for elections).

Paraclete: A title of the Holy Spirit meaning, in Greek, Advocate, Consoler.

Parental Duties: All duties related to the obligation of parents to provide for the welfare of their children. These obligations fall under the Fourth Commandment.

Parish: A community of the faithful served by a pastor charged with responsibility for providing them with full pastoral service. Most parishes are territorial, embracing all of the faithful in a certain area of a diocese: some are personal or national, for certain classes of people, without strict regard for their places of residence.

Parousia: The coming, or saving presence, of Christ which will mark the completion of salvation history and the coming to perfection of God's kingdom at the end of the world.

Paschal Candle: A large candle, symbolic of the risen Christ, blessed and lighted on the Easter Vigil and placed at the Gospel side of the altar until Ascension Day. It is ornamented with five large grains of incense, representing the wounds of Christ, inserted in the form of a cross; the Greek letters Alpha and Omega, symbolizing Christ the beginning and end of all things, at the top and bottom of the shaft of the cross; and the figures of the current year of salvation in the quadrants formed by the cross.

Paschal Precept: The church law requiring the faithful to receive Holy Communion during the Easter time.

Passion of Christ: Sufferings of Christ, recorded in the four Gospels.

Pastor: An ordained minister charged with responsibility for the doctrinal, sacramental and related service of people committed to his care; e.g., a bishop for the people in his diocese, a priest for the people of his parish.

Pater Noster: The initial Latin words, Our Father, of the Lord's Prayer.

Peace, Sign of: A gesture of greeting — e.g., a handshake — exchanged by the ministers and participants at Mass.

Pectoral Cross: A cross worn on a chain about the neck and over the breast by bishops and abbots as a mark of their office.

Penance or Penitence: (1) The spiritual change or conversion of mind and heart by which a person turns away from sin, and all that it implies, toward God, through a personal renewal under the influence of the Holy Spirit. In the apostolic constitution *Paenitemini*, Pope Paul VI called it "a religious, personal act which has as its aim love and surrender to God." Penance involves sorrow and contrition for sin, together with other internal and external acts of atonement. It serves the purposes of reestablishing in one's life the order of God's love and commandments, and of making satisfaction to God for sin. A divine precept states the necessity of penance for salvation: "Unless you do penance, you shall all likewise perish" (Lk. 13:3) . . . "Be converted and believe in the Gospel" (Mk. 1:15).

In the penitential discipline of the Church, the various works of penance have been classified under the headings of prayer (interior), fasting and almsgiving (exterior). The Church has established minimum requirements for the common and social observance of the divine precept by Catholics — e.g., by requiring them to fast and/or abstain on certain days of the year. These observances, however, do not exhaust all the demands of the divine precept, whose fulfillment is a matter of personal responsibility; nor do they have any real value unless they proceed from the internal spirit and purpose of penance.

Related to works of penance for sins actually committed are works of mortification. The purpose of the latter is to develop — through prayer, fasting, renunciations and similar actions — self-control and detachment from things which could otherwise become occasions of sin.

(2) Penance is a virtue disposing a person to turn to God in sorrow for sin and to carry out works of amendment and atonement.

(3) The sacrament of penance and sacramental penance.

Perjury: Taking a false oath, lying under oath, a violation of the honor due to God.

Persecution, Religious: A campaign waged against a church or other religious body by persons and governments intent on its destruction. The best known campaigns of this type against the Christian Church were the Roman persecutions which occurred intermittently from about 54 to the promulgation of the Edict of Milan in 313. The most extensive persecutions took place during the reigns of Nero, the first major Roman persecutor, Domitian, Trajan, Marcus Aurelius, and Diocletian. Besides the Roman persecutions, the Catholic Church has been subject to many others, including those of the 20th century in Communist-controlled countries.

Personal Prelature: A special-purpose jurisdiction — for particular pastoral and missionary work, etc., — consisting of secular priests and deacons and open to lay persons willing to dedicate themselves to its apostolic works. The prelate in charge is an ordinary, with the authority of office; he can establish a national or international seminary, incardinate its students and promote them to holy orders under the title of service to the prelature. The prelature is constituted and governed according to statutes laid down by the Holy See. Statutes define its relationship and mode of operation with the bishops of territories in which members live and work. Opus Dei is a personal prelature (see separate entry).

Peter's Pence: A collection made each year among Catholics for the maintenance of the pope and his works of charity. It was originally a tax of a penny on each house, and was collected on St. Peter's day, whence the name. It originated in England in the eighth century.

Petition: One of the four purposes of prayer. In prayers of petition, persons ask of God the blessings they and others need.

Pharisees: Influential class among the Jews, referred to in the Gospels, noted for their self-righteousness, legalism, strict interpretation of the Law, acceptance of the traditions of the elders as well as the Law of Moses, and beliefs regarding angels and spirits, the resurrection of the dead and judgment. Most of them were laymen, and they were closely allied with the Scribes; their opposite numbers were the Sadducees. The Pharisaic and rabbinical traditions had a lasting influence on Judaism following the destruction of Jerusalem in 70 A.D.

Pious Fund: Property and money originally accumulated by the Jesuits to finance their missionary work in Lower California. When the Jesuits were expelled from the territory in 1767, the fund was appropriated by the Spanish Crown and used to support Dominican and Franciscan missionary work in Upper and Lower California. In 1842 the Mexican government took over administration of the fund, incorporated most of the revenue into the national treasury, and agreed to pay the Church interest of six per cent a year on the capital so incorporated. From 1848 to 1967 the fund was the subject of lengthy negotiations between the U.S. and Mexican governments because of the latter's failure to make payments as agreed. A lump-sum settlement was made in 1967 with payment by Mexico to the U.S. government of more than $700,000, to be turned over to the Archdiocese of San Francisco.

Polytheism: Belief in and worship of many gods or divinities, especially prevalent in pre-Christian religions.

Poor Box: Alms-box; found in churches from the earliest days of Christianity.

Pope Joan: Alleged name of a woman falsely said to have been pope from 855-858, the years of the reign of Benedict III. The myth was not heard of before the 13th century.

Portiuncula: (1) Meaning little portion (of land), the Portiuncula was the chapel of Our Lady of the Angels near Assisi, Italy, which the Benedictines gave to St. Francis early in the 13th century. He repaired the chapel and made it the first church of the Franciscan Order. It is now enshrined in the Basilica of St. Mary of the Angels in Assisi.

(2) The Portiuncula Indulgence, or Pardon of Assisi, was authorized by Honorius III. Originally, it could be gained for the souls in purgatory only in the chapel of Our Lady of the Angels; by later concessions, it could be gained also in other Franciscan and parish churches. The Portiuncula Indulgence can be gained once on the day of Aug. 2, or on the following Sunday with permission of the bishop of the place. The conditions are, in addition to freedom from attachment to sin: reception of the sacraments of penance and the Eucharist on or near the day; a visit to a parish church on the day, during which the Our Father and Creed are offered for the intentions of the pope.

Possession, Diabolical: The extraordinary state of a person who is tormented from within by evil spirits who exercise strong influence over his powers of mind and body.

Postulant: One of several names used to designate a candidate for membership in a religious institute during the period before novitiate.

Poverty: (1) The quality or state of being poor, in actual destitution and need, or being poor in spirit. In the latter sense, poverty means the state of mind and disposition of persons who regard material things in proper perspective as gifts of God for the support of life and its reasonable enrichment, and for the service of others in need. It means freedom from unreasonable attachment to material things as ends in themselves, even though they may be possessed in small or large measure.

(2) One of the evangelical counsels professed as a public vow by members of an institute of consecrated life. It involves the voluntary renunciation of rights of ownership and of independent use and disposal of material goods; or, the right of independent use and disposal, but not of the radical right of ownership. Religious institutes provide their members with necessary and useful goods and services from common resources. The manner in which goods are received and/or handled by religious is determined by poverty of spirit and the rule and constitutions of their institute.

Pragmatism: Theory that the truth of ideas, concepts and values depends on their utility or capacity to serve a useful purpose rather than on their conformity with objective standards; also called utilitarianism.

Prayer: The raising of the mind and heart to God in adoration, thanksgiving, reparation and petition. Prayer, which is always mental because it involves thought and love of God, may be vocal, meditative, private and personal, social, and official. The official prayer of the Church as a worshipping community is called the liturgy.

Precepts: Commands or orders given to individuals or communities in particular cases; they establish law for concerned parties. Preceptive documents are issued by the pope, departments of the Roman Curia and other competent authority in the Church.

Presence of God: A devotional practice of increasing one's awareness of the presence and action of God in daily life.

Presumption: A violation of the theological virtue of hope, by which a person striving for salvation either relies too much on his own capabilities or expects God to do things which he cannot do, in keeping with his divine attributes, or does not will to do, according to his divine plan. Presumption is the opposite of despair.

Preternatural Gifts: Exceptional gifts, beyond

the exigencies and powers of human nature, enjoyed by Adam in the state of original justice: immunity from suffering and death, superior knowledge, integrity or perfect control of the passions. These gifts were lost as the result of original sin; their loss, however, implied no impairment of the integrity of human nature.

Pride: Unreasonable self-esteem; one of the seven capital sins.

Prie-Dieu: A French phrase, meaning pray God, designating a kneeler or bench suitable for kneeling while at prayer.

Priesthood of the Laity: Lay persons share in the priesthood of Christ in virtue of the sacraments of baptism and confirmation. They are not only joined with Christ for a life of union with him but are also deputed by him for participation in his mission, now carried on by the Church, of worship, teaching, witness and apostolic works. St. Peter called Christians "a royal priesthood" (1 Pt. 2:9) in this connection. St. Thomas Aquinas declared: "The sacramental characters (of baptism and confirmation) are nothing else than certain sharings of the priesthood of Christ, derived from Christ himself."

The priesthood of the laity differs from the official ministerial priesthood of ordained priests and bishops — who have the power of holy orders for celebrating the Eucharist, administering the other sacraments, and providing pastoral care. The ministerial priesthood, by divine commission, serves the universal priesthood. (See Role of Sacraments.)

Primary Option: The life-choice of a person for or against God which shapes the basic orientation of moral conduct. A primary option for God does not preclude the possibility of serious sin.

Prior: A superior or an assistant to an abbot in a monastery.

Privilege: A favor, an exemption from the obligation of a law. Privileges of various kinds, with respect to ecclesiastical laws, are granted by the pope, departments of the Roman Curia and other competent authority in the Church.

Probabilism: A moral system for use in cases of conscience which involve the obligation of doubtful laws. There is a general principle that a doubtful law does not bind. Probabilism, therefore, teaches that it is permissible to follow an opinion favoring liberty, provided the opinion is certainly and solidly probable. Probabilism may not be invoked when there is question of: a certain law or the certain obligation of a law; the certain right of another party; the validity of an action; something which is necessary for salvation.

Pro-Cathedral: A church used as a cathedral.

Promoter of the Faith: An official of the Congregation for the Causes of Saints, whose role in beatification and canonization procedures is to establish beyond reasonable doubt the validity of evidence regarding the holiness of prospective saints and miracles attributed to their intercession.

Prophecies of St. Malachy: These so-called prophecies, listing the designations of 102 popes and 10 antipopes, bear the name they have because they have been falsely attributed to St. Malachy, bishop of Armagh, who died in 1148. Actually, they are forgeries by an unknown author and came to light only in the last decade of the 16th century.

The first 75 prophecies cover the 65 popes and 10 antipopes from Celestine II (1143-1144) to Gregory XIV (1590-91), and are exact with respect to names, coats of arms, birthplaces, and other identifying characteristics. This portion of the work, far from being prophetic, is the result of historical knowledge or hindsight. The 37 designations following that of Gregory are vague, fanciful, and subject to wide interpretation. According to the prophecies, John Paul II, from the Labor of the Sun, will have only two successors before the end of the world.

Prophecy: (1) The communication of divine revelation by inspired intermediaries, called prophets, between God and his people. Old Testament prophecy was unique in its origin and because of its ethical and religious content, which included disclosure of the saving will of Yahweh for the people, moral censures and warnings of divine punishment because of sin and violations of the Law and Covenant, in the form of promises, admonitions, reproaches and threats. Although Moses and other earlier figures are called prophets, the period of prophecy is generally dated from the early years of the monarchy to about 100 years after the Babylonian Exile. From that time on the written Law and its interpreters supplanted the prophets as guides of the people. Old Testament prophets are cited in the New Testament, with awareness that God spoke through them and that some of their oracles were fulfilled in Christ. John the Baptist is the outstanding prophetic figure in the New Testament. Christ never claimed the title of prophet for himself, although some people thought he was one. There were prophets in the early Church, and St. Paul mentioned the charism of prophecy in 1 Cor. 14:1-5. Prophecy disappeared after New Testament times. Revelation is classified as the prophetic book of the New Testament.

(2) In contemporary non-scriptural usage, the term is applied to the witness given by persons to the relevance of their beliefs in everyday life and action.

Province: (1) A territory comprising one archdiocese called the metropolitan see and one or more dioceses called suffragan sees. The head of the archdiocese, an archbishop, has metropolitan rights and responsibilities over the province.

(2) A division of a religious order under the jurisdiction of a provincial superior.

Prudence: Practical wisdom and judgment regarding the choice and use of the best ways and means of doing good; one of the four cardinal virtues.

Punishment Due for Sin: The punishment which is a consequence of sin. It is of two kinds:

(1) Eternal punishment is the punishment of hell, to which one becomes subject by the commission of mortal sin. Such punishment is remitted when mortal sin is forgiven.

(2) Temporal punishment is a consequence of venial sin and/or forgiven mortal sin; it is not everlasting and may be remitted in this life by means

of penance. Temporal punishment unremitted during this life is remitted by suffering in purgatory.

Purgatory: The state or condition in which those who have died in the state of grace, but with some attachment to sin, suffer for a time before they are admitted to the glory and happiness of heaven. In this state and period of passive suffering, they are purified of unrepented venial sins, satisfy the demands of divine justice for temporal punishment due for sins, and are thus converted to a state of worthiness of the beatific vision.

R

Racism: A theory which holds that any one or several of the different races of the human family are inherently superior or inferior to any one or several of the others. The teaching denies the essential unity of the human race, the equality and dignity of all men because of their common possession of the same human nature, and the participation of all men in the divine plan of redemption. It is radically opposed to the virtue of justice and the precept of love of neighbor. Differences of superiority and inferiority which do exist are the result of accidental factors operating in a wide variety of circumstances, and are in no way due to essential defects in any one or several of the branches of the one human race. The theory of racism, together with practices related to it, is incompatible with Christian doctrine.

Rash Judgment: Attributing faults to another without sufficient reason; a violation of the obligations of justice and charity.

Rationalism: A theory which makes the mind the measure and arbiter of all things, including religious truth. A product of the Enlightenment, it rejects the supernatural, divine revelation, and authoritative teaching by any church.

Recollection: Meditation, attitude of concentration or awareness of spiritual matters and things pertaining to salvation and the accomplishment of God's will.

Relativism: Theory which holds that all truth, including religious truth, is relative, i.e., not absolute, certain or unchanging; a product of agnosticism, indifferentism, and an unwarranted extension of the notion of truth in positive science. Relativism is based on the tenet that certain knowledge of any and all truth is impossible. Therefore, no religion, philosophy or science can be said to possess the real truth; consequently, all religions, philosophies and sciences may be considered to have as much or as little of truth as any of the others.

Relics: The physical remains and effects of saints, which are considered worthy of veneration inasmuch as they are representative of persons in glory with God. First class relics are parts of the bodies of saints, and instruments of their penance and death; second class relics are objects which had some contact with their persons. Catholic doctrine proscribes the view that relics are not worthy of veneration. In line with norms laid down by the Council of Trent and subsequent enactments, discipline concerning relics is subject to control by the Congregation for the Causes of Saints.

Religion: The adoration and service of God as expressed in divine worship and in daily life. Religion is concerned with all of the relations existing between God and man, and between man and man because of the central significance of God. Objectively considered, religion consists of a body of truth which is believed, a code of morality for the guidance of conduct, and a form of divine worship. Subjectively, it is a person's total response, theoretically and practically, to the demands of faith; it is living faith, personal engagement, self-commitment to God. Thus, by creed, code and cult, a person orders and directs his life in reference to God and, through what the love and service of God implies, to his fellow men and all things.

Reliquary: A vessel for the preservation and exposition of a relic; sometimes made like a small monstrance.

Reparation: The making of amends to God for sin committed; one of the four ends of prayer and the purpose of penance.

Rescript: A written reply by an ecclesiastical superior regarding a question or request; its provisions bind concerned parties only. Papal dispensations are issued in the form of rescripts.

Reserved Case: A sin or censure, absolution from which is reserved to religious superiors, bishops, the pope, or confessors having special faculties. Reservations are made because of the serious nature and social effects of certain sins and censures.

Restitution: An act of reparation for an injury done to another. The injury may be caused by taking and/or retaining what belongs to another or by damaging either the property or reputation of another. The intention of making restitution, usually in kind, is required as a condition for the forgiveness of sins of injustice, even though actual restitution is not possible.

Ring: In the Church a ring is worn as part of the insignia of bishops, abbots, et al.; by sisters to denote their consecration to God and the Church. The wedding ring symbolizes the love and union of husband and wife.

Ritual: A book of prayers and ceremonies used in the administration of the sacraments and other ceremonial functions. In the Roman Rite, the standard book of this kind is the Roman Ritual.

Rogito: The official notarial act or document testifying to the burial of a pope.

Rosary: A form of mental and vocal prayer centered on mysteries or events in the lives of Jesus and Mary. Its essential elements are meditation on the mysteries and the recitation of a number of decades of Hail Marys, each beginning with the Lord's Prayer. Introductory prayers may include the Apostles' Creed, an initial Our Father, three Hail Marys and a Glory be to the Father; each decade is customarily concluded with a Glory be to the Father; at the end, it is customary to say the Hail, Holy Queen and a prayer from the liturgy for the feast of the Blessed Virgin Mary of the Rosary.

The **Mysteries of the Rosary,** which are the subject of meditation, are: (1) Joyful — the Annunciation to Mary that she was to be the Mother of Christ, her visit to Elizabeth, the birth of Jesus, the presentation of Jesus in the Temple, the finding of Jesus in the Temple. (2) Sorrowful — Christ's agony in the Garden of Gethsemani, scourging at the pillar, crowning with thorns, carrying of the Cross to Calvary, and crucifixion. (3) Glorious — the Resurrection and Ascension of Christ, the descent of the Holy Spirit upon the Apostles, Mary's Assumption into heaven and her crowning as Queen of angels and men.

The complete Rosary, called the Dominican Rosary, consists of 15 decades. In customary practice, only five decades are usually said at one time. Rosary beads are used to aid in counting the prayers without distraction.

The Rosary originated through the coalescence of popular devotions to Jesus and Mary from the 12th century onward. Its present form dates from about the 15th century. Carthusians contributed greatly toward its development; Dominicans have been its greatest promoters.

S

Sabbath: The seventh day of the week, observed by Jews and Sabbatarians as the day for rest and religious observance.

Sacramentary: One of the first liturgical books, containing the celebrant's part of the Mass and rites for administration of the sacraments. The earliest book of this kind, the Leonine Sacramentary, dates from the middle or end of the sixth century.

The *Sacramentary* in current use is the same as the *Roman Missal.*

Sacrarium: A basin with a drain leading directly into the ground; standard equipment of a sacristy.

Sacred Heart, Enthronement: An acknowledgment of the sovereignty of Jesus Christ over the Christian family, expressed by the installation of an image or picture of the Sacred Heart in a place of honor in the home, accompanied by an act of consecration.

Sacred Heart, Promises: Twelve promises to persons having devotion to the Sacred Heart of Jesus, which were communicated by Christ to St. Margaret Mary Alacoque in a private revelation in 1675: (1) I will give them all the graces necessary in their state in life. (2) I will establish peace in their homes. (3) I will comfort them in all their afflictions. (4) I will be their secure refuge during life and, above all, in death. (5) I will bestow abundant blessing upon all their undertakings. (6) Sinners shall find in my Heart the source and the infinite ocean of mercy. (7) By devotion to my Heart tepid souls shall grow fervent. (8) Fervent souls shall quickly mount to high perfection. (9) I will bless every place where a picture of my Heart shall be set up and honored. (10) I will give to priests the gift of touching the most hardened hearts. (11) Those who promote this devotion shall have their names written in my Heart, never to be blotted out. (12) I will grant the grace of final penitence to those who communicate (receive Holy Communion) on the first Friday of nine consecutive months.

Sacrilege: Violation of and irreverence toward a person, place or thing that is sacred because of public dedication to God; a sin against the virtue of religion. Personal sacrilege is violence of some kind against a cleric or religious, or a violation of chastity with a cleric or religious. Local sacrilege is the desecration of sacred places. Real sacrilege is irreverence with respect to sacred things, such as the sacraments and sacred vessels.

Sacristy: A utility room where vestments, church furnishings and sacred vessels are kept and where the clergy vest for sacred functions.

Sadducees: The predominantly priestly party among the Jews in the time of Christ, noted for extreme conservatism, acceptance only of the Law of Moses, and rejection of the traditions of the elders. Their opposite numbers were the Pharisees.

Saints, Cult of: The veneration, called dulia, of holy persons who have died and are in glory with God in heaven; it includes honoring them and petitioning them for their intercession with God. Liturgical veneration is given only to saints officially recognized by the Church; private veneration may be given to anyone thought to be in heaven. The veneration of saints is essentially different from the adoration given to God alone; by its very nature, however, it terminates in the worship of God.

According to the Second Vatican Council's *Dogmatic Constitution on the Church* (No. 50): "It is supremely fitting . . . that we love those friends and fellow heirs of Jesus Christ, who are also our brothers and extraordinary benefactors, that we render due thanks to God for them and 'suppliantly invoke them and have recourse to their prayers, their power and help in obtaining benefits from God through his Son, Jesus Christ, our Lord, who is our sole Redeemer and Savior.' For by its very nature every genuine testimony of love which we show to those in heaven tends toward and terminates in Christ, who is the 'crown of all saints.' Through him it tends toward and terminates in God, who is wonderful in his saints and is magnified in them."

Salvation: The liberation of persons from sin and its effects, reconciliation with God in and through Christ, the attainment of union with God forever in the glory of heaven as the supreme purpose of life and as the God-given reward for fulfillment of his will on earth. Salvation-in-process begins and continues in this life through union with Christ in faith professed and in action; its final term is union with God and the whole community of the saved in the ultimate perfection of God's kingdom. The Church teaches that: God wills the salvation of all men; men are saved in and through Christ; membership in the Church established by Christ, known and understood as the community of salvation, is necessary for salvation; men with this knowledge and understanding who deliberately reject this Church, cannot be saved. The Catholic Church is the Church founded by Christ. (See below, Salvation outside the Church.)

Salvation History: The facts and the record of God's relations with men, in the past, present and future, for the purpose of leading them to live in accordance with his will for the eventual attainment after death of salvation, or everlasting happiness with him in heaven.

The essentials of salvation history are: God's love for all men and will for their salvation; his intervention and action in the world to express this love and bring about their salvation; the revelation he made of himself and the covenant he established with the Israelites in the Old Testament; the perfecting of this revelation and the new covenant of grace through Christ in the New Testament; the continuing action-for-salvation carried on in and through the Mystical Body of Christ, the Church; the communication of saving grace to men through the merits of Christ and the operations of the Holy Spirit in the here-and-now circumstances of daily life and with the cooperation of men themselves.

Salvation outside the Church: The Second Vatican Council covered this subject summarily in the following manner: "Those also can attain to everlasting salvation who through no fault of their own do not know the Gospel of Christ or his Church, yet sincerely seek God and, moved by grace, strive by their deeds to do his will as it is known to them through the dictates of conscience. Nor does divine Providence deny the help necessary for salvation to those who, without blame on their part, have not yet arrived at an explicit knowledge of God, but who strive to live a good life, thanks to his grace. Whatever good or truth is found among them is looked upon by the Church as a preparation for the Gospel. She regards such qualities as given by him who enlightens all men so that they may finally have life" *(Dogmatic Constitution on the Church,* No. 16).

Satanism: Worship of the devil, a blasphemous inversion of the order of worship which is due to God alone.

Scandal: Conduct which is the occasion of sin to another person.

Scapular: (1) A part of the habit of some religious orders like the Benedictines and Dominicans; a nearly shoulder-wide strip of cloth worn over the tunic and reaching almost to the feet in front and behind. Originally a kind of apron, it came to symbolize the cross and yoke of Christ.

(2) Scapulars worn by lay persons as a sign of association with religious orders and for devotional purposes are an adaptation of monastic scapulars. Approved by the Church as sacramentals, they consist of two small squares of woolen cloth joined by strings and are worn about the neck. They are given for wearing in a ceremony of investiture or enrollment. There are nearly 20 scapulars for devotional use: the five principal ones are generally understood to include those of Our Lady of Mt. Carmel (the brown Carmelite Scapular), the Holy Trinity, Our Lady of the Seven Dolors, the Passion, the Immaculate Conception.

Scapular Medal: A medallion with a representation of the Sacred Heart on one side and of the Blessed Virgin Mary on the other. Authorized by St. Pius X in 1910, it may be worn or carried in place of a scapular by persons already invested with a scapular.

Scapular Promise: According to a legend of the Carmelite Order, the Blessed Virgin Mary appeared to St. Simon Stock in 1251 at Cambridge and declared that wearers of the brown Carmelite Scapular would be saved from hell and taken to heaven by her on the first Saturday after death. The validity of the legend has never been the subject of official decision by the Church. Essentially, it expresses belief in the intercession of Mary and the efficacy of sacramentals in the context of truly Christian life.

Schism: Derived from a Greek word meaning separation, the term designates formal and obstinate refusal by a baptized person, called a *schismatic,* to be in communion with the pope and the Church. The canonical penalty is excommunication. One of the most disastrous schisms in history resulted in the definitive separation of the Church in the East from union with Rome about 1054.

Scholasticism: The term usually applied to the Catholic theology and philosophy which developed in the Middle Ages.

Scribes: Hebrew intellectuals noted for their knowledge of the Law of Moses, influential from the time of the Exile to about 70 A.D. Many of them were Pharisees. They were the antecedents of rabbis and their traditions, as well as those of the Pharisees, had a lasting influence on Judaism following the destruction of Jerusalem in 70 A.D.

Scruple: A morbid, unreasonable fear and anxiety that one's actions are sinful when they are not, or more seriously sinful than they actually are. Compulsive scrupulosity is quite different from the transient scrupulosity of persons of tender or highly sensitive conscience, or of persons with faulty moral judgment.

Seal of Confession: The obligation of secrecy which must be observed regarding knowledge of things learned in connection with the confession of sin in the sacrament of penance. The seal covers matters whose revelation would make the sacrament burdensome. Confessors are prohibited, under penalty of excommunication, from making any direct revelation of confessional matter; this prohibition holds, outside of confession, even with respect to the person who made the confession unless the person releases the priest from the obligation. Persons other than confessors are obliged to maintain secrecy, but not under penalty of excommunication. General, non-specific discussion of confessional matter does not violate the seal.

Secularism: A school of thought, a spirit and manner of action which ignores and/or repudiates the validity or influence of supernatural religion with respect to individual and social life. In describing secularism in their annual statement in 1947, the bishops of the United States said in part: ". . . There are many men — and their number is daily increasing — who in practice live their lives without recognizing that this is God's world. For the most part they do not deny God. On formal occasions they may even mention his name. Not all of them would subscribe to the statement that all moral values derive from merely human conventions. But they fail to bring an awareness of their responsibility to God into their thought and action as individuals and members of society. This, in essence, is what we mean by secularism."

See: Another name for diocese or archdiocese.

Seminary: A house of study and formation for men, called seminarians, preparing for the priesthood. Traditional seminaries date from the Council of Trent in the middle of the 16th century; before that time, candidates for the priesthood were variously trained in monastic schools, universities under church auspices, and in less formal ways. At the present time, seminaries are undergoing considerable change for the improvement of academic and formation programs and procedures.

Sermon on the Mount: A compilation of sayings of Our Lord in the form of an extended discourse in Matthew's Gospel (5:1 to 7:27) and, in a shorter discourse, in Luke (6:17-49). The passage in Matthew, called the "Constitution of the New Law," summarizes the living spirit of believers in Christ and members of the kingdom of God. Beginning with the Beatitudes and including the Lord's Prayer, it covers the perfect justice of the New Law, the fulfillment of the Old Law in the New Law of Christ, and the integrity of internal attitude and external conduct with respect to love of God and neighbor, justice, chastity, truth, trust and confidence in God.

Servile Work: Work that is mainly physical and done for the sake of material purposes, in distinction from so-called liberal and artistic work which, although involving physical effort, is of a mental and intellectual nature. Commonly classified as servile are such works as farming, manufacturing, commercial operations, mining, etc. Liberal works are those like studying, teaching, designing, writing, typing, etc. The classification of work as servile or otherwise depends in part on custom and cultural interpretation. The reception of pay for work has nothing to do with its classification. Servile work is prohibited on Sundays and holy days of obligation unless there is sound reason for it.

Seven Last Words of Christ: Words of Christ on the Cross. (1) "Father, forgive them; for they do not know what they are doing." (2) To the penitent thief: "I assure you: today you will be with me in Paradise." (3) To Mary and his Apostle John: "Woman, there is your son . . . There is your mother." (4) "My God, my God, why have you forsaken me?" (5) "I am thirsty." (6) "Now it is finished." (7) "Father, into your hands I commend my spirit."

Shrine, Crowned: A shrine approved by the Holy See as a place of pilgrimage. The approval permits public devotion at the shrine and implies that at least one miracle has resulted from devotion at the shrine. Among the best known crowned shrines are those of the Virgin Mary at Lourdes and Fatima.

Shroud of Turin: A strip of brownish linen cloth, 14 feet, three inches in length and three feet, seven inches in width, bearing the front and back imprint of a human body. A tradition dating from the seventh century, which has not been verified beyond doubt, claims that the shroud is the fine linen in which the body of Christ was wrapped for burial. The early history of the shroud is obscure. It was enshrined at Lirey, France, in 1354 and was transferred in 1578 to Turin, Italy, where it has been kept in the cathedral down to the present time. Scientific investigation, which began in 1898, seems to indicate that the markings on the shroud are those of a human body. The shroud, for the first time since 1933, was placed on public view from Aug. 27 to Oct. 8, 1978, and was seen by an estimated 3.3 million people. Scientists conducted intensive studies of it for several days after the end of public viewing.

The shroud, which had been the possession of the House of Savoy, was willed to Pope John Paul II in 1983.

Sick Calls: When a person is confined at home by illness or other cause and is unable to go to church for reception of the sacraments, a parish priest should be informed and arrangements made for him to visit the person at home. Such visitations are common in pastoral practice, both for special needs and for providing persons with regular opportunities for receiving the sacraments.

If a priest cannot make the visitation, arrangements can be made for a Eucharistic minister to bring Holy Communion to the homebound or bedridden person.

Sign of the Cross: A sign, ceremonial gesture or movement in the form of a cross by which a person confesses faith in the Holy Trinity and Christ, and intercedes for the blessing of himself, other persons, and things. In Roman-Rite practice, a person making the sign touches the fingers of the right hand to his forehead, below the breast, left shoulder and right shoulder while saying: "In the name of the Father, and of the Son, and of the Holy Spirit." The sign is also made with the thumb on the forehead, the lips, and the breast. For the blessing of persons and objects, a large sign of the cross is made by movement of the right hand. In Eastern-Rite practice, the sign is made with the thumb and first two fingers of the right hand joined together and touching the forehead, below the breast, the right shoulder and the left shoulder; the formula generally used is the doxology, "O Holy God, O Holy Strong One, O Immortal One." The Eastern manner of making the sign was general until the first half of the 13th century; by the 17th century, Western practice involved the whole right hand and the reversal of direction from shoulder to shoulder.

Signs of the Times: Contemporary events, trends and features in culture and society, the needs and aspirations of people, all the factors that form the context in and through which the Church has to carry on its saving mission. The Second Vatican Council spoke on numerous occasions about these signs and the relationship between them and a kind of manifestation of God's will, positive or negative, and about subjecting them to judgment and action corresponding to the demands of divine revelation through Scripture, Christ, and the experience, tradition and teaching authority of the Church.

Simony: The deliberate intention and act of selling and/or buying spiritual goods or material things so connected with the spiritual that they cannot be separated therefrom; a violation of the virtue of religion, and a sacrilege, because it wrongfully puts a material price on spiritual things, which cannot be either sold or bought. In church law, actual sale or purchase is subject to censure in some cases. The term is derived from the name of Simon Magus, who attempted to buy from Sts. Peter and John the power to confirm people in the Holy Spirit (Acts 8:4-24).

Sin: (1) Actual sin is rejection of God manifested by free and deliberate violation of his law by thought, word or action. (a) Mortal sin — involving serious matter, sufficient reflection and full consent — results in total alienation from God, making a person dead to sanctifying grace, incapable of performing meritorious supernatural acts and subject to everlasting punishment. (b) Venial sin — involving less serious matter, reflection and consent — does not have such serious consequences.

(2) Original sin is the sin of Adam, with consequences for all men. (See separate entry.)

Sins against the Holy Spirit: Despair of salvation, presumption of God's mercy, impugning the known truths of faith, envy at another's spiritual good, obstinacy in sin, final impenitence. Those guilty of such sins stubbornly resist the influence of grace and, as long as they do so, cannot be forgiven.

Sins, Occasions of: Circumstances (persons, places, things, etc.) which easily lead to sin. There is an obligation to avoid voluntary proximate occasions of sin, and to take precautions against the dangers of unavoidable occasions.

Sins That Cry to Heaven for Vengeance: Willful murder, sins against nature, oppression of the poor, widows and orphans, defrauding laborers of their wages.

Sister: Any woman religious, in popular speech; strictly, the title applies only to women religious belonging to institutes whose members never professed solemn vows. Most of the institutes whose members are properly called sisters were established during and since the 19th century. Women religious with solemn vows, or belonging to institutes whose members formerly professed solemn vows, are properly called nuns.

Sisterhood: A generic term referring to the whole institution of the life of women religious in the Church, or to a particular institute of women religious.

Situation Ethics: A subjective, individualistic ethical theory which denies the binding force of ethical principles as universal laws and preceptive norms of moral conduct, and proposes that morality is determined only by situational conditions and considerations and the intention of the person. In an instruction issued on the subject in May, 1956, the Congregation for the Holy Office said:

"It ignores the principles of objective ethics. This 'New Morality,' it is claimed, is not only the equal of objective morality, but is superior to it.

"The authors who follow this system state that the ultimate determining norm for activity is not the objective order as determined by the natural law and known with certainty from this law. It is instead some internal judgment and illumination of the mind of every individual by which the mind comes to know what is to be done in a concrete situation.

"This ultimate decision of man is, therefore, not the application of the objective law to a particular case after the particular circumstances of a 'situation' have been considered and weighed according to the rules of prudence, as the more important authors of objective ethics teach; but it is, according to them, immediate, internal illumination and judgment.

"With regard to its objective truth and correctness, this judgment, at least in many things, is not ultimately measured, is not to be measured or is not measurable by any objective norm found outside man and independent of his subjective persuasion, but it is fully sufficient in itself. . . .

"Much that is stated in this system of 'Situation Ethics' is contrary to the truth of reality and to the dictate of sound reason. It gives evidence of relativism and modernism, and deviates far from the Catholic teaching handed down through the ages."

Slander: Attributing to a person faults which he does not have; a violation of the obligations of justice and charity, for which restitution is due.

Sloth: One of the seven capital sins; spiritual laziness, involving distaste and disgust for spiritual things; spiritual boredom, which saps the vigor of spiritual life. Physical laziness is a counterpart of spiritual sloth.

Sorcery: A kind of black magic in which evil is invoked by means of diabolical intervention; a violation of the virtue of religion.

Soteriology: The division of theology which treats of the mission and work of Christ as Redeemer.

Species, Sacred: The appearances of bread and wine (color, taste, smell, etc.) which remain after the substance has been changed at the Consecration of the Mass into the Body and Blood of Christ. (See Transubstantiation.)

Spiritism: Attempts to communicate with spirits and departed souls by means of seances, table tapping, ouija boards, and other methods; a violation of the virtue of religion. Spiritualistic practices are noted for fakery.

Spiritual Works of Mercy: Works of spiritual assistance, motivated by love of God and neighbor, to persons in need: counseling the doubtful, instructing the ignorant, admonishing sinners, comforting the afflicted, forgiving offenses, bearing wrongs patiently, praying for the living and the dead.

Stational Churches, Days: Churches, especially in Rome, where the clergy and lay people were accustomed to gather with their bishop on certain days for the celebration of the liturgy. The 25 early titular or parish churches of Rome, plus other churches, each had their turn as the site of divine worship in practices which may have started in the third century. The observances were rather well developed toward the latter part of the fourth century, and by the fifth they included a Mass concelebrated by the pope and attendant priests. On some occasions, the stational liturgy was preceded by a procession from another church called a collecta. There were 42 Roman stational churches in the eighth century, and 89 stational services were scheduled annually in connection with the liturgical seasons. Stational observances fell into disuse toward the end of the Middle Ages. Some revival was begun by John XXIII in 1959 and continued by Paul VI.

Stations of the Cross: A series of meditations on the sufferings of Christ: his condemnation to death and taking up of the Cross; the first fall on the way to Calvary; meeting his Mother; being assisted by Simon of Cyrene, and by Veronica who wiped his face; the second fall; meeting the women of Jerusalem; the third fall; being stripped and nailed to the Cross; his death; the removal of his body from the Cross and his burial. Depictions of these scenes are mounted in most churches, chapels and in some other places, beneath small crosses.

A person making the Way of the Cross passes before these Stations, or stopping points, pausing at each for meditation. If the Stations are made by a group of people, only the leader has to pass from Station to Station. Prayer for the intentions of the pope is required for gaining the indulgence granted for the Stations.

Those unable to make the Stations in the ordinary manner, because they are impeded from visiting a church or other place where the Stations are, can still practice the devotion by meditating on the sufferings of Christ; praying the Our Father, Hail Mary and Glory for each Station and five times in commemoration of the wounds of Christ; and praying for the intentions of the pope. This practice has involved the use of a Stations Crucifix.

A recent development in this devotion is toward greater awareness of the relation of the Passion to the Resurrection-Ascension; this trend, in some circles, has led to the erection of a 15th — unofficial — station. The concept amounts to an extension of the whole customary thrust of the devotion.

The Stations originated, remotely, from the practice of Holy Land pilgrims who visited the actual scenes of incidents in the Passion of Christ. Representations elsewhere of at least some of these scenes were known as early as the fifth century. Later, the Stations evolved in connection with and as a consequence of strong devotion to the Passion in the 12th and 13th centuries. Franciscans, who were given custody of the Holy Places in 1342, promoted the devotion widely; one of them, St. Leonard of Port Maurice, became known as the greatest preacher of the Way of the Cross in the 18th century. The general features of the devotion were fixed by Clement XII in 1731.

Statutes: Virtually the same as decrees (see separate entry), they almost always designate laws of a particular council or synod rather than pontifical laws.

Stigmata: Marks of the wounds suffered by Christ in his crucifixion, in hands and feet by nails, and side by the piercing of a lance. Some persons, called stigmatists, have been reported as recipients or sufferers of marks like these. The Church, however, has never issued any infallible declaration about their possession by anyone, even in the case of St. Francis of Assisi whose stigmata seem to be the best substantiated and may be commemorated in the Roman-Rite liturgy. Ninety percent of some 300 reputed stigmatists have been women. Judgment regarding the presence, significance, and manner of causation of stigmata would depend, among other things, on irrefutable experimental evidence.

Stipend, Mass: An offering given to a priest for applying the fruits of the Mass according to the intention of the donor. The offering is a contribution to the support of the priest. The disposition of the fruits of the sacrifice, in line with doctrine concerning the Mass in particular and prayer in general, is subject to the will of God. In the early Christian centuries, when Mass was not offered for the intentions of particular persons, the participants made offerings of bread and wine for the sacrifice and their own Holy Communion, and of other things useful for the support of the clergy and the poor. Some offerings may have been made as early as the fourth century for the celebration of Mass for particular intentions, and there are indications of the existence of this practice from the sixth century when private Masses began to be offered. The earliest certain proof of stipend practice, however, dates from the eighth century. By the 11th century, along with private Mass, it was established custom.

Stole Fee: An offering given on certain occasions; e.g., at a baptism, wedding, funeral, for the support of the clergy who administer the sacraments and perform other sacred rites.

Stoup: A vessel used to contain holy water.

Suffragan See: Any diocese, except the archdiocese, within a province.

Suicide: The taking of one's own life; a violation of God's dominion over human life. Ecclesiastical burial is denied to persons who deliberately commit suicide while in full possession of their faculties; it is permitted in cases of doubt.

Supererogation: Good and virtuous actions which go beyond the obligations of duty and the requirements enjoined by God's law as necessary for salvation. Examples of these works are the profession and observance of the evangelical counsels of poverty, chastity, and obedience, and efforts to practice charity to the highest degree.

Supernatural: Above the natural; that which exceeds and is not due or owed to the essence, exigencies, requirements, powers and merits of created nature. While man has no claim on supernatural things and does not need them in order to exist and act on a natural level, he does need them in order to exist and act in the higher order or economy of grace established by God for his salvation.

God has freely given to man certain things which are beyond the powers and rights of his human nature. Examples of the supernatural are: grace, a kind of participation by man in the divine life, by which man becomes capable of performing acts meritorious for salvation; divine revelation by which God manifests himself to man and makes known truth that is inaccessible to human reason alone; faith, by which man believes divine truth because of the authority of God who reveals it through Sacred Scripture and tradition and the teaching of his Church.

Superstition: A violation of the virtue of religion, by which God is worshipped in an unworthy manner or creatures are given honor which belongs to God alone. False, vain, or futile worship involves elements which are incompatible with the honor and respect due to God, such as error, deception, and bizarre practices. Examples are: false and exaggerated devotions, chain prayers and allegedly unfailing prayers, the mixing of unbecoming practices in worship. The second kind of superstition attributes to persons and things powers and honor which belong to God alone. Examples are: idolatry, divination, magic, spiritism, necromancy.

Suspension: A penalty by which a cleric is forbidden to exercise some or all of his powers of orders and jurisdiction, or to accept the financial support of his benefices.

Swearing: Taking an oath; calling upon God to witness the truth of a statement; a legitimate thing to do for serious reasons and under proper circumstances, as in a court of law. To swear without sufficient reason is to dishonor God's name; to swear falsely in a court of law is perjury.

Swedenborgianism: A doctrine developed in and from the writings of Emmanuel Swedenborg (1688-1772), who claimed that during a number of visions he had in 1745 Christ taught him the spiritual sense of Sacred Scripture and commissioned him to communicate it to others. He held that, just as Christianity succeeded Judaism, so his teaching supplemented Christianity. He rejected belief in the Trinity, original sin, the Resurrection, and all the sacraments except baptism and the Eucharist. His followers are members of the Church of the New Jerusalem or of the New Church.

Syllabus, The: (1) When not qualified, the term refers to the list of 80 errors accompanying Pope Pius IX's encyclical *Quanta Cura,* issued in 1864.

(2) The *Syllabus* of St. Pius X in the decree *Lamentabili,* issued by the Holy Office July 4, 1907, condemning 65 heretical propositions of modernism. This schedule of errors was followed shortly by that pope's encyclical *Pascendi,* the principal ecclesiastical document against modernism, issued Sept. 8, 1907.

Synod, Diocesan: Meeting of representative persons of a diocese — priests, religious, lay persons — with the bishop, called by him for the purpose of considering and taking action on matters affecting the life and mission of the Church in the diocese. Persons taking part in a synod have consultative status; the bishop alone is the legislator, with power to authorize synodal decrees. According to canon law, every diocese should have a synod every 10 years.

T

Te Deum: The opening Latin words, Thee, God,

of a hymn of praise and thanksgiving prescribed for use in the Office of Readings of the Liturgy of the Hours on many Sundays, solemnities and feasts.

Temperance: Moderation, one of the four cardinal virtues.

Temptation: Any enticement to sin, from any source: the strivings of one's own faculties, the action of the devil, other persons, circumstances of life, etc. Temptation itself is not sin. Temptation can be avoided and overcome with the use of prudence and the help of grace.

Thanksgiving: An expression of gratitude to God for his goodness and the blessings he grants; one of the four ends of prayer.

Theism: A philosophy which admits the existence of God and the possibility of divine revelation; it is generally monotheistic and acknowledges God as transcendent and also active in the world. Because it is a philosophy rather than a system of theology derived from revelation, it does not include specifically Christian doctrines, like those concerning the Trinity, the Incarnation and Redemption.

Theological Virtues: The virtues which have God for their direct object: faith, or belief in God's infallible teaching; hope, or confidence in divine assistance; charity, or love of God. They are given to a person with grace in the first instance, through baptism and incorporation in Christ.

Theology: Knowledge of God and religion, deriving from and based on the data of divine Revelation, organized and systematized according to some kind of scientific method. It involves systematic study and presentation of the truths of divine Revelation in Sacred Scripture, tradition, and the teaching of the Church.

The Second Vatican Council made the following declaration about theology and its relation to divine Revelation: "Sacred theology rests on the written word of God, together with sacred tradition, as its primary and perpetual foundation. By scrutinizing in the light of faith all truth stored up in the mystery of Christ, theology is most powerfully strengthened and constantly rejuvenated by that word. For the sacred Scriptures contain the word of God and, since they are inspired, really are the word of God; and so the study of the sacred page is, as it were, the soul of sacred theology" *(Constitution on Revelation.* No. 24).

Theology has been divided under various subject headings. Some of the major fields have been: dogma, moral, pastoral, ascetics (the practice of virtue and means of attaining holiness and perfection), mysticism (higher states of religious experience). Other subject headings include ecumenism (Christian unity, interfaith relations), ecclesiology (the nature and constitution of the Church), Mariology (doctrine concerning the Blessed Virgin Mary), the sacraments, etc.

Tithing: Contribution of a portion of one's income, originally one-tenth, for purposes of religion and charity. The practice is mentioned 46 times in the Bible. In early Christian times, tithing was adopted in continuance of Old Testament practices of the Jewish people, and the earliest positive church legislation on the subject was enacted in 567. Catholics are bound in conscience to contribute to the support of their church, but the manner in which they do so is not fixed by law. Tithing, which amounts to a pledged contribution of a portion of one's income, has aroused new attention in recent years in the United States.

Titular Sees: Dioceses where the Church once flourished but which later were overrun by pagans or Moslems and now exist only in name or title. Bishops without a territorial or residential diocese of their own; e.g., auxiliary bishops, are given titular sees.

Transfinalization, Transignification: Terms coined to express the sign value of consecrated bread and wine with respect to the presence and action of Christ in the Eucharistic sacrifice and the spiritually vivifying purpose of the Eucharistic banquet in Holy Communion. The theory behind the terms has strong undertones of existential and "sign" philosophy, and has been criticized for its openness to interpretations at variance with the doctrine of transubstantiation and the abiding presence of Christ under the appearances of bread and wine after the sacrifice of the Mass and Communion have been completed. The terms, if used as substitutes for transubstantiation, are unacceptable; if they presuppose transubstantiation, they are acceptable as clarifications of its meaning.

Transubstantiation: "The way Christ is made present in this sacrament (Holy Eucharist) is none other than by the change of the whole substance of the bread into his Body, and of the whole substance of the wine into his Blood (in the Consecration at Mass) . . . this unique and wonderful change the Catholic Church rightly calls transubstantiation" (encyclical *Mysterium Fidei* of Paul VI, Sept. 3, 1965). The first official use of the term was made by the Fourth Council of the Lateran in 1215. Authoritative teaching on the subject was issued by the Council of Trent.

Treasury of the Church: The superabundant merits of Christ and the saints from which the Church draws to confer spiritual benefits, such as indulgences.

Triduum: A three-day series of public or private devotions.

U-Z

Usury: Excessive interest charged for the loan and use of money; a violation of justice.

Veronica: A word resulting from the combination of a Latin word for true, *vera*, and a Greek word for image, *eikon*, designating a likeness of the face of Christ or the name of a woman said to have given him a cloth on which he caused an imprint of his face to appear. The veneration at Rome of a likeness depicted on cloth dates from about the end of the 10th century; it figured in a popular devotion during the Middle Ages, and in the Holy Face devotion practiced since the 19th century. A faint, indiscernible likeness said to be of this kind is preserved in St. Peter's Basilica. The origin of the likeness is uncertain, and the identity of the woman is unknown. Before the 14th century, there were no known artistic representations of an incident concerning a woman who wiped the face of Christ with a piece of cloth while He was carrying the Cross to Calvary.

Viaticum: Holy Communion given to those in danger of death. The word, derived from Latin, means provision for a journey through death to life hereafter.

Vicar General: A prelate appointed by a bishop to help him, as a deputy, in the administration of his diocese. Because of his office, he has the same jurisdictional authority as the bishop except in cases reserved to the bishop by himself or by church law.

Virginity: Observance of perpetual sexual abstinence. The state of virginity, which is embraced for the love of God by religious with a public vow or by others with a private vow, was singled out for high praise by Christ (Mt. 19:10-12) and has always been so regarded by the Church. In the encyclical *Sacra Virginitas,* Pius XII stated: "Holy virginity and that perfect chastity which is consecrated to the service of God is without doubt among the most perfect treasures which the founder of the Church has left in heritage to the society which he established."

Paul VI approved in 1970 a rite in which women can consecrate their virginity "to Christ and their brethren" without becoming members of a religious institute. The *Ordo Consecrationis Virginum,* a revision of a rite promulgated by Clement VII in 1596, is traceable to the Roman liturgy of about 500.

Virtue: A habit or established capability for performing good actions. Virtues are *natural* (acquired and increased by repeating good acts) and/or *supernatural* (given with grace by God).

Vocation: A call to a way of life. Generally, the term applies to the common call of all men, from God, to holiness and salvation. Specifically, it refers to particular states of life, each called a vocation, in which response is made to this universal call; viz., marriage, the religious life and/or priesthood, the single state freely chosen or accepted for the accomplishment of God's will. The term also applies to the various occupations in which persons make a living. The Church supports the freedom of each individual in choosing a particular vocation, and reserves the right to pass on the acceptability of candidates for the priesthood and religious life. Signs or indicators of particular vocations are many, including a person's talents and interests, circumstances and obligations, invitations of grace and willingness to respond thereto.

Vow: A promise made to God with sufficient knowledge and freedom, which has as its object a moral good that is possible and better than its voluntary omission. A person who professes a vow binds himself or herself by the virtue of religion to fulfill the promise. The best known examples of vows are those of poverty, chastity and obedience professed by religious (see Evangelical Counsels, individual entries).

Public vows are made before a competent person, acting as an agent of the Church, who accepts the profession in the name of the Church, thereby giving public recognition to the person's dedication and consecration to God and divine worship. Vows of this kind are either solemn, rendering all contrary acts invalid as well as unlawful; or simple, rendering contrary acts unlawful. Solemn vows are for life; simple vows are for a definite period of time or for life. Vows professed without public recognition by the Church are called private vows. The Church, which has authority to accept and give public recognition to vows, also has authority to dispense persons from their obligations for serious reasons.

Week of Prayer for Christian Unity: Eight days of prayer, from Jan. 18 to 25, for the union of all men in the Church established by Christ. On the initiative of Father Paul James Francis, S.A., of Graymoor, N.Y., it originated in 1908 as the Chair of Unity Octave. In recent years, its observance on an interfaith basis has increased greatly.

Witness, Christian: Practical testimony or evidence given by Christians of their faith in all circumstances of life — by prayer and general conduct, through good example and good works, etc.; being and acting in accordance with Christian belief; actual practice of the Christian faith.

Zucchetto: A skullcap worn by bishops and other prelates.

LIBERATION THEOLOGY

Liberation theology deals with the relevance of Christian faith and salvation — and, therefore, of the mission of the Church — to efforts for the promotion of human rights, social justice and human development.

It originated in the religious, social, political and economic environment of Latin America, with its contemporary need for a theory and corresponding action by the Church, in the pattern of its overall mission, for human rights and integral human development.

The pastoral and social doctrine of the Church provides the basic theoretical background of liberation theology worthy of the name. Of particular importance are the expressions of this teaching in: the papal encyclicals *Mater et Magistra* (1961), *Pacem in Terris* (1963) and *Populorum Progressio* (1967); *Gaudium et Spes,* issued by the Second Vatican Council (1965); documents which emanated from the meeting of the Latin American Bishops' Council at Medellin, Colombia, under the title, *The Church in the Present-Day Transformation of Latin America in the Light of the* (Second Vatican) *Council* (1968); statements of the Synod of Bishops (1971 and 1974); the apostolic exhortation of Pope Paul, "Evangelization in Today's World" (1975).

Some versions of liberation theology are at variance with this body of teaching because of their special concept of Christ as liberator, and also because they play down the primary spiritual nature and mission of the Church; they translate sociology — especially Marxism — into theology; they advocate violence in social activism.

Risk in Sociological Commitment

The International Theological Commission said this about the subject in 1976:

"Theological treatments of liberation must deal simultaneously with theories that come from the social sciences, which study objectively what the 'outcry of the people' expresses.

"Theology, however, cannot deduce concrete political norms sheerly from theological principles; and so the theologian cannot settle profound sociological issues by theology's specific resources. Theological treatises which strive to build a more human society must take into account the risks that the use of sociological theories involves. In every instance these theories must be tested for their degree of certitude, inasmuch as they are often no more than conjectures and not infrequently harbor explicit or implicit ideological elements that rest on debatable philosophical assumptions or on an erroneous anthropology. This is true, for instance, of significant segments of analyses inspired by Marxism and Leninism. Anyone who employs such theories and analyses should be aware that these do not achieve a greater degree of truth simply because theology introduces them into its expositions. In fact, theology ought to recognize the pluralism that exists in scientific interpretations of society and realize that it cannot be fettered to any concrete sociological analysis."

Comment by Father Gutierrez

Liberation theology is a Christian theology, not a Marxist manifesto for Latin America. So stated Father Gustavo Gutierrez, coiner of the term and author of *A Theology of Liberation* published in 1973. It is a theology born out of the religious, political and sociological experience of Latin America, he said in July, 1983, while conducting a workshop on liberation spirituality at Xavier University in Cincinnati.

Interviewed by the *Catholic Telegraph,* he said: "People say my book is about political liberation. This is not true. It is one aspect, no more." He referred to what he called a partial and "sometimes not fair" interpretation of the subject matter of the book as purely "social analysis." Rarely quoted, he emphasized, is a major thesis that "the first task of the Church is to celebrate the Eucharist" and that, without contemplation, "we can't have a Christian life." Liberation theology is a "theology of salvation in our historical conditions."

While observing that North Americans were interested in the Latin American theology of liberation, Father Gutierrez said "it is impossible to take a theology born in one context and apply it elsewhere." Although U.S. theologies of liberation as developed by women, blacks and Hispanics may share the Latin American method, it is only by coincidence. "The main point is the presence of God in our people. Maybe liberation theology is helpful for that."

THE CHURCH IN COUNTRIES THROUGHOUT THE WORLD ____

(Principal sources for statistics: *Statistical Yearbook of the Church, 1981* (the latest edition available); *Annuario Pontificio, 1983.* Figures are as of Dec. 31, 1981, or Dec. 31 of the year indicated. See Index under names of countries for additional entries on 1983 events.)

Abbreviation code: archd. — archdiocese; dioc. — diocese; ap. ex. — apostolic exarchate; prel. — prelature; abb. — abbacy; v.a. — vicariate apostolic; p.a. — prefecture apostolic; a.a. — apostolic administration; card. — cardinal; abp. — archbishops (residential and auxiliary); nat. — native; bp. — bishops (residential and auxiliary); priests (dioc. — diocesan or secular priests; rel. — those belonging to religious orders); sem. — major seminarians, diocesan and religious; p.d. — permanent deacons; bros. — brothers; srs. — sisters; bap. — baptisms; Caths. — Catholic population; tot. pop. — total population.

Afghanistan: Republic in south-central Asia; capital, Kabul. Christianity antedated Moslem conquest in the seventh century but was overcome by it. All inhabitants are subject to the law of Islam. Christian missionaries are prohibited. Population (est.), 15,540,000.

Albania: Communist people's republic in the Balkans, bordering the Adriatic Sea; capital, Tirana. Christianity was introduced before the middle of the fourth century. The Byzantine-Rite Church broke from unity with Rome following the schism of 1054; it has been suppressed. The Latin (Roman) Church, which prevailed in the north, has been wiped out by persecution since 1945, with the expulsion of Italian missionaries; a number of death and prison sentences and other repressive measures against bishops, priests, religious and lay persons; the closing of Catholic schools and a seminary; the cutting of lines of communication with the Holy See. In 1967, the government proclaimed itself the first atheist state in the world.

Archd., 2; dioc., 3; abb., 1; a.a. 1; bp., 3 (impeded). No statistics are available. The Catholic population was estimated at 10% of the population in 1969. Tot. pop. (1980 est.), 2,730,000.

Algeria: Republic in northwest Africa: capital, Algiers. Christianity, introduced at an early date, succumbed to Vandal devastation in the fifth century and Moslem conquest in 709, but survived for centuries in small communities into the 12th century. Missionary work was unsuccessful except in service to traders, military personnel and captives along the coast. Church organization was established after the French gained control of the territory in the 1830s. A large number of Catholics were among the estimated million Europeans who left the country after it secured independence from France July 5, 1962. Islam is the state religion. Algeria maintains diplomatic relations with Vatican City.

Archd., 1; dioc., 3; card., 1; abp., 1; bp., 3 (2 nat.); parishes, 83; priests, 201 (85 dioc., *116 rel.); sem. 3; bros., 15; p.d., 3; srs., 501; bap., 61; Caths., 64,000 (.3%); tot. pop., 19,590,000.*

Andorra: Autonomous principality in the Pyrenees, under the rule of co-princes — the French head of state and the bishop of Urgel, Spain; capital, Andorra la Vella. Christianity was introduced at an early date. Catholicism is the state religion. The principality is under the ecclesiastical jurisdiction of the Spanish diocese of Urgel.

Parishes, 7; priests, 19 (13 dioc., 6 rel.); bro., 1; srs., 16; bap., 448; Caths., 26,000; tot. pop., 30,000.

Angola: Independent (Nov. 11, 1975) republic in west Africa; capital, Luanda. Evangelization by Catholic missionaries, dating from about 1570, reached high points in the 17th and 18th centuries. Independence from Portugal in 1975 left the Church with a heavy loss of personnel when about half of the foreign missionaries fled the country. Two ecclesiastical provinces were established in 1977; all but one of the hierarchy are Angolan. In 1983, Abp. Alexandre do Nascimento became the first Angolan cardinal (see Index). Angola has an apostolic delegate.

Archd., 3; dioc., 9; card., 1 (nat.); abp., 2 (nat.); bp., 8 (7 nat.); parishes, 232; priests, 270 (87 dioc., 183 rel.); sem., 101; bros., 51; srs., 624; bap., 67,313; Caths., 3,234,000; tot. pop., 7,260,000.

Anguilla: Self-governing British island territory in the Caribbean; capital, The Valley. Under ecclesiastical jurisdiction of St. John's-Basseterre diocese, Antigua. Statistics included in St. Christopher (Kitts)-Nevis.

Antigua and Barbuda: Independent (Oct. 31, 1981) Caribbean island nation; capital, St. John's, Antigua.

Dioc., 1; bp., 1; parishes, 2; priests, 5 (2 dioc., 3 rel.); sem., 1; bros., 5; srs., 6; sch., 4; bap., 143; Caths., 7,000 (9.2%); tot. pop., 76,000.

Arabian Peninsula: Christianity, introduced in various parts of the peninsula in early Christian centuries, succumbed to Islam in the seventh century. The native population is entirely Moslem. The only Christians are foreigners. Most of the peninsula is under the ecclesiastical jurisdiction of the Vicariate Apostolic of Arabia located in Abu Dhabi, United Arab Emirates. The area has an apostolic delegate (to the Red Sea Region). See individual countries: Bahrain, Oman, Qatar, Saudi Arabia, United Arab Emirates, Yemen, and Peoples Democratic Republic of Yemen.

Argentina: Republic in southeast South America, bordering on the Atlantic; capital, Buenos Aires. Priests were with the Magellan exploration party and the first Mass in the country was celebrated Apr. 1, 1519. Missionary work began in the 1530s, diocesan organization in the late 1540s, and effective evangelization about 1570. Independence from Spain was proclaimed in 1816. Since its establishment in the country, the Church has been influenced by Spanish cultural and institutional forces, antagonistic liberalism, government interference and opposition; the latter reached a climax during the last five years of the first presidency of Juan Peron (1946-1955). Political chaos following military take-over of the government in 1976 resulted in widespread human rights violations including the disappearance of thousands of people. Catholicism is the state religion. Argentina maintains diplomatic relations with Vatican City.

Archd., 12; dioc., 45; prel., 3; ap. ex., 1 (for Armenians of Latin America); ord., 1; card., 3; abp., 10; bp., 65; parishes, 2,178; priests, 5,482 (2,500 dioc., 2,982 rel.); p.d., 31; sem., 1,655; bros., 1,188; srs., 12,552; bap., 610,944; Caths., 26,078,000 (92.8%); tot. pop., 28,090,000.

Australia: Commonwealth; island continent southeast of Asia; capital, Canberra. The first Catholics in the country were Irish under penal sentence, 1795-1804; the first public Mass was celebrated May 15, 1803. Official organization of the Church dates from 1820. The country was officially removed from mission status in March, 1976. Established diplomatic relations with Vatican City, 1973.

Archd., 7; dioc., 21; card., 1; abp., 6; bp., 35; parishes, 1,421; priests, 3,847 (2,287 dioc., 1,560 rel.); p.d., 4; sem., 443; bros., 2,215; srs., 11,685; bap., 70,098; Caths., 3,922,000 (26.3%); tot. pop. 14,860,000.

Austria: Republic in central Europe; capital, Vienna. Christianity was introduced by the end of the third century, strengthened considerably by conversion of the Bavarians from about 600, and firmly established in the second half of the eighth century. Catholicism survived and grew stronger as the principal religion in the country in the post-Reformation period, but suffered from Josephinism in the 18th century. Although liberated from much government harassment in the aftermath of the Revolution of 1848, it came under pressure again some 20 years later in the Kulturkampf. During this time the Church became involved with a developing social movement. The Church faced strong opposition from Socialists after World War I and suffered persecution from 1938 to 1945 during the Nazi regime. Some Church-state matters are regulated by a concordat originally concluded in 1934. Austria maintains diplomatic relations with Vatican City.

Archd., 2; dioc., 7; abb., 1; ord., 1; card., 1; abp., 2; bp., 13; parishes, 3,060; priests, 6,006 (3,518 dioc., 2,488 rel.); p.d., 110; sem., 583; bros., 606; srs., 10,794; bap., 82,655; Caths., 6,605,000 (87.9%); tot. pop., 7,510,000.

Azores: North Atlantic island group 750 miles west of Portugal, of which it is part. Christianity was introduced in the second quarter of the 15th century.

Bahamas: Independent (July 10, 1973) island group consisting of some 700 (30 inhabited) small islands southeast of Florida and north of Cuba; capital, Nassau. On Oct. 12, 1492, Columbus landed on one of these islands, where the first Mass was celebrated in the New World. Organization of the Catholic Church in the Bahamas dates from about

the middle of the 19th century. Established diplomatic relations with Vatican City in 1979.

Dioc., 1; bp., 1; parishes, 28; priests, 40 (12 dioc., 28 rel.); p.d., 4; sem., 3; bros., 5; srs., 58; bap., 2,407; Caths., 48,000 (19.2%); tot. pop., 250,000.

Bahrain: Island state in Persian Gulf; capital, Manama. Under ecclesiastical jurisdiction of Arabia vicariate apostolic.

Priests, 3 (rel); bap., 200; Caths., 6,000; tot. pop., 360,000

Balearic Islands: Spanish province consisting of an island group in the western Mediterranean. Statistics are included in those for Spain.

Bangladesh: Formerly the eastern portion of Pakistan. Officially constituted as a separate nation Dec. 16, 1971; capital, Dacca (Dhaka). Islam is the principal religion; freedom of religion is granted. There were Jesuit, Dominican and Augustinian missionaries in the area in the 16th century. A vicariate apostolic (of Bengali) was established in 1834; the hierarchy was erected in 1950. Established diplomatic relations with Vatican City, 1972.

Archd., 1; dioc., 3; abp., 1 (nat.); bp., 3 (nat.); parishes, 55; priests, 190 (48 dioc., 142 rel.); sem., 126; bros., 54; srs., 476; bap., 5,205; Caths., 165,000 (.18%); tot. pop. 90,630,000.

Barbados: Parliamentary democracy (independent since 1966), easternmost of the Caribbean islands; capital, Bridgetown. About 70 per cent of the people are Anglicans. Established diplomatic relations with Vatican City in 1979.

Dioc., 1; bp., 1; parishes, 7; priests, 10 (4 dioc., 6 rel.); p.d., 2; sem., 4; bros., 5; srs., 31; bap., 227; Caths., 11,000 (4%); tot. pop., 270,000.

Belgium: Constitutional monarchy in north-western Europe; capital, Brussels. Christianity was introduced about the first quarter of the fourth century and major evangelization was completed about 730. During the rest of the medieval period the Church had firm diocesan and parochial organization, generally vigorous monastic life, and influential monastic and cathedral schools. Lutherans and Calvinists made some gains during the Reformation period but there was a strong Catholic restoration in the first half of the 17th century, when the country was under Spanish rule. Jansenism disturbed the Church from about 1640 into the 18th century. Josephinism, imposed by an Austrian regime, hampered the Church late in the same century. Repressive and persecutory measures were enforced during the Napoleonic conquest. Freedom came with separation of Church and state in the wake of the Revolution of 1830, which ended the reign of William I. Thereafter, the Church encountered serious problems with philosophical liberalism and political socialism. Catholics have long been engaged in strong educational, social and political movements. Except for one five-year period (1880-1884), Belgium has maintained diplomatic relations with Vatican City since 1835.

Archd., 1; dioc., 7; card., 2; bp., 17; par-

ishes, 3,974; priests, 12,718 (7,756 dioc., 4,962 rel.); p.d., 216; sem., 333; bros., 2,401; srs., 30,500; bap., 92,712; Caths., 9,009,000 (91.3%); tot. pop., 9,860,000.

Belize (formerly British Honduras): Independent (Sept. 21, 1981) republic on east coast of Central America; capital, Belmopan. Its history has points in common with Guatemala, where evangelization began in the 16th century. Established diplomatic relations with Vatican City, 1983. (See Index for papal visit.)

Dioc., 1; bp., 2; parishes, 12; priests, 37 (10 dioc., 27 rel.); p.d., 1; sem., 2; bros., 8; srs., 84; bap., 3,322; Caths., 90,000; tot. pop., 160,000.

Benin (formerly Dahomey): Republic in west Africa, bordering on the Atlantic; capital, Porto Novo. Missionary work was very limited from the 16th to the 18th centuries. Effective evangelization dates from 1861. The hierarchy was established in 1955. The majority of Christians are Catholics. Benin maintains diplomatic relations with Vatican City.

Archd., 1; dioc., 5; card., 1 (nat.); abp., 2 (nat.); bp., 5 (4 nat.); parishes, 110; priests, 185 (95 dioc., 90 rel.); sem., 63; bros., 18; srs., 315; bap., 11,711; Caths., 590,000 (16.2%); tot. pop., 3,640,000.

Bermuda: British dependency, consisting of 360 islands (20 of them inhabited) nearly 600 miles east of Cape Hatteras; capital, Hamilton. Catholics were not permitted until about 1800. Occasional pastoral care was provided the few Catholics there by visiting priests during the 19th century. Early in the 1900s priests from Halifax began serving the area. A prefecture apostolic was set up in 1953. The first bishop assumed jurisdiction in 1956.

Dioc., 1; bp., 1; parishes, 7; priests, 8 (1 dioc., 7 rel.); p.d., 2; srs., 9; bap., 134; Caths., 9,000 (14.4%); tot. pop., 62,100.

Bhutan: Constitutional monarchy in the Himalayas, northeast of India; capital, Thimphu. Most of the population are Buddhists. Jesuits (1963) and Salesians (1965) were invited to country to direct schools. Salesians were expelled in February, 1982, on disputed charges of proselytism. Jesuits and some Sisters remained *(Fides)*. Ecclesiastical jurisdiction is under the Darjeeling diocese, India.

Priests, 7 (rel.); srs., 4; bap., 15; Caths., 400; tot. pop., 1,328,000.

Bolivia: Republic in central South America; capital, Sucre; seat of government, La Paz. Catholicism, the official religion, was introduced in the 1530s and the first bishopric was established in 1552. Effective evangelization among the Indians, slow to start, reached high points in the middle of the 18th and the beginning of the 19th centuries and was resumed about 1840. Independence from Spain was proclaimed in 1825, at the end of a campaign that started in 1809. The republic inherited the Spanish right of nominating candidates for bishoprics. Church-state relations are regulated by a 1951 concordat with the Holy See. In recent years, human rights violations in conditions of political, economic and social turmoil have occasioned strong protests by members of the hierarchy and

other people of the Church. Bolivia maintains diplomatic relations with Vatican City.

Archd., 4; dioc., 4; prel., 2; v.a., 6; card., 1; abp., 5; bp., 17; parishes, 440; priests, 872 (214 dioc., 658 rel.); p.d., 23; sem., 165; bros., 232; srs., 1,680; bap., 176,529; Caths., 5,420,000 (94%); tot. pop., 5,760,000.

Botswana: Republic (independent since 1966) in southern Africa; capital, Gaborone. Botswana has an apostolic delegate (to Southern Africa).

Dioc., 1; bp., 1; priests, 27 (3 dioc., 24 rel.); p.d., 1; sem., 2; bros., 3; srs., 24; bap., 2.058; Caths., 32,000 (3.7%); tot. pop., 850,000

Brazil: Republic in northeast South America; capital, Brasilia. One of several priests with the discovery party celebrated the first Mass in the country Apr. 26, 1500. Evangelization began some years later and the first diocese was erected in 1551. During the colonial period, which lasted until 1822, evangelization made some notable progress — especially in the Amazon region between 1680 and 1750 — but was seriously hindered by government policy and the attitude of colonists regarding Amazon Indians the missionaries tried to protect from exploitation and slavery. The Jesuits were suppressed in 1782 and other missionaries expelled as well. Liberal anti-Church influence grew in strength. The government gave minimal support but exercised maximum control over the Church. After the proclamation of independence from Portugal in 1822 and throughout the regency, government control was tightened and the Church suffered greatly from dissident actions of ecclesiastical brotherhoods, Masonic anti-clericalism and general decline in religious life. Church and state were separated by the constitution of 1891, proclaimed two years after the end of the empire. The Church carried into the 20th century a load of inherited liabilities and problems amid increasingly difficult political, economic and social conditions affecting the majority of the population. A number of bishops, priests, religious and lay persons have been active in movements for social and religious reform. Brazil maintains diplomatic relations with Vatican City.

Archd., 36; dioc., 187; prel., 17; abb., 2; ord., 1; card., 6; abp., 35; bp., 237; parishes, 6,713; priests, 13,443 (5,210 dioc., 8,233 rel.); p.d., 340; sem., 4,606; bros., 2,638; srs., 36,983; bap., 2,738,381; Caths., 109,540,000 (90.1%); tot. pop., 121,550,000.

Brunei: State under British protection, on the northern coast of Borneo; scheduled for independence by end of 1983; capital, Bandar Seri Begawan. Under ecclesiastical jurisdiction of Miri diocese, Malaysia.

Parishes, 3; priests, 5 (2 dioc., 3 rel.); srs., 4; bap., 102; Caths., 5,000; tot. pop., 240,000.

Bulgaria: People's republic in southeastern Europe on the eastern part of the Balkan peninsula; capital, Sofia. Christianity was introduced before 343 but disappeared with the migration of Slavs into the territory. The baptism of Boris I about 865 ushered in a new period of Christianity which soon became involved in switches of loyalty between Constantinople and Rome. Through it all the

Byzantine, and later Orthodox, element remained stronger and survived under the rule of Ottoman Turks into the 19th century. The few modern Latin Catholics in the country are traceable to 17th century converts from heresy. The Byzantines are products of a reunion movement of the 19th century. In 1947 the constitution of the new republic decreed the separation of Church and state. Catholic schools and institutions were abolished and foreign religious banished in 1948. A year later the apostolic delegate was expelled. Ivan Romanoff, vicar general of Plovdiv, died in prison in 1952. Bishop Eugene Bossilkoff, imprisoned in 1948, was sentenced to death in 1952; his fate remained unknown until 1975 when the Bulgarian government informed the Vatican that he had died in prison shortly after being sentenced. Roman and Bulgarian Rite vicars apostolic were permitted to attend the Second Vatican Council from 1962 to 1965. All church activity is under surveillance and/or control by the government, which professes to be atheistic. Pastoral and related activities are strictly limited. Most of the population is Orthodox. There was some improvement in Bulgarian-Vatican relations in 1975, following a visit of Bulgarian President Todor Zhivkov to Pope Paul VI June 19 and talks between Vatican and Bulgarian representatives at the Helsinki Conference in late July. The needs of the church in Bulgaria were outlined by Pope John Paul II in a private audience with the Bulgarian foreign minister in December, 1978. In 1979, the Sofia-Plovdiv vicariate apostolic was raised to a diocese and a bishop was appointed for the vacant see of Nicopoli.

Dioc., 2; ap. ex., 1; bp., 3; Caths. (est.), 65,000 (.7%); tot. pop., 8,862,000.

Burma: Union of Burma, a republic in southeast Asia, on the Bay of Bengal; capital, Rangoon. Christianity was introduced about 1500. Small-scale evangelization had limited results from the middle of the 16th century until the 1850s when effective organization of the Church began. The hierarchy was established in 1955. Buddhism was declared the state religion in 1961, but the state is now officially secular. In 1965, church schools and hospitals were nationalized. In 1966, all foreign missionaries who had entered the country after 1948 for the first time were forced to leave when the government refused to renew their work permits. Despite these setbacks, the Church has shown some progress in recent years. Burma has an apostolic delegate (pro-nuncio to Bangladesh).

Archd., 2; dioc., 6; p.a., 1; abp., 2 (nat.); bp., 6 (5 nat.); parishes, 144; priests, 215 (187 dioc., 28 rel.); sem., 208; bros., 64; srs., 706; bap., 21,387; Caths., 410,000 (1.1%); tot. pop., 35,200,000.

Burundi: Republic since 1966, near the equator in east-central Africa; capital, Bujumbura. The first permanent Catholic mission station was established late in the 19th century. Large numbers of persons were received into the Church following the ordination of the first Burundi priests in 1925. The first native bishop was appointed in 1959. Most education takes place in schools under Catholic auspices. In 1972-73, the country was torn by tribal

warfare between the Tutsis, the ruling minority, and the Hutus. Since 1979, approximately 100 Catholic missionaries have been expelled. Burundi maintains diplomatic relations with Vatican City.

Archd., 1; dioc., 6; abp., 1 (nat.); bp., 6 (nat.); parishes, 104; priests, 341 (175 dioc., 166 rel.); sem., 84; bros., 151; srs., 740; bap., 73,661; Caths., 2,370,000 (54.4%); tot. pop., 4,350,000.

Cambodia (Peoples Republic of Kampuchea, Democratic Kampuchea): Republic (Oct. 9, 1970) in southeast Asia, bordering on the Gulf of Siam, Thailand, Laos and Vietnam; capital Phnom Penh. Evangelization dating from the second half of the 16th century had limited results, more among Vietnamese than Khmers. Thousands of Catholics of Vietnamese origin were forced to flee in 1970 because of Khmer hostility. The status of the Church remained uncertain following the Khmer Rouge take-over in April, 1975. Foreign missionaries were expelled immediately. Local clergy and religious were sent to work the land; whether they would be able to minister to the faithful was not known. Buddhism is the state religion.

V.a., 1; p.a., 2. No statistics available. Catholics numbered 13,835 (2% of the total population) in 1973. Tot. pop. (est.), 6,830,000.

Cameroon: Republic in west Africa, bordering on the Gulf of Guinea; capital, Yaounde. Effective evangelization began in the 1890s, although Catholics had been in the country long before that time. In the 40-year period from 1920 to 1960, the number of Catholics increased from 60,000 to 700,000. The first native priests were ordained in 1935. Twenty years later the first native bishops were ordained and the hierarchy established. In 1982, three new ecclesiastical provinces and one diocese were established. Cameroon maintains diplomatic relations with Vatican City.

Archd., 4; dioc., 12; abp., 5 (4 nat.); bp., 13 (11 nat.); parishes, 372; priests, 862 (314 dioc., 548 rel.); p.d., 24; sem., 219; bros., 244; srs., 1,303; bap., 76,319; Caths., 2,308,000 (26.6%); tot. pop., 8,650,000.

Canada: Independent federation comprising the northern half of North America; capital, Ottawa. Canada maintains diplomatic relations with Vatican City. (See Church in Canada.)

Archd., 18; dioc., 53; abb., 1; ap. ex., 1; card., 4 (1 is a residential archbishop; 3 are retired); abp., 27 (18 residential, 9 retired); bp., 98 (55 residential, 22 auxiliary, 21 retired); parishes 5,915; priests, 12,375 (7,243 dioc., 5,132 rel.); p.d., 332; sem., 1,021; bros., 3,497; srs., 37,214; bap., 178,777; Caths., 10,433,849 (42.9%); tot. pop., 24,347,400. (Principal source: 1983 Directory of Canadian Conference of Catholic Bishops.)

Canary Islands: Two Spanish provinces, consisting of seven islands, off the northwest coast of Africa. Evangelization began about 1400. Almost all of the one million inhabitants are Catholics. Statistics are included in those for Spain.

Cape Verde: Independent (July 5, 1975) island group in the Atlantic 300 miles west of Senegal; formerly a Portuguese overseas province; capital,

Praia, San Tiago Island. Evangelization began some years before the establishment of the first diocese in 1532. Established diplomatic relations with Vatican City in 1976.

Dioc., 1; bp., 1; parishes, 30; priests, 42 (12 dioc., 30 rel.); sem., 1; bros., 4; srs., 36; bap., 7,662; Caths., 314,000; tot. pop., 330,000.

Carolines and Marshalls, The: U.S. trust territory in the southwest Pacific; scheduled for independence. Effective evangelization began in the late 1880s.

Dioc., 1; bp., 1; parishes, 26; priests, 34 (2 dioc., 32 rel.); p.d., 20; sem., 8; bros., 6; srs., 43; bap., 1,921; Caths., 56,000; tot. pop., 120,000.

Cayman Islands: British colony in Caribbean; capital, George Town on Grand Cayman. Under ecclesiastical jurisdiction of Kingston diocese, Jamaica.

Srs., 2; bap., 19; Caths., 300; tot. pop., 17,000.

Central African Republic: Former French colony (independent since 1960) in central Africa; capital, Bangui. Effective evangelization dates from 1894. The region was organized as a mission territory in 1909. The first native priest was ordained in 1938. The hierarchy was organized in 1955. Established diplomatic relations with Vatican City in 1975.

Archd., 1; dioc., 5; abp., 1 (nat.); bp., 4; parishes, 87; priests, 228 (41 dioc., 187 rel.); p.d., 2; sem., 67; bros., 65; srs., 278; bap., 17,237; Caths., 402,000; tot. pop., 2,370,000.

Ceuta: Spanish possession (city) on the northern tip of Africa, south of Gibraltar. Statistics are included in those for Spain.

Chad: Republic (independent since 1960) in north-central Africa; former French possession; capital, N'Djamena (Fort Lamy). Evangelization began in 1929, leading to firm organization in 1947 and establishment of the hierarchy in 1955. Chad has an apostolic delegate (pro-nuncio, Central African Republic).

Archd., 1; dioc., 3; abp., 1; bp., 3; parishes, 95; priests, 158 (16 dioc., 142 rel.); sem., 29; bros., 45; srs., 184; bap., 10,703; Caths., 255,000 (5.6%); tot. pop., 4,550,000.

Chile: Republic on the southwestern coast of South America; capital, Santiago. Priests were with the Spanish conquistadores on their entrance into the territory early in the 16th century. The first parish was established in 1547 and the first bishopric in 1561. Overall organization of the Church took place later in the century. By 1650 most of the peaceful Indians in the central and northern areas were evangelized. Missionary work was more difficult in the southern region. Church activity was hampered during the campaign for independence, 1810 to 1818, and through the first years of the new government, to 1830. Later gains were made, into this century, but hindering factors were shortages of native clergy and religious and attempts by the government to control church administration through the patronage system in force while the country was under Spanish control. Separation of Church and state were decreed in the constitution of 1925. Church-state relations were strained during the regime of Marxist president Salvador Allende Gossens (1970-73). He was overthrown in a bloody coup and was reported to have committed suicide Sept. 11, 1973. Conditions remained unsettled under the military government which assumed control after the coup. Since 1974, the Chilean bishops have issued several statements criticizing government policies violating human rights and urging release of political prisoners. The Church-backed Vicariate of Solidarity was established in 1976 to give legal aid to political prisoners and aid their families. Human rights situation was again criticized by the bishops in a December, 1982, letter which also called for a return to civilian rule. Chile maintains diplomatic relations with Vatican City.

Archd., 5; dioc., 14; prel., 3; v.a., 2; card., 1; abp., 3; bp., 24; parishes, 816; priests, 2,046 (802 dioc., 1,244 rel.); p.d., 192; sem., 895; bros., 445; srs., 5,091; bap., 185,091; Caths., 9,652,000 (85.5%); tot. pop., 11,290,000.

China *(This article concerns mainland China which has been under Communist control since 1949):* People's Republic in eastern part of Asia; capital, Peking (Beijing), Christianity was introduced by Nestorians who had some influence on part of the area from 635 to 845 and again from the 11th century until 1368. John of Monte Corvino started a Franciscan mission in 1294; he was ordained an archbishop about 1307. Missionary activity involving more priests increased for a while thereafter but the Franciscan mission ended in 1368. The Jesuit Matteo Ricci initiated a remarkable period of activity in the 1580s. By 1700 the number of Catholics was reported to be 300,000. The Chinese Rites controversy, concerning the adaptation of rituals and other matters to Chinese traditions and practices, ran throughout the 17th century, ending in a negative decision by mission authorities in Rome. Bl. Francis de Capillas, the protomartyr of China, was killed in 1648. Persecution, a feature of Chinese history as recurrent as changes in dynasties, occurred several times in the 18th century and resulted in the departure of most missionaries from the country. The Chinese door swung open again in the 1840s and progress in evangelization increased with an extension of legal and social tolerance. At the turn of the 20th century, however, the Boxer Rebellion took one or the other kind of toll among an estimated 30,000 victims. Missionary work in the 1900s reached a new high in every respect before the disaster of persecution initiated by Communists before and especially since they established the republic in 1949. The Reds began a savage persecution as soon as they came into power. Among its results were the expulsion of over 5,000 foreign missionaries, 510 of whom were American priests, brothers and nuns; the arrest, imprisonment and harassment of all members of the native religious, clergy and hierarchy; the forced closing of 3,932 schools, 216 hospitals, 781 dispensaries, 254 orphanages, 29 printing presses and 55 periodicals; denial of the free exercise of religion to all the faithful; the detention of hundreds of priests, religious and lay persons in jail and their employment in slave labor; the proscription of the Legion of Mary and other Catholic Action groups for "counter-revolutionary activities" and "crimes against the new China"; complete outlawing of missionary work and pastoral activity. The government formally established a Patriotic Association of Chinese Catholics in July, 1957. Relatively few priests and lay persons joined the organization, which was condemned by Pius XII in 1958. The government formed the nucleus of what it hoped might become the hierarchy of a schismatic Chinese church in 1958 by "electing" 26 bishops and having them consecrated validly but illicitly between Apr. 13, 1958, and Nov. 15, 1959, without the permission or approval of the Holy See. By 1983, an estimated 60 bishops were consecrated in this manner. In March, 1960, Bishop James E. Walsh, M.M., the last American missionary in China, was sentenced and placed in custody for a period of 20 years. He was released in the summer of 1970. (He died in 1981.) There seemed to be an opening to the West by China in 1979. What this, along with renewed activity of the Patriotic Association in 1980, might mean for the Church in that country is open to question.

Archd., 20; dioc., 92; p.a., 29. No Catholic statistics are available. In 1949 there were between 3,500,000-4,000,000 Catholics, about .7 per cent of the total population. Tot. pop., 988,927,000.

Colombia: Republic in northwest South America, with Atlantic and Pacific borders; capital, Bogota. Evangelization began in 1508. The first two dioceses were established in 1534. Vigorous development of the Church was reported by the middle of the 17th century despite obstacles posed by the multiplicity of Indian languages, government interference through patronage rights and otherwise, rivalry among religious orders and the small number of native priests among the predominantly Spanish clergy. Some persecution, including the confiscation of property, followed in the wake of the proclamation of independence from Spain in 1819. The Church was affected in many ways by the political and civil unrest of the nation through the 19th century and into the 20th. Various aspects of Church-state relations are regulated by a concordat with the Vatican signed July 12, 1973, and ratified July 2, 1975. The new concordat replaced one which had been in effect with some modifications since 1887. In late 1976, the bishops released a statement reaffirming their concern for social justice but rejecting actions of radical Catholic groups such as Priests for Latin America and Christians for Socialism as Marxist-oriented and destructive of Church unity. Colombia maintains diplomatic relations with Vatican City.

Archd., 11; dioc., 30; prel., 2; v.a., 9; p.a., 7; card., 2; abp., 12; bp., 49; parishes, 2,272; priests, 5,196 (3,213 dioc., 1,983 rel.); p.d., 33; sem., 2,174; bros., 939; srs., 18,304; bap., 711,295; Caths., 26,607,000 (95.5%); tot. pop., 27,840,000.

Comoros: Consists of main islands of Grande Comore, Anjouan, Moheli and Mayotte in Indian Ocean off southeast coast of Africa; capital, Moroni, Grande Comore Island. Former French territory; independent (July 6, 1975) except Mayotte which voted to remain part of France. The majority of the population is Moslem. An apostolic administration was established in 1975.

A.a., 1; priests, 4 (1 dioc., 3 rel.); srs., 7; bap., 24; Caths., 1,000 (.2%); tot. pop., 370,000.

Congo Republic: Republic (independent since 1960) in west central Africa; former French possession; capital, Brazzaville. Small-scale missionary work with little effect preceded modern evangelization dating from the 1880s. The work of the Church has been affected by political instability, Communist influence, tribalism and hostility to foreigners. The hierarchy was established in 1955. Established diplomatic relations with the Vatican in 1977.

Archd., 1; dioc., 3; abp., 1 (nat); bp., 2 (nat); parishes, 66; priests, 155 (40 dioc., 115 rel.); p.d., 2; sem., 44; bros., 33; srs., 196; bap., 13,940; Caths., 697,000 (44.1%); tot. pop., 1,580,000.

Cook Islands: Self-governing territory of New Zealand, an archipelago of small islands in Oceania. Evangelization by Protestant missionaries started in 1821, resulting in a predominantly Protestant population. The first Catholic missionary work began in 1894. The hierarchy was established in 1966.

Dioc., 1; bp., 1; parishes, 11; priests, 12 (4 dioc., 8 rel.); sem., 4; bros., 3; srs., 11; bap., 78; Caths., 3,000; tot. pop., 20,000.

Costa Rica: Republic in Central America; capital, San Jose. Evangelization began about 1520 and proceeded by degrees to real development and organization of the Church in the 17th and 18th centuries. The republic became independent in 1838. Twelve years later church jurisdiction also became independent with the establishment of a bishopric in the present capital. Costa Rica maintains diplomatic relations with Vatican City. (See Index for papal visit.)

Archd., 1; dioc., 3; v.a., 1; abp., 1; bp., 5; parishes, 169; priests, 452 (274 dioc., 178 rel.); sem., 226; bros., 29; srs., 1,001; bap., 61,512; Caths., 2,105,000 (92.7%); tot. pop., 2,270,000.

Cuba: Republic under Communist dictatorship, south of Florida; capital, Havana. Effective evangelization began about 1514, leading eventually to the predominance of Catholicism on the island. Native vocations to the priesthood and religious life were unusually numerous in the 18th century but declined in the 19th. The island became independent of Spain in 1902 following the Spanish-American War. Fidel Castro took control of the government Jan. 1, 1959. In 1961, after Cuba was officially declared a socialist state, the University of Villanueva was closed, 350 Catholic schools were nationalized and 136 priests expelled. A greater number of foreign priests and religious had already left the country. Freedom of worship and religious instruction are limited to church premises and no social action is permitted the Church, which survives under surveillance. A new constitution approved in 1976 guaranteed freedom of conscience but restricted its exercise. Cuba maintains diplomatic relations with Vatican City.

Archd., 2; dioc., 5; abp., 2; bp., 5; parishes, 221; priests, 221 (113 dioc., 108 rel.); sem., 47; bros., 20; srs., 218; bap., 20,021; Caths. 4,023,000; tot. pop., 9,770,000.

Cyprus: Republic in the eastern Mediterranean; capital, Nicosia. Christianity was preached on the island in apostolic times and has a continuous history from the fourth century. Latin and Eastern rites were established but the latter prevailed and became Orthodox after the schism of 1054. Roman and Orthodox Christians have suffered under many governments, particularly during the period of Turkish dominion from late in the 16th to late in the 19th centuries, and from differences between the 80 per cent Greek majority and the Turkish minority. About 80 per cent of the population are Orthodox. Cyprus established diplomatic relations with Vatican City in 1973. Maronite-Rite Catholics are under the jurisdiction of the archdiocese of Cyprus (of the Maronites), whose archbishop resides in Lebanon. Roman-Rite Catholics are under the jurisdiction of the Roman-Rite patriarchate of Jerusalem.

Archd., 1 (Maronite); abp., 1 (resides in Lebanon); parishes, 10; priests, 23 (7 dioc., 16 rel.); bros., 3; srs., 92; bap., 61; Caths., 8,000 (1.2%); tot. pop., 640,000.

Czechoslovakia: Federal socialist republic (since 1969) in Central Europe, consisting of the Czech Socialist Republic, capital Prague; and the Slovak Socialist Republic, capital Bratislava. The republics have local autonomy but are subordinate to the Federal Assembly at Prague made up of representatives from both regions. The Czech and Slovak regions of the country have separate religious and cultural backgrounds. Christianity was introduced in Slovakia in the 8th century by Irish and German missionaries and the area was under the jurisdiction of German bishops. In 863, at the invitation of the Slovak ruler Rastislav who wanted to preserve the cultural and liturgical heritage of the people, Sts. Cyril and Methodius began pastoral and missionary work in the region, ministering to the people in their own language. The saints introduced Old Slovak (Old Church Slavonic) into the liturgy and did so much to evangelize the territory that they are venerated as the apostles of Slovakia. A diocese established at Nitra in 880 had a continuous history except for a century ending in 1024. The Church in Slovakia was severely tested by the Reformation and political upheavals. After World War I, when it became part of the Republic of Czechoslovakia, it was 75 per cent Catholic. In the Czech lands, the martyrdom of Prince Wenceslaus in 929 triggered the spread of Christianity. Prague has had a continuous history as a diocese since 973. A parish system was organized about the 13th century in Bohemia and Moravia, the land of the Czechs. Mendicant orders strengthened relations with the Latin Rite in the 13th century. In the next century the teachings of John Hus in Bohemia brought trouble to the Church in the forms of schism and heresy, and initiated a series of religious wars which continued for decades following his death at the stake in 1415. Church property was confiscated, monastic communities were scattered and even murdered, ecclesiastical organization was shattered, and so many of the faithful joined the Bohemian Brethren that Catholics became a minority. The Reformation, with the way prepared by the Hussites and cleared by other factors, affected the Church seriously. A Counter Reformation got under way in the 1560s and led to a gradual restoration through the thickets of Josephinism, the Enlightenment, liberalism and troubled politics. In 1920, two years after the establishment of the Republic of Czechoslovakia, the schismatic Czechoslovak Church was proclaimed at Prague, resulting in numerous defections from the Catholic Church in the Czech region. In Ruthenia, 112,000 became Russian Orthodox between 1918 and 1930. Vigorous persecution of the church began in Slovakia before the end of World War II when Communists mounted a 1944 offensive against bishops, priests and religious. In 1945, church schools were nationalized, youth organizations were disbanded, the Catholic press was curtailed, the training of students for the priesthood was seriously impeded. Msgr. Josef Tiso, president of the Slovak Republic, was tried for "treason" in December, 1947, and was executed the following April. Between 1945 and 1949 approximately 10 per cent of the Slovak population spent some time in jail or a concentration camp. Persecution began later in the Czech part of the country, following the accession of the Gottwald regime to power early in 1948. Hospitals, schools and property were nationalized and Catholic organizations were liquidated. A puppet organization was formed in 1949 to infiltrate the Church and implement an unsuccessful plan for establishing a schismatic church. In the same year Archbishop Josef Beran of Prague was placed under house arrest. (He left the country in 1965, was made a cardinal, and died in 1969 in Rome.) A number of theatrical trials of bishops and priests were staged in 1950. All houses of religious were taken over between March, 1950, and the end of 1951. Pressure was applied on the clergy and faithful of the Eastern Rite in Slovakia to join the Orthodox Church. Diplomatic relations with Vatican City were terminated in 1950. About 3,000 priests were deprived of liberty in 1951 and attempts were made to force "peace priests" on the people. In 1958 it was reported that 450 to 500 priests were in jail; an undisclosed number of religious and Byzantine-Rite priests had been deported; two bishops released from prison in 1956 were under house arrest; one bishop was imprisoned at Leopoldov and two at the Mirov reformatory. In Bohemia, Moravia and Silesia, five of six dioceses were without ruling bishops; one archbishop and two bishops were active but subject to "supervision"; most of the clergy refused to join the "peace priests." In 1962 only three bishops were permitted to attend the first session of the Second Vatican Council. From January to October, 1968, Church-state relations improved to some extent under the Dubcek regime: a number of bishops were reinstated; some 3,000 priests were engaged in the pastoral ministry, although 1,500 were still barred from priestly work; the "peace priests" organization was disbanded; the Eastern-Rite Church, with 147 parishes, was reestablished. In 1969, an end was ordered to rehabilitation trials for priests and religious, but no wholesale restoration of priests and religious to their proper ways of life and work was in prospect. In 1972, the government ordered the removal of nuns from visible but limited apostolates to farms and mental hospitals where they would be out of sight. In 1973, the government allowed the ordination of four bishops — one in the Czech region and three in the Slovak region. Reports from Slovakia late in the same year stated that authorities there had placed severe restrictions on the education of seminarians and the functioning of priests. Government restrictions continued to hamper the work of priests and nuns in recent years. Signatories of the human rights declaration called Charter 77 have been particular objects of government repression and retribution.

Archd., 3; dioc., 10; card., 1; bp., 6 (1 impeded); parishes, 4,444; priests, 3,686 (3,381 dioc., 305 rel.); sem., 295; bros., 72; srs., 5,073; bap., 106,367; Caths., 10,530,000 (68.7%); tot. pop., 15,310,000.

Denmark, including the Faroe Islands and Greenland: Constitutional monarchy in northwestern Europe, north of West Germany; capital, Copenhagen. Christianity was introduced in the ninth century and the first diocese for the area was established in 831. Intensive evangelization and full-scale organization of the Church occurred from the second half of the 10th century and ushered in a period of great development and influence in the 12th and 13th centuries. Decline followed, resulting in almost total loss to the Church during the Reformation when Lutheranism became the national religion. Catholics were considered foreigners until religious freedom was legally assured in 1849. Modern development of the Church dates from the second half of the 19th century. About 95 per cent of the population are Evangelical Lutherans. Established diplomatic relations with Vatican City in 1982.

Dioc., 1; bp., 1; parishes, 60; priests, 111 (38 dioc., 73 rel.); sem., 11; bros., 4; srs., 390; bap., 354; Caths., 27,000 (.5%); tot. pop., 5,120,000.

Djibouti (formerly French Territory of Afars and Issas): Independent (1977) republic in east Africa, on the Gulf of Aden; capital, Djibouti. Christianity in the area, formerly part of Ethiopia, antedated but was overcome by the Arab invasion of 1200. Modern evangelization, begun in the latter part of the 19th century, had meager results. The hierarchy was established in 1955. The territory has an apostolic delegate (to the Red Sea Region).

Dioc., 1; bp., 1; parishes, 7; priests, 9 (1 dioc., 8 rel.); p.d., 1; bros., 7; srs., 28; bap., 36; Caths., 12,000; tot. pop., 250,000.

Dominica: Independent (Nov. 3, 1978) state in Caribbean; capital, Roseau. Evangelization began in 1642. Established diplomatic relations with Vatican City in 1981.

Dioc., 1; bp., 1; parishes, 16; priests, 25 (2 dioc., 23 rel.); p.d., 1; sem., 6; bros., 5; srs., 30; bap., 1,321; Caths., 65,000 (81.2%); tot. pop., 80,000.

Dominican Republic: Caribbean republic on the eastern two-thirds of the island of Hispaniola, bordering on Haiti; capital, Santo Domingo. Evangelization began shortly after discovery by Columbus in 1492 and church organization, the first in America, was established by 1510. Catholicism is the state religion. The Dominican Republic maintains diplomatic relations with Vatican City.

Archd., 1; dioc., 7; card., 1; abp., 2; bp., 8; parishes, 207; priests, 550 (139 dioc., 411 rel.); p.d., 27; sem., 283; bros., 82; srs., 1,320; bap., 88,352; Caths., 5,300,000 (94.8%); tot. pop., 5,584,000.

Ecuador (includes Galapagos Islands): Republic on the west coast of South America; capital, Quito. Evangelization began in the 1530s. The first diocese was established in 1545. A synod, one of the first in the Americas, was held in 1570 or 1594. Multiphased missionary work, spreading from the coastal and mountain regions into the Amazon, made the Church highly influential during the colonial period. The Church was practically enslaved by the constitution enacted in 1824, two years after Ecuador, as part of Colombia, gained independence from Spain. Some change for the better took place later in the century, but from 1891 until the 1930s the Church labored under serious liabilities imposed by liberal governments. The concordat of 1866 was violated; foreign missionaries were barred from the country for some time; the property of religious orders was confiscated; education was taken over by the state; traditional state support was refused; legal standing was denied; attempts to control church offices were made through insistence on rights of patronage. A period of harmony and independence for the Church began after agreement was reached on Church-state relations in 1937. Ecuador maintains diplomatic relations with Vatican City.

Archd., 3; dioc., 10; prel., 1; v.a., 5; p.a., 3; card., 1; abp., 3; bp., 18; parishes, 766; priests, 1,524 (660 dioc., 864 rel.); p.d., 9; sem., 180; bros., 367; srs., 4,133; bap., 203,151; Caths., 7,868,000 (91%); tot. pop., 8,640,000.

Egypt, Arab Republic of: Republic in northeastern Africa, bordering on the Mediterranean; capital, Cairo. Alexandria was the influential hub of a Christian community established by the end of the second century; it became a patriarchate and the center of the Coptic Church, and had great influence on the spread of Christianity in various parts of Africa; Monasticism developed from desert communities of hermits in the third and fourth centuries. Arianism was first preached in Egypt in the 320s. In the fifth century, the Coptic church went Monophysite through failure to accept doctrine formulated by the Council of Chalcedon in 451 with respect to the two natures of Christ. The country was thoroughly Arabized after 640 and was under the rule of Ottoman Turks from 1517 to 1798. English influence was strong during the 19th century. A monarchy established in 1922 lasted about 30 years, ending with the proclamation of a republic in 1953-54. By that time Egypt had become the leader of pan-Arabism against Israel. It waged two unsuccessful wars against Israel in 1948-49 and 1967. Between 1958 and 1961 it was allied with Syria and Yemen, in the United Arab Republic. In 1979, following negotiations initiated by Pres. Anwar el-Sadat in 1977, Egypt and Israel signed a peace agreement. Islam, the religion of some 90 percent of the population, is the state religion. Egypt maintains diplomatic relations with Vatican City.

Patriarchate, 2 (Alexandria for the Copts and for the Melkites); dioc., 9; card., 1; abp., 1; bp., 12; parishes, 195; priests, 350 (178 dioc., 172 rel.); p.d., 1; sem., 63; bros., 67; srs., 1,705; bap., 2,182; Caths., 162,000; tot. pop., 43,470,000.

El Salvador: Republic in Central America; capital, San Salvador. Evangelization affecting the whole territory followed Spanish occupation in the 1520s. The country was administered by the captaincy general of Guatemala until 1821 when independence from Spain was declared and it was annexed to Mexico. El Salvador joined the Central American Federation in 1825, decreed its own independence in 1841 and became a republic formally in 1856. In recent years, Church efforts to achieve social justice have resulted in persecution of the Church. Archbishop Oscar Romero of San Salvador, peace advocate and outspoken champion of human rights, was murdered Mar. 24, 1980, while celebrating Mass. El Salvador maintains diplomatic relations with Vatican City. (See Index for papal visit and coverage of late 1982 and 1983 events.)

Archd., 1; dioc., 4; abp., 1; bp., 6; parishes, 228; priests, 347 (162 dioc., 185 rel.); sem., 110; bros., 76; srs., 852; bap., 105,791; Caths., 4,495,000 (90.9%); tot. pop., 4,940,000.

England: Center of the United Kingdom of Great Britain (England, Scotland, Wales) and Northern Ireland, off the northwestern coast of Europe; capital, London. The arrival of St. Augustine of Canterbury and a band of monks in 597 marked the beginning of evangelization. Real organization of the Church took place some years after the Synod of Whitby, held in 663. Heavy losses were sustained in the wake of the Danish invasion in the 780s, but recovery starting from the time of Alfred the Great and dating especially from the middle of the 10th century led to Christianization of the whole country and close Church-state relations. The Norman Conquest of 1066 opened the Church in England to European influence. The 13th century was climactic, but decline had already set in by 1300 when the country had an all-time high of 17,000 religious. In the 14th century, John Wycliff presaged the Protestant Reformation. Henry VIII, failing in 1529 to gain annulment of his marriage to Catherine of Aragon, refused to acknowledge papal authority over the Church in England, had himself proclaimed its head, suppressed all houses of religious, and persecuted persons — Sts. Thomas More and John Fisher, among others — for not subscribing to the Oath of Supremacy and Act of

Succession. He held the line on other-than-papal doctrine, however, until his death in 1547. Doctrinal aberrations were introduced during the reign of Edward VI (1547-53), through the Order of Communion, two books of Common Prayer, and the Articles of the Established Church. Mary Tudor's attempted Catholic restoration (1553-58) was a disaster, resulting in the deaths of more than 300 Protestants. Elizabeth (1558-1603) firmed up the Established Church with formation of a hierarchy, legal enactments and multi-phased persecution. One hundred and 11 priests and 62 lay persons were among the casualties of persecution during the underground Catholic revival which followed the return to England of missionary priests from France and The Lowlands. Several periods of comparative toleration ensued after Elizabeth's death. The first of several apostolic vicariates was established in 1685; this form of church government was maintained until the restoration of the hierarchy and diocesan organization in 1850. The revolution of 1688 and subsequent developments to about 1781 subjected Catholics to a wide variety of penal laws and disabilities in religious, civic and social life. The situation began to improve in 1791, and from 1801 Parliament frequently considered proposals for the repeal of penal laws against Catholics. The Act of Emancipation restored citizenship rights to Catholics in 1829. Restrictions remained in force for some time afterwards, however, on public religious worship and activity. The hierarchy was restored in 1850. Since then the Catholic Church, existing side by side with the Established Churches of England and Scotland, has followed a general pattern of growth and development. Great Britain established diplomatic relations with Vatican City in 1982.

Archd., 4; dioc., 15; ap. ex., 1; card., 1; abp., 3; bp., 35; parishes, 2,520; priests, 5,877 (3,901 dioc., 1,976 rel.); p.d., 71; sem., 499; bros., 612; srs., 10,472; bap., 77,117; Caths., 3,952,504 (8.5%); tot. pop., 46,220,955 (1983 Annuario Pontificio). The 1983 Catholic Directory of England and Wales reported a total Catholic population of 4,269,019 for the two countries.

Equatorial Guinea: Republic on the west coast of Africa, consisting of Rio Muni on the mainland and the islands of Fernando Po and Annobon in the Gulf of Guinea: capital, Malabo (Santa Isabel). Evangelization began in 1841. The country became independent of Spain in 1968. The Church was severely repressed during the 11-year rule of Pres. Macias (Masie) Nguema. Developments since his overthrow (August 1979) indicated some measure of improvement. An ecclesiastical province was established in October, 1982. Established diplomatic relations with Vatican City in 1981.

Archd., 1; dioc., 2; abp., 1 (nat.); bp., 2 (nat.); parishes, 37; priests, 48 (18 dioc., 30 rel.); sem., 23; bros., 19; srs., 139; bap., 10,535; Caths., 325,000; tot. pop., 370,000.

Estonia: Baltic republic forcibly absorbed by the U.S.S.R. in 1941; capital Tallinn. Catholicism was introduced in the 11th and 12th centuries. Jurisdiction over the area was made directly subject to the

Holy See in 1215. Lutheran penetration was general in the Reformation period and Russian Orthodox influence was strong from early in the 18th century until 1917 when independence was attained. The first of several apostolic administrators was appointed in 1924. The small Catholic community was hard hit during and since Russian occupation in 1941. The Russian takeover of Estonia has not been recognized by the Holy See or the United States.

Ethiopia: Constitutional monarchy in northeast Africa; capital, Addis Ababa. The country was evangelized by missionaries from Egypt in the fourth century and had a bishop by about 340. Following the lead of its parent body, the Egyptian (Coptic) Church, the Church in the area succumbed to the Monophysite heresy in the sixth century. Catholic influence was negligible for centuries. An ordinariate for the Ethiopian Rite was established in Eritrea in 1930. An apostolic delegation was set up in Addis Ababa in 1937 and several jurisdictions were organized, some under the Congregation for the Oriental Churches and others under the Congregation for the Evangelization of Peoples. Most of the Catholics in the country are in the former Italian colony of Eritrea. Ethiopia maintains diplomatic relations with Vatican City.

Archd., 1; dioc., 2; v.a., 5; p.a., 1; abp., 1; bp., 5; parishes, 207; priests, 513 (149 dioc., 364 rel.); p.d., 1; sem. 119; bros., 133; srs., 874; bap., 11,559; Caths., 217,000 (.67%); tot. pop., 32,160,000.

Falkland Islands: British colony off the southern tip of South America; capital, Stanley. The islands are called Islas Malvinas by Argentina which also claims sovereignty.

P.a., 1; parish, 1; priests, 2 (rel.); bap., 5; Caths., 200; tot. pop., 1,900.

Faroe Islands: Self-governing island group in North Atlantic; Danish possession. Under ecclesiastical jurisdiction of Copenhagen diocese.

Priest, 1 (rel.); srs., 12; bap., 1; Caths., 100; tot. pop., 40,000.

Fiji: Independent island group (100 inhabited) in the southwest Pacific; capital, Suva. Marist missionaries began work in 1844 after Methodism had been firmly established. A prefecture apostolic was organized in 1863. The hierarchy was established in 1966. Established diplomatic relations with Vatican City, 1978.

Archd., 1; abp., 1; parishes, 33; priests, 88 (16 dioc., 72 rel.); sem., 45; bros., 45; srs., 257; bap., 2,330; Caths., 54,000 (8.4%); tot. pop., 640,000.

Finland: Republic in northern Europe; capital, Helsinki. Swedes evangelized the country in the 12th century. The Reformation swept the country, resulting in the prohibition of Catholicism in 1595, general reorganization of ecclesiastical life and affairs, and dominance of the Evangelical Lutheran Church. Catholics were given religious liberty in 1781 but missionaries and conversions were forbidden by law. The first Finnish priest since the Reformation was ordained in 1903 in Paris. A vicariate apostolic for Finland was erected in 1920. A law on religious liberty, enacted in 1923, banned the foundation of monasteries. Finland maintains diplomatic relations with Vatican City.

Dioc., 1; bp., 1; parishes, 5; priests, 18 (1 dioc., 17 rel.); p.d., 1; bros., 2; srs., 29; bap., 58; Caths., 3,295 (.06%); tot. pop., 4,813,000.

France: Republic in western Europe; capital, Paris. Christianity was known around Lyons by the middle of the second century. By 250 there were 30 bishoprics. The hierarchy reached a fair degree of organization by the end of the fourth century. Vandals and Franks subsequently invaded the territory and caused barbarian turmoil and doctrinal problems because of their Arianism. The Frankish nation was converted following the baptism of Clovis about 496. Christianization was complete by some time in the seventh century. From then on the Church, its leaders and people, figured in virtually every important development — religious, cultural, political and social — through the periods of the Carolingians, feudalism, the Middle Ages and monarchies to the end of the 18th century. The great University of Paris became one of the intellectual centers of the 13th century. Churchmen and secular rulers were involved with developments surrounding the Avignon residence of the popes and curia from 1309 until near the end of the 14th century and with the disastrous Western Schism that followed. Strong currents of Gallicanism and conciliarism ran through ecclesiastical and secular circles in France; the former was an ideology and movement to restrict papal ¡control of the Church in the country, the latter sought to make the pope subservient to a general council. Calvinism invaded the country about the middle of the 16th century and won a strong body of converts. Jansenism with its rigorous spirit and other aberrations appeared in the next century, to be followed by the highly influential Enlightenment. The Revolution which started in 1789 and was succeeded by the Napoleonic period completely changed the status of the Church, taking a toll of numbers by persecution and defection and disenfranchising the Church in practically every way. Throughout the 19th century the Church was caught up in the whirl of imperial and republican developments and made the victim of official hostility, popular indifference and liberal opposition. In this century, the Church has struggled with problems involving the heritage of the Revolution and its aftermath, the alienation of intellectuals, liberalism, the estrangement of the working classes because of the Church's former identification with the ruling class, and the massive needs of contemporary society. France maintains diplomatic relations with Vatican City.

Archd., 18; dioc., 75; prel., 1; ap. ex., 2; ord., 1; card., 9; abp., 15; bp., 100; parishes, 38,370; priests, 38,449 (30,837 dioc., 7,612 rel.); p.d., 137; sem., 1,305; bros., 5,306; srs., 84,308; bap., 530,385; Caths., 45,720,000 (84.7%); tot. pop., 53,960,000.

Gabon: Republic on the west coast of Equatorial Africa; capital, Libreville. Sporadic missionary effort took place before 1881 when effective evangelization began. The hierarchy was established in 1955. Gabon maintains diplomatic relations with Vatican City.

Archd., 1; dioc., 3; abp., 1 (nat.); bp., 3 (nat.); parishes, 60; priests, 123 (32 dioc., 91 rel.); sem., 11; bros., 37; srs., 154; bap., 8,355; Caths., 435,000 (57.9%); tot. pop., 750,300.

Gambia, The: Republic (1970) on the northwestern coast of Africa, smallest state in Africa; capital, Banjui. The country was under the jurisdiction of a vicariate apostolic until 1931. The hierarchy was established in 1957. Established diplomatic relations with Vatican City, 1978.

Dioc., 1; bp., 1; parishes, 12; priests, 18 (rel.); sem. 6 (dioc.); bros., 2; srs., 21; bap., 376; Caths., 13,000 (2%); tot. pop., 620,000.

Germany: Country in northern Europe partitioned in 1949 into the Communist German Democratic Republic in the East (capital, East Berlin) and the German Federal Republic in the West (capital, Bonn). Christianity was introduced in the third century, if not earlier. Trier, which became a center for missionary activity, had a bishop by 400. Visigoth invaders introduced Arianism in the fifth century but were converted in the seventh century by the East Franks, Celtic and other missionaries. St. Boniface, the apostle of Germany, established real ecclesiastical organization in the eighth century. The Church had great influence during the Carolingian period. Bishops from that time onward began to act in dual roles as pastors and rulers, a state of affairs which led inevitably to confusion and conflict in Church-state relations and perplexing problems of investiture. The Church developed strength and vitality through the Middle Ages but succumbed to abuses which antedated and prepared the ground for the Reformation. Luther's actions from 1517 made Germany a confessional battleground. Religious strife continued until conclusion of the Peace of Westphalia at the end of the Thirty Years' War in 1648. Nearly a century earlier the Peace of Augsburg (1555) had been designed, without success, to assure a degree of tranquillity by recognizing the legitimacy of different religious confessions in different states, depending on the decisions of princes. The implicit principle that princes should control the churches emerged in practice into the absolutism and Josephinism of subsequent years. St. Peter Canisius and his fellow Jesuits spearheaded a Counter Reformation in the second half of the 16th century. Before the end of the century, however, 70 per cent of the population of north and central Germany were Lutheran. Calvinism also had established a strong presence. The Church gained internal strength in a defensive position. Through much of the 19th century, however, its influence was eclipsed by Protestant intellectuals and other influences. It suffered some impoverishment also as a result of shifting boundaries and the secularization of property shortly after 1800. It came under direct attack in the Kulturkampf of the 1870s but helped to generate the opposition which resulted in a dampening of the campaign of Bismarck against it. Despite action by Catholics on the social front and other developments, discrimination against the Church spilled over into the 20th century and lasted beyond World War I. Catholics in politics struggled with others to pull the country through numerous postwar crises. The dissolution of the Center Party, agreed to by the bishops in 1933 without awareness of the ultimate consequences, contributed negatively to the rise of Hitler to supreme power. Church officials protested the Nazi anti-Church and anti-Semitic actions, but to no avail. After World War II Christian leadership had much to do with the recovery of Western Germany. East Germany, gone Communist under Russian auspices, initiated a program of control and repression of the Church in 1948 and 1949. With no prospect of success for measures designed to split bishops, priests, religious and lay persons, the regime has concentrated most of its attention on mind control, especially of the younger generation, by the elimination of religious schools, curtailment of freedom for religious instruction and formation, severe restriction of the religious press, and the substitution since the mid-50's of youth initiation and Communist ceremonies for the rites of baptism, confirmation, marriage, and funerals. Bishops are generally forbidden to travel outside the Republic. The number of priests is decreasing, partly because of reduced seminary enrollments ordered by the government since 1958. In 1973, the Vatican appointed three apostolic administrators and one auxiliary (all titular bishops) for the areas of three West German dioceses located in East Germany. West Germany maintains diplomatic relations with Vatican City.

West Germany: Archd., 5; dioc., 16 (also part of the Berlin diocese); ap., ex., 1; card., 4; abp., 4; bp., 55; parishes, 11,826; priests, 22,985 (17,104 dioc., 5,881 rel.); p.d., 747; sem., 2,624; bros., 3,223; srs., 62,100; bap., 268,248; Caths., 28,600,000 (46.3%); tot. pop., 61,670,000.

East Germany: Dioc., 2 (Dresden-Meissen and Berlin, since most of its territory lies in East Germany); a.a., 1 (Gorlitz; there are also 3 territories with apostolic administrators); card., 1; bps., 8; parishes, 914; priests, 1,509 (1,272 dioc., 237 rel.); p.d., 37; sem., 145; bros., 52; srs., 2,962;- bap., 9,634; Caths., 1,268,000 (7.5%); tot. pop., 16,740,000.

Ghana: Republic on the western coast of Africa, bordering on the Gulf of Guinea; capital, Accra. Priests visited the country in 1482, 11 years after discovery by the Portuguese, but missionary effort — hindered by the slave trade and other factors — was slight until 1880 when systematic evangelization began. A prefecture apostolic was set up in 1879. The hierarchy was established in 1950. Ghana maintains diplomatic relations with Vatican City.

Archd., 2; dioc., 7; abp., 2 (nat.); bp., 7 (nat.); parishes, 208; priests, 438 (203 dioc., 235 rel.); sem., 268; bros., 135; srs., 499; bap., 42,525; Caths., 1,440,000 (11.9%); tot. pop., 12,060,000.

Gibraltar: British colony on the tip of the Spanish Peninsula on the Mediterranean. Evangelization took place after the Moors were driven out near the end of the 15th century. The Church was hindered by the British who acquired the colony in 1713. Most of the Catholics were, and are, Spanish and Italian immigrants and their descendants. A vicariate apostolic was organized in 1817. The diocese was erected in 1910.

Dioc., 1; bp., 1; parishes, 5; priests, 11 (10 dioc., 1 rel.); sem., 3; srs., 18; bap., 318; Caths., 22,000; tot. pop., 30,000.

Greece, including Crete: Kingdom in southeastern Europe on the Balkan Peninsula; capital, Athens. St. Paul preached the Gospel at Athens and Corinth on his second missionary journey and visited the country again on his third tour. Other Apostles may have passed through also. Two bishops from Greece attended the First Council of Nicaea. After the division of the Roman Empire, the Church remained Eastern in rite and later broke ties with Rome as a result of the schism of 1054. A Latin-Rite jurisdiction was set up during the period of the Latin Empire of Constantinople, 1204-1261, but crumbled afterwards. Unity efforts of the Council of Florence had poor results. The country now has Greek Catholic and Latin jurisdictions. The Greek Orthodox Church is predominant. Established diplomatic relations with Vatican City in 1980.

Archd., 4; dioc., 4; v.a., 1; ap. ex., 1; ord., 1; abp., 3; bp., 1; parishes, 73; priests, 101 (57 dioc., 44 rel.); sem., 6; bros., 43; srs., 166; bap., 422; Caths., 49,000 (.5%); tot. pop., 9,710,000.

Greenland (Kalaalit Nunaat): Danish island province northeast of North America; granted self rule in 1979; capital, Nuuk (Godthaab). Catholicism was introduced about 1000. The first diocese was established in 1124 and a line of bishops dated from then until 1537. The first known churches in the western hemisphere, dating from about the 11th century, were on Greenland; the remains of 19 have been unearthed. The departure of Scandinavians and spread of the Reformation reduced the Church to nothing. The Moravian Brethren evangelized the Eskimos from the 1720s to 1901. By 1930 the Danish Church — Evangelical Lutheran — was in full possession. Since 1930 priests have been in Greenland, which is part of the Copenhagen diocese. There are about 60 Catholics in the area.

Grenada: Independent island state in the West Indies; capital, St. George's. Established diplomatic relations with Vatican City in 1979.

Dioc., 1; bp., 1; parishes, 20; priests, 21 (7 dioc., 14 rel.); p.d., 4; sem., 4; bros., 7; srs., 18; bap., 1,207; Caths., 72,000; tot. pop., 110,000.

Guadeloupe: French overseas department in the Leeward Islands of the West Indies; capital, Basse-Terre. Catholicism was introduced in the islands in the 16th century.

Dioc., 1; bp., 1; parishes, 46; priests, 77 (41 dioc., 36 rel.); sem., 7; bros., 8; srs., 201; bap., 5,387; Caths., 299,000 tot. pop., 330,000.

Guam: Outlying area of U.S. in the southwest Pacific; capital, Agana. The first Mass was offered in the Mariana Islands in 1521. The islands were evangelized by the Jesuits, from 1668, and

other missionaries. The first native Micronesian bishop was ordained in 1970.

Dioc., 1 (Agana, suffragan of San Francisco); bp., 1 (nat.); parishes, 27; priests, 50 (18 dioc., 32 rel.); p.d., 7; sem., 18; bros., 4; srs., 135; bap., 1,729; Caths., 102,000; tot. pop., 112,000.

Guatemala: Republic in Central America; capital, Guatemala City. Evangelization dates from the beginning of Spanish occupation in 1524. The first diocese, for all Central American territories administered by the captaincy general of Guatemala, was established in 1534. The country became independent in 1839, following annexation to Mexico in 1821, secession in 1823 and membership in the Central American Federation from 1825. In 1870, a government installed by a liberal revolution repudiated the concordat of 1853 and took active measures against the Church. Separation of Church and state was decreed; religious orders were suppressed and their property seized; priests and religious were exiled; schools were secularized. Full freedom was subsequently granted. The country has been in a virtual state of civil war in recent years, with violence and repression directed at all segments of the population. Since 1976, at least nine priests were reported missing or killed. Guatemala maintains diplomatic relations with Vatican City. (See Index for papal visit.)

Archd., 1; dioc., 8; prel., 2; a.a., 2; bp., 13; parishes, 346; priests, 652 (184 dioc., 468 rel.); p.d., 1; sem., 251; bros., 124; srs., 1,181; bap., 187,698; Caths. 6,270,000 (83.3%); tot. pop. 7,480,000.

Guiana, French (Cayenne): French overseas department on the northeast coast of South America; capital, Cayenne. Catholicism was introduced in the 17th century. The Cayenne diocese was established in 1956.

Dioc., 1; bp., 1; parishes, 22; priests, 30 (9 dioc., 21 rel.); bros., 2; srs., 104; bap., 1,259; Caths., 55,000; tot. pop., 69,000.

Guinea: Republic on the west coast of Africa; capital, Conakry. Occasional missionary work followed exploration by the Portuguese about the middle of the 15th century; organized effort dates from 1877. The hierarchy was established in 1955. Following independence from France in 1958, Catholic schools were nationalized, youth organizations banned and missionaries restricted. Foreign missionaries were expelled in 1967. Archbishop Tchidimbo of Conakry, sentenced to life imprisonment in 1971 on a charge of conspiring to overthrow the government, was released in August, 1979; he resigned his see. Guinea has an apostolic delegate.

Archd., 1; dioc., 1; p.a., 1; abp., 1 (nat.); bp., 1 (nat.); parishes, 28; priests, 19 (18 dioc., 1 rel.); sem., 14 (dioc.); bros., 1; srs., 26; bap., 770; Caths., 51,000 (.9%); tot. pop., 5,150,000.

Guinea-Bissau (formerly Portuguese Guinea): Independent state on the west coast of Africa; capital, Bissau. Catholicism was introduced in the second half of the 15th century but limited missionary work, hampered by the slave trade, had meager results. Missionary work in this century dates from 1933. A prefecture apostolic was established in 1955 (made a diocese in 1977). Guinea-Bissau has an apostolic delegate.

Dioc., 1; bp., 1; parishes, 15; priests, 40 (rel); sem., 4; bros., 10; srs., 29; bap., 612; Caths., 48,000; tot. pop., 660,000.

Guyana: Republic on the northern coast of South America; capital, Georgetown. In 1899 the Catholic Church and other churches were given equal status with the Church of England and the Church of Scotland, which had sole rights up to that time. Most of the Catholics are Portuguese. The Georgetown diocese was established in 1956, 10 years before Guyana became independent of England. The first native bishop was appointed in 1971. Schools were nationalized in 1976. Increased government interference was reported in 1980-81. The Catholic newspaper was forced to close and missionaries were denied access to certain areas.

Dioc., 1; bp., 1; parishes, 23; priests, 56 (6 dioc., 50 rel.); sem., 5; bros., 6; srs., 51; bap., 1,585; Caths., 103,000; tot. pop., 900,000.

Haiti: Caribbean republic on the western third of Hispaniola adjacent to the Dominican Republic; capital, Port-au-Prince. Evangelization followed discovery by Columbus in 1492. Capuchins and Jesuits did most of the missionary work in the 18th century. From 1804, when independence was declared, until 1860, the country was in schism. Relations were regularized by a concordat concluded in 1860, when an archdiocese and four dioceses were established. Factors hindering the development of the Church have been a shortage of native clergy, inadequate religious instruction and the prevalence of voodoo. Political upheavals in the 1960's had serious effects on the Church. Haiti maintains diplomatic relations with Vatican City. (See Index for papal visit.)

Archd., 1; dioc., 6; abp., 1; bp., 6; parishes, 186; priests, 420 (212 dioc., 208 rel.); p.d., 1; sem., 149; bros., 218; srs., 917; bap., 101,165; Caths., 4,410,000; tot. pop. 5,100,000.

Honduras: Republic in Central America; capital, Tegucigalpa. Evangelization preceded establishment of the first diocese in the 16th century. Under Spanish rule and after independence from 1823, the Church held a favored position until 1880 when equal legal status was given to all religions. Harassment of priests and nuns working among peasants and Salvadoran refugees was reported in recent years. Honduras maintains diplomatic relations with Vatican City. (See Index for papal visit.)

Archd., 1; dioc., 4; prel., 1; abp., 1; bp., 7; parishes, 125; priests, 249 (71 dioc., 178 rel.); sem., 29; bros., 16; srs., 341; bap., 97,285; Caths., 3,670,000 (96%); tot. pop., 3,820,000.

Hong Kong: British crown colony at the mouth of the Canton River, adjacent to the southeast Chinese province of Kwangtung. A prefecture apostolic was established in 1841. Members of the Pontifical Institute for Foreign Missions began work there in 1858. The Hong Kong diocese was erected in 1946.

Dioc., 1; bp., 1; parishes, 56; priests, 369 (73

dioc., 296 rel.); sem., 21; bros., 85; srs., 815; bap., 4,874; Caths., 264,000; tot. pop., 5,150,000.

Hungary: People's republic in east central Europe; capital, Budapest. The early origins of Christianity in the country, whose territory was subject to a great deal of change, is not known. Magyars accepted Christianity about the end of the 10th century. St. Stephen I (d. 1038) promoted its spread and helped to organize some of its historical dioceses. Bishops early became influential in politics as well as in the Church. For centuries the country served as a buffer for the Christian West against barbarians from the East, notably the Mongols in the 13th century. Religious orders, whose foundations started from the 1130s, provided the most effective missionaries, pastors and teachers. Outstanding for years were the Franciscans and Dominicans; the Jesuits were noted for their work in the Counter-Reformation from the second half of the 16th century onwards. Hussites and Waldensians prepared the way for the Reformation which struck at almost the same time as the Turks. The Reformation made considerable progress after 1526, resulting in the conversion of large numbers to Lutheranism and Calvinism by the end of the century. Most of them or their descendants returned to the Church later, but many Magyars remained staunch Calvinists. Turks repressed the churches, Protestant as well as Catholic, during a reign of 150 years but they managed to survive. Domination of the Church was one of the objectives of government policy during the reigns of Maria Theresa and Joseph II in the second half of the 18th century; their Josephinism affected Church-state relations until the first World War. More than 100,000 Eastern-Rite schismatics were reunited with Rome about the turn of the 18th century. Secularization increased in the second half of the 19th century, which also witnessed the birth of many new Catholic organizations and movements to influence life in the nation and the Church. Catholics were involved in the social chaos and anti-religious atmosphere of the years following World War I, struggling with their compatriots for religious as well as political survival. After World War II Communist strength, which had manifested itself with less intensity earlier in the century, was great long before it forced the legally elected president out of office in 1947 and imposed a Soviet type of constitution on the country in 1949. The campaign against the Church started with the disbanding of Catholic organizations in 1946. In 1948, "Caritas," the Catholic charitable organization, was taken over and all Catholic schools, colleges and institutions were suppressed. Interference in church administration and attempts to split the bishops preceded the arrest of Cardinal Mindszenty on Dec. 26, 1948, and his sentence to life imprisonment in 1949. (He was free for a few days during the unsuccessful uprising of 1956. He then took up residence at the U.S. Embassy in Budapest where he remained until September, 1971, when he was permitted to leave the country. He died in 1975 in Vienna.) In 1950, religious orders and congregations were suppressed and 10,000 religious were interned. At least 30 priests and monks were assassinated, jailed or deported. About 4,000 priests and religious were confined in jail or concentration camps. The government sponsored a national "Progressive Catholic" church and captive organizations for priests and "Catholic Action," which attracted only a small minority. Signs were clear in 1965 and 1966 that a 1964 agreement with the Holy See regarding episcopal appointments had settled nothing. Six bishops were appointed by the Holy See and some other posts were filled, but none of the prelates were free from government surveillance and harassment. Four new bishops were appointed by the Holy See in January and ordained in Budapest in February, 1969; three elderly prelates resigned their sees. Shortly thereafter, peace priests complained that the "too Roman" new bishops would not deal with them. Talks between Vatican and Hungarian representatives during the past several years have resulted in the appointment of bishops to fill all of Hungary's 11 residential sees.

Archd., 3; dioc., 8; abb., 1; ap. ex., 1; card, 1; abp., 3; bp., 16; parishes, 2,270; priests, 3,193 (3,124 dioc., 69 rel.); p.d., 1; sem., 278; srs., 53; bap., 76,969; Caths., 6,573,000 (61.3%); tot. pop., 10,710,000.

Iceland: Island republic between Norway and Greenland; capital, Reykjavik. Irish hermits were there in the eighth century. Missionaries subsequently evangelized the island and Christianity was officially accepted about 1000. The first bishop was ordained in 1056. The Black Death had dire effects and spiritual decline set in during the 15th century. Lutheranism was introduced from Denmark between 1537 and 1552 and made the official religion. Some Catholic missionary work was done in the 19th century. Religious freedom was granted to the few Catholics in 1874. A vicariate was erected in 1929 (made a diocese in 1968). Iceland maintains diplomatic relations with Vatican City.

Dioc., 1; bp., 1; parishes, 2; priests, 8 (3 dioc., 5 rel.); sem., 6; srs., 36; bap., 26; Caths., 2,000; tot. pop., 230,000.

India: Republic on the subcontinent of south central Asia; capital, New Delhi. Long-standing tradition credits the Apostle Thomas with the introduction of Christianity in the Kerala area. Evangelization followed the establishment of Portuguese posts and the conquest of Goa in 1510. Jesuits, Franciscans, Dominicans, Augustinians and members of other religious orders figured in the early missionary history. An archdiocese for Goa, with two suffragan sees, was set up in 1558. Five provincial councils were held between 1567 and 1606. The number of Catholics in 1572 was estimated to be 280,000. This figure rose to 800,00 in 1700 and declined to 500,000 in 1800. Missionaries had some difficulties with the British East India Co. which exercised virtual government control from 1757 to 1858. They also had trouble because of a conflict that developed between policies of the Portuguese government, which pressed its rights of patronage in episcopal and clerical appointments, and the Congregation for the Propagation of the Faith, which sought greater freedom of ac-

tion in the same appointments. This struggle eventuated in the schism of Goa between 1838 and 1857. In 1886, when the number of Catholics was estimated to be one million, the hierarchy for India and Ceylon was restored. Jesuits contributed greatly to the development of Catholic education from the second half of the 19th century. A large percentage of the Catholic population is located around Goa and Kerala and farther south. The country is predominantly Hindu. So-called anti-conversion laws in effect in several states have had a restrictive effect on pastoral ministry and social service. India maintains diplomatic relations with Vatican City.

Patriarchate, 1 (titular of East Indies); archd., 19; dioc., 88; p.a., 2; card., 2; abp., 19; bp., 101; parishes, 5,159; priests, 12,001 (7,058 dioc., 4,943 rel.); p.d., 24; sem., 5,011; bros., 2,801; srs., 49,956; bap., 288,826; Caths., 11,707,000 (1.7%); tot. pop., 683,810,000.

Indonesia: Republic southeast of Asia, consisting of some 3,000 islands including Kalimantan (most of Borneo), Sulawesi (Celebes), Java, the Lesser Sundas, Moluccas, Sumatra, Timor and West Irian (Irian Jaya, western part of New Guinea); capital, Jakarta. Evangelization by the Portuguese began about 1511. St. Francis Xavier, greatest of the modern missionaries, spent some 14 months in the area. Christianity was strongly rooted in some parts of the islands by 1600. Islam's rise to dominance began at this time. The Dutch East Indies Co., which gained effective control in the 17th century, banned evangelization by Catholic missionaries for some time but Dutch secular and religious priests managed to resume the work. A vicariate of Batavia for all the Dutch East Indies was set up in 1841. About 90 per cent of the population is Moslem. The hierarchy was established in 1961. Indonesia maintains diplomatic relations with Vatican City.

Archd., 7; dioc., 26; card., 1; abp., 6; bp., 26; parishes, 473; priests, 1,731 (249 dioc., 1,482 rel.); p.d., 8; sem., 1,098; bros., 773; srs., 4,106; bap., 164,331; Caths., 3,449,000 (2.2%); tot. pop., 150,520,000. (Statistics for former Portuguese Timor which was annexed by Indonesia in 1976 are listed separately; see Timor, Eastern.)

Iran: Constitutional monarchy in southwestern Asia, between the Caspian Sea and the Persian Gulf; capital, Teheran. Some of the earliest Christian communities were established in this area outside the (then) Roman Empire. They suffered persecution in the fourth century and were then cut off from the outside world. Nestorianism was generally professed in the late fifth century. Islam became dominant after 640. Some later missionary work was attempted but without success. Religious liberty was granted in 1834, but Catholics were the victims of a massacre in 1918. Islam is the religion of perhaps 98 per cent of the population. In 1964 the country had 100,000 Monophysites, the largest group of Christians, and some 20,000 Nestorians. Catholics belong to the Latin, Armenian and Chaldean rites. Iran (Persia until 1935) maintains diplomatic relations with Vatican City.

Archd., 4; dioc., 2; abp., 3; bp., 1; parishes, 32; priests, 33 (6 dioc., 27 rel.); p.d., 9; sem., 5; bro., 1; srs., 41, bap., 265; Caths., 20,000 (.05%); tot. pop., 39,320,000.

Iraq: Republic in southwestern Asia, between Iran and Saudi Arabia; capital, Baghdad. Some of the earliest Christian communities were established in the area, whose history resembles that of Iran. Catholics belong to the Armenian, Chaldean, Latin and Syrian rites; Chaldeans are most numerous. Islam is the religion of some 90 per cent of the population. Iraq maintains diplomatic relations with Vatican City.

Patriarchate, 1; archd., 9; dioc., 5; patriarch, 1; abp., 7; bp., 3; parishes, 103; priests, 148 (109 dioc., 39 rel.); p.d., 4; sem., 17; bros., 18; srs., 250; bap., 5,435; Caths., 374,000; tot. pop., 13,530,000.

Ireland: Republic in the British Isles; capital, Dublin. St. Patrick, who is venerated as the apostle of Ireland, evangelized parts of the island for some years after the middle of the fifth century. Conversion of the island was not accomplished, however, until the seventh century or later. Celtic monks were the principal missionaries. The Church was organized along monastic lines at first, but a movement developed in the 11th century for the establishment of jurisdiction along episcopal lines. By that time many Roman usages had been adopted. The Church gathered strength during the period from the Norman Conquest of England to the reign of Henry VIII despite a wide variety of rivalries, wars, and other disturbances. Henry introduced an age of repression of the faith which continued for many years under several of his successors. The Irish suffered from proscription of the Catholic faith, economic and social disabilities, subjection to absentee landlords and a plantation system designed to keep them from owning property, and actual persecution which took an uncertain toll of lives up until about 1714. Most of those living in the northern part of Ireland became Anglican and Presbyterian in the 1600s but the south remained strong in faith. Some penal laws remained in force until emancipation in 1829. Nearly 100 years later Ireland was divided by two enactments which made Northern Ireland, consisting of six counties, part of the United Kingdom (1920) and gave dominion status to the Irish Free State, made up of the other 26 counties (1922). This state (Eire, in Gaelic) was proclaimed the Republic of Ireland in 1949. The Catholic Church predominates but religious freedom is guaranteed for all. Ireland maintains diplomatic relations with Vatican City.

Archd., 4; dioc., 22; card., 1; abp., 3; bp., 28; parishes, 1,311; priests, 6,091 (3,737 dioc., 2,354 rel.); sem., 1,127; bros., 1,777; srs., 12,504; bap., 88,288 (preceding figures include Northern Ireland); Caths., (approx.), 3,255,000 (93%); tot. pop., 3,440,000.

Ireland, Northern: Part of the United Kingdom, it consists of six of the nine counties of Ulster in the northeast corner of Ireland; capital, Belfast.

History is given under Ireland, above. For recent developments, see Index.

Caths. (approx.), 505,000 (32%); tot. pop., 1,540,000 (other statistics are included in Ireland).

Israel: Parliamentary democracy in the Middle East, at the eastern end of the Mediterranean; capitals, Jerusalem and Tel Aviv (diplomatic). Israel was the birthplace of Christianity, the site of the first Christian communities. Some persecution was suffered in the early Christian era and again during the several hundred years of Roman control. Moslems conquered the territory in the seventh century and, except for the period of the Kingdom of Jerusalem established by Crusaders, remained in control most of the time up until World War I. The Church survived in the area, sometimes just barely, but it did not prosper greatly or show any notable increase in numbers. The British took over the protectorate of the area after World War I. Partition into Israel for the Jews and Palestine for the Arabs was approved by the United Nations in 1947. War broke out a year later with the proclamation of the Republic of Israel. The Israelis won the war and 50 percent more territory than they had originally been ceded. War broke out again for six days in June, 1967, and in October, 1973, resulting in a Middle East crisis which persists to the present time. Caught in the middle of the conflict are hundreds of thousands of dispossessed Palestinian refugees. Judaism is the faith professed by about 85 percent of the inhabitants; approximately one-third of them are considered observants. Most of the Arab minority are Moslems. The Akka archdiocese for Melkites is situated in Israel. Maronites are subject to the bishop of Tyr, Lebanon. Latins are under the jurisdiction of the Roman patriarchate of Jerusalem. Israel has an apostolic delegate. The *1981 Statistical Yearbook of the Church* reported a Catholic population of 128,000 in a total population of 3,950,000.

Italy: Republic in southern Europe; capital, Rome. A Christian community was formed early at Rome, probably by the middle of the first century. St. Peter established his see there. He and St. Paul suffered death for the faith there in the 60s. The early Christians were persecuted at various times there, as in other parts of the empire, but the Church developed in numbers and influence, gradually spreading out from towns and cities in the center and south to rural areas and the north. Organization, in the process of formation in the second century, developed greatly between the fifth and eighth centuries. By the latter date the Church had already come to grips with serious problems, including doctrinal and disciplinary disputes that threatened the unity of faith, barbarian invasions, and the need for the pope and bishops to take over civil responsibilities because of imperial default. The Church has been at the center of life on the peninsula throughout the centuries. It emerged from underground in 313, with the Edict of Milan, and rose to a position of prestige and lasting influence. It educated and converted the barbarians, preserved culture through the early

Middle Ages and passed it on to later times, suffered periods of decline and gained strength through recurring reforms, engaged in military combat for political reasons and intellectual combat for the preservation and development of doctrine, saw and patronized the development of the arts, experienced all human strengths and weaknesses in its members, knew triumph and the humiliation of failure. For long centuries, from the fourth to the 19th, the Church was a temporal as well as spiritual power. This temporal aspect complicated its history in Italy. Since the 1870s, however, when the Papal States were annexed by the Kingdom of Italy, the history became simpler — but remained complicated — as the Church, shorn of temporal power, began to find new freedom for the fulfillment of its spiritual mission. Italy maintains diplomatic relations with Vatican City. (See Index for papal visit to Sicily.)

Patriarchate, 1; archd., 57; dioc., 210; prel., 4; abb., 8; card., 34; abp., and bp., 444 (216 residential; 228 titular, including retired); parishes, 28,656; priests, 62,861 (40,256 dioc., 22,605 rel.); p.d., 246; sem., 4,877; bros., 6,532; srs., 142,733; bap., 639,929; Caths., 55,770,000 (97.5%); tot. pop., 57,200,000.

Ivory Coast: Republic in western Africa; capital, Abidjan. The Holy Ghost Fathers began systematic evangelization in 1895. The first native priests from the area were ordained in 1934. The hierarchy was set up in 1955. Abp. Bernard Yago was named first Ivorian cardinal in 1983. Ivory Coast maintains diplomatic relations with Vatican City.

Archd., 1; dioc., 9; card., 1 (nat.); bp., 8 (nat.); parishes, 168; priests, 419 (132 dioc., 287 rel.); sem., 78; bros., 90; srs., 505; bap., 20,669; Caths., 790,000 (9.9%); tot. pop., 8,300,000.

Jamaica: Parliamentary democracy in the West Indies; capital, Kingston. Franciscans and Dominicans evangelized the island from about 1512 until 1655. Missionary work was interrupted after the English took possession but was resumed by Jesuits about the turn of the 19th century. A vicariate apostolic was organized in 1837. The hierarchy was established in 1967. Established diplomatic relations with Vatican City in 1979.

Archd., 1; dioc., 1; abp., 1; bp., 1; parishes, 30; priests, 92 (13 dioc., 79 rel.); p.d., 3; sem., 5; bros., 9; srs., 201; bap., 3,049; Caths., 215,000 (9.6%); tot. pop., 2,229,000.

Japan: Constitutional monarchy in the northwest Pacific; capital, Tokyo. Jesuits began evangelization in the middle of the 16th century and about 300,000 converts, most of them in Kyushu, were reported at the end of the century. The Nagasaki Martyrs were victims of persecution in 1597. Another persecution took some 4,000 lives between 1614 and 1651. Missionaries, banned for two centuries, returned about the middle of the 19th century and found Christian communities still surviving in Nagasaki and other places in Kyushu. A vicariate was organized in 1866. Religious freedom was guaranteed in 1889. The hierarchy was estab-

lished in 1891. Japan maintains diplomatic relations with Vatican City.

Archd., 3; dioc., 13; p.a., 1; card., 1; abp., 2; bp., 14; parishes, 769; priests, 2,000 (517 dioc., 1,483 rel.); p.d., 2; sem., 187; bros., 424; srs., 7,169; bap., 10,346; Caths., 406,000 (.3%); tot. pop., 117,650,000.

Jerusalem: The entire city, site of the first Christian community, has been under Israeli control since the Israeli-Arab war of June, 1967. There are two patriarchates in the city, Melkite and Latin. Jerusalem has an apostolic delegate.

Jordan: Constitutional monarchy in the Middle East; capital, Amman. Christianity there dates from apostolic times. Survival of the faith was threatened many times under the rule of Moslems from 636 and Ottoman Turks from 1517 to 1918, and in the Islamic Emirate of Trans-Jordan from 1918 to 1949. Since the creation of Israel, some 500,000 Palestinian refugees, some of them Christians, have been in Jordan. Islam is the state religion but religious freedom is guaranteed for all. Jordan has an apostolic delegate.

The Greek Melkite-Rite Archdiocese of Petra and Philadelphia is located in Jordan. Latin (Roman)-Rite Catholics are under the jurisdiction of the Latin patriarchate of Jerusalem.

Archd., 1; abp., 1; parishes, 59; priests, 61 (52 dioc., 9 rel.); sem. 9; bros., 5; srs., 208; bap., 1,111; Caths., 96,000; tot. pop., 3,360,000.

Kenya: Republic in eastern Africa bordering on the Indian Ocean; capital, Nairobi. Systematic evangelization by the Holy Ghost Fathers began in 1892, nearly 40 years after the start of work by Protestant missionaries. The hierarchy was established in 1953. Kenya maintains diplomatic relations with Vatican City.

Archd., 1; dioc., 14; card., 1 (nat.); bp., 14 (10 nat.); parishes, 345; priests, 897 (248 dioc., 649 rel.); p.d., 2; sem., 502; bros., 233; srs., 1,941; bap., 207,597; Caths., 3,354,000 (19.5%); tot. pop., 17,150,000.

Kiribati (Gilbert Islands): Former British colony in Oceania; became independent July 12, 1979; capital Bairiki on Tarawa. French Missionaries of the Sacred Heart began work in the islands in 1888. A vicariate for the islands was organized in 1897. The hierarchy was established in 1966.

Dioc., 1; bp., 1; parishes, 22; priests, 13 (2 dioc., 11 rel.); sem., 5; bros., 2; srs., 45; bap., 384; Caths., 28,000; tot. pop., 57,000 (1983 Annuario Pontificio).

Korea: Peninsula in eastern Asia, east of China, divided into the (Communist) Democratic People's Republic in the North, formed May 1, 1948, with Pyongyang as its capital; and the Republic of Korea in the South, with Seoul as the capital. Some Catholics may have been in Korea before it became a "hermit kingdom" toward the end of the 16th century and closed its borders to foreigners. The real introduction to Catholicism came in 1784 through lay converts. A priest arriving in the country in 1794 found 4,000 Catholics there who had never seen a priest. A vicariate was erected in 1831 but was not manned for several years thereafter. There were 15,000 Catholics by 1857. Four persecutions in the 19th century took a terrible toll; several thousands died in the last one, 1866-69. Freedom of religion was granted in 1883 when Korea opened its borders. Progress was made thereafter. The hierarchy was established in 1962. Since the war of 1950-1953, there have been no signs of Catholic life in the North, which has been blanketed by a news blackout. In July, 1972, both Koreas agreed to seek peaceful means of reunification. The South maintains diplomatic relations with Vatican City. Bishop Tji of Won Ju, South Korea, convicted and sentenced to 15 years' imprisonment in 1974 on a charge of inciting to rebellion, was released in February, 1975.

North Korea: Dioc., 2; abb., 1; bp., 1 (exiled); tot. pop., 18,320,000. No recent Catholic statistics available; there were an estimated 100,000 Catholics reported in 1969.

South Korea: Archd., 3; dioc., 11; card., 1; abp., 2; bp., 12; parishes, 620; priests, 1,113 (793 dioc., 320 rel.); sem., 721; bros., 213; srs., 3,190; bap., 120,618; Caths. 1,397,000 (3.6%); tot. pop., 38,720,000.

Kuwait: Constitutional monarchy (sultanate or sheikdom) in southwest Asia bordering on the Persian Gulf. Remote Christian origins probably date to apostolic times. Islam is the predominant and official religion. Kuwait maintains diplomatic relations with Vatican City.

V.a., 1; bp., 1; parishes, 3; priests, 6 (3 dioc., 3 rel.); srs., 28; bap., 608; Caths., 47,000; tot. pop., 1,460,000.

Laos: Constitutional monarchy in southeast Asia, surrounded by China, Vietnam, Kampuchea, Thailand and Burma; capital, Vientiane. Systematic evangelization by French missionaries started about 1881; earlier efforts ended in 1688. A vicariate apostolic was organized in 1899 when there were 8,000 Catholics and 2,000 catechumens in the country. Most of the foreign missionaries were expelled following the communist take-over in 1975. Buddhism is the state religion. Laos has an apostolic delegate.

V.a., 4; bp., 4 (nat.; a coad. bp. was ordained in 1983). No statistics available. Catholics numbered 35,000 (1% of the total population) in 1974. Tot. pop. (1980), 3,810,000.

Latvia: Baltic republic forcibly absorbed by the U.S.S.R. in the early 1940s; capital, Riga. Catholicism was introduced late in the 12th century. Lutheranism became the dominant religion after 1530. Catholics were free to practice their faith during the long period of Russian control and during independence from 1918 to 1940. The relatively small Catholic community has been repressed since the start of Soviet occupation. The Russian takeover of Latvia has not been recognized by the Holy See or the United States.

Archd., 1; dioc., 1; card., 1 (Bp. Julijans Vaivods, named in 1983); bp., 3 (none residential); parishes, 179; priests, 125 (116 dioc., 9 rel.); sem., 32; bap., 4,413; Caths., 248,000; tot. pop. 2,500,000.

Lebanon: Republic in the Middle East, north of Israel; capital, Beirut. Christianity, introduced in apostolic times, was firmly established by the end of the fourth century and has remained so despite heavy Moslem influence since early in the seventh century. The country is the center of the Maronite Rite. Lebanon maintains diplomatic relations with Vatican City.

Archd. 10 (3 Maronite, 7 Greek Melkite); dioc., 7 (1 Armenian, 1 Chaldean, 5 Maronite); v.a., 1 (Latin); card., 1 (Patr. Antoine Khoraiche of Maronites); patriarchs, 3 (patriarchs of Antioch of the Maronites, a cardinal; Antioch of the Syrians and Cilicia of the Armenians who reside in Lebanon); abp. and bp., 19; priests, 1,428 (635 dioc., 793 rel.); p.d., 1; sem., 349; bros., 120; srs., 3,453; bap., 14,744; Caths., 1,299,000; tot. pop., 3,000,000.

Lesotho: Constitutional monarchy, an enclave in the southeastern part of the Republic of South Africa; capital, Maseru. Oblates of Mary Immaculate, the first Catholic missionaries in the area, started evangelization in 1862. A prefecture apostolic was organized in 1894. The hierarchy was established in 1951. Lesotho maintains diplomatic relations with Vatican City.

Archd., 1; dioc., 3; abp., 1 (nat.); bp., 3 (nat.); parishes, 73; priests, 142 (22 dioc., 120 rel.); sem., 38; bros., 58; srs., 706; bap., 24,860; Caths., 584,000 (43%); tot. pop., 1,370,000.

Liberia: Republic in western Africa, bordering on the Atlantic; capital, Monrovia. Missionary work and influence, dating interruptedly from the 16th century, were slight before the Society of African Missions undertook evangelization in 1906. The hierarchy was established in 1982. Liberia maintains diplomatic relations with Vatican City.

Archd., 1; dioc., 1; abp., 1 (nat.); bp., 1 (nat.); parishes, 45; priests, 49 (8 dioc., 41 rel.); p.d., 3; sem., 25; bros., 29; srs., 84; bap. 1,959; Caths., 38,000 (1.8%); tot. pop., 2,040,000.

Libya: Arab republic in northern Africa, on the Mediterranean between Egypt and Tunisia; capital, Tripoli. Christianity was probably preached in the area at an early date but was overcome by the spread of Islam from the 630's. Islamization was complete by 1067 and there has been no Christian influence since then. The Catholics in the country belong to the foreign colony. Islam is the state religion. Libya has an apostolic delegate.

V.a., 3; p.a., 1; bp., 2; parishes, 3; priests, 12 (1 dioc., 11 rel.); srs., 133; bap., 74; Caths., 43,000 (1.3%); tot. pop., 3,100,000.

Liechtenstein: Constitutional monarchy in central Europe, in the Alps and on the Rhine between Switzerland and Austria; capital, Vaduz. Christianity in the country dates from the fourth century; the area has been under the jurisdiction of Chur, Switzerland, since about that time. The Reformation had hardly any influence in the country. Catholicism is the state religion but religious freedom for all is guaranteed by law.

Parishes, 10; priests, 31 (18 dioc., 13 rel); bros., 11; srs., 102; bap., 350; Caths., 21,000; tot. pop., 30,000.

Lithuania: Baltic republic forcibly absorbed and under Soviet domination since 1945; captial, Vilna (Vilnius). Catholicism was introduced in 1251 and two dioceses were established by 1260. Effective evangelization took place between 1385 and 1417, when Catholicism became the state religion. Losses to Lutheranism in the 16th century were overcome. Efforts of czars to "russify" the Church between 1795 and 1918 were strongly resisted. Concordat relations with the Vatican were established in 1927, nine years after independence from Russia and 13 years before the start of another kind of Russian control with the following results, among others: all convents closed since 1940; four seminaries shut down; appointment to one seminary (Kaunas) only with government approval; priests restricted in pastoral ministry and subject to appointment by government officials; no religious services outside churches; no religious press; religious instruction banned; parish installations and activities controlled by directives enacted in 1976; two bishops — Vincentas Sladkevicius and Julijonas Steponavicius — forbidden to act as bishops and relegated to remote parishes in 1957 and 1961, respectively; arrest, imprisonment or detention in Siberia for four bishops, 185 priests, 275 lay persons between 1945 and 1955. Despite such developments and conditions, there remains a strong and vigorous underground Church in Lithuania, where the Soviet government finds its repressive potential limited by the solidarity of popular resistance. In July, 1982, two episcopal appointments were made: Rev. Antanas Vaicius was named titular bishop of Cubda and apostolic administrator of the Telsiai diocese and Klaipeda prelature; Bishop Vincentas Sladkevicius, titular bishop of Abora and auxiliary bishop of Kaisiadorys, was named apostolic administrator of that diocese. In 1983, four of the five bishops were allowed to go to Rome for their *ad limina* visit. The Soviet takeover of Lithuania is not recognized by the Holy See or the United States.

Archd., 2 (Kaunas and Vilna, which includes territory in political confines of Poland); dioc., 4; prel., 1; bp., 5 (none residential); parishes 630; priests, 707 (698 dioc., 9 rel.); p.d., 1; sem., 94; Caths., 2,542,000; tot. pop., 3,178,000.

Luxembourg: Constitutional monarchy in western Europe, between Belgium, Germany and France; capital, Luxembourg. Christianity, introduced in the fifth and sixth centuries, was firmly established by the end of the eighth century. A full-scale parish system was in existence in the ninth century. Monastic influence was strong until the Reformation, which had minimal influence in the country. The Church experienced some adverse influence from the currents of the French Revolution. Luxembourg maintains diplomatic relations with Vatican City.

Dioc., 1; bp., 1; parishes, 274; priests, 428 (336 dioc., 92 rel.); sem., 18; bros., 28; srs., 1,208; bap., 3,473; Caths. 349,000 (95.3%); tot. pop., 366,000.

Macau: Portuguese-administered territory in southeast Asia across the Pearl River estuary from Hong Kong. Christianity was introduced by the Jesuits in 1557. Diocese was established in 1576. Macau served as a base for missionary work in Japan and China.

Dioc., 1; bp., 1; parishes, 6; priests, 80 (44 dioc., 36 rel.); sem., 7; bros., 16; srs., 189; bap., 528; Caths., 18,000; tot. pop., 290,000.

Madagascar (Malagasy Republic): Republic off the eastern coast of Africa; capital, Antananarivo. Missionary efforts were generally fruitless from early in the 16th century until the Jesuits were permitted to start open evangelization about 1845. A prefecture apostolic was set up in 1850 and a vicariate apostolic in the north was placed in charge of the Holy Ghost Fathers in 1898. There were 100,000 Catholics by 1900. The first native bishop was ordained in 1936. The hierarchy was established in 1955. Madagascar maintains diplomatic relations with Vatican City.

Archd., 3; dioc., 14; card., 1 (nat.); abp., 2 (nat.); bp., 16 (14 nat.); parishes, 228; priests, 687 (164 dioc., 523 rel.); sem., 166; bros., 367; srs., 1,889; bap., 74,834; Caths., 1,993,000 (22.2%); tot. pop. 8,960,000.

Madeira Islands: Portuguese province, an archipelago 340 miles west of the northwestern coast of Africa; capital, Funchal. Catholicism has had a continuous history since the first half of the 15th century. Statistics are included in those for Portugal.

Malawi: Republic in the interior of eastern Africa; capital, Lilongwe. Missionary work, begun by Jesuits in the late 16th and early 17th centuries, was generally ineffective until the end of the 19th century. The White Fathers arrived in 1889 and later were joined by others. A vicariate was set up in 1897. The hierarchy was established in 1959. Malawi maintains diplomatic relations with Vatican City.

Archd., 1; dioc., 6; abp., 1 (nat.); bp., 6 (4 nat.); parishes, 130; priests, 335 (111 dioc., 224 rel.); sem., 147; bros., 97; srs., 635; bap., 48,329; Caths., 1,230,000 (20%); tot. pop., 6,120,000.

Malaysia: Parliamentary democracy in southeastern Asia; federation of former states of Malaya, Sabah (former Br. North Borneo), and Sarawak; capital, Kuala Lumpur. Christianity, introduced by Portuguese colonists about 1511, was confined almost exclusively to Malacca until late in the 18th century. The effectiveness of evangelization increased from then on because of the recruitment and training of native clergy. Singapore (see separate entry), founded in 1819, became a center for missionary work. Seventeen thousand Catholics were in the Malacca diocese in 1888. Effective evangelization in Sabah and Sarawak began in the second half of the 19th century. The hierarchy was established in 1973. Malaysia has an apostolic delegate.

Archd., 2; dioc., 4; abp., 2; bp., 5 (nat.); parishes, 156; priests, 264 (174 dioc., 90 rel.); p.d., 1; sem., 71; bros., 109; srs., 586; bap., 14,306; Caths., 456,000 (3.1%); tot. pop., 14,420,000.

Maldives: Republic, an archipelago 400 miles southwest of India and Ceylon; capital, Male. No serious attempt was ever made to evangelize the area, which is completely Moslem.

Tot. pop., 160,000.

Mali: Republic, inland in western Africa; capital, Bamako. Catholicism was introduced late in the second half of the 19th century. Missionary work made little progress in the midst of the predominantly Moslem population. A vicariate was set up in 1921. The hierarchy was established in 1955. Established diplomatic relations with Vatican City in 1979.

Archd., 1; dioc., 5; abp., 1 (nat.); bp., 5 (3 nat.); parishes, 37; priests, 149 (23 dioc., 126 rel.); sem., 17; bros., 28; srs., 156; bap., 2,243; Caths., 70,000 (.97%); tot. pop., 7,160,000.

Malta: Parliamentary democracy 58 miles south of Sicily; capital, Valletta. Early catacombs and inscriptions are evidence of the early introduction of Christianity. St. Paul was shipwrecked on Malta in 60. Saracens controlled the island(s) from 870 to 1090, a period of difficulty for the Church. The line of bishops extends from 1090 to the present. Passage of a bill in 1983 expropriating most church-owned property was denounced by the bishops as unwarranted interference in spiritual matters. Malta maintains diplomatic relations with Vatican City.

Archd., 1; dioc., 1; abp., 1; bp., 1; parishes, 79; priests, 1,096 (653 dioc., 443 rel.); sem., 132; bros., 108; srs., 1,552; bap., 5,625; Caths., 340,000 (91%); tot. pop., 370,000.

Marianas, The: U.S. Trust territory in Pacific (scheduled to become a U.S. commonwealth). Under ecclesiastical jurisdiction of Agana diocese, Guam.

Parishes, 8; priests, 4 (dioc.); p.d., 2; srs., 19; bap., 730, Caths., 18,000; tot. pop., 24,000.

Martinique: French overseas department in the West Indies, about 130 miles south of Guadeloupe; capital, Fort-de-France. Catholicism was introduced in the 16th century. The hierarchy was established in 1967.

Archd., 1; abp., 1; parishes, 47; priests, 102 (45 dioc., 57 rel.); sem., 7; bros., 12; srs., 226; bap., 4,091; Caths., 308,000; tot. pop., 340,000.

Mauritania: Islamic republic on the northwest coast of Africa; capital, Nouakchott. With few exceptions, the Catholics in the country are members of the foreign colony. Mauritania has an apostolic delegate.

Dioc., 1; bp., 1; parishes, 6; priests, 11 (2 dioc., 9 rel.); bro., 1; srs., 28; bap., 54; Caths., 5,000 (.3%); tot. pop., 1,630,000.

Mauritius: Self-governing island state 500 miles east of Madagascar; capital, Port Louis. Catholicism was introduced by Vincentians in 1722. Port Louis, made a vicariate in 1819, was a jumping-off point for missionaries to Australia, Madagascar and South Africa. Mauritius maintains diplomatic relations with Vatican City.

Dioc., 1; bp., 1; parishes, 44; priests, 163 (85 dioc., 78 rel.); sem., 5; bros., 49; srs., 320;

bap., 7,136; Caths., 350,000 (36%); tot. pop., 970,000.

Melilla: Spanish possession in northern Africa. Statistics are included in those for Spain.

Mexico (United States of Mexico): Republic in Middle America. Christianity was introduced early in the 16th century. Mexico City, made a diocese in 1530, became the missionary and cultural center of the whole country. Missionary work, started in 1524 and forwarded principally by Franciscans, Dominicans, Augustinians and Jesuits, resulted in the baptism of all persons in the central plateau by the end of the century. Progress there and in the rest of the country continued in the following century but tapered off and went into decline in the 18th century, for a variety of reasons ranging from diminishing government support to relaxations of Church discipline. The wars of independence, 1810-21, in which some Catholics participated, created serious problems of adjustment for the Church. Social problems, political unrest and government opposition climaxed in the constitution of 1917 which practically outlawed the Church. Persecution took serious tolls of life and kept the Church underground, under Calles, 1924-1928, again in 1931, and under Cardenas in 1934. President Camacho, 1940-1946, ended persecution and instituted a more lenient policy. The Church, however, still labors under legal and practical disabilities. Mexico has an apostolic delegate; the Mexican president has a personal envoy to the Vatican.

Archd., 12; dioc., 52; card., 3; abp., 10; bp., 74; parishes, 4,072; priests, 10,235 (7,162 dioc., 3,073 rel.); p.d., 42; sem., 3,385; bros., 1,155; srs., 25,468; bap., 1,903,594; Caths., 68,600,000; tot. pop., 71,190,000.

Monaco: Constitutional monarchy, an enclave on the Mediterranean coast of France near the Italian border; capital, Monaco-Ville. Christianity was introduced before 1000. Catholicism is the official religion but freedom is guaranteed for all. Monaco has an ambassador at Vatican City.

Archd., 1; abp., 1; parishes, 5; priests, 32 (15 dioc., 17 rel.); p.d., 1; sem., 4; bros., 24; srs., 61; bap., 220; Caths., 28,000; tot. pop., 30,000.

Mongolia: Republic in north central Asia; capital Ulaanbaatar. Christianity was introduced by Nestorians. Some Franciscans were in the country in the 13th and 14th centuries, en route to China. Limited evangelization efforts from the 18th century had little success among the Mongols in Outer Mongolia, where Buddhism has predominated for hundreds of years. No Christians were known to be there in 1953. There may be a few Catholics in Inner Mongolia. No foreign missionaries have been in the country since 1953.

Pop., 1,670,000.

Montserrat: British island possession in Caribbean; capital, Plymouth. Under ecclesiastical jurisdiction of St. John's-Basseterre diocese, Antigua.

Parishes, 2; priests, 2 (1 dioc., 1 rel.); p.d.; 1; srs., 5; bap., 35; Caths., 1,000; tot. pop., 13,000.

Morocco: Constitutional monarchy in northwest Africa with Atlantic and Mediterranean coastlines; capital, Rabat. Christianity was known in the area by the end of the third century. Bishops from Morocco attended a council at Carthage in 484. Catholic life survived under Visigoth and, from 700, Arab rule; later it became subject to influence from the Spanish, Portuguese and French. Islam is the state religion. The hierarchy was established in 1955. Morocco maintains diplomatic relations with Vatican City.

Archd., 2; parishes, 63; priests, 100 (25 dioc., 75 rel.); bros., 10; srs., 417; bap., 132; Caths., 78,000 (.37%); tot. pop., 20,650,000.

Mozambique: Independent (June 25, 1975) republic in southeast Africa, bordering on the Indian Ocean; former Portuguese territory; capital, Maputo (formerly Lourenco Marques). Christianity was introduced by Portuguese Jesuits about the middle of the 16th century. Evangelization continued from then until the 18th century when it went into decline largely because of the Portuguese government's expulsion of the Jesuits. Conditions worsened in the 1830s, improved after 1881, but deteriorated again during the anticlerical period from 1910 to 1925. Conditions improved in 1940, the year Portugal concluded a new concordat with the Holy See and the hierarchy was established. Outspoken criticism by missionaries of Portuguese policies in Mozambique resulted in Church-state tensions in the years immediately preceding independence. Tension continues to be a factor, although to a smaller degree, in relations between the Church and the Marxist-oriented government in power since 1975. The first two native bishops were ordained March 9, 1975. Mozambique has an apostolic delegate.

Archd., 1; dioc., 8; abp., 1 (nat.); bp., 8 (7 nat.); parishes, 251; priests, 264 (24 dioc., 240 rel.); sem., 19; bros., 77; srs., 501; bap., 22,030; Caths., 1,700,000 (15.7%); tot. pop., 10,760,000.

Namibia (South West Africa): Territory in South Africa in dispute between the Republic of South Africa and the United Nations; capital, Windhoek. The area shares the history of South Africa. Namibia has an apostolic delegate (to Southern Africa).

V.a., 2; bp., 2 (1 nat); parishes, 61; priests, 74 (2 dioc., 72 rel.); p.d., 14; sem., 5; bros., 54; srs., 272; bap., 7,841; Caths., 168,000; tot. pop., 1,028,000.

Nauru: Independent republic in western Pacific; capital, Yaren. Under ecclesiastical jurisdiction of Tarawa and Nauru diocese, (Tarawa).

Srs., 4; bap., 70; Caths., 2,000; tot. pop., 7,000.

Nepal: Constitutional monarchy, the only Hindu kingdom in the world, in central Asia south of the Himalayas between India and Tibet; capital, Kathmandu. Little is known of the country before the 15th century. Some Jesuits passed through from 1628 and some sections were evangelized in the 18th century, with minimal results, before the country was closed to foreigners. Conversions from Hinduism, the state religion, are not recog-

nized in law. Christian missionary work is not allowed. Catholics in the country have been under the jurisdiction of the Patna diocese, India, since 1919.

Priests, 28 (rel); bros., 6; srs., 26; bap., 20; Caths., 300; tot. pop., 15,020,000.

Netherlands: Kingdom in northwestern Europe; capital, Amsterdam (seat of the government, The Hague). Evangelization, begun about the turn of the sixth century by Irish, Anglo-Saxon and Frankish missionaries, resulted in Christianization of the country by 800 and subsequent strong influence on The Lowlands. Invasion by French Calvinists in 1572 brought serious losses to the Catholic Church and made the Reformed Church dominant. Catholics suffered a practical persecution of official repression and social handicap in the 17th century. The schism of Utrecht occurred in 1724. Only one-third of the population was Catholic in 1726. The Church had only a skeleton organization from 1702 to 1853, when the hierarchy was reestablished. Despite this upturn, cultural isolation was the experience of Catholics until about 1914. From then on new vigor came into the life of the Church, and a whole new climate of interfaith relations began to develop. Before and for some years following the Second Vatican Council, the thrust and variety of thought and practice in the Dutch Church moved it to the vanguard position of "progressive" renewal. A particular synod of Dutch bishops held at the Vatican in January, 1980, and aimed at internal improvement of the Church in the Netherlands, had disappointing results, according to reports in 1981. The Netherlands maintains diplomatic relations with Vatican City.

Archd., 1; dioc., 6; card., 3; bp., 10; parishes, 1,794; priests 6,867 (2,617 dioc., 4,250 rel.); p.d., 21; sem., 292; bros., 3,158; srs., 22,300; bap., 56,387; Caths., 5,677,000 (39.8%); tot. pop., 14,240,000.

Netherlands Antilles (Curacao): Autonomous part of the Kingdom of The Netherlands. Consists of two groups of islands in the Caribbean: Curacao, Aruba and Bonaire, off the northern coast of Venezuela; and St. Eustatius, Saba and the southern part of St. Martaan, southeast of Puerto Rico; capital, Willemstad on Curacao. Christianity was introduced in the 16th century. Apostolic delegation was established in 1975.

Dioc., 1; bp., 1; parishes, 47; priests, 60 (11 dioc., 49 rel.); sem., 1; bros., 53; srs., 143; bap., 3,734; Caths., 224,000 (83.8%); tot. pop., 267,000.

New Caledonia: French territory consisting of several islands in Oceania east of Queensland, Australia; capital, Noumea. Catholicism was introduced in 1843, nine years after Protestant missionaries began evangelization. A vicariate was organized in 1847. The hierarchy was established in 1966.

Archd., 1; abp., 1; parishes, 36; priests, 60 (11 dioc., 49 rel.); sem., 5; bros., 75; srs., 199; bap., 1,750; Caths., 91,000; tot. pop., 142,000.

New Zealand: Dominion in the British Commonwealth, a group of islands in Oceania 1,200 miles southeast of Australia: capital, Wellington. Protestant missionaries were the first evangelizers. On North Island, Catholic missionaries started work before the establishment of two dioceses in 1848; their work among the Maoris was not organized until about 1881. On South Island, whose first resident priest arrived in 1840, a diocese was established in 1869. These three jurisdictions were joined in a province in 1896. The Marists were the outstanding Catholic missionaries in the area. Established diplomatic relations with Vatican City, 1973.

Archd., 1; dioc., 5; card., 1 (1983); bp., 6; parishes, 283; priests, 806 (440 dioc., 366 rel.); sem., 93; bros., 306; srs., 1,995; bap., 8,871; Caths. 494,000; tot. pop., 3,130,000.

Nicaragua: Republic in Central America: capital, Managua. Evangelization began shortly after the Spanish conquest about 1524 and eight years later the first bishop took over jurisdiction of the Church in the country. Jesuits were leaders in missionary work during the colonial period, which lasted until the 1820s. Evangelization endeavor increased after establishment of the republic in 1838. In this century it was extended to the Atlantic coastal area where Protestant missionaries had begun work about the middle of the 1900s. Many church leaders, clerical and lay, supported the aims but not necessarily all the methods of the revolution which forced the resignation and flight July 17, 1979, of Anastasio Somoza Debayle, whose family had controlled the government since the early 1930s. Nicaragua maintains diplomatic relations with Vatican City. (See Index for papal visit and 1983 developments.)

Archd., 1; dioc., 4; prel., 2; v.a., 1; abp., 1; bp., 7; parishes, 177; priests, 311 (125 dioc., 216 rel.); p.d., 28; sem., 52; bros., 95; srs., 701; bap., 64,372; Caths., 2,559,000 (90.7%); 2,820,000.

Niger: Republic in west central Africa; capital, Niamey. The first mission was set up in 1831. A prefecture apostolic was organized in 1942 and the first diocese was established in 1961. The country is predominantly Moslem. Niger maintains diplomatic relations with Vatican City.

Dioc., 1; bp., 1; parishes, 11; priests, 27 (4 dioc., 23 rel.); sem., 1; bros., 12; srs., 77; bap., 139; Caths., 14,000 (.25%); tot. pop., 5,430,000.

Nigeria: Republic in western Africa; capital, Lagos. The Portuguese introduced Catholicism in the coastal region in the 15th century. Capuchins did some evangelization in the 17th century but systematic missionary work did not get under way along the coast until about 1840. A vicariate for this area was organized in 1870. A prefecture was set up in 1911 for missions in the northern part of the country where Islam was strongly entrenched. From 1967, when Biafra seceded, until early in 1970 the country was torn by civil war. The hierarchy was established in 1950. Nigeria maintains diplomatic relations with Vatican City.

Archd., 3; dioc., 28; card., 1 (nat.); abp., 3 (nat.); bp., 30 (23 nat.); parishes, 473; priests, 1,350 (778 dioc., 572 rel.); p.d., 11;

sem., 1,205; bros., 199; srs., 1,240; bap., 256,585; Caths., 5,520,000 (6.9%); tot. pop., 79,680,000.

Niue: New Zealand self-governing territory in South Pacific. Under ecclesiastical jurisdiction of Rarotonga diocese, Cook Islands.

Parish, 1; priest, 1 (rel.); srs., 2; Caths., 200; tot. pop., 3,000.

Norway: Constitutional monarchy in northern Europe, the western part of the Scandinavian peninsula; capital, Oslo. Evangelization begun in the ninth century by missionaries from England and Ireland put the Church on a firm footing about the turn of the 11th century. The first diocese was set up in 1153 and development of the Church progressed until the Black Death in 1349 inflicted losses from which it never recovered. Lutheranism, introduced from outside in 1537 and furthered cautiously, gained general acceptance by about 1600 and was made the state religion. Legal and other measures crippled the Church, forcing priests to flee the country and completely disrupting normal activity. Changes for the better came in the 19th century, with the granting of religious liberty in 1845 and the repeal of many legal disabilities in 1897. Norway was administered as a single apostolic vicariate from 1892 to 1932, when it was divided into three jurisdictions under the supervision of the Congregation for the Propagation of the Faith. Established diplomatic relations with Vatican City in 1982.

Dioc., 1; prel., 2; bp., 4; parishes, 27; priests, 62 (17 dioc., 45 rel.); sem., 6; bro., 1; srs., 333; bap., 264; Caths., 16,000; tot. pop., 4,100,000.

Oman: Independent monarchy in eastern corner of Arabian Peninsula; capital, Muscat. Under ecclesiastical jurisdiction of Arabia vicariate apostolic.

Parish, 1; priests, 2 (1 dioc., 1 rel.); srs., 9; bap., 45; Caths., 6,000; tot. pop., 920,000.

Pakistan: Islamic republic in southwestern Asia; capital, Islamabad. (Formerly included East Pakistan which became the independent nation of Bangladesh in 1971.) Islam, firmly established in the eighth century, is the state religion. Christian evangelization of the native population began about the middle of the 19th century, years after earlier scattered attempts. The hierarchy was established in 1950. Pakistan maintains diplomatic relations with Vatican City.

Archd., 1; dioc., 5; card., 1 (nat.); bp., 7 (5 nat.); parishes, 53; priests, 247 (90 dioc., 157 rel.); p.d., 2; sem., 50; bros., 54; srs., 682; bap., 23,964; Caths., 480,000 (.5%); tot. pop., 84,580,000.

Panama: Republic in Central America; capital, Panama City. Catholicism was introduced by Franciscan missionaries and evangelization started in 1514. The Panama diocese, oldest in the Americas, was set up at the same time. The Catholic Church has favored status and state aid for missions, charities and parochial schools, but religious freedom is guaranteed to all religions. Panama maintains diplomatic relations with Vatican City. (See Index for papal visit.)

Archd., 1; dioc., 3; prel., 1; v.a., 1; abp., 1; bp., 6; parishes, 137; priests, 302 (78 dioc., 224 rel.); p.d., 5; sem., 105; bros., 39; srs., 490; bap., 35,247; Caths., 1,727,000 (89%); tot. pop., 1,940,000.

Papua New Guinea: Independent (Sept. 16, 1975) republic (formerly under Australian administration) in southwest Pacific. Consists of the eastern half of the southwestern Pacific island of New Guinea and the Northern Solomon Islands; capital, Port Moresby. (For statistics on the Indonesian portion of New Guinea, see Indonesia.) Marists began evangelization about 1844 but were handicapped by many factors, including "spheres of influence" laid out for Catholic and Protestant missionaries. A prefecture apostolic was set up in 1896 and placed in charge of the Divine Word Missionaries. The territory suffered greatly during World War II. Hierarchy was established for New Guinea and adjacent islands in 1966. Papua New Guinea established diplomatic relations with the Vatican in 1977.

Archd., 4; dioc., 14; abp., 4; bp., 15; parishes, 316; priests, 516 (55 dioc., 461 rel.); p.d., 12; sem., 148; bros., 353; srs., 948; bap., 32,963; Caths., 916,000 (30%); tot. pop., 3,010,000.

Paraguay: Republic in central South America; capital, Asuncion. Catholicism was introduced in 1542, evangelization began almost immediately. A diocese erected in 1547 was occupied for the first time in 1556. On many occasions thereafter dioceses in the country were left unoccupied because of political and other reasons. Jesuits who came into the country after 1609 devised the reductions system for evangelizing the Indians, teaching them agriculture, husbandry, trades and other useful arts, and giving them experience in property use and community life. The reductions were communes of Indians only, under the direction of the missionaries. About 50 of them were established in southern Brazil, Uruguay and northeastern Argentina as well as in Paraguay. They had an average population of three to four thousand. At their peak, some 30 reductions had a population of 100,000. Political officials regarded the reductions with disfavor because they did not control them and feared that the Indians trained in them might foment revolt and upset the established colonial system under Spanish control. The reductions lasted until about 1768 when their Jesuit founders and directors were expelled from Latin America. Church-state relations following independence from Spain in 1811 were tense as often as not because of government efforts to control the Church through continued exercise of Spanish patronage rights and by other means. The Church as well as the whole country suffered a great deal during the War of the Triple Alliance from 1865-70. After that time, the Church had the same kind of experience in Paraguay as in the rest of Latin America with forces of liberalism, anticlericalism, massive educational needs, poverty, a shortage of priests and other personnel. Most recently church leaders have been challenging the government to initiate long-needed economic and social reforms. Paraguay maintains diplomatic relations with Vatican City.

Archd., 1; dioc., 8; prel., 2; v.a., 2; abp., 1; bp., 14; parishes, 266; priests, 554 (185 dioc., 369 rel.); p.d., 13; sem., 172; bros., 96; srs., 977; bap., 90,572; Caths., 2,992,000 (91.4%); tot. pop., 3,270,000.

Peru: Republic on the western coast of South America; capital, Lima. An effective diocese became operational in 1537, five years after the Spanish conquest. Evangelization, already under way, developed for some time after 1570 but deteriorated before the end of the colonial period in the 1820s. The first native-born saint of the new world was a Peruvian, Rose of Lima, a Dominican tertiary who died in 1617 and was canonized in 1671. In the new republic founded after the wars of independence the Church experienced problems of adjustment and many of the difficulties that cropped up in other South American countries: government efforts to control it through continuation of the patronage rights of the Spanish crown; suppression of houses of religious and expropriation of church property; religious indifference and outright hostility. The Church was given special status but was not made the established religion. Repressive measures by the government against labor protests have been condemned by Church leaders in the past several years. Peru maintains diplomatic relations with Vatican City.

Archd., 7; dioc., 12; prel., 13; v.a., 8; card., 1; abp., 5; bp., 44; parishes, 1,200; priests, 2,198 (920 dioc., 1,278 rel.); p.d., 36; sem., 787; bros., 427; srs., 4,944; bap., 447,724; Caths., 16,898,000 (92.4%); tot. pop., 18,280,000.

Philippine Islands: Republic, an archipelago of 7,000 islands off the southeast coast of Asia; capital, Quezon City. Systematic evangelization was begun in 1564 and resulted in firm establishment of the Church by the 19th century. During the period of Spanish rule, which lasted from the discovery of the islands by Magellan in 1521 to 1898, the Church experienced difficulties with the patronage system under which the Spanish crown tried to control ecclesiastical affairs through episcopal and other appointments. This system ended in 1898 when the United States gained possession of the islands and instituted a policy of separation of Church and state. Anticlericalism flared late in the 19th century. The Aglipayan schism, an attempt to set up a nationalist church, occurred a few years later, in 1902. The government of Ferdinand Marcos has been under attack by people of the church for the past several years for violations of human rights. The republic maintains diplomatic relations with Vatican City.

Archd., 16; dioc., 41; prel., 5; v.a., 5; card., 1; abp., 15; bp., 69; parishes, 2,037; priests, 4,969 (2,721 dioc., 2,248 rel.); p.d., 9; sem., 3,997; bros., 341; srs., 8,350; bap., 1,277,281; Caths., 41,520,000 (83.8%); tot. pop., 49,530,000.

Poland: People's republic in eastern Europe; capital, Warsaw. The first traces of Christianity date from the second half of the ninth century. Its spread was accelerated by the union of the Slavs in the 10th century. The first bishopric was set up in 968. The Gniezno archdiocese, with suffragan sees and a mandate to evangelize the borderlands as well as Poland, was established in 1000. Steady growth continued thereafter, with religious orders and their schools playing a major role. Some tensions with the Orthodox were experienced. The Reformation, supported mainly by city dwellers and the upper classes, peaked from about the middle of the 16th century, resulting in numerous conversions to Lutheranism, the Reformed Church and the Bohemian Brethren. A successful Counter-Reformation, with the Jesuits in a position of leadership, was completed by about 1632. The movement served a nationalist as well as religious purpose; in restoring religious unity to a large degree, it united the country against potential invaders, the Swedes, Russians and Turks. The Counter-Reformation had bad side effects, leading to the repression of Protestants long after it was over and to prejudice against Orthodox who returned to allegiance with Rome in 1596 and later. The Church, in the same manner as the entire country, was adversely affected by the partitions of the 18th and 19th centuries. Russification hurt the Orthodox who had reunited with Rome and the Latins who were in the majority. Germans extended their Kulturkampf to the area they controlled. The Austrians exhibited some degree of tolerance. In the republic established after World War I the Church reorganized itself, continued to serve as a vital force in national life, and enjoyed generally harmonious relations with the state. Progressive growth was strong until 1939 when disaster struck in the form of invasion by German and Russian forces and six years of war. In 1945, seven years before the adoption of a Soviet-type of constitution, the Communist-controlled government initiated a policy that included a constant program of atheistic propaganda; a strong campaign against the hierarchy and clergy; the imprisonment in 1948 of 700 priests and even more religious; rigid limitation of the activities of religious; censorship and curtailment of the Catholic press and Catholic Action; interference with church administration and appointments of the clergy; the "deposition" of Cardinal Wyszynski in 1953 and the imprisonment of other members of the hierarchy; the suppression of "Caritas," the Catholic charitable organization; promotion of "Progressive Catholic" activities and a small minority of "patriotic priests." Establishment of the Gomulka regime, the freeing of Cardinal Wyszynski in October, 1956, and the signing of an agreement two months later by bishops and state officials, led to some improvement of conditions. The underlying fact, however, was that the regime conceded to Catholics only so much as was necessary to secure support of the government as a more tolerable evil than the harsh and real threat of a Russian-imposed puppet government like that in Hungary. This has been the controlling principle in Church-state relations. Auxiliary Bishop Ladislaw Rubin of Gniezno sketched the general state of affairs in March, 1968. He said that there was no sign that

the government had any intention of releasing its oppressive grip on the Church. As evidence of the "climate of asphyxiation" in the country he cited: persistent questioning of priests by officials concerning their activities; the prohibition against Catholic schools, hospitals and charitable works; the financial burden of a 60 per cent tax on church income. Cardinal Wyszynski denounced "enforced atheism" in a Lenten pastoral in the same year. In May, 1969, the bishops drafted a list of grievances against the government which, they said, were "only some examples of difficulties which demonstrated the situation of the Church in our homeland." The grievances were: refusal of permits to build new churches and establish new parishes; refusal of permission "for the organization of new religion classes"; pressure on Catholics who attend religious ceremonies; censorship and the lack of an independent Catholic daily newspaper; lack of representation in public life; restriction of "freedom to conduct normal pastoral work" in the western portion of the country. There was a move toward improvement in Church-state relations in 1971-72. In 1973, the Polish bishops issued a pastoral letter urging Catholics to resist the official atheism imposed by the government. In 1974 the Polish bishops expressed approval of renewed Vatican efforts at regularizing Church-state relations but insisted that they (the bishops) be consulted on every step of the negotiations. The bishops have continued their sharp criticism of anti-religious policies and human rights violations of the government. Regular contacts on a working level were established by the Vatican and Poland in 1974. (See Index for papal visit, 1983 events.)

Archd., 7; dioc., 21; card., 3; abp., 3; bp., 79; parishes, 7,641; priests, 19,745 (15,255 dioc., 4,490 rel.); sem., 6,566; bros., 1,129; srs., 25,331; bap., 711,351; Caths., 33,720,000 (93.9%); tot. pop., 35,900,000.

Polynesia, French: French possession in the southern Pacific, including Tahiti and the Marquesas Islands; capital, Papeete. The first phase of evangelization in the Marquesas Islands, begun in 1838, resulted in 216 baptisms in 10 years. A vicariate was organized in 1848 but real progress was not made until after the baptism of native rulers in 1853. Persecution caused missionaries to leave the islands several times. By the 1960s, more than 95 per cent of the population was Catholic. Isolated attempts to evangelize Tahiti were made in the 17th and 18th centuries. Two Picpus Fathers began missionary work in 1831. A vicariate was organized in 1848. By 1908, despite the hindrances of Protestant opposition, disease and other factors, the Church had firm roots.

Archd., 1; dioc., 1; abp., 1 (nat.); bp., 1; parishes, 78; priests, 37 (8 dioc., 29 rel.); p.d., 7; sem., 3; bros., 24; srs., 65; bap., 1,455; Caths., 52,000; tot. pop., 151,000.

Portugal: Republic in the western part of the Iberian peninsula; capital, Lisbon. Christianity was introduced before the fourth century. From the fifth century to early in the eighth century the Church experienced difficulties from the physical invasion of barbarians and the intellectual invasion of doctrinal errors in the forms of Arianism, Priscillianism and Pelagianism. The Church survived under the rule of Arabs from about 711 and of the Moors until 1249. Ecclesiastical life was fairly vigorous from 1080 to 1185, and monastic influence became strong. A decline set in about 1450. Several decades later Portugal became the jumping-off place for many missionaries to newly discovered colonies. The Reformation had little effect in the country. Beginning about 1750, Pombal, minister of foreign affairs and prime minister, mounted a frontal attack on the Jesuits whom he succeeded in expelling from Portugal and the colonies. His anti-Jesuit campaign successful Pombal also attempted, and succeeded to some extent, in controlling the Church in Portugal until his fall from power about 1777. Liberal revolutionaries with anti-Church policies made the 19th century a difficult one for the Church. Similar policies prevailed in Church-state relations in this century until the accession of Salazar to power in 1928. In 1940 he concluded a concordat with the Holy See which regularized Church-state relations but still left the Church in a subservient condition. The prevailing spirit of church authorities in Portugal has been conservative. In 1971 several priests were tried for subversion for speaking out against colonialism and for taking part in guerrilla activities in Angola. A military coup of Apr. 25, 1974, triggered a succession of chaotic political developments which led to an attempt by Communists, after receiving only 18 per cent of the votes cast in a national election, to take over the government in the summer of 1975. Portugal maintains diplomatic relations with Vatican City.

Patriarchate, 1; archd., 2; dioc., 17; card., 1; abp., 2; bp., 24; parishes, 4,278; priests, 4,924 (3,755 dioc., 1,169 rel.); p.d., 2; sem., 520; bros., 524; srs., 7,649; bap., 156,219; Caths., 9,355,000 (94%); tot. pop., 9,930,000.

Puerto Rico: A U.S. commonwealth, the smallest of the Greater Antilles, 885 miles southeast of the southern coast of Florida; capital, San Juan. Following its discovery by Columbus in 1493, the island was evangelized by Spanish missionaries and remained under Spanish ecclesiastical as well as political control until 1898 when it became a possession of the United States. The original diocese, San Juan, was erected in 1511. The present hierarchy was established in 1960. Puerto Rico has an apostolic delegate (nuncio to Dominican Republic).

Archd., 1; dioc., 4; card., 1; bp., 8; parishes, 263; priests, 719 (266 dioc., 453 rel.); p.d., 120; sem., 157; bros., 85; srs., 1,442; bap., 49,045; Caths., 2,990,000 (81.2%); tot. pop., 3,680,000.

Qatar: Independent state in the Persian Gulf; capital, Doha. Under ecclesiastical jurisdiction of Arabia vicariate apostolic.

Priest, 1 (rel.); bap., 54; Caths., 6,000; tot. pop., 250,000.

Reunion: French overseas department, 450 miles east of Madagascar; capital, Saint-Denis. Catholicism was introduced in 1667 and some intermittent missionary work was done through the rest of the century. A prefecture apostolic was organized in 1712. Vincentians began work there in 1817 and were joined later by Holy Ghost Fathers. Reunion has an apostolic delegate.

Dioc., 1; bp., 1; parishes, 67; priests, 114 (60 dioc., 54 rel.); sem., 10; bros., 45; srs., 592; bap., 11,037; Caths., 457,000; tot. pop., 503,000.

Rhodes: Greek island in the Aegean Sea, 112 miles from the southwestern coast of Asia Minor. A diocese was established about the end of the third century. A bishop from Rhodes attended the Council of Nicaea in 325. Most of the Christians followed the Eastern Churches into schism in the 11th century and became Orthodox. Turks controlled the island from 1522 to 1912. The small Catholic population, for whom a diocese existed from 1328 to 1546, lived in crossfire between Turks and Orthodox. After 1719 Franciscans provided pastoral care for the Catholics, for whom an archdiocese was erected in 1928. Statistics are included in Greece.

Romania: Socialist republic in southeastern Europe; capital, Bucharest. Latin Christianity, introduced in the third century, all but disappeared during the barbarian invasions. The Byzantine Rite was introduced by the Bulgars about the beginning of the eighth century and established firm roots. It eventually became Orthodox, but a large number of its adherents returned later to union with Rome. Attempts to reintroduce the Latin Rite on any large scale have been unsuccessful. Communists took over the government following World War II, forced the abdication of Michael I in 1947, and enacted a Soviet type of constitution in 1952. By that time a campaign against religion was already in progress. In 1948 the government denounced a concordat concluded in 1929, nationalized all schools and passed a law on religions which resulted in the disorganization of Church administration. The 1.5 million-member Romanian Byzantine Rite Church, by government decree, was incorporated into the Romanian Orthodox Church, and the Orthodox bishops then seized the cathedrals of Roman Catholic bishops. Five of the six Latin Rite bishops were immediately disposed of by the government, and the last was sentenced to 18 years' imprisonment in 1951, when a great many arrests of priests and laymen were made. Religious orders were suppressed in 1949. Since 1948 more than 50 priests have been executed and 200 have died in prison. One hundred priests were reported in prison at the end of 1958. Some change for the better in Church-state relations was reported after the middle of the summer of 1964, although restrictions were still in effect. About 1,200 priests were engaged in parish work in August, 1965.

Archd., 2; dioc., 8; ord., 1; bp., 2. No recent statistics are available on the number of Catholics. There were an estimated 1,140,000 Catholics (5.9% of the population) in 1969. Tot. pop., 22,460,000.

Rwanda: Republic in east central Africa; capital, Kigali. Catholicism was introduced about the turn of the 20th century. The hierarchy was established in 1959. Intertribal warfare between the ruling Hutus (90 per cent of the population) and the Tutsis (formerly the ruling aristocracy) plagued the country for a number of years. Rwanda maintains diplomatic relations with Vatican City.

Archd., 1; dioc., 7; abp., 1 (nat.); bp., 7 (6 nat.); parishes, 110; priests, 455 (266 dioc., 189 rel.); sem., 143; bros., 210; srs., 749; bap., 98,731; Caths., 2,202,000 (43%); tot. pop., 5,110,000.

Saint Christopher (Kitts)-Nevis: British Associated State in West Indies; capital, Basseterre, on St. Christopher. Under ecclesiastical jurisdiction of St. John's-Basseterre diocese, Antigua.

Parishes, 5; priests, 3 (rel.); bap., 94; Caths., 4,000; tot. pop., 67,000. Statistics include Anguilla.

Saint Lucia: Independent (Feb. 22, 1979) island state in West Indies; capital, Castries.

Archd., 1; abp., 1; parishes, 22; priests, 31 (9 dioc., 23 rel.); p.d., 1; sem., 4; bro., 1; srs., 32; bap., 3,201; Caths., 109,000; tot. pop., 120,000.

Saint Pierre and Miquelon: French overseas department, islands near the southwest coast of Newfoundland. Catholicism was introduced about 1689.

V.a., 1; bp., 1; parishes, 3; priests, 4 (1 dioc., 3 rel.); srs., 13; bap., 102; Caths., 6,000; tot. pop., 6,350.

Saint Vincent and the Grenadines: Independent State in West Indies; capital, Kingstown. Under ecclesiastical jurisdiction of Bridgetown-Kingstown diocese, Barbados.

Parishes, 7; priests, 4 (rel.); bros., 8; srs., 13; bap., 276; Caths., 14,000; tot. pop., 122,000.

Samoa, American: Unincorporated U.S. territory in southwestern Pacific, consisting of six small islands; seat of government, Pago Pago on the Island of Tutuila. Samoa-Pago Pago diocese established in 1982.

Dioc., 1; priests, 7 (3 dioc., 4 rel.); sem., 4; bros., 5; srs., 16; Caths., 7,250; tot. pop., 31,000 (1983 Annuario Pontificio).

Samoa, Western: Independent state in the southwestern Pacific; capital, Apia. Catholic missionary work began in 1845. Most of the missions now in operation were established by 1870 when the Catholic population numbered about 5,000. Additional progress was made in missionary work from 1896. The first Samoan priest was ordained in 1892. A diocese was established in 1966; elevated to a metropolitan see in 1982.

Archd., 1; card., 1; parishes, 24; priests, 41 (12 dioc., 29 rel.); sem., 30; bros., 36; srs., 150; bap., 1,549; Caths., 43,000; tot. pop., 176,000 (1983 Annuario Pontificio).

San Marino: Republic, a 24-square-mile enclave in northeastern Italy; capital, San Marino. The date of initial evangelization is not known, but a diocese was established by the end of the third century. Ecclesiastically, it forms part of the diocese of San Marino-Montefeltro in Italy. San Marino is represented by a minister at Vatican City.

Parishes, 12; priests, 26 (13 dioc., 13 rel.); bro., 1; srs., 33; bap., 219; Caths., 20,000 (95%); tot. pop., 21,000.

Sao Tome and Principe: Independent republic (July 12, 1975), consisting of two islands off the western coast of Africa in the Gulf of Guinea; former Portuguese territory; capital Sao Tome. Evangelization was begun by the Portuguese who discovered the islands in 1471-72. The Sao Tome diocese was established in 1534.

Dioc., 1; parishes, 12; priests, 8 (rel.); bros., 2; srs., 14; bap., 3,542; Caths., 71,000; tot. pop., 90,000.

Saudi Arabia: Monarchy occupying four-fifths of Arabian peninsula; capital, Riyadh (Taif, summer capital). Under ecclesiastical jurisdiction of Arabia vicariate apostolic.

Priests, 6 (rel.); srs., 3; bap., 309; Caths., 198,000; tot. pop., 9,320,000.

Scotland: Part of the United Kingdom, in the northern British Isles; capital, Edinburgh. Christianity was introduced by the early years of the fifth century. The arrival of St. Columba and his monks in 563 inaugurated a new era of evangelization which reached into remote areas by the end of the sixth century. He was extremely influential in determining the character of the Celtic Church, which was tribal, monastic, and in union with Rome. Considerable disruption of church activity resulted from Scandinavian invasions in the late eighth and ninth centuries. By 1153 the Scottish Church took a turn away from its insularity and was drawn into closer contact with the European community. Anglo-Saxon religious and political relations, complicated by rivalries between princes and ecclesiastical superiors, were not always the happiest. Religious orders expanded greatly in the 12th century. From shortly after the Norman Conquest of England to 1560 the Church suffered adverse effects from the Hundred Years' War, the Black Death, the Western Schism and other developments. In 1560 parliament abrogated papal supremacy over the Church in Scotland and committed the country to Protestantism in 1567. The Catholic Church was proscribed, to remain that way for more than 200 years, and the hierarchy was disbanded. Defections made the Church a minority religion from that time on. Presbyterian church government was ratified in 1690. Priests launched the Scottish Mission in 1653, incorporating themselves as a mission body under a prefect apostolic and working underground to serve the faithful in much the same way their confreres did in England. About 100 heather priests, trained in clandestine places in the heather country, were ordained by the early 19th century. Catholics got some relief from legal disabilities in 1793 and more later. Many left the country about that time. Some of their numbers were filled subsequently by immigrants from Ireland. The hierarchy was restored in 1878. Scotland, though predominantly Protestant, has a better record for tolerance than Northern Ireland.

Archd., 2; dioc., 6; card., 1; abp., 1; bp., 8; parishes, 467; priests, 1,043 (800 dioc., 243 rel.); sem., 148; bros., 122; srs., 1,216; bap., 14,672 Caths., 816,557 (15.9%); tot. pop., 5,117,000 (1983 Annuario Pontificio).

Sierra Leone: Republic on the western coast of Africa; capital, Freetown. Catholicism was introduced in 1858. Members of the African Missions Society, the first Catholic missionaries in the area, were joined by Holy Ghost Fathers in 1864. Protestant missionaries were active in the area before their Catholic counterparts. Educational work had a major part in Catholic endeavor. The hierarchy was established in 1950. Sierra Leone has an apostolic delegate.

Archd., 1; dioc., 2; abp., 1; bp., 1; parishes, 27; priests, 118 (12 dioc., 106 rel.); sem., 25; bros., 11; srs., 89; bap., 2,031; Caths., 71,000 (1.9%); tot. pop., 3,570,000.

Singapore: Independent island republic off the southern tip of the Malay Peninsula; capital, Singapore. Christianity was introduced in the area by Portuguese colonists about 1511. Singapore was founded in 1819; the first parish church was built in 1846. Established diplomatic relations with Vatican City, 1981.

Archd., 1; abp., 1 (nat.); parishes, 25; priests, 102 (63 dioc., 39 rel.); sem., 13; bros., 61; srs., 254; bap., 2,952; Caths., 98,000 (4%); tot. pop., 2,440,000.

Solomon Islands: Independent (July 7, 1978) island group in Oceania; capital, Honiara, on Guadalcanal. Evangelization of the Southern Solomons, begun earlier but interrupted because of violence against them, was resumed by the Marists in 1898. A vicariate apostolic was organized in 1912. A similar jurisdiction was set up for the Western Solomons in 1959. World War II caused a great deal of damage to mission installations. Catholic statistics for the Northern Solomons, where Catholic missionary work started in 1899 and a vicariate was set up in 1930, are included in those reported for Papua New Guinea. The area has an apostolic delegate.

Archd., 1; dioc., 1; abp., 1; bp., 2; parishes, 24; priests, 40 (10 dioc., 30 rel.); sem., 2; bros., 29; srs., 130; bap., 1,861; Caths., 42,000; tot. pop., 240,000.

Somalia: Republic on the eastern coast of Africa; capital, Mogadishu. The country has been Moslem for centuries. Pastoral activity has been confined to immigrants. Schools and hospitals were nationalized in 1972, resulting in the departure of some foreign missionaries. Somalia has an apostolic delegate (to the Red Sea Region).

Dioc., 1; bp., 1; parishes, 2; priests, 8 (rel.); bros., 2; srs., 70; bap., 6; Caths., 2,000; tot. pop., 4,600,000.

South Africa: Republic in the southern part of Africa; capitals, Cape Town (legislative) and Pretoria (administrative). Christianity was introduced by the Portuguese who discovered the Cape of Good Hope in 1488. Boers, who founded Cape Town in 1652, expelled Catholics from the region. There was no Catholic missionary activity from that time until the 19th century. After a period of British opposition, a bishop established residence in 1837 and evangelization got under way thereafter among the Bantus and white immigrants. In recent years church authorities have strongly protested the white supremacy policy of apartheid which seriously infringes the human rights of the native blacks and impedes the Church from carrying out its pastoral, educational and social service functions. The hierarchy was established in 1951. South Africa has an apostolic delegate.

Archd., 4; dioc., 19; abb., 1; p.a., 2; card., 1; abp., 3; bp., 20; parishes, 614; priests, 1,194 (301 dioc., 893 rel.); p.d., 70; sem., 165; bros., 364; srs., 3,765; bap., 69,279; Caths., 2,105,000 (6.9%); tot. pop., 30,130,000. Statistics include autonomous homelands of Transkei, Bophuthatswana, Venda and Ciskei.

Spain: Nominal monarchy on the Iberian peninsula in southwestern Europe; capital, Madrid. Christians were on the peninsula by 200; some of them suffered martyrdom during persecutions of the third century. A council held in Elvira about 304/6 enacted the first legislation on clerical celibacy in the West. Vandals invaded the peninsula in the fifth century, bringing with them an Arian brand of Christianity which they retained until their conversion following the baptism of their king Reccared, in 589. One of the significant developments of the seventh century was the establishment of Toledo as the primatial see. The Visigoth kingdom lasted to the time of the Arab invasion, 711-14. The Church survived under Moslem rule but experienced some doctrinal and disciplinary irregularities as well as harassment. Reconquest of most of the peninsula was accomplished by 1248; unification was achieved during the reign of Ferdinand and Isabella. The discoveries of Columbus and other explorers ushered in an era of colonial expansion in which Spain became one of the greatest mission-sending countries in history. In 1492, in repetition of anti-Semitic actions of 694, the expulsion of unbaptized Jews was decreed, leading to mass baptisms but a questionable number of real conversions in 1502. (The Jewish minority numbered about 165,000.) Activity by the Inquisition followed. Spain was not seriously affected by the Reformation. Ecclesiastical decline set in about 1650. Anti-Church actions authorized by a constitution enacted in 1812 resulted in the suppression of religious and other encroachments on the leaders, people and goods of the Church. Political, religious and cultural turmoil recurred during the 19th century and into the 20th. A revolutionary republic was proclaimed in 1931, triggering a series of developments which led to civil war from 1936 to 1939. During the conflict, which pitted leftist Loyalists against the forces of Francisco Franco, 6,632 priests and religious and an unknown number of lay persons perished in addition to thousands of victims of combat. One-man, one-party rule, established after the civil war and with rigid control policies with respect to personal liberties and social and economic issues, continued for more than 35 years before giving way after the death of Franco to democratic reforms. The Catholic Church, long the established religion, was disestablished under a new constitution providing guarantees of freedom for other religions as well. Disestablishment was ratified with modifications of a 1976 revision of the earlier concordat of 1953.

Spain maintains diplomatic relations with Vatican City. (See Index for papal visit.)

Archd., 13; dioc., 52; card., 4; abp., 12; bp., 68; parishes, 21,423; priests, 32,328 (21,778 dioc., 10,550 rel.); p.d., 20; sem., 3,039; bros., 7,695; srs., 79,829; bap., 552,937; Caths., 37,100,000 (98.5%); tot. pop., 37,650,000.

Sri Lanka (formerly Ceylon): Independent socialist republic, island southeast of India; capital, Colombo. Effective evangelization began in 1543 and made great progress by the middle of the 17th century. The Church was seriously hampered during the Dutch period from about 1650 to 1795. Anti-Catholic laws were repealed by the British in 1806. The hierarchy was established in 1886. Leftist governments and other factors have worked against the Church since the country became independent in 1948. The high percentage of indigenous clergy and religious has been of great advantage to the Church. Sri Lanka maintains diplomatic relations with Vatican City.

Archd., 1; dioc., 8; card., 1 (nat.); abp., 1 (nat.); bp., 9 (nat.); parishes, 300; priests, 591 (345 dioc., 246 rel.); p.d., 3; sem., 236; bros., 266; srs., 2,273; bap., 29,577; Caths., 1,064,000 (7%); tot. pop., 14,990,000.

Sudan: Republic in northeastern Africa, the largest country on the continent; capital, Khartoum. Christianity was introduced from Egypt and gained acceptance in the sixth century. Under Arab rule, it was eliminated in the northern region. No Christians were in the country in 1600. Evangelization attempts begun in the 19th century in the south yielded hard-won results. By 1931 there were nearly 40,000 Catholics there, and considerable progress was made by missionaries after that time. In 1957, a year after the republic was established, Catholic schools were nationalized. An act restrictive of religious freedom went into effect in 1962, resulting in the harassment and expulsion of foreign missionaries. By 1964 all but a few Sudanese missionaries had been forced out of the southern region. The northern area, where Islam predominates, is impervious to Christian influence. Late in 1971 some missionaries were allowed to return to work in the South. Southern Sudan was granted regional autonomy within a unified country in March, 1972, thus ending often bitter fighting between the North and South dating back to 1955. The hierarchy was established in 1974. Sudan maintains diplomatic relations with Vatican City.

Archd., 2; dioc., 6; abp., 2 (nat.); bp., 5 (4 nat.); parishes, 90; priests, 146 (39 dioc., 107 rel.); p.d., 1; sem., 50; bros., 40; srs., 221; bap., 17,722; Caths., 953,000 (5%); tot. pop., 18,900,000.

Suriname (formerly Dutch Guiana): Independent (Nov. 25, 1975) state in northern South America; capital, Paramaribo. Catholicism was introduced in 1683. Evangelization began in 1817.

Dioc., 1; bp., 1; parishes, 19; priests, 33 (3 dioc., 30 rel.); p.d., 1; sem., 2; bros., 27; srs., 100; bap., 2,246; Caths., 86,000; tot. pop., 400,000.

Swaziland: Constitutional monarchy in southern Africa; almost totally surrounded by South Africa; capital, Mbabane. Missionary work was entrusted to the Servites in 1913. A prefecture apostolic was organized in 1923. The hierarchy was established in 1951. Swaziland has an apostolic delegate (to Southern Africa).

Dioc., 1; priests, 32 (4 dioc., 28 rel.); sem., 10; bros., 8; srs., 130; bap., 849; Caths., 39,000 (6.8%); tot. pop., 570,000.

Sweden: Kingdom in northwestern Europe; capital, Stockholm. Christianity was introduced by St. Ansgar, a Frankish monk, in 829/30. The Church became well established in the 12th century and was a major influence at the end of the Middle Ages. Political and other factors favored the introduction and spread of the Lutheran Church which became the state religion in 1560. The Augsburg Confession of 1530 was accepted by the government; all relations with Rome were severed; monasteries were suppressed; the very presence of Catholics in the country was forbidden in 1617. A decree of tolerance for foreign Catholics was issued about 1781. Two years later a vicariate apostolic was organized for the country. In 1873 Swedes were given the legal right to leave the Lutheran Church and join another Christian church. (Membership in the Lutheran Church is presumed by law unless notice is given of membership in another church.) In 1923 there were only 11 priests and five churches in the country. Since 1952 Catholics have enjoyed almost complete religious freedom. The hierarchy was reestablished in 1953. Hindrances to growth of the Church are the strongly entrenched established church, limited resources, a clergy shortage and the size of the country. Established diplomatic relations with Vatican City in 1982.

Dioc., 1; bp., 1; parishes, 31; priests, 97 (32 dioc., 65 rel.); sem., 2; bros., 7; srs., 227; bap., 867; Caths., 106,000 (1.2%); tot. pop., 8,320,000.

Switzerland: Republic in central Europe; capital, Bern. Christianity was introduced in the fourth century or earlier and was established on a firm footing before the barbarian invasions of the sixth century. Constance, established as a diocese in the seventh century, was a stronghold of the faith against the pagan Alamanni, in particular, who were not converted until some time in the ninth century. During this period of struggle with the barbarians, a number of monasteries of great influence were established. The Reformation in Switzerland was triggered by Zwingli in 1519 and furthered by him at Zurich until his death in battle against the Catholic cantons in 1531. Calvin set in motion the forces that made Geneva the international capital of the Reformation and transformed it into a theocracy. Catholics mobilized a Counter-Reformation in 1570, six years after Calvin's death. Struggle between Protestant and Catholic cantons was a fact of Swiss life for several hundred years. The Helvetic Constitution enacted at the turn of the 19th century embodied anti-Catholic measures and consequences, among them the dissolution of 130 monasteries. The Church was reorganized later in the century to meet the threats of liberalism, radicalism and the Kulturkampf. In the process, the Church, even though on the defensive, gained the strength and cohesion that characterizes it to the present time. The six dioceses in the country are immediately subject to the Holy See. In 1973, constitutional articles banning Jesuits from the country and prohibiting the establishment of convents and monasteries were repealed. There is a papal nuncio to Switzerland, but Switzerland does not have a diplomatic officer accredited to Vatican City.

Dioc., 6; abb., 2; bp., 7; parishes, 1,696; priests, 4,118 (2,506 dioc., 1,612 rel.); p.d., 12; sem., 218; bros., 368; srs., 10,086; bap., 35,368; Caths., 3,163,000 (48.8%); tot. pop., 6,470,000.

Syria: Arab republic in southwest Asia; capital, Damascus. Christian communities were formed in apostolic times. It is believed that St. Peter established a see at Antioch before going to Rome. Damascus became a center of influence. The area was the place of great men and great events in the early history of the Church. Monasticism developed there in the fourth century. So did the Monophysite and Monothelite heresies to which portions of the Church succumbed. Byzantine Syrians who remained in communion with Rome were given the name Melkites. Christians of various persuasions — Jacobites, Orthodox and Melkites — were subject to various degrees of harassment from the Arabs who took over in 638 and from the Ottoman Turks who isolated the country and remained in control from 1516 to the end of World War II. Syria maintains diplomatic relations with Vatican City.

Patriarchates, 3 (Antioch of Maronites, Greek Melkites and Syrians; patriarchs of Maronites and Syrians reside in Lebanon); Archd., 12 (1 Armenian, 2 Maronite, 5 Greek-Melkite, 4 Syrian); dioc., 3 (Armenian, Chaldean, Maronite); v.a., 1 (Latin); patr., 1; abp., 15; bp., 2; parishes, 185; priests, 225 (148 dioc., 77 rel.); p.d., 2; sem., 36; bros., 9; srs., 384; bap., 2,745; Caths., 238,000 (2.5%); tot. pop., 9,310,000.

Taiwan (Formosa): Location of the Nationalist Government of the Republic of China, an island 100 miles off the southern coast of mainland China; capital, Taipei. Attempts to introduce Christianity in the 17th century were unsuccessful. Evangelization in the 19th century resulted in some 1,300 converts in 1895. Missionary endeavor was hampered by the Japanese who occupied the island following the Sino-Japanese war of 1894-95. Nine thousand Catholics were reported in 1938. Great progress was made in missionary endeavor among the Chinese who emigrated to the island following the Communist take-over of the mainland in 1949. The hierarchy was established in 1952. Nationalist China maintains diplomatic relations with Vatican City.

Archd., 1; dioc., 6; abp., 1; bp., 7; parishes, 452; priests, 757 (207 dioc., 550 rel.); sem., 97; bros., 99; srs., 1,212; bap., 4,629; Caths., 290,000 (1.5%); tot. pop., 18,833,000.

Tanzania: Republic (consisting of former Tan-

ganyika on the eastern coast of Africa and former Zanzibar, an island group off the eastern coast); capital, Dar es Salaam (future capital, Dodoma). The first Catholic mission in the former Tanganyikan portion of the republic was manned by Holy Ghost Fathers in 1868. The hierarchy was established there in 1953. Zanzibar was the landing place of Augustinians with the Portuguese in 1499. Some evangelization was attempted between then and 1698 when the Arabs expelled all priests from the territory. There was no Catholic missionary activity from then until the 1860s. The Holy Ghost Fathers arrived in 1863 and were entrusted with the mission in 1872. Zanzibar was important as a point of departure for missionaries to Tanganyika, Kenya and other places in East Africa. A vicariate for Zanzibar was set up in 1906. Tanzania maintains diplomatic relations with Vatican City.

Archd., 2; dioc., 23; card., 1 (nat.); abp., 1 (nat.); bp., 23 (21 nat.); parishes, 617; priests, 1,543 (767 dioc., 776 rel.); p.d., 1; sem., 343; bros., 391; srs., 3,993; bap., 155,517; Caths., 3,710,000 (20%); tot. pop., 18,510,000.

Thailand (Siam): Constitutional monarchy in southeastern Asia; capital, Bangkok. The first Christians in the region were Portuguese traders who arrived early in the 16th century. A number of missionaries began arriving in 1554 but pastoral care was confined mostly to the Portuguese until the 1660s. Evangelization of the natives got under way from about that time. A seminary was organized in 1665, a vicariate was set up four years later, and a point of departure was established for missionaries to Tonkin, Cochin China and China. Persecution and death for some of the missionaries ended evangelization efforts in 1688. It was resumed, however, and made progress from 1824 onwards. In 1881 missionaries were sent from Siam to neighboring Laos. The hierarchy was established in 1965. Abp., Michai Kitbunchu was named the first Thai cardinal in 1983. Thailand maintains diplomatic relations with Vatican City.

Archd., 2; dioc., 8; card., 1 (nat.); abp., 1 (nat.); bp., 8 (7 nat.); parishes, 238; priests, 396 (181 dioc., 215 rel.); sem., 172; bros., 168; srs., 1,207; bap., 7,062; Caths., 199,000 (.4%); tot. pop., 48,130,000.

Timor, Eastern: Former Portuguese overseas province in the Malay archipelago; annexed by Indonesia in 1976.

Dioc., 1; parishes, 21; priests, 32 (21 dioc., 11 rel.); sem., 17; bros., 7; srs., 46; bap., 35,001; Caths., 240,000; tot. pop., 770,000.

Togo: Republic on the western coast of Africa; capital, Lome. The first Catholic missionaries in the area, where slave raiders operated for nearly 200 years, were members of the African Missions Society who arrived in 1563. They were followed by Divine Word Missionaries in 1914, when a prefecture apostolic was organized. At that time the Catholic population numbered about 19,000. The African Missionaries returned after their German predecessors were deported following World War I. The first native priest was ordained in 1922. The hierarchy was established in 1955. Established diplomatic relations with Vatican City, 1981.

Archd., 1; dioc., 3; abp., 1 (nat.); bp., 3 (2 nat.); parishes, 65; priests, 178 (77 dioc., 101 rel.); sem., 73; bros., 57; srs., 248; bap., 16,014; Caths., 577,000 (21.2%); tot. pop., 2,710,000.

Tokelau: Pacific islands administered by New Zealand. Under ecclesiastical jurisdiction of Samoa-Apia and Tokelau archdiocese, Western Samoa.

Parish, 1; priest, 1 (dioc.); srs., 2; bap., 2; Caths., 900; tot. pop., 2,000.

Tonga: Polynesian monarchy in the southwestern Pacific, consisting of about 150 islands; capital Nuku'alofa. Marists started missionary work in 1842, some years after Protestants had begun evangelization. By 1880 the Catholic population numbered about 1,700. A vicariate was organized in 1937. The hierarchy was established in 1966.

Dioc., 1; bp., 1 (nat); parishes, 13; priests, 26 (12 dioc., 14 rel.); bros., 9; srs., 43; bap., 599; Caths., 17,000 (17%); tot. pop., 100,000.

Trinidad and Tobago: Independent nation, consisting of two islands in the Caribbean; capital, Port-of-Spain. The first Catholic church in Trinidad was built in 1591, years after several missionary ventures had been launched and a number of missionaries killed. Capuchins were there from 1618 until about 1802. Missionary work continued after the British gained control early in the 19th century. Cordial relations have existed between the Church and state, both of which have manifested their desire for the development of native clergy. Established diplomatic relations with Vatican City in 1978.

Archd., 1; abp., 1; parishes, 59; priests, 132 (26 dioc., 106 rel.); p.d., 1; sem., 20; bros., 26; srs., 197; bap., 9,042; Caths., 400,000 (33.6%); tot. pop., 1,190,000.

Tunisia: Republic on the northern coast of Africa; capital, Tunis. There were few Christians in the territory until the 19th century. A prefecture apostolic was organized in 1843 and the Carthage archdiocese was established in 1884. The Catholic population in 1892 consisted of most of the approximately 50,000 Europeans in the country. When Tunis became a republic in 1956, most of the Europeans left the country. The Holy See and the Tunisian government concluded an agreement in 1964 which changed the Carthage archdiocese into a prelacy and handed over some ecclesiastical property to the republic. A considerable number of Moslem students are in Catholic schools, but the number of Moslem converts to the Church has been small. Tunisia maintains diplomatic relations with Vatican City.

Prel., 1; abp., 1; parishes, 13; priests, 52 (23 dioc., 29 rel.); p.d., 1; sem., 1; bros., 4; srs., 210; bap., 50; Caths., 20,000 (.3%); tot. pop., 6,510,000.

Turkey: Republic in Asia Minor and southeastern Europe, capital, Ankara. Christian communities were established in apostolic times, as attested in the Acts of the Apostles, some of the Epistles of St. Paul, and Revelation. The territory was the scene of heresies and ecumenical councils, the place of residence of Fathers of the Church, the area in which ecclesiastical organization reached the dimensions of more than 450 sees in the middle of the seventh century. The region remained generally Byzantine except for the period of the Latin occupation of Constantinople from 1204 to 1261, but was conquered by the Ottoman Turks in 1453 and remained under their domination until establishment of the republic in 1923. Christians, always a minority, numbered more Orthodox than Latins; they were all under some restriction during the Ottoman period. They suffered persecution in the 19th and 20th centuries, the Armenians being the most numerous victims. Turkey is overwhelmingly Moslem. Catholics are tolerated to a degree. Turkey maintains diplomatic relations with Vatican City.

Patriarchate, 1 (Cilicia for the Armenians, the patriarch resides in Lebanon); archd., 3; dioc., 2; v.a., 2; mission "sui juris," 1; ap. ex., 1; abp., 3; bp., 1; parishes, 58; priests, 78 (17 dioc., 61 rel.); p.d., 2; sem., 3; bros., 24; srs., 157; bap., 210; Caths., 17,000; tot. pop., 46,380,000.

Turks and Caicos Islands: British possession in West Indies; capital, Grand Turk. Under ecclesiastical jurisdiction of Nassau diocese, Bahamas.

Caths., 200; tot. pop., 7,000.

Tuvalu (formerly Ellice Islands): Independent state (1978) in Oceania, consisting of 9 islands (8 inhabited); capital, Funafuti.

Mission "sui juris," 1; Caths., 100; tot. pop., 6,000 (Fides).

Uganda: Republic in eastern Africa; capital, Kampala. The White Fathers were the first Catholic missionaries, starting in 1879. Persecution broke out from 1885 to 1887, taking a toll of 22 Catholic martyrs, who were canonized in 1964, and a number of Anglican victims. (Pope Paul honored all those who died for the faith during a visit to Kampala in 1969.) By 1888, there were more than 8,000 Catholics. Evangelization was resumed in 1894, after being interrupted by war, and proceeded thereafter. The first native African bishop was ordained in 1939. The hierarchy was established in 1953. The Church was suppressed during the erratic regime of Pres. Idi-Amin, who was deposed in the spring of 1979. Uganda maintains diplomatic relations with Vatican City.

Archd., 1; dioc., 13; card., 1 (nat.); bp., 14 (12 nat.); parishes, 307; priests, 927 (574 dioc., 353 rel.); p.d., 1; sem., 604; bros., 340; srs., 2,189; bap., 236,592; Caths., 5,504,000 (40%); tot. pop., 13,620,000.

Union of Soviet Socialist Republics: Union of 15 Soviet Socialist Republics in northern Eurasia, from the Baltic Sea to the Pacific; Russian capital, Moscow. The Orthodox Church has been predominant in Russian history. It developed from the Byzantine Church before 1064. Some of its members subsequently established communion with Rome as the result of reunion movements but most of them remained Orthodox. The government has always retained some kind of general or particular control of this church. Latins, always a minority, had a little more freedom. From the beginning of the Communist government in 1917, all churches of whatever kind — including Jews and Moslems — became the targets of official campaigns designed to negate their influence on society and/or to eliminate them entirely. An accurate assessment of the situation of the Catholic Church in Russia is difficult to make. Its dimensions, however, can be gauged from the findings of a team of research specialists made public by the Judiciary Committee of the U.S. House of Representatives in 1964. It was reported: "The fate of the Catholic Church in the USSR and countries occupied by the Russians from 1917 to 1959 shows the following: (a) the number killed: 55 bishops; 12,800 priests and monks; 2.5 million Catholic believers; (b) imprisoned or deported: 199 bishops; 32,000 priests and 10 million believers; (c) 15,700 priests were forced to abandon their priesthood and accept other jobs; and (d) a large number of seminaries and religious communities were dissolved; 1,600 monasteries were nationalized, 31,779 churches were closed. 400 newspapers were prohibited, and all Catholic organizations were dissolved." Several Latin Rite churches are open; e.g., in Moscow, Leningrad, Odessa and Tiflis. An American chaplain is stationed in Moscow to serve Catholics at the U.S. embassy there. Recent reports indicate that, despite repression and attempts at Sovietization, the strongholds of Catholicism in the USSR are Lithuania (incorporated in the USSR in 1940, together with Estonia and Latvia) and the Ukraine. No Catholic statistics are available for the USSR. See separate entries for Estonia, Latvia, Lithuania.

Tot. pop., 268,000,000.

United Arab Emirates: Independent state along Persian Gulf; capital, Abu Dhabi.

V.a., 1; bp., 1; parishes, 4; priests, 9 (3 dioc., 6 rel.); sem. 3; srs., 33; bap., 738; Caths., 30,000; tot. pop., 980,000.

United States: See Catholic History in the United States, Statistics of the Church in the United States.

Upper Volta: Republic inland in western Africa; capital, Ouagadougou. White Fathers started the first missions in 1900 and 1901. White Sisters began work in 1911. A minor and a major seminary were established in 1926 and 1942, respectively. The first native bishop in modern times from West Africa was ordained in 1956 and the first cardinal created in 1965. The hierarchy was established in 1955. Upper Volta established diplomatic relations with Vatican City in 1973.

Archd., 1; dioc., 8; card., 1 (nat.); bp., 10 (nat.); parishes, 101; priests, 406 (161 dioc., 245 rel.); sem., 128; bros., 133; srs., 618; bap., 23,594; Caths., 516,000 (7.2%); tot. pop., 7,090,000.

Uruguay: Republic (called the Eastern Republic of Uruguay) on the southeast coast of South America; capital, Montevideo. The Spanish established a settlement in 1624 and evangelization followed. Missionaries followed the reduction pattern to reach the Indians, form them in the faith and train them in agriculture, husbandry, other useful arts, and the experience of managing property and living in community. Montevideo was made a diocese in 1878. The constitution of 1830 made Catholicism the religion of the state and subsidized some of its activities, principally the missions to the Indians. Separation of Church and state was provided for in the constitution of 1917. Uruguay maintains diplomatic relations with Vatican City.

Archd., 1; dioc., 9; abp., 1; bp., 11; parishes, 222; priests, 586 (197 dioc., 389 rel.); p.d., 18; sem., 89; bros., 148; srs., 1,595; bap., 40,722; Caths., 2,304,000 (78.6%); tot. pop., 2,930,000.

Vanuatu (New Hebrides): Independent (July 29, 1980) island group in the southwest Pacific, about 500 miles west of Fiji; formerly under joint British-French administration; capital, Vila. Effective, though slow, evangelization by Catholic missionaries began about 1887. A vicariate apostolic was set up in 1904. The hierarchy was established in 1966.

Dioc., 1; bp., 1; parishes, 17; priests, 25 (2 dioc., 23 rel.); sem., 18; bros., 14; srs., 62; bap., 585; Caths., 17,000; tot. pop., 120,000.

Vatican City: See separate entry.

Venezuela: Republic in northern South America; capital, Caracas. Evangelization began in 1513-14 and involved members of a number of religious orders who worked in assigned territories, developing missions into pueblos or towns and villages of Indian converts. Nearly 350 towns originated as missions. Fifty-four missionaries met death by violence from the start of missionary work until 1817. Missionary work was seriously hindered during the wars of independence in the second decade of the 19th century and continued in decline through the rest of the century as dictator followed dictator in a period of political turbulence. Restoration of the missions got under way in 1922. The first diocese was established in 1531. Most of the bishops have been native Venezuelans. The first diocesan synod was held in 1574. Church-state relations are regulated by an agreement concluded with the Holy See in 1964. Venezuela maintains diplomatic relations with Vatican City.

Archd., 6; dioc., 18; v.a., 4; card., 2; abp., 5; bp., 31; parishes, 1,000; priests, 2,022 (853 dioc., 1,169 rel.); p.d., 22; sem., 383; bros., 229; srs., 4,270; bap., 350,947; Caths., 13,226,000 (92.4%); tot. pop., 14,310,000.

Vietnam: Country in southeastern Asia, reunited officially July 2, 1976, as the Socialist Republic of Vietnam; capital, Hanoi. Previously, from 1954, partitioned into the Democratic Peoples' Republic of Vietnam in the North (capital, Hanoi) and the Republic of Vietnam in the South (capital, Saigon). Catholicism was introduced in 1533 but missionary work was intermittent until 1615 when Jesuits arrived to stay. One hundred thousand Catholics were reported in 1639. Two vicariates were organized in 1659. A seminary was set up in 1666 and two native priests were ordained two years later. A congregation of native women religious formed in 1670 is still active. Severe persecution broke out in 1698, three times in the 18th century, and again in the 19th. Between 100,000 and 300,000 persons suffered in some way from persecution during the 50 years before 1883 when the French moved in to secure religious liberty for the Catholics. Most of the 117 beatified Martyrs of Vietnam were killed during this 50-year period. After the French were forced out of Vietnam in 1954, the country was partitioned at the 17th parallel. The North went Communist and the Viet Cong, joined by North Vietnamese regular army troops in 1964, fought to gain control of the South. In 1954 there were approximately 1,114,000 Catholics in the North and 480,000 in the South. More than 650,000 fled to the South to avoid the government repression that silenced the Church in the North. In South Vietnam, the Church continued to develop during the war years. Fragmentary reports about the status of the Church since the end of the war in 1975 have been ominous. Freedom of religious belief and practice was promised by the Revolutionary Government in May, 1975, shortly after its capture of Saigon (Ho Chi Min City). The hierarchy was established in 1960. The apostolic delegation, formerly in Saigon, was transferred to Hanoi in 1976; it is presently vacant.

Archd., 3; dioc., 22; card., 1; abp., 4; bp., 37. No statistics are available. There were 2,749,475 Catholics (6.4% of the total population) in 1974. Pop., 54,700,000.

Virgin Islands: Organized unincorporated U.S. territory, about 34 miles east of Puerto Rico; capital, Charlotte Amalie on St. Thomas (one of the three principal islands). The islands were discovered by Columbus in 1493 and named for St. Ursula and her virgin companions. Missionaries began evangelization in the 16th century. A church on St. Croix dates from about 1660; another, on St. Thomas, from 1774. The Baltimore archdiocese had jurisdiction over the islands from 1804 to 1820 when it was passed on to the first of several places in the Caribbean area. Some trouble arose over a pastoral appointment in the 19th century, resulting in a small schism. The Redemptorists took over pastoral care in 1858; normal conditions have prevailed since.

Dioc., 1 (St. Thomas, suffragan of Washington, D.C.); bp., 1; parishes, 6; priests, 18 (3 dioc., 15 rel.); sem., 1; bro., 1; srs., 17; bap., 818; Caths., 25,000; tot. pop., 100,000.

Virgin Islands, British: British crown colony in Caribbean; capital, Road Town.

Parish, 1; priest, 1 (rel.); bap., 10; Caths., 300; tot. pop., 13,000.

Wales: Part of the United Kingdom, on the western part of the island of Great Britain. Celtic missionaries completed evangelization by the end of the sixth century, the climax of what has been called the age of saints. Welsh Christianity received its distinctive Celtic character at this time. Some conflict developed when attempts were made — and proved successful later — to place the Welsh Church under the jurisdiction of Canterbury; the Welsh opted for direct contact with Rome. The Church made progress despite the depredations of Norsemen in the eighth and ninth

centuries. Norman infiltration occurred near the middle of the 12th century, resulting in a century-long effort to establish territorial dioceses and parishes to replace the Celtic organizational plan of monastic centers and satellite churches. The Western Schism produced split views and allegiances. Actions of Henry VIII in breaking away from Rome had serious repercussions. Proscription and penal laws crippled the Church, resulted in heavy defections and touched off a 150-year period of repression in which more than 91 persons died for the faith. Methodism prevailed by 1750. Modern Catholicism came to Wales with Irish immigrants in the 19th century, when the number of Welsh Catholics was negligible. Catholic emancipation was granted in 1829. The hierarchy was restored in 1850.

Archd., 1; dioc., 1; abp., 1; bp., 1; parishes, 169; priests, 312 (179 dioc., 133 rel.); p.d., 4; sem., 22; bros., 84; srs., 652; bap., 3,124; Caths., 149,204 (5.2%); tot. pop., 2,848,800 (1983 Annuario Pontificio).

Wallis and Futuna Islands: French overseas territory in the southwestern Pacific. Marists, who began evangelizing the islands in 1836-7, were the first Catholic missionaries. The entire populations of the two islands were baptized by the end of 1842 (Wallis) and 1843 (Futuna). The first missionary to the latter island was killed in 1841; he was the first martyr of the Pacific. Most of the priests on the islands are native Polynesians. The hierarchy was established in 1966.

Dioc., 1; bp., 1 (nat.); parishes, 5; priests, 13 (8 dioc., 5 rel.); sem., 2; bros., 7; srs., 48; bap., 419; Caths., 10,000; tot. pop., 11,000.

Western Sahara: Former Spanish overseas province (Spanish Sahara) on the northwestern coast of Africa. Territory is under control of Morocco. Islam is the religion of non-Europeans. A prefecture apostolic was established in 1954 for the European Catholics there.

P.a., 1; parishes, 2; priests, 3 (rel.); bap., 2; Caths., 400.

Yemen: Arab republic in southwestern Arabia; capital, Sanaa. Christians perished in the first quarter of the sixth century. Moslems have been in control since the seventh century. The state religion is Islam. In 1973, for the first time in 1,400 years, Catholic personnel — priests, religious, lay persons — were invited to work in the country as staff of a government hospital; they were not to engage in proselytizing. Under ecclesiastical jurisdiction of Arabia vicariate apostolic.

Caths., 3,000; tot. pop., 5,940,000.

Yemen, Peoples Democratic Republic of: Republic in the southern part of the Arabian peninsula; capitals, Aden and Medina as-Shaab. No Christian community has existed there since the Moslem conquest of the seventh century. Catholics are from other countries. Under ecclesiastical jurisdiction of Arabia vicariate apostolic.

Caths., 1,000; tot. pop., 2,030,000.

Yugoslavia: Socialist republic in southeastern Europe; capital, Belgrade. Christianity was introduced from the seventh to ninth centuries in the regions which were combined to form the nation after World War I. Since these regions straddled the original line of demarcation for the Western and Eastern Empires (and churches), and since the Reformation had little lasting effect, the Christians are nearly all either Roman Catholics or Byzantines (some in communion with Rome, the majority Orthodox). Yugoslavia was proclaimed a Socialist republic in 1945. Repression of religion became government policy. Between May, 1945, and December, 1950, persecution took the following toll: almost two-thirds of 22 dioceses lost their bishops; about 348 priests were killed; 200 priests were under arrest and in prison; 12 of 18 seminaries were closed; the Catholic press was confiscated; religious instruction was suppressed in all schools; 300 religious houses and institutions were confiscated, and nuns and other religious driven out; all Church property was expropriated; the ministry of priests was severely restricted and subject to government interference; many thousands of the faithful shared the fate of priests and religious in death, imprisonment and slave labor. Cardinal Stepinac, arrested in 1946 and the symbol of the Church under persecution in Yugoslavia, died Feb. 10, 1960. In an agreement signed June 25, 1966, the government recognized the Holy See's spiritual jurisdiction over the Church in the country and guaranteed to bishops the possibility of maintaining contact with Rome in ecclesiastical and religious matters. The Holy See confirmed the principle that the activity of ecclesiastics, in the exercise of priestly functions, must take place within the religious and ecclesiastical sphere, and that abuse of these functions for political ends would be illegal. Less than two months after the agreement was signed, a group of exiled Croatian priests issued a statement in which they accused the Yugoslav government of failing to abide by it. According to others, an improvement was noticeable. Yugoslavia maintains diplomatic relations with Vatican City.

Archd., 8; dioc., 14; a.a., 1, card., 1; abp., 7; bp., 23; parishes, 2,786; priests, 4,216 (2,768 dioc., 1,448 rel.); p.d., 2; sem., 716; bros., 256; srs., 6,355; bap., 81,934; Caths., 7,147,000 (31.7%); tot. pop., 22,520,000.

Zaire (formerly the Congo): Republic in south central Africa; capital, Kinshasa. Christianity was introduced in 1484 and evangelization began about 1490. The first native bishop in black Africa was ordained in 1518. Subsequent missionary work was hindered by faulty methods of instruction and formation, inroads of the slave trade, wars among the tribes, and Portuguese policy based on the patronage system and having all the trappings of anticlericalism in the 18th and 19th centuries. Modern evangelization started in the second half of the 19th century. The hierarchy was established in 1959. In the civil disorders which followed independence in 1960, some missions and other church installations were abandoned, thousands of people reverted to tribal religions and many priests and religious were killed. Church-state tensions have developed in recent years because of the Church's criticism of the anti-Christian thrust of Pres. Mobutu's "Africanization" policies. Zaire maintains diplomatic relations with Vatican City.

Archd., 6; dioc., 41; card., 1 (nat.); abp., 5 (nat.); bp., 46 (43 nat.); parishes, 998; priests, 2,584 (726 dioc., 1,858 rel.); p.d., 7; sem., 1,790; bros., 941; srs., 4,401; bap., 401,212; Caths., 12,750,000 (46%)· tot. pop., 27,483,000.

Zambia: Republic in central Africa; capital, Lusaka. Portuguese priests did some evangelizing in the 16th and 17th centuries but no results of their work remained in the 19th century. Jesuits began work in the south in the 1880s and White Fathers in the north and east in 1895. Evangelization of the western region began for the first time in 1831. The number of Catholics doubled in the 20 years following World War II. Zambia maintains diplomatic relations with Vatican City.

Archd., 2; dioc., 7; abp., 2 (nat.); bp., 7 (5 nat.); parishes, 211; priests, 518 (90 dioc., 428 rel.); p.d., 1; sem., 114; bros., 166; srs., 684; bap., 45,599; Caths., 1,701,000 (28.5%); tot. pop., 5,960,000.

Zimbabwe (formerly Rhodesia): Independent republic (Apr. 18, 1980) in south central Africa; capital, Harare (Salisbury). Earlier unsuccessful missionary ventures preceded the introduction of Catholicism in 1879. Missionaries began to make progress after 1893. The hierarchy was established in 1955; the first black bishop was ordained in 1973. In 1969, four years after the government of Ian Smith made a unilateral declaration of independence from England, a new constitution was enacted for the purpose of assuring continued white supremacy over the black majority. Catholic and Protestant prelates in the country protested vigorously against the constitution and related enactments as opposed to human rights of the blacks and restrictive of the Church's freedom to carry out its pastoral, educational and social service functions. The Smith regime was ousted in 1979 after seven years of civil war in which at least 25,000 people were killed. Diplomatic relations with the Vatican were established in 1980.

Archd., 1; dioc., 4; p.a., 1; abp., 1 (nat.); bp., 5 (3 nat.); priests, 340 (64 dioc., 276 rel.); p.d., 9; sem., 62; bros., 113; srs., 950; bap., 17,984; Caths., 698,000 (9.1%); tot. pop., 7,600,000.

Senegal: Republic in western Africa; capital, Dakar. The country had its first contact with Catholicism through the Portuguese some time after 1460. Some incidental missionary work was done by Jesuits and Capuchins in the 16th and 17th centuries.

Archd., 1; dioc., 4; p.a., 1; card., 1 (nat.); bp., 4 (nat.); parishes, 57; priests, 219 (65 dioc., 154 rel.); sem., 57; bros., 127; srs., 597; bap., 9,073; Caths., 246,000 (4.2%); tot. pop., 5,810,000.

Seychelles: Independent (1976) group of 92 islands in the Indian Ocean 970 miles east of Kenya; capital, Victoria on Mahe.

Dioc., 1; bp., 1 (nat.); parishes, 17; priests, 23 (6 dioc., 17 rel.); sem. 1; bros., 9; srs., 58; bap., 1,510; Caths., 62,000; tot. pop., 70,000.

CATHOLIC WORLD STATISTICS

(Principal sources: Statistical Yearbook of the Church, 1981, the latest edition available; Annuario Pontificio, 1983. Figures are from Dec. 31, 1981, except for jurisdictions and hierarchy which have been updated to June, 1983, in most cases.)

Patriarchates: 13. Eastern Rites, 8 (Africa, 2; Asia, 6). Roman Rite, 5 (Asia, 2; Europe, 2; West Indies, 1). The West Indies patriarchate has been vacant since 1963.

Archdioceses: 505 (Africa, 57; North and Middle America, 77; South America, 86; Asia, 123; Europe, 145; Oceania, 17).

Dioceses: 1,903 (Africa, 308; North and Middle America, 310; South America, 341; Asia, 358; Europe, 535; Oceania, 51).

Prelatures: 70 (Africa, 1; North and Middle America, 12; South America, 44; Asia, 5; Europe, 8).

Abbacies "nullius": 19 (Africa, 1; North and Middle America, 1; South America, 2; Asia, 1; Europe, 14).

Vicariates Apostolic: 72 (Africa, 12; North and Middle America, 6; South America, 36; Asia, 17; Europe, 1).

Prefectures Apostolic: 55 (Africa, 9; South America, 11; Asia, 35).

Apostolic Administrations: 8 (Africa, 1; North and Middle America, 2; Asia, 1; Europe, 4).

Missions "Sui Juris": 4 (Africa, 1; Asia, 2; Oceania, 1).

Apostolic Exarchates, Ordinariates: 21 (North and Middle America, 3; South America, 3; Asia, 2; Europe, 13).

Military Vicarlates: 27 (Africa, 3; North and Middle America, 4; South America, 7; Asia, 2; Europe, 9; Oceania, 2).

Cardinals (as of Sept. 8, 1983): **133** (Africa, 14; North and Middle America, 19; South America, 17; Asia, 11; Europe, 69; Oceania, 3).

Archbishops: 422 (Africa, 49; North and Middle America, 70; South America, 80; Asia, 94; Europe, 115; Oceania, 14).

Figures for archbishops and bishops (below) include residential and auxiliary prelates only. Titular archbishops and bishops engaged in other apostolates and retired members of the hierarchy are not included. The total number of archbishops and bishops was 695 and 3,017, respectively, according to the "1981 Statistical Yearbook of the Church."

Bishops: 2,435 (Africa, 325; North and Middle America, 486; South America, 510; Asia, 326; Europe, 720; Oceania, 68).

Priests, Total: 411,074 (Africa, 17,578; North and Middle America, 86,205; South America, 34,044; Asia, 27,509; Euorpe, 240,124; Oceania, 5,614).

Priests, Diocesan: 255,904 (Africa, 6,332; North and Middle America, 51,355; South America, 14,772; Europe, 13,822; Europe, 166,731; Oceania, 2,892).

Priests, Religious: 155,170 (Africa, 11,246; North and Middle America, 34,850; South America,

19,272; Asia, 13,687; Europe, 73,393; Oceania, 2,722).

Permanent Deacons: 8,647 (Africa, 156; North and Middle America, 6,026; South America, 716; Asia, 68; Europe, 1,629; Oceania, 52).

Brothers: 70,621 (Africa, 5,305; North and Middle America, 15,496; South America, 6,744; Asia, 5,892; Europe, 34,051; Oceania, 3,133).

Sisters: 952,043 (Africa, 36,165; North and Middle America, 202,427; South America, 90,784; Asia, 87,099; Europe, 519,773; Oceania, 15,795).

Seminarians: 68,633 (Africa, 6,905; North and Middle America, 13,233; South America, 11,113; Asia, 12,499; Europe, 24,032; Oceania, 851).

Baptisms: 17,466,303 (Africa, 2,142,482; North and Middle America, 4,004,563; South America 5,560,451; Asia, 2,039,400; Europe, 3,592,016; Oceania, 127,391). Includes 16,158,149 baptisms up to the age of seven and 1,308,154 over that age.

Marriages: 4,134,512 (Africa, 184,507: North and Middle America, 900,450; South America, 1,101,346; Asia, 386,317; Europe, 1,527,584; Oceania, 34,308). Includes 3,796,073 marriages between Catholis and 338,439 between Catholics and non-Catholics.

Parishes, 207,971 (Africa, 7,412; North and Middle America, 31,150; South America, 15,938; Asia, 12,108; Europe, 139,009; Oceania, 2,354).

Elementary/Primary Schools and Students: 75,470 schools; **20,988,965** students. Africa, 19,082 — 6,006,933; North and Middle America, 12,539 — 3,789,203; South America, 8,807 — 3,160,632; Asia, 11,264 — 3,664,528; Europe, 21,365 — 3,882,505; Oceania, 2,413 — 485,164.

Secondary Schools and Students: 29,919 schools; **11,254,697** students. Africa, 3,609 — 804,712; North and Middle America, 3,608 — 1,468,816; South America, 4,892 — 1,858,045; Asia, 6,235 — 3,310,899; Europe, 10,882 — 3,454,080; Oceania, 693 — 268,145.

Students in Higher Institutes and Universities: 2,143,481 (Africa, 7,872; North and Middle America, 771,787; South America, 463,217; Asia, 662,328; Europe, 233,924; Oceania, 4,353).

Hospitals: 6,475 (Africa, 921; North and Middle America, 1,013; South America, 1,269; Asia, 1,168; Europe, 1,943; Oceania, 161).

Dispensaries: 12,628 (Africa, 3,269; North and Middle America, 1,351; South America, 2,993; Asia, 2,406; Europe, 2,364; Oceania, 245).

Leprosaria; 798 (Africa, 436; North and Middle America, 9; South America, 48; Asia, 295; Europe, 4; Oceania, 6).

Homes for Aged, Chronically Ill, Handicapped: 10,085 (Africa, 295; North and Middle America, 1,024; South America, 1,335; Asia, 550; Europe, 6,711; Oceania, 170).

Orphanages: 6,393 (Africa, 390; North and Middle America, 444; South America, 930; Asia, 1,747; Europe, 2,707; Oceania, 175).

Nurseries: 5,754 (Africa, 583; North and Middle America, 262; South America, 931; Asia, 1,063; Europe, 2,890; Oceania, 25).

Catholic Population: 794,380,000 (17.7% of the total world population of 4,485,462,000). Africa, 60,543,000 (12.5%; total population, 482,056,000). North and Middle America, 169,687,000 (44.8%; total population, 378,474,000). South America, 220,829,000 (90.7%; total population 243,331,000). Asia, 64,575,000 (2.4% total population, 2,674,879,000). Europe, 272,881,000 (39.9%; total population, 683,785,000. Oceania, 5,865,000 (25.5%; total population, 22,937,000).

U.S. VOCATIONAL STATISTICS

Auxiliary Bishop Nicolas Walsh of Seattle, at the annual meeting of the U.S. bishops in November, 1982, called attention to the need for study and action for the promotion of vocations to the priesthood and religious life. The need, he said, was evident in the implications of just a few figures: the median age of priests at that time was 52, there were just a few more than 4,000 seminarians studying theology, and there were estimates that there would be only about 25,000 active priests in the country in 20 years.

Statistics sketching a critical vocational pattern included the following:

• In 1966 there were 126 diocesan seminaries, compared with 86 in 1983; students numbered 22,762 in 1965, and 8,046 in 1983.

• In 1966 there were 481 seminaries or scholasticates of religious orders, compared with 234 in 1983. The number of students declined from 22,657 in 1962 to 4,008 in 1983.

• The total number of students for the priesthood declined from 48,992 in 1965 to 12,054 in 1983.

• The number of brothers declined from 9,201 in 1973 to 7,658 in 1983.

• The number of sisters declined drastically from 143,054 in 1973 to 120,699 in 1983.

The International Fides Service issued a report and table Mar. 16, 1983, on the numbers of seminarians in territories of the Middle East and the rest of Asia under the jurisdiction of the Congregation for the Evangelization of Peoples. The figures were compiled by the Pontifical Society of St. Peter the Apostle for the 1981-82 academic year.

Minor seminarians in all of Asia numbered 11,275 (diocesan) and 5,349 (religious), for a total of 16,624.

Major seminarians numbered 7,421 (diocesan) and 4,769 (religious), for a total of 12,190.

DEATHS SEPTEMBER 1982 TO SEPTEMBER 1983

Alessandrini, Federico, 77, May 2, 1983, Rome, Italy; former director of Vatican Press Office.

Barman, George, 66, Apr. 18, 1983, Dayton, Ohio; retired associate editor of *The Catholic Telegraph* (Cincinnati).

Benelli, Cardinal Giovanni, 61, Oct. 26, 1982, Florence, Italy; archbishop of Florence; undersecretary of state under Paul VI.

Bezy, Rev. Gregory, S.C.J., 68, Sept. 14, 1982, Victorville, Calif.; founder of Sacred Heart League.

Bidault, Georges, 83, Jan. 27, 1983, Cambo-les-Bains, France; former prime minister of France.

Bussard, Rev. Paul, 78, Feb. 22, 1983, St. Paul, Minn.; co-founder of *Catholic Digest*.

Buttimer, Bro. Charles H., F.S.C., 73, Dec. 15, 1982, Narragansett, R.I.; educator; first non-French superior general of Christian Brothers, 1966-76.

Casariego, Cardinal Mario, 74, June 15, 1983, Guatemala City; archbishop of Guatemala.

Casey, Msgr. George W., 87, July 19, 1983, Boston, Mass.; columnist for *The Pilot*, 1950-80.

Cardinale, Archbishop Igino, 66, Mar. 24, 1983, Brussels, Belgium; apostolic nuncio to Belgium, Luxembourg and European Community.

Cassidy, Msgr. Joseph G., 84, Sept. 9, 1982, Decatur, Ga.; rural missioner in Georgia.

Cavanagh, Msgr. John B., 74, July 5, 1983, Denver, Colo.; editor *Register* system; radio personality.

Daley, Bishop Joseph T., 67, Sept. 2, 1983, Harrisburg, Pa.; bishop of Harrisburg from 1971.

Fonseca, Jaime, 66, Jan. 22, 1983, Washington, D.C.; journalist; NC News Service Latin America editor from 1968.

Gallen, Gov. Hugh, 58, Dec. 29, 1982, Boston, Mass.; Democrat governor of New Hampshire.

Garrity, Margaret, 65, May 10, 1983, Lenexa, Mo.; longtime social justice worker.

Gleeson, Bishop Francis D., S.J., 88, Apr. 30, 1983, Fairbanks, Alaska; retired bishop of Fairbanks.

Heckel, Bishop Roger, S.J., 60, Sept. 26, 1982, Strasbourg, France; coadjutor of Strasbourg; former secretary of Pontifical Justice and Peace Commission.

Howard, Archbishop Edward D., 105, Jan. 2, 1983, Beaverton, Ore.; retired archbishop of Portland; world's oldest bishop.

Kennedy, Rev. Robert P., 57, Jan. 19, 1983, New York, N.Y.; social action director of Brooklyn Diocese; associate editor *The Tablet*.

Kern, Msgr. Clement, 76, Aug. 15, 1983, Detroit, Mich.; inner-city pastor; called "Saint of the Slums."

Knox, Cardinal James Robert, 69, June 26, 1983, Rome; Australian Curia official; president of Pontifical Council for Family; former prefect of Congregation for Sacraments and Divine Worship and former archbishop of Melbourne.

Lally, Bro. Alexis V., F.S.C., 90, Feb. 21, 1983, Yonkers, N.Y.; president emeritus of Manhattan College.

Lener, Rev. Salvatore, S.J., 76, Apr. 15, 1983, Rome; member of negotiating team working on revision of 1929 Italy-Vatican concordat.

Leven, Bishop Stephen A., 78, June 28, 1983, San Angelo, Tex.; retired bishop of San Angelo.

McCauley, Bishop Vincent J., C.S.C., 76, Nov. 1, 1982; retired bishop of Fort Portal, Uganda.

McGuire, Rev. Frederick A., C.M., 78, May 22, 1983, Washington, D.C.; missiologist; development director emeritus of CARA; missioner in China.

McGurkin, Bishop Edward A., M.M., 78, Aug. 28, 1983, Maryknoll, N.Y.; missioner; retired bishop of Shinyanga, Tanzania.

McNicholas, Bishop Joseph A., 60, Apr. 17, 1983, Springfield, Ill.; bishop of Springfield from 1975.

Miller, William E., 69, June 24, 1983, Buffalo, N.Y.; former U.S. Representative; running mate of Barry Goldwater in 1964 presidential election.

Motta, Cardinal Carlos Carmelo de Vasconcellos, 92, Sept. 18, 1982, Aparecida, Brazil; archbishop of Aparecida; oldest cardinal.

Pardy, Bishop James V., M.M., 85, Jan. 15, 1983, California; missioner; retired bishop of Cheong-Ju, Korea.

Reynolds, Frank, 59, July 20, 1983, Washington, D.C.; broadcaster, ABC News anchorman.

Roborecki, Bishop Andrew, 72, Oct. 23, 1982, Toronto, Canada; Ukrainian eparch of Saskatoon.

Roche, Msgr. Patrick, 70, Sept. 19, 1982, Los Angeles, Calif.; retired editor of *The Tidings.*

Rosales, Cardinal Julio, 76, June 2, 1983, Cebu, Philippines; retired archbishop of Cebu.

Samore, Cardinal Antonio, 77, Feb. 3, 1983, Rome; librarian and archivist of the Holy Roman Church.

Scanlan, Patrick F., 88, Mar. 27, 1983, Bellmore, N.Y.; managing editor of *The Tablet* (Brooklyn), 1917-68.

Schroeffer, Cardinal Joseph, 80, Sept. 8, 1983, Nurnberg, West Germany; Roman Curia official.

Swigert, John (Jack), 51, Dec. 27, 1982, Washington, D.C.; Republican Congressman-elect from Colorado; former astronaut.

Theall, Rev. D. Bernard, O.S.B., 66, Dec. 3, 1982; librarian, book critic.

Volkomener, Sister Helen, S.P., 59, Nov. 20, 1982, Denver, Colo., in an automobile accident; Colorado Humanities Program director; former director of Catholic Committee on Urban Ministry.

OPUS DEI: PERSONAL PRELATURE

Opus Dei was founded by Msgr. Josemaria Escriva de Belaguer in 1928 in Madrid as "an association of the faithful whose members dedicate themselves entirely to the apostolate (of Christian witness and action) and to the practice of an intense spiritual life without abandoning their own social environment or the exercise of their profession or secular occupation." The association was fully approved by the Vatican as a secular institute in 1950. On Aug. 5, 1982, Pope John Paul II confirmed and ordered publication of a declaration concerning the erection of the secular institute into the Prelature of the Holy Cross and Opus Dei.

Following are excerpts of the Pontiff's declaration of approval of Opus Dei as the first personal prelature established in accord with enactments of the Second Vatican Council.

The text of the declaration was circulated by the N.C. Documentary Service, Origins, Jan. 20, 1983 (Vol. 12, No. 32).

DECLARATION

The Second Vatican Council provided for the setting up of personal prelatures which would engage in "particular pastoral work." These prelatures are a further proof of the sensitiveness with which the Church responds to the specific pastoral and evangelizing needs of our time. For this reason, the pontifical act erecting Opus Dei as a personal prelature, with the name Prelature of the Holy Cross and Opus Dei, is directly aimed at promoting the apostolic activity of the Church.

The chief characteristics of the prelature which has been erected are the following.

I. Organization

a) The Prelature Opus Dei is international. The central offices of the prelate who is the ordinary of the prelature and of his councils are in Rome.

b) The clergy of the prelature, which is incardinated in the prelature, derives from the laity incorporated therein. No candidate to the priesthood, deacon or priest is withdrawn from the local churches.

c) The laity (men and women, single or married, of all professions and social situations) who dedicate themselves to the service of the apostolic purpose of the prelature with a serious commitment do so in virtue of a clearly defined contract and not by vows.

II. Structure

The Prelature Opus Dei is a secular jurisdictional structure, and therefore:

a) As established in the general law of the Church and in the law of the prelature, the clergy incardinated in the prelature belong to the secular clergy to all effects. They therefore maintain close relations with the secular priests of the local church and, with respect to priests' councils, they enjoy an active and passive voice.

b) The laity incorporated to the prelature do not alter their personal situation canonically or theologically. They continue to be ordinary lay faithful and act accordingly in all matters and, specifically, in their apostolate.

c) In the aims and spirit of Opus Dei, stress is laid on the sanctifying value of ordinary work; that is to say, on the obligation to sanctify work, to sanctify oneself in one's work and to turn it into an instrument of apostolate. Therefore, the work and apostolate of those who form part of the prelature are normally carried out in the structure and environment of secular society, bearing in mind the general indications which the Holy See or diocesan bishops may give concerning the apostolate of the laity.

d) As regards decisions in professional, social, political matters, etc., the lay faithful of the prelature enjoy within the limits of Catholic faith and morals and of the discipline of the Church the same freedom as other Catholics, their fellow citizens; hence, the prelature does not make itself responsible for the professional, political or economic activities of any of its members.

III. The Jurisdiction of the Prelate

a) The power of the prelate is an ordinary power of jurisdiction or government, limited to that which refers to the specific finality of the prelature, and differs substantially, by reason of the matter involved, from the jurisdiction of the diocesan bishops in the ordinary spiritual care of the faithful.

b) As well as the government of the clergy of the prelature, the jurisdiction of the prelate includes the general direction of the formation and of the specific apostolic and spiritual attention which the laity incorporated to Opus Dei receive, to help them live a more intense dedication in the service of the Church.

c) Together with the right to incardinate his own candidates to the priesthood, the prelate has the obligation to attend to their specific formation in the centers of the prelature in conformity with the norms established by the competent congregation, and to the spiritual life and the permanent formation of the priests promoted by him to holy orders. He is also obliged to provide for the proper support of his clergy and for their care in old age and in the case of illness, etc.

d) The laity are under the jurisdiction of the prelate in regard to what has to do with the fulfillment of the specific ascetic, formative and apostolic commitments which they have freely undertaken by means of the contractual bond dedicating them to the service of the aims of the prelature.

IV. Relation to Territorial Laws, Bishops

With reference to ecclesiastical territorial laws and to the legitimate rights of local ordinaries:

a) As established by law, the members of the prelature must observe the territorial norms which refer to general directives of a doctrinal, liturgical and pastoral nature; the laws concerning public order, and, in the case of the priests, also the general discipline of the clergy.

b) The priests of the prelature must obtain the ministerial faculties of the competent territorial authority to exercise their ministry with people who do not form part of Opus Dei.

c) The laity incorporated to the Prelature Opus Dei continue to be faithful to the dioceses in which they have their domicile (permanent residence) or quasidomicile, and are therefore under the jurisdiction of the diocesan bishop in what the law lays down for all the ordinary faithful.

V. Pastoral Coordination

In regard to the pastoral coordination with local ordinaries and the fruitful insertion of the Prelature Opus Dei in the local churches, it is also established that:

a) The prior permission of the competent diocesan bishop is required for the erection of each center of the prelature. The diocesan bishop is informed regularly about the activities of those centers and has the right to visit them.

b) As regards parishes, rectoral churches or other churches, and also other ecclesiastical offices which the local ordinary may entrust to the prelature or to the priests incardinated in the prelature, an agreement will be drawn up in each case between the local ordinary and the prelate of Opus Dei or his vicars.

c) In each country the prelature will maintain regular contact with the president and with the organisms of the episcopal conference, and have frequent contact with the bishops of the dioceses in which the prelature is established.

VI. Sacerdotal Society

The Sacerdotal Society of the Holy Cross is an association which is inseparably united to the prelature.

Priests of the diocesan clergy who wish to strive for sanctity in their ministry in accordance with the spirituality of Opus Dei may form part of this association. These priests, by virtue of their membership in the association, do not form part of the clergy of the prelature. They remain, to all effects and purposes, under the jurisdiction of their own ordinary whom they will inform, if he wishes, of their membership in the association.

VII. The prelature is under the Sacred Congregation for Bishops.

VIII. Through the Sacred Congregation for Bishops, the prelate will present to the Roman pontiff every five years a detailed report on the state of the prelature and on the development of its specific apostolate, both from the juridical and from the pastoral points of view.

The Supreme Pontiff by divine providence, Pope John Paul II, in the audience granted to the undersigned prefect of the Sacred Congregation for Bishops Aug. 5, 1982, approved, confirmed and ordered to be published this declaration concerning the erection of the Prelature of the Holy Cross and Opus Dei.

Rome, Sacred Congregation for Bishops, Aug. 23, 1982.

Cardinal Sebastiano Baggio, Prefect; Archbishop Lucas Moreira Neves, Secretary.

FIRST PRELATE, ADDITIONAL FACTS

Msgr. Alvaro del Portillo was invested as the first prelate of the Opus Dei Prelature Mar. 19, 1983.

At the time of his investiture, according to the 1983 edition of *Annuario Pontificio,* the prelacy had 1,043 priests, 62 newly ordained priests, 353 major seminarians and approximately 72,000 lay persons — men and women, married and single, of every class and social condition — in about 80 countries.

General legislation concerning personal prelatures is contained in Canons 294 to 297 of the revised Code of Canon Law, effective Nov. 27, 1983.

In the United States, members of Opus Dei, along with non-member associates, conduct apostolic works corporately in major cities in the East and Midwest, and on the West Coast. Elsewhere, members are engaged in universities, vocational institutes, training schools for farmers and numerous other apostolic initiatives.

An information office is located at 330 Riverside Drive, New York, N.Y. 10025.

EPISCOPAL CONFERENCES

(Principal source: *Annuario Pontificio.*)
Episcopal conferences, organized and operating under general norms and particular statutes approved by the Holy See, are official bodies in and through which the bishops of a given country or territory act together as pastors of the Church.

Listed below according to countries or regions are titles and addresses of conferences and names and sees of presidents (archbishops unless otherwise noted).

Africa, North: Conference Episcopale d'Afrique du Nord, 13 rue Khelifa Boukhalfa, Algiers, Algeria. Card. Leon-Etienne Duval (Algiers).

Africa, South: Southern African Catholic Bishops' Conference (SACBC), P.O. Box 941, Pretoria 0001, S. Africa. Denis Eugene Hurley, O.M.I. (Durban).

Angola and Sao Tome: Conferencia Episcopal de Angola e Sao Tome (CEAST), C.P. 10, Huambo, Angola. Manuel F. da Costa (Huambo).

Antilles: Antilles Episcopal Conference, 27 Maraval Rd., Port of Spain, Trinidad. Gordon Anthony Pantin (Port of Spain).

Arab Countries: Conference des Eveques Latins dans les Regions Arabes (CELRA), Latin Patriarchate, P.O. Box 14152, Jerusalem (Old City). Patriarch Giacomo Beltritti (Jerusalem).

Argentina: Conferencia Episcopal Argentina (CEA), Calle Paraguay 1867, Buenos Aires. Card. Juan Carlos Aramburu (Buenos Aires).

Australia: Australian Episcopal Conference, P.O. Box 297, Kingston, A.C.T., 2604. Card. James Darcy Freeman (Sydney).

Austria: Osterreichische Bischofskonferenz, Rotenturmstrasse 2, A1010 Vienna. Card. Franz Koenig (Vienna).

Bangladesh: Catholic Bishops' Conference (CBCB), P.O. Box 3, Ramna, Dhaka-2. Michael Rozario (Dhaka).

Belgium: Bisschoppenconferentie van Belgie — Conference Episcopale de Belgique, Wollemarkt 15, B-2800 Mechelen. Card. Godfried Danneels (Mechelen-Brussel).

Benin: Conference Episcopale du Benin, B.P. 491, Cotonou. Christophe Adimou (Cotonou).

Bolivia: Conferencia Episcopal de Bolivia (CEB), Casilla 2309, La Paz. Luis Rodriguez Pardo (Santa Cruz de la Sierra).

Brazil: Conferencia Nacional dos Bispos do Brasil (CNBB), C.P. 13-2067, 70000 Brasilia, D.F. Bp. Jose Ivo Lorscheiter (Santa Maria).

Bulgaria: Ulitza Pashovi 10-B, Sofia VI. Bp. Metodio Dimitrow Stratiew (Apostolic Exarch, Sofia).

Burma: Burma Catholic Bishops' Conference (BCBC), 292 Prome Rd., Sanchaung P.O., Rangoon. Bp. Paul Zinghtung Grawng (Myitkyina).

Burundi: Conference Episcopale du Burundi, B. P. 1390, Bujumbura. Joachim Ruhuna (Gitega).

Cameroon: Conference Episcopale Nationale du Cameroun, P.O. Box 207, Yaounde. Jean Zoa (Yaounde).

Canada: See Canadian Conference of Catholic Bishops.

Central African Republic: Conference Episcopale Centrafricaine (CECA), B.P. 798, Bangui. Joachim N'Dayen (Bangui).

Chad: Conference Episcopale du Tchad, B.P., 87, Sarh. Bp. Henri Veniat, S.J. (Sarh).

Chile: Conferencia Episcopal de Chile (CECH), Casilla 13191, Correo 21, Santiago de Chile. Bp. Jose Manuel Santos Ascarza (Valdivia).

China (Republic of China, Taiwan): Regional Episcopal Conference of China, Lane 32, Kuangfu Rd., Taipeh 34, Taiwan. Matthew Kia Yen-Wen (Taipeh).

Colombia: Conferencia Episcopal de Colombia, Apartado 7448, Bogota D.E. Mario Revollo Bravo (Nueva Pamplona).

Congo: Conference Episcopale du Congo, B.P. 2301, Brazzaville. Bp. Georges Singha (Owanda).

Costa Rica: Conference Episcopal de Costa Rica (CECOR), Apartado 497, San Jose. Roman Arrieta Villalobos (San Jose de Costa Rica).

Cuba: Conferencia Episcopal de Cuba (CEC), Apartado 125, Camaguey. Bp. Adolfo Rodriguez Herrera (Camaguey).

Dominican Republic: Conferencia del Episcopado Dominicano (CED), Apartado 1313, Higuey. Abp.-Bp. Hugo Eduardo Polanco Brito (Nuestra Senora de la Altagracia en Higuey).

Ecuador: Conferencia Episcopal Ecuatoriana, Apartado 1081, Quito. Card. Pablo Munoz Vega, S.J. (Quito).

El Salvador: Conferencia Episcopal de El Salvador (CEDES). Apartado Postal 43, San Miguel. Bp. Jose Alvarez Ramirez, C.M. (San Miguel).

Ethiopia: Conferenza Episcopale di Etiopia, P.O. Box 21903, Addis Ababa. Paulos Tzadua (Addis Ababa).

France: Conference Episcopale Francaise, 106 rue du Bac, 75341 Paris CEDEX 07. Bp. Jean Vilnet (Saint-Die).

Gabon: Conference Episcopale du Gabon, B.P. 230, Franceville. Bp. Felicien-Patrice Makouaka (Franceville).

Gambia, Liberia and Sierra Leone: Inter-Territorial Episcopal Conference, P.O. Box 893, Freetown, Sierra Leone. Joseph Ganda (Freetown and Bo.).

Germany: Deutsche Bischofskonferenz, Kaiserstrasse 163, D-5300 Bonn. Card. Joseph Hoeffner (Cologne). Berliner Bischofskonferenz, Franzosische Strasse 34, DDR-108 Berlin. Card. Joachim Meisner (Berlin).

Ghana: Ghana Bishops' Conference, P.O. Box 42, Tamale. Peter Poreku Dery (Tamale).

Great Britain: Bishops' Conference of England and Wales, Archbishop's House, Westminster, London, SWIP 1QJ. Card. George Basil Hume, O.S.B. (Westminster). Bishops' Conference of Scotland, 42 Greenhill Gardens, Edinburgh EH 10 4BJ. Card. Gordon J. Gray (Saint Andrews and Edinburgh).

Greece: Conferenza Episcopale di Grecia,

Archeveche Catholique, Corfu. Antonio Varthalitis (Corfu, Zante and Cefalonia.)

Guatemala: Conferencia Episcopal de Guatemala (CEG), 4 Calle 9-45, zona 1, Ciudad de Guatemala. Bp. Prospero Penados del Barrio (San Marcos).

Guinea: Conference Episcopale de la Guinee, B.P. 1006 Bis, Conakry.

Haiti: Conference Episcopale de Haiti (CEH). Archbishopric, Port-au-Prince. Francois-Wolff Ligonde (Port-au-Prince).

Honduras: Conferencia Episcopal de Honduras (CEH), Arzobispado, Tegucigalpa. Hector Enrique Santos Hernandez, S.D.B. (Tegucigalpa).

Hungary: Magyar Puspoki Kar, Berenyi Zsigmond u. 2, Pf. 25, H-2500 Esztergom. Card. Laszlo Lekai (Esztergom).

India: Catholic Bishops' Conference of India (CBCI), CBCI Centre, Goldakkana, New Delhi-110001. Simeon Ignatius Pimenta (Bombay).

Indonesia: General Conference of the Ordinaries of Indonesia (Majelis Agung Waligerija Indonesia — MAWI), Pusat Jalan Cut Mutiah 10, Jakarta II/14. Bp. Francis Xavier Sudartanto Hadisumarta, O. Carm. (Malang).

Ireland: Episcopal Meetings, "Ara Coeli," Armagh. Card. Tomas O'Fiaich (Armagh).

Italy: Conferenza Episcopale Italiana (CEI), Circonvallazione Aurelia, 50, 00165 Roma. Card. Anastasio Alberto Ballestrero, O.C.D. (Turin).

Ivory Coast: Conference Episcopale de la Cote d'Ivoire, B.P. 1287, Abidjan. Card. Bernard Yago (Abidjan).

Japan: Japan Catholic Bishops' Conference, Catholic Center, 10-34 Uenomachi, Nagasaki-shi. Card. Joseph Asajiro Satowaki (Nagasaki).

Kenya: Kenya Episcopal Conference (KEC), P.O. Box 938, Nakura. Bp. Raphael S. Ndingi Mwana's Nzeki (Nakura).

Korea: Catholic Conference of Korea, Box 16, Seoul. Card. Stephen Sou Hwan Kim (Seoul).

Laos and Cambodia: Conference Episcopale du Laos et du Cambodge, Centre Catholique, Vientiane, Laos. Bp. Thomas Nantha (vic, ap. Vientiane).

Latvia: Pils Jela, 2, Riga. Card. Julijans Vaivods (Ap. Admin., Riga and Liepaja).

Lesotho: Lesotho Catholic Bishops' Conference, P.O. Box 200, Maseru 100. Bp. Sebastian Koto Khoarai, O.M.I. (Mohale's Hoek).

Liberia: See Gambia, Liberia and Sierra Leone.

Lithuania: Vilniaus gatve 4, 233000 Kaunas. Bp. Liudas Povilonis (Ap. Admin., Kaunas and Vilkaviskis).

Madagascar: Conference Episcopale du Madagascar, 102 bis, Av. Marechal Joffre Antanimena, B. P 667, Antananarivo. Card. Victor Razafimahatratra, S.J. (Tananarive).

Malawi: Episcopal Conference of Malawi, Catholic Secretariat of Malawi, P.O. Box 30384, Lilongwe 3. Bp. Felix Mkhori (Chikwawa).

Malaysia-Singapore-Brunei: Catholic Bishops' Conference of Malaysia-Singapore-Brunei, (BCMSB), Archbishop's House, 31 Victoria St., Singapore 0718. Gregory Yong Sooi Nghean (Singapore).

Mali: Conference Episcopale du Mali, B.P. 298, Bamako. Luc Auguste Sangare (Bamako).

Malta: Conferenza Episcopale Maltese, Archbishop's Curia, Floriana. Joseph Mercieca (Malta).

Mexico: Conferencia del Episcopado Mexicano (CEM), Apartado Postal 22-119, Victoria 21, Tlalpan 22, D.F. Sergio Obeso Rivera (Jalapa).

Mozambique: Conferencia Episcopal de Mocambique (CEM), C.P. 286, Maputo. Bp. Jaime Pedro Goncalves (Beira).

Netherlands: Nederlandse Bisschoppenconferentie, Postbus 13049, NL-3507 La, Utrecht. Card. Johannes Willebrands (Utrecht).

New Zealand: New Zealand Episcopal Conference, P.O. Box 198, Wellington. Card. Thomas Stafford Williams (Wellington).

Nicaragua: Conferencia Episcopal de Nicaragua, Apartado 3058, Managua. Miguel Obando Bravo, S.D.B. (Managua).

Niger: See Upper Volta.

Nigeria: National Episcopal Conference of Nigeria, P.O. Box 951, Lagos. Francis Arinze (Onitsha).

Pacific: Conference des Eveques du Pacifique (CEPAC), P.O. Box 1200, Suva, Fiji. Bp. Patelisio Punou-Ki-Hihifo Finau, S.M. (Tonga).

Pakistan: Pakistan Episcopal Conference, St. Patrick's Cathedral, Karachi 3. Card. Joseph Cordeiro (Karachi).

Panama: Conferencia Episcopal de Panama (CEP), Apartado 386, Panama 1. Bp. Jose Maria Carrizo Villareal (Chitre).

Papua New Guinea and Solomon Islands: Bishops' Conference of Papua New Guinea and Solomon Islands, Southern Highlands, P.O. Box 69, Mendi, Papua New Guinea. Bp. Firmin Schmidt, O.F.M. Cap. (Mendi).

Paraguay: Conferencia Episcopal Paraguaya (CEP), Calle Alberdi 782, Casilla Correo 1436, Asuncion. Bp. Felipe Santiago Benitez Avalos (Villarrica).

Peru: Conferencia Episcopal Peruana, Apartado 310, Lima 1. Card. Juan Landazuri Ricketts, O.F.M. (Lima).

Philippine Islands: Catholic Bishops' Conference of the Philippines (CBCP), P.O. Box 1160, Manila. Antonio Mabutas y Lloren (Davao).

Poland: Konferencja Episkopatu Polski, Ul. Wronia 84, 01-015 Warsaw. Card. Jozef Glemp (Gniezno and Warsaw).

Portugal: Conferencia Episcopal Portuguesa, Campo dos martires de Patria, 43-1 Esq., 1198 Lisbon. Bp. Manuel D'Almeida Trindade (Aveiro).

Puerto Rico: Conferencia Episcopal Puertorriquena (CEP), Apartado 5-1967, San Juan de Puerto Rico 00903. Card. Luis Aponte Martinez (San Juan).

Rhodesia: See Zimbabwe.

Rumania: Vacant.

Rwanda: Conference Episcopale du Rwanda (C.Ep.R.), B.P. 715, Kigali. Vincent Nsengiyumva (Kigali).

Scandinavia: Conferentia Episcopalis Scandiae, Akersvejen 5, P.B. 8270 Hammersborg, Oslo 1,

Norway. Bp. John W. Gran, O.C.S.O. (Oslo, Norway).

Senegal-Mauritania: Conference Episcopale du Senegal-Mauritania, B.P. 5082, Dakar, Fann. Senegal. Card. Hyacinthe Thiandoum (Dakar).

Sierra Leone: See Gambia, Liberia and Sierra Leone.

Spain: Conferencia Episcopal Espanola, Calle Anastro 1, Madrid 16. Gabino Diaz Merchan (Oviedo).

Sri Lanka: Catholic Bishops' Conference of Sri Lanka, Bishop's House, Chillaw. Bp. Frank Marcus Fernando (Chilaw).

Sudan: Sudan Episcopal Conference (SEC), P.O. Box 49, Khartoum. Gabriel Zubeir Wako (Khartoum).

Switzerland: Conference des Eveques Suisses, Secretariat, av. Moleson 30, CH-1700 Fribourg 1. Bp. Otmar Mader (Sankt Gallen).

Tanzania: Tanzania Episcopal Conference (TEC), P.O. Box 2133, Dar-es-Salaam. Bp. Anthony Mayala (Musoma).

Thailand: Conference des Eveques de Thailand, P.O. Box 5, Nakhonsawan. Bp. Joseph Banchong Aribarg (Nakhon Sawan).

Togo: Conference Episcopale du Togo, B.P. 348, Lome. Robert Dosseh Anyron (Lome).

Turkey: Conferenza Episcopale di Turchia, Olcek Sokak 83, Harbiya, Istanbul. Bp. Gauthier Pierre Dubois, O.F.M. Cap. (V.A., Istanbul).

Uganda: Uganda Episcopal Conference, P.O. Box 2886, Kampala. Bp. Barnabas Halem 'Imana (Kabale).

United States: See National Conference of Catholic Bishops.

Upper Volta and Niger: Conference des Eveques de la Haute-Volta et du Niger, B.P. 90, Ouagadougou, Upper Volta. Bp. Tatianma Anselm Sanan (Bobo-Dioulasso, Upper Volta).

Uruguay: Conferencia Episcopal Uruguaya (CEU), Avenida Uruguay 1319, Montevideo. Carlos Parteli (Montevideo).

Venezuela: Conferencia Episcopal de Venezuela (CEV), Apartado Postal 954, Caracas 101. Domingo Roa Perez (Maracaibo).

Vietnam: Conference Episcopale du Vietnam, 40 Pho Nha Chung, Hanoi. Card. Joseph-Marie Trinh van-Can (Hanoi).

Yugoslavia: Biskupska Konferencija Jugoslavije, Kaptol 31, P.B. 02-406, Zagreb. Card. Franjo Kuharic (Zagreb).

Zaire: Conference Episcopale du Zaire (CEZ), B.P. 3258, Kinshasa-Gombe. Bp. Kaseba (Kalemie-Kirungu).

Zambia: Zambian Episcopal Conference, P.O. Box 31965, Lusaka. Bp. James Spaita (Mansa).

Zimbabwe: Zimbabwe Catholic Bishops' Conference (ZCBC), P.O. Box 8135, Causeway, Harare. Patrick Chakaipa (Harare).

Territorial Conferences

Territorial as well as national episcopal conferences have been established in some places. Some conferences of this kind are still in the planning stage.

Africa: Association of Member Episcopal Conferences in Eastern Africa (AMECEA): Represents Uganda, Kenya, Tanzania, Zambia and Malawi; Ethiopia was accepted as associate member in 1977. Bishop Medard Joseph Mazombwe, Chipata, Zambia, president. Address: P.O. Box 21191, Nairobi, Kenya.

Symposium of Episcopal Conferences of Africa and Madagascar (SECAM) (Symposium des Conferences Episcopales d'Afrique et de Madagascar, SCEAM): Cardinal Paul Zoungrano, P.A., Ouagadougou, Upper Volta, president. Address: Secretariat, P.O. Box 7530, Accra-North, Ghana.

Regional Episcopal Conference of French-Speaking West Africa (Conference Episcopale Regionale de l'Afrique de l'Ouest Francophone, CERAO): Card. Paul Zoungrana, Ouagadougou, president. Address: B.P. 1471, Ouagadougou, Upper Volta.

Association of Episcopal Conferences of Anglo-Speaking West Africa (AECAWA): Card. Dominic Ignatius Ekandem, Ikot Ekpene, Nigeria, president. Address: P.O. Box 297, Monrovia, Liberia.

Association of Episcopal Conferences of Congo, Central African Republic and Chad (ACECCT): Abp. Joachim N'Dayen, Bangui, Central African Republic, president. Address: Secretariat, B.P. 1518, Bangui, Central African Republic.

Inter-Regional Meeting of Bishops of Southern Africa (IMBISA): Abp. Joseph R. Fitzgerald, O.M.I., bishop of Johannesburg, S. Africa, president. Address: P.O. Box 17054, Hillbrow 2038, Johannesburg, S. Africa.

Asia: Federation of Asian Bishops' Conferences (FABC): Represents 14 Asian episcopal conferences (excluding the Middle East). Headquarters, P.O. Box 2948, Hong Kong. Established in 1970; statutes approved experimentally Dec. 6, 1972. Abp. Mariano Gaviola Garces, Lipa, Philippines, secretary general.

Europe: Council of European Bishops' Conferences (Consilium Conferentiarum Episcopalium Europae, CCEE): Card. George Basil Hume, O.S.B., Westminster, England, president. Address of secretariat: Klosterhof 6b, CH-9000 St. Gallen, Switzerland.

Commission of the Episcopates of the European Community (Commissio Episcopatuum Communitatis Europaeae, COMECE): Established in 1980; represents episcopates of states which belong to European Community. Bishop Franz Hengsbach, Essen, Germany, president. Address of secretariat: 13 Avenue Pere Damien, 1150 Brussels, Belgium.

Central and South America: Latin American Bishops' Conference (Consejo Episcopal LatinoAmericano, CELAM): Established in 1956; statutes approved Nov. 9, 1974. Represents 22 Latin American national bishops' conferences. Bishop Antonio Quarracino, Avellaneda, Argentina, president. Address of the secretariat: Calle 78, no. 11-17, Apartado Aereo 5278, Bogota, D.E., Colombia.

Episcopal Secretariat of Central America and Panama (Secretariado Episcopal de America Central y Panama, SEDAC): Statutes approved experimentally Sept. 26, 1970. Archbishop Roman Arrieta Villalobos, San Jose de Costa Rica, president. Address of secretariat: Apartado 497, San Jose, Costa Rica.

INTERNATIONAL CATHOLIC ORGANIZATIONS

(Principal sources: Conference of International Catholic Organizations; Pontifical Council for the Laity; Almanac survey.)

Guidelines

International organizations wanting to call themselves "Catholic" are required to meet standards set by the Vatican's Council for the Laity and to register with and get the approval of the Papal Secretariat of State, according to guidelines dated Dec. 3 and published in *Acta Apostolicae Sedis* under date of Dec. 23, 1971.

Among conditions for the right of organizations to "bear the name Catholic" are:

• leaders "will always be Catholics," and candidates for office will be approved by the Secretariat of State;

• adherence by the organization to the Catholic Church, its teaching authority and teachings of the Gospel;

• evidence that the organization is really international with a universal outlook and that it fulfills its mission through its own management, meetings and accomplishments.

The guidelines also stated that leaders of the organizations "will take care to maintain necessary reserve as regards taking a stand or engaging in public activity in the field of politics or trade unionism. Abstention in these fields will normally be the best attitude for them to adopt during their term of office."

The guidelines were in line with a provision stated by the Second Vatican Council in the *Decree on the Apostolate of the Laity*: "No project may claim the name 'Catholic' unless it has obtained the consent of the lawful church authority."

They made it clear that all organizations are not obliged to apply for recognition, but that the Church "reserves the right to recognize as linked with her mission and her aims those organizations or movements which see fit to ask for such recognition."

Conference

Conference of International Catholic Organizations: A permanent body for collaboration among various organizations which seek to promote the development of international life along the lines of Christian principles. Eleven international Catholic organizations participated in its foundation and first meeting in 1927 at Fribourg, Switzerland. In 1951, the conference established its general secretariat and adopted governing statutes which were approved by the Vatican Secretariat of State in 1953.

The permanent secretariat is located at 37-39 rue de Vermont, CH-1202 Geneva, Switzerland. Other office addresses are: 1 rue de Varembe, C.P. 43, CH-1211 Geneva 20, Switzerland (Information Center); 9, rue Cler, F-75007 Paris, France (International Catholic Center for UNESCO); ICO Information Center, 323 East 47th St., New York, N.Y. 10017.

International Organizations

International Catholic organizations are listed below. Information includes name, date and place of establishment (when available), address of general secretariat. An asterisk indicates that the organization is a member of the Conference of International Catholic Organizations. Approximately 24 of the organizations have consultative status with other international or regional non-governmental agencies.

Apostleship of Prayer (1849): Borgo Santo Spirito 5, I-00193 Rome, Italy. National secretariat in most countries. (See Index.)

Apostolatus Maris (Apostleship of the Sea) (1922, Glasgow, Scotland): Pontifical Commission for Migration and Tourism, Piazza San Calisto 16, I-00153 Rome, Italy. (See Index.)

Associationes Juventutis Salesianae (Associations of Salesian Youth) (1847): Via della Pisana, 1111, 00163 Rome, Italy.

Blue Army of Our Lady of Fatima: (See Index.)

Caritas Internationalis* (1951, Rome, Italy): Piazza San Calisto 16, I-00153, Rome, Italy. Coordinates relief aid on an international level.

Catholic International Education Office* (1952): 60, rue des Eburons, B-1040 Brussels, Belgium.

Catholic International Federation for Physical and Sports Education* (1911; present name, 1957): 5, rue Cernuschi, F-75017 Paris, France.

Catholic International Union for Social Service* (1925, Milan, Italy): rue de la Poste 111, B-1030 Brussels, Belgium (general secretariat).

Christian Fraternity of the Sick and Handicapped: 9, Avenue de la Gare, CH-1630, Bulle, Switzerland.

"Focolari" (1943, Trent, Italy): Via di Frascati, 302, I-00040 Rocca di Papa (Rome), Italy. (See Index: Focolare Movement.)

International Association of Charities of St. Vincent de Paul* (1617, Chatillon les Dombes, France): 38, rue d'Alsace-Lorraine, B-1050 Brussels, Belgium. (See Index: St. Vincent de Paul Society.)

International Association of Children of Mary (1847): 67 rue de Sèvres, F-75006 Paris, France.

International Catholic Association for Service to Young Women and Girls* (1897): 37-39 rue de Vermont, Case Postale n 22, CH-1211 Geneva 20 CIC, Switzerland. Welfare of Catholic girls living away from home.

International Catholic Auxiliaries (1937, Belgium): 91, rue de la Servette, CH-1202 Geneva, Switzerland.

International Catholic Child Bureau* (1947): 65, rue de Lausanne, CH-1202 Geneva, Switzerland.

International Catholic Conference of Guiding* (1965): Rue Paul-Emile Janson, 35, B-1050 Brussels, Belgium. Founded by member bodies of interdenominational World Association of Guides and Girl Scouts.

International Catholic Conference of Scouting* (1948): 21, rue de Dublin, B-1050 Brussels, Belgium.

International Catholic Film Organization* (1928, The Hague, The Netherlands): 8, rue de l'Orme, B-1040 Brussels, Belgium (general secretariat). Federation of national Catholic film offices.

International Catholic Migration Commission* (1951): 65, rue de Lausanne, CH-1202 Geneva, Switzerland. Coordinates Catholic activities to help migrants.

International Catholic Rural Association (1962, Rome): Piazza San Calisto 16, I-00153 Rome, Italy. International body for agricultural and rural organizations.

International Catholic Union of the Press*: 37-39 rue de Vermont, Case Postale 197 CH-1211 Geneva 20 CIC, Switzerland. Coordinates and represents at the international level the activities of Catholics and Catholic federations or associations in the field of press and information. Has five specialized branches: International Federation of Catholic Dailies and Periodicals (1928); International Federation of Catholic Journalists (1927); International Federation of Catholic Press Agencies (1950); International Catholic Association of Teachers and Scientific or Technical Research Workers on Information (1968); Federation of Church Press Associations (1974).

International Centre for Studies in Religious Education* (1934-35, Louvain, Belgium, under name Catechetical Documentary Centre; present name, 1956): 184, rue Washington, B-1050 Brussels, Belgium. Also referred to as Lumen Vitae Centre; concerned with all aspects of religious formation.

International Committee of Catholic Nurses* (1933): Piazza San Calisto, 16, 00153 Rome, Italy.

International Cooperation for Socio-Economic Development (1965, Rome, Italy): 104, Avenue Princess Elisabeth, B-1030 Brussels, Belgium.

International Council of Catholic Men* (Unum Omnes) (1948): Piazza San Calisto 16, I-00153 Rome, Italy.

International Crusade for the Blind (1957): Chamblious 18, CH-1700 Fribourg, Switzerland. Coordinates action of Catholic groups and associations for the blind and develops their apostolate.

International Federation of Catholic Medical Associations (1954)): 6, Highgate West Hill, London N. 6, England.

International Federation of Catholic Parochial Youth Communities* (1962, Rome, Italy): Kipdorp 30, B-2000 Antwerp, Belgium.

International Federation of Catholic Pharmacists* (1954): 59, Bergstrasse, B-4700 Eupen, Belgium.

International Federation of Catholic Rural Movements* (1964, Lisbon, Portugal): 92, rue Africaine, B-1050 Brussels, Belgium.

International Federation of Catholic Universities* (1949): 78A, rue de Sevres, F-75341 Paris Codex 7, France.

International Federation of Institutes for Social and Socio-Religious Research (1952): Vlamingenstraat, 116, B-3000 Leuven, Belgium.

International Military Apostolate (1967): 20, rue Notre-Dame des Champs, F-75006 Paris, France. Comprised of organizations of military men.

International Movement of Apostolate of Children* (1929, France): 8, rue Duguay-Trouin, F-75006 Paris, France.

International Movement of Apostolate in Middle and Upper Classes* (1963): Piazza San Calisto 16, I-00153 Rome, Italy. Evangelization of adults of the independent milieus (that part of population known as old or recent middle class, aristocracy, bourgeoisie or "white collar").

International Movement of Catholic Agricultural and Rural Youth (1954, Annevoie, Belgium): Tiensevest 68, B-3000 Leuven, Belgium (permanent secretariat).

International Young Catholic Students* (1946, Fribourg, Switzerland; present name, 1954): 171 rue de Rennes, F-75006 Paris, France.

International Young Christian Workers* (1925, Belgium): 11, rue Plantin, B-1070 Brussels, Belgium.

Laity and Christian Community (1966, Algiers, Algeria): 80, rue de Tourbillon, CH-1950 Sion, Switzerland. Universal brotherhood.

Legion of Mary* (1921, Dublin, Ireland): De Montfort House, North Brunswick St., Dublin, Ireland. (See Index.)

Medicus Mundi: P.O. Box 1547, 6501 BN Nijmegen, Netherlands. Place medicine at service of poor.

Movement for a Better World (1952): Via Vinovo, 58, 00166, Rome, Italy. (See Index.)

Our Lady's Teams (Equipes Notre-Dame) (1937, France): 49, rue de la Glacière, F-75013 Paris, France. Movement for spiritual formation of couples.

Pax Christi (1950): Kerkstraat, 150, B-2000 Antwerp, Belgium. (See Index.)

Pax Romana* (1921, Fribourg, Switzerland, divided into two movements, 1947):

International Movement of Catholic Students* (1921): 171, rue de Rennes, F-75006, Paris, France. For undergraduates.

International Catholic Movement for Intellectual and Cultural Affairs* (1947): 37-39 rue de Vermont, Case Postale n 85, CH-1211 Geneva 20 CIC, Switzerland. For university graduates. Has professional secretariats at: Stradhouderskade 86, Amsterdam, The Netherlands (artists); Biesseltsebaan, 40, Nijmegen, The Netherlands (teachers); 18 rue de Varenne, F-75007 Paris, France (engineers); via della Conciliazione 4d, I-00193 Rome, Italy (lawyers).

St. Joan's International Alliance (1911 in England; present title, 1931): 7, Hayes Lane, Kenley, Surrey, England CR2 5LE.

Salesian Cooperators (1876): Don Bosco College, Newton, N.J. 07860. Third Salesian family founded by St. John Bosco. Members commit themselves to an apostolate at the service of the Church, giving particular attention to youth in the Salesian spirit and style.

Secular Franciscan Order (1221, first Rule approved): Via Piemonte, 70, 00187, Rome, Italy. (See Index.)

Serra International (1953, in U.S.): (See Index.)

Society of St. Vincent de Paul* (1933): 5, rue Pré-aux-Clercs, F-75007 Paris, France.

The Grail (1921, Nijmegen, The Netherlands): Duisburgerstrasse 470, D-4330, Mulheim, West Germany. (See Index.)

Third Order of St. Dominic (1285): Convento Santa Sabina, Piazza Pietro d'Illiria, Aventino, I-00153 Rome, Italy. (See Index.)

Unda: International Catholic Association for Radio and Television* (1928, Cologne, Germany): rue de l'Orme, 12, B-1040 Brussels, Belgium. (See Index.)

Unio Internationalis Laicorum in Servitio Ecclesiae (1965, Aachen, Germany): Postfach 990125, Am Kielshof 2, 5000 Cologne, Germany 91. Consists of national and diocesan associations of persons who give professional services to the Church.

Union of Adorers of the Blessed Sacrament (1937): Largo dei Monti Parioli 3, I-00197, Rome, Italy.

World Catholic Federation for the Biblical Apostolate (1969, Rome): Mittelstrasse, 12, D 7000, Stuttgart 1, Germany.

World Federation of Christian Life Communities* (1953): 8, Borgo Santo Spirito, I-00193, Rome, Italy. First Sodality of Our Lady founded in 1563.

World Movement of Christian Workers* (1961): 90, rue des Palais, B-1030 Brussels, Belgium.

World Organization of Former Students of Catholic Schools (1967, Rome): Largo Nazareno 25, I-00167 Rome, Italy.

World Union of Catholic Philosophical Societies (1948, Amsterdam, The Netherlands): The Catholic University of America, Washington, D.C. 20064.

World Union of Catholic Teachers* (1951): Piazza San Calisto 16, I-00153, Rome, Italy.

World Union of Catholic Women's Organizations* (1910): 20, rue Notre Dame des Champs, F-75006 Paris, France.

Regional Organizations

European Federation for Catholic Adult Education (1963, Lucerne, Switzerland): Bildunghaus Turnseestrasse 24, D-7800, Freiburg 1. B2, Germany.

European Forum of National Committees of the Laity (1968): 12, Brookwood Lawn Artane, Dublin 5, Ireland.

Movimiento Familiar Cristiano (1949-50, Montevideo and Buenos Aires): Carrera 17 n. 4671, Bogota, D.E., Colombia. Christian Family Movement of Latin America.

COMMUNISM

The substantive principles of modern Communism, a theory and system of economics and social organization, were stated about the middle of the 19th century by Karl Marx, author of *The Com-*munist Manifesto* and, with Friedrich Engels, *Das Kapital.*

The elements of Communist ideology include: radical materialism; dialectical determinism; the inevitability of class struggle, which is to be furthered for the ultimate establishment of a worldwide, classless society; common ownership of productive and other goods; the subordination of all persons and institutions to the dictatorship of the collectivity; denial of the rights, dignity and liberty of persons; militant atheism and hostility to religion; utilitarian morality.

Communism in theory and practice has been the subject of many papal documents and statements. Pius IX condemned it in 1846. Leo XIII dealt with it at length in the encyclicals *Quod Apostolici Muneris* in 1878 and *Rerum Novarum* in 1891. Pius XI wrote on the same subject the encyclicals *Quadragesimo Anno* in 1931 and *Divini Redemptoris* in 1937. These writings were updated and developed in new directions by Pius XII, John XXIII, Paul VI and John Paul II.

OUR LADY OF CZESTOCHOWA

The Black Madonna, the icon of Our Lady of Czestochowa, is enshrined on the "Hill of Light," Jasna Gora, above the city of Czestochowa in south central Poland. Long the center and focus of Marian devotion since it was brought there in 1382, it is the primary symbol of Polish religious faith and freedom.

The icon is a portrayal of Mary holding the Child Jesus. Their faces and hands are dark, as though they had been burned or stained by smoke. Three cuts are on one of Mary's cheeks, put there by robbers who desecrated the icon in 1430.

The origin of the icon is not clear. Elements of the legend say it was painted by St. Luke on a panel made by St. Joseph for the home of the Holy Family in Nazareth; that it was transported from the Holy Land to Constantinople; that it was given in 988 to a Ukrainian princess, Anna, the wife of Vladimir of Kiev; and that it eventually was brought to Czestochowa in 1382. The *Catholic Encyclopedia* notes another possibility, that the icon was of Greek-Italian origin in the ninth century.

The location of the icon on the hill above Czestochowa was related to the establishment of a priory of Pauline monks there, also in 1382. A shrine was built some time after 1386. A church was erected in 1644, and a 344-foot tower was raised in 1702.

Our Lady of Czestochowa was declared the Queen of Poland in 1656, and the icon was solemnly crowned in 1717 during the pontificate of Pope Clement XI.

The shrine has a long history as the greatest pilgrimage and religious center in Central Europe.

The shrine has undergone changes, some of them violent, in the years since 1382. Even in this century it has been a target of search and harassment by officials of the Communist government in control of the country since the end of World War II.

One thing has not changed, however; that is the significance of the icon and Czestochowa in the religious and patriotic life of the Polish people.

THE CATHOLIC CHURCH IN CANADA

The first date in the remote background of the Catholic history of Canada was July 7, 1534, when a priest in the exploration company of Jacques Cartier celebrated Mass on the Gaspe Peninsula.

Successful colonization and the significant beginnings of the Catholic history of the country date from the foundation of Quebec in 1608 by Samuel Champlain and French settlers. Montreal was established in 1642.

The earliest missionaries were Franciscan Recollects and Jesuits who arrived in 1615 and 1625, respectively. They provided some pastoral care for the settlers but worked mainly among the 100,000 Indians — Algonquins and Huron-Iroquois — in the interior and in the Lake Ontario region. Five Jesuits of the group of eight North American Martyrs were killed in the 1640s; Isaac Jogues and two lay missionaries were martyred at Ossernenon (Auriesville, N.Y.). Sulpician Fathers, who arrived in Canada late in the 1640's, played a part in the great missionary period which ended about 1700.

Kateri Tekakwitha, "Lily of the Mohawks," who was baptized in 1676 and died in 1680, was declared "Blessed" June 22, 1980.

The communities of women religious with the longest histories in Canada are the Canonesses of St. Augustine, since 1637; the Ursulines, since 1639; and the Hospitallers of St. Joseph, since 1642. Communities of Canadian origin are the Congregation of Notre Dame, founded by St. Marguerite Bourgeoys in 1658, and the Grey Nuns, formed by Bl. Marie Marguerite d'Youville in 1738.

Mother Marie (Guyard) of the Incarnation, an Ursuline nun, was one of the first three women missionaries to New France; called "Mother of the Church in Canada," she was declared "Blessed" June 22, 1980.

Start of Church Organization

Ecclesiastical organization began with the appointment in 1658 of Francois De Montmorency-Laval, "Father of the Church in Canada," as vicar apostolic of New France. He was the first bishop of Quebec from 1674 to 1688, with jurisdiction over all French-claimed territory in North America. He was declared "Blessed" June 22, 1980.

In 1713, the French Canadian population numbered 18,000. In the same year, the Treaty of Utrecht ceded Acadia, Newfoundland and the Hudson Bay Territory to England. The Acadians were scattered among the American Colonies in 1755.

The English acquired possession of Canada and its 70,000 French-speaking inhabitants in virtue of the Treaty of Paris in 1763. Anglo-French and Anglican-Catholic differences and tensions developed. The pro-British government at first refused to recognize the titles of church officials, hindered the clergy in their work and tried to install a non-Catholic educational system. Laws were passed which guaranteed religious liberties to Catholics (Quebec Act of 1774, Constitutional Act of 1791, legislation approved by Queen Victoria in 1851), but it took some time before actual respect for these liberties matched the legal enactments. The initial moderation of government antipathy toward the Church was caused partly by the loyalty of Catholics to the Crown during the American Revolution and the War of 1812.

Growth

The 15 years following the passage in 1840 of the Act of Union, which joined Upper and Lower Canada, were significant. New communities of men and women religious joined those already in the country. The Oblates of Mary Immaculate, missionaries par excellence in Canada, advanced the penetration of the West which had been started in 1818 by Abbe Provencher. New jurisdictions were established, and Quebec became a metropolitan see in 1844. The first Council of Quebec was held in 1851. The established Catholic school system enjoyed a period of growth.

Laval University was inaugurated in 1854 and canonically established in 1876.

Archbishop Elzear-Alexandre Taschereau of Quebec was named Canada's first cardinal in 1886.

The apostolic delegation to Canada was set up in 1899. It became a nunciature October 16, 1969, with the establishment of diplomatic relations with the Vatican.

Early in this century, Canada had eight ecclesiastical provinces, 23 dioceses, three vicariates apostolic, 3,500 priests, 2.4 million Catholics, about 30 communities of men religious, and 70 or more communities of women religious. The Church in Canada was phased out of mission status and removed from the jurisdiction of the Congregation for the Propagation of the Faith in 1908.

Diverse Population

The greatest concentration of Catholics is in the eastern portion of the country. In the northern and western portions, outside metropolitan centers, there are some of the most difficult parish and mission areas in the world. Bilingual (English-French) differences in the general population are reflected in the Church; for example, in the parallel structures of the Canadian Conference of Catholic Bishops, which was established in 1943. Quebec is the center of French cultural influence. Many language groups are represented among Catholics, who include about 211,265 members of Eastern Rite in a metropolitan see, six eparchies and an apostolic exarchate.

Education, a past source of friction between the Church and the government, is administered by the civil provinces in a variety of arrangements authorized by the Canadian Constitution. Denominational schools have tax support in one way in Quebec and Newfoundland, and in another way in Alberta, Ontario and Saskatchewan. Several provinces provide tax support only for public schools, making private financing necessary for separate church-related schools.

ECCLESIASTICAL JURISDICTIONS OF CANADA

Provinces

Names of ecclesiastical provinces and metropolitan sees in bold face: suffragan sees in parentheses.

Edmonton (Calgary, St. Paul).

Grouard-McLennan (Mackenzie-Ft. Smith, Prince George, Whitehorse).

Halifax (Antigonish, Charlottetown, Yarmouth).

Keewatin-LePas (Churchill-Hudson Bay, Labrador-Schefferville, Moosonee).

Kingston (Alexandria-Cornwall, Peterborough, Sault Ste. Marie).

Moncton (Bathurst, Edmundston, St. John).

Montreal (Joliette, St. Jean-Longueuil, St. Jerome, Valleyfield).

Ottawa (Gatineau-Hull, Hearst, Mont-Laurier, Pembroke, Rouyn-Noranda, Timmins).

Quebec (Amos, Chicoutimi, Ste.-Anne-de-la-Pocatiere, Trois Rivieres).

Regina (Gravelbourg, Prince Albert, Saskatoon, Abbey of St. Peter).

Rimouski (Gaspe, Hauterive).

St. Boniface (no suffragans).

St. John's (Grand Falls, St. George).

Sherbrooke (Nicolet, St. Hyacinthe).

Toronto (Hamilton, London, St. Catharines, Thunder Bay).

Vancouver (Kamloops, Nelson, Victoria).

Winnipeg — Ukrainian (Edmonton, New Westminster, Saskatoon, Toronto).

Jurisdictions immediately subject to the Holy See: Roman-Rite Archdiocese of Winnipeg, Byzantine-Rite Eparchy of Sts. Cyril and Methodius for Slovaks, Byzantine-Rite Apostolic Exarchate for Greek Melkites; Antiochene-Rite Eparchy of St. Maron of Montreal for Maronites.

Archdioceses, Archbishops

Edmonton, Alta. (St. Albert, 1871; archdiocese, transferred Edmonton, 1912): Joseph N. MacNeil, archbishop, 1973.

Grouard-McLennan, Alta. (v.a. Athabaska-Mackenzie, 1862; Grouard, 1927; archdiocese Grouard-McLennan, 1967); Henri Legare, O.M.I., archbishop, 1972.

Halifax, N.S. (1842; archdiocese, 1852): James M. Hayes, archbishop, 1967.

Keewatin-Le Pas, Man. (v.a., 1910; archdiocese, 1967): Paul Dumouchel, O.M.I., archbishop, 1967.

Kingston, Ont. (1826; archdiocese, 1889): Francis J. Spence, archbishop, 1982.

Moncton, N.B. (1936): Donat Chiasson, archbishop, 1972.

Montreal, Que. (1836; archdiocese, 1886): Paul Gregoire, archbishop, 1968. Valerien Belanger, Andre Cimichella, O.S.M., Leonard Crowley, Gerard Tremblay, Jude Saint-Antoine, Jean-Claude Turcotte, auxiliaries.

Ottawa, Ont. (Bytown, 1847, name changed, 1854; archdiocese, 1886): Joseph Aurele Plourde, archbishop, 1967. John Beahen, Gilles Belisle, auxiliaries.

Quebec, Que. (v.a., 1658; diocese, 1674; archdiocese, 1819; metropolitan, 1844; primatial see, 1956): Louis-Albert Vachon, archbishop, 1981. Jean-Paul Labrie, Maurice Couture, Marc Leclerc, auxiliaries.

Regina, Sask. (1910; archdiocese, 1915): Charles A. Halpin, archbishop, 1973.

Rimouski, Que. (1867; archdiocese, 1946): Gilles Ouellet, P.M.E., archbishop, 1973.

St. Boniface, Man. (1847; archdiocese, 1871): Antoine Hacault, archbishop, 1974.

St. John's, Nfld. (p.a., 1784; v.a., 1796; diocese, 1847; archdiocese, 1904): Alphonsus Penney, archbishop, 1979.

Sherbrooke, Que. (1874; archdiocese, 1951); J.-M. Fortier, archbishop, 1968.

Toronto, Ont. (1841; archdiocese, 1870): Cardinal G. Emmett Carter, archbishop, 1978. Aloysius M. Ambrozic, Michael Pearse Lacey, Robert B. Clune, Leonard J. Wall, auxiliaries.

Vancouver, B. C. (v.a. British Columbia, 1863; diocese New Westminster, 1890; archdiocese Vancouver, 1908): James F. Carney, archbishop, 1969.

Winnipeg, Man. (1915): Adam Exner, O.M.I, archbishop, 1982.

Winnipeg, Man. (Ukrainian Byzantine Rite) (Ordinariate of Canada, 1912; ap. ex. Central Canada, 1948; ap. ex. Manitoba, 1951; archdiocese Winnipeg, 1956): Maxim Hermaniuk, C.SS.R., archbishop, 1956. Myron Daciuk, O.S.B.M., auxiliary.

Dioceses, Bishops

Alexandria-Cornwall, Ont. (1890): Eugene Philippe LaRocque, bishop, 1974.

Amos, Que. (1938): Gerard Drainville, bishop, 1978.

Antigonish, N.S. (Arichat, 1844; transferred, 1886): William E. Power, bishop, 1960.

Bathurst, N.B. (Chatham, 1860; transferred, 1938): Edgar Godin, bishop, 1969.

Calgary, Alta. (1912): Paul J. O'Byrne, bishop, 1968.

Charlottetown, P.E.I. (1829): James H. MacDonald, C.S.C., bishop, 1982.

Chicoutimi, Que. (1878): Jean-Guy Couture, bishop, 1979. Roch Pedneault, auxiliary.

Churchill-Hudson Bay, Man. (p.a., 1925; v.a. Hudson Bay, 1931; diocese Churchill, 1967; Churchill-Hudson Bay, 1968): Omer Robidoux, O.M.I., bishop, 1970.

Edmonton, Alta. (Ukrainian Byzantine Rite) (ap. ex., 1948; diocese, 1956): Nile Nicholas Savaryn, O.S.B.M., bishop, 1948. Martin Greschuk, auxiliary.

Edmundston, N.B. (1944): Vacant as of June 29, 1983.

Gaspe, Que. (1922): Bertrand Blanchet, bishop, 1973.

Gatineau-Hull, Que. (1963 as Hull; name changed, 1982); Adolphe E. Proulx, bishop, 1974.

Grand Falls, Nfld. (Harbour Grace, 1856; present title, 1964): Joseph Faber MacDonald, bishop, 1980.

Gravelbourg, Sask. (1930): Noel Delaquis, bishop, 1974.

Hamilton, Ont. (1856): Paul F. Reding, bishop, 1973. Anthony Tonnos, auxiliary.

Hauterive, Que. (p.a., 1882; v.a., 1905; diocese Gulf of St. Lawrence, 1945; name changed, 1960): Roger Ebacher, bishop, 1979.

Hearst, Ont. (p.a., 1918; v.a., 1920; diocese, 1938): Roger Despatie, bishop, 1973.

Joliette, Que. (1904): Rene Audet, bishop, 1968.

Kamloops, B.C. (1945): Lawrence Sabatini, C.S., bishop, 1982.

Labrador (Nfld.)-Schefferville, Que. (v.a. Labrador, 1945; diocese, 1967): Peter A. Sutton, O.M.I., bishop, 1974.

London, Ont. (1855; transferred Sandwich, 1859; London, 1869): John Sherlock, bishop, 1978. Marcel Gervais, auxiliary.

Mackenzie-Fort Smith, N.W.T. (v.a. Mackenzie, 1901; diocese Mackenzie-Fort Smith, 1967): Paul Piché, O.M.I., bishop, 1967.

Mont-Laurier, Que. (1913): Jean Gratton, bishop, 1978.

Moosonee, Ont. (v.a. James Bay, 1938; diocese Moosonee, 1967): Jules LeGuerrier, O.M.I., bishop, 1967.

Nelson, B.C. (1936): Wilfred Emmett Doyle, bishop, 1958.

New Westminster, B.C. (Ukrainian Byzantine Rite) (1974): Jerome Chimy, O.S.B.M., bishop, 1974.

Nicolet, Que. (1885): Albertus Martin, bishop, 1950.

Pembroke, Ont. (v.a. 1882; diocese, 1898): Joseph R. Windle, bishop, 1971.

Peterborough, Ont. (1882): James L. Doyle, bishop, 1976.

Prince Albert, Sask. (v.a., 1890; diocese, 1907): Blaise Morand, bishop, 1983.

Prince George, B.C. (p.a., 1908; v.a. Yukon and Prince Rupert, 1944; diocese Prince George, 1967): J. Fergus O'Grady, O.M.I., bishop, 1967.

Rouyn-Noranda, Que. (1973): Jean-Guy Hamelin, bishop, 1974.

St. Catharines, Ont. (1958): Thomas B. Fulton, bishop, 1978.

St. George's, Nfld. (p.a., 1870; v.a., 1890; diocese, 1904): Richard T. McGrath, bishop, 1970.

St. Hyacinthe, Que. (1852): Louis-de-Gonzague Langevin, bishop, 1979.

Saint-Jean-Longueuil, Que. (1933 as St.-Jean-de-Quebec; named changed, 1982): Bernard Hubert, bishop, 1978.

St. Jerome, Que. (1951): Charles Valois, bishop, 1977. Raymond Saint-Gelais, auxiliary.

Saint John, N.B. (1842): Arthur J. Gilbert, bishop, 1974.

St. Maron of Montreal (Maronites) (1982); Elias Shaheen, eparch, 1982.

St. Paul in Alberta (1948): Raymond Roy, bishop, 1972.

Sts. Cyril and Methodius, Toronto, Ont. (Slovakian Byzantine Rite) (1981): Michael Rusnak, C.Ss.R., bishop, 1981.

Sainte-Anne-de-la-Pocatiere, Que. (1951): C.-H. Levesque, bishop, 1968.

Saskatoon, Sask. (1933): James P. Mahoney, bishop, 1967.

Saskatoon, Sask. (Ukrainian Byzantine Rite) (ap. ex., 1951; diocese, 1956): Vacant as of June 29, 1983.

Sault Ste. Marie, Ont. (1904): Alexander Carter, bishop, 1958. Bernard F. Pappin, Gerard Dionne, auxiliaries.

Thunder Bay, Ont. (Ft. William, 1952; transferred, 1970): John A. O'Mara, bishop, 1976.

Timmins, Ont. (v.a. Temiskaming, 1908; diocese Haileybury, 1915; present title, 1938): Jacques Landriault, bishop, 1971.

Toronto, Ont. (Ukrainian Byzantine Rite) (ap. ex., 1948; diocese, 1956): Isidore Borecky, bishop, 1948.

Trois-Rivieres, Que. (1852): Laurent Noel, bishop, 1975.

Valleyfield, Que. (1892): Robert Lebel, bishop, 1976.

Victoria, B.C. (diocese Vancouver Is., 1846; archdiocese, 1903; diocese Victoria, 1908): Remi J. De Roo, bishop, 1962.

Whitehorse, Y.T. (v.a., 1944; diocese 1967): Hubert P. O'Connor, O.M.I., bishop, 1971.

Yarmouth, N.S. (1953): Austin-Emile Burke, bishop, 1968.

Apostolic Exarchate for Greek Melkites (Montreal, Que.) (1980): Archbishop Michel Hakim, B.S., exarch, 1980.

Military Vicariate of Canada (1951): Archbishop Francis J. Spence, military vicar.

Abbacy of St. Peter, Muenster, Sask. (1921): Jerome Weber, O.S.B. (blessed, 1960).

An **Apostolic Exarchate for Armenian-Rite Catholics in Canada and the United States** was established in July, 1981, with headquarters in New York City.

Dioceses with Interprovincial Lines

The following dioceses, indicated by + in the table, have interprovincial lines.

Churchill-Hudson Bay includes part of Northwest Territories.

Keewatin-Le Pas includes part of Manitoba and Saskatchewan provinces.

Labrador-Schefferville includes the Labrador region of Newfoundland and the northern part of Quebec province.

MacKenzie-Fort Smith, Northwest Territories, includes part of Alberta and Saskatchewan provinces.

Moosonee, Ont., includes part of Quebec province.

Pembroke, Ont., includes one county of Quebec province.

Whitehorse, Y.T., includes part of British Columbia.

The Administrative Committee of the National Conference of Catholic Bishops, at a meeting Sept. 13 to 15, 1983, authorized continuation of a project for the preparation of uniform liturgical texts in Spanish for use in the United States.

STATISTICS OF CATHOLIC CHURCH IN CANADA

(Principal source: *1983 Directory of the Canadian Conference of Catholic Bishops.* Permanent deacon statistics are from the *1983 Annuario Pontificio.* Archdioceses are indicated by an asterisk. For dioceses marked +, see Canadian Dioceses with Interprovincial Lines.)

Canada's 10 civil provinces and two territories are divided into 17 ecclesiastical provinces consisting of 17 metropolitan sees (archdioceses) and 52 suffragan sees (51 dioceses and one abbacy); there are also one archdiocese, one eparchy and one exarchate immediately subject to the Holy See. (See listing of Ecclesiastical Provinces elsewhere in this section.)

This table presents a regional breakdown of Catholic statistics. In some cases, the totals are approximate because diocesan boundaries fall within several civil provinces.

Civil Province Diocese	Cath. Pop.	Dioc. Priests	Rel. Priests	Total Priests	Perm. Deacs.	Bros.	Srs.	Parishes
Newfoundland.............	199,370	123	38	161	—	92	514	279
*St. John's................	111,280	57	19	76	—	61	333	88
Grand Falls..............	34,365	32	2	34	—	15	72	106
Labrador-Schefferville+..........	15,703	3	16	19	—	8	36	24
St. George's.............	38,022	31	1	32	—	8	73	61
Prince Edward Island								
Charlottetown............	51,084	75	1	76	1	—	263	57
Nova Scotia...............	283,400	287	54	341	13	10	1,052	219
*Halifax.................	120,000	76	28	104	13	3	448	51
Antigonish..............	126,400	188	9	197	—	6	537	127
Yarmouth...............	37,000	23	17	40	—	1	67	41
New Brunswick...........	347,967	309	101	410	2	46	1,207	272
*Moncton................	76,430	80	49	129	—	22	400	64
Bathurst................	112,435	85	26	111	—	11	377	70
Edmundston.............	54,102	57	14	71	—	11	195	37
St. John................	105,000	87	12	99	2	2	235	101
Quebec....................	5,560,075	4,188	2,814	7,002	124	2,727	25,417	1,911
*Montreal...............	1,506,220	700	1,237	1,937	25	875	8,113	292
*Quebec.................	953,283	830	510	1,340	43	183	6,021	274
*Rimouski...............	162,737	230	63	293	1	45	975	117
*Sherbrooke.............	254,169	314	134	448	5	117	1,450	147
Amos...................	104,983	92	23	115	—	23	299	82
Chicoutimi..............	272,388	290	80	370	4	119	911	95
Gaspe..................	106,007	103	21	124	1	11	280	63
Gatineau-Hull............	145,000	83	71	154	2	16	360	61
Hauterive..............	110,840	60	31	91	3	26	254	52
Joliette.................	160,820	145	55	200	1	147	618	58
Mont Laurier.............	74,168	71	19	90	—	55	219	59
Nicolet.................	166,840	228	37	265	9	142	1,115	85
Rouyn-Noranda...........	55,410	31	24	55	—	14	165	41
Ste.-Anne-de-la-Pocatiere............	93,056	184	10	194	—	9	401	54
St. Hyacinthe............	303,541	239	122	361	22	399	1,583	115
St. Jean-Longueuil........	431,434	161	112	273	—	97	727	88
St. Jerome..............	244,850	114	120	234	2	147	329	36
Trois Rivieres...........	241,479	202	95	297	5	213	1,213	97
Valleyfield..............	172,850	111	50	161	1	89	384	65
Ontario..................	2,582,696	1,302	1,212	2,514	144	403	5,218	1,185
*Kingston...............	62,651	73	5	78	—	—	258	68
*Ottawa.................	293,936	155	221	376	10	121	1,252	113
*Toronto................	1,000,000	239	505	744	88	145	1,048	189
Alexandria-Cornwall......	43,805	46	8	54	1	13	119	39
Hamilton...............	305,000	146	148	294	1	52	554	120
Hearst.................	34,645	21	5	26	—	2	54	40
London.................	337,806	245	122	367	—	23	754	175

Civil Province Diocese	Cath. Pop.	Dioc. Priests	Rel. Priests	Total Priests	Perm. Deacs.	Bros.	Srs.	Par- ishes
Ontario								
Moosonee+	2,500	—	11	11	1	8	9	8
Pembroke+	55,498	58	13	71	—	3	300	72
Peterborough	54,085	67	5	72	—	2	176	77
St. Catharines	100,000	63	38	101	—	2	83	47
Sault Ste. Marie	175,000	130	72	202	42	10	445	115
Thunder Bay	58,000	24	43	67	—	1	68	88
Timmins	59,770	35	16	51	1	21	98	34
Manitoba	205,700	146	203	349	21	59	1,018	231
*Keewatin-LePas+	23,000	1	32	33	2	8	49	32
*St. Boniface	80,000	97	71	168	6	38	605	108
*Winnipeg	97,500	48	83	131	13	10	355	68
Churchill-Hudson Bay+	5,200	—	17	17	—	3	9	23
Saskatchewan	208,219	188	143	331	—	20	791	408
*Regina	90,000	86	44	130	—	3	245	181
Gravelbourg	13,798	29	5	34	—	—	90	49
Prince Albert	47,421	38	28	66	—	6	190	88
Saskatoon	45,000	35	37	72	—	1	172	66
St. Peter Muenster (Abb.)	12,000	—	29	29	—	10	94	24
Alberta	367,765	231	243	474	1	45	916	422
*Edmonton	165,000	102	114	216	—	23	605	179
*Grouard-McLennan	30,000	3	41	44	—	4	64	81
Calgary	130,000	94	76	170	1	18	168	88
St. Paul	42,765	32	12	44	—	—	79	74
British Columbia	317,742	173	181	354	1	54	620	302
*Vancouver	175,000	94	109	203	—	31	326	70
Kamloops	28,000	17	14	31	1	6	48	76
Nelson	40,519	30	13	43	—	1	61	57
Prince George	30,223	4	23	27	—	8	56	40
Victoria	44,000	28	22	50	—	8	129	59
Yukon Territory								
Whitehorse+	7,738	2	16	18	—	2	12	16
Northwest Territories								
MacKenzie-Ft. Smith+	18,390	1	34	35	—	22	42	50
Eastern Rite (Ukrainians) ...	211,265	168	72	240	25	17	138	503
*Winnipeg	55,000	38	17	55	8	2	30	166
Edmonton	41,065	31	15	46	5	9	35	98
New Westminster	7,000	10	4	14	1	—	6	23
Saskatoon	25,000	16	20	36	2	4	42	129
Toronto	83,200	73	16	89	9	2	25	87
Other Eastern Rites								
Sts. Cyril and Methodius of Toronto (Slovaks)	30,000	(See Note below.)						
St. Maron of Montreal (Maronites)	—	(See Note below.)						
Greek Melkites (Ap. Ex.) ...	17,000	(See Note below.)						
Military Vicariate	72,438	50	20	70	—	—	6	60
TOTALS 1983	10,433,849	7,243	5,132	12,375	332	3,497	37,214	5,915
Totals 1982	10,425,087	7,340	5,286	12,626	277	4,195	37,982	5,787

Note: Statistics for the Slovak Eparchy of Sts. Cyril and Methodius and the Greek Melkite Apostolic Exarchate are from the *1983 Annuario Pontificio* and are not included in totals. No statistics were available at press time for the Maronite Eparchy of St. Maron. The apostolic exarchate for Armenian Rite Catholics of the United States and Canada reported a total of 38,000, with no indication of the number residing in Canada.

CANADIAN CONFERENCE OF CATHOLIC BISHOPS

The *Canadian Conference of Catholic Bishops was established Oct. 12, 1943, as a permanent voluntary association of the bishops of Canada, was given official approval by the Holy See in 1948, and acquired the status of an episcopal conference after the Second Vatican Council.*

The CCCB acts in two ways: (1) as a strictly ecclesiastical body through which the bishops act together with pastoral authority and responsibility for the Church throughout the country; (2) as an operational secretariat through which the bishops act on a wider scale for the good of the Church and society.

At the top of the CCCB organizational table are the president, an executive committee, an administrative board and a plenary assembly. The membership consists of all the bishops of Canada.

Departments and Offices

The CCCB's work is planned and co-ordinated by a Pastoral Team of 14 members — six bishops and six staff members (lay and clergy) and the two general secretaries.

The CCCB has six departments all of which work in both French and English: (I) Department for Theology and Canon Law; (II) Department for Christian Education and Migration and Tourism; (III) Department for Social Affairs and Laity; (IV) Department for Missions, Clergy and Religious; (V) Department for Ecumenism and Non-Believers; (VI) Department for Liturgy and Social Communications.

The general secretariat consists of a French and an English general secretary and their assistants and directors of public relations.

Administrative services for purchasing, archives and library, accounting, personnel, publications, printing and distribution are supervised by directors who relate to the general secretaries.

Various advisory councils and committees with mixed memberships of lay persons, religious, priests and bishops also serve the CCCB on a variety of topics.

Operations

Meetings for the transaction of business are held at least once a year by the plenary assembly, eight times a year by the executive committee, and four times a year by the administrative board.

Archbishop Henri Legare, O.M.I., of Grouard-McLennan, Alta., is president of the CCCB; Bishop Paul Reding of Hamilton, Ont., is vice-president.

Headquarters are located at 90 Parent Ave., Ottawa, K1N 7B1, Canada.

ORGANIZATIONS

The Catholic Church Extension Society of Canada supports home missions. Address: 67 Bond St., Toronto, Ontario M5B 1X6.

The Oblate Indian-Eskimo Council of Canada, 238 Argyle St., Ottawa.

The Canadian Catholic Women's League, with a membership of more than 100,000. Address: 3081 Ness Ave., Winnipeg, Man. R2Y 2G3.

G. K. Chesterton Society, 1437 College Dr., Saskatoon, Sask. S7N OW8.

PERCENTAGE OF CATHOLICS

Catholic population statistics are from the *1983 Directory of the Canadian Conference of Catholic Bishops;* total population figures are 1982 estimates.

The table presents a regional breakdown of Catholic percentage in total population. In some cases, the Catholic totals are approximate because diocesan boundaries fall within several civil provinces. See Index: Canadian Dioceses with Interprovincial Lines.

Civil Province Territory	Cath. Pop.	Total Pop.	Cath. Pct.
Alberta	367,765	2,212,300	16.6
British Columbia	317,742	2,737,700	11.6
Manitoba	205,700	1,034,400	19.9
New Brunswick	347,967	712,500	48.8
Newfoundland	199,370	588,300	33.9
Nova Scotia	283,400	859,400	32.9
Ontario	2,582,696	8,664,600	29.8
Prince Edward Is.	51,084	124,900	40.9
Quebec	5,560,075	6,358,200	87.4
Saskatchewan	208,219	988,400	21.1
Northwest Territories	18,390	44,100	41.7
Yukon	7,738	22,600	34.2
Eastern Rites	211,265	—	—
Military Vicariate	72,438	—	—
TOTALS 1983	**10,433,849**	**24,347,400**	**42.9**
Totals 1982	10,425,087	24,088,500	43.3

BIOGRAPHIES OF CANADIAN BISHOPS

(Sources: Almanac survey; *1983 Directory of Canadian Conference of Catholic Bishops; Annuario Pontificio.* Data as of July 10, 1982.)

Ambrozic, Aloysius M.: b. Jan. 27, 1930; ord. priest June 4, 1955; ord. titular bishop of Valabria and auxiliary bishop of Toronto, May 27, 1976.

Audet, Lionel: b. May 22, 1908, Ste. Marie de Beauce, Que.; ord. priest July 8, 1934; ord. titular bishop of Tibari and auxiliary bishop of Quebec, May 1, 1952; retired Mar. 26, 1983.

Audet, Rene: b. Jan. 18, 1920, Montreal, Que.; ord. priest May 30, 1948; ord. titular bishop of

Chonochora and auxiliary bishop of Ottawa, July 31, 1963; bishop of Joliette, Jan. 3, 1968.

Baudoux, Maurice: b. July 10, 1902, Louviere, Belgium; ord. priest July 17, 1929; ord. bishop of St. Paul in Alberta, Oct. 28, 1948; titular archbishop of Preslavus and coadjutor archbishop of St. Boniface, Mar. 4, 1952; archbishop of St. Boniface, Sept. 14, 1955; retired Sept. 7, 1974.

Beahen, John: b. Feb. 14, 1922, Ottawa, Ont.; ord. priest June 15, 1946; ord. titular bishop of

Ploaghe and auxiliary bishop of Ottawa, June 21, 1977.

Belanger, Valerien: b. Apr. 6, 1902, Valleyfield, Que.; ord. priest May 29, 1926; ord titular bishop of Cyrene and auxiliary bishop of Montreal, May 11, 1956.

Belisle, Gilles: b. Oct. 7, 1923, Clarence Creek, Ont.; ord. priest Feb. 2, 1950; ord. titular bishop of Uccula and auxiliary bishop of Ottawa, June 21, 1977.

Blais, Leo: b. Apr. 28, 1904, Dollar Bay, Mich.; ord. priest June 14, 1930; ord. bishop of Prince Albert, Aug. 28, 1952; titular bishop of Geron and auxiliary bishop of Montreal, 1959-64. Retired.

Blanchet, Bertrand: b. Sept. 19, 1932, Saint Thomas de Montmagny, Que.; ord. priest May 20, 1956; ord. bishop of Gaspe, Dec. 8, 1973.

Borecky, Isidore: b. Oct. 1, 1911, Ostrovec, Ukraine; ord. priest July 17, 1938; ord. titular bishop of Amathus in Cypro and exarch of Toronto, May 27, 1948; bishop of Toronto (Ukrainians), Nov. 3, 1956.

Brodeur, Rosario L.: b. Oct. 30, 1889, Acton Vale, Que.; ord. priest June 17, 1916; ord. titular bishop of Mideo and coadjutor bishop of Alexandria, June 30, 1941; bishop of Alexandria, July 27, 1941; retired Oct. 15, 1966.

Burke, Austin-Emile: b. Jan. 22, 1922, Sluice Point, N.S.; ord. priest Mar. 25, 1950; ord. bishop of Yarmouth, May 14, 1968.

Cabana, Georges: b. Oct. 23, 1894, Notre Dame de Granby, Que; ord. priest July 28, 1918; ord. titular archbishop of Anchialo and coadjutor archbishop of St. Boniface, June 30, 1941; coadjutor archbishop of Sherbrooke, Jan. 20, 1952; archbishop of Sherbrooke, May 28, 1952; retired Feb. 7, 1968.

Carew, William A.: b. Oct. 23, 1922, St. John's, Nfld., ord. priest June 15, 1947; ord. titular archbishop of Telde, Jan. 4, 1970; nuncio to Rwanda and Burundi, 1970-74; apostolic delegate to Jerusalem and Palestine and pro-nuncio to Cyprus, 1974.

Carney, James F.: b. June 28, 1915, Vancouver, B.C.; ord. priest Mar. 21, 1942; ord. titular bishop of Obori and auxiliary bishop of Vancouver, Feb. 11, 1966; archbishop of Vancouver, Jan. 8, 1969.

Carter, Alexander: b. Apr. 16, 1909, Montreal, Que.; ord. priest June 6, 1936; ord. titular bishop of Sita and coadjutor bishop of Sault Ste. Marie, Feb. 2, 1957; bishop of Sault Ste. Marie, Nov. 22, 1958.

Carter, G. Emmett: (See Cardinals, Biographies.)

Charbonneau, Paul E.: b. May 4, 1922, Ste. Therese de Blainville, Que.; ord. priest May 31, 1947; ord. titular bishop of Thapsus and auxiliary bishop of Ottawa, Jan. 18, 1961; first bishop of Hull, May 21, 1963; retired Apr. 12, 1973, because of ill health.

Chiasson, Donat: b. Jan. 2, 1930, Paquetville, N.B.; ord. priest May 6, 1956; ord. archbishop of Moncton, June 1, 1972.

Chimy, Jerome I., O.S.B.M.: b. Mar. 12, 1919, Radway, Alta.; ord. priest, June 29, 1944; ord. first bishop of New Westminster, B.C., for the Ukrainians, Sept. 5, 1974.

Cimichella, Andre, O.S.M.: b. Feb. 21, 1921, Grotte Santo Stefano, Italy; ord. priest May 26, 1945; ord. titular bishop of Quiza and auxiliary of Montreal, July 16, 1964.

Clune, Robert B.: b. Sept. 18, 1920, Toronto, Ont.; ord. priest May 26, 1945; ord. titular bishop of Lacubaza and auxiliary bishop of Toronto, June 21, 1979.

Coderre, Gerard Marie: b. Dec. 19, 1904, St. Jacques de Montcalm, Que.; ord. priest May 30, 1931; ord. titular bishop of Aegae and coadjutor bishop of St.-Jean-de-Quebec, Sept. 12, 1951; bishop of St.-Jean-de-Quebec, Feb. 3, 1955. Retired May 3, 1978.

Couture, Jean-Guy: b. May 6, 1929, St.-Jean-Baptiste de Quebec, Que.; ord. priest May 30, 1953; ord. bishop of Hauterive, Que., Aug. 15, 1975; bishop of Chicoutimi, Apr. 5, 1979.

Couture, Maurice, R.S.V.: b. Nov. 3, 1926, Saint-Pierre-de-Broughton, Que.; ord. priest June 17, 1951; ord. titular bishop of Talaptula and auxiliary bishop of Quebec, Oct. 22, 1982.

Couturier, Gerard: b. Jan. 12, 1913, St. Louis du Ha Ha, Que; ord. priest Mar. 25, 1938; ord. bishop of Hauterive, Feb. 28, 1957; resigned see Sept. 7, 1974.

Crowley, Leonard: b. Dec. 28, 1921, Montreal, Que.; ord. priest May 31, 1947; ord. titular bishop of Mons and auxiliary bishop of Montreal, Mar. 24, 1971.

Daciuk, Myron, O.S.B.M.: b. Nov. 16, 1919, Mundare, Alta; ord. priest June 10, 1945; ord. titular bishop of Thyatira and auxiliary bishop of Winnipeg (Ukrainians), Oct. 14, 1982.

Decosse, Aime: b. June 21, 1903, Somerset, Man.; ord. priest July 4, 1926; ord. bishop of Gravelbourg, Jan. 20, 1954; retired May 12, 1973.

Delaquis, Noel: b. Dec. 25, 1934, Notre-Dame-de Lourdes, Man.; ord. priest June 5, 1958; ord. bishop of Gravelbourg, Feb. 19, 1974.

De Roo, Remi J.: b. Feb. 24, 1924, Swan Lake, Man.; ord. priest June 8, 1950; ord. bishop of Victoria, Dec. 14, 1962.

Despatie, Roger: b. Apr. 12, 1927, Sudbury, Ont.; ord. priest Apr. 12, 1952; ord. titular bishop of Usinaza and auxiliary bishop of Sault Ste. Marie, June 28, 1968; bishop of Hearst, Feb. 8, 1973.

Dionne, Gerard: b. June 19, 1919, Saint-Basile, N.B.; ord. priest May 1, 1948; ord. titular bishop of Garba and auxiliary bishop of Sault Ste. Marie, Apr. 8, 1975.

Douville, Arthur: b. July 22, 1894, St. Casimir de Portneuf, Que.; ord. priest May 25, 1919; ord. titular bishop of Vita and auxiliary bishop of St. Hyacinthe, Jan. 29, 1940; coadjutor bishop of St. Hyacinthe, Mar. 21, 1942; bishop of St. Hyacinthe, Nov. 27, 1942; retired June 13, 1967.

Doyle, James L.: b. June 20, 1929, Chatham, Ont.; ord. priest June 12, 1954; ord. bishop of Peterborough June 28, 1976.

Doyle, W. Emmett: b. Feb. 18, 1913, Calgary, Alta.: ord. priest June 5, 1938; ord. bishop of Nelson, Dec. 3, 1958.

Drainville, Gerard: b. May 20, 1930, L'Isle-du-

Pas, Que.; ord. priest May 30, 1953; ord. bishop of Amos, June 12, 1978.

Dumouchel, Paul, O.M.I.: b. Sept. 19, 1911, St. Boniface, Man.; ord. priest June 24, 1936; ord. titular bishop of Sufes and vicar apostolic of Keewatin, May 24, 1955; archbishop of Keewatin-Le Pas, July 13, 1967.

Ebacher, Roger: b. Oct. 6, 1936, Amos, Que.; ord. priest May 27, 1961; ord. bishop of Hauterive, July 31, 1979.

Exner, Adam, O.M.I.: b. Dec. 24, 1928, Killaly, Sask.; ord. priest July 7, 1957; ord. bishop of Kamloops, B.C., Mar. 12, 1974; archbishop of Winnipeg, April, 1982.

Flahiff, George F.: (See Cardinals Biographies.)

Fortier, Jean-Marie: b. July 1, 1920, Quebec, Que.; ord. priest June 16, 1944; ord. titular bishop of Pomaria and auxiliary bishop of Ste. Anne-de-la-Pocatiere, Jan. 23, 1961; bishop of Gaspe, Jan. 19, 1965; archbishop of Sherbrooke, Apr. 20, 1968.

Fulton, Thomas B.: b. Jan. 13, 1918, St. Catharines, Ont.; ord. priest June 7, 1941; ord. titular bishop of Cursola and auxiliary bishop of Toronto, Jan. 6, 1969; bishop of St. Catharines, July 7, 1978.

Gagnon, Edouard, P.S.S.: b. Jan. 15, 1918, Port Daniel, Que.; ord. priest Aug. 15, 1940; ord. bishop Mar. 25, 1969; bishop of St. Paul in Alberta 1969-72; rector of Canadian College in Rome, 1972-77; vice-president and secretary of Vatican Committee for the Family, 1973-80; pro-president of Pontifical Council for Family, 1983.

Gervais, Marcel A.: b. Sept. 21, 1931, Elie, Man.; ord. priest May 31, 1958; ord. titular bishop of Rosmarkaeum and auxiliary bishop of London, Ont., June 11, 1980.

Gilbert, Arthur J.: b. Oct. 26, 1915, Oromocto, N.B.; ord. priest June 3, 1943; ord. bishop of St. John, N.B., June 19, 1974.

Godin, Edgar: b. May 31, 1911, Neguac, N.B.; ord. priest June 15, 1941; ord. bishop of Bathurst, July 25, 1969.

Gratton, Jean: b. Dec. 4, 1924, Wendover, Ont.; ord. priest Apr. 27, 1952; ord. bishop of Mont Laurier, June 29, 1978.

Gregoire, Paul: b. Oct. 24, 1911, Verdun, Que.; ord. priest May 22, 1937; ord. titular bishop of Curubis and auxiliary bishop of Montreal, Dec. 27, 1961; archbishop of Montreal, Apr. 20, 1968.

Greschuk, Martin: b. Nov. 7, 1923, Innisfree, Alta.; ord. priest June 11, 1950; ord. titular bishop of Nazianus and auxiliary bishop of Edmonton of the Ukrainians, Oct. 3, 1974.

Hacault, Antoine: b. Jan. 17, 1926, Bruxelles, Man.; ord. priest May 20, 1951; ord. titular bishop of Media and coadjutor of St. Boniface, Sept. 8, 1964; archbishop of St. Boniface, Sept. 7, 1974.

Hains, Gaston: b. Sept. 10, 1921, Drummondville, Que.; ord. priest June 15, 1946; ord. titular bishop of Belesana and auxiliary bishop of St. Hyacinthe, Oct. 10, 1964; coadjutor bishop of

Amos, 1967; bishop of Amos, Oct. 31, 1968; retired 1978.

Hakim, Michel: b. Apr. 21, 1921, Magdouche, South Lebanon; ord. priest Nov. 10, 1947; ord. archbishop of Saida of Greek Melkites, Sept. 10, 1977; app. titular archbishop of Caesarea in Cappadocia and apostolic exarch of Greek Melkite Catholics in Canada, Oct. 13, 1980.

Halpin, Charles A.: b. Aug. 30, 1930, St. Eustache, Man.; ord. priest May 27, 1956; ord. archbishop of Regina, Nov. 26, 1973.

Hamelin, Jean-Guy: b. Oct. 8, 1925, St. Severin-de-Proulxville, Que.; ord. priest June 11, 1949; ord. first bishop of Rouyn-Noranda, Que., Feb. 9, 1974.

Hayes, James M.: b. May 27, 1924, Halifax, N.S.; ord. priest June 15, 1947; ord. titular bishop of Reperi and apostolic administrator of Halifax, Apr. 20, 1965; archbishop of Halifax, June 22, 1967.

Hermaniuk, Maxim, C.Ss.R.: b. Oct. 30, 1911, Nove Selo, Ukraine; ord. priest Sept. 4, 1938; ord. titular bishop of Sinna and exarch of Manitoba (Ukrainians), June 29, 1951; archbishop of Winnipeg (Ukrainians), Nov. 3, 1956.

Hubert, Bernard: b. June 1, 1929, Beloeil, Que.; ord. priest May 30, 1953; ord. bishop of St. Jerome, Sept. 12, 1971; coadjutor bishop of Saint-Jean-de-Quebec, 1977; succeeded as bishop of Saint-Jean-de-Quebec, May 3, 1978; title of see changed to St. Jean-Longueuil, 1982.

Jette, Edouard: b. Aug. 9, 1898, St. Jacques, Que.; ord. priest May 31, 1923; ord. titular bishop of Tabe and auxiliary of Joliette, Apr. 14, 1948; retired 1968.

Labrie, Jean-Paul: b. Nov. 4, 1922, Laurieville, Que.; ord. priest May 20, 1951; ord. titular bishop of Urci and auxiliary bishop of Quebec, May 14, 1977.

Lacey, Michael Pearse: b. Nov. 27, 1916, Toronto, Ont.; ord. priest May 23, 1943; ord. titular bishop of Diana and auxiliary bishop of Toronto, June 21, 1979.

Lacroix, Fernand, C.J.M.: b. Oct. 16, 1919, Quebec; ord. priest Feb. 10, 1946; ord. bishop of Edmundston, Oct. 20, 1970; retired May 31, 1983.

Landriault, Jacques: b. Sept. 23, 1921, Alfred, Ont.; ord. priest Feb. 9, 1947; ord. titular bishop of Cadi and auxiliary bishop of Alexandria, July 25, 1962; bishop of Hearst, May 27, 1964; app. bishop of Timmins, Mar. 24, 1971.

Langevin, Louis-de-Gonzague, P.B.: b. Oct. 31, 1921, Oka, Que.; ord. priest Feb. 2, 1950; ord. titular bishop of Rosemarkie and auxiliary of St. Hyacinthe Sept. 23, 1974; bishop of St. Hyacinthe, July 18, 1979.

LaRocque, Eugene Philippe: b. Mar. 27, 1927, Windsor, Ont.; ord. priest June 7, 1952; ord. bishop of Alexandria, Ont., Sept. 3, 1974; title of see changed to Alexandria-Cornwall, 1976.

Lebel, Robert: b. Nov. 8, 1924, Trois-Pistoles, Que.; ord. priest June 18, 1950; ord. titular bishop of Alinda and auxiliary of St. Jean de Quebec, May 12, 1974; bishop of Valleyfield, May 12, 1976.

Le Blanc, Camille A.: b. Aug. 25, 1898, Barachois, N.B.; ord. priest Apr. 5, 1924; ord. bishop of Bathurst, Sept. 8, 1942; retired Jan. 8, 1969.

Leclerc, Marc: b. Jan. 9, 1933, Saint-Gregoire de Montmorency, Que; ord. priest, May 31, 1958; ord. titular bishop of Eguga and auxiliary bishop of Quebec, Oct. 22, 1982.

Legare, Henri, O.M.I.: b. Feb. 20, 1918, Willow Bunch, Sask.; ord. priest June 29, 1943; ord. first bishop of Labrador-Schefferville, Sept. 9, 1967; archbishop of Grouard-McLennan, Nov. 21, 1972. President of Canadian Conference of Catholic Bishops, 1981.

Leger, Paul-Emile: (See Cardinals, Biographies).

Leguerrier, Jules, O.M.I.: b. Feb. 18, 1915, Clarence Creek, Ont.; ord. priest June 19, 1943; ord. titular bishop of Bavagaliana and vicar apostolic of James Bay, June 29, 1964; first bishop of Moosonee, July 13, 1967.

Lemieux, Marie Joseph, O.P.: b. May 10, 1902, Quebec, Que.; ord. priest Apr. 15, 1928; ord. bishop of Sendai, Japan, June 29, 1936; titular bishop of Calydon, 1941; apostolic administrator of Gravelbourg, 1942; bishop of Gravelbourg, Apr. 15, 1944; archbishop of Ottawa, June 20, 1953; retired Sept. 16, 1966 (titular archbishop of Salde).

Levesque, Charles Henri: b. Dec. 29, 1921, St. Andre de Kamouraska, Que.; ord. priest June 13, 1948; ord. titular bishop of Guzabeta and auxiliary bishop of Ste.-Anne-de-la-Pocatiere, Dec. 27, 1965; bishop of Ste.-Anne-de-la-Pocatiere, Aug. 17, 1968.

Levesque, Louis: b. May 27, 1908, Amqui, Que.; ord. priest June 26, 1932; ord. bishop of Hearst, Aug. 15, 1952; titular archbishop of Egnatia and coadjutor of Rimouski, Apr. 13, 1964; archbishop of Rimouski, Feb. 25, 1967; retired May 14, 1973.

Lussier, Philippe, C.Ss.R.: b. Oct. 3, 1911, Weedon, Que.; ord. priest Sept. 18, 1937; ord. bishop of St. Paul in Alberta, Aug. 17, 1952; retired Aug. 17, 1968.

MacDonald, James H., C.S.C.: b. Apr. 28, 1925, Wycogama, N.S.; ord. priest June 28, 1953; ord. titular bishop of Gibba and auxiliary bishop of Hamilton April 17, 1978; app. bishop of Charlottetown, Aug. 12, 1982.

MacDonald, Joseph Faber: b. Jan. 20, 1932, Little Pond, P.E.I.; ord. priest Mar. 9, 1963; ord. bishop of Grand Falls, Mar. 19, 1980.

McGrath, Richard T.: b. June 17, 1912, Oderin, Placentia Bay, Nfld.; ord. priest June 24, 1936; ord. bishop of St. George's, Nfld., July 22, 1970.

MacNeil, Joseph N.: b. Apr. 15, 1924, Sydney, N.S.; ord. priest May 23, 1948; ord. bishop of St. John, N.B., June 24, 1969; archbishop of Edmonton, July 6, 1973. President Canadian Conference of Catholic Bishops, 1979-81.

Mahoney, James P.: b. Dec. 7, 1927, Saskatoon, Sask.; ord. priest June 7, 1952; ord. bishop of Saskatoon, Dec. 13, 1967.

Martin, Albertus: b. Oct. 4, 1913, Southbridge, Mass.; ord. priest May 18, 1939; ord. titular bishop of Bassiana and coadjutor bishop of Nicolet, Oct. 7, 1950; bishop of Nicolet, Nov. 8, 1950.

Morand, Blaise E.: b. Sept. 12, 1932, Tecumseh, Ont.; ord. priest Mar. 22, 1958; ord. coadjutor bish-

op of Prince Albert, June 29, 1981; bishop of Prince Albert, Apr. 9, 1983.

Morin, Laurent: b. Feb. 14, 1908, Montreal, Que.; ord. priest May 27, 1934; ord. titular bishop of Arsamosata and auxiliary bishop of Montreal, Oct. 30, 1955; bishop of Prince Albert, Feb. 28, 1959; retired Apr. 9, 1983.

Noel, Laurent: b. Mar. 19, 1920, Saint-Just-de-Bretenieres, Que.; ord. priest June 16, 1944; ord. titular bishop of Agathopolis and auxiliary bishop of Quebec, Aug. 29, 1963; bishop of Trois Rivieres, Nov. 5, 1975.

O'Byrne, Paul J.: b. Dec. 21, 1922, Calgary, Alta.; ord. priest Feb. 21, 1948; ord. bishop of Calgary, Aug. 22, 1968.

O'Connor, Hubert P., O.M.I.: b. Feb. 17, 1928, Huntingdon, Que.; ord. priest June 5, 1955; ord. bishop of Whitehorse, Dec. 8, 1971.

O'Grady, John Fergus, O.M.I.: b. July 27, 1908, Macton, Ont.; ord. priest June 29, 1934; ord. titular bishop of Aspendus and vicar apostolic of Prince Rupert, Mar. 7, 1956; first bishop of Prince George, July 13, 1967.

O'Mara, John A.: b. Nov. 17, 1924, Buffalo, N.Y.; ord. priest June 1, 1951; ord. bishop of Thunder Bay, June 29, 1976.

O'Neill, Michael C.: b. Feb. 15, 1898, Kemptville, Ont.; ord. priest Dec. 21, 1927; ord. archbishop of Regina, Apr. 14, 1948; retired Sept. 26, 1973.

Ouellet, Gilles, P.M.E.: b. Aug. 14, 1922, Bromptonville, Que.; ord. priest June 30, 1946; ord. bishop of Gaspe, Nov. 23, 1968; app. archbishop of Rimouski, Apr. 27, 1973. President Canadian Conference of Catholic Bishops, 1977-79.

Ouellette, Andre: b. Feb. 4, 1913, Salem, Mass.; ord. priest June 11, 1938; ord. titular bishop of Carre and auxiliary bishop of Mont-Laurier, Feb. 25, 1957; bishop of Mont-Laurier, Mar. 27, 1965; retired Feb. 1978.

Pappin, Bernard F.: b. July 10, 1928, Westmeath, Ont.; ord. priest May 27, 1954; ord. titular bishop of Aradi and auxiliary bishop of Sault Ste. Marie, Apr. 11, 1975.

Pare, Marius: b. May 22, 1903, Montmagny, Que.; ord. priest July 3, 1927; ord. titular bishop of Aegae and auxiliary bishop of Chicoutimi, May 1, 1956; bishop of Chicoutimi, Feb. 18, 1961. Retired Apr. 5, 1979.

Pedneault, Roch: b. Apr. 10, 1927, Saint Joseph d'Alma, Que.; ord. priest Feb. 8, 1953; ord. titular bishop of Aggersel and auxiliary of Chicoutimi, Que., June 29, 1974.

Pelletier, Georges Leon: b. Aug. 19, 1904, Saint-Epiphane, Que.; ord. priest June 24, 1931; ord. titular bishop of Hephaestus and auxiliary bishop of Quebec, Feb. 24, 1943; bishop of Trois Rivieres, July 26, 1947; retired Oct. 31, 1975.

Penney, Alphonsus L.: b. Sept. 17, 1924, St. John's, Nfld.; ord. priest June 29, 1949; ord. bishop of Grand Falls, Jan. 18, 1973; archbishop of St. John's, Nfld., Apr. 5, 1979.

Piche, Paul, O.M.I.: b. Sept. 14, 1909, Gravelbourg, Sask.; ord. priest Dec. 23, 1934; ord. titular bishop of Orcistus and vicar apostolic of Mackenzie, June 11, 1959; first bishop of Mackenzie-Fort Smith, July 13, 1967.

Plourde, Joseph Aurele: b. Jan. 12, 1915, St. Francois de Madawaska, N.B.; ord. priest May 7, 1944; ord. titular bishop of Lapda and auxiliary bishop of Alexandria, Aug. 26, 1964; archbishop of Ottawa, Jan. 2, 1967.

Pocock, Philip: b. July 2, 1906, St. Thomas, Ont.; ord. priest June 14, 1930; ord. bishop of Saskatoon, June 29, 1944; titular archbishop of Aprus and coadjutor archbishop of Winnipeg, Aug. 6, 1951; archbishop of Winnipeg, Jan. 14, 1952; titular archbishop of Isauropolis and coadjutor archbishop of Toronto, Feb. 18, 1961; archbishop of Toronto, Mar. 30, 1971; retired Apr. 29, 1978.

Power, William E.: b. Sept. 27, 1915; Montreal, Que.; ord. priest June 7, 1941; ord. bishop of Antigonish, July 20, 1960; president Canadian Conference of Catholic Bishops, 1971-73.

Proulx, Adolphe J.: b. Dec. 12, 1927, Hanmer, Ont., Canada; ord. priest Apr. 17, 1954; ord. titular bishop of Missua and auxiliary bishop of Sault Ste. Marie, Feb. 24, 1965; bishop of Alexandria, Apr. 28, 1967; bishop of Hull, Feb. 13, 1974; title of see changed to Gatineau-Hull, 1982.

Reding, Paul F.: b. Feb. 14, 1925, Hamilton, Ont.; ord. priest June 3, 1950; ord. titular bishop of Liberalia and auxiliary bishop of Hamilton, Sept. 14, 1966; bishop of Hamilton, Sept. 14, 1973.

Robidoux, Omer, O.M.I.: b. Nov. 19, 1913 Saint-Pierre-Jolys, Man.; ord. priest June 29, 1939; ord. bishop of Churchill-Hudson Bay, May 20, 1970.

Routhier, Henri, O.M.I.: b. Feb. 28, 1900, Pincher Creek, Alta.; ord. priest Sept. 7, 1924; ord. titular bishop of Naissus and coadjutor vicar apostolic of Grouard, Sept. 8, 1945; vicar apostolic of Grouard, 1953; archbishop of Grouard-McLennan, July 13, 1967; retired Nov. 2 1, 1972.

Roy, Maurice: (Cardinals, Biographies.)

Roy, Raymond: b. May 3, 1919, St. Boniface, Man.; ord. priest May 31, 1947; ord. bishop of St. Paul in Alberta, July 18, 1972.

Rusnak, Michael, C.Ss.R.: b. Aug. 21, 1921, Beaverdale, Pa.; ord. priest July 3, 1949; ord. titular bishop of Tzernicus and auxiliary bishop of Toronto eparchy and apostolic visitator to Slovak Catholics of Byzantine rite in Canada, Jan. 2, 1965; first bishop of Sts Cyril and Methoduis Eparchy for Slovaks of Byzantine Rite, Feb. 28, 1981.

Ryan, Joseph F.: b. Mar. 1, 1897, Dundas, Ont.; ord. priest May 21, 1921; ord. bishop of Hamilton, Oct. 19, 1937; retired Mar. 27, 1973.

Sabatini, Lawrence, C.S.: b. May 15, 1930, Chicago, Ill.; ord. priest Mar. 19, 1957; ord. titular bishop of Nasai and auxiliary bishop of Vancouver, Sept. 21, 1978; bishop of Kamloops, Sept. 30, 1982.

Saint-Antoine, Jude: b. Oct. 29, 1930, Montreal, Que.; ord. priest May 31, 1956; ord. titular bishop of Scardona and auxiliary bishop of Montreal, May 22, 1981. Episcopal vicar of west central region.

Saint-Gelais, Raymond: b. Mar. 23, 1936, Baie St. Paul, Que.; ord. priest June 12, 1960; ord.

titular bishop of Diana and auxiliary bishop of St. Jerome, July 31, 1980.

Sanschagrin, Albert, O.M.I.: b. Aug. 5, 1911, Saint-Tite, Que.; ord. priest May 24, 1936; ord. titular bishop of Bagi and coadjutor bishop of Amos Sept. 14, 1957; bishop of Saint-Hyacinthe, June 13, 1967. Retired July 18, 1979.

Savaryn, Nile Nicholas, O.S.B.M.: b. May 19, 1905, Stary Sambir, Ukraine; ord. priest Aug. 23, 1931; ord. titular bishop of Jos and auxiliary bishop of the Catholic Ukrainian diocese in Canada, July 1, 1943; bishop of apostolic exarchate for western Canada, 1948; bishop of Edmonton (Ukrainians), Nov. 3, 1956.

Setian, Nerses Mikael: Apostolic Exarch of Armenian Catholics in Canada and the U.S. (see Index).

Shaheen, Elias: b. July 20, 1914, Ebrine, Patriarchate of Antioch of Maronites; ord. priest Mar. 25, 1939; ord. first eparch of St. Maron of Montreal for the Maronites, Nov. 7, 1982.

Sherlock, John M.: b. Jan. 20, 1926, Regina, Sask.; ord. priest June 3, 1950; ord. titular bishop of Macriana and auxiliary bishop of London, Ont., Aug. 28, 1974; bishop of London, July 7, 1978.

Skinner, Patrick J., C.J.M.: b. Mar. 9, 1904, St. John's, Nfld.; ord. priest May 30, 1929; ord. titular bishop of Zenobia and auxiliary bishop of St. John's, Mar. 17, 1950; archbishop of St. John's, Mar. 23, 1951. Retired Apr. 5, 1979.

Smith, William J.: b. Jan. 2, 1897, Greenfield, Ont.; ord. priest June 16, 1927; ord. bishop of Pembroke, July 25, 1945; retired Feb. 8, 1971.

Spence, Francis J.: b. June 3, 1926, Perth, Ont.; ord. priest Apr. 16, 1950; ord. titular bishop of Nova and auxiliary bishop of the military vicariate, June 15, 1967; bishop of Charlottetown, Aug. 15, 1970; military vicar of Canada, March 1982; archbishop of Kingston, May, 1982.

Sutton, Peter A., O.M.I.: b. Oct. 18, 1934, Chandler, Que.; ord. priest Oct. 22, 1960; ord. bishop of Labrador-Schefferville, July 18, 1974.

Tessier, Maxime: b. Oct. 9, 1906, St. Sebastien, Que.; ord. priest June 14, 1930; ord. titular bishop of Christopolis and auxiliary bishop of Ottawa, Aug. 2, 1951; coadjutor bishop of Timmins, 1953; bishop of Timmins, May 8, 1955; retired Mar. 24, 1971.

Tonnos, Anthony: b. Aug. 1, 1935, Port Colborne, Ont.; ord. priest May 27, 1961; app. auxiliary bishop of Hamilton, May 18, 1983.

Tremblay, Gerard, P.S.S.: b. Oct. 27, 1918, Montreal, Que.; ord. priest June 16, 1946; ord. titular bishop of Trisipa and auxiliary bishop of Montreal, May 22, 1981.

Turcotte, Jean-Claude: b. June 26, 1936, Montreal, Que.; ord. priest May 24, 1959; ord. titular bishop of Suas and auxiliary bishop of Montreal, June 29, 1982.

Vachon, Louis-Albert: b. Feb. 4, 1912, Saint-Frederic, Que.; ord. priest June 11, 1938; ord. titular bishop of Mesarfelta and auxiliary bishop of Quebec, May 14, 1977; archbishop of Quebec and primate of Canada, Apr. 4, 1981.

Valois, Charles: b. Apr. 24, 1924, Montreal, Que.; ord. priest June 3, 1950; ord. bishop of St. Jerome, June 29, 1977.

Wall, Leonard J.: b. Sept. 27, 1924, Windsor, Ont.; ord. priest June 11, 1949; ord. titular bishop of Leptiminus and auxiliary bishop of Toronto, June 21, 1979.

Wilhelm, Joseph L.: b. Nov. 16, 1909, Walkerton, Ont.; ord. priest June 9, 1934; ord. titular bishop of Saccaea and auxiliary bishop of Calgary, Aug. 22, 1963; archbishop of Kingston, Dec. 14, 1966; retired Mar. 12, 1982.

Windle, Joseph R.: b. Aug. 28, 1917, Ashdad, Ont.; ord. priest May 16, 1943; ord. titular bishop of Uzita and auxiliary bishop of Ottawa, Jan. 18, 1961; coadjutor bishop of Pembroke, 1969; bishop of Pembroke, Feb. 15, 1971.

CANADIAN SHRINES

Our Lady of the Cape (Cap de la Madeleine), Queen of the Most Holy Rosary: The Three Rivers, Quebec, parish church, built of fieldstone in 1714 and considered the oldest stone church on the North American continent preserved in its original state, was rededicated June 22, 1888, as a shrine of the Queen of the Most Holy Rosary. Thereafter, the site increased in importance as a pilgrimage and devotional center, and in 1904 St. Pius X decreed the crowning of a statue of the Blessed Virgin which had been donated 50 years earlier to commemorate the dogma of the Immaculate Conception. In 1909, the First Plenary Council of Quebec declared the church a shrine of national pilgrimage. In 1964, the church at the shrine was given the status and title of minor basilica.

St. Anne de Beaupre: The devotional history of this shrine in Quebec, began with the reported cure of a cripple, Louis Guimont, on Mar. 16, 1658, the starting date of construction work on a small chapel of St. Anne. The original building was successively enlarged and replaced by a stone church which was given the rank of minor basilica in 1888. The present structure, a Romanesque-Gothic basilica, houses the shrine proper in its north transept. The centers of attraction are an eight-foot-high oaken statue and the great relic of St. Anne, a portion of her forearm.

St. Joseph's Oratory: The massive oratory basilica standing on the western side of Mount Royal and overlooking the city of Montreal had its origin in a primitive chapel erected there by Blessed Andre Bessette, C.S.C., in 1904. Eleven years later, a large crypt was built to accommodate an increasing number of pilgrims, and in 1924 construction work was begun on the large church. A belfry, housing a 60-bell carillon and standing on the site of the original chapel, was dedicated May 15, 1955, as the first major event of the jubilee year observed after the oratory was given the rank of minor basilica.

Martyrs' Shrine: A shrine commemorating several of the Jesuit Martyrs of North America who were killed between 1642 and 1649 in the Ontario and northern New York area is located on the former site of old Forte Sainte Marie. Before its loca-

tion was fixed near Midland, Ont., in 1925, a small chapel had been erected in 1907 at old Mission St. Ignace to mark the martyrdom of Fathers Jean de Brebeuf and Gabriel Lalemant. This sanctuary has a U.S. counterpart in the Shrine of the North American Martyrs near Auriesville, N.Y., under the care of the Jesuits.

Others

Other shrines and historic churches in Canada include the following.

In Quebec City: the Basilica of Notre Dame, dating from 1650, once the cathedral of a diocese stretching from Canada to Mexico; Notre Dame des Victoires, on the waterfront, dedicated in 1690; the Ursuline Convent, built in 1720, on du Parloir St.

In Montreal: Notre Dame Basilica, patterned after the famous basilica of the same name in Paris, constructed in 1829; the Shrine of Mary, Queen of All Hearts.

Near Montreal: the Chapel of Mother d'Youville, foundress of the Grey Nuns; Notre Dame de Lourdes, at Rigaud.

CONFERENCE OF RELIGIOUS

The Canadian Religious Conference, founded in 1954, is a union of major superiors of men and women in Canada. Offices are located at 324 E. Laurier Ave., Ottawa, Ont. KIN 6P6.

CANADIAN CATHOLIC PUBLICATIONS

(Sources: *Catholic Press Directory*, Canadian Conference of Catholic Bishops.)

Newspapers

British Columbia Catholic, The, w; 150 Robson St., Vancouver, B.C. V6B 2A7.

Catholic New Times (national), biweekly; 80 Sackville St., Toronto, Ont. M5A 3E5.

Catholic Register, The (national), w; 67 Bond St., Toronto, Ont. M5B 1X6.

Catholic Times, The, 10 times a year; 2005 St. Marc St., Montreal, Que. H3H 2G8.

Diocesan News, m; P.O. Box 1689, Charlottetown, P.E.I. CIA 7N4.

Hamilton Diocesan News, 3 or 4 times a year; 700 King St., West Hamilton, Ont. L8P 1C7.

L'Informateur Catholique, semimonthly; 1915 Est-Boulevard Gouin, Montreal, Que. H2B 1W7.

Monitor, The, m; P.O. Box 986, St. John's, Nfld. A1C 5M3.

New Freeman, The, w; Box 6609, Sta. A, St. John, N.B. E2L 4S1.

Our Diocese, bm; 22 Sutherland Dr., Grand Falls, Nfld. A2A 2G1.

Pastoral Reporter, The, 4 times a year; 1916 Second St. S.W., Calgary. Alta. T2S 153.

Prairie Messenger, w; Box 190, Muenster, Sask. SOK 2Y0.

Teviskes, Ziburiai (Lithuanian), w; 2185 Stavebank Rd., Mississauga, Ont. L5C 1T3.

Western Catholic Reporter, w; 10562 109th St., Edmonton, Alta. T5H 3B2.

Magazines

Annals of St. Anne de Beaupre, m; Box 1000, St. Anne de Beaupre, Que. GOA 3CO; Basilica of St. Anne.

Apostolat, bm; 460, Primiere Rue, Richelieu, Que. J3L 4B5, Oblates of Mary Immaculate.

Bulletin (French-English), m; 324 E. Laurier Ave., Ottawa, Ont. K1N 6P6. Canadian Religious Conference.

Canadian Catholic Review, 11 times a year; 1437 College Dr., Saskatoon, Saskatchewan S7N 0W6.

Canadian League, The, 4 times a year; 3081 Ness Ave., Winnipeg, Man. R2Y 2G3. Catholic Women's League of Canada.

Chesterton Review, q; 1437 College Dr., Saskatoon, Sask. S7N 0W6.

Companion of St. Francis and St. Anthony, m; P.O. Box 535, Sta. F., Toronto, Ont. M4Y 2L8; Conventual Franciscan Fathers.

Global Village Voice, The, 4 times a year; 3028 Danforth Ave., Toronto, Ont. M4C 1N2. Canadian Catholic Organization for Development and Peace.

Indian Record, 4 times a year; 503-480 Aulneau, Winnipeg, Man. R2H 2V2.

Kateri (English-French), q; P.O. Box 70, Caughnawaga, Que. JOL 1BO.

Logos (Ukrainian, English and French), q; 165 Catherine St., P.O. Box 220, Yorkton, Sask. S3N 2V7.

Martyrs' Shrine Message, q; Midland, Ont. L4R 4K5.

Messager de Saint Antoine, Le, 10 times a year; Lac-Bouchette, Que. GOW 1VO.

Messenger of the Sacred Heart, m; 661 Greenwood Ave., Toronto, Ont. M4J 4B3.

Missions Etrangeres, 6 times a year; 160 Place Juge-Desnoyers, Laval, Que. H7G 1A4.

Oblate Missions, q; 17 Graham Ave., Ottawa, Ont. K1S 0B6.

Oratory, 6 times a year; 3800 Ch. Reine-Marie, Montreal, Que. H3V 1H6.

Our Family, m; P.O. Box 249, Battleford, Sask.; S0M 0E0; Oblates of Mary Immaculate.

Prete et Pasteur, m; 4450 St. Hubert St., Montreal, Que. H2J 2W9.

Redeemer's Voice, m; 165 Catherine St., P.O. Box 220, Yorkton, Sask. S3N 2V7.

Regard de Foi, 6 times a year; 5875 Est. rue Sherbrooke, Montreal, Que. H1N 1B6.

Relations, m; 8100 Blvd., Saint-Laurent, Montreal Que. H2P 2L9; Jesuit Fathers.

Restoration, m; Madonna House, Combermere, Ont., KOJ 1LO.

Sainte Anne de Beaupre, m; Basilica of St. Anne, Que. GOA 3CO.

Scarboro Missions, m; 2685 Kingston Rd., Scarboro, Ont. M1M 1M4.

Spiritan News, 4 times a year; 2475 Queen St., Toronto, Ont. M4E 1H8.

Unity, bm; 308 Young St., Montreal, Que. H3C 2G2.

MISSIONARIES TO THE AMERICAS

Allouez, Claude Jean (1622-1689): French Jesuit; missionary in Canada and midwestern U.S.; preached to 20 different tribes of Indians and baptized over 10,000; vicar general of Northwest.

Altham, John (1589-1640): English Jesuit; missionary among Indians in Maryland.

Anchieta, Jose de, Bl. (1534-1597): Portuguese Jesuit, b. Canary Islands; missionary in Brazil; writer; beatified 1980; feast, June 9.

Andreis, Felix de (1778-1820): Italian Vincentian; missionary and educator in western U.S.

Aparicio, Sebastian, Bl. (1502-1600): Franciscan brother, born Spain; settled in Mexico, c. 1533; worked as road builder and farmer before becoming Franciscan at about the age of 70; beatified, 1787; feast, Feb. 25.

Badin, Stephen T. (1768-1853): French missioner; came to U.S., 1792, when Sulpician seminary in Paris was closed; ordained, 1793, Baltimore, the first priest ordained in U.S.; missionary in Kentucky, Ohio and Michigan; bought land on which Notre Dame University now stands; buried on its campus.

Baraga, Frederic (1797-1868): Slovenian missionary bishop in U.S.; studied at Ljubljana and Vienna, ordained, 1823; came to U.S., 1830; missionary to Indians of Upper Michigan; first bishop of Marquette, 1857-1868; wrote Chippewa grammar, dictionary, prayer book and other works.

Bertran, Louis, St. (1526-1581): Spanish Domini-can; missionary in Colombia and Caribbean, 1562-69; canonized, 1671; feast, Oct. 9.

Betancur, Pedro de San Jose, Bl. (1626-1667): Secular Franciscan, b. Canary Islands; arrived in Guatemala, 1651; established hospital, school and homes for poor; beatified 1980; feast, Apr. 25.

Bourgeoys, Marguerite, St. (1620-1700): French foundress, missionary; settled in Canada, 1653; founded Congregation of Notre Dame de Montreal, 1658; beatified, 1950; canonized 1982; feast, Jan. 19.

Brebeuf, John de, St. (1593-1649): French Jesuit; missionary among Huron Indians in Canada; martyred by Iroquois, Mar. 16, 1649; canonized, 1930; one of Jesuit North American martyrs; feast, Oct. 19.

Cancer de Barbastro, Louis (1500-1549): Spanish Dominican; began missionary work in Middle America, 1533; killed at Tampa Bay, Fla.

Castillo, John de, Bl. (1596-1628): Spanish Jesuit; worked in Paraguay Indian mission settlements (reductions); martyred; beatified, 1934; feast, Nov. 17.

Catala, Magin (1761-1830): Spanish Franciscan; worked in California mission of Santa Clara for 36 years.

Chabanel, Noel, St. (1613-1649): French Jesuit; missionary among Huron Indians in Canada; murdered by renegade Huron, Dec. 8, 1649; canonized, 1930; one of Jesuit North American martyrs; feast, Oct. 19.

Chaumonot, Pierre Joseph (1611-1693): French Jesuit; missionary among Indians in Canada.

Claver, Peter, St. (1581-1654): Spanish Jesuit; missionary among Negroes of South America and West Indies; canonized, 1888; patron of Catholic missions among black people; feast, Sept. 9.

Daniel, Anthony, St. (1601-1648): French Jesuit; missionary among Huron Indians in Canada; martyred by Iroquois, July 4, 1648; canonized, 1930; one of Jesuit North American martyrs; feast, Oct. 19.

De Smet, Pierre Jean (1801-1873): Belgian-born Jesuit; missionary among Indians of northwestern U.S.; served as intermediary between Indians and U.S. government; wrote on Indian culture.

Duchesne, Rose Philippine, Bl. (1769-1852): French nun; educator and missionary in the U.S.; established first convent of the Society of the Sacred Heart in the U.S., at St. Charles, Mo. (later Florissant); founded schools for girls; did missionary work among Indians; beatified, 1940; feast, Nov. 17.

Farmer, Ferdinand (family name, Steinmeyer) (1720-1786): German Jesuit; missionary in Philadelphia, where he died; one of the first missionaries in New Jersey.

Flaget, Benedict J. (1763-1850): French Sulpician bishop; came to U.S., 1792; missionary and educator in U.S.; first bishop of Bardstown, Ky. (now Louisville), 1810-32; 1833-50.

Gallitzin, Demetrius (1770-1840): Russian prince, born The Hague; convert, 1787; ordained priest at Baltimore, 1795; frontier missionary, known as Father Smith; Gallitzin, Pa., named for him.

Garnier, Charles, St. (c. 1606-1649): French Jesuit; missionary among Hurons in Canada; martyred by Iroquois, Dec. 7, 1649; canonized, 1930; one of Jesuit North American martyrs; feast, Oct. 19.

Gibault, Pierre (1737-1804): Canadian missionary in Illinois and Indiana; aided in securing states of Ohio, Indiana, Illinois, Michigan and Wisconsin for the Americans during Revolution.

Gonzalez, Roch, Bl. (1576-1628): Paraguayan Jesuit; worked in Paraguay Indian mission settlements (reductions); martyred; beatified, 1934; feast, Nov. 17.

Goupil, Rene, St. (1607-1642): French Jesuit brother; missionary companion of St. Isaac Jogues among the Hurons; martyred, Sept. 29, 1642; canonized, 1930; one of Jesuit North American martyrs; feast, Oct. 19.

Gravier, Jacques (1651-1708): French Jesuit; missionary among Indians of Canada and midwestern U.S.

Jesuit North American Martyrs: Isaac Jogues, Anthony Daniel, John de Brebeuf, Gabriel Lalemant, Charles Garnier, Noel Chabanel (Jesuit priests), and Rene Goupil and John Lalande (lay missionaries) who were martyred between Sept. 29, 1642, and Dec. 9, 1649, in the missions of New France; canonized June 29, 1930; feast, Oct. 19. See separate entries.

Jogues, Isaac, St. (1607-1646): French Jesuit; missionary among Indians in Canada; martyred near present site of Auriesville, N.Y., by Mohawks, Oct. 18, 1646; canonized, 1930; one of Jesuit North American martyrs; feast, Oct. 19.

Kino, Eusebio (1645-1711): Italian Jesuit; missionary and explorer in U.S.; arrived Southwest, 1681; established 25 Indian missions, took part in 14 exploring expeditions in northern Mexico, Arizona and southern California; helped develop livestock raising and farming in the area. He was selected in 1965 to represent Arizona in Statuary Hall.

Lalande, John, St. (d. 1646): French lay missionary, companion of Isaac Jogues; martyred by Mohawks at Auriesville, N.Y., Oct. 19, 1646; canonized, 1930; one of Jesuit North American martyrs; feast, Oct. 19.

Lalemant, Gabriel, St. (1610-1649): French Jesuit; missionary among the Hurons in Canada; martyred by the Iroquois, Mar. 17, 1649; canonized, 1930; one of Jesuit North American martyrs; feast, Oct. 19.

Lamy, Jean Baptiste (1814-1888): French prelate; came to U.S., 1839; missionary in Ohio and Kentucky; bishop in Southwest from 1850; first bishop (later archbishop) of Santa Fe, 1850-1885. He was nominated in 1951 to represent New Mexico in Statuary Hall.

Las Casas, Bartolome (1474-1566): Spanish Dominican; missionary in Haiti, Jamaica and Venezuela; reformer of abuses against Indians and black people; bishop of Chalapas, Mexico, 1544-47; historian.

Laval, Francoise de Montmorency, Bl. (1623-1708): French Jesuit; named vicar apostolic of Canada, 1658; first bishop of Quebec, 1674; jurisdiction extended over all French-claimed territory in New World; beatified 1980; feast, May 6.

Manogue, Patrick (1831-1895): Missionary bishop in U.S., b. Ireland; migrated to U.S.; minor in California; studied for priesthood at St. Mary's of the Lake, Chicago, and St. Sulpice, Paris; ordained, 1861; missionary among Indians of California and Nevada; coadjutor bishop, 1881-84, and bishop, 1884-86, of Grass Valley; first bishop of Sacramento, 1886-1895, when see was transferred there.

Margil, Antonio (1657-1726): Spanish Franciscan; missionary in Middle America; apostle of Guatemala; established missions in Texas.

Marie of the Incarnation, Bl. (Marie Guyard Martin) (1599-1672): French widow; joined Ursuline Nuns; arrived in Canada, 1639; first superior of Ursulines in Quebec; missionary to Indians; writer; beatified 1980; feast, Apr. 30.

Marquette, Jacques (1637-1675): French Jesuit; missionary and explorer in America; sent to New France, 1666; began missionary work among Ottawa Indians on Lake Superior, 1668; accompanied Joliet down the Mississippi to mouth of the Arkansas, 1673, and returned to Lake Michigan by way of Illinois River; made a second trip over the same route; his diary and map are of historical significance. He was selected in 1895 to represent Wisconsin in Statuary Hall.

Massias (Macias), John de, St. (1585-1645): Dominican brother, a native of Spain; entered Dominican Friary at Lima, Peru, 1622; served as doorkeeper until his death; beatified, 1837; canonized 1975; feast, Sept. 16.

Mazzuchelli, Samuel C. (1806-1864): Italian Dominican; missionary in midwestern U.S.; called builder of the West; writer.

Membre, Zenobius (1645-1687): French Franciscan; missionary among Indians of Illinois; accompanied LaSalle expedition down the Mississippi (1681-1682) and Louisiana colonizing expedition (1684) which landed in Texas; murdered by Indians.

Nerinckx, Charles (1761-1824): Belgian priest; missionary in Kentucky; founded Sisters of Loretto at the Foot of the Cross.

Nobrega, Manoel (1517-1570): Portuguese Jesuit; leader of first Jesuit missionaries to Brazil, 1549.

Padilla, Juan de (d. 1542): Spanish Franciscan; missionary among Indians of Mexico and southwestern U.S.; killed by Indians in Kansas; protomartyr of the U.S.

Palou, Francisco (c. 1722-1789): Spanish Franciscan; accompanied Junipero Serra to Mexico, 1749; founded Mission Dolores in San Francisco; wrote history of the Franciscans in California.

Pariseau, Mother Mary Joseph (1833-1902): Canadian Sister of Charity of Providence; missionary in state of Washington from 1856; founded first hospitals in northwest territory; artisan and architect. Represents Washington in National Statuary Hall.

Peter of Ghent (d. 1572): Belgian Franciscan brother; missionary in Mexico for 49 years.

Porres, Martin de, St. (1579-1639): Peruvian Dominican oblate; his father was a Spanish soldier and his mother a black freedwoman from Panama; called wonder worker of Peru; beatified, 1837; canonized, 1962; feast, Nov. 3.

Quiroga, Vasco de (1470-1565): Spanish missionary in Mexico; founded hospitals; bishop of Michoacan, 1537.

Ravalli, Antonio (1811-1884): Italian Jesuit; missionary in far-western United States, mostly Montana, for 40 years.

Raymbaut, Charles (1602-1643): French Jesuit; missionary among Indians of Canada and northern U.S..

Richard, Gabriel (1767-1832): French Sulpician; missionary in Illinois and Michigan; a founder of University of Michigan; elected delegate to Congress from Michigan, 1823; first priest to hold seat in the House of Representatives.

Rodriguez, Alonso, Bl. (1598-1628): Spanish Jesuit; missionary in Paraguay; martyred; beatified, 1934; feast, Nov. 17.

Rosati, Joseph (1789-1843): Italian Vincentian; missionary bishop in U.S. (vicar apostolic of Mississippi and Alabama, 1822; coadjutor of Louisiana and the Two Floridas, 1823-26; administrator of New Orleans, 1826-29; first bishop of St. Louis, 1826-1843).

Sahagun, Bernardino de (c. 1500-1590): Spanish Franciscan; missionary in Mexico for over 60 years; expert on Aztec archaeology.

Seelos, Francis X. (1819-1867): Redemptorist

missionary, born Bavaria; ordained, 1844, at Baltimore; missionary in Pittsburgh and New Orleans.

Serra, Junipero (1713-1784): Spanish Franciscan, b. Majorca; missionary in America; arrived Mexico, 1749, where he did missionary work for 20 years; began work in Upper California in 1769 and established nine of the 21 Franciscan missions along the Pacific coast; baptized some 6,000 Indians and confirmed almost 5,000; a cultural pioneer of California. Represents California in Statuary Hall.

Seghers, Charles J. (1839-1886): Belgian missionary bishop in North America; Apostle of Alaska; archbishop of Oregon City (now Portland), 1880-1884; murdered by berserk companion.

Solanus, St. Francis (1549-1610): Spanish Franciscan; missionary in Paraguay, Argentina and Peru; wonder worker of the New World; canonized, 1726; feast, July 13.

Sorin, Edward F. (1814-1893): French priest; member of Congregation of Holy Cross; sent to U.S. in 1841; founder and first president of the University of Notre Dame; missionary in Indiana and Michigan.

Todadilla, Anthony de (1704-1746): Spanish Capuchin; missionary to Indians of Venezuela; killed by Motilones.

Turibius de Mogrovejo, St. (1538-1606): Spanish archbishop of Lima, Peru, c. 1580-1606; canonized 1726; feast, Apr. 27.

Twelve Apostles of Mexico (early 16th century): Franciscan priests; arrived in Mexico, 1524: Fathers Martin de Valencia (leader), Francisco de Soto, Martin de la Coruna, Juan Suares, Antonio de Ciudad Rodrigo, Toribio de Benevente, Garcia de Cisneros, Luis de Fuensalida, Juan de Ribas, Francisco Ximenes; Brothers Andres de Coroboda, Juan de Palos.

Valdivia, Luis de (1561-1641): Spanish Jesuit; defender of Indians in Peru and Chile.

Vasques de Espinosa, Antonio (early 17th century): Spanish Carmelite; missionary and explorer in Mexico, Panama and western coast of South America.

Vieira, Antonio (1608-1687): Portuguese Jesuit; preacher; missionary in Peru and Chile; protector of Indians against exploitation by slave owners and traders; considered foremost prose writer of 17th-century Portugal.

White, Andrew (1579-1656): English Jesuit; missionary among Indians in Maryland.

Wimmer, Boniface (1809-1887): German Benedictine; missionary among German immigrants in the U.S..

Youville, Marie Marguerite d', Bl. (1701-1771): Canadian widow; foundress of Sisters of Charity (Grey Nuns), 1738, at Montreal: beatified, 1959; feast, Dec. 23.

Zumarraga, Juan de (1468-1548): Spanish Franciscan; missionary; first bishop of Mexico; introduced first printing press in New World, published first book in America, a catechism for Aztec Indians; extended missions in Mexico and Central America; vigorous opponent of exploitation of Indians; approved of devotions at Guadalupe; leading figure in early church history in Mexico.

The starting point of the mainstream of Catholic history in the United States was Baltimore at the end of the Revolutionary War, although before that time Catholic explorers had traversed much of the country and missionaries had done considerable work among the Indians in the Southeast, Northeast and Southwest.

Beginning of Organization

Father John Carroll's appointment as superior of the American missions on June 9, 1784, was the first step toward organization of the Church in this country.

At that time, according to a report he made to Rome in 1785, there were approximately 25,000 Catholics in the general population of four million. Many of them had been in the Colonies for several generations. Among them were such outstanding figures as Charles Carroll, a member of the Continental Congress and signer of the Declaration of Independence; Thomas FitzSimons of Philadelphia and Oliver Pollock, the Virginia agent, who raised funds for the militia; Commander John Barry, father of the American Navy, and numerous high-ranking army officers. For the most part, however, Catholics were an unknown minority laboring under legal and social handicaps.

Father Carroll, the cousin of Charles Carroll, was named the first American bishop in 1789 and placed in charge of the Diocese of Baltimore, whose boundaries were coextensive with those of the United States. He was consecrated in England Aug. 15, 1790, and installed in his see the following Dec. 12.

Ten years later, Father Leonard Neale became his coadjutor and the first bishop ordained in the United States. Bishop Carroll became an archbishop in 1808 when Baltimore was designated a metropolitan see and the new dioceses of Boston, New York, Philadelphia and Bardstown were established. These jurisdictions were later subdivided, and by 1840 there were, in addition to Baltimore, 15 dioceses, 500 priests and 663,000 Catholics in the general population of 17 million.

Priests and First Seminaries

The number of the 24 original priests was gradually augmented with the arrival of others from France, after the Civil Constitution on the Clergy went into effect there, and other countries. Among the earliest arrivals were several Sulpicians who established the first seminary in the U.S., St. Mary's, Baltimore, in 1791. By 1815, 30 alumni of the school had been ordained to the priesthood. By that time, two additional seminaries were in operation: Mt. St. Mary's, established in 1809 at Emmitsburg, Md., and St. Thomas, founded two years later, at Bardstown, Ky. These and similar institutions founded later played key roles in the development and growth of the American clergy.

Early Schools

Early educational enterprises included the establishment in 1791 of a school at Georgetown which later became the first Catholic university in the U.S.; the opening of a secondary school for girls, conducted by Visitation Nuns, in 1792 at Georgetown; and the start of a similar school in the first decade of the 19th century at Emmitsburg, Md., by Saint Elizabeth Ann Seton and the Sisters of Charity of St. Joseph, the first religious community of American foundation.

By the 1840s, which saw the beginnings of the present public school system, more than 200 Catholic elementary schools, half of them west of the Alleghenies, were in operation. From this start, the Church subsequently built the greatest private system of education in the world.

Trusteeism

The initial lack of organization in ecclesiastical affairs, nationalistic feeling among Catholics and the independent action of some priests were factors involved in several early crises.

In Philadelphia, some German Catholics withdrew from one parish in 1789 and founded one of their own, Holy Trinity, which they maintained until 1802. Controversy over the affair reached the point of schism in 1796. Philadelphia was also the scene of the Hogan Schism, which developed in the 1820's when Father William Hogan, with the aid of lay trustees, seized control of St. Mary's Cathedral. His movement, for churches and parishes controlled by other than canonical procedures and run in extra-legal ways, was nullified by a decision of the Pennsylvania Supreme Court in 1822.

Similar troubles seriously disturbed the peace of the Church in other places, principally New York, Baltimore, Buffalo, Charleston and New Orleans.

Dangers arising from the exploitation of lay control were gradually diminished with the extension and enforcement of canonical procedures and with changes in civil law about the middle of the century.

Bigotry

Bigotry against Catholics waxed and waned during the 19th century and into the 20th. The first major campaign of this kind, which developed in the wake of the panic of 1819 and lasted for about 25 years, was mounted in 1830 when the number of Catholic immigrants began to increase to a noticeable degree. Nativist anti-Catholicism generated a great deal of violence, represented by climaxes in loss of life and property in Charlestown, Mass., in 1834, and in Philadelphia 10 years later. Later bigotry was fomented by the Know-Nothings, in the 1850s; the Ku Klux Klan, from 1866; the American Protective Association, from 1887, and the Guardians of Liberty. Perhaps the last eruption of virulently overt anti-Catholicism occurred during the campaign of Alfred E. Smith for the presidency in 1928. Observers feel the issue was muted to a considerable extent in the political area with the election of John F. Kennedy to the presidency in 1960.

Growth and Immigration

Between 1830 and 1900, the combined factors of

natural increase, immigration and conversion raised the Catholic population to 12 million. A large percentage of the growth figure represented immigrants: some 2.7 million, largely from Ireland, Germany and France, between 1830 and 1880; and another 1.25 million during the 1880s when Eastern and Southern Europeans came in increasing numbers. By the 1860s the Catholic Church, with most of its members concentrated in urban areas, was one of the largest religious bodies in the country.

The efforts of progressive bishops to hasten the acculturation of Catholic immigrants occasioned a number of controversies, which generally centered around questions concerning national or foreign-language parishes. One of them, called Cahenslyism, arose from complaints that German Catholic immigrants were not being given adequate pastoral care.

Immigration continued after the turn of the century, but its impact was more easily cushioned through the application of lessons learned earlier in dealing with problems of nationality and language.

Councils of Baltimore

The bishops of the growing U.S. dioceses met at Baltimore for seven provincial councils between 1829 and 1849.

In 1846, they proclaimed the Blessed Virgin Mary patroness of the United States under the title of the Immaculate Conception, eight years before the dogma was proclaimed.

After the establishment of the Archdiocese of Oregon City in 1846 and the elevation to metropolitan status of St. Louis, New Orleans, Cincinnati and New York, the first of the three plenary councils of Baltimore was held.

The first plenary assembly was convoked on May 9, 1852, with Archbishop Francis P. Kenrick of Baltimore as papal legate. The bishops drew up regulations concerning parochial life, matters of church ritual and ceremonies, the administration of church funds and the teaching of Christian doctrine.

The second plenary council, meeting from Oct. 7 to 21, 1866, under the presidency of Archbishop Martin J. Spalding, formulated a condemnation of several current doctrinal errors and established norms affecting the organization of dioceses, the education and conduct of the clergy, the management of ecclesiastical property, parochial duties and general education.

Archbishop (later Cardinal) James Gibbons called into session the third plenary council which lasted from Nov. 9 to Dec. 7, 1884. Among highly significant results of actions taken by this assembly were the preparation of the line of Baltimore catechisms which became a basic means of religious instruction in this country; legislation which fixed the pattern of Catholic education by requiring the building of elementary schools in all parishes; the establishment of the Catholic University of America in Washington, D.C., in 1889; and the determination of six holy days of obligation for observance in this country.

The enactments of the three plenary councils have had the force of particular law for the Church in the United States.

The Holy See established the Apostolic Delegation in Washington, D.C., on Jan. 24, 1893.

Slavery

In the Civil War period, as before, Catholics reflected attitudes of the general population with respect to the issue of slavery. Some supported it, some opposed it, but none were prominent in the Abolition Movement. Gregory XVI had condemned the slave trade in 1839, but no contemporary pope or American bishop published an official document on slavery itself. The issue did not split Catholics in schism as it did Baptists, Methodists and Presbyterians.

Catholics fought on both sides in the Civil War. Five hundred members of 20 or more sisterhoods served the wounded of both sides.

One hundred thousand of the four million slaves emancipated in 1863 were Catholics; the highest concentrations were in Louisiana, about 60,000, and Maryland, 16,000. Three years later, their pastoral care was one of the subjects covered in nine decrees issued by the Second Plenary Council of Baltimore. The measures had little practical effect with respect to integration of the total Catholic community, predicated as they were on the proposition that individual bishops should handle questions regarding segregation in churches and related matters as best they could in the pattern of local customs.

Long entrenched segregation practices continued in force through the rest of the 19th century and well into the 20th. The first effective efforts to alter them were initiated by Cardinal Joseph Ritter of St. Louis in 1947, Cardinal (then Archbishop) Patrick O'Boyle of Washington in 1948, and Bishop Vincent Waters of Raleigh in 1953.

Friend of Labor

The Church became known during the 19th century as a friend and ally of labor in seeking justice for the working man. Cardinal Gibbons journeyed to Rome in 1887, for example, to defend and prevent a condemnation of the Knights of Labor by Leo XIII. The encyclical *Rerum Novarum* was hailed by many American bishops as a confirmation, if not vindication, of their own theories. Catholics have always formed a large percentage of union membership, and some have served unions in positions of leadership.

The American Heresy

Near the end of the century some controversy developed over what was characterized as Americanism or the phantom heresy. It was alleged that Americans were discounting the importance of contemplative virtues, exalting the practical virtues, and watering down the purity of Catholic doctrine for the sake of facilitating convert work.

The French translation of Father Walter Elliott's *Life of Isaac Hecker,* which fired the controversy, was one of many factors that led to the issuance of Leo XIII's *Testem Benevolentiae* in

January, 1899, in an attempt to end the matter. It was the first time the orthodoxy of the Church in the U.S. was called into question.

Schism

In the 1890s, serious friction developed between Poles and Irish in Scranton, Buffalo and Chicago, resulting in schism and the establishment of the Polish National Church. A central figure in the affair was Father Francis Hodur, who was excommunicated by Bishop William O'Hara of Scranton in 1898. Nine years later, his ordination by an Old Catholic Archbishop of Utrecht gave the new church its first bishop.

Another schism of the period led to formation of the American Carpatho-Russian Orthodox Greek Catholic Church.

Coming of Age

In 1900, there were 12 million Catholics in the total U.S. population of 76 million, 82 dioceses in 14 provinces, and 12,000 priests and members of about 40 communities of men religious. Many sisterhoods, most of them of European origin and some of American foundation, were engaged in Catholic educational and hospital work, two of their traditional apostolates.

The Church in the United States was removed from mission status with promulgation of the apostolic constitution *Sapienti Consilio* by Pope St. Pius X on June 29, 1908.

Before that time, and even into the early 1920s, the Church in this country received financial assistance from mission-aid societies in France, Bavaria and Austria. Already, however, it was making increasing contributions of its own. At the present time, it is the heaviest national contributor to the worldwide Society for the Propagation of the Faith.

American foreign missionary personnel increased from 14 or less in 1906 to 7,148 by 1975 (197 diocesan priests, 3,692 religious priests and brothers, 2,850 sisters, 65 seminarians, 344 lay persons). The first missionary seminary in the U.S. was in operation at Techny, Ill., in 1909, under the auspices of the Society of the Divine Word. Maryknoll, the first American missionary society, was established in 1911 and sent its first priests to China in 1918. Despite these contributions, the Church in the U.S. has not matched the missionary commitment of some other nations.

Bishops' Conference

A highly important apparatus for mobilizing the Church's resources was established in 1917 under the title of the National Catholic War Council. Its name was changed to National Catholic Welfare Conference several years later, but its objectives remained the same: to serve as an advisory and coordinating agency of the American bishops for advancing works of the Church in fields of social significance and impact — education, communications, immigration, social action, legislation, youth and lay organizations.

The forward thrust of the bishops' social thinking was evidenced in a program of social re-construction they recommended in 1919. By 1945, all but one of their twelve points had been enacted into legislation.

The NCWC was renamed the United States Catholic Conference (USCC) in November, 1966, when the hierarchy also organized itself as a territorial conference with pastoral-juridical authority under the title, National Conference of Catholic Bishops. The USCC is carrying on the functions of the former NCWC.

Pastoral Concerns

The potential for growth of the Church in this country by immigration was sharply reduced but not entirely curtailed after 1921 with the passage of restrictive federal legislation. As a result, the Catholic population became more stabilized and, to a certain extent and for many reasons, began to acquire an identity of its own.

Some increase from outside has taken place in the past 50 years, however; from Canada, from Central and Eastern European countries, and from Puerto Rico and Latin American countries since World War II. This influx, while not as great as that of the 19th century and early 20th, has enriched the Church here with a sizable body of Eastern-Rite Catholics for whom eight ecclesiastical jurisdictions were established between 1924 and 1969. It has also created a challenge for pastoral care of millions of Hispanics in urban centers and in agricultural areas where migrant workers are employed.

The Church continues to grapple with serious pastoral problems in rural areas, where about 600 counties are no-priest land. The National Catholic Rural Life Conference was established in 1922 in an attempt to make the Catholic presence felt on the land, and the Glenmary Society since its foundation in 1939 has devoted itself to this single apostolate. Religious communities and diocesan priests are similarly engaged.

Other challenges lie in the cities and suburbs where 75 percent of the Catholic population lives. Conditions peculiar to each segment of the metropolitan area have developed in recent years as the flight to the suburbs has not only altered some traditional aspects of parish life but has also, in combination with many other factors, left behind a complex of special problems in inner city areas.

Contemporary Factors

The Church in the U.S. is in a stage of transition from a relatively stable and long established order of life and action to a new order of things. Some of the phenomena of this period are:

• differences in trends and emphasis in theology, and in interpretation and implementation of directives of the Second Vatican Council, resulting in situations of conflict;

• the changing spiritual formation, professional education, style of life and ministry of priests and religious (men and women), which are altering influential patterns of pastoral and specialized service;

• vocations to the priesthood and religious life, which are generally in decline;

- departures from the priesthood and religious life which, while small percentage-wise, are numerous enough to be a matter of serious concern;
- decline of traditional devotional practices;
- exercise of authority along the lines of collegiality and subsidiarity;
- structure and administration, marked by a trend toward greater participation in the life and work of the Church by its members on all levels, from the parish on up;
- alienation from the Church, leading some persons into the catacombs of an underground church,

"anonymous Christianity" and religious indifferentism;
- education, undergoing crisis and change in Catholic schools and seeking new ways of reaching out to the young not in Catholic schools and to adults;
- social witness in ministry to the world, which is being shaped by the form of contemporary needs — e.g., race relations, poverty, the peace movement, the Third World;
- ecumenism, involving the Church in interfaith relations on a wider scale than before.

BACKGROUND DATES IN U.S. CATHOLIC CHRONOLOGY

Dates in this section refer mostly to earlier "firsts" and developments in the background of Catholic history in the United States. For other dates, see various sections of the Almanac.

Alabama

1540: Priests crossed the territory with De Soto's expedition.
1560: Five Dominicans in charge of mission at Santa Cruz des Nanipacna.
1682: La Salle claimed territory for France.
1704: First parish church established at Fort Louis de la Mobile under the care of diocesan priests.
1829: Mobile diocese established (redesignated Mobile-Birmingham, 1954-69).
1830: Spring Hill College, Mobile, established.
1834: Visitation Nuns established an academy at Summerville.
1969: Birmingham diocese established.
1980: Mobile made metropolitan see.

Alaska

1779: Mass celebrated for first time on shore of Port Santa Cruz on lower Bucareli Bay on May 13 by Franciscan Juan Riobo.
1868: Alaska placed under jurisdiction of Vancouver Island.
1879: Father John Althoff became first resident missionary.
1886: Archbishop Charles J. Seghers, "Apostle of Alaska," murdered by a guide; had surveyed southern and northwest Alaska in 1873 and 1877, respectively.
Sisters of St. Ann first nuns in Alaska.
1887: Jesuits enter Alaska territory.
1894: Alaska made prefecture apostolic.
1902: Sisters of Providence opened hospital at Nome.
1916: Alaska made vicariate apostolic.
1917: In first ordination in territory, Rev. G. Edgar Gallant raised to priesthood.
1951: Juneau diocese established.
1962: Fairbanks diocese established.
1966: Anchorage archdiocese established.

Arizona

1539: Franciscan Marcos de Niza explored the state.
1540: Franciscans Juan de Padilla and Marcos de Niza accompanied Coronado expedition through the territory.

1629: Spanish Franciscans began work among Moqui Indians.
1632: Franciscan Martin de Arvide killed by Indians.
1680: Franciscans Jose de Espeleta, Augustin de Santa Maria, Jose de Figueroa and Jose de Trujillo killed in Pueblo Revolt.
1700: Jesuit Eusebio Kino established mission at San Xavier del Bac, near Tucson.
1767: Jesuits expelled; Franciscans took over 10 missions.
1828: Spanish missionaries expelled by Mexican government.
1863: Jesuits returned to San Xavier del Bac briefly.
1869: Sisters of Loretto arrived to conduct schools at Bisbee and Douglas.
1897: Tucson diocese established.
1969: Phoenix diocese established.

Arkansas

1541: Priests accompanied De Soto expedition through the territory.
1673: Marquette visited Indians in east.
1686: Henri de Tonti established trading post, first white settlement in territory.
1700-1702: Fr. Nicholas Foucault working among Indians.
1805: Bishop Carroll of Baltimore appointed Administrator Apostolic of Arkansas.
1838: Sisters of Loretto opened first Catholic school.
1843: Little Rock diocese established. There were about 700 Catholics in state, two churches, one priest.
1851: Sisters of Mercy founded St. Mary's Convent in Little Rock.

California

1542: Cabrillo discovered Upper (Alta) California; name of priest accompanying expedition unknown.
1602: On Nov. 12 Carmelite Andres de la Ascencion offered first recorded Mass in California on shore of San Diego Bay.
1697: Missionary work in Lower and Upper Californias entrusted to Jesuits.
1767: Jesuits expelled from territory. Spanish Crown confiscated their property, including the Pious Fund for Missions. Upper California missions entrusted to Franciscans.
1769: Franciscan Junipero Serra began establish-

ment of Franciscan missions in California, in present San Diego. (See Franciscan Missions of Upper California.)

1775: Franciscan Luis Jayme killed by Indians at San Diego Mission.

1779: Diocese of Sonora, Mexico, which included Upper California, established.

1781: On Sept. 4 an expedition from San Gabriel Mission founded present city of Los Angeles — Pueblo "de Nuestra Senora de los Angeles."

Franciscans Francisco Hermenegildo Garces, Juan Antonio Barreneche, Juan Marcello Diaz and Jose Matias Moreno killed by Indians.

1812: Franciscan Andres Quintana killed at Santa Cruz Mission.

1822: Dedication on Dec. 8 of Old Plaza Church, "Assistant Mission of Our Lady of the Angels."

1833: Missions secularized, finally confiscated.

1840: Pope Gregory XVI established Diocese of Both Californias.

1846: Peter H. Burnett, who became first governor of California in 1849, received into Catholic Church.

1848: Mexico ceded California to the United States.

1850: Monterey diocese erected; title changed to Monterey-Los Angeles, 1859; and to Los Angeles-San Diego, 1922.

1851: University of Santa Clara chartered.

Sisters of Notre Dame de Namur opened women's College of Notre Dame at San Jose; chartered in 1868; moved to Belmont, 1923.

1852: Baja California detached from Monterey diocese.

1853: San Francisco archdiocese established.

1855: Negotiations inaugurated to restore confiscated California missions to Church.

1868: Grass Valley diocese established; transferred to Sacramento in 1886.

1922: Monterey-Fresno diocese established; became separate dioceses, 1967.

1934: Sesquicentennial of Serra's death observed; Serra Year officially declared by Legislature and Aug. 24 observed as Serra Day.

1936: Los Angeles made archdiocese. San Diego diocese established.

1952: Law exempting non-profit, religious-sponsored elementary and secondary schools from taxation upheld in referendum, Nov. 4.

1953: Archbishop James Francis McIntyre of Los Angeles made cardinal by Pius XII.

1962: Oakland, Santa Rosa and Stockton dioceses established.

1973: Archbishop Timothy Manning of Los Angeles made cardinal by Pope Paul VI.

1976: Orange diocese established.

1978: San Bernardino diocese established.

1981: San Jose diocese established.

Byzantine-Rite eparchy of Van Nuys established.

Colorado

1858: First parish in Colorado established.

1864: Sisters of Loretto at the Foot of the Cross, first nuns in the state, established academy at Denver.

1868: Vicariate Apostolic of Colorado and Utah established.

1887: Denver diocese established.

1888: Regis College founded.

1941: Denver made archdiocese.

Pueblo diocese established.

Connecticut

1651: Probably first priest to enter state was Jesuit Gabriel Druillettes; ambassador of Governor of Canada, he participated in a New England Colonial Council at New Haven.

1756: Catholic Acadians, expelled from Nova Scotia, settled in the state.

1791: Rev. John Thayer, first native New England priest, offered Mass at the Hartford home of Noah Webster, his Yale classmate.

1808: Connecticut became part of Boston diocese.

1818: Religious freedom established by new constitution, although the Congregational Church remained, in practice, the state church.

1829: Father Bernard O'Cavanaugh became first resident priest in state.

Catholic Press of Hartford established.

1830: First Catholic church in state dedicated at Hartford.

Father James Fitton (1805-81), New England missionary, was assigned to Hartford for six years. He ministered to Catholics throughout the state.

1843: Hartford diocese established.

1882: Knights of Columbus founded by Father Michael J. McGivney.

1942: Fairfield University founded.

1953: Norwich and Bridgeport dioceses established. Hartford made archdiocese.

1956: Byzantine Rite Exarchate of Stamford established; made eparchy, 1958.

Delaware

1730: Mount Cuba, New Castle County, the scene of Catholic services.

1750: Jesuit mission at Apoquiniminck administered from Maryland.

1772: First permanent parish established at Coffee Run.

1792: French Catholics from Santo Domingo settled near Wilmington.

1816: St. Peter's Church, later the cathedral of the diocese, erected at Wilmington.

1830: Daughters of Charity opened school and orphanage at Wilmington.

1868: Wilmington diocese established.

1869: Visitation Nuns established residence in Wilmington.

District of Columbia

1641: Jesuit Andrew White evangelized Anacostia Indians.

1774: Father John Carroll ministered to Catholics.

1789: Georgetown, first Catholic college in U.S., established.

1791: Pierre Charles L'Enfant designed the Federal City of Washington. His plans were not fully implemented until the early 1900's.

1792: James Hoban designed the White House.

1794: Father Anthony Caffrey began St. Patrick's

Church, first parish church in the new Federal City.

1801: Poor Clares opened school for girls in Georgetown; first school established by nuns in U.S..

1802: First mayor of Washington, appointed by President Jefferson, was Judge Robert Brent.

1889: Catholic University of America founded.

1893: Apostolic Delegation established with Archbishop Francesco Satolli as the first delegate.

1919: National Catholic Welfare Conference (now the United States Catholic Conference) organized by American hierarchy to succeed National Catholic War Council.

1920: Cornerstone of National Shrine of Immaculate Conception laid.

1939: Washington made archdiocese of equal rank with Baltimore, under direction of same archbishop.

1947: Washington archdiocese received its own archbishop, was separated from Baltimore; became a metropolitan see in 1965.

1967: Archbishop Patrick A. O'Boyle of Washington made cardinal by Pope Paul VI.

1976: Archbishop William Baum of Washington made a cardinal by Pope Paul VI; transferred to Roman Curia in 1980 as prefect of Sacred Congregation for Catholic Education.

Florida

1513: Ponce de Leon discovered Florida.

1521: Missionaries accompanying Ponce de Leon and other explorers probably said first Masses within present limits of U.S..

1528: Franciscans landed on western shore.

1539: Twelve missionaries landed with De Soto at Tampa Bay.

1549: Dominican Luis Cancer de Barbastro and two companions slain by Indians near Tampa Bay.

1565: City of St. Augustine, oldest in U.S., founded by Pedro Menendez de Aviles, who was accompanied by four secular priests.

America's oldest mission, Nombre de Dios, was established.

Father Martin Francisco Lopez de Mendoza Grajales became the first parish priest of St. Augustine, where the first parish in the U.S. was established.

1572: St. Francis Borgia, general of the Society, withdrew Jesuits from Florida.

1606: Bishop Juan de las Cabeyas de Altamirano, O.P., conducted the first episcopal visitation in the U.S..

1620: The chapel of Nombre de Dios was dedicated to Nuestra Senora de la Leche y Buen Parto (Our Nursing Mother of the Happy Delivery); oldest shrine to the Blessed Mother in the U.S..

1704: Destruction of Florida's northern missions by English and Indian troops led by Governor James Moore of South Carolina. Franciscans Juan de Parga, Dominic Criodo, Tiburcio de Osorio, Augustine Ponze de Leon, Marcos Delgado and two Indians, Anthony Enixa and Amador Cuipa Feliciano, were slain by the invaders.

1735: Bishop Francis Martinez de Tejadu Diaz de Velasco, auxiliary of Santiago, was the first bishop to take up residence in U.S., at St. Augustine.

1793: Florida and Louisiana were included in Diocese of New Orleans.

1857: Eastern Florida made a vicariate apostolic.

1870: St. Augustine diocese established.

1917: Convent Inspection Bill passed; repealed 1935.

1958: Miami diocese established.

1968: Miami made metropolitan see; Orlando and St. Petersburg dioceses established.

1976: Pensacola-Tallahassee diocese established.

Georgia

1540: First priests to enter were chaplains with De Soto. They celebrated first Mass within territory of 13 original colonies.

1566: Pedro Martinez, first Jesuit martyr of the New World, was slain by Indians on Cumberland Island.

1569: Jesuit mission was opened at Guale Island by Father Antonio Sedeno.

1572: Jesuits withdrawn from area.

1595: Five Franciscans assigned to Province of Guale.

1597: Five Franciscan missionaries (Fathers Pedro de Corpa, Blas de Rodriguez, Miguel de Anon, Francisco de Berascolo and Brother Antonio de Badajoz) killed in coastal missions.

1606: Bishop Altamirano, O.P., conducted visitation of the Georgia area.

1612: First Franciscan province in U.S. erected under title of Santa Elena; it included Georgia, South Carolina and Florida.

1655: Franciscans had nine flourishing missions among Indians.

1742: Spanish missions ended as result of English conquest at Battle of Bloody Marsh.

1796: Augustinian Father Le Mercier was first post-colonial missionary to Georgia.

1798: Catholics granted right of refuge.

1800: First church erected in Savannah on lot given by city council.

1810: First church erected in Augusta on lot given by State Legislature.

1850: Savannah diocese established; became Savannah-Atlanta, 1937; divided into two separate sees, 1956.

1864: Father Emmeran Bliemel, of the Benedictine community of Latrobe, Pa., was killed at the battle of Jonesboro while serving as chaplain of the Confederate 10th Tennessee Artillery.

1962: Atlanta made metropolitan see.

Hawaii

1825: Pope Leo XII entrusted missionary efforts in Islands to Sacred Hearts Fathers.

1827: The first Catholic missionaries arrived — Fathers Alexis Bachelot, Abraham Armand and Patrick Short, along with three lay brothers. After three years of persecution, the priests were forcibly exiled.

1836: Father Arsenius Walsh, SS. CC., a British subject, was allowed to remain in Islands but was not permitted to proselytize or conduct missions.

1839: Hawaiian government signed treaty with France granting Catholics freedom of worship and same privileges as Protestants.

1844: Vicariate Apostolic of Sandwich Islands (Hawaii) erected.

1873: Father Damien de Veuster of the Sacred Hearts Fathers arrived in Molokai and spent the remainder of his life working among lepers.

1941: Honolulu diocese established, made a suffragan of San Francisco.

Idaho

1840: Jesuit Pierre de Smet preached to the Flathead and Pend d'Oreille Indians; probably offered first Mass in state.

1842: Jesuit Nicholas Point opened a mission among Coeur d'Alene Indians near St. Maries.

1863: Secular priests sent from Oregon City to administer to incoming miners.

1867: Sisters of Holy Names of Jesus and Mary opened first Catholic school at Idaho City.

1868: Idaho made a vicariate apostolic.

1870: First church in Boise established.

Church lost most of missions among Indians of Northwest Territory when Commission on Indian Affairs appointed Protestant missionaries to take over.

1893: Boise diocese established.

Illinois

1673: Jesuit Jacques Marquette, accompanying Joliet, preached to Indians.

1674: Father Marquette set up a cabin for saying Mass in what later became City of Chicago.

1675: Father Marquette established Mission of the Immaculate Conception among Kaskaskia Indians, near present site of Utica; transferred to Kaskaskia, 1703.

1679: La Salle brought with him Franciscans Louis Hennepin, Gabriel de la Ribourde, and Zenobius Membre.

1680: Father Ribourde was killed by Kickapoo Indians.

1689: Jesuit Claude Allouez died after 32 years of missionary activity among Indians of Midwest; he had evangelized Indians of 20 different tribes. Jesuit Jacques Gravier succeeded Allouez as vicar general of Illinois.

1699: Mission established at Cahokia, first permanent settlement in state.

1730: Father Gaston, a diocesan priest, was killed at the Cahokia Mission.

1763: Jesuits were banished from the territory.

1778: Father Pierre Gibault championed Colonial cause in the Revolution and aided greatly in securing states of Ohio, Indiana, Illinois, Michigan and Wisconsin for Americans.

1827: The present St. Patrick's Parish at Ruma, oldest English-speaking Catholic congregation in state, was founded.

1833: Visitation Nuns established residence in Kaskaskia.

1843: Chicago diocese established.

1853: Quincy diocese established; transferred to Alton, 1857; Springfield, 1923.

1860: Quincy College founded.

1877: Peoria diocese established.

1880: Chicago made archdiocese.

1887: Belleville diocese established.

1894: Franciscan Sisters of Bl. Kunegunda (now the Franciscan Sisters of Chicago) founded by Mother Marie Therese (Josephine Dudzik).

1908: Rockford diocese established.

First American Missionary Congress held in Chicago.

1924: Archbishop Mundelein of Chicago made cardinal by Pope Pius XI.

1926: The 28th International Eucharistic Congress, first held in US, convened in Chicago.

1946: Blessed Frances Xavier Cabrini, former resident of Chicago, was canonized; first U.S. citizen raised to dignity of altar.

Archbishop Samuel A. Stritch of Chicago made cardinal by Pope Pius XII.

1948: Joliet diocese established.

1958: Cardinal Stritch appointed Pro-Prefect of the Sacred Congregation for the Propagation of the Faith — the first U.S.-born prelate to be named to the Roman Curia.

1959: Archbishop Albert G. Meyer of Chicago made cardinal by Pope John XXIII.

1961: Eparchy of St. Nicholas of the Ukrainians established at Chicago.

1967: Archbishop John P. Cody of Chicago made cardinal by Pope Paul VI.

1983: Archbishop Joseph L. Bernardin of Chicago made cardinal by Pope John Paul II.

Indiana

1679: Recollects Louis Hennepin and Gabriel de la Ribourde passed through state.

1686: Land near present Notre Dame University at South Bend given by French government to Jesuits for mission.

1749: Beginning of the records of St. Francis Xavier Church, Vincennes. These records continue with minor interruptions to the present.

1778: Father Gibault aided George Rogers Clark in campaign against British in conquest of Northwest Territory.

1824: Sisters of Charity of Nazareth, Ky., opened St. Clare's Academy in Vincennes.

1825: Laying of cornerstone of third church of St. Francis Xavier, which later (from 1834-98) was the cathedral of the Vincennes diocese. The church was designated a minor basilica in 1970 and is still in use as a parish church.

1834: Vincennes diocese established with Simon Gabriel Brute as bishop; title changed to Indianapolis, 1898.

1840: Sisters of Providence founded St. Mary-of-the-Woods College for women.

1842: University of Notre Dame founded by Holy Cross Father Edward Sorin and Brothers of St. Joseph on land given the diocese of Vincennes by Father Stephen Badin.

1853: First Benedictine community established in state at St. Meinrad. It became an abbey in 1870 and an archabbey in 1954.

1857: Fort Wayne diocese established; changed to Fort Wayne-South Bend, 1960.
1944: Indianapolis made archdiocese. Lafayette and Evansville dioceses established.
1957: Gary diocese established.

Iowa

1673: A Peoria village on Mississippi was visited by Father Marquette.
1679: Fathers Louis Hennepin and Gabriel de la Ribourde visited Indian villages.
1836: First permanent church, St. Raphael's, founded at Dubuque by Dominican Samuel Mazzuchelli.
1837: Dubuque diocese established.
1838: St. Joseph's Mission founded at Council Bluffs by Jesuit Father De Smet.
1843: Sisters of Charity of the Blessed Virgin Mary were first sisterhood in state.
Sisters of Charity opened Clarke College, Dubuque.
1850: First Trappist Monastery in state, Our Lady of New Melleray, was begun.
1881: Davenport diocese established.
1882: St. Ambrose College, Davenport, established.
1893: Dubuque made archdiocese.
1902: Sioux City diocese established.
1911: Des Moines diocese established.

Kansas

1542: Franciscan Juan de Padilla, first martyr of the United States, was killed in central Kansas.
1858: St. Benedict's College founded.
1863: Sisters of Charity opened orphanage at Leavenworth, and St. John's Hospital in following year.
1877: Leavenworth diocese established; transferred to Kansas City in 1947.
1887: Dioceses of Concordia (transferred to Salina in 1944) and Wichita established.
1888: Oblate Sisters of Providence opened an orphanage for Negro boys at Leavenworth, first west of Mississippi.
1951: Dodge City diocese established.
1952: Kansas City made archdiocese.

Kentucky

1775: First Catholic settlers came to Kentucky.
1787: Father Charles Maurice Whelan, first resident priest, ministered to settlers in the Bardstown district.
1793: Father Stephen T. Badin began missionary work in Kentucky.
1806: Dominican Fathers built Priory at St. Rose of Lima.
1808: Bardstown diocese established with Benedict Flaget as its first bishop; transferred to Louisville, 1841.
1811: Rev. Guy I. Chabrat first priest ordained west of the Allegheny Mountains.
St. Thomas Seminary founded.
1812: Sisters of Loretto founded by Rev. Charles Nerinckx; first religious community in the United States without foreign affiliation.
Sisters of Charity of Nazareth founded, the second

native community of women founded in the West.
1814: Nazareth College for women established.
1816: Cornerstone of St. Joseph's Cathedral, Bardstown, laid.
1836: Hon. Benedict J. Webb founded *Catholic Advocate* first Catholic weekly newspaper in Kentucky.
1848: Trappist monks took up residence in Gethsemani.
1849: Cornerstone of Cathedral of the Assumption laid at Louisville.
1852: Know-Nothing troubles in state.
1853: Covington diocese established.
1937: Louisville made archdiocese. Owensboro diocese established.

Louisiana

1682: La Salle's expedition, accompanied by two priests, completed discoveries of De Soto at mouth of Mississippi. LaSalle named territory Louisiana.
1699: French Catholics founded colony of Louisiana.
First recorded Mass offered Mar. 3, by Franciscan Father Anastase Douay.
1706: Father John Francis Buisson de St. Cosme was killed near Donaldsonville.
1717: Franciscan Anthony Margil established first Spanish mission in north central Louisiana.
1718: City of New Orleans founded by Jean Baptiste Le Moyne de Bienville.
1720: First resident priest in New Orleans was the French Recollect Prothais Boyer.
1725: Capuchin Fathers opened school for boys.
1727: Ursuline Nuns founded convent in New Orleans, oldest convent in what is now U.S.; they conducted a school, hospital and orphan asylum.
1793: New Orleans diocese established.
1850: New Orleans made archdiocese.
1853: Natchitoches diocese established; transferred to Alexandria in 1910; became Alexandria-Shreveport in 1977.
1892: Sisters of Holy Family, a black congregation, established at New Orleans.
1912: Loyola University of South established.
1918: Lafayette diocese established.
1925: Xavier University established in New Orleans.
1961: Baton Rouge diocese established.
1962: Catholic schools on all levels desegregated in New Orleans archdiocese.
1977: Houma-Thibodaux diocese established.
1980: Lake Charles diocese established.

Maine

1604: First Mass in territory celebrated by Father Nicholas Aubry, accompanying De Monts' expedition which was authorized by King of France to begin colonizing region.
1605: Colony founded on St. Croix Island; two secular priests served as chaplains.
1613: Four Jesuits attempted to establish permanent French settlement near mouth of Kennebec River.
1619: French Franciscans began work among set-

tlers and Indians; driven out by English in 1628.

1630: New England made a prefecture apostolic in charge of French Capuchins.

1633: Capuchin Fathers founded missions on Penobscot River.

1646: Jesuits established Assumption Mission on Kennebec River.

1688: Church of St. Anne, oldest in New England, built at Oldtown.

1704: English soldiers destroyed French missions.

1724: English forces again attacked French settlements, killed Jesuit Sebastian Rale.

1853: Portland diocese established.

1854: Know-Nothing uprising resulted in burning of church in Bath.

1856: Anti-Catholic feeling continued; church at Ellsworth burned.

1864: Sisters of Congregation of Notre Dame from Montreal opened academy at Portland.

1875: James A. Healy, first bishop of Negro blood consecrated in U.S., became second Bishop of Portland.

Maryland

1634: Maryland established by Lord Calvert. Two Jesuits among first colonists.

First Mass offered on Island of St. Clement in Lower Potomac by Jesuit Father Andrew White.

St. Mary's founded by English and Irish Catholics.

1641: St. Ignatius Parish founded by English Jesuits at Chapel Point, near Port Tobacco.

1649: Religious Toleration Act passed by Maryland Assembly. It was repealed in 1654 by Puritan-controlled government.

1651: Cecil Calvert, second Lord Baltimore, gave Jesuits 10,000 acres for use as Indian mission.

1658: Lord Baltimore restored Toleration Act.

1672: Franciscans came to Maryland under leadership of Father Massius Massey.

1688: Maryland became royal colony as a result of the Revolution in England; Anglican Church became the official religion (1692); Toleration Act repealed; Catholics disenfranchised and persecuted until 1776.

1784: Father John Carroll appointed prefect apostolic for the territory embraced by new Republic.

1789: Baltimore became first diocese established in U.S., with John Carroll as first bishop.

1790: Carmelite Nuns founded convent at Port Tobacco, the first in the English-speaking Colonies.

1791: First Synod of Baltimore held.

St. Mary's Seminary, first seminary in U.S., established.

1793: Rev. Stephen T. Badin first priest ordained by Bishop Carroll.

1800: Jesuit Leonard Neale became first bishop consecrated in present limits of U.S..

1806: Cornerstone of Assumption Cathedral, Baltimore, was laid.

1808: Baltimore made archdiocese.

1809: St. Joseph's College, first women's college in U.S., founded.

Sisters of Charity of St. Joseph founded by St. Elizabeth Ann Seton; first native American sisterhood.

1821: Assumption Cathedral, Baltimore, formally opened.

1829: Oblate Sisters of Providence, a Negro congregation, established at Baltimore.

First Provincial Council of Baltimore held; six others followed, in 1833, 1837, 1840, 1843, 1846 and 1849.

1836: Roger B. Taney appointed Chief Justice of Supreme Court by President Jackson.

1852: First of the three Plenary Councils of Baltimore convened. Subsequent councils were held in 1866 and 1884.

1855: German Catholic Central Verein founded.

1886: Archbishop James Gibbons of Baltimore made cardinal by Pope Leo XIII.

1965: Archbishop Lawrence Shehan of Baltimore made cardinal by Pope Paul VI.

Massachusetts

1630: New England made a prefecture apostolic in charge of French Capuchins.

1647: Massachusetts Bay Company enacted an anti-priest law.

1732: Although Catholics were not legally admitted to colony, a few Irish families were in Boston; a priest was reported working among them.

1755-56: Acadians landing in Boston were denied services of a Catholic priest.

1775: General Washington discouraged Guy Fawkes Day procession in which pope was carried in effigy, and expressed surprise that there were men in his army "so void of common sense as to insult the religious feelings of the Canadians with whom friendship and an alliance are being sought."

1780: The Massachusetts State Constitution granted religious liberty, but required a religious test to hold public office and provided for tax to support Protestant teachers of piety, religion and morality.

1788: First public Mass said in Boston on Nov. 2 by Abbe de la Poterie, first resident priest.

1803: Church of Holy Cross erected in Boston with financial aid given by Protestants headed by John Adams.

1808: Boston diocese established.

1831: Irish Catholic immigration increased.

1832: St. Vincent's Orphan Asylum, oldest charitable institution in Boston, opened by Sisters of Mercy.

1834: Ursuline Convent in Charlestown burned by a Nativist mob.

1843: Holy Cross College founded.

1855: Catholic militia companies disbanded; nunneries' inspection bill passed.

1859: St. Mary's, first parochial school in Boston, opened.

1860: Portuguese Catholics from Azores settled in New Bedford.

1870: Springfield diocese established.

1875: Boston made archdiocese.

1904: Fall River diocese established.

1911: Archbishop O'Connell of Boston made cardinal by Pope Pius X.
1950: Worcester diocese established.
1958: Archbishop Richard J. Cushing of Boston made cardinal by Pope John XXIII.
1966: Apostolic Exarchate for Melkites in the U.S. established, with headquarters in Boston; made an eparchy in 1976.
1973: Archbishop Humberto S. Medeiros of Boston made cardinal by Pope Paul VI.

Michigan

1641: Jesuits Isaac Jogues and Charles Raymbaut preached to Chippewas; named the rapids Sault Sainte Marie.
1660: Jesuit Rene Menard opened first regular mission in Lake Superior region.
1668: Father Marquette founded Sainte Marie Mission at Sault Sainte Marie.
1671: Father Marquette founded St. Ignace Mission at Michilimackinac.
1701: Fort Pontchartrain founded on present site of Detroit and placed in command of Antoine de la Mothe Cadillac. The Chapel of Sainte-Anne-de-Detroit founded.
1706: Franciscan Father Delhalle killed by Indians at Detroit.
1823: Father Gabriel Richard elected delegate to Congress from Michigan territory; he was the first priest chosen for the House of Representatives.
1833: Father Frederic Baraga celebrated first Mass in present Grand Rapids.
Detroit diocese established, embracing whole Northwest Territory.
1843: *Western Catholic Register* founded at Detroit.
1845: St. Vincent's Hospital, Detroit, opened by Sisters of Charity.
1848: Cathedral of Sts. Peter and Paul, Detroit, consecrated.
1853: Vicariate Apostolic of Upper Michigan established.
1857: Sault Ste. Marie diocese established; later transferred to Marquette.
1877: University of Detroit founded.
1882: Grand Rapids diocese established.
1897: Nazareth College for women founded.
1937: Detroit made archdiocese. Lansing diocese established.
1938: Saginaw diocese established.
1946: Archbishop Edward Mooney of Detroit created cardinal by Pope Pius XII.
1949: Opening of St. John's Theological (major) Seminary at Plymouth; this was first seminary in U.S. serving an entire ecclesiastical province (Detroit).
1966: Apostolic Exarchate for Maronites in the United States established, with headquarters in Detroit; made an eparchy in 1972; transferred to Brooklyn, 1977.
1969: Archbishop John Dearden of Detroit made cardinal by Pope Paul VI.
1971: Gaylord and Kalamazoo dioceses established.
1982: Apostolic Exarchate for Chaldean-Rite Catholics in United States established. Detroit designated see city.

Minnesota

1680: Falls of St. Anthony discovered by Franciscan Louis Hennepin.
1727: First chapel, St. Michael the Archangel, erected near town of Frontenac and placed in charge of French Jesuits.
1732: Fort St. Charles built; Jesuits ministered to settlers.
1736: Jesuit Jean Pierre Aulneau killed by Indians.
1839: Swiss Catholics from Canada settled near Fort Snelling; Bishop Loras of Dubuque, accompanied by Father Pellamourgues, visited the Fort and administered sacraments.
1841: Father Lucian Galtier built Church of St. Paul, thus forming nucleus of modern city of same name.
1850: St. Paul diocese established.
1851: Sisters of St. Joseph arrived in state.
1857: St. John's University founded.
1888: St. Paul made archdiocese; name changed to St. Paul and Minneapolis in 1966.
1889: Duluth, St. Cloud and Winona dioceses established.
1909: Crookston diocese established.
1957: New Ulm diocese established.

Mississippi

1540: Chaplains with De Soto expedition entered territory.
1682: Franciscans Zenobius Membre and Anastase Douay preached to Taensa and Natchez Indians. Father Membre offered first recorded Mass in the state on Mar. 29, Easter Sunday.
1698: Priests of Quebec Seminary founded missions near Natchez and Fort Adams.
1702: Father Nicholas Foucault murdered by Indians near Fort Adams.
1721: Missions practically abandoned, with only Father Juif working among Yazoos.
1725: Jesuit Mathurin de Petit carried on mission work in northern Mississippi.
1729: Indians tomahawked Jesuit Paul du Poisson near Fort Rosalie; Father Jean Souel shot by Yazoos.
1736: Jesuit Antoine Senat burned at stake by Chickasaws.
1822: Vicariate Apostolic of Mississippi and Alabama established.
1825: Mississippi made a separate vicariate apostolic.
1837: Natchez diocese established; became Natchez-Jackson in 1956; transferred to Jackson in 1977.
1848: Sisters of Charity opened orphan asylum and school in Natchez.
1977: Biloxi diocese established.

Missouri

1700: Jesuit Gabriel Marest established a mission among Kaskaskia Indians near St. Louis.
1734: French Catholic miners and traders settled Old Mines and Sainte Genevieve.
1750: Jesuits visited French settlers.

1762: Mission established at St. Charles.

1767: Carondelet mission established.

1770: First church founded at St. Louis.

1811: Jesuits established Indian mission school at Florissant.

1818: Bishop Dubourg arrived at St. Louis, with Vincentians Joseph Rosati and Felix de Andreis. St. Louis University, the diocesan (Kenrick) seminary and the Vincentian Seminary in Perryville trace their origins to them.

1826: St. Louis diocese established.

1828: Sisters of Charity opened first hospital west of the Mississippi, at St. Louis.

1832: *The Shepherd of the Valley,* first Catholic paper west of the Mississippi.

1845: First conference of Society of St. Vincent de Paul in U.S. founded at St. Louis.

1847: St. Louis made archdiocese.

1865: A Test Oath Law passed by State Legislature (called Drake Convention) to crush Catholicism in Missouri. Law declared unconstitutional by Supreme Court in 1866.

1867: College of St. Teresa for women founded at Kansas City.

1868: St. Joseph diocese established.

1880: Kansas City diocese established.

1946: Archbishop John J. Glennon of St. Louis made cardinal by Pope Pius XII.

1956: Kansas City and St. Joseph dioceses combined into one see. Jefferson City and Springfield-Cape Girardeau dioceses established.

1961: Archbishop Joseph E. Ritter of St. Louis made cardinal by Pope John XXIII.

1969: Archbishop John J. Carberry of St. Louis made cardinal by Pope Paul VI.

Montana

1743: Pierre and Francois Verendrye, accompanied by Jesuit Father Coquart, may have explored territory.

1833: Indian missions handed over to care of Jesuits by Second Provincial Council of Baltimore.

1840: Jesuit Pierre De Smet began missionary work among Flathead and Pend d'Oreille Indians.

1841: St. Mary's Mission established by Father De Smet and two companions on the Bitter Root River in present Stevensville.

1845: Jesuit Antonio Ravalli arrived at St. Mary's Mission; Ravalli County named in his honor.

1859: Fathers Point and Hoecken established St. Peter's Mission near the Great Falls.

1869: Sisters of Charity founded a hospital and school in Helena.

1884: Helena diocese established.

1904: Great Falls diocese established; redesignated Great Falls-Billings in 1980.

1910: Carroll College founded.

1935: Rev. Joseph M. Gilmore became first Montana priest elevated to hierarchy.

Nebraska

1541: Coronado expedition, accompanied by Franciscan Juan de Padilla, reached the Platte River.

1673: Father Marquette visited Nebraska Indians.

1720: Franciscan Juan Miguel killed by Indians near Columbus.

1855: Father J. F. Tracy administered to Catholic settlement of St. Patrick and to Catholics in Omaha.

1856: Land was donated by Governor Alfred Cumming for a church in Omaha.

1857: Nebraska vicariate apostolic established.

1878: Creighton University established.

1881: Poor Clares, first contemplative group in state, arrived in Omaha.

Duchesne College established.

1885: Omaha diocese established.

1887: Lincoln diocese established.

1912: Kearney diocese established; name changed to Grand Island, 1917.

1917: Father Flanagan founded Boy's Town for homeless boys, an institution which gained national and international recognition in subsequent years.

1945: Omaha made archdiocese.

Nevada

1774: Franciscan missionaries passed through Nevada on way to California missions.

1860: First parish, serving Genoa, Carson City and Virginia City, established.

1862: Rev. Patrick Manogue appointed pastor of Virginia City. He established a school for boys and girls, an orphanage and hospital.

1871: Church erected at Reno.

1931: Reno diocese established; name changed to Reno-Las Vegas, 1977.

New Hampshire

1630: Territory made part of a prefecture apostolic embracing all of New England.

1784: State Constitution included a religious test which barred Catholics from public office; local support was provided for local Protestant teachers of religion.

1818: The Barber family of Claremont was visited by their son Virgil (converted to Catholicism in 1816) accompanied by Father Charles Ffrench, O.P. The visit led to the conversion of the entire Barber family.

1823: Father Virgil Barber, minister who became a Jesuit priest, built first Catholic church and school at Claremont.

1830: Church of St. Aloysius dedicated at Dover.

1853: New Hampshire made part of the Portland diocese.

1858: Sisters of Mercy began to teach school at St. Anne's, Manchester.

1877: Catholics obtained full civil liberty and rights.

1884: Manchester diocese established.

1893: St. Anselm's College opened; St. Anselm's Abbey canonically erected.

1937: Francis P. Murphy became first Catholic governor of New Hampshire.

New Jersey

1668: William Douglass of Bergen was refused a

seat in General Assembly because he was a Catholic.

1672: Fathers Harvey and Gage visited Catholics in Woodbridge and Elizabethtown.

1701: Tolerance granted to all but "papists."

1744: Jesuit Theodore Schneider of Pennsylvania visited German Catholics of New Jersey.

1762: Fathers Ferdinand Farmer and Robert Harding working among Catholics in state.

1765: First Catholic community organized in New Jersey at Macopin in Passaic County.

1776: State Constitution tacitly excluded Catholics from office.

1799: Foundation of first Catholic school in state, St. John's at Trenton.

1814: First church in Trenton erected.

1820: Father Richard Bulger, of St. John's, Paterson, first resident pastor in state.

1844: Catholics obtained full civil liberty and rights.

1853: Newark diocese established.

1856: Seton Hall University established.

1878: John P. Holland, teacher at St. John's School, Paterson, invented first workable submarine.

1881: Trenton diocese established.

1937: Newark made archdiocese. Paterson and Camden dioceses established.

1947: U.S. Supreme Court ruled on N.J. bus case, permitting children attending non-public schools to ride on buses and be given other health services provided for those in public schools.

1957: Seton Hall College of Medicine and Dentistry established: the first medical school in state; it was run by Seton Hall until 1965.

1963: Byzantine Eparchy of Passaic established.

New Mexico

1539: Territory explored by Franciscan Marcos de Niza.

1581: Franciscans Agustin Rodriguez, Juan de Santa Maria and Francisco Lopez named the region "New Mexico"; they later died at hands of Indians.

1598: Juan de Onate founded a colony at Chamita, where first chapel in state was built.

1609-10: Santa Fe founded.

1631: Franciscan Pedro de Miranda was killed by Indians.

1632: Franciscan Francisco Letrado was killed by Indians.

1672: Franciscan Pedro de Avila y Ayala was killed by Indians.

1675: Franciscan Alonso Gil de Avila was killed by Indians.

1680: Pueblo Indian revolt; 21 Franciscan missionaries massacred; missions destroyed.

1692: Franciscan missions refounded and expanded.

1696: Indians rebelled, five more Franciscan missionaries killed.

1850: Jean Baptiste Lamy appointed head of newly established Vicariate Apostolic of New Mexico.

1852: Sisters of Loretto arrived in Santa Fe.

1853: Santa Fe diocese established.

1859: Christian Brothers arrived, established first school for boys in New Mexico (later St. Michael's College).

1865: Sisters of Charity started first orphanage and hospital in Santa Fe. It was closed in 1966.

1875: Santa Fe made archdiocese.

1939: Gallup diocese established.

1982: Las Cruces diocese established.

New York

1524: Giovanni da Verrazano was first white man to enter New York Bay.

1642: Jesuits Isaac Jogues and Rene Goupil were mutilated by Mohawks; Rene Goupil was killed by them shortly afterwards. Dutch Calvinists rescued Father Jogues.

1646: Jesuit Isaac Jogues and John Lalande were martyred by Iroquois at Ossernenon, now Auriesville.

1654: The Onondagas were visited by Jesuits from Canada.

1655: First permanent mission established near Syracuse.

1656: Church of St. Mary erected on Onondaga Lake, in first French settlement within state.

Kateri Tekakwitha, "Lily of the Mohawks," was born at Ossernenon, now Auriesville (d. in Canada, 1680). She was beatified in 1980.

1658: Indian uprisings destroyed missions among Cayugas, Senecas and Oneidas.

1664: English took New Amsterdam. Freedom of conscience allowed by the Duke of York, the new Lord Proprietor.

1667: Missions were restored under protection of Garaconthie, Onondaga chief.

1678: Franciscan Louis Hennepin, first white man to describe Niagara Falls, celebrated Mass there.

1682: Thomas Dongan appointed governor by Duke of York.

1683: English Jesuits came to New York, later opened a school.

1700: Although Assembly enacted a bill calling for religious toleration of all Christians in 1683, other penal laws were now enforced against Catholics; all priests were ordered out of the province.

1709: French Jesuit missionaries obliged to give up their central New York missions.

1741: Because of an alleged popish plot to burn city of New York, four whites were hanged and 11 blacks burned at stake.

1774: Elizabeth Bayley Seton, foundress of the American Sisters of Charity, was born in New York City on Aug. 28. She was canonized in 1975.

1777: State Constitution gave religious liberty, but the naturalization law required an oath to renounce allegiance to any foreign ruler, ecclesiastical as well as civil.

1785: Cornerstone was laid for St. Peter's Church, New York City, first permanent structure of Catholic worship in state.

Trusteeism began to cause trouble at New York.

1806: Anti-Catholic 1777 Test Oath for naturalization repealed.

1808: New York diocese established.

1828: New York State Legislature enacted a law upholding sanctity of seal of confession.

1834: First native New Yorker to become a secular priest, Rev. John McCloskey, was ordained.

1836: John Nepomucene Neumann arrived from Bohemia and was ordained a priest in Old St. Patrick's Cathedral, New York City. He was canonized in 1977.

1841: Fordham University and Manhattanville College established.

1847: Albany and Buffalo dioceses established.

1850: New York made archdiocese.

1853: Brooklyn diocese established.

1856: Present St. Bonaventure University and Christ the King Seminary founded at Allegany.

1858: Cornerstone was laid of second (present) St. Patrick's Cathedral, New York City. The cathedral was completed in 1879.

1868: Rochester diocese established.

1872: Ogdensburg diocese established.

1875: Archbishop John McCloskey of New York made first American cardinal by Pope Pius IX.

1878: Franciscan Sisters of Allegany were first native American community to send members to foreign missions.

1880: William R. Grace was first Catholic mayor of New York City.

1886: Syracuse diocese established.

1889: Mother Frances Xavier Cabrini arrived in New York City to begin work among Italian immigrants. She was canonized in 1946.

1911: Archbishop John M. Farley of New York made cardinal by Pope Pius X.

Catholic Foreign Mission Society of America (Maryknoll) opened a seminary for foreign missions, the first of its kind in U.S. The Maryknollers were also unique as the first U.S.-established foreign mission society.

1917: Military Ordinariate established with headquarters at New York.

1919: Alfred E. Smith became first elected Catholic governor.

1924: Archbishop Patrick Hayes of New York made cardinal by Pope Pius XI.

1930: Jesuit Martyrs of New York and Canada were canonized on June 29.

1946: Archbishop Francis J. Spellman of New York made cardinal by Pope Pius XII.

1957: Rockville Centre diocese established.

1969: Archbishop Terence Cooke of New York made cardinal by Pope Paul VI.

1981: Apostolic Exarchate for Armenian-Rite Catholics in the United States and Canada established. New York designated see city.

North Carolina

1526: The Ayllon expedition attempted to establish a settlement on Carolina coast.

1540: De Soto expedition, accompanied by chaplains, entered state.

1776: State Constitution denied office to "those who denied the truths of the Protestant religion."

1805: The few Catholics in state were served by visiting missionaries.

1821: Bishop John England celebrated Mass in the ballroom of the home of William Gaston at New Bern, marking the start of organization of the first parish, St. Paul's, in the state.

1835: William Gaston, State Supreme Court Justice, succeeded in having repealed the article denying religious freedom.

1852: First Catholic church erected in Charlotte.

1868: North Carolina vicariate apostolic established.

Catholics obtained full civil liberty and rights.

1874: Sisters of Mercy arrived, opened an academy, several schools, hospitals and an orphanage.

1876: Benedictine priory and school (later Belmont Abbey College) founded at Belmont; priory designated an abbey in 1884.

1910: Belmont Abbey established as an abbacy nullius; abbacy nullius status suppressed in 1977.

1924: Raleigh diocese established.

1971: Charlotte diocese established.

North Dakota

1742: Pierre and Francois Verendrye, accompanied by Jesuit Father Coquart, explored territory.

1818: Canadian priests ministered to Catholics in area.

1840: Jesuit Father De Smet made first of several trips among Mandan and Gros Ventre Indians.

1848: Father George Belcourt, first American resident priest in territory, reestablished Pembina Mission.

1874: Grey Nuns arrived at Fort Totten to conduct a school.

1889: Jamestown diocese established; transferred to Fargo in 1897.

1893: Benedictines founded St. Gall Monastery at Devil's Lake. (It was moved to Richardton in 1899 and became an abbey in 1903.)

1909: Bismarck diocese established.

1959: Archbishop Aloysius J. Muench, bishop of Fargo, made cardinal by Pope John XXIII.

Ohio

1749: Jesuits in expedition of Céleron de Blainville preached to Indians.

First religious services were held within present limits of Ohio. Jesuit Joseph de Bonnecamps celebrated Mass at mouth of Little Miami River and in other places.

1751: First Catholic settlement founded among Huron Indians near Sandusky by Jesuit Father de la Richardie.

1790: Benedictine Pierre Didier ministered to French immigrants.

1812: Bishop Flaget of Bardstown visited and baptized Catholics of Lancaster and Somerset Counties.

1818: Dominican Father Edward Fenwick (later first bishop of Cincinnati) built St. Joseph's Church and established first Dominican convent in Ohio.

1821: Cincinnati diocese established.

1831: Xavier University founded.

1843: Members of Congregation of Most Precious Blood arrived in Cincinnati from Switzerland.

1845: Cornerstone laid for St. Peter's Cathedral, Cincinnati.

1847: Cleveland diocese established.

1850: Cincinnati made archdiocese.

Marianists opened St. Mary's Institute, now University of Dayton.

1865: Sisters of Charity opened hospital in Cleveland, first institution of its kind in city.

1868: Columbus diocese established.

1871: Ursuline College for women opened at Cleveland.

1910: Toledo diocese established.

1935: Archbishop John T. McNicholas, O.P., founded the Institutum Divi Thomae in Cincinnati for fundamental research in natural sciences.

1943: Youngstown diocese established.

1944: Steubenville diocese established.

1969: Byzantine Rite Eparchy of Parma established.

1982: Apostolic Exarchate for Romanian Byzantine-Rite Catholics in the United States established. Canton designated see city.

Oklahoma

1540: De Soto expedition, accompanied by chaplains, explored territory.

1541: Coronado expedition, accompanied by Franciscan Juan de Padilla, explored state.

1630: Spanish Franciscan Juan de Salas labored among Indians.

1700: Scattered Catholic families were visited by priests from Kansas and Arkansas.

1874: First Catholic church built by Father Smyth at Atoka.

1876: Prefecture Apostolic of Indian Territory established with Benedictine Isidore Robot as its head.

1886: First Catholic day school for Choctaw and white children opened by Sisters of Mercy at Krebs.

1891: Vicariate Apostolic of Oklahoma and Indian Territory established.

1905: Oklahoma diocese established; title changed to Oklahoma City and Tulsa, 1930.

1917: Benedictine Heights College for women founded.

Carmelite Sisters of St. Theresa of the Infant Jesus founded at Oklahoma City.

1972: Oklahoma City made archdiocese. Tulsa diocese established.

Oregon

1603: Vizcaino explored northern Oregon coast.

1774: Franciscan missionaries accompanied Juan Perez on his expedition to coast, and Heceta a year later.

1811: Catholic Canadian trappers and traders with John J. Astor expedition founded first American settlement — Astoria.

1834: Indian missions in Northwest entrusted to Jesuits by Holy See.

1838: Abbe Blanchet appointed vicar general to Bishop of Quebec with jurisdiction over area which included Oregon Territory.

1839: First Mass celebrated at present site of St. Paul.

1843: Oregon vicariate apostolic established.

St. Joseph's College for boys opened.

1844: Jesuit Pierre de Smet established Mission of St. Francis Xavier near St. Paul.

Sisters of Notre Dame de Namur, first to enter Oregon, opened an academy for girls.

1846: Vicariate made an ecclesiastical province with Bishop Blanchet as first Archbishop of Oregon City (now Portland).

Walla Walla diocese established; suppressed in 1853.

1847: First priest was ordained in Oregon.

1848: First Provincial Council of Oregon.

1857: Death of Dr. John McLoughlin, "Father of Oregon."

1865: Rev. H. H. Spalding, a Protestant missionary, published the Whitman Myth to hinder work of Catholic missionaries.

1874: Catholic Indian Mission Bureau established.

1875: St. Vincent's Hospital, first in state, opened at Portland.

1903: Baker diocese established.

1922: Anti-private school bill sponsored by Scottish Rite Masons was passed by popular vote, 115,506 to 103,685.

1925: U.S. Supreme Court declared Oregon anti-private school bill unconstitutional.

1953: First Trappist monastery on West Coast established in Willamette Valley north of Lafayette.

Pennsylvania

1673: Priests from Maryland ministered to Catholics in the Colony.

1682: Religious toleration was extended to members of all faiths.

1720: Jesuit Joseph Greaton became first resident missionary of Philadelphia.

1734: St. Joseph's Church, first Catholic church in Philadelphia, was opened.

1741: Jesuit Fathers Schneider and Wappeler ministered to German immigrants.

Conewego Chapel, a combination chapel and dwelling, was built by Father William Wappeler, S.J., a priest sent to minister to the German Catholic immigrants who settled in the area in the 1730's.

1782: St. Mary's Parochial School opened at Philadelphia.

1788: Holy Trinity Church, Philadelphia, was incorporated; first exclusively national church organized in U.S.

1797: Augustinian Matthew Carr founded St. Augustine parish, Philadelphia.

1799: Prince Demetrius Gallitzin (Father Augustine Smith) built church in western Pennsylvania, at Loretto.

1808: Philadelphia diocese established.

1814: St. Joseph's Orphanage was opened at Philadelphia; first Catholic institution for children in U.S.

1842: University of Villanova founded by Augustinians.

1843: Pittsburgh diocese established.

1844: Thirteen persons killed, two churches and a

school burned in Know-Nothing riots at Philadelphia.

1846: First Benedictine Abbey in New World founded near Latrobe by Father Boniface Wimmer.

1852: Redemptorist John Nepomucene Neumann became fourth bishop of Philadelphia. He was beatified in 1963 and canonized in 1977.

1853: Erie diocese established.

1868: Scranton and Harrisburg dioceses established.

1871: Chestnut Hill College, first for women in state, founded.

1875: Philadelphia made archdiocese.

1901: Altoona-Johnstown diocese established.

1913: Byzantine Rite Apostolic Exarchate of Philadelphia established; became metropolitan see, 1958.

1921: Archbishop Dennis Dougherty made cardinal by Pope Benedict XV.

1924: Byzantine Rite Apostolic Exarchate of Pittsburgh established; made an eparchy in 1963; raised to metropolitan status and transferred to Munhall, 1969; transferred back to Pittsburgh in 1977.

1951: Greensburg diocese established.

1958: Archbishop John O'Hara, C.S.C., of Philadelphia made cardinal by Pope John.

1961: Allentown diocese established.

1967: Archbishop John J. Krol of Philadelphia made cardinal by Pope Paul VI.

1969: Bishop John J. Wright of Pittsburgh made cardinal by Pope Paul VI and transferred to Curia post.

1976: The 41st International Eucharistic Congress, the second held in the U.S. convened in Philadelphia, August 1-8.

Rhode Island

1663: Colonial Charter granted freedom of conscience.

1719: Laws denied Catholics the right to hold public office.

1829: St. Mary's Church, Pawtucket, was first Catholic church in state.

1837: Parochial schools inaugurated in state. First Catholic church in Providence was built.

1851: Sisters of Mercy began work in Rhode Island.

1872: Providence diocese established.

1900: Trappists took up residence in state.

1917: Providence College founded.

South Carolina

1569: Jesuit Juan Rogel was the first resident priest in the territory.

1573: First Franciscans arrived in southeastern section.

1606: Bishop Altamirano conducted visitation of area.

1655: Franciscans had two missions among Indians; later destroyed by English.

1697: Religious liberty granted to all except "papists."

1790: Catholics given right to vote.

1820: Charleston diocese established.

1822: Bishop England founded *U.S. Catholic Miscellany,* first Catholic paper of a strictly religious nature in U.S.

1830: Sisters of Our Lady of Mercy, first in state, took up residence at Charleston.

1847: Cornerstone of Cathedral of St. John the Baptist, Charleston, was laid.

1861: Cathedral and many institutions destroyed in Charleston fire.

South Dakota

1842: Father Augustine Ravoux began ministrations to French and Indians at Fort Pierre, Vermilion and Prairie du Chien; printed devotional book in Sioux language the following year.

1867: Parish organized among the French at Jefferson.

1878: Benedictines opened school for Sioux children at Fort Yates.

1889: Sioux Falls diocese established.

1902: Lead diocese established; transferred to Rapid City, 1930.

1950: Mount Marty College for women founded.

1952: Blue Cloud Abbey, first Benedictine foundation in state, was dedicated.

Tennessee

1541: Cross planted on shore of Mississippi by De Soto; accompanying the expedition were Fathers John de Gallegos and Louis De Soto.

1682: Franciscan Fathers Membre and Douay accompanied La Salle to present site of Memphis; may have offered the first Masses in the territory.

1800: Catholics were served by priests from Bardstown, Ky.

1822: Non-Catholics assisted in building church in Nashville.

1837: Nashville diocese established.

1843: Sisters of Charity opened a school for girls in Nashville.

1921: Sisters of St. Dominic opened Siena College for women at Memphis; closed in 1971.

1940: Christian Brothers College founded at Memphis.

1970: Memphis diocese established.

Texas

1541: Missionaries with Coronado expedition probably entered territory.

1553: Dominicans Diego de la Cruz, Hernando Mendez, Juan Ferrer, Brother Juan de Mina killed by Indians.

1675: Bosque-Larios missionary expedition entered region; Father Juan Larios offered first recorded high Mass.

1682: Mission Corpus Christi de Isleta (Ysleta) founded by Franciscans near El Paso, first mission in present-day Texas.

1690: Mission San Francisco de los Tejas founded in east Texas.

1703: Mission San Francisco de Solano founded on Rio Grande; rebuilt in 1718 as San Antonio de Valero or the Alamo.

1717: Franciscan Antonio Margil founded six missions in northeast.

1720: San Jose y San Miguel de Aguayo Mission founded by Fray Antonio Margil de Jesus.

1721: Franciscan Brother Jose Pita killed by Indians at Carnezeria.

1728: Site of San Antonio settled.

1738: Construction of San Fernando Cathedral at San Antonio.

1744: Mission church of the Alamo built.

1750: Franciscan Francisco Xavier was killed by Indians; so were Jose Ganzabal in 1752, and Alonzo Ferrares and Jose San Esteban in 1758.

1793: Mexico secularized missions.

1825: Governments of Cohuila and Texas secularized all Indian missions.

1838-39: Irish priests ministered to settlements of Refugio and San Patricio.

1841: Vicariate of Texas established.

1847: Ursuline Sisters established their first academy in territory at Galveston.
Galveston diocese established.

1852: Oblate Fathers and Franciscans arrived in Galveston to care for new influx of German Catholics.
St. Mary's College founded at San Antonio.

1854: Know-Nothing Party began to stir up hatred against Catholics.

1858: Texas Legislature passed law entitling all schools granting free scholarships and meeting state requirements to share in school fund.

1874: San Antonio diocese established.
Vicariate of Brownsville established.

1881: St. Edward's College founded: became first chartered college in state in 1889.
Sisters of Charity founded Incarnate Word College at San Antonio.

1890: Dallas diocese established; changed to Dallas-Ft. Worth, 1953; made two separate dioceses, 1969.

1912: Corpus Christi diocese established.

1914: El Paso diocese established.

1926: San Antonio made archdiocese. Amarillo diocese established.

1947: Austin diocese established.

1959: Galveston diocese redesignated Galveston-Houston.

1961: San Angelo diocese established.

1965: Brownsville diocese established.

1966: Beaumont diocese established.

1982: Victoria diocese established.

1983: Lubbock diocese established.

Utah

1776: Franciscans Silvestre de Escalante and Atanasio Dominguez reached Utah (Salt) Lake; first white men known to enter the territory.

1858: Jesuit Father De Smet accompanied General Harney as chaplain on expedition sent to settle troubles between Mormons and U.S. Government.

1866: On June 29 Father Edward Kelly offered first Mass in Salt Lake City in Mormon Assembly Hall.

1886: Utah vicariate apostolic established.

1891: Salt Lake City diocese established.

1926: College of St. Mary-of-the-Wasatch for women was founded.

Vermont

1609: Champlain expedition passed through territory.

1666: Captain La Motte built fort and shrine of St. Anne on Isle La Motte; Sulpician Father Dollier de Casson celebrated first Mass.

1668: Bishop Laval of Quebec (beatified in 1980), administered confirmation in region; this was the first area in northeastern U.S. to receive an episcopal visit.

1710: Jesuits ministered to Indians near Lake Champlain.

1793: Discriminatory measures against Catholics were repealed.

1830: Father Jeremiah O'Callaghan became first resident priest in state.

1853: Burlington diocese established.

1854: Sisters of Charity of Providence arrived to conduct St. Joseph's Orphanage at Burlington.

1904: St. Michael's College founded.

1951: First Carthusian foundation in America established at Whitingham.

Virginia

1526: Dominican Antonio de Montesinos offered first Mass on Virginia soil.

1561: Dominicans visited the coast.

1571: Father John Baptist de Segura and seven Jesuit companions killed by Indians.

1642: Priests outlawed and Catholics denied right to vote.

1689: Capuchin Christopher Plunket was captured and exiled to a coastal island where he died in 1697.

1776: Religious freedom granted.

1791: Father Jean Dubois arrived at Richmond with letters from Lafayette. The House of Delegates was placed at his disposal for celebration of Mass.

1796: A church was built at Alexandria.

1820: Richmond diocese established.

1822: Trusteeism created serious problems in diocese; Bishop Kelly resigned the see.

1848: Sisters of Charity opened an orphan asylum at Norfolk.

1866: School Sisters of Notre Dame and Sisters of Charity opened academies for girls at Richmond.

1974: Arlington diocese established.

Washington

1774: Spaniards explored the region.

1838: Fathers Blanchet and Demers, "Apostles of the Northwest," were sent to territory by archbishop of Quebec.

1840: Cross erected on Whidby Island, Puget Sound.

1843: Vicariate Apostolic of Oregon, including Washington, was established.

1844: Mission of St. Paul founded at Colville.
Six Sisters of Notre Dame de Namur began work in area.

1850: Nesqually diocese established; transferred to Seattle, 1907.

1856: Providence Academy, the first permanent Catholic school in the Northwest, was built at Fort Vancouver by Mother Joseph Pariseau of the Sisters of Charity of Providence.
1887: Gonzaga University founded.
1913: Spokane diocese established.
1951: Seattle made archdiocese. Yakima diocese established.

West Virginia

1749: Father Joseph de Bonnecamps, accompanying the Bienville expedition, may have offered first Mass in the territory.
1821: First Catholic church in Wheeling.
1838: Sisters of Charity founded school at Martinsburg.
1848: Visitation Nuns established academy for girls in Wheeling.
1850: Wheeling diocese established; name changed to Wheeling-Charleston, 1974.
Wheeling Hospital incorporated, the oldest Catholic charitable institution in territory.
1955: Wheeling College established.

Wisconsin

1661: Jesuit Rene Menard, first known missionary in the territory, was killed or lost in the Black River district.
1665: Jesuit Claude Allouez founded Mission of the Holy Ghost at La Pointe Chegoimegon, now Bayfield; was the first permanent mission in region.
1673: Father Marquette and Louis Joliet traveled from Green Bay down the Wisconsin and Mississippi rivers.
1762: Suppression of Jesuits in French Colonies closed many missions for 30 years.
1843: Milwaukee diocese established.
1853: St. John's Cathedral, Milwaukee, was built.
1864: State charter granted for establishment of Marquette University. First students admitted, 1881.
1868: Green Bay and La Crosse dioceses established.
1875: Milwaukee made archdiocese.
1905: Superior diocese established.
1946: Madison diocese established.

Wyoming

1840: Jesuit Pierre de Smet offered first Mass near Green River.
1851: Father De Smet held peace conference with Indians near Fort Laramie.
1867: Father William Kelly, first resident priest, arrived in Cheyenne and built first church a year later.
1873: Father Eugene Cusson became first resident pastor in Laramie.
1875: Sisters of Charity of Leavenworth opened school and orphanage at Laramie.
1884: Jesuits took over pastoral care of Shoshone and Arapaho Indians.
1887: Cheyenne diocese established.
1949: Weston Memorial Hospital opened near Newcastle.

Puerto Rico

1493: Island discovered by Columbus on his second voyage; he named it San Juan de Borinquen (the Indian name for Puerto Rico).
1509: Juan Ponce de Leon, searching for gold, colonized the island and became its first governor; present population descended mainly from early Spanish settlers.
1511: Diocese of Puerto Rico established as suffragan of Seville, Spain; Bishop Alonso, Manso, sailing from Spain in 1512, became first bishop to take up residence in New World.
1645: Synod held in Puerto Rico to regulate frequency of Masses according to distances people had to walk.
1898: Puerto Rico ceded to U.S. (became self-governing Commonwealth in 1952); inhabitants granted U.S. citizenship in 1917.
1924: Diocese of Puerto Rico renamed San Juan de Puerto Rico and made immediately subject to the Holy See; Ponce diocese established.
1948: Catholic University of Puerto Rico founded at Ponce through efforts of Bishop James E. McManus, C.SS.R., 1947-63.
1960: San Juan made metropolitan see. Arecibo diocese established.
1964: Caguas diocese established.
1973: Archbishop Luis Aponte Martinez of San Juan made first native Puerto Rican cardinal by Pope Paul VI.
1976: Mayaguez diocese established.
Virgin of Providence officially approved as Patroness of Puerto Rico by Pope Paul VI.

CATHOLICS IN STATUARY HALL

Statues of 13 Catholics deemed worthy of national commemoration by the donating states are among the more than 90 enshrined in National Statuary Hall and other places in the U.S. Capitol. The Hall, formerly the chamber of the House of Representatives, was erected by Act of Congress July 2, 1864.

Donating states, names and years of placement are listed. An asterisk indicates placement of a statue in the Hall itself.

Arizona: Rev. Eusebio Kino, S. J., missionary, 1965.
California: Rev. Junipero Serra, O. F. M.* missionary, 1931.
Hawaii: Father Damien, missionary, 1969.
Illinois: Gen. James Shields, statesman, 1893.
Louisiana: Edward D. White, Justice of the U.S. Supreme Court (1894-1921), 1955.
Maryland: Charles Carroll,* statesman, 1901.
Nevada: Patrick A. McCarran,* statesman, 1960.
New Mexico: Dennis Chavez, statesman, 1966. (Archbishop Jean B. Lamy, pioneer prelate of Santa Fe, was nominated for Hall honor in 1951.)
North Dakota: John Burke,* U.S. treasurer, 1963.
Oregon: Dr. John McLoughlin, pioneer, 1953.
Washington: Mother Mary Joseph Pariseau, pioneer missionary and humanitarian.
West Virginia: John E. Kenna, statesman, 1901.
Wisconsin: Rev. Jacques Marquette, S.J., missionary, explorer, 1895.

CATHOLICS IN PRESIDENTS' CABINETS

Roger B. Taney, Attorney General 1831-33, Secretary of Treasury 1833-34; app. by Andrew Jackson.

James Campbell, Postmaster General 1853-57; app. by Franklin Pierce.

John B. Floyd, Secretary of War 1857-61; app. by James Buchanan.

Joseph McKenna, Attorney General 1897-98; app. by William McKinley.

Robert J. Wynne, Postmaster General 1904-05; app. by Theodore Roosevelt.

Charles Bonaparte, Secretary of Navy 1905-06, Attorney General 1906-09; app. by Theodore Roosevelt.

James A. Farley, Postmaster General 1933-40; app. by Franklin D. Roosevelt.

Frank Murphy, Attorney General 1939-40; app. by Franklin D. Roosevelt.

Frank C. Walker, Postmaster General 1940-45; app. by Franklin D. Roosevelt.

Robert E. Hannegan, Postmaster General 1945-47; app. by Harry S. Truman.

J. Howard McGrath, Attorney General 1949-52; app. by Harry S. Truman.

Maurice J. Tobin, Secretary of Labor; 1949-53; app. by Harry S. Truman.

James P. McGranery, Attorney General 1952-53; app. by Harry S. Truman.

Martin P. Durkin, Secretary of Labor 1953; app. by Dwight D. Eisenhower.

James P. Mitchell, Secretary of Labor 1953-61; app. by Dwight D. Eisenhower.

Robert F. Kennedy, Attorney General 1961-65; app. by John F. Kennedy, reapp. by Lyndon B. Johnson.

Anthony Celebrezze, Secretary of Health, Education and Welfare 1962-65; app. by John F. Kennedy, reapp. by Lyndon B. Johnson.

John S. Gronouski, Postmaster General 1963-65; app. by John F. Kennedy, reapp. by Lyndon B. Johnson.

John T. Connor, Secretary of Commerce 1965-67; app. by Lyndon B. Johnson.

Lawrence O'Brien, Postmaster General 1965-68; app. by Lyndon B. Johnson.

Walter J. Hickel, Secretary of Interior 1969-71; app. by Richard M. Nixon.

John A. Volpe, Secretary of Transportation 1969-72; app. by Richard M. Nixon.

Maurice H. Stans, Secretary of Commerce, 1969-72; app. by Richard M. Nixon.

Peter J. Brennan, Secretary of Labor, 1973-75; app. by Richard M. Nixon, reapp. by Gerald R. Ford.

William E. Simon, Secretary of Treasury, 1974-76; app. by Richard M. Nixon, reapp. by Gerald R. Ford.

Joseph A. Califano, Jr., Secretary of Health, Education and Welfare, 1977-79; app. by Jimmy Carter.

Benjamin Civiletti, Attorney General, 1979-81; app. by Jimmy Carter.

Moon Landrieu, Secretary of Housing and Urban Development, 1979-81; app. by Jimmy Carter.

Edmund S. Muskie, Secretary of State, 1980-81; app. by Jimmy Carter.

Alexander M. Haig, Secretary of State, 1981-82; app. by Ronald Reagan.

Raymond J. Donovan, Secretary of Labor, 1981; app. by Ronald Reagan.

Margaret M. Heckler, Secretary of Health and Human Services, 1983-; app. by Ronald Reagan.

Men who became Catholics after leaving Cabinet posts: Thomas Ewing, Secretary of Treasury under William A. Harrison, and Secretary of Interior under Zachary Taylor; Luke E. Wright, Secretary of War under Theodore Roosevelt; Albert B. Fall, Secretary of Interior under Warren G. Harding.

CATHOLIC SUPREME COURT JUSTICES

Roger B. Taney, Chief Justice 1836-64; app. by Andrew Jackson.

Edward D. White, Associate Justice 1894-1910, app. by Grover Cleveland; Chief Justice 1910-21, app. by William H. Taft.

Joseph McKenna, Associate Justice 1898-1925; app. by William McKinley.

Pierce Butler, Associate Justice 1923-39; app. by Warren G. Harding.

Frank Murphy, Associate Justice 1940-49; app. by Franklin D. Roosevelt.

William Brennan, Associate Justice 1956-; app. by Dwight D. Eisenhower.

Sherman Minton, Associate Justice from 1949 to 1956, became a Catholic several years before his death in 1965.

CHURCH-STATE DECISIONS OF THE SUPREME COURT

(Among sources of this listing of U.S. Supreme Court decisions was *The Supreme Court on Church and State,* Joseph Tussman, editor; Oxford University Press, New York, 1962.)

Terrett v. Taylor, 9 Cranch 43 (1815): The Court declared unconstitutional an act of the Virginia Legislature which denied property rights to Protestant Episcopal churches in the state. Religious corporations, like other corporations, have rights to their property.

Vidal v. Girard's Executors, 2 Howard 205 (1844): The Court upheld the will of Stephen Girard, which barred ministers of any religion from serving as faculty members or visitors in a school he established for orphans.

Watson v. Jones, 13 Wallace 679 (1872): The Court declared that a member of a religious organization may not appeal to secular courts against a decision made by a church tribunal within the area of its competence.

Reynolds v. United States, 98 US 145 (1879): The Court declared, in reference to the Mormon practice of polygamy, that one may not knowingly violate by external practices the law of the land on religious grounds, since such conduct would make the professed doctrines of belief superior to federal or state law. One must keep the external practice of religion within the framework of laws enacted for the common welfare. This was the first decision rendered on the Free Exercise Clause of the First Amendment.

Davis v. Beason, 133 US 333 (1890): The Court upheld the denial of the right of Mormons to vote in Idaho if they refused to sign a registration oath stating that they were not bigamists or polygamists and would not encourage or preach bigamy or polygamy.

Church of Latter-Day Saints v. United States, 136 US 1 (1890): The Court upheld an Act of Congress which annulled the charter of the Corporation of the Church of Jesus Christ of Latter-Day Saints, and declared "forfeited to the government all its real estate except a small portion used exclusively for public worship" (Tussman, op. cit., p. 33). The Court held that the Corporation continually used its power to violate US laws prohibiting polygamy.

Church of the Holy Trinity v. United States, 143 US 457 (1892): The Court declared it is not "a misdemeanor for a church of this country to contract for the services of a Christian minister residing in another nation" (from the text of the decision).

Bradfield v. Roberts, 175 US 291 (1899): The Court denied that an appropriation of government funds for an institution (Providence Hospital, Washington, D.C.) run by Roman Catholic sisters violated the No Establishment Clause of the First Amendment.

Pierce v. Society of Sisters, 268 US 510 (1925): The Court denied that a state can require children to attend public schools only. The Court held that the liberty of the Constitution forbids standardization by such compulsion, and that the parochial schools involved had claims to protection under the Fourteenth Amendment.

Cochran v. Board of Education, 281 US 370 (1930): The Court upheld a Louisiana statute providing textbooks at public expense for children attending public or parochial schools. The Court held that the children and state were beneficiaries of the appropriations, with incidental secondary benefit going to the schools.

United States v. MacIntosh, 283 US 605 (1931): The Court denied that anyone can place allegiance to the will of God above his allegiance to the government, since such a person could make his own interpretation of God's will the decisive test as to whether he would or would not obey the nation's law. The Court stated that the nation, which has a duty to survive, can require citizens to bear arms in its defense.

Hamilton v. Regents of University of California, 293 US 245 (1934): The Court rejected a "claim to exemption from R.O.T.C. based on conscientious objection to war" (Tussman op. cit., p. 64). If such an exemption were allowed, the liberties of the objector might be extended to the point of refusal to pay taxes in furtherance of a war or any other end condemned by his conscience. This would be an undue exaltation of the right of private judgment.

Cantwell v. Connecticut, 310 US 296 (1940): The Court declared that the right to religious freedom is violated by a statute requiring a person to secure a permit from a government official before soliciting money for alleged religious purposes from someone not of his or her sect. Such a practice would constitute censorship of religion.

Minersville School District v. Gobitis, 310 US 586 (1940): The Court upheld the right of a state to require the salute to the national flag from school children, even from those who refused to do so for sincere religious reasons.

Jones v. City of Opelika, 316 US 584 (1942): The court upheld licensing ordinances in three municipalities against "the claim by Jehovah's Witnesses that they interfere with the free exercise of religion" (Tussman, op. cit., p. 91).

Murdock v. Commonwealth of Pennsylvania, 319 US 105 (1943): In a reversal of the decision handed down in Jones v. City of Opelika, the Court declared the licensing unconstitutional since it violated a freedom guaranteed under the First Amendment. The selling of religious literature by traveling preachers does not make evangelism the equivalent of a commercial enterprise taxable by the State.

Jones v. City of Opelika, 316 US 584 105 (1943): The Court declared that the Constitution denies a city the right to control the expression of men's minds and denies also the right of men to win others to their views through a program of taxes levied against such activity.

Douglas v. City of Jeannette, 319 US 157 (1943): The Court again upheld the proselytizing rights of Jehovah's Witnesses, ruling unconstitutional the action of any public authority in regulating or taxing such activity.

West Virginia State Board of Education v. Barnette, 319 US 624 (1943): In a reversal of the decision handed down in Minersville School District v. Gobitis, the Court declared unconstitutional a state statute requiring of all children a salute to the national flag and a pledge of allegiance which a child may consider contrary to sincere religious beliefs.

Prince v. Commonwealth of Massachusetts, 321 US 158 (1944): The Court upheld a "child-labor regulation against the claim that it prevents a child from performing her religious duty" (Tussman, op. cit., p. 170). The Court asserted a general principle that the state has a wide range of power for limiting parental freedom and authority in things affecting the child's welfare.

United States v. Ballard, 322 US 78 (1944): The Court upheld the general principle that "the truth of religious claims is not for secular authority to determine" (Tussman, op. cit., p. 181).

In Re Summers, 325 US 561 (1945): The Court upheld "the denial, to an otherwise qualified applicant, of admission to the bar on the basis of the applicant's religiously motivated 'conscientious scruples against participation in war' " (Tussman, op. cit., p. 192). The petitioner was barred because he could not in good faith take the prescribed oath to support the Constitution of Illinois which required service in the state militia in times of necessity.

Girouard v. United States, 328 US 61 (1946): In a ruling related to that handed down in United States v. MacIntosh, the Court affirmed the opinion that the refusal of an alien to bear arms does not deny him citizenship.

Everson v. Board of Education, 330 US 1 (1947): The Court upheld the constitutionality of a New Jersey statute authorizing free school bus transportation for parochial as well as public school students. The Court expressed the opinion that the benefits of public welfare legislation, included under such bus transportation, do not run contrary to the concept of separation of Church and State.

McCollum v. Board of Education, 333 US 203 (1948): The Court declared unconstitutional a program for releasing children, with parental consent, from public school classes so they could receive religious instruction on public school premises from representatives of their own faiths.

Zorach v. Clauson, 343 US 306 (1952): The Court upheld the constitutionality of a New York statute permitting, on a voluntary basis, the release during school time of students from public school classes for religious instruction given off public school premises.

Kedroff v. St. Nicholas Cathedral, 344 US 94 (1952): The Court ruled against an action of New York in taking "control of St. Nicholas Cathedral away from the Moscow hierarchy" (Tussman, *op. cit.*, p. 292), on the ground that the controversy involved a matter of church government.

Fowler v. Rhode Island, 345 US 67 (1953): The Court upheld the right of a Jehovah's Witness to preach in a public park against a city ordinance which forbade such preaching. The Court held that the ordinance, as construed and applied, discriminated against the Witness and therefore amounted to preferment by the state of other religious groups.

Torcaso v. Watkins, 367 US 488 (1961): The Court declared unconstitutional a Maryland requirement that one must make a declaration of belief in the existence of God as part of the oath of office for notaries public.

McGowan v. Maryland, 81 Sp Ct 1101; Two Guys from Harrison v. McGinley, 81 Sp Ct 1135; Gallagher v. Crown Kosher Super Market, 81 Sp Ct 1128; Braunfield v. Brown, 81 Sp Ct 1144 (1961): The Court ruled that Sunday closing laws do not violate the No Establishment of Religion Clause of the First Amendment, even though the laws were religious in their inception and still have some religious overtones. The Court held that, "as presently written and administered, most of them, at least, are of a secular rather than of a religious character, and that presently they bear no relationship to establishment of religion as those words are used in the Constitution of the United States."

Engel v. Vitale, 370 US 42 (1962): The Court declared that the voluntary recitation in public schools of a prayer composed by the New York State Board of Regents is unconstitutional on the ground that it violates the No Establishment of Religion Clause of the First Amendment.

Abington Township School District v. Schempp and **Murray v. Curlett, 83 Sp Ct 1560 (1963):** The Court ruled that Bible reading and recitation of the Lord's Prayer in public schools, with

voluntary participation by students, are unconstitutional on the ground that they violate the No Establishment of Religion Clause of the First Amendment.

Sherbert v. Verner, 83 A Sp Ct 1790 (1963): The Court ruled that individuals of any religious faith may not, because of their faith or lack of it, be deprived of the benefits of public welfare legislation.

Chamberlin v. Dade County, 83 Sp Ct 1864 (1964): The Court reversed a decision of the Florida Supreme Court concerning the constitutionality of prayer and devotional Bible reading in public schools during the school day, as sanctioned by a state statute which specifically related the practices to a sound public purpose.

Board of Education v. Allen, No. 660 (1968): The Court declared constitutional the New York school book loan law which requires local school boards to purchase books with state funds and lend them to parochial and private school students.

Flast v. Cohen, No. 416 (1968): The Court held that individual taxpayers can bring suits to challenge federal expenditures on grounds that they violate the principle of separation of Church and State even though generally taxpayers cannot challenge federal expenditures in court.

Walz v. Tax Commission of New York (1970): The Court upheld the constitutionality of a New York statute exempting church-owned property from taxation.

Earle v. DiCenso, Robinson v. DiCenso, Lemon v. Kurtzman, Tilton v. Richardson (1971): In Earle v. DiCenso and Robinson v. DiCenso, the Court ruled unconstitutional a 1969 Rhode Island statute which provided salary supplements to teachers of secular subjects in parochial schools; in Lemon v. Kurtzman, the Court ruled unconstitutional a 1968 Pennsylvania statute which authorized the state to purchase services for the teaching of secular subjects in nonpublic schools. The principal argument against constitutionality in these cases was that the statutes and programs at issue entailed excessive entanglement of government with religion. In Tilton v. Richardson, the Court held that this argument did not apply to a prohibitive degree with respect to federal grants, under the Higher Education Facilities Act of 1963, for the construction of facilities for nonreligious purposes by four church-related institutions of higher learning, three of which were Catholic, in Connecticut.

Amish Decision (1972): In a case appealed on behalf of Yoder, Miller and Yutzy, the Court ruled that Amish parents were exempt from a Wisconsin statute requiring them to send their children to school until the age of 16. The Court said in its decision that secondary schooling exposed Amish children to attitudes, goals and values contrary to their beliefs, and substantially hindered "the religious development of the Amish child and his integration into the way of life of the Amish faith-community at the crucial adolescent state of development."

Committee for Public Education and Religious Liberty, et al., v. Nyquist, et al., No. 72-694 (1973): The Court ruled that provisions of a 1972 New York statute were unconstitutional on the grounds that they were violative of the No Establishment Clause of the First Amendment and had the "impermissible effect" of advancing the sectarian activities of church-affiliated schools. The programs ruled unconstitutional concerned: (1) maintenance and repair grants, for facilities and equipment, to ensure the health, welfare and safety of students in nonpublic, non-profit elementary and secondary schools serving a high concentration of students from low income families; (2) tuition reimbursement ($50 per grade school child, $100 per high school student) for parents (with income less than $5,000) of children attending nonpublic elementary or secondary schools; tax deduction from adjusted gross income for parents failing to qualify under the above reimbursement plan, for each child attending a nonpublic school.

Sloan, Treasurer of Pennsylvania, et al., v. Lemon, et al., No. 72-459 (1973): The Court ruled unconstitutional a Pennsylvania Parent Reimbursement Act for Nonpublic Education which provided funds to reimburse parents (to a maximum of $150) for a portion of tuition expenses incurred in sending their children to nonpublic schools. The Court held that there was no significant difference between this and the New York tuition reimbursement program (above), and declared that the Equal Protection Clause of the Fourteenth Amendment cannot be relied upon to sustain a program held to be violative of the No Establishment Clause.

Levitt, et al., v. Committee for Public Education and Religious Liberty, et al., No. 72-269 (1973): The Court ruled unconstitutional the Mandated Services Act of 1970 under which New York provided $28 million ($27 per pupil from first to seventh grade, $45 per pupil from seventh to 12th grade) to reimburse nonpublic schools for testing, recording and reporting services required by the state. The Court declared that the act provided "impermissible aid" to religion in contravention of the No Establishment Clause.

In related decisions handed down June 25, 1973, the Court: (1) affirmed a lower court decision against the constitutionality of an Ohio tax credit law benefiting parents with children in nonpublic schools; (2) reinstated an injunction against a parent reimbursement program in New Jersey; (3) affirmed South Carolina's right to grant construction loans to church-affiliated colleges, and dismissed an appeal contesting its right to provide loans to students attending church-affiliated colleges (**Hunt v. McNair, Durham v. McLeod**).

Wheeler v. Barrera (1974): The Court ruled that nonpublic school students in Missouri must share in federal funds for educationally deprived students on a comparable basis with public school students under Title I of the Elementary and Secondary Education Act of 1965.

Norwood v. Harrison (93 S. Ct. 2804): The Court ruled that public assistance which avoids the prohibitions of the "effect" and "entanglement" tests (and which therefore does not substantially promote the religious mission of sectarian schools) may be confined to the secular functions of such schools.

Wiest v. Mt. Lebanon School District (1974): The Court upheld a lower court ruling that invocation and benediction prayers at public high school commencement ceremonies do not violate the principle of separation of Church and state.

Meek v. Pittenger (1975): The Court ruled unconstitutional portions of a Pennsylvania law providing auxiliary services for students of nonpublic schools; at the same time, it ruled in favor of provisions of the law permitting textbook loans to students of such schools. In denying the constitutionality of auxiliary services, the Court held that they had the "primary effect of establishing religion" and involved "excessive entanglement" of Church and state officials with respect to supervision; objection was also made against providing such services only on the premises of non-public schools and only at the request of such schools.

Roemer v. Board of Public Works of Maryland, 96 S. Ct. 2337 (1976): The Court ruled that a Maryland statute which authorized state funds to any private institution meeting certain minimal criteria was constitutional. The Court said the statute met the test previously outlined in Lemon v. Kurtzman because the colleges were not pervasively sectarian and the aid was in fact intended only for secular purposes.

Serbian Eastern Orthodox Diocese v. Milivojevich, 96 S. Ct. 2372 (1976): The Court held unconstitutional the decision of the Illinois Supreme Court that the Serbian Orthodox Church had arbitrarily removed one of its bishops and that its reorganization of the diocese was beyond the power of the church. The Court declared that the First Amendment does not permit civil courts to make ecclesiastical decisions.

TWA, Inc., v. Hardison, 75-1126; **International Association of Machinists and Aero Space Workers v. Hardison,** 75-1385 (1977): The Court ruled that federal civil rights legislation does not require employers to make more than minimal efforts to accommodate employees who want a particular working day off as their religion's Sabbath Day, and that an employer cannot accommodate such an employee by violating seniority systems determined by a union collective bargaining agreement. The Court noted that its ruling was not a constitutional judgment but an interpretation of existing law.

Wolman v. Walter (1977): The Court ruled constitutional portions of an Ohio statute providing tax-paid textbook loans and some auxiliary services (standardized and diagnostic testing, therapeutic and remedial services, off school premises) for nonpublic school students. It decided that other portions of the law, providing state funds for nonpublic school field trips and instructional materials (audio-visual equipment, maps, tape recorders), were unconstitutional.

Decisions since 1977

Clergymen (1978): The Court struck down the last state ban against the holding of public office by clergymen, nullifying the 182-year-old provision of the Tennessee constitution which held that involvement in politics might affect the clergy's "dedication to God and the care of souls."

Lay Teachers (1979): The Court ruled that lay teachers in church-related schools are not covered by the National Labor Relations Act. The decision was based, not on church-state grounds, but on the lack of any affirmative decision of the Congress to include such teachers in coverage of the law.

Church Property (1979): The Court ruled, in Jones v. Wolf, that civil courts are not always bound to yield to decisions of church courts in settling local church property disputes.

Parochiaid (1979): The Court decided, in Byrne v. Public Funds for Public Schools, against the constitutionality of a 1976 New Jersey law providing state income tax deductions for tuition paid by parents of students attending parochial and other private schools.

Religious Belief v. Union (1979): The Court supported the claim of a San Diego man that his right to religious freedom was violated when he was fired from his job because his Seventh Day Adventist beliefs prevented him from belonging to a union.

Student Bus Transportation (1979): The Court upheld a Pennsylvania law providing bus transportation at public expense for students to non-public schools up to 10 miles away from the boundaries of the public school districts in which they lived.

Reimbursement (1980): The Court upheld the constitutionality of a 1974 New York law providing direct cash payment to non-public schools for the costs of state-mandated testing and record-keeping.

Solicitation of Funds (1980): The Court struck down a Schaumburg, Ill., ordinance permitting the solicitation of funds only by groups spending a specific percentage of their funds for charitable purposes.

Remedial Teaching (1980): The Court refused to hear an appeal from a lower court ruling in support of a New York law permitting the use of federal funds to pay for remedial teaching in non-public schools.

Ten Commandments (1980): The Court struck down a 1978 Kentucky law requiring the posting of the Ten Commandments in public school classrooms in the state.

Christmas Carols (1980): The Court refused to hear an appeal from a lower court ruling permitting the singing of Christmas carols in public school holiday programs in Sioux City, S.D.

Highway Prayer (1981): The Court ruled that North Carolina could not publish a prayer for highway safety on official state maps.

Unemployment Benefits (1981): The Court decided, in Thomas v. Review Board, that a worker who, for religious reasons, quits his job rather than help to produce armaments cannot be denied state unemployment benefits.

Unemployment Taxes (1981): The Court ruled, in St. Martin Evangelical Lutheran Church v. South Dakota, that church-run schools do not have to pay state unemployment compensation taxes for their employees, because the relevant 1976 law

did not "reveal any clear intent to repeal" their tax-exempt status.

Campus Worship (1981): The Court ruled, in Widmar v. Vincent, that the University of Missouri at Kansas City could not deny student religious groups the use of campus facilities for worship services. The Court also, in Brandon v. Board of Education of Guilderland Schools, declined without comment to hear an appeal for reversal of lower court decisions denying a group of New York high school students the right to meet for prayer on public school property before the beginning of the school day.

Americans United (1982): The Court ruled that Americans United for the Separation of Church and State did not have legal standing to challenge in court the transfer of government property to a Protestant college in Pennsylvania.

Social Security Taxes (1982): The Court ruled that Amish businessmen must pay Social Security taxes for their employees even if such payments violate their religious beliefs.

Unification Church (1982): The Court struck down a Minnesota law, aimed at the Unification Church, which required detailed financial reports from religious groups which raise more than half of their funds from non-members.

No Meeting on Public School Property (1983): By refusing to hear an appeal in Lubbock v. Lubbock Civil Liberties Union, the Court upheld a lower court ruling against a public policy of permitting student religious groups to meet on public school property before and after school hours.

Tuition Tax Deduction (1983): In Mueller v. Allen, the Court upheld a Minnesota law allowing parents of students in public and non-public (including parochial) schools to take a tax deduction for the expenses of tuition, textbooks and transportation. Maximum allowable deductions were $500 per child in elementary school and $700 per child in grades seven through 12.

Pay for Chaplain (1983): The Court ruled in Marsh v. Chambers that it was not against the Constitution for the Nebraska Legislature to pay a chaplain to open each day's session with a prayer.

THE WALL OF SEPARATION

Thomas Jefferson, in a letter written to the Danbury (Conn.) Baptist Association Jan. 1, 1802, coined the metaphor, "a wall of separation between Church and State," to express a theory concerning interpretation of the religion clauses of the First Amendment: "Congress shall make no law respecting an establishment of religion or prohibiting the free exercise thereof."

The metaphor was cited for the first time in judicial proceedings in 1879, in the opinion by Chief Justice Waite in Reynolds v. United States. It did not, however, figure substantially in the decision.

Accepted as Rule

In 1947 the wall of separation gained acceptance as a constitutional rule, in the decision handed down in Everson v. Board of Education. Associate Justice Black, in describing the principles involved in the No Establishment Clause, wrote:

"Neither a state nor the Federal Government can set up a church. Neither can pass laws which aid one religion, aid all religions, or prefer one religion over another. Neither can force nor influence a person to go to or to remain away from church against his will or force him to profess a belief or disbelief in any religion. No person can be punished for entertaining or professing religious beliefs or disbeliefs, for church attendance or non-attendance. No tax in any amount, large or small, can be levied to support any religious activities or institutions, whatever they may be called, or whatever form they may adopt to teach or practice religion. Neither a state nor the Federal Government can, openly or secretly, participate in the affairs of any religious organizations or groups and vice versa. In the words of Jefferson, the clause against establishment of religion by law was intended to erect 'a wall of separation between Church and State.' "

Mr. Black's associates agreed with his statement of principles, which were framed without reference to the Freedom of Exercise Clause. They disagreed, however, with respect to application of the principles, as the split decision in the case indicated. Five members of the Court held that the benefits of public welfare legislation — in this case, free bus transportation to school for parochial as well as public school students — did not run contrary to the concept of separation of Church and State embodied in the First Amendment.

Different Opinions

Inside and outside the legal profession, opinion is divided concerning the wall of separation and the balance of the religion clauses of the First Amendment.

The view of absolute separationists, carried to the extreme, would make government the adversary of religion. The bishops of the United States, following the McCollum decision in 1948, said that the wall metaphor had become for some persons the "shibboleth of doctrinaire secularism."

Proponents of governmental neutrality toward religion are of the opinion that such neutrality should not be so interpreted as to prohibit incidental aid to religious institutions providing secular services.

In the realm of practice, federal and state legislatures have enacted measures involving incidental benefits to religious bodies. Examples of such measures are the tax exemption of church property; provision of bus rides, book loans and lunch programs to students in church-related as well as public schools; military chaplaincies; loans to church-related hospitals; the financing of studies by military veterans at church-related colleges under GI bills of rights.

CHURCH TAX EXEMPTION

The exemption of church-owned property was ruled constitutional by the U.S. Supreme Court May 4, 1970, in the case of Walz v. The Tax Commission of New York.

Suit in the case was brought by Frederick Walz, who purchased in June, 1967, a 22-by-29-foot plot of ground in Staten Island valued at $100 and taxable at $5.24 a year. Shortly after making the purchase, Walz instituted a suit in New York State, contending that the exemption of church property from taxation authorized by state law increased his own tax rate and forced him indirectly to support churches in violation of his constitutional right to freedom of religion under the First Amendment. Three New York courts dismissed the suit, which had been instituted by mail. The Supreme Court, judging that it had probable jurisdiction, then took the case.

In a 7-1 decision affecting Church-state relations in every state in the nation, the Court upheld the New York law under challenge.

For and Against

Chief Justice Warren E. Burger, who wrote the majority opinion, said that Congress from its earliest days had viewed the religion clauses of the Constitution as authorizing statutory real estate tax exemption to religious bodies. He declared: "Nothing in this national attitude toward religious tolerance and two centuries of uninterrupted freedom from taxation has given the remotest sign of leading to an established church or religion, and on the contrary it has operated affirmatively to help guarantee the free exercise of all forms of religious beliefs."

Justice William O. Douglas wrote in dissent that the involvement of government in religion as typified in tax exemption may seem inconsequential but: "It is, I fear, a long step down the establishment path. . . Perhaps I have been misinformed. But, as I read the Constitution and the philosophy, I gathered that independence was the price of liberty."

Burger rejected Douglas' "establishment" fears. If tax exemption is the first step toward establishment, he said, "the second step has been long in coming."

The basic issue centered on the following question: Is there a contradiction between federal constitutional provisions against the establishment of religion, or the use of public funds for religious purposes, and state statutes exempting church property from taxation?

In the Walz' decision, the Supreme Court ruled that there is no contradiction.

NFPC

The National Federation of Priests' Councils was organized by 233 delegates from 127 priests' organizations at a charter meeting held in Chicago May 20 and 21, 1968. Its stated purpose is to give priests' councils, official or unofficial, a representative voice in matters of presbyteral, pastoral and ministerial concern to the U.S. and the universal Church. The NFPC has a membership of 110 senates (councils and associations), religious institutes, PADRES and the National Black Catholic Clergy Caucus.

Headquarters are located at 1307 S. Wabash Ave., Chicago, Ill. 60605.

The organizational structure of the Catholic Church in the United States consists of 33 provinces with as many archdioceses (metropolitan sees), 142 suffragan sees (dioceses), two jurisdictions immediately subject to the Holy See (the Eparchy of St. Maron for the Maronites and the Melkite Eparchy of Newton), two apostolic exarchates (for Chaldean-Rite Catholics and for Romanians of Byzantine Rite) and the Military Ordinariate. An Armenian-Rite apostolic exarchate for the United States and Canada has its seat in New York. Each of these jurisdictions is under the direction of an archbishop or bishop, called an ordinary, who has apostolic responsibility and authority for the pastoral service of the people in his care.

The structure includes the territorial episcopal conference known as the National Conference of Catholic Bishops. In and through this body, which is strictly ecclesiastical and has defined juridical authority, the bishops exercise their collegiate pastorate over the Church in the entire country (see Index).

Related to the NCCB is the United States Catholic Conference, a civil corporation and operational secretariat through which the bishops, in cooperation with other members of the Church, act on a wider-than-ecclesiastical scale for the good of the Church and society in the United States (see Index).

The representative of the Holy See to the Church in this country is an Apostolic Delegate.

ECCLESIASTICAL PROVINCES

(Sources: *The Official Catholic Directory,* NC News Service.)

The 33 ecclesiastical provinces bear the names of archdioceses, i.e., of metropolitan sees.

Anchorage: Archdiocese of Anchorage and suffragan sees of Fairbanks, Juneau. Geographical area: Alaska.

Atlanta: Archdiocese of Atlanta (Ga.) and suffragan sees of Savannah (Ga.), Charlotte and Raleigh (N.C.), Charleston (S.C.). Geographical area: Georgia, North Carolina, South Carolina.

Baltimore: Archdiocese of Baltimore (Md.) and suffragan sees of Wilmington (Del.), Arlington and Richmond (Va.), Wheeling-Charleston (W. Va.). Geographical area: Maryland (except five counties), Delaware, Virginia, West Virginia.

Boston: Archdiocese of Boston (Mass.) and suffragan sees of Fall River, Springfield and Worcester (Mass.), Portland (Me.), Manchester (N.H.), Burlington (Vt.). Geographical area: Massachusetts, Maine, New Hampshire, Vermont.

Chicago: Archdiocese of Chicago and suffragan sees of Belleville, Joliet, Peoria, Rockford, Springfield. Geographical area: Illinois.

Cincinnati: Archdiocese of Cincinnati and suffragan sees of Cleveland, Columbus, Steubenville, Toledo, Youngstown. Geographical area: Ohio.

Denver: Archdiocese of Denver (Colo.) and suffragan sees of Pueblo (Colo.), Cheyenne (Wyo.). Geographical area: Colorado, Wyoming.

Detroit: Archdiocese of Detroit and suffragan sees of Gaylord, Grand Rapids, Kalamazoo, Lansing, Marquette, Saginaw. Geographical area: Michigan.

Dubuque: Archdiocese of Dubuque and suffragan sees of Davenport, Des Moines, Sioux City. Geographical area: Iowa.

Hartford: Archdiocese of Hartford (Conn.) and suffragan sees of Bridgeport and Norwich (Conn.), Providence (R.I.). Geographical area: Connecticut, Rhode Island.

Indianapolis: Archdiocese of Indianapolis and suffragan sees of Evansville, Fort Wayne-South Bend, Gary, Lafayette. Geographical area: Indiana.

Kansas City (Kans.): Archdiocese of Kansas City and suffragan sees of Dodge City, Salina, Wichita. Geographical area: Kansas.

Los Angeles: Archdiocese of Los Angeles and suffragan sees of Fresno, Monterey, Orange, San Bernardino, San Diego. Geographical area: Southern and Central California.

Louisville: Archdiocese of Louisville (Ky.) and suffragan sees of Covington and Owensboro (Ky.), Memphis and Nashville (Tenn.). Geographical area: Kentucky, Tennessee.

Miami: Archdiocese of Miami and suffragan sees of Orlando, Pensacola-Tallahassee, St. Augustine, St. Petersburg. Geographical area: Florida.

Milwaukee: Archdiocese of Milwaukee and suffragan sees of Green Bay, La Crosse, Madison, Superior. Geographical area: Wisconsin.

Mobile: Archdiocese of Mobile, Ala., and suffragan sees of Birmingham (Ala.) and Biloxi and Jackson (Miss.). Geographical area: Alabama, Mississippi.

Newark: Archdiocese of Newark and suffragan sees of Camden, Metuchen, Paterson, Trenton. Geographical area: New Jersey.

New Orleans: Archdiocese of New Orleans and suffragan sees of Alexandria-Shreveport, Baton Rouge, Houma-Thibodaux, Lafayette and Lake Charles. Geographical area: Louisiana.

New York: Archdiocese of New York and suffragan sees of Albany, Brooklyn, Buffalo, Ogdensburg, Rochester, Rockville Centre, Syracuse. Geographical area: New York.

Oklahoma City: Archdiocese of Oklahoma City (Okla.) and suffragan sees of Tulsa (Okla.) and Little Rock (Ark.). Geographical area: Oklahoma, Arkansas.

Omaha: Archdiocese of Omaha and suffragan sees of Grand Island, Lincoln. Geographical area: Nebraska.

Philadelphia: Archdiocese of Philadelphia and suffragan sees of Allentown, Altoona-Johnstown, Erie, Greensburg, Harrisburg, Pittsburgh, Scranton. Geographical area: Pennsylvania.

Philadelphia (Byzantine Rite): Metropolitan See of Philadelphia (Byzantine Rite) and Eparchies of

St. Nicholas of the Ukrainians in Chicago and Stamford, Conn. The jurisdiction extends to all Ukrainian Catholics in the U.S. from the ecclesiastical province of Galicia in the Ukraine.

Pittsburgh (Byzantine Rite): Metropolitan See of Pittsburgh, Pa. and Eparchies of Passaic (N.J.), Parma (Ohio), Van Nuys (Calif.).

Portland: Archdiocese of Portland (Ore.) and suffragan sees of Baker (Ore.), Boise (Ida.), Great Falls-Billings and Helena (Mont.). Geographical area: Oregon, Idaho, Montana.

St. Louis: Archdiocese of St. Louis and suffragan sees of Jefferson City, Kansas City-St. Joseph, Springfield-Cape Girardeau. Geographical area: Missouri.

St. Paul and Minneapolis: Archdiocese of St. Paul and Minneapolis (Minn.) and suffragan sees of Crookston, Duluth, New Ulm, St. Cloud and Winona (Minn.), Bismarck and Fargo (N.D.), Rapid City and Sioux Falls (S.D.). Geographical area: Minnesota, North Dakota, South Dakota.

San Antonio: Archdiocese of San Antonio (Tex.)

and suffragan sees of Amarillo, Austin, Beaumont, Brownsville, Corpus Christi, Dallas, El Paso, Fort Worth, Galveston-Houston, Lubbock, San Angelo and Victoria (Tex.). Geographical area: Texas.

San Francisco: Archdiocese of San Francisco (Calif.) and suffragan sees of Oakland, Sacramento, San Jose, Santa Rosa and Stockton (Calif.), Agaña (Guam), Honolulu (Hawaii), Reno-Las Vegas (Nev.), Salt Lake City (Utah). Geographical area: Northern California, Nevada, Utah, Hawaii, Guam, the Marianas Islands and Ryukyus Islands.

Santa Fe: Archdiocese of Santa Fe (N.M.) and suffragan sees of Gallup and Las Cruces (N.M.), Phoenix and Tucson (Ariz.). Geographical area: New Mexico, Arizona.

Seattle: Archdiocese of Seattle and suffragan sees of Spokane, Yakima. Geographical area: Washington.

Washington: Archdiocese of Washington, D.C., and suffragan see of St. Thomas (Virgin Islands). Geographical area: District of Columbia, five counties of Maryland, Virgin Islands.

ARCHDIOCESES, DIOCESES, ARCHBISHOPS, BISHOPS

(Sources: *The Official Catholic Directory;* NC News Service. As of Aug. 15, 1983.)

Information includes name of diocese, year of foundation (as it appears on the official document erecting the see), present ordinaries and auxiliaries (for biographies, see Index), former ordinaries.

Archdioceses are indicated by an asterisk.

Albany, N.Y. (1847): Howard J. Hubbard, bishop, 1977.

Former bishops: John McCloskey, 1847-64; John J. Conroy, 1865-77; Francis McNeirny, 1877-94; Thomas M. Burke, 1894-1915; Thomas F. Cusack, 1915-18; Edmund F. Gibbons, 1919-54; William A. Scully, 1954-09, Edwin B. Broderick, 1969-76.

Alexandria-Shreveport, La. (1853): William B. Friend, bishop, 1983.

Established at Natchitoches, transferred to Alexandria 1910; present title 1977.

Former bishops: Augustus M. Martin, 1853-75; Francis X. Leray, 1877-79, administrator, 1879-83; Anthony Durier, 1885-1904; Cornelius Van de Ven, 1904-32; D. F. Desmond, 1933-45; Charles P. Greco, 1946-73; Lawrence P. Graves, 1973-82.

Allentown, Pa. (1961): Thomas J. Welsh, bishop, 1983.

Former bishop: Joseph McShea, 1961-83.

Altoona-Johnstown, Pa. (1901): James J. Hogan, bishop, 1966.

Established as Altoona, name changed, 1957.

Former bishops: Eugene A. Garvey, 1901-20; John J. McCort, 1920-36; Richard T. Guilfoyle, 1936-57; Howard J. Carroll, 1958-60; J. Carroll McCormick, 1960-66.

Amarillo, Tex. (1926): Leroy T. Matthiesen, bishop, 1980.

Former bishops; Rudolph A. Gerken, 1927-33; Robert E. Lucey, 1934-41; Laurence J. Fitzsimon, 1941-58; John L. Morkovsky, 1958-63; Lawrence M. De Falco, 1963-79.

Anchorage,* Alaska (1966): Francis T. Hurley, archbishop, 1976.

Former archbishop: Joseph T. Ryan, 1966-75.

Arlington, Va. (1974): John R. Keating, bishop, 1983.

Former bishop: Thomas J. Welsh, 1974-83.

Atlanta,* Ga. (1956; archdiocese, 1962): Thomas A. Donnellan, archbishop, 1968.

Former ordinaries: Francis E. Hyland, 1956-61; Paul J. Hallinan, first archbishop, 1962-68.

Austin, Tex. (1947): Vincent M. Harris, bishop, 1971.

Former bishop: Louis J. Reicher, 1947-71.

Baker, Ore. (1903): Thomas J. Connolly, bishop, 1971.

Established as Baker City, name changed, 1952.

Former bishops: Charles J. O'Reilly, 1903-18; Joseph F. McGrath, 1919-50; Francis P. Leipzig, 1950-71.

Baltimore,* Md. (1789; archdiocese, 1808): William D. Borders, archbishop, 1974. T. Austin Murphy, P. Francis Murphy, auxiliaries.

Former ordinaries: John Carroll, 1789-1815, first archbishop; Leonard Neale, 1815-17; Ambrose Marechal, S.S., 1817-28; James Whitfield, 1828-34; Samuel Eccleston, S.S., 1834-51; Francis P. Kenrick, 1851-63; Martin J. Spalding, 1864-72; James R. Bayley, 1872-77; Cardinal James Gibbons, 1877-1921; Michael J. Curley, 1921-47; Francis P. Keough, 1947-61; Cardinal Lawrence J. Shehan, 1961-74.

Baton Rouge, La. (1961): Stanley J. Ott, bishop, 1983.

Former bishops: Robert E. Tracy, 1961-74; Joseph V. Sullivan, 1974-82.

Beaumont, Tex. (1966): Bernard J. Ganter, bishop, 1977.

Former bishops: Vincent M. Harris, 1966-71; Warren L. Boudreaux, 1971-77.

Belleville, Ill. (1887): John N. Wurm, bishop, 1981.

Former bishops: John Janssen, 1888-1913; Henry Althoff, 1914-47; Albert R. Zuroweste, 1948-76; William M. Cosgrove, 1976-81.

Biloxi, Miss. (1977): (Joseph) Lawson E. Howze, bishop, 1977.

Birmingham, Ala. (1969): Joseph G. Vath, bishop, 1969.

Bismarck, N. Dak. (1909): John F. Kinney, bishop, 1982.

Former bishops: Vincent Wehrle, O.S.B., 1910-39; Vincent J. Ryan, 1940-51; Lambert A. Hoch, 1952-56; Hilary B. Hacker, 1957-82.

Boise, Ida. (1893): Sylvester Treinen, bishop, 1962.

Former bishops: Alphonse J. Glorieux, 1893-1917; Daniel M. Gorman, 1918-27; Edward J. Kelly, 1928-56; James J. Byrne, 1956-62.

Boston,* Mass. (1808; archdiocese, 1875): Cardinal Humberto S. Medeiros, archbishop, 1970. Lawrence J. Riley, Thomas V. Dailey, John M. D'Arcy, John J. Mulcahy, Daniel A. Hart, Alfred C. Hughes, auxiliaries.

Former ordinaries: John L. de Cheverus, 1810-23; Benedict J. Fenwick, S.J., 1825-46; John B. Fitzpatrick, 1846-66; John J. Williams, 1866-1907, first archbishop; Cardinal William O'Connell, 1907-44; Cardinal Richard Cushing, 1944-70.

Bridgeport, Conn. (1953): Walter W. Curtis, bishop, 1961.

Former bishop: Lawrence J. Shehan, 1953-61.

Brooklyn, N.Y. (1853): Francis J. Mugavero, bishop, 1968. Anthony Bevilacqua, Joseph M. Sullivan, Rene Valero, auxiliaries.

Former bishops: John Loughlin, 1853-91; Charles E. McDonnell, 1892-1921; Thomas E. Molloy, 1921-56; Bryan J. McEntegart, 1957-68.

Brownsville, Tex. (1965): John J. Fitzpatrick, bishop, 1971.

Former bishops: Adolph Marx, 1965; Humberto S. Medeiros, 1966-70.

Buffalo, N.Y. (1847): Edward D. Head, bishop, 1973. Pius A. Benincasa, Bernard J. McLaughlin, auxiliaries.

Former bishops: John Timon, C.M., 1847-67; Stephen V. Ryan, C.M., 1868-96; James E. Quigley, 1897-1903; Charles H. Colton, 1903-15; Dennis J. Dougherty, 1915-18; William Turner, 1919-36; John A. Duffy, 1937-44; John F. O'Hara, C.S.C., 1945-51; Joseph A. Burke, 1952-62; James McNulty, 1963-72.

Burlington, Vt. (1853): John A. Marshall, bishop, 1972.

Former bishops: Louis De Goesbriand, 1853-99; John S. Michaud, 1899-1908; Joseph J. Rice, 1910-38; Matthew F. Brady, 1938-44; Edward F. Ryan, 1945-56; Robert F. Joyce, 1957-71.

Camden, N.J. (1937): George H. Guilfoyle, bishop, 1968. James L. Schad, auxiliary.

Former bishops: Bartholomew J. Eustace, 1938-56; Justin J. McCarthy, 1957-59; Celestine J. Damiano, 1960-67.

Charleston, S.C. (1820): Ernest L. Unterkoefler, bishop, 1964.

Former bishops: John England, 1820-42; Ignatius W. Reynolds, 1844-55; Patrick N. Lynch, 1858-82; Henry P. Northrop, 1883-1916; William T.

Russell, 1917-27; Emmet M. Walsh, 1927-49; John J. Russell, 1950-58; Paul J. Hallinan, 1958-62; Francis F. Reh, 1962-64.

Charlotte, N.C. (1971): Michael J. Begley, bishop, 1972.

Cheyenne, Wyo. (1887): Joseph Hart, bishop, 1978.

Former bishops: Maurice F. Burke, 1887-93; Thomas M. Lenihan, 1897-1901; James J. Keane, 1902-11; Patrick A. McGovern, 1912-51; Hubert M. Newell, 1951-78.

Chicago,* Ill. (1843; archdiocese, 1880): Cardinal Joseph L. Bernardin, archbishop, 1982. Alfred L. Abramowicz, Nevin W. Hayes, O. Carm., auxiliaries.

Former ordinaries: William Quarter, 1844-48; James O. Van de Velde, S.J., 1849-53; Anthony O'Regan, 1854-58; James Duggan, 1859-70; Thomas P. Foley, administrator, 1870-79; Patrick A. Feehan, 1880-1902, first archbishop; James E. Quigley, 1903-15; Cardinal George Mundelein, 1915-39; Cardinal Samuel Stritch, 1939-58; Cardinal Albert Meyer, 1958-65; Cardinal John Cody, 1965-82.

Cincinnati,* Ohio (1821; archdiocese, 1850): Daniel E. Pilarczyk, archbishop, 1982. Nicholas Elko (titular archbishop), auxiliary.

Former ordinaries: Edward D. Fenwick, O.P., 1822-32; John B. Purcell, 1833-83, first archbishop; William H. Elder, 1883-1904; Henry Moeller, 1904-1925; John T. McNicholas, O.P., 1925-50; Karl J. Alter, 1950-69; Paul F. Leibold, 1969-72; Joseph L. Bernardin, 1972-82.

Cleveland, Ohio (1847): Anthony M. Pilla, bishop, 1980. Gilbert I. Sheldon, James P. Lyke, O.F.M., A. Edward Pevec, auxiliaries.

Former bishops: L. Amadeus Rappe, 1847-70; Richard Gilmour, 1872-91; Ignatius F. Horstmann, 1892-1908; John P. Farrelly, 1909-21; Joseph Schrembs, 1921-45; Edward F. Hoban, 1945-66; Clarence G. Issenmann, 1966-74; James A. Hickey, 1974-80.

Columbus, Ohio (1868): James A. Griffin, bishop, 1983.

Former bishops: Sylvester H. Rosecrans, 1868-78; John A. Watterson, 1880-99; Henry Moeller, 1900-03; James J. Hartley, 1904-44; Michael J. Ready, 1944-57; Clarence Issenmann, 1957-64; John J. Carberry, 1965-68; Clarence E. Elwell, 1968-73; Edward J. Herrmann, 1973-82.

Corpus Christi, Tex. (1912): Rene H. Gracida, bishop, 1983.

Former bishops: Paul J. Nussbaum, C.P., 1913-20; Emmanuel B. Ledvina, 1921-49; Mariano S. Garriga, 1949-65; Thomas J. Drury, 1965-83.

Covington, Ky. (1853): William A. Hughes, bishop, 1979.

Former bishops: George A. Carrell, S.J., 1853-68; Augustus M. Toebbe, 1870-84; Camillus P. Maes, 1885-1914; Ferdinand Brossart, 1916-23; Francis W. Howard, 1923-44; William T. Mulloy, 1945-59; Richard Ackerman, C.S.Sp., 1960-78.

Crookston, Minn. (1909): Victor Balke, bishop, 1976.

Former bishops: Timothy Corbett, 1910-38; John H. Peschges, 1938-44; Francis J. Schenk, 1945-60;

Laurence A. Glenn, 1960-70; Kenneth J. Povish, 1970-75.

Dallas, Tex. (1890): Thomas Tschoepe, bishop, 1969.

Established 1890, as Dallas, title changed to Dallas-Ft. Worth 1953; redesignated Dallas, 1969, when Ft. Worth was made diocese.

Former bishops: Thomas F. Brennan, 1891-92; Edward J. Dunne, 1893-1910; Joseph P. Lynch, 1911-54; Thomas K. Gorman, 1954-69.

Davenport, Ia. (1881): Gerald F. O'Keefe, bishop, 1966.

Former bishops: John McMullen, 1881-83; Henry Cosgrove, 1884-1906; James Davis, 1906-26; Henry P. Rohlman, 1927-44; Ralph L. Hayes, 1944-66.

Denver,* Colo. (1887; archdiocese, 1941): James V. Casey, archbishop, 1967. George R. Evans, Richard C. Hanifen, auxiliaries.

Former ordinaries: Joseph P. Machebeuf, 1887-89; Nicholas C. Matz, 1889-1917; J. Henry Tihen, 1917-31; Urban J. Vehr, 1931-67, first archbishop.

Des Moines, Ia. (1911): Maurice J. Dingman, bishop, 1968.

Former bishops: Austin Dowling, 1912-19; Thomas W. Drumm, 1919-33; Gerald T. Bergan, 1934-48; Edward C. Daly, O.P., 1948-64; George J. Biskup, 1965-67.

Detroit,* Mich. (1833; archdiocese, 1937): Edmund C. Szoka, archbishop, 1981. Thomas J. Gumbleton, Walter J. Schoenherr, Moses B. Anderson, Patrick R. Cooney, Dale C. Melczek, auxiliaries.

Former ordinaries: Frederic Rese, 1833-71; Peter P. Lefevere, administrator, 1841-69; Caspar H. Borgess, 1871-88; John S. Foley, 1888-1918; Michael J. Gallagher, 1918-37; Cardinal Edward Mooney, 1937-58, first archbishop; Cardinal John F. Dearden, 1958-80.

Dodge City, Kans. (1951): Stanley G. Schlarman, bishop, 1983.

Former bishops: John B. Franz, 1951-59; Marion F. Forst, 1960-76; Eugene J. Gerber, 1976-82.

Dubuque,* Iowa (1837; archdiocese, 1893): Vacant as of late August, 1983. Francis J. Dunn, auxiliary.

Former ordinaries: Mathias Loras, 1837-58; Clement Smyth, O.C.S.O., 1858-65; John Hennessy, 1866-1900, first archbishop; John J. Keane, 1900-11; James J. Keane, 1911-29; Francis J. Beckman, 1930-46; Henry P. Rohlman, 1946-54; Leo Binz, 1954-61; James J. Byrne, 1962-83.

Duluth, Minn. (1889): Robert H. Brom, bishop, 1982.

Former bishops: James McGolrick, 1889-1918; John T. McNicholas, O.P., 1918-25; Thomas A. Welch, 1926-59; Francis J. Schenk, 1960-69; Paul F. Anderson, 1969-82.

El Paso, Tex. (1914): Raymond J. Pena, bishop, 1980.

Former bishops: Anthony J. Schuler, S.J., 1915-42; Sidney M. Metzger, 1942-78. Patrick F. Flores, 1978-79.

Erie, Pa. (1853): Michael J. Murphy, bishop, 1982.

Former bishops: Michael O'Connor, 1853-54; Josue M. Young, 1854-66; Tobias Mullen, 1868-99;

John E. Fitzmaurice, 1899-1920; John M. Gannon, 1920-66; John F. Whealon, 1966-69; Alfred M. Watson, 1969-82.

Evansville, Ind. (1944): Francis Raymond Shea, bishop, 1970.

Former bishops: Henry J. Grimmelsman, 1944-65; Paul F. Leibold, 1966-69.

Fairbanks, Alaska (1962): Robert L. Whelan, S.J., bishop, 1968.

Former bishop: Francis D. Gleeson, S.J., 1962-68.

Fall River, Mass. (1904): Daniel A. Cronin, bishop, 1970.

Former bishops: William Stang, 1904-07; Daniel F. Feehan, 1907-34; James E. Cassidy, 1934-51; James L. Connolly, 1951-70.

Fargo, N. Dak. (1889): Justin A. Driscoll, bishop, 1970.

Established at Jamestown, transferred, 1897.

Former bishops: John Shanley, 1889-1909; James O'Reilly, 1910-34; Aloysius J. Muench, 1935-59; Leo F. Dworschak, 1960-70.

Fort Wayne-South Bend, Ind. (1857): William E. McManus, bishop, 1976. Joseph R. Crowley, auxiliary.

Established as Fort Wayne, name changed, 1960.

Former bishops: John H. Luers, 1858-71; Joseph Dwenger, C.Pp. S., 1872-93; Joseph Rademacher, 1893-1900; Herman J. Alerding, 1900-24; John F. Noll, 1925-56; Leo A. Pursley, 1957-76.

Fort Worth, Tex. (1969): Joseph P. Delaney, bishop, 1981.

Former bishop: John J. Cassata, 1969-80.

Fresno, Calif. (1967): Joseph J. Madera, M.Sp.S., bishop, 1980.

Formerly Monterey-Fresno, 1922.

Former bishops (Monterey-Fresno): John J. Cantwell, administrator, 1922-24; John B. MacGinley, first bishop, 1924-32; Philip G. Sher, 1933-53; Aloysius J. Willinger, 1953-67.

Former bishops (Fresno): Timothy Manning, 1967-69; Hugh A. Donohoe, 1969-80.

Gallup, N. Mex. (1939): Jerome J. Hastrich, bishop, 1969.

Former bishop: Bernard T. Espelage, O.F.M., 1940-69.

Galveston-Houston, Tex. (1847): John L. Morkovsky, bishop, 1975. John E. McCarthy, auxiliary.

Established as Galveston, name changed, 1959.

Former bishops: John M. Odin, C.M., 1847-61; Claude M. Dubuis, 1862-92; Nicholas A. Gallagher, 1892-1918; Christopher E. Byrne, 1918-50; Wendelin J. Nold, 1950-75.

Gary, Ind. (1956): Andrew G. Grutka, bishop, 1957.

Gaylord, Mich. (1971): Robert J. Rose, bishop, 1981.

Former bishop: Edmund C. Szoka, 1971-81.

Grand Island, Neb. (1912): Lawrence McNamara, bishop, 1978.

Established at Kearney, transferred, 1917.

Former bishops: James A. Duffy, 1913-31; Stanislaus V. Bona, 1932-44; Edward J. Hunkeler, 1945-51; John L. Paschang, 1951-72; John J. Sullivan, 1972-77.

Grand Rapids, Mich. (1882): Joseph M. Breitenbeck, bishop, 1969. Joseph C. McKinney, auxiliary.

Former bishops: Henry J. Richter, 1883-1916; Michael J. Gallagher, 1916-18; Edward D. Kelly, 1919-26; Joseph G. Pinten, 1926-40; Joseph C. Plagens, 1941-43; Francis J. Haas, 1943-53; Allen J. Babcock, 1954-69.

Great Falls-Billings, Mont. (1904): Thomas J. Murphy, bishop, 1978.

Established as Great Falls; name changed, 1980.

Former bishops: Mathias C. Lenihan, 1904-30; Edwin V. O'Hara, 1930-39; William J. Condon, 1939-67; Eldon B. Schuster, 1968-77.

Green Bay, Wis. (1868): Vacant as of Aug. 15, 1983. Robert F. Morneau, auxiliary.

Former bishops: Joseph Melcher, 1868-73; Francis X. Krautbauer, 1875-85; Frederick X. Katzer, 1886-91; Sebastian G. Messmer, 1892-1903; Joseph J. Fox, 1904-14; Paul P. Rhode, 1915-45; Stanislaus V. Bona, 1945-67; Aloysius J. Wycislo, 1968-83.

Greensburg, Pa. (1951): William G. Connare, bishop, 1960. Norbert F. Gaughan, auxiliary.

Former bishop: Hugh L. Lamb, 1951-59.

Harrisburg, Pa. (1868): Joseph T. Daley, bishop, 1971. William H. Keeler, auxiliary.

Former bishops: Jeremiah F. Shanahan, 1868-86; Thomas McGovern, 1888-98; John W. Shanahan,1899-1916; Philip R. McDevitt, 1916-35; George L. Leech, 1935-71.

Hartford,* Conn. (1843; archdiocese, 1953): John F. Whealon, archbishop, 1969. John F. Hackett, Peter A. Rosazza, auxiliaries.

Former ordinaries: William Tyler, 1844-49; Bernard O'Reilly, 1850-56; F. P. MacFarland, 1858-74; Thomas Galberry, O.S.A., 1876-78; Lawrence S. McMahon, 1879-93; Michael Tierney, 1894-1908; John J. Nilan, 1910-34; Maurice F. McAuliffe, 1934-44; Henry J. O'Brien, 1945-68, first archbishop.

Helena, Mont. (1884): Elden F. Curtiss, bishop, 1976.

Former bishops: John B. Brondel, 1884-1903; John P. Carroll, 1904-25; George J. Finnigan, C.S.C., 1927-32; Ralph L. Hayes, 1933-35; Joseph M. Gilmore, 1936-62; Raymond Hunthausen, 1962-75.

Honolulu, Hawaii (1941): Joseph A. Ferrario, bishop, 1982.

Former bishops: James J. Sweeney, 1941-68; John J. Scanlan, 1968-81.

Houma-Thibodaux, La. (1977): Warren L. Boudreaux, bishop, 1977.

Indianapolis,* Ind. (1834; archdiocese, 1944): Edward T. O'Meara, archbishop, 1980.

Established at Vincennes, transferred, 1898.

Former ordinaries: Simon G. Bruté, 1834-39; Celestine de la Hailandiere, 1839-47; John S. Bazin, 1847-48; Maurice de St. Palais, 1849-77; Francis S. Chatard, 1878-1918; Joseph Chartrand, 1918-33; Joseph E. Ritter, 1934-46, first archbishop; Paul C. Schulte, 1946-70; George J. Biskup, 1970-79.

Jackson, Miss. (1837): Joseph B. Brunini, bishop, 1968. William R. Houck, auxiliary.

Established at Natchez; title changed to Natchez-Jackson, 1956; transferred to Jackson, 1977 (Natchez made titular see).

Former bishops: John J. Chanche, S.S., 1841-52;

James Van de Velde, S.J., 1853-55; William H. Elder, 1857-80; Francis A. Jansens, 1881-88; Thomas Heslin, 1889-1911; John E. Gunn, S.M., 1911-24; Richard O. Gerow, 1924-67.

Jefferson City, Mo. (1956): Michael F. McAuliffe, bishop, 1969.

Former bishop: Joseph Marling, C.Pp.S., 1956-69.

Joliet, Ill. (1948): Joseph I. Imesch, bishop, 1979. Raymond J. Vonesh, Daniel L. Ryan, auxiliaries.

Former bishop: Martin D. McNamara, 1949-66. Romeo Blanchette, 1966-79.

Juneau, Alaska (1951): Michael H. Kenny, bishop, 1979.

Former bishops: Dermot O'Flanagan, 1951-68; Joseph T. Ryan, administrator, 1968-71; Francis T. Hurley, 1971-76, administrator, 1976-79.

Kalamazoo, Mich. (1971): Paul V. Donovan, bishop, 1971.

Kansas City,* Kans. (1877; archdiocese, 1952): Ignatius J. Strecker, archbishop, 1969. Marion F. Forst, auxiliary.

Established as vicariate apostolic, 1850, became Diocese of Leavenworth, 1877, transferred to Kansas City 1947.

Former ordinaries: J. B. Miege, vicar apostolic, 1851-74; Louis M. Fink, O.S.B., vicar apostolic, 1874-77, first bishop, 1877-1904; Thomas F. Lillis, 1904-10; John Ward, 1910-29; Francis Johannes, 1929-37; Paul C. Schulte, 1937-46; George J. Donnelly, 1946-50; Edward Hunkeler, 1951-69, first archbishop.

Kansas City-St. Joseph, Mo. (Kansas City, 1880; St. Joseph, 1868; united 1956): John J. Sullivan, bishop, 1977. George K. Fitzsimons, auxiliary.

Former bishops: John J. Hogan, 1880-1913; Thomas F. Lillis, 1913-38; Edwin V. O'Hara, 1939-56; John P. Cody, 1956-61; Charles H. Helmsing, 1962-77.

Former bishops (St. Joseph): John J. Hogan, 1868-80, administrator, 1880-93; Maurice F. Burke, 1893-1923; Francis Gilfillan, 1923-33; Charles H. Le Blond, 1933-56.

La Crosse, Wis. (1868): Vacant as of Aug. 15, 1983. John J. Paul, auxiliary.

Former bishops: Michael Heiss, 1868-80; Kilian C. Flasch, 1881-91; James Schwebach, 1892-1921; Alexander J. McGavick, 1921-48; John P. Treacy, 1948-64; Frederick W. Freking, 1965-83.

Lafayette, Ind. (1944): George A. Fulcher, bishop, 1983.

Former bishops: John G. Bennett, 1944-57; John J. Carberry, 1957-65; Raymond J. Gallagher, 1965-82.

Lafayette, La. (1918): Gerard L. Frey, bishop, 1973.

Former bishops: Jules B. Jeanmard, 1918-56; Maurice Schexnayder, 1956-72.

Lake Charles, La. (1980): Jude Speyrer, bishop, 1980.

Lansing, Mich. (1937): Kenneth J. Povish, bishop, 1975. James Sullivan, auxiliary.

Former bishops: Joseph H. Albers, 1937-65; Alexander Zaleski, 1965-75.

Las Cruces, N. Mex. (1982): Ricardo Ramirez, C.S.B., bishop, 1982.

Lincoln, Neb. (1887): Glennon P. Flavin, bishop, 1967.

Former bishops: Thomas Bonacum, 1887-1911; J. Henry Tihen, 1911-17; Charles J. O'Reilly, 1918-23; Francis J. Beckman, 1924-30; Louis B. Kucera, 1930-57; James V. Casey, 1957-67.

Little Rock, Ark. (1843): Andrew J. McDonald, bishop, 1972.

Former bishops: Andrew Byrne, 1844-62; Edward Fitzgerald, 1867-1907; John Morris, 1907-46; Albert L. Fletcher, 1946-72.

Los Angeles,* Calif. (1840; archdiocese, 1936): Cardinal Timothy Manning, archbishop, 1970. John J. Ward, Juan A. Arzube, William Levada, Donald Montrose, auxiliaries.

Former ordinaries: Francisco Garcia Diego y Moreno, O.F.M., 1840-46; Joseph S. Alemany, O.P., 1850-53; Thaddeus Amat, C.M., 1854-78; Francis Mora, 1878-96; George T. Montgomery, 1896-1903; Thomas J. Conaty, 1903-15; John J. Cantwell, 1917-47, first archbishop; Cardinal James McIntyre, 1948-70.

Louisville,* Ky. (1808; archdiocese, 1937): Thomas C Kelly, O.P., archbishop, 1982. Charles G. Maloney, auxiliary.

Established at Bardstown, transferred, 1841.

Former ordinaries: Benedict J. Flaget, S.S. 1810-32; John B. David, S.S., 1832-33; Benedict J. Flaget, S.S., 1833-50; Martin J. Spalding, 1850-64; Peter J. Lavialle, 1865-67; William G. McCloskey, 1868-1909; Denis O'Donaghue, 1910-24; John A. Floersh, 1924-67, first archbishop; Thomas J. McDonough, 1967-81.

Lubbock, Tex. (1983): Michael Sheehan, bishop, 1983.

Madison, Wis. (1946): Cletus F. O'Donnell, bishop, 1967. George O. Wirz, auxiliary.

Former bishop: William P. O'Connor, 1946-67.

Manchester, N.H. (1884): Odore J. Gendron, bishop, 1974 Robert Mulvee, auxiliary.

Former bishops: Denis M. Bradley, 1884-1903; John B. Delany, 1904-06; George A. Guertin, 1907-32; John B. Peterson, 1932-44; Matthew F. Brady, 1944-59; Ernest J. Primeau, 1960-74.

Marquette, Mich. (1857): Mark F. Schmitt, bishop, 1978.

Former bishops: Frederic Baraga, 1857-68; Ignatius Mrak, 1869-78; John Vertin, 1879-99; Frederick Eis, 1899-1922; Paul J. Nussbaum, C.P., 1922-35; Joseph C. Plagens, 1935-40; Francis Magner, 1941-47; Thomas L. Noa, 1947-68; Charles A. Salatka, 1968-77.

Memphis, Tenn. (1970): J. Francis Stafford, bishop, 1982.

Former bishop: Carroll T. Dozier, 1971-82.

Metuchen, N.J. (1981): Theodore E. McCarrick, bishop, 1981.

Miami,* Fla. (1958; archdiocese, 1968): Edward A. McCarthy, archbishop, 1977. John J. Nevins, Agustin A. Roman, auxiliaries.

Former ordinary: Coleman F. Carroll, 1958-77, first archbishop.

Milwaukee,* Wis. (1843; archdiocese, 1875): Rembert G. Weakland, O.S.B., archbishop, 1977. Leo J. Brust, Richard J. Sklba, auxiliaries.

Former ordinaries: John M. Henni, 1844-81, first archbishop; Michael Heiss, 1881-90; Frederick X. Katzer, 1891-1903; Sebastian G. Messmer, 1903-30; Samuel A. Stritch, 1930-39; Moses E. Kiley, 1940-53; Albert G. Meyer, 1953-58; William E. Cousins, 1959-77.

Mobile,* Ala. (1829; archdiocese, 1980): Oscar H. Lipscomb, first archbishop, 1980.

Former bishops: Michael Portier, 1829-59; John Quinlan, 1859-83; Dominic Manucy, 1884; Jeremiah O'Sullivan, 1885-96; Edward P. Allen, 1897-1926; Thomas J. Toolen, 1927-69; John L. May, 1969-80.

Monterey in California (1967): Thaddeus A. Shubsda, bishop, 1982.

Formerly Monterey-Fresno, 1922.

Former bishops (Monterey-Fresno): John J. Cantwell, administrator, 1922-24; John B. MacGinley, first bishop, 1924-32; Philip G. Sher, 1933-53; Aloysius J. Willinger, 1953-67.

Former bishop (Monterey): Harry A. Clinch, 1967-82.

Nashville, Tenn. (1837): James D. Niedergeses, bishop, 1975.

Former bishops: Richard P. Miles, O.P., 1838-60; James Whelan, O.P., 1860-64; Patrick A. Feehan, 1865-80; Joseph Rademacher, 1883-93; Thomas S. Byrne, 1894-1923; Alphonse J. Smith, 1924-35; William L. Adrian, 1936-69; Joseph A. Durick, 1969-75.

Newark,* N.J. (1853; archdiocese, 1937): Peter L. Gerety, archbishop, 1974. Jerome Pechillo, T.O.R., Robert F. Garner, Joseph A. Francis, S.V.D., Dominic A. Marconi, David Arias, auxiliaries.

Former ordinaries: James R. Bayley, 1853-72; Michael A. Corrigan, 1873-80; Winand M. Wigger, 1881-1901; John J. O'Connor, 1901-27; Thomas J. Walsh, 1928-52, first archbishop; Thomas A. Boland, 1953-74.

New Orleans,* La. (1793; archdiocese, 1850): Philip M. Hannan, archbishop, 1965. Harold R. Perry, S. V. D., auxiliary.

Former ordinaries: Luis Penalver y Cardenas, 1793-1801; John Carroll, administrator, 1809-15; W. Louis Dubourg, S.S., 1815-25; Joseph Rosati, C.M., administrator, 1826-29; Leo De Neckere, C.M., 1829-33; Anthony Blanc, 1835-60, first archbishop; Jean Marie Odin, C.M., 1861-70; Napoleon J. Perche, 1870-83; Francis X. Leray, 1883-87; Francis A. Janssens, 1888-97; Placide L. Chapelle, 1897-1905; James H. Blenk, S.M., 1906-17; John W. Shaw, 1918-34; Joseph F. Rummel, 1935-64; John P. Cody, 1964-65.

Newton, Mass. (Melkite Rite) (1966; eparchy, 1976): Archbishop Joseph Tawil, exarch, 1969, first eparch, 1976.

Former ordinary: Justin Najmy, 1966-68.

New Ulm, Minn. (1957): Raymond A. Lucker, bishop, 1976.

Former bishop: Alphonse J. Schladweiler, 1958-75.

New York,* N.Y. (1808; archdiocese, 1850): Cardinal Terence J. Cooke, archbishop, 1968. Patrick V. Ahern, James P. Mahoney, Anthony F. Mestice, Austin Vaughan, Francisco Garmendia, Joseph T. O'Keefe, Emerson Moore, auxiliaries.

Former ordinaries: Richard L. Concanen, O.P.,

1808-10; John Connolly, O.P., 1814-25; John Dubois, S.S., 1826-42; John J. Hughes, 1842-64, first archbishop; Cardinal John McCloskey, 1864-85; Michael A. Corrigan, 1885-1902; Cardinal John Farley, 1902-18; Cardinal Patrick Hayes, 1919-38; Cardinal Francis Spellman, 1939-67.

Norwich, Conn. (1953): Daniel P. Reilly, bishop, 1975.

Former bishops: Bernard J. Flanagan, 1953-59; Vincent J. Hines, 1960-75.

Oakland, Calif. (1962): John S. Cummins, bishop, 1977.

Former bishop: Floyd L. Begin, 1962-77.

Ogdensburg, N.Y. (1872): Stanislaus J. Brzana, bishop, 1968.

Former bishops: Edgar P. Wadhams, 1872-91; Henry Gabriels, 1892-1921; Joseph H. Conroy, 1921-39; Francis J. Monaghan, 1939-42; Bryan J. McEntegart, 1943-53; Walter P. Kellenberg, 1954-57; James J. Navagh, 1957-63; Leo R. Smith, 1963; Thomas A. Donnellan, 1964-68.

Oklahoma City,* Okla. (1905; archdiocese, 1972): Charles A. Salatka, archbishop, 1977.

Former ordinaries: Theophile Meerschaert, 1905-24; Francis C. Kelley, 1924-48; Eugene J. McGuinness, 1948-57; Victor J. Reed, 1958-71; John R. Quinn, 1971-77, first archbishop.

Omaha,* Nebr. (1885; archdiocese, 1945): Daniel E. Sheehan, archbishop, 1969. Anthony Milone, auxiliary.

Former ordinaries: James O'Gorman, O.C.S.O., 1859-74, vicar apostolic; James O'Connor, vicar apostolic, 1876-85, first bishop, 1885-90; Richard Scannell, 1891-1916; Jeremiah J. Harty, 1916-27; Francis Beckman, administrator, 1926-28; Joseph F. Rummel, 1928-35; James H. Ryan, 1935-47, first archbishop; Gerald T. Bergan, 1948-69.

Orange, Calif. (1976): William R. Johnson, bishop, 1976.

Orlando, Fla. (1968): Thomas J. Grady, bishop, 1974.

Former bishop: William Borders, 1968-74.

Owensboro, Ky. (1937): John J. McRaith, bishop, 1982.

Former bishops: Francis R. Cotton, 1938-60, Henry J. Soenneker, 1961-82.

Parma, Ohio (Byzantine Rite) (1969): Emil Mihalik, eparch, 1969.

Passaic, N.J. (Byzantine Rite) (1963): Michael J. Dudick, eparch, 1968 Andrew Pataki, auxiliary.

Former bishop: Stephen Kocisko, 1963-68.

Paterson, N.J. (1937): Frank J. Rodimer, bishop, 1978.

Former bishops: Thomas H. McLaughlin, 1937-47; Thomas A. Boland, 1947-52; James A. McNulty, 1953-63; James J. Navagh, 1963-65; Lawrence B. Casey, 1966-77.

Pensacola-Tallahassee, Fla. (1975): Vacant as of Aug. 15, 1983.

Former bishop: Rene H. Gracida, 1975-83.

Peoria, Ill. (1877): Edward W. O'Rourke, bishop, 1971.

Former bishops: John L. Spalding, 1877-1908; Edmund M. Dunne, 1909-29; Joseph H. Schlarman, 1930-51; William E. Cousins, 1952-58; John B. Franz, 1959-71.

Philadelphia,* Pa. (1808; archdiocese, 1875): Cardinal John Krol, archbishop, 1961. John J. Graham, Martin J. Lohmuller, Edward T. Hughes, Francis B. Schulte, Louis A. De Simone, auxiliaries.

Former ordinaries: Michael Egan, O.F.M., 1810-14; Henry Conwell, 1820-42; Francis P. Kenrick, 1842-51; John N. Neumann, C.SS.R., 1852-60; James F. Wood, 1860-83, first archbishop; Patrick J. Ryan, 1884-1911; Edmond F. Prendergast, 1911-18; Cardinal Dennis Dougherty, 1918-51; Cardinal John O'Hara, C.S.C., 1951-60.

Philadelphia,* Pa. (Byzantine Rite) (1924; metropolitan, 1958): Stephen Sulyk, archbishop, 1981. Robert Moskal, auxiliary.

Former ordinaries: Stephen Ortynsky, O.S.B.M., 1907-16; Constantine Bohachevsky, 1924-61; Ambrose Senyshyn, O.S.B.M., 1961-76; Joseph Schmondiuk, 1977-78; Myroslav J. Lubachivsky, 1979-80, apostolic administrator, 1980-81.

Phoenix, Ariz. (1969): Thomas J. O'Brien, bishop, 1982.

Former bishops: Edward A. McCarthy, 1969-76; James S. Rausch, 1977-81.

Pittsburgh,* Pa. (Byzantine Rite) (1924; metropolitan, 1969): Stephen J. Kocisko, eparch, 1968, first metropolitan, 1969. John M. Bilock, auxiliary.

Former ordinaries: Basil Takach 1924-48; Daniel Ivancho, 1948-54; Nicholas T. Elko, 1955-67.

Pittsburgh, Pa. (1843): Vacant as of Aug. 15, 1983. John B. McDowell, Anthony G. Bosco, auxiliaries.

Former bishops: Michael O'Connor, 1843-53, 1854-60; Michael Domenec, C.M., 1860-76; J. Tuigg, 1876-89; Richard Phelan, 1889-1904; J.F. Regis Canevin, 1904-20; Hugh C. Boyle, 1921-55; John F. Dearden, 1950-58; John J. Wright, 1959-69; Vincent M. Leonard, 1969-83.

Portland, Me. (1853): Edward C. O'Leary, bishop, 1974. Amedee W. Proulx, auxiliary.

Former bishops: David W. Bacon, 1855-74; James A. Healy, 1875-1900; William H. O'Connell, 1901-06; Louis S. Walsh, 1906-24; John G. Murray, 1925-31; Joseph E. McCarthy, 1932-55; Daniel J. Feeney, 1955-69; Peter L. Gerety, 1969-74.

Portland,* Ore. (1846): Cornelius M. Power, archbishop, 1974. Paul E. Waldschmidt, C.S.C., Kenneth D. Steiner, auxiliaries.

Established as Oregon City, name changed, 1928.

Former ordinaries: Francis N. Blanchet, 1846-80 vicar apostolic, first archbishop; Charles J. Seghers, 1880-84; William H. Gross, C.SS.R., 1885-98; Alexander Christie, 1899-1925; Edward D. Howard, 1926-66; Robert J. Dwyer, 1966-74.

Providence, R.I. (1872): Louis E. Gelineau, bishop, 1972. Kenneth A. Angell, auxiliary.

Former bishops: Thomas F. Hendricken, 1872-86; Matthew Harkins, 1887-1921; William A. Hickey, 1921-33; Francis P. Keough, 1934-47; Russell J. McVinney, 1948-71.

Pueblo, Colo. (1941): Arthur N. Tafoya, bishop, 1980.

Former bishops: Joseph C. Willging, 1942-59; Charles A. Buswell, 1959-79.

Raleigh, N.C. (1924): F. Joseph Gossman, bishop, 1975. George E. Lynch, auxiliary.

Former bishops: William J. Hafey, 1925-37; Eugene J. McGuinness, 1937-44; Vincent S. Waters, 1945-75.

Rapid City, S. Dak. (1902): Harold J. Dimmerling, bishop, 1969.

Established at Lead, transferred, 1930.

Former bishops: John Stariha, 1902-09; Joseph F. Busch, 1910-15; John J. Lawler, 1916-48; William T. McCarty, C.SS.R., 1948-69.

Reno-Las Vegas, Nev. (1931): Norman F. McFarland, bishop, 1976.

Established at Reno; title changed to Reno-Las Vegas, 1976.

Former bishops: Thomas K. Gorman, 1931-52; Robert J. Dwyer, 1952-66; Joseph Green, 1967-74.

Richmond, Va. (1820): Walter F. Sullivan, bishop, 1974.

Former bishops: Patrick Kelly, 1820-22; Richard V. Whelan, 1841-50; John McGill, 1850-72; James Gibbons, 1872-77; John J. Keane, 1878-88; Augustine Van de Vyver, 1889-1911; Denis J. O'Connell, 1912-26; Andrew J. Brennan, 1926-45; Peter L. Ireton, 1945-58; John J. Russell, 1958-73.

Rochester, N.Y. (1868): Matthew H. Clark, bishop, 1979. Dennis W. Hickey, auxiliary.

Former bishops: Bernard J. McQuaid, 1868-1909; Thomas F. Hickey, 1909-28; John F. O'Hern, 1929-33; Edward F. Mooney, 1933-37; James E. Kearney, 1937-66; Fulton J. Sheen, 1966-69; Joseph L. Hogan, 1969-78.

Rockford, Ill. (1908): Arthur J. O'Neill, bishop, 1968.

Former bishops: Peter J. Muldoon, 1908-27; Edward F. Hoban, 1928-42; John J. Boylan, 1943-53; Raymond P. Hillinger, 1953-56; Loras T. Lane, 1956-68.

Rockville Centre, N.Y. (1957): John R. McGann, bishop, 1976. Gerald Ryan, James Daly, auxiliaries.

Former bishop: Walter P. Kellenberg, 1957-76.

Sacramento, Calif. (1886): Francis A. Quinn, bishop, 1979. Alphonse Gallegos, O.A.R., auxiliary.

Former bishops: Patrick Manogue, 1886-95; Thomas Grace, 1896-1921; Patrick J. Keane, 1922-28; Robert J. Armstrong, 1929-57; Joseph T. McGucken, 1957-62; Alden J. Bell, 1962-79.

Saginaw, Mich. (1938): Kenneth E. Untener, bishop, 1980.

Former bishops: William F. Murphy, 1938-50; Stephen S. Woznicki, 1950-68; Francis F. Reh, 1969-80.

St. Augustine, Fla. (1870): John J. Snyder, bishop, 1979.

Former bishops: Augustin Verot, S.S., 1870-76; John Moore, 1877-1901; William J. Kenny, 1902-13; Michael J. Curley, 1914-21; Patrick J. Barry, 1922-40; Joseph P. Hurley, 1940-67; Paul F. Tanner, 1968-79.

St. Cloud, Minn. (1889): George H. Speltz, bishop, 1968.

Former bishops: Otto Zardetti, 1889-94; Martin Marty, O.S.B., 1895-96; James Trobec, 1897-1914; Joseph F. Busch, 1915-53; Peter Bartholome, 1953-68.

St. Louis,* Mo. (1826; archdiocese, 1847): John L. May, archbishop, 1980. George J. Gottwald, Charles R. Koester, auxiliaries.

Former ordinaries: Joseph Rosati, C.M., 1827-43; Peter R. Kenrick, 1843-95, first archbishop; John J. Kain, 1895-1903; Cardinal John Glennon, 1903-46; Cardinal Joseph Ritter, 1946-67; Cardinal John J. Carberry, 1968-79.

St. Maron, Brooklyn, N.Y. (Maronite Rite) (1966; diocese, 1971): Francis Zayek, (titular archbishop), exarch, 1966, first eparch, 1972. John Chedid, auxiliary.

Established at Detroit; transferred to Brooklyn, 1977.

St. Nicholas in Chicago (Byzantine Rite Eparchy of St. Nicholas of the Ukrainians) (1961): Innocent H. Lotocky, O.S.B.M., bishop, 1981.

Former bishop: Jaroslav Gabro, 1961-80.

St. Paul and Minneapolis,* Minn. (1850; archdiocese, 1888): John R. Roach, archbishop, 1975. William H. Bullock, J. Richard Ham, M.M., auxiliaries.

Former ordinaries: Joseph Cretin, 1851-57; Thomas L. Grace, O.P., 1859-84; John Ireland, 1884-1918, first archbishop; Austin Dowling, 1919-30; John G. Murray, 1931-56; William O. Brady, 1956-61; Leo Binz, 1962-75.

St. Petersburg, Fla. (1968): W. Thomas Larkin, bishop, 1979. J. Keith Symons, auxiliary.

Former bishop: Charles McLaughlin, 1968-78.

Salina, Kans. (1887): Daniel W. Kucera, O.S.B., bishop, 1980.

Established at Concordia, transferred, 1944.

Former bishops: Richard Scannell, 1887-91; John J. Hennessy, administrator, 1891-98; John F. Cunningham, 1898-1919; Francis J. Tief, 1921-38; Frank A. Thill, 1938-57; Frederick W. Freking, 1957-64; Cyril J. Vogel, 1965-79.

Salt Lake City, Utah (1891): William K. Weigand, bishop, 1980.

Former bishops: Lawrence Scanlan, 1891-1915; Joseph S. Glass, C.M., 1915-26; John J. Mitty, 1926-32; James E. Kearney, 1932-37; Duane G. Hunt, 1937-60; J. Lennox Federal, 1960-80.

San Angelo, Tex. (1961): Joseph A. Fiorenza, bishop, 1979.

Former bishops: Thomas J. Drury, 1962-65; Thomas Tschoepe, 1966-69; Stephen A. Leven, 1969-79.

San Antonio,* Tex. (1874; archdiocese, 1926): Patrick F. Flores, archbishop, 1979. Bernard Popp, auxiliary.

Former ordinaries: Anthony D. Pellicer, 1874-80; John C. Neraz, 1881-94; John A. Forest, 1895-1911; John W. Shaw, 1911-18; Arthur Jerome Drossaerts, 1918-40, first archbishop; Robert E. Lucey, 1941-69; Francis Furey, 1969-79.

San Bernardino, Calif. (1978): Phillip F. Straling, bishop, 1978.

San Diego, Calif. (1936): Leo T. Maher, bishop, 1969. Gilbert Espinoza Chavez, auxiliary.

Former bishops: Charles F. Buddy, 1936-66; Francis J. Furey, 1966-69.

San Francisco,* Calif. (1853): John R. Quinn, archbishop, 1977. Daniel F. Walsh, auxiliary.

Former ordinaries: Joseph S. Alemany, O.P.,

1853-84; Patrick W. Riordan, 1884-1914; Edward J. Hanna, 1915-35; John Mitty, 1935-61; Joseph T. McGucken, 1962-77.

San Jose, Calif. (1981): R. Pierre DuMaine, first bishop, 1981.

Santa Fe,* N. Mex. (1850; archdiocese, 1875): Robert Sanchez, archbishop, 1974.

Former ordinaries: John B. Lamy, 1850-85, first archbishop; John B. Salpointe, 1885-94; Placide L. Chapelle, 1894-97; Peter Bourgade, 1899-1908; John B. Pitaval, 1909-18; Albert T. Daeger, O.F.M., 1919-32; Rudolph A. Gerken, 1933-43; Edwin V. Byrne, 1943-63; James P. Davis, 1964-74.

Santa Rosa, Calif. (1962): Mark J. Hurley, bishop, 1969.

Former bishop: Leo T. Maher, 1962-69.

Savannah, Ga. (1850): Raymond W. Lessard, bishop, 1973.

Former bishops: Francis X. Gartland, 1850-54; John Barry, 1857-59; Augustin Verot, S.S., 1861-70; Ignatius Persico, O.F.M. Cap., 1870-72; William H. Gross, C.SS.R., 1873-85; Thomas A. Becker, 1886-99; Benjamin J. Keiley, 1900-22; Michael Keyes, S.M., 1922-35; Gerald P. O'Hara, 1935-59; Thomas J. McDonough, 1960-67; Gerard L. Frey, 1967-72.

Scranton, Pa. (1868): John J. O'Connor, bishop, 1983. James C. Timlin, auxiliary.

Former bishops: William O'Hara, 1868-99; Michael J. Hoban, 1899-1926; Thomas C. O'Reilly, 1928-38; William J. Hafey, 1938-54; Jerome D. Hannan, 1954-65; J. Carroll McCormick, 1966-83.

Seattle,* Wash. (1850; archdiocese, 1951): Raymond G. Hunthausen, archbishop, 1975. Nicholas E. Walsh, auxiliary.

Established as Nesqually, name changed, 1907.

Former ordinaries; Augustin M. Blanchet, 1850-79; Aegidius Junger, 1879-95; Edward J. O'Dea, 1896-1932; Gerald Shaughnessy, S.M., 1933-50; Thomas A. Connolly, first archbishop, 1950-75.

Sioux City, Ia. (1902): Lawrence D. Soens, bishop, 1983.

Former bishops: Philip J. Garrigan, 1902-19; Edmond Heelan, 1919-48; Joseph M. Mueller, 1948-70; Frank H. Greteman, 1970-83.

Sioux Falls, S. Dak. (1889): Paul V. Dudley, bishop, 1978. Paul F. Anderson, auxiliary.

Former bishops: Martin Marty, O.S.B., 1889-94; Thomas O'Gorman, 1896-1921; Bernard J. Mahoney, 1922-39; William O. Brady, 1939-56; Lambert A. Hoch, 1956-78.

Spokane, Wash. (1913): Lawrence H. Welsh, bishop, 1978.

Former bishops: Augustine F. Schinner, 1914-25; Charles D. White, 1927-55; Bernard J. Topel, 1955-78.

Springfield, Ill. (1853): Vacant as of Aug. 15, 1983.

Established at Quincy, transferred to Alton 1857; transferred to Springfield 1923.

Former bishops: Henry D. Juncker, 1857-68; Peter J. Baltes, 1870-86; James Ryan, 1888-1923; James A. Griffin, 1924-48; William A. O'Connor, 1949-75; Joseph A. McNicholas, 1975-83.

Springfield, Mass. (1870): Joseph F. Maguire, bishop, 1977. Leo E. O'Neil, auxiliary.

Former bishops: Patrick T. O'Reilly, 1870-92; Thomas D. Beaven, 1892-1920; Thomas M. O'Leary, 1921-49; Christopher J. Weldon, 1950-77.

Springfield-Cape Girardeau, Mo. (1956): Bernard F. Law, bishop, 1973.

Former bishops: Charles Helmsing, 1956-62; Ignatius J. Strecker, 1962-69; William Baum, 1970-73.

Stamford, Conn. (Byzantine Rite) (1956); Basil Losten, eparch, 1977.

Former eparchs: Ambrose Senyshyn, O.S.B.M., 1956-61; Joseph Schmondiuk, 1961-77.

Steubenville, Ohio (1944): Albert H. Ottenweller, bishop, 1977.

Former bishop: John K. Mussio, 1945-77.

Stockton, Calif. (1962): Roger M. Mahony, bishop, 1980.

Former bishops: Hugh A. Donohoe, 1962-69; Merlin J. Guilfoyle, 1969-79.

Superior, Wis. (1905): George A. Hammes, bishop, 1960. Raphael M. Fliss, coadjutor.

Former bishops: Augustine F. Schinner, 1905-13; Joseph M. Koudelka, 1913-21; Joseph G. Pinten, 1922-26; Theodore M. Reverman, 1926-41; William P. O'Connor, 1942-46; Albert G. Meyer, 1946-53; Joseph Annabring, 1954-59.

Syracuse, N.Y. (1886): Francis J. Harrison, bishop, 1976. Thomas J. Costello, auxiliary.

Former bishops: Patrick A. Ludden, 1887-1912; John Grimes, 1912-22; Daniel J. Curley, 1923-32; John A. Duffy, 1933-37; Walter A. Foery, 1937-70; David F. Cunningham, 1970-76.

Toledo, Ohio (1910): James R. Hoffman, bishop, 1980.

Former bishops: Joseph Schrembs, 1911-21; Samuel A. Stritch, 1921-30; Karl J. Alter, 1931-50; George J. Rehring, 1950-67; John A. Donovan, 1967-80.

Trenton, N.J. (1881): John C. Reiss, bishop, 1980. Edward U. Kmiec, auxiliary.

Former bishops: Michael J. O'Farrell, 1881-94; James A. McFaul, 1894-1917; Thomas J. Walsh, 1918-28; John J. McMahon, 1928-32; Moses E. Kiley, 1934-40; William A. Griffin, 1940-50; George W. Ahr, 1950-79.

Tucson, Ariz. (1897): Manuel D. Moreno, bishop, 1982.

Former bishops: Peter Bourgade, 1897-99; Henry Granjon, 1900-22; Daniel J. Gercke, 1923-60; Francis J. Green, 1960-81.

Tulsa, Okla. (1972): Eusebius J. Beltran, bishop, 1978.

Former bishop: Bernard J. Ganter, 1973-77.

Van Nuys, Calif. (Byzantine Rite) (1981): Thomas Dolinay, bishop, 1982.

Victoria, Tex. (1982): Charles Grahmann, bishop, 1982.

Washington,* D.C. (1939): James A. Hickey, archbishop, 1980. Thomas W. Lyons, Eugene A. Marino, S.S.J., auxiliaries.

Former ordinaries: Michael J. Curley, 1939-47; Cardinal Patrick O'Boyle, 1948-73; Cardinal William Baum, 1973-80.

Wheeling-Charleston, W. Va. (1850): Joseph H.

Hodges, bishop, 1962. James E. Michaels, S.S.C., auxiliary.
Established as Wheeling; name changed, 1974.
Former bishops: Richard V. Whelan, 1850-74; John J. Kain, 1875-93; Patrick J. Donahue, 1894-1922; John J. Swint, 1922-62.
Wichita, Kans. (1887): Eugene J. Gerber, bishop, 1982.
Former bishops: John J. Hennessy, 1888-1920; Augustus J. Schwertner, 1921-39; Christian H. Winkelmann, 1940-46; Mark K. Carroll, 1947-67; David M. Maloney, 1967-82.
Wilmington, Del. (1868): Thomas J. Mardaga, bishop, 1968.
Former bishops: Thomas A. Becker, 1868-86; Alfred A. Curtis, 1886-96; John J. Monaghan, 1897-1925; Edmond Fitzmaurice, 1925-60; Michael Hyle, 1960-67.
Winona, Minn. (1889): Loras J. Watters, bishop, 1969.
Former bishops: Joseph B. Cotter, 1889-1909; Patrick R. Heffron, 1910-27; Francis M. Kelly, 1928-49; Edward A. Fitzgerald, 1949-69.
Worcester, Mass. (1950): Vacant as of Aug. 15, 1983. Timothy J. Harrington, auxiliary.
Former bishops: John J. Wright, 1950-59; Bernard J. Flanagan, 1959-83.
Yakima, Wash. (1951): William Skylstad, bishop, 1977.
Former bishops: Joseph P. Dougherty, 1951-69; Cornelius M. Power, 1969-74; Nicholas E. Walsh, 1974-76.
Youngstown, Ohio (1943): James W. Malone, bishop, 1968. Benedict C. Franzetta, auxiliary.
Former bishops: James A. McFadden, 1943-52; Emmet M. Walsh, 1952-68.

Apostolic Exarchate for Armenian-Rite Catholics in the United States and Canada, New York, N.Y. (1981); Nerses Mikail Setian, exarch, 1981.
Apostolic Exarchate for Chaldean-Rite Catholics in the United States, Detroit, Mich. (1982): Ibrahim Ibrahim, exarch, 1982.
Apostolic Exarchate for Romanians of Byzantine Rite in the United States, Canton, O. (1982): Louis Puscas, exarch, 1983.
Military Ordinariate (1917): Cardinal Terence J. Cooke, military vicar, 1968. Joseph T. Ryan, coadjutor archbishop, 1975. Lawrence Kenney, Francis Roque, Joseph T. Dimino, military delegates.
Former military vicars: Cardinal Patrick Hayes, 1917-38; Cardinal Francis Spellman, 1939-67.

Military Ordinariate

The Military Ordinariate or Vicariate, is the diocese which serves members of the armed forces of the United States wherever they serve. It has jurisdiction over: military and Veterans Administration hospital chaplains; personnel of the armed forces and members of their families and dependents habitually living with them; members of the Coast Guard, National Guard, Air National Guard and Civil Air Patrol when on active duty; persons living on military installations and/or attached to military offices or VA facilities.
The ordinariate was canonically established on a permanent basis by a decree of the Sacred Consistorial Congregation dated Sept. 8, 1957. Cardinal Terence J. Cooke, Archbishop of New York, is Military Vicar. Offices of the ordinariate are located at 1011 First Ave., New York, N.Y. 10022.

MISSIONARY BISHOPS

Africa

Namibia (South West Africa): Keetmanshoop (vicariate apostolic), Edward F. Schlotterback, O.S.F.S.
Nigeria: Sokoto (diocese), Michael J. Dempsey, O.P.
South Africa: De Aar (diocese), Joseph A. De Palma, S.C.J.
Keimos (diocese), John Minder, O.S.F.S.
Tanzania: Arusha (diocese), Dennis V. Durning, C.S.Sp.
Nachingwea (diocese), 'Arnold R. Cotey, S.D.S.

Asia

China: Chowtsun (diocese), Henry A. Pinger, O.F.M. Expelled.
Wuchow (diocese), Frederick A. Donaghy, M.M. Expelled.
India: Bhagalpur (diocese), Urban McGarry, T.O.R.
Indonesia: Agats (diocese), Alphonse A. Sowada, O.S.C.
Iraq: Mossul (Chaldean-rite archdiocese), George Garmo.
Korea: Inchon (diocese), William J. McNaughton, M.M.

Pakistan: Multan (diocese), Ernest B. Boland, O.P.
Philippine Islands: Cotabato (archdiocese), Philip F. Smith, O.M.I.
Jolo (vicariate apostolic), Georges Dion, O.M.I.
Taiwan: Taichung (diocese), William F. Kupfer, M.M.

Central America, West Indies

Belize: Belize (diocese), Robert L. Hodapp, S.J.
Dominican Republic: San Juan de la Maguana (diocese), Ronald G. Connors, C.SS.R.,
Honduras: Comayagua (diocese), Gerald Scarpone, O.F.M.
Nicaragua: Bluefields (vicariate apostolic), Salvator Schlaefer, O.F.M.Cap.
Virgin Islands: St. Thomas (diocese), Edward Harper, C.SS.R.

North America

Mexico: Mexico City (archdiocese), Ricardo Watty Urquidi, M.Sp.S., auxiliary.

Oceania

Caroline and Marshall Islands (diocese), Martin J. Neylon, S.J.

Papua New Guinea: Goroko (diocese), Raymond R. Caesar, S.V.D.
Madang (archdiocese), Leo Arkfeld, S.V.D.
Mendi (diocese), Firmin Schmidt, O.F.M.Cap.
Mount Hagen (archdiocese), George Bernarding, S.V.D.
Wewak (diocese), Raymond P. Kalisz, S.V.D.
Vanuatu (New Hebrides): Port Vila (diocese), Francis Lambert, S.M.

South America

Bolivia: Coroico (diocese), Thomas R. Manning, O.F.M.
La Paz (archdiocese), Andrew B. Schierhoff, auxiliary.
Santa Cruz (archdiocese), Charles A. Brown, M.M., auxiliary.

Brazil: Abaetetuba (diocese), Angelo Frosi, S.X.
Belem do Para (archdiocese), Jude Prost, O.F.M., auxiliary.
Borba (prelacy), Adrian J. M. Veigle, T.O.R.
Cristalandia (prelacy), James A. Schuck, O.F.M.
Jatai (diocese), Benedict D. Coscia, O.F.M. Michael P. Mundo, auxiliary.
Paranagua (diocese), Bernard Nolker, C.SS.R.
Rui Barbosa (diocese), Mathias Schmidt, O.S.B.
Santarem (diocese), James C. Ryan, O.F.M.
Sao Paulo (archdiocese), Alfred Novak, C.SS.R., auxiliary.
Sao Salvador da Bahia (archdiocese), Thomas W. Murphy, C.SS.R., auxiliary.
Peru: Chulucanas (prelacy), John McNabb, O.S.A.

CATHOLIC POPULATION OF THE UNITED STATES

(Source: *The Official Catholic Directory, 1983;* figures as of Jan. 1, 1983. Archdioceses are indicated by an asterisk; for dioceses marked +, see Dioceses with Interstate Lines.)

Section, State Diocese	Catholics	Dioc. Priests	Rel. Priests	Total Priests	Perm. Deacons	Bros.	Sisters	Par- ishes
NEW ENGLAND	5,672,727	4,065	2,561	6,626	594	693	13,003	1,703
Maine, Portland	331,537	219	117	336	1	36	816	144
New Hampshire, Manchester	294,384	290	112	402	1	63	1,124	130
Vermont, Burlington	148,713	161	70	231	19	27	375	100
Massachusetts	2,949,377	2,013	1,765	3,778	215	376	6,946	784
*Boston	1,925,042	1,175	1,224	2,399	126	197	4,542	408
Fall River	340,000	229	201	430	25	38	726	112
Springfield	351,585	261	138	399	19	24	920	136
Worcester	332,750	348	202	550	45	117	758	128
Rhode Island, Providence	623,694	394	200	594	80	158	1,258	159
Connecticut	1,325,022	988	297	1,285	278	33	2,484	386
*Hartford	790,795	587	105	692	213	—	1,492	222
Bridgeport	334,366	254	112	366	37	8	655	88
Norwich+	199,861	147	80	227	28	25	337	76
MIDDLE ATLANTIC	13,326,271	9,449	5,533	14,982	1,259	1,802	32,685	3,905
New York	6,674,424	4,352	3,065	7,417	582	1,093	14,972	1,713
*New York	1,839,000	982	1,547	2,529	208	436	5,178	411
Albany	408,648	401	222	623	60	93	1,250	201
Brooklyn	1,380,957	923	471	1,394	82	255	2,218	221
Buffalo	811,950	589	382	971	59	81	2,313	295
Ogdensburg	169,534	194	39	233	16	34	351	122
Rochester	376,475	380	139	519	24	54	921	163
Rockville Centre	1,287,860	490	152	642	91	109	1,993	129
Syracuse	400,000	393	113	506	42	31	748	171
New Jersey	2,969,795	1,915	920	2,835	552	343	4,885	696
*Newark	1,368,400	831	443	1,274	237	167	2,521	247
Camden	354,250	372	42	414	67	19	—	127
Metuchen	409,398	141	70	211	59	24	600	96
Paterson	359,829	296	247	543	79	50	1,107	106
Trenton	447,918	275	118	393	110	83	657	120
Pennsylvania	3,682,052	3,182	1,548	4,730	125	366	12,828	1,496
*Philadelphia	1,359,005	967	649	1,616	24	222	5,482	305
Allentown	262,714	309	109	418	33	18	872	153
Altoona-Johnstown	149,093	180	99	279	1	29	270	122
Erie	234,791	273	54	327	1	8	709	128
Greensburg	223,084	196	121	317	—	11	448	117
Harrisburg	193,710	175	85	260	39	15	822	110
Pittsburgh	911,421	620	308	928	27	54	3,069	321
Scranton	348,234	462	123	585	—	9	1,156	240

Section, State Diocese	Catholics	Dioc. Priests	Rel. Priests	Total Priests	Perm. Deacons	Bros.	Sisters	Par- ishes
SOUTH ATLANTIC	**3,251,143**	**2,288**	**2,075**	**4,363**	**473**	**560**	**6,591**	**1,308**
Delaware, Wilmington+	125,369	122	108	230	21	38	443	55
Maryland, *Baltimore	431,693	335	399	734	113	105	1,737	152
District of Columbia								
*Washington+	393,517	356	650	1,006	114	174	1,018	130
Virginia	307,895	245	148	393	49	29	563	163
Arlington	188,000	82	106	188	47	23	226	56
Richmond	119,895	163	42	205	2	6	337	107
West Virginia								
Wheeling-Charleston	106,502	130	78	208	15	8	435	126
North Carolina	110,217	130	96	226	2	16	321	124
Charlotte	59,537	64	67	131	—	11	211	64
Raleigh	50,680	66	29	95	2	5	110	60
South Carolina, Charleston	67,138	83	55	138	22	28	243	79
Georgia	173,793	163	136	299	34	39	399	102
*Atlanta	117,562	95	97	192	17	29	180	57
Savannah	56,231	68	39	107	17	10	219	45
Florida	1,535,019	724	405	1,129	103	123	1,432	377
*Miami	896,702	397	214	581	45	63	643	135
Orlando	196,000	106	34	140	—	1	174	68
Pensacola-Tallahassee	45,408	60	14	74	42	—	71	38
St. Augustine	73,462	66	30	96	3	7	109	45
St. Petersburg	323,447	125	113	238	13	52	435	91
EAST NORTH CENTRAL	**10,390,578**	**7,765**	**4,658**	**12,423**	**1,324**	**1,868**	**29,453**	**4,199**
Ohio	2,246,743	2,013	956	2,969	271	501	7,108	970
*Cincinnati	489,000	460	417	877	65	247	1,943	256
Cleveland	865,190	646	273	919	48	162	2,407	246
Columbus	199,058	222	71	293	31	12	654	108
Steubenville	53,913	146	14	160	1	9	127	77
Toledo	347,724	277	126	403	107	26	1,512	166
Youngstown	291,858	262	55	317	19	45	465	117
Indiana	710,290	727	574	1,301	64	297	2,966	451
*Indianapolis	201,353	218	182	400	—	80	1,086	142
Evansville	89,973	129	22	151	16	3	422	74
Ft. Wayne-South Bend	137,387	124	234	358	16	180	1,033	89
Gary	194,657	144	78	222	26	25	294	83
Lafayette	86,920	112	58	170	6	9	131	63
Illinois	3,571,708	2,230	1,758	3,988	618	701	8,701	1,101
*Chicago	2,365,843	1,231	1,230	2,461	434	309	4,939	443
Belleville	122,381	176	48	224	25	11	542	130
Joliet	411,000	213	171	384	54	319	1,055	113
Peoria	245,848	252	111	363	36	16	632	169
Rockford	237,542	174	91	265	69	15	593	102
Springfield	189,094	184	107	291	—	31	940	144
Michigan	2,261,571	1,309	611	1,920	206	130	4,643	806
*Detroit	1,446,043	607	412	1,019	123	100	2,531	331
Gaylord	89,596	59	21	80	2	4	150	59
Grand Rapids	155,574	157	42	199	16	2	601	91
Kalamazoo	96,461	59	31	90	19	8	283	47
Lansing	219,309	157	56	213	21	14	744	85
Marquette	86,968	123	23	146	1	—	136	88
Saginaw	167,620	147	26	173	24	2	198	105
Wisconsin	1,600,266	1,486	759	2,245	165	239	6,035	871
*Milwaukee	706,170	628	478	1,106	105	154	3,507	268
Green Bay	347,277	285	187	472	60	56	1,113	211
La Crosse	231,965	261	33	294	—	14	553	167
Madison	223,302	213	39	252	—	13	634	138
Superior	91,552	99	22	121	—	2	228	87
EAST SOUTH CENTRAL	**705,035**	**966**	**417**	**1,383**	**198**	**307**	**3,869**	**663**
Kentucky	365,625	521	152	673	74	138	2,700	288
*Louisville	208,306	256	105	361	74	110	1,634	131

Section, State Diocese	Catholics	Dioc. Priests	Rel. Priests	Total Priests	Perm. Deacons	Bros.	Sisters	Par- ishes
Kentucky								
Covington	105,500	188	24	212	—	17	782	85
Owensboro	51,819	77	23	100	—	11	284	72
Tennessee	**126,188**	**145**	**59**	**204**	**73**	**74**	**334**	**123**
Memphis	50,597	69	24	93	34	54	161	44
Nashville	75,591	76	35	111	39	20	173	79
Alabama	**117,946**	**153**	**129**	**282**	**33**	**27**	**459**	**135**
*Mobile	61,788	87	67	154	14	23	276	76
Birmingham	56,158	66	62	128	19	4	183	59
Mississippi	**95,276**	**147**	**77**	**224**	**18**	**68**	**376**	**117**
Biloxi	53,700	68	33	101	6	49	91	44
Jackson	41,576	79	44	123	12	19	285	73
WEST NORTH CENTRAL	**3,424,307**	**4,003**	**1,937**	**5,940**	**461**	**715**	**15,090**	**2,764**
Minnesota	**1,057,908**	**992**	**440**	**1,432**	**102**	**188**	**4,173**	**697**
*St. Paul and Minneapolis	577,923	408	194	602	76	83	1,829	219
Crookston	42,600	51	22	73	—	1	303	46
Duluth	90,213	94	32	126	9	1	320	79
New Ulm	71,977	106	5	111	2	—	159	93
St. Cloud	153,844	160	170	330	15	70	849	136
Winona	121,351	173	17	190	—	33	713	124
Iowa	**556,195**	**858**	**125**	**983**	**91**	**56**	**2,264**	**538**
*Dubuque	245,366	348	80	428	36	35	1,352	198
Davenport	110,900	190	20	210	18	19	423	117
Des Moines	88,348	120	10	130	18	1	202	83
Sioux City	111,581	200	15	215	19	1	287	140
Missouri	**817,019**	**948**	**772**	**1,720**	**158**	**360**	**4,452**	**506**
*St. Louis	535,230	566	511	1,077	55	217	3,426	249
Jefferson City	86,536	134	19	153	44	12	168	94
Kansas City-St. Joseph	147,638	166	167	333	59	56	650	100
Springfield-Cape Girardeau	47,615	82	75	157	—	75	208	63
North Dakota	**178,263**	**215**	**99**	**314**	**27**	**24**	**486**	**184**
Bismarck	79,032	75	63	138	11	20	167	73
Fargo	99,231	140	36	176	16	4	319	111
South Dakota	**135,623**	**174**	**110**	**284**	**11**	**20**	**690**	**204**
Rapid City	35,824	40	46	86	11	—	127	82
Sioux Falls	99,799	134	64	198	—	20	563	122
Nebraska	**331,953**	**421**	**214**	**635**	**72**	**39**	**948**	**275**
*Omaha	209,264	215	188	403	72	25	680	139
Grand Island	52,393	87	2	89	—	—	125	50
Lincoln	70,296	119	24	143	—	14	143	86
Kansas	**347,346**	**395**	**177**	**572**	**—**	**28**	**2,077**	**360**
*Kansas City	147,045	125	103	228	—	25	1,071	122
Dodge City	39,354	59	11	70	—	—	177	46
Salina	61,049	79	35	114	—	2	354	98
Wichita	99,898	132	28	160	—	1	475	94
WEST SOUTH CENTRAL	**4,296,566**	**2,085**	**1,696**	**3,781**	**829**	**613**	**6,843**	**1,595**
Arkansas, Little Rock	**62,052**	**103**	**70**	**173**	**27**	**60**	**525**	**88**
Louisiana	**1,338,909**	**700**	**549**	**1,249**	**188**	**280**	**2,002**	**483**
*New Orleans	529,127	242	315	557	80	205	1,202	139
Alexandria-Shreveport	83,283	115	40	155	3	10	208	83
Baton Rouge	183,625	87	78	165	21	18	183	70
Houma-Thibodaux	127,682	52	11	63	26	10	65	36
Lafayette	325,088	162	74	236	40	33	296	120
Lake Charles	90,104	42	31	73	18	4	48	35
Oklahoma	**136,961**	**173**	**71**	**244**	**35**	**24**	**473**	**126**
*Oklahoma City	81,698	111	30	141	16	14	242	71
Tulsa	55,263	62	41	103	19	10	231	55
Texas	**2,758,644**	**1,109**	**1,006**	**2,115**	**579**	**249**	**3,843**	**898**
*San Antonio	487,477	159	220	379	105	121	1,273	132
Amarillo	84,372	70	28	98	50	2	152	66
Austin	135,120	94	57	151	6	35	160	84

Section, State Diocese	Catholics	Dioc. Priests	Rel. Priests	Total Priests	Perm. Deacons	Bros.	Sisters	Par- ishes
Texas								
Beaumont	93,000	53	31	84	6	—	117	43
Brownsville	409,373	49	76	125	23	11	170	61
Corpus Christi	314,812	88	87	175	18	22	356	77
Dallas	190,639	113	94	207	112	3	300	64
El Paso	179,560	100	49	149	35	14	300	50
Fort Worth	99,349	68	61	129	23	14	153	81
Galveston-Houston	592,346	206	247	453	135	26	633	140
Lubbock	No separate statistics available.							
San Angelo	75,420	56	39	95	63	—	55	53
Victoria	97,176	53	17	70	3	1	174	47
MOUNTAIN	**1,921,523**	**1,213**	**820**	**2,033**	**377**	**257**	**3,039**	**848**
Montana	**131,117**	**205**	**45**	**250**	**8**	**12**	**253**	**136**
Great Falls-Billings	66,092	85	30	115	1	6	173	74
Helena	65,025	120	15	135	7	6	80	62
Idaho, Boise	**76,443**	**91**	**25**	**116**	**18**	**4**	**198**	**71**
Wyoming, Cheyenne+	**60,000**	**59**	**9**	**68**	**3**	**5**	**76**	**39**
Colorado	**439,574**	**301**	**264**	**565**	**82**	**59**	**1,107**	**193**
*Denver	328,507	205	212	417	77	43	906	134
Pueblo	111,067	96	52	148	5	16	201	59
New Mexico	**461,812**	**239**	**183**	**422**	**91**	**109**	**722**	**188**
*Santa Fe	300,677	148	103	251	60	86	465	87
Gallup+	43,320	54	46	100	11	20	183	58
Las Cruces	117,815	37	34	71	20	3	74	43
Arizona	**546,820**	**208**	**186**	**394**	**143**	**40**	**439**	**135**
Phoenix	273,267	116	118	234	73	29	285	78
Tucson	273,553	92	68	160	70	11	154	57
Utah, Salt Lake City	**61,757**	**58**	**60**	**118**	**31**	**18**	**121**	**43**
Nevada, Reno-Las Vegas	**144,000**	**52**	**48**	**100**	**1**	**10**	**123**	**43**
PACIFIC	**6,410,750**	**2,966**	**2,702**	**5,668**	**520**	**830**	**9,673**	**1,544**
Washington	**423,417**	**381**	**334**	**715**	**115**	**45**	**1,296**	**228**
*Seattle	287,367	225	210	435	88	38	793	130
Spokane	78,150	96	111	207	25	7	444	58
Yakima	57,900	60	13	73	2	—	59	40
Oregon	**328,156**	**233**	**249**	**482**	**5**	**75**	**895**	**155**
*Portland	300,857	187	240	427	4	74	810	126
Baker	27,299	46	9	55	1	1	85	29
California	**5,399,937**	**2,261**	**1,969**	**4,230**	**347**	**642**	**7,027**	**1,041**
*Los Angeles	2,370,000	612	685	1,297	129	161	2,866	283
*San Francisco	365,762	304	322	626	15	59	1,038	104
Fresno	320,000	124	58	182	2	12	190	86
Monterey	130,000	85	45	130	—	28	181	43
Oakland	403,473	156	242	398	47	165	610	87
Orange	408,200	130	86	216	29	15	450	51
Sacramento	257,350	187	76	263	17	51	310	93
San Bernardino	281,302	192	85	277	30	16	201	86
San Diego	333,857	227	92	319	47	25	492	90
San Jose	307,338	113	224	337	20	60	504	47
Santa Rosa	95,468	83	22	105	2	43	111	40
Stockton	127,187	48	32	80	9	7	74	31
Alaska	**44,240**	**41**	**62**	**103**	*44	**14**	**100**	**56**
*Anchorage	23,737	21	19	40	10	7	40	18
Fairbanks	14,775	6	41	47	27	7	42	29
Juneau	5,728	14	2	16	7	—	18	9
Hawaii, Honolulu	**215,000**	**50**	**88**	**138**	**9**	**54**	**355**	**64**
EASTERN RITES	**564,844**	**556**	**115**	**671**	**31**	**13**	**453**	**510**
*Philadelphia	167,612	112	13	125	1	—	203	111
St. Nicholas	19,121	38	7	45	3	—	10	32
Stamford	46,000	58	20	78	2	3	49	48
*Pittsburgh	152,100	85	10	95	—	5	136	87
Parma	24,659	48	12	60	1	—	25	41

Section, State Diocese	Catholics	Dioc. Priests	Rel. Priests	Total Priests	Perm. Deacons	Bros.	Sisters	Par- ishes
Eastern Rites								
Passaic	96,558	95	22	117	5	1	25	90
Van Nuys	5,299	15	2	17	5	—	2	14
St. Maron	30,588	66	1	67	—	—	—	50
Newton	22,907	39	28	67	14	4	3	37
Romanians (Ap. Ex.)	No separate statistics available							
Chaldeans (Ap. Ex.)	No separate statistics available							
Armenians (Ap. Ex.)	No separate statistics available							
MILITARY ORDINARIATE	**2,125,000**	—	—	—	—	—	—	—
TOTALS 1983	**52,088,744**	**35,356**	**22,514**	**57,870**	**6,066**	**7,658**	**120,699**	**19,039**
Totals 1982	**51,207,579**	**35,513**	**22,572**	**58,085**	**5,471**	**7,880**	**121,370**	**18,903**
Totals 1973	**48,460,427**	**36,223**	**20,746**	**56,969**	—	**9,201**	**143,054**	**18,384**

Dioceses with Interstate Lines

Diocesan lines usually fall within a single state and in some cases include a whole state.

The following dioceses, with their statistics as reported in tables throughout the Almanac, are exceptions.

Norwich, Conn., includes Fisher's Island, N.Y.

Wilmington, Del., includes all of Delaware and nine counties of Maryland.

Baltimore, includes all of Maryland except nine counties under the jurisdiction of Wilmington and five under Washington.

Washington, D.C., includes five counties of Maryland.

Gallup, N.M., has jurisdiction over several counties of Arizona.

Cheyenne, Wyo., includes all of Yellowstone National Park.

PERCENTAGE OF CATHOLICS IN U.S. POPULATION

(Source: *The Official Catholic Directory, 1983;* figures are as of Jan. 1, 1983. Total general population figures at the end of the table are U.S. Census Bureau estimates for Jan. 1 of the respective years. Archdioceses are indicated by an asterisk; for dioceses marked +, see Dioceses with Interstate Lines.)

Section, State Diocese	Catholic Pop.	Total Pop.	Cath. Pct.	Section, State Diocese	Catholic Pop.	Total Pop.	Cath. Pct.
NEW ENGLAND	**5,672,727**	**11,500,987**	**49.32**	New Jersey			
				Camden	354,250	1,145,494	30.93
Maine, Portland	331,537	1,025,030	32.34	Metuchen	409,398	970,812	42.17
New Hampshire				Paterson	359,829	971,370	37.04
Manchester	294,384	920,610	31.98	Trenton	447,918	1,519,616	31.45
Vermont, Burlington	148,713	517,000	28.76	Pennsylvania	3,682,052	11,815,045	31.16
Massachusetts	2,949,377	4,977,383	59.26	*Philadelphia	1,359,005	3,662,506	37.11
*Boston	1,925,042	3,012,690	63.90	Allentown	262,714	1,027,302	25.57
Fall River	340,000	530,000	64.15	Altoona-Johnstown	149,093	654,338	22.79
Springfield	351,585	790,725	44.47	Erie	234,791	892,564	26.31
Worcester	332,750	643,968	51.67	Greensburg	223,084	718,242	31.06
Rhode Island, Providence	623,694	947,154	65.84	Harrisburg	193,710	1,723,961	11.24
Connecticut	1,325,022	3,113,810	42.56	Pittsburgh	911,421	2,165,361	42.09
*Hartford	790,795	1,725,892	45.82	Scranton	348,234	970,771	35.87
Bridgeport	334,366	812,000	41.18				
Norwich+	199,861	575,918	34.70	**SOUTH ATLANTIC**	**3,251,143**	**37,694,825**	**8.62**
				Delaware, Wilmington+	125,369	890,608	14.08
MIDDLE ATLANTIC	**13,326,271**	**37,154,968**	**35.87**	Maryland, *Baltimore	431,693	2,508,418	17.21
				District of Columbia			
New York	6,674,424	17,975,064	37.13	*Washington+	393,517	2,098,200	18.75
*New York	1,839,000	5,124,853	35.89	Virginia	307,895	5,643,617	5.46
Albany	408,648	1,472,684	27.75	Arlington	188,000	1,472,000	12.77
Brooklyn	1,380,957	4,122,261	33.50	Richmond	119,895	4,171,617	2.87
Buffalo	811,950	1,636,300	49.62	West Virginia			
Ogdensburg	169,534	395,873	42.83	Wheeling-Charleston	106,502	1,949,644	5.46
Rochester	376,475	1,419,843	26.52	North Carolina	110,217	5,867,054	1.88
Rockville Centre	1,287,860	2,595,597	49.62	Charlotte	59,537	3,101,207	1.92
Syracuse	400,000	1,207,653	33.12	Raleigh	50,680	2,765,847	1.83
New Jersey	2,969,795	7,364,859	40.32	South Carolina			
*Newark	1,368,400	2,757,567	49.62	Charleston	67,138	3,167,000	2.12

Section, State Diocese	Catholic Pop.	Total Pop.	Cath. Pct.
Georgia	173,793	5,599,833	3.10
*Atlanta	117,562	3,675,283	3.20
Savannah	56,231	1,924,550	2.92
Florida	1,535,019	9,970,451	15.40
*Miami	896,702	3,450,641	25.99
Orlando	196,000	2,173,000	9.02
Pensacola-Tallahassee	45,408	862,237	5.27
St. Augustine	73,462	1,088,000	6.75
St. Petersburg	323,447	2,396,573	13.50
EAST NORTH CENTRAL	**10,390,578**	**41,609,997**	**24.98**
Ohio	2,246,743	10,844,164	20.72
*Cincinnati	489,000	2,770,516	17.65
Cleveland	865,190	2,841,792	30.45
Columbus	199,058	1,940,333	10.26
Steubenville	53,913	541,093	9.96
Toledo	347,724	1,486,614	23.40
Youngstown	291,858	1,263,816	23.09
Indiana	710,290	5,476,673	12.97
*Indianapolis	201,353	2,127,915	9.46
Evansville	89,973	466,821	19.27
Ft. Wayne-S. Bend	137,387	1,044,602	13.15
Gary	194,657	772,235	25.21
Lafayette	86,920	1,065,100	8.16
Illinois	3,571,708	11,418,485	31.28
*Chicago	2,365,843	5,693,562	41.56
Belleville	122,381	861,986	14.20
Joliet	411,000	1,200,000	34.25
Peoria	245,848	1,501,917	16.37
Rockford	237,542	1,027,342	23.12
Springfield	189,094	1,133,678	16.68
Michigan	2,261,571	9,151,920	24.71
*Detroit	1,446,043	4,362,312	33.15
Gaylord	89,596	391,840	22.87
Grand Rapids	155,574	906,483	17.16
Kalamazoo	96,461	863,911	11.17
Lansing	219,309	1,593,926	13.76
Marquette	86,968	320,028	27.18
Saginaw	167,620	713,420	23.50
Wisconsin	1,600,266	4,718,755	33.91
*Milwaukee	706,170	2,029,553	34.79
Green Bay	347,277	736,053	47.18
La Crosse	231,965	751,203	30.88
Madison	223,302	893,208	25.00
Superior	91,552	308,738	29.65
EAST SOUTH CENTRAL	**705,035**	**14,850,170**	**4.75**
Kentucky	365,625	3,657,669	9.10
*Louisville	208,306	1,301,024	16.01
Covington	105,500	1,591,000	6.63
Owensboro	51,819	765,645	6.77
Tennessee	126,188	4,778,469	2.64
Memphis	50,597	1,500,000	3.37
Nashville	75,591	3,278,469	2.31
Alabama	117,946	3,872,670	3.05
*Mobile	61,788	1,422,835	4.34
Birmingham	56,158	2,449,835	2.30
Mississippi	95,276	2,541,362	3.75
Biloxi	53,700	631,362	8.51
Jackson	41,576	1,910,000	2.18

Section, State Diocese	Catholic Pop.	Total Pop.	Cath. Pct.
WEST NORTH CENTRAL	**3,424,307**	**17,080,510**	**20.05**
Minnesota	1,057,908	4,072,371	25.98
*St. Paul and Minneapolis	577,923	2,173,572	26.59
Crookston	42,600	239,045	17.82
Duluth	90,213	425,987	21.18
New Ulm	71,977	291,014	24.73
St. Cloud	153,844	409,791	37.54
Winona	121,351	532,962	22.77
Iowa	556,195	2,909,826	19.11
*Dubuque	245,366	995,648	24.64
Davenport	110,900	733,591	15.12
Des Moines	88,348	667,726	13.23
Sioux City	111,581	512,861	21.76
Missouri	817,019	4,907,409	16.65
*St. Louis	535,230	1,919,042	27.90
Jefferson City	86,536	730,592	11.84
Kansas City-St. Joseph	147,638	1,260,051	11.72
Springfield-Cape Girardeau	47,615	997,724	4.77
North Dakota	178,263	652,633	27.31
Bismarck	79,032	269,310	29.35
Fargo	99,231	383,323	25.89
South Dakota	135,623	663,208	20.45
Rapid City	35,824	178,208	20.10
Sioux Falls	99,799	485,000	20.58
Nebraska	331,953	1,492,825	22.24
*Omaha	209,264	750,582	27.88
Grand Island	52,393	230,600	22.72
Lincoln	70,296	511,643	13.74
Kansas	347,346	2,382,238	14.58
*Kansas City	147,045	952,000	15.45
Dodge City	39,354	221,575	17.76
Salina	61,049	348,953	17.49
Wichita	99,898	859,710	11.62
WEST SOUTH CENTRAL	**4,296,566**	**23,776,682**	**18.07**
Arkansas, Little Rock	62,052	2,284,037	2.72
Louisiana	1,338,909	4,085,617	32.77
*New Orleans	529,127	1,326,512	39.89
Alexandria-Shreveport	82,283	1,083,132	7.69
Baton Rouge	183,625	717,855	25.58
Houma-Thibodaux	127,682	201,222	63.45
Lafayette	325,088	530,051	61.33
Lake Charles	90,104	226,845	39.72
Oklahoma	139,961	2,927,151	4.68
*Oklahoma City	81,698	1,670,551	4.89
Tulsa	55,263	1,256,600	4.40
Texas	2,758,644	14,479,877	19.05
*San Antonio	487,477	1,365,384	35.70
Amarillo	84,372	733,400	11.50
Austin	135,120	1,289,794	10.48
Beaumont	93,000	675,600	13.77
Brownsville	409,373	537,607	76.12
Corpus Christi	314,812	596,393	52.79
Dallas	190,639	2,840,600	6.71
El Paso	179,560	598,514	30.00
Fort Worth	99,349	1,631,228	6.09
Galveston-Houston	592,346	3,331,817	17.79

Section, State Diocese	Catholic Pop.	Total Pop.	Cath. Pct.
Texas			
Lubbock	No separate statistics available.		
San Angelo	75,420	656,440	11.49
Victoria	97,176	223,100	43.56
MOUNTAIN	**1,921,523**	**11,600,667**	**16.56**
Montana	131,117	755,465	17.36
Great Falls-Billings	66,092	351,858	18.78
Helena	65,025	403,607	16.11
Idaho, Boise	76,443	959,000	7.97
Wyoming, Cheyenne+	60,000	420,000	14.29
Colorado	439,574	2,887,151	15.23
*Denver	328,507	2,414,825	13.60
Pueblo	111,067	472,326	23.51
New Mexico	461,812	1,518,226	30.42
*Santa Fe	300,677	800,000	37.58
Gallup+	43,320	355,340	12.19
Las Cruces	117,815	362,886	32.47
Arizona	546,820	2,650,100	20.63
Phoenix	273,267	1,759,100	15.53
Tucson	273,553	891,000	30.70
Utah, Salt Lake City	61,757	1,520,000	4.06
Nevada, Reno-Las Vegas	144,000	890,725	16.17
PACIFIC	**6,410,750**	**32,385,737**	**19.79**
Washington	423,417	4,060,161	10.43
*Seattle	287,367	3,091,138	9.30
Spokane	78,150	574,023	13.61
Yakima	57,900	395,000	14.66
Oregon	328,156	2,630,441	12.48
*Portland	300,857	2,276,341	13.22
Baker	27,299	354,100	7.71
California	5,399,937	24,239,150	22.28
*Los Angeles	2,370,000	8,548,900	27.72
*San Francisco	365,762	1,488,871	24.57
Fresno	320,000	1,463,878	21.86
Monterey	130,000	650,000	20.00
Oakland	403,473	1,786,204	22.59
Orange	408,200	1,993,831	20.47
Sacramento	257,350	2,085,300	12.34
San Bernardino	281,302	1,558,939	18.04
San Diego	333,857	2,021,735	16.51
San Jose	307,338	1,295,071	23.73
Santa Rosa	95,468	628,371	15.19
Stockton	127,187	718,050	17.71
Alaska	44,240	455,985	9.70
*Anchorage	23,737	275,000	8.63
Fairbanks	14,775	125,000	11.82
Juneau	5,728	55,985	10.23
Hawaii, Honolulu	215,000	1,000,000	21.5
EASTERN RITES	**564,844**	—	—
MILITARY ORDINARIATE	**2,125,000**	—	—
TOTALS 1983	**52,088,744**	**233,267,000**	**22.33**
Totals 1982	51,207,579	231,009,000	22.17
Totals 1973	48,460,427	209,712,000	23.11

INFANT BAPTISMS AND CONVERTS IN THE UNITED STATES

(Source: *The Official Catholic Directory, 1983;* figures as of Jan. 1, 1983. Archdioceses are indicated by an asterisk; for dioceses marked +, see Dioceses with Interstate Lines.)

Section, State Diocese	Infant Baptisms	Converts
NEW ENGLAND	**82,584**	**3,384**
Maine, Portland	4,548	453
New Hampshire, Manchester	4,838	263
Vermont, Burlington	2,512	248
Massachusetts	43,689	1,383
*Boston	27,518	802
Fall River	5,707	118
Springfield	5,334	252
Worcester	5,130	211
Rhode Island, Providence	7,529	310
Connecticut	19,468	727
*Hartford	11,566	379
Bridgeport	4,765	142
Norwich+	3,137	206
MIDDLE ATLANTIC	**212,363**	**11,450**
New York	110,318	4,472
*New York	31,632	1,418
Albany	6,663	—
Brooklyn	25,119	699
Buffalo	10,161	598
Ogdensburg	3,104	279
Rochester	6,945	615
Rockville Centre	19,332	304
New York		
Syracuse	7,362	559
New Jersey	45,217	1,632
*Newark	17,340	435
Camden	6,837	410
Metuchen	5,646	180
Paterson	6,610	229
Trenton	8,784	378
Pennsylvania	56,828	5,346
*Philadelphia	20,754	1,843
Allentown	4,184	178
Altoona-Johnstown	2,568	322
Erie	4,005	553
Greensburg	3,287	404
Harrisburg	4,126	770
Pittsburgh	12,298	910
Scranton	5,606	366
SOUTH ATLANTIC	**61,238**	**9,751**
Delaware, Wilmington+	2,679	300
Maryland, *Baltimore	8,455	1,344
District of Columbia, *Washington+	7,269	1,041
Virginia	6,893	1,200
Arlington	3,977	472
Richmond	2,916	728
West Virginia, Wheeling-Charleston	1,925	683

Section, State Diocese	Infant Baptisms	Converts
North Carolina	2,359	611
Charlotte	1,176	385
Raleigh	1,183	226
South Carolina, Charleston	1,567	488
Georgia	3,593	1,178
*Atlanta	2,370	622
Savannah	1,223	556
Florida	26,498	2,906
*Miami	15,551	995
Orlando	3,823	621
Pensacola-Tallahassee	1,151	279
St. Augustine	1,505	300
St. Petersburg	4,468	711
EAST NORTH CENTRAL	**174,533**	**24,065**
Ohio	38,673	6,988
*Cincinnati	9,789	1,589
Cleveland	12,748	2,309
Columbus	4,068	1,219
Steubenville	1,249	290
Toledo	6,227	909
Youngstown	4,592	672
Indiana	14,209	3,209
*Indianapolis	4,499	1,278
Evansville	1,954	483
Ft. Wayne-South Bend	2,852	519
Gary	3,261	453
Lafayette	1,643	476
Illinois	60,208	6,270
*Chicago	35,921	2,692
Belleville	2,260	618
Joliet	8,354	479
Peoria	4,902	1,111
Rockford	5,198	556
Springfield	3,573	814
Michigan	33,471	5,125
*Detroit	17,697	2,027
Gaylord	1,574	261
Grand Rapids	3,332	725
Kalamazoo	1,771	369
Lansing	4,536	1,034
Marquette	1,663	188
Saginaw	2,898	521
Wisconsin	27,972	2,473
*Milwaukee	12,529	906
Green Bay	5,266	372
La Crosse	4,551	563
Madison	3,556	421
Superior	2,070	211
EAST SOUTH CENTRAL	**15,434**	**4,121**
Kentucky	7,686	1,376
*Louisville	4,111	659
Covington	2,289	443
Owensboro	1,286	274
Tennessee	3,542	1,367
Memphis	2,000	892
Nashville	1,542	475
Alabama	2,145	761
*Mobile	1,211	376
Birmingham	934	385

Section, State Diocese	Infant Baptisms	Converts
Mississippi	2,061	617
Biloxi	1,180	241
Jackson	881	376
WEST NORTH CENTRAL	**74,527**	**11,874**
Minnesota	23,381	1,990
*St. Paul and Minneapolis	12,227	1,066
Crookston	1,066	133
Duluth	1,872	226
New Ulm	1,715	167
St. Cloud	3,670	213
Winona	2,831	185
Iowa	11,697	2,267
*Dubuque	4,741	757
Davenport	2,498	636
Des Moines	1,865	541
Sioux City	2,593	333
Missouri	15,286	3,393
*St. Louis	9,814	1,795
Jefferson City	1,679	310
Kansas City-St. Joseph	2,803	867
Springfield-Cape Girardeau	990	421
North Dakota	4,344	260
Bismarck	2,043	143
Fargo	2,301	117
South Dakota	3,213	794
Rapid City	1,110	327
Sioux Falls	2,103	467
Nebraska	7,978	1,394
*Omaha	4,896	705
Grand Island	1,290	330
Lincoln	1,792	359
Kansas	8,628	1,776
*Kansas City	3,280	659
Dodge City	1,034	152
Salina	1,571	299
Wichita	2,743	666
WEST SOUTH CENTRAL	**111,582**	**8,498**
Arkansas, Little Rock	1,374	428
Louisiana	29,079	2,363
*New Orleans	10,283	797
Alexandria-Shreveport	2,055	460
Baton Rouge	4,091	462
Houma-Thibodaux	2,755	86
Lafayette	7,790	285
Lake Charles	2,105	273
Oklahoma	3,507	1,042
*Oklahoma City	2,380	590
Tulsa	1,127	452
Texas	77,622	4,665
*San Antonio	14,533	421
Amarillo	4,025	195
Austin	3,583	380
Beaumont	2,092	261
Brownsville	8,845	125
Corpus Christi	6,515	122
Dallas	6,614	1,027
El Paso	6,859	88
Fort Worth	3,580	474
Galveston-Houston	15,316	1,279

Section, State Diocese	Infant Baptisms	Converts
Texas		
Lubbock	No separate statistics available.	
San Angelo	3,277	147
Victoria	2,383	146
MOUNTAIN	**49,574**	**4,899**
Montana	3,297	641
Great Falls-Billings	1,847	274
Helena	1,450	367
Idaho, Boise	2,174	551
Wyoming, Cheyenne+	1,665	310
Colorado	12,563	1,184
*Denver	9,827	960
Pueblo	2,736	224
New Mexico	11,561	813
*Santa Fe	7,126	430
Gallup+	1,390	258
Las Cruces	3,045	125
Arizona	13,958	552
Phoenix	8,093	521
Tucson	5,865	31
Utah, Salt Lake City	1,725	337
Nevada, Reno-Las Vegas	2,631	511
PACIFIC	**161,808**	**13,658**
Washington	9,407	2,337
*Seattle	5,917	1,519
Spokane	1,789	660
Yakima	1,701	158
Oregon	4,634	1,107
*Portland	3,858	937
Baker	776	170
California	141,655	9,607
*Los Angeles	65,415	2,297
*San Francisco	6,159	1,539

Section, State Diocese	Infant Baptisms	Converts
California		
Fresno	12,303	538
Monterey	4,255	280
Oakland	7,152	714
Orange	10,319	887
Sacramento	6,659	712
San Bernardino	6,842	867
San Diego	8,713	873
San Jose	7,806	374
Santa Rosa	2,252	255
Stockton	3,780	271
Alaska	1,302	224
*Anchorage	708	155
Fairbanks	433	32
Juneau	161	37
Hawaii, Honolulu	4,810	383
EASTERN RITES	**4,214**	**321**
*Philadelphia	826	22
St. Nicholas	307	10
Stamford	348	15
*Pittsburgh	637	53
Parma	441	70
Passaic	622	42
Van Nuys	71	17
St. Maron	565	37
Newton	397	55
Romanians (Ap. Ex.)	No separate statistics available.	
Chaldeans (Ap. Ex.)	No separate statistics available.	
Armenians (Ap. Ex.)	No separate statistics available.	
MILITARY ORDINARIATE	**17,192**	**2,230**
TOTALS 1983	**965,049**	**94,251**
Totals 1982	**982,586**	**92,861**
Totals 1973	**975,071**	**73,925**

STATISTICAL SUMMARY OF THE CHURCH IN THE U.S.

(Principal source: *The Official Catholic Directory, 1983.* Comparisons are with figures reported in the previous edition.)

Catholic Population: 52,088,744; increase, 881,165. Percent of total population: 1983 — 22.3; 1982 — 22.1.

Jurisdictions: 33 archdioceses, 144 dioceses (including Guam), 3 apostolic exarchates; the military vicariate.

Cardinals: 10 (5 head archiepiscopal sees, 1 is a Roman Curia official, 4 are retired). As of Aug. 25, 1983.

Archbishops: 54. Residential, in U.S., 32 (includes 5 cardinals); coadjutor, 1; retired, 16 (includes 4 cardinals); serving outside U.S., 5. As of Aug. 25, 1983.

Bishops: 380. Residential, in U.S., 135; coadjutor, 1; exarchs, 3; auxiliaries, 110; retired, 89; serving outside U.S., 42. As of Aug. 25, 1983.

Abbots: 89.

Priests: 57,870; decrease, 215. Diocesan or secular priests, 35,356 (decrease, 157); religious order priests, 22,514 (decrease, 58).

Permanent Deacons: 6,066; increase, 595.

Brothers: 7,658; decrease, 222.

Sisters: 120,699; decrease, 671.

Seminarians: 12,054; increase, 409. Diocesan seminarians, 8,046 (increase, 421); religious order seminarians, 4,008 (decrease, 12).

Infant Baptisms: 965,049; decrease, 17,537.

Converts: 94,251; increase, 1,390.

Marriages: 347,445; decrease, 5,930.

Deaths: 414,460; decrease, 10,781.

Parishes: 19,039; increase, 136.

Seminaries, Diocesan: 86 (no change).

Religious Seminaries, Novitiates, Scholasticates: 234; increase, 17.

Colleges and Universities: 238; students, 544,136.

High Schools: 1,470 (no change). Students, 814,068; decrease, 19,834.

Elementary Schools: 7,969; decrease, 110. Students, 2,268,453; decrease, 65,016.

Teachers: 168,382; decrease, 4,910. Priests, 4,718 (decrease, 393); scholastics, 162 (increase, 2); brothers, 2,884 (decrease, 5); sisters, 33,310 (decrease, 2,756); lay teachers, 127,308 (decrease, 1,706).

Public School Students in Religious Instruction

Programs: 4,205,311; decrease, 95,183. High school students, 986,707 (increase, 9,609); elementary school students, 3,218,606 (decrease, 104,792).

Catholic Hospitals: 729; increase, 19. Patients treated, 38,295,193; increase 1,116,620.

Nurses' Schools: 125; increase, 4. Student Nurses, 21,316; increase, 1,289.

Homes for Aged: 579; increase, 19. Residents, 72,707; increase, 1,846.

Orphanages: 191; children, 10,422. Children in Foster Homes, 15,952.

CATHEDRALS IN THE UNITED STATES

A cathedral is the principal church in a diocese, the one in which the bishop has his seat *(cathedra).* He is the actual rector, although many functions of the church, which usually serves a parish, are the responsibility of a priest serving as the administrator. Because of the dignity of a cathedral, the dates of its dedication and its patronal feast are observed throughout a diocese.

The pope's cathedral, the Basilica of St. John Lateran, is the highest-ranking church in the world.

(Archdioceses are indicated by asterisk.)

Albany, N.Y.: Immaculate Conception.

Alexandria-Shreveport, La.: St. Francis Xavier. (Alexandria); St. John Berchmans (Shreveport Co-Cathedral).

Allentown, Pa.: St. Catherine of Siena.

Altoona-Johnstown, Pa.: Blessed Sacrament (Altoona); St. John Gualbert (Johnstown Co-Cathedral).

Amarillo, Tex.: St. Laurence.

Anchorage,* Alaska: Holy Family.

Arlington, Va: St. Thomas More.

Atlanta,* Ga.: Christ the King.

Austin, Tex.: St. Mary (Immaculate Conception).

Baker, Ore.: St. Francis de Sales.

Baltimore,* Md.: Mary Our Queen; Basilica of the Assumption of the Blessed Virgin Mary (Co-Cathedral).

Baton Rouge, La.: St. Joseph.

Beaumont, Tex.: St. Anthony (of Padua).

Belleville, Ill.: St. Peter.

Biloxi, Miss.: Nativity of the Blessed Virgin Mary.

Birmingham, Ala.: St. Paul.

Bismarck, N.D.: Holy Spirit.

Boise, Ida.: St. John the Evangelist.

Boston,* Mass.: Holy Cross.

Bridgeport, Conn.: St. Augustine.

Brooklyn, N.Y.: St. James (Minor Basilica).

Brownsville, Tex.: Immaculate Conception.

Buffalo, N.Y.: St. Joseph.

Burlington, Vt.: Immaculate Conception.

Camden, N.J.: Immaculate Conception.

Charleston, S.C.: St. John the Baptist.

Charlotte, N.C.: St. Patrick.

Cheyenne, Wyo.: St. Mary.

Chicago,* Ill.: Holy Name (of Jesus).

Cincinnati,* Ohio: St. Peter in Chains.

Cleveland, Ohio: St. John the Evangelist.

Columbus, Ohio: St. Joseph.

Corpus Christi, Tex.: Corpus Christi.

Covington, Ky.: Basilica of the Assumption.

Crookston, Minn.: Immaculate Conception.

Dallas, Tex.: Cathedral-Santuario de Guadalupe.

Davenport, Ia.: Sacred Heart.

Denver,* Colo.: Immaculate Conception (Minor Basilica).

Des Moines, Ia.: St. Ambrose.

Detroit,* Mich.: Blessed Sacrament.

Dodge City, Kans.: Sacred Heart.

Dubuque,* Ia.: St. Raphael.

Duluth, Minn.: Holy Rosary.

El Paso, Tex.: St. Patrick.

Erie, Pa.: St. Peter.

Evansville, Ind.: Most Holy Trinity (Pro-Cathedral).

Fairbanks, Alaska: Sacred Heart.

Fall River, Mass.: St. Mary of the Assumption.

Fargo, N.D.: St. Mary.

Fort Wayne-S. Bend, Ind.: Immaculate Conception (Fort Wayne); St. Matthew (South Bend Co-Cathedral).

Fort Worth, Tex.: St. Patrick.

Fresno, Calif.: St. John the Baptist.

Gallup, N.M.: Sacred Heart.

Galveston-Houston, Tex.: St. Mary (Minor Basilica, Galveston); Sacred Heart (Houston Co-Cathedral).

Gary, Ind.: Holy Angels.

Gaylord, Mich.: St. Mary, Our Lady of Mt. Carmel.

Grand Island, Nebr.: Nativity of Blessed Virgin Mary.

Grand Rapids, Mich.: St. Andrew.

Great Falls-Billings, Mont.: St. Ann (Great Falls); St. Patrick (Billings Co-Cathedral).

Green Bay, Wis.: St. Francis Xavier.

Greensburg, Pa.: Blessed Sacrament.

Harrisburg, Pa.: St. Patrick.

Hartford,* Conn.: St. Joseph.

Helena, Mont.: St. Helena.

Honolulu, Hawaii: Our Lady of Peace.

Houma-Thibodaux, La.: St. Francis de Sales (Houma); St. Joseph (Thibodaux Co-Cathedral).

Indianapolis,* Ind.: Sts. Peter and Paul.

Jackson, Miss.: St. Peter.

Jefferson City, Mo.: St. Joseph.

Joliet, Ill.: St. Raymond Nonnatus.

Juneau, Alaska: Nativity of the Blessed Virgin Mary.

Kalamazoo, Mich.: St. Augustine.

Kansas City,* Kans.: St. Peter the Apostle.

Kansas City-St. Joseph, Mo.: Immaculate Conception (Kansas City); St. Joseph (St. Joseph Co-Cathedral).

La Crosse, Wis.: St. Joseph.

Lafayette, Ind.: St. Mary.

Lafayette, La.: St. John the Evangelist.

Lake Charles, La.: Immaculate Conception.

Lansing, Mich.: St. Mary.

Las Cruces, N. Mex.: Immaculate Heart of Mary.

Lincoln, Nebr.: Cathedral of the Risen Christ.

Little Rock, Ark.: St. Andrew.

Los Angeles,* Calif.: St. Vibiana.

Louisville,* Ky.: Assumption.

Lubbock, Tex.: Christ the King.
Madison, Wis.: St. Raphael.
Manchester, N.H.: St. Joseph.
Marquette, Mich.: St. Peter.
Memphis, Tenn.: Immaculate Conception.
Metuchen, N.J.: St. Francis (of Assisi).
Miami,* Fla.: St. Mary (Immaculate Conception).
Milwaukee,* Wis.: St. John.
Mobile,* Ala.: Immaculate Conception (Minor Basilica).
Monterey, Calif.: San Carlos Borromeo.
Nashville, Tenn.: Incarnation.
Newark,* N.J.: Sacred Heart.
New Orleans,* La.: Cathedral (Basilica) of St. Louis.
Newton, Mass. (Melkite Rite): Our Lady of the Annunciation (Boston).
New Ulm, Minn.: Holy Trinity.
New York,* N.Y.: St. Patrick.
Norwich, Conn.: St. Patrick.
Oakland, Calif.: St. Francis de Sales.
Ogdensburg, N.Y.: St. Mary (Immaculate Conception).
Oklahoma City,* Okla.: Our Lady of Perpetual Help.
Omaha,* Nebr.: St. Cecilia.
Orange, Calif.: Holy Family.
Orlando, Fla.: St. James.
Owensboro, Ky.: St. Stephen.
Parma, Ohio (Byzantine Rite): St. John the Baptist.
Passaic, N.J. (Byzantine Rite): St. Michael.
Paterson, N.J.: St. John the Baptist.
Pensacola-Tallahassee, Fla.: Sacred Heart (Pensacola); St. Thomas More (Tallahassee Co-Cathedral).
Peoria, Ill.: St. Mary.
Philadelphia,* Pa.: Sts. Peter and Paul (Minor Basilica).
Philadelphia,* Pa. (Byzantine Rite): Immaculate Conception.
Phoenix, Ariz.: Sts. Simon and Jude.
Pittsburgh,* Pa. (Byzantine Rite): St. John the Baptist, Munhall.
Pittsburgh, Pa.: St. Paul.
Portland, Me.: Immaculate Conception.
Portland,* Ore.: Immaculate Conception.
Providence, R.I.: Sts. Peter and Paul.
Pueblo, Colo.: Sacred Heart.
Raleigh, N.C.: Sacred Heart.
Rapid City, S.D.: Our Lady of Perpetual Help.
Reno-Las Vegas, Nev.: St. Thomas Aquinas (Reno), Guardian Angel (Las Vegas Co-Cathedral).
Richmond, Va.: Sacred Heart.
Rochester, N.Y.: Sacred Heart.
Rockford, Ill.: St. Peter.
Rockville Centre, N.Y.: St. Agnes.
Sacramento, Calif.: Blessed Sacrament.
Saginaw, Mich.: St. Mary.
St. Augustine, Fla.: St. Augustine (Minor Basilica).
St. Cloud, Minn.: St. Mary.
St. Louis,* Mo.: St. Louis.
St. Maron, Brooklyn, N.Y. (Maronite Rite): Our Lady of Lebanon.

St. Nicholas in Chicago (Byzantine Rite): St. Nicholas.
St. Paul and Minneapolis,* Minn.: St. Paul (St. Paul); Basilica of St. Mary (Minneapolis Co-Cathedral).
St. Petersburg, Fla.: St. Jude the Apostle.
Salina, Kans.: Sacred Heart.
Salt Lake City, Utah: The Madeleine.
San Angelo, Tex.: Sacred Heart.
San Antonio,* Tex.: San Fernando.
San Bernardino, Calif: Our Lady of the Rosary.
San Diego, Calif.: St. Joseph.
San Francisco,* Calif.: St. Mary (Assumption).
San Jose, Calif.: St. Patrick.
Santa Fe,* N.M.: San Francisco de Asis.
Santa Rosa, Calif.: St. Eugene.
Savannah, Ga.: St. John the Baptist.
Scranton, Pa.: St. Peter.
Seattle,* Wash.: St. James.
Sioux City, Ia.: Epiphany.
Sioux Falls, S.D.: St. Joseph.
Spokane, Wash.: Our Lady of Lourdes.
Springfield, Ill.: Immaculate Conception.
Springfield, Mass.: St. Michael.
Springfield-Cape Girardeau, Mo.: St. Agnes (Springfield); St. Mary (Cape Girardeau Co-Cathedral).
Stamford, Conn. (Byzantine Rite): St. Vladimir.
Steubenville, Ohio: Holy Name.
Stockton, Calif: Annunciation.
Superior, Wis.: Christ the King.
Syracuse, N.Y.: Immaculate Conception.
Toledo, Ohio: Blessed Virgin Mary of the Holy Rosary.
Trenton, N.J.: St. Mary (Assumption).
Tucson, Ariz.: St. Augustine.
Tulsa, Okla.: Holy Family.
Van Nuys, Calif. (Byzantine Rite). St. Mary.
Victoria, Tex.: Our Lady of Victory.
Washington,* D.C.: St. Matthew.
Wheeling-Charleston, W. Va.: St. Joseph (Wheeling); Sacred Heart (Charleston Co-Cathedral).
Wichita, Kans.: Immaculate Conception.
Wilmington, Del.: St. Peter.
Winona, Minn.: Sacred Heart.
Worcester, Mass.: St. Paul.
Yakima, Wash.: St. Paul.
Youngstown, Ohio: St. Columba.
Apostolic Exarchate for Chaldean-Rite Catholics in the United States: Our Lady of Chaldeans Cathedral (Mother of God Church), Southfield, Mich.
Apostolic Exarchate for Romanian Catholics of Byzantine Rite in U.S.: St. George, Canton, O. (Pro-Cathedral).
Apostolic Exarchate for Armenian-Rite Catholics in the U.S. and Canada: St. Ann (110 E. 12th St., New York, N.Y. 10003).

BASILICAS IN U.S. AND CANADA

Basilica is a title assigned to certain churches because of their antiquity, dignity, historical importance or significance as centers of worship. Major basilicas have the papal altar and holy door, which is opened at the beginning of a Jubilee Year;

minor basilicas enjoy certain ceremonial privileges.

Among the major basilicas are the patriarchal basilicas of St. John Lateran, St. Peter, St. Paul Outside the Walls and St. Mary Major in Rome; St. Francis and St. Mary of the Angels in Assisi, Italy. The patriarchal basilica of St. Lawrence, Rome, is a minor basilica.

The dates in the listings below indicate when the churches were designated as basilicas.

Minor Basilicas in U.S., Puerto Rico

Alabama: Mobile, Cathedral of the Immaculate Conception (Mar. 10, 1962).

California: San Francisco, Mission Dolores (Feb. 8, 1952); Carmel, Old Mission of San Carlos (Feb. 5, 1960); Alameda, St. Joseph (Jan. 21, 1972); San Diego, Mission San Diego de Alcala (Nov. 17, 1975).

Colorado: Denver, Cathedral of the Immaculate Conception (Nov. 3, 1979).

Florida: St. Augustine, Cathedral of St. Augustine (Dec. 4, 1976).

Illinois: Chicago, Our Lady of Sorrows (May 4, 1956), Queen of All Saints (Mar. 26, 1962).

Indiana: Vincennes, Old Cathedral (Mar. 14, 1970).

Iowa: Dyersville, St. Francis Xavier (May 11, 1956).

Kentucky: Trappist, Our Lady of Gethsemani (May 3, 1949); Covington, Cathedral of Assumption (Dec. 8, 1953).

Louisiana: New Orleans, St. Louis King of France (Dec. 9, 1964).

Maryland: Baltimore, Assumption of the Blessed Virgin Mary (Sept. 1, 1937).

Massachusetts: Roxbury, Perpetual Help ("Mission Church") (Sept. 8, 1954).

Michigan: Grand Rapids, St. Adalbert (Aug. 22, 1979).

Minnesota: Minneapolis, St. Mary (Feb. 1, 1926).

Missouri: Conception, Basilica of Immaculate Conception (Sept. 14, 1940); St. Louis, St. Louis King of France (Jan. 27, 1961).

New York: Brooklyn, Our Lady of Perpetual Help (Sept. 5, 1969), Cathedral-Basilica of St. James (June 22, 1982); Lackawanna, Our Lady of Victory (1926); Youngstown, Blessed Virgin Mary of the Rosary of Fatima (Oct. 7, 1975).

Ohio: Carey, Shrine of Our Lady of Consolation (Oct. 21, 1971).

Pennsylvania: Latrobe, St. Vincent Basilica, Benedictine Archabbey (Aug. 22, 1955); Conewago, Basilica of the Sacred Heart (June 30, 1962); Philadelphia, Sts. Peter and Paul (Sept. 27, 1976).

Texas: Galveston, St. Mary Cathedral (Aug. 11, 1979).

Wisconsin: Milwaukee, St. Josaphat (Mar. 10, 1929).

Puerto Rico: San Juan, Cathedral of San Juan (Jan. 25, 1978).

Minor Basilicas in Canada

Manitoba: St. Boniface, Cathedral Basilica of St. Boniface (June 10, 1949).

Newfoundland: St. John's, Cathedral Basilica of St. John the Baptist.

Nova Scotia: Halifax, St. Mary's Basilica (June 14, 1950).

Ontario: Ottawa, Basilica of Notre Dame; London, St. Peter's Cathedral (Dec. 13, 1961).

Prince Edward Island: Charlottetown, Basilica of St. Dunstan.

Quebec: Sherbrooke, Cathedral Basilica of St. Michael (July 31, 1959). Montreal, Cathedral Basilica of St. James the Greater; St. Joseph of Mount Royal; Basilica of Notre Dame (Feb. 15, 1982). Cap-de-la-Madeleine, Basilica of Our Lady of the Cape (Aug. 15, 1964). Quebec, Basilica of Notre Dame; St. Anne de Beaupre, Basilica of St. Anne.

CHANCERY OFFICES OF U.S. ARCHDIOCESES AND DIOCESES

A chancery office, under this or another title, is the central administrative office of an archdiocese or diocese.

(Archdioceses are indicated by asterisk.)

Albany, N.Y.: 465 State St., Box 6297, Quail Station. 12206.

Alexandria-Shreveport, La.: 2417 Texas Ave., P.O. Box 7417, Alexandria. 71306.

Allentown, Pa.: 202 N. 17th St., P.O. Box F. 18105.

Altoona-Johnstown, Pa.: Box 126, Logan Blvd., Hollidaysburg, Pa. 16648.

Amarillo, Tex.: 1800 N. Spring St., P.O. Box 5644. 79107.

Anchorage,* Alaska: P.O. Box 2239. 99510.

Arlington, Va.: 200 N. Glebe Rd. 22203.

Atlanta,* Ga.: Catholic Center, 680 W. Peachtree St. N.W. 30308.

Austin, Tex.: N. Congress and 16th, P.O. Box 13327. Capitol Sta. 78711.

Baker, Ore.: Baker and First Sts., P.O. Box 826, 97814.

Baltimore,* Md.: 320 Cathedral St. 21201.

Baton Rouge, La.: P.O. Box 2028. 70821.

Beaumont, Tex.: 703 Archie St., P.O. Box 3948. 77704.

Belleville, Ill.: The Catholic Center, 220 W. Lincoln St. 62221.

Biloxi, Miss.: P.O. Box 1189. 39533.

Birmingham, Ala.: P.O. Box 2086. 35201.

Bismarck, N.D.: 420 Raymond St., Box 1575. 58501.

Boise, Ida.: Box 769. 83701.

Boston,* Mass.: 2121 Commonwealth Ave., Brighton, Mass. 02135.

Bridgeport, Conn.: The Catholic Center, 238 Jewett Ave. 06606.

Brooklyn, N.Y.: 75 Greene Ave., P.O. Box C. 11202.

Brownsville, Tex.: P.O. Box 2279. 78520.

Buffalo, N.Y.: 35 Lincoln Parkway. 14222.

Burlington, Vt.: 351 North Ave. 05401.

Camden, N.J.: 1845 Haddon Ave., P.O. Box 709, 01801.

Charleston, S.C.: 119 Broad St., P.O. Box 818. 29402.

Charlotte, N.C.: P.O. Box 36776. 28236.

Cheyenne, Wyo.: Box 426. 82001.

Chicago,* Ill,: P.O. Box 1979. 60690.

Cincinnati,* O.: 100 E. 8th St. 45202.

Cleveland, O.: Chancery Bldg., 1027 Superior Ave. 44114.

Columbus, O.: 198 E. Broad St. 43215.

Corpus Christi, Tex.: 620 Lipan St. 78401.

Covington, Ky.: 1140 Madison Ave., P.O. Box 192. 41012.

Crookston, Minn.: 1200 Memorial Dr., P.O. Box 610. 56716.

Dallas, Tex.: 3915 Lemmon Ave., P.O. Box 190507. 75219.

Davenport, Ia.: St. Vincent Center, 2706 Gaines St. 52804.

Denver,* Colo.: 200 Josephine St. 80206.

Des Moines, Ia.: 2910 Grand Ave., P.O. Box 1816. 50306.

Detroit,* Mich.: 1234 Washington Blvd. 48226.

Dodge City, Kans.: 910 Central Ave., P.O. Box 849. 67801.

Dubuque,* Ia.: 1229 Mt. Loretta Ave. 52001.

Duluth, Minn.: 215 W. 4th St. 55806.

El Paso, Tex.: 499 St. Matthews. 79907.

Erie, Pa.: 205 W. 9th St. 16501.

Evansville, Ind.: P.O. Box 4169. 47711.

Fairbanks, Alaska: 1316 Peger Rd. 99701.

Fall River, Mass.: 47 Underwood St., Box 2577. 02722.

Fargo, N.D.: 1310 Broadway, Box 1750. 58107.

Fort Wayne-South Bend, Ind.: P.O. Box 390, Fort Wayne. 46801.

Fort Worth, Tex.: 411 E. Bolt St. 76110.

Fresno, Calif.: P.O. Box 1668, 1550 N. Fresno St. 93717.

Gallup, N. Mex.: 711 S. Puerco Dr., P.O. Box 1338. 87301.

Galveston-Houston, Tex.: 1700 San Jacinto St., Houston. 77002.

Gary, Ind.: 975 W. Sixth Ave., P.O. Box M-474. 46401.

Gaylord, Mich.: M-32 West, P.O. Box 700. 49735.

Grand Island, Nebr.: 311 W. 17th St., P.O. Box 996. 68801.

Grand Rapids, Mich.: 660 Burton St., 49507.

Great Falls-Billings, Mont.: P.O. Box 1399, Great Falls. 59403.

Green Bay, Wis.: Box 66. 54305.

Greensburg, Pa.: 723 E. Pittsburgh St. 15601.

Harrisburg, Pa.: P.O. Box 2153. 17105.

Hartford,* Conn.: 134 Farmington Ave. 06105.

Helena, Mont.: 515 North Ewing, P.O. Box 1729. 59624.

Honolulu, Hawaii: 1184 Bishop St. 96813.

Houma-Thibodaux, La.: 1220 Aycock St., P.O. Box 9077, Houma, La. 70361.

Indianapolis,* Ind.: 1400 N. Meridian St., P.O. Box 1410, 46206.

Jackson, Miss.: 237 E. Amite St., P.O. Box 2248. 39205.

Jefferson City, Mo.: 605 Clark Ave. P.O. Box 417. 65101.

Joliet, Ill.: 425 Summit St. 60435.

Juneau, Alaska: 419 6th St. 99801.

Kalamazoo, Mich.: 215 N. Westnedge. Ave., P.O. Box 949, 49005.

Kansas City,* Kans.: 2220 Central Ave., P.O. Box 2328. 66110.

Kansas City-St. Joseph, Mo.: P.O. Box 1037, Kansas City. 64141.

La Crosse, Wis.: P.O. Box 69. 54601.

Lafayette in Indiana: P.O. Box 260, 47902.

Lafayette, La.: P.O. Drawer 3387. 70502.

Lake Charles, La.: P.O. Box 3223. 70602.

Lansing, Mich.: 300 W. Ottawa. 48933.

Las Cruces, N. Mex.: P.O. Box 16318. 88004.

Lincoln, Nebr.: 3400 Sheridan Blvd., P.O. Box 80328. 68501.

Little Rock, Ark.: 2415 N. Tyler St. 72217.

Los Angeles,* Calif.: 1531 W. 9th St. 90015.

Louisville,* Ky.: 212 E. College St., P.O. Box 1073. 40201.

Lubbock, Tex.: P.O. Box 10238. 79408.

Madison, Wis.: 15 E. Wilson St. 53701.

Manchester, N. H.: 153 Ash St. 03105.

Marquette, Mich.: 444 S. Fourth St., P.O. Box 550. 49855.

Memphis, Tenn.: 1325 Jefferson Ave., 38104.

Metuchen, N.J.: P.O. Box 191. 08840.

Miami,* Fla.: 9401 Biscayne Blvd., Miami Shores. 33138.

Milwaukee,* Wis.: 345 N. 95th St., P.O. Box 2018. 53201.

Mobile,* Ala.: 400 Government St., P.O. Box 1966. 36633.

Monterey, Calif.: 580 Fremont Blvd. 93940.

Nashville, Tenn.: 2400 21st Ave. S. 37212.

Newark,* N.J.: 31 Mulberry St. 07102.

New Orleans,* La.: 7887 Walmsley Ave. 70125.

Newton, Mass. (Melkite Rite): 19 Dartmouth St., W. Newton, Mass. 02165.

New Ulm, Minn.: 1400 Chancery Drive. 56073.

New York,* N.Y.: 1011 First Ave. 10022.

Norwich, Conn.: 201 Broadway, P.O. Box 587. 06360.

Oakland, Calif.: 2900 Lakeshore Ave. 94610.

Ogdensburg, N.Y.: 622 Washington St. 13669.

Oklahoma City,* Okla.: P.O. Box 18838. 73154.

Omaha,* Nebr.: 100 N. 62nd St. 68132.

Orange, Calif.: 2811 E. Villa Real Dr. 92667.

Orlando, Fla.: P.O. Box 1800. 32802.

Owensboro, Ky.: 4003 Frederica St. 42301.

Parma, Ohio (Byzantine Rite): 1900 Carlton Rd. 44134.

Passaic, N.J. (Byzantine Rite): 101 Market St. 07055.

Paterson, N.J.: 777 Valley Rd., Clifton. 07013.

Pensacola-Tallahassee, Fla.: P.O. Drawer 17329, Pensacola. 32522.

Peoria, Ill.: 607 N.E. Madison Ave., P.O. Box 1406. 61655.

Philadelphia,* Pa.: 222 N. 17th St. 19103.

Philadelphia,* Pa. (Byzantine Rite): 815 N. Franklin St. 19123.

Phoenix, Ariz.: 400 E. Monroe St. 85004.

Pittsburgh,* Pa. (Byzantine Rite): 54 Riverview Ave. 15214.

Pittsburgh, Pa.: 111 Blvd. of the Allies. 15222.

Portland, Me.: 510 Ocean Ave., Woodfords P.O. Box 6750. 04103.

Portland in Oregon*: P.O. Box 351, 97207.

Providence, R.I.: One Cathedral Sq. 02903.

Pueblo, Colo.: 1426 Grand Ave. 81003.

Raleigh, N.C.: 300 Cardinal Gibbons Dr. 27606.

Rapid City, S.D.: 606 Cathedral Dr., P.O. Box 678. 57709.

Reno-Las Vegas, Nev.: 515 Court St., Reno 89509. (Mailing address: P.O. Box 1211, Reno. 89504.)

Richmond, Va.: 811 Cathedral Pl., Suite C. 23220.

Rochester, N.Y.: 1150 Buffalo Rd. 14624.

Rockford, Ill.: 1245 N. Court St. 61101.

Rockville Centre, N.Y.: 50 N. Park Ave. 11570.

Sacramento, Calif.: 1119 K St., P.O. Box 1706. 95808.

Saginaw, Mich.: 5800 Weiss St. 48603.

St. Augustine, Fla.: P.O. Box 24000, Jacksonville, Fla. 32241.

St. Cloud, Minn.: P.O. Box 1248. 56302.

St. Louis,* Mo.: 4445 Lindell Blvd. 63108.

St. Maron (Maronite Rite), Brooklyn, N.Y.: 8120 15th Ave., Brooklyn. 11228.

St. Nicholas in Chicago (Byzantine Rite): 2245 W. Rice St. 60622.

St. Paul and Minneapolis,* Minn.: 226 Summit Ave., St. Paul. 55102.

St. Petersburg, Fla.: 6363 9th Ave. N. 33710. P.O. Box 40200. 33743.

Salina, Kans.: P.O. Box 999. 67401.

Salt Lake City, Utah: 27 C St., 84103.

San Angelo, Tex.: 116 S. Oakes. Box 1829. 76902.

San Antonio,* Tex.: 9123 Lorene Lane, P.O. Box 32648. 78284.

San Bernardino, Calif.: 1450 North D St. 92405.

San Diego, Calif.: P.O. Box 80428. 92138.

San Francisco,* Calif.: 445 Church St. 94114.

San Jose, Calif.: 7600 St. Joseph Ave., Los Altos 94022.

Santa Fe,* N. Mex.: 202 Morningside Dr. S.E., Albuquerque. 87108.

Santa Rosa, Calif.: 547 "B" St., P.O. Box 1297. 95402.

Savannah, Ga.: 225 Abercorn St., P.O. Box 8789, 31412.

Scranton, Pa.: 300 Wyoming Ave. 18503.

Seattle,* Wash.: 910 Marion St. 98104.

Sioux City, Ia.: P.O. Box 1530. 51102.

Sioux Falls, S.D.: 423 N. Duluth Ave., Box 5033. 57117.

Spokane, Wash.: 1023 W. Riverside Ave. 99201.

Springfield, Illinois: 524 E. Lawrence Ave., P.O. Box 1667. 62705.

Springfield, Mass.: 76 Elliot St. 01105. P.O. Box 1730, 01101.

Springfield-Cape Girardeau, Mo.: 200 McDaniel Bldg., Springfield. 65806.

Stamford, Conn. (Byzantine Rite): 161 Glenbrook Rd. 06902.

Steubenville, Ohio: 422 Washington St., P.O. Box 969. 43952.

Stockton, Calif.: 1105 N. Lincoln St. 95203. P.O. Box 4237. 95204.

Superior, Wis.: 1201 Hughitt Ave. 54880.

Syracuse, N.Y.: 240 E. Onondaga St., 13202.

Toledo, Ohio: 2544 Parkwood Ave. 43610.

Trenton, N.J.: 701 Lawrenceville Rd. 08648.

Tucson, Ariz.: 192 S. Stone Ave., Box 31, 85702.

Tulsa, Okla.: P.O. Box 2009. 74101.

Van Nuys, Calif. (Byzantine Rite): 5335 Sepulveda Blvd. 91411.

Victoria, Tex.: P.O. Box 4708. 77903.

Washington,* D.C.: 5001 Eastern Ave., P.O. Box 29260. 20017..

Wheeling-Charleston, W. Va.: 1300 Byron St., Wheeling. 26003.

Wichita, Kans.: 424 N. Broadway. 67202.

Wilmington, Del.: P.O. Box 2030. 19899.

Winona, Minn.: P.O. Box 588. 55987.

Worcester, Mass.: 49 Elm St. 01609.

Yakima, Wash.: 222 Washington Mutual Bldg., P.O. Box 505 98907.

Youngstown, Ohio: 144 W. Wood St. 44503.

Armenian-Rite Apostolic Exarchate for the United States and Canada: St. Ann Church, 110 E. 12th St., New York, N.Y. 10003.

Chaldean-Rite Apostolic Exarchate for the United States: Our Lady of Chaldeans Cathedral, 25585 Berg Rd., Southfield, Mich. 48034.

Romanian Catholic Apostolic Exarchate for the United States (Byzantine Rite): 1121 44th St. N.E., Canton, O. 44714.

NATIONAL CATHOLIC CONFERENCES

The two conferences described below are related in membership and directive control but distinct in nature, purpose and function.

The National Conference of Catholic Bishops (NCCB) is a strictly ecclesiastical body in and through which the bishops of the United States act together, officially and with authority as pastors of the Church. It is the sponsoring organization of the United States Catholic Conference.

The United States Catholic Conference (USCC) is a civil corporation and operational secretariat in and through which the bishops, together with other members of the Church, act on a wider scale for the good of the Church and society. It is sponsored by the National Conference of Catholic Bishops.

The principal officers of both conferences are: Archbishop John R. Roach, president; Bishop James W. Malone, vice president; Archbishop Edmund C. Szoka, treasurer; Archbishop Thomas C. Kelly, O.P., secretary.

The membership of the Administrative Committee of the NCCB and the Administrative Board of the USCC is identical.

Headquarters of both conferences are located at 1312 Massachusetts Ave. N.W., Washington, D.C. 20005.

NCCB

The National Conference of Catholic Bishops, established by action of the U.S. hierarchy Nov. 14, 1966, is a strictly ecclesiastical body with defined juridical authority over the Church in this country. It was set up with the approval of the Holy See and in line with directives from the Second Vatican Council. Its constitution was formally ratified during the November, 1967, meeting of the U.S. hierarchy.

The NCCB is a development from the Annual Meeting of the Bishops of the United States, whose pastoral character was originally approved by Pope Benedict XV Apr. 10, 1919.

The address of the Conference is 1312 Massachusetts Ave. N.W., Washington, D.C. 20005. Rev. Msgr. Daniel F. Hoye is general secretary.

Pastoral Council

The conference, one of many similar territorial conferences envisioned in the conciliar *Decree on the Pastoral Office of Bishops in the Church* (No. 38), is "a council in which the bishops of a given nation or territory (in this case, the United States) jointly exercise their pastoral office to promote the greater good which the Church offers mankind, especially through the forms and methods of the apostolate fittingly adapted to the circumstances of the age."

Its decisions, "provided they have been approved legitimately and by the votes of at least two-thirds of the prelates who have a deliberative vote in the conference, and have been recognized by the Apostolic See, are to have juridically binding force only in those cases prescribed by the common law or determined by a special mandate of the Apostolic See, given either spontaneously or in response to a petition of the conference itself."

All bishops who serve the Church in the U.S., its territories and possessions, have membership and voting rights in the NCCB.

Officers, Committees

The conference operates through a number of bishops' committees with functions in specific areas of work and concern. Their basic assignments are to prepare materials on the basis of which the bishops, assembled as a conference, make decisions, and to put suitable action plans into effect.

The principal officers are: Archbishop John R. Roach, president; Bishop James W. Malone, vice president; Archbishop Edmund C. Szoka, treasurer; Archbishop Thomas C. Kelly, O.P., secretary.

These officers, with several other bishops, hold positions on executive-level committees — Executive Committee, the Committee on Budget and Finance, the Committee on Personnel and Administrative Services, and the Committee on Research, Plans and Programs. They also, with other bishops, serve on the NCCB Administrative Board.

The standing committees and their chairmen (Archbishops and Bishops) are as follows.

American Board of Catholic Missions, Robert F. Sanchez.

Bishops' Welfare Emergency Relief, John R. Roach.

Boundaries of Dioceses and Provinces, John R. Roach.

Canonical Affairs, Anthony J. Bevilacqua.

Church in Latin America, Patrick F. Flores.

Conciliation and Arbitration, Roger M. Mahony.

Doctrine, John R. Quinn.

Ecumenical and Interreligious Affairs, John F. Whealon.

Human Values, Howard J. Hubbard.

Laity, James R. Hoffman.

Liaison with Priests, Religious and Laity, John J. Nevins.

Liturgy, John S. Cummins.

Men Religious, Paul E. Waldschmidt, C.S.C.

Missions, Edward T. O'Meara.

North American College, Louvain, Peter L. Gerety.

North American College, Rome, Oscar H. Lipscomb.

Pastoral Research and Practices, Raymond W. Lessard.

Permanent Diaconate, John J. Snyder.

Priestly Formation, Thomas J. Murphy.

Priestly Life and Ministry, Michael J. Murphy.

Selection of Bishops, John R. Roach.

Vocations, Anthony F. Mestice.

Women Religious, Amedee W. Proulx.

Ad hoc committees and their chairmen are as follows.

Bicentennial of Establishment of U.S. Hierarchy, William D. Borders.

Campaign for Human Development, William B. Friend.

Catholic Charismatic Renewal, Kenneth J. Povish.

Christianity and Capitalism, Rembert G. Weakland, O.S.B.

Church-Government Issues, John L. May.

Collegeville Follow-Up, James W. Malone.

Conference-Wide Priorities, James W. Malone.

Evangelization, Edward T. O'Meara.

Farm Labor, Roger M. Mahony.

Hispanic Affairs, Robert F. Sanchez.

Inter-Rite, William G. Connare.

Liaison with National Office for Black Catholics, Eugene A. Marino, S.S.J.

Migration and Tourism, Anthony J. Bevilacqua.

Mission Statement, Daniel Pilarczyk.

Nomination of Conference Offices, Thomas W. Lyons.

Pro-Life Activities, Cardinal Terence J. Cooke.

Sapientia Christiana, Paul E. Waldschmidt, C.S.C.

Synod, John R. Roach.

War and Peace Issues, Cardinal Joseph L. Bernardin.

Women in Society and Church, Joseph L. Imesch.

USCC

The United States Catholic Conference, Inc. (USCC), is the operational secretariat and service agency of the National Conference of Catholic Bishops for carrying out the civic-religious work of the Church in this country. It is a civil corporation related to the NCCB in membership and directive control but distinct from it in purpose and function.

The address of the Conference is 1312 Massachusetts Ave. N.W., Washington, D.C. 20005. Rev. Msgr. Daniel F. Hoye is general secretary.

Service Secretariat

The USCC, as of Jan. 1, 1967, took over the general organization and operations of the former National Catholic Welfare Conference, Inc., whose origins dated back to the National Catholic War Council of 1917. The council underwent some change after World War I and was established on a permanent basis Sept. 24, 1919, as the National Catholic Welfare Council to serve as a central agency for organizing and coordinating the efforts of U.S. Catholics in carrying out the social mission of the Church in this country. In 1923, its name was changed to National Catholic Welfare Conference, Inc., and clarification was made of its nature as a service agency of the bishops and the Church rather than as a conference of bishops with real juridical authority in ecclesiastical affairs.

The Official Catholic Directory states that the USCC assists "the bishops in their service to the Church in this country by uniting the people of God where voluntary collective action on a broad interdiocesan level is needed. The USCC provides an organizational structure and the resources needed to insure coordination, cooperation, and assistance in the public, educational and social concerns of the Church at the national or interdiocesan level."

Officers, Departments

The principal officers of the USCC are Archbishop John R. Roach, president; Bishop James W. Malone, vice president; Archbishop Edmund C. Szoka, treasurer; Archbishop Thomas C. Kelly, O.P., secretary. These officers, with several other bishops, hold positions on executive-level committees — the Executive Committee; the Committee on Research, Plans and Programs; the Committee on Budget and Finance; the Committee on Personnel and Administrative Services. They also serve on the Administrative Board.

The Executive Committee, organized in 1969, is authorized to handle matters of urgency between meetings of the Administrative Board and the general conference, to coordinate items for the agenda of general meetings, and to speak in the name of the USCC.

The major departments and their chairmen (Archbishops and Bishops) are: Communications, R. Pierre Du Maine; Education, Edward T. Hughes; Social Development and World Peace, Mark J. Hurley. Each department is supervised by a committee composed of an equal number of episcopal and non-episcopal members, including lay persons.

A national Advisory Council of bishops, priests, men and women religious, lay men and women advises the Administrative Board on overall plans and operations of the USCC.

The administrative general secretariat, in addition to other duties, supervises staff-service offices of Finance and Administration, General Counsel, Government Liaison, and Research, Plans and Programs.

Most of the organizations and associations affiliated with the USCC are covered in separate Almanac entries.

NCCB-USCC REGIONS

For meeting and other operational purposes, the members of the National Conference of Catholic Bishops and the U.S. Catholic Conference are grouped in the following geographical regions.

I. Maine, Vermont, New Hampshire, Massachusetts, Rhode Island, Connecticut.

II. New York.

III. New Jersey, Pennsylvania.

IV. Delaware, District of Columbia, Florida, Georgia, Maryland, North Carolina, South Carolina, Virgin Islands, Virginia, West Virginia.

V. Alabama, Kentucky, Louisiana, Mississippi, Tennessee.

VI. Michigan, Ohio.

VII. Illinois, Indiana, Wisconsin.

VIII. Minnesota, North Dakota, South Dakota.

IX. Iowa, Kansas, Missouri, Nebraska.

X. Arkansas, Oklahoma, Texas.

XI. California, Hawaii, Nevada, Guam.

XII. Idaho, Montana, Alaska, Washington, Oregon.

XIII. Utah, Arizona, New Mexico, Colorado, Wyoming.

1982 MEETING OF THE U.S. BISHOPS

Nearly 300 bishops attended the annual meeting of the National Conference of Catholic Bishops and the U.S. Catholic Conference Nov. 15 to 18, 1982, in Washington, D.C.

Discussion of a semifinal draft of a pastoral letter on nuclear arms dominated the meeting more than any other subject on the agenda. Final action on the letter was put off until a special meeting scheduled for May, 1983.

Presidential Address

Archbishop John R. Roach set the tone of the meeting with a presidential address in which he said that the bishops' concern over abortion and the bomb — among other issues — stemmed from respect for human life. "Concern for human life," he declared, "is the nexus between our positions on these two large issues. Respect for the right to life is basic to the realization of all other human rights."

Items of Business

Items on the agenda of the meeting included the following.

Budget: A budget of $22.6 million was approved for 1983, along with an increase of 25 percent on the tax levied on dioceses (to 12 and one-half cents per Catholic) for support of the conferences and their programs.

Communications: Bishop Louis E. Gelineau of Burlington, Vt., reported that the Catholic Telecommunications Network of America, in operation since the previous Sept. 20, was providing three hours of radio and television programming a day and had 33 dioceses affiliated with it.

Films: Bishop Stanislaus J. Brzana of Ogdensburg asked the bishops and other Catholics to consider doing more "to influence movie-makers and television networks to avoid films and programs which are morally offensive, and to produce more films and programs which reflect higher moral values."

Liturgy: Approval was voted for:

• a document containing revised rites, entitled "Pastoral Care of the Sick: Rites of Anointing and Viaticum," requiring ratification by the Vatican;

• experimental use of a new, ecumenically developed lectionary, requiring ratification by the Vatican;

• new dates for memorial observances honoring Blessed Kateri Tekakwitha (July 14), Marie-Rose Durocher (Oct. 6) and Andre Bessette (Jan. 6), requiring ratification by the Vatican.

Natural Family Planning: Archbishop Thomas A. Donnellan reported that the program approved by the bishops to introduce natural family planning as a continuing service to dioceses had undergone "significant growth and development" during the previous year. One hundred and 43 dioceses had coordinators to oversee the program, and "about one-third" of more than 600 Catholic hospitals had some type of program on natural family planning.

Officers: Elected during the meeting were: Archbishop Thomas C. Kelly of Louisville, secretary; Archbishop John R. Quinn of San Francisco, chairman of the Committee on Doctrine; Bishop Roger M. Mahony of Stockton, chairman of the Committee on Conciliation and Arbitration; Archbishop Patrick F. Flores of San Antonio, chairman of the Committee on the Church in Latin America; Coadjutor Bishop Michael Murphy of Erie, chairman of the Committee on Priestly Life and Minis-

try; Bishop R. Pierre Du Maine of San Jose, head of the Communications Committee; Auxiliary Bishop Paul E. Waldschmidt of Portland, Ore., for Liaison with Men Religious; Auxiliary Bishop Amedee W. Proulx of Portland, Me., for Liaison with Women Religious.

Pastoral Statements To Come: The bishops approved requests for the writing of pastoral letters on ministry to Hispanics, campus ministry, prayer and worship. Archbishop Robert F. Sanchez said the Hispanic pastoral would be a "beacon of hope" to Hispanic Catholics. Auxiliary Bishop Edward T. Hughes of Philadelphia called the campus ministry pastoral necessary because of the large numbers of Catholics on secular campuses and the increase in proselytizing on campuses by other religious groups, especially biblical fundamentalists. A prayer and worship statement would mark the 20th anniversary of the Second Vatican Council's *Constitution on the Sacred Liturgy* and would also encourage spirituality among Catholics.

Synod of Bishops: General discussion during one of the sessions of the meeting elicited comment related to "Reconciliation and Penance in the Mission of the Church," the subject of the assembly of the Synod of Bishops scheduled to be held in the fall of 1983.

Vocations to the Priesthood: Auxiliary Bishop Nicolas E. Walsh of Seattle said the bishops should "initiate, encourage and otherwise support a study of the real causes" of the critical decline in the numbers of vocations to the priesthood.

STATE CATHOLIC CONFERENCES

These conferences are agencies of bishops and dioceses in the various states. Their general purposes are to develop and sponsor cooperative programs designed to cope with pastoral and common-welfare needs, and to represent the dioceses before governmental bodies, the public, and in private sectors. Their membership consists of representatives from the dioceses in the states — bishops, clergy and lay persons in various capacities.

The **National Association of State Catholic Conference Directors** maintains liaison with the general secretariat of the United States Catholic Conference. Bro. Richard Daly, C.S.C., executive director of the Texas Catholic Conference, is president.

Arizona Catholic Conference, 400 E. Monroe St., Phoenix, Ariz. 85004; exec. dir., Thomas F. Allt.

California Catholic Conference, 926 J St., Suite 1100, Sacramento, Calif. 95814; exec. dir., Most Rev. William J. Levada.

Colorado Catholic Conference, 200 Josephine St., Denver, Colo. 80206; exec. dir., Sr. Loretto Anne Madden, S.L.

Connecticut Catholic Conference, 134 Farmington Ave., Hartford, Conn. 06105; exec. dir., William Wholean.

Florida Catholic Conference, P.O. Box 1571, Tallahassee, Fla. 32302; exec. dir., Thomas A. Horkan, Jr.

Georgia Catholic Conference, Sussex Pl., Suite

520, 148 International Blvd., Atlanta, Ga. 30303; exec. dir., Cheatham E. Hodges, Jr.

Hawaii Catholic Conference, 1184 Bishop St., Honolulu, H.I. 96813; exec. sec., Mrs. Maggie Bunson.

Illinois Catholic Conference, One East Superior St., Chicago, Ill. 60611; 300 E. Monroe St., Springfield, Ill. 62701; exec. dir., Rev. John J. Quinn.

Indiana Catholic Conference, 1400 N. Meridian St., P.O. Box 1410, Indianapolis, Ind. 46206; exec. dir., M. Desmond Ryan.

Iowa Catholic Conference, 818 Insurance Exchange Building, Des Moines, Iowa 50309; exec. dir., Timothy McCarthy.

Kansas Catholic Conference, 702 Commercial National Bank Bldg., Kansas City, Kan. 66101; exec. dir., Robert Runnels, Jr.

Kentucky Catholic Conference, P.O. Box 1073, Louisville, Ky. 40201; exec. dir., Ken Dupre.

Louisiana Catholic Conference: P.O. Box 52948, New Orleans, La. 70152; exec. dir., Emile Comar. (Office of Governmental Programs and Planning). FNB Tower, Box 19, 666 Jefferson St., Lafayette 70501; exec. dir., Rev. Msgr. Robert Angelle (Office of Church Ministry and Development).

Maryland Catholic Conference, 5400 Roland Ave., Baltimore, Md. 21210; exec. dir., Francis X. McIntyre.

Massachusetts Catholic Conference, 60 School St., Boston, Mass. 02107; exec. dir., Gerald D. D'Avolio, Esq.

Michigan Catholic Conference, 505 N. Capitol

Ave., Lansing, Mich. 48933; acting dir., Sr. Monica Kostielney.

Minnesota Catholic Conference, 296 Chester St., St. Paul, Minn. 55107; exec. dir., Rev. Msgr. James D. Habiger.

Missouri Catholic Conference, P.O. Box 1022, Jefferson City, Mo. 65102; exec. dir., Louis C. DeFeo, Jr.

Montana Catholic Conference, P.O. Box 1708, Helena, Mont. 59624; exec. dir., John Frankino.

Nebraska Catholic Conference, 521 S. 14th St., Lincoln, Nebr. 68508; exec. dir., James R. Cunningham.

New Jersey Catholic Conference, 211 N. Warren St., Trenton, N.J. 08618; exec. dir., Edward J. Leadem.

New York State Catholic Conference, 11 N. Pearl St., Albany, N.Y. 12207; exec. dir., J. Alan Davitt.

North Dakota Catholic Conference, 107 N. 4th St. — Room 25, Bismarck, N. Dak. 58501; exec. dir., Mrs. Corrine Engelstad.

Ohio, Catholic Conference of, 35 E. Gay St., Suite 502, Columbus, Ohio 43215; exec. dir., Nelson N. Harper.

Oregon Catholic Conference, 2838 E. Burnside, Portland, Ore. 97214; sec., Rev. Joseph Jacobberger.

Pennsylvania Catholic Conference, 223 North St., Box 2835, Harrisburg, Pa. 17105; exec. dir., Howard J. Fetterhoff.

Texas Catholic Conference, 3001 S. Congress Ave., Austin, Tex. 78704; exec. dir., Bro. Richard Daly, C.S.C.

Washington State Catholic Conference, 1402 3rd Ave., Suite 618, Seattle, Wash. 98101; exec. dir. Rev. D. Harvey McIntyre.

Wisconsin Catholic Conference, 30 W. Mifflin St., Suite 910, Madison, Wis. 53703; exec. dir., Charles M. Phillips.

BIOGRAPHIES OF AMERICAN BISHOPS

(Sources: Almanac survey, *The Official Catholic Directory*, NC News Service. As of Aug. 15, 1983.)

A

Abramowicz, Alfred L.: b. Jan. 27, 1919, Chicago, Ill.; educ. St. Mary of the Lake Seminary (Mundelein, Ill.), Gregorian Univ. (Rome); ord. priest May 1, 1943; ord. titular bishop of Paestum and auxiliary bishop of Chicago, June 13, 1968.

Ackerman, Richard Henry, C.S.Sp.: b. Aug. 30, 1903, Pittsburgh, Pa.; educ. Duquesne Univ. (Pittsburgh, Pa.), St. Mary's Scholasticate (Norwalk, Conn.), Univ. of Fribourg (Switzerland); ord. priest Aug. 28, 1926; ord. titular bishop of Lares and auxiliary bishop of San Diego, May 22, 1956; app. bishop of Covington, Apr. 4, 1960; resigned Nov. 28, 1978.

Ahern, Patrick V.: b. Mar. 8, 1919, New York, N.Y.; educ. Manhattan College and Cathedral College (New York City), St. Joseph's Seminary (Yonkers, N.Y.), St. Louis Univ. (St. Louis, Mo.), Notre Dame Univ. (Notre Dame, Ind.); ord. priest Jan. 27, 1945; ord. titular bishop of Naiera and auxiliary bishop of New York, Mar. 19, 1970.

Ahr, George William: b. June 23, 1904, Newark, N.J.; educ. St. Vincent College (Latrobe, Pa.), Seton Hall College (S. Orange, N.J.), North American College (Rome); ord. priest July 29, 1928; ord. bishop of Trenton, Mar. 20, 1950; resigned June 23, 1979.

Anderson, Moses B., S.S.E.: b. Sept. 9, 1928, Selma, Ala.; educ. St. Michael's College (Winooski, Vt.), St. Edmund Seminary (Burlington, Vt.), Univ. of Legon (Ghana); ord. priest May 30, 1958; ord. titular bishop of Vatarba and auxiliary bishop of Detroit, Jan. 27, 1983.

Anderson, Paul F.: b. Apr. 20, 1917, Roslindale, Mass.; educ. Boston College (Chestnut Hill, Mass.), St. John's Seminary (Brighton, Mass.); ord. priest Jan. 6, 1943; ord. titular bishop of Polignano and coadjutor bishop of Duluth, Oct. 17, 1968; bishop of Duluth, Apr. 30, 1969; resigned August 17, 1982; app. auxiliary bishop of Sioux Falls.

Angell, Kenneth A.: b. Aug. 3, 1930, Providence, R.I.; educ. St. Mary's Seminary (Baltimore, Md.); ord. priest May 26, 1956; ord. titular bishop of Septimunicia and auxiliary bishop of Providence, R.I., Oct. 7, 1974.

Arias, David, O.A.R.: b. July 22, 1929, Leon, Spain; educ. St. Rita's College (San Sebastian, Spain), Our Lady of Good Counsel Theologate (Granada, Spain), Teresianum Institute (Rome, Italy); ord. priest May 31, 1952; ord. titular bishop of Badie and auxiliary bishop of Newark, Apr. 7, 1983; episcopal vicar for Hispanic affairs.

Arkfeld, Leo, S.V.D.: b. Feb. 4, 1912, Butte, Nebr.; educ. Divine Word Seminary (Techny, Ill.), Sacred Heart College (Girard, Pa.); ord. priest Aug. 15, 1943; ord. titular bishop of Bucellus and vicar apostolic of Central New Guinea, Nov. 30, 1948; name of vicariate changed to Wewak, May 15, 1952; first bishop of Wewak, Nov. 15, 1966; app. archbishop of Madang, Papua New Guinea, Dec. 19, 1975.

Arliss, Reginald, C.P.: b. Sept. 8, 1906, East Orange, N.J.; educ. Immaculate Conception Seminary (Jamaica, N.Y.) and other Passionist houses of study; ord. priest Apr. 28, 1934; missionary in China for 16 years, expelled 1951; missionary in Philippines; rector of the Pontifical Philippine College Seminary in Rome, 1961-69; ord. titular bishop of Cerbali and prelate of Marbel, Philippines (now a diocese), Jan. 30, 1970; resigned from titular see and prelature, Oct. 1, 1981.

Arzube, Juan: b. June 1, 1918, Guayaquil, Ecuador; educ. Rensselaer Polytechnic Institute (Troy, N.Y.), St. John's Seminary (Camarillo, Calif.); ord. priest May 5, 1954; ord. titular bishop of Civitate and auxiliary bishop of Los Angeles, Mar. 25, 1971.

B

Balke, Victor: b. Sept. 29, 1931, Meppen, Ill.; educ. St. Mary of the Lake Seminary (Mundelein, Ill.), St. Louis Univ. (St. Louis, Mo.); ord. priest May 24, 1958; ord. bishop of Crookston, Sept. 2, 1976.

Baum, William W.: (See Cardinals, Biographies.)

Begley, Michael J.: b. Mar. 12, 1909, Mattineague, Mass.; educ. Mt. St. Mary Seminary (Emmitsburg, Md.); ord. priest May 26, 1934; ord. first bishop of Charlotte, N.C., Jan. 12, 1972.

Beltran, Eusebius J.: b. Aug. 31, 1934, Ashley, Pa.; educ. St. Charles Seminary (Philadelphia, Pa.); ord. priest May 14, 1960; ord. bishop of Tulsa, Apr. 20, 1978.

Benincasa, Pius A.: b. July 8, 1913, Niagara Falls, N.Y.: educ. Propaganda Univ. and Lateran Univ. (Rome); ord. priest Mar. 27, 1937; served in Vatican Secretariat of State, 1954-64; ord. titular bishop of Buruni and auxiliary bishop of Buffalo, June 29, 1964.

Bernardin, Joseph L: (See Cardinals, Biographies.)

Bernarding, George, S.V.D.: b. Feb. 15, 1912, Carrick, Pa.; educ. Divine Word Seminary (Girard, Pa.); ord. priest Aug. 13, 1939; ord. titular bishop of Belabitene and first vicar apostolic of Mount Hagen, New Guinea, Apr. 21, 1960; first bishop of Mount Hagen, Nov. 15, 1966; app. first archbishop Mar. 29, 1982, when see was elevated to metropolitan rank.

Bevilacqua, Anthony J.: b. June 17, 1923, Brooklyn, N.Y.; educ. Cathedral College (Brooklyn, N.Y.), Immaculate Conception Seminary (Huntington, N.Y.), Gregorian Univ. (Rome), Columbia Univ. and St. John's Univ. (New York); ord. priest June 11, 1949; ord. titular bishop of Aquae Albae in Byzacena and auxiliary bishop of Brooklyn, Nov. 24, 1980.

Bilock, John M.: b. June 20, 1916, McAdoo, Pa.; educ. St. Procopius College and Seminary (Lisle, Ill.); ord. priest Feb. 3, 1946; vicar general of Byzantine archdiocese of Munhall, 1969; ord. titular bishop of Pergamum and auxiliary bishop of Munhall, May 15, 1973; title of see changed to Pittsburgh, 1977.

Boccella, John H., T.O.R.: b. June 25, 1912, Castelfranci, Italy; came to U.S. at the age of two; educ. St. Francis College and Seminary (Loretto, Pa.), Angelicum Univ. (Rome), Catholic Univ. (Washington, D.C.); ord. priest Mar. 29, 1941; minister general of Third Order Regular, 1947-65; ord. archbishop of Izmir, Turkey, Apr. 17, 1968; transferred to titular see of Ephesus, Dec. 7, 1978 (resides in Rome).

Boland, Ernest B., O.P.: b. July 10, 1925, Providence, R.I.; educ. Providence College (Rhode Island), Dominican Houses of Study (Somerset, Ohio; Washington, D.C.); ord. priest June 9, 1955; ord. bishop of Multan, Pakistan, July 25, 1966.

Borders, William D.: b. Oct. 9, 1913, Washington, Ind.; educ. St. Meinrad Seminary (St. Meinrad, Ind.), Notre Dame Seminary (New Orleans, La.), Notre Dame Univ. (Notre Dame, Ind.); ord. priest May 18, 1940; ord. first bishop of Orlando, June 14, 1968; app. archbishop of Baltimore, Apr. 2, 1974, installed June 26, 1974.

Bosco, Anthony G.: b. Aug. 1, 1927, New Castle, Pa.; educ. St. Vincent Seminary (Latrobe, Pa.), Lateran Univ. (Rome); ord. priest June 7, 1952; ord. titular bishop of Labicum and auxiliary of Pittsburgh, June 30, 1970.

Boudreaux, Warren L: b. Jan. 25, 1918,

Berwick, La.; educ. St. Joseph's Seminary (St. Benedict, La.), St. Sulpice Seminary (Paris, France), Notre Dame Seminary (New Orleans, La.), Catholic Univ. (Washington, D.C.); ord. priest May 30, 1942; ord. titular bishop of Calynda and auxiliary bishop of Lafayette, La., July 25, 1962; app. bishop of Beaumont, June 5, 1971; app. first bishop of Houma-Thibodaux, installed June 5, 1977.

Breitenbeck, Joseph M.: b. Aug. 3, 1914, Detroit, Mich.; educ. University of Detroit, Sacred Heart Seminary (Detroit, Mich.), North American College and Lateran Univ. (Rome), Catholic Univ. (Washington, D.C.); ord. priest May 30, 1942; ord. titular bishop of Tepelta and auxiliary bishop of Detroit, Dec. 20, 1965; app. bishop of Grand Rapids, Oct. 15, 1969, installed Dec. 2, 1969.

Brizgys, Vincas: b. Nov. 10, 1903, Plyniai, Lithuania; ord. priest June 5, 1927; ord. titular bishop of Bosano and auxiliary bishop of Kaunas, Lithuania, May 10, 1940; taken into custody and deported to Germany, 1944; liberated by Americans, 1945; U.S. citizen, 1958.

Broderick, Edwin B.: b. Jan. 16, 1917, New York, N.Y.; educ. Cathedral College (New York City), St. Joseph's Seminary (Yonkers, N.Y.), Fordham Univ. (New York City); ord. priest May 30, 1942; ord. titular bishop of Tizica and auxiliary of New York, Apr. 21, 1967; bishop of Albany, 1969-76; executive director of Catholic Relief Services, 1976-82.

Brom, Robert H.: b. Sept. 18, 1938, Arcadia, Wis.; educ. St. Mary's College (Winona, Minn.), Gregorian Univ. (Rome); ord. priest Dec. 18, 1963, in Rome; ord. bishop of Duluth, May 23, 1983.

Brown, Charles, A., M.M.: b. Aug. 20, 1919, New York, N.Y.; educ. Cathedral College (New York City), Maryknoll Seminary (Maryknoll, N.Y.); ord. priest June 9, 1946; ord. titular bishop of Vallis and auxiliary bishop of Santa Cruz, Bolivia, Mar. 27, 1957.

Brunini, Joseph B.: b. July 24, 1909, Vicksburg, Miss.; educ. Georgetown Univ. (Washington, D.C.), North American College (Rome), Catholic Univ. (Washington, D.C.); ord. priest Dec. 5, 1933; ord. titular bishop of Axomis and auxiliary bishop of Natchez-Jackson, Jan. 29, 1957; apostolic administrator of Natchez-Jackson, 1966; app. bishop of Natchez-Jackson, Dec. 2, 1967, installed Jan. 29, 1968; title of see changed to Jackson, 1977.

Brust, Leo J.: b. Jan. 7, 1916, St. Francis, Wis.; educ. St. Francis Seminary (Milwaukee, Wis.), Canisianum (Innsbruck, Austria), Catholic Univ. (Washington, D.C.); ord. priest May 30, 1942; ord. titular bishop of Suelli and auxiliary bishop of Milwaukee. Oct. 16, 1969.

Brzana, Stanislaus J.: b. July 1, 1917, Buffalo, N.Y.; educ. Christ the King Seminary (St. Bonaventure, N.Y.), Gregorian Univ. (Rome); ord. priest June 7, 1941; ord. titular bishop of Cufruta and auxiliary bishop of Buffalo, June 29, 1964; bishop of Ogdensburg, Oct. 22, 1968.

Bullock, William H.: b. Apr. 13, 1927, Maple Lake, Minn.; educ. St. Thomas College and St. Paul Seminary (St. Paul, Minn.), Notre Dame Univ. (Notre Dame, Ind.); ord. priest June 7, 1952;

ord. titular bishop of Natchez and auxiliary bishop of St. Paul and Minneapolis, Aug. 12, 1980.

Burke, James C., O.P.: b. Nov. 30, 1926, Philadelphia, Pa.; educ. King's College (Wilkes-Barre, Pa.), Providence College (R.I.); ord. priest June 8, 1956; ord. titular bishop of Lamiggiga and prelate of Chimbote, Peru, May 25, 1967, resigned from prelature, June 8, 1978. Vicar for urban affairs, Wilmington, Del., diocese.

Buswell, Charles A.: b. Oct. 15, 1913, Homestead, Okla.; educ. St. Louis Preparatory Seminary (St. Louis, Mo.), Kenrick Seminary (Webster Groves, Mo.), American College, Univ. of Louvain (Belgium); ord. priest July 9, 1939; ord. bishop of Pueblo, Sept. 30, 1959; resigned Sept. 18, 1979.

Byrne, James J.: b. July 28, 1908, St. Paul, Minn.; educ. Nazareth Hall Preparatory Seminary and St. Paul Seminary (St. Paul, Minn.), Univ. of Minnesota (Minneapolis, Minn.); Louvain Univ. (Belgium); ord. priest June 3, 1933; ord. titular bishop of Etenna and auxiliary bishop of St. Paul, July 2, 1947; app. bishop of Boise, June 16, 1956; app. archbishop of Dubuque, Mar. 19, 1962, installed May 8, 1962; retired 1983.

C

Caesar, Raymond R., S.V.D.: b. Feb. 14, 1932, Eunice, La.; educ. Divine Word Seminary (Bay St. Louis, Miss.); Catholic Univ. (Washington, D.C.); ord. priest June 4, 1961; missionary in New Guinea from 1962; ord. coadjutor bishop of Goroka, Papua New Guinea, Oct. 25, 1978; bishop of Goroko, Aug. 30, 1980.

Caillouet, L. Abel.: b. Aug. 2, 1900, Thibodaux, La.; educ. St. Joseph's Preparatory Seminary (St. Benedict, La.), St. Mary's Seminary (Baltimore, Md.), North American College (Rome); ord. priest Mar. 7, 1925; ord. titular bishop of Setea and auxiliary bishop of New Orleans, Oct. 28, 1947; retired July 7, 1976.

Carberry, John J.: (See Cardinals, Biographies.)

Carroll, Mark K.: b. Nov. 19, 1896, St. Louis, Mo.; educ. St. Louis Preparatory Seminary and Kenrick Seminary (St. Louis, Mo.); ord. priest June 10, 1922; ord. bishop of Wichita, Apr. 23, 1947; retired, 1963, but retained title; resigned, 1967.

Casey, James V.: b. Sept. 22, 1914, Osage, Ia.; educ. Loras College (Dubuque, Ia.), North American College (Rome), Catholic Univ. (Washington, D.C.); ord. priest Dec. 8, 1939; ord. titular bishop of Citium and auxiliary bishop of Lincoln, Apr. 24, 1957; bishop of Lincoln, June 14, 1957; app. archbishop of Denver, Feb. 22, 1967, installed May 17, 1967.

Cassata, John J.: b. Nov. 8, 1908, Galveston, Tex.; educ. St. Mary's Seminary (La Porte, Tex.), North American College, Urban Univ. and Gregorian Univ. (Rome); ord. priest Dec. 8, 1932; ord. titular bishop of Bida and auxiliary bishop of Dallas-Fort Worth, June 5, 1968; app. bishop of Fort Worth, Aug. 27, 1969, installed Oct. 21, 1969; retired Sept. 16, 1980.

Chavez, Gilbert Espinoza: b. May 9, 1932, Ontario, Calif.; educ. St. Francis Seminary (El Cajon, Calif.), Immaculate Heart Seminary (San Diego), Univ. of California; ord. priest Mar. 19, 1960;

ord. titular bishop of Magarmel and auxiliary of San Diego, June 21, 1974.

Chedid, John: b. July 4, 1923, Eddid, Lebanon; educ. seminaries in Lebanon and Pontifical Urban College (Rome); ord. priest Dec. 21, 1951, in Rome; ord. titular bishop of Callinico and auxiliary bishop of St. Maron of Brooklyn for the Maronites, Jan. 25, 1981.

Clark, Matthew H.: b. July 15, 1937, Troy, N.Y.; educ. St. Bernard's Seminary (Rochester, N.Y.), Gregorian Univ. (Rome); ord. priest Dec. 19, 1962; ord. bishop of Rochester, May 27, 1979; installed June 26, 1979.

Clinch, Harry A.: b. Oct. 27, 1908, San Anselmo, Calif.; educ. St. Patrick's College (Mountain View, Calif.), St. Patrick's Seminary (Menlo Park, Calif.); ord. priest June 6, 1936; ord. titular bishop of Badiae and auxiliary bishop of Monterey-Fresno, Feb. 27, 1957; app. first bishop of Monterey in California, installed Dec. 14, 1967; resigned Jan. 19, 1982.

Cohill, John Edward, S.V.D.: b. Dec. 13, 1907, Elizabeth, N.J.; educ. Divine Word Seminary (Techny, Ill.); ord. priest Mar. 20, 1936; ord. first bishop of Goroko, Papua New Guinea, Mar. 11, 1967; resigned Aug. 30, 1980.

Comber, John W., M.M.: b. Mar. 12, 1906, Lawrence, Mass.; educ. St. John's Preparatory College (Danvers, Mass.), Boston College (Boston, Mass.), Maryknoll Seminary (Maryknoll, N.Y.); ord. priest Feb. 1, 1931; superior general of Maryknoll, 1956-66; ord. titular bishop of Foratiana, Apr. 9, 1959.

Connare, William G.: b. Dec. 11, 1911, Pittsburgh, Pa.; educ. Duquesne Univ. (Pittsburgh, Pa.), St. Vincent Seminary (Latrobe, Pa.); ord. priest June 14, 1936; ord. bishop of Greensburg, May 4, 1960.

Connolly, James L.: b. Nov. 15, 1894, Fall River, Mass.; educ. St. Charles College (Catonsville, Md.), St. Mary's Seminary (Baltimore, Md.), Catholic Univ. (Washington, D.C.), Louvain Univ. (Belgium); ord. priest Dec. 21, 1923; rector of St. Paul (Minn.) minor seminary 1940-43, major seminary 1943-45; ord. titular bishop of Mylasa and coadjutor of Fall River, May 24, 1945; bishop of Fall River, May 17, 1951, resigned Oct. 30, 1970.

Connolly, Thomas Arthur: b. Oct. 5, 1899, San Francisco, Calif.; educ. St. Patrick's Seminary (Menlo Park, Calif.), Catholic Univ. (Washington, D.C.); ord. priest June 11, 1926; ord. titular bishop of Sila and auxiliary bishop of San Francisco, Aug. 24, 1939; app. coadjutor bishop of Seattle, Feb. 28, 1948; succeeded as bishop of Seattle, May 18, 1950; first archbishop of Seattle, June 23, 1951; retired Feb. 25, 1975.

Connolly, Thomas J.: b. July 18, 1922, Tonopah, Nev.; educ. St. Patrick's Seminary (Menlo Park, Calif.), Catholic Univ. (Washington, D.C.), Lateran Univ. (Rome); ord. priest Apr. 8, 1947; ord. bishop of Baker, June 30, 1971.

Connors, Ronald G., C.SS.R.: b. Nov. 1, 1915, Brooklyn, N.Y.; ord. priest June 22, 1941; ord. titular bishop of Equizetum and coadjutor bishop of San Juan de la Maguana, Dominican Republic,

July 20, 1976; succeeded as bishop of San Juan de la Maguana, July 20, 1977.

Cooke, Terence J.: (See Cardinals, Biographies.)

Cooney, Patrick R.: b. Mar. 10, 1934, Detroit, Mich.; educ. Sacred Heart Seminary (Detroit), Gregorian Univ. (Rome), Notre Dame Univ. (Notre Dame, Ind.); ord. priest Dec. 20, 1959; ord. titular bishop of Hodelm and auxiliary bishop of Detroit, Jan. 27, 1983.

Coscia, Benedict Dominic, O.F.M.: b. Aug. 10, 1922, Brooklyn, N.Y.; educ. St. Francis College (Brooklyn, N.Y.), Holy Name College (Washington, D.C.); ord. priest June 11, 1949; ord. bishop of Jatai, Brazil, Sept. 21, 1961.

Cosgrove, William M.: b. Nov. 26, 1916, Canton, Ohio; educ. John Carroll Univ. (Cleveland, O.); ord. priest Dec. 18, 1943; ord. titular bishop of Trisipa and auxiliary bishop of Cleveland, Sept. 3, 1968; app. bishop of Belleville, installed Oct. 28, 1976; retired May 19, 1981.

Costello, Thomas J.: b. Feb. 23, 1929, Camden, N.Y.; educ. Niagara Univ. (Niagara Falls, N.Y.), St. Bernard's Seminary (Rochester, N.Y.), Catholic Univ. (Washington, D.C.); ord. priest June 5, 1954; ord. titular bishop of Perdices and auxiliary bishop of Syracuse Mar. 13, 1978.

Cotey, Arnold R., S.D.S.: b. June 15, 1921, Milwaukee, Wis.; educ. Divine Savior Seminary (Lanham, Md.), Marquette Univ. (Milwaukee, Wis.); ord. priest June 7, 1949; ord. first bishop of Nachingwea, Tanzania, Oct. 20, 1963.

Cousins, William E.: b. Aug. 20, 1902, Chicago, Ill.; educ. Quigley Seminary (Chicago, Ill.), St. Mary of the Lake Seminary (Mundelein, Ill.); ord. priest Apr. 23, 1927; ord. titular bishop of Forma and auxiliary bishop of Chicago, Mar. 7, 1949; app. bishop of Peoria, May 21, 1952; archbishop of Milwaukee, Jan. 27, 1959; retired Jan. 17, 1977.

Cronin, Daniel A.: b. Nov. 14, 1927, Newton, Mass.; educ. St. John's Seminary (Boston, Mass.), North American College and Gregorian Univ. (Rome); ord. priest Dec. 20, 1952; attaché apostolic nunciature (Addis Ababa), 1957-61; served in papal Secretariat of State, 1961-68; ord. titular bishop of Egnatia and auxiliary bishop of Boston, Sept. 12, 1968; bishop of Fall River, Dec. 16, 1970.

Crowley, Joseph R.: b. Jan. 12, 1915, Fort Wayne, Ind.; educ. St. Mary's College (St. Mary, Ky.), St. Meinrad Seminary (St. Meinrad, Ind.); served in US Air Force, 1942-46; ord. priest May 1, 1953; editor of *Our Sunday Visitor* 1958-67; ord. titular bishop of Maraguis and auxiliary bishop of Fort Wayne-South Bend, Aug. 24, 1971.

Cummins, John S.: b. Mar. 3, 1928, Oakland, Calif.; educ. St. Patrick's Seminary (Menlo Park, Calif.), Catholic Univ. (Washington, D.C.), Univ. of California; ord. priest Jan. 24, 1953; executive director of the California Catholic Conference 1971-76; ord. titular bishop of Lambaesis and auxiliary bishop of Sacramento, May 16, 1974; app. bishop of Oakland, installed June 30, 1977.

Curtis, Walter W.: b. May 3, 1913, Jersey City, N.J.; educ. Fordham Univ. (New York City), Seton Hall Univ. (South Orange, N.J.), Immaculate Conception Seminary (Darlington, N.J.),

North American College and Gregorian Univ. (Rome), Catholic Univ. (Washington, D.C.); ord. priest Dec. 8, 1937; ord. titular bishop of Bisica and auxiliary bishop of Newark, Sept. 24, 1957; app. bishop of Bridgeport, 1961, installed Nov. 21, 1961.

Curtiss, Elden F.: b. June 16, 1932, Baker, Ore.; educ. St. Edward Seminary College and St. Thomas Seminary (Kenmore, Wash.); ord. priest May 24, 1958; ord. bishop of Helena, Mont., Apr. 28, 1976.

D

Daily, Thomas V.: b. Sept. 23, 1927, Belmont, Mass.; educ. Boston College, St. John's Seminary (Brighton, Mass.); ord. priest Jan. 10, 1952; missionary in Peru for five years as a member of the Society of St. James the Apostle; ord. titular bishop of Bladia and auxiliary bishop of Boston, Feb. 11, 1975.

Daley, Joseph T.: b. Dec. 21, 1915, Connerton, Pa.; educ. St. Charles Borromeo Seminary (Philadelphia, Pa.); ord. priest June 7, 1941; ord. titular bishop of Barca and auxiliary bishop of Harrisburg, Pa., Jan. 7, 1964; coadjutor bishop of Harrisburg, Aug. 2, 1967; bishop of Harrisburg, Oct. 19, 1971.

Daly, James: b. Aug. 14, 1921, New York, N.Y.; educ. Cathedral College (Brooklyn, N.Y.), Immaculate Conception Seminary (Huntington, L.I.); ord. priest May 22, 1948; ord. titular bishop of Castra Nova and auxiliary bishop of Rockville Centre, May 9, 1977.

Danglmayr, Augustine: b. Dec. 11, 1898, Muenster, Tex.; educ. Subiaco College (Arkansas), St. Mary's Seminary (La Porte, Tex.), Kenrick Seminary (St. Louis, Mo.); ord. priest June 10, 1922; ord. titular bishop of Olba, Oct. 7, 1942; auxiliary bishop of Dallas-Ft. Worth, 1942-69.

D'Antonio, Nicholas, O.F.M.: b. July 10, 1916, Rochester, N.Y.; educ. St. Anthony's Friary (Catskill, N.Y.); ord. priest June 7, 1942; ord. titular bishop of Giufi Salaria and prelate of Olancho, Honduras, July 25, 1966; resigned 1977; app. vicar general of New Orleans archdiocese and episcopal vicar for Spanish Speaking, August, 1977.

D'Arcy, John M.: b. Aug. 18, 1932, Brighton, Mass.; educ. St. John's Seminary (Brighton, Mass.), Angelicum Univ. (Rome); ord. priest Feb. 2, 1957; spiritual director of St. John's Seminary; ord. titular bishop of Mediana and auxiliary bishop of Boston, Feb. 11, 1975.

Davis, James Peter: b. June 9, 1904, Houghton, Mich.; educ. St. Joseph's College (Mountain View, Calif.), St. Patrick's Seminary (Menlo Park, Calif.); ord. priest May 19, 1929; ord. bishop of San Juan, Puerto Rico, Oct. 6, 1943; app. first archbishop of San Juan, July 30, 1960; app. archbishop of Santa Fe, installed Feb. 25, 1964; resigned June 4, 1974.

Dearden, John Francis: (See Cardinals, Biographies.)

Deksnys, Antanas L.: b. May 9, 1906, Buteniskiai, Lithuania; educ. Metropolitan Seminary and Theological and Philosophical Faculty at Vytautas the Great Univ. (all at Kaunas, Lithuania), Univ. of Fribourg (Switzerland); ord. priest

May 30, 1931; served in US parishes at Mt. Carmel, Pa., and East St. Louis, Ill.; ord. titular bishop of Lavellum, June 15, 1969; assigned to pastoral work among Lithuanians in Western Europe.

Delaney, Joseph P.: b. Aug. 29, 1934, Fall River, Mass.; educ. Cardinal O'Connell Seminary (Boston, Mass.), Theological College (Washington, D.C.), North American College (Rome), Rhode Island College (Providence, R.I.); ord. priest Dec. 18, 1960; ord. bishop of Fort Worth, Tex., Sept. 13, 1981.

Dempsey, Michael J., O.P.: b. Feb. 22, 1912, Providence, R.I.; entered Order of Preachers (Dominicans), Chicago province, 1935; ord. priest June 11, 1942; ord. bishop of Sokoto, Nigeria, Aug. 15, 1967.

Denning, Joseph P.: b. Jan. 4, 1907, Flushing, L.I.; educ. Cathedral College (Brooklyn, N.Y.), Immaculate Conception Seminary (Huntington, L.I.), St. Mary's Seminary (Baltimore, Md.); ord. priest May 21, 1932; ord. titular bishop of Mallus and auxiliary bishop of Brooklyn, Apr. 22, 1959; resigned Apr. 13, 1982.

De Palma, Joseph A., S.C.J.: b. Sept. 4, 1913, Walton, N.Y.; ord. priest May 20, 1944; superior general of Congregation of Priests of the Sacred Heart, 1959-67; ord. first bishop of De Aar, South Africa, July 19, 1967.

De Simone, Louis A.: b. Feb. 21, 1922, Philadelphia, Pa.; educ. Villanova Univ. (Villanova, Pa.), St. Charles Borromeo Seminary (Overbrook, Pa.); ord. priest May 10, 1952; ord. titular bishop of Cillium and auxiliary bishop of Philadelphia, Aug. 12, 1981.

Dimino, Joseph T.: b. Jan. 7, 1923, New York, N.Y.; educ. Cathedral College (New York, N.Y.), St. Joseph's Seminary (Yonkers, N.Y.), Catholic Univ. (Washington, D.C.); ord. priest June 4, 1949; ord. titular bishop of Carini and auxiliary bishop of the Military Vicariate, May 10, 1983.

Dimmerling, Harold J.: b. Sept. 23, 1914, Braddock, Pa.; educ. St. Fidelis Preparatory Seminary (Herman, Pa.), St. Charles Seminary (Columbus, O.), St. Francis Seminary (Loretto, Pa.); ord. priest May 2, 1940; ord. bishop of Rapid City, Oct. 30, 1969.

Dingman, Maurice J.: b. Jan. 20, 1914, St. Paul, Ia.; educ. St. Ambrose College (Davenport, Ia.), North American College and Gregorian Univ. (Rome), Catholic Univ. (Washington, D.C.); ord. priest Dec. 8, 1939; ord. bishop of Des Moines, June 19, 1968.

Dion, Georges E., O.M.I.: b. Sept. 25, 1911, Central Falls, R.I.; educ. Holy Cross College (Worcester, Mass.), Oblate Juniorate (Colebrook, N.H.), Oblate Scholasticates (Natick, Mass., and Ottawa, Ont.); ord. priest June 24, 1936; ord. titular bishop of Arpaia and vicar apostolic of Jolo, Philippine Islands, Apr. 23, 1980.

Dolinay, Thomas V.: b. July 24, 1923, Uniontown, Pa.; educ. St. Procopius College (Lisle, Ill.); ord. priest May 16, 1948; editor *Eastern Catholic Life*, 1966-82; ord. titular bishop of Tiatira and auxiliary bishop of Byzantine-Rite diocese of Passaic, Nov. 23, 1976; app. first bishop Byzantine-Rite diocese of Van Nuys, Calif., Dec. 3, 1981, installed Mar. 9, 1982.

Donaghy, Frederick Anthony, M.M.: b. Jan. 13, 1903, New Bedford, Mass.; educ. Holy Cross College (Worcester, Mass.), St. Mary's Seminary (Baltimore, Md.), Maryknoll Seminary (Maryknoll, N.Y.); ord. priest Jan. 29, 1929; ord. titular bishop of Setea and vicar apostolic of Wuchow, China, Sept. 21, 1939; title changed to bishop of Wuchow, Apr. 11, 1946; expelled by Communists.

Donnellan, Thomas A.: b. Jan. 24, 1914, New York, N.Y.; educ. Cathedral College and St. Joseph's Seminary (New York, N.Y.), Catholic Univ. (Washington, D.C.); ord. priest June 3, 1939; ord. bishop of Ogdensburg, Apr. 9, 1964; app. archbishop of Atlanta, installed July 16, 1968.

Donohoe, Hugh A.: b. June 28, 1905, San Francisco, Calif.; educ. St. Patrick's Preparatory and Major Seminaries (Menlo Park, Calif.), Catholic Univ. (Washington, D.C.); ord. priest June 14, 1930; ord. titular bishop of Taium and auxiliary bishop of San Francisco, Oct. 7, 1947; app. first bishop of Stockton, Jan. 27, 1962; app. bishop of Fresno, Aug. 27, 1969, installed Oct. 7, 1969; retired July 1, 1980.

Donovan, John A.: b. Aug. 5, 1911, Chatham, Ont., Canada; educ. Sacred Heart Seminary (Detroit, Mich.), North American College and Gregorian Univ. (Rome); ord. priest Dec. 8, 1935; ord. titular bishop of Rhasus and auxiliary bishop of Detroit, Oct. 26, 1954; app. bishop of Toledo, installed Apr. 18, 1967; retired July 29, 1980.

Donovan, Paul V.: b. Sept. 1, 1924, Bernard, Iowa; educ. St. Gregory's Seminary (Cincinnati, Ohio), Mt. St. Mary's Seminary (Norwood, Ohio), Lateran Univ. (Rome); ord. priest May 20, 1950; ord. first bishop of Kalamazoo, Mich., July 21, 1971.

Dougherty, John J.: b. Sept. 16, 1907, Jersey City, N.J.; educ. Seton Hall Univ. (S. Orange, N.J.), Immaculate Conception Seminary (Darlington, N.J.), North American College, Gregorian Univ., Pontifical Biblical Institute (Rome); ord. priest July 23, 1933; ord. titular bishop of Cotenna and auxiliary bishop of Newark, Jan. 24, 1963; retired Sept. 18, 1982.

Dozier, Carroll T.: b. Aug. 18, 1911, Richmond, Va.; educ. Holy Cross College (Worcester, Mass.), Gregorian Univ. (Rome); ord. priest, Mar. 19, 1937, Rome; ord. first bishop of Memphis, Jan. 6, 1971; resigned July 27, 1982.

Driscoll, Justin A.: b. Sept. 30, 1920, Bernard, Ia.; educ. Loras College (Dubuque, Ia.), Catholic Univ. (Washington, D.C.); ord. priest July 28, 1945; president of Loras College, 1967-70; ord. bishop of Fargo, Oct. 28, 1970.

Drury, Thomas J.: b. Jan. 4, 1908, Co. Sligo, Ireland; educ. St. Benedict's College (Atchison, Kans.), Kenrick Seminary (St. Louis, Mo.); ord. priest June 2, 1935; ord. first bishop of San Angelo, Tex., Jan. 24, 1962; app. bishop of Corpus Christi, installed Sept. 1, 1965; resigned May 24, 1983.

Dudick, Michael J.: b. Feb. 24, 1916, St. Clair, Pa.; educ. St. Procopius College and Seminary (Lisle, Ill.); ord. priest Nov. 13, 1945; ord. bishop of Byzantine Rite Eparchy of Passaic, Oct. 24, 1968.

Dudley, Paul: b. Nov. 27, 1926, Northfield, Minn.; educ. Nazareth College and St. Paul Seminary (St. Paul, Minn.); ord. priest June 2, 1951; ord. titular bishop of Ursona and auxiliary bishop of St. Paul and Minneapolis, Jan. 25, 1977; app. bishop of Sioux Falls, installed Dec. 13, 1978.

Duhart, Clarence James, C.SS.R.: b. Mar. 23, 1912, New Orleans, La.; ord. priest June 29, 1937; ord. bishop of Udon Thani, Thailand, Apr. 21, 1966; resigned Oct. 2, 1975.

DuMaine, (Roland) Pierre: b. Aug. 2, 1931, Paducah, Ky.; educ. St. Joseph's College (Mountain View, Calif.), St. Patrick's College and Seminary (Menlo Park, Calif.), Univ. of California (Berkeley), Catholic Univ. (Washington, D.C.); ord. priest June 15, 1957; ord. titular bishop of Sarda and auxiliary bishop of San Francisco, June 29, 1978; app. first bishop of San Jose, Jan. 27, 1981; installed Mar. 18, 1981.

Dunn, Francis J.: b. Mar. 22, 1922, Elkader, Ia.; educ. Loras College (Dubuque, Ia.), Kenrick Seminary (St. Louis, Mo.), Angelicum (Rome, Italy); ord. priest Jan. 11, 1948; chancellor of Dubuque, Aug. 27, 1960; ord. titular bishop of Turris Tamallani and auxiliary bishop of Dubuque, Aug. 27, 1969, app. vicar general, Aug. 28, 1969.

Durick, Joseph Aloysius: b. Oct. 13, 1914, Dayton, Tenn.; educ. St. Bernard Minor Seminary (St. Bernard, Ala.), St. Mary's Seminary (Baltimore, Md.), Urban Univ. (Rome); ord. priest May 23, 1940; ord. titular bishop of Cerbal and auxiliary bishop of Mobile-Birmingham, Mar. 24, 1955; app. coadjutor bishop of Nashville, Tenn., installed Mar. 3, 1964; apostolic administrator, 1966; bishop of Nashville, Sept. 10, 1969; resigned Apr. 4, 1975, to work with inmates of Federal correctional institutions and their families.

Durning, Dennis V., C.S.Sp.: b. May 18, 1923, Germantown, Pa.; educ. St. Mary's Seminary (Ferndale, Conn.); ord. priest June 3, 1949; ord. first bishop of Arusha, Tanzania, May 28, 1963.

E

Elko, Nicholas T.: b. Dec. 14, 1909, Donora, Pa.; educ. Duquesne Univ. (Pittsburgh, Pa.), Seminary of Uzhorod (Czechoslovakia) Louvain Univ. (Belgium); ord. priest Sept. 30, 1934; ord. titular bishop of Apollonias and apostolic administrator of Byzantine-Rite exarchy of Pittsburgh, Mar. 6, 1955; succeeded as exarch of Pittsburgh, Sept. 5, 1955; became eparch when Pittsburgh was raised to eparchy, July, 1963; app. titular archbishop of Dara, 1967, and ordaining prelate for Byzantine Rite in Rome; head of Oriental liturgical commission; app. auxiliary bishop of Cincinnati, Aug. 10, 1971.

Etteldorf, Raymond P.: b. Aug. 12, 1911, Ossian, Ia.; educ. Loras College (Dubuque, Ia.), Gregorian Univ. (Rome); ord. priest Dec. 8, 1937; secretary general of Supreme Council for direction of Pontifical Missionary Works, 1964-68; secretary of Pontifical Commission for Economic Affairs, 1968-69; ord. titular archbishop of Tindari, Jan. 6, 1969; papal representative to New Zealand and the Pacific Islands, 1968-74; pro-nuncio to Ethiopia, 1974-82; nuncio-at-large; app. consultor to Congregation for Evangelization of Peoples and Secretariat for Promoting Christian Unity, 1983.

Evans, George R.: b. Sept. 25, 1922, Denver, Colo.; educ. Notre Dame Univ. (Notre Dame, Ind.), St. Thomas Seminary (Denver, Colo.), Apollinare Univ. (Rome, Italy); ord. priest May 31, 1947; ord. titular bishop of Tubyza and auxiliary bishop of Denver, Apr. 23, 1969.

F

Federal, Joseph Lennox: b. Jan. 13, 1910, Greensboro, N.C.; educ. Belmont Abbey College (Belmont Abbey, N.C.), Niagara Univ. (Niagara Falls, N.Y.), Univ. of Fribourg (Switzerland), North American College and Gregorian Univ. (Rome); ord. priest Dec. 8, 1934; ord. titular bishop of Appiaria and auxiliary bishop of Salt Lake City, Apr. 11, 1951; app. coadjutor with right of succession, May, 1958; bishop of Salt Lake City, Mar. 31, 1960; retired Apr. 22, 1980.

Ferrario, Joseph A.: b. Mar. 3, 1926, Scranton, Pa.; educ. St. Charles College (Catonsville, Md.), St. Mary's Seminary (Baltimore, Md.), Catholic Univ. (Washington, D.C.); Univ. of Scranton; ord. priest May 19, 1951; ord. titular bishop of Cuse and auxiliary bishop of Honolulu Jan. 13, 1978; bishop of Honolulu, May 13, 1982.

Fiorenza, Joseph A.: b. Jan. 25, 1931, Beaumont, Tex.; educ. St. Mary's Seminary (LaPorte, Tex.); ord. priest May 29, 1954; ord. bishop of San Angelo, Oct. 25, 1979.

Fitzpatrick, John J.: b. Oct. 12, 1918, Trenton, Ont., Canada; educ. Urban Univ. (Rome), Our Lady of the Angels Seminary (Niagara Falls, N.Y.); ord. priest Dec. 13, 1942; ord. titular bishop of Cenae and auxiliary bishop of Miami, Aug. 28, 1968; bishop of Brownsville, Tex., May 28, 1971.

Fitzsimons, George K.: b. Sept. 4, 1928, Kansas City, Mo.; educ. Rockhurst College (Kansas City, Mo.), Immaculate Conception Seminary (Conception, Mo.); ord. priest Mar. 18, 1961; ord. titular bishop of Pertusa and auxiliary bishop of Kansas City-St. Joseph, July 3, 1975.

Flanagan, Bernard Joseph: b. Mar. 31, 1908, Proctor, Vt.; educ. Holy Cross College (Worcester, Mass.), North American College (Rome), Catholic Univ. (Washington, D.C.); ord. priest Dec. 8, 1931; ord. first bishop of Norwich, Nov. 30, 1953; app. bishop of Worcester, installed, Sept. 24, 1959; resigned Apr. 12, 1983.

Flavin, Glennon P.: b. Mar. 2, 1916, St. Louis, Mo.; educ. Kenrick Seminary (St. Louis, Mo.); ord. priest Dec. 20, 1941; ord. titular bishop of Joannina and auxiliary bishop of St. Louis, May 30, 1957; app. bishop of Lincoln, installed Aug. 17, 1967.

Fliss, Raphael M.: b. Oct. 25, 1930, Milwaukee, Wis.; educ. St. Francis Seminary (Milwaukee, Wis.), Catholic University (Washington, D.C.), Pontifical Lateran Univ. (Rome); ord. priest May 26, 1956; ord. coadjutor bishop of Superior with right of succession, Dec. 20, 1979.

Flores, Felixberto C.: b. Jan. 13, 1921, Agana, Guam; educ. St. John's Seminary (Brighton,

Mass.), Fordham Univ. (New York); ord. priest Apr. 30, 1949; ord. titular bishop of Stonj, May 17, 1970, and apostolic administrator of the diocese of Agana, Guam; installed second residential bishop of Agana, July 12, 1972.

Flores, Patrick F.: b. July 26, 1929, Ganado, Tex.; educ. St. Mary's Seminary (Houston, Tex.); ord. priest May 26, 1956; ord. titular bishop of Itolica and auxiliary bishop of San Antonio, May 5, 1970 (first Mexican-American bishop); app. bishop of El Paso, Apr. 4, 1978, installed May 29, 1978; app. archbishop of San Antonio 1979.

Forst, Marion F.: b. Sept. 3, 1910, St. Louis, Mo.; educ. St. Louis Preparatory Seminary (St. Louis, Mo.), Kenrick Seminary (Webster Groves, Mo.); ord. priest June 10, 1934; ord. bishop of Dodge City, Mar. 24, 1960; app. titular bishop of Scala and auxiliary bishop of Kansas City, Kans. Oct. 16, 1976.

Francis Joseph A., S.V.D.: b. Sept. 30, 1923, Lafayette, La.; educ. St. Augustine Seminary (Bay St. Louis, Miss.), St. Mary Seminary (Techny, Ill.), Catholic Univ. (Washington, D.C.); ord. priest Oct. 7, 1950; president Conference of Major Superiors of Men, 1974-76, and the National Black Catholic Clergy Caucus; ord. titular bishop of Valliposita and auxiliary bishop of Newark, June 25, 1976.

Franz, John B.: b. Oct. 29, 1896, Springfield, Ill.; educ. Quincy College (Quincy, Ill.), Kenrick Seminary (Webster Groves, Mo.), Catholic Univ. (Washington, D.C.); ord. priest June 13, 1920; ord. first bishop of Dodge City, Aug. 29, 1951; app. bishop of Peoria, installed Nov. 4, 1959; resigned May 24, 1971.

Franzetta, Benedict C.: b. Aug. 1, 1921, East Liverpool, O.; educ. St. Charles College (Catonsville, Md.), St. Mary Seminary (Cleveland, O.); ord. priest Apr. 29, 1950; ord. titular bishop of Oderzo and auxiliary bishop of Youngstown, Sept 4, 1980.

Freking, Frederick W.: b. Aug. 11, 1913, Heron Lake, Minn.; educ. St. Mary's College (Winona, Minn.), North American College and Gregorian Univ. (Rome), Catholic Univ. (Washington, D.C.); ord. priest July 31, 1938; ord. bishop of Salina, Nov. 30, 1957; app. bishop of La Crosse, Dec. 30, 1964, installed Feb. 24, 1965; resigned May 10, 1983.

Frey, Gerard L.: b. May 10, 1914, New Orleans, La.; educ. Notre Dame Seminary (New Orleans, La.); ord. priest Apr. 2, 1938; ord. bishop of Savannah, Aug. 8, 1967; app. bishop of Lafayette, La., Nov. 7, 1972, installed Jan, 7, 1973.

Friend, William B.: b. Oct. 22, 1931, Miami, Fla.; educ. St. Mary's College (St. Mary, Ky.), Mt. St. Mary Seminary (Emmitsburg, Md.), Catholic Univ. (Washington, D.C.), Notre Dame Univ. (Notre Dame, Ind.); ord. priest May 7, 1959; ord. titular bishop of Pomaria and auxiliary bishop of Alexandria-Shreveport, La., Oct. 30, 1979; app. bishop of Alexandria-Shreveport, Nov. 17, 1982, installed Jan 11, 1983.

Frosi, Angelo, S. X.: b. Jan. 31, 1924, Baffano Cremona, Italy; ord. priest May 6, 1948; U.S. citizen; ord. titular bishop of Magneto, May 1, 1970, and prelate of Abaete do Tocantins, Brazil; app. first bishop of Abaetetuba, Brazil, Sept. 17, 1981.

Fulcher, George A.: b. Jan. 30, 1922, Columbus, Ohio; educ. St. Charles Borromeo Seminary (Columbus, O.), Mt. St. Mary of the West Seminary (Norwood, O.), North American College and Angelicum (Rome); ord. priest Feb. 28, 1948; ord. titular bishop of Morosbisdus and auxiliary bishop of Columbus, July 18, 1976; app. bishop of Lafayette in Indiana, Feb. 8, 1983, installed Apr. 14, 1983.

Furlong, Philip J.: b. Dec. 8, 1892, New York, N.Y.; educ. Cathedral College (New York, N.Y.), St. Joseph's Seminary (Yonkers, N.Y.); ord. priest May 18, 1918; ord. titular bishop of Araxa and auxiliary to military vicar, Jan. 25, 1956. Retired 1971.

G

Gallagher, Raymond J.: b. Nov. 19, 1912, Cleveland, Ohio; educ. John Carroll Univ. and Our Lady of the Lake Seminary (Cleveland, O.); ord. priest Mar. 25, 1939; secretary of the National Conference of Catholic Charities 1961-65; ord. bishop of Lafayette in Indiana, Aug. 11, 1965; resigned Oct. 26, 1982.

Gallegos, Alphonse, O.A.R.: b. Feb. 20, 1931, Albuquerque, N. Mex., ord priest May 24, 1958; ord. titular bishop of Sasabe and auxiliary bishop of Sacramento, Nov. 4, 1981.

Ganter, Bernard J.: b. July 17,1928, Galveston, Tex.; educ. Texas A & M Univ. (College Sta., Tex.), St. Mary's Seminary (La Porte, Tex.), Catholic Univ. (Washington, D.C.); ord. priest May 22, 1952; chancellor of Galveston-Houston diocese, 1966-73; ord. first bishop of Tulsa, Feb. 7, 1973; app. bishop of Beaumont, Tex., Oct. 18, 1977, installed Dec. 13, 1977.

Garmendia, Francisco: b. Nov. 6, 1924, Lozcano, Spain; ord. priest June 29, 1947, in Spain; came to New York in 1964; became naturalized citizen; ord. titular bishop of Limisa and auxiliary bishop of New York, June 29, 1977. Vicar for Spanish pastoral development in New York archdiocese.

Garmo, George: b. Dec. 8, 1921, Telkaif, Iraq; educ. St. Peter Chaldean Patriarchal Seminary (Mossul, Iraq), Pontifical Urban Univ. (Rome); ord. priest Dec. 8, 1945; pastor of Chaldean parish in Detroit archdiocese, 1960-64, 1966-80; ord. archbishop of Chaldean-Rite archdiocese of Mossul, Iraq, Sept. 14, 1980.

Garner, Robert F.: b. Apr. 27, 1920, Jersey City, N.J.; educ. Seton Hall Univ. (S. Orange, N.J.), Immaculate Conception Seminary (Darlington, N.J.); ord. priest June 15, 1946; ord. titular bishop of Blera and auxiliary bishop of Newark, June 25, 1976.

Gaughan, Norbert F.: b. May 30, 1921, Pittsburgh, Pa.; educ. St. Vincent College (Latrobe, Pa.), Univ. of Pittsburgh; ord. priest Nov. 4, 1945; ord. titular bishop of Taraqua and auxiliary bishop of Greensburg, June 26, 1975.

Gelineau, Louis E.: b. May 3, 1928, Burlington, Vt.; educ. St. Michael's College (Winooski, Vt.), St. Paul's Univ. Seminary (Ottawa, Ont.), Catholic

Univ. (Washington, D.C.); ord. priest June 5, 1954; ord. bishop of Providence, R.I., Jan. 26, 1972.

Gendron, Odore: b. Sept. 13, 1921, Manchester, N.H.; educ. St. Charles Borromeo Seminary (Sherbrooke, Que., Canada), Univ. of Ottawa, St. Paul Univ. Seminary (Ottawa, Ont., Canada); ord. priest May 31, 1947; ord. bishop of Manchester, Feb. 3, 1975.

Gerber, Eugene J.: b. Apr. 30, 1931, Kingman, Kans.; educ. St. Thomas Seminary (Denver, Colo.), Wichita State Univ.; Catholic Univ. (Washington, D.C.), Angelicum (Rome); ord. priest May 19, 1959; ord. bishop of Dodge City, Dec. 14, 1976; app. bishop of Wichita, Nov. 17, 1982.

Gerbermann, Hugo, M.M.: b. Sept. 11, 1913, Nada, Tex.; educ. St. John's Minor and Major Seminary (San Antonio, Tex.), Maryknoll Seminary (Maryknoll, N.Y.); ord. priest Feb. 7, 1943; missionary work in Ecuador and Guatemala; ord. titular bishop of Amathus and prelate of Huehuetenango, Guatemala, July 22, 1962; first bishop of Huehuetenango, Dec. 23, 1967; app. titular bishop of Pinkel and auxiliary bishop of San Antonio, July 24, 1975; resigned June 30, 1982.

Gerety, Peter L: b. July 19, 1912, Shelton, Conn.; educ. Sulpician Seminary (Paris, France); ord. priest June 29, 1939; ord. titular bishop of Crepedula and coadjutor bishop of Portland, Me., with right of succession, June 1, 1966; app. apostolic administrator of Portland, 1967; bishop of Portland, Me., Sept. 15, 1969; app. archbishop of Newark, Apr. 2, 1974; installed June 28, 1974.

Gerrard, James J.: b. June 9, 1897, New Bedford, Mass.; educ. St. Laurent College (Montreal, Que.), St. Bernard's Seminary (Rochester, N.Y.); ord. priest May 26, 1923; ord. titular bishop of Forma and auxiliary bishop of Fall River, Mar. 19, 1959. Retired January, 1976.

Glenn, Laurence A.: b. Aug. 25, 1900, Bellingham, Wash.; educ. St. John's Univ. (Collegeville, Minn.), Catholic Univ. (Washington, D.C.); ord. priest June 11, 1927; ord. titular bishop of Tuscamia and auxiliary bishop of Duluth, Sept. 12, 1956; app. bishop of Crookston, Jan. 27, 1960, installed Apr. 20, 1960; resigned 1970.

Glennie, Ignatius T., S.J.: b. Feb. 5, 1907, Mexico City; educ. Mt. St. Michael's Scholasticate (Spokane, Wash.), Pontifical Seminary (Kandy, Ceylon), St. Mary's College (Kurdeong, India); entered Society of Jesus, 1924; ord. priest Nov. 21, 1938; ord. bishop of Trincomalee, Ceylon, Sept. 21, 1947; title of see changed to Trincomalee-Batticaloa (Sri Lanka), 1967; resigned Feb. 15, 1974.

Gossman, F. Joseph: b. Apr. 1, 1930, Baltimore, Md.; educ. St. Charles College (Catonsville, Md.), St. Mary's Seminary (Baltimore, Md.), North American College (Rome), Catholic Univ. (Washington, D.C.); ord. priest Dec. 17, 1955; ord. titular bishop of Agunto and auxiliary bishop of Baltimore, Sept. 11, 1968; named urban vicar, June 13, 1970; app. bishop of Raleigh April 8, 1975.

Gottwald, George J.: b. May 12, 1914, St. Louis, Mo.; educ. Kenrick Seminary (Webster Groves, Mo.); ord. priest June 9, 1940; ord. titular bishop of Cedamusa and auxiliary bishop of St. Louis, Aug. 8, 1961.

Gracida, Rene H.: b. June 9, 1923, New Orleans, La.; educ. Rice Univ. and Univ. of Houston (Houston, Tex.), Univ. of Fribourg (Switzerland); ord. priest May 23, 1959; ord. titular bishop of Masucaba and auxiliary bishop of Miami, Jan. 25, 1972; app. first bishop of Pensacola-Tallahassee, Oct. 1, 1975, installed Nov. 6, 1975; app. bishop of Corpus Christi, May 24, 1983, installed July 11, 1983.

Grady, Thomas J.: b. Oct. 9, 1914, Chicago, Ill.; educ. St. Mary of the Lake Seminary (Mundelein, Ill.), Gregorian Univ. (Rome), Loyola Univ. (Chicago, Ill.); ord. priest Apr. 23, 1938; ord. titular bishop of Vamalla and auxiliary bishop of Chicago, Aug. 24, 1967; app. bishop of Orlando, Fla., Nov. 11, 1974, installed Dec. 16, 1974.

Graham, John J.: b. Sept. 11, 1913, Philadelphia, Pa.; educ. St. Charles Borromeo Seminary (Philadelphia, Pa.), Pontifical Roman Seminary (Rome, Italy); ord. priest Feb. 26, 1938; ord. titular bishop of Sabrata and auxiliary bishop of Philadelphia, Jan. 7, 1964.

Grahmann, Charles V.: b. July 15, 1931, Halletsville, Tex.; educ. The Assumption-St. John's Seminary (San Antonio, Tex.); ord. priest Mar. 17, 1956; ord. titular bishop of Equilium and auxiliary bishop of San Antonio, Aug. 20, 1981; app. first bishop of Victoria, Tex., Apr. 13, 1982.

Graves, Lawrence P.: b. May 4, 1916, Texarkana, Ark.; educ. St. John's Seminary (Little Rock, Ark.), North American College (Rome), Catholic Univ. (Washington, D.C.); ord. priest June 11, 1942; ord. titular bishop of Vina and auxiliary bishop of Little Rock, Apr. 25, 1969; app. bishop of Alexandria, May 22, 1973, installed Sept. 18, 1973; title of see changed to Alexandria-Shreveport, Jan. 12, 1977; resigned July 20, 1982.

Graziano, Lawrence, O.F.M.: b. Apr. 5, 1921, Mt. Vernon, N.Y.; educ. Mt. Alvernia Seminary (Wappingers Falls, N.Y.); ord. priest Jan. 26, 1947; ord. titular bishop of Limata and auxiliary bishop of Santa Ana, El Salvador, Sept. 21, 1961; app. coadjutor bishop of San Miguel, El Salvador, with right of succession, 1965; bishop of San Miguel, Jan. 10, 1968; resigned June 27, 1969.

Greco, Charles Paschal: b. Oct. 29, 1894, Rodney, Miss.; educ. St. Joseph's Seminary (St. Benedict, La.), Louvain Univ. (Belgium), Dominican Univ. (Fribourg, Switzerland); ord. priest July 25, 1918; ord. bishop of Alexandria Feb. 25, 1946; retired May 22, 1973.

Green, Francis J.: b. July 7, 1906, Corning, N.Y.; educ. St. Patrick's Seminary (Menlo Park, Calif.); ord. priest May 15, 1932; ord. titular bishop of Serra and auxiliary bishop of Tucson, Sept. 17, 1953; named coadjutor of Tucson with right of succession, May 11, 1960; bishop of Tucson, Oct. 26, 1960; retired July 27, 1981.

Grellinger, John B.: b. Nov. 5, 1899, Milwaukee, Wis.; educ. Marquette Univ. and St. Francis Seminary (Milwaukee, Wis.), Urban Univ. and Gregorian Univ. (Rome); ord. priest July 14, 1929; ord. titular bishop of Syene and auxiliary bishop of Green Bay, July 14, 1949; retired Sept. 22, 1974.

Greteman, Frank H.: b. Dec. 25, 1907, Willey, Ia.; educ. Loras Academy and Loras College (Dubuque, Ia.), North American College (Rome),

Catholic Univ. (Washington, D.C.); ord. priest Dec. 8, 1932; ord. titular bishop of Vissalsa and auxiliary bishop of Sioux City, May 26, 1965; bishop of Sioux City, Dec. 9, 1970; resigned Jan. 23, 1983.

Griffin, James A.: b. June 13, 1934, Fairview Park, O.; educ. St. Charles College (Baltimore, Md.), Borromeo College (Wicklife, O.); St. Mary Seminary (Cleveland, O.); Lateran Univ. (Rome); Cleveland State Univ.; ord. priest May 28, 1960; ord. titular bishop of Holar and auxiliary bishop of Cleveland, Aug. 1, 1979; app. bishop of Columbus, Feb. 8, 1983.

Grutka, Andrew G.: b. Nov. 17, 1908, Joliet, Ill.; educ. St. Procopius College and Seminary (Lisle, Ill.), Urban Univ. and Gregorian Univ. (Rome); ord. priest Dec. 5, 1933; app. moderator of lay activities in Gary diocese, 1955; ord. first bishop of Gary, Feb. 25, 1957; app. member of Pontifical Marian Academy, Jan. 5, 1970.

Guilfoyle, George H.: b. Nov. 13, 1913, New York, N.Y.; educ. Georgetown Univ. (Washington, D.C.), Fordham Univ. (New York City), St. Joseph's Seminary (Dunwoodie, N.Y.), Columbia Univ. Law School (New York City); ord. priest Mar. 25, 1944; ord. titular bishop of Marazane and auxiliary bishop of New York, Nov. 30, 1964; app. bishop of Camden, installed Mar. 4, 1968.

Gumbleton, Thomas J.: b. Jan. 26, 1930, Detroit, Mich.; educ. St. John Provincial Seminary (Detroit, Mich.), Pontifical Lateran Univ. (Rome); ord. priest June 2, 1956; ord. titular bishop of Ululi and auxiliary bishop of Detroit, May 1, 1968.

H

Hacker, Hilary B.: b. Jan. 10, 1913, New Ulm, Minn.; educ. St. Paul Seminary (St. Paul, Minn.), Gregorian Univ. (Rome); ord. priest June 4, 1938; ord. bishop of Bismarck, N. Dak., Feb. 27, 1957; resigned June 30, 1982.

Hackett, John F.: b. Dec. 7, 1911, New Haven, Conn.; educ. St. Thomas Seminary (Bloomfield, Conn.), Seminaire Ste. Sulpice (Paris); ord. priest June 29, 1936; ord. titular bishop of Helenopolis in Palaestina and auxiliary bishop of Hartford, Mar. 19, 1953.

Hagarty, Paul Leonard, O.S.B.: b. Mar. 20, 1909, Greene, Ia.; educ. Loras College (Dubuque, Ia.), St. John's Seminary and St. John's Univ. (Collegeville, Minn.); entered Order of St. Benedict, 1931; ord. priest June 6, 1936; ord. titular bishop of Arba and vicar apostolic of the Bahamas, Oct. 19, 1950; first bishop of Nassau, July 5, 1960; retired 1981.

Ham, J. Richard, M.M.: b. July 11, 1921, Chicago, Ill.; educ. Maryknoll Seminary (New York); ord. priest June 12, 1948; missionary to Guatemala, 1958; ord. titular bishop of Puzia di Numidia and auxiliary bishop of Guatemala, Jan. 6, 1968; resigned see 1979; app. vicar for Hispanic ministry in St. Paul and Minneapolis archdiocese, January, 1980; auxiliary bishop of St. Paul and Minneapolis, October, 1980.

Hammes, George A.: b. Sept. 11, 1911, St. Joseph Ridge, Wis.; educ. St. Lawrence Seminary (Mt. Calvary. Wis.), St. Louis Preparatory Seminary (St. Louis, Mo.), Kenrick Seminary (Webster Groves, Mo.), Sulpician Seminary, Catholic Univ. (Washington, D.C.); ord. priest May 22, 1937; ord. bishop of Superior, May 24, 1960.

Hanifen, Richard C.: b. June 15, 1931, Denver, Colo,; educ. Regis College and St. Thomas Seminary (Denver, Colo.), Catholic Univ. (Washington, D.C.), Lateran Univ. (Rome); ord. priest June 6, 1959; ord. titular bishop of Abercorn and auxiliary bishop of Denver, Sept. 20, 1974.

Hannan, Philip M.: b. May 20, 1913, Washington, D.C.; educ. St. Charles College (Catonsville, Md.), Catholic Univ. (Washington, D.C.), North American College (Rome); ord. priest Dec. 8, 1939; ord. titular bishop of Hieropolis and auxiliary bishop of Washington, D.C., Aug. 28, 1956; app. archbishop of New Orleans, installed Oct. 13, 1965.

Harper, Edward, C.SS.R.: b. July 23, 1910, Brooklyn, N.Y.; educ. Redemptorist Houses of Study; ord. priest June 18, 1939; ord. titular bishop of Heraclea Pontica and first prelate of Virgin Islands, Oct. 6, 1960; became first bishop, 1977, when prelacy was made diocese of St. Thomas.

Harrington, Timothy J.: b. Dec. 19, 1918, Holyoke, Mass.; educ. Holy Cross College (Worcester, Mass.), Grand Seminary (Montreal, Que.), Boston College School of Social Work; ord. priest Jan. 19, 1946; ord. titular bishop of Rusuca and auxiliary bishop of Worcester, Mass., July 2, 1968.

Harris, Vincent M.: b. Oct. 14, 1913, Conroe, Tex.; educ. St. Mary's Seminary (La Porte, Tex.), North American College and Gregorian Univ. (Rome), Catholic Univ. (Washington, D.C.); ord. priest Mar. 19, 1938; ord. first bishop of Beaumont, Tex., Sept. 28, 1966; app. titular bishop of Rotaria and coadjutor bishop of Austin, Apr. 27, 1971; bishop of Austin, Nov. 16, 1971.

Harrison, Francis J.: b. Aug. 12, 1912; Syracuse, N.Y.; educ. Notre Dame Univ. (Notre Dame, Ind.), St. Bernard's Seminary (Rochester, N.Y.), ord. priest June 4, 1937; ord. titular bishop of Aquae in Numidia and auxiliary bishop of Syracuse, Apr. 22, 1971; app. bishop of Syracuse, Nov. 9, 1976, installed Feb. 6, 1977.

Hart, Daniel A.: b. Aug. 24, 1927, Lawrence, Mass.; educ. St. John's Seminary (Brighton, Mass.); ord. priest Feb. 2, 1953; ord. titular bishop of Tepelta and auxiliary bishop of Boston, Oct. 18, 1976.

Hart, Joseph: b. Sept. 26, 1931, Kansas City, Missouri; educ. St. John Seminary (Kansas City, Mo.), St. Meinrad Seminary (Indianapolis, Ind.); ord. priest May 1, 1956; ord. titular bishop of Thimida Regia and auxiliary bishop of Cheyenne, Wyo., Aug. 31, 1976; app. bishop of Cheyenne, installed June 12, 1978.

Hastrich, Jerome J.: b. Nov. 13, 1914, Milwaukee, Wis.; educ. Marquette Univ., St. Francis Seminary (Milwaukee, Wis.); ord. priest Feb. 9, 1941; ord. titular bishop of Gurza and auxiliary bishop of Madison, Sept. 3, 1963; app. bishop of Gallup, N.Mex., Sept. 3, 1969.

Hayes, Nevin W., O.Carm: b. Feb. 17, 1922, Chicago, Ill.; entered Carmelite novitiate Aug. 15, 1939; educ. Mt. Carmel College (Niagara Falls, Canada), Whitefriars Hall and Catholic Univ.

(Washington, D.C.); ord. priest June 8, 1946; prelate nullius of Sicuani, Peru, 1959; ord. titular bishop of Nova Sinna and prelate of Sicuani, Aug. 5, 1965; resigned November 1970; app. auxiliary bishop of Chicago, Feb. 2, 1971.

Head, Edward D.: b. Aug. 5, 1919, White Plains, N.Y.; educ. Cathedral College, St. Joseph's Seminary, Columbia Univ. (New York City); ord. priest Jan. 27, 1945; director of New York Catholic Charities; ord. titular bishop of Ardsratha and auxiliary bishop of New York, Mar. 19, 1970; app. bishop of Buffalo, Jan. 23, 1973, installed Mar. 19, 1973.

Helmsing, Charles H.: b. Mar. 23, 1908, Shrewsbury, Mo.; educ. St. Louis Preparatory Seminary (St. Louis, Mo.), Kenrick Seminary (Webster Groves, Mo.); ord. priest June 10, 1933; ord. titular bishop of Axomis and auxiliary bishop of St. Louis, Apr. 19, 1949; first bishop of Springfield-Cape Girardeau, Aug. 24, 1956; bishop of Kansas City-St. Joseph, 1962, installed Apr. 3, 1962; resigned June 25, 1977.

Herrmann, Edward J.: b. Nov. 6, 1913, Baltimore, Md.; educ. Mt. St. Mary's Seminary (Emmitsburg, Md.), Catholic Univ. (Washington, D.C.); ord. priest June 12, 1947; ord. titular bishop of Lamzella and auxiliary bishop of Washington, D.C., Apr. 26, 1966; app. bishop of Columbus, June 26, 1973; resigned Sept. 18, 1982.

Hettinger, Edward Gerhard: b. Oct. 14, 1902, Lancaster, O.; educ. St. Vincent's College (Beatty, Pa.); ord. priest June 2, 1928; ord. titular bishop of Teos and auxiliary bishop of Columbus, Feb. 24, 1942; retired Oct. 18, 1977.

Hickey, Dennis W.: b. Oct. 28, 1914, Dansville, N.Y.; educ. Colgate Univ. and St. Bernard's Seminary (Rochester, N.Y.); ord. priest June 7, 1941; ord. titular bishop of Rusuccuru and auxiliary bishop of Rochester, N.Y., Mar. 14, 1968.

Hickey, James A.: b. Oct. 11, 1920, Midland, Mich.; educ. Sacred Heart Seminary (Detroit, Mich.), Catholic Univ. (Washington, D.C.), Lateran Univ. and Angelicum (Rome), Michigan State Univ.; ord. priest June 15, 1946; ord. titular bishop of Taraqua and auxiliary bishop of Saginaw, Apr. 14, 1967; rector of North American College, Rome, 1969-74; app. bishop of Cleveland, June 5, 1974; installed July 16, 1974; app. archbishop of Washington, D.C., installed Aug. 5, 1980.

Hines, Vincent J.: b. Sept. 14, 1912, New Haven, Conn.; educ. St. Thomas Seminary (Bloomfield, Conn.), St. Sulpice Seminary (Paris), Lateran Univ. (Rome); ord. priest May 2, 1937; ord. bishop of Norwich, Conn., Mar. 17, 1960; retired June 17, 1975.

Hoch, Lambert A.: b. Feb. 6, 1903, Elkton, S.D.; educ. Creighton Univ. (Omaha, Nebr.), St. Paul Seminary (St. Paul, Minn.); ord. priest May 30, 1928; ord. bishop of Bismarck, Mar. 25, 1952; app. bishop of Sioux Falls Dec. 5, 1956; retired June 13, 1978.

Hodapp, Robert L., S.J.: b. Oct. 1, 1910. Mankato, Minn.; educ. St. Stanislaus Seminary (Florissant, Mo.), St. Louis Univ. (St. Louis, Mo.); ord. priest June 18, 1941; ord. bishop of Belize, June 26, 1958.

Hodges, Joseph H.: b. Oct. 8, 1911, Harper's

Ferry, W.Va.; educ. St. Charles College (Catonsville, Md.), North American College (Rome); ord. priest Dec. 8, 1935; ord. titular bishop of Rusadus and auxiliary bishop of Richmond, Oct. 15, 1952; named coadjutor bishop of Wheeling with right of succession, May 24, 1961; bishop of Wheeling, Nov. 23, 1962; title of see changed to Wheeling-Charleston 1974.

Hoffman, James R.: b. June 12, 1932, Fremont, O.; educ. Our Lady of the Lake Minor Seminary (Wawasee, Ind.), St. Meinrad College (St. Meinrad, Ind.); Mt. St. Mary Seminary (Norwood, O.); Catholic Univ. (Washington, D.C.); ord. priest July 28, 1957; ord. titular bishop of Italica and auxiliary bishop of Toledo, June 23, 1978; bishop of Toledo, Dec. 16, 1980.

Hogan, James J.: b. Oct. 17, 1911, Philadelphia, Pa.; educ. St. Charles College (Catonsville, Md.), St. Mary's Seminary (Baltimore), Gregorian Univ. (Rome), Catholic Univ. (Washington, D.C.); ord. priest Dec. 8, 1937; ord. titular bishop of Philomelium and auxiliary bishop of Trenton, Feb. 25, 1960; app. bishop of Altoona-Johnstown, installed July 6, 1966.

Hogan, Joseph L.: b. Mar. 11, 1916, Lima, N.Y.; educ. St. Bernard's Seminary (Rochester, N.Y.), Canisius College (Buffalo, N.Y.), Angelicum (Rome); ord. priest June 6, 1942; ord. bishop of Rochester, Nov. 28, 1969; resigned Nov. 28, 1978.

Houck, William Russell: b. June 26, 1926, Mobile Ala.; educ. St. Bernard Junior College (Cullman, Ala.), St. Mary's Seminary College and St. Mary's Seminary (Baltimore, Md.), Catholic Univ. (Washington, D.C.); ord. priest May 19, 1951; ord. titular bishop of Alessano and auxiliary bishop of Jackson, Miss., May 27, 1979, by Pope John Paul II.

Howze, (Joseph) Lawson E.: b. Aug. 30, 1923, Daphne, Ala.; convert to Catholicism, 1948; educ. St. Bonaventure Univ. (St. Bonaventure, N.Y.); ord. priest May 7, 1959; ord. titular bishop of Massita and auxiliary bishop of Natchez-Jackson, Jan. 28, 1973; app. first bishop of Biloxi, Miss., Mar. 8, 1977; installed June 6, 1977.

Hubbard, Howard J.: b. Oct. 31, 1938, Troy, N.Y.; educ. St. Joseph's Seminary (Dunwoodie, N.Y.); North American College and Gregorian Univ. (Rome), Catholic Univ. (Washington, D.C.); ord. priest Dec. 18, 1963; ord. bishop of Albany, Mar. 27, 1977.

Hughes, Alfred C.: b. Dec. 2, 1932, Boston, Mass.; educ. St. John Seminary (Brighton, Mass), Gregorian Univ. (Rome); ord. priest Dec. 15, 1957, in Rome; ord. titular bishop of Maximiana in Byzacena and auxiliary bishop of Boston, Sept. 14, 1981.

Hughes, Edward T.: b. Nov. 13, 1920, Landowne, Pa.; educ. St. Charles Seminary, Univ. of Pennsylvania (Philadelphia, Pa.); ord. priest May 31, 1947; ord. titular bishop of Segia and auxiliary bishop of Philadelphia, July 21, 1976.

Hughes, William A.: b. Sept. 23, 1921, Youngstown, O.; educ. St. Charles College (Catonsville, Md.), St. Mary's Seminary (Cleveland, O.) Notre Dame Univ. (Notre Dame, Ind.); ord. priest Apr. 6, 1946; ord. titular bishop of Inis Cathaig and auxiliary bishop of Youngstown, Sept. 12, 1974; app. bishop of Covington, installed May 8, 1979.

Hunthausen, Raymond G.: b. Aug. 21, 1921, Anaconda, Mont.; educ. Carroll College (Helena, Mont.), St. Edward's Seminary (Kenmore, Wash.), St. Louis Univ. (St. Louis, Mo.), Catholic Univ. (Washington, D.C.), Fordham Univ. (New York City), Notre Dame Univ. (Notre Dame, Ind.); ord. priest June 1, 1946; ord. bishop of Helena, Aug. 30, 1962; app. archbishop of Seattle, Feb. 25, 1975.

Hurley, Francis T.: b. Jan. 12, 1927, San Francisco, Calif.; educ. St. Patrick's Seminary (Menlo Park, Calif.), Catholic Univ. (Washington, D.C.); ord. priest June 16, 1951; assigned to NCWC in Washington, D.C., 1957; assistant (1958) and later (1968) associate secretary of NCCB and USCC; ord. titular bishop of Daimlaig and auxiliary bishop of Juneau, Alaska, Mar. 19, 1970; app. bishop of Juneau, July 20, 1971, installed Sept. 8, 1971; app. archbishop of Anchorage, May 4, 1976, installed July 8, 1976.

Hurley, Mark J.: b. Dec. 13, 1919, San Francisco, Calif.; educ. St. Patrick's Seminary (Menlo Park, Calif.), Univ. of California (Berkeley), Catholic Univ. (Washington, D.C.), Lateran Univ. (Rome), Univ. of Portland (Portland, Ore.); ord. priest Sept. 23, 1944; ord. titular bishop of Thunusuda and auxiliary bishop of San Francisco, Jan. 4, 1968; app. bishop of Santa Rosa, Nov. 19, 1969.

I-J

Ibrahim, Ibrahim N.: b. Oct. 1, 1937, Telkaif, Mosul, Iraq.; educ. Patriarchal Seminary (Mosul, Iraq), St. Sulpice Seminary (Paris, France); ord. priest Dec. 30, 1962, in Baghdad, Iraq; ord. titular bishop of Anbar and apostolic exarch for Chaldean-Rite Catholics in the United States, Mar. 8, 1982, in Baghdad; installed in Detroit, Apr. 18, 1982.

Imesch, Joseph L.: b. June 21, 1931, Detroit, Mich.; educ. Sacred Heart Seminary (Detroit, Mich.), North American College, Gregorian Univ. (Rome); ord. priest Dec. 16, 1956; ord. titular bishop of Pomaria and auxiliary bishop of Detroit, Apr. 3, 1973; app. bishop of Joliet, June 30, 1979.

Iranyi, Ladislaus A., Sch.P.: b. Apr. 9, 1923, Szeged, Hungary; educ. Pazmany Univ. (Budapest, Hungary), Angelicum and Gregorian Univ. (Rome); ord. priest Mar. 13, 1948, in Rome; becamse U.S. citizen, 1958; ord. titular bishop of Castel Mediano, July 27, 1983; responsible for spiritual care of Hungarian Catholics living outside Hungary.

Johnson, William R.: b. Nov. 19, 1918, Tonopah, Nev.; educ. Los Angeles College and St. John's Seminary (Camarillo, Calif.), National Catholic School of Social Service, Catholic Univ. (Washington, D.C.); ord. priest May 28, 1944; ord. titular bishop of Blera and auxiliary bishop of Los Angeles, Mar. 25, 1971; app. first bishop of Orange, Calif., Mar. 30, 1976, installed June 18, 1976.

Joyce, Robert F.: b. Oct. 7, 1896, Proctor, Vt.; educ. Univ. of Vermont (Burlington, Vt.), Grand Seminary (Montreal, Canada); ord. priest May 26, 1923; ord. titular bishop of Citium and auxiliary bishop of Burlington, Oct. 28, 1954; installed as bishop of Burlington, Feb. 26, 1957; resigned Dec. 14, 1971.

K

Kalisz, Raymond P., S.V.D.: b. Sept. 25, 1927, Melvindale, Mich.; educ. St. Mary's Seminary (Techny, Ill.); ord. priest Aug. 15, 1954; ord. bishop of Wewak, Papua New Guinea, August 15, 1980.

Keating, John Richard: b. July 20, 1934, Chicago, Ill.; educ. Quigley Preparatory Seminary (Chicago, Ill.), St. Mary of the Lake Seminary (Mundelein, Ill.), Gregorian Univ. (Rome); ord. priest Dec. 20, 1958; ord. bishop of Arlington, Aug. 4, 1983.

Keeler, William Henry: b. Mar. 4, 1931, San Antonio, Tex.; educ. St. Charles Seminary (Overbrook, Pa.), North American College, Pontifical Gregorian Univ. (Rome); ord. priest July 17, 1955; ord. titular bishop of Ulcinium and auxiliary bishop of Harrisburg, Sept. 21, 1979.

Kellenberg, Walter P.: b. June 3, 1901, New York, N.Y.; educ. Cathedral College (New York, City), St. Joseph Seminary (Dunwoodie, N.Y.); ord. priest June 2, 1928; ord. titular bishop of Joannina and auxiliary bishop of New York, Oct. 5, 1953; app. bishop of Ogdensburg, Jan. 19, 1954; app. first bishop of Rockville Centre Apr. 16, 1957, installed May 27, 1957; retired May 4, 1976.

Kelly, Thomas C., O.P.: b. July 14, 1931, Rochester, N.Y.; educ. Providence College (Providence, R.I.), Immaculate Conception College (Washington, D.C.), Angelicum (Rome); professed in Dominicans, Aug. 26, 1952; secretary, apostolic delegation, Washington, D.C., 1965-71; associate general secretary, 1971-77, and general secretary, 1977-81, NCCB/USCC; ord. titular bishop of Tusurus and auxiliary bishop of Washington, D.C., Aug. 15, 1977; app. archbishop of Louisville, Dec. 28, 1981, installed Feb. 18, 1982.

Kenny, Lawrence J.: b. Aug. 30, 1930, New Rochelle, N.Y.; educ. Cathedral College (New York, N.Y.), St. Joseph's Seminary (Yonkers, N.Y.), Iona College (New Rochelle, N.Y.); ord. priest June 2, 1956; ord. titular bishop of Holar and auxiliary bishop of the Military Vicariate, May 10, 1983.

Kenny, Michael H.: b. June 26, 1937, Hollywood, Calif.; educ. St. Joseph College (Mountain View, Calif.), St. Patrick's Seminary (Menlo Park, Calif.), Catholic Univ. (Washington, D.C.); ord. priest Mar. 30, 1963; ord. bishop of Juneau, May 27, 1979.

Kinney, John: b. June 11, 1937, Oelwein, Iowa; educ. Nazareth Hall and St. Paul Seminaries (St. Paul, Minn.); Pontifical Lateran University (Rome); ord. priest Feb. 2, 1963; ord. titular bishop of Caorle and auxiliary bishop of St. Paul and Minneapolis, Jan. 25, 1977; app. bishop of Bismarck June 30, 1982.

Kmiec, Edward U.: b. June 4, 1936, Trenton, N.J.; educ. St. Charles College (Catonsville, Md.), St. Mary's Seminary (Baltimore, Md.), Gregorian Univ. (Rome); ord. priest Dec. 20, 1961; ord. titular bishop of Simidicca and auxiliary bishop of Trenton, Nov. 3, 1982.

Kocisko, Stephen: b. June 11, 1915, Minneapolis,

Minn.; educ. Nazareth Hall Minor Seminary (St. Paul, Minn.), Pontifical Ruthenian College, Urban Univ. (Rome); ord. priest Mar. 30, 1941; ord. titular bishop of Teveste and auxiliary bishop of apostolic exarchate of Pittsburgh, Oct. 23, 1956; installed as first eparch of the eparchy of Passaic, Sept. 10, 1963; app. eparch of Byzantine-Rite diocese of Pittsburgh, installed Mar. 5, 1968; app. first metropolitan of Munhall, installed June 11, 1969; title of see changed to Pittsburgh, 1977.

Koester, Charles R.: b. Sept. 16, 1915, Jefferson City, Mo.; educ. Conception Academy (Conception, Mo.), St. Louis Preparatory Seminary and Kenrick Seminary (St. Louis, Mo.), North American College (Rome); ord. priest Dec. 20, 1941; ord. titular bishop of Suacia and auxiliary bishop of St. Louis, Feb. 11, 1971.

Krawczak, Arthur H.: b. Feb. 2, 1913, Detroit, Mich.; educ. Sacred Heart Seminary, Sts. Cyril and Methodius Seminary (Orchard Lake, Mich.), Catholic Univ. (Washington, D.C.); ord. priest May 18, 1940; ord. titular bishop of Subbar and auxiliary bishop of Detroit, Apr. 3, 1973; retired Aug. 17, 1982.

Krol, John J.: (See Cardinals, Biographies.)

Kucera, Daniel, O.S.B.: b. May 7, 1923, Chicago, Ill.; educ. St. Procopius College (Lisle, Ill.), Catholic Univ. (Washington, D.C.); professed in Order of St. Benedict, June 16, 1944; ord. priest May 26, 1949; abbot, St. Procopius Abbey, 1964-71; pres. Illinois Benedictine College, 1959-65 and 1971-76; ord. titular bishop of Natchez and auxiliary bishop of Joliet, July 21, 1977; app. bishop of Salina, Mar. 5, 1980.

Kupfer, William F., M.M.: b. Jan. 28, 1909, Brooklyn, N.Y.; educ. Cathedral College (Brooklyn, N.Y.), Maryknoll Seminary (Maryknoll, N.Y.); ord. priest June 11, 1933; missionary in China; app. prefect apostolic of Taichung, Formosa, 1951; ord. first bishop of Taichung, July 25, 1962.

L

Lambert, Francis, S.M.: b. Feb. 7, 1921, Lawrence, Mass.; educ. Marist Seminary (Framingham, Mass.); ord. priest, June 29, 1946; served in Marist missions in Oceania; provincial of Marist Oceania province, 1971; ord. bishop of Port Vila, Vanuatu (New Hebrides), Mar. 20, 1977.

Larkin, W. Thomas: b. Mar. 31, 1923, Mt. Morris, N.Y.; educ. St. Andrew Seminary and St. Bernard Seminary (Rochester, N.Y.); Angelicum Univ. (Rome); ord. priest May 15, 1947; ord. bishop of St. Petersburg, May 27, 1979.

Law, Bernard F.: b. Nov. 4, 1931, Torreon, Mexico; educ. Harvard Univ. (Cambridge, Mass.), St. Joseph Seminary (St. Benedict, La.), Pontifical College Josephinum (Worthington, O.); ord. priest May 21, 1961; editor of *Mississippi Register* (now *Mississippi Today*), 1963-68; director of NCCB Committee on Ecumenical and Inter-religious Affairs, 1968-71; vicar general of Natchez-Jackson diocese, 1971-73; ord. bishop of Springfield-Cape Girardeau, Mo., Dec. 5, 1973.

Leech, George Leo: b. May 21, 1890, Ashley, Pa.; educ. St. Charles Borromeo Seminary

(Overbrook, Pa.), Catholic Univ. (Washington, D.C.); ord. priest May 29, 1920; ord. titular bishop of Mela and auxiliary bishop of Harrisburg, Oct. 17, 1935; bishop of Harrisburg Dec. 19, 1935; resigned Oct. 19, 1971; app. titular bishop of Allegheny.

Lemay, Leo, S.M.: b. Sept. 23, 1909, Lawrence, Mass.; educ. Marist College (Washington, D.C.), Gregorian Univ. (Rome); ord. priest Apr. 15, 1933; ord. titular bishop of Agbia and vicar apostolic of North Solomon Islands, Sept. 21, 1960; first bishop of Bougainville, Nov. 15, 1966; resigned July 1, 1974.

Leonard, Vincent M.: b. Dec. 11, 1908, Pittsburgh, Pa.; educ. Duquesne Univ. (Pittsburgh, Pa.), St. Vincent Seminary (Latrobe, Pa.); ord. priest June 16, 1935; ord. titular bishop of Arsacal and auxiliary bishop of Pittsburgh, Apr. 21, 1964; app. bishop of Pittsburgh, installed July 2, 1969; resigned June 30, 1983.

Lessard, Raymond W.: b. Dec. 21, 1930, Grafton, N.D.; educ. St. Paul Seminary (St. Paul, Minn.), North American College (Rome); ord. priest Dec. 16, 1956; served on staff of the Congregation for Bishops in the Roman Curia, 1964-73; ord. bishop of Savannah, Apr. 27, 1973.

Levada, William J.: b. June 15, 1936, Long Beach, Calif.; educ. St. John's College (Camarillo, Calif.), Gregorian Univ. (Rome); ord. priest Dec. 20, 1961; ord. titular bishop of Capri and auxiliary bishop of Los Angeles, May 12, 1983.

Lipscomb, Oscar H.: b. Sept. 21, 1931, Mobile, Ala.; educ. McGill Institute, St. Bernard College (Cullman, Ala.), North American College and Gregorian Univ. (Rome), Catholic Univ. (Washington, D.C.); ord. priest July 15, 1956; ord. first archbishop of Mobile, Nov. 16, 1980.

Lohmuller, Martin J.: b. Aug. 21, 1919, Philadelphia, Pa.; educ. St. Charles Borromeo Seminary (Philadelphia, Pa.), Catholic Univ. (Washington, D.C.); ord. priest June 3, 1944; ord. titular bishop of Ramsbury and auxiliary bishop of Philadelphia, Apr. 2, 1970.

Losten, Basil: b. May 11, 1930, Chesapeake City, Md.; educ. St. Basil's College (Stamford, Conn.), Catholic University (Washington, D.C.); ord. priest June 10, 1957; ord. titular bishop of Arcadiopolis in Asia and auxiliary bishop of Ukrainian archeparchy of Philadelphia, May 25, 1971; app. apostolic administrator of archeparchy, 1976; app. bishop of Ukrainian eparchy of Stamford, Sept. 20, 1977.

Lotocky, Innocent Hilarius, O.S.B.M.: b. Nov. 3, 1915, Petlykiwci, Ukraine; educ. seminaries in Ukraine, Czechoslovakia and Austria; ord. priest Nov. 24, 1940; ord. bishop of St. Nicholas of Chicago for the Ukrainians, Mar. 1, 1981.

Lubachivsky, Myroslav J.: b. June 24, 1914, Dolynian, Ukraine; educ. Innsbruck Univ. (Austria), Gregorian Univ. and Biblicum (Rome); began pastoral work in U.S. in 1947; ord. archbishop of Ukrainian-Rite archeparchy of Philadelphia, Nov. 12, 1979; app. coadjutor archbishop of Lwow of the Ukrainians, Mar. 27, 1980.

Lucker, Raymond A.: b. Feb. 24, 1927, St. Paul, Minn.; educ. St. Paul Seminary (St. Paul, Minn.);

University of Minnesota (Minneapolis), Angelicum (Rome); ord. priest June 7, 1952; director of USCC department of education, 1968-71; ord. titular bishop of Meta and auxiliary bishop of St. Paul and Minneapolis, Sept. 8, 1971; app. bishop of New Ulm, Dec. 23, 1975, installed Feb. 19, 1976.

Lyke, James Patterson, O.F.M.: b. Feb. 18, 1939, Chicago, Ill.; educ. Quincy College (Quincy, Ill.), Antonianum (Rome), Union Graduate School (Cincinnati, O.); professed in Order of Friars Minor, June 21, 1963; ord. priest June 24, 1966; president of National Black Catholic Clergy Caucus; ord. titular bishop of Furnos Maior and auxiliary bishop of Cleveland, Aug. 1, 1979.

Lynch, George E.: b. Mar. 4, 1917, New York, N.Y.; educ. Fordham Univ. (New York), Mt. St. Mary's Seminary (Emmitsburg, Md.), Catholic Univ. (Washington, D.C.); ord. priest May 29, 1943; ord. titular bishop of Satafi and auxiliary bishop of Raleigh Jan. 6, 1970.

Lyons, Thomas W.: b. Sept. 26, 1923, Washington, D.C.; educ. St. Charles College (Catonsville, Md.), St. Mary's Seminary (Baltimore, Md.); ord. priest May 22, 1948; ord. titular bishop of Mortlach and auxiliary bishop of Washington, D.C., Sept. 12, 1974.

M

McAuliffe, Michael F.: b. Nov. 22, 1920, Kansas City, Mo.; educ. St. Louis Preparatory Seminary (St. Louis, Mo.), Catholic Univ. (Washington, D.C.); ord. priest May 31, 1945; ord. bishop of Jefferson City, Aug. 18, 1969.

McCarrick, Theodore E.: b. July 7, 1930, New York, N.Y.; educ. Fordham Univ. (Bronx, N.Y.), St. Joseph's Seminary (Dunwoodie, N.Y.), Catholic Univ. (Washington, D.C.); ord. priest May 31, 1958; dean of students Catholic Univ. of America, 1961-63; pres., Catholic Univ. of Puerto Rico, 1965-69; secretary to Cardinal Cooke, 1970; ord. titular bishop of Rusubisir and auxiliary bishop of New York, June 29, 1977; app. first bishop of Metuchen, N.J., Nov. 19, 1981, installed Jan. 31, 1982.

McCarthy, Edward A.: b. Apr. 10, 1918, Cincinnati, O.; educ. Mt. St. Mary Seminary (Norwood, O.), Catholic Univ. (Washington, D.C.), Lateran and Angelicum (Rome); ord. priest May 29, 1943; ord. titular bishop of Tamascani and auxiliary bishop of Cincinnati, June 15, 1965; first bishop of Phoenix, Ariz., Dec. 2, 1969; app. coadjutor archbishop of Miami, Fla., July 7, 1976; succeeded as archbishop of Miami, July 26, 1977.

McCarthy, John E., b. June 21, 1930, Houston, Tex.; educ. Univ. of St. Thomas (Houston, Tex.); ord. priest May 26, 1956; assistant director Social Action Dept. USCC, 1967-69; executive director Texas Catholic Conference; ord. titular bishop of Pedena and auxiliary bishop of Galveston-Houston, Mar. 14, 1979.

McCormick, J. Carroll: b. Dec. 15, 1907, Philadelphia, Pa.; educ. College Ste. Marie (Montreal), St. Charles Seminary (Overbrook, Pa.), Minor and Major Roman Seminary (Rome); ord. priest July 10, 1932; ord. titular bishop of Ruspae and auxiliary bishop of Philadelphia, Apr. 23, 1947; app.

bishop of Altoona-Johnstown, installed Sept. 21, 1960; app. bishop of Scranton, installed May 25, 1966; resigned Feb. 15, 1983.

McDonald, Andrew J.: b. Oct. 24, 1923, Savannah, Ga.; educ. St. Mary's Seminary (Baltimore, Md.), Catholic Univ. (Washington, D.C.), Lateran Univ. (Rome); ord. priest May 8, 1948; ord. bishop of Little Rock, Sept. 5, 1972.

McDonald, William J.: b. June 17, 1904, Mooncoin, Ireland; educ. St. Kieran's College and Seminary (Kilkenny, Ireland), Catholic Univ. (Washington, D.C.); ord. priest June 10, 1928; rector of Catholic Univ. of America, 1957-67; ord. titular bishop of Aquae Regiae and auxiliary bishop of Washington, May 19, 1964; app. auxiliary bishop of San Francisco, July 26, 1967; retired June 5, 1979.

McDonough, Thomas J.: b. Dec. 5, 1911, Philadelphia, Pa.; educ. St. Charles Seminary (Overbrook, Pa.), Catholic Univ. (Washington, D.C.); ord. priest May 26, 1938; ord. titular bishop of Thenae and auxiliary bishop of St. Augustine, Apr. 30, 1947; app. auxiliary bishop of Savannah, Jan. 2, 1957; named bishop of Savannah, installed Apr. 27, 1960; app. archbishop of Louisville, installed May 2, 1967; resigned Sept. 29, 1981.

McDowell, John B.: b. July 17, 1921, New Castle, Pa.; educ. St. Vincent College, St. Vincent Theological Seminary (Latrobe, Pa.), Catholic Univ. (Washington, D.C.); ord. priest Nov. 4, 1945; superintendent of schools, Pittsburgh diocese, 1955-70; ord. titular bishop of Tamazuca, and auxiliary bishop of Pittsburgh, Sept. 8, 1966.

McEleney, John J., S.J.: b. Nov. 13, 1895, Woburn, Mass.; educ. Boston College (Boston, Mass.), Jesuit Scholasticate (New England Province); entered Society of Jesus, 1918; ord. priest June 18, 1930; app. provincial of New England Province, 1944; ord. titular bishop of Zeugma and vicar apostolic of Jamaica, Apr. 15, 1950; title changed to bishop of Kingston, Feb. 29, 1956; archbishop of Kingston, Sept. 14, 1967; retired Sept. 1, 1970.

McFarland, Norman F.: b. Feb. 21, 1922, Martinez, Calif.; educ. St. Patrick's Seminary (Menlo Park, Calif.), Catholic Univ. (Washington, D.C.); ord. priest June 15, 1946; ord. titular bishop of Bida and auxiliary bishop of San Francisco, Sept. 8, 1970; apostolic adminstrator of Reno, 1974; app. bishop of Reno, Feb. 10, 1976, installed Mar. 31, 1976; title of see changed to Reno-Las Vegas.

McGann, John R.: b. Dec. 2, 1924, Brooklyn, N.Y.; educ. Cathedral College (Brooklyn, N.Y.), Immaculate Conception Seminary (Huntington, L.I.); ord. priest June 3, 1950; ord. titular bishop of Morosbisdus and auxiliary bishop of Rockville Centre, Jan. 7, 1971; vicar general and episcopal vicar; app. bishop of Rockville Centre May 3, 1976, installed June 24, 1976.

McGarry, Urban, T.O.R.: b. Nov. 11, 1911, Warren, Pa.; ord. priest Oct. 3, 1942, in India; prefect apostolic of Bhagalpur, Aug. 7, 1956; ord. first bishop of Bhagalpur, India, May 10, 1965.

McGucken, Joseph T.: b. Mar. 13, 1902, Los Angeles, Calif.; educ. St. Patrick's Seminary (Menlo Park, Calif.), North American College (Rome); ord. priest Jan. 15, 1928; ord. titular bishop of Sanavus and auxiliary bishop of Los Angeles, Mar. 19, 1941; app. coadjutor bishop of Sacramento with right of succession, Oct. 26, 1955; bishop of Sacramento, Jan. 14, 1957; archbishop of San Francisco, installed Apr. 3, 1962; resigned Feb. 22, 1977.

McGurkin, Edward A., M.M.: b. June 22, 1905, Hartford, Conn.; educ. Maryknoll Seminary (Maryknoll, N.Y.); ord. priest Sept. 14, 1930; ord. first bishop of Maswa, Tanganyika, Oct. 3, 1956; title of see changed to Shinyanga (Tanzania), 1957; resigned Jan. 30, 1975.

McKinney, Joseph C.: b. Sept. 10, 1928, Grand Rapids, Mich.: educ. St. Joseph's Seminary (Grand Rapids, Mich.), Seminaire de Philosophie (Montreal, Canada), Urban Univ. (Rome, Italy); ord. priest Dec. 20, 1953; ord. titular bishop of Lentini and auxiliary bishop of Grand Rapids, Sept. 26, 1968.

McLaughlin, Bernard J.: b. Nov. 19, 1912, Buffalo, N.Y.; educ. Urban Univ. (Rome, Italy); ord. priest Dec. 21, 1935, at Rome; ord. titular bishop of Mottola and auxiliary bishop of Buffalo, Jan. 6, 1969.

McManus, William E.: b. Jan. 27, 1914, Chicago, Ill.; educ. St. Mary of the Lake Seminary (Mundelein, Ill.), Catholic Univ. (Washington, D.C.); ord. priest Apr. 15, 1939; ord. titular bishop of Mesarfelta and auxiliary bishop of Chicago, Aug. 24, 1967; app. bishop of Fort Wayne-South Bend, Aug. 31, 1976, installed Oct. 19, 1976.

McNabb, John C., O.S.A.: b. Dec. 11, 1925, Beloit, Wis.; educ. Villanova Univ. (Villanova, Pa.), Augustinian College and Catholic Univ. (Washington, D.C.), De Paul Univ. (Chicago, Ill.); ord. priest May 24, 1952; ord. titular bishop of Saia Maggiore, June 17, 1967 (resigned titular see, Dec. 27, 1977); prelate of Chulucanas, Peru, 1967.

McNamara, Lawrence J.: b. Aug. 5, 1928, Chicago, Ill.; educ. St. Paul Seminary (St. Paul, Minn.), Catholic Univ. (Washington, D.C.); ord. priest May 30, 1953; executive director of Campaign for Human Development 1973-77; ord. bishop of Grand Island, Nebr., Mar. 28, 1978.

McNaughton, William J., M.M.: b. Dec. 7, 1926, Lawrence, Mass.; educ. Maryknoll Seminary (Maryknoll, N.Y.); ord. priest June 13, 1953; ord. titular bishop of Thuburbo Minus and vicar apostolic of Inchon, Korea, Aug. 24, 1961; title changed to bishop of Inchon, Mar. 10, 1962.

McRaith, John Jeremiah: b. Dec. 6, 1934, Hutchinson, Minn.; educ. St. John Preparatory School (Collegeville, Minn.), Loras College, St. Bernard Seminary (Dubuque, Ia); ord. priest Feb. 21, 1960; exec. dir. of Catholic Rural Life Conference, 1971-78; ord. bishop of Owensboro, Ky., Dec. 15, 1982.

McShea, Joseph M.: b. Feb. 22, 1907, Latimer, Pa.; educ. St. Charles Seminary (Philadelphia, Pa.), Major Pontifical Roman Seminary (Rome); ord. priest Dec. 6, 1931; ord. titular bishop of Mina and auxiliary bishop of Philadelphia, Mar. 19, 1952; app. first bishop of Allentown, installed Apr. 11, 1961; resigned Feb. 8, 1983.

Madera, Joseph J., M.Sp.S.: b. Nov. 27, 1927, San Francisco, Calif.; educ. Domus Studiorum of the Missionaries of the Holy Spirit (Coyoacan, D.F.

Mexico); ord. priest June 15, 1957; ord. coadjutor bishop of Fresno, Mar. 4, 1980; bishop of Fresno, July 1, 1980.

Maginn, Edward J.: b. Jan. 4, 1897, Glasgow, Scotland; educ. Holy Cross College (Worcester, Mass.), St. Joseph's Seminary (Yonkers, N.Y.); ord. priest June 10, 1922; ord. titular bishop of Curium and auxiliary bishop of Albany, Sept. 12, 1957; apostolic administrator of Albany, 1966-69; retired July 8, 1972.

Maguire, John J.: b. Dec. 11, 1904, New York, N.Y.; educ. Cathedral College (New York City), St. Joseph's Seminary (Dunwoodie, N.Y.), North American College (Rome); ord. priest Dec. 22, 1928; ord. titular bishop of Antiphrae and auxiliary bishop of New York, June 29, 1959; app. titular archbishop of Tabalta and coadjutor archbishop of New York, Sept. 15, 1965; retired Jan. 8, 1980.

Maguire, Joseph F.: b. Sept. 4, 1919, Boston, Mass.; educ. Boston College, St. John's Seminary (Boston, Mass.); ord. priest June 29, 1945; ord. titular bishop of Macteris and auxiliary bishop of Boston, Feb. 2, 1972; app. coadjutor bishop of Springfield, Mass., Apr. 13, 1976; succeeded as bishop of Springfield, Mass., Oct. 15, 1977.

Maher, Leo T.: b. July 1, 1915, Mount Union, Ia.; educ. St. Joseph's College (Mountain View, Calif.); St. Patrick's Seminary (Menlo Park, Calif.); ord. priest Dec. 18, 1943; ord. first bishop of Santa Rosa, April 5, 1962; bishop of San Diego, Oct. 4, 1969.

Mahoney, James P.: b. Aug. 16, 1925, Kingston, N.Y.; educ. St. Joseph's Seminary (Dunwoodie, N.Y.); ord. priest May 19, 1951; ord. titular bishop of Ipagro and auxiliary bishop of New York, Sept. 15, 1972.

Mahony, Roger M.: b. Feb. 27, 1936, Hollywood, Calif.; educ. St. John's Seminary (Camarillo, Calif.), National Catholic School of Social Service (Catholic Univ., Washington, D.C.); ord. priest May 1, 1962; ord. titular bishop of Tamascani and auxiliary bishop of Fresno, Mar. 19, 1975; app. bishop of Stockton, installed Apr. 25, 1980.

Malone, James W.: b. Mar. 8, 1920, Youngstown, O.; educ. St. Charles Preparatory Seminary (Catonsville, Md.), St. Mary's Seminary (Cleveland, O.), Catholic Univ. (Washington, D.C.); ord. priest May 26, 1945; ord. titular bishop of Alabanda and auxiliary bishop of Youngstown, Mar. 24, 1960; apostolic administrator, 1966; bishop of Youngstown, installed June 20, 1968.

Maloney, Charles G.: b. Sept. 9, 1912, Louisville, Ky.; educ. St. Joseph's College (Rensselaer, Ind.), North American College (Rome); ord. priest Dec. 8, 1937; ord. titular bishop of Capsa and auxiliary bishop of Louisville, Feb. 2, 1955.

Maloney, David M.: b. Mar. 15, 1912, Littleton, Colo.; educ. St. Thomas Seminary (Denver, Colo.), Gregorian Univ. and Apollinare Univ. (Rome); ord. priest Dec. 8, 1936; ord. titular bishop of Ruspe and auxiliary bishop of Denver, Jan. 4, 1961; app. bishop of Wichita, Kans., Dec. 6, 1967; resigned July 16, 1982.

Manning, Thomas R., O.F.M.: b. Aug. 29, 1922, Baltimore, Md.; educ. Duns Scotus College (Southfield, Mich.), Holy Name College (Washington,

D.C.); ord. priest June 5, 1948; ord. titular bishop of Arsamosata, July 14, 1959 (resigned titular see Dec. 30, 1977); prelate of Coroico, Bolivia, July 14, 1959; became first bishop, 1983, when prelature was raised to diocese.

Manning, Timothy: (See Cardinals, Biographies.)

Marcinkus, Paul C.: b. Jan. 15, 1922, Cicero, Ill.; ord. priest May 3, 1947; served in Vatican secretariat from 1952; ord. titular bishop of Orta, Jan. 6, 1969; secretary (1968-71) and president (1971-   ) of Institute for Works of Religion (Vatican Bank); titular archbishop, Sept. 26, 1981; pro-president of Pontifical Commission for the State of Vatican City.

Marconi, Dominic A.: b. Mar. 13, 1927, Newark, N.J.; educ. Seton Hall Univ. (S. Orange, N.J.), Immaculate Conception Seminary (Darlington, N.J.), Catholic Univ. (Washington, D.C.); ord. priest May 30, 1953; ord. titular bishop of Bure and auxiliary bishop of Newark, June 25, 1976.

Mardaga, Thomas J.: b. May 14, 1913, Baltimore, Md.; educ. St. Charles College (Catonsville, Md.), St. Mary's Seminary (Baltimore, Md.); ord. priest May 14, 1940; ord. titular bishop of Mutugenna and auxiliary bishop of Baltimore, Jan. 25, 1967; app. bishop of Wilmington, installed Apr. 6, 1968.

Marino, Eugene A., S.S.J.: b. May 29, 1934, Biloxi, Miss.; educ. Epiphany Apostolic College and Mary Immaculate Novitiate (Newburgh, N.Y.), St. Joseph's Seminary (Washington, D.C.), Catholic Univ. (Washington, D.C.), Loyola Univ. (New Orleans, La.), Fordham Univ. (New York City); ord. priest June 9, 1962; ord. titular bishop of Walla Walla and auxiliary bishop of Washington, D.C., Sept. 12, 1974.

Marshall, John A.: b. Apr. 26, 1928, Worcester, Mass.; educ. Holy Cross College (Worcester, Mass.), Sulpician Seminary (Montreal), North American College and Gregorian Univ. (Rome), Assumption College (Worcester); ord. priest Dec. 19, 1953; ord. bishop of Burlington, Jan. 25, 1972.

Matthiesen, Leroy Theodore: b. June 11, 1921, Olfen, Tex.; educ. Josephinum College (Columbus, O.), Catholic Univ. (Washington, D.C.), Register School of Journalism; ord. priest Mar. 10, 1946; ord. bishop of Amarillo, May 30, 1980.

May, John L.: b. Mar. 31, 1922, Evanston, Ill.; educ. St. Mary of the Lake Seminary (Mundelein, Ill.); ord. priest May 3, 1947; general secretary and vice-president of the Catholic Church Extension Society, 1959; ord. titular bishop of Tagarbala and auxiliary bishop of Chicago, Aug. 24, 1967; bishop of Mobile, Ala., Sept. 29, 1969; app. archbishop of St. Louis, installed Mar. 25, 1980.

Medeiros, Humberto S.: (See Cardinals, Biographies.)

Melczek, Dale J.: b. Nov. 9, 1938, Detroit, Mich.; educ. St. Mary's College (Orchard Lake, Mich.), St. John's Provincial Seminary (Plymouth, Mich.), Univ. of Detroit; ord. priest June 6, 1964; ord. titular bishop of Trau and auxiliary bishop of Detroit, Jan. 27, 1983; vicar general; regional bishop of northwest region of Detroit archdiocese.

Mendez, Alfred, C.S.C.: b. June 3, 1907, Chica-

go, Ill.; educ. Notre Dame Univ. (Notre Dame, Ind.), Institute of Holy Cross (Washington, D.C.); ord. priest June 24, 1935; ord. first bishop of Arecibo, Puerto Rico, Oct. 28, 1960; resigned Jan. 24, 1974.

Mestice, Anthony F.: b. Dec. 6, 1923, New York, N.Y.; educ. St. Joseph Seminary (Yonkers, N.Y.); ord. priest June 4, 1949; ord. titular bishop of Villa Nova and auxiliary bishop of New York Apr. 27, 1973.

Metzger, Sidney Matthew: b. July 11, 1902, Fredericksburg, Tex.; educ. St. John's Seminary (San Antonio, Tex.), North American College (Rome); ord. priest Apr. 3, 1926; ord. titular bishop of Birtha and auxiliary bishop of Santa Fe, Apr. 10, 1940; app. coadjutor bishop of El Paso, Dec. 26, 1941; bishop of El Paso, Dec. 1, 1942; retired May 29, 1978.

Michaels, James E., S.S.C.: b. May 30, 1926, Chicago, Ill.; educ. Columban Seminary (St. Columban, Neb.), Gregorian Univ. (Rome); ord. priest Dec. 21, 1951; ord. titular bishop of Verbe and auxiliary bishop of Kwang Ju, Korea, Apr. 14, 1966; app. auxiliary bishop of Wheeling, Apr. 3, 1973; title of see changed to Wheeling-Charleston, 1974.

Mihalik, Emil J.: b. Feb. 6, 1920, Pittsburgh, Pa.; educ. St. Procopius Seminary (Lisle, Ill.), Duquesne Univ. (Pittsburgh, Pa.); ord. priest Sept. 21, 1945; ord. first bishop of Byzantine Rite diocese of Parma, O., June 12, 1969.

Milone, Anthony: b. Sept. 24, 1932, Omaha, Nebr.; educ. North American College (Rome); ord. priest Dec. 15, 1957, in Rome; ord. titular bishop of Plestia and auxiliary bishop of Omaha, Jan. 6, 1982.

Minder, John, O.S.F.S.: b. Nov. 1, 1923, Philadelphia, Pa.; ord. priest June 3, 1950; ord. bishop of Keimos, South Africa, Jan. 10, 1968.

Montrose, Donald: b. May 13, 1923, Denver, Colo.; educ. St. John's Seminary (Camarillo, Calif.); ord. priest May 7, 1949; ord. titular bishop of Forum Novum and auxiliary bishop of Los Angeles, May 12, 1983.

Moore, Emerson John: b. May 16, 1938, New York, N.Y.; educ. Cathedral College (New York City), St. Joseph's Seminary (Yonkers, N.Y.); New York University, Columbia Univ. School of Social Work (New York City); ord. priest May 30, 1964; ord. auxiliary bishop of Curubi and auxiliary bishop of New York, Sept. 8, 1982.

Moran, William J.: b. Jan. 15, 1906, San Francisco, Calif.; educ. St. Patrick's Seminary (Menlo Park, Calif.); ord. priest June 20, 1931; Army chaplain, 1933; ord. titular bishop of Centuria and auxiliary to the military vicar, Dec. 13, 1965; retired Jan. 15, 1981.

Moreno, Manuel D.: b. Nov. 27, 1930, Placentia, Calif.; educ. Univ. of California (Los Angeles), Our Lady Queen of Angels (San Fernando, Calif.), St. John's Seminary (Camarillo, Calif.); ord. priest Apr. 25, 1961; ord. titular bishop of Tanagra and auxiliary bishop of Los Angeles, Feb. 19, 1977; bishop of Tucson, Jan. 12, 1982, installed Mar. 11, 1982.

Morkovsky, John Louis: b. Aug. 16, 1909, Praha, Tex.; educ. St. John's Seminary (San Antonio,

Tex.), North American College, Urban Univ. and Gregorian Univ. (Rome), Catholic Univ. (Washington, D.C.); ord. priest Dec. 5, 1933; ord titular bishop of Hieron and auxiliary bishop of Amarillo, Feb. 22, 1956; app. bishop of Amarillo, Aug. 27, 1958; titular bishop of Tigava and coadjutor bishop of Galveston-Houston with right of succession, June 11, 1963; apostolic administrator; president Texas Conference of Churches, 1970-72; bishop of Galveston-Houston, Apr. 22, 1975.

Morneau, Robert F.: b. Sept. 10, 1938, New London, Wis.; educ. St. Norbert's College (De Pere, Wis.), Sacred Heart Seminary (Oneida, Wis.), Catholic Univ. (Washington, D.C.); ord. priest May 28, 1966; ord. titular bishop of Massa Lubrense and auxiliary bishop of Green Bay, Feb. 22, 1979.

Morrow, Louis La Ravoire, S.D.B.: b. Dec. 24, 1892, Weatherford, Tex.; educ. Salesian School and Palafox (Puebla, Mexico); professed in Salesians of St. John Bosco, Sept. 29, 1912; ord. priest May 21, 1921; ord. bishop of Krishnagar, India, Oct. 29, 1939; resigned Oct. 31, 1969.

Moskal, Robert: b. Oct. 24, 1937, Carnegie, Pa.; educ. St. Basil Minor Seminary (Stamford, Conn.), St. Josaphat Seminary and Catholic Univ. (Washington, D.C.); ord. priest Mar. 25, 1963; ord. titular bishop of Agatopoli and auxiliary bishop of the Ukrainian-Rite archeparchy of Philadelphia, Oct. 13, 1981.

Mugavero, Francis John: b. June 8, 1914, Brooklyn, N.Y.; educ. Cathedral College (Brooklyn, N.Y.), Immaculate Conception Seminary (Huntington, N.Y.), Fordham Univ. (New York City); ord. priest May 18, 1940; ord. bishop of Brooklyn, Sept. 12, 1968.

Mulcahy, John J.: b. June 26, 1922, Dorchester, Mass.; educ. St. John's Seminary (Brighton, Mass.); ord. priest May 1, 1947; rector Pope John XXIII Seminary for Delayed Vocations, 1969-73; ord. titular bishop of Penafiel and auxiliary bishop of Boston, Feb. 11, 1975.

Mulrooney, Charles R.: b. Jan. 13, 1906, Brooklyn, N.Y.; educ. Cathedral College (Brooklyn, N.Y.), St. Mary's Seminary (Baltimore, Md.), Sulpician Seminary (Washington, D.C.); ord. priest June 10, 1930; ord. titular bishop of Valentiniana and auxiliary bishop of Brooklyn, Apr. 22, 1959; retired Jan. 13, 1981.

Mulvee, Robert E.: b. Feb. 15, 1930, Boston, Mass.; educ. St. Thomas Seminary (Bloomfield, Conn.), University Seminary (Ottawa, Ont., Canada), American College (Louvain, Belgium), Lateran Univ. (Rome); ord. priest June 30, 1957; ord. titular bishop of Summa and auxiliary bishop of Manchester, N.H., Apr. 14, 1977.

Mundo, Michael P.: b. July 25, 1937, New York, N.Y.; educ. Fordham Univ. (Bronx, N.Y.), St. Jerome's College (Kitchener, Ont., Canada), St. Francis Seminary (Loretto, Pa.); ord. May 19, 1962; missionary in Brazil from 1963; ord. titular bishop of Blanda Julia and auxiliary bishop of Jatai, Brazil, June 2, 1978.

Murphy, Michael J.: b. July 1, 1915, Cleveland, O.; educ. Niagara Univ. (Niagara Falls, N.Y.); North American College (Rome), Catholic Univ.

(Washington, D.C.); ord. priest Feb. 28, 1942; ord. titular bishop of Ariendela and auxiliary bishop of Cleveland, June 11, 1976; app. coadjutor bishop of Erie, Nov. 20, 1978; bishop of Erie, July 16, 1982.

Murphy, Philip Francis: b. Mar. 25, 1933, Cumberland, Md.; educ. St. Mary Seminary (Baltimore, Md.), North American College (Rome); ord. priest Dec. 20, 1958; ord. titular bishop of Tacarata and auxiliary bishop of Baltimore, Feb. 29, 1976.

Murphy, T. Austin: b. May 11, 1911, Baltimore, Md.; educ. St. Charles College (Catonsville, Md.), St. Mary's Seminary (Baltimore, Md.); ord priest June 10, 1937; ord. titular bishop of Appiaria and auxiliary bishop of Baltimore, July 3, 1962.

Murphy, Thomas J.: b. Oct. 3, 1932, Chicago, Ill.; educ. Quigley Preparatory Seminary (Chicago, Ill.), St. Mary of the Lake Seminary (Mundelein, Ill.); ord. priest Apr. 12, 1958; ord. bishop of Great Falls, Mont. Aug. 21, 1978; title of see changed to Great Falls-Billings, 1980.

Murphy, Thomas W., C.SS.R.: b. Dec. 17, 1917, Omaha, Nebr.; educ. St. Joseph's College (Kirkwood, Mo.); ord. priest June 29, 1943; ord. first bishop of Juazeiro, Brazil, Jan. 2, 1963; resigned Dec. 29, 1973; app. titular bishop of Sululos and auxiliary bishop of Sao Salvador da Bahia, Brazil, Jan. 31, 1974.

N

Nelson, Knute Ansgar, O.S.B.: b. Oct. 1, 1906, Copenhagen, Denmark; educ. Abbey of Maria Laach (Germany), Brown Univ. (Providence, R.I.); professed in the Order of St. Benedict, May 30, 1932; ord. priest May 22, 1937; became an American citizen, Mar. 4, 1941; ord. titular bishop of Bilta and coadjutor bishop of Stockholm, Sweden, Sept. 8, 1947; succeeded as bishop of Stockholm, Oct. 1, 1957; retired; titular bishop of Dura. 1962.

Nevins, John J.: b. Jan. 19, 1932, New Rochelle, N.Y.; educ. Iona College (New Rochelle, N.Y.), Catholic Univ. (Washington, D.C.); ord. priest June 6, 1959; ord. titular bishop of Rusticana and auxiliary bishop of Miami, Mar. 24, 1979.

Newell, Hubert M.: b. Feb. 16, 1904, Denver, Colo.; educ. Regis College and St. Thomas Seminary (Denver, Colo.), Catholic Univ. (Washington, D.C.); ord. priest June 15, 1930; ord. titular bishop of Zapara and coadjutor bishop of Cheyenne, Sept. 24, 1947; bishop of Cheyenne, Nov. 10, 1951; retired Jan. 3, 1978.

Neylon, Martin J., S.J.: b. Feb. 13, 1920, Buffalo, N.Y.; ord. priest June 18, 1950; ord. titular bishop of Libertina and coadjutor vicar apostolic of the Caroline and Marshall Islands, Feb. 2, 1970; vicar apostolic of Caroline and Marshall Is., Sept. 20, 1971; first bishop when vicarate apostolic was raised to diocese, 1979.

Niedergeses, James D.: b. Feb. 2, 1917, Lawrenceburg, Tenn.; educ. St. Bernard College (St. Bernard, Ala.), St. Ambrose College (Davenport, Ia.), Mt. St. Mary Seminary of the West and Athenaeum (Cincinnati, Ohio); ord. priest May 20, 1944; ord. bishop of Nashville May 20, 1975.

Nolker, Bernard, C.SS.R.: b. Sept. 25, 1912, Baltimore, Md.; educ. St. Mary's College (North East, Pa.), St. Mary's College (Ilchester, Md.), Mt. St. Alphonsus Seminary (Esopus, N.Y.); ord. priest June 18, 1939; ord. first bishop of Paranagua, Brazil, Apr. 25, 1963.

Novak, Alfred, C.SS.R.: b. June 2, 1930, Dwight, Nebr.; educ. Immaculate Conception Seminary (Oconomowoc, Wis.); ord. priest July 2, 1956; ord. titular bishop of Vardimissa and auxiliary bishop of Sao Paulo, Brazil, May 25, 1979.

O

O'Boyle, Patrick A.: (See Cardinals, Biographies.)

O'Brien, Thomas Joseph: b. Nov. 29, 1935, Indianapolis, Ind.; educ. St. Meinrad High School Seminary, St. Meinrad College Seminary (St. Meinrad, Ind); ord. priest May 7, 1961; ord. bishop of Phoenix, Jan. 6, 1982.

O'Connor, John J.: b. Jan. 15, 1920, Philadelphia, Pa.; educ. St. Charles Borromeo Seminary (Philadelphia, Pa.), Catholic Univ., Georgetown Univ. (Washington, D.C.); ord. priest Dec. 15, 1945; U.S. Navy chief of chaplains, 1975; ord. titular bishop of Cursola and auxiliary to the military vicar, May 27, 1979; app. bishop of Scranton, May 10, 1983, installed June 29, 1983.

O'Connor, Martin J.: b. May 18, 1900, Scranton, Pa.; educ. St. Thomas College (Scranton, Pa.), St. Mary's Seminary (Baltimore, Md.), North American College, Urban Univ. and Apollinaris (Rome); ord. priest Mar. 15, 1924; ord. titular bishop of Thespia and auxiliary bishop of Scranton, Jan. 27, 1943; rector of North American College 1946-1964; app. titular archbishop of Laodicea in Syria, Sept. 5, 1959; apostolic nuncio to Malta, 1965-69; president emeritus Pontifical Commission for Social Communication.

O'Connor, William A.: b. Dec. 27, 1903, Chicago, Ill.; educ. Quigley Seminary (Chicago, Ill.), St. Mary of the Lake Seminary (Mundelein, Ill.), Urban Univ. (Rome); ord. priest Sept. 24, 1927; ord. bishop of Springfield, Ill., Mar. 7, 1949; retired July 22, 1975.

O'Donnell, Cletus F.: b. Aug. 22, 1917, Waukon, Ia.; educ. St. Mary Seminary (Mundelein, Ill.), Catholic Univ. (Washington, D.C.); ord. priest May 3, 1941; ord. titular bishop of Abritto and auxiliary bishop of Chicago, Dec. 21, 1960; app. bishop of Madison, Feb. 22, 1967, installed Apr. 25, 1967.

O'Keefe, Gerald F.: b. Mar. 30, 1918, St. Paul, Minn.; educ. College of St. Thomas, St. Paul Seminary (St. Paul, Minn.); ord. priest Jan. 29, 1944; ord. titular bishop of Candyba and auxiliary bishop of St. Paul July 2, 1961; bishop of Davenport, Oct. 20, 1966, installed Jan. 4, 1967.

O'Keefe, Joseph Thomas: b. Mar. 12, 1919, New York, N.Y.; educ. Cathedral College (New York City), St. Joseph's Seminary (Yonkers, N.Y.), Catholic Univ. (Washington, D.C.); ord. priest Apr. 17, 1948; ord. titular bishop of Tre Taverne and auxiliary bishop of New York, Sept. 8, 1982.

O'Leary, Edward C.: b. Aug. 21, 1920, Bangor, Me.; educ. Holy Cross College (Worcester, Mass.), St. Paul's Seminary (Ottawa, Canada); ord. priest June 15, 1946; ord. titular bishop of

Moglena and auxiliary bishop of Portland, Me., Jan. 25, 1971; app. bishop of Portland, installed Dec. 18, 1974.

O'Meara, Edward T.: b. Aug. 3, 1921, St. Louis, Mo.; educ. Cardinal Glennon College and Kenrick Seminary (St. Louis, Mo.), Angelicum (Rome); ord. priest Dec. 21, 1946; app. national director of Society for the Propagation of the Faith, 1967; ord. titular bishop of Thisiduo and auxiliary bishop of St. Louis, Feb. 13, 1972; app. archbishop of Indianapolis, installed Jan. 10, 1980.

O'Neil, Leo E.: b. Jan. 31, 1928, Holyoke, Mass.; educ. Maryknoll Seminary (Maryknoll, N.Y.), St. Anselm's College (Manchester, N.H.), Grand Seminary (Montreal, Canada); ord. priest June 4, 1955; ord. titular bishop of Bencenna and auxiliary bishop of Springfield, Mass., Aug. 22, 1980.

O'Neill, Arthur J.: b. Dec. 14, 1917, East Dubuque, Ill.; educ. Loras College (Dubuque, Ia.), St. Mary's Seminary (Baltimore, Md.); ord. priest Mar. 27, 1943; ord. bishop of Rockford, Oct. 11, 1968.

O'Rourke, Edward W.: b. Oct. 31, 1917, Downs, Ill.; educ. St. Mary's Seminary (Mundelein, Ill.), Aquinas Institute of Philosophy and Theology (River Forest, Ill.); ord. priest May 28, 1944; exec. dir. National Catholic Rural Life Conference, 1960-71; ord. bishop of Peoria, July 15, 1971.

Ott, Stanley J.: b. June 29, 1927, Gretna, La.; educ. Notre Dame Seminary (New Orleans, La.), North American College and Gregorian Univ. (Rome); ord. priest Dec. 8, 1951; ord. titular bishop of Nicives and auxiliary bishop of New Orleans, June 29, 1976; app. bishop of Baton Rouge, Jan 17, 1983, installed Mar. 24, 1983.

Ottenweller, Albert H.: b. Apr. 5, 1916, Stanford, Mont.; educ. St. Joseph's Seminary (Rensselaer, Ind.), Catholic Univ. (Washington, D.C.); ord. priest June 19, 1943; ord. titular bishop of Perdices and auxiliary bishop of Toledo, May 20, 1974; app. bishop of Steubenville, Oct. 11, 1977, installed Nov. 22, 1977.

P

Paschang, John L.: b. Oct. 5, 1895, Hemingford, Nebr.; educ. Conception College (Conception, Mo.), St. John Seminary (Collegeville, Minn.), Catholic Univ. (Washington, D.C.); ord. priest June 12, 1921; ord. bishop of Grand Island, Oct. 9, 1951; resigned July 25, 1972.

Pataki, Andrew: b. Aug. 30, 1927, Palmerton, Pa.; educ. St. Vincent College (Latrobe, Pa.), St. Procopius College, St. Procopius Seminary (Lisle, Ill.), Sts. Cyril and Methodius Byzantine Catholic Seminary (Pittsburgh, Pa.), Gregorian Univ. and Oriental Pontifical Institute (Rome, Italy); ord. priest Feb. 24, 1952; ord. titular bishop of Telmisso and auxiliary bishop of Byzantine diocese of Passaic, Aug. 23, 1983; vicar general; episcopal vicar of Pennsylvania.

Paul, John J.: b. Aug. 17, 1918, La Crosse, Wis.; educ. Loras College (Dubuque, Iowa), St. Mary's Seminary (Baltimore, Md.), Marquette Univ. (Milwaukee, Wis.), ord. priest Jan. 24, 1943; ord. titular bishop of Lambaesis and auxiliary bishop of La Crosse, Aug. 4, 1977.

Pearce, George H., S.M.: b. Jan. 9, 1921, Brighton, Mass.; educ. Marist College and Seminary (Framington, Mass.); ord. priest Feb. 2, 1947; ord. titular bishop of Attalea in Pamphylia and vicar apostolic of the Samoa and Tokelau Islands, June 29, 1956; title changed to bishop of Apia, June 21, 1966; app. archbishop of Suva, Fiji Islands, June 22, 1967; resigned Apr. 10, 1976.

Pechillo, Jerome, T.O.R.: b. May 16, 1919, Brooklyn, N.Y.; educ. Catholic Univ. (Washington, D.C.); ord. priest June 10, 1947; ord. titular bishop of Novasparsa and prelate of Coronel Oviedo, Paraguay, Jan. 25, 1966; app. auxiliary bishop of Newark, N.J., Mar. 6, 1976.

Pena, Raymond J.: b. Feb. 19, 1934, Robstown, Tex.; educ. Assumption Seminary (San Antonio, Tex.); ord. priest May 25, 1957; ord. titular bishop of Trisipa and auxiliary bishop of San Antonio, Dec. 13, 1976; app. bishop of El Paso, Apr. 29, 1980.

Pernicone, Joseph M.: b. Nov. 4, 1903, Regalbuto, Sicily; educ. Cathedral College (New York City), St. Joseph's Seminary (Dunwoodie, N.Y.), Catholic Univ. (Washington, D.C.); ord. priest Dec. 18, 1926; ord. titular bishop of Hadrianapolis and auxiliary bishop of New York, May 5, 1954; app. episcopal vicar, 1966; retired Nov. 28, 1978.

Perry, Harold R., S.V.D.: b. Oct. 9, 1916, Lake Charles, La.; educ. St. Augustine Seminary (Bay St. Louis, Miss.), St. Mary's Seminary (Techny, Ill.); ord. priest Jan. 6, 1944; app. provincial of southern province of Society of the Divine Word, 1964; ord. titular bishop of Mons in Mauretania and auxiliary bishop of New Orleans, Jan. 6, 1966.

Pevec, A. Edward: b. Apr. 16, 1925, Cleveland, O.; educ. St. Mary's Seminary, John Carroll Univ. (Cleveland, O.); ord. priest Apr. 29, 1950; ord. titular bishop of Mercia and auxiliary bishop of Cleveland, July 2, 1982.

Pilarczyk, Daniel E.: b. Aug. 12, 1934, Dayton, Ohio; educ. St. Gregory's Seminary (Cincinnati, O.), Urban Univ. (Rome), Xavier Univ. and Univ. of Cincinnati (Cincinnati, O.); ord. priest Dec. 20, 1959; ord. titular bishop of Hodelm and auxiliary bishop of Cincinnati, Dec. 20, 1974; app. archbishop of Cincinnati, Oct. 30, 1982.

Pilla, Anthony M.: b. Nov. 12, 1932, Cleveland, O.; educ. St. Gregory College Seminary (Cincinnati, O.), Borromeo College Seminary (Wickliffe, O.), St. Mary Seminary and John Carroll Univ. (Cleveland, O.); ord. priest May 23, 1959; ord. titular bishop of Scardona and auxiliary bishop of Cleveland, Aug. 1, 1979; app. apostolic administrator of Cleveland, 1980; bishop of Cleveland, Nov. 13, 1980.

Pinger, Henry A., O.F.M.: b. Aug. 16, 1897, Lindsay, Nebr.; educ. Our Lady of Angels Seminary (Cleveland, O.), St. Anthony's Seminary (St. Louis, Mo.); professed in the Order of Friars Minor, June 18, 1918; ord. priest June 27, 1924; ord. titular bishop of Capitolias and vicar apostolic of Chowtsun, China, Sept. 21, 1937; title changed to bishop of Chowtsun, Apr. 11, 1946; imprisoned by Reds in 1951, released in 1956; expelled.

Popp, Bernard F.: b. Dec. 6, 1917, Nada, Tex.; educ. St. John's Seminary and St. Mary's Univ.

(San Antonio, Tex.); ord. priest Feb. 24, 1943; ord. titular bishop of Capsus and auxiliary bishop of San Antonio, July 25, 1983.

Povish, Kenneth J.: b. Apr. 19, 1924, Alpena, Mich.; educ. St. Joseph's Seminary (Grand Rapids, Mich.), Sacred Heart Seminary (Detroit, Mich.), Catholic Univ. (Washington, D.C.); ord. priest June 3, 1950; ord. bishop of Crookston, Sept. 29, 1970; app. bishop of Lansing, Oct. 8, 1975, installed Dec. 11, 1975.

Power, Cornelius M.: b. Dec. 18, 1913, Seattle, Wash.; educ. St. Patrick's College (Menlo Park, Calif.), St. Edward's Seminary (Kenmore, Wash.), Catholic Univ. (Washington, D.C.); ord. priest June 3, 1939; ord. bishop of Yakima, May 1, 1969, installed May 20, 1969; app. archbishop of Portland, Ore., Jan. 22, 1974, installed Apr. 17, 1974.

Primeau, Ernest J.: b. Sept. 17, 1909, Chicago, Ill.; educ. Loyola Univ. (Chicago, Ill.), St. Mary of the Lake Seminary (Mundelein, Ill.), Lateran Univ. (Rome); ord. priest Apr. 7, 1934; ord. bishop of Manchester, Feb. 25, 1960; resigned Jan. 30, 1974; director of Villa Stritch, Rome, 1974-79.

Prost, Jude, O.F.M.: b. Dec. 6, 1915, Chicago, Ill.; educ. Our Lady of the Angels Seminary (Cleveland, O.), St. Joseph's Seminary (Teutopolis, Ill.); ord. priest June 24, 1942; ord. titular bishop of Fronta and auxiliary bishop of Belem do Para, Brazil, Nov. 1, 1962.

Proulx, Amedee W.: b. Aug. 31, 1932, Sanford, Me.; educ. St. Hyacinthe Seminary (Quebec), St. Paul Univ. Seminary (Ottawa), Catholic Univ. (Washington, D.C.); ord. priest May 31, 1958; ord. titular bishop of Clipia and auxiliary bishop of Portland, Me., Nov. 12, 1975.

Pursley, Leo A.: b. Mar. 12, 1902, Hartford City, Ind.; educ. Mt. St. Mary's Seminary (Cincinnati, O.); ord. priest June 11, 1927; ord. titular bishop of Hadrianapolis in Pisidia and auxiliary bishop of Fort Wayne, Sept. 19, 1950; app. apostolic administrator of Fort Wayne, Mar. 9, 1955; installed as bishop of Fort Wayne, Feb. 26, 1957; title of see changed to Fort Wayne-South Bend, 1960; resigned Aug. 31, 1976.

Puscas, Louis: b. Sept. 13, 1915, Aurora, Ill.; educ. Quigley Preparatory Seminary (Chicago, Ill.), seminary in Oradea-Mare (Romania), Propaganda Fide Seminary (Rome), Illinois Benedictine College (Lisle, Ill.); ord. priest May 14, 1942; app. titular bishop of Leuce and first exarch of apostolic exarchate for Romanians of the Byzantine Rite in the U.S., Dec. 21, 1982 (seat of the exarchate is Canton, Ohio).

Q

Quinn, Francis A.: b. Sept. 11, 1921, Los Angeles, Calif.; educ. St. Joseph's College (Mountain View, Calif.), St. Patrick's Seminary (Menlo Park, Calif.), Catholic Univ. (Washington, D.C.); Univ. of California (Berkley); ord. priest June 15, 1946; ord. titular bishop of Numana and auxiliary bishop of San Francisco, June 29, 1978; app. bishop of Sacramento Dec. 18, 1979.

Quinn, John R.: b. Mar. 28, 1929, Riverside, Calif.; educ. St. Francis Seminary (El Cajon,

Calif.), North American College (Rome); ord. priest July 19, 1953; ord. titular bishop of Thisiduo and auxiliary bishop of San Diego, Dec. 12, 1967; bishop of Oklahoma City and Tulsa, Nov. 30, 1971; first archbishop of Oklahoma City, Dec. 19, 1972; app. archbishop of San Francisco Feb. 22, 1977, installed Apr. 26, 1977; president NCCB, USCC, 1977-80.

R

Ramirez, Ricardo, C.S.B.: b. Sept. 12, 1936, Bay City, Tex.; educ. Univ. of St. Thomas (Houston, Tex.), Univ. of Detroit (Detroit, Mich.), St. Basil's Seminary (Toronto, Ont.); Seminario Concilium (Mexico City, Mexico), East Asian Pastoral Institute (Manila, Philippines); ord. priest Dec. 10, 1966; ord titular bishop of Vatarba and auxiliary of San Antonio, Dec. 6, 1981; app. first bishop of Las Cruces, N. Mex., Aug. 17, 1982.

Raya, Joseph M.: b. July 20, 1917, Zahle, Lebanon; educ. St. Louis College (Paris, France), St. Anne's Seminary (Jerusalem); ord. priest July 20, 1941; came to U.S., 1949, became U.S. citizen; ord. archbishop of Acre, Israel, of the Melkites, Oct. 20, 1968; resigned Aug. 20, 1974; assigned titular metropolitan see of Scytopolis.

Regan, Joseph W., M.M.: b. Apr. 5, 1905, Boston, Mass.; educ. Boston College (Boston, Mass.), St. Bernard's Seminary (Rochester, N.Y.), Maryknoll Seminary (Maryknoll, N.Y.); ord. priest Jan. 27, 1929; missionary in China 15 years; in Philippines since 1952; ord. titular bishop of Isinda and prelate of Tagum, Philippine Islands, Apr. 25, 1962; resigned May 16, 1980.

Reh, Francis F.: b. Jan. 9, 1911, New York, N.Y.; educ. St. Joseph's Seminary (Dunwoodie, N.Y.), North American College and Gregorian Univ. (Rome); ord. priest Dec. 8, 1935; ord. bishop of Charleston, S.C., June 29, 1962; named titular bishop of Macriana in Mauretania, 1964; rector of North American College, 1964-68; bishop of Saginaw, installed Feb. 26, 1969; resigned Apr. 28, 1980.

Reicher, Louis J.: b. June 14, 1890, Piqua, O.; educ. St. Mary's Seminary (Cincinnati, O.), St. Mary's Seminary (La Porte, Tex.): ord. priest Dec. 6, 1918; ord. first bishop of Austin, Apr. 14, 1948; resigned Nov. 15, 1971.

Reilly, Daniel P.: b. May 12, 1928, Providence, R.I.; educ. Our Lady of Providence Seminary (Warwick, R.I.), St. Brieuc Major Seminary (Cotes du Nord, France); ord. priest May 30, 1953; ord. bishop of Norwich, Aug. 6, 1975.

Reilly, Thomas F., C.SS.R.: b. Dec. 20, 1908, Boston, Mass.; educ. Mt. St. Alphonsus Seminary (Esopus, N.Y.), Catholic Univ. (Washington, D.C.); ord. priest June 10, 1933; ord. titular bishop of Themisonium and prelate of San Juan de la Maguana, Dominican Republic, Nov. 30, 1956; first bishop of San Juan de la Maguana, Nov. 21, 1969; retired July 20, 1977.

Reiss, John C.: b. May 13, 1922, Red Bank, N.J.; educ. Catholic Univ. (Washington, D.C.), Immaculate Conception Seminary (Darlington, N.J.); ord. priest May 31, 1947; ord. titular bishop of Sim-

idicca and auxiliary bishop of Trenton, Dec. 12, 1967; app. bishop of Trenton, Mar. 11, 1980.

Riley, Lawrence J.: b. Sept. 6, 1914; Boston, Mass.; educ. Boston College and St. John's Seminary (Boston, Mass.), North American College and Gregorian Univ. (Rome), Catholic Univ. (Washington, D.C.); ord. priest Sept. 21, 1940; ord. titular bishop of Daimlaig and auxiliary bishop of Boston, Feb. 2, 1972.

Roach, John R.: b. July 31, 1921, Prior Lake, Minn.; educ. St. Paul Seminary (St. Paul, Minn.), Univ. of Minnesota (Minneapolis); ord. priest June 18, 1946; ord. titular bishop of Cenae and auxiliary bishop of St. Paul and Minneapolis, Sept. 8, 1971; app. archbishop of St. Paul and Minneapolis, May 28, 1975; vice-president NCCB/USCC, 1977-80; president, 1980.

Rodimer, Frank J.: b. Oct. 25, 1927, Rockaway, N.J.; educ. Seton Hall Prep (South Orange, N.J.), St. Charles College (Catonsville, Md.), St. Mary's Seminary (Baltimore, Md.), Immaculate Conception Seminary (Darlington, N.J.), Catholic Univ. (Washington, D.C.); ord. priest May 19, 1951; ord. bishop of Paterson, Feb. 28, 1978.

Rodriguez, Migúel, C.SS.R.: b. Apr. 18, 1931, Mayaguez, P.R.; educ. St. Mary's Minor Seminary (North East, Pa.), Mt. St. Alphonsus Major Seminary (Esopus, N.Y.); ord. priest June 22, 1958; ord. bishop of Arecibo, P.R., Mar. 23, 1974.

Roman, Agustin: b. May 5, 1928, San Antonio de los Banos, Havana, Cuba; educ. San Alberto Magno Seminary (Matanzas, Cuba), Missions Etrangeres (Montreal, Canada), Barry College (Miami, Fla.); ord. priest July 5, 1959, Cuba; vicar for Spanish speaking in Miami archdiocese, 1976; ord. titular bishop of Sertei and auxiliary bishop of Miami, Mar. 24, 1979.

Roque, Francis: b. Oct. 9, 1928, Providence R.I.; educ. St. John's Seminary (Brighton, Mass.); ord. priest Sept. 19, 1953; became chaplain in U.S. Army 1961; ord. titular bishop of Bagai and auxiliary bishop of Military Vicariate, May 10, 1983.

Rosazza, Peter Anthony: b. Feb. 13, 1935, New Haven, Conn.; educ. St. Thomas Seminary (Bloomfield, Conn.), Dartmouth College (Hanover, N.H.), St. Bernard's Seminary (Rochester, N.Y.), St. Sulpice (Issy, France); ord. priest June 29, 1961; ord. titular bishop of Oppido Nuovo and auxiliary bishop of Hartford, June 24, 1978.

Rose, Robert John: b. Feb. 28, 1930, Grand Rapids, Mich.; educ. St. Joseph's Seminary (Grand Rapids, Mich.), Seminaire de Philosophie (Montreal, Canada), Pontifical Urban University (Rome), Univ. of Michigan (Ann Arbor, Mich.); ord. priest Dec. 21, 1955; ord. bishop of Gaylord, Dec. 6, 1981.

Rudin, John J., M.M.: b. Nov. 27, 1916, Pittsfield, Mass.; educ. Maryknoll Seminary (Maryknoll, N.Y.), Gregorian Univ. (Rome); ord. priest June 11, 1944; ord. first bishop of Musoma, Tanzania, Oct. 3, 1957; retired Jan. 12, 1979.

Russell, John J.: b. Dec. 1, 1897, Baltimore, Md.; educ. St. Charles College (Catonsville, Md.), St. Mary's Seminary (Baltimore, Md.), North American College (Rome); ord. priest July 8, 1923; ord.

bishop of Charleston, Mar. 14, 1950; bishop of Richmond, July 3, 1958; retired Apr. 30, 1973.

Ryan, Daniel L.: b. Sept. 28, 1930, Mankato, Minn.; educ. St. Procopius Seminary (Lisle, Ill.), Lateran Univ. (Rome); ord. priest May 3, 1956; ord. titular bishop of Surista and auxiliary bishop of Joliet, Sept. 30, 1981.

Ryan, Gerald: b. Aug. 24, 1923, Brooklyn, N.Y.; educ. Cathedral College (Brooklyn, N.Y.), Immaculate Conception Seminary (Huntington, L.I.), Fordham Univ. Graduate School of Social Work (Bronx, N.Y.); ord. priest June 3, 1950; ord. titular bishop of Munatiana and auxiliary bishop of Rockville Centre, May 9, 1977.

Ryan, James C., O.F.M.: b. Nov. 17, 1912, Chicago, Ill.; educ. St. Joseph's Seraphic Seminary (Westmont, Ill.), Our Lady of the Angels Seminary (Cleveland, O.); ord. priest June 24, 1938; ord. titular bishop of Margo and prelate of Santarem, Brazil, April 9, 1958; first bishop of Santarem, Dec. 4, 1979.

Ryan, Joseph T.: b. Nov. 1, 1913, Albany, N.Y.; educ. Manhattan College (New York City); ord. priest June 3, 1939; national secretary of Catholic Near East Welfare Assn. 1960-65; ord. first archbishop of Anchorage, Alaska, Mar. 25, 1966; app. titular archbishop of Gabi and coadjutor archbishop of the military ordinariate, Oct. 24, 1975, installed Dec. 13, 1975.

S

Salatka, Charles A.: b. Feb. 26, 1918, Grand Rapids, Mich.; educ. St. Joseph's Seminary (Grand Rapids, Mich.), Catholic Univ. (Washington, D.C.), Lateran Univ. (Rome); ord. priest Feb. 24, 1945; ord. titular bishop of Cariana and auxiliary bishop of Grand Rapids, Mich., Mar. 6, 1962; app. bishop of Marquette, installed Mar. 25, 1968; app. archbishop of Oklahoma City, Sept. 27, 1977; installed Dec. 15, 1977.

Sanchez, Robert: b. Mar. 20, 1934, Socorro, N.M.; educ. Immaculate Heart Seminary (Santa Fe, N.M.), Gregorian Univ. (Rome), Catholic Univ. (Washington, D.C.); ord. priest Dec. 20, 1959; ord. archbishop of Santa Fe, N.M., July 25, 1974.

Scanlan, John J.: b. May 24, 1906, County Cork, Ireland; educ. National Univ. of Ireland (Dublin), All Hallows College (Dublin); ord. priest June 22, 1930; U.S. citizen 1938; ord. titular bishop of Cenae and auxiliary bishop of Honolulu, Sept. 21, 1954; bishop of Honolulu, installed May 1, 1968; retired June 30, 1981.

Scarpone, Gerald, O.F.M.: b. Oct. 1, 1928, Watertown, Mass.; ord. priest June 24, 1956; ord. coadjutor bishop of Comayagua, Honduras, Feb. 21, 1979; succeeded as bishop of Comayagua, May 30, 1979.

Schad, James L.: b. July 20, 1917, Philadelphia, Pa.; educ. St. Mary's Seminary (Baltimore, Md.); ord. priest Apr. 10, 1943; ord. titular bishop of Panatoria and auxiliary bishop of Camden, Dec. 8, 1966.

Schierhoff, Andrew B.: b. Feb. 10, 1922, St. Louis, Mo.; ord. priest Apr. 14, 1948; missionary in Bolivia from 1956; ord. titular bishop of Cerenza and auxiliary of La Paz, Bolivia, Jan. 6, 1969.

Schladweiler, Alphonse: b. July 18, 1902, Milwaukee, Wis.; educ. St. Joseph College (Teutopolis, Ill.), St. Paul's Seminary (St. Paul, Minn.), Univ. of Minnesota (Minneapolis, Minn.); ord. priest June 9, 1929; ord. first bishop of New Ulm, Jan. 29, 1958; retired Dec. 23, 1975.

Schlaefer, Salvator, O.F.M. Cap.: b. June 27, 1920, Campbellsport, Wis.; ord. priest June 5, 1946; missionary in Bluefields, Nicaragua from 1947; ord. titular bishop of Fiumepiscense and vicar apostolic of Bluefields, Nicaragua, Aug. 12, 1970.

Schlarman, Stanley Gerard: b. July 27, 1933, Belleville, Ill.; educ. St. Henry Prep Seminary (Belleville, Ill.), Gregorian Univ. (Rome), St. Louis Univ. (St. Louis, Mo.); ord. priest July 13, 1958, Rome; ord. titular bishop of Capri and auxiliary bishop of Belleville, May 14, 1979; app. bishop of Dodge City, Mar. 1, 1983.

Schlotterback, Edward F., O.S.F.S.: b. Mar. 2, 1912, Philadelphia, Pa.; educ. Catholic Univ. (Washington, D.C.); ord. priest Dec. 17, 1938; ord. titular bishop of Balanea and vicar apostolic of Keetmanshoop, Namibia, June 11, 1956.

Schmidt, Firmin M., O.F.M.Cap.: b. Oct. 12, 1918, Catherine, Kans.; educ. Catholic Univ. (Washington, D.C.); ord. priest June 2, 1946; app. prefect apostolic of Mendi, Papua New Guinea, Apr. 3, 1959; ord. titular bishop of Conana and first vicar apostolic of Mendi, Dec. 15, 1965; became first bishop of Mendi when vicariate apostolic was raised to a diocese, Nov. 15, 1966.

Schmidt, Mathias, O.S.B.: b. Apr. 21, 1931, Wortonville, Kans.; ord. priest May 30, 1957; missionary in Brazil; ord. titular bishop of Mutugenna and auxiliary bishop of Jatai, Brazil, Sept. 10, 1972; bishop of Rui Barbosa, Brazil, May 14, 1976.

Schmitt, Mark: b. Feb. 14, 1923, Algoma, Wis., educ. Salvatorian Seminary (St. Nazianz, Wis.), St. John's Seminary (Collegeville, Minn.); ord. priest May 22, 1948; ord. titular bishop of Ceanannus Mor and auxiliary bishop of Green Bay, June 24, 1970; app. bishop of Marquette, Mar. 21, 1978, installed May 8, 1978.

Schoenherr, Walter J.: b. Feb. 28, 1920, Detroit, Mich.; educ. Sacred Heart Seminary (Detroit, Mich.), Mt. St. Mary Seminary (Norwood, O.); ord. priest Oct. 27, 1945; ord. titular bishop of Timidana and auxiliary bishop of Detroit, May 1, 1968.

Schuck, James A., O.F.M.: b. Jan. 17, 1913, Treverton, Pa.; educ. St. Joseph's Seminary (Callicoon, N.Y.), St. Bonaventure's University (St. Bonaventure, N.Y.). Holy Name College (Washington, D.C.); ord. priest June 11, 1940; ord. titular bishop of Avissa, Feb. 24, 1959 (resigned titular see May 26, 1978); prelate of Cristalandia, Brazil, 1959.

Schulte, Francis B.: b. Dec. 23, 1926, Philadelphia, Pa.; educ. St. Charles Borromeo Seminary (Overbrook, Pa.): ord. priest May 10, 1952; ord. titular bishop of Afufenia and auxiliary bishop of Philadelphia, Aug. 12, 1981.

Schulte, Paul Clarence: b. Mar. 18, 1890, Fredericktown, Mo.; educ. St. Francis Solanus

College (Quincy, Ill.), Kenrick Seminary (Webster Groves, Mo.); ord. priest June 11, 1915; ord. bishop of Leavenworth, Sept. 21, 1937; archbishop of Indianapolis, July 27, 1946; resigned Jan. 14, 1970; assigned titular see of Elicrora.

Schuster, Eldon B.: b. Mar. 10, 1911, Calio, N. Dak.; educ. Loras College (Dubuque, Ia.), Catholic Univ. (Washington, D.C.), Oxford Univ. (England), St. Louis Univ. (St. Louis, Mo.); ord. priest May 27, 1937; ord. titular bishop of Ambladaand auxiliary bishop of Great Falls, Mont., Dec. 21, 1961; app. bishop of Great Falls, Dec. 2, 1967, installed Jan. 23, 1968; resigned Dec. 28, 1977.

Setian, Nerses Mikail: b. Oct. 18,1918, Sebaste, Turkey; educ. Armenian Pontifical College and Gregorian Univ. (Rome); ord. priest Apr. 13, 1941, in Rome; ord. titular bishop of Ancira of the Armenians and first exarch of the apostolic exarchate for Armenian-Rite Catholics in Canada and the United States (see city New York), Dec. 5, 1981.

Shea, Francis R.: b. Dec. 4, 1913, Knoxville, Tenn.; educ. St. Mary's Seminary (Baltimore, Md.), North American College (Rome), Peabody College (Nashville, Tenn.); ord. priest Mar. 19, 1939; ord. bishop of Evansville, Ind., Feb. 3, 1970.

Sheehan, Daniel E.: b. May 14, 1917, Emerson, Nebr.; educ. Creighton Univ. (Omaha, Nebr.), Kenrick Seminary (Webster Groves, Mo.), Catholic Univ. (Washington, D.C.): ord. priest May 23, 1942; ord. titular bishop of Capsus and auxiliary bishop of Omaha, Mar. 19, 1964; app. archbishop of Omaha, installed Aug. 11, 1969.

Sheehan, Michael J.: b. July 9, 1939, Wichita, Kans.; educ. Assumption Seminary (San Antonio, Tex.), Gregorian Univ. and Lateran Univ. (Rome); ord. priest July 12, 1964; ord. first bishop of Lubbock, Tex., June 17, 1983.

Shehan, Lawrence Joseph: (See Cardinals, Biographies.)

Sheldon, Gilbert I.: b. Sept. 20, 1926, Cleveland, O.; educ. John Carroll Univ. and St. Mary Seminary (Cleveland, O.); ord. priest Feb. 28, 1953; ord. titular bishop of Taparura and auxiliary bishop of Cleveland, June 11, 1976.

Shubsda, Thaddeus A.: b. Apr. 2, 1925, Los Angeles, Calif.; educ. St. John's Seminary (Camarillo, Calif.); ord. priest Apr. 26, 1950; ord. titular bishop of Trau and auxiliary bishop of Los Angeles, Feb. 19, 1977; app. bishop of Monterey, June 1, 1982.

Sklba, Richard J.: b. Sept. 11, 1935, Racine, Wis.; educ. Old St. Francis Minor Seminary (Milwaukee, Wis.), North American College, Gregorian Univ., Pontifical Biblical Institute, Angelicum (Rome); ord. priest Dec. 20, 1959; ord. titular bishop of Castra and auxiliary bishop of Milwaukee, Dec. 19, 1979.

Skylstad, William: b. Mar. 2, 1934, Omak, Wash.; educ. Pontifical College Josephinum (Worthington, Ohio), Washington State Univ. (Pullman, Wash.), Gonzaga Univ. (Spokane, Wash.); ord. priest May 21, 1960; ord. bishop of Yakima, May 12, 1977.

Smith, Philip F., O.M.I.: b. Oct. 16, 1924, Lowell, Mass.; ord. priest Oct. 29, 1950; ord. titular bishop of Lamfua and vicar apostolic of Jolo, Philippine Islands, Sept. 8, 1972; app. coadjutor archbishop of Cotabato, Philippines, April 11, 1979; archbishop of Cotabato, Mar. 14, 1980.

Snyder, John J.: b. Oct. 25, 1925, New York, N.Y.; educ. Cathedral College (Brooklyn, N.Y.), Immaculate Conception Seminary (Huntington, N.Y.); ord. priest June 9, 1951; ord. titular bishop of Forlimpopli and auxiliary bishop of Brooklyn, Feb. 2, 1973; app. bishop of St. Augustine, installed Dec. 5, 1979.

Soenneker, Henry J.: b. May 27, 1907, Melrose, Minn.; educ. Pontifical Josephinum College (Worthington, O.), Catholic Univ. (Washington, D.C.); ord. priest May 26, 1934; ord. bishop of Owensboro, Apr. 26, 1961; resigned June 30, 1982.

Soens, Lawrence D.: b. Aug. 26, 1926, Iowa City, Ia.; educ. Loras College (Dubuque, Ia.), St. Ambrose College (Davenport, Ia.), Kenrick Seminary (St. Louis, Mo.), Univ. of Iowa; ord. priest May 6, 1950; ord. bishop of Sioux City, Aug. 17, 1983.

Sowada, Alphonse A., O.S.C.: b. June 23, 1933, Avon, Minn.; educ. Holy Cross Scholasticate (Fort Wayne, Ind.), Catholic Univ. (Washington, D.C.), ord. priest May 31, 1958; missionary in Indonesia from 1958; ord. bishop of Agats, Indonesia, Nov. 23, 1969.

Speltz, George H.: b. May 29, 1912, Altura, Minn.; educ. St. Mary's College, St. Paul's Seminary (St. Paul, Minn.), Catholic Univ. (Washington, D.C.); ord. priest June 2, 1940; ord. titular bishop of Claneus and auxiliary bishop of Winona, Mar. 25, 1963; app. coadjutor bishop of St. Cloud, Apr. 4, 1966; bishop of St. Cloud, Jan. 31, 1968.

Speyrer, Jude: b. Apr. 14, 1929, Leonville, La.; educ. St. Joseph Seminary (Covington, La), Notre Dame Seminary (New Orleans, La.), Gregorian Univ. (Rome), Univ. of Fribourg (Switzerland); ord. priest July 25, 1953; ord. first bishop of Lake Charles, La., Apr. 25, 1980.

Stafford, James Francis: b. July 26, 1932, Baltimore, Md.; educ. St. Mary's Seminary (Baltimore, Md.), North American College and Gregorian Univ. (Rome); ord. priest Dec. 15, 1957; ord. titular bishop of Respecta and auxiliary bishop of Baltimore, Feb. 29, 1976; app. bishop of Memphis, Nov. 17, 1982.

Steiner, Kenneth Donald: b. Nov. 25, 1936, David City, Nebr.; educ. Mt. Angel Seminary (St. Benedict, Ore.), St. Thomas Seminary (Seattle, Wash.); ord. priest, May 19, 1962; ord. titular bishop of Avensa and auxiliary bishop of Portland, Ore., Mar. 2, 1978.

Stemper, Alfred M., M.S.C.: b. Jan. 2, 1913, Black Hammer, Minn.; ord. priest June 26, 1940; ord. titular bishop of Eleutheropolis and vicar apostolic of Kavieng, New Guinea, Oct. 28, 1957; first bishop of Kavieng, Nov. 15, 1966; retired Oct. 24, 1980.

Straling, Phillip F.: b. Apr. 25, 1933, San Bernardino, Calif.; educ. Immaculate Heart Seminary, St. Francis Seminary, Univ. of San Diego and San Diego State University (San Diego, Calif.), North American College (Rome); ord. priest Mar. 19, 1959; ord. first bishop of San Bernardino, Nov. 6, 1978.

Strecker, Ignatius J.: b. Nov. 23, 1917, Spearville, Kans.; educ. St. Benedict's College (Atchison, Kans.), Kenrick Seminary (Webster Groves, Mo.), Catholic Univ. (Washington, D.C.); ord. priest Dec. 19, 1942; ord. bishop of Springfield-Cape Girardeau, Mo., June 20, 1962; archbishop of Kansas City, Kans., Oct. 28, 1969.

Sullivan, James S.: b. July 23, 1929, Kalamazoo, Mich.; educ. Sacred Heart Seminary (Detroit, Mich.), St. John Provincial Seminary (Plymouth, Mich.); ord. priest June 4, 1955; ord. titular bishop of Siccessi and auxiliary bishop of Lansing, Sept. 21, 1972.

Sullivan, John J.: b. July 5, 1920, Horton, Kans.; educ. Kenrick Seminary (St. Louis, Mo.); ord. priest Sept. 23, 1944; vice-president of Catholic Church Extension Society and national director of Extension Lay Volunteers, 1961-68; ord. bishop of Grand Island, Sept. 19, 1972; app. bishop of Kansas City-St. Joseph, June 27, 1977, installed Aug. 17, 1977.

Sullivan, Joseph M.: b. Mar. 23, 1930, Brooklyn, N.Y.; educ. Immaculate Conception Seminary (Huntington, N.Y.), Fordham Univ. (New York); ord. priest June 2, 1956; ord. titular bishop of Suliana and auxiliary bishop of Brooklyn, Nov. 24, 1980.

Sullivan, Walter F.: b. June 10, 1928, Washington, D.C.; educ. St. Mary's Seminary (Baltimore, Md.), Catholic Univ. (Washington, D.C.); ord. priest May 9, 1953; ord. titular bishop of Selsea and auxiliary bishop of Richmond, Va., Dec. 1, 1970; app. bishop of Richmond, June 4, 1974.

Sulyk, Stephen: b. Oct. 2, 1924, Balnycia, Western Ukraine; migrated to U.S. 1948; educ. Ukrainian Catholic Seminary of the Holy Spirit (Hirschberg, Germany), St. Josaphat's Seminary and Catholic Univ. (Washington, D.C.); ord. priest June 14, 1952; ord. archbishop of the Ukrainian-Rite archeparcy of Philadelphia, Mar. 1, 1981.

Swanstrom, Edward E.: b. Mar. 20, 1903, New York, N.Y.; educ. Fordham Univ. (New York City), St. John's Seminary (Brooklyn, N.Y.), New York School of Social Work; ord. priest June 2, 1928; director of Catholic Relief Services 1947-76; ord. titular bishop of Arba and auxiliary bishop of New York, Oct. 28, 1960; retired Mar. 20, 1978.

Symons, J. Keith: b. Oct. 14, 1932, Champion, Mich.; educ. St. Thomas Seminary (Bloomfield, Conn.), St. Mary Seminary (Baltimore, Md.); ord. priest May 18, 1958; ord. titular bishop of Sigus and auxiliary bishop of St. Petersburg, Mar. 19, 1981.

Szoka, Edmund C.: b. Sept. 14, 1927, Grand Rapids, Mich.; educ. Sacred Heart Seminary (Detroit, Mich.), St. John's Provincial Seminary (Plymouth, Mich.), Lateran Univ. (Rome); ord. priest June 5, 1954; ord. first bishop of Gaylord, Mich., July 20, 1971; app. archbishop of Detroit, Mar. 28, 1981, installed May 17, 1981.

T

Tafoya, Arthur N.: b. Mar. 2, 1933, Alameda, N.M.; educ. St. Thomas Seminary (Denver, Colo.), Conception Seminary (Conception, Mo.); ord. priest May 12, 1962; ord. bishop of Pueblo, Sept. 10, 1980.

Tanner, Paul F.: b. Jan. 15, 1905, Peoria, Ill.; educ. Marquette Univ. (Milwaukee, Wis.), Kenrick Seminary (Webster Groves, Mo.), St. Francis Seminary (Milwaukee, Wis.), Catholic Univ. (Washington, D.C.): ord. priest May 30, 1931; assistant director NCWC Youth Department 1940-45; assistant general secretary of NCWC 1945-58; general secretary of NCWC (now USCC) 1958-68; ord. titular bishop of Lamasba, Dec. 21, 1965; bishop of St. Augustine, Mar. 27, 1968; resigned Apr. 21, 1979.

Tawil, Joseph: b. Dec. 25, 1913, Damascus, Syria; ord. priest July 20, 1936; ord. titular archbishop of Mira and patriarchal vicar for eparchy of Damascus of the Patriarchate of Antioch for the Melkites, Jan. 1, 1960; apostolic exarch for faithful of the Melkite rite in the U.S., Oct. 31, 1969; app. first eparch when exarchate was raised to eparchy, July 15, 1976; title of see changed to Newton, 1977.

Timlin, James C.: b. Aug. 5, 1927, Scranton, Pa.; educ. St. Charles College (Catonsville, Md.), St. Mary's Seminary (Baltimore, Md.), North American College (Rome); ord. priest July 16, 1951; ord. titular bishop of Gunugo and auxiliary bishop of Scranton, Sept. 21, 1976.

Topel, Bernard J.: b. May 31, 1903, Bozeman, Mont.; educ. Carroll College (Helena, Mont.), Grand Seminary (Montreal), Catholic Univ. (Washington, D.C.), Harvard Univ. (Cambridge, Mass.), Notre Dame Univ. (Notre Dame, Ind.); ord. priest June 7, 1927; ord. titular bishop of Binda and coadjutor bishop of Spokane, Sept. 21, 1955; bishop of Spokane, Sept. 25, 1955; retired Apr. 11, 1978.

Treinen, Sylvester: b. Nov. 19, 1917, Donnelly, Minn.; educ. Crosier Seminary (Onamia, Minn.), St. Paul Seminary (St. Paul, Minn.); ord. priest June 11, 1946; ord. bishop of Boise, July 25, 1962.

Tschoepe, Thomas: b. Dec. 17, 1915, Pilot Point, Tex.; educ. Pontifical College Josephinum (Worthington, O.); ord. priest May 30, 1943; ord. bishop of San Angelo, Tex., Mar. 9, 1966; app. bishop of Dallas, Tex., Aug. 27, 1969.

U-V

Untener, Kenneth E.: b. Aug. 3, 1937, Detroit, Mich.; educ. Sacred Heart Seminary (Detroit, Mich.), St. John's Provincial Seminary (Plymouth, Mich.), Gregorian Univ. (Rome); ord. priest June 1, 1963; ord. bishop of Saginaw, Nov. 24, 1980.

Unterkoefler, Ernest L.: b. Aug. 17, 1917, Philadelphia, Pa.; educ. Catholic Univ. (Washington, D.C.); ord. priest May 18, 1944; ord. titular bishop of Latopolis and auxiliary bishop of Richmond, Va., Feb. 22, 1962; app. bishop of Charleston, Dec. 12, 1964, installed Feb. 22, 1965.

Valero, René A.: b. Aug. 15, 1930, New York, N.Y.; educ. Cathedral College, Immaculate Conception Seminary (Huntington, N.Y.), Fordham Univ. (New York); ord. priest June 2, 1956; ord. titular bishop of Turris Vicus and auxiliary bishop of Brooklyn, Nov. 24, 1980.

Vath, Joseph G.: b. Mar. 12, 1918, New Orleans, La.; educ. Notre Dame Seminary (New Orleans,

La.), Catholic Univ. (Washington, D.C.); ord. priest June 7, 1941; ord. titular bishop of Novaliciana and auxiliary bishop of Mobile-Birmingham, May 26, 1966; app. first bishop of Birmingham, Oct. 8, 1969.

Vaughan, Austin B.: b. Sept. 27, 1927, New York, N.Y.; educ. North American College and Gregorian Univ. (Rome), ord. priest Dec. 8, 1951; pres. Catholic Theological Society of America, 1967; rector of St. Joseph's Seminary (Dunwoodie, N.Y.), 1973; ord. titular bishop of Cluain Iraird and auxiliary bishop of New York, June 29, 1977.

Veigle, Adrian J.M., T.O.R.: b. Sept. 15, 1912, Lilly, Pa.; educ. St. Francis College (Loretto, Pa.), Pennsylvania State College; ord. priest May 22, 1937; ord. titular bishop of Gigthi June 9, 1966 (resigned titular see May 26, 1978); prelate of Borba, Brazil, 1966.

Vonesh, Raymond J.: b. Jan. 25, 1916, Chicago, Ill.; educ. St. Mary of the Lake Seminary (Mundelein, Ill.). Gregorian Univ. (Rome); ord. priest May 3, 1941; ord. titular bishop of Vanariona and auxiliary bishop of Joliet, Ill., Apr. 3, 1968.

W

Waldschmidt, Paul E., C.S.C.: b. Jan. 7, 1920, Evansville, Ind.; educ. Notre Dame Univ. (Notre Dame, Ind.), Holy Cross College (Washington, D.C.), Laval Univ. (Quebec), Angelicum (Rome), Louvain (Belgium), Sorbonne (Paris), ord. priest June 24, 1946; president University of Portland, 1962-77; ord. titular bishop of Citium and auxiliary bishop of Portland, Ore., Mar. 2, 1978.

Walsh, Daniel Francis: b. Oct. 2, 1937, San Francisco, Calif.; educ. St. Joseph Seminary (Mountain View, Calif.), St. Patrick Seminary (Menlo Park, Calif.) Catholic Univ. (Washington, D.C.); ord. priest Mar. 30, 1963; ord.titular bishop of Tigia and auxiliary bishop of San Francisco, Sept. 24, 1981.

Walsh, Nicholas E.: b. Oct. 20, 1916, Burnsville, Minn.; educ. St. Paul Seminary (St. Paul, Minn.), Catholic Univ. (Washington, D.C.), Pontifical Palafoxianum Seminary (Puebla, Mexico), Register College of Journalism (Denver, Colo.); ord. priest June 6, 1942; first editor of *Idaho Register;* diocesan vicar for Mexican Americans; ord. bishop of Yakima, Oct. 28, 1974; app. titular bishop of Bolsena and auxiliary bishop of Seattle, Aug. 10, 1976.

Ward, John J.: b. Sept. 28, 1920, Los Angeles, Calif.; educ. St. John's Seminary (Camarillo, Calif.), Catholic Univ. (Washington, D.C.); ord. priest May 4, 1946; ord. titular bishop of Bria and auxiliary bishop of Los Angeles, Dec. 12, 1963.

Watson, Alfred M.: b. July 11, 1907, Erie, Pa.; educ. St. Mary's Seminary (Baltimore, Md.), Catholic Univ. (Washington, D.C.); ord. priest May 10, 1934; ord. titular bishop of Nationa and auxiliary bishop of Erie, June 29, 1965; app. bishop of Erie, 1969, installed May 13, 1969; resigned July 16, 1982.

Watters, Loras J.: b. Oct. 14, 1915, Dubuque, Ia.; educ. Loras College (Dubuque, Ia.), Gregorian Univ. (Rome), Catholic Univ. (Washington, D.C.); ord. priest June 7, 1941; ord. titular bishop of Fidoloma and auxiliary bishop of Dubuque, Aug.

26, 1965; bishop of Winona, installed Mar. 13, 1969.

Watty Urquidi, Ricardo, M.Sp.S.: b. July 16, 1938, San Diego, Calif.; ord. priest June 8, 1968; ord. titular bishop of Macomedes and auxiliary bishop of Mexico City, July 19, 1980.

Weakland, Rembert G., O.S.B.: b. Apr. 2, 1927, Patton, Pa.; joined Benedictines, 1945; ord. priest June 24, 1951; abbot-primate of Benedictine Confederation, 1967-77; ord. archbishop of Milwaukee, Nov. 8, 1977.

Weigand, William K.: b. May 23, 1937, Bend, Ore.; educ. Mt. Angel Seminary (St. Benedict, Ore.), St. Edward's Seminary and St. Thomas Seminary (Kenmore, Wash.); ord. priest May 25, 1963; ord. bishop of Salt Lake City, Nov. 17, 1980.

Welsh, Lawrence H.: b. Feb. 1, 1935, Winton, Wyo.; educ. Univ. of Wyoming (Laramie, Wyo.), St. John's Seminary (Collegeville, Minn.), Catholic Univ. (Washington, D.C.); ord. priest May 26, 1962; ord. bishop of Spokane, Dec. 14, 1978.

Welsh, Thomas J.: b. Dec. 20, 1921, Weatherly, Pa.; educ. St. Charles Borromeo Seminary (Philadelphia, Pa.), Catholic Univ. (Washington, D.C.); ord. priest May 30, 1946; ord. titular bishop of Scattery Island and auxiliary bishop of Philadelphia, Apr. 2, 1970; app. first bishop of Arlington, Va., June 4, 1974, installed Aug. 13, 1974; app. bishop of Allentown, Feb. 8, 1983, installed Mar. 21, 1983.

Whealon, John F.: b. Jan. 15, 1921, Barberton, O.; educ. St. Charles College (Catonsville, Md.), St. Mary's Seminary (Cleveland, O.); ord. priest May 26, 1945; ord. titular bishop of Andrapa and auxiliary bishop of Cleveland, July 6, 1961; app. bishop of Erie, Dec. 9, 1966, installed Mar. 7, 1967; archbishop of Hartford, installed Mar. 19, 1969.

Whelan, Robert L., S.J.: b. Apr. 16, 1912, Wallace, Ida.; educ. St. Michael's College (Spokane, Wash.), Alma College (Alma, Calif.); ord. priest June 17, 1944; ord. titular bishop of Sicilibba and coadjutor bishop of Fairbanks, Alaska, with right of succession, Feb. 22, 1968; bishop of Fairbanks, Nov. 30, 1968.

Wildermuth, Augustine F., S.J.: b. Feb. 20, 1904, St. Louis, Mo.; educ. St. Stanislaus Seminary (Florissant, Mo.), St. Michael's Scholasticate (Spokane, Wash.), Sacred Heart College (Shembaganur, S. India), St. Mary's College (Kurseong, India), Gregorian Univ. (Rome); entered Society of Jesus, 1922; ord. priest July 25, 1935; ord. bishop of Patna, India, Oct. 28, 1947; retired Mar. 6, 1980.

Wirz, George O.: b. Jan. 17, 1929, Monroe, Wis.; educ. St. Francis Seminary and Marquette Univ. (Milwaukee, Wis.); Cath. Univ. (Washington, D.C.); ord. priest May 31, 1952; ord. titular bishop of Municipa and auxiliary bishop of Madison, Mar. 9, 1978.

Wurm, John N.: b. Dec. 6, 1927, Overland, Mo.; educ. Kenrick Seminary and St. Louis Univ. (St. Louis, Mo.); ord. priest Apr. 3, 1954; ord. titular bishop of Plestia and auxiliary bishop of St. Louis, Aug. 17, 1976; app. bishop of Belleville, Sept. 21, 1981, installed Nov. 4, 1981.

Wycislo, Aloysius John: b. June 17, 1908, Chicago, Ill.; educ. St. Mary's Seminary (Mundelein, Ill.), Catholic Univ. (Washington, D.C.); ord. priest Apr. 4, 1934; ord. titular bishop of Stadia and auxiliary bishop of Chicago, Dec. 21, 1960; app. bishop of Green Bay, installed Apr. 16, 1968; resigned May 10, 1983.

Z

Zayek, Francis: b. Oct. 18, 1920, Manzanillo, Cuba; ord. priest Mar. 17, 1946; ord. titular bishop of Callinicum and auxiliary bishop for Maronites in Brazil, Aug. 5, 1962; named apostolic exarch for Maronites in U.S., with headquarters in Detroit; installed June 11, 1966; first eparch of St. Maron of Detroit, Mar. 25, 1972; see transferred to Brooklyn, June 27, 1977; given personal title of archbishop, Dec. 22, 1982.

Zuroweste, Albert R.: b. Apr. 26, 1901, East St. Louis, Ill.; educ. St. Francis College (Quincy, Ill.), Kenrick Seminary (Webster Groves, Mo.), Catholic Univ. (Washington, D.C.); ord. priest June 8, 1924; ord. bishop of Belleville, Jan. 29, 1948; retired Oct. 29, 1976.

RETIRED U.S. PRELATES

Information, as of Aug. 15, 1983, includes name of the prelate and see held at the time of retirement or resignation; archbishops are indicated by an asterisk. Most of the prelates listed below resigned their sees because of age in accordance with church law. See Index: Biographies of American Bishops.

The usual form of address of retired residential prelates (unless they have a titular see) is *Former Archbishop or Bishop of* (last see held).

Richard H. Ackerman, C.S.Sp. (Covington), George W. Ahr (Trenton), Reginald Arliss, C.P. (Marbel, Philippines, prelate), John H. Boccella, T.O.R.* (Izmir, Turkey), James C. Burke, O.P. (Chimbote, Peru, prelate), Charles A. Buswell (Pueblo), James J. Byrne* (Dubuque), L. Abel Caillouet (New Orleans, auxiliary), Cardinal John Carberry* (St. Louis), Mark K. Carroll (Wichita), John J. Cassata (Fort Worth), Harry A. Clinch (Monterey), John E. Cohill, S.V.D. (Goroka, Papua New Guinea), James L. Connolly (Fall River), Thomas Connolly* (Seattle), William M. Cosgrove (Belleville), William E. Cousins* (Milwaukee), Augustine Danglmayr (Ft. Worth, auxiliary), Nicholas D'Antonio, O.F.M. (Olancho, Honduras).

James P. Davis* (Santa Fê), Cardinal John F. Dearden* (Detroit), Joseph P. Denning (Brooklyn, auxiliary), Hugh A. Donohoe (Fresno), John A. Donovan (Toledo), John J. Dougherty (Newark, auxiliary), Carroll T. Dozier (Memphis), Thomas J. Drury (Corpus Christi), Clarence J. Duhart, C.SS.R. (Udon Thani, Thailand), Joseph A. Durick (Nashville), J. Lennox Federal (Salt Lake City), Bernard J. Flanagan (Worcester), John B. Franz (Peoria), Frederick W. Freking (La Crosse), Philip J. Furlong (Military Vicariate, delegate).

Raymond J. Gallagher (Lafayette, Ind.), Hugo Gerbermann, M.M. (San Antonio, auxiliary), James J. Gerrard (Fall River, auxiliary), Laurence A. Glenn (Crookston), Ignatius T. Glennie, S.J. (Trincomalee-Batticaloa, Sri Lanka), Lawrence P. Graves (Alexandria-Shreveport), Lawrence Graziano, O.F.M. (San Miguel, El Salvador), Charles P. Greco (Alexandria), Francis J. Green (Tucson), John B. Grellinger, (Green Bay, auxiliary), Frank J. Greteman (Sioux City).

Hilary B. Hacker (Bismarck), Paul L. Hagarty (Nassau, Bahamas), Charles H. Helmsing (Kansas City-St. Joseph), Edward J. Herrmann (Columbus), Edward G. Hettinger (Columbus, auxiliary), Vincent J. Hines (Norwich), Lambert A. Hoch (Sioux Falls), Joseph L. Hogan (Rochester), Robert F. Joyce (Burlington), Walter P. Kellenberg (Rockville Centre), Arthur H. Krawczak (Detroit, auxiliary), George L. Leech (Harrisburg; titular bishop of Allegheny), Leo Lemay, S.M. (Bougainville, Solomon Is.), Vincent M. Leonard (Pittsburgh).

J. Carroll McCormick (Scranton), William McDonald (San Francisco, auxiliary), Thomas J. McDonough* (Louisville), John J. McEleney, S.J.* (Kingston, Jamaica), Joseph T. McGucken* (San Francisco), Edward A. McGurkin, M.M. (Shinyanga, Tanzania), Joseph H. McShea (Allentown), Edward J. Maginn (Albany, auxiliary), John J. Maguire* (New York, coadjutor), David M. Maloney (Wichita), Alfred Mendez, C.S.C. (Arecibo, P.R.), Sidney M. Metzger (El Paso), William J. Moran (Military Vicariate, delegate).

Louis La Ravoire Morrow, S.D.B. (Krishnagar, India), Charles R. Mulrooney (Brooklyn, auxiliary), Knute Ansgar Nelson, O.S.B. (Stockholm, Sweden), Hubert M. Newell (Cheyenne), Cardinal Patrick O'Boyle* (Washington, D.C.).

Martin J. O'Connor* (Prefect Emeritus, Pontifical Commission for Social Communications), William A. O'Connor (Springfield, Ill.), John L. Paschang (Grand Island), George H. Pearce, S.M.* (Suva, Fiji Islands), Joseph M. Pernicone (New York, auxiliary), Ernest J. Primeau (Manchester), Leo A. Pursley (Fort Wayne-South Bend), Joseph M. Raya* (Acre), Joseph W. Regan, M.M. (Tagum, P.I., Prelate), Francis F. Reh (Saginaw).

Louis J. Reicher (Austin), Thomas F. Reilly, C.SS.R. (San Juan de la Maguana, Dominican Republic), John J. Rudin, M.M. (Musoma, Tanzania), John J. Russell (Richmond), John J. Scanlan (Honolulu), Alphonse Schladweiler (New Ulm), Paul C. Schulte* (Indianapolis; titular archbishop of Elicora), Eldon B. Schuster (Great Falls).

Cardinal Lawrence J. Shehan* (Baltimore), Henry J. Soenneker (Owensboro), Alfred M. Stemper, M.S.C. (Kavieng, Papua New Guinea), Edward E. Swanstrom (New York, auxiliary), Paul F. Tanner (St. Augustine), Bernard J. Topel (Spokane), Alfred M. Watson (Erie), Augustine Wildermuth, S.J. (Patna, India), Aloysius J. Wycislo (Green Bay), Albert R. Zuroweste (Belleville).

HEALING

The Church has never had an ordained ministry of healing, although the charism of healing has always been recognized as a free gift of the Holy Spirit for the good of both individuals and the community of faith. Underlying all aspects of healing are faith in the power and providence of God and a readiness to accept his permissive will.

Institutes of consecrated life — religious orders and congregations — are special societies in the Church. Their members, called religious, commit themselves by public vows to observance of the evangelical counsels of poverty, chastity and obedience in a community kind of life in accordance with rules and constitutions approved by church authority.

(See also Essential Elements in Church Teaching on Religious Life.)

Institutes of Consecrated Life

The particular goal of each institute and the means of realizing it in practice are stated in the rule and constitutions proper to the institute. Local bishops can give approval for rules and constitutions of institutes of diocesan rank. Pontifical rank belongs to institutes approved by the Holy See. General jurisdiction over all religious is exercised by the Congregation for Religious and Secular Institutes. General legislation concerning religious is contained in Canons 573 to 709 in Book II, Part III, of the revised Code of Canon Law, effective Nov. 27, 1983.

All religious institutes are commonly called religious orders, despite the fact that there are differences between orders and congregations. The best known orders include the Benedictines, Trappists, Franciscans, Dominicans, Carmelites and Augustinians, for men; and the Carmelites, Benedictines, Poor Clares, Dominicans of the Second Order and Visitation Nuns, for women. The orders are older than the congregations, which did not appear until the 16th century.

Contemplative institutes are oriented to divine worship and service within the confines of their communities, by prayer, penitential practices, other spiritual activities and self-supporting work. Examples are the Trappists and Carthusians, the Carmelite and Poor Clare nuns. Active institutes are geared primarily for the ministry and various kinds of apostolic work. Mixed institutes combine elements of the contemplative and active ways of life. While most institutes of men and women can be classified as active, all of them have contemplative aspects.

Historical Development

The basis of the life of religious institutes was the invitation Christ extended to men (Mt. 19:16ff.) to follow him with special dedication in a life like his own, which was that of a poor and chaste man under obedience to the Father.

In the earliest years of Christianity, some men and women dedicated themselves to the service of God in a special manner. Among them were holy women, deaconesses and virgins mentioned in the Acts of the Apostles, and confessors and ascetics like St. Clement of Rome, St. Ignatius of Antioch and St. Polycarp.

In the third and fourth centuries, there were traces of a kind of religious profession, and the root idea of the life began to produce significant results in the solitary and community hermitages of Egypt and Syria under the inspiration of men like St. Paul of Thebes, St. Anthony the Abbot and St. Pachomius.

St. Basil, "Father of Monasticism in the East," exerted a deep and still continuing influence on the development of religious life among men and women. His opposite number in the West was St. Benedict, whose rule or counsels, dating from about 530, set the pattern of monastic life for men and women which prevailed for nearly six centuries and which still endures. Before his time, St. Augustine framed guidelines for community life which are still being followed by some men and women religious.

Non-Monastic Institutes

Mendicant orders, whose members were freer than the monks for works of the active ministry, made their appearance early in the 13th century and began to change some of the established aspects of religious life. Religious women, however, continued to live in the monastic manner.

A significant change in religious life developed in the 16th century when several communities of men with simple rather than solemn vows were approved; among them were clerics regular like the Jesuits and Barnabites. Some of these communities are considered to be orders, although they differ in some respects from the older orders.

The Sisters of Charity, in 1633, were the first community of women with simple vows to gain church approval. Since that time, the number and variety of female communities have greatly increased. Women religious, no longer restricted to the hidden life of prayer, became engaged in many kinds of work including education, health and social service, and missionary endeavor.

Clerical communities of men — i. e., those whose membership is predominantly composed of priests — are similarly active in many types of work. Their distinctive fields are education, home and foreign missions, retreats, special assignments and the communications media, as well as the internal life and conduct of their own communities. They also engage in the ordinary pastoral ministry which is the principal work of diocesan or secular priests. They are generally called regular clergy because of the rule of life (regula in Latin) they follow.

Non-clerical or lay institutes of men are the various brotherhoods whose non-ordained members (called lay brothers, or simply brothers) are engaged in educational and hospital work, missionary endeavors, and other special fields.

Some of the institutes of men listed below have a special kind of status because their members, while living a common life like that which is characteristic of religious, do not profess the vows of religious. Examples are the Maryknoll Fathers, the Oratorians of St. Philip Neri, the Paulists and Sulpicians. They are called societies of apostolic life and are the subject of Canons 731 to 746 in the revised Code of Canon Law.

RELIGIOUS INSTITUTES OF MEN IN THE UNITED STATES

(Sources: *Official Catholic Directory;* Catholic Almanac survey.)

African Missions, Society of, S.M.A.: Founded 1856, at Lyons, France, by Bishop Melchior de Marion Brésillac. Generalate, Rome, Italy; American provincialate, 23 Bliss Ave., Tenafly, N.J. 07670. Missionary work.

Assumptionists (Augustinians of the Assumption), AA.: Founded 1845, at Nimes, France, by Rev. Emmanuel d'Alzon; in U.S., 1946. General motherhouse, Rome, Italy; U.S. province, 328 Adams St., Milton, Mass. 02186. Educational, parochial, ecumenical, retreat, foreign mission work.

Atonement, Franciscan Friars of the, S.A.: Founded as an Anglican Franciscan community in 1898 at Garrison, N.Y., by Rev. Paul Wattson. Community corporately received into the Catholic Church in 1909. Motherhouse, St. Paul Friary, Graymoor, Garrison N.Y. 10524. Ecumenical, mission, retreat and charitable works.

Augustinian Recollects, O.A.R.: Founded 1588: in U.S., 1944. General motherhouse, Rome, Italy. Missionary, parochial, education work.

St. Augustine Province (1944), 29 Ridgeway Ave., W. Orange, N.J. 07052.

St. Nicholas Province (Madrid): U.S. Delegate, 2800 Schurz Ave., Bronx, N.Y. 10465.

Augustinians (Order of St. Augustine), O.S.A.: Established canonically in 1256 by Pope Alexander IV; in U.S., 1796. General motherhouse, Rome, Italy.

St. Thomas of Villanova Province (1796), Villanova, Pa. 19085.

Our Mother of Good Counsel Province (1941), Tolentine Center, 20300 Governors Hwy., Olympia Fields, Ill. 60461.

St. Augustine Province (1969), 2060 N. Vermont Ave., Los Angeles, Calif. 90027.

Good Counsel Vice-Province, St. Augustine Priory, Richland, N.J. 08350.

U.S. Vicariate of Castile, Spain, Province, P.O. Box 190, Waxachachie, Tex. 75165.

Barnabites (Clerics Regular of St. Paul), C.R.S.P.: Founded 1530, in Milan, Italy, by St. Anthony M. Zaccaria. Generalate, Rome, Italy; American headquarters, 1023 Swann Rd., Youngstown, N.Y. 14174. Parochial, educational, mission work.

Basil the Great, Order of St. (Ukrainian), O.S.B.M.: General motherhouse, Rome, Italy; U.S. province, 31-12 30th St., Long Island City, N.Y. 11106. Parochial work among Byzantine Ukrainian Rite Catholics.

Basilian Fathers (Congregation of the Priests of St. Basil), C.S.B.: Founded 1822, at Annonay, France. General motherhouse, 20 Humewood Dr., Toronto, Ont. M6C 2W2, Canada. Educational, parochial work.

Basilian Salvatorian Fathers: Founded 1684, at Saida, Lebanon, by Eftimios Saifi; in U.S., 1953. General motherhouse, Saida, Lebanon; American headquarters, 30 East St., Methuen, Mass. 01844. Educational, parochial work among Eastern Rite peoples.

Benedictine Monks (Order of St. Benedict), O.S.B.: Founded 529, in Italy, by St. Benedict of Nursia; in U.S., 1846.

• American Cassinese Federation (1855). Rt. Rev. Martin Burne, O.S.B., pres., St. Mary's Abbey, Delbarton, Morristown, N.J. 07960. Abbeys and Priories belonging to the federation:

St. Vincent Archabbey, Latrobe, Pa. 15650; St. John's Abbey, Collegeville, Minn. 56321; St. Benedict's Abbey, Atchison, Kans. 66002; St. Mary's Abbey, Delbarton, Morristown, N.J. 07960; Belmont Abbey, Belmont, N.C. 28012; St. Bernard Abbey, St. Bernard, Cullman, Ala. 35055; St. Procopius Abbey, Lisle, Ill. 60532; St. Gregory's Abbey, Shawnee, Okla. 74801; St. Leo Abbey, St. Leo, Fla. 33574; Assumption Abbey, Richardton, N. Dak. 58652;

St. Bede Abbey, Peru, Ill. 61354; St. Martin's Abbey, Lacey, Wash. 98503; Holy Cross Abbey, Canon City, Colo. 81212; St. Anselm's Abbey, Manchester, N.H. 03102; St. Andrew's Abbey, 2900 East Blvd., Cleveland, O. 44104; Holy Trinity Monastery, Butler, Pa. 16001; St. Maur Priory, 4545 Northwestern Ave., Indianapolis, Ind. 46208; Newark Abbey, 528 High St., Newark, N.J. 07102; St. Mark's Priory, South Union, Ky. 42283; Benedictine Priory, 6502 Seawright Dr., Savannah, Ga. 31406; Woodside Priory, 302 Portola Rd., Portola Valley, Calif. 94025.

• Swiss-American Federation (1870), Rt. Rev. Raphael De Salvo O.S.B., pres., New Subiaco Abbey, New Subiaco, Ark. 72865. Abbeys and priory belonging to the federation:

St. Meinrad Archabbey, St. Meinrad, Ind. 47577; Conception Abbey, Conception, Mo. 64433; Mt. Michael Abbey, Elkhorn, Nebr. 68022; New Subiaco Abbey, Subiaco, Ark. 72865; St. Joseph's Abbey, St. Benedict, La. 70457; Mt. Angel Abbey, St. Benedict, Ore. 97373; Marmion Abbey, Butterfield Rd., Aurora, Ill. 60504;

St. Benedict's Abbey, Benet Lake, Wis. 53102; Glastonbury Abbey, 16 Hull St., Hingham, Mass. 02043; Westminster Abbey, Mission, B.C., Canada; St. Pius X Abbey, Pevely, Mo. 63070; Blue Cloud Abbey, Marvin, S. Dak. 57251; Corpus Christi Abbey, Star Route, Box A-38-A, Sandia, Tex. 78383; Our Lady of Guadalupe Abbey, Pecos N. Mex. 87552; Prince of Peace Abbey, Benet Hill, Oceanside, Calif. 92054.

• English Benedictine Congregation: St. Anselm's Abbey, 4501 S. Dakota Ave. N.E., Washington, D.C. 20017; Abbey of St. Gregory, Cory's Lane, Portsmouth, R.I. 02871; Priory of St. Mary and St. Louis, 500 S. Mason Rd., St. Louis, Mo. 63141.

• Congregation of St. Ottilien for Foreign Missions, St. Paul's Abbey, Newton, N.J. 07860; Benedictine Mission House, Schuyler, Neb. 68661.

• Congregation of the Annunciation, St. Andrew Priory, Valyermo, Calif. 93563.

• Houses not in Congregations: Mount Saviour Monastery, Pine City, N.Y. 14871; Conventual Priory of St. Gabriel the Archangel, Weston, Vt. 05161.

Benedictines, Olivetan, O.S.B.: General motherhouse, Siena, Italy. U.S. foundation, Our Lady of Mt. Olivet Monastery, 4029 Ave. G, Lake Charles, La. 70601.

Benedictines, Sylvestrine, O.S.B.: Founded 1231, in Italy by Sylvester Gozzolini. General motherhouse, Rome, Italy; U.S. foundations; 17320 Rosemont Rd., Detroit, Mich. 48219; 2711 E. Drahner Rd., Oxford, Mich. 48051; 1697 State Highway 3, Clifton, N.J. 07012.

Bethlehem Missionaries, Society of, S.M.B.: Founded 1921, at Immensee, Switzerland, by Rt. Rev. Canon Peter Bondolfi. General motherhouse, Immensee, Switzerland; U.S. headquarters, 5630 E. 17th Ave., Denver, Colo. 80220. Foreign mission work.

Blessed Sacrament, Congregation of the, S.S.S.: Founded 1856, at Paris, France, by St. Pierre Julien Eymard; in U.S., 1900. General motherhouse, Rome, Italy; U.S. province, 5384 Wilson Mills Rd., Cleveland, O. 44143. Eucharistic apostolate.

Brigittine Monks (Order of the Most Holy Savior), O.Ss.S.: Monastery of the Most Holy Savior, 125 Northgate Dr., Woodside, Calif. 94062.

Camaldolese Congregation, Cam. O.S.B.: Founded 1012, at Camaldoli, near Arezzo, Italy, by St. Romuald; in U.S. 1958. General motherhouse, Arezzo, Italy; U.S. foundation, Immaculate Heart Hermitage, Big Sur, Calif. 93920.

Camaldolese Hermits of the Congregation of Monte Corona, Er. Cam.: Founded 1520, from Camaldoli, Italy, by Bl. Paul Giustiniani. General motherhouse, Frascati (Rome), Italy; U.S. foundation, Holy Family Hermitage, Rt. 2, Box 36, Bloomingdale, O. 43910.

Camillian Fathers and Brothers (Order of St. Camillus; Order of Ministers of the Sick), O.S.Cam.: Founded 1582, at Rome, by St. Camillus de Lellis; in U.S., 1923. General motherhouse, Rome, Italy; North American province, 10213 W. Wisconsin Ave., Wauwatosa, Wis. 53226.

Carmelites (Order of Our Lady of Mt. Carmel), O. Carm.: General motherhouse, Rome, Italy. Educational, charitable work.

Most Pure Heart of Mary Province (1864), 45 E. Dundee Rd., Barrington, Ill. 60010.

St. Elias Province (1931), 249 9th St., Brooklyn, N.Y. 11215.

Mt. Carmel Hermitage, Pineland, R.D. 1, Box 36, New Florence, Pa. 15944 (immediately subject to Prior General.)

Carmelites, Order of Discalced, O.C.D.: Established 1562, a Reform Order of Our Lady of Mt. Carmel; in U.S., 1935. Generalate, Rome, Italy. Spiritual direction, retreat, parochial work.

St. Therese of Oklahoma Province (1935), 1125 S. Walker St., P.O. Box 26127, Oklahoma City, Okla. 73126.

Immaculate Heart of Mary Province (1947), P.O. Box 67, Hubertus, Wis. 53033.

Anglo-Irish Province (1924), 510 N. El Molino St., Alhambra, Calif. 91801.

Polish Province of the Holy Spirit, 1628 Ridge Rd., Munster, Ind. 46321.

Carthusians, Order of, O. Cart.: Founded 1084, in France, by St. Bruno; in U.S., 1951. General motherhouse, St. Pierre de Chartreuse, France; U.S. charterhouse, Arlington, Vt. 05250. Cloistered contemplatives; semi-eremitic.

Charity, Servants of, S.C.: Founded 1908, in Italy, by Bl. Luigi Guanella. General motherhouse, Rome, Italy; U.S. headquarters, Don Guanella School, Sproul Rd., Springfield, Pa. 19064.

Christ, Society of, S.Ch.: Founded 1932, General Motherhouse, Poznan, Poland; U.S. address, 3000 Eighteen Mile Rd., Sterling Heights, Mich. 48078.

Cistercians, Order of, O. Cist.: Founded 1098, by St. Robert. Headquarters, Rome, Italy.

Our Lady of Spring Bank Abbey, 34639 W. Fairview Rd., Oconomowoc, Wis. 53066.

Our Lady of Gerowval Monastery, Rose Hill, Miss. 39356.

Our Lady of Dallas Monastery, Rt. 2, Box 1, Irving, Tex. 75062.

Cistercian Monastery of Our Lady of Fatima, Hainesport-Mt. Laurel Rd., Mt. Laurel, N.J. 08054.

Cistercian Monastery of Saint Mary, R.D. 1, New Ringgold, Pa. 17960.

Cistercians of the Strict Observance, Order of (Trappists), O.C.S.O.: Founded 1098, in France, by St. Robert; in U.S., 1848. Generalate, Rome, Italy.

Our Lady of Gethsemani Abbey (1848), Trappist P.O., Ky. 40073.

Our Lady of New Melleray Abbey (1849), Dubuque, Iowa 52001.

St. Joseph's Abbey (1825), Spencer, Mass. 01562.

Holy Spirit Monastery (1944), Conyers, Ga. 30208.

Our Lady of Guadalupe Abbey (1947), Lafayette, Ore. 97127.

Our Lady of the Holy Trinity Abbey (1047), Huntsville, Utah 84317.

Abbey of the Genesee (1951), Piffard, N.Y. 14533.

Our Lady of Mepkin Abbey (1949), Route 3, Box 800, Moncks Corner, S. Car. 29461.

Our Lady of the Holy Cross Abbey (1950), Berryville, Va. 22611.

Our Lady of the Assumption Abbey (1950), Rt. 5, Box 193, Ava, Mo. 65608.

Abbey of New Clairvaux (1955), Vina, Calif. 96092.

St. Benedict's Monastery (1956), Snowmass, Colo. 81654.

Claretians (Missionary Sons of the Immaculate Heart of Mary), C.M.F.: Founded 1849, at Vich, Spain, by St. Anthony Mary Claret. General headquarters, Rome, Italy. Missionary, parochial, educational, retreat work.

Western Province, 1119 Westchester Pl., Los Angeles, Calif. 90019.

Eastern Province, 400 N. Euclid Ave. Oak Park, Ill. 60302.

Clerics Regular Minor (Adorno Fathers) C.R.M.: Founded 1588, at Naples, Italy, by Ven. Augustine Adorno and St. Francis Caracciolo. General motherhouse, Rome, Italy; U.S. address, 575 Darlington Ave., Ramsey, N.J. 07446.

Columban, Society of St. (St. Columban Foreign Mission Society, S.S.C.): Founded 1918. General headquarters, Dublin, Ireland. U.S. headquarters, St. Columbans, Nebr. 68056. Foreign mission work.

Comboni Missionaries of the Heart of Jesus (Verona Fathers), **M.C.C.J.:** Founded 1885, in Italy by Bp. Daniele Comboni. General motherhouse, Rome, Italy; North American headquarters, Comboni Mission Center, 8108 Beechmont Ave., Cincinnati, O. 45230. Mission work in Africa and the Americas.

Consolata Society for Foreign Missions, I.M.C.: Founded 1901, at Turin, Italy, by Father Joseph Allamano. General motherhouse, Rome, Italy; U.S. headquarters, P.O. Box C, Lincoln Hwy., Somerset, N.J. 08873.

Crosier Fathers (Canons Regular of the Order of the Holy Cross), O.S.C.: Founded 1210, in Belgium by Bl. Theodore De Celles. Generalate, Amersfoort, Netherlands; U.S. province, 711 Lincoln Ave., St. Paul, Minn. 55105. Mission, retreat, educational work.

Cross, Priests of the Congregation of Holy, C.S.C.: Founded 1837, in France; in U.S., 1841. Generalate, Rome, Italy. Educational and pastoral work; home missions and retreats; foreign missions; social services and apostolate of the press.

Indiana Province (1841), 1304 E. Jefferson Blvd., South Bend, Ind. 46617.

Eastern Province (1952), 835 Clinton Ave., Bridgeport, Conn. 06604.

Southern Province (1968), 1828 S. Carrollton Ave., New Orleans, La. 70118.

Divine Word, Society of the, S.V.D.: Founded 1875, in Holland, by Bl. Arnold Janssen. North American Province founded 1897 with headquarters in Techny, Ill. General motherhouse, Rome, Italy.

Province of the Blessed Virgin (Northern Province), (1964), Techny, Ill. 60082.

Sacred Heart Province (Eastern Province) (1940), 1025 Michigan Ave. N.E., Washington, D.C. 20017.

St. Augustine's Province (Southern Province) (1940), 201 Ruella Ave., Bay St. Louis, Miss. 39520.

St. Therese Province (Western Province) (1964), 2181 W. 25th St., Los Angeles, Calif. 90018.

Dominicans (Order of Friars Preachers), O.P.: Founded early 13th century by St. Dominic de Guzman. General headquarters, Santa Sabina, Rome, Italy. Preaching, teaching, missions, research, parishes.

St. Joseph Province (1806), 141 E. 65th St., New York, N.Y. 10021.

Holy Name of Jesus Province (1912), 5877 Birch Ct., Oakland, Calif. 94618.

St. Albert the Great Province (1939), 1909 S. Ashland Ave., Chicago, Ill. 60608.

Southern Dominican Province (1979), 3407 Napoleon Ave., New Orleans, La. 70125.

St. Dominic Province (1873), 5353 Notre Dame de Grace Ave., Montreal, Que. H4A 1L2, Canada.

Spanish Province, U.S. foundation (1933), P.O. Box 279, San Diego, Tex. 78384.

Edmund, Society of St., S.S.E.: Founded 1843, in France, by Fr. Jean Baptiste Muard. General motherhouse, Edmundite Generalate, Fairholt, S.

Prospect St., Burlington, Vt. 05401. Educational, missionary work.

Eudists (Congregation of Jesus and Mary), C.J.M.: Founded 1643, in France, by St. John Eudes. General motherhouse, Rome, Italy; North American province, 6125 Première Ave., Charlesbourg, Quebec G1H 2V9, Canada. Parochial, educational, pastoral, missionary work.

Francis, Third Order Regular of St., T.O.R.: Founded 1221, in Italy; in U.S., 1910. General motherhouse, Rome, Italy. Educational, parochial, missionary work.

Most Sacred Heart of Jesus Province (1910), 601 Pitcairn Pl., Pittsburgh, Pa. 15232.

Immaculate Conception Province (1925), 2006 Edgewater Parkway, Silver Springs, Md. 20903.

Commissariat of the Spanish Province (1924), 301 Jefferson Ave., Waco, Tex. 76702.

Francis de Sales, Oblates of St., O.S.F.S.: Founded 1871, by Fr. Louis Brisson. General motherhouse, Rome, Italy. Educational, missionary, parochial work.

Wilmington-Philadelphia Province (1906), 2200 Kentmere Parkway, Box 1452, Wilmington, Del. 19899.

Toledo-Detroit Province (1966), Box 4683, Toledo, Ohio 43620.

Franciscans (Order of Friars Minor), O.F.M.: A family of the First Order of St. Francis (of Assisi) founded in 1209 and established as a separate jurisdiction in 1517; in U.S., 1844. General headquarters, Rome, Italy. Preaching, missionary, educational, parochial, charitable work.

St. John the Baptist Province (1844), 1615 Vine St., Cincinnati, Ohio 45210.

Sacred Heart Province (1858), 3140 Meramec St., St. Louis, Mo. 63118.

Assumption of the Blessed Virgin Mary Province (1887), Pulaski, Wis. 54162.

Most Holy Name of Jesus Province (1901), 135 W. 31st St., New York, N.Y. 10001.

St. Barbara Province (1915), 1500 34th Ave., Oakland, Calif. 94601.

Immaculate Conception Province (1855), 147 Thompson St., New York, N.Y. 10012.

Holy Cross Custody (1912), 1400 Main St., P.O. Box 608, Lemont, Ill. 60439.

Most Holy Savior Custody, 232 S. Home Ave., Pittsburgh, Pa. 15202.

St. John Capistran Custody (1928), 1290 Hornberger Ave., Roebling, N.J. 08554.

St. Stephen Transylvanian Commissariat (1948), 517 S. Belle Vista Ave., Youngstown, Ohio 44509.

Holy Family Croatian Custody, (1927), 4848 S. Ellis Ave., Chicago, Ill. 60615.

St. Casimir Lithuanian Vicariate, Kennebunkport, Me. 04046.

Holy Gospel Province (Mexico), U.S. foundation, 2400 Marr St., El Paso, Tex. 79903.

Saints Francis and James Province (Jalisco, Mexico), U.S. foundation, 504 E. Santa Clara St., Hebbronville, Tex. 78361.

Commissariat of the Holy Land, Mt. St. Sepulchre, 14th and Quincy Sts. N.E., Washington, D.C. 20017.

St. Mary of the Angels Custody, Byzantine

Slavonic Rite, P.O. Box 270, Sybertsville, Pa. 18251.

Academy of American Franciscan History, P.O. Box 34440, West Bethesda, Md. 20817.

Franciscans (Order of Friars Minor Capuchin), O.F.M. Cap.: A family of the First Order of St. Francis (of Assisi) founded in 1209 and established as a separate jurisdiction in 1528. General motherhouse, Rome, Italy. Missionary, parochial work, chaplaincies.

St. Joseph Province (1857), 1740 Mt. Elliott Ave., Detroit, Mich. 48207.

St. Augustine Province (1873), 220 37th St., Pittsburgh, Pa. 15201.

St. Mary Province (1952), 30 Gedney Park Dr., White Plains, N.Y. 10605.

Province of the Stigmata (1918), St. Francis Friary, Box 549, Orange, N.J. 07051.

Western American Capuchin Province, Our Lady of the Angels, 1721 Hillside Dr., Burlingame, Calif. 94010.

Sts. Adalbert and Stanislaus Province (Warsaw, Poland), Manor Dr., Oak Ridge, N.J. 07438.

Province of Mid-America (1977), St. Conrad Friary, 2 E. 75th St., Kansas City, Mo. 64114.

Texas Capuchin Fraternity (Province of Navarre, Spain), 5605 Bernal Dr., Dallas, Tex. 75212.

Franciscans (Order of Friars Minor Conventual), O.F.M. Conv.: A family of the First Order of St. Francis (of Assisi) founded in 1209 and established as a separate jurisdiction in 1517; first U.S. foundation, 1852. General curia, Rome, Italy. Missionary, educational, parochial work.

Immaculate Conception Province (1872), P.O. Box 830, Union City, N.J. 07087.

St. Anthony of Padua Province (1905), 1300 Dundalk Ave., Baltimore, Md. 21222.

St. Bonaventure Province (1939), 6107 Kenmore Ave., Chicago, Ill.

Our Lady of Consolation Province (1926), Mt. St. Francis, Ind. 47146.

Our Lady of Guadalupe Custody (vice-province), St. Cecilia Friary, P.O. Box 430, Jal, N. Mex. 88252.

St. Joseph Cupertino Province (1981), P.O. Box 1113, Arroyo Grande, Calif. 93420.

Glenmary Missioners (The Home Missioners of America): Founded 1939, in U.S. General headquarters, Fairfield, Ohio; mailing address, P.O. Box 46404, Cincinnati, Ohio 45246. Home mission work.

Holy Family, Congregation of the Missionaries of the, M.S.F.: Founded 1895, in Holland, by Rev. John P. Berthier. General motherhouse, Rome, Italy; U.S. provincial house, 10415 Midland Blvd., St. Louis, Mo. 63114. Belated vocations for the missions.

Holy Family, Sons of the, S.F.: Founded 1864, at Barcelona, Spain, by Joseph Mañanet y Vives; in U.S., 1920. General motherhouse, Barcelona, Spain; U.S. address, 401 Randolph Rd., Silver Spring, Md. 20904.

Holy Ghost Fathers, C.S.Sp.: Founded 1703, in Paris, by Claude Francois Poullart des Places; in U.S., 1872. Generalate, Rome, Italy. Missions, education.

Eastern Province (1872), 6230 Brush Run Rd., Bethel Park, Pa. 15102.

Western Province (1968), 919 Briarcliff, San Antonio, Tex. 78213.

Holy Ghost Fathers of Ireland (1971), U.S. delegate (East), 48-49 37th St., Long Island City, N.Y. 11101.

Holy Spirit, Missionaries of the, M.Sp.S.: Founded 1914, at Mexico City, Mexico, by Felix Rougier. General motherhouse, Mexico City; U.S. headquarters, 1005 Colonia Rd., Oxnard, Calif. 93030. Missionary work.

Jesuits (Society of Jesus), S.J.: Founded 1534, in France, by St. Ignatius of Loyola; received papal approval, 1540; first U.S. province, 1833. Generalate, Rome, Italy. Missionary, educational, literary work.

Maryland Province (1833), 5704 Roland Ave., Baltimore, Md. 21210.

New York Province (1943), 501 E. Fordham Rd., Bronx, N.Y. 10458.

Missouri Province (1823), 4511 W. Pine Blvd., St. Louis, Mo. 63108.

New Orleans Province (1907), 500 S. Jefferson Davis Pkwy., New Orleans, La. 70119.

California Province (1909), College at Prospect Aves., P.O. Box 519, Los Gatos, Calif. 95030.

New England Province (1926), 761 Harrison Ave., Boston, Mass. 02118.

Chicago Province, 2058 N. Clark St., Chicago, Ill. 60614.

Oregon Province (1932), 2222 N.W. Hoyt, Portland, Ore. 97210.

Detroit Province (1955), 7303 W. Seven Mile Rd., Detroit, Mich. 48221.

Wisconsin Province (1955), 1434 W. State St., Milwaukee, Wis. 53233.

Joseph, Congregation of St., C.S.J.: General motherhouse, Rome, Italy; U.S. vice province, 12021 Mayfield Rd., Cleveland, O. 44106. Parochial, missionary, educational work.

Joseph, Oblates of St., O.S.J.: Founded 1878, in Italy, by Bishop Joseph Marello. General motherhouse, Rome, Italy. Parochial, educational work.

Eastern Province, 62 W. Oak St., Pittston, Pa. 18640.

Western Province, 544 W. Cliff Dr., Santa Cruz, Calif. 95060.

Josephite Fathers, C.J.: General motherhouse, Ghent, Belgium; U.S. foundation, 989 Brookside Ave., Santa Maria, Calif. 93454.

Josephites (St. Joseph's Society of the Sacred Heart), S.S.J.: Founded 1866, in England, by Cardinal Vaughan; in U.S., 1871. General motherhouse, 1130 N. Calvert St., Baltimore, Md. 21202. Work in black missions.

LaSalette, Missionaries of Our Lady of, M.S.: Founded 1852, by Msgr. de Bruillard; in U.S., 1892. Motherhouse, Rome, Italy.

Our Lady of Seven Dolors Province (1933), P.O. Box 6127, Hartford, Conn. 06106.

Immaculate Heart of Mary Province (1945), P.O. Box 538, Attleboro, Mass. 02703.

Mary Queen Province (1958), 4650 S. Broadway, St. Louis, Mo. 63111.

Mary Queen of Peace Vice Province (1967), P.O. Box 95, Georgetown, Ill. 61846.

Legionaries of Christ, L.C.: Founded 1941, in Mexico, by Rev. Marcial Maciel. General headquarters, Rome, Italy; U.S. novitiate, 393 Derby Ave., Orange, Conn. 06477.

Marian Fathers and Brothers, M.I.C.: Founded 1673; U.S. foundation, 1913. General motherhouse, Rome, Italy. Educational, parochial, mission, publication work.

St. Casimir Province (1930), 6336 S. Kilbourn Ave., Chicago, Ill. 60629.

St. Stanislaus Kostka Province (1948), Eden Hill, Stockbridge, Mass. 01262.

Marianists (Society of Mary; Brothers of Mary), S.M.: Founded 1817, at Bordeaux, France, by Rev William-Joseph Chaminade; in U.S., 1849. General motherhouse, Rome, Italy. Educational work.

Cincinnati Province (1849), 4435 E. Patterson Rd., Dayton, Ohio 45430.

St. Louis Province (1908), 4538 Maryland Ave., St. Louis, Mo. 63156.

Pacific Province (1948), P.O. Box AC, Cupertino, Calif. 95015.

New York Province (1961), 4301 Roland Ave., Baltimore, Md. 21210.

Province of Meribah (1976), 240 Emory Rd., Mineola, N.Y. 11501.

Mariannhill, Congregation of the Missionaries of, C.M.M.: Trappist monastery, begun in 1882 by Abbot Francis Pfanner in Natal, South Africa, became an independent modern congregation in 1909; in U.S., 1920. Generalate, Rome, Italy; U.S.-Canadian province, St. Joseph Mission House, Route 1, Center Valley, Pa. 18034. Foreign mission work.

Marist Fathers (Society of Mary), S.M.: Founded 1816, at Lyons, France, by Jean Claude Colin; in U.S., 1863. General motherhouse, Rome, Italy. Educational, foreign mission, pastoral work.

Washington Province (1924), 4408 8th St. N.E., Washington D.C. 20017.

Northeast Province (1924), 72 Beacon St., Chestnut Hill, Mass. 02167.

San Francisco Western Province (1961), 625 Pine St., San Francisco, Calif. 94108.

Maronite Hermits of St. Francis (of Assisi), **O.P.C.:** Holy Trinity Monastery, Dunhampton Rd., Palmer, Mass. 01069.

Mary Immaculate, Missionary Oblates of, O.M.I.: Founded 1816, in France, by Bl. Charles Joseph Eugene de Mazenod; in U.S., 1849. General motherhouse, Rome, Italy. Parochial, foreign mission, educational work; ministry to marginal.

Southern U.S. Province (1904), 7711 Madonna Rd., San Antonio, Tex. 78216.

Our Lady of Hope, Eastern Province (1883), 350 Jamaicaway, Boston, Mass. 02130.

St. John the Baptist Province (1921), 45 Kenwood Ave., Worcester, Mass. 01605.

Central Province (1924), 267 E. 8th St., St. Paul, Minn. 55101.

Western Province (1953), 290 Lenox Ave., Oakland, Calif. 94610.

Italian Province, U.S. foundation, St. Nicholas Church, 442 Brinkerhoff Ave., Palisades Park, N.J. 07650.

Maryknoll (Catholic Foreign Mission Society of America), M.M.: Founded 1911, in U.S., by Frs. Thomas F. Price and James A. Walsh. General Center, Maryknoll, N.Y. 10545.

Mekhitarist Order of Vienna, C.M.Vd.: Established 1773. General headquarters, Vienna, Austria. U.S. addresses: Holy Cross Church, 100 Mt. Auburn St., Cambridge, Mass. 02138; Our Lady Queen of Martyrs Church, 1327 Pleasant Ave., Los Angeles, Calif. 90033. Work among Armenians in U.S..

Mercedarians (Order of Our Lady of Mercy), O. de M.: Founded 1218, in Spain, by St. Peter Nolasco. General motherhouse, Rome, Italy; U.S. headquarters, 8692 Lake St., LeRoy, N.Y. 14482.

Mercy, Congregation of Priests of (Fathers of Mercy), C.P.M.: Founded 1808, in France, by Rev. Jean Baptiste Rauzan; in U.S., 1839. General mission house, Cold Spring, N.Y. 10516. Mission work.

Mill Hill Missionaries (St. Joseph's Society for Foreign Missions), M.H.M.: Founded 1866, in England, by Cardinal Vaughan; in U.S., 1951. General motherhouse, London, England; American headquarters, Albany, N.Y. 12203.

Missionhurst — CICM (Congregation of the Immaculate Heart of Mary): Founded 1862, at Scheut, Brussels, Belgium, by Very Rev. Theophile Verbist. General motherhouse, Rome, Italy; U.S. province, 4651 N. 25th St., Arlington, Va. 22207. Home and foreign mission work.

Missionaries of St. Charles, Congregation of the, C.S.: Founded 1887, at Piacenza, Italy, by Bishop John Baptist Scalabrini. General motherhouse, Rome, Italy.

St. Charles Borromeo Province (1888), 27 Carmine St., New York, N.Y. 10014.

St. John Baptist Province (1903), 546 N. East Ave., Oak Park, Ill. 60302.

Missionaries of the Holy Apostles, M.Ss.A.: Founded 1962, Washington, D.C., by Eusebe M. Menard. North American headquarters, 33 Prospect Hill Rd., Cromwell, Conn. 06416.

Montfort Missionaries (Missionaries of the Company of Mary), S.M.M.: Founded 1715, by St. Louis Marie Grignon de Montfort; in U.S., 1948. General motherhouse, Rome, Italy; U.S. headquarters, 101-18 104th St., Ozone Park, N.Y. 11416, Mission work.

Mother Co-Redemptrix, Congregation of, C.M.C.: Founded 1953 at Lein-Thuy, Vietnam (North), by Fr. Dominic Mary Tran Dinh Thu; in U.S., 1975. General house, Hochiminhville, Vietnam; U.S. provincial house, 1900 Grand Ave., Carthage, Mo. 64836. Work among Vietnamese Catholics in U.S.

Oratorians (Congregation of the Oratory of St. Philip Neri), C.O.: Founded 1575, at Rome, by St. Philip Neri. A confederation of autonomous houses. U.S. addresses: P.O. Box 11586, Rock Hill, S.C. 29730; P.O. Box 1688, Monterey, Calif. 93940; 4040 Bigelow Blvd., Pittsburgh, Pa. 15213; P.O. Box 211, Yarnell, Ariz. 85362; P.O. Drawer J, Pharr, Tex. 78577.

Pallottines (Society of the Catholic Apostolate), S.A.C.: Founded 1835, at Rome, by St. Vincent Pallotti. Generalate, Rome, Italy. Charitable, educational, parochial, mission work.

Immaculate Conception Province (1953), P.O. Box 573, Pennsauken, N.J. 08810.

Mother of God Province (1946), 5424 W. Blue Mound Rd., Milwaukee, Wis. 53208.

Irish Province, U.S. address: 3352 4th St., Wyandotte, Mich. 48192.

Queen of Apostles Province (1909), 448 E. 116th St., New York, N.Y. 10029.

Christ the King Province, 3452 Niagara Falls, Blvd., N. Tonawanda, N.Y. 14120.

Paraclete, Servants of the, s.P.: Founded 1947, Santa Fe, N.M., archdiocese. General motherhouse, Rome, Italy; U.S. motherhouse, Via Coeli, Jemez Springs, N.M. 87025. Devoted to care of priests.

Paris Foreign Missions Society, M.E.P.: Founded 1662, at Paris, France. Headquarters, Paris, France; U.S. establishment, 930 Ashbury St., San Francisco, Calif. 94117. Mission work and training of native clergy.

Passionists (Congregation of the Passion), C.P.: Founded 1720, in Italy, by St. Paul of the Cross. General motherhouse, Rome, Italy.

St. Paul of the Cross Province (1852), 80 David St., South River, N.J. 08882.

Holy Cross Province (Western Province), 5700 N. Harlem Ave., Chicago, Ill. 60631.

Patrick's Missionary Society, St., S.P.S.: Founded 1932, at Wicklow, Ireland, by Msgr. Patrick Whitney; in U.S., 1953. International headquarters, Kiltegan Co., Wicklow, Ireland. U.S. foundations: 70 Edgewater Rd., Cliffside Park, N.J. 07010; 19536 Eric Dr., Saratoga, Calif. 95070; 1347 W. Granville Ave., Chicago, Ill. 60660.

Pauline Fathers (Order of St. Paul the First Hermit), O.S.P.: Founded 1215; established in U.S., 1955. General motherhouse, Czestochowa, Jasna Gora, Poland; U.S. headquarters, P.O. Box 151, Doylestown, Pa. 18901.

Pauline Fathers and Brothers (Society of St. Paul for the Apostolate of Communications), S.S.P.: Founded 1914, by Very Rev. James Alberione; in U.S., 1932. Motherhouse, Rome, Italy; American province, 6746 Lake Shore Rd., Derby, N.Y. 14047. Social communications work.

Paulists (Missionary Society of St. Paul the Apostle), C.S.P.: Founded 1858, in New York, by Fr. Isaac Thomas Hecker. General offices, 86 Dromore Rd., Scarsdale, N.Y. 10583. Missionary, ecumenical, pastoral work.

Piarists (Order of the Pious Schools), Sch.P.: Founded 1617, at Rome, Italy, by St. Joseph Calasanctius. General motherhouse, Rome, Italy. American provincial, 4605 Bayview Dr., Fort Lauderdale, Fla. 33308. New York-Puerto Rico vice-province (Calasanzian Fathers), 88 Convent Ave., New York, N.Y. 10027. Educational work.

Pontifical Institute for Foreign Missions, P.I.M.E.: Founded 1850, in Italy, at request of Pope Pius IX. General motherhouse, Rome, Italy; U.S. headquarters,17330 Quincy Ave., Detroit, Mich. 48221. Foreign mission work.

Precious Blood, Society of, C.Pp.S.: Founded 1815, in Italy, by St. Gaspar del Bufalo. General motherhouse, Rome, Italy.

Cincinnati Province, 431 E. Second St., Dayton, O. 45402.

Kansas City Province, Ruth Ewing Rd., Liberty, Mo. 64068.

Pacific Province, 1427 Sixth St., Alameda, Calif. 94501.

Atlantic Vicariate, 381 Robbins Ave., Niles, O. 44446.

Premonstratensians (Order of the Canons Regular of Premontre; Norbertines), O. Praem.: Founded 1120, at Premontre, France, by St. Norbert. Generalate, Rome, Italy. Educational, parish work.

St. Norbert Abbey, 1016 N. Broadway, DePere, Wis. 54115.

Daylesford Abbey, 220 S. Valley Rd., Paoli, Pa. 19301.

St. Michael's Priory, 1042 Star Route, Orange, Calif. 92667.

Providence, Sons of Divine, F.D.P.: Founded 1893, at Tortona, Italy, by Bl. Luigi Orione; in U.S., 1933. General motherhouse, Tortona, Italy; U.S. address, 111 Orient Ave., E. Boston, Mass. 02128.

Redemptorists (Congregation of the Most Holy Redeemer), C.SS.R.: Founded 1732, in Italy, by St. Alphonsus Mary Liguori. Generalate, Rome, Italy. Mission work.

Baltimore Province (1850), 7509 Shore Rd., Brooklyn, N.Y. 11209.

St. Louis Province (1875), Box 6, Glenview, Ill. 60025.

Oakland Province (1952), 3696 Clay St., San Francisco, Calif. 94118.

New Orleans Vice-Province, 1527 3rd St., New Orleans, La., 70130.

Resurrectionists (Congregation of the Resurrection), C.R.: Founded 1836, in France, under direction of Bogdan Janski. Motherhouse, Rome, Italy;

Chicago Province, 2250 N. Latrobe Ave., Chicago, Ill. 60639.

Ontario Kentucky Province, Resurrection College, Westmont Rd., N., Waterloo, Ont. N2L 3G7, Canada.

Rogationist Fathers, R.C.J.: Founded 1926. General motherhouse, Rome, Italy. U.S. addresses: P.O. Box 248, Mendota, Calif. 93640; P.O. Box 335, Sanger, Calif. 93657.

Rosminians (Institute of Charity), I.C.: Founded 1828, in Italy, by Antonio Rosmini-Serbati. General motherhouse, Rome, Italy; U.S. address, 2327 W. Heading Ave., Peoria, Ill. 61604. Charitable work.

Sacerdotal Fraternity, Congregation of the, C.F.S.: Founded 1901, at Paris, France. General house, 500 Ave. Claremont, Montreal (Westmount), Que. H3Y 2N5 Canada. Care of priests.

Sacred Heart, Missionaries of the, M.S.C.: Founded 1854, by Rev. Jules Chevelier. General motherhouse, Rome, Italy; U.S. province, 305 S. Lake St., P.O. Box 270, Aurora, Ill. 60507.

Sacred Heart of Jesus, Congregation of the (Sacred Heart Fathers and Brothers), S.C.J.: Founded

1877, in France. General motherhouse, Rome, Italy; U.S. headquarters, Sacred Heart Monastery, Hales Corners, Wis. 53130. Educational, preaching, mission work.

Sacred Hearts, Fathers of the (Picpus Fathers), SS.CC.: Founded 1805, in France, by Fr. Coudrin. General motherhouse, Rome, Italy. Mission, educational work.

Eastern Province (1946), 3 Adams St. (Box 111), Fairhaven, Mass. 02719.

Western Province (1970), 32481 Sage Rd., Hemet, Calif. 92343.

Hawaiian Province, Box 797, Kaneohe, Oahu, Hawaii 96744.

Sacred Hearts of Jesus and Mary, Missionaries of the, M.SS.CC.: Founded at Naples, Italy, by Ven. Cajetan Errico. General motherhouse, Rome, Italy; U.S. headquarters, 2249 Shore Rd., Linwood, N.J. 08221.

Salesians of St. John Bosco (Society of St. Francis de Sales), S.D.B.: Founded 1859, by St. John (Don) Bosco. General motherhouse, Rome, Italy.

St. Philip the Apostle Province (1902), 148 Main St., New Rochelle, N.Y. 10802.

San Francisco Province (1926), 1100 Franklin St., San Francisco, Calif. 94109.

Salvatorians (Society of the Divine Savior), S.D.S.: Founded 1881, in Rome, by Fr. Francis Jordan; in U.S., 1896. General headquarters, Rome, Italy; U.S. province, 1735 Hi-Mount Blvd., Milwaukee, Wis. 53208. Educational, parochial, mission work; campus ministries, chaplaincies.

Scalabrinians: See Missionaries of St. Charles, Congregation of the.

Servites (Order of Friar Servants of Mary), O.S.M.: Founded 1233, at Florence, Italy, by Seven Holy Founders. Generalate, Rome, Italy. General apostolic ministry.

Eastern Province (1967) 3401 S. Home Ave., Berwyn, Ill. 60402.

Western Province (1967), 5210 Somerset St., Buena Park, Calif. 90621.

Somascan Fathers, C.R.S.: Founded 1534, at Somasca, Italy, by St. Jerome Emiliani. General motherhouse, Rome, Italy; U.S. addresses: 628 Hanover St., Manchester, N.H. 03104; Pine Haven Boys Center, River Rd., Allenstown, P.O. Suncook, N.H. 03275.

Sons of Mary Missionary Society (Sons of Mary, Health of the Sick), F.M.S.I.: Founded 1952, in the Boston archdiocese, by Rev. Edward F. Garesche, S.J. Headquarters, 567 Salem End Rd., Framingham, Mass. 01701. Dedicated to health of the sick; medical, catechetical and social work in home and foreign missions.

Stigmatine Fathers and Brothers (Congregation of the Sacred Stigmata), C.S.S.: Founded 1816, by Bl. Gaspare Bertoni. General motherhouse, Rome, Italy; U.S. headquarters, 36 Fairmont Ave., Newton, Mass. 02158. Parish work.

Sulpicians (Society of Priests of St. Sulpice), S.S.: Founded 1641, at Paris, by Rev. Jean Jacques Olier. General motherhouse, Paris, France; U.S. province, 5408 Roland Ave., Baltimore, Md. 21210. Education of seminarians and priests.

Theatines (Congregation of Clerics Regular):

C.R.: Founded 1524, at Rome, by St. Cajetan. General motherhouse, Rome, Italy; U.S. headquarters, 1050 S. Birch St., Denver, Colo. 80222.

Trappists: See Cistercians of the Strict Observance.

Trinitarians (Order of the Most Holy Trinity), O.SS.T.: Founded 1198, by St. John of Matha. General motherhouse, Rome, Italy; U.S. headquarters, P.O. Box 5719, Baltimore, Md. 21208.

Trinity Missions (Missionary Servants of the Most Holy Trinity), S.T.: Founded 1929, by Fr. Thomas Augustine Judge. Generalate, 1215 N. Scott St., Arlington, Va. 22209. Home mission work.

Viatorian Fathers (Clerics of St. Viator), C.S.V.: Founded 1831, in France, by Fr. Louis Joseph Querbes. General motherhouse, Rome, Italy: U.S. headquarters, 1212 E. Euclid St., Arlington Hts., Ill. 60004. Educational work.

Vincentians (Congregation of the Mission; Lazarists), C.M.: Founded 1625, in Paris, by St. Vincent de Paul; in U.S., 1817. General motherhouse, Rome, Italy. Educational work.

Eastern Province (1867), 500 E. Chelten Ave., Philadelphia, Pa. 19144.

Midwest Province (1888), 1723 Pennsylvania Ave., St. Louis, Mo. 63104.

New England Province (1975), 1109 Prospect Ave., W. Hartford, Conn. 06105.

American Italian Branch, Our Lady of Pompei Church, 3600 Claremont St., Baltimore, Md. 21224.

American Spanish Branch (Barcelona, Spain), 134 Vernon Ave., Brooklyn, N.Y. 11206.

American Spanish Branch (Zaragoza, Spain), Holy Agony Church, 1834 3rd Ave., New York, N.Y. 10029.

Western Province (1975), 649 W. Adams Blvd., Los Angeles, Calif. 90007.

Southern Province (1975), 1302 Kipling St., Houston, Tex. 77006.

Puerto Rico Province (1955), Box 8361, Santurce, P.R. 00910.

Vocationist Fathers (Society of Divine Vocations), S.D.V.: Founded 1920, in Italy; in U.S., 1962. General motherhouse, Naples, Italy; U.S. address, 170 Broad St., Newark, N.J. 07104.

White Fathers of Africa (Society of Missionaries of Africa), W.F.: Founded 1868, at Algiers, by Cardinal C.M.A. Lavigerie. Generalate, Rome, Italy; U.S. headquarters, 1624 21st St. N.W., Washington, D.C. 20009. Missionary work in Africa.

Xaverian Missionary Fathers, S.X.: Founded 1895, by Archbishop Conforti, at Parma, Italy. General motherhouse, Rome, Italy; U.S. province, 12 Helene Ct., Wayne, N.J. 07470. Foreign mission work.

INSTITUTES OF BROTHERS

Alexian Brothers, C.F.A.: Founded 14th century in western Germany and Belgium during the Black Plague. Motherhouse, Aachen, Germany; generalate, Signal Mountain, Tenn. 37377. Hospital and general health work.

Carmelite Brothers of the Holy Eucharist, C.F.S.E.: Founded 1975 by Bro. Aloysius Scafidi. Motherhouse, 2264 Marshall Ave., Elm Grove,

Wheeling, W. Va. 26003. Educational, clerical, social, nursing work.

Charity, Brothers of, F.C.: Founded 1807, in Belgium, by Canon Peter J. Triest. General motherhouse, Rome, Italy: American District, 7720 Doe Lane, Philadelphia, Pa. 19118. Charitable, educational work.

Charity, Missionary Brothers of, M.C.: Founded 1963. U.S. address, 600 Ingraham St., Los Angeles, Calif. 90017. Work among poor and outcast.

Christian Brothers, Congregation of, C.F.C. (formerly Christian Brothers of Ireland): Founded 1802 at Waterford, Ireland, by Edmund Ignatius Rice. General motherhouse, Rome, Italy. Educational work.

American Province, Eastern U.S. (1916), 21 Pryer Terr., New Rochelle, N.Y. 10804. 354.

American Province, Western U.S. (1966), P.O. Box 85R, Romeoville, Ill. 60441.

Christian Instruction, Brothers of (La Mennais Brothers), F.I.C.: Founded 1817, at Ploermel, France, by Abbe Jean Marie de la Mennais and Abbe Gabriel Deshayes. General motherhouse, Rome, Italy; American province, Notre Dame Institute, Alfred, Me. 04002.

Christian Schools, Brothers of the (Christian Brothers), F.S.C.: Founded 1680, at Reims, France, by St. Jean Baptiste de la Salle. General motherhouse, Rome, Italy; U.S. Conference, 100 De La Salle Dr., Romeoville, Ill. 60441. Educational, charitable work.

Baltimore Province (1845), Box 29, Adamstown, Md. 21710.

Chicago Province (1966), 200 De La Salle Dr., Romeoville, Ill. 60441.

New York Province (1848), 820 Newman Springs Rd., Lincroft, N.J. 07738.

Long Island-New England Province (1957), Christian Brothers Center, 635 Ocean Ave., Narragansett, R.I. 02882.

St. Louis Province (1849), 1886 Rue de la Salle, Glencoe, Mo. 63038.

San Francisco Province (1868), P.O. Box A-D, Saint Mary's College, Moraga, Calif. 94575.

New Orleans-Santa Fe Province (1921), De La Salle Christian Brothers, 1522 Breaux Bridge Rd., Lafayette, La. 70501.

Winona Province (1963), 807 Summit Ave., St. Paul, Minn. 55105.

Cross, Congregation of Holy, C.S.C.: Founded 1837, in France, by Rev. Basil Moreau; U.S. province, 1841. Generalate, Rome, Italy. Educational, social work; missions.

Midwest Province (1841), Box 460, Notre Dame, Ind. 46556.

Southwest Province (1956), St. Edward's University, Austin, Tex. 78704.

Eastern Province (1956), 85 Overlook Circle, New Rochelle, N.Y. 10804.

Francis, Brothers of Poor of St., C.F.P.: Founded 1857. Motherhouse, Aachen, Germany; U.S. province, 6942 Windward St., Cincinnati, Ohio. 45227. Educational work, especially with poor and emotionally disturbed youth.

Francis Xavier, Brothers of St. (Xaverian Brothers), C.F.X.: Founded 1839, in Belgium, by Theodore J. Ryken. Generalate, Rome, Italy. Educational work.

Sacred Heart Province, 10516 Summit Ave., Kensington, Md. 20895.

St. Joseph Province, 704 Brush Hill Rd., Milton, Mass. 02186.

Franciscan Brothers of Brooklyn, O.S.F.: Founded in Ireland; established at Brooklyn, 1858. Generalate, 135 Remsen St., Brooklyn, N.Y. 11201. Educational work.

Franciscan Brothers of Christ the King, O.S.F.: Founded 1961. General motherhouse, 1310 W. Pleasant St., Davenport, Ia. 52808.

Franciscan Brothers of the Good News, O.S.F.: Founded 1970 in Archdiocese of New York. Central friary, Mount Road, Cummington, Mass. 01026. Combine volunteer works of mercy with contemplative life of prayer in hermitages.

Franciscan Brothers of the Holy Cross, F.F.S.C.: Founded 1862, in Germany. Generalate, Hausen, Linz Rhein, West Germany; U.S. region, R.R. 1, Springfield, Ill. 62707. Educational work.

Franciscan Missionary Brothers of the Sacred Heart of Jesus, O.S.F.: Founded 1927, in the St. Louis, Mo., archdiocese. Motherhouse, R.R. 3, Box 39, Eureka, Mo. 63025. Care of aged, infirm, homeless men and boys.

Good Shepherd, Society of Brothers of the, B.G.S.: Founded 1951, by Bro. Mathias Barrett. Motherhouse, P.O. Box 389, Albuquerque, N.M. 87102. Operate shelters and refuges for aged and homeless; homes for handicapped men and boys, alcoholic rehabilitation center.

Guadalupe, Brothers of Our Lady of, H.N.S.G.: Founded 1974 in Gallup, N. Mex., by Bishop Jerome Hastrich. Motherhouse, 500 S. Woodrow Dr., Gallup, N. Mex. 87301. Team ministry apostolate.

Holy Eucharist, Brothers of the, F.S.E.: Founded in U.S., 1957. Generalate, P.O. Box 25, Plaucheville, La. 71362. Teaching, social, clerical, nursing work.

Immaculate Heart of Mary, Brothers of the, F.I.C.M.: Founded 1948, at Steubenville, Ohio, by Bishop John K. Mussio. Motherhouse, Villa Maria, 609 N. 7th St., Steubenville, Ohio 43952. Educational, charitable work.

John of God, Brothers of the Hospitaller Order of St., O.H.: Founded 1537, in Spain. General motherhouse, Rome, Italy; American province, 2425 S. Western Ave., Los Angeles, Calif. 90018; Irish Province of Immaculate Conception, 532 Delsea Dr., Westville Grove, N.J. 08093. Nursing work and related fields.

Little Brothers of Jesus: Generalate, London, England; U.S. foundation, 2833 Cochrane, Detroit, Mich. 48216.

Little Brothers of St. Francis, O.S.F.: Founded 1970 in Archdiocese of Boston. General fraternity, 789 Parker St., Mission Hill (Boston), Mass. 02120. Combine contemplative life with evangelical street ministry

Marist Brothers, F.M.S.: Founded 1817, in France, by Bl. Marcellin Champagnat. General motherhouse, Rome, Italy. Educational, social, catechetical work.

Province of St. Joseph, P.O. Box 186, Esopus, N.Y. 12429.

Poughkeepsie Province, 38 N. Clinton St., Poughkeepsie, N.Y. 12601.

Mercy, Brothers of, F.M.M.: Founded 1856, in Germany. General motherhouse, Montabaur, Germany. American headquarters, 4520 Ransom Rd., Clarence, N.Y. 14031. Hospital work.

Mercy, Brothers of Our Lady of, C.F.M.M.: Founded 1844, in The Netherlands by Abp. J. Zwijsen. Generalate, Tilburg, The Netherlands; U.S. region, 2336 South "C" St., Oxnard, Calif. 93030.

Patrician Brothers (Brothers of St. Patrick), F.S.P.: Founded 1808, in Ireland, by Bishop Daniel Delaney; U.S. novitiate, 7820 Bolsa Ave., Midway City, Calif. 92655. Educational work.

Pius X, Brothers of St.: Founded 1952, at La Crosse, Wis., by Bishop John P. Treacy. Mother-house, 3710 East Ave. S., La Crosse, Wis. 54601. Education.

Presentation Brothers of Mary, F.P.M.: Founded 1802, at Waterford, Ireland, by Edmund Ignatius Rice. General motherhouse, Cork, Ireland. U.S. foundation (Canadian Province), 368 S. Ellsworth, Marshall, Mo. 65340.

Rosary, Brothers of the Holy, F.S.R.: Founded 1956, in U.S., Motherhouse and novitiate, 1725 S. McCarran Blvd., Reno, Nev. 89502.

Sacred Heart, Brothers of the, S.C.: Founded 1821, in France, by Rev. Andre Coindre. General motherhouse, Rome, Italy, Educational work.

New Orleans Province (1847), P.O. Box 89, Bay St. Louis, Miss. 39520.

New England Province (1945), Rt. 98, R.R. 1, Pascoag, R.I. 02859.

New York Province (1960), P.O. Box 68, Belvidere, N.J. 07823.

MEMBERSHIP OF RELIGIOUS INSTITUTES OF MEN

(Principal source: *Annuario Pontificio*. Statistics as of Jan. 1, 1982, unless indicated otherwise.)

Listed below are world membership statistics of institutes of men of pontifical right with 500 or more members; the number of priests is in parentheses. Also listed are institutes with less than 500 members with houses in the United States.

Jesuits (19,671)	26,778
Franciscans (Friars Minor) (14,028)	20,666
Salesians (11,029)	16,893
Franciscans (Capuchins) (8,500)	11,830
Brothers of Christian Schools	10,011
Benedictines (6,046)	9,614
Dominicans (5,439)	7,062
Marist Brothers	6,825
Redemptorists (4,932)	6,596
Oblates of Mary Immaculate (4,513)	5,837
Society of the Divine Word (3,275)	5,311
Franciscans (Conventuals) (2,675)	4,038
Vincentians (3,587)	4,014
Holy Spirit, Congregation (2,958)	3,723
Augustinians (2,593)	3,397
Discalced Carmelties (2,337)	3,297
Trappists (1,452)	3,084
Passionists (2,313)	3,023
White Fathers (2,567)	2,956
Claretians (1,952)	2,956
Christian Brothers	2,771
Priests of the Sacred Heart (1,902)	2,706
Missionaries of the Sacred Heart of Jesus (1,830)	2,497
Pallottines (1,473)	2,178
Holy Cross, Congregation (920)	2,093
Marianists (618)	2,051
Carmelites (Ancient Observance) (*1980*) (1,560)	1,989
Marists (1,594)	1,972
Brothers of the Sacred Heart (55)	1,894
Combonian Missionaries of the Heart of Jesus (1,271)	1,828
Hospitallers of St. John of God (118)	1,685
Piarists (1,341)	1,674
Brothers of Christian Instruction	1,562

Congregation of the Immaculate Heart of Mary (1,275)	1,539
Sacred Hearts, Congregation (Picpus) (1,192)	1,421
Carmelites of BVM (870)	1,397
Cistercians (Common Observance) (876)	1,372
Brothers of Christian Instruction of St. Gabriel (31)	1,366
Montfort Missionaries (1,037)	1,349
Society of African Missions (1,183)	1,347
Premonstratensians (1,034)	1,316
Augustinians (Recollects) (999)	1,270
Salvatorians (846)	1,248
Servants of Mary (931)	1,223
Assumptionists (1,007)	1,213
Society of St. Paul (524)	1,203
Blessed Sacrament, Congr. of (804)	1,159
Viatorians (449)	1,113
Little Workers of Divine Providence (747)	1,074
Missionaries of Holy Family (752)	1,047
Consolata Missionaries (833)	1,040
Ministers of Sick (667)	1,013
Mill Hill Missionaries (827)	963
Oblates of St. Francis de Sales (719)	958
Columbans (841)	899
Maryknollers (748)	886
LaSalette Missionaries (636)	879
Brothers of Charity	878
Xaverian Missionaries (645)	878
Franciscans (Third Order Regular) (605)	861
Canons Regular of St. Augustine (695)	844
Legionaries of Christ (155)	836
Mercedarians (530)	746
Scalabrinians (595)	744
Congregation of St. Joseph (566)	735
Pontifical Institute for Foreign Missions (601)	735
Missionaries of the Most Precious Blood (578)	729

Brothers of the Immaculate Conception (6)	657	Rogationists (186)	293
Brothers of Our Lady of Mercy	620	Paulists (243)	276
Trinitarians (402)	603	Order of St. Paul the First Hermit (135)	274
Paris Foreign Mission Society (581)	583	Little Brothers of Jesus (75)	270
Crosier Fathers and Brothers (431)	570	Brothers of St. Patrick	216
Sulpicians (529)	529	Vocationist Fathers (169)	206
Missionaries of St. Francis de Sales of Annecy (329)	528	Missionary Servants of the Most Holy Trinity (149)	201
Eudists (443)	520	Josephite Fathers (S.S.J.) (174)	199
Servants of Charity (374)	500	Atonement Friars (129)	199
Barnabites (383)	488	Alexian Brothers (1)	192
Brothers of Our Lady of Lourdes	458	Presentation Brothers	178
Resurrection, Congregation of (337)	454	Sons of the Holy Family (122)	171
Xaverian Brothers	451	Josephites (C.J.) (119)	151
Mariannhill Missionaries (269)	451	Theatines (105)	141
Congr. of St. Basil (Canada) (414)	444	Bros. of Poor of St. Francis	138
Oratorians (356)	441	Basilian Salvatorian Fathers (1977) (84)	121
Somascan Fathers (304)	434	Glenmary Missioners (74)	115
St. Patrick's Mission Society (389)	432	Brothers of Mercy	114
Society of Christ (241)	428	Society of St. Edmund (86)	105
Stigmatine Fathers and Brothers (344)	408	Franciscan Bros. of Holy Cross (3)	83
Order of St. Basil the Great (274)	408	Congr. of Sacerdotal Fraternity (42)	79
Rosminians (304)	407	Camaldolese (29)	79
Carthusians (223)	397	Servants of Holy Paraclete (1980) (31)	46
Oblates of St. Joseph (260)	377	Clerics Regular Minor (Adorno Fathers) (34)	40
Marian Fathers and Brothers (222)	356	Mekhitarist Order of Vienna (20)	26
Missionaries of the Holy Spirit (219)	341		
Bethlehem Missionaries (251)	317		

RELIGIOUS INSTITUTES OF WOMEN IN THE UNITED STATES

(Sources: Catholic Almanac survey; *Official Catholic Directory*.)

Africa, Missionary Sisters of Our Lady of (Sisters of Africa), S.A.: Founded 1869, at Algiers, Algeria, by Cardinal Lavigerie; in U.S., 1929. General motherhouse, Frascati, Italy; U.S. headquarters, 5335 16th St., N.W., Washington, D.C. 20011. Medical, educational, catechetical and social work in Africa.

Agnes, Sisters of St., C.S.A.: Founded 1858, in U.S., by Caspar Rehrl. General motherhouse, 475 Gillett St., Fond du Lac, Wis. 54935. Education, health care, social services.

Ann, Sisters of St., S.S.A.: Founded 1834, in Italy; in U.S., 1952. General motherhouse, Rome, Italy; U.S. headquarters, Mount St. Ann, Ebensburg, Pa. 15931.

Anne, Sisters of St., S.S.A.: Founded 1850, at Vaudreuil, Que., Canada; in U.S., 1866. General motherhouse, Lachine, Que., Canada; U.S. address, 720 Boston Post Rd., Marlboro, Mass. 01752. Retreat work, pastoral ministry, religious education.

Anthony, Missionary Servants of St., M.S.S.A.: Founded 1929, in U.S., by Rev. Peter Baque. General motherhouse, 100 Peter Baque Rd., San Antonio, Tex. 78209. Social work.

Apostolate, Sisters Auxiliaries of the, A.A.: Founded 1903, in Canada; in U.S., 1911. General motherhouse, 689 Maple Terr., Monongah, W. Va. 26554. Education, nursing.

Assumption, Little Sisters of the, L.S.A.: Founded 1865, in France; in U.S., 1891. General motherhouse, Paris, France; U.S. provincialate, 1195 Lexington Ave., New York, N.Y. 10028. Social work, nursing, family life education.

Assumption, Religious of the, R.A.: Founded 1839, in France; in U.S., 1919. General motherhouse, Paris, France; U.S. province, 227 N. Bowman Ave., Merion, Pa. 19066. Educational work.

Assumption of the Blessed Virgin, Sisters of the, S.A.S.V.: Founded 1853, in Canada; in U.S., 1891. General motherhouse, Nicolet, Que., Canada; American province, North Main St., Box 128, Petersham, Mass. 01366. Education, mission, pastoral ministry.

Basil the Great, Sisters of St. (Pittsburgh Byzantine Rite), O.S.B.M.: Founded fourth century, by St. Basil the Great. Motherhouse, Mount St. Macrina. 500 W. Main St., Uniontown, Pa. 15401. Education, health care.

Basil the Great, Sisters of the Order of St. (Ukrainian Byzantine Rite), O.S.B.M.: Founded fourth century, in Cappadocia, by St. Basil the Great; in U.S., 1911. Generalate, Rome, Italy; U.S. motherhouse, 710 Fox Chase Rd., Philadelphia, Pa. 19111. Education.

Benedict, Sisters of the Order of St., O.S.B.: Our Lady of Mount Caritas Monastery (founded 1979, Ashford, Conn.), RR No. 2 Seckar Rd., West Willington, Conn. 06279. Contemplative.

Benedict, Sisters of the Order of St. (of the Congregation of Solesmes), O.S.B.: U.S. establishment, 1981, in Burlington diocese. Monastery of the Immaculate Heart of Mary, Westfield, Vt. 05874. Cloistered, papal enclosure.

Benedictine Nuns of the Primitive Observance, O.S.B.; Founded c. 529, in Italy; in U.S., 1948. Abbey of Regina Laudis, Flanders Rd., Bethlehem, Conn. 06751. Cloistered.

Benedictine Sisters, O.S.B.: Founded c. 529, in Italy; in U.S., 1852. General motherhouse, Eichstatt, Bavaria, Germany. U.S. addresses: St. Vincent's Archabbey, Latrobe, Pa. 15650; St. Emma's Retreat House and Convent, 1001 Harvey St., Greensburg, Pa. 15601; St. Walburga Convent, 6717 S. Boulder Rd., Boulder, Colo. 80302.

Benedictine Sisters (Bedford, N.H.), **O.S.B.:** Founded 1627, in Lithuania as cloistered community; reformed 1918 as active community; established in U.S. 1957, by Mother M. Raphaela Simonis. Regina Pacis, 333 Wallace Rd., Bedford, N.H. 03102.

Benedictine Sisters, Missionary, O.S.B.: Founded 1885. Generalate, Rome, Italy; U.S. motherhouse, 300 N. 18th St., Norfolk, Nebr. 68701.

Benedictine Sisters, Olivetan, O.S.B.: Founded 1887, in U.S.. General motherhouse, Holy Angels Convent, Jonesboro, Ark. 72401. Educational, hospital work.

Benedictine Sisters of Perpetual Adoration of Pontifical Jurisdiction, Congregation of the, O.S.B.: Founded in U.S., 1874, from Maria Rickenbach, Switzerland. General motherhouse, 8300 Morganford Rd., St. Louis, Mo. 63123.

Benedictine Sisters of Pontifical Jurisdiction, O.S.B.: Founded c. 529, in Italy. No general motherhouse in U.S.. Three federations.

• Federation of St. Scholastica (1922). Pres., Sister Johnette Putnam, O.S.B., St. Scholastica Priory, Box 1118, Covington, La. 70433. Motherhouses belonging to the federation:

Emmanuel Priory, 3812 Fifth St., Baltimore, Md. 21225; Mt. St. Scholastica, Atchison, Kans. 66002; Benedictine Sisters of Elk Co., St. Joseph's Convent, St. Mary's, Pa. 15857; Mt. St. Benedict Priory, 6101 E. Lake Rd., Erie, Pa. 16511; Benedictine Sisters of Chicago, St. Scholastica Priory, 7430 Ridge Blvd., Chicago, Ill. 60645; Benedictine Convent of the Sacred Heart, 1910 Maple Ave., Lisle, Ill. 60532; Our Lady of Sorrows Convent, 5900 W. 147th St., Oak Forest, Ill. 60452; St. Walburga Convent, 851 N. Broad St., Elizabeth, N.J. 07208; Benedictine Sisters, Mt. St. Mary Priory, 4530 Perrysville Ave., Pittsburgh, Pa. 15229;

Red Plains Priory, P.O. Box 60165, Oklahoma City, Okla. 73146; St. Joseph's Convent, 2200 S. Lewis, Tulsa, Okla. 74114; St. Gertrude's Priory, Ridgely P.O., Md. 21660; St. Walburga Convent, Villa Madonna, 2500 Amsterdam Rd., Covington, Ky. 41016; Sacred Heart Convent, Cullman, Ala. 35055; St. Scholastica Priory, Box 1118, Covington, La. 70434; Holy Family Convent, Benet Lake, Wis. 53102; St. Benedict's Convent, Bristow, Va. 22013; St. Scholastica Convent, P.O. Box 700, Boerne, Tex. 78006; St. Lucy's Priory, Glendora, Calif. 91740; Holy Name Priory, St. Leo, Fla. 33574; Benet Hill Priory, 2555 N. Chelton Rd., Colorado Springs, Colo. 80909; Queen of Heaven Convent

(Byzantine Rite), 8640 Squires Lane N.E., Warren, O. 44484.

• Federation of St. Gertrude the Great (1937). Pres., Sister Anselm Hammerling, O.S.B., St. Benedict Priory, 225 Masters Ave., RR 1, Winnipeg, Man. R3C 4A3, Canada. Motherhouses belonging to the federation:

Mother of God Priory, Watertown, S. Dak. 57201; Sacred Heart Convent, Yankton, S. Dak. 57078; Mt. St. Benedict Convent, Crookston, Minn. 56716; Sacred Heart Priory, Richardton, N. Dak. 58652; St. Martin's Priory of the Black Hills, R.R. 4, Box 253, Rapid City, S. Dak. 57701; Convent of the Immaculate Conception, 802 E. 10th St., Ferdinand, Ind. 47532; Priory of St. Gertrude, Cottonwood, Ida. 83522;

St. Benedict Priory, Fox Bluff, Box 5070, Madison, Wis. 53705; Queen of Angels Priory, Mt. Angel, Ore. 97362; St. Scholastica's Convent, Albert Pike and Rogers Ave., Fort Smith, Ark. 72913; Our Lady of Peace Convent, 1511 Wilson, Columbia, Mo. 65201; Queen of Peace Priory, 701 Rolla, Belcourt, N. Dak. 58316. Convent of Our Lady of Grace, Beech Grove, Ind. 46107; Holy Spirit Convent, 9725 Pigeon Pass Rd., Sunnymead, Calif. 92388; St. Benedict's Priory, Winnipeg, Manitoba, R3C 4A3, Canada.

• Federation of St. Benedict (1947). Pres., Sister Margaret Michaud, O.S.B., St. Bede Priory, Eau Claire, Wis. 54702. Motherhouses belonging to the federation:

St. Benedict's Convent, St. Joseph, Minn. 56374; St. Scholastica Priory, Kenwood Ave., Duluth, Minn. 55811; St. Bede Priory, Priory Rd., Eau Claire, Wis. 54702; St. Mary Priory, Nauvoo, Ill. 62354; Annunciation, Priory, Apple Creek Rd., Bismarck, N. Dak. 58501; St. Paul's Priory, 2675 Larpenteur Ave. E., St. Paul, Minn. 55109; St. Placid Priory, 4600 Martin Way, Olympia, Wash. 98506.

Bethany, Sisters of, C.V.D.: Founded 1928, in El Salvador; in U.S. 1949. General motherhouse, Santa Tecla, El Salvador. U.S. address: 850 N. Hobart Blvd., Los Angeles, Calif. 90029.

Bethlemita Sisters, Daughters of the Sacred Heart of Jesus, S.C.I.F.: Founded 1861, in Guatemala. Motherhouse, Bogota, Colombia; U.S. address, St. Joseph Residence, 330 W. Pembroke St., Dallas, Tex. 75208.

Blessed Virgin Mary, Institute of the (Loreto Sisters), I.B.V.M.: Founded 17th century in Belgium; in U.S., 1954. Motherhouse, Rathfarnham, Dublin, Ireland; U.S. addresses: 6351 N. 27th Ave., Phoenix, Ariz. 85017; 810 Patrick Lane, Prescott, Ariz. 86301; 202 S. Kendrick, Flagstaff, Ariz. 86001.

Blessed Virgin Mary, Institute of the (Loretto Sisters), I.B.V.M.: Founded 1609, in Belgium; in U.S., 1880. U.S. address, Loretto Convent, Box 508, Wheaton, Ill. 60187. Educational work.

Bon Secours, Sisters of, C.B.S.: Founded 1824, in France; in U.S., 1881. Generalate, Rome, Italy; U.S. provincial house, Marriottsville Rd., Marriottsville, Md. 21104. Hospital work.

Brigid, Congregation of St., C.S.B.: Founded 1807, in Ireland; in U.S., 1953. U.S. regional house,

5118 Loma Linda Dr., San Antonio, Tex. 78201.

Brigittine Sisters (Order of the Most Holy Savior), O.SS.S.: Founded 1344, at Vadstena, Sweden, by St. Bridget; in U.S., 1957. General motherhouse, Rome, Italy; U.S. address, Vikingsborg, Darien, Conn. 06820.

Carmel, Congregation of Our Lady of Mount, O. Carm.: Founded 1825, in France; in U.S., 1833. General motherhouse, P.O. Box 476, Lacombe, La. 70445. Education, social services, pastoral ministry, retreat work.

Carmel, Institute of Our Lady of Mount, O. Carm.: Founded 1854, in Italy; in U.S., 1947. General motherhouse, Rome, Italy; U.S. novitiate, 5 Wheatland St., Peabody, Mass. 01960. Apostolic work.

Carmel Community, C.C.: Founded 1975, Columbus, O. Address, 2065 Barton Pl., Columbus, O. 43209. Contemplative.

Carmelite Missionaries of St. Theresa, C.M.S.T.: Founded 1903, in Mexico. General motherhouse, Mexico City, Mexico; U.S. foundation, 9600 Deertrail Rd., Houston, Tex. 77003.

Carmelite Nuns, Byzantine: Holy Annunciation Monastery, R.D. 1, P.O. Box 245, Sugarloaf, Pa. 18249.

Carmelite Sisters (Corpus Christi), O. Carm.: Founded 1908, in England; in U.S., 1920. General motherhouse, Tunapuna, Trinidad, W.I. U.S. addresses: Carmelite Retreat House, 21 Battery St., Newport, R.I. 02840; Mt. Carmel Home, 412 W. 18th St., Kearney, Nebr. 68847; Carmelite Sisters, 765 W. 18th St., Eugene, Ore. 97405. Home and foreign mission work.

Carmelite Sisters for the Aged and Infirm, O. Carm.: Founded 1929, at New York, by Mother M. Angeline Teresa, O. Carm. Motherhouse, Avila-on-Hudson, Germantown, N.Y. 12526. Social work, nursing and educating in the field of gerontology.

Carmelite Sisters of Charity, C.a.Ch.: Founded 1826 at Vich, Spain, by St. Joaquina de Vedruna. General motherhouse, Rome, Italy; U.S. address, 4200 16th St. N.W., Washington, D.C. 20011.

Carmelite Sisters of St. Therese of the Infant Jesus, C.S.T.: Founded 1917, in U.S.. General motherhouse, 1300 Classen Dr., Oklahoma City, Okla. 73103. Educational work.

Carmelite Sisters of the Divine Heart of Jesus, D.C.J.: Founded 1891, in Germany; in U.S., 1912. General motherhouse, Sittard, Netherlands. U.S. provincial houses: 1230 Kavanaugh Pl., Milwaukee, Wis. 52313 (Northern Province); 10341 Manchester Rd., St. Louis, Mo. 63122 (Central Province); 8585 La Mesa Blvd., La Mesa, Calif. 92041 (South Western Province). Social services, mission work.

Carmelite Sisters of the Sacred Heart, O.C.D.: Founded 1904, in Mexico. General motherhouse, Guadalajara, Mexico; U.S. provincialate and novitiate, 920 E. Alhambra Rd., Alhambra, Calif. 91801. Social services, retreat and educational work.

Carmelites, Calced (Carmelite Nuns of the Ancient Observance), O. Carm.: Founded 1452, in The Netherlands; in U.S., 1930, from Naples, Italy, convent. U.S. monasteries: Carmel of Mary,

Wahpeton, N.D. 58075; Carmel of the Sacred Heart, 430 Laurel Ave., Hudson, Wis. 54016. Papal enclosure.

Carmelites, Discalced, O.C.D.: Founded 1562, Spain. First foundation in U.S. in 1790, at Charles County, Md.; this monastery was moved to Baltimore. Monasteries in U.S. are listed below, according to states.

Alabama: 716 Dauphin Island Pkwy., Mobile 36606. Arkansas: 7201 W. 32nd St., Little Rock 72204. California: 215 E. Alhambra Rd., Alhambra 91801; 27601 Highway 1, Carmel 93923; 68 Rincon Rd., Kensington 94707; 3361 E. Ocean Blvd., Long Beach 90803; 6981 Teresian Way, Georgetown 95634; 5158 Hawley Blvd., San Diego 92116; 721 Parker Ave., San Francisco 94118; 530 Blackstone Dr., San Rafael 94903; 1000 Lincoln St., Santa Clara 95050.

Colorado: 6138 S. Gallup St., Littleton 80120. Georgia: Coffee Bluff, 11 W. Back St., Savannah 31406; Illinois: River Rd. and Central, Des Plaines 60016. Indiana: 2500 Cold Springs Rd., Indianapolis 46222; 63 Allendale Pl., Terre Haute 47802. Iowa: Carmelite Rd., Eldridge 52748; 2901 S. Cecilia St., Sioux City 51106. Kansas: 3535 Wood Ave., Kansas City, 66102. Kentucky: 1740 Newburg Rd., Louisville 40205. Louisiana: Carmel Ave., Lafayette 70507; 1611 Mirabeau Ave., New Orleans 70122.

Maryland: 1318 Dulaney Valley Rd., Towson, Baltimore 21204; R.R. 4, Box 4035A, LaPlata, Md. 20646. Massachusetts: 61 Mt. Pleasant Ave., Roxbury, Boston 02119; 15 Mt. Carmel Rd., Danvers 01923; Sol-E-Mar Rd., S. Dartmouth 02748. Michigan: 16630 Wyoming Ave., Detroit 48221; 1036 Valley Ave. N.W., Grand Rapids 49504; U.S. 2 Highway, P.O. Box 397, Iron Mountain 49801; 3501 Silver Lake Rd., Traverse City 49684. Minnesota: 8251 De Montreville Trail N., Lake Elmo 55042. Mississippi: 2155 Terry Rd., Jackson 39204.

Missouri: 2201 W. Main St., Jefferson City 65101; 9150 Clayton Rd., Ladue, St. Louis Co. 63124; 424 E. Republic Rd., Springfield 65807. Nevada: 1950 La Fond Dr., Reno 89509. New Hampshire: 275 Pleasant St., Concord, 03301. New Jersey: P.O. Box 785, Flemington 08822; 189 Madison Ave., Morristown 07960. New Mexico: Mt. Carmel Rd., Santa Fe 87501. New York: 745 St. John's Pl., Brooklyn 11216; 139 De Puyster Ave., Beacon 12500; 75 Carmel Rd., Buffalo 14214; 1931 W. Jefferson Rd., Pittsford 14534; 68 Franklin Ave., Saranac Lake 12983; 428 Duane Ave., Schenectady 12304.

Ohio: 3176 Fairmount Blvd., Cleveland Heights 44118. Oklahoma: 4200 N. Meridian Ave., Oklahoma City 73112. Oregon: 87609 Green Hill Rd., Eugene 97402. Pennsylvania: Thornbrow, Elysburg 17824; 510 E. Gore Rd., Erie 16509; R.D. 6, Box 28, Center Dr., Latrobe 15650; P.O. Box 57, Loretto 15940; 66th Ave. and Old York Rd. (Oak Lane), Philadelphia 19126. Rhode Island: Watson Ave. at Nayatt Rd., Barrington 02806.

Texas: 600 South Flowers Ave., Dallas 75211; 1600 Sunset Terr., Ft. Worth 76102; 1100 Parthenon Pl., Roman Forest, New Caney 77357. 1104 Kentucky Ave., San Antonio 78201. Utah: 5714 Holladay Blvd., Salt Lake City 84121. Vermont: Beckley Hill, Barre, 05641. Washington: 2215 N.E. 147th St.,

Seattle 98155. Wisconsin: W267 N2517 Meadowbrook Rd., Pewaukee 53072.

Casimir, Sisters of St., S.S.C.: Founded 1907, in U.S. by Mother Maria Kaupas. General motherhouse, 2601 W. Marquette Rd., Chicago, Ill. 60629. Education, missions, social services.

Cenacle, Congregation of Our Lady of the Retreat in the, R.C.: Founded 1826, in France; in U.S., 1892. General motherhouse, Rome, Italy. U.S. provinces: 154-27 Horace Harding Expressway, Flushing, N.Y. 11367; 284 Foster St., Brighton, Mass. 02135; 513 Fullerton Pkwy., Chicago, Ill. 60614.

Charity, Daughters of Divine, F.D.C.: Founded 1868, at Vienna, Austria; in U.S., 1913. General motherhouse, Rome, Italy. U.S. provinces: 56 Meadowbrook Rd., White Plains, N.Y. 10605; 39 Portage Path, Akron, O. 44303; 1315 N. Woodward Ave., Bloomfield Hills, Mich. 48013. Education, social services.

Charity, Little Missionary Sisters of, P.M.C.: Founded 1915, in Italy; in U.S., 1949. General motherhouse, Rome, Italy; U.S. headquarters, 201 Washington St., S. Groveland, Mass. 01834.

Charity, Missionaries of, M.C.: Founded 1950, in Calcutta, India, by Mother Teresa. General motherhouse, 54A Acharya Jagadish C. Bose Road, Calcutta 16, India. U.S. address, 335 E. 145th St., Bronx, N.Y. 10451. Service of the poor.

Charity, Religious Sisters of, R.S.C.: Founded 1815, in Ireland; in U.S., 1953. Motherhouse, Dublin, Ireland; U.S. headquarters, Marycrest Manor, 10664 St. James Dr., Culver City, Calif. 90230.

Charity, Sisters of (of Seton Hill), S.C.: Founded 1870, at Altoona, Pa., from Cincinnati foundation. Administrative Offices, De Paul Center, Mt. Thor Rd., Greensburg, Pa. 15601. Educational, hospital, social, foreign mission work.

Charity, Sisters of (Grey Nuns of Montreal), S.G.M.: Founded 1737, in Canada by Bl. Marie Marguerite d'Youville; in U.S., 1855. General administration, Montreal, Que. H2Y 2L7, Canada; U.S. provincial house, 10 Pelham Rd., Lexington, Mass. 02173.

Charity, Sisters of (of Leavenworth), S.C.L.: Founded 1858, in U.S.. Motherhouse, Leavenworth, Kans. 66048.

Charity, Sisters of (of Nazareth), S.C.N.: Founded 1812, in U.S.. General motherhouse, Nazareth P. O., Nelson Co., Ky. 40048.

Charity, Sisters of (of St. Augustine), C.S.A.: Founded 1851, at Cleveland, O. Motherhouse, 5232 Broadview Rd., Richfield, O. 44286.

Charity, Sisters of Christian, S.C.C.: Founded 1849, in Paderborn, Germany; in U.S., 1873. General motherhouse, Rome, Italy. U.S. provinces: Mallinckrodt Convent, Mendham, N.J. 07945; Maria Immaculata Convent, 1041 Ridge Rd., Wilmette, Ill. 60091, Education, health services, other apostolic work.

Charity, Vincentian Sisters of, V.S.C.: Founded 1835, in Austria; in U.S., 1902. General motherhouse, 8200 McKnight Rd., Pittsburgh, Pa. 15237.

Charity, Vincentian Sisters of, V.S.C.: Founded 1928, at Bedford, O. General motherhouse, 1160 Broadway, Bedford, O. 44146.

Charity of Cincinnati, Ohio, Sisters of, S.C.: Founded 1829. General motherhouse, Mt. St. Joseph, Ohio 45051. Educational, hospital, social work.

Charity of Ottawa, Sisters of (Grey Nuns of the Cross), S.C.O.: Founded 1845, at Ottawa, Canada; in U.S., 1857. General motherhouse, Ottawa, Canada; U.S. provincial house, 975 Varnum Ave., Lowell, Mass. 01854. Educational, hospital work, extended health care.

Charity of Our Lady, Mother of Mercy, Sisters of, S.C.M.M.: Founded 1832, in Holland; in U.S., 1874. General motherhouse, Rome, Italy; U.S. provincialate, 520 Thompson Ave., East Haven Conn. 06512.

Charity of Our Lady of Mercy, Sisters of, O.L.M.: Founded 1829, in U.S. Generalate and motherhouse, Charleston, S.C. 29412. Education, campus ministry, social services.

Charity of Quebec, Sisters of (Grey Nuns), S.C.Q.: Founded 1849, at Quebec; in U.S., 1890. General motherhouse, 2655 rue Le Pelletier, Beauport, Quebec GIC 3X7, Canada. Social work.

Charity of St. Elizabeth, Sisters of (Convent, N.J.), S.C.: Founded 1859, at Newark, N. J. Generalate, Convent Station, N. J. 07961. Education, pastoral ministry, social services.

Charity of St. Hyacinthe, Sisters of (Grey Nuns), S.C.S.H.: Founded 1840, at St. Hyacinthe, Canada; in U.S., 1878. General motherhouse, 665 Avenue Bourdages, SUD, St. Hyacinthe, Quebec J2T 4J8, Canada. Regional house, 98 Campus Ave., Lewiston Me. 04240.

Charity of St. Joan Antida, Sisters of, S.C.S.J.A.: Founded 1799, in France; in U.S., 1932. General motherhouse, Rome, Italy; U.S. provincial house, 8560 N. 76th Pl., Milwaukee, Wis. 53223.

Charity of St. Louis, Sisters of, S.C.S.L.: Founded 1803, in France; in U.S., 1910. General motherhouse, Rome, Italy; U.S. provincial house, 29 Casablanca Court, Clifton Park, N.Y. 12065.

Charity of St. Vincent de Paul, Daughters of, D.C.: Founded 1633, in France; in U.S. 1809, at Emmitsburg, Md., by St. Elizabeth Ann Seton. General motherhouse, Paris, France. U.S. provinces: Emmitsburg, Md. 21727; 7800 Natural Bridge Rd., St. Louis, Mo. 63121; 9400 New Harmony Rd., Evansville, Ind. 47712; 96 Menands Rd., Albany, N.Y. 12204; 26000 Altamont Rd., Los Altos Hills, Calif. 94022.

Charity of St. Vincent de Paul, Sisters of, S.V.Z.: Founded 1845, in Croatia; in U.S., 1955. General motherhouse, Zagreb, Yugoslavia; U.S. foundation, 171 Knox Ave., West Seneca, N.Y. 14224.

Charity of St. Vincent de Paul, Sisters of, Halifax, S.C.H.: Founded 1856, at Halifax, N. S., from Emmitsburg, Md., foundation. Generalate, Mt. St. Vincent, Halifax, N. S., Canada. U.S. addresses: Commonwealth of Massachusetts, 125 Oakland St., Wellesley Hills, Mass. 02181; Boston Province, 26 Phipps St., Quincy, Mass. 02169; New York Province, 410 Grant Ave., Brooklyn, N.Y. 11208. Educational, hospital, social work.

Charity of St. Vincent de Paul, Sisters of, New York, S.C.: Founded 1817, from Emmitsburg, Md. General motherhouse, Mt. St. Vincent on Hudson,

New York, N.Y. 10471. Educational, hospital work.

Charity of the Blessed Virgin Mary, Sisters of, B.V.M.: Founded 1833, in U.S. General motherhouse, Mt. Carmel, Dubuque, Ia. 52001. Education, pastoral ministry, social services.

Charity of the Immaculate Conception of Ivrea, Sisters of, S.C.I.C.: General motherhouse, Rome, Italy; U.S. address, Immaculate Virgin of Miracles Convent, R.D. 2, Mt. Pleasant, Pa. 15666.

Charity of the Incarnate Word, Congregation of the Sisters of, C.C.V.I.: Founded 1869, at San Antonio, Tex., by Bishop C. M. Dubuis. General motherhouse, 4503 Broadway, San Antonio, Tex. 78209.

Charity of the Incarnate Word, Congregation of the Sisters of (Houston, Tex.), C.C.V.I.: Founded 1866, in U.S., by Bishop C. M. Dubuis. General motherhouse, 6510 Lawndale Ave., Houston, Tex. 77023. Educational, hospital, social work.

Charity of the Sacred Heart, Daughters of, F.C.S.C.J.: Founded 1823, at La Salle de Vihiers, France; in U.S., 1905. General motherhouse, La Salle de Vihiers, France; U.S. address, Sacred Heart Province, P.O. Box 642, Littleton, N.H. 03561.

Charles Borromeo, Missionary Sisters of St. (Scalabrini Srs.): Founded 1895, in Italy; in U.S., 1941. American novitiate, 1414 N. 37th Ave., Melrose Park, Ill. 60601.

Child Jesus, Sisters of the Poor, P.C.J.: Founded 1844, at Aix-la-Chapelle, Germany; in U.S., 1924. General motherhouse, Simpelveld, Holland; American provincialate, 4567 Olentangy River Rd., Columbus, O. 43214.

Chretienne, Sisters of Ste., S.S.CH.: Founded 1807, in France; in U.S., 1903. General motherhouse, Metz, France; American provincial house, 297 Arnold St., Wrentham, Mass. 02093. Educational, hospital, mission work.

Christ, Adorers of the Blood of, A.S.C.: Founded 1834, in Italy; in U.S., 1870. General motherhouse, Rome, Italy. U.S. provinces: Ruma Province, Rt. 1, Box 115, Red Bud, Ill. 62278; 1400 South Sheridan, Wichita, Kans. 67213; Columbia, Pa. 17512. Education, retreats, social services, pastoral ministry.

Christ the King, Sister Servants of, S.S.C.K.: Founded 1936, in U.S. General motherhouse, Loretto Convent, Mt. Calvary, Wis. 53057. Social services.

Christian Doctrine, Sisters of Our Lady of, R.C.D.: Founded 1910, at New York. Motherhouse, Marydell, Montebello Rd., Suffern, N.Y. 10901.

Christian Education, Religious of, R.C.E.: Founded 1817, in France; in U.S., 1905. General motherhouse, Paris, France; U.S. provincial residence, 36 Hillcrest Rd., Belmont, Mass. 02178.

Cistercian Nuns, O. Cist.: Headquarters, Rome, Italy; U.S. address, Valley of Our Lady Monastery, Rt. 1, Box 136, Prairie du Sac, Wis. 53578.

Cistercian Nuns of the Strict Observance, Order of, O.C.S.O.: Founded 1125, in France, by St. Stephen Harding; in U.S., 1949. U.S. addresses: Mt. St. Mary's Abbey, Arnold St., Wrentham, Mass. 02093; Our Lady of the Santa Rita Abbey, Box 97, Sonoita, Ariz. 85637; Our Lady of the Redwoods Abbey, Whitethorn, Calif. 95489; Abbey of Our Lady of the Mississippi, R.R. 3, Dubuque, Ia. 52001.

Clergy, Congregation of Our Lady, Help of the, C.L.H.C.: Founded 1961, in U.S. Motherhouse, Maryvale Convent, Rt. 1, Box 164, Vale, N.C. 28168.

Clergy, Servants of Our Lady Queen of the, S.R.C.: Founded 1929, in Canada; in U.S., 1936. General motherhouse, Lac-au-Saumon, Que., GOJ 1MO, Canada.

Colettines: See Franciscan Poor Clare Nuns.

Columban, Missionary Sisters of St., S.S.C.: Founded 1922, in Ireland; in U.S., 1930. General motherhouse, Wicklow, Ireland; U.S. region, 1250 W. Loyola Ave., Chicago, Ill. 60626.

Comboni Missionary Sisters (Missionary Sisters of Verona), C.M.S.: Founded 1872, in Italy; in U.S., 1950. U.S. address, 1307 S. Lakeside Ave., Richmond, Va. 23228.

Consolata Missionary Sisters, M.C.: Founded 1910, in Italy; in U.S., 1954. General motherhouse, Turin, Italy; U.S. headquarters, 6801 Belmont Rd., Belmont, Mich. 49306.

Cross, Daughters of the, D.C.: Founded 1640, in France; in U.S., 1855. General motherhouse, 1000 Fairview St., Shreveport, La. 71104. Educational work.

Cross, Daughters of, of Liege, F.C.: Founded 1833, in Liege, Belgium; in U.S., 1958. U.S. address, 165 W. Eaton Ave., Tracy, Calif. 95376.

Cross, Sisters, Lovers of the Holy (Phat Diem): Founded 1670, in Vietnam; in U.S. 1976. U.S. address, Mary Immaculate Seminary Convent, Northampton, Pa. 18067.

Cross, Sisters of the Holy, C.S.C.: Founded 1841, at Le Mans, France; in U.S., 1843. General motherhouse, Saint Mary's, Notre Dame, Ind. 46556. Education, health care, social services, pastoral ministry.

Cross, Sisters of the Holy (Sisters of the Holy Cross and Seven Dolors), C.S.C.: Founded 1841, at La Mans, France, established 1847, in Canada; in U.S., 1881. General motherhouse, St. Laurent, Montreal, Que., Canada; U.S. provincial house, Fairview Rd., Pittsfield, N.H. 03263. Educational work.

Cross and Passion, Sisters of the (Passionist Sisters), C.P.: Founded 1852; in U.S., 1924. General motherhouse, Bolton, England; U.S. address: Mt. St. Joseph, 670 Tower Hill Rd., Wakefield, R.I. 02880.

Cross and Passion of Our Lord Jesus Christ, Nuns of the (Passionist Nuns), C.P.: Founded 1771, in Italy, by St. Paul of the Cross; in U.S., 1910. U.S. convents: 2715 Churchview Ave., Pittsburgh, Pa. 15227; 631 Griffin Pond Rd., Clarks Summit, Pa. 18411; 1420 Benita Ave., Owensboro, Ky. 42301; 751 Donaldson Hwy., Erlanger, Ky. 41018; 1032 Clayton Rd., Ellisville, Mo. 63011. Contemplatives.

Cyril and Methodius, Sisters of Sts., SS.C.M.: Founded 1909, in U.S., by Rev. Matthew Jankola. General motherhouse, Danville, Pa. 17821. Education, care of aged.

Disciples of the Divine Master, Sister, P.D.D.M.: Founded 1924; in U.S., 1948. General motherhouse, Rome, Italy; U.S. headquarters, 12830 Warren Ave., Dearborn, Mich. 48126.

Divine Compassion, Sisters of, R.D.C.: Founded 1886, in U.S. General motherhouse, 52 N. Broadway, White Plains, N.Y. 10603. Education, other ministries.

Divine Love, Oblates to, Sisters, R.O.D.A.: Founded 1923, in Italy; in U.S., 1947. General motherhouse, Rome, Italy; U.S. provincial house, St. Clare's Convent, 1925 Hone Ave., Bronx, N.Y. 10461.

Divine Spirit, Congregation of the, C.D.S.: Founded 1956, in U.S., by Archbishop John M. Gannon. Motherhouse, 409 W. 6th St., Erie, Pa. 16507. Education, social services.

Dominicans

Nuns of the Order of Preachers (Dominican Nuns), O.P.: Founded 1206 by St. Dominic at Prouille, France. Cloistered, contemplative. Two branches in the United States:

• Dominican Nuns having perpetual adoration. First monastery established 1880, in Newark, N.J., from Oullins, France, foundation (1869). Seven autonomous monasteries.

St. Dominic, 13th Ave. and S. 10th St., Newark, N.J. 07103; Corpus Christi, 1230 Lafayette Ave., Bronx, N.Y. 10474; Blessed Sacrament, 29575 Middlebelt Rd., Farmington Hills, Mich. 48018; Holy Name, 3020 Erie Ave., Hyde Park, Cincinnati, O. 45208; Monastery of the Angels, 1977 Carmen Ave., Los Angeles, Calif. 90068; Corpus Christi, 215 Oak Grove Ave., Menlo Park, Calif. 94025; Infant Jesus, 1501 Lotus Lane, Lufkin, Tex. 75901.

• Dominican Nuns devoted to the perpetual Rosary. First monastery established 1891, in Union City, N.J., from Calais, France, foundation (1880). Thirteen autonomous monasteries (some also observe perpetual adoration).

Dominican Nuns of Perpetual Rosary, 14th and West Sts., Union City, N.J. 07087; 217 N. 68th St., Milwaukee, Wis. 53213; Dominican Monastery, 720 Maiden Choice Lane, Catonsville, Baltimore, Md. 21228; Perpetual Rosary, 1500 Haddon Ave., Camden, N.J. 08103; Our Lady of the Rosary, 335 Doat St., Buffalo, N.Y. 14211; St. Dominic, 3000 South Ave., La Crosse, Wis. 54601; Our Lady of the Rosary, 543 Springfield Ave., Summit, N.J. 07901; Mother of God, 1430 Riverdale St., W. Springfield, Mass. 01089; Perpetual Rosary, 802 Court St., Syracuse, N.Y. 13208; Immaculate Heart of Mary, 1834 Lititz Pike, Lancaster, Pa. 17601; Mary the Queen, 1310 W. Church St., Elmira, N.Y. 14905; St. Jude, Marbury, Ala. 36051; Our Lady of Grace, North Guilford, Conn. 06437.

Dominican Rural Missionaries, O.P.: Founded 1932, in France; in U.S., 1951, at Abbeville, La. General motherhouse, Luzarches, France; U.S. address, 1318 S. Henry St., Abbeville, La. 70510.

Dominican Sisters of Bethany, Congregation, O.P.: Founded 1866, in France. Motherhouse, France; U.S. novitiate, 204 Ridge St., Millis, Mass. 02054.

Dominican Sisters of the Presentation, O.P.: Founded 1684, in France; in U.S., 1906. General motherhouse, Tours, France; U.S. headquarters,

3012 Elm St., Dighton, Mass. 02715. Hospital work.

Dominican Sisters of the Roman Congregation of St. Dominic, O.P.: Founded 1621, in France; in U.S., 1904. General motherhouse, Rome, Italy; U.S. province, 2624 Fillmore St., Davenport, Ia. 52804. Educational work.

Eucharistic Missionaries of St. Dominic, O.P.: Founded 1927, in Louisiana. General motherhouse, 1101 Aline St., New Orleans, La. 70115. Parish work, social services .

Maryknoll Sisters of St. Dominic, M.M.: Founded 1912, in New York. Center, Maryknoll, N.Y. 10545.

Religious Missionaries of St. Dominic, O.P.: General motherhouse, Rome, Italy. U.S. foundations: 808 S. Wright St., Alice, Texas 78332; 47 E. Gramman St., Beeville, Tex. 78102; 432 N. Oak St., Santa Paula, Calif. 93060.

Sisters of St. Dominic, O.P.: Thirty congregations in the U.S. Educational, hospital work. Names of congregations are given below, followed by the date of foundation, and location of motherhouse.

St. Catharine of Siena, 1822. St. Catharine, Ky. 40061.

St. Mary of the Springs, 1830. Columbus Ohio 43219.

Most Holy Rosary, 1847. Sinsinawa, Wis. 53824.

Most Holy Name of Jesus, 1850. San Rafael, Calif. 94901.

Holy Cross, 1853. Albany Ave., Amityville, N.Y. 11701.

Most Holy Rosary, 1859. Mt. St. Mary on Hudson, Newburgh, N.Y. 12550.

St. Cecilia, 1860. Eighth Ave. N. and Clay St., Nashville, Tenn. 37208.

St. Mary, 1860. 580 Broadway, New Orleans, La. 70118.

St. Catherine of Siena, 1862. 5635 Erie St., Racine, Wis. 53402.

Our Lady of the Sacred Heart, 1873. 1237 W. Monroe St., Springfield, Ill. 62704.

Our Lady of the Rosary, 1876. Sparkill, N.Y. 10976.

Queen of the Holy Rosary, 1876. Mission San Jose, Calif. 94538.

Most Holy Rosary, 1892. 1257 Siena Heights Dr., Adrian, Mich. 49221.

Our Lady of the Sacred Heart, 1877. 2025 E. Fulton St., Grand Rapids, Mich. 49503.

St. Dominic, 1878. Blauvelt, N.Y. 10913.

Immaculate Conception (Dominican Sisters of the Sick Poor), 1879. Ossining, N.Y. 10562. Social work.

St. Catherine de Ricci, 1880. 2850 N. Providence Rd., Media, Pa. 19063.

Sacred Heart of Jesus, 1881. Mt. St. Dominic, Caldwell, N.J. 07006.

Sacred Heart, 1882. 6501 Almeda Rd., Houston, Tex. 77021.

St. Thomas Aquinas, 1888. 423 E. 152nd St., Tacoma, Wash. 98445.

Holy Cross, 1890. P.O. Box 280, Edmonds, Wash. 98020.

St. Catherine of Siena, 1891. 37 Park St., Fall River, Mass. 02721.

St. Rose of Lima (Servants of Relief for Incurable Cancer), 1896. Hawthorne, N.Y. 10532.

Immaculate Conception, 1902. 3600 Broadway, Great Bend, Kans. 67530.

St. Catherine of Siena, 1911. 4600 93rd St., Kenosha, Wis. 53140.

St. Rose of Lima, 1923. 775 Drahner Rd., Oxford, Mich. 48051.

Immaculate Conception, 1929. 9000 W. 81st St., Justice, Ill. 60458.

Immaculate Heart of Mary, 1929. Akron, Ohio 44313.

Immaculate Heart of Mary Province (Dominican Sisters of Spokane). W. 3102 Fort George Wright Dr., Spokane, Wash. 99204.

Dominican Sisters of Oakford (St. Catherine of Siena), 1889. Motherhouse, Oakford, Natal, South Africa. U.S. regional house, 1965. Villa Siena, 1855 Miramonte Ave., Mountain View, Calif. 94040.

(End, Listing of Dominicans)

Dorothy, Institute of the Sisters of St., S.S.D.: Founded 1834, in Italy; in U.S., 1911. General motherhouse, Rome, Italy; U.S. provincialate, Villa Fatima, Taunton, Mass. 02780.

Eucharist, Religious of the, R.E.: Founded 1857, in Belgium; in U.S., 1900. General motherhouse, Belgium; U.S. foundation, 2907 Ellicott Terr., N.W., Washington, D.C. 20008.

Eucharistic Missionary Sisters, E.M.S.: Founded 1943, in Mexico. Motherhouse, Our Lady of Loretto Convent, 267 N. Belmont Ave., Los Angeles, Calif. 90026.

Family, Congregation of the Sisters of the Holy, S.S.F.: Founded 1842, in U.S. General motherhouse, 6901 Chef Menteur Hway., New Orleans, La. 70126. Educational, hospital work.

Family, Little Sisters of the Holy, P.S.S.F.: Founded 1880, in Canada; in U.S., 1900. General motherhouse, Sherbrooke, Que., Canada. U.S. novitiate, 285 Andover St., Lowell, Mass. 01852.

Family, Sisters of the Holy, S.H.F.: Founded 1872, in U.S. General motherhouse, P.O. Box 3248, Mission San Jose, Calif. 94538. Educational, social work.

Family of Nazareth, Sisters of the Holy, C.S.F.N.: Founded 1875, in Italy; in U.S., 1885. General motherhouse, Rome, Italy. U.S. provinces: 353 N. River Rd., Des Plaines, Ill. 60016; Grant and Torresdale Aves., Torresdale, Philadelphia, Pa. 19114; 285 Bellevue Rd., Pittsburgh, Pa. 15229; Marian Heights, 1428 Monroe Turnpike, Monroe, Conn. 06468; 1814 Egyptian Way, Box 757, Grand Prairie, Tex. 75050.

Filippini, Religious Teachers, M.P.F.: Founded 1692, in Italy; in U.S., 1910. General motherhouse, Rome, Italy; U.S. provinces: St. Lucy Filippini Province, Villa Walsh, Morristown, N.J. 07960; Queen of Apostles Province, 474 East Rd., Bristol, Conn. 06010. Educational work.

Francis de Sales, Oblate Sisters of St., O.S.F.S.: Founded 1866, in France; in U.S., 1951. General motherhouse, Troyes, France; U.S. headquarters, Villa Aviat Convent, Childs, Md. 21916. Educational, social work.

Franciscans

Bernardine Sisters of the Third Order of St. Francis, O.S.F.: Founded 1457, at Cracow, Poland; in U.S., 1894. Generalate, 647 Spring Mill Rd., Villanova, Pa. 19085. Educational, hospital, social work.

Capuchin Sisters of St. Clare (Madres Clarisas Capuchinas): U.S. establishment, 1981, Amarillo diocese. Convent of the Blessed Sacrament and Our Lady of Guadalupe, 4201 N.E. 18th St., Amarillo, Tex. 79107. Cloistered.

Congregation of the Servants of the Holy Infancy of Jesus, O.S.F.: Founded 1855, in Germany; in U.S., 1929. General motherhouse, Wuerzburg, Germany; American motherhouse, Villa Maria, P.O. Box 708, North Plainfield, N.J. 07061.

Congregation of the Third Order of St. Francis of Mary Immaculate, O.S.F.: Founded 1865, in U.S., by Fr. Pamphilus da Magliano, O.F.M. General motherhouse, 520 Plainfield Ave., Joliet, Ill. 60435. Educational and pastoral work.

Daughters of St. Francis of Assisi, D.S.F.: Founded 1890, in Austria-Hungary; in U.S., 1946. Provincial motherhouse, 507 N. Prairie St., Lacon, Ill. 61540. Nursing, CCD work.

Felician Sisters (Congregation of the Sisters of St. Felix), C.S.S.F.: Founded 1855, in Poland; in U.S., 1874. General motherhouse, Rome, Italy. U.S. provinces: 36800 Schoolcraft Rd., Livonia, Mich. 48150; 600 Doat St., Buffalo, N.Y. 14211; 3800 Peterson Ave., Chicago, Ill. 60659; 260 South Main St., Lodi, N.J. 07644; 1500 Woodcrest Ave., Coraopolis, Pa. 15108; 1315 Enfield St., Enfield, Conn. 06082; 4210 Meadowlark Lane, S.E., Rio Rancho, N. Mex. 87174.

Franciscan Handmaids of the Most Pure Heart of Mary, F.H.M.: Founded 1917, in U.S.. General motherhouse, 15 W. 124th St., New York, N.Y. 10027. Educational, social work.

Franciscan Hospitaller Sisters of the Immaculate Conception, F.H.I.C.: Founded 1876, in Portugal; in U.S., 1960. General motherhouse, Oporto, Portugal; U.S. novitiate, 300 S. 17th St., San Jose, Calif. 95112.

Franciscan Missionaries of Mary, F.M.M.: Founded 1877, in India; in U.S., 1904. General motherhouse, Rome, Italy; U.S. provincialate, 225 E. 45th St., New York, N.Y. 10017. Mission work.

Franciscan Missionaries of Our Lady, O.S.F.: Founded 1854, at Calais, France; in U.S., 1913. General motherhouse, Desvres, France; U.S. motherhouse, 4200 Essen Lane, Baton Rouge, La. 70809. Hospital work.

Franciscan Missionaries of St. Joseph (Mill Hill Sisters), F.M.S.J.: Founded 1883, at Rochdale, Lancashire, England; in U.S., 1952. General motherhouse, Eccleshall, Stafford, England; U.S. headquarters, Franciscan House, 1006 Madison Ave., Albany, N.Y. 12208.

Franciscan Missionaries of the Infant Jesus: Generalate, Rome, Italy. U.S. provincialate, 1215 Kresson Rd., Cherry Hill, N.J. 08003.

Franciscan Missionary Sisters for Africa, O.S.F.: American foundation, 1953. Generalate, Ireland;

U.S. headquarters, 172 Foster St., Brighton, Mass. 02135.

Franciscan Missionary Sisters of Assisi, F.M.S.A.: First foundation in U.S., 1961. General motherhouse, Assisi, Italy; U.S. address, St. Francis Convent, 1039 Northampton St., Holyoke, Mass. 01040.

Franciscan Missionary Sisters of Our Lady of Sorrows, O.S.F.: Founded 1937, in China, by Bishop R. Palazzi, O.F.M.; in U.S., 1949. U.S. address, 2385 Laurel Glen Rd., Santa Cruz, Calif. 95065. Educational, social, domestic, retreat and foreign mission work.

Franciscan Missionary Sisters of the Divine Child, F.M.D.C.: Founded 1927, at Buffalo, N.Y., by Bishop William Turner. General motherhouse, 6380 Main St., Williamsville, N.Y. 14221. Educational, social work.

Franciscan Missionary Sisters of the Immaculate Conception, O.S.F.: Founded 1874, in Mexico; in U.S., 1926. U.S. provincial house, 11306 Laurel Canyon Blvd., San Fernando, Calif. 91340.

Franciscan Missionary Sisters of the Immaculate Heart of Mary, F.M.I.H.M.: Founded at Cairo, Egypt by Mother Catarino di S. Rosa (Costanzo Troiano). Generalate, Rome, Italy; U.S. address, Ave Maria House, 3501 Good Intent Rd., Deptford, N.J. 08096.

Franciscan Missionary Sisters of the Sacred Heart, F.M.S.C.: Founded 1860, in Italy; in U.S., 1865. Generalate, Rome, Italy; U.S. provincialate, 250 South St., Peekskill, N.Y. 10566. Educational and social welfare apostolates and specialized services.

Franciscan Poor Clare Nuns (Poor Clares, Order of St. Clare, Poor Clares of St. Colette), P.C., O.S.C., P.C.C.: Founded 1212, at Assisi, Italy, by St. Francis of Assisi; in U.S., 1875. Proto-monastery, Assisi, Italy. Addresses of autonomous motherhouses in U.S. are listed below.

3626 N. 65th Ave., Omaha, Nebr. 68104; 720 Henry Clay Ave., New Orleans, La. 70118; 509 S. Kentucky Ave., Evansville, Ind. 47714; 1310 Dellwood Ave., Memphis Tenn. 38127; 920 Centre St., Jamaica Plain, Mass. 02130; 201 Crosswicks St., Bordentown, N.J. 08505; 1271 Langhorne-Newton Rd., Langhorne, Pa. 19047; 4419 N. Hawthorne St., Spokane, Wash. 99205; 142 Hollywood Ave., Bronx, N.Y. 10465; 421 S. 4th St., Sauk Rapids, Minn. 56379; 8650 Russell Ave. S., Minneapolis, Minn. 55431; 3501 Rocky River Dr., Cleveland, O. 44111; 89th and Kean Ave., Hickory Hills, Ill. 60457; 280 State Park Dr., Aptos, Calif. 95003; 2111 S. Main St., Rockford, Ill. 61102; 215 E. Los Olivos St., Santa Barbara, Calif. 93105; P.O. Box 333, Lowell, Mass. 01853; 809 E. 19th St., Roswell, N. Mex. 88201; 28210 Natoma Rd., Los Altos Hills. Calif. 94022; 1916 N. Pleasantburg Dr., Greenville, S.C. 29609; 28 Harpersville Rd., Newport News, Va. 23601; 805 N. Malfalfa Rd., Kokoma, Ind. 46901; 4000 Sherwood Blvd., Delray Beach, Fla. 33445; 200 Marycrest Dr., St. Louis, Mo. 63129.

Franciscan Sisters, Daughters of the Sacred Hearts of Jesus and Mary, O.S.F.: Founded 1860, in Germany; in U.S., 1872. Generalate, Rome, Italy; U.S. motherhouse, P.O. Box 667, Wheaton, Ill.

60187. Educational, hospital, foreign mission, social work.

Franciscan Sisters of Allegany, N.Y., O.S.F.: Founded 1859, at Allegany, N.Y., by Fr. Pamphilus da Magliano, O.F.M. General motherhouse Allegany, N.Y. 14706. Educational, hospital, foreign mission work.

Franciscan Sisters of Baltimore, O.S.F.: Founded 1868, in England; in U.S., 1881. General motherhouse, 3725 Ellerslie Ave., Baltimore, Md. 21218. Educational work; social services.

Franciscan Sisters of Chicago, O.S.F.: Founded 1894, in U.S., by Mother Mary Therese (Josephine Dudzik). General motherhouse, 1220 Main St., Lemont, Ill. 60439. Educational work, social services.

Franciscan Sisters of Christian Charity, O.S.F.: Founded 1869, in U.S. Holy Family Convent, 2409 S. Alverno Rd., Manitowoc, Wis. 54220. Educational, hospital work.

Franciscan Sisters of Little Falls, Minn., O.S.F.: Founded 1891, in U.S. General motherhouse, Little Falls, Minn. 56345. Health, education, social services, pastoral ministry, mission work.

Franciscan Sisters of Mary Immaculate of the Third Order of St. Francis of Assisi, F.M.I.: Founded 16th century, in Switzerland; in U.S., 1932. General motherhouse, Bogota, Colombia; U.S. provincial house, 4301 N.E. 18th Ave., Amarillo, Tex. 79107. Education.

Franciscan Sisters of Our Lady of Perpetual Help, O.S.F.: Founded 1901, in U.S., from Joliet, Ill., foundation. General motherhouse, 201 Brotherton Lane, St. Louis, Mo. 63135. Educational, hospital work.

Franciscan Sisters of Ringwood, F.S.R.: Founded 1927, at Passaic, N.J. General motherhouse, Mt. St. Francis, Ringwood, N.J. 07456. Educational work.

Franciscan Sisters of St. Elizabeth, F.S.S.E.: Founded 1866, at Naples, Italy; in U.S., 1919. General motherhouse, Rome; U.S. novitiate, 449 Park Rd., Parsippany, N.J. 07054. Educational work, social services.

Franciscan Sisters of St. Joseph, F.S.S.J.: Founded 1897, in U.S. General motherhouse, 5286 S. Park Ave., Hamburg, N.Y. 14075. Educational, hospital work.

Franciscan Sisters of the Atonement, Third Order Regular of St. Francis (Graymoor Sisters), S.A.: Founded 1898, in U.S., as Anglican community; entered Church, 1909. General motherhouse, Graymoor, Garrison P.O., N.Y. 10524. Mission work.

Franciscan Sisters of the Blessed Virgin Mary of the Holy Angels, B.M.V.A.: Founded 1863, at Neuwied, Germany; in U.S., 1923. General motherhouse, Rhine, Germany; U.S. motherhouse, 1388 Prior Ave. S., St. Paul, Minn. 55116. Educational, hospital, social work.

Franciscan Sisters of the Immaculate Conception, O.S.F.: Founded in Germany; in U.S., 1928. General motherhouse, Kloster, Bonlanden, Germany; U.S. province, 291 W. North St., Buffalo, N.Y. 14201.

Franciscan Sisters of the Immaculate Conception, O.S.F.: Founded 1901, in U.S. General motherhouse, 1000 30th St., Rock Island, Ill. 61201. Health care.

Franciscan Sisters of the Immaculate Conception, Missionary, O.S.F.: Founded 1873, in U.S. General motherhouse, Rome, Italy; U.S. address, 790 Centre St., Newton, Mass. 02158. Educational work.

Franciscan Sisters of the Immaculate Conception and St. Joseph for the Dying, O.S.F.: Founded 1919, in U.S. General motherhouse, 485 Church St., Monterey, Calif. 93940.

Franciscan Sisters of the Poor, S.F.P.: Founded 1845, at Aachen, Germany, by Bl. Frances Schervier; in U.S., 1858. Community service center, 23 Middagh St., Brooklyn, N.Y. 11201. Hospital, social work and foreign missions.

Franciscan Sisters of the Sacred Heart, O.S.F.: Founded 1866, in Germany; in U.S., 1876. General motherhouse, Mokena, Ill. 60448. Education, health care, other service ministries.

Hospital Sisters of the Third Order of St. Francis, O.S.F.: Founded 1844, in Germany; in U.S., 1875. General motherhouse, Muenster, Germany; U.S. motherhouse, Box 42, Springfield, Ill. 62705. Hospital work.

Institute of the Franciscan Sisters of the Eucharist, F.S.E.: Founded 1973. Motherhouse, 405 Allen Ave., Meriden, Conn. 06450.

Little Franciscan Sisters of Mary, P.F.M.: Founded 1889, in U.S. General motherhouse, Baie St. Paul, Que., Canada. U.S. province, 55 Moore Ave., Worcester, Mass. 01602. Educational, hospital, social work.

Little Sisters of St. Francis, O.S.F.: Founded 1979, in Boston archdiocese. Address, 785 Parker St., Mission Hill, Mass. 02120. Combine contemplative life with street ministry apostolate.

Missionaries of the Third Order of St. Francis of Our Lady of the Prairies, O.L.P.: Founded 1960, in U.S. General motherhouse, Powers Lake, N.D. 58773.

Missionary Sisters of the Immaculate Conception of the Mother of God, S.M.I.C.: Founded 1910, in Brazil; in U.S., 1922, Generalate, 779 Broadway, Paterson, N.J. 07514; provincialate, P.O. Box 3026, Paterson, N.J. 07509. Mission, educational, health work, social services.

Mothers of the Helpless, M.D.: Founded 1873, in Spain; in U.S., 1916. General motherhouse, Valencia, Spain; U.S. address, San Jose Day Nursery, 432 W. 20th St., New York, N.Y. 10011.

Philip Neri Missionary Teachers, Sisters of St., R.F.: Founded 1858, in Spain; in U.S., 1956. Motherhouse, Madrid, Spain; U.S. address: Sisters of St. Philip Neri, St. Albert's Convent, 1259 St. Alberts St., Reno, Nev. 89503.

Poor Clares of Perpetual Adoration, P.C.P.A.: Founded 1854, at Paris, France; in U.S., 1921, at Cleveland, Ohio. U.S. monasteries: 4200 N. Market Ave., Canton, O. 44714; 2311 Timlin Rd., Portsmouth, O. 45662; 4108 Euclid Ave., Cleveland, O. 44103; 3900 13th St. N.E., Washington, D.C. 20017; 5817 Old Leeds Rd., Birmingham, Ala. 35210. Contemplative, cloistered, perpetual adoration.

School Sisters of St. Francis, O.S.F.: Founded 1874, in U.S. General motherhouse, 1501 Layton Blvd., Milwaukee, Wis. 53215.

School Sisters of St. Francis (Bethlehem, Pa.), O.S.F.: Founded in Austria, 1843; in U.S., 1913. General motherhouse, Rome, Italy; U.S. province, 395 Bridle Path Rd., Bethlehem, Pa. 18017. Educational, mission work.

School Sisters of St. Francis, (Pittsburgh, Pa.), O.S.F.: Established 1913, in U.S. Motherhouse, Mt. Assisi Convent, 934 Forest Ave., Pittsburgh, Pa. 15202. Education, health care services and related ministries.

School Sisters of the Third Order of St. Francis (Panhandle, Tex.), O.S.F.: Founded 1845, in Austria; in U.S., 1942. General motherhouse, Vienna, Austria; U.S. center and novitiate, Sancta Maria Convent, Panhandle, Tex. 79068. Educational, social work.

Sisters of Charity of Our Lady, Mother of the Church, S.C.M.C.: Established 1970, in U.S. Motherhouse, Baltic, Conn. 06330. Teaching, nursing, care of aged, and dependent children.

Sisters of Our Lady of Mercy (Mercedarians), S.O.L.M.: General motherhouse, Rome, Italy; U.S. addresses: 133 27th Ave., Brooklyn, N.Y. 11214; St. Edward School, Pine Hill, N.J. 08021.

Sisters of Mercy of the Holy Cross, S.C.S.C.: Founded 1856, in Switzerland; in U.S. 1912. General motherhouse, Ingenbohl, Switzerland; U.S. provincial house, 1500 O'Day St., Merrill, Wis. 54452.

Sisters of St. Elizabeth, S.S.E.: Founded 1931, at Milwaukee, Wis. General motherhouse, 745 N. Brookfield Rd., Brookfield, Wis. 53005.

Sisters of St. Francis (Clinton, Iowa), O.S.F.: Founded 1868, in U.S. General motherhouse, Bluff Blvd. and Springdale Dr., Clinton, Ia. 57232. Educational, hospital, social work.

Sisters of St. Francis (Maryville, Mo.), O.S.F.: Founded 1894, in U.S. Motherhouse, Mt. Alverno Convent, R.R. 3, Box 64, Maryville, Mo. 64468. Hospital work.

Sisters of St. Francis (Millvale, Pa.), O.S.F.: Founded 1865, Pittsburgh, Pa. General motherhouse, 146 Hawthorne Rd., Millvale P.O., Pittsburgh, Pa. 15209. Educational, hospital work.

Sisters of St. Francis, Hastings-on-Hudson, O.S.F.: Founded 1893, in New York. General motherhouse, Hastings-on-Hudson, N.Y. 10706. Education, parish ministry, social services.

Sisters of St. Francis of Christ the King, O.S.F.: Founded 1869, in Austria. General motherhouse, Rome, Italy; U.S. provincial house, 1600 Main St., Lemont, Ill. 60439. Educational work, home for aged.

Sisters of St. Francis of Penance and Christian Charity, O.S.F.: Founded 1835, in Holland; in U.S., 1874. General motherhouse, Rome, Italy. U.S. provinces: 4421 Lower River Rd., Stella Niagara, N.Y. 14144; 2851 W. 52nd Ave., Denver, Colo. 80221; 3910 Bret Harte Dr., P.O. Box 1028, Redwood City, Calif. 94064.

Sisters of St. Francis of Philadelphia, O.S.F.: Founded 1855, at Philadelphia, by Mother Mary Francis Bachmann and St. John N. Neumann. General motherhouse, Convent of Our Lady of the

Angels, Glen Riddle, Aston, Pa. 19014. Education, health care, social services.

Sisters of St. Francis of Savannah, Mo., O.S.F.: Founded 1850, in Austria; in U.S., 1922. Provincial house, La Verna Heights, Savannah, Mo. 64485. Educational, hospital work.

Sisters of St. Francis of the Congregation of Our Lady of Lourdes, O.S.F.: Founded 1916, in U.S. General motherhouse, 6832 Convent Blvd., Sylvania, O. 43560. Education, health care, social services, pastoral ministry.

Sisters of St. Francis of the Holy Cross, O.S.F.: Founded 1881, in U.S., by Rev. Edward Daems, O.S.C. General motherhouse, 3025 Bay Settlement Rd., Green Bay, Wis. 54301. Educational, nursing work, pastoral ministry, foreign missions.

Sisters of St. Francis of the Holy Eucharist, O.S.F.: Founded 1424, in Switzerland; in U.S., 1893. General motherhouse, 2100 N. Noland Rd., Independence, Mo. 64050. Education, health care, social services, foreign missions.

Sisters of St. Francis of the Holy Family, O.S.F.: Founded 1875, in U.S. Motherhouse, Mt. St. Francis, Dubuque, Ia. 52001. Varied apostolates.

Sisters of St. Francis of the Immaculate Conception, O.S.F.: Founded 1890, in U.S. General motherhouse, 2408 W. Heading Ave., Peoria, Ill. 61604. Education, care of aging, pastoral ministry.

Sisters of St. Francis of the Immaculate Heart of Mary, O.S.F.: Founded 1241, in Bavaria; in U.S., 1913. General motherhouse, Rome, Italy; U.S. motherhouse, Hankinson, N.D. 58041. Education, social services.

Sisters of St. Francis of the Martyr St. George, O.S.F.: Founded 1859, in Germany; in U.S., 1923. General motherhouse, Thuine, West Germany; U.S. provincial house, Alton, Ill. 62002. Education, social services, foreign mission work.

Sisters of St. Francis of the Perpetual Adoration, O.S.F.: Founded 1863, in Germany; in U.S., 1875. General motherhouse, Olpe, Germany. U.S. provinces: Box 766, Mishawaka, Ind. 46544; P.O. Box 1060, Colorado Springs, Colo. 80901. Educational, hospital work.

Sisters of St. Francis of the Providence of God, O.S.F.: Founded 1922, in U.S., by Msgr. M. L. Krusas. General motherhouse, Grove and McRoberts Rds., Pittsburgh, Pa. 15234. Education, varied apostolates.

Sisters of St. Joseph of the Third Order of St. Francis, S.S.J.: Founded 1901, in U.S. Administrative office, 231 S. Michigan Ave., P.O. Box 688, South Bend, Ind. 46624. Education, health care, social services.

Sisters of St. Mary of the Third Order of St. Francis, S.S.M.: Founded 1872, in St. Louis, Mo. General motherhouse, 1100 Bellevue Ave., St. Louis, Mo. 63117. Health care, social services.

Sisters of the Infant Jesus, I.J.: Founded 1662, at Rouen, France; in U.S., 1950. Motherhouse, Paris, France. Generalate, Rome, Italy. U.S. addresses: 20 Reiner St., Colma, Calif. 94014; St. John the Baptist School, Healdsburg, Calif. 95448; 60 Bellevue Ave., Daly City, Calif. 94014.

Sisters of the Sorrowful Mother (Third Order of St. Francis), S.S.M.: Founded 1883, in Italy; in U.S., 1889. General motherhouse, Rome, Italy. U.S. provinces: 6618 N. Teutonia Ave., Milwaukee, Wis. 53209; 9 Pocono Rd., Denville, N.J. 07834; Tulsa Provincialate, 17600 E. 51st St. S., Broken Arrow, Okla. 74012. Educational, hospital work.

Sisters of the Third Franciscan Order Minor Conventuals, O.S.F.: Founded 1860, at Syracuse, N.Y. Generalate offices, 100 Michaels Ave., Syracuse, N.Y. 13208. Educational, hospital work.

Sisters of the Third Order of St. Francis, O.S.F.: Founded 1877, in U.S., by Bishop John L. Spalding. Motherhouse, Edgewood Hills, E. Peoria, Ill. 61611. Hospital work.

Sisters of the Third Order of St. Francis, O.S.F.: Founded 1861, at Buffalo, N.Y., from Philadelphia foundation. General motherhouse, 400 Mill St., Williamsville, N.Y. 14221. Educational, hospital work.

Sisters of the Third Order of St. Francis (Oldenburg, Ind.), O.S.F.: Founded 1851, in U.S. General motherhouse, Convent of the Immaculate Conception, Oldenburg, Ind. 47036. Education, social services, pastoral ministry, foreign missions.

Sisters of the Third Order of St. Francis of Assisi, O.S.F.: Founded 1849, in U.S. General motherhouse, 3221 S. Lake Dr., Milwaukee, Wis. 53207. Education, other ministries.

Sisters of the Third Order of St. Francis of Penance and Charity, O.S.F.: Founded 1869, in U.S., by Rev. Joseph Bihn. Motherhouse, St. Francis Convent, St. Francis Ave., Tiffin, O. 44883. Education, social services.

Sisters of the Third Order of St. Francis of the Perpetual Adoration, F.S.P.A.: Founded 1849, in U.S. Generalate, 912 Market St., La Crosse, Wis. 54601. Education, health care.

Sisters of the Third Order Regular of St. Francis of the Congregation of Our Lady of Lourdes, O.S.F.: Founded 1877, in U.S. General motherhouse, Assisi Heights, Rochester, Minn. 55901. Education, health care, social services.

(End, Listing of Franciscans)

Good Shepherd Sisters (Servants of the Immaculate Heart of Mary), S.C.I.M.: Founded 1850, in Canada; in U.S., 1882. General motherhouse, Quebec, Canada; Provincial House, Bay View, Saco, Maine 04072. Educational, social work.

Good Shepherd, Sisters of Our Lady of Charity of the, R.G.S.: Founded 1641, in France; in U.S., 1843. Generalate, Rome, Italy. U.S. provinces: 9517 Leebrook Dr., Cincinnati, O. 45231; 82-31 Doncaster Pl., Jamaica, N.Y. 11432; 504 Hexton Hill Rd., Silver Spring, Md. 20904; 7654 Natural Bridge Rd., St. Louis, Mo. 63121; 2041 Laurel Ave., St. Paul, Minn. 55104.

Graymoor Sisters: See Franciscan Sisters of the Atonement.

Grey Nuns of the Sacred Heart, G.N.S.H.: Founded 1921, in U.S. General motherhouse, Quarry Rd., Yardley, Pa. 19067.

Guadalupe, Sisters of, O.L.G.: Founded 1946, in Mexico City. General motherhouse, Mexico City, Mexico; U.S. address, St. Mary's College, Winona, Minn. 55987.

Guardian Angels, Sisters of the Holy, S.A.C.:

Founded 1839, in France. General motherhouse, Madrid, Spain; U.S. foundation, 1245 S. Van Ness, Los Angeles, Calif. 90019.

Handmaids of Mary Immaculate, A.M.I.: Founded 1952 in Helena, Mont. Address: Ave Maria Institute, Washington, N.J. 07882.

Handmaids of the Precious Blood, Congregation of, H.P.B.: Founded 1947, at Jemez Springs, N.M. Motherhouse and novitiate, Cor Jesu Monastery, Jemez Springs, N.M. 87025.

Helpers, Society of, H.H.S.: Founded 1856, in France; in U.S., 1892. General motherhouse, Paris, France; American province, 303 W. Barry Ave., Chicago, Ill. 60657.

Hermanas Catequistas Guadalupanas, H.C.G.: Founded 1923, in Mexico; in U.S., 1950. General motherhouse, Mexico; U.S. foundation, 4110 S. Flores, San Antonio, Tex. 78214.

Holy Child Jesus, Society of the, S.H.C.J.: Founded 1846, in England; in U.S., 1862. General motherhouse, Rome, Italy. U.S. province: 620 Edmonds Ave., Drexel Hill, Pa. 19026.

Holy Faith, Congregation of the Sisters of the, C.H.F.: Founded 1856, in Ireland; in U.S., 1953. General motherhouse, Dublin, Ireland; U.S. regional superior, 13817 S. Pioneer Blvd., Norwalk, Calif. 90650.

Holy Ghost, Sisters of the, C.H.G.: Founded 1913, in U.S., by Most Rev. J. F. Regis Canevin. General motherhouse, 5246 Clarwin Ave., Ross Township, Pittsburgh, Pa. 15229. Educational, nursing work; care of aged.

Holy Ghost and Mary Immaculate, Sister Servants of, S.H.G.: Founded 1893, in U.S. Motherhouse, 301 Yucca St., San Antonio, Tex. 78203. Education, hospital work.

Holy Heart of Mary, Servants of the, S.S.C.M.: Founded 1860, in France; in U.S., 1889. General motherhouse, Montreal, Que., Canada; U.S. province, 145 S. 4th Ave., Kankakee, Ill. 60901. Educational, hospital, social work.

Holy Names of Jesus and Mary, Sisters of the, S.N.J.M.: Founded 1843, in Canada; in U.S., 1859. General motherhouse, Pierrefonds H9K 1C6, P.Q., Canada. U.S. addresses: Oregon Province, Marylhurst, Ore. 97036; California Province, P.O. Box 907, Los Gatos, Calif. 95031; New York Province, 1061 New Scotland Rd., Albany, N.Y. 12208; Washington Province, W. 2911 Ft. Wright Dr., Spokane, Wash. 99204.

Holy Spirit, Daughters of the, D.H.S.: Founded 1706, in France; in U.S., 1902. Generalate, Rennes, France; U.S. motherhouse, 72 Church St., Putnam, Conn. 06260. Educational work, district nursing; pastoral ministry.

Holy Spirit, Mission Sisters of the, M.S.Sp.: Founded 1932, at Cleveland, O. Motherhouse, 1030 N. River Rd., Saginaw, Mich. 48603.

Holy Spirit, Missionary Sisters, Servants of the: Founded 1889, in Holland; in U.S., 1901. Generalate, Rome, Italy; U.S. motherhouse, Convent of the Holy Spirit, Techny, Ill. 60082.

Holy Spirit, Sisters of the, C.S.Sp.: Founded 1890, in Rome, Italy; in U.S., 1929. General motherhouse, 10102 Granger Rd., Garfield Hts., Ohio 44125. Educational, social, nursing work.

Holy Spirit of Perpetual Adoration, Sister Servants of the: Founded 1896, in Holland; in U.S., 1915. General motherhouse, Steyl, Holland; U.S. motherhouse, 2212 Green St., Philadelphia, Pa. 19130.

Home Mission Sisters of America (Glenmary Sisters): Founded 1952, in U.S. Motherhouse, Morning Star, P.O. Box 39188, Cincinnati, O. 45239.

Home Visitors of Mary, Sisters, H.V.M.: Founded 1949, in Detroit, Mich. Motherhouse, 356 Arden Park, Detroit, Mich. 48202.

Humility of Mary, Congregation of, C.H.M.: Founded 1854, in France; in U.S., 1864. U.S. address, Convent of Humility of Mary, Ottumwa, Ia. 52501.

Humility of Mary, Sisters of the, H.M.: Founded 1854, in France; in U.S., 1864. U.S. address, Villa Maria, Pa. 16155.

Immaculate Conception, Little Servant Sisters of the: Founded 1850, in Poland; in U.S., 1926. General motherhouse, Poland; U.S. provincial house, 184 Amboy Ave., Woodbridge, N.J. 07095. Education, social services, African missions.

Immaculate Conception, Sisters of the, R.C.M.: Founded 1892, in Spain; in U.S., 1962. General motherhouse, Madrid, Spain; U.S. foundation, 867 Oxford, Clovis, Calif. 93612.

Immaculate Conception, Sisters of the, C.I.C.: Founded 1874, in U.S. General motherhouse, 4920 Kent St., Metairie, La. 70002.

Immaculate Conception of the Blessed Virgin Mary, Sisters of the (Lithuanian): Founded 1918, at Mariampole, Lithuania; in U.S., 1936. General motherhouse, Lithuania; U.S. headquarters, Immaculate Conception Convent, Putnam, Conn. 06260.

Immaculate Heart of Mary, Missionary Sisters, I.C.M.: Founded 1897, in India; in U.S., 1919. Generalate, Rome, Italy; U.S. address, 1710 N. Glebe Rd., Arlington, Va. 22207. Educational social, foreign mission work.

Immaculate Heart of Mary, Sisters of the: Founded 1848, in Spain; in U.S., 1878. General motherhouse, Rome, Italy. U.S. province, 4100 Sabino Canyon Rd., Tucson, Ariz. 85715. Educational work.

Immaculate Heart of Mary, Sisters of the (California Institute of the Most Holy and Immaculate Heart of the B.V.M.), I.H.M.: Founded 1848, in Spain; in U.S., 1871. Generalate, 3431 Waverly Dr., Los Angeles, Calif. 90027.

Immaculate Heart of Mary, Sisters, Servants of the, I.H.M.: Founded 1845, at Monroe, Mich., by Rev. Louis Florent Gillet. Three independent branches: Generalate, 610 W. Elm St., Monroe, Mich. 48161; Villa Maria, Immaculata, Pa. 19345; Immaculate Heart of Mary Generalate, Marywood, Scranton, Pa. 18509.

Incarnate Word and Blessed Sacrament, Congregation of, V.I.: Founded 1625, in France; in U.S., 1853. Incarnate Word Convent, 3400 Bradford Pl., Houston, Tex. 77028.

Incarnate Word and Blessed Sacrament, Congregation of the, of the Archdiocese of San Antonio, I.W.B.S.: Motherhouses: 1101 Northeast

Water St., Victoria, Tex. 77901; 2930 S. Alameda, Corpus Christi, Tex. 78404.

Incarnate Word and Blessed Sacrament, Sisters of the, S.I.W.: Founded 1625, in France; in U.S. 1853. Motherhouse, 6618 Pearl Rd., Parma Heights, Cleveland, O. 44130.

Infant Jesus, Congregation of the (Nursing Sisters of the Sick Poor), C.I.J.: Founded 1835, in France; in U.S., 1905. General motherhouse, 310 Prospect Park W., Brooklyn, N.Y. 11215.

Jeanne d'Arc, Sisters of Ste.: Founded 1914, in America, by Rev. Marie Clement Staub, A.A. General motherhouse, 1505, rue de l'Assomption Sillery, Que. G1S 4T3, Canada. Spiritual and temporal service of priests.

Jesus, Daughters of, F.I.: Founded 1871, in Spain; in U.S., 1950. General motherhouse, Rome, Italy; U.S. address, South Side Mission, 329 S. 4th St., Brooklyn, N.Y. 11211.

Jesus, Daughters of (Filles de Jesus), F.J.: Founded 1834, in France; in U.S., 1904. General motherhouse, Kermaria, Locmine, France; American provincial house, 9040 84th Ave., Edmonton, Alberta T6C 1E4, Canada. Educational, hospital, parish and social work.

Jesus, Little Sisters of: Founded 1939, in Sahara; in U.S., 1952. General motherhouse, Rome, Italy; U.S. headquarters, 700 Irving St. N.E., Washington, D.C. 20017.

Jesus, Society of the Sisters, Faithful Companions of, F.C.J.: Founded 1820, in France; in U.S., 1896. General motherhouse, Kent, England. U.S. convents: 20 Atkins St., Providence, R.I. 02908; St. Philomena Convent, Cory's Lane, Portsmouth, R.I. 02871.

Jesus Crucified, Congregation of: Founded 1930, in France; in U.S., 1955. General motherhouse, Brou, France; U.S. foundations: Regina Mundi Priory, Devon, Pa. 19333; St. Paul's Priory, 61 Narragansett, Newport, R.I. 02840.

Jesus Crucified and the Sorrowful Mother, Poor Sisters of, C.J.C.: Founded 1924, in U.S., by Rev. Alphonsus Maria, C.P. Motherhouse, 261 Thatcher St., Brockton, Mass. 02402. Education, nursing homes, catechetical centers.

Jesus-Mary, Religious of, R.J.M.: Founded 1818, at Lyons, France; in U.S., 1877. General motherhouse, Rome, Italy; U.S. province, 8908 Riggs Rd., Hyattsville, Md. 20783. Educational work.

Jesus, Mary and Joseph, Missionaries of, M.J.M.J.: Founded 1942, in Spain; in U.S., 1956. General motherhouse, Madrid, Spain; U.S. regional house, 12940 Up River Rd., Corpus Christi, Tex. 78410.

John the Baptist, Sisters of St., C.S.J.B.: Founded 1878, in Italy; in U.S., 1906. General motherhouse, Rome, Italy; U.S. provincialate, Anderson Hill Rd., Purchase, N.Y. 10577. Education, parish and retreat work; social services.

Joseph, Missionary Servants of St., M.S.S.J.: Founded 1874, in Spain; in U.S., 1957. General motherhouse, Salamanca, Spain; U.S. address, 203 N. Spring St., Falls Church, Va. 22046.

Joseph, Poor Sisters of St.: Founded 1880, in Argentina. General motherhouse, Muniz, Argentina; U.S. addresses, Casa Belen, 305 E. 4th St., Bethle-

hem, Pa. 78015; St. Gabriel Convent, 4319 Sano St., Alexandria, Va. 22312.

Joseph, Religious Daughters of St., F.S.J.: Founded 1875, in Spain. General motherhouse, Spain; U.S. foundation, 319 N. Humphreys Ave., Los Angeles, Calif. 90022.

Joseph, Religious Hospitallers of St., R.H.S.J.: Founded 1636, in France; in U.S., 1894. Generalate, 5621 Canterbury Ave., Montreal, Que., H3T 15B, Canada. Hospital work.

Joseph, Sisters of St., C.S.J.: Founded 1650, in France; in U.S., 1836, at St. Louis. U.S. independent motherhouses:

637 Cambridge St., Brighton, Mass. 02135; 1515 W. Ogden Ave., La Grange Park, Ill., 60525; 480 S. Batavia St., Orange, Calif. 92668; Mt. St. Joseph Convent, Chestnut Hill, Philadelphia, Pa. 19118.

St. Joseph Convent, Brentwood, N.Y. 11717; 23 Agassiz Circle, Buffalo, N.Y. 14214; Avila Hall, Clement Rd., Rutland, Vt. 05701; 3430 Rocky River Dr., Cleveland, O. 44111; Main St. and Division Rd., Tipton, Ind. 46072; Nazareth, Mich. 49074; 1425 Washington St., Watertown, N.Y. 13601; St. Joseph Motherhouse, Baden, Pa. 15005; 819 W. 8th St., Erie, Pa. 16502.

4095 East Ave., Rochester, N.Y. 14610; 215 Court St., Concordia, Kans. 66901; Holyoke, Mass. 01040; 1412 E. 2nd St., Superior, Wis. 54880; Pogue Run Rd., Wheeling, W. Va. 26003; 3700 E. Lincoln St., Wichita, Kans. 67218.

Joseph, Sisters of St. (Lyons, France), C.S.J.: Founded 1650, in France; in U.S., 1906. General motherhouse, Lyons, France; U.S. provincialate, 93 Halifax St., Winslow, Me. 04901. Educational, hospital work.

Joseph, Sisters of St., of Peace, C.S.J.: Founded 1884, in England. Generalate, 1234 Massachusetts Ave. N.W., Washington, D.C. 20005. Educational, hospital, social service work

Joseph of Carondelet, Sisters of St., C.S.J.: Founded 1650, in France; in U.S., 1836, at St. Louis, Mo. U.S. headquarters, 2307 S. Lindbergh Blvd., St. Louis, Mo. 63131.

Joseph of Chambery, Sisters of St.: Founded 1650, in France; in U.S., 1885. Generalate, Rome, Italy; U.S. provincial house, 27 Park Rd., West Hartford, Conn. 06119. Educational, hospital, social work.

Joseph of Cluny, Sisters of St., S.J.C.: Founded 1807, in France. Generalate, Paris, France; U.S. provincial house, Brenton Rd., Newport, R.I. 02840.

Joseph of Medaille, Sisters of, C.S.J.: Founded 1823, in France; in U.S., 1855. Became an American congregation Nov. 30, 1977. Central office, 5108 Reading Rd., Cincinnati, Ohio 45237.

Joseph of St. Augustine, Fla., Sisters of St., S.S.J.: General motherhouse, 241 St. George St., St. Augustine, Fla. 32084. Educational, hospital, pastoral, social work.

Joseph of St. Mark, Sisters of St., S.S.J.S.M.: Founded 1845, in France; in U.S., 1937. General motherhouse, 21800 Chardon Rd., Euclid, Cleveland, O. 44117. Nursing homes.

Joseph the Worker, Sisters of St., S.J.W.: General motherhouse, St. Joseph Convent, 143 S. Main St., Walton, Ky. 41094.

Lamb of God, Sisters of the, A.D.: Founded 1945, in France; in U.S., 1958. General motherhouse, France; U.S. address, Rt. 1, No. 260, Philpot, Ky 42366.

Living Word, Sisters of the, S.L.W.: Founded 1975, in U.S. Motherhouse, The Center, 7200 N. Osceola Ave., Chicago, Ill. 60648. Education, hospital, parish ministry work.

Loretto at the Foot of the Cross, Sisters of, S.L.: Founded 1812 in U.S., by Rev. Charles Nerinckx. General motherhouse, Nerinx, Ky. 40049. Educational work.

Louis, Congregation of Sisters of St., S.S.L.: Founded 1842, in France; in U.S., 1949. General motherhouse, Monaghan, Ireland; U.S. regional house, 22300 Mulholland Dr., Woodland Hills, Calif. 91364. Educational, medical, parish, foreign mission work.

Marian Sisters of the Diocese of Lincoln: Founded 1954. Motherhouse, Marycrest, Waverly, Nebr. 68462.

Marian Society of Dominican Catechists, O.P.: Founded 1954 in Louisiana. General motherhouse, Boyce, La. 71409. Community of Alexandria-Shreveport, La., diocese.

Marianites of Holy Cross, Congregation of the Sisters, M.S.C.: Founded 1841, in France; in U.S., 1843. Motherhouse, Le Mans, Sarthe, France. U.S. provinces: 4123 Woodland Dr., New Orleans, La. 70114; Great Rd. and Drakes Corner, Princeton, N.J. 08540; Cresci Blvd., Hazlet, N.J. 07730 (vice province).

Marist Sisters, Congregation of Mary, S.M.: Founded 1824, in France. General motherhouse, Rome, Italy; U.S. convents: St. Albert the Great, Dearborn Hts., Mich. 48125; St. Barnabas, E. Detroit, Mich. 48021; Our Lady of Peace, Wheeling, W. Va. 26002.

Maronite Antonine Sisters: Established in U.S., 1966. U.S. address, 2961 N. Lipkey Rd., R.D. 2, North Jackson, Ohio 44451.

Martha of Prince Edward Island, Sisters of St., C.S.M.: Founded 1916, in Canada; in U.S., 1961. General motherhouse, 141 Mt. Edward Rd., Charlottetown, P.E.I., CIA 7M8, Canada.

Marthe, Sisters of Sainte (of St. Hyacinthe), S.M.S.H.: Founded 1883, in Canada; in U.S., 1929. General motherhouse 675 ouest, rue St.-Pierre, Hyacinthe, Que., Canada J2T IN7.

Mary, Company of, O.D.N.: Founded 1607, in France; in U.S., 1926. General motherhouse, Rome, Italy; U.S. motherhouse, 16791 E. Main St., Tustin, Calif. 92680.

Mary, Daughters of the Heart of, D.H.M.: Founded 1790, in France; in U.S., 1851. Generalate, Paris, France; U.S. provincialate, 1339 Northampton St., Holyoke, Mass. 01040. Education retreat work.

Mary, Little Company of, Nursing Sisters, L.C.M.: Founded 1877, in England; in U.S., 1893. General motherhouse, Rome, Italy; U.S. provincial house, 9350 S. California Ave., Evergreen Park, Ill. 60642.

Mary, Missionary Sisters of the Society of

(Marist Sisters), S.M.S.M.: Founded 1845, at St. Brieuc, France; in U.S., 1922. General motherhouse, Rome, Italy; U.S. regional house, 357 Grove St., Waltham, Mass. 02154. Foreign missions.

Mary, Servants of, O.S.M.: Founded 13th century, in Italy; in U.S., 1893. Generalate, Rome, Italy; U.S. provincial motherhouse, 7400 Military Ave., Omaha, Nebr. 68134.

Mary, Servants of (Servite Sisters), O.S.M.: Founded 13th century, in Italy; in U.S., 1912. General motherhouse, Our Lady of Sorrows Convent, Ladysmith, Wis. 54848.

Mary, Servants of, of Blue Island, O.S.M.: Founded 1861, in Italy; in U.S., 1916. Generalate, Rome, Italy; U.S. motherhouse, 13811 S. Western Ave., Blue Island, Ill. 60406. Educational work.

Mary, Sisters of St., of Oregon, S.S.M.O.: Founded 1886, in Oregon, by Bishop William H. Gross, C.Ss.R. General motherhouse, 4440 S.W. 148th Ave., Beaverton, Ore. 97007. Educational, nursing work.

Mary, Sisters Servants of (Trained Nurses), S.M.: Founded 1851, at Madrid, Spain; in U.S., 1914. General motherhouse, Rome, Italy; U.S. motherhouse, 800 N. 18th St., Kansas City, Kans. 66102. Home nursing.

Mary and Joseph, Daughters of, D.M.J.: Founded 1817, in Belgium; in U.S., 1926. Generalate, Rome, Italy; American novitiate, 6037 W. 78th St., Los Angeles, Calif. 90045.

Mary Help of Christians, Daughters of (Salesian Sisters of St. John Bosco), F.M.A.: Founded 1872, in Italy, by St. John Bosco and St. Mary Dominic Mazzarello; in U.S., 1908. General motherhouse, Rome, Italy; U.S. motherhouse, Haledon, N.J. 07508. Education, youth work.

Mary Immaculate, Daughters of (Marianist Sisters), F.M.I.: Founded 1816, in France, by Very Rev. William-Joseph Chaminade. General motherhouse, Rome, Italy; U.S. foundation, 251 W. Ligustrum Dr., San Antonio, Tex. 78228. Educational work.

Mary Immaculate, Religious of, R.M.I.: Founded 1876, in Spain; in U.S., 1954. General motherhouse, Rome, Italy; U.S. foundations, 719 Augusta St., San Antonio, Tex. 78215; 539 W. 54th St., New York, N.Y. 10019.

Mary Immaculate, Sisters Servants of, S.M.I: Founded 1892, in Ukraine; in U.S., 1935. General motherhouse, Rome, Italy; U.S. province, Immaculate Conception Province, Table Rock, Sloatsburg, N.Y. 10974. Educational, hospital work.

Mary Immaculate of Mariowka, Sister Servants of, S.S.M.I.: Founded 1878 in Poland. General motherhouse, Poland; American provincialate, 1220 Tugwell Dr., Catonsville, Md. 21228.

Mary of Namur, Sisters of St., S.S.M.N.: Founded 1819, at Namur, Belgium; in U.S., 1863. General motherhouse, Namur, Belgium. U.S. provinces: 3756 Delaware Ave., Kenmore, N.Y. 14217; 3300 Hemphill St., Ft. Worth, Tex. 76110.

Mary of Providence, Daughters of St., D.S.M.P.: Founded 1872, at Como, Italy; in U.S., 1913. General motherhouse, Rome, Italy; U.S. provincial house, 4200 N. Austin Ave., Chicago, Ill.

60634. Special education for mentally handicapped.

Mary of the Immaculate Conception, Daughters of, D.M.: Founded 1904, in U.S., by Msgr. Lucian Bojnowski. General motherhouse, 314 Osgood Ave., New Britain, Conn. 06053. Educational, hospital work.

Mary Reparatrix, Society of, S.M.R.: Founded 1857, in France; in U.S., 1908. Generalate, Rome, Italy. U.S. province, 14 E. 29th St., New York, N.Y. 10016.

Medical Mission Sisters (Society of Catholic Medical Missionaries, Inc.), S.C.M.M.: Founded 1925, in U.S., by Mother Anna Dengel. Generalate, Rome, Italy; U.S. headquarters, 8400 Pine Rd., Philadelphia, Pa. 19111. Medical work, health education, especially in mission areas.

Medical Missionaries of Mary, M.M.M.: Founded 1937, in Ireland, by Mother Mary Martin; in U.S., 1950. General motherhouse, Drogheda, Ireland; U.S. headquarters, 563 Minneford Ave., City Island, Bronx, N.Y. 10464. Medical aid in missions.

Mercedarian Missionaries of Berriz, M.M.B.: Founded 1930, in Spain; in U.S., 1946. General motherhouse, Rome, Italy. U.S. headquarters, 918 E. 9th St., Kansas City, Mo. 64106.

Mercy, Daughters of Our Lady of, D.M.: Founded 1837, in Italy, by St. Mary Joseph Rossello; in U.S., 1919. General motherhouse, Savona, Italy; U.S. motherhouse, Villa Rossello, Catawba Ave., Newfield, N.J. 08344. Educational, hospital work.

Mercy, Missionary Sisters of Our Lady of, M.O.M.: Founded 1938, in Brazil; in U.S., 1955. General motherhouse, Brazil; U.S. address, 388 Franklin St., Buffalo, N.Y. 14202.

Mercy, Sisters of, R.S.M.: Founded 1831, in Ireland, by Mother Mary Catherine McAuley. U.S. motherhouses:

634 New Scotland Ave., Albany, N.Y. 12208; 273 Willoughby Ave., Brooklyn, N.Y. 11205; S. 5245 Murphy Rd., Orchard Park, N.Y. 14127; 100 Mansfield Ave., Burlington, Vt. 05401; 1125 Prairie Dr., N.E., Cedar Rapids, Ia. 52402; 444 E. Grandview Blvd., Erie, Pa. 16504; 249 Steele Rd., W. Hartford, Conn. 06117.

Windham, N.H. 03087; Merion, Pa. 10966; 3333 Fifth Ave., Pittsburgh, Pa. 15213; 605 Stevens Ave., Portland, Me. 04103; Belmont, N. Car. 28012; 1437 Blossom Rd., Rochester, N.Y. 14610; 535 Sacramento St., Auburn, Calif. 95603.

2300 Adeline Dr., Burlingame, Calif. 94010; U.S. Route 22 at Terrill Rd., Plainfield, N.J. 07061; 101 Barry Rd., Worcester, Mass. 01609.

Mercy, Sisters of, of the Union in the United States of America, R.S.M.: Founded 1831 in Ireland, by Mother M. Catherine McAuley; union formed in 1929. U.S. provinces:

P.O. Box 11448, Baltimore, Md. 21239; 10024 S. Central Park Ave., Chicago, Ill. 60642; 2301 Grandview Ave., Cincinnati, Ohio 45206; 29000 Eleven Mile Rd., Farmington Hills, Mich. 48024; 541 Broadway, Dobbs Ferry, N.Y. 10522; 1801 S. 72nd St., Omaha, Nebr. 68124; R.D. 3, Cumberland, R.I. 02864; 2039 N. Geyer Rd., St. Louis, Mo. 63131; Dallas, Pa. 18612.

Mercy, Sisters of, Daughters of Christian Chari-

ty of St. Vincent de Paul, S.M.D.C.: Founded 1842, in Hungary; U.S. foundation, Rt. 1, Box 353, Hewitt, N.J. 07421.

Mercy of the Blessed Sacrament, Sisters of: Founded 1910 in Mexico. U.S. foundation, 555 E. Mountain View, Barstow, Calif. 92311.

Mill Hill Sisters; See Franciscan Missionaries of St. Joseph.

Minim Sisters of Mary Immaculate, C.F.M.M.: Founded 1886, in Mexico; in U.S. 1926. General motherhouse, Leon, Guanajuato, Mexico; U.S. address, St. Joseph Hospital Convent, Target Range Rd., Nogales, Ariz. 85621.

Misericordia Sisters, S.M.: Founded 1848, in Canada; in U.S., 1887. General motherhouse. 12435 Ave. Misericorde, Montreal H4J 2G3, Canada. Social work with unwed mothers and their children; hospital work.

Mission Helpers of the Sacred Heart, M.H.S.H.: Founded 1890, in U.S. General motherhouse, 1001 W. Joppa Rd., Baltimore, Md. 21204. Religious education, evangelization.

Missionary Catechists of the Sacred Hearts of Jesus and Mary (Violetas), M.C.: Founded 1918, in Mexico; in U.S., 1943. Motherhouse, Tlalpan, Mexico; U.S. address, 209 W. Murray St., Victoria, Tex. 77901.

Missionary Sisters of the Catholic Apostolate (Pallottine Missionary Sisters), S.A.C.: Founded in Rome, 1843; in U.S., 1912. Generalate, Rome, Italy; U.S. provincialate, Rt. 2, 15270 Old Halls Ferry Rd., Florissant, Mo. 63034.

Mother of God, Missionary Sisters of the, M.S.M.G.: Byzantine, Ukrainian Rite, Stamford. Motherhouse, 711-719 N. Franklin St., Philadelphia, Pa. 19123.

Mother of God, Sisters Poor Servants of the, S.M.G.: Founded 1869, at London, England; in U.S., 1947. General motherhouse, Maryfield, Roehampton, London. U.S. addresses: Maryfield Nursing Home, Greensboro Rd., High Point, N.C. 27260; St. Mary's Hospital, 916 Virginia Ave., Norton, Va. 24273; Holy Spirit School, 1800 Geary St., Philadelphia, Pa. 19145. Hospital, educational work.

Nazareth, Poor Sisters of: Founded in England; U.S. foundation, 1924. General motherhouse, Hammersmith, London, England; U.S. novitiate, 3333 Manning Ave., Los Angeles, Calif. 90064. Social services, education.

Notre Dame, School Sisters of, S.S.N.D.: Founded 1833, in Germany; in U.S., 1847. General motherhouse, Rome, Italy. U.S. provinces: 700 W. Highland Rd., Mequon, Wis. 53092; 6401 N. Charles St., Baltimore, Md. 21212; 320 E. Ripa Ave., St. Louis, Mo. 63125; Good Counsel Hill, Mankato, Minn. 56001; 345 Belden Hill Rd., Wilton, Conn. 06897; 1451 E. Northgate, Irving, Tex. 75062; 1431 Euclid Ave., Berwyn, Ill. 60402.

Notre Dame, Sisters of, S.N.D.: Founded 1850, at Coesfeld, Germany; in U.S., 1874. General motherhouse, Rome, Italy. U.S. provinces: 13000 Auburn Rd., Chardon, O. 44024; 1601 Dixie Highway, Covington, Ky. 41011; 3837 Secor Rd., Toledo, O. 43623; 1776 Hendrix Ave., Thousand Oaks, Calif. 91360.

Notre Dame, Sisters of the Congregation of, C.N.D.: Founded 1653, in Canada; in U.S., 1860. General motherhouse, Montreal, Que., Canada; U.S. province, 223 West Mountain Rd., Ridgefield, Conn. 06877. Education.

Notre Dame de Namur, Sisters of, S.N.D.: Founded 1803, in France; in U.S., 1840. General motherhouse, Rome, Italy. U.S. provinces: 328 Dartmouth St., Boston, Mass. 02116; Jeffrey's Neck Rd., Ipswich, Mass. 01938; 1561 N. Benson Rd., Fairfield, Conn. 06431; Landing Rd., Ilchester, Md. 21083; 701 E. Columbia Ave., Cincinnati, O. 45215; 14800 Bohlman Rd., Saratoga, Calif. 95070. Educational work.

Notre Dame de Sion, Congregation of, N.D.S.: Founded 1843, in France; in U.S., 1892. Generalate, Rome, Italy; U.S. provincial house, 3823 Locust St., Kansas City, Mo. 64109. Creation of better understanding and relations between Christians and Jews.

Notre Dame des Anges, Missionary Sisters of, M.N.D.A.: Founded 1922, in Canada; in U.S., 1949. General motherhouse, Lennoxville, Canada; U.S. address, St. Mary's Catechetical School, 320 N. Main St., Union City, Conn. 06770.

Notre Dame Sisters: Founded 1853, in Czechoslovakia; in U.S., 1910. General motherhouse, Javornik, Czechoslovakia; U.S. motherhouse, 3501 State St., Omaha, Nebr. 68112. Educational work.

Our Lady of Charity, North American Union of Sisters of, Eudist Sisters (Sisters of Our Lady of Charity of the Refuge), O.L.C.: Founded 1641, in Caen, France, by St. John Eudes; in U.S., 1855. Autonomous houses were federated in 1944 and in May, 1978, the North American Union of the Sisters of Our Lady of Charity was established. General motherhouse and administrative center, Box 327, Wisconsin Dells, Wis. 53965. Primarily devoted to re-education and rehabilitation of women and girls in residential and non-residential settings.

Our Lady of Mercy, Sisters of: General motherhouse, Wexford, Ireland; U.S. foundation, St. Peter's Convent, 445 W. New York Ave., DeLand, Fla. 32720.

Our Lady of Sorrows, Sisters of, O.L.S.: Founded 1839, in Italy; in U.S., 1947. General motherhouse, Rome, Italy; U.S. headquarters, 10450 Ellerbe Rd., Shreveport, La. 71106.

Our Lady of the Garden, Sisters of, O.L.G.: Founded 1829, in Italy, by St. Anthony Mary Gianelli. Motherhouse, Rome, Italy; U.S. address, St. Brendan School, 445½ Whalley Ave., New Haven, Conn. 06511.

Pallottine Sisters of the Catholic Apostolate, C.S.A.C.: Founded 1843, at Rome, Italy; in U.S., 1889. General motherhouse, Rome; U.S. motherhouse, St. Patrick's Villa, Harriman Heights, Harriman, N.Y. 10926. Educational work.

Parish Visitors of Mary Immaculate, P.V.M.I.: Founded 1920, in New York. General motherhouse, Box 658, Monroe, N.Y. 10950. Mission work.

Passionist Sisters: See Cross and Passion, Sisters of the.

Paul, Angelic Sisters of St.: Founded 1535, in Milan, Italy; U.S. address, Fatima Shrine, Swan Rd., Youngstown, N.Y. 14174.

Paul, Daughters of St. (Missionary Sisters of the Media of Communication), D.S.P.: Founded 1915, at Alba, Piedmont, Italy; in U.S., 1932. General motherhouse, Rome, Italy; U.S. provincial house, 50 St. Paul's Ave., Jamaica Plain, Mass. 02130. Apostolate of the communications arts.

Paul of Chartres, Sisters of St., S.P.C.: Founded 1696, in France. General house, Rome, Italy; U.S. address, County Road 492, Marquette, Mich. 49855.

Peter Claver, Missionary Sisters of St., S.S.P.C.: Founded 1894; in U.S., 1914. General motherhouse, Rome, Italy; U.S. address, 667 Woods Mill Rd. S., Chesterfield, Mo. 63017.

Pious Schools, Sisters of, Sch. P.: Founded 1829 in Spain; in U.S., 1954. General motherhouse, Rome, Italy; U.S. headquarters, 9925 Mason Ave., Chatsworth, Calif. 91311.

Poor, Little Sisters of the, L.S.P.: Founded 1839, in France; in U.S., 1868. General motherhouse, St. Pern, France. U.S. provinces: 110-30 221st St., Queens Village, N.Y. 11429; 601 Maiden Choice Lane, Baltimore, Md. 21228; 2325 N. Lakewood Ave.; Chicago, Ill. 60614. Care of aged.

Poor Clare Missionary Sisters (Misioneras Clarisas), M.C.: Founded Mexico. General motherhouse, Rome, Italy; U.S. novitiate, 1019 N. Newhope, Santa Ana, Calif. 92703.

Poor Clare Nuns: See Franciscan Poor Clare Nuns.

Poor Clares (Sisters of St. Clare), P.C.: General motherhouse, Dublin, Ireland; U.S. foundation, 37 E. Emerson, Chula Vista, Calif. 92011.

Poor Handmaids of Jesus Christ (Ancilla Domini Sisters), P.H.J.C.: Founded 1851, in Germany; in U.S., 1868. General motherhouse, Dernbach, Westerwald, Germany; U.S. motherhouse, Donaldson, Ind. 46513. Educational, hospital work, social services.

Precious Blood, Daughters of Charity of the Most: Founded 1872, at Pagani, Italy; in U.S., 1908. General motherhouse, Rome, Italy; U.S. convent, 1482 North Ave., Bridgeport, Conn. 06604.

Precious Blood, Missionary Sisters of the, C.P.S.: Founded 1885, at Mariannhill, South Africa; in U.S., 1925. Generalate, Rome, Italy: U.S. novitiate, New Holland Ave., P.O. Box 97, Shillington, Pa. 19607. Home and foreign mission work.

Precious Blood, Sisters Adorers of the, A.P.B.: Founded 1861, in Canada; in U.S., 1890. General motherhouses: 2520, rue Girouard, St. Hyacinthe, Que. J2S 7B8, Canada (French); 301 Ramsay Rd., London, Ont. N6G 1N7, Canada (English). Contemplatives.

Precious Blood, Sisters of the, C.Pp.S.: Founded 1834, in Switzerland; in U.S., 1844. Generalate, 4000 Denlinger Rd., Dayton, Ohio 45426. Education, health care, other ministries.

Precious Blood, Sisters of the Most, C.Pp.S.: Founded 1845, in Steinerberg, Switzerland; in U.S., 1870. General motherhouse, 204 N. Main St., O'Fallon, Mo. 63366. Education, other ministries.

Presentation, Sisters of St. Mary of the, S.M.P.: Founded 1829, in France; in U.S., 1903. General motherhouse, Broons, Cotes-du-Nord, France. U.S. address, Maryvale Novitiate, Valley City, N. Dak. 58072. Educational, hospital work.

Presentation of Mary, Sisters of the, P.M.: Founded 1796, in France; in U.S., 1873. General motherhouse, Castel Gandolfo, Italy. U.S. provincial houses: 495 Mammoth Rd., Manchester, N.H. 03104; 209 Lawrence St., Methuen, Mass. 01844.

Presentation of the B.V.M., Sisters of the, P.B.V.M.: Founded 1775, in Ireland; in U.S., 1854, in San Francisco. U.S. motherhouses: 2360 Carter Rd., Dubuque, Ia. 52001; R.D. 2, Box 101, Newburgh, N.Y. 12550; 8931 Callaghan Rd., San Antonio, Tex. 78230; 2340 Turk Blvd., San Francisco, Calif. 94118; Watervliet, N.Y. 12189.

Route 1, Fargo, N. Dak. 58103; 250 S. Davis Dr., P.O. Box 1113, Warner Robbins, Ga. 31093; 1500 N. Main, Aberdeen, S. Dak. 57401; 1300 E. Cedar, Globe, Ariz. 85501; 1555 E. Dana, Mesa, Ariz. 85201; 366 South St., Fitchburg, Mass. 01420; 419 Woodrow Rd., Annadale, Staten Island, N.Y. 10312.

Providence, Daughters of Divine, F.D.P.: Founded 1832, Italy; in U.S., 1964. General motherhouse, Rome, Italy; U.S. address, 1625 Missouri St., Chalmette, La. 70043.

Providence, Missionary Catechists of Divine, M.C.D.P.: Founded 1930, as a filial society; adjunct branch of Sisters of Divine Providence (Helotes, Tex.). Motherhouse, 2318 Castroville Rd., San Antonio, Tex. 78237.

Providence, Oblate Sisters of, O.S.P.: Founded 1829, in U.S. General motherhouse, 701 Gun Rd., Baltimore, Md. 21227. Educational work.

Providence, Sisters of, S.P.: Founded 1861, in Canada; in U.S., 1873. General motherhouse, Our Lady of Victory Convent, Brightside, Holyoke, Mass. 01040.

Providence, Sisters of, S.P.: Founded 1843, in Canada; in U.S., 1854. General motherhouse, Montreal, Canada. U.S. provinces: 1511 Third Ave., Seattle, Wash. 98101; 9 E. 9th Ave., Spokane, Wash. 99202.

Providence, Sisters of (of St. Mary-of-the-Woods), S.P.: Founded 1806, in France; in U.S., 1840. Generalate, St. Mary-of-the-Woods, Ind. 47876.

Providence, Sisters of Divine, C.D.P.: Founded 1762, in France; in U.S., 1866. Generalate, Box 197, Helotes, Tex. 78023. Educational, hospital work.

Providence, Sisters of Divine, C.D.P.: Founded 1851, in Germany; in U.S., 1876. Generalate, Rome, Italy. U.S. provinces: 9000 Babcock Blvd., Allison Park, Pa. 15101; 8351 Florissant Rd., St. Louis, Mo. 63121; Box 2, Rte. 80, Kingston, Mass. 02364. Educational, hospital work.

Providence, Sisters of Divine (of Kentucky), C.D.P.: Founded 1762, in France; in U.S., 1889. General motherhouse, Moselle, France; U.S. province, Melbourne, Ky. 41059. Education, social services, other ministries.

Redeemer, Oblates of the Most Holy, O.SS.R.: Founded 1864, in Spain. General motherhouse, Spain; U.S. foundation, 60-80 Pond St., Jamaica Plain, Mass. 02130.

Redeemer, Order of the Most Holy, O.SS.R.: Founded 1731, by St. Alphonsus Liguori; in U.S.,

1957. U.S. addresses: Mother of Perpetual Help Monastery, Esopus, N.Y. 12429; St. Alphonsus Monastery, Liguori, Mo. 63057.

Redeemer, Sisters of the Divine, S.D.R.: Founded 1849, in Niederbronn, France; in U.S., 1912. General motherhouse, Rome, Italy; U.S. province, 999 Rock Run Road, Elizabeth, Pa. 15037. Educational, hospital work; care of the aged.

Redeemer, Sisters of the Holy, S.H.R.: Founded 1849, in Alsace; in U.S., 1924. General motherhouse, Wuerzburg, Germany; U.S. provincial house, Huntingdon Valley, Pa. 19006. Personalized medical care in hospitals, homes for aged, private homes; retreat work.

Reparation of the Congregation of Mary, Sisters of, S.R.C.M.: Founded 1903, in U.S. Motherhouse, St. Zita's Villa, Monsey, N.Y. 10952.

Resurrection, Sisters of the, C.R.: Founded 1891, in Italy; in U.S., 1900. General motherhouse, Rome, Italy. U.S. provinces: 7432 Talcott Ave., Chicago, Ill. 60631; Mt. St. Joseph, Castleton-on-Hudson, N.Y. 12033. Education, nursing.

Rita, Sisters of St., O.S.A.: General motherhouse, Wurzburg, Germany. U.S. foundation, St. Monica's Convent, 3920 Green Bay Rd., Racine, Wis. 53404.

Rosary, Congregation of Our Lady of the Holy, R.S.R.: Founded 1874, in Canada; in U.S., 1899. General motherhouse, C.P. 2020, Rimouski, Que., Canada. U.S. regional house, 20 Thomas St., Portland, Me. 04102. Educational work.

Rosary, Missionary Sisters of Our Lady of the Holy, H.R.S.: Founded 1924, in Ireland; in U.S., 1954. Motherhouse, Dublin, Ireland. U.S. regional address, P.O. Box 304, Bryn Mawr, Pa. 19010. African missions.

Sacrament, Missionary Sisters of the Most Blessed, M.SS.S.: General motherhouse, Madrid, Spain; U.S. foundation: 1111 Wordin Ave., Bridgeport, Conn. 06605.

Sacrament, Nuns of the Perpetual Adoration of the Blessed, A.P.: Founded 1807, in Rome, Italy; in U.S., 1925. U.S. monasteries: 145 N. Cotton Ave., El Paso, Tex. 79901; 771 Ashbury St., San Francisco, Calif. 94117.

Sacrament, Oblate Sisters of the Blessed, O.S.B.S.: Founded 1935, in U.S.; motherhouse, St. Sylvester Convent, Marty, S.D. 57361. Care of American Indians.

Sacrament, Religious Sisters of the Blessed, R.M.S.S.: Founded 1910, in Mexico; in U.S., 1926. General motherhouse, Mexico City, Mexico; U.S. convent, 222 W. Cevallos St., San Antonio, Tex. 78204.

Sacrament, Servants of the Blessed, S.S.S.: Founded 1858, in France, by St. Pierre Julien Eymard; in U.S., 1947. General motherhouse, Rome, Italy; American vice-provincial house, 101 Silver St., Waterville, Me. 04901. Contemplative.

Sacrament, Sisters of the Blessed, for Indians and Colored People, S.B.S.: Founded 1891, in U.S. General motherhouse, Bensalem, Pa. 19020.

Sacrament, Sisters of the Most Holy, M.H.S.: Founded 1851, in France; in U.S., 1872. General motherhouse, 409 W. St. Mary Blvd. (P.O. Box 2429), Lafayette, La. 70502.

Sacrament, Sisters Servants of the Blessed, S.S.B.S.: Founded 1904, in Mexico. General motherhouse, Guadalajara, Mexico. U.S. address, Our Lady of Guadalupe School, 536 Rockwood Ave., Calexico, Calif. 92231.

Sacramentine Nuns (Religious of the Order of the Blessed Sacrament and Our Lady), O.S.S.: Founded 1639, in France; in U.S., 1912. U.S. monasteries: 23 Park Ave., Yonkers, N.Y. 10703; US 31, Conway, Mich. 49722. Perpetual adoration of the Holy Eucharist.

Sacred Heart, Daughters of Our Lady of the: Founded 1882, in France; in U.S., 1955. General motherhouse, Rome, Italy; U.S. address, 424 E. Browning Rd., Bellmawr, N.J. 08031. Educational work.

Sacred Heart, Missionary Sisters of the (Cabrini Sisters), M.S.C.: Founded 1880, in Italy, by St. Frances Xavier Cabrini; in U.S., 1889. General motherhouse, Rome, Italy; U.S. provinces: 223 E. 19th St., New York, N.Y. 10003 (Eastern); 434 W. Deming Pl., Chicago, Ill. 60614 (Western). Educational, health, social and catechetical work.

Sacred Heart, Religious of the Apostolate of the, R.A.: General motherhouse, Madrid, Spain; U.S. address, 1120 6th St., Miami Beach, Fla., 33139.

Sacred Heart, Society Devoted to the, S.D.S.H.: Founded 1940, in Hungary; in U.S., 1956. U.S. motherhouse, 2121 W. Olive Dr., Burbank, Calif. 91506. Educational work.

Sacred Heart, Society of the, R.S.C.J.: Founded 1800, in France; in U.S., 1818. General motherhouse, Rome, Italy. U.S. provincial house, 4389 W. Pine Blvd., St. Louis, Mo. 63108. Educational work.

Sacred Heart of Jesus, Apostles of, A.S.C.J.: Founded 1894, in Italy; in U.S., 1902. General motherhouse, Rome, Italy; U.S. motherhouse, 265 Benham St., Hamden, Conn. 06514. Educational, social work.

Sacred Heart of Jesus, Handmaids of the, A.C.J.: Founded 1877, in Spain. General motherhouse, Rome, Italy; U.S. province, 616 Coopertown Rd., Haverford, Pa. 19041. Educational, retreat work.

Sacred Heart of Jesus, Missionary Sisters of the Most (Hiltrup), M.S.C.: Founded 1899, in Germany; in U.S., 1908. General motherhouse, Rome, Italy; U.S. province, Hyde Park, Reading, Pa. 19605. Education, health care, pastoral ministry.

Sacred Heart of Jesus, Oblate Sisters of the, O.S.H.J.: Founded 1894; in U.S., 1949. General motherhouse, Rome, Italy; U.S. headquarters, 50 Warner Rd., Hubbard, Ohio 44425. Educational, social work.

Sacred Heart of Jesus, Servants of the Most: Founded 1894, in Poland; in U.S., 1959. General motherhouse, Cracow, Poland; U.S. address, 231 Arch St., Cresson, Pa. 16630. Education, health care, social services.

Sacred Heart of Jesus, Sisters of the, S.S.C.J.: Founded 1816, in France; in U.S., 1903. General motherhouse, St. Jacut, Brittany, France; U.S. provincial house, 5922 Blanco Rd., San Antonio,

Tex. 78216. Educational, hospital, domestic work.

Sacred Heart of Jesus and of the Poor, Servants of the (Mexican), S.S.H.J.P.: Founded 1885, in Mexico; in U.S., 1907. General motherhouse, Apartado 92, Puebla, Pue., Mexico; U.S. regional house, 237 Tobin Pl., El Paso, Tex. 79905.

Sacred Heart of Jesus for Reparation, Congregation of the Handmaids of the: Founded 1918, in Italy; in U.S., 1958. U.S. address, Sunshine Park, R.D. 3, Steubenville, Ohio 43952.

Sacred Heart of Mary, Religious of the, R.S.H.M.: Founded 1848, in France; in U.S., 1877. Generalate, Rome, Italy. U.S. provinces: 50 Wilson Park Dr., Tarrytown, N.Y. 10591; 8008 Loyola Blvd., Los Angeles, Calif. 90045.

Sacred Hearts, Religious of the Holy Union of the, S.U.S.C.: Founded 1826, in France; in U.S., 1886. Generalate, Rome, Italy. U.S. provinces: 550 Rock St., Fall River, Mass. 02720; Main St., Groton, Mass. 01450. Varied ministries.

Sacred Hearts and of Perpetual Adoration, Sisters of the, SS.CC.: Founded 1797, in France; in U.S., 1908. General motherhouse, Rome, Italy; U.S. provincial house, 53 Ocean St., New Bedford, Mass. 02740. Varied ministries.

Sacred Hearts of Jesus and Mary, Sisters of the, S.H.J.M.: Established 1953, in U.S. General motherhouse, Essex, England; U.S. address, 310 San Carlos Ave., El Cerrito, Calif. 94530.

Savior, Company of the, C.S.: Founded 1952, in Spain; in U.S., 1962. General motherhouse, Madrid, Spain; U.S. foundation, 820 Clinton Ave., Bridgeport, Conn. 06608.

Savior, Sisters of the Divine, S.D.S.: Founded 1888, in Italy; in U.S., 1895. General motherhouse, Rome, Italy; U.S. province, 4311 N. 100th St., Milwaukee, Wis. 53222. Educational, hospital work.

Social Service, Sisters of, S.S.S.: Founded in Hungary, 1923, by Sr. Margaret Slachta. U.S. address, 440 Linwood Ave., Buffalo, N.Y. 14209. Social work.

Social Service, Sisters of, of Los Angeles, S.S.S.: Founded 1908, in Hungary; in U.S., 1926. General motherhouse, 1120 Westchester Pl., Los Angeles, Calif. 90019.

Teresa of Jesus, Society of St., S.T.J.: Founded 1876, in Spain; in U.S., 1910. General motherhouse, Rome, Italy; U.S. provincial house, 154 Fair Ave., San Antonio, Tex. 78223.

Thomas of Villanova, Congregation of Sisters of St., S.S.T.V.: Founded 1661, in France; in U.S., 1948. General motherhouse, Neuilly-sur-Seine, France; U.S. foundation W. Rocks Rd., Norwalk, Conn. 06851.

Trinity, Missionary Servants of the Most Blessed, M.S.B.T.: Founded 1912, in U.S., by Very Rev. Thomas A. Judge. General motherhouse, 3501 Solly St., Philadelphia, Pa. 19136. Educational, social work; health services.

Trinity, Sisters of the Most Holy, O.Ss.T.: Founded 1198, in Rome; in U.S., 1920. General motherhouse, Rome, Italy; U.S. address, Immaculate Conception Province, 21320 Euclid Ave., Euclid, Ohio 44117. Educational work.

Ursula of the Blessed Virgin, Society of the Sisters of St., S.U.: Founded 1606, in France; in U.S.,

1902. General motherhouse, France; U.S. novitiate, Rhinebeck, N.Y. 12572. Educational work.

Ursuline Nuns (Roman Union), O.S.U.: Founded 1535, in Italy; in U.S., 1727. Generalate, Rome, Italy. U.S. provinces: 323 E. 198th St., Bronx, N.Y. 10458; Crystal Heights Rd., Crystal City, Mo. 63019; 639 Angela Dr., Santa Rosa, Calif. 95401; 71 Lowder St., Dedham, Mass. 02026,

Ursuline Nuns of the Congregation of Paris, O.S.U.: Founded 1535, in Italy; in U.S., 1727, in New Orleans. U.S. motherhouses: St. Martin, O. 45170; East and Miami Sts., Paola, Kans. 66071; 3115 Lexington Rd., Louisville, Ky. 40206; 2600 Lander Rd., Cleveland, O. 44124; Maple Mount, Ky. 42356; 2413 Collingwood Blvd., Toledo, O. 43620; 4250 Shields Rd., Canfield, O. 44406; 1339 E. McMillan St., Cincinnati, O. 45206.

Ursuline Nuns of the Congregation of Tildonk, Belgium, R.U.: Founded 1535, in Italy; in U.S., 1924. Generalate, Tildonk, Belgium; U.S. address, 81-15 Utopia Parkway, Jamaica, N.Y. 11432. Educational, foreign mission work.

Ursuline Sisters, O.S.U.: Founded 1535, in Italy; in U.S., 1910. General motherhouse, Mount Calvary, Germany; U.S. motherhouse, 1026 N. Douglas Ave., Belleville, Ill. 62221. Educational work.

Ursuline Sisters (Irish Ursuline Union), O.S.U.: General motherhouse, Blackrock, Cork, Ireland; U.S. address, 1973 Torch Hill Rd., Columbus, Ga. 31903.

Venerini Sisters, Religious, M.P.V.: Founded 1685, in Italy; in U.S., 1909. General motherhouse, Rome, Italy; U.S. provincialate; 23 Edward St., Worcester, Mass. 01605.

Victory Missionary Sisters, Our Lady of, O.L.V.M.: Founded 1922, in U.S. Motherhouse, Victory Noll, Box 109, Huntington, Ind. 46750. Educational, social work.

Vincent de Paul, Sisters: See Charity of St. Vincent de Paul, Sisters of.

Visitation Nuns, V.H.M.: Founded 1610, in France; in U.S. (Georgetown, D.C.), 1799. Contemplative, educational work. Two federations in U.S.

First Federation of North America. Major pontifical enclosure. Pres., Mother Mary Gabriella Muth, Monastery of the Visitation, 9001 Old Georgetown Rd., Bethesda, Md. 20014. Addresses of monasteries belonging to the federation: 2300

Springhill Ave., Mobile, Ala. 36607; 9001 Old Georgetown Rd., Bethesda, Md. 20014; 2002 Bancroft Pkwy., Wilmington, Del. 19806; 2209 E. Grace St., Richmond, Va. 23223; 5820 City Ave., Philadelphia, Pa. 19131; 1745 Parkside Blvd., Toledo, O. 43607; 2055 Ridgedale Dr., Snellville, Ga. 30278.

Second Federation of North America. Constitutional enclosure. Pres., Rev. Mother Anne Madeline Ernstmann, Visitation Monastery, 3200 S.W. Dash Point Rd., Federal Way, Wash. 98003. Addresses of monasteries belonging to the federation: 1500 35th St., Washington, D.C. 20007; 3020 N. Ballas Rd., St. Louis, Mo. 63131; 200 E. Second St., Frederick, Md. 21701; Mt. St. Chantal Monastery of the Visitation, Wheeling, W. Va. 26003; Ridge Blvd. and 89th St., Brooklyn, N.Y. 11209; 1600 Murdock Ave., Parkersburg, W. Va. 26101; 2000 Sixteenth Ave., Rock Island, Ill. 61201; 2475 Dodd Rd., Mendota Heights, St. Paul, Minn. 55120; Visitation Monastery, Georgetown, Ky. 40324; 3200 S.W. Dash Point Rd., Federal Way, Wash. 98003.

Visitation of the Congregation of the Immaculate Heart of Mary, Sisters of the, S.V.M.: Founded 1952, in U.S. Motherhouse, 900 Alta Vista St., Dubuque, Ia. 52001. Educational work, parish ministry.

Vocationist Sisters (Sisters of the Divine Vocations): Founded 1921, in Italy. General motherhouse, Naples, Italy; U.S. foundation, Perpetual Help Nursery, 172 Broad St., Newark, N.J. 07104.

White Sisters: See Africa, Missionary Sisters of Our Lady of.

Wisdom, Daughters of, D.W.: Founded 1703, in France, by St. Louis Marie Grignion de Montfort; in U.S., 1904. General motherhouse, Vendee, France; U.S. province, 385 S. Ocean Ave., Islip, N.Y. Education, health care, parish ministry, social services.

Xaverian Missionary Society of Mary, Inc., X.M.M.: Founded 1945, in Italy; in U.S., 1954. General motherhouse, Parma, Italy; U.S. address, 242 Salisbury St., Worcester, Mass. 01609.

Xavier Mission Sisters (Catholic Mission Sisters of St. Francis Xavier), X.M.S.: Founded 1946, at Warren, Mich., by Cardinal Edward Mooney. General motherhouse, 37179 Moravian Dr., Mount Clemens, Mich. 48043. Educational, hospital, social work in missions.

ORGANIZATIONS OF RELIGIOUS

Men

Conference of Major Superiors of Men: An association of major superiors of religious institutes of men, founded in 1956 and established officially Mar. 23, 1960, by decree of the Congregation for Religious and Secular Institutes. Its purposes are to assist religious to fulfill their proper prophetic role in the Church and the world; to provide liaison opportunities among religious and with church officials; to exert Christian influence through its operations, and to serve as a national voice for the corporate views of superiors. Conference membership consists of 263 major superiors of institutes with a combined total of approximately 30,000 members. The principal officers are Rev. Ronald Carignan, O.M.I., president, and Rev. Donald P. Skwor, S.D.S., executive director. The national office is located at 8808 Cameron St., Silver Spring, Md. 20910.

National Assembly of Religious Brothers: Founded in 1972 as a grassroots organization open to members of all-brother institutes as well as mixed institutes of priests and brothers. It is a service organization for its members and those affected by their apostolates. The primary objectives of the NARB are: to publicize the unique vocations of brothers, to encourage the development of the spiritual life of all brothers; to promote increased awareness among brothers of their ministerial power for good; to provide a corporate voice for brothers in shaping the future of religious life; to heighten their concern with and involvement in the needs of the Church and society; and to further communication among brothers and provide liaison with various organizations of the Church. Membership in the assembly is open to brothers in the U.S. and Canada. Sacred Heart Brother Adrian Gaudin is president of the assembly. Brother Gerard Clark, C.SS.R., executive secretary, is located at 1 Liguori Drive, P.O. Box 26, Liguori, Mo. 63057.

Women

Association of Contemplative Sisters: Founded by nearly 140 representatives of 57 communities in the U.S. and Canada in August, 1969. Its principal purpose is development of the contemplative lifestyle for effective service to the Church. It has a membership of approximately 400. Sister Annamae Dannes, O.C.D., is president. The central office is located at 3176 Fairmount Blvd., Cleveland Heights, O. 44118.

Consortium Perfectae Caritatis: Named Association of Perfect Love after the Latin title of the Second Vatican Council's *Decree on the Appropriate Renewal of Religious Life,* and organized in March, 1971, at a meeting of nearly 150 sisters from 48 communities in the U.S. and Canada. Its purposes are to encourage the development of religious life in line with Vatican II guidelines and related directives, and to share experiences in the renewal of religious life. Sister Mary Elise, S.N.D., is executive director. The association is administered by a group of 14 superiors from 12 states and Canada. The mailing address is 13000 Auburn Rd., Chardon, Ohio 44024. Rev. James A. Viall is coordinator.

Las Hermanas: A national organization of Hispanic women formed in 1971 for the purpose of being "actively present to the ever changing needs" of Hispanics in the U.S. through programs of cultural awareness, leadership training, peace and justice concerns. The organization, with non Hispanic associates, is directed by a national coordinating team consisting of Olga Villa-Parra and Sisters Veronica Mendez, R.C.D., and Sylvia Sedillo, S.L. The address is P.O. Box 4274, Denver, Colo., 80204.

Leadership Conference of Women Religious: An association of major superiors of religious communities of women, with the purpose of promoting the spiritual and apostolic calling and works of sisterhoods in the U.S. Organized in the late 50s and approved by the Congregation for Religious and Secular Institutes June 13, 1962, it has a membership of approximately 700. Its original name, changed in 1971, was the Conference of Major Superiors of Women. With its formerly affiliated Sister Formation Conference, it inaugurated measures for the religious and professional development of sisters and has contributed to the renewal of religious life in this country. Sister Helen Flaherty, S.C., is president; Sister Lora Ann Quinonez, C.D.P., is executive director. The national secretariat is located at 8808 Cameron St., Silver Spring, Md. 20910.

National Assembly of Religious Women: Formed in 1970 and with the title, National Assembly of Women Religious, until August, 1982, a movement of feminist women committed to prophetic tasks of giving witness, raising awareness, and engaging in public action and advocacy for justice. Membership is both organizational and individual. Sister Marjorie Tuite, O.P., is national coordinator. Offices are located at 1307 S. Wabash Ave., Chicago, Ill. 60605.

National Black Sisters' Conference: Organized in August, 1968, for the purposes of determining priorities in service to black people, of promoting black vocations and the development of religious life in the unique black life-style, and to influence the formational and recruitment practices of white religious communities. Its members include 700 black sisters belonging to 123 religious communities. Sister Marie de Porres Taylor, S.N.J.M., is the executive director. The mailing address of the conference is 6226 Camden St., Oakland, Calif. 94605.

National Coalition of American Nuns: Organized under the leadership of Sister Margaret Traxler, S.S.N.D., in July, 1969, for efforts to secure recognition and development of the role of women in the Church and society, along with advocacy for social activism. Sister Donna Quinn, O.P., is president. Offices are located at 1307 S. Wabash Ave., Chicago, Ill 60605.

National Sisters' Vocation Conference: Formed in September, 1970, as a national organization dedicated to promoting understanding of the role of women, especially religious, in the Church through work in the vocation apostolate. It coordinates and provides informational and other services to persons and organizations in the vocation apostolate, and assists prospective candidates for religious life. Its membership includes approximately 1,200 women and men. Sister Gertrude Wemhoff, O.S.B., is executive director. The national office is located at 1307 S. Wabash Ave., Chicago, Ill. 60605.

Religious Formation Conference: Originally organized with the title of the Sister Formation Conference in 1953, for the purpose of promoting the spiritual and professional formation of sisters in the U.S. In 1976, the name was changed to Religious Formation Conference to reflect openness to a membership including men and persons belonging to non-canonical religious groups. Sister Carol Ann Jokerst, C.C.V.I., is executive director. The national office is located at 1234 Massachusetts Ave. N.W., Washington, D.C. 20005.

Other Conferences

International Union of Superiors General (Women): Established in 1965, with approval of its statutes by the Congregation for Religious and Secular Institutes in 1967. Sister Regina Casey, M.S.C., is president.

Latin American Confederation of Religious: Established in 1959, with approval of its statutes by the Congregation for Religious and Secular Institutes in 1967. Father Mateo Perdia, C.P., is president.

National Conference of Vicars for Religious: Established in 1967 as a national organization of diocesan officials concerned with relations between their respective dioceses and religious communities engaged therein. A service and informational agency for vicars, it also carries on liaison with the Congregation for Religious and Secular Institutes, the National Conference of Catholic Bishops and other organizations concerned with religious. The president is Rev. Angelo Caligiuri, 100 S. Elmwood Ave., Buffalo, N.Y. 14202.

National Conferences: Conferences of religious superiors, generally separate for men and women, have been established in 19 countries in Europe, 14 in North and Central America, 10 in South America, 24 in Africa, and 20 in Asia and Oceania.

Union of Superiors General (Men): Established in 1957, with approval of its statutes by the Congregation for Religious and Secular Institutes in 1967. Father Vincent de Couesnongle, O.P., is president. Fathers John Vaughn, superior general of the Order of Friars Minor, and Paul Boyle, superior general of the Passionists, are American councillors of the union.

World Conference of Secular Institutes: Established in 1974.

Vocation Council

The National Catholic Vocation Council replaced the National Center for Church Vocations in 1977. The principal purpose of the council is to give the Church in the U.S. visible witness of the mutual collaboration of national vocation organizations in their effort to promote awareness and understanding of dedication to the Church, especially through the ordained ministry and vowed life. The council also services efforts of mutual concern and benefit to membership organizations in the recruitment and development of vocations to the priesthood, diaconate and vowed life.

Member organizations with representatives on the council are: the National Sisters Vocation Conference, the National Conference of Diocesan Vocation Directors, the National Conference of Religious Vocation Directors, Serra International, the Bishops' Committee on Vocations (National Conference of Catholic Bishops), the Leadership Conference of Women Religious and the Conference of Major Superiors of Men and the Conference of Secular Institutes.

Brother James Gaffney, C.F.C., is president; Sr. Margaret M. Kopish, A.S.C., is administrator.

Offices are located at 1307 S. Wabash Ave., Suite 350, Chicago, Ill. 60605

SECULAR INSTITUTES

(Sources: Almanac survey; United States Conference of Secular Institutes; *Annuario Pontificio.*)

Secular institutes are societies of men and women living in the world who dedicate themselves to observe the evangelical counsels and to carry on apostolic works suitable to their talents and opportunities in the areas of their everyday life.

"Secular institutes are not religious communities but they carry with them in the world a profession of evangelical counsels which is genuine and complete, and recognized as such by the Church. This profession confers a consecration on men and women, laity and clergy, who reside in the world. For this reason they should chiefly strive for total self-dedication to God, one inspired by perfect charity. These institutes should preserve their proper and particular character, a secular one, so that they may everywhere measure up successfully to that apostolate which they were designed to exercise, and which is both in the world and, in a sense, of the world" (*Decree on the Appropriate Renewal of Religious Life,* No. 11; Second Vatican Council).

Secular institutes are under the jurisdiction of the Congregation for Religious and Secular Institutes. General legislation concerning them is contained in Canons 710 to 730 of the revised Code of Canon Law, effective Nov. 27, 1983.

A secular institute reaches maturity in several stages. It begins as an association of the faithful, technically called a pious union, with the approval of a local bishop. Once it has proved its viability, he can give it the status of an institute of diocesan

right, in accordance with norms and permission emanating from the Congregation for Religious and Secular Institutes. On issuance of a separate decree from this congregation, an institute of diocesan right becomes an institute of pontifical right.

Secular institutes, which originated in the latter part of the 18th century, were given full recognition and approval by Pius XII Feb. 2, 1947, in the apostolic constitution *Provida Mater Ecclesia.* On Mar. 25 of the same year a special commission for secular institutes was set up within the Congregation for Religious. Institutes were commended and confirmed by Pius XII in a motu proprio of Mar. 12, 1948, and were the subject of a special instruction issued a week later, Mar. 19, 1948.

The **United States Conference of Secular Institutes** (CSI) was established in October, 1972, following the organization of the World Conference of Secular Institutes in Rome. Its membership is open to all canonically erected secular institutes with members living in the United States. The conference was organized to offer secular institutes an opportunity to exchange experiences, to do research in order to help the Church carry out its mission, and to search for ways and means to make known the existence of secular institutes in the U.S. Address: c/o Claudette Cyr, president, 121 Greenwood St., Watertown, Conn. 06795.

Institutes in the U.S.

Caritas Christi: Originated in Marseilles, 1937; for women. Established as a secular institute of pontifical right Mar. 19, 1955. Address: P.O. Box 162, River Forest, Ill. 60305.

Company of St. Paul: Originated in Milan, Italy, 1920; for lay people and priests. Approved as a secular institute of pontifical right June 30, 1950. Address: 52 Davis Ave., White Plains, N.Y. 10605.

Company of St. Ursula, Secular Institute of St. Angela Merici: Founded in Brescia, Italy, 1535; for women. Approved as a secular institute of pontifical right 1958. Addresses: Lina Moser, President, Via Rosmini 128, 38100 Trento, Italy; J. Lamb, P.O. Box 17670, Fort Worth, Tex. 76102. International membership of 3,000.

DeSales Secular Institute: Founded in Vienna, Austria, 1940; for women. Pontifical right, 1964. Address: Rev. John Conmy, O.S.F.S., National Assistant, 24 S. Cliffe Ave., Wilmington, Del. 19809.

Diocesan Laborer Priests: Approved as a secular institute of pontifical right, 1952. The specific aim of the institute is the promotion, sustenance and cultivation of apostolic, religious and priestly vocations. Address: c/o Rev. Ovid Percharroman, 3706 15th St. N.E., Washington, D.C. 20017.

Don Bosco Volunteers: Founded 1917; for women. Approved as a secular institute of pontifical right Aug. 5, 1978. Address: Don Bosco Volunteers, 202 Union Ave., Paterson, N.J. 07502. International membership of over 800 in 25 countries.

Handmaids of Divine Mercy: Founded in Bari, Italy, 1951; for women. Approved as an institute of pontifical right 1972. Address: Mary I. DiFonzo, 2410 Hughes Ave., Bronx, N.Y. 10458. International membership of 980.

Institute of Secular Missionaries: Founded in Vitoria, Spain, 1939; for women. Approved as a secular institute, 1955. Address: 2710 Ruberg Ave., Cincinnati, O. 45211, Att. E. Dilger.

Institute of the Heart of Jesus: Originated in France Feb. 2, 1791; restored Oct. 29, 1918; for diocesan priests and lay people. Received final approval from the Holy See as a secular institute of pontifical right Feb. 2, 1952. Rev. Jean Grebouval, superior general. Addresses: Central House, 202 Avenue du Maine, Paris 14me, France; U.S. address, Rev. John Lorenz, P.O. Box 4692, Des Moines, Iowa 50306. International membership of approximately 1,400.

Mission of Our Lady of Bethany: Founded in Plessis-Chenet, France, 1948; for women. Approved as an institute of diocesan right 1965. Address: Box 207, Jamaica Plain, Mass. 02130.

Missionaries of the Kingship of Christ the King: Under this title are included three distinct and juridically separate institutes founded by Agostino Gemelli, O.F.M. (1878-1959).

(1) Women Missionaries of the Kingship of Christ — Founded in 1919, in Italy; definitively approved as an institute of pontifical rite 1953. Established in 15 countries. U.S. branch established 1950. Age at time of entrance, 21 to 40.

(2) Men Missionaries of the Kingship of Christ — Founded 1928, in Italy, as an institute of diocesan right. U.S. branch established 1962.

(3) Priest Missionaries of the Kingship of Christ — Established in U.S., 1954; approved as institute

of pontifical right July 15, 1978. For diocesan priests.

Address: Rev. Stephen Hartdegen, O.F.M., Holy Name College, 14th and Shepherd Sts. N.E., Washington, D.C. 20017.

Oblate Missionaries of Mary Immaculate: Founded, 1952, and approved as a secular institute Feb. 2, 1962; for women. Addresses: Oblate Missionaries of Mary Immaculate, 49J Forest Acres Dr., Bradford, Mass. 01830; 7535 Boulevard Parent, Trois Rivieres, P. Q. G9A 5E1, Canada. International membership.

Rural Parish Workers of Christ the King: Originated in Cottleville, Mo., 1942; for women. An approved lay institute of apostolic action of the Archdiocese of St. Louis. Dedicated to the service of neighbor, especially in rural areas. Address: Box 300, Rt. 1, Cadet, Mo. 63630.

Schoenstatt Sisters of Mary: Originated in Schoenstatt, Germany, 1926; for women. Established as a secular institute of diocesan right May 20, 1948; of pontifical right Oct. 18, 1948. Addresses: Schoenstatt Sisters of Mary, W. 284 N. 698 Cherry Lane, Waukesha, Wis. 53186; House Schoenstatt, Star Rt. 1, Box 100, Rockport, Tex. 78382. International membership of more than 2,800.

Secular Institute of Pius X: Originated in Manchester, N.H., 1940; for priests and laymen. Approved as a secular institute, 1959 (first secular institute of diocesan right founded in the U.S. to be approved by the Holy See). Also admits married and unmarried men as associate members. Addresses: Lynchville Park, Goffstown, N.H. 03045. C.P. 1815, Quebec City, P.Q. G1K 7K7, Canada.

Servitium Christi Secular Institute of the Blessed Sacrament: Founded in Holland, 1952; for women. Approved as a secular institute of diocesan right May 8, 1963. Address: Miss Olympia Panagatos, 260 E. 77th St., Apt. 3B, New York, N.Y. 10021.

Society of Our Lady of the Way: Originated, 1936; for women. Approved as a secular institute of pontifical right Jan. 3, 1953. Addresses: 2701 14th Ave., San Francisco, Calif. 94127; 2339 N. Catalina St., Los Angeles, Calif. 90027; P.O. Box 412, Stamford, Conn. 06904; 2738 Noble Rd., No. 13B, Cleveland Heights, O. 44121. International membership, 300.

Teresian Institute: Founded in Spain 1911 by Pedro Poveda. Approved as an institute of pontifical right Jan. 11, 1924. Mailing Address: P.O. Box 14-3407, Coral Gables, Fla. 33114.

Voluntas Dei: Originated in Canada, 1958; for secular priests, laymen and couples. Approved as a secular institute May 6, 1965. Addresses: Institute Voluntas Dei, 7385, Blvd. Parent, Trois-Rivieres, Que., Canada G9A 5E1. David J. McDonald, 615 West Alturas St., No. 397, Tucson, Ariz. 85705. International membership of approximately 210.

The *Annuario Pontificio* lists the following secular institutes of pontifical right which are not established in the U.S.:

For men: Christ the King; Institute of Our Lady of Life; Institute of Prado; Priests of the Sacred Heart of Jesus.

For women: Alliance in Jesus through Mary; Apostles of the Sacred Heart; Catechists of Mary, Virgin and Mother; Catechists of the Sacred Heart of Jesus (Ukrainian); Cordimarian Filiation; Daughters of the Nativity of Mary; Daughters of the Queen of the Apostles; Daughters of the Sacred Heart; Evangelical Crusade; Faithful Servants of Jesus; Handmaids of Our Mother of Mercy; Institute of the Blessed Virgin Mary (della Strada); Institute of Notre Dame du Travail; Institute of Our Lady of Life; Institute of St. Boniface; Little Apostles of Charity; Life and Peace in Christ Jesus; Missionaries of Royal Priesthood; Missionaries of the Sick; Oblates of Christ the King; Oblates of the Sacred Heart of Jesus; Servants of Jesus the Priest; Servite Secular Institute; Union of the Daughters of God; Workers of Divine Love; Workers of the Cross; Handmaids of Holy Church.

Associations

Association of Mary Immaculate: Founded 1963. Received diocesan approval Jan. 28, 1977. For mature men and women, widows and widowers; separate section for married couples. Training on cassette tape for blind or handicapped. Address: 8804 Arlington Expressway, Jacksonville, Fla. 32211.

Caritas: Originated in New Orleans, 1950; for women. Follow guidelines of secular institutes. Small self-supporting groups who live and work among the poor and oppressed; work in Louisiana and Guatemala. Address: Box 308, Abita Springs, La. 70420.

Daughters of Our Lady of Fatima: Originated in Lansdowne, Pa., 1949; for women. Received diocesan approval, Jan., 1952. Address: Fatima House, Rolling Hills Rd., Ottsville, Pa. 18942.

Focolare Movement: Inaugurated in Trent, Italy, in 1943, by Chiara Lubich and a small group of companions; for men and women. Approved as an association of the faithful, 1962. Address for information: P.O. Box 496, New York, N.Y. 10021 (indicate men's or women's branch).

Institute of Apostolic Oblates: Founded in Rome, Italy, 1947; for women. Address: 2125 W. Walnut Ave., Fullerton, Calif. 92633.

Jesus Caritas — Fraternity of Priests: An international association of priests who strive to live in the spirit of Charles de Foucauld, combining an active life with a contemplative calling. U.S. address: Rev. Howard W. Calkins (National Responsible), St. Jerome Church, 230 Alexander Ave., Bronx, N.Y. 10454

Madonna House Apostolate: Originated in Toronto, Canada, 1930; for priests and lay persons. Diocesan pious union. Address: Madonna House, Combermere, Ontario, Canada KOJ ILO — Catherine Doherty (women), Jim Guinan (men), Rev. J. Callahan (priests). International membership and missions.

Pax Christi: Lay institute of men and women dedicated to witnessing to Christ, with special emphasis on service to the poor in Mississippi. Addresses: St. Francis Center, 708 Ave. I, Greenwood, Miss. 38930; LaVerna House, 2108 Altawoods Blvd., Jackson, Miss. 39204.

SECULAR ORDERS

Secular orders (commonly called third orders) are societies of the faithful living in the world who seek to deepen their Christian life and apostolic commitment in association with and according to the spirit of various religious institutes. The orders are called "third" because their foundation followed the establishment of the first (for men) and second (for women) religious orders with which they are associated.

Augustine, Third Order Secular of St.: Founded, 13th century; approved Nov. 7, 1400.

Carmel (The Lay Carmelite Order) (Calced): Founded, 13th century; approved by Pope Nicholas V, Oct. 7, 1452. Revised rule aproved November, 1977. Address: Aylesford, National Scapular Center, I-55 ahd Cass Ave. N. Darien, Ill. 60559. Approximately 16,500 members in U.S.

Carmelites, The Secular Order of Discalced (formerly the Third Order Secular of the Blessed Virgin Mary of Mt Carmel and of St. Teresa of Jesus): Rule based on the Carmelite reform established by St. Teresa and St. John of the Cross, 16th century; approved Mar. 23, 1594. Revised rule approved May 10, 1979. Office of National Secretariat, U.S.A.; P.O. Box 3079, San Jose, Calif. 95116. Approximately 22,245 throughout the world; 1,800 in U.S.

Dominican Laity: Founded in the 13th century. Addresses of provincial coordinators: 487 Michigan Ave. N.E., Washington, D.C. 20017; 1909 S. Ashland Ave., Chicago, Ill. 60608; 2390 Bush St., San Francisco, Calif. 94115, P.O. Box 3894, Little Rock, Ark. 72203.

Franciscan Order, Secular (SFO): Founded, 1209 by St. Francis of Assisi; approved Aug. 30, 1221. National minister, James David Lynch, 4143 "J" St., Juniata Park, Philadelphia, Pa. 19124. Approximately 780,000 throughout the world; 40,000 in U.S.

Mary, Third Order of: Founded, Dec. 8, 1850; rule approved by the Holy See, 1857. Addresses of provincial directors: 4408 — 8th St. N.E., Washington, D.C. 20017; 7 Harvard St., P.O. Box 66, Charlestown, Mass. 02129; P.O. Box 158, Kekaha, Kauai, Hawaii 96752. Approximately 14,000 in the world, 5,600 in U.S.

Mary, Third Order Secular of Servants of (Servite): Founded, 1233; approved, 1304. Address: Director of Third Order, 3401 S. Home Ave., Berwyn, Ill. 60402.

Mercy, Secular Third Order of Our Lady of (Mercedarian): Founded, 1219 by St. Peter Nolasco; approved the same year.

Norbert, Third Order of St.: Founded, 1122 by St. Norbert; approved by Pope Honorius II, 1126. Address: St. Norbert Abbey, De Pere, Wis. 54115.

Trinity, Third Order Secular of the Most Holy: Founded 1198; approved, 1219.

Oblates of St. Benedict are lay persons affiliated with a Benedictine abbey or monastery who strive to direct their lives, as circumstances permit, according to the spirit and Rule of St. Benedict.

MISSIONARY ACTIVITY OF THE CHURCH

UNITED STATES FOREIGN MISSIONARIES

Data on U.S. foreign missionary personnel in the following tables were gathered by, and are reproduced with permission of, the United States Catholic Mission Association, 1233 Lawrence St. N.E., Washington, D.C. 20017.

For additional information about the Church in mission areas, see News Events and other Almanac entries.

Field Distribution, 1983

Under this and following headings, Alaska, Hawaii, etc., are considered abroad because they are outside the 48 contiguous states.

Africa: 990 (519 men, 471 women). Largest numbers in Kenya, 173; Tanzania, 171; Ghana, 104; Zambia, 83; Nigeria, 66.

Near East: 68 (44 men, 24 women). Largest numbers in Israel, 43; Egypt, 12; Lebanon, 9.

Far East: 1,468 (1,007 men, 461 women). Largest numbers in Philippines, 385; Japan, 327; Taiwan, 167; Korea, 139; India, 116; Hong Kong, 78.

Oceania: 640 (328 men, 312 women). Largest groups in Papua New Guinea, 205; Hawaii, 202; Australia, 61; Mariana Islands, 43; Caroline Islands, 37; Samoa, 36.

Europe: 34 (20 men, 14 women). Largest groups in Sweden, 11; Finland, 9; Denmark, 6.

North America: 346 (147 men, 199 women). Largest group in Alaska, 199.

Caribbean Islands: 517 (284 men, 233 women). Largest groups in Puerto Rico, 231; Jamaica, 119; Haiti, 42.

Central America: 650 (305 men, 205 women). Largest groups in Mexico, 211; Guatemala, 159.

South America: 1,533 (811 men, 722 women). Largest groups in Peru, 459; Brazil, 456; Bolivia, 217; Chile, 173.

TOTAL: 6,246 (3,545 men, 2,701 women).

Men Religious, 1983

Eighty-nine mission-sending groups had 3,285 priests and brothers in overseas assignments.

Jesuits: 561 in 41 countries; largest group, 90 in the Philippines.

Maryknoll Fathers: 542 in 26 countries; largest group, 55 in Tanzania.

Franciscans (O.F.M.): 210 in 26 countries; largest group, 67 in Brazil.

Divine Word Missionaries: 161 in 13 countries; largest group, 53 in Papua New Guinea.

Redemptorists: 151 in 8 countries; largest group, 60 in Brazil.

Oblates of Mary Immaculate: 135 in 18 countries; largest group, 26 in Brazil.

Marianists: 133 in 15 countries; largest group, 33 in Hawaii.

Capuchins (O.F.M. Cap): 131 in 9 countries; largest group, 31 in Papua New Guinea.

Benedictines: 91 in 14 countries; largest group, 21 in Guatemala.

Brothers of the Christian Schools: 69 in 12 countries; largest group, 25 in the Philippines.

Columbans: 66 in 10 countries; largest group, 27 in the Philippines.

Conventual Franciscans (O.F.M. Conv): 65 in 9 countries; largest group, 16 in Canada.

Holy Cross Fathers: 61 in 10 countries; largest group, 19 in Bangladesh.

Dominicans: 59 in 8 countries; largest group, 15 in Pakistan.

Holy Ghost Fathers: 57 in 7 countries; largest group, 24 in Tanzania.

Holy Cross Brothers: 55 in 7 countries; largest group, 18 in Brazil.

Passionists: 48 in 6 countries; largest group, 22 in the Philippines.

Vincentians: 43 in 8 countries; largest group, 18 in Panama.

La Salette Fathers: 39 in 6 countries; largest group, 12 each in Argentina and the Philippines.

Marist Fathers: 36 in 10 countries; largest group, 11 in Hawaii.

Augustinians: 34 in 3 countries; largest group, 22 in Peru.

Missionaries of the Sacred Heart: 31 in 4 countries; largest group, 23 in Papua New Guinea.

White Fathers: 29 in 11 countries: largest group, 6 in Uganda.

Salesians: 27 in 10 countries; largest group, 11 in Canada.

Brothers of the Sacred Heart: 22 in 4 countries; largest group, 10 in Zambia.

Sixty-four other mission-sending institutes had 19 or less members in overseas assignments.

Diocesan Priests, 1983

One hundred and 74 diocesan priests from 75 dioceses were in overseas assignments in 1983.

The largest groups were from Boston (19 in 4 countries) and St. Louis (8 in 2 countries).

Fifty-three of the diocesan priests in overseas assignments were members of the Missionary Society of St. James the Apostle, founded by Cardinal Richard J. Cushing of Boston in 1958. Its director is Rev. George F. Emerson, 24 Clark St., Boston, Mass. 02109.

Fifteen other diocesan priests in overseas assignments were working as priest associates with the Maryknoll Fathers, whose headquarters are in Maryknoll, New York 10545.

Sisters, 1983

Two hundred and 21 mission-sending groups had 2,540 sisters in overseas assignments.

Maryknoll Sisters: 399 in 26 countries; largest group, 56 in Hawaii.

School Sisters of Notre Dame: 100 in 18 countries; largest group, 15 in Puerto Rico.

Marists: 82 in 14 countries; largest group, 13 in Papua New Guinea.

Medical Mission Sisters: 77 in 14 countries; largest group, 15 in Ghana.

Sisters of Notre Dame de Namur: 61 in 10 countries; largest group, 16 in Kenya.

Daughters of Charity: 60 in 9 countries; largest group, 33 in Bolivia.

Sisters of St. Joseph (Carondelet): 52 in 4 countries; largest group, 23 in Hawaii.

Benedictines: 48 in 10 countries: largest group, 12 in Colombia.

Franciscan Missionaries of Mary: 44 in 18 countries; largest groups, 7 in Japan.

Sisters of the Holy Cross: 44 in 6 countries; largest group, 17 in Brazil.

Servants of the Immaculate Heart of Mary (Philadelphia): 43 in 2 countries; largest group, 32 in Peru.

Ursulines of the Roman Union: 39 in 12 countries; largest group, 8 in Thailand.

Society of the Sacred Heart: 33 in 7 countries; largest group, 13 in Japan.

Franciscan Sisters of Allegany: 32 in 3 countries; largest group, 19 in Jamaica.

Servants of the Holy Spirit: 31 in 7 countries; largest group, 11 in Ghana.

Religious Sisters of Mercy of the Union in the U.S.A.: 27 in 8 countries; largest group, 13 in Jamaica.

Sisters of Notre Dame: 25 in 3 countries; largest group, 13 in India.

Sisters of the Third Franciscan Order, Minor Conventuals (Syracuse): 25 in 3 countries; largest group, 15 in Hawaii.

Little Sisters of the Poor: 24 in 12 countries; largest group, 5 in Hong Kong.

Sisters of St. Joseph (Brentwood): 23 in 3 countries; largest group, 20 in Puerto Rico.

Adorers of the Blood of Christ: 22 in 5 countries; largest group, 8 in Liberia.

Sisters of the Holy Child Jesus: 21 in 7 countries; largest group, 8 in Nigeria.

One hundred and 98 other mission-sending institutes had 19 or less members in overseas assignments.

Lay Volunteers, 1983

Two hundred and 47 lay volunteers of 24 sponsoring organizations were in overseas assignments in 1983.

Maryknoll Lay Missioners: 61 in 17 countries; largest group, 10 in Venezuela.

Jesuit Volunteer Corps: 55 in Alaska.

Lay Mission Helpers: 34 in 11 countries; largest group, 10 in Samoa.

Frontier Apostolate: 21 in Canada.

Catholic Medical Mission Board: 16 in 8 countries; largest group, 5 in Papua New Guinea. (This figure represents those whose term of service was for at least one year. In addition, 43 short-term volunteers served in 9 countries during the year.)

Milwaukee Latin American Office: 9 in 5 countries; largest group, 4 in Colombia.

Diocese of Davenport: 9 in 5 countries; largest groups, 3 in Mexico.

The other 17 sponsoring organizations had 8 members or less in overseas assignments.

U.S. MISSION ASSOCIATION

The United States Catholic Mission Association, juridically established Sept. 1, 1981, continues the activities and functions of the former U.S. Catholic Mission Council.

According to existing bylaws approved by the general assembly May 25, 1982, the USCMA is "open to all those who seek to promote global mission in community with others. It is envisioned to be an experience of the renewed Church, in which all members are equal. The methods of decision-making, of financial support, and of committee service reflect the underlying ecclesiology." The purpose of the association is the "promotion of global mission. Its primary focus is cross-cultural mission, with special emphasis on international justice."

Typical activities of the association are educational efforts related to the Church's teaching about its missionary nature, sponsorship of conferences on theological and pastoral foundations of missionary endeavor, liaison and cooperation with missionary bodies of other Christian churches, training programs and refresher courses for departing and returning missionaries, and general mission animation. The association is also responsible for gathering and publishing annual statistical data on U.S. missionary personnel overseas. It publishes the data in the annual, *Mission Handbook.* The association also publishes ten times a year *Mission Intercom,* a newsletter with brief information on the life and activities of the Church in the six continents.

Officers of the association are: Sister Mary Ann Dillon, R.S.M., president; Rev. Simon Smith, S.J., vice president; Rev. Anthony Bellagamba, I.M.C., executive director.

The office of the association is located at 1233 Lawrence St. N.E., Washington, D.C. 20017.

BISHOP-BROTHERS

(The asterisk indicates brothers who were bishops at the same time.)

There have been nine pairs of brother-bishops in the history of the U.S. hierarchy.

Living: Francis T. Hurley,* archbishop of Anchorage and Mark J. Hurley* of Santa Rosa.

Deceased: Francis Blanchet* of Oregon City (Portland) and Augustin Blanchet* of Walla Walla; John S. Foley of Detroit and Thomas P. Foley of Chicago; Francis P. Kenrick,* apostolic administrator of Philadelphia, bishop of Philadelphia and Baltimore, and Peter R. Kenrick* of St. Louis; Matthias C. Lenihan of Great Falls and Thomas M. Lenihan of Cheyenne; James O'Connor, vicar apostolic of Nebraska and bishop of Omaha, and Michael O'Connor of Pittsburgh and Erie; Jeremiah F. and John W. Shanahan, both of Harrisburg; Sylvester J. Espelage, O.F.M.,* of Wuchang, China, who died 10 days after the ordination of his brother, Bernard T. Espelage,* O.F.M., of Gallup; Coleman F. Carroll* of Miami and Howard Carroll* of Altoona-Johnstown.

U.S. FOREIGN MISSIONARIES, 1960-1983

Year	Diocesan Priests	Religious Priests	Religious Brothers	Religious Sisters	Seminarians	Lay Persons	Total
1960	14	3018	575	2827	170	178	6782
1962	31	3172	720	2764	152	307	7146
1964	80	3438	782	3137	157	532	8126
1966	215	3731	901	3706	201	549	9303
1968	282	3727	869	4150	208	419	9655
1970	373	3117	666	3824	90	303	8373
1972+	246	3182	634	3121	97	376	7656
1973	237	3913*		3012		529	7691
1974	220	3084	639	2916	101	458	7418
1975	197	3023	669	2850	65	344	7148
1976	193	2961	691	2840	68	257	7010
1977	182	2882	630	2781	42	243	6760
1978	166	2830	610	2673	43	279	6601
1979	187	2800	592	2568	50	258	6455
1980	188	2750	592	2592	50	221	6393
1981	187	2702	584	2574	43	234	6324
1982	178	2668	578	2560	44	217	6245
1983	174	2668	569	2540	48	247	6246

+A corrected total for 1972 should read 7937, indicating losses of 436 from 1970 to 1972 and 246 from 1972 to 1973.
*Includes religious brothers and seminarians.

FIELD DISTRIBUTION BY AREAS, 1960-1983

Year	Africa	Far East	Near East	Oceania	Europe	N. Amer.	Carib. Is.	Cent. Amer.	S. Amer.	Total
1960	781	1959	111	986	203	337	991	433	981	6782
1962	901	2110	75	992	93	224	967	537	1247	7146
1964	1025	2332	122	846	69	220	1056	660	1796	8126
1966	1184	2453	142	953	38	211	1079	857	2386	9303
1968	1157	2470	128	1027	33	251	1198	936	2455	9655
1970	1141	2137	39	900	38	233	1067	738	2080	8373
1972	1107	1955	59	826	39	234	819	728	1889	7656
1973	1229	1962	54	811	40	253	796	763	1783	7691
1974	1121	1845	60	883	43	241	757	752	1716	7418
1975	1065	1814	71	808	37	252	698	734	1669	7148
1976	1042	1757	68	795	34	313	671	712	1618	7010
1977	1003	1659	62	784	34	296	629	702	1591	6760
1978	066	1001	57	789	34	339	603	705	1537	6601
1979	923	1562	65	743	37	332	562	686	1545	6455
1980	909	1576	65	711	35	294	548	699	1556	6393
1981	946	1529	70	696	36	315	511	693	1528	6324
1982	956	1501	62	673	32	319	522	669	1511	6245
1983	990	1468	68	640	34	346	517	650	1533	6246

HOME MISSIONS

The expression "home missions" is applied to places in the U.S. where the local church does not have its own resources, human and otherwise, which are needed to begin or, if begun, to survive and grow. These areas share the name "missions" with their counterparts in foreign lands because they too need outside help to provide the personnel and means for making the Church present and active there in carrying out its mission for the salvation of people.

Dioceses in the Southeast, the Southwest, and the Far West are most urgently in need of outside help to carry on the work of the Church. Millions of persons live in counties in which there are no resident priests. Many others live in rural areas beyond the reach and influence of a Catholic center. According to recent statistics compiled by the Glenmary Research Center, there are approximately 550 priestless counties in the United States. Many states generally thought to be well off from a pastoral standpoint include areas in which the Catholic Church and the ministry of priests are virtually unknown.

About 20 per cent of the total U.S. population and less than three per cent of the Catholic population live within the boundaries of the 17 "most missionary" dioceses of the country. A "Survey of the Catholic Weakness" conducted by the National Catholic Rural Life Conference disclosed that the Catholic Church ranked near the bottom of about 40 religious bodies in percentage of rural membership.

Mission Workers

A number of forces are at work to meet the pastoral needs of these missionary areas and to establish permanent churches and operating institutions where they are required. In many dioceses, one or more missions and stations are attended from established parishes and are gradually growing to independent status. Priests, brothers and sisters belonging to scores of religious institutes are engaged full-time in the home missions. Lay persons, some of them in affiliation with special groups and movements, are also involved.

The Society for the Propagation of the Faith, which conducts an annual collection for mission support in all parishes of the U.S., allocates 40 per cent of this sum for disbursement to home missions through the American Board of Catholic Missions.

The Catholic Church Extension Society provides one million dollars or more a year for the building of mission installations and related needs.

Special mission support is the purpose of the Commission for the Catholic Missions among the Colored People and the Indians.

Diocesan, parochial and high school mission societies frequently undertake projects in behalf of the home missions.

The **Glenmary Home Missioners,** founded by Father W. Howard Bishop in 1939, is the only home mission society established for the sole purpose of carrying out the pastoral ministry in small towns and the rural districts of the United States. With 72 priests and 23 professed brothers as of March 24, 1983, the Glenmary Missioners had 38 mission bases and 45 satellite missions in the archdioceses of Atlanta and Cincinnati, and in the dioceses of Birmingham, Charlotte, Covington, Dallas, Little Rock, Nashville, Jackson, Tulsa, Owensboro, Savannah, Richmond and Wheeling-Charleston. National headquarters are located in Fairfield, O. The mailing address is P.O. Box 46404, Cincinnati, O. 45246.

Black Missions

The Commission for Catholic Missions among the Colored People and the Indians reported the following (January, 1982), statistics for 80 dioceses and six religious communities to whom it supplied financial assistance: 993,000 Catholics; 658 churches; 860 priests; 141 predominantly black schools with 34,800 students; 255 integrated schools with 4,700 students.

Dioceses reporting the largest numbers of black Catholics were: Brooklyn, N.Y., 132,000; New Orleans, La., 90,000; Washington, D.C., 75,000; Lafayette, La., 67,427; New York, N.Y., 50,000; Baltimore, Md., 47,000; Galveston-Houston, 45,885; Philadelphia, Pa., 40,000; Detroit, Mich., 37,000; St. Louis, Mo., 31,000; San Diego, Calif., 28,000; Lake Charles, La., 20,000; Kansas City-St. Joseph, Mo., 18,000; Baton Rouge, La., 16,000; Rockville Centre, N.Y., 15,320; San Francisco, Calif., 14,300; Cleveland, O., 11,000; Newark, N.J., 10,000. The total black Catholic population of these 18 mainly urban dioceses numbered 733,155; they comprised nearly 74 per cent of the total black Catholic population of the 86 dioceses covered in the report.

The report noted that it was impossible to determine "whether, or to what extent, lapsed Catholics are included in a parish or diocesan report."

The commission report, which was limited in scope, did not cover all aspects of the Church's ministry to the black population, which was estimated to number more than 22 million. (See Index: Black Catholics.)

Indian Missions

The Commission for Catholic Missions among the Colored People and the Indians reported the following statistics (January, 1982) for 53 dioceses and one religious community to whom it supplied financial assistance: 264,000 Catholics, 346 churches and chapels, 268 priests, 23 elementary schools, four high schools.

The states with the largest number of missions and Catholic Indians are Arizona, New Mexico, North and South Dakota, Oklahoma and Montana, where almost two-thirds of the reservation Indians now live. Sixty-nine churches and chapels and four schools were maintained with 117 priests engaged in serving more than 163,000 Catholic Indians in these areas. Forty-five missions and three schools are located in the states of California, Minnesota, Wisconsin and Wyoming where 35 priests are serving the estimated 33,420 Catholic Indians there. Alaska has 45 mission churches and chapels and 32 priests to minister to approximately 27,000 Indians, Aleuts, Eskimos. In other states, the Commission reported, reservations were small; consequently only several schools and from one to five missions were maintained in most of them.

According to 1980 census reports, an estimated 376,000 of the total U.S. Indian population of 1,418,195 were living on federal reservations. An estimated 25,000 Catholic Indians were not on reservations.

Bishops Statement: The bishops of the United States, in a statement approved during a May 3 to 5, 1977, meeting in Chicago, urged American Catholics to increase their "understanding of the present needs, aspirations and values of the American Indian peoples." They recommended:

• that dioceses and Catholic organizations make efforts to improve their ministry with American Indians;

• that church property adjacent to Indian lands or in the midst of urban Indian neighborhoods be made more available for use by Indian communities;

• that Catholic educational institutions examine textbooks and curricula, and promote programs in the appreciation of American Indian history, culture and spirituality;

• that special attention be given to government policy and legislation affecting Indians.

This special attention, the statement said, should focus on "advocacy of the speedy and equitable resolution of treaty and statute questions; protection of Indian land and resource rights; more adequate housing and delivery of social, education and health-care services; and increased levels of funding and technical assistance necessary to aid American Indians in achieving political and economic self-determination and full employment."

The bishops said, in conclusion: "We hope to fashion a renewed commitment to serve Indian peoples. In turn, their participation in and challenge to the Christian community will strengthen our common witness to Jesus and the gospel message."

Organizations

The Catholic Church Extension Society: This society was established for the purpose of preserving and extending the Church in the U.S. and its dependencies principally through the collection and disbursement of funds for missions. Since the time of its founding in 1905, approximately $93 million have been received and expended for this purpose. Disbursements in fiscal year 1982 were in excess of $7 million.

Works of the society are supervised by a board of governors consisting of twelve members: Cardinal Joseph Bernardin, archbishop of Chicago, chancellor; Very Rev. Edward J. Slattery, president; five bishops or priests, and five laymen. Society headquarters are located at 35 E. Wacker Drive, Chicago, Ill. 60601.

Commission for Catholic Missions among the Colored People and the Indians: Organized in 1886, this commission provides financial support ($4,211,000 allocated in 1981-82 year to 127 dioceses) for religious works among Blacks and Indians in the United States. Funds are raised by an annual collection in all parishes of the country.

Cardinal John J. Krol is head of the board of directors. Msgr. Paul A. Lenz is secretary. Commission headquarters are located at 2021 H St. N.W., Washington, D.C. 20006.

Bureau of Catholic Indian Missions: Established in 1874 as the representative of Catholic Indian missions before the federal government and the public; made permanent organization in 1883 by Third Plenary Council of Baltimore. After a remarkable history of rendering important services to the Indian people, the bureau continues to represent the Catholic Church in the U.S. in her apostolate to the American Indian. Concerns are evangelization, catechesis, liturgy, family life, education, advocacy. Cardinal John Krol is president of the board; Msgr. Paul A. Lenz is secretary. Address: 2021 H St., Washington, D.C. 20006.

Rural Ministry Institute: The Edwin Vincent O'Hara Institute for Rural Ministry Education was founded in 1978 to provide training and other resource services for priests, seminarians religious and lay persons beginning or already involved in rural ministry. Brother David Andrews, C.S.C., is director. Address: 14th and Shepherd Sts. N.E., Washington, D.C. 20017.

Tekakwitha Conference: Established in 1939, the Conference includes active and former Catholic missionaries among Native American people and Native American people recognized as leaders in their respective communities. The primary focus is evangelization in these areas of concern: development of Native American ministry, catechesis, liturgy, family life, social justice ministry, education, ecumenical cooperation, urban ministry spirituality and vocations. The annual Conference serves as an opportunity for exchange of ideas, approaches and mutual support. Publications include a quarterly Newsletter and the annual Proceedings. President is Rev. Gilbert F. Hemauer, O.F.M. Cap. Address: 1818 Ninth Ave., South No. 5, Great Falls, Mont. 59405.

BLACK CATHOLICS

The National Office for Black Catholics, organized in August, 1970, is a central agency with the general purposes of promoting active and full participation by black Catholics in the Church and of making more effective the presence and ministry of the Church in the black community.

Its operations are in support of the aspirations and calls of black Catholics for a number of objectives, including the following:

• representation and voice for blacks among bishops and others with leadership and decision-making positions in the Church;

• vocational recruitment for the priesthood and religious life;

• recognition of the black heritage in liturgy, community life, theology and education.

The NOBC office is located at 1234 Massachusetts Ave. N.W., Washington, D.C. 20005.

1983 Meetings

Parish outreach to the black community was the focus of concern at the meeting of the National Association of Black Catholic Administrators, held in April in Pittsburgh. Eight organizations of black Catholics were represented at the meeting.

The National Catholic Conference for Interracial Justice sponsored a conference on "The Morality of Equity" June 1 to 4 at Xavier University, New Orleans. The NCCIJ, under the executive direction of Father Frederick M. Hinton, has its office at 1200 Varnum St. N.E., Washington, D.C. 20017.

Joint Conference

The National Black Sisters' Conference, the National Black Catholic Clergy Caucus and the National Black Catholic Seminarians' Association convened for their third annual joint conference Aug. 8 to 12 at Jackson State University in Jackson, Miss.

Benedictine Father Cyprian Davis, professor of church history at St. Meinrad Archabbey, told the delegates in a keynote address: "As men and women of God, we find ourselves at some time or other . . . caught in a no-man's land — too far along to go back, too far back to go forward."

"One of the things that any spirituality should do is provide a road map for those who travel in the peculiar circumstances of their own age. I believe that within the framework of our traditionally Catholic spirituality, bolstered by the strength of our own black spiritual tradition, there is a place for such a road map."

'To be a black religious or priest is to partake of this mystery of Christ as mediator. It is to become a bridge. The price of mediatorship . . . the cost of being a bridge — is that one must be stretched to reach both sides. . . . It is also the cost of being placed on the cross — to be suspended between heaven and earth and to join the one with the other."

Black Gifts

Another speaker, Discalced Carmelite Sister Barbara Jean LaRochester of Towson, Md., said blacks could use their "roots" to help in their ministry: "The gifts black religious women and men have to offer those who seek us out . . . are our examples of love and concern for self and family — a love grounded in the sweat, blood and tears of our ancestors . . . our innate empathy and sympathy . . . patient endurance . . . and liberation."

Black ministers face a tremendous challenge because they must be prepared to educate their people and be educated by them, said Marist Brother Cyprian R. Rowe, outgoing executive director of the National Black Catholic Clergy Conference: "This education is so different because it implies that the minister must know the positive elements of the culture: the writings, the music, the history, the folklore — all the elements that can tell people what they need to know in order to grow to what they can be. This means study. Without this, the minister is not really ministering but posturing."

Honors and Officers

Brother Rowe offered congratulations to Capuchin Brother Booker T. Ashe, recipient of the clergy group's Brother Joseph Morgan Davis Award for 20 years of service as director of the House of Peace Community Center in Milwaukee.

Delegates also honored Bishop Joseph Brunini of Jackson for his contributions to the cause of racial justice.

During the meeting, Sister Elizabeth Harris of the Home Visitors of Mary, Detroit, was re-elected president of the National Black Sisters' Conference.

Father Donald M. Clark of the Detroit archdiocese assumed office as president of the National Black Catholic Clergy Conference.

Capuchin Brother Robert Smith of Chicago became president of the National Black Catholic Seminarians' Association.

Statistics

In 1983, there were a million or more black Catholics in the U.S., comprising about four per cent of the total black population and two per cent of the Catholic population. Black priests and religious numbered, respectively, about 250 and 700. There were seven black bishops: Bishop Joseph L. Howze, head of the Diocese of Biloxi, and Auxiliary Bishops Joseph A. Francis, S.V.D., of Newark, Eugene A. Marino, S.S.J., of Washingotn, Harold R. Perry, S.V.D., of New Orleans, James P. Lyke, O.F.M., of Cleveland, Emerson Moore of New York and Moses Anderson of Detroit.

Various dioceses have agencies like New York's Office of Black Ministry for pastoral and related service to the black community.

Josephite Pastoral Center

The Josephite Pastoral Center was established in September, 1968, as an educational and pastoral service agency for the Josephites in their mission work, specifically in the black community. St. Joseph's Society of the Sacred Heart, the sponsoring body, has about 185 priests and 20 brothers in 80 mostly southern parishes in 18 dioceses.

The staff of the center includes Father John G. Harfman, S.S.J., director, and Brother Damian Wilson, S.S.J., and Maria M. Lannon, associate directors. The center is located at St. Joseph Seminary, 1200 Varnum St. N.E., Washington, D.C. 20017.

HISPANICS

U.S. Census Bureau figures indicate that there were 14,605,883 persons of Hispanic origin in the United States in 1980. (Not counted were undocumented Hispanic aliens estimated to number between three and six million).

Between 1970 and 1980, there was a nationwide increase of 5,037,440 persons.

Regional increases for the same period were: Northeast, 709,381 for a total of 2,604,261; North Central, 228,144 for a total of 1,276,405; South, 1,707,365 for a total of 4,473,172; West, 2,884,291 for a total of 6,252,045.

Most persons of Hispanic origin in the United States have been baptized in the Catholic Church and comprise, probably, between 25 and 30 per cent of the Catholic population.

In the U.S., as of April, 1983, there were 15 Hispanic bishops (eight heads of dioceses and seven auxiliaries, all named since 1970). Other recent figures indicated there were 1,485 Hispanic priests, 450 Hispanic permanent deacons, 854 Hispanics in seminaries, and an estimated total of 724 Hispanic women religious.

Pastoral Patterns

Pastoral ministry to Hispanics varies, depending on differences among the people and the availability of personnel to carry it out.

The pattern in cities with large numbers of Spanish-speaking is built around special churches, centers or other agencies where pastoral and additional forms of service are provided in a manner suited to the needs, language and culture of the people. Services in some places are extensive and include legal advice, job placement, language instruction, recreational and social assistance, specialized counseling, replacement services. In many places, however, even where there are special ministries, the needs are generally greater than the means required to meet them.

Some of the urban dwellers have been absorbed into established parishes and routines of church life and activity. Many Spanish-speaking communities, especially those with transients, remain in need of special ministries.

An itinerant form of ministry best meets the needs of the thousands of migrant workers who follow the crops.

Special ministries for the Spanish-speaking have been in operation for a long time in dioceses of the Southwest. The total number of dioceses with such ministries is more than 75.

Pastoral care for Hispanics was the central concern of two national meetings, *Encuentros,* held in 1972 and 1977. In line with recommendations made then, particular emphasis has since been focused on meetings and actions for increasing language capability among persons involved in ministry, awareness of Hispanic cultural elements in liturgy and practice, leadership development, and moves for the formation of basic Christian communities (*comunidades de base*). A task force for implementation is chaired by Archbishop Robert F. Sanchez of Santa Fe, N.M.

At the time of writing, preparations were under way for a third *Encuentro* in 1985.

In November, 1982, the National Conference of Catholic Bishops approved the preparation of a pastoral statement on Hispanic ministry and entrusted the project to its Ad Hoc Committee for Hispanic Affairs. A draft written by a team of bishops headed by Bishop Ricardo Ramirez, O.S.B., of Las Cruces, N.M., was due for consideration and possible approval at the NCCB meeting scheduled for Nov. 14 to 17, 1983.

Secretariat for Hispanic Affairs

The national secretariat was established by the U.S. Catholic Conference for service in promoting and coordinating pastoral ministry to the Spanish-speaking. Its basic orientation is toward integral evangelization, combining religious ministry with development efforts in programs geared to the culture and needs of Hispanics. Its concerns are urban and migrant Spanish-speaking people; communications and publications in line with secretariat purposes and the service of people; bilingual and bicultural religious and general education; liaison for and representation of Hispanics with church, civic and governmental agencies.

The secretariat publishes a biweekly newsletter, *En Marcha,* available on request to interested parties. In addition, a weekly column available in English and Spanish, written by a variety of Hispanic Catholic authors, is syndicated to Catholic newspapers.

Paul Sedillo, Jr., is director of the national office at 1312 Massachusetts Ave. N.W., Wasington, D.C. 20005.

The secretariat has working relationships with regional offices in the Northeast, Southeast, Midwest, Southwest, Far West and Northwest. Each office shares the objectives of the secretariat. In addition, the Northeast, Southeast and Midwest offices have established pastoral institutes for formation, training and program development.

The Northeast regional office, officially the Northeast Pastoral Center for Hispanics, was established in 1976 and is supported by bishops in 14 states from Maine to Virginia. The office consists of five professional staff members in the fields of evangelization, vocation, pastoral work, communications and publications. It has established the Conference of Diocesan Directors of the Hispanic Apostolate, Association of Hispanic Deacons, Regional Youth Task Force and a regional committee of Diocesan Coordinators of Religious Educators for the Hispanics. The executive director is Mario J. Paredes. The center is located at 1011 First Ave., New York, N.Y. 10022.

The Southeast regional office serves the entire South. Its South East Pastoral Institute offers courses in pastoral ministry, reaches out to communities throughout the region with its Evangelization Mobile Team and distributes audio-visual and print resources for Hispanic ministry. Father Mario Vizcaino, Sch. P., is director of the region and institute. The office is located at 2900 S.W. 87th Ave., Miami, Fla. 33165.

Five states of the Midwest are served by a Spanish Speaking Catholic Commission and the Midwest Institute for Hispanic Ministry. The executive director of the commission is Olga Villa Parra. The office is located at P.O. Box 703 (Holy Cross Annex), Notre Dame, Ind. 46556.

In the Southwest, a reorganized regional office serving Arkansas, Oklahoma, and Texas was reopened Mar. 1, 1983. Sister Elisa Rodriguez is director of the office which is located at 3019 French Pl., San Antonio, Tex. 78228.

California and Nevada are served by the Far West office, which is a component of the California Catholic Conference. The regional director is Father Ricardo A. Chavez. The office is located at 926 J St., Suite 1100, Sacramento Calif. 95814.

A two-year-old regional office serves the northwestern corner of the U.S. and Alaska. The director of the region is Sister Elisa Martinez. The office is located at P.O. Box 1062, Yakima, Wash. 98907.

A new Hispanic region, comprising Arizona, Colorado and New Mexico, was being organized during 1983.

PADRES, Las Hermanas

In the Southwest, 55 Mexican-American priests organized PADRES in February, 1970, to help the Church identify more closely with the pastoral, social, economic and educational needs of the Spanish-speaking. The present membership exceeds 500, mainly in California, Texas, New Mexico and on the East Coast. PADRES is an acronym for the Spanish title, "Padres Asociados para Derechos Religiosos, Educativos y Sociales."

Leadership development of Hispanos is one of the principal concerns of PADRES, now a national organization with membership open to priests, brothers and deacons working in Hispanic ministry. Seminarians and others interested in working with the Hispanic community are eligible for honorary membership. Father Ramon Gaitan, O.A.R., is the national president. The national office is located at 3310 Garfield Ave., Kansas City, Kan. 66104.

An analogous organization of Chicano sisters, **Las Hermanas,** was organized in 1971 (see separate entry).

Mexican American Cultural Center

This center was founded in 1972 as a pastoral institute with a variety of programs focused on the evangelization of Hispanics in the United States, particularly through lay leadership and liaison between North, Central and South America. It has been named a center of liturgical research by the National Conference of Catholic Bishops.

Father Virgil Elizondo is president of the center, which is located at 3019 French Pl., P.O. Box 28185, San Antonio, Tex. 78228.

A National Resource Center for Hispanic Ministry, begun in 1981 at the Cultural Center by initiative of the U.S. Bishops' Committee on Hispanic Affairs, collects information on personnel and resources available to the Hispanic apostolate. John Diercksmeier is director of the center located at 3019 French Pl., San Antonio, Tex. 78228.

Miami Apostolate

The Spanish-Speaking Apostolate in metropolitan Miami is one of the most extensive in the country. It serves a population of well over 650,000 people — including Cubans who have established residence there since Fidel Castro rose to power Jan. 1, 1959; an increasing permanent Latin American population, and migrant workers.

Directly involved in the apostolate are 110 Spanish-speaking priests and 121 religious sisters. Spanish-speaking priests are assigned to 47 parishes. All pastoral programs of the archdiocese are duplicated in Spanish, and the social service agencies have Spanish-speaking personnel.

Bishop Agustin A. Roman is episcopal vicar for Spanish-speaking people in the Archdiocese of Miami.

CAMPUS MINISTRY

"Campus ministry is a pastoral apostolate of service to the members of the entire university and college community through concern and care for persons, the proclamation of the Gospel, and the celebration of the liturgy," according to a set of guidelines drawn up by an eight-member commission of the National Catholic Educational Association. The general purpose of the ministry is to make the Church present and active in the academic community.

Ideally, according to the guidelines, elements of the ministry — carried on by teams of priests, men and women religious, and lay persons — include liturgical leadership; pastoral counseling; coordination of expressions and energies for religious life on campus; Christian witness on social and moral issues; objective and independent mediation between various groups on campus; participation in religious aspects of the work of the administration, faculty and students.

Status, Agencies

The dimensions and challenge of the campus ministry are evident from estimates that approximately 75 to 80 per cent of 2.4 million Catholics in colleges and universities are on non-Catholic public and private campuses. Serving them are about 1,200 full-time and 700 part-time campus ministry personnel.

The Office of Campus and Young Adult Ministry, under the Department of Education of the U.S. Catholic Conference, has responsibility for continuing support of ministry in this field. The office, headed by Father Joseph J. Kenna, is located at 1312 Massachusetts Ave. N.W., Washington, D.C. 20005.

The autonomous Catholic Campus Ministry Association, is headquartered at 3700 West 103rd St., Chicago, Ill. 60655. Sister Margaret M. Ivers, I.B.V.M., is executive director.

NCEA

The National Catholic Educational Association, founded in 1904, is a voluntary organization of educational institutions and individuals concerned with Catholic education in the U.S. Its objectives are to promote and encourage the principles and ideals of Christian education and formation by suitable service and other activities.

The NCEA has 14,000 institutional and individual members. Its official publication is *Momentum*. Numerous service publications are issued to members.

Bishop John F. Cummins of Oakland, Calif., is chairman of the association. Msgr. John F. Meyers is president.

Headquarters are located at: 1077 30th St. N.W., Washington, D.C. 20007.

SCHOOL STATISTICS

The status of Catholic educational institutions and programs in the United States at the beginning of 1983, 1982 and 1973 was reflected in figures (as of Jan. 1) reported by "The Official Catholic Directory, 1983."

Colleges and Universities: 238 (1 more than in 1982 and 24 less than in 1973).

College and University Students: 544,136.

High Schools: 1,470 (same as in 1982 and 283 less than in 1973).

High School Students: 814,068 (19,834 less than in 1982 and 115,606 less than in 1973).

Public High School Students Receiving Religious Instruction: 986,707 (9,609 more than in 1982 and 304,467 less than in 1973).

Elementary Schools: 7,969 (110 less than in 1982 and 863 less than in 1973).

Elementary School Students: 2,268,453 (65,016 less than in 1982 and 605,798 less than in 1973).

Public Elementary School Students Receiving Religious Instruction: 3,218,606 (104,792 less than in 1982 and 1,015,038 less than in 1973).

Teachers: 168,382 (4,910 less than in 1982 and 14,876 less than in 1973).

Lay Teachers: 127,308 (1,706 less than in 1982 and 23,525 more than in 1973).

Sisters Teaching: 33,310 (2,756 less than in 1982 and 33,688 less than in 1973).

Priests Teaching (full time): 4,718 (393 less than in 1982 and 3,323 less than in 1973).

Brothers Teaching: 2,884 (5 less than in 1982 and 1,177 less than in 1973).

Scholastics Teaching: 162 (2 more than in 1982 and 213 less than in 1973).

EDUCATION

LEGAL STATUS OF CATHOLIC EDUCATION

The right of private schools to exist and operate in the United States is recognized in law. It was confirmed by the U.S. Supreme Court in 1925 when the tribunal ruled (Pierce v. Society of Sisters, see Church-State Decisions of the Supreme Court) that an Oregon state law requiring all children to attend public schools was unconstitutional.

Private schools are obliged to comply with the education laws in force in the various states regarding such matters as required basic curricula, periods of attendance, and standards for proper accreditation.

The special curricula and standards of private schools are determined by the schools themselves. Thus, in Catholic schools, the curricula include not only the subject matter required by state educational laws but also other fields of study, principally, education in the Catholic faith.

The Supreme Court has ruled that the First Amendment to the U.S. Constitution, in accordance with the No Establishment of Religion Clause of the First Amendment, prohibits direct federal and state aid from public funds to church-affiliated schools. (See several cases in Church-State Decisions of the Supreme Court.)

Public Aid

This prohibition does not extend to all child-benefit and public-purpose programs of aid to students of non-public elementary and secondary schools.

Statutes authorizing such programs have been ruled constitutional on the grounds that they:

• have a "secular legislative purpose";
• neither inhibit nor advance religion as a "principal or primary effect";
• do not foster "excessive government entanglement with religion."

Aid programs considered constitutional have provided bus transportation, textbook loans, school lunches and health services, and "secular, neutral or non-ideological services, facilities and materials provided in common to all school children," public and non-public.

The first major aid to education program in U.S. history containing provisions benefitting nonpublic school students was enacted by the 89th Congress and signed into law by President Lyndon B. Johnson Apr. 11, 1965. The Elementary and Secondary Education Act was designed to avoid the separation of Church and state impasse which had blocked all earlier aid proposals pertaining to non-

public, and especially church-affiliated, schools. The objective of the program, under public control, is to serve the public purpose by aiding disadvantaged pupils in nonpublic as well as public schools.

In a highly significant 5-to-4 decision June 29, 1983, the U.S. Supreme Court upheld the constitutionality of a Minnesota tuition tax credit for the parents of students attending parochial, other private and public schools. The majority opinion rejected arguments that the law benefitted religion in an unconstitutional manner, and said that the program did not involve excessive church-state entanglement. Supporters of the measure called it sound tax policy.

With respect to college and university education in church-affiliated institutions, the Supreme Court has upheld the constitutionality of statutes providing student loans and, under the Federal Higher Education Facilities Act of 1963, construction loans and grants for secular-purpose facilities.

Catholic schools are exempt from real estate taxation in all of the states. Since Jan. 1, 1959, nonprofit parochial and private schools have also been exempt from several federal excise taxes.

Shared and Released Time

In a shared time program of education, students enrolled in Catholic or other church-related schools take some courses (e.g., religion, social studies, fine arts) in their own schools and others (e.g., science, mathematics, industrial arts) in public schools. Such a program has been given serious consideration in recent years by Catholic and other educators. Its constitutionality has not been seriously challenged, but practical problems — relating to teacher and student schedules, transportation, adjustment to new programs, and other factors — are knotty.

Several million children of elementary and high school age of all denominations have the opportunity of receiving religious instruction on released time. Under released time programs they are permitted to leave their public schools during school hours to attend religious instruction classes held off the public school premises. They are released at the request of their parents. Public school authorities merely provide for their dismissal, and take no part in the program.

CATHOLIC SCHOOLS AND STUDENTS IN THE UNITED STATES

(Source: *The Official Catholic Directory, 1983;* figures as of Jan. 1, 1983. Archdioceses are indicated by an asterisk.)

Section, State Diocese	Univs. Colleges	High Students	High Schools	Elem. Students	Elem. Schools	Students
NEW ENGLAND	26	61,670	136	66,887	541	145,881
Maine, Portland	1	500	3	1,009	21	5,492
New Hampshire, Manchester	5	8,154	6	2,563	30	8,134
Vermont, Burlington	3	2,830	3	1,170	11	2,753

513

Section, State Diocese	Univs. Colleges	Students	High Schools	Students	Elem. Schools	Students
Massachusetts	9	30,431	78	35,169	249	71,478
*Boston	4	19,975	61	24,158	166	48,123
Fall River	1	2,710	5	3,381	24	6,721
Springfield	1	746	4	3,243	35	10,796
Worcester	3	7,000	8	4,387	24	5,838
Rhode Island, Providence	2	7,775	13	6,333	64	17,595
Connecticut	6	11,980	33	20,643	166	40,429
*Hartford	3	1,878	18	11,047	97	22,969
Bridgeport	2	10,032	10	6,004	48	13,142
Norwich	1	70	5	3,592	21	4,318
MIDDLE ATLANTIC	62	167,215	364	236,514	2,120	663,368
New York	28	87,730	156	105,511	920	305,751
*New York	11	41,143	64	38,635	290	92,603
Albany	4	5,844	13	5,145	58	15,154
Brooklyn	2	20,511	23	25,498	176	86,821
Buffalo	6	14,185	21	9,565	141	31,332
Ogdensburg	1	426	3	953	26	5,043
Rochester	—	—	8	6,433	78	21,188
Rockville Centre	2	2,957	16	15,051	87	39,539
Syracuse	2	2,664	8	4,231	64	14,071
New Jersey	8	17,828	90	51,791	451	133,151
*Newark	4	15,375	45	22,136	201	55,612
Camden	—	—	11	8,131	67	19,470
Metuchen	—	—	8	5,016	52	16,217
Paterson	3	954	14	6,347	65	17,057
Trenton	1	1,499	12	10,161	66	24,795
Pennsylvania	26	61,657	118	79,212	749	224,466
*Philadelphia	10	29,400	51	47,674	279	116,467
Allentown	2	1,860	10	4,893	68	14,662
Altoona-Johnstown	2	2,106	—	1,859	38	7,730
Erie	3	6,309	10	4,141	55	14,599
Greensburg	2	2,028	2	1,377	48	8,969
Harrisburg	—	—	10	4,586	57	12,447
Pittsburgh	3	8,924	24	9,739	143	38,834
Scranton	4	11,030	11	4,943	61	12,758
SOUTH ATLANTIC	16	41,038	126	65,538	535	164,773
Delaware, Wilmington	—	—	8	5,130	29	11,143
Maryland, *Baltimore	4	10,117	24	12,518	87	28,456
District of Columbia, *Washington	3	19,835	25	11,634	83	26,234
Virginia	3	1,859	14	6,118	57	17,940
Arlington	3	1,859	4	3,262	29	10,026
Richmond	—	—	10	2,856	28	7,914
West Virginia, Wheeling-Charleston	1	988	9	2,162	35	5,951
North Carolina	2	1,085	3	1,196	33	7,685
Charlotte	2	1,085	2	968	15	3,904
Raleigh	—	—	1	228	18	3,781
South Carolina, Charleston	—	—	4	1,470	29	5,668
Georgia	—	—	7	3,818	29	8,789
*Atlanta	—	—	2	1,724	13	4,402
Savannah	—	—	5	2,094	16	4,387
Florida	3	7,154	32	21,492	153	52,907
*Miami	2	5,994	17	12,385	65	24,884
Orlando	—	—	5	2,716	29	8,662
Pensacola-Tallahassee	—	—	1	547	10	2,686
St. Augustine	—	—	2	1,431	16	5,114
St. Petersburg	1	1,160	7	4,413	33	11,561
EAST NORTH CENTRAL	51	131,406	313	197,501	2,141	593,953
Ohio	11	29,328	89	57,237	513	165,418
*Cincinnati	4	19,875	22	16,957	120	40,364
Cleveland	3	5,754	26	20,288	168	62,570

Section, State Diocese	Univs. Colleges	Students	High Schools	Students	Elem. Schools	Students
Ohio	**11**	**29,328**	**89**	**57,237**	**513**	**165,418**
Columbus	1	1,019	15	5,903	53	14,757
Steubenville	1	890	4	1,179	17	3,096
Toledo	1	640	16	8,638	94	27,778
Youngstown	1	1,150	6	4,272	61	16,853
Indiana	**9**	**16,994**	**25**	**13,876**	**210**	**48,022**
*Indianapolis	2	1,599	9	5,258	73	16,504
Evansville	—	—	5	1,879	30	4,811
Ft. Wayne-South Bend	5	13,164	5	3,474	43	11,743
Gary	1	1,269	4	2,937	42	11,761
Lafayette	1	962	2	428	22	3,203
Illinois	**14**	**43,974**	**99**	**73,771**	**665**	**200,093**
*Chicago	8	35,250	61	53,076	380	133,595
Belleville	1	1,051	4	2,234	54	8,932
Joliet	3	5,377	9	6,919	64	19,376
Peoria	—	—	8	3,668	58	12,896
Rockford	—	—	8	4,099	47	11,607
Springfield	2	2,296	9	3,775	62	13,687
Michigan	**8**	**17,992**	**67**	**34,845**	**340**	**94,705**
*Detroit	5	13,275	44	24,172	164	56,932
Gaylord	—	—	5	924	20	3,563
Grand Rapids	1	2,743	4	2,874	46	9,491
Kalamazoo	1	576	3	1,249	21	4,479
Lansing	1	1,398	5	3,266	41	10,718
Marquette	—	—	1	81	12	2,336
Saginaw	—	—	5	2,279	36	7,186
Wisconsin	**9**	**23,118**	**33**	**17,772**	**413**	**85,715**
*Milwaukee	5	19,093	15	10,409	173	41,424
Green Bay	2	2,067	9	3,479	95	18,902
La Crosse	1	1,105	7	2,893	76	13,128
Madison	1	793	2	991	47	8,349
Superior	—	—	—	—	22	3,912
EAST SOUTH CENTRAL	**8**	**8,801**	**54**	**23,354**	**286**	**65,807**
Kentucky	**5**	**6,070**	**29**	**12,889**	**159**	**35,537**
*Louisville	3	3,934	11	7,547	79	20,244
Covington	1	1,224	13	3,724	53	10,338
Owensboro	1	912	5	1,618	27	4,955
Tennessee	**2**	**1,836**	**10**	**4,587**	**42**	**9,995**
Memphis	1	1,513	5	2,368	16	4,423
Nashville	1	323	5	2,219	26	5,572
Alabama	**1**	**895**	**5**	**3,013**	**48**	**12,196**
*Mobile	1	895	3	1,715	27	7,087
Birmingham	—	—	2	1,298	21	5,109
Mississippi	**—**	**—**	**10**	**2,865**	**37**	**8,079**
Biloxi	—	—	5	1,679	17	3,527
Jackson	—	—	5	1,186	20	4,552
WEST NORTH CENTRAL	**34**	**57,961**	**159**	**67,528**	**911**	**199,464**
Minnesota	**9**	**16,448**	**25**	**11,865**	**226**	**50,860**
*St. Paul and Minneapolis	3	9,029	14	8,847	110	30,936
Crookston	—	—	1	170	11	1,859
Duluth	1	1,155	—	—	16	2,202
New Ulm	—	—	3	585	26	3,992
St. Cloud	3	4,307	3	967	37	6,779
Winona	2	1,957	4	1,296	26	5,092
Iowa	**7**	**9,071**	**29**	**12,358**	**158**	**31,370**
*Dubuque	3	3,843	11	5,125	59	14,377
Davenport	3	3,935	7	1,932	38	5,100
Des Moines	—	—	2	2,089	23	4,317
Sioux City	1	1,293	9	3,212	38	7,576

Section, State Diocese	Univs. Colleges	Students	High Schools	Students	Elem. Schools	Students
Missouri	6	18,795	46	23,902	280	67,808
*St. Louis	4	13,714	32	18,253	179	48,113
Jefferson City	—	—	2	885	36	6,018
Kansas City-St. Joseph	2	5,081	9	4,110	43	11,045
Springfield-Cape Girardeau	—	—	3	654	22	2,632
North Dakota	2	1,311	7	1,883	33	6,211
Bismarck	1	1,121	6	1,389	18	3,482
Fargo	1	190	1	494	15	2,729
South Dakota	2	904	5	1,441	27	4,817
Rapid City	—	—	2	400	3	739
Sioux Falls	2	904	3	1,041	24	4,078
Nebraska	2	6,823	30	9,307	95	18,896
*Omaha	2	6,823	17	6,383	63	13,743
Grand Island	—	—	7	1,523	8	1,033
Lincoln	—	—	6	1,401	24	4,120
Kansas	6	4,609	17	6,772	92	19,502
*Kansas City	3	2,522	7	3,158	38	9,570
Dodge City	1	618	—	—	12	1,696
Salina	1	706	6	946	12	2,003
Wichita	1	763	4	2,668	30	6,233
WEST SOUTH CENTRAL	12	22,434	122	50,685	504	156,810
Arkansas, Little Rock	—	—	6	1,918	34	5,518
Louisiana	4	8,451	63	29,662	202	82,316
*New Orleans	4	8,451	28	17,907	95	43,924
Alexandria-Shreveport	—	—	7	2,192	24	6,567
Baton Rouge	—	—	9	3,443	28	12,065
Houma-Thibodaux	—	—	3	1,288	12	4,940
Lafayette	—	—	14	4,012	33	11,327
Lake Charles	—	—	2	820	10	3,493
Oklahoma	1	338	5	2,270	31	6,022
*Oklahoma City	1	338	2	943	17	3,181
Tulsa	—	—	3	1,327	14	2,841
Texas	7	13,645	48	16,835	237	62,954
*San Antonio	4	6,346	10	3,634	35	13,323
Amarillo	—	—	2	211	12	2,050
Austin	1	2,575	1	223	15	3,456
Beaumont	—	—	2	671	10	1,897
Brownsville	—	—	2	810	8	2,103
Corpus Christi	—	—	2	961	27	5,801
Dallas	1	2,684	9	3,125	34	10,383
El Paso	—	—	3	1,154	14	3,476
Fort Worth	—	—	4	1,420	15	3,785
Galveston-Houston	1	2,040	9	4,126	51	13,230
Lubbock	No separate statistics available.					
San Angelo	—	—	—	—	4	791
Victoria	—	—	4	500	12	2,659
MOUNTAIN	5	6,456	34	14,155	170	47,325
Montana	1	2,592	5	1,115	20	3,853
Great Falls-Billings	1	1,272	3	507	18	3,419
Helena	—	1,320	2	608	2	434
Idaho, Boise	1	48	1	389	12	1,780
Wyoming, Cheyenne	—	—	1	126	7	1,366
Colorado	1	1,045	9	3,426	54	13,621
*Denver	1	1,045	6	3,054	42	11,937
Pueblo	—	—	3	372	12	1,684
New Mexico	2	2,771	5	1,736	37	7,978
*Santa Fe	2	2,771	3	1,563	23	5,482
Gallup	—	—	2	173	9	1,684
Las Cruces	—	—	—	—	5	812

Section, State Diocese	Univs. Colleges	Students	High Schools	Students	Elem. Schools	Students
Arizona	—	—	9	4,884	20	12,999
Phoenix	—	—	6	3,553	—	8,172
Tucson	—	—	3	1,331	20	4,827
Utah, Salt Lake City	—	—	2	964	9	2,680
Nevada, Reno-Las Vegas	—	—	2	1,515	11	3,048
PACIFIC	22	46,749	157	91,193	717	224,432
Washington	3	8,590	12	7,297	84	19,217
*Seattle	2	5,058	9	5,873	58	14,805
Spokane	1	3,532	2	1,148	19	2,711
Yakima	—	—	1	276	7	1,701
Oregon	2	3,922	10	3,889	56	10,402
*Portland	2	3,922	9	3,809	52	9,726
Baker	—	—	1	80	4	676
California	16	33,330	125	75,603	544	183,821
*Los Angeles	5	8,488	57	35,439	231	74,105
*San Francisco	3	9,043	19	10,059	15	22,603
Fresno	—	—	2	1,387	25	6,505
Monterey	—	—	2	917	14	3,639
Oakland	4	3,492	11	6,508	54	15,528
Orange	1	100	5	4,108	36	13,853
Sacramento	—	—	9	4,063	42	11,286
San Bernardino	—	—	2	1,466	29	7,885
San Diego	1	4,976	5	3,295	44	13,239
San Jose	2	7,231	6	4,801	28	8,813
Santa Rosa	—	—	5	2,034	14	3,208
Stockton	—	—	2	1,526	12	3,157
Alaska	—	—	2	241	4	781
*Anchorage	—	—	—	—	2	283
Fairbanks	—	—	2	241	1	352
Juneau	—	—	—	—	1	146
Hawaii, Honolulu	1	907	8	4,163	29	10,211
EASTERN RITES	2	406	5	713	44	6,640
*Philadelphia	1	390	1	369	15	2,682
St. Nicholas of Chicago	—	—	1	104	2	369
Stamford	1	16	3	240	9	897
*Pittsburgh	—	—	—	—	6	1,020
Parma	—	—	—	—	5	814
Passaic	—	—	—	—	7	858
Van Nuys	—	—	—	—	—	—
St. Maron	—	—	—	—	—	—
Newton	—	—	—	—	—	—
Romanians (Ap. Ex.)	No separate statistics available.					
Chaldeans (Ap. Ex.)	No separate statistics available.					
Armenians (Ap. Ex.)	No separate statistics available.					
MILITARY VICARIATE	—	—	—	—	—	—
TOTALS 1983	238	544,136	1,470	814,068	7,969	2,268,453
Totals 1982	237	533,086	1,470	833,902	8,079	2,333,469
Totals 1973	262	418,083	1,753	929,674	8,832	2,874,251

Educational Associations

National Association of Boards of Education: Founded in 1971 and made a department of the National Catholic Educational Association in 1973, to develop and promote policy-making boards for the advancement of Catholic education. Has a national membership of 1,204. Publishes *PolicyMaker* four times a year. Office: 1077 30th St. N.W., Washington, D.C. 20007.

National Forum of Catholic Parent Organizations: Founded in 1976 as a commission of the National Catholic Educational Association, to support and promote the role of parents as primary educators of their children. Has a national membership of 400 affiliates. Publishes *Parentcator* 5 five times a year. Office: 1077 30th St. N.W., Washington, D.C. 20007.

UNIVERSITIES AND COLLEGES IN THE UNITED STATES

(Sources: Almanac survey; *The Official Catholic Directory.*)

Listed below are institutions of higher learning established under Catholic auspices. Some of them are now independent.

Information includes: name of each institution; indication of male (m), female (w), coeducational (c) student body; name of founding group or group with which the institution is affiliated; year of foundation; number of students, in parentheses.

Albertus Magnus College (w): 700 Prospect St., New Haven, Conn. 06511. Dominican Sisters; 1925 (500).

Albuquerque, University of (c): St. Joseph Pl. N.W., Albuquerque, N.M. 87140. Sisters of St. Francis; 1920 (1,180).

Allentown College of St. Francis de Sales (c): Center Valley, Pa. 18034. Oblates of St. Francis de Sales; 1965 (1,101).

Alvernia College (c): Reading, Pa. 19607. Bernardine Sisters; 1958 (721).

Alverno College (w): 3401 S. 39th St. Milwaukee, Wis. 53215. School Sisters of St. Francis; 1936; independent (1,359).

Anna Maria College (c): Sunset Lane, Paxton, Mass. 01612. Sisters of St. Anne; 1946; independent (1,742).

Aquinas College (c): 1607 Robinson Rd. S.E., Grand Rapids, Mich. 49506. Sisters of St. Dominic; 1922 (2,800).

Assumption College (c): 500 Salisbury St., Worcester, Mass. 01609. Assumptionist Fathers; 1904 (2,664).

Avila College (c): 11901 Wornall Rd., Kansas City, Mo. 64145. Sisters of St. Joseph of Carondelet; 1916 (1,876).

Barat College (c): 700 E. Westleigh Rd., Lake Forest, Ill. 60045. Society of the Sacred Heart; 1919; independent (655).

Barry University (c): 11300 N.E. 2nd Ave., Miami, Fla. 33161. Dominican Sisters; 1940 (3,018).

Bellarmine College (c): Newburg Rd., Louisville, Ky. 40205; Louisville archdiocese, 1950 (2,730).

Belmont Abbey College (c): Belmont, N.C. 28012. Benedictine Fathers; 1876 (801).

Benedictine College (c): Atchison, Kans. 66002. Benedictines, 1971 (965).

Biscayne College (c): 16400 N.W. 32nd Ave., Miami, Fla. 33054. Augustinian Fathers; 1962 (3,000).

Boston College (University Status) (c): Chestnut Hill, Mass. 02167. Jesuit Fathers; 1863 (14,069).

Brescia College (c): 120 W. 7th St., Owensboro, Ky. 42301. Ursuline Sisters; 1925 (912).

Briar Cliff College (c): W. 3303 Rebecca St., Sioux City, Ia. 51104. Sisters of St. Francis of the Holy Family; 1930 (1,342).

Cabrini College (c): Radnor, Pa. 19087. Missionary Srs. of Sacred Heart; 1957 (606).

Caldwell College (w): Caldwell, N.J. 07006. Dominican Sisters; 1939 (758).

Calumet College (c): 2400 New York Ave.,

Whiting, Ind. 46394. Society of the Precious Blood, 1951 (1,287).

Canisius College (c): 2001 Main St., Buffalo, N.Y. 14208. Jesuit Fathers; 1870; independent (4,418).

Cardinal Newman College (c): 7701 Florissant Rd., St. Louis, Mo. 63121. Catholic college with autonomous board of trustees; 1976.

Cardinal Stritch College (c): 6801 N. Yates Rd., Milwaukee, Wis. 53217. Sisters of St. Francis of Assisi; 1932; independent (1,350).

Carlow College (w): 3333 5th Ave., Pittsburgh, Pa. 15213. Sisters of Mercy; 1929 (963).

Carroll College (c): Helena, Mont. 59625. Diocesan; 1909 (1,370).

Catholic University of America, The (c): 620 Michigan Ave. N.E., Washington, D.C. 20064. Hierarchy of the United States; 1887. Pontifical University (7,200).

Catholic University of Puerto Rico (c): Ponce, P.R. Hierarchy of Puerto Rico; 1948; Pontifical University (13,048).

Chaminade University (c): 3140 Waialae Ave., Honolulu, Hawaii 96816. Marianists; 1955 (1,907).

Chestnut Hill College (w): Philadelphia, Pa. 19118. Sisters of St. Joseph; 1871 (1,100).

Christendom College (c): Rt. 3, Box 87, Front Royal, Va. 22630 (98).

Christian Brothers College (c): 650 E. Parkway S., Memphis, Tenn. 38104. Brothers of the Christian Schools; 1871 (1,483).

Clarke College (c): 1550 Clarke Dr., Dubuque, Iowa 52001. Sisters of Charity, BVM; 1843 (850).

Creighton University (c): 2500 California St., Omaha, Neb. 68178. Jesuit Fathers; 1878 (5,600).

Dallas, University of (c): Irving, Tex. 75061. Private; 1956; independent (2,684).

Dayton, University of (c): 300 College Park Ave., Dayton, Ohio 45409. Marianists; 1850 (10,700).

De Lourdes College (w): 353 N. River Rd., Des Plaines, Ill. 60016. Sisters of the Holy Family of Nazareth; 1927; independent (278).

DePaul University (c): 2323 N. Seminary Ave., Chicago, Ill. 60614. Vincentians; 1898 (13,000).

Detroit, University of (c): 4001 W. McNichols Rd. at Livernois, Detroit, Mich. 48221. Jesuit Fathers; 1877 (6,270).

Dominican College of Blauvelt (c): Orangeburg, N.Y. 10962. Dominican Sisters; 1952; independent (1,731).

Dominican College of San Rafael (c): 1520 Grand Ave.; San Rafael, Calif. 94901. Dominican Sisters; 1890; independent (600).

Duquesne University (c): Bluff St., Pittsburgh, Pa. 15282. Holy Ghost Fathers; 1878 (6,400).

D'Youville College (c): One D'Youville Square, Buffalo, N.Y. 14201. Grey Nuns of the Sacred Heart; 1908; independent (1,200).

Edgecliff College of Xavier University (c): 2220 Victory Pkwy., Cincinnati, Ohio 45206. Sisters of Mercy; 1935 (667).

Edgewood College (c): 855 Woodrow St.,

Madison, Wis. 53711. Dominican Sisters; 1927 (793).

Elms College (w): Chicopee, Mass. 01013. Sisters of St. Joseph; 1928 (700).

Emmanuel College (w): 400 The Fenway, Boston, Mass. 02115. Sisters of Notre Dame de Namur; independent (1,067).

Fairfield University (c): North Benson Rd., Fairfield, Conn. 06430. Jesuit Fathers; 1942 (4,960).

Felician College (w): S. Main St., Lodi, N.J. 07644. Felician Sisters; 1942 (610). Coed in nursing and evening programs.

Fontbonne College (c): 6800 Wydown Blvd., St. Louis, Mo. 63105. Sisters of St. Joseph of Carondelet; 1917 (900).

Fordham University (c): Fordham Rd. and Third Ave., New York, N.Y. 10458. Society of Jesus (Jesuits); 1841; independent (14,000).

Gannon University (c): University Square, Erie, Pa. 16541. Diocese of Erie; 1933 (4,200).

Georgetown University (c): Post Office Box 37455, Washington, D.C. 20013. Jesuit Fathers; 1789 (11,960).

Georgian Court College (w): Lakewood, N.J. 08701. Sisters of Mercy; 1908 (1,499). Coed in evening and graduate divisions.

Gonzaga University (c): Spokane, Wash. 99258. Jesuit Fathers; 1887 (3,532).

Great Falls, College of (c): 1301 20th St. S., Great Falls, Mont. 59405. Sisters of Providence; 1932 (750).

Gwynedd-Mercy College (c): Gwynedd Valley, Pa. 19437. Sisters of Mercy; 1948; independent (2,200).

Holy Cross, College of the (c): Worcester, Mass. 01610. Jesuit Fathers; 1843 (2,494).

Holy Family College (c): Grant and Frankford Aves., Philadelphia, Pa. 19114. Sisters of Holy Family of Nazareth; 1954 (1,309).

Holy Names College (c): 3500 Mountain Blvd., Oakland, Calif. 94619. Sisters of the Holy Names of Jesus and Mary; 1868 (678).

Illinois Benedictine College (c): Lisle, Ill. 60532. Benedictine Fathers of St. Procopius Abbey; 1887 (1,630).

Immaculata College (w): Immaculata, Pa 19345. Sisters, Servants of the Immaculate Heart of Mary; 1920 (823).

Incarnate Word College (c): 4301 Broadway, San Antonio, Tex. 78209. Sisters of Charity of the Incarnate Word; 1881 (1,400).

Iona College (c): 715 North Ave., New Rochelle, N.Y. 10801. Congregation of Christian Brothers; 1940; independent (6,200).

John Carroll University (c): North Park and Miramar Blvds., Cleveland, Ohio. 44118. Jesuit Fathers; 1886 (3,954).

Kansas Newman College (formerly Sacred Heart College) (c): 3100 McCormick Ave., Wichita, Kans. 67213. Sisters Adorers of the Blood of Christ; 1933 (763).

King's College (c): Wilkes-Barre, Pa. 18711. Holy Cross Fathers; 1946 (2,306).

La Roche College (c): 9000 Babcock Blvd.,

Pittsburgh, Pa. 15237. Sisters of Divine Providence; 1963 (1,613).

La Salle College (c): 20th St. and Olney Ave., Philadelphia, Pa. 19141. Brothers of the Christian Schools; 1863 (7,065).

Le Moyne College (c): Syracuse, N.Y. 13214. Jesuit Fathers; 1946; independent (1,800).

Lewis University (c): Romeoville, Ill. 60441. Christian Brothers; 1932 (2,700).

Loras College (c): 1450 Alta Vista St., Dubuque, Ia. 52001. Archdiocese of Dubuque; 1839 (1,882).

Lourdes College (c): Sylvania, Ohio 43560. Franciscan Srs.; 1958 (720).

Loyola College (c): 4501 N. Charles St., Baltimore, Md. 21210, Jesuits; 1852; combined with Mt. St. Agnes College, 1971 (6,211).

Loyola Marymount University (c): 7101 W. 80th St., Los Angeles, Calif. 90045. Society of Jesus; Religious of Sacred Heart of Mary, Sisters of St. Joseph of Orange; 1911 (6,359).

Loyola University (c): 6363 St. Charles Ave., New Orleans, La. 70118. Jesuit Fathers; 1904 (4,347).

Loyola University of Chicago (c): 820 N. Michigan Ave., Chicago, Ill. 60611. Jesuit Fathers; 1870 (15,857).

Madonna College (c): 36600 Schoolcraft Rd., Livonia, Mich. 48150. Felician Sisters; 1947 (3,505).

Magdalen College (c): 270 D.W. Highway So., RFD No. 5, Bedford, N.H. 03102; Magdalen College Corporation; 1973 (70).

Mallinckrodt College (c): 1041 Ridge Rd., Wilmette, Ill. 60091. Sisters of Christian Chrity; 1918; independent. (285).

Manhattan College (c): 4513 Manhattan College Pkwy., New York, N.Y. 10471. Brothers of the Christian Schools; 1853; independent (5,000). Cooperative program with College of Mt. St. Vincent.

Manhattanville College (c): Purchase, N.Y. 10577. Society of the Sacred Heart; 1841; independent (1,585).

Marian College (c): Fond du Lac, Wis. 54935. Sisters of St. Agnes; 1936 (563).

Marian College (c): 3200 Cold Spring Rd., Indianapolis, Ind. 46222. Sisters of St. Francis (Oldenburg, Ind.); 1851 (850).

Marist College (c): Poughkeepsie, N.Y. 12601. Marist Brothers of the Schools; 1946; independent (1,899).

Marquette University (c): 615 N. 11th St., Milwaukee, Wis. 53233. Jesuit Fathers; 1881; independent (12,000).

Mary College (c): Bismarck, N.D. 58501. Benedictine Sisters; 1959 (1,153).

Marycrest College (c): 1607 W. 12th St., Davenport, Iowa 52804. Congregation of the Humility of Mary; 1939; independent (1,400).

Marygrove College (c): 8425 W. McNicholas Rd., Detroit, Mich. 48221. Sisters, Servants of the Immaculate Heart of Mary; 1910 (1,153).

Marylhurst Education Center, College for Lifelong Learning (c): Marylhurst, Ore. 97036. Srs. of Holy Names of Jesus and Mary; 1893; independent (453).

Marymount College (w): Tarrytown, N.Y. 10591. Religious of the Sacred Heart of Mary; 1907;

independent (1,300). Coed in weekend degree programs.

Marymount College of Kansas (c): Salina, Kans. 67401. Salina diocese; 1922 (706).

Marymount College of Virginia (w): 2807 N. Glebe Rd., Arlington, Va. 22007. Religious of the Sacred Heart of Mary; 1950; independent (1,650).

Marymount Manhattan College (w): 221 E. 71st St., New York, N.Y. 10021. Religious of the Sacred Heart of Mary; 1936; independent (2,214).

Maryville College (c): 13550 Conway Rd., St. Louis, Mo. 63141. Religious of the Sacred Heart; 1872; independent (1,927).

Marywood College (w): Scranton, Pa. 18509. Sisters, Servants of the Immaculate Heart of Mary; 1915 (3,191). Coed in graduate division.

Mater Dei College (c): Riverside Dr., Ogdensburg, N.Y. 13669. Sisters of St. Joseph; 1960; independent (400).

Mercy College of Detroit (c): 8200 W. Outer Dr., Detroit, Mich. 48219. Sisters of Mercy; 1941 (2,210).

Mercyhurst College (c): 501 E. 38th St., Erie, Pa. 16546. Sisters of Mercy; 1926 (1,441).

Merrimack College (c): North Andover, Mass. 01845. Augustinians; 1947 (2,205).

Misericordia (College Misericordia) (c): Dallas, Pa. 18612. Religious Sisters of Mercy of the Union; 1924 (897).

Molloy College (c): 1000 Hempstead Ave., Rockville Centre, N.Y. 11570. Dominican Sisters; 1955 (1,636).

Mount Marty College (c): Yankton, S.D. 57078. Benedictine Sisters; 1936 (570).

Mount Mary College (w): 2900 W. Menomonee River Pkwy., Milwaukee, Wis. 53222. School Sisters of Notre Dame; 1913 (1,111).

Mt. Mercy College (c): 1330 Elmhurst Dr. N.E., Cedar Rapids, Ia. 52402. Sisters of Mercy; 1928 (1,167).

Mt. St. Clare College (c): Bluff Blvd. and Springdale Dr., Clinton, Ia. 52732. Clinton Franciscans; 1928 (379).

Mt. St. Joseph on the Ohio, College of (w): Mt. St. Joseph, Ohio 45051. Sisters of Charity; 1920 (1,887).

Mt. St. Mary College (c): Newburgh, N.Y. 12550. Dominican Sisters; 1959; independent (1,015).

Mount St. Mary College (c): Emmitsburg, Md. 21727. Diocesan Clergy; 1808; independent (1,358).

Mt. St. Mary's College (w): 12001 Chalon Rd., Los Angeles, Calif. 90049 and 10 Chester Pl., Los Angeles, Calif. 90007 (Doheny Campus). Sisters of St. Joseph of Carondelet; 1925 (1,144). Coed in music, nursing and graduate programs.

Mt. St. Vincent, College of (c): Mt. St. Vincent-on-Hudson, New York, N.Y. 10471. Sisters of Charity; 1847; independent (1,200). Cooperative program with Manhattan College.

Mundelein College (w): 6363 N. Sheridan Rd., Chicago, Ill. 60660. Sisters of Charity of the Blessed Virgin Mary; 1929 (1,282).

Nazareth College (c): Nazareth, Mich. 49074. Sisters of St. Joseph; 1924; independent (540).

Nazareth College (c): East Ave., Rochester,

N.Y. 14610. Sisters of St. Joseph of Rochester; 1924; independent (2,422).

Neumann College (formerly Our Lady of Angels) (c): Aston, Pa. 19014. Sisters of St. Francis; 1965 (847).

New Rochelle, College of (w): 29 Castle Pl., New Rochelle, N.Y. 10801 (main campus). Ursuline Nuns; 1904; independent (5,729). Coed in nursing, graduate, new resources divisions.

Niagara University (c): Niagara Univ., N.Y. 14109. Vincentian Fathers; 1856 (3,954).

Notre Dame, College of (c): Belmont, Calif. 94002. Sisters of Notre Dame de Namur; 1868; independent (1,420).

Notre Dame, University of (c): Notre Dame, Ind. 46556. Congregation of Holy Cross; 1842 (9,050).

Notre Dame College (w): 4545 College Rd., Cleveland, Ohio 44121. Sisters of Notre Dame; 1922 (729).

Notre Dame College (w): Manchester, N.H. 03104. Sisters of the Holy Cross; 1950 (716).

Notre Dame of Maryland, College of (w): 4701 N. Charles St., Baltimore, Md. 21210. School Sisters of Notre Dame; 1873 (575).

Ohio Dominican College (c): Columbus, Ohio 43219. Dominican Sisters of St. Mary of the Springs; 1911 (1,019).

Our Lady of Holy Cross College (c): 4123 Woodland Dr., New Orleans, La. 70114. Congregation of Sisters Marianites of Holy Cross (758).

Our Lady of the Lake University of San Antonio (c): 411 S.W. 24th St., San Antonio, Tex. 78285. Sisters of Divine Providence; 1911 (1,695).

Parks College of St. Louis University (c): Cahokia, Ill. 62206. Jesuits; 1927; independent (1,051).

Portland, University of (c): 5000 N. Willamette Blvd., Portland, Ore. 97203. Holy Cross Fathers; 1901; independent (2,872).

Providence College (c): River Ave. and Eaton St., Providence, R.I. 02918. Dominican Friars; 1917 (3,400).

Quincy College (c): 1831 College Ave., Quincy, Ill. 62301. Franciscan Friars; 1859 (1,940).

Regis College (c): W. 50th Ave. and Lowell Blvd. Denver, Colo. 80221. Jesuit Fathers; 1887 (1,070).

Regis College (w): Weston, Mass. 02193. Sisters of St. Joseph; 1927; independent (1,189).

Rivier College (w): Nashua, N.H. 03060. Sisters of the Presentation of Mary; 1933; independent (2,261). Coed continuing education and graduate school.

Rockhurst College (c): 5225 Troost Ave., Kansas City, Mo. 64110. Jesuit Fathers; 1910 (3,205).

Rosary College (c): 7900 Division St., River Forest, Ill. 60305. Dominican Sisters; 1901 (1,692).

Rosemont College (w): Rosemont, Pa. 19010. Society of the Holy Child Jesus; 1921 (600).

Sacred Heart College (c): Belmont, N.C. 28012. Sisters of Mercy; 1935 (395).

Sacred Heart University (c): Fairfield (P.O. Bridgeport), Conn. 06606. Diocese of Bridgeport; 1963; independent (5,072).

St. Ambrose College (c): Davenport, Ia. 52803. Diocese of Davenport; 1882 (2,060).

Saint Anselm College (c): Manchester N.H. 03102. Benedictine Monks; 1889 (1,901).

St. Basil's College (m): 195 Glenbrook Rd., Stamford, Conn. 06902. Byzantine-Ukrainian Rite Diocese of Stamford; 1939 (15).

Saint Benedict, College of (w): St. Joseph, Minn. 56374. Benedictine Sisters; 1913 (1,951).

St. Bonaventure University (c): St. Bonaventure, N.Y. 14778. Franciscan Friars; 1856; independent (2,900).

St. Catherine, College of (w): 2004 Randolph St., St. Paul, Minn. 55105. Sisters of St. Joseph of Carondelet; 1905 (1,953).

St. Edward's University (c): Austin, Tex. 78704. Holy Cross Brothers; 1885; independent (2,474).

St. Elizabeth, College of (w): Convent Station, N.J. 07961. Sisters of Charity; 1899; independent (880).

St. Francis, College of (c): 500 N. Wilcox St., Joliet, Ill. 60435. Sisters of St. Francis of Mary Immaculate; 1925; independent (940).

St. Francis College (c): 180 Remsen St., Brooklyn, N.Y. 11201. Franciscan Brothers; 1884; private, independent in the Franciscsan tradition (2,882).

St. Francis College (c): 2701 Spring St., Fort Wayne, Ind. 46808. Sisters of St. Francis; 1890 (1,275).

St. Francis College (c): Loretto, Pa. 15940. Franciscan Fathers; 1847; independent (1,503).

St. John Fisher College (c): 3690 East Ave., Rochester, N.Y. 14618. Basilian Fathers; 1951; independent (1,700).

St. John's University (c): Grand Central and Utopia Pkwys., Jamaica, N.Y. 11439 (Queens Campus); 300 Howard Ave., Grymes Hill, Staten Island, N.Y. 10301 (Staten Island Campus). Vincentian Fathers; 1870 (18,490).

St. John's University (m): Collegeville, Minn. 56321. Benedictines; 1857 (2,000). Coed in graduate school.

Saint Joseph College (w): 1678 Asylum Ave., West Hartford, Conn. 06117. Sisters of Mercy; 1932 (1,212). Coed in graduate school.

Saint Joseph's College (c): N. Windham, Me. 04062. Sisters of Mercy; 1912 (500).

Saint Joseph's College (c): Rensselaer, Ind. 47978. Society of the Precious Blood; 1889 (982).

St. Joseph's College (c): 245 Clinton Ave., Brooklyn, N.Y. 11205 and 155 Roe Blvd., Patchogue, N.Y. 11772. Sisters of St. Joseph; 1916; independent (1,735).

St. Joseph's University (c): 5600 City Ave., Philadelphia, Pa. 19131. Jesuit Fathers; 1851 (5,587).

St. Joseph the Provider, College of (c): Clement Rd., Rutland, Vt. 05701. Sisters of St. Joseph; 1954; independent (154).

Saint Leo College (c): Saint Leo, Fla. 33574. Order of St. Benedict; 1889; independent (1,200).

St. Louis University (c): 221 N. Grand Blvd., St. Louis, Mo. 63103. Jesuit Fathers; 1818 (10,179).

Saint Martin's College (c): Lacey, Wash. 98503. Benedictine Monks; 1895 (550).

St. Mary, College of (w): 1901 S. 72nd St., Oma-

ha, Neb. 68124. Sisters of Mercy; 1923; independent (1,141).

Saint Mary College (w): Leavenworth, Kans. 66048. Sisters of Charity of Leavenworth; 1923 (863).

St. Mary of the Plains College (c): Dodge City, Kans. 67801. Sisters of St. Joseph of Wichita; 1952 (667).

St. Mary-of-the-Woods College (w): St. Mary-of-the-Woods, Ind. 47876. Sisters of Providence; 1840 (770).

St. Mary's College (w): Notre Dame, Ind. 46556. Sisters of the Holy Cross; 1844 (1,853).

St. Mary's College (c): Orchard Lake, Mich. 48033. Secular Clergy; 1885 (240).

St. Mary's College (c): Moraga, Calif. 94575. Brothers of the Christian Schools; 1863 (2,779).

St. Mary's College (c): Winona, Minn. 55987. Brothers of the Christian Schools; 1912 (1,404).

St. Mary's Dominican College (w): 7214 St. Charles Ave., New Orleans, La. 70118. Dominican Sisters; 1910 (880).

St. Mary's University (c): One Camino Santa Maria, San Antonio, Tex. 78284. Society of Mary (Marianists); 1852 (3,311).

St. Michael's College (c): Winooski, Vt. 05404. Society of St. Edmund; 1904 (1,638).

St. Norbert College (c): De Pere, Wis. 54115. Norbertine Fathers; 1898; independent (1,733).

St. Peter's College (c): 2641 Kennedy Blvd., Jersey City, N.J. 07306. Jesuit Fathers; independent; 1872 (4,036).

Saint Rose, College of (c): 432 Western Ave., Albany, N.Y. 12203. Sisters of St. Joseph of Carondelet; 1920; independent (2,728).

St. Scholastica, College of (c): 1200 Kenwood Ave., Duluth, Minn. 55811. Benedictine Sisters; 1912 (1,161).

Saint Teresa, College of (w): Winona, Minn. 55907. Sisters of St. Francis; 1907 (609).

St. Thomas, College of (c): St. Paul, Minn. 55101. Archdiocese of St. Paul; 1885 (5,854).

St. Thomas, University of (c): 3812 Montrose Blvd., Houston, Tex. 77006. Basilian Fathers; 1947 (1,929).

St. Thomas Aquinas College (c): Sparkill, N.Y. 10976. Dominican Sisters of Sparkill; 1952; independent, corporate board of trustees (1,973).

St. Vincent College (c): Latrobe, Pa. 15650. Benedictine Fathers; 1846 (1,060).

St. Xavier College (c): 3700 W. 103rd St., Chicago, Ill. 60655. Sisters of Mercy; chartered 1847 (2,300).

Salve Regina — The Newport College (c): Ochre Point Ave., Newport, R.I. 02840. Sisters of Mercy; 1934 (1,960).

San Diego, University of (c): Alcala Park, San Diego, Calif. 92110. San Diego diocese and Religious of the Sacred Heart; 1949; independent (5,003).

San Francisco, University of (c): Ignation Heights, San Francisco, Calif. 94117. Jesuit Fathers; 1855 (7,065).

Santa Clara, University of (c): Santa Clara, Calif. 95053. Jesuit Fathers; 1851 (7,266).

Santa Fe, College of (c): Santa Fe, N. Mex.

87501. Brothers of the Christian Schools; 1947 (1,000).

Scranton, University of (c): Scranton, Pa. 18510. Society of Jesus; 1888 (4,517).

Seattle University (c): Broadway and East Madison, Seattle, Wash. 98122. Jesuit Fathers; 1891 (4,467).

Seton Hall University (c): South Orange, N.J. 07079. Diocesan Clergy; 1856 (10,157).

Seton Hill College (w): Greensburg, Pa. 15601. Sisters of Charity of Seton Hill; 1883 (937).

Siena College (c): Loudonville, N.Y. 12211. Franciscan Friars; 1937 (2,818).

Siena Heights College (c): Adrian, Mich. 49221. Dominican Sisters; 1919; independent (1,485).

Silver Lake College of Holy Family (c): 2406 S. Alverno Rd., Manitowoc, Wis. 54220. Franciscan Sisters of Christian Charity; 1935 (425).

Spalding College (c): 851 S. 4th Ave., Louisville, Ky. 40203. Sisters of Charity of Nazareth; 1814; independent (1,015).

Spring Hill College (c): Mobile, Ala. 36608. Jesuit Fathers; 1830 (898).

Steubenville, University of (c): Steubenville, Ohio 43952. Franciscan Fathers; 1946 (915).

Stonehill College (c): North Easton, Mass. 02356. Holy Cross Fathers; 1948; independent (2,710).

Thomas Aquinas College (c): 1000 N. Ojai Rd., Santa Paula, Calif. 93060. (108).

Thomas More College (c): Crestview Hills, Covington, Ky. 41017. Diocese of Covington; 1921 (1,229).

Trinity College (w): Colchester Ave., Burlington, Vt. 05401. Sisters of Mercy; 1925 (869).

Trinity College (w): Michigan Ave. and Franklin St. N.E., Washington, D.C. 20017. Sisters of Notre Dame de Namur; 1897 (758). Coed in graduate school.

Ursuline College (w): 2550 Lander Rd., Cleveland, Ohio 44124. Ursuline Nuns; 1871 (1,300).

Villa Maria College (w): 2551 W. Lake Rd., Erie, Pa. 16505. Sisters of St. Joseph; 1925 (693).

Villanova University (c): Villanova, Pa. 19085. Order of St. Augustine; 1842 (11,190).

Viterbo College (c): La Crosse, Wis. 54601. Franciscan Sisters; 1890 (1,160).

Walsh College (c): 2020 Easton St. N.W., Canton, Ohio 44720. Brothers of Christian Instruction; 1958 (1,150).

Wheeling College (c): 316 Washington Ave., Wheeling, W. Va. 26003. Jesuit Fathers; 1954 (990).

Xavier University (c): 3800 Victory Pkwy., Cincinnati, Ohio 45207. Jesuit Fathers; 1831 (6,950).

Xavier University of Louisiana (c): 7325 Palmetto St., New Orleans, La. 70125. Sisters of Blessed Sacrament; 1925; lay religious administration board (2,194).

Catholic Junior Colleges

Ancilla Domini College (c): Donaldson, Ind. 46513. Ancilla Domini Sisters; 1937 (420).

Aquinas Junior College (c): Harding Rd., Nashville, Tenn. 37205. Dominican Sisters; 1961 (350).

Assumption College for Sisters: Hilltop Rd.,

Mendham, N.J. 07945. Sisters of Christian Charity; 1953 (30).

Chatfield College (c): St. Martin, O. 45118. Ursulines; 1971 (314).

Donnelly College (c): 1236 Sandusky Ave., Kansas City, Kans. 66102. Archdiocesan College; 1949 (710).

Don Bosco Technical Institute (m): 1151 San Gabriel Blvd., Rosemead, Calif. 91770. Salesians; 1969 (324).

Elizabeth Seton College (c): 1061 N. Broadway, Yonkers, N.Y. 10701. Sisters of Charity; 1960; independent (1,432).

Felician College (c): 3800 W. Peterson Ave., Chicago, Ill. 60659.

Hilbert College (c): 5200 S. Park Ave., Hamburg, N.Y. 14075. Franciscan Sisters of St. Joseph; 1957; independent (607).

Holy Cross Junior College (c): Notre Dame, Ind. 46556. Brothers of Holy Cross; 1966 (265).

Manor Junior College (w): Fox Chase Manor, Jenkintown, Pa. 19046. Sisters of St. Basil the Great; 1947 (390).

Maria College (c): 700 New Scotland Ave., Albany, N.Y. 12208. Sisters of Mercy; 1963 (841).

Maria Regina College (w): 1024 Court St., Syracuse, N.Y. 13208. Franciscan Sisters; 1963; independent (622).

Marymount Palos Verdes College (c): Rancho Palos Verdes, Calif. 90274. Religious of the Sacred Heart of Mary (534).

Mt. Aloysius Junior College (c): Cresson, Pa. 16630. Sisters of Mercy; 1939 (449).

Presentation College (c): Aberdeen, S.D. 57401. Sisters of the Presentation; 1951 (325).

St. Catharine College (c); St. Catharine, Ky. 40061. Dominican Sisters; 1931 (243).

St. Gertrude, College of (c): Cottonwood, Ida. 83522. Benedictine Sisters.

St. Gregory's College (c): Shawnee, Okla. 74801. Benedictine Monks; 1876 (341).

St. Mary's College of O'Fallon (c): 200 N. Main St., O'Fallon, Mo. 63366. Sisters of the Most Precious Blood; 1921 (617).

St. Mary's Junior College (c): 2500 S. 6th St., Minneapolis, Minn. 55454. Sisters of St. Joseph of Carondelet (889).

Springfield College in Illinois (c): 1500 N. Fifth St., Springfield, Ill. 62702. Ursuline Nuns; 1929 (441).

Trocaire College (c): 110 Red Jacket Pkwy., Buffalo, N.Y. 14220. Sisters of Mercy; 1958; independent (1,044).

Villa Julie College (c): Green Spring Valley Rd., Stevenson, Md. 21153. Sisters of Notre Dame de Namur; 1952; independent (870).

Villa Maria College of Buffalo (c): 240 Pine Ridge Rd., Buffalo, N.Y. 14225. Felician Srs.; 1960 (850).

A report, entitled "Catholic Higher Education: Trends in Enrollment and Finances 1978-82," indicated that within that period Catholic colleges had increases in total enrollment, enrollment of full-time and part-time students, men and women, undergraduate and graduate students.

DIOCESAN AND INTERDIOCESAN SEMINARIES

(Sources: Almanac survey; *Official Catholic Directory;* NC News Service.)

Information, according to states, includes names of archdioceses and dioceses, and names and addresses of seminaries. Types of seminaries, when not clear from titles, are indicated in most cases. Interdiocesan seminaries are generally conducted by religious orders for candidates for the priesthood from several dioceses. The list does not include houses of study only for members of religious communities. Archdioceses are indicated by an asterisk.

California: Los Angeles* — St. John's Seminary (major), 5012 E. Seminary Rd., Camarillo. 93010; St. John's College Seminary, 5118 E. Seminary Rd., Camarillo. 93010; Seminary of Our Lady, Queen of Angels (minor, high school), Box 1071, San Fernando. 91341.

San Diego — St. Francis Seminary (college residence), 1667 Santa Paula Dr., San Diego 92111.

San Francisco* — St. Patrick's Seminary (major), 320 Middlefield Rd., Menlo Park. 94025.

San Jose — St. Joseph's College, P.O. Box 7009, Mountain View 94039.

Colorado: Denver* — St. Thomas Theological Seminary (major), 1300 S. Steele St., Denver 80210.

Connecticut: Hartford* — St. Thomas Seminary (minor), 467 Bloomfield Ave., Bloomfield. 06002.

Norwich — Holy Apostles College (delayed vocation seminary), 33 Prospect Hill Rd., Cromwell 06416.

Stamford Byzantine Rite — Ukrainian Catholic Seminary: St. Basil College (minor), 195 Glenbrook Rd., Stamford 06902; St. Basil's Preparatory School (minor), 39 Clovelly Rd., Stamford 06902.

District of Columbia: Washington* — Theological College, The Catholic University of America, 401 Michigan Ave., N.E. 20064.

Florida: Miami*, Pensacola-Tallahassee, St. Augustine, St. Petersburg — St. John Vianney College Seminary, 2900 S.W. 87th Ave., Miami 33165; St. Vincent de Paul Regional Seminary (major), Military Trail, P.O. Box 460, Boynton Beach. 33435.

Hawaii: Honolulu — St. Stephen's Seminary (college level), P.O. Box 699, Kaneohe. 96744.

Illinois: Belleville — St. Henry's Preparatory Seminary, 5901 W. Main St., Belleville 62223.

Chicago* — Quigley Preparatory Seminary (North), 103 East Chestnut St., Chicago 60611; Quigley Preparatory Seminary (South), 7740 South Western Ave., Chicago 60620; Niles College of Loyola University, 7135 N. Harlem Ave., Chicago 60631; St. Mary of the Lake Seminary, Mundelein. 60060.

Springfield — Immaculate Conception Seminary, 1903 E. Lake Dr., Springfield 62707.

Indiana: Indianapolis* — St. Meinrad Seminary, College and School of Theology (interdiocesan), St. Meinrad. 47577.

Iowa: Davenport — St. Ambrose College Seminary, 518 W. Locust St., Davenport 52803.

Dubuque* — Seminary of St. Pius X, Loras College, Dubuque 52001.

Kansas: Kansas City* — Savior of the World Seminary (minor), 12601 Parallel Ave., Kansas City 66109.

U.S. SEMINARIES AND STUDENTS, 1962-1983

(Source: *The Official Catholic Directory.*)

Year	Dioc. Seminaries	Total Dioc. Students	Religious Seminaries Scholasticates	Total Rel. Students	Total Seminarians
1962	98	23,662	447	22,657	46,319
1963	107	25,247	454	22,327	47,574
1964	112	26,701	459	22,049	48,750
1965	117	26,762	479	22,230	48,992
1966	126	26,252	481	21,862	48,114
1967	123	24,293	452	21,086	45,379
1968	124	22,232	437	17,604	39,836
1969	122	19,573	407	14,417	33,990
1970	118	17,317	383	11,589	28,906
1971	110	14,987	340	10,723	25,710
1972	106	13,554	326	9,409	22,963
1973	107	12,925	304	8,855	21,780
1974	109	11,765	293	7,583	19,348
1975	104	11,223	269	6,579	17,802
1976	102	11,015	269	6,232	17,247
1977	100	10,344	287	5,599	15,943
1978	98	9,560	278	5,438	14,998
1979	92	8,694	258	5,266	13,960
1980	92	8,552	252	4,674	13,226
1981	88	7,954	240	4,514	12,468
1982	86	7,625	217	4,020	11,645
1983	86	8,046	234	4,008	12,054

Kentucky: Covington — Seminary of St. Pius X, Erlanger. 41018.

Louisiana: New Orleans* — Notre Dame Seminary Graduate School of Theology, 2901 S. Carrollton Ave., New Orleans 70118; St. John Vianney Preparatory School, 3801 Monroe St., New Orleans 70118; St. Joseph Seminary College (interdiocesan), St. Benedict 70457.

Maryland: Baltimore* — St. Mary's Seminary and University, 5400 Roland Ave., Baltimore 21210; Mt. St. Mary's Seminary, Emmitsburg. 21727.

Massachusetts: Boston* — St. John's Seminary School of Theology, 127 Lake St., Brighton. 02135; St. John's Seminary, College of Liberal Arts, 197 Foster St., Brighton 02135; Pope John XXIII National Seminary, 558 South Ave., Weston. 02193.

Melkite Eparchy of Newton — St. Gregory the Theologian Seminary, 233 Grant Ave., Newton 02159; St. Basil's Seminary, 30 East St., Methuen 01844.

Michigan: Detroit* — Sacred Heart Seminary College, Inc., 2701 Chicago Blvd., Detroit 48206; Sts. Cyril and Methodius Seminary (independent institution primarily serving Polish-American community), Orchard Lake 48033; St. John's Provincial Seminary (major, for dioceses in Detroit province), 44011 Five Mile Rd., Plymouth. 48170.

Grand Rapids — St. Joseph's Minor Seminary, 600 Burton St., S.E., Grand Rapids 49507.

Minnesota: Seminary of the Diocese of St. Cloud, Collegeville. 56321.

St. Paul and Minneapolis* — St. Paul Seminary, 2260 Summit Ave., St. Paul. 55105; St. John Vianney College Seminary, 2115 Summit Ave., St. Paul. 55105.

Winona — Immaculate Heart of Mary Seminary, St. Mary's College, Winona 55987.

Missouri: Jefferson City — St. Thomas Aquinas Preparatory Seminary, 245 N. Levering Ave. Hannibal. 63401.

Kansas City-St. Joseph — St. John's Diocesan Seminary (high school), 2015 E. 72nd St. Kansas City. 64132.

St. Louis* — St. Louis Roman Catholic Theological Seminary (Kenrick Seminary), 7800 Kenrick Rd., St. Louis 63119; Cardinal Glennon College, 5200 Glennon Dr., St. Louis 63119; St. Louis Preparatory Seminary, 5200 Shrewsbury Ave., St. Louis 63119 (South), 3500 St. Catherine St., Florissant 63033 (North).

Montana: Helena — Diocesan Pre-Seminary Program, Carroll College, Helena 59601.

New Jersey: Newark* — Immaculate Conception Seminary (major), Darlington, Mahwah. 07430 (scheduled to be transferred to Seton Hall University by the end of 1983); Seton Hall University College Seminary of the Immaculate Conception, Divinity School, South Orange. 07079.

New Mexico: Gallup — Cristo Rey College and High School Seminary, 205 E. Wilson, Gallup 87301.

Santa Fe* — Immaculate Heart of Mary Seminary (college house of formation), Mt. Carmel Rd., Santa Fe 87501.

New York: Brooklyn — Cathedral Preparatory Seminary of the Immaculate Conception, 555 Washington Ave., Brooklyn 11238; Cathedral Preparatory Seminary of the Immaculate Conception, 56-25 92nd St., Elmhurst. 11373; Cathedral College of the Immaculate Conception, 7200 Douglaston Parkway, Douglaston. 11362.

Buffalo — Christ the King Seminary (interdiocesan), 711 Knox Rd., East Aurora. 14052.

New York* — St. Joseph's Seminary (major), Dunwoodie, Yonkers. 10704: Cathedral Preparatory Seminary, 555 West End Ave., New York 10024.

Ogdensburg — Wadhams Hall, Riverside Dr., Ogdensburg 13669.

Rochester — Becket Hall College Seminary, 80 Fairport Rd., E. Rochester. 14445.

Rockville Centre — Immaculate Conception Diocesan Seminary, Lloyd Harbor, Huntington, L.I. 11743; St. Pius X Preparatory Seminary, 1220 Front St., Uniondale, L.I. 11553.

St. Maron Diocese, Brooklyn — Our Lady of Lebanon Maronite Seminary, 7164 Alaska Ave. N.W., Washington, D.C. 20012.

Syracuse — Syracuse-Aquinas House, 702 Danforth St., Syracuse 13208.

North Dakota: Fargo — Cardinal Muench Seminary, 100 35th Ave. N.E., Fargo 58102.

Ohio: Cincinnati* — Mt. St. Mary's Seminary of the West, 6616 Beechmont Ave., Cincinnati. 45230 (division of the Athenaeum of Ohio).

Cleveland — St. Mary Seminary, 1227 Ansel Rd., Cleveland 44108; Borromeo College of Ohio, 28700 Euclid Ave. Wickliffe. 44092.

Columbus — Pontifical College Josephinum (interdiocesan), theologate and college, Columbus. 43085.

Toledo — Holy Spirit Seminary High School, 5201 Airport Highway, Toledo 43615.

Oregon: Portland* — Mt. Angel Seminary (college, pre-theology program, graduate school of theology), St. Benedict 97373; St. John Vianney House of Studies, 1538 Southwest Montgomery St., Portland 97201.

Pennsylvania: Allentown — Mary Immaculate Seminary (interdiocesan), Northampton 18067.

Erie — St. Mark's Seminary, 429 E. Grandview Blvd., Erie 16504.

Greensburg — St. Vincent Seminary (interdiocesan), Latrobe 15650.

Philadelphia* — Theological Seminary of St. Charles Borromeo, Overbrook. 19151.

Philadelphia Byzantine Rite (Ukrainians)* — St. Josaphat's Seminary, 201 Taylor St. N.E., Washington, D.C. 20017.

Pittsburgh Byzantine Rite (Ruthenians)* — Byzantine Catholic Seminary of Sts. Cyril and Methodius, 3605 Perrysville Ave., Pittsburgh. 15214.

Pittsburgh — St. Paul Seminary, 2900 Noblestown Rd. 15205.

Scranton — St. Pius X Seminary (college division), Dalton. 18414.

Rhode Island: Providence — Our Lady of Providence College Seminary, Warwick Neck Ave., Warwick. 02889.

Texas: Corpus Christi — Corpus Christi Minor Seminary, Rt. 1, Box 500. 78415.

Dallas — Holy Trinity Seminary (major), P.O. Box 3068, Irving. 75061.

El Paso — St. Charles Seminary High School, P.O. Box 17548, El Paso 79917.

Galveston-Houston — St. Mary's Seminary (major), 9845 Memorial Dr. Houston. 77024.

San Antonio* — The Assumption-St. John's Seminary (major), 2600 W. Woodlawn Ave., San Antonio 78284.

Washington: Spokane — Bishop White Seminary, E. 429 Sharp Ave., Spokane 99202.

West Virginia: Wheeling-Charleston — St. Joseph Preparatory Seminary, Rt. 6, Vienna. 26101; Seminary House of Studies (college residence), 1252 National Rd., Wheeling. 26003.

Wisconsin: Madison — Holy Name Seminary (High School), 3577 High Point Rd., Madison 53711.

Milwaukee* — St. Francis Seminary, 3257 S. Lake Dr., Milwaukee 53207. De Sales Preparatory Seminary, 3501 S. Lake Dr., Milwaukee 53207.

PONTIFICAL UNIVERSITIES

(Principal source: *Annuario Pontificio.*)

These universities, listed according to country of location, have been canonically erected and authorized by the Sacred Congregation for Catholic Education to award degrees in stated fields of study.

New laws and norms governing ecclesiastical universities and faculties were promulgated in the apostolic constitution *Sapientia Christiana*, issued Apr. 15, 1979.

Argentina: Catholic University of S. Maria of Buenos Aires (June 16, 1960): Juncal 1912, Buenos Aires.

Belgium: Catholic University of Louvain (Dec. 9, 1425; 1834), with autonomous institutions for French- (Louvain) and Flemish- (Leuven) speaking: Place de l'Universite I, 1348 Louvain-La-Neuve (French); Naamsestraat 22B, 3000 Leuven (Flemish).

Brazil: Pontifical Catholic University of Rio de Janeiro (Jan. 20, 1947). Rua Marques de Sao Vicente 209, Rio de Janeiro, Est. de Guanabara.

Pontifical Catholic University of Rio Grande do Sul (Nov. 1, 1950): Praca Dom. Sebastiao 2, Porto Alegre, Estado do Rio Grande do Sul.

Pontifical Catholic University of Sao Paulo (Jan. 25, 1947): Rua Monte Alegre 984, Sao Paulo.

Pontifical University of Campinas (Sept. 8, 1956): Rua Marechal Deodoro 1099, Campinas, Sao Paulo.

Canada: Laval University (Mar. 15, 1876): Case Postale 460, Quebec G1K 7P4.

St. Paul University (formerly University of Ottawa) (Feb. 5, 1889): 223, Rue Main, Ottawa, K1S 1C4, Ontario.

University of Sherbrooke (Nov. 21, 1957): Chemin Ste.-Catherine, Cite Universitaire, Sherbrooke, Que. J1K 2R1.

Chile: Catholic University of Chile (June 21, 1888): Avenida Bernardo O'Higgins 340, Casilla 114D, Santiago de Chile.

Catholic University of Valparaiso (Nov. 1, 1961): Avenida Brasil 2950, Casilla 4059, Valparaiso.

Colombia: Bolivarian Pontifical Catholic University (Aug. 16, 1945): Calle 52, N. 43-53, Medellin.

Pontifical Xaverian University (July 31, 1937): Carrera 7, N. 40-62, Bogota D.E.

Cuba: Catholic University of St. Thomas of Villanueva (May 4, 1957): Avenida Quenta 16,660, Marianao, Havana. Taken over by the Castro government in May, 1961.

Ecuador: Catholic University of Ecuador (July 16, 1954): Doce de Octubre, N. 1076, Apartado 2184, Quito.

Ethiopia: University of Asmara (Sept. 8, 1960): Via Menelik II, 45, Post Office Box 1220, Asmara.

France: Catholic University of Lille (Nov. 18, 1875): Boulevard Vauban 60, 59046 Lille.

Catholic Faculties of Lyon (Nov. 22, 1875): 25, Rue du Plat, 69288 Lyon.

Catholic Institute of Paris (Aug. 11, 1875): 21, Rue d'Assas, 75270 Paris.

Catholic Institute of Toulouse (Nov. 15,1877): Rue de la Fonderie 31, 31068 Toulouse.

Catholic University of the West (Sept. 16, 1875): 3, Place Andre Leroy, B.P. 808, 49005 Angers.

Germany: Eichstatt Catholic University (Apr. 1, 1980): Ostenstrasse 26-28, D-8078, Eichstatt.

Guatemala: Rafael Landivar University (Oct. 18, 1961): 17 Calle 8-64, Z 10 Guatemala.

Ireland: St. Patrick's College (Mar. 29, 1896): Maynooth, Co. Kildare.

Italy: Catholic University of the Sacred Heart (Dec. 25, 1920): Largo Gemelli 1, 20123 Milan.

Japan: *Jochi Daigaku* (Sophia University) (Mar. 29, 1913): Chiyoda-Ku, Kioi-cho 7, Tokyo.

Lebanon: St. Joseph University of Beirut (Mar. 25, 1881): Rue de l'Universite St.-Joseph, Boite Postale 293, Beyrouth.

Netherlands: Nijmegen Roman Catholic University (June 29, 1923): Wilhelminasingel 13, Nijmegen.

Panama: University of S. Maria la Antigua (May 27, 1965): Apartado 2143, Panama 1.

Paraguay: Catholic University of Our Lady of the Assumption (Feb. 2, 1965): Comuneros e Independencia Nacional, Asuncion.

Peru: Catholic University of Peru (Sept. 30, 1942): Apartado 1761, Lima.

Philippine Islands: Pontifical University of Santo Tomas (Nov. 20, 1645): Espana Street, Manila.

Poland: Catholic University of Lublin (July 25, 1920): Aleje Raclawickie 14, Skr. Poczt. 279, 20-950, Lublin.

Pontifical Academy of Theology of Crakow (Dec. 8, 1981): Ul. Podzamcze 8, 31-003 Crakow.

Portugal: Portuguese Catholic University (Nov. 1, 1967): Palma de Cima, 1600 Lisbon.

Puerto Rico: Catholic University of Puerto Rico (Aug. 15, 1972): Ponce, Puerto Rico 00731.

Spain: Catholic University of Navarra (Aug. 6, 1960): Ciudad Universitaria, Pamplona.

Pontifical University "Comillas" (Mar. 29, 1904): Canto Blanco, Apartado Postal 3082, Madrid 34.

Pontifical University of Salamanca (Sept. 25,

1940): Compania 1, Apartado 541, Salamanca.
University of Deusto (Aug. 10, 1963): Avenida de las Universidades, 28, Apartado 1, Bilbao.

Taiwan (China): Fu Jen Catholic University (Nov. 15, 1923, at Peking; reconstituted at Taipeh, Sept. 8, 1961): Hsinchuang, Taipeh Hsien.

United States: Catholic University of America (Mar. 7, 1889): Washington, D.C. 20064.
Georgetown University (Mar. 30, 1833): 37th and O Sts. N.W., Washington, D.C. 20057.
Niagara University (June 21, 1956): Niagara University, N.Y. 14109.

Venezuela: Catholic University "Andres Bello" (Sept. 29, 1963): Esquina Jesuitas, Apartado 422, Caracas.

ECCLESIASTICAL FACULTIES

(Source: *Annuario Pontificio*)

These faculties in Catholic seminaries and universities, listed according to country of location, have been canonically erected and authorized by the Sacred Congregation for Catholic Education to award degrees in stated fields of study. In addition to those listed here, there are other faculties of theology or philosophy in state universities and for members of certain religious orders only.

Argentina: Faculties of Philosophy and Theology, San Miguel (Sept. 8, 1932).

Australia: Institute of Theology, Sydney (Feb. 2, 1954).

Austria: Theological Faculty, Linz (Dec. 25, 1978).

Brazil: Ecclesiastical Faculty of Philosophy "John Paul II," Rio de Janeiro Aug. 6, 1981.
Philosophical and Theological Faculties of the Company of Jesus, Belo Horizonte (July 15, 1941 and Mar. 30, 1945).

Canada: Pontifical Institute of Medieval Studies, Toronto (Oct. 18, 1939).
Dominican Faculty of Theology of Canada, Ottawa (1965; Nov. 15, 1975).
Regis College — Toronto Section of the Jesuit Faculty of Theology in Canada, Toronto (Feb. 17, 1956; Dec. 25, 1977).
College of Immaculate Conception — Montreal Section of Jesuit Faculties in Canada (Sept. 8, 1932).

France: Centre Sevres — Faculties of Theology and Philosophy of the Jesuits, Paris (Sept. 8, 1932).

Germany: Theological Faculty, Paderborn (June 11, 1966).
Theological Faculty of the Major Episcopal Seminary, Trier (Sept. 8, 1955)
Philosophical Faculty, Munich (1932; Oct. 25, 1971).
Theological-Philosophical Faculty, Frankfurt (1932; June 7, 1971).
Theological Faculty, Fulda (Dec. 22, 1978).

Great Britain: Heythrop College, University of London, London (Nov. 1, 1964). Theology, philosophy.

India: "Jnana Deepa" (Pontifical Athenaeum), Institute of Philosophy and Religion, Poona (July 27, 1926).
Pontifical Institute of Theology and Philosophy, Alwaye, Kerala (Feb. 24, 1972).

"Vidyajyoti," Institute of Religious Studies, Faculty of Theology, Delhi (1932; Dec. 9, 1974).
Dharmaran Pontifical Institute of Theology and Philosophy, Bangalore (Jan. 6, 1976).
Faculty of Theology, Ranchi (Aug. 15, 1982).
Pontifical Oriental Institute of Religious Studies, Kottayam (July 3, 1982).
St. Peter's Pontifical Institute of Theology, Bangalore (Jan. 6, 1976).
"Satya Nilayam," Institute of Philosophy and Culture. Faculty of Philosophy, Shembaganur (Sept. 8, 1932; Dec. 15, 1976).

Italy: Interregional Theological Faculty, Milan (Aug. 8, 1935).
Pontifical Theological Faculty of the Most Sacred Heart of Jesus, Cagliari, of the Pontifical Regional Seminary of Sardinia (July 5, 1927).
Pontifical Ambrosian Institute of Sacred Music, Milan (Mar. 12, 1940).
Theological Faculty of Sicily, Palermo (Dec. 8, 1980).
Theological Faculty of Southern Italy, Naples. Two sections: St. Thomas Aquinas Capodimonte (Oct. 31, 1941) and St. Louis Posillipo (Mar. 16, 1918). Pastoral Ignatian Institute, Messina (July 31, 1972).
Faculty of Philosophy "Aloisianum," Gallarate (1937; Mar. 20, 1974).

Ivory Coast: Catholic Institute of West Africa, Abidjan (Aug. 12, 1975).

Lebanon: Faculty of Theology, University of the Holy Spirit, Kaslik (May 30, 1982).

Madagascar: Superior Institute of Theology, at the Regional Seminary of Antananarivo, Ambatoroka-Antananarivo (Apr. 21, 1960).

Malta: Faculty of Theology, Tal-Virtu (Nov. 22, 1769).

Mexico: Theological Faculty of Mexico, Mexico City (June 29, 1982).

Nigeria: Catholic Institute of West Africa, Port Harcourt (Nov. 30, 1981).

Peru: Pontifical and Civil Faculty of Theology, Lima (July 25, 1571).

Poland: Theological Faculty, Poznan (1969; pontifical designation, June 2, 1974).

Spain: Theological Faculty of Barcelona, of the Major Seminary of Barcelona and the College of St. Francis Borgia of San Cugat del Valles (Mar. 7, 1968).
Theological Faculty, Granada (1940; July 31, 1973).
Theological Faculty of the North, of the Metropolitan Seminary of Burgos and the Diocesan Seminary of Vitoria (Feb. 6, 1967).
Theological Faculty "San Vicente Ferrer" (two sections), Valencia (Jan. 23, 1974).

Switzerland: Theological Faculty, Chur (Jan. 1, 1974).
Theological Faculty, Luzerne (Dec. 25, 1973).

United States: St. Mary's Seminary and University. School of Theology, Baltimore (May 1, 1822).
St. Mary of the Lake Faculty of Theology, Chicago (Sept. 30, 1929).
The Jesuit School of Theology, Berkeley, Calif. (Feb. 2, 1934, as "Alma College," Los Gatos, Calif.).

Vietnam: Theological Faculty of the Pontifical National Seminary of St. Pius X, Dalat (July 31, 1965). Activities suppressed.

The Pontifical College Josephinum (Theologate and College) at Columbus, Ohio, is a regional pontifical seminary. Established Sept. 1, 1888, it is immediately subject to the Holy See.

PONTIFICAL UNIVERSITIES AND INSTITUTES IN ROME

(Source: *Annuario Pontificio*.)

Pontifical Gregorian University (1552): Piazza della Pilotta, 4, 00187 Rome. Associated with the university are:

The **Pontifical Biblical Institute** (May 7, 1909): Via della Pilotta, 25, 00187 Rome.

The **Pontifical Institute of Oriental Studies** (Oct. 15, 1917): Piazza S. Maria Maggiore, 7, 00185 Rome.

Pontifical Lateran University (1773). Piazza S. Giovanni in Laterano, 4, 00184 Rome.

Pontifical Urban University (1627): Via Urban VIII, 16, 00165 Rome.

Pontifical University of St. Thomas Aquinas (Angelicum) (1580), of the Order of Preachers: Largo Angelicum, 1, 00184 Rome.

Pontifical University Salesianum (May 3, 1940; university designation May 24, 1973), of the Salesians of Don Bosco: Piazza dell' Ateneo Salesiano, 1, 00139 Rome. Associated with the university is

the **Pontifical Institute of Higher Latin Studies** (Feb. 22, 1964).

Pontifical Athenaeum of St. Anselm (1687), of the Benedictines: Piazza dei Cavalieri di Malta, 5, 00153 Rome.

Pontifical Athenaeum Antonianum (of St. Anthony) (May 17, 1933), of the Order of Friars Minor: Via Merulana, 124, 00185 Rome.

Pontifical Institute of Sacred Music (1911; May 24, 1931): Piazza S. Agostino, 20-A, 00186, Rome.

Pontifical Institute of Christian Archeology (Dec. 11, 1925): Via Napoleone III, 1, 00185 Rome.

Pontifical Theological Faculty "St. Bonaventure" (Dec. 18, 1587), of the Order of Friars Minor Conventual: Via del Serafico, 1, 00142 Rome.

Pontifical Theological Faculty, Pontifical Institute of Spirituality "Teresianum" (1935), of the Discalced Carmelites: Piazza San Pancrazio, 5-A, 00152 Rome.

Pontifical Theological Faculty "Marianum" (1398), of the Servants of Mary: Viale Trente Aprile, 6, 00153 Rome.

Pontifical Institute of Arabic and Islamic Studies (1926), of the White Fathers: Piazza S. Apollinare, 49, 00186 Rome.

Pontifical Faculty of Educational Science "Auxilium" (June 27, 1970), of the Daughters of Mary, Help of Christians: Via di Selva Candida, 267, 00166 Rome.

Pontifical Institute "Regina Mundi" (1954): Lungotevere Tor di Nona, 7, 00186 Rome.

PONTIFICAL ACADEMY OF SCIENCES

(Sources: *Annuario Pontificio*, NC News Service. Membership as of May 24, 1983.)

The Pontifical Academy of Sciences was constituted in its present form by Pius XI Oct. 28, 1936, in virtue of *In Multis Solaciis*, a document issued on his own initiative.

The academy is the only supranational body of its kind in the world, with a pope-selected, life-long membership of outstanding mathematicians and experimental scientists from many countries. The normal complement of members is 70; the total number, however, includes additional honorary and supernumerary members. Non-Catholics as well as Catholics belong to the academy.

Purposes of the academy are to honor pure science and its practitioners, to promote the freedom of pure science and to foster research.

The academy traces its origin to the *Linceorum Academia* (Academy of the Lynxes — its symbol) founded in Rome Aug. 17, 1603. Pius IX reorganized this body and gave it a new name — *Pontificia Accademia dei Nuovi Lincei* — in 1847. It was taken over by the Italian state in 1870 and called the *Accademia Nationale dei Lincei*. Leo XIII reconstituted it with a new charter in 1887. Pius XI designated the Vatican Gardens as the site of academy headquarters in 1922 and gave it its present title and status in 1936. Four years later he gave the title of Excellency to its members.

Members in U.S.

Scientists in the U.S. who presently hold membership in the Academy are listed below according to year of appointment.

1936 (Oct. 28): Franco Rasetti, professor emeritus of physics at John's Hopkins University, Baltimore, Md.; George Speri-Sperti, president and director of the Institute Divi Thomae in the Athanaeum of Ohio.

1948 (May 29): Adelbert Doisy, professor emeritus of biochemistry at St. Louis University.

1964 (Sept. 24): William Wilson Morgan, professor emeritus of astronomy at the University of Chicago.

1970 (Apr. 10): Albert Szent-Gyorgyi, director of Institute for Muscle Research at the Marine Biological Laboratory, Woods Hole, Mass.

1974 (June 24): Rita Levi-Montalcini, professor of biology at Washington University, St. Louis, Mo.; Severo Ochoa, professor emeritus of the Roche Institute of Molecular Biology, Nutley, N.J.; Marshall Warren Nirenberg, professor of genetics and biochemistry at the National Institutes of Health, Bethesda, Md.

1975 (Dec. 2): George Palade, professor of cellular biology at Yale University, New Haven, Conn.; Victor Weisskopf, professor of physics at the Massachusetts Institute of Technology, Cambridge, Mass.

1978 (Apr. 17): David Baltimore, professor of biology, Har Gobind Khorana, professor of biochemistry, and Alexander Rich, professor of biophysics — all at the Massachusetts Institute of Technology, Cambridge, Mass.; Roger Walcott

Sperry, professor of psychobiology, California Institute of Technology, Pasadena, Calif.

1981 (May 13): Christian Anfinsen, professor of biochemistry at the National Institutes of Health, Bethesda, Md.

1983 (Feb. 12): Charles Townes, professor of physics at the University of California at Berkley.

Deceased U.S. members of the Academy were: George D. Birkhoff, Alexis Carrel, Herbert Sidney Langfeld, Robert A. Millikan, Thomas H. Morgan, Theodore von Karman, Victor F. Hess, Peter Debye, Hugh Stott Taylor.

Members in Other Countries

Other members of the Academy are listed below according to country of location; dates of their selection are given in parentheses.

Argentina: Luis F. Leloir (Apr. 22, 1968).

Austria: Hans Tuppy (Apr. 10, 1970).

Belgium: Christian de Duve (Apr. 10, 1970).

Brazil: Carlos Chagas (Aug. 18, 1961); Johanna Dobereiner (Apr. 17, 1978); Crodowaldo Pavan (Apr. 17, 1978).

Canada: Gerhard Herzberg (Sept. 24, 1964); Karel Wiesner (Apr. 17, 1978).

Chile: Hector Croxatto Rezzio (Dec. 2, 1975).

Denmark: Bengt Georg Stromgren (Dec. 2, 1975); Aage Bohr (Apr. 17, 1978).

France: Louis de Broglie (Apr. 5, 1955); Pierre Raphael Lepine (Sept. 24, 1964); Louis Leprince-Ringuet (Aug. 18, 1961); Jerome Lejeune (June 24, 1974); Andre Blanc-LaPierre (Apr. 17, 1978), Anatole Abragam (May 13, 1981), Andre Lichnerowicz (May 13, 1981), Bernard Pullman (May 13, 1981).

Germany: Rudolf L. Mossbauer (Apr. 10, 1970), Manfried Eigen (May 13, 1981).

Great Britain: Hermann Alexander Bruck (Apr. 5, 1955); Paul Adrien Dirac (Aug. 18, 1961); Alan Lloyd Hodgkin (Apr. 22, 1968); Alfred R. Ubbelohde (Apr. 22, 1968); Percy C. C. Garnham (Apr. 10, 1970); George Porter (June 24, 1974);

Martin Ryle (Dec. 2, 1975), Max Ferdinand Perutz (May 13, 1981); Stanley Keith Runcorn (Sept. 13, 1981).

Hungary: Janos Zsentagothai (May 13, 1981).

India: Mambillikalathil Dovind Kumar Menon (May 13, 1981).

Israel: Michael Sela (Dec. 2, 1975).

Italy: Giovanni Battista Bonino (May 23, 1942); Bettolo Giovanni Battista Marini (Apr. 22, 1968); Giuseppe Colombo (Apr. 17, 1978); Giuseppe Moruzzi (Apr. 17, 1978); Giampietro Puppi (Apr. 17, 1978), Ennio De Giorgi (May 13, 1981), Abdus Salam (May 13, 1981).

Japan: Sanichiro Paul Mizushima (Aug. 18, 1961).

Kenya: Thomas R. Odhiambo (May 13, 1981).

Netherlands: Jan Hendrik Oort (Aug. 18, 1961).

New Zealand: Albert William Liley (Apr. 17, 1978).

Pakistan: Salimuzzaman Siddiqui (Sept. 24, 1964).

Peru: Alberto Hurtado (Aug. 18, 1961).

Poland: Stanislao Lojasiewicz (Feb. 12, 1983).

Portugal: Antonio De Almeida (Apr. 8, 1961).

Spain: Manuel Lora Tomayo (Sept. 24, 1964).

Sweden: Sven Horstadius (Aug. 18, 1961).

Switzerland: John Carew Eccles (Apr. 8, 1961), Thomas Lambo (June 24, 1974), Werner Arber (May 13, 1981).

Venezuela: Marcel Roche (Apr. 10, 1970).

Ex officio members: Rev. George V. Coyne, S.J., director of Vatican Observatory; Alfons Stickler, S.D.B., prefect of the Vatican Library; Msgr. Martino Giusti, prefect of the Secret Vatican Archives.

Honorary members: Silvio Ranzi, professor emeritus of biology and zoology of the University of Milan (May 13, 1981); Pietro Salviucci, former chancellor of the Pontifical Academy of Sciences (Nov. 18, 1982).

President: Carlos Chagas (Nov. 9, 1972).

ECCLESIAL COMMUNITIES

The concept and operational model of basic Christian communities — comunidades de base, basic ecclesial communities — envision relatively small, basic communities of the faithful integrated for religious and secular life, with maximum potential for pastoral ministry, liturgical participation, apostolic activity and human, spiritual and social development.

Communities of this type originated mainly in Latin America, where it is estimated that they number more than 150,000. They have also developed in the United States and other places.

Basic communities were the subject of a message from the Pope to their leaders when he was in Brazil July 10, 1980. Its main theme was the need for such communities to maintain their sense of being church bodies.

He referred to the "enormous importance that basic communities have in the pastoral activity of the Church in Brazil." He warned, however, that it would be easy for a community to lose sight of its ecclesial or church-related base if it were formed

and/or conducted for a political reason and purpose.

With respect to the leader of a basic community, the Pope said he "does not transmit his thoughts or doctrines but that which he learns and receives from the Church." He also said the leader should provide a "persuasive example of Christian life, of radiant and active faith."

AGRIMISSIO

Agrimissio is a service office established for the purpose of assisting missionaries in rural development work. Founded in 1970 by Msgr. Luigi Ligutti, its honorary president, it is sponsored by the Union of Superiors General (of male religious), the International Union of Superiors General (of female religious), and the National Catholic Rural Life Conference in the U.S. It promotes cooperation among missionaries, the Rome headquarters of religious orders, governmental and non-governmental organizations, especially the international Food and Agriculture Organization.

Headquarters are located at the Palazzo S. Calisto, 00120, Vatican City.

The **National Conference of Catholic Charities:** Established in 1910 to help advance and promote the charitable programs and activities of Catholic community and social service agencies in the United States. As the central and national organization for this purpose, it services member agencies and institutions by consultation, information and assistance in planning and evaluating social service programs under Catholic auspices.

The principal fields of service in which Catholic Charities agencies are engaged are family counseling, child welfare, services for unmarried mothers, community services, day care centers, neighborhood center programs, and care of the aged. Community organization and social action are also functions of Catholic Charities.

The NCCC conducts research with respect to service to the aging, community self-help programs, the institutional care of children, and other social service projects. It represents the Catholic philosophy of social service to government agencies and personnel, and to professional organizations in the field. Its publications include *Charities USA*, a monthly membership magazine, and *Social Thought*, a quarterly co-sponsored with the National School of Social Service of the Catholic University of America.

The NCCC membership includes 575 diocesan agencies and branches, 200 institutions and 3,000 individuals.

Rev. Thomas J. Harvey is executive director of the conference, with offices at 1346 Connecticut Ave. N.W., Washington, D.C. 20036.

The Society of St. Vincent de Paul, originally called the Conference of Charity: An association of Catholic laity devoted to personal service of the poor through the spiritual and corporal works of mercy. The first conference was formed at Paris in 1833 by Frederic Ozanam and his associates.

The first conference in the U.S. was organized in 1845 at St. Louis. There are now approximately 4,300 units of the society in this country, with a membership of about 34,000.

In the past 50 years, members of the society in this country have distributed among poor persons financial and other forms of assistance valued at approximately $350 million.

U.S. Vincentian councils and conferences participating in "twinning" programs assist their poorer counterparts abroad by sending them correspondence, information and financial aid on a continuing basis.

Under the society's revised regulations, women are being admitted to membership. Increasing emphasis is being given to stores and rehabilitation workshops of the society through which persons with marginal income can purchase refurbished goods at minimal cost. Handicapped persons are employed in renovating goods and store operations.

Amin A. de Tarrazi of Paris, France, is president of the Council General, the governing body of the society. There are approximately 750,000 members in the world.

The office of the U.S. Superior Council is located at 4140 Lindell Blvd., St. Louis, Mo. 63108.

Catholic Health Association of the United States, formerly Catholic Hospital Association: Founded in 1915, is a service organization for about 900 Catholic-sponsored health care facilities located throughout the United States.

The association is dedicated to the healing mission of the Church by promoting health of those who are sick or infirm because of age or disability; by respecting human dignity in the experience of sickness and death; and by fostering physical, psychological, emotional, spiritual and social well-being of people.

John E. Curley, Jr., is president. Executive offices are located at 4455 Woodson Rd., St. Louis, Mo. 63134.

The Official Catholic Directory, 1983, reported 635 Catholic general hospitals with 170,676 beds treating 37,832,614 patients; 94 special hospitals with 6,520 beds treating 452,579; and 125 nurses' schools with 21,316 students.

National Association of Catholic Chaplains: Founded in 1965. Membership is approximately 3,000.

Rev. Timothy J. Toohey is executive director. Address: 3257 S. Lake Dr., Milwaukee Wis. 53207.

FACILITIES FOR RETIRED AND AGED PERSONS

(Sources: Almanac survey, *The Official Catholic Directory.*)

This list covers residence, health care and other facilities for the retired and aged under Catholic auspices. Information includes name, type of facility if not evident from the title, address, and total capacity (in parentheses); unless noted otherwise, facilities are for both men and women. Many facilities for the aged offer intermediate nursing care.

Alabama: Allen Memorial Home (Nursing Home), 735 S. Washington Ave., Mobile 36603 (94).

Good Samaritan Skilled Nursing Home, 1107 Voeglin Ave., Selma 36701 (26).

Sacred Heart Residence Little Sisters of the Poor, 1655 McGill Ave., Mobile 36604 (120).

Villa Mercy (Skilled Nursing Facility, Hospice, Home Health Agency), P.O. Box 1096, Daphne 36526.

Arizona: Sacred Heart Home for the Aged, Little Sisters of the Poor, 1110 N. 16th St., Phoenix 85006 (128).

Villa Maria de Guadalupe Geriatric Center (Skilled Nursing Facility and Apartments), 4310 E. Grant Rd., Tucson 85712 (93 beds, 50 apartments).

Arkansas: Benedictine Manor (Retirement Home), 2nd and Grand Sts., Hot Springs 71901 (100).

California: Casa Manana Inn, 3700 N. Sutter St., Stockton 95204 (175).

Cathedral Plaza, 1551 Third Ave., San Diego 92101 (221 apartments).

Catholic Women's Center (Residence for Retired Senior Women), 195 E. San Fernando St., San Jose 95112 (50).

Ellis Seniors Residence, 3263 First Ave., Sacramento 95817 (18).

Francis of Assisi Community, 148 Guerrero St., San Francisco 94103 (140); for elderly and handicapped.

Guadalupe Plaza, P.O. Box 80428, San Diego 92138.

Little Flower Haven (Residential Care Facility for Retired), 8585 La Mesa Blvd., La Mesa 92041 (93).

Little Sisters of the Poor, 300 Lake St., San Francisco 94118 (120).

Little Sisters of the Poor, Jeanne Jugan Residence, 2100 South Western Ave., San Pedro, Calif. 90732 (120).

Madonna Residence (Retirement Home for Women over 60), 1055 Pine St., San Francisco 94109 (46).

Marian Residence (Retirement Home), 124 S. College Dr., Santa Maria 93454 (58).

Nazareth House, 2121 N. 1st St., Fresno 93703 (80).

Nazareth House, 3333 Manning Ave., Los Angeles 90064 (107).

Nazareth House, 245 Nova Albion Way, Terra Linda, San Rafael 94903 (145).

Nazareth House Retirement Home, 6333 Rancho Mission Rd., San Diego 92108 (122).

Our Lady of Fatima Villa (Skilled Nursing Facility, Women), 20400 Saratoga/Los Gatos Rd., Saratoga 95070 (85).

Our Lady's Home, 3431 Foothill Blvd., Oakland 94601 (154).

St. Francis Home (Elderly and Retired Women), 1718 W. 6th St., Santa Ana 92703 (87).

St. John of God Nursing Hospital and Residence, 2035 W. Adams Blvd., Los Angeles 90018.

Villa Scalabrini (Retirement Center), 10631 Vinedale St., Sun Valley 91352 (125).

Villa Siena (Residence and Intermediate Care), 1855 Miramonte Ave., Mountain View 94040 (50, residence; 20, intermediate care).

Colorado: Little Sisters of the Poor, 3629 W. 29th Ave., Denver 80211 (118).

St. Elizabeth Center (Retirement Home), 2825 W. 32nd Ave., Denver 80211 (187).

Connecticut: Augustana Homes, Simeon Rd., Bethel 06801.

Matulaitis Nursing Home, Putnam 06260.

Monsignor Bojnowski Manor, Inc., 50 Pulaski St., New Britain 06053 (60).

Notre Dame Convalescent Home, 76 West Rocks Rd., Norwalk 06851 (60).

Regina Pacis Villa (Residence), RFD No. 1, Pomfret Center 06259 (16).

St. Joseph Guest Home (Women, Employed and Retired), 311 Greene St., New Haven 06511 (86).

St. Joseph's Home for the Aged, 88 Jackson St., Willimantic 06226 (37).

St. Joseph's Manor, Carmelite Srs. for Aged and Infirm, 6448 Main St., Trumbull 06611 (285).

St. Joseph's Residence, Little Sisters of the Poor, 1365 Enfield St., Enfield, Conn. 06082 (94)

St. Lucian's Home for the Aged, 532 Burritt St., New Britain 06053 (65).

St. Mary's Home (Residence and Health Care Facility), 291 Steele Rd., W. Hartford 06117 (177).

Villa Maria Rest Home for the Aged, West St., Thompson 06277 (30).

Delaware: The Antonican, 1701 W. 10th St., Wilmington 19805 (136).

Jeanne Jugan Residence, Little Sisters of the Poor, 185 Salem Church Rd., Newark 19713.

St. Patrick's House, Inc., 14th and French Sts., Wilmington 19801 (14).

District of Columbia: Jeanne Jugan Residence—St. Joseph' Villa, Little Sisters of the Poor, 4200 Harewood Rd., N.E. 20017.

Florida: All Saints Home for the Aged, 2040 Riverside Ave., Jacksonville 32204 (57).

Carroll Manor, 3667 S. Miami Ave., Miami 33133

Casa Calderón, Inc., 800 W. Virginia St., Tallahassee 32304. Apartments (111).

Cor Jesu Retirement Center, 4918 N. Habana Ave., Tampa 33614 (75).

Haven of Our Lady of Peace (Residence and Health Care Facility), 5203 9th Ave., Pensacola 32504 (88).

Maria Manor Health Care Center, 10300 4th St. N., St. Petersburg 33702 (274).

Marian Towers, Inc. (Retirement Apartments), 17505 North Bay Rd., Miami Beach 33160.

Noreen McKeen Residence for Geriatric Care, 315 Flagler Dr. S., W. Palm Beach 33401.

Pennsylvania Retirement Residence, 208 Evernia St., W. Palm Beach 33401 (176).

St. Andrew Towers (Retirement Apartments), 2700 N.W. 99th Ave., Coral Springs 33065.

St. Dominic Gardens, 5849 N.W. 7th St., Miami 33126.

St. Elizabeth Gardens, Inc. (Retirement Apartments), 801 N.E. 33rd St., Pompano Beach 33064.

St. Joseph's Residence, 3485 N.W. 30th St., Ft. Lauderdale 33311.

St. Vincent de Paul Home for Aged, 1618 Polk St., Hollywood 33020.

Illinois: Addolorato Villa (Home for Aged), Highway 83, McHenry Rd., Wheeling 60090 (103).

Alvernia Manor (Residence), 1598 Main St., Lemont 60439 (56).

Carlyle Healthcare Center, 501 Clinton St., Carlyle 62231 (124).

Carmelite Carefree Village, 8419 Bailey Rd., Darien 60559 (96 units, 150 residents).

Cortland Manor Retirement Home, 1900 N. Karlow, Chicago 68639. (52).

Holy Family Health Center, 2380 Dempster, Des Plaines 60016 (272).

Holy Family Villa (Residence and Health Care,), Lemont 60439 (102).

Huber Memorial Home (Women), 1000 30th St., Rock Island 61201 (16).

Jugan Terrace, Little Sisters of the Poor, 2300 N. Racine, Chicago 60614.

Little Sisters of the Poor Center for the Aging, 2325 N. Lakewood Ave., Chicago, Ill. 60614 (120).

Marian Heights Apartments (Elderly, Infirm, Handicapped), 20 Oak St., Alton 62002 (133).

Marian Park, Inc., 2126 W. Roosevelt Rd., Wheaton 60187 (118 apartments).

Maryhaven, Inc. (Intermediate Care Facility), 1700 E. Lake Ave., Glenview 60025 (147).

Mayslake Village (Retirement Apartments), 1801 35th St., Oak Brook 60521 (630 Apartments).

Meredith Memorial Home, Public Square, Belleville 62220 (90).

Merkle-Knipprath Nursing Home, Rt. 1, Franciscan Brothers. Clifton 60927 (100).

Mother Theresa Home, 1270 Main St., Lemont 60439 (58).

Nazarethville, 300 River Rd., Des Plaines 60016 (84).

Our Lady of Angels Retirement Home, 1201 Wyoming, Joliet 60435 (100).

Our Lady of the Snows Apartment Community (Retirement Apartment Community; Health Care Program), 9500 W. Ill., Rt. 15, Belleville 62223 (200).

Pope John Paul I Apartments (Elderly, Infirm, Handicapped), 1 Pope John Paul Plaza, Springfield 62703 (160).

Resurrection Retirement Community, 7266 W. Peterson Ave., Chicago, 60631 (232 Apartments).

Rosary Hill Home, 9000 W. 81st St., Justice 60458 (60).

St. Andrew Home, 7000 N. Newark Ave., Chicago 60648 (198).

St. Ann's Health Care Center, 770 State St.. Chester 62233 (92).

St. Benedict Home, 6930 W. Touhy Ave., Niles 60648 (52).

St. Joseph's Home (Sheltered and Intermediate Care), 3306 S. 6th St. Rd., Springfield 62703 (121).

St. Joseph's Home, 2223 W. Heading Ave., Peoria 61604 (200).

St. Joseph's Home for the Aged, 649 E. Jefferson St., Freeport 61032 (109).

St. Joseph's Home for the Elderly, 80 W. Northwest Hwy., Palatine 60067 (135).

St. Joseph's Home of Chicago, Inc., 2650 N. Ridgeway Ave., Chicago 60647 (173).

St. Patrick's Residence (Sheltered and Intermediate Care; Skilled Nursing Facility), 22 E. Clinton St., Joliet 60431 (202).

Villa Saint Cyril (Residence), 1111 St. John's Ave., Highland Park 60035 (80).

Villa Scalabrini (Residence), 480 N. Wolf Rd., Northlake 60164 (249).

Indiana: Little Company of Mary Health Facility, San Pierre 46374 (180).

Providence Retirement Home, 703 E. Spring St., New Albany 47150 (85).

Regina Pacis Home (Skilled Nursing and Intermediate Care Facility), 3900 Washington Ave., Evansville 47715 (154).

Sacred Heart Home (Comprehensive Nursing), R.R. 2, Avilla 46710 (130). LaVerna Terrace (for well elderly), same address (51 units).

St. Anne Home (Residence and Comprehensive Nursing), 1900 Randalia Dr., Ft. Wayne 46805 (154).

St. Anthony's Medical Center, Nursing Home, Main and Franciscan Rd., Crown Point 46307 (211).

St. Augustine Home for the Aged, Little Sisters of the Poor, 2345 W. 86th St., Indianapolis 46260 (120).

St. John's Home for the Aged, Little Sisters of the Poor, 1236 Lincoln Ave., Evansville 47714 (130).

St. Paul Hermitage, 501 N. 17th St., Beech Grove 46107 (105).

Iowa: The Alverno Health Care Facility, 849 13th Ave. N., Clinton 52732 (136).

Bishop Drumm Retirement Center, 5387 Winwood Dr., Des Moines 50324 (120 beds; 95 apartments).

Hallmar-Mercy Hospital (Home for the Aged), 701 Tenth St. S.E., Cedar Rapids 52403.

Holy Spirit Retirement Home (Nursing Home), 1701 W. 25th St., Sioux City 51103 (94).

Kahl Home for the Aged and Infirm (Intermediate Care Facility), 1101 W. 9th St., Davenport 52804 (125).

The Marian Home, 2400 6th Ave. North, Fort Dodge 50501 (97) and Marian Village (Apartments), 2320 6th Ave. North, Fort Dodge 50501.

Mary of the Angels Home (Women, Employed and Retired), 605 Bluff St., Dubuque 52001 (85).

Padre Pio Health Care Center, Stonehill Care Center (Residence, Nursing Home), 3485 Windsor, Dubuque 52001 (250).

Ritter Home for Retired Women, 1837 Sunnyside Ave., Burlington 52601 (6).

St. Anthony Nursing Home, 406 E. Anthony St., Carroll 51401 (80).

St. Francis Continuation Care and Nursing Home, Burlington 52601 (82).

Kansas: Catholic Center for the Aging, 3411 E. Zimmerly, Wichita 67218 (150).

Mt. Joseph (Intermediate Care Facility), 1110 W. 11, R.R. 1, Concordia 66901 (100).

St. John Rest Home (Intermediate Care Facility), 701 Seventh St., Victoria 67671 (60).

St. Joseph Home (Skilled Care Facility), 759 Vermont Ave., Kansas City 66101.

Villa Maria, Inc. (Intermediate Care Facility), 116 S. Central, Mulvane 67110 (66).

Kentucky: Cardome Residence for Women, Georgetown 40324 (30).

Carmel Home (Residence and Nursing Home), Old Hartford Rd., Owensboro 42301 (84).

Carmel Manor (Personal Care Home), Carmel Manor Rd., Ft. Thomas, 41075 (99).

Knottsville Home for Senior Citizens, P.O. Box R. 1, Philpot 42366 (59).

Madonna Manor Nursing Home, 2344 Amsterdam Rd., Covington 41016 (38). (Cottages for Senior Citizens: 9, with 48 apartments.

St. Charles Nursing Home, 500 Farrell Dr., Covington 41011 (147).

St. Margaret of Cortona Home (Women, Personal Care Home), 1310 Leestown Pike, Lexington 40508 (24).

Taylor Manor Nursing Home, Versailles 40383 (82).

Louisiana: Annunciation Inn, 1220 Spain St., New Orleans 70117 (106 residential units).

Bethany M.H.S. Health Care Center (Women), P.O. Box 2308, Lafayette 70501 (42).

Chateau de Notre Dame (Residence and Nursing Home), 2832 Burdette St., New Orleans 70125 (110 residential units, 180 nursing beds).

Christopher Inn Apartments, 2110 Royal St., New Orleans 70116.

Consolata Home (Nursing Home), 2319 E. Main St., New Iberia 70560.

Lafon Nursing Home of the Holy Family, 6900 Chef Menteur Hwy., New Orleans 70126 (171).

Mary-Joseph Residence for the Elderly, 4201 Woodland Dr., New Orleans 70114 (123).

Mater Dolorosa Adult Group Home, 1215 Dublin St., New Orleans 70118.

Metairie Manor, 4929 York St., Metairie 70001 (200 residential units).

Nazareth Inn, 9630 Haynes Blvd., New Orleans 70127 (150 Apartments).

Ollie Steele Burden Manor (Nursing Home), 4200 Essen Lane, Baton Rouge 70809 (60).

Our Lady of Prompt Succor Home (Nursing and Extended Care Facility), 751 E. Prudhomme Lane, Opelousas 70570.

Place Dubourg, 201 Rue Dubourg, LaPlace 70068 (115 residential units).

Rouquette Lodge, 4300 Hwy 22, Mandeville 70448 (119 residential units).

St. Charles Nursing Home, P.O. Box 508, Newellton 71357.

St. John Berchman's Manor, 3400 St. Anthony St., New Orleans 70122.

St. Joseph's Home (Nursing Home), 2301 Sterlington Rd., Monroe 71201 (130).

St. Margaret's Daughters Nursing Home, (Women), 6220 Chartres St., New Orleans 70117 (110).

St. Martin Manor, 1501 N. Johnson St., New Orleans 70116 (140 residential units).

Villa St. Maurice, 500 St. Maurice Ave., New Orleans 70117. (110 residential units).

Wynhoven Apartments (Residence for Senior Citizens), 4600 - 10th St., Marrero 70072 (350).

Maine: Deering Pavilion (Apartments for Senior Citizens), 800 Forest Ave., Portland 04103 (200 units).

Marcotte Nursing Home, 100 Campus Ave., Lewiston 04240 (376).

Mt. St. Joseph (Nursing Home), Highwood St., Waterville 04901 (77).

St. Andre Health Care Facility, Inc. (Nursing Home), 407 Pool Rd., Biddeford 04005 (96).

St. Joseph's Manor, 1133 Washington Ave., Portland 04103 (200).

Seton Village, Inc., 1 Carver St., Waterville 04901 (140 housing units.)

Villa Muir, Home for Women, Bay View, Saco 04072 (15).

Maryland: Cardinal Shehan Center for the Aging, Inc., 2300 Dulaney Valley Rd., Towson 21204. Five services: 400-bed long-term care facility; 200 apartments for elderly; residence for elderly in urban area; outreach programs to elderly in homes; retirement residence for priests.

Carroll Manor (Residence and Nursing Home), 4922 La Salle Rd., Hyattsville 20782 (232).

Little Sisters of the Poor, St. Martin's Home (for the Aged), 601 Maiden Choice Lane, Baltimore 21228 (120).

Sacred Heart Home, 5805 Queens Chapel Rd., Hyattsville 20782 (102).

St. Joseph Nursing Home, 1222 Tugwell Dr., Baltimore 21228 (40).

Villa Rosa (Nursing Home), Lottsford Vista Rd., Mitchellville 20716 (99).

Massachusetts: Beaven-Kelly Home for Men (Rest Home), 1245 Main St., Brightside, Holyoke 01040 (55).

Catholic Memorial Home (Nursing Home), 2446 Highland Ave., Fall River 02720 (288).

Don Orione Nursing Home, 111 Orient Ave., East Boston 02128 (200). Adult day care center (30).

D'Youville Manor (Nursing Home), 981 Varnum St., Lowell 01854 (196). Day care program (20).

Jeanne Jugan Residence, Little Sisters of the Poor (Nursing Home), 186 Highland Ave., Somerville 02143 (120). Jeanne Jugan Pavilion, 190 Highland Ave., Somerville 02143. Apartments (33 residents).

Madonna Manor (Nursing Home), N. Washington St., N. Attleboro 02760 (121).

Marian Manor, Carmelite Sisters for the Aged and Infirm (Nursing Home), 130 Dorchester St., S. Boston, 02127 (376).

Marian Manor of Taunton Nursing Home, 33 Summer St., Taunton 02780 (83).

Maristhill Nursing Home, 66 Newton St., Waltham 02154 (120).

Mary Immaculate Nursing Home, Bennington St., Lawrence 01841 (250). Adult Day Health Care Center (30).

Mt. St. Vincent Nursing Home, Holy Family Rd., Holyoke 01040 (116).

Our Lady's Haven (Nursing Home), 71 Center St., Fairhaven 02719 (110).

The Protectory, Inc., 189 Maple St., Lawrence 01841. (111 units). The Second Protectory, Inc., 191 Maple St., Lawrence (106 units). The Third Protectory, Inc., 193 Maple St., Lawrence 01841 (88 units). Congregate Housing; Apartments.

Sacred Heart Nursing Home, 359 Summer St., New Bedford 02740 (215).

St. Francis Home for Aged, 37 Thorne St., Worcester 01604 (83). Adult Day Health Care (30).

St. Joseph Manor Nursing Home, 215 Thatcher St., Brockton 02402 (120).

St. Joseph's Manor (Rest Home, Women), 321 Centre St., Dorchester, Boston 02122 (95).

St. Luke's Home (Rest Home, Women), 85 Spring St., Springfield 01105 (92).

St. Patrick's Manor (Nursing Home), 863 Central St., Framingham 01701 (292).

Michigan: Bishop Noa Home for Senior Citizens, Escanaba 49829 (109).

Burtha M. Fisher Home, Little Sisters of the Poor (Residence and Nursing Home), 17550 Southfield Rd., Detroit 48235 (130).

Casa Maria (Residence), 600 Maple Vista, Imlay City 48444 (96).

Kundig Center (Residence), 3300 Jefferies Freeway, Detroit 48208 (180). Rooms and apartments.

Lourdes Nursing Home (Skilled Facility), 2300 Watkins Lake Rd., Pontiac 48054 (108).

Madonna Villa Senior Residence, 17825 Fifteen Mile Rd., Fraser, 48026 (90).

Marian Hall (Residence), 529 Detroit St., Flint 48502 (124).

Marian-Oakland West, 29250 W. Ten Mile Rd., Farmington Hills 48024 (100).

Marian Place (Residence), 408 W. Front St., Monroe 48161 (52).

Marycrest Manor (Skilled Nursing Facility), 15475 Middlebelt Rd., Livonia 48154 (55).

Marydale Center for Senior Citizens (Board and Apartments), 3147 Tenth Ave., Port Huron 48060 (74).

Maryhaven (Residence), 11350 Reeck Rd., Southgate 48195 (93).

St. Ann's Home, (Residence and Nursing Home), 2161 Leonard St. N.W., Grand Rapids 49504 (112).

St. Catherine Cooperative House for Elderly Women, 1641 Webb Ave., Detroit 48206.

St. Elizabeth Briarbank (Residence), P.O. Box O, 1315 N. Woodward Ave., Bloomfield Hills 48013 (55).

St. Francis Home (Nursing Home), 915 N. River Rd., Saginaw 48603 (100).

St. John Vianney Cooperative House for Men, 4806 Mt. Elliot, Detroit 48207 (30).

St. Joseph's Home for the Aged, 4800 Cadieux Rd., Detroit 48224 (104).

Stapleton Center (Residence), 9341 Agnes St., Detroit 48214 (65).

Villa Elizabeth (Nursing Home), 2100 Leonard St. N.E., Grand Rapids 49505 (136).

Villa Francesca (Residence, Women), 565 W. Long Lake Rd., Bloomfield Hills 48013 (18).

Villa Marie (Board and Apartments), 15131 Newburgh Rd., Livonia 48154.

Minnesota: Assumption Home, Cold Spring 56320 (68).

Bethany Home, Onamia 56359 (80).

Divine Providence Community Home (Intermediate Care), 700 Third Ave. N.W., Sleepy Eye 56085 (58).

Divine Providence Home (Skilled Nursing Home), Ivanhoe 56142 (51).

John Paul Apartments, Cold Spring 56320 (61). For elderly and handicapped.

Little Sisters of the Poor, Holy Family Residence (Skilled Nursing and Intermediate Care),

330 S. Exchange St., St. Paul 55102 (143).

Madonna Towers (Retirement Apartments and Nursing Home), 4001 19th Ave. N.W., Rochester 55901 (200).

Mary Rondorf Retirement Home, 222 N. 5th St., Staples 56479 (84).

Mother of Mercy Nursing Home, Albany 56307 (62).

Regina Nursing Home and Retirement Residence, Hastings 55033. Nursing home (61); retirement home (86).

Sacred Heart Hospice (Nursing Home), 1200 Twelfth St. S.W., Austin 55912 (59).

St. Ann's Residence, 330 E. 3rd St., Duluth 55805 (200).

St. Anne Hospice (Residence and Nursing Care), 1347 W. Broadway, Winona 55987 (121).

St. Benedict's Center (Nursing Home), 1810 Minnesota Blvd. S.E., St. Cloud 56301 (220).

St. Elizabeth's Hospital and Nursing Home, 1200-5th Grant Blvd., Wabasha 55981 (52).

St. Francis Home, Breckenridge 56520 (124).

St. Mary's Home (Nursing Home), 1925 Norfolk Ave., St. Paul 55116 (140).

St. Mary's Hospital and Nursing Home, Winsted 55395 (95).

St. Mary's Nursing Center, Detroit Lakes 56501 (103).

St. Mary's Rehabilitation Center, 2512 S. 7th St., Minneapolis 55454 (240).

St. Mary's Villa (Nursing Home), Pierz 56364 (66).

St. Otto's Home (Nursing Home), Little Falls 56345 (159).

St. Therese Home (Residence and Health Care Facility) (302) and St. Therese Retirement Apartments (220), 8000 Bass Lake Rd., New Hope 55428.

St. William's Nursing Home, Parkers Prairie 56361 (61).

Villa of St. Francis Nursing Home, Morris 56267 (144).

Villa St. Vincent (Skilled Nursing Home and Residence), 516 Walsh St., Crookston 56726. Nursing home (80); residence (95).

Mississippi: Santa Maria Retirement Apartments, 305 E. Beach St., Biloxi, 39530.

Villa Maria Retirement Apartments, 921 Porter Ave., Ocean Springs 39564.

Missouri: The Alverne (Retirement Home), 1014 Locust St., St. Louis 63101 (251).

Cathedral Square Towers, 444 W. 12th St., Kansas City 64105. Apartments for elderly and handicapped.

Chariton Apartments (Retirement Apartments), 4249 Michigan Ave., St. Louis 63111 (122 units; 132 residents).

DePaul Community Health Center — St. Anne's Division (Nursing Home), 12349 DePaul Dr., Bridgeton 63044 (114).

LaVerna Heights Retirement Home (Women), 104 E. Park Ave., Savannah 64485 (40).

LaVerna Village Apartments, 1000-1005 Hall Ave., Savannah 64485 (20).

LaVerna Village Nursing Home, 904 Hall Ave., Savannah 64485 (120).

Little Sisters of the Poor (Home for Aged), 3225 N. Florissant Ave., St. Louis 63107 (210).

Mary, Queen and Mother Center (Skilled-Intermediate Nursing Care), 7601 Watson Rd., St. Louis 63119 (220).

Mercy Villa (Nursing Home), Division of St. John's Regional Health Center, 1100 E. Montclair, Springfield 65807 (150).

Mother of Good Counsel Home (Nursing Home, Women), 6825 Natural Bridge Rd., Normandy, 63121.

Our Lady of Mercy Home (Residence and Nursing Home), 918-24 E. 9th St., Kansas City 64106 (153).

Our Lady of Mercy Country House, Box 451, R.R. No. 4, Liberty 64038 (39).

Price Memorial Skilled Nursing Facility Forby Rd., P.O. Box 476, Eureka 63025 (120.

St. Agnes Home for the Aged, 10341 Manchester Rd., Kirkwood 63122 (130).

St. Joseph Hill Nursing Care Facility (Men), Highway FF, Eureka 63025 (130).

St. Joseph's Home, 723 First Capitol Dr., St. Charles 63301 (101).

St. Joseph's Home for the Aged, 1306 W. Main St., Jefferson City 65101 (75).

Nebraska: Bergen Mercy Care Center (Health Care), 1870 S. 75th St., Omaha 68124 (250).

Madonna Professional Care Center, 2200 S. 52nd St., Lincoln 68506 (182).

Mt. Carmel Home, Keens' Memorial (Nursing Home), 412 W. 18th St., Kearney 68847 (76).

New Cassel Retirement Center, 900 N. 90th St., Omaha 68114. (156).

St. Joseph's Home (Residential Care), 320 E. Decatur St., West Point 68788 (48).

St. Joseph's Home, 401 N. 18th St., Norfolk 68701 (70).

St. Joseph's Villa, David City 68632. (65).

New Hampshire: Mount Carmel Nursing Home, 235 Myrtle St., Manchester 03104 (120).

St. Ann Home, 195 Dover Point Rd., Dover 03820 (53).

St. Francis Home (Nursing Home), Court St., Laconia 03246 (51).

St. Teresa Manor (Nursing Home), 519 Bridge St., Manchester 03104 (51).

St. Vincent de Paul Nursing Home, Providence Ave., Berlin 03570 (80).

New Jersey: Holy Family Residence (Women), 44 Rifle Camp Rd., P.O. Box 536, W. Paterson 07424 (64).

Little Sisters of the Poor, St. Joseph Home, 140 Shepherd Lane, Totowa 07512 (247).

Mater Dei Nursing Home, RD 3, Box 164, Rt. 40, P.O. Newfield 08344 (64).

Morris Hall, Home for the Aged (Residence and Skilled Nursing Home), 2361 Lawrenceville Rd., Lawrenceville 08648 (127).

Mount St. Andrew Villa (Residence), 55 W. Midland Ave., Paramus 07652 (59).

Our Lady's Residence (Nursing Home), Glendale and Clematis Aves., Pleasantville 08232 (104).

St. Ann's Home for the Aged (Skilled Nursing Home, Women), 198 Old Bergen Rd., Jersey City 07305 (106). Adult Medical Day Care.

St. Joseph's Home (Women), 240 Longhouse Dr., Hewitt 07421.

St. Joseph's Rest Home for Aged Women, 46 Preakness Ave., Paterson 07502 (30).

St. Joseph's Senior Residence, 1 St. Joseph Terr., Woodbridge 07095.

St. Joseph's Villa (Residence, Women), Peapack 07977 (18).

St. Mary's Catholic Home (Skilled Nursing Home), 1730 Kresson Rd., Cherry Hill 08003 (215).

St. Vincent's Nursing Home, 45 Elm St., Montclair 07042 (135).

Villa Maria (Residence and Infirmary, Women), 641 Somerset St., N. Plainfield 07061 (70).

New Mexico: Good Shepherd Manor (Residential Care for Aged Persons), Little Brothers of the Good Shepherd, P.O. Box 10248, Albuquerque 87114 (43).

New York: Bernardine Apartments, 417 Churchill Ave., Syracuse 13205.

Consolation Residence, 111 Beach Dr., West Islip 11795 (250).

Ferncliff Nursing Home, P.O. Box 386, River Rd., Rhinebeck 12572 (320).

Frances Schervier Home and Hospital, 2975 Independence Ave., New York 10463 (364).

Good Samaritan Nursing Home, Sayville, N.Y. 11782.

The Heritage (Residence), 1450 Portland Ave., Rochester 14621.

Holy Family Home, 410 Mill St., Williamsville 14221 (90).

Kateri Residence, 150 Riverside Dr., New York 10024.

Little Sisters of the Poor, Jeanne Jugan Residence (Skilled Nursing and Health Related), 3200 Baychester Ave., Bronx 10475 (203).

Little Sisters of the Poor, Holy Family Home, 1740-84th St., Brooklyn 11214 (146).

Little Sisters of the Poor, Queen of Peace Residence, 110-30 221st St., Queens Village 11429 (202).

Madonna Home of Mercy Hospital (Nursing Home and Extended Care Facility) (140), and Mercy Hospital Health Related Facility (Residence) (58), Watertown 13601.

Madonna Residence, 1 Prospect Park W., Brooklyn, 11215 (290).

Mary Manning Walsh Home (Nursing Home), 1339 York Ave., New York 10021 (362).

Mercy General Hospital Nursing Home Unit, Tupper Lake 12986 (31).

Mt. Loretto Nursing Home, (Skilled Nursing Facility), R.D., 3, Amsterdam 12010 (82).

Nazareth Nursing Home, and Health Related Facility, 291 W. North St., Buffalo 14201 (122).

Our Lady of Hope Residence (Home for the Aged), Little Sisters of the Poor, 1 Jeanne Jugan Lane, Latham 12210 (250).

Ozanam Hall of Queens Nursing Home, Inc.

(Skilled Nursing and Health-Related Facilities), 42-41 201st St., Bayside 11361 (432).

Providence Rest, 3304 Waterbury Ave., Bronx 10465 (200).

Resurrection Rest Home (Nursing Home and Health Related Facility, Women), Castleton 12033 (50).

Sacred Heart Home (Residence) 4520 Ransom Rd., Clarence 10431. Brothers of Mercy Nursing Home, 10570 Bergtold Rd., Clarence 14031. Brothers of Mercy Housing Co., Inc. (Apartments), 10500 Bergtold Rd., Clarence 14031.

Sacred Heart Nursing Home, 8 Mickle St., Plattsburgh 12901 (89).

St. Ann's Home (Nursing Home and Extended Care Facility), 1500 Portland Ave., Rochester 14621 (354).

St. Anthony's Home for the Aged, 5285 S. Park Ave., Hamburg 14075 (68).

St. Clare Manor, 543 Locust St., Lockport 14094 (28).

St. Columban's on the Lake (Retirement Home), Silver Creek 14136 (50).

St. Elizabeth Home, 5539 Broadway, Lancaster 14086 (102).

St. Francis Home (Nursing and Health Related Facility), 147 Reist St., Williamsville 14221 (98).

St. Joseph Manor, W. State St., Olean 14760 (22).

St. Joseph's Guest Home, Missionary Sisters of St. Benedict,, 350 Cuba Hill Rd., Huntington 11743 (60).

St. Joseph's Home, Table Rock Sloatsburg 10974 (20).

St. Joseph's Home (Nursing Home), 420 Lafayette St., Ogdensburg 13669 (82).

St. Joseph's Nursing Home, 2535 Genesee St., Utica 13501 (120).

St. Joseph's Villa (Residence), 38 Prospect Ave., Catskill 12414 (60).

St. Luke Manor for Chronically Ill, 17 Wiard St., Batavia 14020 (20).

St. Mary's Manor, 515 Sixth St., Niagara Falls 14301 (119).

St. Patrick's Home for the Aged and Infirm, 66 Van Cortland Park S., Bronx 10463 (226).

St. Vincent's Home for the Aged, 319 Washington Ave., Dunkirk 14048 (36).

St. Zita's Home (Women), 143 W. 14th St., New York 10011 (46).

Teresian House, Washington Ave. Extension, Albany 12203 (300).

Uihlein Mercy Center (Nursing Home), Lake Placid 12946 (96).

North Carolina: Maryfield Nursing Home (116 beds) and Maryfield Acres (16 retirement homes), Greensboro Rd., High Point 27260 (115).

North Dakota: Holy Family Guest Home (Nursing Home), Carrington 58421 (38).

Manor St. Joseph Home for Aged and Infirm; Edgeley 58433 (40).

Marillac Manor (Retirement Apartments), 1016 N. 28th St., Bismarck 58501 (42 apartments).

St. Anne's Guest Home (Retirement), 524 N.

17th St., 813 Lewis Blvd., Grand Forks 58201 (56) Apartments (30).

St. Olaf Guest (Retirement) Home, Powers Lake 58773 (20).

St. Vincent's Nursing Home, 1021 N. 26th St., Bismarck 58501 (94).

Ohio: Archbishop Leibold Home for the Aged, Little Sisters of the Poor, 476 Riddle Rd., Cincinnati 45220 (125).

Assumption Nursing Home, 550 W. Chalmers Ave., Youngstown 44511 (126).

Francesca Residence, 39 N. Portage Path, Akron 44303 (50).

Franciscan Terrace (Residence and Nursing Care), 80 Compton Rd., Cincinnati 45215 (90).

House of Loreto (Nursing Home), 2812 Harvard Ave. N.W., Canton 44709 (98).

Jennings Hall, Inc. (Intermediate Care Facility), 10204 Granger Rd., Garfield Heights 44125 (105).

Kirby Manor (Retirement Apartments), 11500 Detroit Ave., Cleveland 44102 (202 suites).

Little Sisters of the Poor, Sacred Heart Home, 4900 Navarre Ave., Oregon 43616 (158).

Little Sisters of the Poor, Sts. Joseph and Mary Home for Aged, 4291 Richmond Rd., Cleveland 44122 (140).

The Maria-Joseph Living Care Center, 4830 Salem Ave., Dayton 45416 (388).

Mount Alverna (Residence and Nursing Care for Aged), 6765 State Rd., Parma 44134 (200).

Mt. St. Joseph (Skilled Nursing Facility, Dual Certified), 21800 Chardon Rd., Cleveland 44117 (100).

Nazareth Towers, 300 E. Rich St., Columbus 43215. Hi-rise apartments for independent living.

St. Augustine Manor (Nursing Home), 7818 Detroit Ave., Cleveland 44102 (194).

St Edward Nursing Home, 3131 Smith Rd., Akron 44313 (100).

St. Francis Home for the Aged, 182 St. Francis Ave., Tiffin 44883 (111).

St. Francis Rehabilitation Hospital and Nursing Home, 401 N. Broadway St., Green Springs 44836.

St. Joseph's Hospice (Nursing Home), 2308 Reno Dr., Louisville 44641 (100).

St. Margaret Hall (Residence and Nursing Facility), 1960 Madison Rd., Cincinnati 45206 (145).

St. Raphael Home (Nursing Home), 1550 Roxbury Rd., Columbus 43212 (80).

St. Rita's Home (Skilled Nursing Home), 880 Greenlawn Ave., Columbus 43223 (100).

St. Theresa Home for the Aged, 6760 Belkenton Pl., Cincinnati 45236 (110).

Schroder Manor (Residence and Skilled Nursing Care), Franciscan Sisters of the Poor, 1302 Millville Ave., Hamilton 45013 (85).

The Siena Home (Skilled Nursing Home), 235 W. Orchard Spring Dr., Dayton 45415 (99).

The Villa Sancta Anna Home for the Aged, 25000 Chagrin Blvd., Beachwood 44122 (68).

Oklahoma: Franciscan Villa, 17110 E. 51st St. S., Broken Arrow 74012. Intermediate nursing care (60); apartments (66).

St. Ann's Nursing Home, 3825 N.W. 19th St., Oklahoma City 73107 (82).

Oregon: Benedictine Nursing Center, S. Main St., Mt. Angel 97362 (127).

Maryville Nursing Home, 14645 S.W. Farmington, Beaverton 97007 (132).

Mt. St. Joseph's Residence and Extended Care Center, 3060 S.E. Stark St., Portland 97214 (317).

St. Catherine's Residence and Nursing Center, 3959 Sheridan Ave., North Bend 97459 (166).

St. Elizabeth's Nursing Home, 2365 4th St., Baker 97814 (93).

Pennsylvania: Ascension Manor I (Senior Citizen Housing), 911 N. Franklin St., Philadelphia 19123 (140 units).

Ascension Manor II (Senior Citizen Housing), 970 N. 7th St., Philadelphia 19123 (140 units).

Benetwood Apartments for Elderly and Handicapped, 640 Troupe Rd., Erie 16421 (83).

Christ the King Manor, 1100 W. Long Ave., Du Bois 15801 (160).

Corpus Christi Residence, 7165 Churchland St., Pittsburgh 15206 (27).

Drueding Infirmary, 413 W. Master St., Philadelphia 19122 (52).

Garvey Manor (Nursing Home), Logan Blvd., Hollidaysburg, 16648 (150).

Holy Family Home, Little Sisters of the Poor, 5300 Chester Ave., Philadelphia 19143 (1600).

Holy Family Manor (Skilled Nursing Facility), 1200 Spring St., Bethlehem 18018 (200).

Holy Ghost Guest Home (Women), 4537 Wm. Flynn Hwy., Allison Park 15101 (15).

Immaculate Mary Home, (Skilled and Intermediate Nursing Care), Holme Circle and Welsh Rd., Philadelphia 19136 (300).

John XXIII Home, 2250 Shenango Freeway, Hermitage 16146 (100).

Little Flower Manor Nursing Home, 1201 Springfield Rd., Darby 19023 (122).

Little Flower Manor of Diocese of Scranton, (Long-Term Skilled Nursing and Intermediate Care Facility), 200 S. Meade St., Wilkes-Barre 18702.

Little Sisters of the Poor, 1028 Benton Ave. N.S., Pittsburgh 15212 (140).

Little Sisters of the Poor, Holy Family Residence, 2500 Adams Ave., Scranton 18509 (82).

Maria Joseph Manor, Danville 17821 (94).

Marian Manor (Residence and Nursing Care), 2695 Winchester Dr., Pittsburgh 15220 (172).

Mount Macrina Manor (Women), Uniontown 15401 (46).

Mt. Trexler Skilled Nursing Unit of Sacred Heart Hospital, Limeport 18060 (65).

Redeemer Village, Huntingdon Pike, Huntingdon Valley 19006 (150 apartments).

Sacred Heart Manor (Nursing Home), 6445 Germantown Ave., Philadelphia 19119 (153).

St. Anne Home (Intermediate and Skilled Nursing Care), R.D. 2, Columbia 17512 (120).

St. Anne Home for the Elderly (Skilled Nursing Facility), 685 Angela Dr., Greensburg 15601 (125).

St. Basil's Home for Aged Women (Residential), Box 878, Uniontown 15401 (8).

St. Ignatius Nursing Home, 4401 Haverford Ave., Philadelphia 19104 (176).

St. John Neumann Nursing Home, 10400 Roosevelt Blvd. Philadelphia 19116 (196).

St. Joseph Home for the Aged, 1182 Holland Rd., Holland 18966 (96).

St. Joseph Home for the Aged (Skilled Nursing Facility), 5324 Penn Ave., Pittsburgh 15224 (150).

St. Joseph's House of Hospitality (Low Income Senior Citizen Residence for Men and Women), 1635 Bedford Ave., Pittsburgh 15219 (65).

St. Joseph Manor (Skilled Nursing Facility), 1616 Huntingdon Pike, Meadowbrook 19046 (250).

St. Joseph's Residence, 1111 S. Cascade St., New Castle 16101.

St. Leonard's Guest Home, 601 N. Montgomery St., Hollidaysburg 16648 (22).

St. Mary's Home of Erie, 607 E. 26th St., Erie 16504. Residential facility (110); geriatric nursing facility (196).

St. Mary's Manor for Sighted and Blind, 701 Lansdale Ave., Lansdale 19446 (160).

St. Mary's Villa (Nursing Home), Elmhurst 18416 (121).

Villa de Marillac Nursing Home, 5300 Stanton Ave., Pittsburgh 15206 (50).

Villa St. Teresa (Residence), 1215 Springfield Rd., Darby 19023 (53).

Villa Teresa (Nursing Home), 1051 Avila Rd., Harrisburg 17109 (178).

Vincentian Home for the Chronically Ill., Perrymont Rd., Pittsburgh 15237 (219).

Rhode Island: Jeanne Jugan Residence of the Little Sisters of the Poor, 964 Main St., Pawtucket 02860 (132).

L'Hospice St. Antoine (Home for Aged), 400 Mendon Rd., North Smithfield 02895 (244).

St. Clare Home for the Aged, 309 Spring St., Newport 02840 (44).

Scalabrini Villa (Convalescent, Rest — Nursing Home). 860 N. Quidnessett Rd., North Kingstown 02852 (70).

South Carolina: Carter-May Home, 1660 Ingram Rd., Charleston 29407 (12). Personal care home for elderly ladies.

South Dakota: Brady Memorial Home (Skilled Nursing Facility), 500 S. Ohlman St., Mitchell 57301 (60). Independent living units (2).

Maryhouse, Inc. (Skilled Nursing Facility), 717 E. Dakota, Pierre 57501 (82).

Mother Joseph Manor (Skilled Nursing Facility), 1002 North Jay St., Aberdeen 57401 (80). Apartment units (7). Adult day care program. Respite nursing care.

St. William's Home for the Aged (Intermediate Care, 60), and Angela Hall (Supervised Living, 15), 901 E. Virgil, Box 432, Milbank 57252.

Tekakwitha Nursing Home (Skilled and Intermediate Care). Sisseton 57262 (101).

Tennessee: Alexian Brothers Rest Home (Retired Men and Women), Signal Mountain 37377 (150).

Ave Maria Home, Inc., 2805 Charles Bryan Rd., Memphis 38134 (73).

St. Mary Manor, 1771 Highway 45 Bypass, Jackson 38301.

St. Peter Manor, 108 N. Aubrundale, Memphis 38104.

St. Peter Villa (Nursing Home), 141 N. McLean, Memphis 38104.

Texas: Casa Apartment Complex for Elderly and Handicapped, 3201 Sondra Dr., Fort Worth 76107.

Home for Aged Women-Men, 920 S. Oregon St., El Paso 79901 (24).

Laboure Care Center, 1950 Record Crossing Rd., Dallas 75235.

Mother of Perpetual Help Home (Intermediate Care Facility), 519 E. Madison Ave., Brownsville 78520 (39).

Mt. Carmel Home (Personal Care Home), 4130 S. Alameda St., Corpus Christi 78411 (92).

The Regis (Retirement Center), 400 Austin Ave., Waco 76701 (210).

The Retirement Residence, Inc., 2819 Rio Grande, Austin 78705 (100).

St. Ann's Home (Skilled Nursing Facility), P.O. Box 1179, Panhandle 79068 (52).

St. Anthony's Center (Skilled Nursing, Rehabilitation, Geriatric), 6301 Almeda Rd., Houston 77021 (372).

St. Benedict's Nursing Home, Alamo and Johnson Sts., San Antonio 78204 (197).

St. Dominic Residence Hall, 2401 E. Holcombe Blvd., Houston 77021 (180).

St. Dominic Nursing Home, 6502 Grand Ave., Houston 77021 (120).

St. Elizabeth Nursing Home, 400 Austin Ave., Waco 76701 (179).

St. Francis Nursing Home (Home for Aged and Convalescents), 2717 N. Flores St., San Antonio 78212 (143).

St. Francis Village, Inc. (Retired and Elderly), Crowley. Mailing address — P.O. Box 16310, Ft. Worth 76133 (425).

St. Joseph Residence, 330 W. Pembroke St., Dallas 75200 (49).

San Juan Nursing Home (Skilled Care Facility), 300 N. Nebraska Ave., P.O. Box 1238, San Juan 78589 (52).

Utah: St. Joseph Villa (Skilled Nursing Home), 474 Westminster Ave., Salt Lake City 84115 (98).

Vermont: Loretto Home for Aged, 59 Meadow St., Rutland 05701 (54).

Michaud Memorial Manor (Home for Aged), Derby Line 05830 (24).

St. Joseph's Home for Aged, 243 N. Prospect St., Burlington 05401 (53).

Virginia: Madonna Home, 814 W. 37th St., Norfolk 23508 (15).

Russell House, 900 First Colonial Rd., Virginia Beach 23454 (127).

St. Francis Home, 2511 Wise St., Richmond 23225 (25).

St. Joseph's Home for the Aged, Little Sisters of the Poor, 1503 Michael Rd., Richmond 23229 (126).

Washington: Cathedral Plaza Apartments (Retirement Apartments), W. 1120 Sprague Ave., Spokane 99204 (150).

The Delaney, W. 242 Riverside Ave., Spokane 99201 (84).

The De Paul Retirement Apartments, 4831 35th Ave. S.W., Seattle 98126 (111 units).

Fahy Garden Apartments, W. 1403 Dean Ave., Spokane 99201 (31).

Fahy West Apartments, W. 1523 Dean Ave., Spokane 99201 (55).

The Josephinum (Retirement Home), 1902 2nd Ave., Seattle 98101 (228).

Mt. St. Vincent Nursing Center, 4831 35th Ave., S.W., Seattle 98126 (198).

The O'Malley, E. 707 Mission, Spokane 99202 (100).

St. Joseph Nursing Home, 1006 North H St., Aberdeen 98520 (33).

St. Joseph Care Center (Skilled Long-Term Care), West 20 — 90th Ave., Spokane 99204 (103). Adult day care center (35).

West Virginia: Knights of St. George Home, Wellsburg 26070 (44).

Welty Home for the Aged (Women), 21 Washington Ave., Wheeling 26003 (44).

Wisconsin: Alexian Village of Milwaukee (Retirement Community/Skilled Nursing Home), 9301 N. 76th St., Milwaukee 53223 (197 apartments).

Bethany-St. Joseph Health Care Center, 2507 Shelby Rd., La Crosse 54601 (226).

Clement Manor (Retirement Community Skilled Nursing), 3939 S. 92nd St., Greenfield 53228 (70).

Divine Savior Nursing Home, 715 W. Pleasant St., Portage 53901 (111).

Franciscan Villa, 3601 S. Chicago Ave., S. Milwaukee 53172 (150).

Hope Nursing Home, 439 Ashford Ave., Lomira 53048 (40).

McCormick Memorial Home for the Aged, 212 Iroquois St., Green Bay 54301 (70).

Marian Catholic Home, 3333 W. Highland Blvd., Milwaukee 53208 (360).

Maryhill Manor Nursing and Retirement Home, 973 Main St., Niagara 54151 (45).

Milwaukee Catholic Home, Inc., 2462 N. Prospect Ave., Milwaukee 53211 (185).

Nazareth House (Skilled Nursing Facility), Stoughton 53589 (100).

St. Ann Rest Home (Intermediate Care Facility, Women), 2020 S. Muskego Ave., Milwaukee 53204 (54).

St. Anne's Home for the Elderly (Aged Poor), 3800 N. 92nd St., Milwaukee 53222 (156).

St. Camillus Health Center (Skilled Nursing Home), 10100 W. Bluemound Rd., Wauwatosa 53226 (188).

St. Catherine Infirmary (Nursing Home), 5635 Erie St., Racine 53402 (40).

St. Elizabeth Home, 502 St. Lawrence Ave., Janesville 53545.

St. Elizabeth's Nursing Home (Women), 745 N. Brookfield Rd., Brookfield 53005 (16).

St. Francis Home, 700 West Ave. S., La Crosse 54601 (95).

St. Francis Home (Skilled Nursing Facility), 1800 New York Ave., Superior 54880 (192).

St. Francis Home (Skilled Nursing), 365 Gillett St., Fond du Lac 54935 (70).

St. Francis Manor (Retirement Residence), 3553 S. 41st St., Milwaukee 53221 (5).

St. Joan Antida Home (Women), 6640 W. Beloit Rd., W. Allis 53219 (76).

St. Joseph's Home, 705 Clyman St., Watertown 53094 (28).

St. Joseph's Home, 9244 29th Ave., Kenosha 53140 (89).

St. Joseph's Home, 5301 W. Lincoln Ave., W. Allis 53219 (124).

St. Joseph's Nursing Home, 464 S. St. Joseph Ave., Arcadia 54612 (72).

St. Joseph's Nursing Home, 2415 Cass St., La Crosse 54601 (62).

St. Joseph's Nursing Home, 400 Water Ave., Hillsboro 54634 (65).

St. Joseph Residence, Inc. (Nursing Home), 1925 Division St., New London 54961 (107).

St. Mary's Home for the Aged (Residence and Nursing Care), 2005 Division St., Manitowoc 54220 (172).

St. Mary's Nursing Home, 3516 W. Center St., Milwaukee 53210 (121).

St. Monica's Senior Citizens Home, 3920 N. Green Bay Rd., Racine 53404 (90).

St. Paul Home (Residence and Skilled Nursing Home), 509 W. Wisconsin Ave., Kaukauna 54130 (52).

Villa Clement (Nursing and Convalescent Center), 9047 W. Greenfield Ave., W. Allis 53214 (190).

Villa Loretto Nursing Home, Mount Calvary 53057 (52).

FACILITIES FOR HANDICAPPED CHILDREN AND ADULTS

Sources: Almanac survey; *Directory of Catholic Special Facilities and Programs for Handicapped Children and Adults,* published by the National Catholic Educational Association; *Official Catholic Directory.*

This listing covers facilities and programs with educational and training orientation. Information about other services for the handicapped can generally be obtained from the Catholic Charities Office or its equivalent (c/o Chancery Office) in any diocese. (See Index for listing of addresses of chancery offices in the U.S.)

Abbreviation code: b, boys; c, coeducational; d, day; g, girls; r, residential. Other information includes chronological age for admission. The number in parentheses at the end of an entry indicates total capacity or enrollment.

Deaf and Hard of Hearing

California: St. Joseph's Center for Deaf and Hard of Hearing (d,c; 3-14 yrs.), 4025 Grove St., Oakland 94609 (mailing address).

Illinois: Holy Trinity Day Classes for the Deaf (c; 3-14 yrs.) 1910 Taylor, Chicago 60612 (45).

Louisiana: Chinchuba Institute (d,c; 16 yrs.), 1131 Barataria Blvd., Marrero. 70072 (101).

Massachusetts: Boston School for the Deaf (r,d,c; 3-21 yrs.), 800 N. Main St., Randolph. 02368 (236). Psycho-Education Center (PEC) for emotionally disturbed deaf children (r, d; 3-10 yrs.).

Missouri: St. Joseph Institute for the Deaf (r,d,c; birth to 15 yrs.), 1483 82nd Blvd., St. Louis 63132 (150).

New York: Cleary School for the Deaf (d,c; infancy through high school), 301 Smithtown Blvd., Lake Ronkonkoma, L.I. 11779 (105).

St. Francis de Sales School for the Deaf (d,c; parent-infant programs through age 14), 260 Eastern Parkway, Brooklyn 11225.

St. Joseph's School for the Deaf (d,c; birth-13 yrs.), 1000 Hutchinson River Pkwy, Bronx. 10465 (230).

St. Mary's School for the Deaf (r,d,c; birth to 21 yrs.), 2253 Main St., Buffalo. 14214 (220).

Ohio: St. Rita School for the Deaf (r,c; 4 yrs. and older), 1720 Glendale-Milford Rd., Cincinnati. 45215 (120).

Pennsylvania: Abp. Ryan Memorial Institute for Deaf (d,c; parent-infant programs through 8th grade), 3509 Spring Garden St., Philadelphia. 19104 (80).

De Paul Institute (d,c; birth-21 yrs.), Castlegate Ave., Pittsburgh. 15226 (132).

Emotionally And/Or Socially Maladjusted

This listing includes facilities for abused, abandoned and neglected as well as emotionally disturbed children and youth.

California: Gracenter, Convent of the Good Shepherd (r, women), 501 Cambridge, San Francisco 94134 (16).

Hanna Boys Center (r; 9-16 yrs.), Box 100, Sonoma. 95476 (72).

Rancho San Antonio (r,b; 12-16 yrs.), 21000 Plummer St., Chatsworth. 91311 (118).

Stanford Lathrop Memorial Home and Group Homes, Sisters of Social Service, 800 N. Street, Sacramento 95814. Conduct six homes for boys and girls.

Colorado: Excelsior Youth Centers (r,g; 12-21 yrs.), 15001 E. Oxford Ave., Aurora 80014 (96).

Mt. St. Vincent Home (r,c; 5-13 yrs.), 4159 Lowell Blvd., Denver. 80211 (45).

Connecticut: Highland Heights — St. Francis Home for Children (r,d,c; 8-13 yrs.), 651 Prospect St., New Haven. 06505 (38). Also conducts Ken-Mar Group Home (r,d,c; 14-17 yrs.), 682 Prospect St., New Haven 06505 (10).

Mt. St. John (r,b; 11-16 yrs.), Kirtland St., Deep River. 06417 (75).

Delaware: Our Lady of Grace Home for Children (r,c; 6-12 yrs.), 487 Chestnut Hill Rd., Newark 19713 (28).

Florida: Boystown of Florida (r; 13-17 yrs.), 11400 SW 137th Ave., Miami 33186 (45).

Georgia: Village of St. Joseph (r,d,c; 6-16 yrs.), 2969 Butner Rd. S.W., Atlanta 30331 (40 r; 48 d). Residential treatment center and therapeutic special school for children with emotional problems, behavior disorders, learning disabilities.

Illinois: Charles I. Doyle, S.J., Center and Day School of Loyola University (d, c; pre-school to 19 yrs.), 1043 Loyola Ave., Chicago 60626 (25 in day school, unlimited in guidance center).

Guardian Angel (r,d,c; 5-15 yrs.), Plainfield at Theodore St., Joliet 60435 (20 r, 30 d).

St. Joseph Carondelet Child Center (r,b; 5-16 yrs. and d,c; 5-15 yrs.); 739 E. 35th St., Chicago 60616 (32 r, 20 d).

Indiana: Gibault School for Boys (r; 10-16 yrs.), 5901 Dixie Bee Rd., Terre Haute. 47802 (104).

Hoosier Boys Town (r; 9-18 yrs.), Schererville. 46375 (65).

Kentucky: Boys' Haven (r; 13 18 yrs.), 3201 Bardstown Rd., Louisville. 40205 (51).

Maryhurst School (r,g; 13-17 yrs.), 1015 Dorsey Lane, Louisville 40223 (42).

Louisiana: Hope Haven — Madonna Manor School and Home (r,b; 6-17 yrs.), 1101 Barataria Blvd., Marrero 70072 (176).

Maison Marie Group Home (r,g; 13-18 yrs.), 3020 Independence St., Metairie 70002 (12).

Maryland: Good Shepherd Center (r,d,g; 14-18 yrs.), 4100 Maple Ave., Baltimore. 21227 (90r, 15d).

Massachusetts: Cushing Hall (r,b; 11-14½ yrs.), 279 Tilden Rd., Scituate. 02066 (40). Diagnostic treatment center.

McAuley Nazareth Home for Boys (r; 6-14 yrs.), 77 Mulberry St., Leicester. 01524 (27).

Madonna Hall (r,g, 12-17 yrs.), Cushing Hill Dr., Marlboro 01752 (48). Diagnostic treatment program (12) and Secure Assessment Treatment Center (12).

Nazareth Child Care Center (r,d,c; 5-14 yrs.), 420 Pond St., Jamaica Plain, Mass. 02130 (96).

Our Lady of Providence Children's Center (r,d,c; 5-15 yrs.), 2112 Riverdale St., W. Springfield. 01089 (50). Diagnostic treatment program also.

St. Vincent Home (r,c), 2425 Highland Ave., Fall River 02720 (85).

Michigan: Barat House, Barat Human Services, League of Catholic Women (r,g; 13-17 yrs.), 5250 John R. St., Detroit. 48202 (24).

Boysville of Michigan, Inc. (r; 13-18 yrs.), 8744 Clinton-Macon Rd., Clinton. 49236 (180).

Don Bosco Hall (r,b; 13-17 years.), 10001 Petoskey Ave., Detroit. 48204 (38).

St. John's Home (r,c; 9-16 yrs.), 385 E. Leonard N.E., Grand Rapids 49503 (40).

St. Vincent Home for Children (r,c; 5-15 yrs.), 2800 W. Willow St., Lansing 48917 (36).

Villa Maria, Sisters of the Good Shepherd (r,g; 13-17 yrs.), 1315 Walker Ave. N.W., Grand Rapids. 49504 (30).

Vista Maria (r,d, g; 13-17 yrs.), 20651 W. Warren Ave., Dearborn Heights. 48127 (107 r; 20 d).

Minnesota: Home of the Good Shepherd (r.g; 12-17 yrs.), 5100 Hodgson Rd., St. Paul. 55112 (48).

St. Cloud Children's Home (r,c; 8-17 yrs.), 1726 7th Ave. S., St. Cloud. 56301 (72).

St. James Children's Home (r,c), Woodland Hills, Duluth 55803 (60).

Tiffany House Group Home (c), 374 4th Ave. S., St. Cloud 56301 (11).

Missouri: Child Center of Our Lady (r,c; 4-12 yrs. — d,c; 4-17 yrs.), 7900 Natural Bridge Rd., St. Louis. 63121 (79).

Marillac Center for Children (r,d,c; 4-14 yrs.), 310 W. 106th St., Kansas City. 64114 (28 r; 60 d).

Marygrove (r,g; d,c; 13-17 yrs.), 2705 Mullanphy Lane, Florissant. 63031 (44).

Nebraska: Father Flanagan's Boys' Home (r; 10-18 yrs.), Boys Town, Nebr. 68010 (r, 390; d, 307).

Nevada: St. Yves School (r,g; 13-17 yrs.), 7000 North Jones Blvd., Las Vegas, 89131 (60).

New Jersey: Christopher House (c; 18 and over), 55 N. Clinton Ave., Trenton 08607 (90). Psychiatric day treatment.

Collier Group Home (r,g; 14-18 yrs.), 47 Reckless Pl., Red Bank 07701 (10).

Collier School (d,c; 13-18 yrs.), Wickatunk 07765.

Guidance Clinic of Catholic Welfare Bureau (c), 39 N. Clinton Ave., Trenton 08607. Psychiatric counseling for children and adults.

Mt. St. Joseph Children's Center (r,d,c; 6-12 yrs.), Shepherd Lane, Totowa 07512 (32).

New Jersey's Boystown (r; adolescents), 499 Belgrove Dr., Kearney 07032 (100).

New York: The Astor Home for Children (r,d,c; 5-12 yrs.), 36 Mill St., Rhinebeck 12572 (75). Group Homes (7-18 yrs.), 1200 Zerega Ave., Bronx 10462 (52). Child Guidance Clinics/Day Treatment (Rhinebeck, Poughkeepsie, Beacon, Bronx). Head start — Day Care (Poughkeepsie, Beacon, Hyde Park, Dover, Millerton).

Baker Hall (r,d,b; 10-18 yrs.), 150 Martin Rd., Lackawanna. 14218 (250). Special services, institution, group homes, foster homes, preventive services, special education school.

LaSalle School (r,d,b, 12-18 yrs.), 391 Western Ave., Albany. 12203 (145). Also conducts group homes.

Madonna Heights Services (r,d,g; 11-17 yrs.), Burrs Lane, Huntington. 11743 (110). Also conducts group homes on Long Island and outpatient programs.

Saint Anne Institute (r,d,g; 12-18 yrs.), 160 N. Main Ave., Albany. 12206 (140). Critical level, preventive services, group home.

St. Helena's Residence (r,g; 12-17 yrs.), 120 W. 60th St., New York. 10023 (20).

St. John's of Rockaway Beach (r,b; 10-18 yrs.), 144 Beach 111th St., Rockaway Park. 11694 (112). Also conducts group homes in Far Rockaway and Richmond Hill.

North Dakota: Home on the Range for Boys (r; 12-18 yrs.), Box 41, Sentinel Butte. 58654 (46).

Ohio: Diocesan Child Guidance Center, Inc. (d,c; preschool) Outpatient counseling program (c; 2-18 yrs.), 840 W. State St., Columbus 43222.

Marycrest (r,g; 13-18 yrs.), 7800 Brookside Rd., Independence. 44131 (70).

Parmadale/St. Anthony's Youth Services Village (r,c; 7-21 yrs.), 6753 State Rd., Parma 44134.

Rosemont (r,g;d,c; 12-18 yrs.), 2440 Dawnlight Ave., Columbus 43211 (150).

Oregon: St. Mary's Home for Boys (r; 9-17 yrs.), 16535 S.W. Tualatin Valley Highway, Beaverton 97006 (43).

Pennsylvania: De LaSalle in Towne (d,b; 12-17 yrs.), 25 S. Van Pelt St., Philadelphia 19103 (110).

De LaSalle Vocational Day Treatment (b; 15-17 yrs.), P.O. Box 344 — Street Rd. and Bristol Pike, Bensalem 19020 (120).

Gannondale School for Girls (r; 12-17 yrs.), 4635 E. Lake Rd., Erie 16511 (57).

Harborcreek School for Boys (r; 10-17 yrs.), 5712 Iroquois Ave., Harborcreek 16421 (135). Also conducts group homes.

Lourdesmont Good Shepherd Adolescent Services (r,g;d,c; 13-17 yrs.), 537 Venard Rd., Clarks Summit 18411 (100).

Pauline Auberle Foundation, The Auberle Home for Boys (r,b; 13-18 yrs.), 1101 Hartman St., McKeesport 15132 (50).

St. Gabriel Hall (r,b; 12-17 yrs.), P.O. Box 13, Audobon 19407 (220). Also conducts group homes.

St. Michael's School for Boys (r,b; d,c; 12-17 yrs.), Hoban Heights, Tunkhannock 18657 (120). Also conducts group homes.

Tennessee: DeNeuville Heights School for Girls (r; 12-18 yrs.), 3060 Baskin St., Memphis 38127 (52).

Texas: St. Joseph Youth Center (r,c; 12-17 yrs.), 901 S. Madison St., Dallas 75208 (48).

Washington: Morning Star Boys Ranch (Spokane Boys' Ranch, Inc.), (r,b; 9-18 yrs.), Box 8087 Manito Station, Spokane 99203 (30).

Wisconsin: Eudes Corporation at Our Lady of Charity Center (r,c; 10-17 yrs.), 2640 West Point Rd., Green Bay 54303 (50).

St. Aemilian Child Care Center, Inc. (r,b; 6-12 yrs.), 8901 W. Capitol Dr., Milwaukee 53222 (57).

St. Charles Boys Home (r; 12-18 yrs.), 151 S. 84th St., Milwaukee 53214 (56).

Wyoming: St. Joseph's Children's Home (r,c; 6-18 yrs.), P.O. Box 1117, Torrington 82240 (48). Also conducts group home.

Developmentally Handicapped

This listing includes facilities for children, youth and adults with learning disabilities and/or mental retardation.

Alabama: Father Walter Memorial Child Care Center (r,c; birth-12 yrs.), 2815 Forbes Dr., Montgomery 36199 (34). Skilled nursing facility.

California: Catholic Charities "Empower" Services to Developmentally Disabled Persons, 433 Jefferson St., Oakland 94607. Services include (in various locations): Evergreen Center (d; adults); Concord House (r; adults); C.O.R.E. (d; adults outreach program for homebound); Case Management (d; adults, children — social workers); Religious Nurture Program (d; adults, children).

Child Study Center (d,c; 5-13 yrs.), 1339 - 20th St., Santa Monica. 90404 (80). Also conducts a developmental nursery (18 mos.-3 yrs.) and a preschool for children from culturally deprived areas (3-5 yrs.).

Helpers of the Mentally Retarded, Inc., 2626 Fulton St., San Francisco 94118. Conducts three homes: Helpers Home for Girls (18 years and older), 2608 Fulton St. and 2626 Fulton St., San Francisco 94118; Helpers Home for Men (18 years and older), 2750 Fulton St., San Francisco 94118.

St. Madeleine Sophie's Training Center (d,c; 18 yrs. and older), 2111 E. Madison Ave., El Cajon 92021 (102).

St. Vincent's (r,d,c; 8-21 yrs.), P.O. Drawer V, 4200 Calle Real, Santa Barbara 93102 (116).

Tierra del Sol (d,c; 18 yrs. and older), 9919 Sunland Blvd., Sunland 91040 (100).

Connecticut: Gengras Center (d,c; 8-21 yrs.), St. Joseph College, 1678 Asylum Ave., W. Hartford 06117 (70).

Special Education Department, Diocese of Bridgeport, 238 Jewett Ave., Bridgeport 06606.

Villa Maria Education Center (d,c), 159 Sky Meadow Dr., Stamford 06903 (31). For children with learning disabilities.

District of Columbia: Lt. Joseph P. Kennedy Jr. Institute (d,c; 5-20 yrs.), 801 Buchanan St. N.E., Washington 20017 (120). Also conducts group homes, continuing education and life skills training programs, contract employment and job placement.

St. Gertrude's School of Arts and Crafts (r,d,g; 6-19 yrs.), 4801 Sargent Rd. N.E., Washington 20017 (40).

Florida: Marian Center Services for Developmentally Handicapped and Mentally Retarded (r,d,c), 15701 Northwest 37th Ave., Opa Locka 33054. Offers variety of services.

Marian School for Exceptional Children (d,c; 2-5 yrs.), 326 Pine Terr., W. Palm Beach 33401.

Morning Star School (d,c; 4-12 yrs.), 725 Mickler Rd., Jacksonville 32211 (70).

Morning Star School (d,c; 3-12 yrs.), 954 Leigh Ave., Orlando 32804 (45).

Morning Star School (d,c; 6-13 yrs.), 4661 - 80th Ave., N., Pinellas Park 33565 (50).

Morning Star School (d,c; 6-13 yrs.), 210 E. Linebaugh Ave., Tampa 33612. For children with learning disabilities.

Illinois: Bartlett Learning Center (r,d,c; 5-21 yrs.), 801 W. Bartlett Rd., Bartlett 60103 (124).

Good Shepherd Manor (permanent home for men; 18 yrs. and older), P.O. Box 260, Momence. 60954 (120).

Lt. Joseph P. Kennedy, Jr., School (r,b;d,c; 6-21 yrs.) and Job Training Center (c; 16 yrs. and older), 123rd and Wolf Rd., Palos Park. 60464 (101).

Misericordia Home South (r,c; 1 mo.-6 yrs.), 2916 W. 47th St., Chicago 60632 (122).

Misericordia Home North (r,c; 4-21 yrs.), 6300 North Ridge, Chicago 60660 (82).

Mt. St. Joseph (mentally handicapped women; 20-45 yrs.), 24955 N. Highway 12, Lake Zurich 60047 (160).

St. Francis School for Exceptional Children (r,c; 4-12 yrs.), 1209 S. Walnut Ave., Freeport 61032 (32).

St. Jude Special Education Center (d,c), 2nd and Spring Ave., Aviston 62216.

St. Mary of Providence (r,d,g; 4-21 yrs.), 4200 N. Austin Ave., Chicago 60634 (190).

St. Rose Center (d,c; 3-21 yrs.), 4911 S. Hoyne Ave., Chicago 60609 (60).

St. Vincent Residential School (c; 12 yrs. and older) (30), and St. Vincent Community Living Facility (adults) (20), and St. Vincent Supported Living Arrangement (adults) (60), 659 E. Jefferson St., Freeport 61032.

Special Education Program of the East St. Louis Deanery (d,c; 5-16 yrs.), 8213 Church Lane, East St. Louis 62203 (60).

Indiana: Marian Day Program (d,c; 6-16 yrs.), 700 Herndon Dr., Evansville 47711 (20).

Providence House (r, men; 18 yrs. and up), 520 W. 9th St., Jasper 47546 (66).

St. Bavo Special Class (d,c; 6-15 yrs.), 512 W. 8th St., Mishawaka 46544 (12).

St. Mary Child Center School (d,c; 3-16 yrs.), 311 N. New Jersey St., Indianapolis 46204 (32). Developmentally Disabled.

Kansas: Holy Family Center (d,c; 6-21 yrs.), 619 S. Maize Rd., Wichita 67209 (65).

Lakemary Center, Inc. (r,d,c; 3-16 yrs.), 100 Lakemary Dr., Paola 66071 (72r,35d).

Kentucky: Ursuline-Pitt School (d,c), 10715 Ward Ave., Louisville 40223 (62).

Ursuline Speech Clinic (d,c), 3105 Lexington Rd., Louisville 40206 (105).

Louisiana: Department of Special Education, Archdiocese of New Orleans, St. Michael Special School, 1522 Chippewa St., New Orleans 70130.

Holy Angels School (r,c; teen-age, 14 yrs. and older; nursery, 2 mo. to kindergarten age), 10450 Ellerbe Rd., Shreveport 71106 (200).

Our Lady of Fatima School (d,c; 6-18 yrs.), 2315 Johnston St., Lafayette 70503 (50).

Padua House (r,c; birth-21 yrs.), 200 Beta St., Belle Chase 70037 (44).

Regina Caeli Center (d,c; 6-16 yrs.), 3903 Kingston, Lake Charles. 70605 (50).

St. Agnes Vocational Evaluation and Training Center (d,c), P.O. Box 53326, 715 East Blvd., Baton Rouge 70802 (140).

St. Mary's Training School (r,c: 3-22 yrs.), P.O. Drawer 7768, Alexandria 71306 (150).

Maryland: The Benedictine School for Exceptional Children (r,c; 6-21 yrs.), Ridgely 21660 (100). Also conducts Habilitation Center (r,c; 17 yrs. and older) (50).

Francis X. Gallagher Center (r), 2520 Pot Spring Rd., Timonium 21093 (76).

St. Elizabeth School and Habilitation Center (d,c; 12-21 yrs.), 801 Argonne Dr., Baltimore 21218 (125).

St. Francis School for Special Education (d,c; 3-12 yrs.), 2226 Maryland Ave., Baltimore 21218 (60).

Massachusetts: Cardinal Cushing School and Training Center (r,d,c; 6-22 yrs.), Hanover 02339 (130 r; 65 d).

Mercy Centre for Developmental Disabilities (d,c; 3-22 yrs. and over), 25 West Chester St., Worcester 01605 (160).

Nazareth Hall (d,c; 7-22 yrs.), 887 Highland Ave., Fall River, 02720 (45).

Nazareth on the Cape (d,c; 6-15 yrs.), 261 South St., Hyannis 02601 (25).

St. Coletta Day School (d,c; 6-20 yrs., admission age), 85 Washington St., Braintree 02184 (132).

Michigan: Our Lady of Providence Center (r,d,g; 5-17 yrs., child caring; 18-26, adult foster care), 16115 Beck Rd., Northville. 48167 (100).

St. Louis Center and School (r,d,b; 6-18 yrs. child care; 18-26 yrs. adult foster care), 16195 Old U.S. 12, Chelsea 48118 (80).

Minnesota: Mother Teresa Home (r,c; adults), 101-10th Ave. N., Cold Spring 56320 (14).

St. Elizabeth Home (r,c; adults), 306 15th Ave. N., St. Cloud 56301 (14).

St. Francis Home (r,c; 9-12 yrs.) 25-2nd St. N., Waite Park 56387 (6).

Missouri: Department of Special Education, Archdiocese of St. Louis, 4472 Lindell Blvd., St. Louis. 63108. Conducts 31 special day classes (c; 5-16 yrs.).

Good Shepherd Manor (residential for developmentally disabled men; 16 yrs. and up), Little Brothers of the Good Shepherd, 3220 E. 23rd St., Kansas City 64127 (43).

Mt. Carmel Group Home (r,c; 16-21 yrs.), 8757 Annetta Ave., St. Louis 63147.

St. Joseph's Vocational Center (d,c; 15-21 yrs.), 5341 Emerson Ave., St. Louis 63120 (147).

St. Mary's Special School (r,c; 5-16 yrs.), 5341 Emerson Ave., St. Louis 63120 (135).

St. Peter's Special Classes (d,c; 5-21 yrs.), 314 W. High St., Jefferson City 65101 (30).

Universal Sheltered Workshop (c, adults), 6912 W. Florissant Ave., St. Louis 63136. Sheltered employment (80).

Nebraska: Madonna School for Exceptional Children (d,c; 5-21 yrs.), 2537 N. 62nd St., Omaha 68104 (65).

Villa Marie School (r,d,c; 7-16 yrs.), P. O. Box 80328, Waverly 68501 (25).

New Jersey: Alhambra Child Study Center (d,c; 3-12 yrs.), 31 Contro St., Newark 07103 (36).

Archbishop Boland Rehabilitation Center (d,c; 16-60 yrs.), 450 Market St. Newark 07105 (350).

Archbishop Damiano School (d,c; 5-21 yrs.), 532 Delsea Dr., Westville Grove 08093.

Catholic Community Services, Multi-Service Center, 17 Mulberry St., Newark 07102.

Department of Special Education, Diocese of Camden, 1845 Haddon Ave., Camden 08108. Services include: Archbishop Damiano School (above), and full time programs at 6 Catholic Schools; adult evening classes (18-65 yrs.); religious education programs.

Department of Special Education, Diocese of Paterson. Murray House (r; adults), 389 Main St., Paterson 07501. Also conducts four other adult group homes and one adult opportunity center.

Felician School for Exceptional Children (r,d,c; 2½-14 yrs.), 260 S. Main St., Lodi 07644 (120).

McAuley School for Exceptional Children (d,c; 5-9 yrs.), 1633 Rt. 22 at Terrill Rd., Plainfield-Watchung 07060 (40).

Mt. Carmel Guild Special Education School (d,c; 6-15 yrs.), 241 Erie St., Jersey City 07302 (80).

Mt. Carmel Guild Special Education School (d,c; 6-12 yrs.), 550 E. Broad St., Westfield 07079 (45).

St. Anthony's Special Education School (d,c; 10-20 yrs.), 25 N. 7th St., Belleville 07109 (60).

Sr. Georgine Learning Center (d,c; 6-17 yrs.), 544 Chestnut Ave., Trenton 08611 (30).

St. John of God Community Services (d,c; birth to adults), 532 Delsea Dr., Westville Grove 05093.

St. Patrick's Special Education School (d,c; 6-17 yrs.), 72 Central Ave., Newark 07109 (60).

New Mexico: St. Joseph's Manor (r,b; 18-35 yrs.), P.O. Box 610, Bernalillo 87004. Little Brothers of the Good Shepherd, P.O. Box 610, Bernalillo 87004. Twenty-four-hour adult care center for mentally retarded men.

New York: Cantalician Center for Learning (d,c; birth-21 yrs.), 3233 Main St., Buffalo 14214 (300).

Cantalician Center Workshop (d,c; 18 yrs. and older), 129A Central Park Plaza, Buffalo 14214 (150). Also conducts a vocational evaluation and rehabilitation training program.

Catholic Charities, Diocese of Rockville Centre — Services for Retarded Adults, 50 N. Park Ave., Box X, Rockville Centre 11570. Conducts four residences for retarded adults (Christopher Residence; Neumann Residence for Deaf Retarded; Alhambra House; Seton Residence — r,c; 21 yrs. and up).

Cobb Memorial School (r,c; 6-10 yrs.), Altamont 12009 (40).

Friends of L'Arche of Greater Syracuse, Inc. (r, adults), 1701 James St., Syracuse 13206 (12). Long-term facility for mentally retarded adults following philosophy of Jean Vanier and L'Arche movement.

Maryhaven Center of Hope (r,d,c; pre-school to adult), Myrtle Ave., Port Jefferson 11777. Offers variety of services.

Mercy Home for Children (r,c), 273 Willoughby Ave., Brooklyn 11205.

Office for the Handicapped, Diocese of Brooklyn, 191 Joralemon St., Brooklyn 11201. Services include day care center and community residences for retarded adults.

Office of the Handicapped, Archdiocese of New York, 1011 First Ave., New York 10022.

St. Catherine Center for Children (r,c; birth to 12 yrs. and d,c; 3-12 yrs.), 30 N. Main St., Albany 12203 (140). Also conducts group home and specialized foster care programs.

St. Joseph School for Exceptional Children (r,d,c; 5-21 yrs.), 10807 Bennett Rd., Dunkirk 14048 (26 r, 14 d). Residents must return home weekends and vacations.

School of the Holy Childhood (d,c; 5-21 yrs.), 1150 Buffalo Rd., Rochester 14624 (94). Adult program, 18-50 yrs.

North Carolina: Holy Angels Nursery (r,c; birth to 12 yrs.), Belmont 28012 (66).

Ohio: Good Shepherd Manor (permanent care of men 18 years and older), P.O. Box 387, Wakefield 45687 (104).

Mary Immaculate School (d,c; 7-14 yrs.), 3837 Secor Rd., Toledo 43623 (60). For children with learning disabilities.

Mt. Aloysius (r, men; 21 yrs. and over), Tile Plant Rd., New Lexington 43764 (100).

Our Lady of Angels Special School (d,c; 6-16 yrs.), 3570 Rocky River Dr., Cleveland 44111 (30).

Our Lady of the Elms Special School (d,c; 6-15 yrs.), 1230 W. Market St., Akron 44313 (74).

Rose Mary, The Johanna Graselli Rehabilitation and Education Center (r,c; 3-12 yrs.), 19350 Euclid Ave., Cleveland 44117 (40).

St. John's Villa (r,c,b, 6-14 yrs; g, 6-18 yrs., continued care, g, 18 yrs. and over), 620 Roswell Rd. N.W., Carrollton 44615 (221).

St. Joseph Center (d,c; 6-16 yrs.), 2346 W. 14th St., Cleveland 44113 (70).

Sheltered Workshop and Training Center (c; 16 yrs. and older), 1890 W. 22nd St., Cleveland 44113 (35).

Oregon: Emily School for Multi-Handicapped Children (d,c; 2½-5 yrs.), 830 N.E. 47th Ave., Portland 97213 (12).

Providence Children's Nursing Center (r, c; nursing care), 830 N. E. 47th Ave., Portland 97213 (54).

Pennsylvania: Clelian Heights School for Exceptional Children (r,d,c; 5-21 yrs.), R.D. 9, Box 607, Greensburg 15601 (140). Also conducts re-socialization program (r,d,c; young adults).

Don Guanella School (r,d,b; 6-21 yrs.) and C. K. Center (r,c; adults, post-school age), Sproul Rd., Springfield 19064.

McGuire Memorial (r,d,c; infancy to 7 yrs.), 2119 Mercer Rd., New Brighton 15066 (99).

Mercy Day School: Center for Special Learning (d,c; 2-21 yrs.), 830 S. Woodward St., Allentown 18103 (69).

Our Lady of Confidence Day School (d,c; 5-18 yrs.), 10th and Lycoming Sts., Philadelphia 19140 (120).

St. Anthony School for Exceptional Children (r,d,c; 5-21 yrs.), 13th St. and Hulton Rd., Oakmont 15139 (135).

St. Joseph Day School Center for Special Learning (d,c; 6-21 yrs.), 619 Mahantongo St., Pottsville 17901 (40).

St. Joseph's Center (r,c; birth-20 yrs.), 2010 Adams Ave., Scranton 18509 (85).

St. Katherine School (d,c; 4-18 yrs.), William Rd. and Bowman Ave., Philadelphia 19151 (150)

St. Mary of Providence Center (r,d,g; 6-14 yrs.), Elverson 19520 (120).

Tennessee: Madonna Day School for Retarded Children (d,c; 5-16 yrs.), 4189 Leroy, Memphis 38108 (50).

St. Bernard School for Exceptional Children, (c; 4-8 yrs.), 2021 21st Ave. S., Nashville 37212 (25).

Texas: Notre Dame of Dallas Special School (d,c; 3-16 yrs.), 1451 E. Northgate Dr., Irving 75062. (115). Notre Dame Vocational Center (d,c; 16 yrs. and over), same address, provides work-study program for exceptional people over 16 (60).

Virginia: St. Coletta School (d,c; 3-25 yrs.), 1305 N. Jackson St., Arlington 22201 (45).

St. Mary's Infant Home (r,c; 3 days-9 yrs.), 317 Chapel St., Norfolk 23504 (50).

Wisconsin: St. Coletta School (r,c), Jefferson 53549 (372). Offers the following programs: a complete program of special education from kindergarten through elementary and advanced levels (r,d,c);

a work training center in preparation for job placement (r,c; 18-25 yrs.);

a residential care center (r,c; 45-85 yrs.);

a half-way house to give guidance and assist with problems (r; 18-24 yrs.);

sheltered workshop employment for the mentally retarded in a homelike environment (r,c; 25-45 yrs.).

St. Coletta Day School (c; 8-16 yrs.), 1725 N. 54th St., Milwaukee. 53208 (12).

Orthopedically Handicapped

Alabama: Father Purcell Memorial (r,c; birth to 14 yrs.), 2048 W. Fairview Ave., Montgomery 36108 (52). Skilled nursing home.

Kentucky: Redwood School and Rehabilitation Center (d,c; birth and up), 71 Orphanage Rd., Fort Mitchell 41017 (200).

Pennsylvania: St. Edmond's Home for Crippled Children (r,c; 2-10 yrs.)., 320 S. Roberts Rd., Rosemont 19010 (50).

Visually Handicapped

Illinois: Department of Vision, Catholic Charities, 721 N. LaSalle St., Chicago 60610. Itinerant education services for visually impaired students attending regular Catholic elementary and high schools in Chicago archdiocese (30).

Maine: Visually Handicapped Services: 47 High St., Portland 04101; 15 Vaughn St., Caribou 04736; 382 Sabattus St., Lewiston 04240; 95 Main St., Orono 04472; 333 Lincoln St., Saco 04072; 224 Main St., Waterville. Itinerant teacher and other services.

New Jersey: St. Joseph's School for the Multiple Handicapped Blind (r,d,c; 3-21 yrs.), 253 Baldwin Ave., Jersey City 07306 (25).

New York: Catholic Charities Services for Visually Impaired Persons (c), 272 Merrick Rd., Lynbrook 11563. All ages, differing programs.

Lavelle School for the Blind (r,d,c; 3-21 yrs.), 221st St. and Paulding Ave., Bronx 10469 (120).

Pennsylvania: St. Lucy Day School (d,c; 3½-14 yrs.), 929 S. Farragut St., Philadelphia. 19143.

ORGANIZATIONS

(See separate article for a listing of facilities for the handicapped.)

Blind

The Carroll Center for the Blind (formerly the Catholic Guild for All the Blind): Located at 770 Centre St., Newton, Mass. 02158, the center conducts diagnostic evaluation and rehabilitation programs for blind people over 16 years of age, and maintains programs in community services for all ages, volunteer and special services, casework and counseling, low-vision training and professional training. It offers a large range of services for blind people who are not in residence, and maintains an office of public education and information. *AAR Review* is the quarterly publication of the center. The executive director is Rachel Rosenbaum.

Xavier Society for the Blind: The Society is located at 154 E. 23rd St., New York, 10010. Founded in 1900 by Rev. Joseph Stadelman, S.J., it is a center for publications for the blind and maintains a circulating library of approximately 7,000 volumes in Braille, large type and on tape. Its many publications include *The Catholic Review,* a monthly selection of articles of current interest from the Catholic press presented for the visually handicapped in Braille, on tape, and in large print. The director of Xavier is Rev. Anthony F. La Bau, S.J.

The Deaf

According to the National Catholic Office for the Deaf, there are approximately 95,000 Catholics among the total deaf population of 410,522. (The deaf were defined by the 1974 National Census of the Deaf Population as "those persons who could not hear and understand speech and who had lost — or never had — that ability prior to 19 years of age.) Reported statistics indicated: Students in Catholic schools for the deaf, 1,969; teachers, 570 (147 were religious). Personnel involved in out-of-school pastoral ministry to the deaf included: priests, 73 (41 full-time, 32 part-time); permanent deacons, 6 (part-time); sisters, 45 (40 full-time, 5 part-time); brothers, 3 (1 full-time, 2 part-time); lay people, 23 (19 full-time, 4 part-time).

Organizations involved in work for the deaf include the following.

International Catholic Deaf Association: Established by deaf adults in Toronto, Canada, in 1949, the association has more than 3,000 members in 121 chapters, mostly in the U.S. It is the only international lay association founded and controlled by deaf Catholic adults. It is affiliated with the World Federation of the Deaf. Home office address: 814 Thayer Ave., Silver Spring, Md. 20910. The ICDA publishes *The Deaf Catholic,* a bimonthly, and sponsors regional conferences, workshops and an annual convention.

National Catholic Office for the Deaf: Formally established in 1976, at Washington, D.C., to provide pastoral service to those who teach deaf children and adults, to the parents of deaf children, to pastors of deaf persons, and to organizations of the deaf. The office develops liturgical and religious education materials; organizes workshops, pastoral weeks, community weeks, leadership programs, cursillos; and serves as a clearinghouse for information concerning ministry to the deaf. It publishes *Listening,* a pastoral service for the hearing impaired, five times a year. The executive director is Sister Alverna Hollis, O.P. Address: 814 Thayer Ave., Silver Spring, Md. 20910.

Mentally Retarded

National Apostolate with Mentally Retarded Persons: Established in 1968, the apostolate has headquarters at Trinity College, P.O. Box 4588, Washington, D.C. 20017. It publishes the quarterly *NAMRP Journal* and a monthly newsletter, and has available a bibliography on the religious education of the retarded. Sr. Mary Catherine Widger is president of the apostolate; the executive director is Bro. Joseph Moloney, O.S.F., 191 Joralemon St., Brooklyn, N.Y. 11201.

Service Agencies

National Catholic Office for Persons with Disabilities: Established in 1982 to assist dioceses in developing pastoral services with handicapped persons. The executive director is Sister Rita Baum, S.S.J. Address: 1200 5th St. N.W., Suite 102, Washington, D.C. 20005.

Special Education Department, National Catholic Educational Association: Established in 1954 to coordinate under one agency information and service functions for all areas of special education under Catholic auspices. The executive director is Sr. Suzanne Hall, S.N.D. de N. Address: 1077 30th St. N.W., Washington, D.C. 20007.

OTHER SOCIAL SERVICES

Cancer Hospitals or Homes: The following homes or hospitals specialize in the care of cancer patients. They are listed according to state.

Penrose Cancer Hospital, Sisters of Charity of Cincinnati, 2215 N. Cascade Ave., Colorado Springs, Colo. 80907.

Our Lady of Perpetual Help Home, Servants of Relief for Incurable Cancer, 760 Washington St., S.W., Atlanta, Ga. 30315 (54).

Rose Hawthorne Lathrop Home, Servants of Relief for Incurable Cancer, 1600 Bay St., Fall River, Mass. 02724 (35).

Our Lady of Good Counsel Free Cancer Home, Servants of Relief for Incurable Cancer, 2076 St. Anthony Ave., St. Paul, Minn. 55104 (40).

Calvary Hospital, Inc., 1740-70 Eastchester Rd., Bronx, N.Y. 10461 (200). Sponsored by Catholic Charities, Department of Health and Hospitals, Archdiocese of New York.

St. Rose's Free Home for Incurable Cancer, Servants of Relief for Incurable Cancer, 71 Jackson St., New York, N.Y. 10002 (45).

Rosary Hill Home, Servants of Relief for Incurable Cancer, Hawthorne, N.Y. 10532 (72).

Holy Family Home, Servants of Relief for Incurable Cancer, 6707 State Rd., Parma, O. 44134 (50).

Sacred Heart Free Home for Incurable Cancer, Servants of Relief for Incurable Cancer, 1315 W. Hunting Park Ave., Philadelphia, Pa. 19140 (59).

Drug Abuse: Rehabilitation centers and outpatient clinics have been established in several dioceses. Facilities include:

Alpha House for Drug Rehabilitation (women) and Dismas House for Drug Rehabilitation (men), 396 Straight St., Paterson, N.J. 07501 (residential rehabilitation programs). Cedar Outpatient Clinic and Cedar Day Care Center, 101-105 Cedar St., Paterson, N.J. 07501 (outpatient services).

Daytop Village, Inc., 54 W. 40th St., New York, N.Y. 10018. Msgr. William B. O'Brien. Five residential facilities and six outreach centers in New York.

New Hope Manor (live in therapeutic community for rehabilitation of female drug addicts), Graymoor, Garrison, N.Y. 10524.

St. Joseph's Hospital, L. E. Phillips Center for the Chemically Dependent, 2661 County Trunk I, Chippewa Falls, Wis. 54729 (46).

St. Luke's Center/Bethesda Manor, 3290 N.W. 7th St., Miami, Fla. 33125. Residential and outpatient detoxification programs for drug abusers; day care services for children of addicts in treatment.

Alcoholics: Some priests and religious throughout the U.S. are committed in a special way to the personal rehabilitation and pastoral care of alcoholics through participation in Alcoholics Anonymous and other programs. Facilities for the rehabilitation of alcoholics include:

Matt Talbot Inn, 2270 Professor St., Cleveland, Ohio 44113 (capacity 23 men; Halfway House; residential treatment for male alcoholics).

Straight and Narrow Hospital for Alcoholism (20 beds), and Straight and Narrow Rehabilitation Center for Male Alcoholics (50 beds), 396 Straight St., Paterson, N.J. 07501. McNulty House for Male Alcoholics (10 beds), 101 Cedar St., Paterson, N.J. 07501. Straight and Narrow Alcohol Abuse Services (outpatient services), 896 E. 19th St., Paterson, N.J. 07501.

Sacred Heart Rehabilitation Center, Inc., 569 E. Elizabeth St., Detroit, Mich. 48201 (13 beds, detoxification; 60 beds, early treatment); 400 Stoddard Rd., Memphis, Mich. 48041 (123 beds, advance treatment). Both facilities serve male and female live-in clients.

The National Clergy Conference on Alcoholism and Related Drug Problems, 3112 - 7th St. N.E., Washington, D.C. 20017, offers educational material to those involved in pastoral ministry on ways of dealing with problems related to alcoholism and medication dependency.

Convicts: Priests serve as full- or part-time chaplains in penal and correctional institutions throughout the country. Limited efforts have been made to assist in the rehabilitation of released prisoners in Halfway House establishments.

Dining Rooms; Facilities for Homeless: Representative of places where meals are provided, and in some cases lodging and other services as well, are:

St. Anthony's Dining Room, 121 Golden Gate Ave., San Francisco, Calif. 94102. Founded in 1950 by Rev. Alfred Boeddeker, O.F.M. More than 15 million free meals have been served. Director, Rev. Floyd A. Lotito, O.F.M.

St. Vincent de Paul Free Dining Room, 675 23rd St., Oakland, Calif. 94604. Administered by Little Brothers of the Good Shepherd, under sponsorship of St. Vincent de Paul Society. Hot meals served at lunch time 7 days a week; clothing, lodging provided those in need.

St. Vincent's Dining Room, 505 W. 3rd St., Reno, Nev. 89503.

St. Vincent Dining Room, 650 S. Main St., Las Vegas, Nev. 89101. Hot meal every day at noon.

Good Shepherd Refuge, Little Brothers of the Good Shepherd, 601 2nd St. S.W., Albuquerque, N.M. 87103.

Holy Name Centre for Homeless Men, Inc., 18 Bleeker St., New York, N.Y. 10012. A day shelter for alcoholic, homeless men. Provides social services and aid to transients and those in need. Affiliated with New York Catholic Charities.

St. Francis Inn, 2441 Kensington Ave., Philadelphia, Pa. 19125. Serves hot meals. Temporary shelter.

St. John's Hospice for Men, Little Brothers of the Good Shepherd, 1221 Race St., Philadelphia, Pa. 19107. Founded in 1963. Hot breakfast and dinner served to all in need; accommodations for 35 men for night shelter; clothing distributed daily to needy.

Camillus House, Little Brothers of the Good Shepherd, 726 N.E. First Ave., Miami, Fla. 33132. Breakfast, lunch and dinner served to all in need; accommodations for 61 men for night lodging; clothing distributed daily.

Temporary Shelters: Facilities for runaways, the abused, exploited and homeless include:

Anthony House, under sponsorship of St. Anthony's Guild (see Index). Four locations: 246 2nd St., Jersey City, N.J. 07302 (for homeless women and children); 38 Roosevelt Ave., Roosevelt, N.Y. 11575 (with St. Vincent de Paul Society — for homeless men); P.O. Box 880, Zellwood, Fla. 32798 (for migrant workers and their families); 2130 N. Hancock St., Philadelphia, Pa. 19122 (for homeless youth).

Covenant House, 460 W. 41st St., New York, N.Y. 10036. Non-sectarian. President, Rev. Bruce Ritter, O.F.M. Conv. Provides shelter and services for homeless, runaway and exploited youth under the age of 21, in New York. Toronto (Canada) and Antigua (Guatemala).

Crescent House, 1231 Prytania St., New Orleans, La. 70130. Temporary residence for abused women and their children.

The Dwelling Place, 409 W. 40th St., New York, N.Y. 10018. For homeless women.

Francis House, 1902 Cuming St., Omaha, Nebr. 68102. For homeless men.

The Good Shepherd Shelter, 1126 W. Grace St., Chicago, Ill. 60613. For abused women with children.

Good Shepherd Shelter, 2561 Venice Blvd., Los Angeles, Calif. 90019. For battered women with children.

Mercy Hospice, Sisters of Mercy, 334 S. 13th St., Philadelphia, Pa. 19107. Temporary shelter and relocation assistance for homeless women and children.

Mt. Carmel House, Carmelite Sisters, 471 G Pl., N.W., Washington, D.C. 20001. For homeless women.

Ozanam Inn, Little Brothers of the Good Shepherd, 843 Camp St., New Orleans, La. 70130. Under sponsorship of the St. Vincent de Paul Society. Hospice for homeless men.

St. Christopher Inn, Graymoor, Garrison, N.Y. 10524. Temporary shelter for homeless and needy men.

Siena House of Hospitality, 804 N. 19th St., Omaha, Nebr. 68102. For homeless women and children.

Unwed Mothers: Residential and care services for unwed mothers are available in many dioceses.

CHARISMATIC RENEWAL

(Written with the assistance of the staff of the Service Committee of the Catholic Charismatic Renewal of the U.S.)

The movement originated with a handful of Duquesne University students and faculty members in the 1966-67 academic year and spread from there to Notre Dame, Michigan State University, the University of Michigan and to other campuses and cities throughout the country.

According to a Gallup poll reported in the Feb. 22, 1980, issue of *Christianity Today*, 18 per cent of adult Catholics in the U.S. — nearly 6 million — considered themselves charismatic. More than 4,660 U.S. groups are listed in the latest issue of the *International Directory of Catholic Charismatic Prayer Groups*. Findings of a survey conducted by Father Kenneth Metz of the Archdiocese of Milwaukee and reported in August, 1981, estimated that there were 6,364 Catholic charismatic prayer groups in the U.S.

The movement is strong in Canada and some 110 other countries, probably involving more than a million participants. The Catholic charismatic renewal is growing rapidly in South America.

Keys to the Movement

Scriptural keys to the renewal are:
• Christ's promise to send the Holy Spirit upon the Apostles;
• the description, in the Acts of the Apostles, of the effects of the coming of the Holy Spirit upon the Apostles on Pentecost;

• St. Paul's explanation, in the Letter to the Romans, of the charismatic gifts (for the good of the Church and persons) the Holy Spirit would bestow on Christians;
• New Testament evidence concerning the effects of charismatic gifts in and through the early Church.

The personal key to the renewal is baptism of the Holy Spirit. This is not a new sacrament but the personally experienced actualization of grace already sacramentally received.

The experience of baptism of the Holy Spirit is often accompanied by the reception of one or more charismatic gifts.

Among the movement's strongest points of emphasis are prayer, openness to the Holy Spirit, community experience and the sharing of spiritual gifts.

The characteristic form of the renewal is the weekly prayer meeting, a gathering which includes periods of spontaneous prayer, singing, sharing of experience and testimony, fellowship and teaching.

Father Fio Mascarenhas, S.J., is director of the movement's International Communication Office, Via Feruccio, 19, 00185 Rome, Italy. Kevin M. Ranaghan is executive director of the National Service Committee, 237 N. Michigan St., South Bend, Ind. 46601. Auxiliary Bishop Joseph McKinney of Grand Rapids is episcopal consultant.

There is great variety in retreat and renewal programs, with orientations ranging from the traditional to teen encounters. Central to all of them are celebration of the liturgy and deepening of a person's commitment to faith and witness in life.

Features of many of the forms are as follows.

Traditional Retreats: Centered around conferences and the direction of a retreat master; oriented to the personal needs of the retreatants; including such standard practices as participation in Mass, reception of the sacraments, private and group prayer, silence and meditation, discussions.

Team Retreat: Conducted by a team of several leaders or directors (priests, religious, lay persons) with division of subject matter and activities according to their special skills and the nature and needs of the group.

Closed Retreat: Involving withdrawal for a period of time — overnight, several days, a weekend — from everyday occupations and activities.

Open Retreat: Made without total disengagement from everyday involvements, on a part-time basis.

Private Retreat: By one person, on a kind of do-it-yourself basis with the one-to-one assistance of a director.

Special Groups: With formats and activities geared to particular groups; e.g., members of Alcoholics Anonymous, vocational groups and apostolic groups.

Marriage Encounters: Usually weekend periods of husband-wife reflection and dialogue; introduced into the U.S. from Spain in 1967.

Charismatic Renewal: Featuring elements of the movement of the same name; "Spirit-oriented"; communitarian and flexible, with spontaneous and shared prayer, personal testimonies of faith and witness.

Christian Community: Characterized by strong community thrust.

Teens Encounter Christ (TEC), SEARCH: Formats adapted to the mentality and needs of youth, involving experience of Christian faith and commitment in a community setting.

Christian Maturity Seminars: Similar to teen encounters in basic concept but different to suit persons of greater maturity.

Cursillo: see separate entry.

House of Prayer Experience: see separate entry.

Movement for a Better World: see separate entry.

Conference

Retreats International Inc.: The first organization for promoting retreats in the U.S. was started in 1904 in California. Its initial efforts and the gradual growth of the movement led to the formation in 1927 of the National Catholic Laymen's Retreat Conference, the forerunner of the men's division of Retreats International. The women's division developed from the National Laywomen's Retreat Movement which was founded in Chicago in 1936. The men's and women's divisions merged July 9, 1977. The services of the organization include an annual summer institute for retreat and pastoral ministry, regional conferences for retreat center leadership and area meetings of directors and key leadership in the retreat movement. The officers are: Auxiliary Bishop Robert Morneau of Green Bay, episcopal advisor; Mr. John Van den Wymelenberg, president; Rev. Thomas W. Gedeon, S.J., executive director. National office: 1112 Memorial Library, Notre Dame, Ind. 46556.

HOUSES OF RETREAT AND RENEWAL

(Principal sources: Almanac survey; *The Official Catholic Directory.*)

Abbreviation code: m, men; w, women; mc, married couples; y, youth. Houses and centers without code generally offer facilities to most groups. An asterisk after an abbreviation indicates that the facility is primarily for the group designated but that special groups are also accommodated. Houses furnish information concerning the types of programs they offer.

Alabama: Blessed Trinity Shrine Retreat, Holy Trinity 36859.

Visitation Sacred Heart Retreat House, 2300 Spring Hill Ave., Mobile 36607.

Alaska: Holy Spirit Retreat House, Star Route A, Box 2388, Anchorage 99507.

Arizona: Franciscan Renewal Center, Casa de Paz y Bien, 5802 E. Lincoln Dr., Box 220, Scottsdale 85252.

Mount Claret Cursillo Center, 4633 N. 54th St., Phoenix 85018.

Picture Rocks Retreat — A Christian Renewal Center, 7101 W. Picture Rocks Rd., Tucson 85704. Mailing address, Box 569, Cortaro 85230.

Arkansas: The Abbey Retreat (Coury House), Subiaco 72865.

California: Angela Center, 535 Angela Dr., Santa Rosa 95401.

Camp Mariastella (y*, families, ecumenical), Wrightwood 92397. Office, 1120 Westchester Pl., Los Angeles 90019.

Cenacle Retreat House 5340 Fair Oaks Blvd., Carmichael 95608.

Christ the King Retreat Center, Box 156, Citrus Heights 95610.

Christian Brothers Retreat House (y*), 2233 Sulphur Springs Ave., St. Helena 94574.

Claretian Retreat Center, 1119 Westchester Pl., Los Angeles 90019.

El Carmelo Retreat House, 926 E. Highland Ave., Redlands 92373.

Holy Spirit Retreat Center, 4316 Lanai Rd., Encino 91436.

Immaculate Heart Retreat House, 3431 Waverly Dr., Los Angeles 90027. (Days of Recollection only.)

Jesuit Retreat House, P.O. Box 128, Los Altos 94022.

Manresa Retreat House (m*), P.O. Box K, Azusa 91702.

Mary and Joseph Retreat Center, 5300 Crest Rd., Rancho Palos Verdes 90274.

Mater Dolorosa Retreat House (m*), 700 N. Sunnyside Ave., Sierra Madre 91024.

Mission San Luis Rey Retreat, P.O. Box 409, San Luis Rey 92068.

Mount Mary Immaculate, 3254 Gloria Terr., Lafayette 94549.

Mt. Tabor Monastery, 17001 Tomki Rd., Redwood Valley 95470.

New Camaldoli Immaculate Heart Hermitage Big Sur 93920.

Poverello of Assisi Retreat House, 1519 Woodworth St., San Fernando 91340.

Prince of Peace Abbey, 650 Benet Hill, Oceanside 92054.

Sacred Heart Retreat House (w*), 920 E. Alhambra Rd., Alhambra 91801.

St. Andrew's Priory Retreat House, Valyermo 93563.

St. Anthony's Retreat House, P.O. Box 248, Three Rivers 93271.

St. Clare's Retreat, 2381 Laurel Glen Rd. Santa Cruz 95065.

St. Francis Retreat, P.O. Box 1070, San Juan Bautista 95045.

St. Joseph's Salesian Youth Center (St. Dominic Savio Retreat House) (y), 8301 Arroyo Dr., Rosemead 91770.

San Damiano Retreat, P.O. Box 767, Danville 94526.

San Miguel Retreat House, P.O. Box 69, San Miguel 93451.

Santa Sabina Center, 1520 Grand Ave., San Rafael 94901.

Serra Retreat, 3401 S. Serra Rd., Malibu 90265.

Starcross Monastery, House of Prayer, Annapolis, Calif. 95412.

Vallombrosa Center, 250 Oak Grove Ave., Menlo Park 94025.

Villa Maria del Mar, Santa Cruz. Mailing address, 2-1918 E. Cliff Dr., Santa Cruz 95062.

Colorado: Convent of St. Walburga, 6717 S. Boulder Rd., Boulder 80303.

El Pomar Center, 1661 Mesa Ave., Colorado Springs 80906.

Sacred Heart Retreat House, Box 185, Sedalia 80135.

Spiritual Life Institute (individuals only), Nada Hermitage, Crestone 81131.

Connecticut: Cenacle Center for Meditation and Spiritual Renewal, Wadsworth St., P.O. Box 550, Middletown 06457.

Edmundite Apostolate and Conference Center, Enders Island, Mystic 06355.

Holy Family Retreat (m, mc*), 303 Tunxis Rd., West Hartford 06107.

Immaculata Retreat House, Route 32, Box 55, Windham Rd., Willimantic 06226.

Mercy Center, P.O. Box 191, 167 Neck Rd., Madison 06443.

Our Lady of Calvary Retreat (w*), Colton St., Farmington 06032.

Villa Maria Retreat House, 159 Sky Meadow Dr., Stamford 06903.

Delaware: St. Francis Renewal Center, 1901 Prior Rd., Wilmington 19809.

District of Columbia: Washington Retreat House (w*), 4000 Harewood Rd. N.E., Washington 20017.

Florida: Cenacle Retreat House, 1400 S. Dixie Highway, Lantana 33462.

Dominican Retreat House, Inc., 7275 S.W. 124th St., Kendall 33156.

Franciscan Center, 3010 Perry Ave., Tampa 33603.

Holy Name Priory, P.O. Drawer H, St. Leo 33574.

Our Lady of Florida Retreat House, 1300 US Hwy. No. 1, North Palm Beach 33408.

Pilgrim Center of St. Leo Abbey, P.O. Drawer "L," St. Leo 33574.

Georgia: Ignatius House, 6700 Riverside Dr. N.W., Atlanta 30328.

Monastery of the Holy Spirit (m), 3780 Hwy. 212 S.W., Conyers 30207.

Idaho: Nazareth, 4450 N. Five Mile Rd., Boise 83704.

Illinois: Aylesford Carmelite Spiritual Center, I-55 at Cass Ave. N., Darien 60559.

Bellarmine Hall (m*), Box 268, Barrington 60010.

Bishop Lane Retreat House, R.R. 2, Box 214 A, Rockford 61102.

Cabrini Retreat Center, 9430 Golf Rd., Des Plaines 60016.

Cenacle Retreat House, 513 Fullerton Parkway, Chicago 60614.

Cenacle Retreat and Conference Center, P.O. Box 340, Warrenville 60555.

Childerley Retreat House, 506 McHenry Rd., Wheeling 60090.

Christian Life Center, 1209 W. Ogden Ave., La Grange Park 60525.

Divine Word International, 2001 Waukegan Rd., Techny 60082.

Franciscan Apostolic Center, P.O. Box 42, Sangamon Ave., Springfield 67205.

King's House, N. 66th St., Belleville 62223.

King's House of Retreats, Box 165, Henry 61537.

La Salle Manor, Christian Brothers Retreat House, Plano 60545.

Longwood Cenacle, 11600 Longwood Dr., Chicago 60643.

National Shrine of Our Lady of the Snows, 9500 W. Illinois Route 15, Belleville 62223.

Our Lady of Angels Retreat and Renewal Center, 1901 E. 18th St., Quincy 62301.
Resurrection Center, 2710 S. Country Club Rd., Woodstock 60098.
Sacred Heart Center, 3000 Central Rd., Rolling Meadows 60008.
St. Francis Retreat, House at Mayslake, 1717 31st St., Oak Brook 60521.
St. Mary's Retreat House, P.O. Box 608, 1400 Main St., Lemont 60439.
Tolentine Center, 20300 Governors Highway, Olympia Fields 60461.
Villa Desiderata Retreat House, 3015 N. Bayview Lane, McHenry 60050.
Villa Center for Renewal, 35 W. 076 Villa Maria Rd., St. Charles 60174.
Villa Redeemer, Box 6, Glenview 60025.

Indiana: Alverna Center, 8140 Spring Mill Rd., Indianapolis 46260.
Crosier Center, 2620 E. Wallen Rd., Ft. Wayne 46825.
John XXIII Center, 407 W. McDonald St., Hartford City 47348.
Kordes Enrichment Center, R.R. 3, Box 200, Ferdinand 47532.
Lourdes Retreat House (m*), Box 156, Cedar Lake 46303.
Mount Saint Francis Retreat Center, Mount Saint Francis 47146.
Our Lady of Fatima Retreat House, 5353 E. 56th St., Indianapolis 46226.
Our Lady of Fatima Retreat Center, Notre Dame 46556.
St. Jude Guest House, St. Meinrad 47577.
Saint Maur Hospitality Center, 4545 Northwestern Ave., Indianapolis 46208.
Sarto Retreat House, 4200 N. Kentucky Ave., Evansville 47711.
Solitude of St. Joseph, Notre Dame, Ind. 46556.

Iowa: American Martyrs Retreat House, 2209 N. Union Rd., Cedar Falls 50613.
Colfax Interfaith Spiritual Center, Box 37, Colfax, 50054.

Kansas: St. Augustine Retreat Center, A 3301 Parallel Parkway, Kansas City 66104.
Villa Christi Retreat House, 3033 W. Second St., Wichita 67203.

Kentucky: Marydale Retreat Center, 695 Donaldson Rd., Erlanger 41018.
Our Lady of Gethsemani (m, private), The Guestmaster, Abbey of Gethsemani, Trappist 40073.
Saint Thomas Center, 170 Crabbs Lane, Louisville 40206.

Louisiana: Abbey Christian Life Center, St. Joseph's Abbey, St. Benedict 70457.
Ave Maria Retreat House, Route 1, Box 0368 AB, Marrero 70072.
Cenacle Retreat House (w*), 5500 St. Mary St., P.O. Box 8115, Metairie 70011.

Manresa House of Retreats (m), P.O. Box 89, Convent 70723.
Maryhill Renewal Center, 600 Maryhill Rd., Pineville 71360.
Our Lady of the Oaks Retreat House, P.O. Drawer D, Grand Coteau 70541.

Maine: St. Paul's Center, Oblate Fathers Retreat House (French-English), 136 State St., Augusta 04330.

Maryland: Bon Secours Spiritual Center, Marriottsville 21104.
CYO Retreat Center, 5625 Edson Lane, Rockville 20852.
Christian Brothers Spiritual Center, 2535 Buckeyestown Pike, Adamstown 21710.
Loyola Retreat House-on-Potomac, Faulkner 20632.
Manresa-on-Severn, P.O. Box 9, Annapolis 21404.
Monsignor Clare J. O'Dwyer Youth Retreat House, 15523 York Rd., Sparks 21152.
St. Joseph Spiritual Center, 3800 Frederick Ave., Baltimore 21229.

Massachusetts: Calvary Retreat Center, Passionist Community, 59 South St., Shrewsbury 01545.
Campion Renewal Center, 319 Concord Rd., Weston 02193.
Cenacle Retreat House, 200 Lake St., Brighton, Boston 02135.
Eastern Point Retreat House, Gonzaga Hall, Gloucester 01930.
Espousal Center, 554 Lexington St., Waltham 02154.
Esther House of Spiritual Renewal, Sisters of St. Anne, 1015 Pleasant St., Worcester 01602.
Genesis Spiritual Life Center, 53 Mill St., Westfield 01085.
Glastonbury Abbey (Benedictine Monks), 16 Hull St., Hingham 02043.
Holy Cross Fathers Retreat House, 490 Washington St., N. Easton 02356.
Jesuit Center, Sullivan Square, Charlestown, Boston 02129.
Julie Center of Spirituality, Jeffrey's Neck Rd., Ipswich 01938.
La Salette Center for Christian Living, 947 Park St., Attleboro 02703.
Marian Center (w*), 1365 Northampton St., Holyoke 01040.
Mater Dei Retreat House (boys), Old Groveland Rd., Bradford 01830.
Miramar Retreat House, Duxbury, 02332.
Mother of Sorrows Retreat House, 110 Monastery Ave., W. Springfield 01089.
Mt. Carmel Christian Life Center, Oblong Rd., Williamstown 01267.
Sacred Heart Retreat House, Salesians of St. John Bosco, P.O. Box 271, Ipswich 01938.
St. Joseph's Abbey Retreat House (m) (Trappist Monks), Spencer 01562.
St. Stephen Priory (Dominican), 20 Glen St., Box 370, Dover, Mass. 02030.

Michigan: Blessed Sacrament Retreat House, Sacramentine Sisters, Conway 49722.

Capuchin Retreat, Box 188, Washington 48094.

Colombiere Retreat/Conference Center, Box 139, 9075 Big Lake Rd., Clarkston 48016.

Manresa Jesuit Retreat House, 1390 Quarton Rd., Bloomfield Hills 48013.

Marygrove Center, Garden 49835.

Portiuncula in the Pines, 703 E. Main St., De Witt 48820.

Queen of Angels Retreat, Box 2026, 3400 S. Washington Blvd., Saginaw 48605.

Retreat Center (w*), Sisters of Mary Reparatrix, 13600 Virgil Ave., Detroit 48223.

St. Basil's Center, 3990 Giddings Rd., Pontiac 48055.

St. Clare Capuchin Retreat, 1975 N. River Rd., St. Clair 48079.

St. Lazare Retreat House, W. Spring Lake Rd., Spring Lake 49456.

St. Mary's Retreat House (w*), 775 W. Drahner Rd., Oxford 48051.

St. Paul of the Cross Retreat Center, 23333 Schoolcraft, Detroit 48223.

Weber Center, 1257 E. Siena Heights Dr., Adrian 49221.

Minnesota: The Cenacle, 1221 Wayzata Blvd., Wayzata 55391.

Center for Spiritual Development, Box 538, 211 Tenth St., Bird Island 55310.

Christian Brothers Retreat Center, 15525 St. Croix Trail North, Marine-on-St. Croix 55047.

Christian Community Center, Assisi Heights, Box 4900, Rochester 55903.

The Dwelling Place, 210 3rd Ave. S., Sauk Rapids 56379.

Epiphany House of Prayer, 266 Summit Ave., St. Paul 55102.

Franciscan Retreats, Conventual Franciscan Friars, 16385 St. Francis Lane, Prior Lake 55372.

Jesuit Retreat House, 8243 De Montreville Trail North, Lake Elmo 55109.

King's House of Retreats, 621 S. First Ave., Buffalo 55313.

Maryhill Retreat House, Society of Daughters of the Heart of Mary, 260 Summit Ave., St. Paul 55102.

Minneapolis Catholic Youth Center (y, mc), 2120 Park Ave. S., Minneapolis 55404.

Villa Maria Center, Frontenac 55026.

Welch Center, 605 N. Central Ave., Duluth 55807.

Missouri: Cenacle Retreat House, 900 S. Spoede Rd., St. Louis 63131.

Maria Fonte Solitude (private), P.O. Box 322, High Ridge 63049.

Marian Hall Retreat Center, Conception Seminary College, Conception 64433.

Marianist Apostolic Center, P.O. Box 127, Glencoe 63038.

Our Lady of Assumption Abbey (m, w), Trappists, Rt. 5, Box 193, Ava 65608.

Pallottine Renewal Center, R.R. 2, 15270 Old Halls Ferry Rd., Florissant 63034.

Passionist Retreat of Our Lady, Retreat House, Passionist Fathers and Brothers, 3036 Bellerive Dr., St. Louis 63121.

Queen of Heaven Solitude (private), Rt. 1, Box 107A, Marionville 65705.

St. Pius X Abbey, Abbey Rd., Pevely 63070.

The White House Retreat (m), 7400 Christopher Dr., St. Louis 63129.

Montana: Emmaus Retreat House, 438 7th Ave., Havre 59501.

Ursuline Retreat Center, 2300 Central Ave., Great Falls 59401.

Nebraska: Crosier Renewal Center, 223 E. 14th St., P.O. Box 789, Hastings 68901.

Good Counsel, R.R. 1, Box 110, Waverly 68462.

St. Columbans Foreign Mission Society, St. Columbans 68056.

New Hampshire: The Common - St. Joseph Monastery, Discalced Carmelite Friars, Peterborough 03458.

New Hampshire Monastery, Hundred Acres, New Boston 03070.

Oblate Fathers Retreat House, Rt. 3A, Lowell Rd., Hudson 03051.

St. Francis Retreat Center, 860 Central Rd., Rye Beach 03871.

New Jersey: Bethlehem Hermitage, Pleasant Hill Rd., Box 315, Chester 07930.

Blackwood Center, St. Pius X House, Box 216, Blackwood 08012.

Carmel Retreat House, 1071 Ramapo Valley Rd., Mahwah 07430.

Cenacle Retreat House, 411 River Rd., Highland Park 08904.

Good Shepherd Center, 74 Kahdena Rd., Morristown 07960.

Loyola House of Retreats, 161 James St., Morristown 07960.

Marianist Christian Family Living Center (families), Cape and Yale Ave., Cape May Point 08212.

Mt. St. John Academy, Gladstone, N.J. 07934.

Queen of Peace Retreat House, St. Paul's Abbey, P.O. Box 7, Newton 07860.

St. Joseph's Villa (w), Srs. of St. John the Baptist, Peapack 07977.

San Alfonso Retreat House, 755 Ocean Ave., Long Branch 07740.

Villa Pauline Retreat and Guest House (w*), Hilltop Rd., Mendham 07945.

Xavier Center, Convent Station 07961.

New Mexico: Holy Cross Retreat House, P.O. Box 158, Mesilla Park 88047.

Our Lady of Guadalupe Monastery (families - pentecostal), Pecos 87552.

Our Lady Queen of Peace, 5825 Coors Rd. S.W., Albuquerque 87105.

New York: Bethany Retreat House, County Road 105, Highland Mills 10930.

Bethlehem Retreat House (m*), Abbey of the Genesee, Piffard 14533.

Bishop Molloy Retreat House, 86-45 178th St., Jamaica, L.I. 11432.

Cabrini-on-the Hudson, West Park, N.Y. 12493.

Cardinal Spellman Retreat House, Passionist Fathers, 5801 Palisade Ave., Bronx (Riverdale) 10471.

Cenacle Center for Spiritual Renewal, Cenacle Rd., Lake Ronkonkoma 11779.

The Cenacle: Center for Spiritual Renewal, 693 East Ave., Rochester 14607.

Cenacle Retreat House, State Rd., P.O. Box 467, Bedford Village 10506.

Christ the King Retreat House, 500 Brookford Rd., Syracuse 13224.

Cormaria Retreat House, Sag Harbor, L.I. 11963.

Diocesan Cursillo Center (Spanish), 118 Congress St., Brooklyn 11201.

Dominican Retreat House, 1945 Union St., Schenectady 12309.

Don Bosco Retreat Center, Filor's Lane, West Haverstraw 10993.

Graymoor Christian Unity Center, Graymoor, Garrison 10524.

Jesuit Retreat House, North American Martyrs Shrine, Auriesville 12016.

Mary Reparatrix Retreat Center, 14 E. 29th St., New York 10016.

Monastery of the Precious Blood (w), Ft. Hamilton Parkway and 54th St., Brooklyn 11219.

Mount Alvernia Retreat House, Box 858, Wappingers Falls 12590.

Mount Manresa Retreat House, 239 Fingerboard Rd., Staten Island 10305.

Notre Dame Retreat House, Box 342, Foster Rd., Canandaigua 14424.

Queen of Apostles Retreat House, North Haven, Sag Harbor 11963.

Regina Maria Retreat House (w*), 77 Brinkerhoff St., Plattsburgh 12901.

Retreat House, Basilian Monastery, East Beach Rd., Glen Cove 11542.

St. Andrew's House, 89 A St. Andrew's Rd., Walden 12586.

St. Columban's Retreat House, P.O. Box 816, Derby 14047.

St. Gabriel Retreat House, 64 Burns Rd., P.O. Box P, Shelter Island 11965.

St. Ignatius Renewal Center, Diocese of Buffalo, 6969 Strickler Rd., Clarence Center 14032. Poustinia available.

St. Ignatius Retreat House, Searington Rd., Manhasset, L.I. 11030.

St. Joseph Center (Spanish Center), 523 W. 142nd St., New York 10031.

Stella Maris Retreat House and Center for Renewal, 130 E. Genesee St., Skaneateles 13152.

Stella Niagara Center of Renewal, 4421 Lower River Rd., Stella Niagara 14144.

Tagaste Monastery Retreat House (m, y), Suffern 10901.

North Carolina: Maryhurst Retreat House, P.O. Box 38, Pinehurst 28374.

North Dakota: Queen of Peace Retreat, Redemptorist Fathers, 1310 N. Broadway, Fargo 58102.

Ohio: Bergamo Conference Center, 4435 E. Patterson Rd., Dayton 45430.

Friarhurst Retreat House, 8136 Wooster Pike, Cincinnati 45227.

Jesuit Renewal Center, 5361 S. Milford Rd., Milford 45150.

Jesuit Retreat House, 5629 State Rd., Cleveland 44134.

Loyola of the Lakes, 700 Killinger Rd., Clinton 44216.

Maria Stein Center, 2365 St. Johns Rd., Maria Stein 45860.

Men of Milford Retreat House, Box 348, Milford 45150.

MSC Center, Rt. 4, Shelby 44875.

Our Lady of Consolation Renewal Center, 320 West St., Carey 43316.

Our Lady of the Pines, 1250 Tiffin St., Fremont 43420.

Sacred Heart, 3128 Logan Ave., Box 6074, Youngstown 44501.

St. Anthony Pilgrim House, 321 Clay St., Carey 43316. (Facilities only.)

St. Joseph Christian Life Center, 18485 Lake Shore Blvd., Cleveland 44119.

Shrine Center for Renewal, Diocese of Columbus, 5277 E. Broad St., Columbus 43213.

Oklahoma: St. Gregory's Abbey, Shawnee 74801.

Oregon: Loyola Retreat House (Jesuit Center for Spiritual Renewal), 3220 S.E. 43rd St., Portland 97206.

Mt. Angel Abbey Guest-Retreat Center, St. Benedict 97373.

Our Lady of Peace Retreat (m, w); 3600 S. W. 170th Ave., Beaverton 97005.

Shalom Prayer Center, Benedictine Sisters, Mt. Angel 97362.

Trappist Abbey Retreat (m*, private), P.O. Box 97, Lafayette 97127.

Pennsylvania: Byzantine Catholic Seminary (m), 3605 Perrysville Ave., Pittsburgh 15214.

Cenacle Retreat House (w*), 4721 Fifth Ave., Pittsburgh 15213.

Dominican Retreat House, Ashbourne Rd. and Juniper Ave., Elkins Park 19117.

Family Life Center, P.O. Box 306, Route 219 North, Ebensburg 15931.

Fatima House, Rolling Hills Rd., Ottsville 18942.

Jesuit Center for Spiritual Growth, Box 223, Church Rd., Wernersville 19565.

Malvern Retreat House (m*), St. Joseph's in the Hills, Malvern 19355.

Maria Wald Retreat House, Convent of the Precious Blood, New Holland Ave., Shillington 19607.

Marian Hall, St. Joseph Convent/Academy, R.D. 2, Columbia 17512.

Mercy Center, Box 370, Dallas 18612.

Mount St. Macrina Retreat Center, Mt. St. Macrina, Box 878, Uniontown 15401.

Our Lady of Fatima Center, Griffin Rd., Box 163, Elmhurst 18416.

St. Alphonsus Retreat House (m*), Box 218, Tobyhanna 18466 (1,200).

St. Emma Retreat House, 1001 Harvey St., Greensburg 15601.

St. Fidelis Retreat Center, Herman 16039.

St. Francis Retreat House, 3918 Chipman Rd., Easton 18042.

St. Francis Retreat House (w), Monocacy Manor, 395 Bridle Path Rd., Bethlehem 18017.

St. Gabriel's Retreat House (w), 631 Griffin Pond Rd., Clarks Summit 18411.

St. Paul of the Cross Retreat House, 148 Monastery Ave., Pittsburgh 15203.

Saint Raphaela Mary Retreat House, 616 Coopertown Rd., Haverford 19041.

St. Vincent Archabbey (m*, summer), Latrobe 15650.

Villa Maria Retreat Center, Box 208, Wernersville 19565.

Villa of Our Lady Retreat House (w, mc), Mt. Pocono 18344.

Rhode Island: Carmel Renewal Center, 21 Battery St., Newport 02840.

Ephpheta House — A Center for Renewal, 10 Manville Hill Rd; mailing address, P.O. Box 1, Manville 02838.

Our Lady of Peace Spiritual Life Center, Ocean Rd., Narragansett 02882.

St. Dominic Savio Youth Center (y*), Broad Rock Rd., Box 67, Peace Dale 02883.

South Carolina: Springbank Christian Center, Dominican Retreat House, Kingstree 29556.

South Dakota: St. Martin's Community Center, R.R. 4, Box 253, Rapid City 57701.

Sioux Spiritual Center (for Native Americans), Diocese of Rapid City, Howes Star Route Box 271, Plainview 57748.

Tennessee: House of the Lord, 1306 Dellwood Ave., Memphis 38127.

House of the Lord, Rt. 4, Box 251, Paris 38242.

Texas: Catholic Renewal Center of North Texas, 4503 Bridge St., Ft. Worth 76103.

Cenacle Retreat House, 420 N. Kirkwood, Houston 77079.

Christian Holiday House and Renewal Center, Oblate Fathers, P.O. Box 635, Dickinson 77539.

Holy Name Retreat Center (m*), 430 Bunker Hill Rd., Houston 77024.

Montserrat Jesuit Retreat House, P.O. Box 398, Lake Dallas 75065.

Our Lady of the Pillar Christian Renewal Center, 2507 N.W. 36th St., San Antonio 78228.

Saint Joseph Retreat House (Casa San Jose), 127 Oblate Dr., San Antonio 78216.

San Juan Retreat House, Diocese of Brownsville, P.O. Box 998, San Juan 78589.

Utah: Our Lady of the Holy Trinity Retreat House (m), Huntsville 84317.

Our Lady of the Mountains, 1794 Lake St., Ogden 84401.

Virginia: Dominican Retreat, 7103 Old Dominion Dr., McLean 22101.

The Franciscan Center, Rt. 642, Box 825, Winchester 22601.

Holy Family Retreat House, Redemptorist Fathers, 1414 N. Mallory St., Hampton 23363.

Missionhurst CICM Mission Center, 4651 N. 25th St., Arlington 22207.

Spiritual Renewal Center (Genesis House), Rt. 2, Box 388 B, Richmond 23233.

Washington: Camp Field Retreat Center, P.O. Box 128, Leavenworth 98826.

Immaculate Heart Retreat House, Route 3, Box 653, Spokane 99203.

Redemptorist Palisades Retreat, P.O. Box 3739, Federal Way 98003.

St. Peter the Apostle Diocesan Retreat Center, Route 1, Box 86, Cowiche 98923.

Visitation Retreat Center (w), 3200 S.W. Dash Point Rd., Federal Way 98003.

West Virginia: Cenacle Retreat House, 1114 Virginia St. E., Charleston 25301.

St. Joseph Pastoral Center, Rt. 6, Vienna 26101.

Wisconsin: Cardoner Jesuit Retreat Center, 1501 S. Layton Blvd., Milwaukee 53215.

Chapel House of Prayer, Route 1, New Franken, Wis. 54229.

Holy Name Retreat House, Chambers Island; mailing address, 1825 Riverside Drive, P.O. Box 337, Green Bay 54305.

Jesuit Retreat House, 4800 Fahrnwald Rd., Oshkosh 54901.

Marynook — House of the Lord, 500 S. 12th St., P.O. Box 6, Galesville 54630.

Monte Alverno Retreat Center, 1000 N. Ballard Rd., Appleton 54911.

Perpetual Help Retreat Center, 1800 N. Timber Trail Lane, Oconomowoc 53066.

St. Anthony Retreat Center, Marathon 54448.

St. Benedict Center (ecumenical retreat and conference center), Fox Bluff, P.O. Box 5070, Madison 53705.

St. Francis Friary and Retreat Center, 503 S. Browns Lake Dr., Burlington 53105.

St. Joseph's Retreat Center, Bailey's Harbor 54202.

St. Vincent Pallotti Center, Rt. 3, Box 61, Elkhorn 53121.

Schoenstatt Center, W. 284 N. 698 Cherry Lane, Waukesha 53186.

HOUSE OF PRAYER EXPERIENCE

The purpose of the House of Prayer Experience is to help active religious, priests and lay persons to acquire a contemporary style of contemplative life for renewal, inner growth and a more joyful personal and communal life in the light of the Gospel. The result sought is an apostolic spirituality integrating prayer with action in ministry and witness, especially for justice and peace.

SPECIAL AGENCIES

Some of the following agencies are engaged in carrying out programs of the United States Catholic Conference. Additional agencies are reported in other Almanac entries.

Religious Education/Catechesis/CCD (Confraternity of Christian Doctrine): Its objective is the catechesis of persons from early childhood through adult life.

The modern expansion of catechesis dates from publication of the encyclical letter *Acerbo Nimis* by Pope St. Pius X in 1905. His directive, that CCD programs be established in every parish, was incorporated in the 1917 Code of Canon Law, reaffirmed by the Second Vatican Council in the *Decree on the Bishops' Pastoral Office in the Church,* and given direction by the publication of the *National Catechetical Directory* in 1971.

Programs for catechesis are parish-based. Policies are developed by parish boards or commissions, and responsibility for administering programs rests ideally with a coordinator or director who is a trained professional.

On the diocesan level, religious education is coordinated by a director with a staff operating under the title of an office of religious education or a similar title. The diocesan office coordinates and acts as consultant to the work of local parish and regional programs; it conducts teacher-training courses, issues guidelines for unified programs, provides overall in-service aid and resources for local staffs and programs.

On the national level, Religious Education/Catechetical Ministry/CCD (formerly called the National Center for the Confraternity of Christian Doctrine, and since 1969 under the Department of Education, U.S. Catholic Conference) provides representation and service for local diocesan staffs and programs. On the international level, it participates in programs which find their roots with the Vatican congregations that deal with religious education or catechesis. Publications include *The Living Light,* Catechetical Sunday material and other related programs.

Sister Mariella Frye, M.H.S.H., is representative for Catechetical Ministry in the Department of Education, U.S. Catholic Conference.

Offices are located at 1312 Massachusetts Ave. N.W., Washington, D.C. 20005.

National Council of Catholic Men: A federation of Catholic organizations through which Catholic men may be heard nationally on matters of common interest. NCCM is a constituent of the National Council of Catholic Laity.

Offices are located at 4712 Randolph Dr., Annandale, Va. 22003.

National Council of Catholic Women: A federation of some 10,000 organizations of Catholic women in the U.S.; founded in 1920. NCCW unites Catholic organizations and individual Catholic women of the U.S., develops their leadership potential, assists them to act upon current issues in the Church and society, provides a medium through which Catholic women may speak and act upon matters of common interest, and relates to other national and international organizations in the solution of present-day problems. It is an affiliate of the World Union of Catholic Women's Organizations.

The official publication is *Catholic Woman,* issued 6 times a year.

National office: 1312 Massachusetts Ave. N.W., Washington, D.C. 20005.

National Council of Catholic Laity: Formed in 1971 by the National Council of Catholic Men and the National Council of Catholic Women to provide direction and guidance to existing and new lay organizations. It sponsors conferences and is a contact agency for information about specialized groups in the Church.

The mailing address is P.O. Box 14525, Cincinnati, Ohio 45214.

National Catholic Rural Life Conference: Founded in 1923 through the efforts of Bishop Edwin V. O'Hara for the purpose of promoting the general welfare of rural people by a program of extensive services, publications and rural-related activities. Publications include a newsletter and *Catholic Rural Life.*

The conference has approximately 5,000 members among rural pastors, farmers, teachers, sociologists, economists, agricultural agents and officials. There are 144 officially appointed diocesan rural life directors.

Most Rev. Lawrence J. McNamara, bishop of Grand Island, Neb., is president. Mr. Gregory Cusack is executive director.

National headquarters are located at 4625 N.W. Beaver Dr., Des Moines, Ia. 50322.

Catholic Relief Services — USCC: The official overseas aid and development agency of American Catholics; it is a separately incorporated organization of the U.S. Catholic Conference.

CRS was founded in 1943 by the bishops of the United States to help civilians in Europe and North Africa caught in the disruption and devastation of World War II.

Initially, CRS collected, purchased and shipped to war-torn countries huge quantities of food, clothing, medicines and other relief supplies which were distributed to hundreds of thousands of displaced persons, prisoners of war, bombed-out families, widows, orphans and other war victims.

As conditions in Europe improved in the late 1940s and early 1950s, the works conducted by CRS spread to other continents and areas — Asia, Africa and Latin America.

CRS staffs offices in 50 countries and has local representatives in another 20 countries. The agency works with local counterpart organizations to provide humanitarian assistance and emergency relief. Help is given strictly in response to need; race, creed, color and political affiliation are no consideration.

Although best known for its record of disaster response, compassionate aid to refugees and commitment to reconstruction and rehabilitation, CRS places primary focus on long-term development projects designed to help people to help themselves and to determine their own future.

Administrative funding for CRS comes from an annual collection, the Catholic Relief Services Annual Appeal (known variously as Bishops' Relief or American Catholic Overseas Aid Appeal), held during Lent in most of the 18,000 Catholic parishes of the U.S.

Major support is derived from private, individual donors through direct contributions and through a program of sacrificial giving called Operation Rice Bowl. Funds are also received from philanthropic foundations and humanitarian organizations in the U.S. and Europe. Clothing is collected each year, generally at Thanksgiving, for distribution overseas. More than 7 million pounds of used clothing, blankets and bolt goods are contributed annually through Catholic churches.

Assistance is received from the U.S. Government in several forms: foodstuffs available under Title II of Public Law 480, ocean-freight subsidies for government food and other privately generated relief supplies, and grants for both emergency programs and community development projects.

In 1982, the CRS global program in 70 countries employed 1,100 people and was valued at $325 million.

Lawrence Pezzullo is executive director.

CRS headquarters are located at 1011 First Ave., New York, N.Y. 10022.

SPECIAL APOSTOLATES AND GROUPS

Apostleship of the Sea: An international Catholic organization for the moral, social and spiritual welfare of seafarers and those involved in the maritime industry. It was founded in 1920 in Glasgow, Scotland, and formally approved by the Holy See in 1922. It is promoted and directed by the Pontifical Commission for Migrants and Tourism, Piazza San Calisto 16, Rome, Italy 00153. The U.S. unit is the Apostleship of the Sea in the United States, an affiliate of the NCCB-USCC, established in 1947. It serves 70 port chaplains in 58 U.S. ports on the seacoasts and the Great Lakes. Operations include a hospitality and welcoming program as well as counseling and spiritual services carried on by individual port chaplains through Catholic maritime clubs in Alabama (Mobile); California (Oakland, San Francisco, Wilmington); Florida (Miami); New York (Brooklyn); Washington (Seattle); and interfaith clubs located in Alaska (Ketchikan); Florida (Pensacola); Georgia (Savannah); Maryland (Baltimore); New Jersey (Newark, Port Elizabeth); Texas (Beaumont, Brownsville, Corpus Christi, Galveston, Houston); Washington (Tacoma); Wisconsin (Milwaukee). Recent developments have emphasized the interfaith cooperation on the port level in seamen's ministry. The episcopal promoter of the conference is Most Rev. Rene Gracida, 620 Lipan St., Corpus Christi, Tex. 78401. Rev. James E. Dillenburg is national director. Address of the national office is P.O. Box 12824, Pensacola, Fla. 32575. Also affiliated with the Apostleship of the Sea in the United States is the **National Catholic Conference for Seafarers.** The president is Rev. Mario Balbi, S.D.B., 222 E. Harris, P.O. Box 8307, Savannah, Ga. 31412.

Auxiliaries of Our Lady of the Cenacle (1878, France): An association of Catholic laywomen, under the direction of the Congregation of Our Lady of the Cenacle, who serve God through their own professions and life styles by means of vows. Members live a fully secular life consecrated according to the spirituality of the Cenacle and pursue individual apostolates. They number approximately 150 throughout the world. U.S. regional director: Sister Barbara Whittemore, r.c., 310 Cenacle Rd., Lake Ronkonkoma, N.Y. 11779.

Catholic Central Union of America (1855): One of the oldest Catholic lay organizations in the U.S., the Union is devoted to the development and vigor of Christian principles in personal, social, cultural, economic and civic life. It was the first society ever given an official mandate for Catholic Action by a committee of the American bishops, in 1936. The Central Bureau in St. Louis is the center for the separate but coordinated direction of the National Catholic Women's Union. The headquarters is also a publishing house (*Social Justice Review*, other publications), a library of German-Americana and Catholic Americana, a clearinghouse for information, and a center for works of charity. Aid is given to the missions, and maintenance and direction are provided for St. Elizabeth's Settlement and Day Nursery in St. Louis. Union membership is approximately 11,500. Harvey J. Johnson is director of the Central Bureau located at 3835 Westminster Place, St. Louis, Mo. 63108. (See also: National Catholic Women's Union.)

Catholic Medical Mission Board (1928): Founded by Dr. Paluel Flagg and the Rev. Edward Garesche, S.J. Its purposes are to gather and ship medical supplies for the sick poor in mission lands, and to recruit and assign medical and paramedical personnel to overseas mission hospitals and dispensaries. Since its foundation, it has shipped approximately 46 million pounds of supplies. In 1982, more than $9.8 million in medicines were shipped to 1,608 mission distribution centers in 52 countries. Also in 1982, 52 medical volunteers were placed in 12 countries. Rev. Joseph J. Walter, S.J., is the director. Office: 10 W. 17th Street, New York, N.Y. 10011.

Center for Applied Research in the Apostolate (CARA): A research and development agency in the field of the Church's worldwide religious and social mission. Its purpose is to gather information for the use of decision-makers in evaluating the present status of the Church's mission of service and in planning programs of development toward greater effectiveness of its multiphased ministry in the future. CARA has research and planning programs focused on: church personnel (recruitment, selection training, utilization, effectiveness), overseas areas, diocesan planning, religious life, health care ministry, and other subjects. CARA was incorporated as a non-profit corporation in the District of Columbia Aug. 5, 1964. Rev. Cassian J. Yuhaus, C.P., is president. Offices are located at 3700 Oakview Terrace, N.E., Washington, D.C. 20017.

Christian Family Movement (CFM) (1947): Originating in Chicago and having a membership of married couples and individuals, its purpose is to Christianize family life and create communities conducive to Christian family life. Since 1968, CFM in the U.S. has included couples from all Christian churches. The International Confederation of Christian Family Movements embraces a worldwide membership. National and international headquarters: Box 272, Ames, Iowa 50010. Spanish-speaking, CFM was organized in 1969 under the title **Movimiento Familiar Cristiano (MFC)**. National spiritual director: Msgr. Teodoro de la Torre, 1618 Texas Ave., Box 214, Houston, Tex. 77001.

Christian Life Communities: Formerly known as Sodalities of Our Lady, they are groups of men and women, adults and youth, joined with other people involved in living their full Christian vocation and commitment in the world. The governing principles and operating norms of Sodalities, revised in the spirit of documents of the Second Vatican Council, were promulgated and approved by Pope Paul VI in 1971. The Spiritual Exercises of St. Ignatius remain a specific source and characteristic of the spirituality of the movement. Christian Life Communities are located in more than 50 countries; the U.S. Federation is comprised of approximately 150 communities. Eileen C. Burke is executive director. National office: 3721 Westminster Blvd., St. Louis, Mo. 63108. The World Federation office is located in Rome.

Cursillo Movement: An instrument of Christian renewal designed to form and stimulate persons to engage in apostolic action individually and in the organized apostolate, in accordance with the mission which individuals have to transform the environments in which they live into Christian environments. The movement originated in Spain, where the first cursillo was held near Palma, Mallorca, in 1949. It was introduced in the U.S. in 1957 and is functioning in more than 140 dioceses. The method of the movement involves a three-day weekend called a cursillo and a follow-up program known as the post-cursillo.

The weekend is an intensive experience in Christian community living centered on Christ and built around 15 talks (10 by laymen, five by priests), active participation in discussions and related activities, the celebration of the liturgy. The follow-up program focuses on small weekly reunions of three to five persons and larger group reunions, called ultreyas, in which participants share experiences and insights derived from their prayer life, study and apostolic action. The movement operates within the framework of diocesan and parish pastoral plans, and functions autonomously in each diocese under the direction of the bishop. Responsibility for growth and effectiveness rests with a

diocesan leaders' school, a diocesan secretariat, or both. Most Rev. James S. Sullivan, auxiliary bishop of Lansing, is episcopal advisor to the movement. Gerald P. Hughes is executive director of the National Cursillo Center, P.O. Box 210226, Dallas, Tex. 75211.

Frontier Apostolate (1956): Volunteers for a minimum of two years' service in their professional line (teachers, secretaries, houseparents, etc.) in the Diocese of Prince George, British Columbia, Canada. More than 2,600 have served since the start of the corps by Bishop Fergus O'Grady. There are about 150 men and women from 8 different countries actively engaged in works throughout the diocese. Address: Bishop O'Grady, College Rd., P.O. Box 7000, Prince George, B.C., Canada V2N 3Z2.

Grail, The (1921): An international movement of women concerned about the full development of all peoples, working in education, religious, social and cultural areas. Founded by Rev. Jacques van Ginneken, S.J., in The Netherlands, it was introduced in the U.S. in 1940. The Grail is at work in: Australia, Brazil, Canada, Costa Rica, Egypt, France, Germany, India, Italy, Kenya, The Netherlands, Nigeria, Philippines, Portugal, South Africa. Tanzania, Uganda, United States. U.S. headquarters: Grailville, Loveland, Ohio 45140. International Secretariat: Duisburger Strasse 470, 4330 Mulheim, West Germany.

Group Seven (1971): Started by the Glenmary Home Missioners to recruit Catholic men and women (married, single, religious, permanent deacon), 21 years of age and older for periods of two years or more in the U.S. home mission apostolate, particularly in the 17-state area of Appalachia, the South and Southeast. Members support themselves in their own profession or trade. They are given orientation and opportunity for ongoing mission training. Address: P.O. Box 1376, Wise, Va. 24293.

International Liaison, Inc. (1963): The U.S. Catholic Coordinating Center for Lay Volunteer Ministries, an affiliate of the U.S. Catholic Conference, is engaged in the promotion, recruiting and referral of lay volunteer personnel with church missions, interdenominational and private volunteer agencies throughout the U.S. The organization also assists mission agencies to facilitate participation by lay persons in ministries of the Church. Publications include *The Response,* an annual directory of lay volunteer ministry opportunities, and a quarterly newsletter. David J. Suley is the executive director. National office: 1234 Massachusetts Ave. N.W., Washington, D.C. 20005.

Jesuit Volunteer Corps (1956): Established by the Oregon Province of the Jesuits, for service to the poor and oppressed. Regional offices are located in Portland, Ore., Oakland, Calif., Houston, Tex., Detroit, Mich., and Philadelphia, Pa. There are 250 volunteers working among Eskimos, on Indian reservations and in inner-city areas. Address for information: P.O. Box 3928, Portland Ore. 97208.

Lay Mission-Helpers Association (1955): It trains and assigns men and women for work in overseas apostolates for periods of three years. Approximately 600 members of the association have served in overseas assignments since 1955. The Rev. Msgr. Lawrence O'Leary is director of the association. Headquarters: 1531 West Ninth St., Los Angeles, Calif. 90015.

The **Mission Doctors Association** recruits, trains and sends Catholic physicians and their families to mission hospitals and clinics throughout the world for tours of two to three years. Address: 1531 W. Ninth St., Los Angeles, Calif. 90015.

Legion of Mary (1921): Founded in Dublin, its purposes are the sanctification of its members and service to others. It is one of the largest lay organizations in the Church. U.S. address for information: The Legion of Mary, St. Louis Regional Senatus, Box 1313, St. Louis, Mo. 63188. The supreme governing body has offices at De Montfort House, North Brunswick St., Dublin 7, Ireland.

Movement for a Better World (1952): An international movement founded by Rev. Riccardo Lombardi, S.J. The U.S. promoting group, like its counterparts in other countries, conducts various types of renewal programs with a distinctive communitarian thrust for the purpose of motivating Christian witness and action for making a better world in accordance with the plan of God. Address for information: Sr. Mary Byrnes, 78 Grand St., Jersey City, N.J. 07302. The movement is a non-governmental organization with the United Nations and has a U.N. office at 777 U.N. Plaza, New York, N.Y. 10017.

Pax Christi (1948): International Catholic peace movement. Originated in Lourdes, France, as a union of French and German Catholics to symbolize a mutual effort to heal wounds inflicted by World War II, spread to Poland and Italy, and acquired its international title when it merged with the English organization Pax. A general secretariat is located at Antwerp, Belgium. **Pax Christi USA**, was founded in 1973 to establish peace-making as a priority for the American Catholic Church, to work for disarmament, primacy of conscience, a just world order, education for peace, and alternatives to violence. A newsletter is published bimonthly; membership, 7,500. Paul Mazur is national coordinator. Address: 6337 West Cornelia, Chicago, Ill. 60634.

Pax Romana — American Graduate and Professional Commission: The U.S. affiliate of Pax Romana, an international Catholic movement for intellectual and cultural affairs (see Catholic International Organizations). The president is Professor James E. Dougherty, St. Joseph University, Philadelphia, Pa. 19131. The Pax Romana representative to the United Nations is Professor W. Hilary Lee, Stevens Institute of Technology, Hoboken, N.J. 07030.

Regis College Lay Apostolate (1950): Founded by Sister Mary John Sullivan, C.S.J., it enlists college graduates for a year of teaching service in home and overseas missions. More than 250 lay apostles from Regis College and more than 400 from other colleges have served since the beginning of the program. Headquarters: Regis College, Weston, Mass. 02193

Southwest Volunteer Apostolate: Recruits and places volunteers for work among the Indians and Spanish-speaking of the Diocese of Gallup. Mailing address: P. O. Box 626, Gallup, N.M. 87301.

Center of Concern (1971): An independent, public-interest group engaged in analysis, education and advocacy relating to issues of global concern. Discussion is carried on within the framework of social justice. A newsletter, *Center Focus*, is published bimonthly. Peter J. Henriot, S.J., is director. Address: 3700 13th St. N.E., Washington, D.C. 20017.

CATHOLIC YOUTH ORGANIZATIONS

Boy Scouts in the Catholic Church: The National Catholic Committee on Scouting works with the Boy Scouts of America in developing the character and spiritual life of 600,000 members in units chartered to Catholic and non-Catholic organizations. *Boy's Life.* Committee Chairman, Gerard O. Rocque, West Main Rd., Silver Creek, N.Y. 14136.

Camp Fire, Inc. (1910): 4601 Madison Ave., Kansas City, Mo. 64112. The National Catholic Committee for Girl Scouts and Camp Fire, a standing committee of the National Federation for Catholic Youth Ministry, cooperates with Camp Fire. To help young people learn and grow in their individual ways through participation in enjoyable activities. Open to youth up to 21 years of age. Membership: approximately 500,000 (no exact statistics available on number of Catholics participating).

Catholic Forester Youth Program, Catholic Order of Foresters: 305 W. Madison Street, Chicago, Ill. 60606. To develop Christian leadership and promote the moral, intellectual, social and physical growth of its youth members. *Catholic Forester.* Membership: youth up to 16 years of age — about 22,000 in 776 local courts in U.S. the High Chief Ranger is John A. Gorski.

Catholic Youth Organization (CYO): Name of parish-centered diocesan Catholic youth programs throughout the country. CYO promotes a program of spiritual, social and physical activities. The original CYO was organized by Bishop Bernard Sheil of Chicago in 1930.

Columbian Squires (1925): P.O. Drawer 1670, New Haven, Conn. 06507. Junior organization of the Knights of Columbus. To train and develop leadership through active participation in a well-organized program of activities. Membership: 12- to 18-year-old Catholic boys. More than 20,000 in 1,000 circles (local units) active in the U.S., Canada, Puerto Rico, Mexico, Guam and the Philippines. *Squires Newsletter,* monthly.

Girl Scouts of the U.S.A.: 830 Third Ave., New York, N.Y. 10022. Girls from most archdioceses and dioceses in the U.S. and its possessions participate in Girl Scouting. The National Catholic Committee for Girl Scouts and Camp Fire, a standing committee of the National Federation for Catholic Youth Ministry, cooperates with Girl Scouts of the U.S.A. *Girl Scout Leader.* Membership: approximately three million (no exact statistics available on number of Catholic girls participating).

Holy Childhood Association (Pontifical Association of the Holy Childhood) (1843): 1720 Massachusetts Ave. N.W., Washington, D.C. 20036. The official children's mission-aid society of the Church; provides assistance to children in 94 mission countries. Furnishes mission education programs and materials to pupils in Catholic elementary schools and religious education programs. *It's Our World,* four times a year. National Director, Rev. Francis W. Wright, C.S.Sp.

Junior Catholic Daughters of the Americas: 10 W. 71st St., New York, N.Y. 10023. A major department of the Catholic Daughters of the Americas. To promote development of the whole person, service to others, spiritual growth. Membership: Juniors (11 to 18 years old); Juniorettes (6 to 10 years old).

Knights of the Altar (1937): P.O. Drawer 5476, Lakeland, Fla. 33803 (national office). Society for altar boys. *Young Heralds,* 6 times a year. Membership: 3,000 units in the U.S. and foreign countries.

National Catholic Forensic League (1952): To develop articulate Catholic leaders through an inter-diocesan program of speech and debate activities. *Newsletter,* quarterly. Membership: 600 schools; membership open to Catholic, private and public schools through the local diocesan league. Secretary-Treasurer, Richard Gaudette, 21 Nancy Rd., Milford, Mass. 01757.

National Catholic Young Adult Ministry Association (1982): 4665 Willowbrook Ave., Los Angeles, Calif 90029. To strengthen the professional competence of those engaged in campus and young adult ministry. President, Rev. Paul Ojibway, S.A.

National Christ Child Society Inc. (1887): 5100 Wisconsin Ave. N.W., Washington, D.C. 20016. Founder, Mary V. Merrick. A welfare organization for the care of underprivileged adults and children. Membership: approximately 10,000 adult and junior members in 31 cities in U.S. President, Mrs. John W. Wilson.

National Federation for Catholic Youth Ministry (1982): 3025 4th St. N.E., Washington, D.C. 20017. To foster the development of youth ministry

in the United States through CYO and other expressions of ministry to, with, by and for youth. *Emmaus Newsletter,* quarterly. Executive Director, Mrs. Maggie Brown.

St. Dominic Savio Club (1950): Marian Shrine, Filor's Lane, West Haverstraw, N.Y. 10993. To promote a program of spiritual, intellectual and recreational activities. *Savio Notes,* six times a year. Membership: students in grades three through nine — more than 1,500,000 since its founding. Director, Rev. Peter Malloy, S.O.B. members in U.S., Canada and nine foreign countries.

Young Christian Students: 7436 W. Harrison, Forest Park, Ill. 60130. A student movement for Christian personal and social change. Membership: 500 in high schools and parishes.

Fraternities and Sororities

Alpha Delta Gamma (1924): P.O. Box 54321, Los Angeles, Calif. 90054. Fraternity. *Alphadelity.* Membership: 7,260 in 12 college chapters and 11 alumni associations.

Delta Epsilon Sigma (1939): College of Great Falls, Great Falls, Mont. 59405. National scholastic honor society for students, faculty and alumni of colleges and universities with a Catholic tradition. Membership: 26,500 in 100 chapters. Secretary, Dr. Charles M. Hepburn.

Kappa Gamma Pi (1926): A national Catholic college women's honor society for graduates who, in addition to academic excellence, have shown outstanding leadership in extra-curricular activities. *Kappa Gamma Pi News,* quarterly. Membership: approximately 16,000 in 123 colleges; 40 alumnae chapters in metropolitan areas. President, Dr. Sally Ann Vonderbrink, 5747 Colerain Ave., Cincinnati, O. 45239.

Phi Kappa Theta: 332 Main St., Worcester, Mass. 01608. National collegiate fraternity with a Catholic heritage. Merger (1959) of Phi Kappa Fraternity, founded at Brown Univ. in 1889, and Theta Kappa Phi Fraternity, founded at Lehigh Univ. in 1919. *The Temple Magazine* quarterly, and newsletter, *The Sun.* Membership: 3,000 undergraduate and 36,000 alumni in 55 collegiate and 15 alumni chapters. Executive Director, Kirk Thomas.

ASSOCIATIONS, MOVEMENTS, SOCIETIES IN THE U.S.

(Principal source: Almanac survey.)

See Index for other associations, movements and societies covered elsewhere.

A

Academy of American Franciscan History (1944), Box 34440, West Bethesda, Md. 20817. Dir., Rev. John-Marie Cassese, O.F.M.

Academy of California Church History (1946), P.O. Box 1668, Fresno, Calif. 93717.

American Benedictine Academy (1947). Scholarly Benedictine society. Pres., Sr. Dorothy Neuhofer, O.S.B., Holy Name Priory, San Antonio, Fla. 33574.

American Catholic Correctional Chaplains Association (1952), 275 in 475 institutions. Pres., Rev.

Kloman Riggie; Sec., Rev. Dismas Boeff, O.S.B., 2900 East Blvd., Cleveland, O. 44104.

American Catholic Historical Association (1919), Catholic University of America, Washington, D.C. 20064. *The Catholic Historical Review,* quarterly. Sec.-Treas., Rev. Robert Trisco.

American Catholic Philosophical Association (1926), Catholic University of America, Washington, D.C. 20064; 1,500. *New Scholasticism,* quarterly, *Proceedings,* annually.

American Committee on Italian Migration (1952), 42 E. 23rd St., New York, N.Y. 10010; 6,000. *ACIM Newsletter* and *ACIM Nuova Via,* 6 times a year. Sec., Rev. Joseph A. Cogo, C.S.

Ancient Order of Hibernians in America, Inc. (1836); 120,000. *National Hibernian Digest,* bimonthly. Nat. Pres., Joseph A. Roche; Nat.

Sec., John K. Henry, 10 Stonehedge Rd., Norwalk, Conn. 06851.

Apostleship of Prayer (1849-France; 1861-U.S.): 3 Stephen Ave., New Hyde Park, N.Y. 11040. Promotes Daily Offering and Sacred Heart devotion.

Apostolate for Family Consecration (1975), The House of St. Joseph, Box 220, Kenosha, Wis. 53141; 26,000 members. Family reinforcement by transforming neighborhoods into God-centered communities Pres., Jerome F. Coniker.

Apostolate of Christian Action, (1956), P.O. Box 24, Fresno, Calif. 93707. *Divine Love,* quarterly.

Archconfraternity of Christian Mothers (Christian Mothers) (1881), 220 37th St., Pittsburgh, Pa. 15201; over 3,400 branches. Dir., Rev. Bertin Roll, O.F.M. Cap.

Archconfraternity of Our Lady of Perpetual Help and St. Alphonsus (1871), 526 59th St., Brooklyn, N.Y. 11220.

Archconfraternity of the Holy Ghost (1912), Holy Ghost Preparatory School, Bensalem, Pa. 19020 (U.S. headquarters). Nat. Dir., Very Rev. Henry J. Brown, C.S.Sp.

Association for Religious and Value Issues in Counseling (1962), division of American Personnel and Guidance Association. *Counseling and Values,* quarterly. Address, 2 Skyline Pl., Suite 400, 5203 Leesburg Pike, Falls Church, Va. 22041.

Association for Social Economics (formerly the Catholic Economic Association) (1941), De Paul University, 25 E. Jackson Blvd., Chicago, Ill. 60604; 1,300. *Review of Social Economy,* triannually.

Association of Catholic Diocesan Archivists (1983), c/o Archives, Archdiocese of Boston, 2121 Commonwealth Ave., Brighton, Mass. 02135; 125 members. To work for establishment of an archival program in every American diocese; to provide for professional training and development of diocesan archivists; to work toward formation of national archival standards for the Church in the U.S. Pres., James M. O'Toole, Archivist, Archdiocese of Boston.

Association of Catholic Trade Unionists (1937), 12 Holly Hills Dr., Woodstock, N.Y. 12498. Exec. Sec., John C. Donohue.

Association of Marian Helpers (1946), Stockbridge, Mass. 01262; 1,100,000, mostly in U.S. *The Marian Helpers Bulletin,* quarterly.

Association of Romanian Catholics of America (1948), 4309 Olcott Ave., E. Chicago, Ind. 46312.

B

Blue Army of Our Lady of Fatima (1946), Washington, N.J. 07882; worldwide membership. *Soul,* bimonthly. U.S. Pres., Most Rev. Jerome Hastrich, bishop of Gallup, N. Mex.

C

Calix Society (1947), 7601 Wayzata Blvd., Minneapolis, Minn. 55426; 2,000 members in U.S. and Canada; *Chalice,* bimonthly. Association of Catholic alcoholics maintaining their sobriety through affiliation with and participation in Alcoholics Anonymous. Dir., R. D. Dickinson.

Campaign for Surplus Rosaries (1948) and the Mid-America Rosary Museum (1976), 1821 W. Short 17th St., North Little Rock, Ark. 72114. Collect rosaries and religious articles for free distribution to the poor throughout the world. Lay Internatl. Chairman, P. Marion Chudy, S.F.O.

Canon Law Society of America (1939), Catholic University, Washington, D.C. 20064. To further research and study in canon law; 1,600. Exec. Coord., Rev. James H. Provost.

Cardinal Mindszenty Foundation (CMF) (1958), P.O. Box 11321, St. Louis, Mo. 63105. To combat communism with knowledge and facts. Exec. Sec., Eleanor Schlafly.

Catholic Aid Association (1878), 49 W. Ninth St., St. Paul, Minn. 55102; 80,000. *Catholic Aid News,* monthly. Fraternal life insurance society. Pres., F. L. Spanier.

Catholic Alumni Clubs International (1957), To advance social, cultural and spiritual well-being of members. Membership limited to single Catholics with professional education; 7,000 in 50 clubs in U.S. International Pres., Jeanette Hess, Apt. 7, 396 Emerson Rd., Eggertsville, N.Y. 14226. International Chaplain, Rev. Peter Campbell, M.S.C., P.O. Box 6074, Youngstown, O. 44501.

Catholic Biblical Association of America (1936), Catholic University of America, Washington, D.C. 20064; 947. *The Catholic Biblical Quarterly.* Pres., Most Rev. Richard J. Sklba.

Catholic Big Brothers, Inc. (of Archdiocese of New York) (1911), 1011 First Ave., New York, N.Y. 10022; Newsletter, quarterly. To provide opportunities for male identification to fatherless boys, 7-15 years of age, through services of qualified adult male volunteers. Exec. Dir., Sr. Cecile Kaval, R.S.H.M.

Catholic Big Sisters, Inc. (of the Archdiocese of New York), 60 Lafayette St., New York, N.Y. 10013. Voluntary organization providing adjunctive services to Family Court, for girls up to 16 and boys up to 10 years of age. Dir., Hortense Baffa.

Catholic Commission on Intellectual and Cultural Affairs (CCICA) (1946), P.O. Box 21, Notre Dame, Ind. 46556; 268. Exec. Dir. Rev. Konrad Schaum.

Catholic Daughters of the Americas (1903), 10 W. 71st St., New York, N.Y. 10023; 170,000. *Share Magazine.* Nat. Regent, Miss Loretta J. Knebel.

Catholic Evidence Guild (1918, in England; 1931, in US), c/o 127 W. 31st St., New York, N.Y. 10001. Lay movement for spread of Catholic truth by means of outdoor speaking.

Catholic Family Life Insurance (1868), 1572 E. Capitol Dr., Milwaukee, Wis. 53211; 48,000. *The Family Friend,* quarterly. Pres., David L. Springob.

Catholic Golden Age: National Headquarters, Scranton, Pa. 18503; 350,000. *CGA World Magazine,* bimonthly. Assist Catholics over 50 years of age in their religious and secular needs.

Catholic Guardian Society (1913), 1011 First Ave., New York, N.Y. 10022. Exec. Dir., James P. O'Neill.

Catholic Home Bureau for Dependent Chil-

dren (1898), 1011 First Ave., New York, N.Y. 10022. Exec. Dir., Sr. Una McCormack.

Catholic Interracial Council of New York, Inc. (1934), 286 Fifth Ave., New York, N.Y. 10001. Sponsors conferences, forums and workshops; educational and research projects on racism, bigotry and discrimination, Newsletter, published periodically. Exec. Dir., John J. Garra.

Catholic Interracial Councils: See National Catholic Conference for Interracial Justice.

Catholic Knights of America (1877), 217 E. 8th St., Cincinnati, O. 45202; 10,200. *Catholic Knights of America Journal,* monthly. Fraternal insurance society.

Catholic Knights of St. George (1881), 709 Brighton Rd., Pittsburgh, Pa. 15233; 67,000. Fraternal insurance society. Pres., John F. Kenawell.

Catholic Kolping Society of America (1923), 22515 Masonic Blvd., St. Clair Shores, Mich. 48082. *Kolping Banner,* monthly. International society concerned with spiritual, educational and physical development of members.

Catholic Lawyers' Guild. Organization usually on a diocesan basis, under different titles.

Catholic League (1943), 1200 N. Ashland Ave., Chicago, Ill. 60622. Exec. Dir., Most Rev. Alfred Abramowicz.

Catholic Library Association (1921), 461 W. Lancaster Avenue, Haverford, Pa., 19041; 3,162. *Catholic Library World,* monthly (Sept.-April), bimonthly (May-June, July-Aug.); *Catholic Periodical and Literature Index.* Pres., Sr. Dennis Lynch, S.H.C.J., Exec. Dir., Matthew R. Wilt.

Catholic Near East Welfare Association (Near East Missions) (1926), 1011 First Ave., New York, N.Y. 10022. *Near East Missions,* weekly column in 132 diocesan and four national newspapers. Aids missionary activity in 18 countries (under jurisdiction of the Sacred Congregation for the Oriental Church) in Europe, Africa and Asia, including the Holy Land. Nat. Sec., Rev. Msgr. John G. Nolan; Assoc. Sec., Rev. Msgr. Edward C. Foster.

Catholic Negro-American Mission Board (1907), 2021 H. St. N.W., Washington, D.C. 20006.15,000. *Educating in Faith,* quarterly. Exec. Sec., Msgr. Paul A. Lenz.

Catholic One Parent Organization (COPO): To give widows and widowers an opportunity to meet others in the same situation, blending social and spiritual programs. Organized in various dioceses.

Catholic Order of Foresters (1883), 305 W. Madison St., Chicago, Ill. 60606; 163,000. *The Catholic Forester,* bimonthly. Fraternal insurance society. High Chief Ranger, John A. Gorski.

Catholic Pamphlet Society (1938), 2171 Fillmore Ave., Buffalo, N.Y. 14214. Parish pamphlet rack distributors. Dir., Rev. Msgr. Paul T. Cronin.

Catholic Peace Fellowship (1964), 339 Lafayette St., New York, N.Y. 10012; 6,500, *CPF Bulletin.* Peace education and action projects, development of the nonviolent tradition within the Catholic Church; draft counseling. Nat. Sec., Thomas C. Cornell.

Catholic Press Association of the U.S., Inc. (1911), 119 N. Park Ave., Rockville Centre, N.Y. 11570. *The Catholic Journalist* monthly; *Catho-*

lic Press Directory, annually. Pres., Rev. Norman Muckerman, C.SS.R. Exec. Dir., James A. Doyle.

Catholic Theological Society of America (1946), Office of Secretary, St. Mary of the Lake Seminary, Mundelein, Ill. 60060; 1,200. *Proceedings,* annually. Pres. (1983-84), Michael Fahey.

Catholic Union of the Sick in America, Inc. (CUSA) (1947), 63 Wall St., New York, N.Y. 10005 (legal office); 1,200. Admin. Leader, Miss Anna Marie Sopko, 176 W. 8th St., Bayonne, N.J. 07002 (national central office).

Catholic War Veterans (1935), 2 Massachusetts Ave. N.W., Washington, D.C. 20001; 500 posts, *Catholic War Veteran,* bimonthly.

Catholic Worker Movement (1933), 36 E. First St., New York, N.Y. 10003. *The Catholic Worker,* 9 times a year. Lay apostolate founded by Peter Maurin and Dorothy Day; has Houses of Hospitality in 29 U.S. cities and several communal farms in various parts of the country. Promotes pacifism and anarchism in that it is decentralist, and believes in what the popes have termed the principle of subsidiarity, urging decentralization in the school system, community control, and in the economic field credit unions, cooperatives and unions of workers and mutual aid.

Catholic Workman (Katolicky Delnik) (1891), New Prague, Minn. 56071; 18,023. *Catholic Workman,* monthly. Fraternal and insurance society. Pres. Rudy G. Faimon.

Catholic Writers' Guild of America (1919), 65 East 89th St., New York, N.Y. 10028.

Catholics United for the Faith (1968), 222 North Ave., Box S, New Rochelle, N.Y. 10801; 15,000 worldwide, *Lay Witness,* monthly. Lay apostolate founded in response to Vatican II's call to the laity. Pres., Mrs. Madeleine F. Stebbins.

Center for Pastoral Liturgy (1975), Catholic University of America, Washington, D.C. 20064. Concerned with promotion of pastoral-liturgical action in the U.S.; sponsors programs, publications, conferences, and workshops oriented toward the service of local churches. Dir., Rev. G. Thomas Ryan.

Central Association of the Miraculous Medal (1915), 475 E. Chelten Ave., Philadelphia, Pa. 19144. *Miraculous Medal,* quarterly. Dir., Rev. Robert P. Cawley, C.M.

Chaplains' Aid Association, Inc. (1917), 1011 First Ave., New York, N.Y. 10022. Pres., Most Rev. Philip J. Furlong.

Christopher Movement (1945), 12 E. 48th St., New York, N.Y. 10017. Without formal organization or meetings, the movement stimulates personal initiative and responsible action in line with Christian principles, particularly in the fields of education, government, industrial relations and communications. Christopher radio and TV programs are broadcast by more than 2,250 radio and TV stations; 600,000 copies of *Christopher News Notes* are distributed seven times a year without subscription fee; 152 weekly and 12 daily newspapers carry Christopher columns. Dir., Rev. John Catoir.

Citizens for Educational Freedom (1959): Non-sectarian group concerned with parents' right to educational choice by means of tuition tax credits and vouchers. National office: Suite 854 Washington Bldg., 15th St. and New York Ave. N.W., Washington, D.C. 20005.

Confraternity of Catholic Clergy (1976), 21-72 43rd St., Astoria, N.Y. 11105; *C.C.C. Newsletter*, bimonthly. To support priests by mutual prayer for personal holiness, loyalty to Pope and adherence to teaching of magisterium. Pres., Rev. Vincent J. Rigdon.

Confraternity of the Immaculate Conception of Our Lady of Lourdes (1874), Box 561, Notre Dame, Ind. 46556. Distributors of Lourdes water.

Confraternity of the Most Holy Rosary: See Rosary Altar Society.

Convert Movement Our Apostolate (CMOA) (1945), formerly Convert Makers of America, c/o Our Lady of Grace Rectory, 430 Avenue W, Brooklyn, N.Y. 11223. *Bulletin* quarterly. To train and assist lay persons on a parish level to discuss and present the Faith to interested persons on a one-to-one basis. Dir., Msgr. Erwin A. Juraschek.

Czech Catholic Union of Texas (K.J.T.) (1889), 214 Colorado St., La Grange, Tex. 78945; 16,616. *Nasinec*, weekly, and *K. J. T. News*, monthly. Fraternal and insurance society. Pres., Amos Pavlik.

D

Damien-Dutton Society for Leprosy Aid, Inc. (1944), 616 Bedford Ave., Bellmore, N.Y. 11710; 25,000. *Damien Dutton Call*, quarterly. Provides medicine, rehabilitation and research for conquest of leprosy. Pres., Howard E. Crouch, Dir., Sr. Mary Augustine, S.M.S.M.

Daughters of Isabella (1897), 375 Whitney Ave., New Haven, Conn. 06511; 120,000. International Regent, Mrs. Mary R. Bergman.

E

Edith Stein Guild, Inc. (1955), Our Lady of Victory Church, 60 William St., New York, N.Y. 10005; quarterly newsletter. Promotes Judaeo-Christian understanding, extends friendship to Catholics of Jewish background, spreads knowledge of life and writings of Edith Stein (Sister Benedicta of the Cross).

Enthronement of the Sacred Heart in the Home (1907), 3 Adams St., Fairhaven, Mass. 02719; over 2,500,000.

Eucharistic Guard for Nocturnal Adoration (1938), 800 North Country Club Rd., Tucson, Ariz. 85716.

Eymard League (1948), 194 E. 76 St., New York, N.Y. 10021; approximately 24,000. Dir., Rev. Ralph A. Lavigne, S.S.S.

F

Families for Christ (1977), 6026 W. Harwood Ave., Orlando, Fla., 32811; 8,000. Promote social reign of Christ. Pres., Albert Barone.

Families for Prayer (1982), 775 Madison Ave., Albany, N.Y. 12208. Dir., Rev. John J. Gurley, C.S.C.

Family Rosary, Inc. (1942), Executive Park Drive, Albany, N.Y. 12203. Pres., Rev. Patrick Peyton, C.S.C.

Federation of Diocesan Liturgical Commissions (FDLC) (1969), 3033 4th St. N.E., Washington, D.C. 20017. Voluntary association of personnel from diocesan liturgical commissions of the U.S. The main purpose is promotion of the liturgy as the heart of Christian life, especially in the parish community. Exec. Sec., Mr. Lawrence J. Johnson.

Fellowship of Catholic Scholars (1977), Msgr. George A. Kelly, Newsletter editor, St. John's University, Jamaica, N.Y. 11439; 400 members. Interdisciplinary research and publications of Catholic scholars in accord with the magisterium of the Catholic Church. Pres., Rev. William Smith.

First Catholic Slovak Ladies' Association, USA (1892), 24950 Chagrin Blvd., Beachwood, Ohio 44122; 105,000. *Fraternally Yours*, monthly. Fraternal insurance society. Pres., Louise M. Yash.

First Catholic Slovak Union (Jednota) (1890), 3289 E. 55th St., Cleveland, Ohio 44127; 115,097. *Jednota*, weekly. Exec. Sec., Joseph R. Vehec.

First Friday Clubs (1936). Organized on local basis; about 90 clubs in US, others elsewhere. Objectives are to spread devotion to the Sacred Heart, encourage members to receive Holy Communion on First Fridays and to meet at breakfast, luncheon or dinner for discussions of Catholic interest.

Franciscan Apostolate of the Way of the Cross (1949), St. Anthony Friary, 63 Bartholdi Ave., Butter, N.J. 07405. Stations Crucifix available on request. Dir., Rev. Cassian J. Kirk, O.F.M.

Friendship House (1938), 1746 W. Division, Chicago, Ill. 60622. *Community*, quarterly. Work for social justice through nonviolence and simple living; promote Catholic interracial apostolate.

G

Gabriel Richard Institute (1949), 2315 Orleans Ave., Detroit, Mich. 48207. Conducts Christopher leadership courses in 18 dioceses.

Gelasian Guild (1976), Association of Catholic attorneys working with the USCC; concerned with scholarly study of legal questions affecting Church-state relations. Pres., Rev. Charles Whelan, S.J., 106 W. 56th St., New York, N.Y. 10019.

Guard of Honor of the Immaculate Heart of Mary (1932), 135 West 31st St., New York, N.Y. 10001. An archconfraternity approved by the Holy See whose members cultivate devotion to the Blessed Virgin Mary, particularly through a daily Guard Hour of Prayer.

Guild of Catholic Lawyers (1928), 220 E. 23rd St., New York, N.Y. 10010; 600.

Guild of Our Lady of Ransom (1948), c/o St. Timothy's Rectory, 650 Nichols St., Norwood, Mass. 02062. Boston archdiocesan ministry for spiritual aid and rehabilitation of inmates of penal institutions. Exec. Dir. and Treas., Rev. Dr. Joseph P. McDermott.

Guild of St. Paul (1937), Visitation Monastery, Georgetown, Ky. 40324; Nat. Spir. Dir., Rev. Msgr. Leonard Nienaber; Pres., Bert Oram.

H

Holy Name Society: Founded in 1274 by Blessed John Vercelli, master general of the Dominicans, to promote reverence for the Holy Name of Jesus; this is still the principal purpose of the society, which also develops lay apostolic programs in line with directives of the Second Vatican Council. Introduced in the U.S. by Dominican Father Charles H. McKenna in 1870-71, the society has about 5 million members on diocesan and parochial levels. With approval of the local bishop and pastor, women as well as men may be members.

Holy Name Society, National Association (NAHNS) (1970), 516 N. Front St., Minersville, Pa. 17954. Association of diocesan and parochial Holy Name Societies. Spir. Dir., Rev. James F. Lanergan, 140 Shawmut Ave., Boston, Mass. 02118. Pres., John H. Farmerie.

Hungarian Catholic League of America, Inc. (1945), 30 E. 30th St., New York, N.Y. 10016. Member of the National Catholic Resettlement Council. *Catholic Hungarian Sunday,* weekly. Pres., Rev. Msgr. John S. Sabo.

I

Institute on Religious Life (1974), 4200 N. Austin Ave., Chicago, Ill. 60634. *Consecrated Life,* semiannually; *Religious Life,* 10 issues a year. To foster more effective understanding and implementation of teachings of the Church on religious life, promote vocations to religious life and the priesthood, and promote growth in sanctity of all the faithful according to their state in life.

International Institute of the Heart of Jesus (1972), 7700 Blue Mound Rd., Milwaukee Wis. 53213 (corporate headquarters); 14 Borgo Angelico, 00193 Rome, Italy (executive offices). Promote awareness and appreciation of the mystery of the Heart of Christ and establish an international forum for the apostolate. Pres., Harry G. John.

Italian Catholic Federation of California, Central Council (1924), 1801 Van Ness Ave., San Francisco, Calif. 94109; 30,000; *Bollettino,* monthly. Sec., Robert Aquistapace.

J

John Carroll Society, The (1951), 1870 Wyoming Ave. N.W., Washington, D.C. 20009. Pres. Hon. Dr. James E. Boland.

Judean Society, Inc., The (1966), 1075 Space Park Way No. 336, Mt. View, Calif. 94043; over 800. International organization for divorced Catholic women. Self-help, mutual-help counseling groups. Foundress/Internatl., Dir., Frances A. Miller.

K

Knights of Peter Claver (1909), 554 Palmetto St., P.O. Box 204, Mobile, Ala. 36601; 17,000. *The Claverite,* biannually. Fraternal and aid society.

Knights of St. John, Supreme Commandery (1886), 6517 Charles Ave., Parma, O. 44129; Sup. Sec., Brig. Gen. Salvatore La Bianca.

Knights of the Immaculata (Militia Immaculatae, M.I.) (1917), National Center, 1600 W. Park Ave., Libertyville, Ill. 60048; canonically es-

tablished with international headquarters in Rome. A pious association for evangelization and catechesis beginning with members' own inner renewal, through the intercession of the Blessed Virgin Mary.

L

Ladies of Charity of the United States, Association of (1960), 7806 Natural Bridge Rd., P.O. Box 5730, St. Louis, Mo. 63121; 40,000. International Association founded by St. Vincent de Paul in 1617. Pres., Mrs. John J. Buckley, 232 Main St., Binghamton, N.Y. 13905.

Lithuanian Groups: Ateitininkai, members of Lithuanian Catholic Federation Ateitis (1910), 9610 Singleton Dr., Bethesda, Md. 20817; to promote Catholic action and uphold Lithuanian heritage among youth; *Ateitis,* monthly; Pres., Joseph Laucka. Knights of Lithuania (1913), educational-fraternal organization; *Vytis,* monthly; Pres., Loretta T. Stukas, 234 Sunlit Dr., Watchung, N.J. 07060. Lithuanian Catholic Alliance (1886), 73 S. Washington St., Wilkes-Barre, Pa. 18701; 118 branches; *Garsas,* monthly; fraternal insurance organization; Pres., Thomas E. Mack. Lithuanian Roman Catholic Federation of America (1906), umbrella organization for Lithuanian parishes and organizations; Pres., Saulius Kuprys, 4545 W. 63rd St., Chicago, Ill. 60629. Lithuanian Roman Catholic Priests' League (1909): religious-professional association; Pres., Albert Contons, 50 Orton-Marotta Way, Boston, Mass. 02127. Two organizations with offices at 351 Highland Blvd., Brooklyn, N.Y. 11207 — Lithuanian American Catholic Services (1975); religious, educational, research and service association; Exec. Dir., Rev. Casimir Pugevicius. Lithuanian Catholic Religious Aid, Inc. (1961); to assist persecuted Catholics in Lithuania; Pres., Most Rev. Vincent Brizgys.

Little Flower Mission League (1957), P.O. Box 25, Plaucheville, La. 71362. Sponsored by the Brothers of the Holy Eucharist.

Little Flower Society (1923), 1313 Frontage Rd.; Darien, Ill. 60539; 200,000 Nat. Dir., Rev. Terrence L. Sempowski, O. Carm.

Liturgical Conference, The, 806 Rhode Island Ave. N.E., Washington, D.C. 20018. *Liturgy, Accent on Worship, Homily Service.* Education, research and publication programs for renewing and enriching Christian liturgical life. Ecumenical. Exec. Dir., Rachel Reeder.

Loyal Christian Benefit Association (1890), 700 Peach St., Erie, Pa. 16512; 56,623. *The Fraternal Leader,* bimonthly. Pres., Mrs. Catherine T. Kelly.

M

Marian Movement of Priests, Inc. Nat. Dir., Rev. Albert G. Roux, P.O. Box 8, St. Francis, Me. 04774.

Mariological Society of America (1949), Sec., Rev. Theodore A. Koehler, S.M., Marian Library, University of Dayton, Dayton, O. 45469: 300. *Marian Studies,* annually.

Markham Prayer Card Apostolate (Apostolate To Aid the Dying) (1931), Franciscan Sisters of the Poor, 60 Compton Rd., Cincinnati, Ohio 45215. Dir., Rev. Herman H. Kenning.

Maryheart Crusaders, The (1964), 22 Button St., Meriden, Conn. 06450; 2,000. *The Maryheart Crusader*, 4 times a year. To reunite fallen-away Catholics and promote religious education for adults. Pres., Louise D'Angelo.

Men of the Sacred Hearts (1964), Shrine of the Sacred Heart, Harleigh, Pa. 18225. Promote enthronement of Sacred Heart.

Missionary Association of Catholic Women (1916), 3521 W. National Ave., Milwaukee, Wis. 53215. Pres., Mrs. Elizabeth Schneider.

Missionary Cenacle Apostolate (MCA) (1909), 3501 Solly Ave., Philadelphia, Pa. 19136; 350. To foster spiritual and apostolic life of the laity through prayer, instruction, example and service.

Missionary Vehicle Association, Inc. (MIVA-America) (1971), 1326 Perry St., N.E., Washington, D.C. 20017. To raise funds and distribute them annually as grants to missionaries working with the poor in Third World countries. Nat. Dir., Rev. Philip De Rea, M.S.C.

Morality in Media, Inc. (1962), 475 Riverside Dr., New York, N.Y. 10115; 50,000 members. Newsletter, 8 times a year *The Obscenity Law Reporter*, bimonthly. To stop traffic in pornography constitutionally and effectively, and promote principles of love, truth and taste in the media. A major project is the National Obscenity Law Center which provides legal information for prosecutors and other attorneys. Pres., Rev. Morton A. Hill, S.J.

N

National Alliance of Czech Catholics (1917), 2657-59 S. Lawndale Ave., Chicago, Ill. 60623; 450 parishes. Pres., Mr. Vaclav Hyvnar.

National Association of Church Personnel Administrators (1973), 100 E. 8th St., Cincinnati, O. 45202. Pres., Rev. George Crespin, Exec. Dir., Sr. Mary Ann Barnhorn, S.N.D.

National Association of Diocesan Ecumenical Officers, Pres., Rev. Alex J. Brunett, 17500 Farmington Rd., Livonia, Mich. 48152.

National Association of Pastoral Musicians (1976), 225 Sheridan St., N.W., Washington, D.C. 20011; 7,000. *Pastoral Music*, six times a year. For clergy and musicians. Pres. and Exec. Dir., Rev. Virgil C. Funk.

National Association of Priest Pilots (1964), Pres., Rev. John Hemann, 204 S. Jackson, Eagle Grove, Iowa 50533.

National Catholic Bandmasters' Association (1953), Box 523, Notre Dame University, Notre Dame, Ind. 46556. *The School Musician Magazine*.

National Catholic Cemetery Conference (1949), 710 N. River Rd., Des Plaines, Ill. 60016. *The Catholic Cemetery*, monthly. Pres., Rev. Joseph P. Minturn.

National Catholic Conference for Interracial Justice (NCCIJ) (1960), 1200 Varnum St. N.E., Washington, D.C. 20017. National resource center and coordinator for Catholic interracial councils

and individual members. Exec. Dir. Rev. Frederick M. Hinton.

National Catholic Development Conference (1968), 119 N. Park Ave., Rockville Centre, N.Y. 11570. Professional association of organizations and individuals engaged in raising funds for Catholic charitable activities. Pres., Rev. Richard K. Knuge, S.M.; Exec. Dir., George T. Holloway.

National Catholic Disaster Relief Committee, 1346 Connecticut Ave. N.W., Suite 307, Washington, D.C. 20036.

National Catholic Pharmacists Guild of the United States (1962), 400 members; *The Catholic Pharmacist*. Pres., John P. Winkelmann, 1012 Surrey Hills Dr., St. Louis, Mo. 63117.

National Catholic Society of Foresters (1891), 35 E. Wacker, Chicago, Ill. 60601; 71,791; *National Catholic Forester*, quarterly. A fraternal insurance society. Pres., Mrs. Dolores M. Johnson.

National Catholic Stewardship Council (1962), 1 Columbia Place, Albany, N.Y. 12207. To promote the total concept of stewardship. Exec. Dir. Rev. James M. Mackey.

National Catholic Women's Union (1916), 3835 Westminster Pl., St. Louis, Mo. 63108; 14,500. *The Catholic Woman's Journal*, 10 times a year.

National Center for Urban Ethnic Affairs (1971): 1523 "O" St. N.W., Washington, D.C. 20005. To continue the expression of the Church's concern for problems of urban society. An affiliate of the USCC. Pres., Dr. John A. Kromkowski.

National Church Goods Association, 1114 Greenfield Lane, Mt. Prospect, Ill. 60056. Pres., Robert A. Tonini.

National Clergy Conference on Alcoholism and Related Drug Problems, 3112-7th St. N.E., Washington, D.C. 20017. Exec. Dir., Rev. John F. X. O'Neill.

National Conference of Diocesan Vocation Directors (NCDVD) (1961), 1307 S. Wabash, Suite 350, Chicago, Ill. 60605. Coordinate diocesan awareness and discernment of vocations to the diocesan or religious priesthood and the religious life for both men and women. Provide information services. Exec. Dir., Rev. Timothy K. Johnson.

National Conference of Religious Vocation Directors (NCRVD), 1307 S. Wabash Ave., Suite 350, Chicago, Ill. 60605. *Call to Growth/Ministry*, *NCRVD Newsletter*, quarterlies. Service organization for men and women religious assigned to vocational ministry. Exec. Dir., Rev. Steven Mudd, C.P.

National Federation of Catholic Physicians' Guilds (1927), 850 Elm Grove, Suite 11, Elm Grove, Wis. 53122; 6,700 in 88 autonomous guilds in U.S. and Canada, *Linacre Quarterly*. Pres., William Fitzsimmons, M.D.

National Federation of Spiritual Directors (1972). Pres., Rev. Msgr. Henry F. Fawcett, St. Francis Seminary, 1667 Santa Paula Drive, San Diego, Calif. 92111.

National Guild of Catholic Psychiatrists, Inc. (1949). Integration of psychiatry and Roman Catholic theology. *The Bulletin*. Pres. (1983-1984), Louis M. Vuksinick, M.D. Mailing address: Exec. Sec., 120 Hill St., Whitinsville, Mass. 01588.

National Organization for Continuing Education of Roman Catholic Clergy, Inc. (1973). Membership, 130 dioceses, 71 religious provinces, 30 affiliated institutions. Pres., Rev. Robert Pearson, 304 S. Adams Rd., Spokane, Wash. 99216. Exec. Dir., Rev. Jerome Thompson, Catholic Theological Union, 5401 S. Cornell, Chicago, Ill. 60615 (national office).

Network (1971), 806 Rhode Island Ave. N.E., Washington, D.C. 20018. A Catholic social justice lobby.

Nocturnal Adoration Society of the United States (1882), 194 E. 76th St., New York, N.Y. 10021; 57,000 in 540 units.

North American Academy of Liturgy, c/o David Truemper, Valparaiso Univ., Valparaiso, Ind. 46383. *Proceedings,* annually. Foster liturgical research, publication and dialogue on a scholarly level. Pres., Dr. Mark Searle.

O

Order of the Alhambra (1904), 4200 Leeds Ave., Baltimore, Md. 21229. 11,000 in U.S. and Canada. Fraternal society dedicated to assisting retarded children. Supreme Commander, Sam Spatafore.

P

Paulist League (1924), 415 W. 59th St., New York, N.Y. 10019; 23,700. Dir., Rev. Robert A. O'Donnell, C.S.P.

Philangeli (Friends of the Angels) (1949 in England; 1956 in U.S.), Viatorian Fathers, 1115 E. Euclid St., Arlington Heights, Ill. 60004; approximately 750,000 in 60 countries. To encourage devotion to the angels.

Pious Union of Prayer (1898), St. Joseph's Home, P.O. Box 288, Jersey City, N.J. 07303; 51,000. *St. Joseph's Messenger and Advocate of the Blind,* quarterly.

Pious Union of the Holy Spirit (1900), 30 Gedney Park Dr., White Plains, N.Y. 10605. Pres., Rev. Jerome McHugh, O.F.M. Cap.

Pontifical Mission for Palestine (1949), c/o Catholic Near East Welfare Association, 1011 First Ave., New York, N.Y. 10022. Field offices in Beirut, Lebanon, Jerusalem and Amman, Jordan. The papal relief agency for 1.5 million Palestinian refugees in Lebanon, Syria, Jordan, and the Gaza Strip. Distributes food, clothing, other essentials; maintains medical clinics, orphanages, libraries, refugee camp schools and chapels, the Pontifical Mission Center for the Blind (Gaza), the Pontifical Mission Libraries (Jerusalem, Bethlehem, Nazareth), the Epheta Institute for Deaf-Mutes (Bethlehem). Pres., Rev. Msgr. John G. Nolan, Exec. Vice-Pres., Rev. Msgr. Edward C. Foster.

Pontifical Missionary Union in the USA (1936), 366 Fifth Ave., New York, N.Y. 10001. Pontifical organization to promote mission awareness among clergy, religious, candidates to priestly and religious life, and others engaged in pastoral ministry of the Church. Pres., Cardinal Terence Cooke, Nat. Dir., Rev. Msgr. William J. McCormack.

Priests' Eucharistic League (1887), 194 E. 76th St., New York, N.Y. 10021; 17,500. *Emmanuel,*

monthly. Nat. Dir., Rev. Eugene La Verdiere, S.S.S.

Pro Ecclesia Foundation (1970), 663 Fifth Ave., New York, N.Y. 10022. *Pro Ecclesia,* 10 times a year; other publications; Manhattan Cable-TV program. To answer attacks against Church and promote Church teachings. Pres., Dr. Timothy A. Mitchell.

Pro Maria Committee (1952), 22 Second Ave., Lowell, Mass. 01854. Promote devotion to Our Lady of Beauraing (See Index).

The Providence Association of the Ukrainian Catholics in America (Ukrainian Catholic Fraternal Benefit Society) (1912), 817 N. Franklin St., Philadelphia, Pa. 19123. *America* (Ukrainian-English).

R

Raskob Foundation for Catholic Activities, Inc. (1945), Kennett Pike and Montchanin Rd., P.O. Box 4019, Wilmington, Del. 19807. Exec. Vice Pres., Gerard S. Garey.

Reparation Society of the Immaculate Heart of Mary, Inc. (1946), 100 E. 20th St., Baltimore, Md. 21218. *Fatima Findings,* monthly. Dir. Rev. John Ryan, S.J.

Rosary Altar Society (Confraternity of the Most Holy Rosary) (1891, in US), 141 E. 65th St., New York, N.Y. 10021; 3,000,000. Prov. Dir., Rev. Jovian Lacey, O.P.

Rosary League (1901), Franciscan Sisters of the Atonement, Graymoor, Garrison, N.Y. 10524.

S

Sacred Heart League, Walls, Miss. 38686; 700,000. Promote devotion to the Sacred Heart. Its program services include the Sacred Heart Auto League for careful, prayerful driving and the Apostolate of the Printed Word. Pres., Rev. Robert Hess, S.C.J.

St. Ansgar's Scandinavian Catholic League (1910), 40 W. 13th St., New York, N.Y. 10011; 1,000. *St. Ansgar's Bulletin,* annually.

St. Anthony's Guild (1924), Paterson, N.J. 07509. *Anthonian,* quarterly. Dir., Rev. Salvator Fink, O.F.M.

St. Jude League (1929), 221 W. Madison St., Chicago, Ill. 60606. *St. Jude Journal,* bi-monthly. Dir., Rev. Mark J. Brummel, C.M.F.

St. Margaret of Scotland Guild, Inc. (1938), Graymoor, Garrison, N.Y. 10524; 2,200. Moderator, Bro. Pius MacIsaac, S.A.

St. Martin de Porres Guild (1935), 141 E. 65th St., New York, N.Y. 10021. Gen. Dir., Rev. Theodore Breslin, O.P.

St. Thomas Aquinas Foundation of the Dominican Fathers of the United States (STAF). Mod., Very Rev. Thomas H. McBrien, O.P., Providence College, Providence, R.I. 02918

Serra International (1938), 22 W. Monroe St., Chicago, Ill. 60603; 14,500 members in 475 clubs in 33 countries. *Serran,* bimonthly. Fosters vocations to the priesthood, and religious life, trains Catholic lay leadership. Formally aggregated to the Pontifical Society for Priestly Vocations, 1951. Pres., Kevin J. Lynch.

Slovak Catholic Federation (1911): Founded by Rev. Joseph Murgas to promote and coordinate religious activities among Slovak Catholic fraternal societies, religious communities and Slovak ethnic parishes in their effort to address themselves to the special needs of Slovak Catholics in the U.S. and Canada. Pres., Rev. Joseph V. Adamec, 1515 Cass Ave., Bay City, Mich. 48706.

Slovak Catholic Sokol (1905), 205 Madison St., Passaic, N.J. 07055; 48,500. *Katolicky Sokol (Catholic Falcon)*, biweekly; *Priatel Dietok (Children's Friend)*, bimonthly.

Society for the Propagation of the Faith (1822), 366 Fifth Ave., New York, N.Y. 10001; established in 171 dioceses. Church's principal instrument for promoting mission awareness and generating financial support for the missions. General fund for ordinary and extraordinary subsidies for all mission diocese. *Mission*, 5 times a year; *Director's Newsletter*. Is subject to Sacred Congregation for the Evangelization of Peoples. Nat. Dir., Rev. Msgr. William J. McCormack.

Society of St. Peter the Apostle (1898), 366 Fifth Ave., New York, N.Y. 10001; 171 dioceses. Church's central fund for support of seminaries, seminarians and novices in all mission dioceses. Nat. Dir., Rev. Msgr. William J. McCormack.

Spiritual Life Institute of America (1960), Box 260, Crestone, Colo. 81131. *Desert Call,* seasonal. An eremetical movement to foster the contemplative spirit in America. Founder, Rev. William McNamara, O.C.D. Second foundation: Primitive Wilderness Hermitage, Kemptville, Nova Scotia, Canada B0W 1Y0.

T

Theresians of America (1961), 5326 E. Pershing Ave., Scottsdale, Ariz. 85254; 5,000. Spiritual, intellectual and apostolic organization concerned with the vocation to Christian womanhood. Exec. Dir., Sr. Patricia Mullen.

U

United Societies of U.S.A. (1903), 613 Sinclair St., McKeesport, Pa. 15132; 3,899 members. *Prosvita-Enlightenment,* monthly newspaper.

United States Catholic Historical Society (1884). 300. *Journal,* quarterly; and *Monograph Series,* annually. Exec. Sec., James J. Mahoney, St. Joseph's Seminary, Yonkers, N.Y. 10704.

W-Y

Western Catholic Union (1877), W.C.U. Bldg., 506-510 Maine St., Quincy, Ill. 62301; 27,537 members. *Western Catholic Union Record,* bimonthly.

Word of God Institute (1972), 487 Michigan Ave. N.E., Washington, D.C. 20017. For renewed biblical preaching, Bible sharing and evangelization. Dir., Rev. John Burke, O.P.

Young Ladies' Institute (1887), P.O. Box 99687, San Francisco, Calif. 94109. Grand Sec. Mrs. Sylvia Sharman.

Young Men's Institute (1883), 50 Oak St., San Francisco, Calif. 94102; 4,500. *Institute Journal,* bimonthly. Grand Sec., R. A. Bettencourt.

Knights of Columbus

The Knights of Columbus, which originated as a fraternal benefit society of Catholic men, was founded by Father Michael J. McGivney and chartered by the General Assembly of Connecticut Mar. 29, 1882.

In line with their general purpose to be of service to the Church, the Knights are active in many apostolic works and community programs.

Since January, 1947, the Knights have sponsored a program of Catholic advertising in secular publications with national circulation. This has brought some 7 million inquiries and led to more than 650,000 enrollments in courses in the Catholic faith. In recent years the Knights have broadened this program to include other media for spreading Christian and religious ideals. As a result substantial contributions have been made to support the work of the John LaFarge Institute in New York, the Catholic Communications Foundation in New York, and the Center for Applied Research in the Apostolate (CARA) in Washington. In 1975 the Knights also undertook funding of the up-link costs for telecasting papal ceremonies throughout the world via satellite.

K. of C. scholarship funds — two at the Catholic University of America, another for disbursement at other Catholic colleges in the U.S., one at Canadian colleges and others for the Philippines, Mexico and Puerto Rico — have provided college educations for some 1,600 students since 1914.

The order promotes youth activity through sponsorship of the Columbian Squires and through cooperation with other organized youth groups.

Recent programs undertaken by the Knights include: promotion of vocations to the priesthood and religious life; promotion of rosary devotion with free distribution of more than 100,000 rosaries a year; efforts to halt the increased killing of the unborn; assistance to the retarded and other disadvantaged people.

In 1981, local units of the Knights contributed more than $41.7 million to charitable and benevolent causes, and gave more than 10.4 million hours of community service.

K. of C. membership, as of Mar. 1, 1983, was 1,378,078 in 7,447 councils in the U.S., Canada, the Philippines, Cuba, Mexico, Puerto Rico, Panama, Guatemala, Guam, the Dominican Republic and the Virgin Islands. Assets, as of Dec. 31, 1982, amounted to $1,155,605,416 and total insurance in force, $7,553,538,732.

The Knights' publication, *Columbia,* has the greatest circulation (over 1.3 million) of any Catholic monthly in North America.

Virgil C. Dechant is Supreme Knight.

International headquarters are located at One Columbus Plaza, New Haven, Conn. 06507.

During the final session of the 101st annual meeting of the Supreme Council Aug. 2 to 4 in Columbus, O., delegates called for a broad-based educational program about the teaching of the Church on war, nuclear weapons and the arms race. They also urged all members and their families "to pray often for world peace, especially to Our Lady of Fatima."

COMMUNICATIONS

CATHOLIC PRESS STATISTICS

The *1983 Catholic Press Directory*, published by the Catholic Press Association, reported a total of 547 periodicals in North America with a circulation of 26,838,983. The figures included 178 English-language newspapers with a circulation of 5,843,924 and 13 other-language newspapers (including 7 Spanish) with a circulation of approximately 145,000. Magazines numbered 328 in the English language with a circulation of 20,481,185 and 28 in other languages with a circulation of more than 350,000.

Newspapers in the U.S.

There were 159 English-language newspapers (circulation 5,570,795); 7 Spanish-language (circulation almost 85,000) and 6 other-languages (circulation, over 60,000). Ten of these had national circulation; 150 (including 4 editions of *Our Sunday Visitor*) were diocesan newspapers. Listed below, according to circulation figures, are the national weekly newspapers and diocesan weekly newspapers with large circulations.

National: *Our Sunday Visitor*, 211,694; *National Catholic Register*, 69,945; *Catholic Twin Circle*, 65,596; *National Catholic Reporter*, 44,650; *The Wanderer*, 36,866; *Jednota* (Slovak and English), 36,035; *El Visitante Dominical* (Spanish), 31,000.

Diocesan: *Chicago Catholic*, 162,254; *Long Island Catholic*, (Rockville Centre), 149,067; *Catholic New York* (New York), 133,000; *Pittsburgh Catholic*, 121,000; *St. Louis Review*, 98,788; *The Tablet* (Brooklyn, N.Y.), 94,453;

Catholic Voice (Oakland), 87,000; *Catholic Standard and Times* (Philadelphia), 79,292; *Denver Catholic Register*, 77,843; *Clarion Herald* (New Orleans), 77,373; *The Evangelist* (Albany, N.Y.), 72,500; *The Monitor* (Trenton), 61,162; *Catholic Herald* (Milwaukee), 59,120; *The Record* (Louisville), 58,827; *Catholic Witness* (Harrisburg), 58,045; *Catholic Bulletin* (St. Paul and Minneapolis), 57,139; *Catholic Voice* (Omaha), 56,403; *Florida Catholic* (Orlando), 56,244; *The Pilot* (Boston), 56,229; *The Voice* (Miami), 55,000.

The oldest Catholic newspaper in the United States is *The Pilot* of Boston, established in 1829 (under a different title).

Magazines

The *Catholic Press Directory* reported 328 English-language magazines in the U.S. and Canada with a circulation of 20,481,185 and 28 other-language magazines with a circulation of more than 350,000.

America (circulation, 32,831) and *Commonweal* (circulation, 18,126), are the only weekly and biweekly magazines, respectively, of general interest.

The monthly magazine with the largest circulation is *Columbia* (1,295,918), the official organ of the Knights of Columbus.

General-interest monthly magazines with large circulations include: *Catholic Digest* (614,734); *Liguorian* (575,000); *St. Anthony's Messenger* (345,214); *U.S. Catholic* (48,498).

CATHOLIC NEWSPAPERS AND MAGAZINES IN THE U.S.

(Sources: *Catholic Press Directory, 1983*; Almanac survey; NC News Service.)

Abbreviation code: a, annual; bm, bimonthly; m, monthly; q, quarterly; w, weekly.

Circulation figures for some of these newspapers and magazines are given in the article, Catholic Press Statistics.

Newspapers

Advocate, The, w; 37 Evergreen Pl., E. Orange, N.J. 07018; Newark archdiocese.

Alaskan Shepherd, 6 times a year; 1312 Peger Rd., Fairbanks, Alaska 99701; Fairbanks diocese.

Alive, m; 400 East Monroe, Phoenix, Ariz. 85004; Phoenix diocese.

America (Ukrainian-English), daily; 817 N. Franklin St., Philadelphia, Pa. 19123.

Anchor, The w; P.O. Box 7, Fall River, Mass. 02722; Fall River diocese.

Arizona Catholic Lifetime, biweekly; 64 W. Ochoa St., Tucson, Ariz. 85701; Tucson diocese.

Arlington Catholic Herald, w; 200 N. Glebe Rd., Suite 614, Arlington, Va. 22203; Arlington diocese.

Bayou Catholic, The, w; P.O. Box 9077, Houma, La. 70361; Houma-Thibodaux diocese.

Beacon, The, w; Box A, Pequannock, N.J. 07440; Paterson diocese.

Bishop's Bulletin, m; P.O. Box 665, Yankton, S. Dak. 57078.

Bolletino, m; 1801 Van Ness Ave., San Francisco, Calif. 94109; Central Council of Italian Catholic Federation.

Byzantine Catholic World, biweekly; 3643 Perrysville Ave., Pittsburgh, Pa. 15214; Pittsburgh Byzantine archdiocese.

Catholic Accent, w; P.O. Box 850, Greensburg, Pa. 15601; Greensburg diocese.

Catholic Advance, The, w; 424 N. Broadway, Wichita, Kans. 67202; Wichita diocese.

Catholic Banner, w; P.O. Box 818, Charleston, S.C. 29402; Charleston diocese.

Catholic Bulletin, w; 244 Dayton Ave., St. Paul, Minn. 55102; St. Paul and Minneapolis archdiocese.

Catholic Chronicle, biweekly; P.O. Box 1866, Toledo, O. 43603; Toledo diocese.

Catholic Commentary, w; P.O. Box 2239, Anchorage, Alaska 99510; one-page supplement in local newspaper; Anchorage archdiocese.

Catholic Commentator, The, w; P.O. Box

14746, Baton Rouge, La. 70808; Baton Rouge diocese.

Catholic Communicator, w; 202 Morningside Dr. S.E., Albuquerque, N.M. 87108. Santa Fe archdiocese.

Catholic Crosswinds, semi-monthly; 1001 N. Grand Ave., Pueblo, Colo. 81003; Pueblo diocese.

Catholic Exponent, biweekly; 315 Ohio One Bldg., Youngstown, O. 44503; Youngstown diocese.

Catholic Free Press, w; 47 Elm St., Worcester, Mass. 01609; Worcester diocese.

Catholic Herald, w; P.O. Box 26587, Milwaukee, Wis. 53226; Milwaukee archdiocese.

Catholic Herald — Madison Edition, w; P.O. Box 1176, Middleton, Wis. 53701.

Catholic Herald — Superior Edition, w; P.O. Box 310, Superior, Wis. 54880.

Catholic Herald, The, w; 5890 Newman Ct., Sacramento, Calif. 95819; Sacramento diocese.

Catholic Hungarian's Sunday, w; 1739 Mahoning Ave., Youngstown, O. 44509.

Catholic Key to the News, The, w; P.O. Box 1037, Kansas City, Mo. 64141; Kansas City-St. Joseph diocese.

Catholic Lantern, m; P.O. Box 4237, Stockton, Calif. 95204; Stockton diocese.

Catholic Light, biweekly; 300 Wyoming Ave., Scranton, Pa. 18503; Scranton diocese.

Catholic Messenger, w; 201 W. 2nd St., Davenport, Ia. 52801; Davenport diocese.

Catholic Mirror, biweekly; 200 Jewett Bldg., Des Moines, Ia. 50309.

Catholic Missourian, w; P.O. Box 1107, Jefferson City, Mo. 65102; Jefferson City diocese.

Catholic New York, w; P.O. Box 5133, New York, N.Y. 10150; New York archdiocese.

Catholic Observer, biweekly; Box 1570, Springfield, Mass. 01101; Springfield diocese.

Catholic Outlook, m; 215 W. 4th St., Duluth, Minn. 55806; Duluth diocese.

Catholic Post, The, w; P.O. Box 1722, Peoria, Ill. 61656; Peoria diocese.

Catholic Register, biweekly; Box 126-C, Logan Blvd., Hollidaysburg, Pa. 16648; Altoona-Johnstown diocese.

Catholic Review, w; 320 Cathedral St., Baltimore, Md. 21203; Baltimore archdiocese.

Catholic Sentinel, w; 2816 E. Burnside St., Portland, Ore. 97214; Portland archdiocese, Baker diocese.

Catholic Spirit, The, m; P.O. Box 13327, Capitol Sta., Austin, Tex. 78711; Austin diocese.

Catholic Spirit, The, w; 161 Edgington Lane, Wheeling, W. Va. 26003; Wheeling-Charleston diocese.

Catholic Standard, w; 1721 Rhode Island Ave., N.W., Washington, D.C. 20036; Washington archdiocese.

Catholic Standard and Times, w; 222 N. 17th St., Philadelphia, Pa. 19103; Philadelphia archdiocese; Allentown diocese.

Catholic Star Herald, w; 1845 Haddon Ave., Camden, N.J. 08103; Camden diocese.

Catholic Sun, The, w; 257 E. Onondaga St., Syracuse, N.Y. 13202; Syracuse diocese.

Catholic Telegraph, w; 100 E. 8th St., Cincinnati, O. 45202; Cincinnati archdiocese.

Catholic Times, w; P.O. Box 636, Columbus, O. 43216; Columbus diocese.

Catholic Transcript, w; 785 Asylum Ave., Hartford, Conn. 06105; Hartford archdiocese, Bridgeport and Norwich dioceses.

Catholic Twin Circle, w; 1901 Avenue of the Stars, Suite 1511, Los Angeles, Calif. 90067.

Catholic Universe Bulletin, biweekly; 1027 Superior Ave. N.E., Cleveland, O. 44114; Cleveland diocese.

Catholic Virginian, biweekly; 14 N. Laurel St., Box 26843, Richmond, Va. 23261; Richmond diocese.

Catholic Voice, The, w; 2918 Lakeshore Ave., Oakland, Calif. 94610; Oakland diocese.

Catholic Voice, The, w; P.O. Box 4010, Omaha, Nebr. 68104; Omaha archdiocese.

Catholic Week, w; P.O. Box 349, Mobile, Ala. 36601; Mobile diocese.

Catholic Weekly, The, w; P.O. Box 1405, Saginaw, Mich. 48605; Saginaw and Gaylord dioceses.

Catholic Weekly, The, w; 1628 Lambden Rd., Flint, Mich. 48501; Lansing diocese.

Catholic Witness, The, w; P.O. Box 2555, Harrisburg, Pa. 17105; Harrisburg diocese.

Central California Register, biweekly; P.O. Box 1668, 1550 N. Fresno St., Fresno, Calif. 93717; Fresno diocese.

Central Washington Catholic, m; P.O. Box 505, Yakima, Wash. 90907. Yakima diocese.

Challenge, The, semimonthly; P.O. Box 14082, Jefferson Sta., Detroit, Mich. 48214. St. Maron diocese.

Chicago Catholic, The w; 155 E. Superior St., Chicago, Ill. 60611; Chicago archdiocese.

Church Today, biweekly; P.O. Box 7417, Alexandria, La. 71306; Alexandria Shreveport diocese.

Church World, w; Industry Rd., Brunswick, Me. 04011; Portland diocese.

Clarion Herald, w; 523 Natchez St., New Orleans, La. 70130; New Orleans archdiocese.

Common Sense, w; 1325 Jefferson Ave., Memphis, Tenn. 38104; Memphis diocese.

Community, w; P.O. Box 10607, Jacksonville, Fla. 32207; one-page weekly in Sunday editions of two daily newspapers; St. Augustine diocese.

Compass, The, w; P.O. Box 909; Green Bay, Wis. 54305; Green Bay diocese.

Courier, The, m; P.O. Box 949, Winona, Minn. 55987; Winona diocese.

Courier-Journal, w; 114 S. Union St., Rochester, N.Y. 14607; Rochester diocese.

Criterion, The, w; P.O. Box 174, Indianapolis, Ind. 46206; Indianapolis archdiocese.

Dakota Catholic Action, 9 times a year; P.O. Box 128, Wilton, N.D. 58579; Bismarck diocese.

Darbininkas (Lithuanian), w; 341 Highland Blvd., Brooklyn, N.Y. 11207; Lithuanian Franciscan Fathers.

Denver Catholic Register, w; P.O. Box 1620, Denver, Colo. 80201; Denver archdiocese.

Dialog, The, w; 1925 Delaware Ave., Wilmington, Del. 19806; Wilmington diocese.

Diocese of Orange Bulletin, m; 2811 E. Villa Real Dr., Orange, Calif. 92667.

Draugas (Lithuanian), daily; 4545 W. 63rd St., Chicago, Ill. 60629; Lithuanian Catholic Press Society.

East Texas Catholic, The, biweekly; P.O. Box 3948, Beaumont, Tex. 77704; Beaumont diocese.

Eastern Catholic Life, w; 101 Market St., Passaic, N.J. 07055; Passaic Byzantine eparchy.

* **Eastern Montana Catholic Register,** w; P.O. Box 2107, Great Falls, Mont. 59403; Great Falls-Billings diocese.

Eastern Oklahoma Catholic, biweekly; Box 520, Tulsa, Okla. 74101; Tulsa diocese.

El Heraldo Catolico (Spanish), bm; P.O. Box 19312, Sacramento, Calif. 95819; Sacramento diocese.

El Pregonero (Spanish), semi-monthly; 1015 University Blvd. East, Silver Springs, Md. 20903; Centro Catolico Hispano of Washington archdiocese.

El Visitante de Puerto Rico (Spanish), w; Box 1967, San Juan, P.R. 00903; Bishops of Puerto Rico.

El Visitante Dominical (Spanish), w; P.O. Box 96, San Antonio, Tex. 78291; Missionary Society of Oblate Fathers of Texas, Inc.

Evangelist, The, w; 39 Philip St., Albany, N.Y. 12207; Albany diocese.

Florida Catholic, The, w; 321 Hillman Ave., P.O. Box 3551, Orlando, Fla. 32802; Orlando and St. Petersburg dioceses.

Gary Sunday Visitor, w; P.O. Box M-356, Gary, Ind. 46401; Gary diocese.

Georgia Bulletin, w; 680 W. Peachtree St. N.W., Atlanta, Ga. 30308; Atlanta archdiocese.

Globe, The, w; 1821 Jackson St., Sioux City, Ia. 51105; Sioux City diocese.

Guardian, The, w; P.O. Box 7417, Little Rock, Ark. 72217; Little Rock diocese.

Harmonizer, The (Edition O.S.V.), w; Cathedral Center, P.O. Box 11169, Fort Wayne, Ind. 46856; Fort Wayne-S. Bend diocese.

Hawaii Catholic Herald, w; 1184 Bishop St., Honolulu, H.I. 96813; Honolulu diocese.

Hlas Naroda (Voice of the Nation) (Czech-English), w; 2657-59 S. Lawndale Ave., Chicago. 60623.

Horizons, semimonthly; 1900 Carlton Rd., Parma, O. 44134; Parma diocese.

Idaho Register, w; P.O. Box 2835, Boise, Idaho 83701; Boise diocese.

IDEA Ink, q; 4716 Verona Rd., P.O. Box 4010, Madison, Wis. 53711; Dominican Educational Assn., Inc.

Impact! 4 to 6 times a year; 1234 Massachusetts Ave. N.W. Suite 1004, Washington, D.C. 20005; National Office for Black Catholics.

Inland Catholic, The, w; P.O. Box 2788, San Bernardino, Calif. 92405. San Bernardino diocese.

Inland Register, w; P.O. Box 48, Spokane, Wash. 99210; Spokane diocese.

Inside Passage, w; 419 6th St., Juneau, Alaska 99801; Juneau diocese.

Intermountain Catholic, The, w; P.O. Box 2489, Salt Lake City, Utah 84110; Salt Lake City diocese.

Jednota (Slovak-Eng.), w; Jednota and Rosedale Aves., Middletown, Pa. 17057; First Catholic Slovak Union.

Joliet Catholic Explorer, w; St. Charles Borromeo Pastoral Center, Rt. 53 and Airport Rd., Romeoville, Ill. 60441. Joliet diocese.

Lafayette Sunday Visitor, w; P.O. Box 5808, Lafayette, Ind. 47903; Lafayette diocese.

Lake Shore Visitor, w; P.O. Box 4047, Erie, Pa. 16512; Erie diocese.

La Voz (Spanish), w; 9401 Biscayne Blvd., Miami, Fla 33138; Miami archdiocese.

Leaven, The, w; 2220 Central, Kansas City, Kans. 66110; Kansas City archdiocese.

Long Island Catholic, The, w; P.O. Box 700, Hempstead, N.Y. 11551; Rockville Centre diocese.

Message, The, w; P.O. Box 4169, Evansville, Ind. 47711; Evansville diocese.

Messenger, The, w; 220 W. Lincoln St., Belleville, Ill. 62221; Belleville diocese.

Messenger, The, w; P.O. Box 268, Covington, Ky. 41012; Covington diocese.

Michigan Catholic, The, w; 2701 Chicago Blvd., Detroit, Mich. 48206; Detroit archdiocese.

Mirror, The, weekly; M.P.O. Box 847, Springfield, Mo. 65801; Springfield-Cape Girardeau diocese.

Mississippi Today, w; P.O. Box 2130, Jackson, Miss. 39205; Jackson and Biloxi dioceses.

Monitor, The, w; 441 Church St., San Francisco, Calif. 94114; San Francisco archdiocese.

Monitor, The, w; P.O. Box 3095, Trenton, N.J. 08619; Trenton diocese.

Morning Star, The, w; P.O. Box 3223, Lafayette, La. 70502; Lafayette diocese.

Narod Polski (Polish-Eng.) semi-monthly; 984 Milwaukee Ave., Chicago, Ill. 60622.

Nasa Nada (Eng.-Croatian), m; 4848 S. Ellis Ave., Chicago, Ill. 60615; Croatian Catholic Union.

National Catholic Register, w; 1901 Avenue of the Stars, Suite 1511, Los Angeles, Calif. 90067.

National Catholic Reporter, The, w; P.O. Box 281, Kansas City, Mo. 64141.

New Earth, The, m (Oct-June); P.O. Box 1750, Fargo, N.D. 58107; Fargo diocese.

New Star, The, w; 2208 W. Chicago Ave., Chicago, Ill. 60622; St. Nicholas of Chicago Ukrainian diocese.

North Carolina Catholic, w; 300 Cardinal Gibbons Dr., Raleigh, N.C. 27606 and 1524 E. Morehead St., Charlotte, N.C. 28207; Raleigh and Charlotte dioceses.

North Country Catholic, w; Box 326, Ogdensburg, N.Y. 13669; Ogdensburg diocese.

Northwestern Kansas Register, w; P.O. Box 958, Salina, Kans. 67401; Salina diocese.

Nuevo Amanecer, m; P.O. Box 155, Brooklyn,

N.Y. 11243; for Hispanic Catholic community of Brooklyn diocese.

Observer, The, w; P.O. Box 2079, Monterey, Calif. 93940; Monterey diocese.

Observer, The, biweekly; 921 W. State St., Rockford, Ill. 61102; Rockford diocese.

One Voice, w; P.O. Box 10822, Birmingham, Ala. 35202; Birmingham diocese.

Our Northland Diocese, 22 issues annually; P.O. Box 610, Crookston, Minn. 56716; Crookston diocese.

Our Sunday Visitor, w; 200 Noll Plaza, Huntington, Ind. 46750; national edition and official publication for 4 dioceses.

P.A.D.R.E.S. National Bulletin, q; 3310 Garfield Ave., Kansas City, Kans. 66104.

Pilot, The, w; 49 Franklin St., Boston, Mass. 02110; Boston archdiocese.

Pittsburgh Catholic, The, w; 110 Third Ave., Pittsburgh, Pa. 15222; Pittsburgh diocese.

Polish American Journal, m; 413 Cedar Ave., Scranton, Pa. 18505.

Progress, The, w; 907 Terry Ave., Seattle, Wash. 98104; Seattle archdiocese.

Pueblo de Dios (Spanish), biweekly; 37 Evergreen Pl., E. Orange N.J. 07018; Newark archdiocese.

Record, The, w; 701 W. Jefferson St., Louisville, Ky. 40202; Louisville archdiocese.

Redwood Crozier, The, biweekily, P.O. Box 1297, Santa Rosa, Calif. 95402; Santa Rosa diocese.

St. Cloud Visitor, w; P. O. Box 1068, St. Cloud, Minn. 56302; St. Cloud diocese.

St. Joseph's-Blatt (German-Eng.), m; St. Benedict, Ore. 97373; Manfred F. Ellenberger.

St. Louis Review, w; 462 N. Taylor Ave., St. Louis, Mo. 63108; St. Louis archdiocese.

Shlakh — The Way, w; 805 N. Franklin St., Philadelphia, Pa. 19123; Philadelphia archeparchy. Stamford and Chicago eparchies.

Sooner Catholic, The, biweekly; P.O. Box 32180, Oklahoma City, Okla. 73123; Oklahoma City archdiocese.

South Texas Catholic, w; 1200 Lantana St., Corpus Christi, Tex. 78407; Corpus Christi diocese.

Southern Catholic, The, m; 855 W. Carolina St., Tallahassee, Fla. 32304. Pensacola-Tallahassee diocese.

Southern Cross, The, w; P.O. Box 81869, San Diego, Calif. 92138; San Diego diocese.

Southern Cross, The, w; 601 E. 6th St., Waynesboro, Ga. 30830; Savannah diocese.

Southern Nebraska Register, w; P.O. Box 80329, Lincoln, Nebr. 68501; Lincoln diocese.

Southwest Kansas Register, w; P.O. Box 1317, Dodge City, Kans. 67801; Dodge City diocese.

Steubenville Register, w; P.O. Box 160, Steubenville, O. 43952; Steubenville diocese.

Tablet, w; 1 Hanson Pl., Brooklyn, N.Y. 11243; Brooklyn diocese.

Tennessee Register, The, w; 2400 21st Ave. S., Nashville, Tenn. 37212; Nashville diocese.

Texas Catholic, w; 3915 Lemmon Ave., Dallas, Tex. 75219; Dallas and Fort Worth dioceses.

Texas Catholic Herald, The, semi-monthly; 1700 San Jacinto St., Houston, Tex. 77002; Galveston-Houston diocese.

Tidings, The, w; 1530 W. 9th St., Los Angeles, Calif. 90015; Los Angeles archdiocese.

Time and Eternity, w; 514 E. Lawrence St., Springfield, Ill. 62703; Springfield diocese.

Times-Review, The, w; P.O. Box 937, La Crosse, Wis. 54601; La Crosse diocese.

Today's Catholic, w; P.O. Box 12429, San Antonio, Tex. 78212; San Antonio archdiocese.

Upper Peninsula Catholic, biweekly; P.O. Box 548, Marquette, Mich. 49855; Marquette diocese.

Valley Catholic, m; 7600 Y St. Joseph Ave., Los Altos, Calif. 94022; San Jose diocese.

Valley Catholic Witness, 208 Iris, McAllen, Tex. 78501; one page every other week in three area newspapers; Brownsville diocese.

Vermont Catholic Tribune, biweekly; 351 North Ave., Burlington, Vt. 05401; Burlington diocese.

Visitor, The, w; 184 Broad St., Providence, R.I. 02903; Providence diocese.

Voice, The, w; 6201 Biscayne Blvd., Miami, Fla. 33138; Miami archdiocese.

Voice of the Southwest, w; P.O. Box 7, San Fidel, N. Mex. 87049; Gallup diocese.

Wanderer, The, w; 201 Ohio St., St. Paul, Minn. 55107.

WestMont Word, biweekly; P.O. Box 1729, Helena, Mont. 59624; Helena diocese.

West Nebraska Register, w; P.O. Box 608, Grand Island, Nebr. 68801; Grand Island diocese.

West River Catholic, m; P.O. Box 678, Rapid City, S. Dak. 57709; Rapid City diocese.

West Texas Angelus, biweekly; 116 S. Oakes, San Angelo, Tex. 76903; San Angelo diocese.

West Texas Catholic, w; 1800 N. Spring, Amarillo, Tex. 79107; Amarillo and Lubbock dioceses.

Western Michigan Catholic, w; 650 Burton S.E., Grand Rapids, Mich. 49507; Grand Rapids diocese.

Western New York Catholic Visitor, m; 100 S. Elmwood Ave., Buffalo, N.Y. 14202; Buffalo diocese.

Witness, The, w; 1229 Mt. Loretta, Dubuque, Ia. 52001; Dubuque archdiocese.

Wyoming Catholic Register, w; 128 W. 11th St., Caspar, Wyo. 82601.

Magazines, Other Periodicals

ADRIS Newsletter, q; Department of Theology, Fordham University, Bronx, N.Y. 10458. Association for the Development of Religious Information Services.

AIM (Aids in Ministry), q; 1800 W. Winnemac Ave., Chicago, Ill. 60640.

Alaskan Shepherd, 6 times a year; 1312 Peger Rd., Fairbanks, Alaska 99701.

America, w; 106 W. 56th St., New York, N.Y. 10019.

American Benedictine Review, Assumption Abbey, Richardton, N.D. 58652.

American Midland Naturalist, q; Notre Dame, Ind. 46556.

Americas, The, q; Box 34440, W. Bethesda, Md. 20817; Academy of American Franciscan History.

Amerikanski Slovenec (Slovenian), w; 6117 St. Clair Ave., Cleveland, O. 44103; Slovenian Catholic Union.

Angel Guardian Home Quarterly, The, q; 6301 12th Ave., Brooklyn, N.Y. 11219.

Anthonian, q; Paterson, N.J. 07509; St. Anthony's Guild.

Anthropological Quarterly, q; 620 Michigan Ave. N.E., Washington, D.C. 20064.

Apostolate of Our Lady, m; 315 Clay St., Carey, O. 43316; Our Lady of Consolation National Shrine.

Apostolate of the Little Flower, bm; P.O. Box 5280, 906 Kentucky Ave., San Antonio, Tex. 78201; Discalced Carmelite Fathers.

Archeparchal Bulletin, q; 815 N. Franklin St., Philadelphia, Pa. 19123; Philadelphia archeparchy.

Atchison Benedictine Community News (ABC News), bm; Mount St. Scholastica Convent, Atchison, Kans. 66002.

Ateitis (The Future) (Lithuanian), m; 9610 Singleton Dr., Bethesda, Md. 20807; for youth.

Ave Maria (Polish), 6 times a year; 600 Doat St., Buffalo, N.Y. 14211; Felician Srs.

Benedictine Orient, bm; 2400 Maple Ave., Lisle, Ill. 60532.

Benedictines, semiannually; Mt. St. Scholastica, Atchison, Kans. 66002.

Bernardine Bulletin, The, semiannually; 647 Spring Mill Rd., Villanova, Pa. 19085; Bernardine Srs..

Best Sellers, m; Univ. of Scranton, Scranton, Pa. 18510.

Better World, q; Belford, N.J. 07718; Mary Productions Guild.

Bible Today, The, bm; Liturgical Press, Collegeville, Minn. 56321.

BLUEPRINT for Social Justice, 10 times a year; Institute of Human Relations, Loyola University, New Orleans, La. 70118.

Bringing Religion Home, m; 221 W. Madison St., Chicago, Ill. 60606.

Brothers, q; P.O. Box 26, Liguori, Mo. 63057. National Assembly of Religious Brothers.

Call Board, The, 5 times a year; 1501 Broadway, Suite 2400, New York, N.Y. 10036; Catholic Actors' Guild.

Camillian: Journal of the National Association of Catholic Chaplains, q; 325 S. Lake Dr., Milwaukee, Wis. 53207; National Association of Catholic Chaplains.

Carmelite Review, The, m; 29 N. Broadway, Joliet, Ill. 60435; Canadian-American Province of Carmelite Order.

Catechist, The, m (exc. Dec., June-Aug.); 2451 E. River Rd., Dayton, O. 45439.

Catholic Aid News, m; 49 W. 9th St., St. Paul, Minn. 55102.

Catholic Biblical Quarterly, q; Catholic University of America, Washington, D.C. 20064; Catholic Biblical Assn.

Catholic Cemetery, The, m; 710 N. River Rd., Des Plaines, Ill. 60016; National Catholic Cemetery Conference.

Catholic Digest, The, m; P.O. Box 43090, St. Paul, Minn. 55164.

Catholic Evangelist, The, six times a year; 119 N.W. 11th St., P. O. Box 1282, Boca Raton, Fla. 33432. Catholic Evangelism, Inc.

Catholic Forester Magazine, bm; 305 W. Madison St., Chicago, Ill. 60606; Catholic Order of Foresters.

CGA World Magazine, bm; National Headquarters, Catholic Golden Age, Scranton, Pa. 18503.

Catholic Historical Review, q; 620 Michigan Ave. N.E., Washington, D.C. 20064; American Catholic Historical Assn.

CHA in Washington, The, m; 4455 Woodson Rd., St. Louis, Mo. 63134; Catholic Health Association.

Catholic Journalist, The, m; 119 N. Park Ave., Rockville Centre, N.Y. 11570; Catholic Press Association.

C.K. of A. Journal, m; 217 E. 8th St., Cincinnati, O. 45202; Catholic Knights of America.

C.L. of C. Index, m; 2770 E. Main St., Columbus, O. 43209.

Catholic Lawyer, q; St. John's University, Jamaica, N.Y. 11439; St. Thomas More Institute for Legal Research.

Catholic League Newsletter, m; 1100 W. Wells St., Milwaukee, Wis. 53233; Catholic League for Religious and Civil Rights.

Catholic Library World, 10 times a year; 461 W. Lancaster Ave., Haverford, Pa. 19041; Catholic Library Association.

Catholic Life Magazine, m (exc. July-Aug.); 35750 Moravian Dr., Fraser, Mich. 48026; PIME Missionaries.

Catholic Mind, The, m (exc. July-Aug.); 106 W. 56th St., New York, N.Y. 10019.

Catholic Near East Magazine, q; 1011 First Ave., New York, N.Y. 10022; Catholic Near East Welfare Assn.

Catholic Periodical and Literature Index, bm; 461 W. Lancaster Ave., Haverford, Pa. 19041; Catholic Library Association.

Catholic Pharmacist, q; 1012 Surrey Hills Dr., St. Louis, Mo. 63117; National Catholic Pharmacists Guild.

Catholic Press Directory, a; 119 N. Park Ave. Rockville Centre, N.Y. 11570; Catholic Press Assn.

Catholic Quote, m; Valparaiso, Nebr. 68065; Rev. Jerome Pokorny.

CRS News, q; 1011 First Ave., New York, N.Y. 10022. Catholic Relief Services.

Catholic Review (Braille), m; 154 E. 23rd St., New York, N.Y. 10010; Xavier Society for the Blind.

Catholic Rural Life, m; 4625 N.W. Beaver Dr., Des Moines, Ia. 50322; National Catholic Rural Life Conference.

Catholic Trends, biweekly; 1312 Massachusetts

Ave. N.W. Washington, D.C. 20005; NC News Service.

Catholic University of America Law Review, q; Washington, D.C. 20064.

Catholic Update, m; 1615 Republic St., Cincinnati, O. 45210.

Catholic War Veteran, bm; 2 Massachusetts Ave. N.W., Washington, D.C. 20001.

Catholic Woman, bm; 1312 Massachusetts Ave. N.W., Washington, D.C. 20005. National Council of Catholic Women.

Catholic Woman's Journal, 10 times a year; 3835 Westminster Pl., St. Louis, Mo. 63108; National Catholic Women's Union.

Catholic Worker, 9 times a year; 36 E. First St., New York, N.Y. 10003.

Catholic Workman, m; 111 W. Main, P.O. Box 47, New Prague, Minn. 56071.

Catholic Youth Ministry, 10 times a year; 22 Willow St., Mystic, Conn. 06355.

Celebration, m; 115 East Armour Blvd., Kansas City, Mo. 64111; National Catholic Reporter Publishing Co.

Center Journal, q; 237 N. Michigan St., P.O. Box A, Notre Dame, Ind. 46556; Center for Christian Studies.

Charities USA, m; 1346 Connecticut Ave. N.W., Washington, D.C. 20036; National Conference of Catholic Charities.

Chicago Studies, 3 times a year; P.O. Box 665, Mundelein, Ill. 60060.

Christian Life Communities Harvest, 6 times a year; 3721 Westminster Pl., St. Louis, Mo. 63108; National Federation of Christian Life Communities.

Christian Renewal News, P.O. Box 467, La Puente, Calif. 91747. Apostolate of Christian Renewal.

Christopher News Notes, 7 times a year; 12 E. 48th St., New York, N.Y. 10017; The Christophers, Inc.

City of God, The, 3 times a year; 4545 Northwestern Ave., Indianapolis, Ind. 46208; St. Maur Theological Center.

Clarion, The, 6 times a year; Notre Dame, Alfred, Maine 04002; Brothers of Christian Instruction.

Claverite, The, biannually; 554 Palmetto St., P.O. Box 204, Mobile, Ala. 36601; Knights of Peter Claver.

Columban Mission, m (exc. June, Aug.); St. Columbans, Nebr. 68056; Columban Fathers.

Columbia, m; One Columbus Plaza, New Haven, Conn. 06507; Knights of Columbus.

Columbian, The, w; 188 W. Randolph St., Chicago, Ill. 60601.

Comboni Missions, 6 times a year; 8108 Beechmont Ave., Cincinnati, O. 45230.

Commitment, q; 1200 Varnum St. N.E., Washington, D.C. 20017; National Catholic Conference for Interracial Justice.

Commonweal, biweekly; 232 Madison Ave., New York, N.Y. 10016.

Communio — International Catholic Review, q; Gonzaga University, Spokane, Wash. 99202.

Community, irregularly; 1746 W. Division St., Chicago, Ill. 60622; Friendship House.

Consecrated Life, semi-annually; 4200 N. Austin Ave., Chicago, Ill. 60634; Institute on Religious Life. English edition of *Informationes,* official publication of Sacred Congregation for Religious and Secular Institutes.

Consolata, 6 times a year; P.O. Box C, Somerset, N.J. 08873.

Contact, 10 times a year; 123-15 14 Ave., College Point, N.Y. 11356; Sisters of St. Dominic.

Contemplative Review, q; Beckley Hill, Barre, Vt. 05641; Association of Contemplative Sisters.

Context, 22 issues a year; 221 W. Madison St., Chicago, Ill. 60606.

Cord, The, m; P.O. Drawer F, St. Bonaventure, N.Y. 14778.

Counseling and Values, q; 2 Skyline Place, Suite 400, 5203 Leesburg Pike, Falls Church, Va. 22041; Association for Religious and Value Issues in Counseling.

Crescat, 3 times a year; Belmont Abbey, Belmont, N.C. 28012; Benedictine Monks.

Cross Currents, q; Mercy College, 555 Broadway, Dobbs Ferry, N.Y. 10522.

Crossroads Radio Centre, bm; 1089 Elm St., W. Springfield, Mass. 01089.

Crusader's Almanac, The, biannually; 1400 Quincy St. N.E., Washington, D.C. 20017; Commissariat of the Holy Land.

CRUX of the News, w; 75 Champlain St., Albany, N.Y. 12204.

Damien-Dutton Call, q; 616 Bedford Ave., Bellmore, N.Y. 11710.

Damien Report, The, m; 131 Kuulei Rd., Kailua, H.I. 96734.

Daystar, a; 172 Foster St., Brighton, Mass. 02135; Franciscan Missionary Sisters for Africa.

Deaf Blind Weekly, The (Braille), w; 154 E. 23rd St., New York, N.Y. 10010; Xavier Society for the Blind.

Desert Call, q; SLIA-Nada, Box 260, Crestone, Colo. 81131; Spiritual Life Institute of America.

Diakonia, 3 times a year; Fordham Univ., Bronx, N.Y. 10458; John XXIII Center for Eastern Christian Studies.

Dimensions, m; 119 N. Park Ave., Rockville Centre, N.Y. 11570; National Catholic Development Conference.

Divine Love, q; P.O. Box 24, Fresno, Calif. 93707.

Divine Word Messenger, semiannually; Bay St. Louis, Miss. 39520.

Divine Word Missionaries, q; Techny, Ill. 60082.

Ecumenical Trends, m (exc. July-Aug.); Graymoor Ecumenical Institute, Garrison, N.Y. 10524.

Ecumenist, The, 6 times a year; Paulist Press, 545 Island Rd., Ramsey, N.J. 07446.

Educating in Faith, q; 2021 H St. N.W., Washington, D.C. 20006. Catholic Negro-American Mission Board.

Emmanuel, m (bm July-Aug.); 194 E. 76th St., New York, N.Y. 10021; Blessed Sacrament Fathers.

Emmaus Letter, q; 3025 Fourth St. N.E., Washington, D.C. 20017. Federation for Catholic Youth Ministry.

Envoy, q; Office of Public Affairs, Catholic University of America, Washington, D.C. 20064.

Envoy, Journal of Formative Reading, bm; Institute of Formative Spirituality, Duquesne Univ., Pittsburgh, Pa. 15282.

Extension, m; 35 E. Wacker Dr., Suite 400, Chicago, Ill. 60601; Catholic Church Extension Society.

Family, m; 50 St. Paul's Ave., Boston, Mass. 02130; Daughters of St. Paul.

Family Festivals, bm; Resource Publications, 7291 Cornoado Dr., San Jose, Calif. 95129.

Family Friend, q; P.O. Box 11563, Milwaukee, Wis. 53211; Catholic Family Life Insurance.

Fatima Findings, m; 100 E. 20th St., Baltimore, Md. 21218; Reparation Society of the Immaculate Heart of Mary.

Fellowship of Catholic Scholars Newsletter, q; St. John's University, Jamaica, N.Y. 11439.

Filipino Catholic Newsmagazine, semimonthly; 114 E. 2nd St., Los Angeles, Calif. 90012; Filipino Catholic Publications, Inc.

Franciscan Herald, m; 1434 W. 51st St., Chicago, Ill. 60609.

F.M.A. Focus, q; 274-280 W. Lincoln Ave., Mt. Vernon, N.Y. 10550; Franciscan Mission Associates.

Franciscan Reporter, q; 3140 Meramec St., St. Louis, Mo. 63138.

Franciscan Studies, a; St. Bonaventure, N.Y. 14778; Franciscan Institute.

Fraternal Leader, bm; 305 W. 6th St., Erie, Pa. 16512; Loyal Christian Benefit Association.

Fund Raising Forum, m; 119 N. Park Ave., Rockville Centre, N.Y. 11570; National Catholic Development Conference.

Garsas (Lithuanian-English), m; 341 Highland Blvd., Brooklyn, N.Y. 11207; Lithuanian Roman Catholic Alliance of America.

Generation, m; 221 W. Madison St., Chicago, Ill. 60606.

Glenmary Challenge, The, q; P.O. Box 46404, Cincinnati, O. 45246; Glenmary Home Missioners.

God's Word Today, m; Box 40664, St. Petersburg, Fla. 33743.

Good News, m; 3003 S. Congress Ave., Lake Worth, Fla. 33461; Sunday Publications, Inc.

Good Shepherd (Dobry Pastier) (Slovak and English), a; 425 W. 12th Ave., Gary, Ind. 46407; Slovak Catholic Federation of America.

Goose Corn, 10 issues a year; 221 W. Madison St., Chicago, Ill. 60606.

Harmony, 4 or 5 times a year; 8300 Morganford Rd., St. Louis, Mo. 63123; Benedictine Srs. of Perpetual Adoration.

Holy Land, The, q; 1400 Quincy St. N.E., Washington, D.C. 20017; Custody of Holy Land.

Holy Name Newsletter, m (exc. July and Dec.); P.O. Box 4033, Rocky Mount, N.C. 27801; National Association of the Holy Name Society.

Homiletic and Pastoral Review, m; 86 Riverside Dr., New York, N.Y. 10024.

Horizons: Journal of the College Theology Society, biannual; Villanova University, Villanova, Pa. 19085.

Hospital Progress, m; 4455 Woodson Rd., St. Louis, Mo. 63134; Catholic Health Association.

Human Development, q; Jesuit Educational Center, 53 Park Pl., New York, N.Y. 10007.

Human Life Issues, q; St. John's University. Collegeville, Minn. 56321; Human Life Center.

I.C. Good News, q; Loyola Center, 5600 City Ave., Philadelphia, Pa. 19131; North City Catholic Conference, Inc.

Immaculata, m; 1600 W. Park Ave., Libertyville, Ill. 60048; Franciscan Fathers.

In-Formation, 8 times a year; 1234 Massachusetts Ave., N.W., Washington, D.C. 20005; Religious Formation Conference.

Institute Journal, bm; 50 Oak St., San Francisco, Calif. 94102; Young Men's Institute.

Integrity, m; 6243 S. Fairfield Ave., Chicago, Ill. 60629; Rev. L. Dudley Day, O.S.A.

International Philosophical Quarterly; Fordham University, Bronx, N.Y. 10458.

International Review — Natural Family Planning, q; St. John's University, Collegeville, Minn. 56321.

It's Our World, 4 times a year; 1720 Massachusetts Ave. N.W., Washington, D.C. 20036. Holy Childhood Association.

Jesuit, The, q; 39 E. 83rd St., New York, N.Y. 10028.

Jesuit Blackrobe, q; 3601 W. Fond du Lac Ave., Milwaukee, Wis. 53216.

Jesuit Bulletin, 4 times a year; 4511 W. Pine Blvd., St. Louis, Mo. 63108; Jesuit Seminary Aid Association.

Josephite Harvest, The, q; 1130 N. Calvert St., Baltimore, Md. 21202; Josephite Missionaries.

Jurist, The, semiannually; Catholic University of America, Washington, D.C. 20064; School of Canon Law.

Katolicky Sokol (Catholic Falcon) (Slovak-English), biweekly; 205 Madison St., Passaic, N.J. 07055; Slovak Catholic Sokol.

Kinship, q; P.O. Box 39188, Cincinnati, O. 45239; Glenmary Sisters.

KIT — Keeping in Touch, m; 1820 Mt. Elliott Ave., Detroit, Mich. 48207; Capuchin Province of St. Joseph.

Knights of St. John, q; 6517 Charles Ave., Cleveland, O. 44129.

Kolping Banner, m; 115-14 227th St., Cambria Heights., N.Y. 11411; Catholic Kolping Society.

Laivas (Lithuanian), m; 4545 W. 63rd St., Chicago, Ill. 60629.

Land of Cotton, q; 2048 W. Fairview Ave., Montgomery, Ala. 39196; City of St. Jude.

Law Briefs, m; 1312 Massachusetts Ave. N.W., Washington, D.C. 20005; Office of General Counsel, USCC.

Law Reports, m; 4455 Woodson Rd., St. Louis, Mo. 63134.

Laywitness, m; 222 North Avenue, P.O. Box S, New Rochelle, N.Y. 10801; Catholics United for the Faith.

Leaven, q; Convent of the Holy Spirit, Techny, Ill. 60082.

Leaves, bm; 23715 Ann Arbor Trail, Dearborn Heights, Mich. 48127; Mariannhill Fathers.

Let's Pray Together, w; 775 Madison Ave., Albany, N.Y. 12208; Families for Prayer.

Liguorian, m; 1 Liguori Rd., Liguori, Mo. 63057; Redemptorist Fathers.

Linacre Quarterly, q; 850 Elm Grove Rd., Elm Grove, Wis. 53122; Federation of Catholic Physicians Guilds.

Listening, 5 times a year; 814 Thayer Ave., Silver Spring, Md. 20910. National Catholic Office for the Deaf.

Liturgy, q; 810 Rhode Island Ave. N.E. Washington, D.C. 20018.

Living Light, The, q; 11 Park Place, New York, N.Y. 10007; Department of Education, USCC.

Marian Helpers Bulletin, q; Stockbridge, Mass. 01262; Association of Marian Helpers and of the Congregation of Marian Fathers.

Marriage and Family Living, m; Abbey Press, St. Meinrad, Ind. 47577.

Marriage Encounter, m; 955 Lake Dr., St. Paul, Minn. 55120; National Marriage Encounter.

Mary Magazine and Aylesford News, bm; Cass Ave. N. at I-55, P.O. Box 65, Darien Ill. 60559; Carmelite Fathers.

Maryknoll, m; Maryknoll, N.Y. 10545; Catholic Foreign Mission Society.

Media and Values, q; 1962 S. Shenandoah, Los Angeles, Calif. 90034; Center for Communications Ministry.

Medical Mission News, bm; 10 W. 17th St., New York, N.Y. 10011; Catholic Medical Mission Board, Inc.

Medical Mission Sisters News, 4 times a year; 8400 Pine Road, Philadelphia, Pa. 19111.

Men of Malvern, bm; Malvern, Pa. 19355; Laymen's Retreat League of Philadelphia.

Messenger of St. Joseph's Union, The, 108 Bedell St., Staten Island, N.Y. 10309.

MHS Review (Franciscanews), q; 232 S. Home Ave., Pittsburgh, Pa. 15202.

Mid-America, 3 times a year; Loyola University, Chicago, Ill. 60626.

Miesiecznik Franciszkanski (Polish), m; 165 E. Pulaski St., Pulaski, Wis. 54162; Franciscan Fathers.

Migration Today, 5 times a year; 209 Flagg Pl., Staten Island, N.Y. 10304; Center for Migration Studies.

Miraculous Medal, The, q; 475 E. Chelten Ave., Philadelphia, Pa. 19144; Central Association of the Miraculous Medal.

Mission, 5 times a year; 366 Fifth Ave., New York, N.Y. 10001; Society for Propagation of the Faith.

Mission, bm; 1663 Bristol Pike, Bensalem, Pa. 19020; Sisters of the Blessed Sacrament.

Mission Handbook, a; 1233 Lawrence St. N.E.;

Washington, D.C. 20017. United States Catholic Mission Association.

Mission Helper, The, q; 1001 W. Joppa Rd., Baltimore, Md. 21204; Mission Helpers of the Sacred Heart.

Missionhurst, 6 times a year; 4651 N. 25th St., Arlington, Va. 22207; Immaculate Heart of Mary Mission Society, Inc.

Mission Intercom, 10 times a year; 1233 Lawrence St., N.E., Washington, D.C. 20017; U.S. Catholic Mission Association.

Missionaries of Africa Report, bm; 1622 21st St. N.W., Washington, D.C. 20009; Society of Missionaries of Africa (White Fathers).

Modern Liturgy, 9 times a year; Resource Publications, 7291 Coronado Dr., San Jose, Calif. 95129.

Modern Schoolman, The, q; 3700 W. Pine Blvd., St. Louis, Mo. 63108; St. Louis University.

Momentum, 4 times a year; Suite 100, 1077 30th St., Washington, D.C. 20017; National Catholic Educational Asssociation.

Mother Cabrini Messenger, bm; 434 W. Deming Pl., Chicago, Ill. 60614; Mother Cabrini League.

Mountain Spirit, The, 6 times a year; 322 Crab Orchard Rd., Lancaster, Ky. 40446; ecumenical; Christian Appalachian Project.

MSC Spotlite, q; 305 S. Lake St., Aurora, Ill. 60507; Missionaries of the Sacred Heart.

My Daily Visitor, bm; 200 Noll Plaza, Huntington, Ind. 46750; Our Sunday Visitor, Inc.

My Friend, 10 times a year; 50 St. Paul's Ave., Jamaica Plain, Boston, Mass. 02130; for children.

National Catholic Forester, q; 35 E. Wacker Dr., Chicago, Ill. 60601.

NFPC News, 8 times a year; 1307 S. Wabash, Chicago, Ill. 60605; National Federation of Priests' Councils.

National Jesuit News, m; St. Joseph's University, Philadelphia, Pa. 19131.

National Service Committee Newsletter, 10 times a year; 237 N. Michigan St., South Bend, Ind. 46601; Catholic Charismatic Renewal.

Network Quarterly; Newsletter, bm; 806 Rhode Island Ave. N.E., Washington, D.C. 20018; Network.

New Catholic World, bm; 545 Island Rd., Ramsey, N.J. 07446.

New Covenant, m; P.O. Box 8617, Ann Arbor, Mich. 48107; Catholic Charismatic Renewal.

New Scholasticism, q; 715 Memorial Library, Notre Dame, Ind. 46556. American Catholic Philosophical Association.

News/Views, 5 times a year; 1307 S. Wabash Ave., Chicago, Ill. 60605; National Sisters Vocation Conference.

News and Views, q; 3900 Westminster Pl.; St. Louis, Mo. 63108; Sacred Heart Program.

Newsletter of the Bureau of Catholic Indian Missions, 10 times a year; 2021 H St. N.W., Washington, D.C. 20006.

North American Voice of Fatima, m; 1023 Swann Rd., Youngstown, N.Y. 14174.

Notre Dame Magazine, 5 times a year; Notre Dame Univ., Notre Dame, Ind. 46556.

Nursing Sisters Today, q; 310 Prospect Park W., Brooklyn, N.Y. 11215; Congregation of Infant Jesus.

Oblate World and Voice of Hope, bm; 350 Jamaica Way, Boston, Mass. 02130; Oblates of Mary Immaculate.

Origins, 48 times a year; 1312 Massachusetts Ave., N.W., Washington, D.C. 20005; NC News Service.

Our Lady of the Snows Newsletter, bm; 15 S. 59th St., Belleville, Ill. 62222; Shrine of Our Lady of the Snows.

Our Lady's Digest, q; Box 777, Twin Lakes, Wis. 53181; La Salette Fathers.

Our Lady's Missionary, m; 315 Topsfield Rd., Ipswich, Mass. 01938; La Salette Fathers.

Pacer, bm; 500 17th Ave., Seattle, Wash. 98124; Providence Medical Center.

Padres' Trail, 4 times a year; St. Michael's Mission, St. Michael, Ariz. 86511; Franciscan Fathers.

Paraclete, 4 times a year; P.O. Box 2000, Wheaton, Md. 20902; Holy Ghost Fathers.

Parish Communication, 10 times a year, 22 Willow St., Mystic, Conn. 06355.

Pastoral Life, m; Route 224, Canfield, Ohio 44406; Society of St. Paul.

Pastoral Music, 6 times a year; 225 Sheridan St., N.W. Washington, D.C. 20011; National Association of Pastoral Musicians.

Paulist Fathers News, 6 times a year; 301 Island Rd., Mahwah, N.J. 07430.

People of God Messenger, 10 times a year; 202 Morningside Dr. S.E., Albuquerque, N.M. 87108; Santa Fe archdiocesan office of communications.

Perpetual Help World, q; 294 E. 150th St., Bronx, N.Y. 10451; Redemptorists.

Philosophy Today, q; Carthagena Station, Celina, Ohio 45822.

Pilgrim, q; Jesuit Fathers, Auriesville, N.Y. 12016; Shrine of North American Martyrs.

Pope Speaks, The, q; Our Sunday Visitor, Inc., 200 Noll Plaza, Huntington, Ind. 46750.

Priatel Dietok (Children's Friend) (Slovak), bm; 205 Madison St., Passaic, N.J. 07055; Slovak Catholic Sokol.

Priest, The, 11 times a year; 200 Noll Plaza, Huntington, Ind. 46750; Our Sunday Visitor, Inc.

Probe, bm (Sept.-June); 1307 S. Wabash Ave., Chicago, Ill. 60605; NAWR.

Professional Placement Newsnotes, bm; 10 W. 17th St., New York, N.Y. 10011; Catholic Medical Mission Board, Inc.

Program Supplement, 18 times a year; Columbus Plaza, New Haven, Conn. 06507; Knights of Columbus.

Provincial Annals, irregularly; Siena College, Loudonville, N.Y. 12211. Holy Name Province, Order of Friars Minor.

Quarterly, The, 2021 H St. N.W., Washington, D.C. 20006; Commission for Catholic Missions Among the Colored People and the Indians.

Queen; bm; 26 S. Saxon Ave., Bay Shore, N.Y. 11706; Montfort Fathers.

Reign of the Sacred Heart, m; Hales Corners, Wis. 53130.

Religion Teacher's Journal, m (Sept.-May); P.O. Box 180, Mystic, Conn. 06355.

Religious Life, m (bm, May-Aug.); 4200 N. Austin Ave., Chicago, Ill. 60634; Institute on Religious Life.

Renascence, q; Marquette University, Milwaukee, Wis. 53233.

Respect Life Report, m; 1312 Massachusetts Ave. N.W., Washington, D.C. 20005; Committee for Pro-Life Activities, NCCB.

Response, The, annual; 1234 Massachusetts Ave. N.W., Washington, D.C. 20005; International Liaison.

Review for Religious, bm; Room 428, 3601 Lindell Blvd., St. Louis, Mo. 63108.

Review of Politics, q; Box B, Notre Dame, Ind. 46556.

Review of Social Economy, 3 times a year; 25 E. Jackson Blvd., Chicago, Ill. 60604; Association for Social Economics.

Revista Maryknoll (Spanish-English), m; Maryknoll, N.Y. 10545; Catholic Foreign Mission Society of America.

Roze Maryi (Polish), m; Eden Hill, Stockbridge, Mass. 01262; Marian Fathers.

Sacred Music, q; 548 Lafond Ave., St. Paul, Minn. 55103.

St. Anthony Messenger, m; 1615 Republic St., Cincinnati, O. 45210; Franciscan Fathers.

St. Anthony's Newsletter, m; Mt. St. Francis, Ind. 47146.

St. Joseph's Messenger and Advocate of the Blind, q; St. Joseph Home, P.O. Box 288, Jersey City, N.J. 07303.

Salesian Bulletin, bm; 148 Main St., New Rochelle, N.Y. 10802; Salesian Fathers.

Salesian Missions, q; 148 Main St., New Rochelle, N.Y. 10802; Salesians of St. John Bosco.

Salt, m; 221 W. Madison St., Chicago, Ill. 60606; Claretians.

Salvatorian Newsletter, The, q; Society of the Divine Savior, Salvatorian Center, Wis. 53062.

Sandal Prints, bm; 1820 Mt. Elliott Ave., Detroit, Mich. 48207; Capuchin Fathers.

Scalabrinians, 3 times a year; 209 Flagg Pl., Staten Island, N.Y. 10304.

School Guide, a; 80 W. Broad St., Mt. Vernon, N.Y. 10552.

School Sister, The, q; Notre Dame of the Lake, Mequon, Wis. 53092; Sisters of Notre Dame.

SCRC Vision, The, m; 5730 W. Manchester Ave., Los Angeles, Calif. 90045; Southern California Renewal Communities.

Scripture in Church, 4 times a year; P.O. Box 9, Northport, N.Y. 11768.

Serenity, q; 601 Maiden Choice Lane, Baltimore, Md. 21228; Little Sisters of the Poor.

Serran, The, bm; 22 W. Monroe St., Chicago, Ill. 60603; Serra International.

Share, 1312 Massachusetts Ave. N.W., Washington, D.C. 20005; Dept. of Communications, USCC.

Share, q; 4545 Connecticut Ave. N.W., Washington, D.C. 20008. Catholic Daughters of the Americas.

Share the Word, bm; 3031 Fourth St. N.E., Washington, D.C. 20017; Paulist Catholic Evangelist Center.

Shepherd's Call, The, q; 901 Thirteenth St., N.W., Albuquerque, N.M. 87103; Brothers of Good Shepherd.

Silent Advocate, bm; St. Rita School for the Deaf, 1720 Glendale-Milford Rd., Cincinnati, O. 45215.

Sister Miriam Teresa League of Prayer Bulletin, q; League Headquarters, Convent Station, N.J. 07961.

SC News, m (Sept.-May); 4400 Churchman Ave., Louisville, Ky. 40215; Sisters of Charity of Nazareth.

Sisters Today, m (exc. July-Aug.); Liturgical Press, Collegeville, Minn. 56321.

Social Justice Review, bm; 3835 Westminster Pl., St. Louis, Mo. 63108; Catholic Central Union of America.

Social Thought, q; 1346 Connecticut Ave. N.W., Washington, D.C. 20036; National Conference of Catholic Charities.

Sophia, m; P.O. Box 265, Newton Center, Mass. 02159; Newton Melkite eparchy.

Soul, bm; Mountain View Rd., Washington, N.J. 07882; Blue Army.

Southern Jesuits, The, 3 times a year; 211 Pere Marquette Bldg., New Orleans, La. 70112.

Spectrum, q; 1011 First Ave., New York, N.Y. 10022; Catholic Relief Services.

Spirit, biannually; Seton Hall University, South Orange, N.J. 07079; poetry magazine.

Spirit and Life, 6 times a year; 8300 Morganford Rd., St. Louis, Mo. 63123; Benedictine Srs. of Perpetual Adoration.

Spirit and the Bride, The, 10 times a year; 4140 Lindell Blvd., St. Louis, Mo. 63108; Catholic Charismatic Renewal Office.

Spiritual Book News, 8 times a year; Notre Dame, Ind. 46556.

Spiritual Life, q; 2131 Lincoln Rd. N.E., Washington, D.C. 20002; Discalced Carmelites.

Spirituality Today (formerly Cross and Crown), q; 1909 S. Ashland Ave., Chicago, Ill. 60608, Dominican Fathers.

Squires Newsletter, m; Columbus Plaza, New Haven, Conn. 06507; Columbian Squires.

Star, 10 times a year; 18 W. Bijou, Colorado Springs, Colo. 80903.

Strain Forward, 11 times a year; 50 St. Paul's Avenue, Jamaica Plain, Boston, Mass. 02130; Daughters of St. Paul.

Studies in Formative Spirituality, 3 times a year; Institute of Formative Spirituality, Duquesne Univ., Pittsburgh, Pa. 15282.

Studies in the Spirituality of Jesuits, 5 times a year; 3700 W. Pine Blvd., St. Louis, Mo. 63108.

Tekakwitha Conference Newsletter, q; 1818 Ninth Ave. So. No. 5, Great Falls, Mont. 59405.

Theological Studies, q; Georgetown Univ., 37th and O Sts., N.W., Washington, D.C. 20057.

Theology Digest, q; 3634 Lindell Blvd., St. Louis, Mo. 63108.

Theresian News, The, 6 times a year; 5326 E. Pershing Ave., Scottsdale, Ariz. 85254.

Thirsting for Justice, q; 1312 Massachusetts Ave. N.W. Washington, D.C. 20005, Campaign for Human Development.

This Week, w; 135 W. 31st St., New York, N.Y. 10001; Franciscan Communication Office, Holy Name Province.

Thomist, The, q; 487 Michigan Ave. N.E., Washington, D.C. 20017; Dominican Fathers.

Thought, q; Fordham University Press, Box L, Bronx, N.Y. 10458; Fordham University.

Today's Catholic Teacher, m (Sept.-May); 2451 E. River Rd., Suite 200, Dayton, O. 45439.

Today's Parish, m (Sept.-May); P.O. Box 180, Mystic, Conn. 06355.

To Him She Leads, q; Michigan Ave. and 4th St. E., Washington, D.C.; National Shrine of the Immaculate Conception.

Topic, semi-annually; 151 Thompson St., New York, N.Y. 10012. Secular Franciscan Order, Province of Immaculate Conception.

Trinity Missions Magazine, q; P.O. Box 7130, Silver Springs, Md. 20907.

Trinity Review, bm; 3606 Coolcrest Dr., P.O. Box 169, Jefferson, Md. 21755.

Ultreya Magazine, m; 4500 W. Davis St., Dallas, Tex. 75211. Cursillo Movement.

L'Union (French), bm; 1 Social St., Woonsocket, R.I. 02895.

UNIREA, The Union (Romanian and English), m; 4309 Olcott Ave., East Chicago, Ind. 46312.

U.S. Catholic, m; 221 W. Madison St., Chicago, Ill. 60606; Claretian Fathers and Brothers.

Venture, 26 times during school year; 2451 E. River Rd., Dayton, O. 45439, Pflaum Press. Intermediate grades.

Vision, 3 times a year; P.O. Box 28185, San Antonio, Tex. 78228. Mexican American Cultural Center.

Visions, 26 times during school year; 2451 E. River Rd., Dayton, O. 45439; Pflaum Press.

Vox Regis Alumni Newsletter, 3 times a year; 711 Knox Rd., East Aurora, N.Y. 14052; Christ the King Seminary.

Waif's Messenger, q; 1140 W. Jackson Blvd., Chicago, Ill. 60607; Mission of Our Lady of Mercy.

Way — of St. Francis, bm; 109 Golden Gate Ave., San Francisco, Calif. 94102; Franciscan Friars of California, Inc.

Western Catholic Union Record, m; 906 W.C.U. Bldg., Quincy, Ill. 62301; Western Catholic Union.

Wheeling College Chronicle, 4 times a year; 316 Washington Ave., Wheeling, W. Va. 26003.

Word of God, w; 2187 Victory Blvd., Staten Island, N.Y. 10314; Society of St. Paul.

Working for Boys, q; Box A, Danvers, Mass. 01923; Xaverian Brothers.

Worship, 6 times a year; St. John's Abbey, Collegeville, Minn. 56321. North American Academy of Liturgy.

Xaverian Missions Newsletter, 101 Summer St., Holliston, Mass. 01746; Xaverian Missionary Fathers.

Your Edmundite Missions Newsletter, bm; 1428 Broad St., Selma, Ala. 36701; Southern Missions of Society of St. Edmund.

Zeal Magazine, q; St. Elizabeth Mission Society of the Sisters of St. Francis, N. Main St., Allegany, N.Y. 14706.

FOREIGN CATHOLIC PERIODICALS

Principal source: Catholic Almanac survey. Included are English-language Catholic periodicals published outside the U.S.

African Ecclesial Review (AFER), bm; Gaba Publications, P.O. Box 908, Eldoret, Kenya.

Australasian Catholic Record, q; St. Patrick's Seminary, Manly, New South Wales, Australia.

Christ to the World, bm; Via di Propaganda 1-C, 00187, Rome, Italy.

Clergy Review, m; 48 Great Peter St., London, SW1P 2HB, England.

Doctrine and Life, m, and Supplement to Doctrine and Life, bm; Dominican Publications, St. Saviour's, Dublin 1, Ireland.

Downside Review, q; Newman Bookshop, 87 St. Aldates, Oxford, England.

Dublin Review, q; 14 Howick Place, London, S.W. 1, England.

East Asian Pastoral Review, q; East Asian Pastoral Institute, P.O. Box 1815, Manila, Philippines.

Eastern Churches Review, semi-annual; 9 Alfred St., Oxford, England.

Faith Today, 10 times a year; Dominican Publications, St. Saviour's, Dublin 1, Ireland.

Furrow, m; St. Patrick's College, Maynooth, Ireland.

Heythrop Journal q; Heythrop College, 11 Cavendish Sq., London W1M, OAN, England (Editorial Office).

Irish Biblical Studies, q; Union Theological College, Belfast BT7 1JT, N. Ireland.

Irish Theological Quarterly, q; St. Patrick's College, Maynooth, Ireland.

L'Osservatore Romano, w; Vatican City.

Louvain Studies, semi-annual; Naamsestraat 100 B-3000, Louvain, Belgium.

Lumen Vitae, q; International Center for Studies in Religious Education, 184, rue Washington, 1050 Brussels, Belgium.

Maynooth Review, q; St. Patrick's College, Maynooth, Ireland.

Mediaeval Studies, annual; Pontifical Institute of Mediaeval Studies, 59 Queen's Park Crescent East, Toronto, Ont., Canada M5S 2C4.

Month, m; 114 Mount St., London, WIY, 6AH, England.

Music and Liturgy, q; Barnsthorn, Ockham Rd., North, West Horsley, Leatherhead, Surrey, England.

New Blackfriars, m; edited by English Dominicans, Blackfriars, Oxford, England.

One in Christ, q; Turvey Abbey, Turvey, Beds. MK43 8DE, England.

Recusant History, biannual; Catholic Record Society, 114 Mount St., London, W1Y 6AH, England.

Religion and Society, q; Christian Institute for the Study of Religion and Society, 17 Miller Rd., P.O. Box 4600, Bangalore 560 046, India.

Social Studies, q; St. Patrick's College, Maynooth, Ireland.

Studies in Religion/Sciences Religieuses (bilingual), q; Wilfrid Laurier University Press, Waterloo, Ont., Canada N2L 3C5.

Sursum Corda—Lift Up Your Hearts, bm; Box 79, Box Hill, Victoria, Australia 3128.

Tablet, The w; 48 Great Peter St., SW1P 2HB, London, England.

Teilhard Review, The, 3 times a year; The Teilhard Centre for the Future of Man, 23 Kensington Square, London W8 5 HN, England.

Theology, bm; S.P.C.K. Holy Trinity Church, Marylebone Rd., London, NW1 4DU, England.

Way, The, q; and Supplements to The Way, triannual: 39 Fitzjohn's Ave., London NW3 5JT, England.

CATHOLIC NEWS AGENCIES

(Sources: International Catholic Union of the Press, Geneva; Catholic Press Association, U.S.)

Argentina: Agencia Informativa Catolica Argentina (AICA), Rodriguez Pena 846, 4º Casilla de Correo Central 2886, Buenos Aires.

Austria: Katholische Presse-Agentur (Kathpress), Singerstrasse 6.2, 1010 Vienna 1.

Belgium: Centre d'Information de Presse (CIP), 1 Bd. Charlemagne, 1041 Bruxelles (Brussels).

Germany: Katholische Nachrichten Agentur (KNA), Adenauer Allee 134, 5300 Bonn 1.

Great Britain: Catholic Information Office of England and Wales (CIOEW), St. Vincent's Convent, Carlisle Place, London SW1P 1NL.

Greece: Agence TYPOS Rue Acharnon 246, Athenes 815.

Hong Kong: UCA-News, P.O. Box 9791, Hong Kong.

Hungary: Magyar Kurir, Karolyi w 4-8, Postafiok 41, Budapest V.

India: South Asia Religious News (SAR-News), P.O. Box 4228, New Delhi 110.048.

Italy: Servizio Informazioni Settimanali (SIS-Roma) 1, via della Conciliazione, I-00193 Roma.

Centrum Informationis Catolicae (CIC-Roma), via Domenico Silveri, 30, I-00165 Roma.

Spain: Prensa Asociada (PA), Alfonso XI, 4—Apartado 14530, Madrid 14.

Switzerland: Katholische Internationale Presse-Agentur (KIPA), Case Postale 1054 CH 1701, Fribourg.

Centre International de Reportages et d'Information Culturelle (CIRIC), 10, av. de la Gare-des-Eaux Vives, CH-1207 Geneva.

United States of America: NC News Service (NC), 1312 Massachusetts Ave. N.W., Washington, D.C. 20005.

Yugoslavia: Aktusinosti Krscanska Sadasnjost

(AKSA), Marulicev TRG 14, Zagreb p.p. 02-748.
Zaire: Documentation et Information Africaine (DIA), B.P. 2598, Kinshasa I.
Missions: Agenzia Internationale Fides (AIF), Palazzo di Propagande Fide, Via di Propaganda I-c, 00187 Rome, Italy.

Agencies distributing news related to Catholicism as well as other news are:
France: Agence France Presse (AFP), 13 Place de la Bourse, Paris 2e.
Italy: Agenzia Nazionale Stampa Associata (ANSA), Via Propaganda 27, Rome.
United States of America: Religious News Service (RNS), 43 W. 57th St., New York, N.Y. 10019.

U.S. PRESS SERVICES

National Catholic News Service (NC), established in 1920, provides a worldwide daily news report by wire throughout the U.S. and into Canada, Europe and Australia, and by mail to other subscribers, serving Catholic publications and broadcasters including Vatican Radio, and institutional subscribers in more than 40 countries. NC also provides feature and photo services and a weekly religious education package, "Know Your Faith." It publishes "Origins," a weekly documentary service, and "Catholic Trends," a fortnightly newsletter. NC maintains a full-time bureau in Rome. It is a division of the United States Catholic Conference, with offices at 1312 Massachusetts Ave. N.W., Washington, D.C. 20005. The director and editor-in-chief is Richard W. Daw.
Religious News Service (RNS) provides domestic and foreign Catholic and other religious

news in daily photos and features; "The Religious News Reporter," a weekly 15-minute radio and/or TV package; "The Week in Religion," a feature. RNS was inaugurated in 1933 by the National Conference of Christians and Jews as an independent news agency. Its offices are located at 43 W. 57th St., New York, N.Y. 10019.
Eastern Rite Information Service (ER), for Eastern Church news; 2208 W. Chicago Ave., Chicago, Ill. 60622.
Spanish-Language Service: A weekly news summary, *Resumen Semanal de Noticias,* provided by NC News Service, is used by a number of diocesan newspapers. Some papers carry features of their own in Spanish.

BOOKS

The Official Catholic Directory, annual, P. J. Kenedy and Sons, 866 Third Ave., New York, N.Y. 10022. First edition, 1817.
The Catholic Almanac, annual; Our Sunday Visitor, Inc., 200 Noll Plaza, Huntington, Ind. 46750, publisher; editorial offices, 620 Route 3, Clifton, N.J. 07013. First edition, 1904.

BOOK CLUBS

Catholic Book Club (1928), 106 W. 56th St., New York, N.Y. 10019. Sponsors the Campion Award.
Catholic Digest Book Club (1954), Catholic Digest Magazine, P.O. Box 43090, St. Paul, Minn. 55164.
Herald Book Club (1958), Franciscan Herald Press, 1434 W. 51st St., Chicago, Ill. 60609.
Thomas More Book Club (1939), Thomas More Association, 225 W. Huron St., Chicago, Ill. 60610.

CATHOLIC WRITERS' MARKET

(Source: Almanac survey.)
Editors call the following suggestions to the attention of writers:
Manuscripts should be typewritten, double-spaced, on one side of the page.
Writers should know the editorial policy, purpose and style of the publication to which they submit manuscripts. Sample copies may easily be obtained, often for the mere cost of postage. Some editors suggest that writers send outlines of proposed material, in order to facilitate editorial decision and direction. "Timely" copy should be submitted considerably in advance of the date of proposed publication; some editors advise a period of three months. Authors are urged to avoid sermonizing. Writers should not expect extensive criticism of their work, although they should profit from advice and direction when these are given. Editors are not required to state their reasons for rejecting manuscripts. Replies regarding the acceptance or rejection of copy are usually made within a few weeks.
All writers should send to editors stamped, self-addressed envelopes for the return of material. Those who write to Canadian editors may use international reply coupons, not U.S. stamps.
Payment is made on acceptance or publication. Rates are sometimes variable because of the reputation of the writer, the quality and length of the

manuscript, the amount of editorial work required for its final preparation.
America: 106 W. 56th St., New York, N.Y. 10019. Ed., Rev. Joseph A O'Hare, S.J. Weekly, circulation 37,000; $21 per year.
ARTICLES on important public issues evaluated scientifically and morally; serious and authenticated articles on family life, education, religion, and social and political issues with ethical or religious implications; occasionally, "thought" pieces; 1,000-2,000 words — 3¢ a word. VERSE, short and modern, befitting a Catholic publication but not necessarily religious—$7.50 and up. No fiction.
Annals of St. Anne de Beaupre, The: P.O. Box 1000, St. Anne de Beaupre, Que., Canada G0A 3C0. Ed., Rev. Roch Achard, C.Ss.R. Monthly, circulation 65,000; $6 per year.
FICTION: Stories of general Catholic interest, preferably with slant on devotion to St. Anne; 700-1,200 words — 2-4¢ a word. ARTICLES of solid general interest to Catholics: on aspects of devotion to St. Anne, relative to history of the devotion in North America or elsewhere; on educational or social problems, or situations that should be of concern to all — especially Christians: 700-1,200 words — 2-4¢ a word, Payment on acceptance.
BLUEPRINT for Social Justice: Institute for Human Relations, Loyola University, New Orleans,

La. 70118. Ed., John J. Mawhinney, S.J. Ten times a year, circulation 4,500; sent free on request.

ARTICLES on current social-justice issues; length, about 2,000 words.

Catechist: 2451 E. River Rd., Dayton, O. 45439. Ed., Patricia Fischer. Monthly August through April (exc. Dec.), circulation 45,620; $14.95 per year.

ARTICLES of interest to teachers of religion in parochial schools and CCD programs: 1,200-1,800 words — rate varies. PHOTOGRAPHS, black and white — rate varies. Payment on publication.

Catholic Digest: P.O. Box 43090, St. Paul, Minn. 55164. Ed., Henry Lexau. Monthly, circulation 606,827; $9.97 per year.

ARTICLES of close-to-home interest for average Catholic — rates vary; most frequent payments are $200 for originals, $100 for reprints; payment on acceptance. FILLERS, short features and jokes — rates vary; payment on publication. Cover pictures — $150. No fiction or verse. No queries necessary.

Columban Mission: St. Columbans, Nebr. 68056. Ed., Rev. Richard Steinhilber. Monthly (exc. June, Aug.); circulation 228,975; $3 per year.

ARTICLES mostly from missions or staff written: occasionally accept feature or factual articles on social and religious aspects of Asian and Latin American life: 2,000 words — $100 and up. PHOTOGRAPHS of Asian and Latin American subjects and photo stories — $10 each.

Columbia: Columbus Plaza, New Haven, Conn. 06507. Ed., Elmer Von Feldt. Monthly, circulation 1,342,575; $6 per year. Official organ of the Knights of Columbus.

ARTICLES dealing with current events, social problems, Catholic apostolic activities: 2,500-3,500 words (must be accompanied by glossy photos) — $400 to $600. FICTION, Christian viewpoint: up to 3,000 words — up to $500. SATIRE: 1,000 words — $200. CARTOONS, pungent, wordless humor — $25. COVERS — $750.

Commonweal: 232 Madison Ave., New York, N.Y. 10016. Ed., James O'Gara. Biweekly, circulation 18,000; $24 per year.

ARTICLES, political, religious and literary subjects: 1,000-3,000 words — 2¢ a word. VERSE, serious poetry of high literary merit — about 40¢ a line.

Crusader's Almanac: Franciscan Monastery, 1400 Quincy St. N.E., Washington, D.C. 20017. Ed., Rev. Bartholomew Bengisser, O.F.M. Biannually, circulation 85,000; $1 per year.

ARTICLES about the Holy Land, Bible and Crusades given preference — 1¢ a word.

Emmanuel: 194 E. 76th Street, New York, N.Y. 10021. Editor-in-Chief, Rev. Eugene La Verdiere, S.S.S. Monthly (combined Jan.-Feb., July-Aug. issues), circulation 8,300; $15 per year.

ARTICLES, spirituality for those in Church ministry, Eucharistic, pastoral, theological, Scriptural: 2,000-3,000 words — $40-$50.

Family Festivals: 23 Madison Dr., Laurel Springs, N.J. 08021. Ed., Sam Mackintosh. Bimonthly, circulation, 9,000; $16 per year.

ARTICLES, examples of family ritual or customs; 500-1,000 words — 3¢ a word. BOOK REVIEWS — $1 plus book. All material should be queried (send S.A.S.E. if reply expected.) Writers' guidelines available with S.A.S.E. Sample copies, $2.50 each.

Franciscan Herald: 1434 W. 51st St., Chicago, Ill. 60609. Monthly, circulation 8,000; $11 per year.

ARTICLES concerning St. Francis of Assisi and related subjects; application of Gospel principles to living Catholicism today; 2,000 words — $35. BOOK REVIEWS related to Franciscan topics — $10.

Hospital Progress: 4455 Woodson Rd., St. Louis, Mo. 63134. Ed., C. S. Boyer. Monthly, circulation 14,000; $25 per year (U.S. and Canada); $30 (foreign).

Official journal of the Catholic Health Association of the United States.

ARTICLES, health-care oriented; administrative procedures and theories; hospital departmental services: 1,500-3,000 words — payment by agreement. BOOK REVIEWS, hospital oriented — payment by agreement.

Immaculata: 1600 W. Park Ave., Libertyville, Ill. 60048. Ed., Rev. Bernard M. Geiger, O.F.M. Conv. Ten issues a year, circulation 19,000; $12 per year.

Official publication of Knights of the Immaculata.

ARTICLES: seasonal, following liturgical calendar of the Church; conversion stories, profiles of saints; analyses of contemporary Catholic events; 700-1,200 words — $35 and up. POETRY, 8-40 lines — payment varies. PHOTOS, DRAWINGS, CARTOONS with accompanying article or separately — $10 to $30. BOOK REVIEWS — $15 to $35. Query preferred. Payment on publication.

Institute Journal: 50 Oak St., San Francisco, Calif. 94102. Ed., Thomas P. Brady. Bimonthly, $1 per year.

FICTION — no fixed rate. PHOTOGRAPHS — $15.

Josephite Harvest, The: 1130 N. Calvert St., Baltimore, Md. 21202. Ed., Rev. Earle A. Newman, S.S.J. Quarterly; circulation 40,000; $2 per year.

ARTICLES concerning apostolate of Catholic Church in U.S. to the black community.

Liguorian: One Liguori Dr., Liguori, Mo. 63057. Ed., Norman J. Muckerman, C.SS.R. Monthly, circulation over 570,000; $12 per year.

FICTION concerning current situations; stories with a Christian influence yet without maudlin sentimentality; 1,500-2,000 words — 7-10¢ a word. ARTICLES on family, Scripture, liturgy; material for older readers and those under 21 needed; 1,500-2,000 words — 7-10¢ a word. POETRY, $25. ILLUSTRATIONS and BOOK REVIEWS on assignment only.

Living Light, The: Editorial offices, Department of Education, 1312 Massachusetts Ave. N.W., Washington D.C. 20005. Quarterly, circulation 2,000; $12 per year.

ARTICLES on Catholic education, catechesis, pastoral ministry; under 3,000 words — $15 per published page.

Marriage and Family Living: St. Meinrad, Ind.

47577. Ed., Keith McClellan, O.S.B. Monthly, circulation 45,000; $12.50 per year.

ARTICLES: (1) aimed at enriching the husband-wife and parent-child relationship by expanding religious and psychological insights or sensitivity: 1,000-2,000 words; (2) informative, aimed at helping couple cope, in practical ways, with problems of modern living: maximum 2,000 words; (3) personal essays relating amusing and/or heartwarming incidents that point up the human side of marriage and family life: maximum 1,500 words — 7¢ a word. PHOTOS: 8x11 b & w glossies, color transparencies — $10 minimum. 4-color cover photo — $150; b & w cover photo — $50; 2-page spread in contents — $35; 1-page in contents — $30. Photos of couples especially desired. Model releases required.

Buys North American serial rights only. Report on submissions in 3 to 4 weeks. Sample copy available for 50¢. Payment on acceptance.

Maryknoll: Maryknoll, N.Y. 10545. Ed., Moises Sandoval. Monthly, circulation more than 300,000; $1 per year.

ARTICLES must apply in some way to the hopes and aspirations, the culture, the problems and challenges of peoples in Asia, Africa and Latin America: 1,000-1,500 words — average payment, $100. Outline wanted before submission of material. PHOTOS: More interested in photo stories than in individual black and whites and color transparencies. Photo stories — up to $150, black and white; up to $200, color. Individual photos — $20, black and white, $35, color. Transparencies returned after use. Query to be made before sending photos.

Messenger of the Sacred Heart, The: 833 Broadview Ave., Toronto, Ont., Canada, M4K 2P9. Ed., Rev. F. J. Power, S.J. Monthly, circulation 21,000; $5 per year.

FICTION: stories which appeal to men, written with humor—good family reading: maximum, 2,000 words — 2¢ a word. ARTICLES of Catholic interest: 2,500 words — 2¢ a word. Payment upon acceptance.

Miraculous Medal, The: 475 E. Chelten Ave., Philadelphia, Pa. 19144. Ed., Rev. Robert P. Cawley, C.M. Quarterly, circulation 100,000.

FICTION, of general interest. Catholic in principle: 1,500-2,000 words — 2¢ a word and up. VERSE, religious in theme or turn; preferably about Our Lady: maximum 20 lines — 50¢ a line and up. Payment on acceptance. No articles.

Modern Liturgy: 7291 Coronado Dr., San Jose, Calif. 95129. Ed. William Burns. Nine issues a year, circulation, 15,000; $27 per year.

FICTION: parables, fantasy, fables; 1,000 words — 3¢ a word. ARTICLES: how-to, sample services, skills for liturgical artists; 1,200 words — 3¢ a word. POETRY, up to 50 lines — $10. BOOK REVIEWS appropriate for liturgy or religious education — $1 plus book.

Writers' guidelines available, send S.A.S.E.; or, for $3, a recent issue of magazine.

My Daily Visitor: Noll Plaza, Huntington, Ind. 46750. Ed., Patrick R. Moran. Bimonthly, circulation 14,747; $6.75 per year.

A pocket-sized booklet of reflections for each day of the month.

MATERIAL: Daily reflections based on spiritual meditation, the feast of the day or the liturgical season: maximum 165 words per page (each day's reflection is printed on a separate page) — $100 for series of reflections.

New Catholic World: 545 Island Rd., Ramsey, N.J. 07446. Mng. Ed., Robert Heyer. Bimonthly, circulation 14,000; $10 per year. Thematic issues.

ARTICLES, related to themes of issue (query editor): about 1,800-2,000 words. Rates of payment supplied.

Our Family: Box 249,Dept. C, Battleford, Sask., Canada SOM OEO. Ed., Rev. Albert Lalonde, O.M.I. Monthly, circulation 13,200; $9 per year; $12 in U.S.

FICTION, adult only; stories that reflect lives, problems and concerns of audience; anything true to human nature; no sentimentality or blatant moralizing; stories with "woven in" Christian message: 1,000-3,000 words — 7¢ to 10¢ a word. ARTICLES related to family living; religion, education, social, biographical, marriage, courtship, domestic, institutional: 1,000-3,000 words — 7¢ to 10¢ a word. POETRY, in the market for many more poems; should deal with man in search for himself, for God, for others, for love, for meaning in life, for commitment: 8-30 lines — 75¢-$1.00 per line. PHOTOS — purchased with manuscript as package (extra payment for photos); also in search of individual photos for editorial use. FILLERS — anecdotes of inspirational value, straight exposition, short humor. Writers' guide and photo specification sheet available on request (free; please enclose SASE). A sample copy is available for $1.50. Usually buys first North American serial rights; will consider purchasing second or reprint rights.

Our Sunday Visitor Magazine: Noll Plaza, Huntington, Ind. 46750. Ed., Rev. Vincent J. Giese. Weekly, circulation 290,000; $16 per year.

ARTICLES, no limitation on subjects other than those imposed by good taste and orthodoxy. Picture and text stories, profiles of individuals and organizations; articles that reflect moral, cultural, historical, social, economic and certain political concerns about the U.S. and the world; articles on current problems. Practical, factual and anecdotal material is sought: 750-1,000 words — $75-$100, usual payment. Queries are preferred to unsolicited completed manuscripts. PHOTOGRAPHS, picture stories preferred rather than individual photos. Picture stories (color) — $100 and up.No fiction or poetry.

Parish Family Digest: Noll Plaza, Huntington, Ind. 46750. Ed., Patrick R. Moran. Bimonthly, circulation 150,000.

ARTICLES of timely interest to the young and growing Catholic family as a unit of the Catholic parish — personality profiles, interviews, social concerns, education, humor, inspiration and family and parish-family interrelationships; 1,000 words or less — 5¢ a word. REPRINTS — $25. CARTOONS — $10 each for exclusives. FILLERS

— $5 each for exclusives based on personal experience.

Pastoral Music: 225 Sheridan St. N.W., Washington, D.C. 20011. Ed. Daniel Connors. Bimonthly, circulation 8,000; $18 per year.
FICTION and ARTICLES — 4¢ a word.

Priest, The: 200 Noll Plaza, Huntington, Ind. 46750. Ed., Rev. Vincent J. Giese. Eleven issues a year, circulation 10,000; $16.50 per year.
ARTICLES of benefit to priests and seminarians in any of the following areas: priestly spirituality, contemporary theology, liturgy, apostolate and ministry, pastoral notes, Scripture. Controversial subject matter acceptable provided it does not go beyond the realm of orthodoxy or respect for authority or demands of fraternal charity: 6-15 double-spaced pages — $25 to $100 (about $6 per manuscript page).

Queen of All Hearts: 40 S. Saxon Ave., Bay Shore, N.Y. 11706. Ed., Rev. James McMillan, S.M.M.; Mng. Ed., Rev. Roger M. Charest S.M.M. Bimonthly; circulation 8,500; $8 per year (U.S.), $9 (Canada and foreign).
FICTION: short stories, preferably with a Marian theme: 1,000-2,000 words. ARTICLES that bring out the importance of devotion to Mary. Payment varies. VERSE with Marian theme — payment, two years' subscription. No artwork or fillers.

Religion Teacher's Journal: Twenty-Third Publications, P.O. Box 180, Mystic, Conn. 06355. Ed., Gwen Costello. Seven issues a year, circulation 40,000; $12 per year.
FICTION about teachers relating to children, children and liturgical seasons; maximum length, 7 typewritten, double-spaced pages — $100 maximum. ARTICLES on catechesis, methods, theology, sample programs, how-to ideas, etc.; length and rates same as above. ILLUSTRATIONS, black and white — $15 each; covers/color slides — $25.

Review for Religious: Room 428, 3601 Lindell Blvd., St. Louis, Mo. 63108. Ed., D.F.X. Meenan, S.J. Bimonthly, circulation 18,618; $9 per year.
ARTICLES, of interest to religious: 3,000-6,000 words — $6 per printed page.

St. Anthony Messenger: 1615 Republic St., Cincinnati, O. 45210. Ed., Rev. Norman Perry, O.F.M. Monthly, circulation 360,000; $10 per year.
FICTION: Written out of a totally Christian background, illuminating the truth of human nature for adults. No preachiness, sentimentality. FACT ARTICLES: 3,000-3,500 words. Outstanding personalities (must be based on personal interview). Information and comment on major movements in the Church: application of Christian faith to daily life; real-life solutions in the areas of a) family life, education; b) personal living (labor, leisure, art, psychology, spirituality). Human interest narrative. Humor. Photos and picture stories. Query letters welcome.

St. Joseph's Messenger and Advocate of the Blind: St. Joseph's Home, P.O. Box 288, Jersey City, N.J. 07303. Ed., Sr. Ursula Maphet, C.S.J. Quarterly, circulation 51,000; $2 per year.
FICTION, and ARTICLES, contemporary, mainstream themes, 500-1,500 words — 1¢ to 3¢ a word.

Salesian Missions: 148 Main St., New Rochelle, New York 10802. Ed., Rev. Edward J. Cappelletti, S.D.B. Quarterly, circulation 1,000,000; $1 per year.
ARTICLES: mission interest; pertaining to Salesian Society, life, spirit and educational system of St. John Bosco; adolescent interest and education — 5¢ a word and up. PHOTOGRAPHS — $6. Suggest queries before submitting material. Payment on acceptance. Early report.

Social Justice Review: 3835 Westminster Pl., St. Louis, Mo. 63108. Ed., Harvey J. Johnson. Bimonthly, circulation 1,300; $12 per year.
ARTICLES: research, editorial and review: 2,000-4,000 words — $4 per column. No fiction.

Spiritual Life: 2131 Lincoln Rd., N.E., Washington, D.C. 20002. Ed., Rev. Christopher Latimer, O.C.D. Quarterly, circulation 18,000; $9 per year.
ARTICLES, must follow scope of magazine: 3,000-5,000 words — rate varies. Sample copy and instructions for writers sent upon request.

Spirituality Today: 1909 S. Ashland Ave., Chicago, Ill. 60608. Ed., Rev. Christopher Kiesling, O.P. Quarterly, circulation 5,000; $9 per year.
ARTICLES concerning any phase of the spiritual life: minimum 3,000-4,000 words — 1¢ a word. No fiction or poetry.

Today's Catholic Teacher: 2451 E. River Rd., Suite 200, Dayton, O. 45439. Monthly Sept. through May (exc. Dec.), circulation 50,000; $14.95 per year.
ARTICLES of professional and personal interest to teachers, administrators, pastors, parish councils and school board members concerning Catholic schools and CCD programs: 600-800 words, 1,500-3,000 words — $15-$75. Premium payment for superior content and writing presentation. Black and white photos helpful. Payment on publication.

Today's Parish: Twenty-Third Publications, P.O. Box 180, Mystic, Conn. 06355. Ed., Carol Clark. Seven issues a year, circulation 20,000; $15 per year.
ARTICLES, 1,200-1,500 words — $60 to $100. PHOTOS — $15.

WAY — of St. Francis: 109 Golden Gate Ave. San Francisco, Calif. 94102. Ed., Simon Scanlon, O.F.M. Bimonthly, circulation 8,000; $5 per year.
ARTICLES, in keeping with the purpose of the magazine, to bear effective witness to the ideals and aims of the Order of St. Francis: to view the world through Christian eyes; to point up the relationship between abstract belief and concrete action in the modern world: 1,500-2,200 words — $30 to $50. PHOTOGRAPHS: bought with articles.

Working for Boys: Box A, Danvers, Mass. 01923. Ed., Brother Alphonsus Dwyer, C.F.X. (Mss. to Bro. Alois, C.F.X., Assoc. Ed., St. John's High School, Shrewsbury, Mass, 01545.) Quarterly, circulation 16,000; $2 per year.
FICTION, preferably seasonal: 800-1,000 words — 4¢ a word. ARTICLES, preferably seasonal: All Souls, Christmas, Easter, Summer: 800-1,000 words — 4¢ a word. VERSE, seasonal, 4-16 lines — 25¢-50¢ a line.

Worship: St. John's Abbey, Collegeville, Minn.

56321. Ed., Rev. Aelred Tegels, O.S.B. Bimonthly, circulation 7,594; $14 per year.

ARTICLES related to the engagement of the magazine in ongoing study of both the theoretical and pastoral dimensions of liturgy; examines historical traditions of worship in their doctrinal context, the experience of worship in Christian churches, the findings of contemporary theology, psychology, communications, cultural anthropology, and sociology insofar as they have a bearing on public worship: 5,000-8,000 words. No fiction or poetry.

RADIO, TELEVISION, THEATRE

Radio and Television

Christopher Radio Program: 15-minute interview-discussion series, "Christopher Closeup," weekly, on 236 stations; a one-minute "Christopher Thought for Today," daily, on 1,598 stations. Address: 12 E. 48th St., New York, N.Y. 10017.

Christopher TV Series, "Christopher Closeup": Originated in 1951. Half-hour and quarter-hour interviews in color, weekly, on 52 commercial stations, 500 American Forces Network outlets, CBN and PTL syndicate stations and 41 cable systems, Address; 12 E. 48th St., New York, N.Y. 10017.

Crossroads (Radio): Originated in 1954 as the Hour of the Crucified, produced by the Passionist Priests and Brothers. Weekly, on nearly 130 stations. Address: 1089 Elm St., West Springfield, Mass. 01089.

Directions (TV): Originated in 1960, this weekly half-hour program is a news-oriented approach to reporting social, moral and religious issues within a Catholic context. The Department of Communication, NCCB/USCC, cooperates in the production of some 15 segments a year, in addition to interfaith and seasonal specials; carried at variable dates on more than 80 stations (ABC).

For Our Times (TV): Originated in April 1979, this weekly half-hour series produced by CBS in a unique joint cooperative consultation with the Department of Communication, NCCB/USCC, the National Council of Churches and the New York Board of Rabbis focuses on the ethical and social challenges confronting American society today. Format: documentary and studio discussion (CBS).

Guideline (Radio): Produced in cooperation with the Department of Communication, NCCB/USCC. Weekly program designed to set forth the teachings of the Catholic Church and to discuss issues the Church faces in the contemporary world; heard on approximately 65 stations (NBC).

On This Rock (Radio): Originated in 1941, produced in cooperation with the Department of Communication, NCCB/USCC. A 15-minute weekly program currently employing a youth-oriented music and commentary format; heard on more than 950 stations (ABC).

Sacred Heart Program (Radio, TV): Originated in 1939, operated by the Jesuits. Produces and syndicates nationally one TV program and eight radio programs each week on more than 1,300 stations. Address: 3900 Westminster Place, St. Louis, Mo. 63108.

Religious Specials (TV): The Department of Communication, NCCB/USCC, cooperates in the production of four one-hour Catholic specials a year and occasional seasonal or tri-faith presentations. These programs offer a varied format: film, dramatizations, panel discussions, music and commentary, etc. Catholic portions are telcast on approximately 140 stations (NBC).

Theatre

Catholic University Drama Department: Established in 1937. Offers degree courses in theatre arts, produces five plays a year in The Hartke Theatre. Affiliated with National Players and Olney Theatre. Chairman of the department, William H. Graham. Address: Catholic University of America, Washington, D.C. 20064.

National Players: An operation of University Players, a non-profit organization affiliated with the Drama Department of the Catholic University. It originated in 1949 and is the oldest classical touring company in the U.S.

Olney Theatre Corporation: A non-profit organization affiliated with the Drama Department of Catholic University. It operates Olney Theatre, Olney, Md., an Equity theatre designated the State Summer Theatre of Maryland in 1978.

Catholic Actors' Guild of America, Inc.: Established in 1914 to provide material and spiritual assistance to people in the theatre. Has more than 500 members; publishes *The Call Board* bimonthly. Address: 1501 Broadway, Suite 2400, New York, N.Y. 10036.

Communications Services

Clemons Productions, Inc., P.O. Box 440, Pelham, N.Y. 10803.

Cross Current Communications: Dedicated to producing quality Catholic TV programming covering all phases of movements and personalities in the contemporary Church. Produces and distributes CROSSFIRE, a 13-part documentary series for TV. Address: 3220 Geronimo Dr., Oxnard, Calif. 93033.

Eternal Word Television Network, Inc., 5817 Old Leeds Rd., Birmingham, Ala. 35210. Mother M. Angelica, P.C.P.A., foundress.

Father Justin Rosary Hour: Station F — Box 217, Buffalo, N.Y. 14212.

Father Peyton's Family Theater Productions: Films for TV, for sale and rental. Address: 7201 Sunset Blvd., Hollywood, Calif. 90046.

Franciscan Advertising and Media Enterprises (F.A.M.E.): Produces and distributes media and advertising programs for religious education and evangelization. Address: 620 Route 3, Clifton, N.J. 07014.

Franciscan Communications: An audio-visual media center dedicated to the production of public service broadcasting material and audio-visual media for religious education. Creators and producers of TeleSPOTS and AudioSPOTS, 10- to 60-second public service messages for radio and TV; TeleKETICS films and media kits, filmstrips, slide programs, video cassettes, phonograph records and tapes, for religious, moral and value education. Address: 1229 South Santee St., Los Angeles, Calif. 90015.

Hispanic Telecommunications Network, Inc. (HTN): Produces *Nuestra Familia,* a national weekly Spanish-language TV series. Address: 1828 Grandstand Dr., San Antonio, Tex. 78238.

Mary Productions "Airtime": Originated in 1950. Offers royalty-free scripts for stage, film, radio and tape production. Audio and video tapes of lives of the saints and historical characters. Address: Mary Productions Guild, 58 Lenison Ave., Belford, N.J. 07718.

Oblate Centro de Comunicación, Oblates of Mary Immaculate: Publishes religious educational books, audio-visual materials and a weekly Spanish newspaper. Address: P.O. Box 96, San Antonio, Tex. 78291.

Passionist Communications Center, 117 Harmon Ave., P.O. Box 440, Pelham, N.Y. 10803. Sunday Mass on TV; publish TV Prayer Guide.

Paulist Communications: Contracts with dioceses and parishes to provide public service programs and spot series free to radio stations and scripts to priest-broadcasters; contacts stations for dioceses. Address: 2257 Barry Ave., Los Angeles, Calif. 90064.

Paulist Productions: Producers and distributors of the INSIGHT Film Series (available for TV) and educational film series. Purchase and rental information available. Address: P.O. Box 1057, Pacific Palisades, Calif. 90272.

Catholic Telecommunications Network of America (CTNA): 95 Madison Avenue, Suite 804, New York, N.Y. 10016.

Catholic Television Network (CTN): Instructional TV operations have been established in the following archdioceses and dioceses. Archdioceses are indicated by an asterisk.

Boston,* Mass.: Rev. James Hawker, Director, 1 Lake St., Brighton 02135.

Brooklyn, N.Y.: Rev. Msgr. Michael J. Dempsey, Director, 1712 10th Ave., 11215.

Chicago,* Ill.: Mr. Charles E. Hinds, Executive Director, One N. Wacker Dr. 60606.

Los Angeles,* Calif.: Mr. Steven J. Gorski, 1520 W. Ninth St. 90015.

New York,* N.Y.: Sr. M. Irene Fugazy, Director, Seminary Ave., Yonkers, N.Y. 10704.

Rockville Centre, N.Y.: Rev. Thomas Hartman, Director, 1345 Admiral Lane, Uniondale, N.Y. 11553.

San Francisco,* Calif.: Mr. Thomas A. Combellick, 324 Middlefield Rd., Menlo Park, Calif. 94025.

Unda-USA: A national professional Catholic association for broadcasters and allied communicators organized in 1972. It succeeded the Catholic Broadcasters Association of America which in 1948 had replaced the Catholic Forum of the Air organized in 1938. It is a member of the international Catholic association for radio and television known as Unda (the Latin word for "wave," symbolic of air waves of communication). Subgroups include Catholic Television Network, the Association of Catholic Radio and Television Syndicators, and the Association of Diocesan Directors. Unda-USA publishes a newsletter six times a year for members, produces "Real to Reel," a Catholic TV magazine, sponsors an annual general assembly and presents the Gabriel Awards annually for excellence in broadcasting. President, Rev. John Geaney, C.S.P. National office: 3035 Fourth St. N.E., Washington, D.C. 20017.

The Catholic Communications Foundation (CCF) was established by the Catholic Fraternal Benefit Societies in 1966 to lend support and assistance to development of the broadcasting apostolate of the Church. The CCF, promotes the development of diocesan communications capabilities and funds a scholarship program at the Annual Institute for Religious Communications. CCF officers include Bishop Anthony G. Bosco, chairman of the board. Address: Suite 198, Box 9000, Carlsbad, Calif. 92008.

DIOCESAN COMMUNICATIONS OFFICES, DIRECTORS

(Sources: *1983 Directory of Catholic Communications Personnel,* published by the Office of Public Affairs, USCC; *Official Catholic Directory;* NC News Service. Archdioceses are designated by an asterisk.)

Alabama: Birmingham — Rev. Martin Muller (Communications), Box 6147, Birmingham 35209.

Mobile* — Rev. Robert L. Anderson, S.J. (Ed., *The Catholic Week),* 400 Government St., Mobile 36601.

Alaska: Anchorage* — Bro. Charles P. McBride, C.S.C. (Communications), P.O. Box 2239, Anchorage 99510.

Fairbanks — Rev. Vincent G. Wissman, C.S.P. (Radio-TV), P.O. Box 55091, North Pole 99705. Rev. James Poole, S.J., Box 101, Nome 99762.

Juneau — Miss Carol Crater (Ed., *Inside Passage),* 419 Sixth St., Juneau 99801.

Arizona: Phoenix — Ms. Marge Injasoulian (Communications), 400 E. Monroe St., Phoenix 85004.

Tucson — Mr. Robert Nordmeyer (Ed., *Arizona Catholic Lifetime),* 64 W. Ochoa St., Tucson 85701.

Arkansas: Little Rock — Mr. William W. O'Donnell (Assoc. Dir., Communications), 2500 N. Tyler St., Little Rock 72217.

California: Fresno — Mr. Joseph Jasmin (Information), Box 4273, Fresno 93744.

Los Angeles* — Rev. Joseph Battaglia (Communications), Sr. Gail Tenney, O.S.F., Mr. Steven Gorski (ETV), 1530 W. 9th St., Los Angeles 90015.

Monterey — Rev. Dennis M. Gilbert (Communications Commission), Old Mission, 941 Chorro, P.O. Box 1483, San Luis Obispo 93406; Rev. Felix

Migliazzo (Ed., *The Observer*), Box 2079, Monterey 93940.

Oakland — Mrs. Reggie Finney (Public Relations), Dan Morris (Ed., *The Catholic Voice*), 2918 Lakeshore Ave., Oakland 94610.

Orange — Mr. Thomas A. Fuentes (Communications), P.O. Box 2590, Newport Beach 92663.

Sacramento — Rev. Brendan Considine (Communications and Media), 1002 Natoma St., Folsom 95630.

San Bernardino — Dan E. Pitre (Ed., *Inland Catholic*), P.O. Box 2788, San Bernardino 92405. Rev. Vincent Connor (Electronic Media), P.O. Box 847, Highland 92346.

San Diego — Rev. George A. Byrne (Communications), Box 80428, San Diego 92138.

San Francisco* — Rev. Michael Reis (Producer, Creative Services), Rev. Harry Schlitt (Director, Archdiocesan Communications Center), Mr. Jack Kelly (Radio-TV), 2655 Van Ness Ave., San Francisco 94109; Rev. Miles O'Brien Riley (Director, Information), 441 Church St., San Francisco 94114.

San Jose — Arlene Goetze (Communications), 7600 Y St. Joseph Ave., Los Altos 94022.

Santa Rosa — Msgr. Walter J. Tappe (Communications), P.O. Box 1297, Santa Rosa 95402.

Stockton — Yvonne Goodman (Communications), Box 4237, Stockton 95204.

Colorado: Denver* — Rev. C. B. Woodrich (Information), 200 Josephine St., Denver 80206.

Pueblo — Ms. Geraldine Carrigan (Communications; Ed., *Catholic Crosswinds*), 1001 N Grand Ave., Pueblo 81003.

Connecticut: Bridgeport — Rev. Nicholas V. Grieco (Communications), 238 Jewett Ave., Bridgeport 06606; Rev. Alfred J. Sienkiewicz (Radio-TV), 385 Scofieldtown Rd., Stamford 06903.

Hartford* — Rev. Edmund S. Nadolny (Radio-TV), 785 Asylum Ave., Hartford 06105.

Norwich — Jacqueline M. Keller (Communications), 201 Hickory St., Norwich 06360.

Stamford (Ukrainian Diocese) — Rev. Lew Lubynsky, 303 Eddy Glover Blvd., New Britain 06053.

Delaware: Wilmington — Mr. F. Eugene Donnelly (Secretary, Communications), Box 2030, Wilmington 19899.

District of Columbia: Washington* — Rev. Maurice T. Fox (Delegate, Communications), Mr. Jay Cormier (Director, Communications), Box 29260, Washington 20017.

Florida: Miami* — Rev. Donald F. Connolly (Communications), Marjorie Donohue (Public Information), Rev. Jose P. Nickse (Radio-TV), 9401 Biscayne Blvd., Miami 33138.

Orlando — Mr. John Filimon (Communications), Box 2728, Orlando 32802.

Pensacola-Tallahassee — Mr. Gerald Butterfield (Communications), 855 W. Carolina St., Tallahassee 32304.

St. Augustine — Sr. Carol Stovall, S.S.J. (Communications), Box 24000, Jacksonville 32207. Msgr. R. Joseph James (Radio-TV), 1649 Kingsley Ave., Orange Park 32073.

St. Petersburg — Catholic Media Center, Box

18081, Tampa 33679.

Georgia: Atlanta* — Msgr. Noel C. Burtenshaw (Communications), 680 W. Peachtree St. N.W., Atlanta 30308.

Savannah — Rev. Joseph Stranc (Communications), 12 W. Jones Ave., Statesboro 30458. Mrs. Gillian Brown (Information), P.O. Box 8789, Savannah 31412.

Hawaii: Honolulu — Rev. James Drew (Communications), 1525 Waimano Home Rd., Pearl City 96782.

Idaho: Boise — Rev. David L. Riffle (Communications Center), 6003 Overland, Boise 83709.

Illinois: Belleville — John T. Myler, (Communications), 220 W. Lincoln St., Belleville 62221.

Chicago* — Mr. Peter Foote (Communications), P.O. Box 1979, Chicago 60690. Rev. James Moriarty (Radio-TV), One N. Wacker Dr., Suite 1100, Chicago 60606.

Joliet — Rev. William F. Irwin (Communications), St. Charles Borromeo Pastoral Center, Rt. 53 and Airport Rd., Romeoville 60441.

Peoria — Mr. Robert England (Communications), 1301 N.E. Glendale,, Peoria 61603.

Rockford — Rev. David D. Kagan (Communications), 850 N. Church St., Rockford 61103.

St. Nicholas in Chicago for Ukrainians — Msgr. Jaroslav Swyschuk (Eastern Rite Information Bureau), 2208 W. Chicago Ave., Chicago 60622.

Springfield — Rev. Richard L. Paynic (Ed., *Time and Eternity*), Rev. Neal Dee (Radio-TV), 514 E. Lawrence, Springfield 62703.

Indiana: Evansville — Rev. Joseph L. Ziliak (Information), P.O. Box 4169, Evansville 47711.

Fort Wayne-South Bend — Mr. Lou Jacquet (Ed., *The Harmonizer*), P.O. Box 11169, Ft. Wayne 46856.

Gary — Rev. John F. Morales (Communications), P.O. Box M474, Gary 46401.

Indianapolis* — Mr. Charles J. Schisla (Communications), Box 1410, Indianapolis 46206.

Lafayette — Office of Information. 3104 W. County Rd., 100 North, Kokomo 46901.

Iowa: Davenport — Rev. Francis C. Henricksen (Communications), Suite 500, First Natl. Bldg., 201 W. 2nd St., Davenport 52805.

Des Moines — Sr. Mira Mosle, B.V.M. (Communications), 818 Fifth Ave., Box 1816, Des Moines 50306.

Dubuque* — Sr. Carol Hoverman (Communications), 1229 Mt. Loretta Ave. Dubuque 52001.

Sioux City — Mr. Joe Maher (Ed., *The Globe*), 1821 Jackson St., Sioux City 51105; Msgr. Frank Brady (Radio-TV), 1212 Morningside Ave., Sioux City 51106.

Kansas: Dodge City — Rev. Daniel V. Heim, Our Lady of Guadalupe Church, 805 Avenue J, Dodge City 67801.

Kansas City* — Rev. William Maher (Ed., *The Leaven*), Box 2329, Kansas City 66110.

Salina — Msgr. Raymond Menard (Information), Box 958, Salina 67401.

Wichita — Rev. Arthur A. Busch (Communications), 424 N. Broadway, Wichita 67202.

Kentucky: Covington — Sr. Colleen Winston,

O.S.B. (Communications), Box 192, Covington 41012.

Louisville* — Mr. Nick Rice (Communications), 3940 Poplar Level Rd., Louisville 40204.

Owensboro — Msgr. George Hancock (Information), 4005 Frederica St., Owensboro 42301; Rev. Leonard Reisz (Radio-TV), 1001 W. 7th St., Owensboro 42301.

Louisiana: Alexandria-Shreveport — Mr. Al Nassif (Information), Box 7417, Alexandria 71306.

Baton Rouge — Mr. Thomas Barbarie (Ed., *Catholic Commentator*), Box 14746, Baton Rouge 70898.

Houma-Thibodaux — Mr. Louis Aguirre (Communications, Ed., *The Bayou Catholic*), P.O. Box 9077, Houma 70361.

Lafayette — Mr. John Jungkind (Communications), Box 3223, Lafayette 70502.

Lake Charles — Mr. Truman Stacey (Diocesan News), 1100 16th St., Lake Charles 70601.

New Orleans* — Mr. Thomas M. Finney (Communications, Public Relations), 7887 Walmsley Ave., New Orleans 70125.

Maine: Portland — Mr. Clarence F. McKay (Communications), 510 Ocean Ave., Portland 04103.

Maryland: Baltimore* — Rev. Leo A. Murray, S.J. (Communications), 320 Cathedral St., Baltimore 21201.

Massachusetts: Boston* — Rev. Peter V. Conley (Communications), 49 Franklin St., Boston 02110; Rev. Francis T. McFarland (Radio-TV), 55 Chapel St., Newton 02160.

Fall River — Rev. John F. Moore (Communications), 410 Highland Ave., Fall River 02722; Rev. John F. Hogan, (TV), 494 Slocum Rd., N. Dartmouth 02747.

Springfield — Msgr. David P. Welch (Ed., *Catholic Observer*), Box 1570, Springfield 01101; Rev. John P. Moore, C.P. (Radio-TV), 1089 Elm St., W. Springfield 01089.

Worcester — Rev. John W. Barrett (Communications), 49 Elm St., Worcester 01609.

Melkite Eparchy of Newton — Rev. Ronald Golini (Communications), Box 265, Newton 02159.

Michigan: Detroit* — Mr. Jay M. Berman (Communications), 305 Michigan Ave., Detroit 48226.

Gaylord — Betty J. Ballou (Communications), 202 W. Mitchell Ave., Gaylord 49735.

Grand Rapids — Rev. Joseph J. Pettit, 267 Sheldon Ave. S.E., Grand Rapids 49503.

Kalamazoo — Mrs. A. Carole Smith (Communications), 215 N. Westnedge Ave., Kalamazoo 49005.

Lansing — Rev. Donald L. Eder (Communications), 300 W. Ottawa St., Lansing 48933.

Marquette — Gregory B. Bell (Communications), Box 550, Marquette 49855.

Saginaw — Rev. Donald L. Eder (Communications), 5800 Weiss St., Saginaw 48603.

Minnesota: Crookston — Rev. Michael Patnode (Information), Rev. Gerald Noesen (Radio-TV), Box 610, Crookston 56716.

Duluth — Mr. Francis J. Shane (Information), 215 W. 4th St., Duluth 55806.

New Ulm — Rev. Dennis Labat (Communica-

tions), 1400 Chancery Dr., New Ulm 56073.

St. Cloud — Ms. Rosemary Borgert (Information), 305 7th Ave. N., Suite 207, St. Cloud 56301.

St. Paul and Minneapolis* — Ms. Joan Bernet (Communications), 226 Summit Ave., St. Paul 55102.

Winona — Miss Marian O'Keefe (Communications), Box 588, Winona 55987.

Mississippi: Biloxi — Rev. James Russell (Communications), P.O. Box 1189, Biloxi 39533.

Jackson — Mrs. Janna Avalon (Ed., *Mississippi Today*), Box 2248, Jackson 39205.

Missouri: Jefferson City — Mr. Mark Saucier (Communications), Box 417, Jefferson City 65101.

Kansas City-St. Joseph — Rev. John C. Weiss (Communications), 1357 N.E. 42nd Terr., Kansas City 64116.

St. Louis* — Msgr. Edward O'Donnell (Information), 4445 Lindell Blvd., St. Louis 63108; Mr. Ronald Coleman (Public Relations), 2249 S. Brentwood Blvd., St. Louis 63144. Rev. Joseph M. O'Brien (Radio-TV), 9229 Lackland Rd., St. Louis 63108.

Springfield-Cape Girardeau — Mrs. Marilyn Vydra (Communications), 200 McDaniel Bldg., Springfield 65806.

Montana: Great Falls-Billings — Box 2107, Great Falls 59403.

Helena — Rev. Robert J. O'Donnell (Chancellor, Communications), Box 1729, Helena 59624.

Nebraska: Grand Island — Most Rev. Lawrence McNamara (Communications), P.O. Box 1531, Grand Island 68801.

Lincoln — Rev. James D. Dawson (Information), Box 80328, Lincoln 68501.

Omaha* — Rev. Mel Rempe (Communications), 100 N. 62nd St., Omaha 68132.

Nevada: Reno-Las Vegas — Msgr. Thomas Meger, Chancellor, Box 1211, Reno 89504; Mr. Gerard E. Sherry (Information), 953 Sahara Ave., Las Vegas 89104.

New Hampshire: Manchester — Rev. John Poirier (Radio-TV), 153 Ash St., Manchester 03105.

New Jersey: Camden — Msgr. Charles Giglio (Information), Box 709, Camden 08101.

Newark* — Michael S. McGraw (Information, Public Affairs), 31 Mulberry St., Newark 07102.

Passaic (Byzantine Rite Eparchy) — Msgr. Robert G. Moneta (Ed., *Eastern Catholic Life*), 101 Market St., Passaic 07055.

Paterson — Sister Pat Kowalski, O.S.M. (Communications), 597 Valley Rd., Clifton, N.J. 07013.

Trenton — Rev. Leonard F. Troiano (Communications), 315 Lowell Ave., Trenton 08619.

New Mexico: Gallup — Rev. Cormac Antram, O.F.M. (Communications, Radio-TV), P.O. Box 39, Tohatchi 87325.

Santa Fe* — Rev. Albert Gallegos (Communications-Media), 202 Morningside Dr. S.E., Albuquerque 87108.

New York: Albany — Rev. Michael Farano (Information), 465 State St., Albany 12206.

Brooklyn — Mr. Frank DeRosa (Information), Box C, Brooklyn 11202.

Buffalo — Rev. David M. Lee (Communications), 100 S. Elmwood Dr., Buffalo 14202.

New York* — Rev. Peter G. Finn (Communications), Rev. Lester S. Avestruz, O.S.A. (Spanish Media), 1011 First Ave., New York, N.Y. 10022. Sr. Irene Fugazy (Instructional TV), Seminary Ave., Yonkers, 10704.

Ogdensburg — Rev. David W. Stinebrickner (Information), 622 Washington St., Ogdensburg 13669; Rev. Donald Kramberg (Radio-TV), Wadhams Hall, RFD No. 4, Ogdensburg 13669.

Rochester — Rev. Louis A. Vasile (Information), 1150 Buffalo Rd., Rochester 14624.

Rockville Centre — Rev. Msgr. Daniel S. Hamilton (Information), Box 700, Hempstead 11551; Rev. Thomas J. Hartman (Radio-TV), 1345 Admiral Lane, Uniondale 11553.

St. Maron Diocese (Maronite Rite) — Rev. Richard Saad, 836 8th St. S., Birmingham, Ala. 35256.

Syracuse — Mr. Ron Smith (Communications), 240 E. Onondaga St., Syracuse 13202.

North Carolina: Charlotte — Ms. Mary C. Coyne (Asst. Ed., *North Carolina Catholic*), 1524 E. Moorehead St., Charlotte 28207.

Raleigh — Rev. Joseph G. Vetter (Communications), 300 Cardinal Gibbons Dr., Raleigh 27606.

North Dakota: Bismarck — Rev. John J. Owens, Box 128, Wilton 58579.

Fargo — Deacon Matt Lanz (Ed., *The New Earth*), Box 1750, Fargo 58107.

Ohio: Cincinnati* — Mr. Daniel J. Kane (Communications), Rev. Theodore Kosse (Radio-TV), 100 E. 8th St., Cincinnati 45202.

Cleveland — Rev. Frank P. Kosem (Communications), Mr. J. Jerome Lackamp (Radio-TV), Mr. Patrick DiSalvatore (Catholic Communications Center), 1027 Superior Ave., Cleveland 44114.

Columbus — Rev. James P. Hanley (Vicar, Communications), Mr. Richard J. Hatem (Radio-TV), Sr. Mary LaVernne, O.S.F. (Public Relations, Information), 197 E. Gay St., Columbus 43215.

Parma (Byzantine Rite Eparchy) — Rev. Donald Petyo, 5500 W. 54th St., Parma 44129.

Steubenville — Rev. Michael Gromczewski, Box 969, Steubenville 43952.

Toledo — Mr. Jim Richards (Communications), 2544 Parkwood Ave., Toledo 43610.

Youngstown — Rev. Bernard Bonnot (Communications), Miss Joan M. Nero (Public/Media Relations), 144 W. Wood St., Youngstown 44503.

Oklahoma: Oklahoma City* — Rev. David F. Monahan (Communications), Box 32180, Oklahoma City 73123.

Tulsa — Rev. Dennis C. Dorney, Chancellor, 820 S. Boulder St., Box 2009, Tulsa 74101.

Oregon: Baker — Rev. Joseph B. Hayes, Sacred Heart Church, 815 High St., Klameth Falls 97601.

Portland* — Robert Riler (Communications), 2838 E. Burnside St., Portland 97214.

Pennsylvania: Allentown — Rev. Stanley T. Sosnowski (Information), 202 N. 17th St., Box F, Allentown 18105.

Altoona-Johnstown — Msgr. Philip Saylor (Information), Box 413 Logan Blvd., Hollidaysburg 16648.

Erie — Rev. Thomas McSweeney (Communications), Gannon University, 703 Peach St. Erie 16541.

Greensburg — Mrs. Alice Laurich (Communications), Box 850, Greensburg 15601.

Harrisburg — Sr. Arlene Ronollo, S.S.J. (Communications), 4800 Union Deposit Rd., Box 3557, Harrisburg 17105.

Philadelphia* — Rev. John J. Sibel (Communications), 222 North 17th St., Philadelphia 19103.

Philadelphia* (Ukrainian) — Rev. Ronald Popivchak, Box 126, Bridgeport 19405.

Pittsburgh* (Byzantine Rite) — Msgr. Edward V. Rosack (Information), 624 Park Rd., Ambridge 15003; Most Rev. John M. Bilock (Radio-TV), 54 Riverview Ave., Pittsburgh 15214.

Pittsburgh — Rev. Ronald P. Lengwin (Communications), 111 Boulevard of the Allies, Pittsburgh 15222.

Scranton — Rev. Joseph P. Gilgallon, 300 Wyoming Ave., Scranton 18503.

Rhode Island: Providence — Marianne Postiglione, R.S.M. (Communications), Gilles D. Dery (Media Center), One Cathedral Square, Providence 02903.

South Carolina: Charleston — Dr. Paul C. Beach (Communications), Box 818, Charleston 29402.

South Dakota: Rapid City — Mr. Brian T. Olszewski, Box 678, Rapid City 57709.

Sioux Falls — Rev. Leonard Thury, Holy Family Catholic Church, 321 E. 3rd St., Mitchell 57301; Rev. Thomas J. Ryan, 509 Capital, Yankton 57078.

Tennessee: Memphis — Msgr. Paul W. Clunan (Communications), 203 S. White Station Rd., Memphis 38117.

Nashville — Mr. Joseph A. Sweat (Communications, Public Relations), 2400 21st Ave. S., Nashville 37212.

Texas: Amarillo — Terri Goodman (Information), 1800 N. Spring St., Box 5644, Amarillo 79107.

Austin — Rev. Thomas J. Holohan, C.S.P., Box 13327, Austin 78711.

Beaumont — Rev. James Vanderholt (Communications), P.O. Box 3948, Beaumont 77704.

Brownsville — Rev. Jon McMahon, O.M.I., Box 547, Brownsville 78516.

Corpus Christi — Joseph Michael Feist (Public Information), Sr. Janie Barrera (Communications Coordinator), Rev. Robert E. Freeman (Communications), 620 Lipan St., Corpus Christi 78401.

Dallas — Deacon Steve Landregan (Communications), Patricia Hasbrouck (ETV), 3915 Lemmon Ave., Dallas 75219.

El Paso — Mr. Andrew Sparke (Parochial Schools TV), 1101 Birch St., El Paso 79930.

Fort Worth — Rev. Reynold Matus, St. Vincent de Paul Church, 5819 W. Pleasant Ridge Rd., Arlington 76016.

Galveston-Houston — Msgr. John L. Fos, 1700 San Jacinto St., Box 1878, Houston 77001; Rev. Bert Akers, S.J. (Radio-TV), Box 907, Houston 77001.

San Angelo — Rev. Maurice J. Voity (Communications), Box 1829, San Angelo 76902.

San Antonio* — Rev. John W. Yanta (Communications), Box 12429, San Antonio 78212.

Utah: Salt Lake City — Sr. Margaret Andre

Stechschulte, O.P. (Communications Media), 27C St., Salt Lake City 84103.

Vermont: Burlington — Rev. Joseph T. Sullivan (Communications), 351 North Ave., Burlington 05401.

Virginia: Arlington — Ellen McCloskey (Communications), 200 N. Glebe Rd., Arlington 22203.

Richmond — Mr. Bob Edwards (Communications), 811 Cathedral Pl., Richmond 23220.

Washington: Seattle* — Dr. Maury Sheridan, 910 Marion St., Seattle 98104.

Spokane — Rev. Michael J. Savelesky (Communications), Box 1453, Spokane 99210.

Yakima — Rev. P. J. Auve, Pastoral Office, Box 505, Yakima 98907.

West Virginia: Wheeling-Charleston — Mr. W. C. Hehr, 1300 Byron St., Box 230, Wheeling 26003.

Wisconsin: Green Bay — Mr. Tony Kuick (Communications), Box 66, Green Bay 54305.

La Crosse — Rev. Bernard McGarty (Communications), Box 69, La Crosse 54601.

Madison — Maureen Quinn Hartin (Communications), 3577 High Point Rd., Rt. 2, Madison 53711.

Milwaukee* — Sr. Mary Luke Baldwin, S.S.N.D. (Communications), 345 N. 95th, Box 2018, Milwaukee 53201.

Superior — Rev. Robert Urban (Information), 1512 N. 12th St., Superior 54880.

Wyoming: Cheyenne — Mr. Roy Lansing (Information), P.O. Box 1387, Cheyenne 82001.

Catholic Communications Northwest: Regional communications center serving dioceses in Alaska, Idaho, Montana, Oregon and Washington. Executive Director, Dr. Maury Sheridan, 910 Marion St., Seattle, Wash. 98104.

Delaware Valley Catholic Office for Television and Radio: Interdiocesan agency of the Archdiocese of Philadelphia, the dioceses of Camden and Trenton, N.J. and Wilmington, Del. Address: 222 North 17th St., Philadelphia, Pa. 19103.

National Office

The National Catholic Office for Information (NCOI), successor to the NCWC Bureau of Information, serves as the official spokesman for both the United States Catholic Conference and the National Conference of Catholic Bishops in relating to the news media. The NCOI is part of the NCCB USCC Office for Public Affairs.

William Ryan is director of the office, which is located at 1312 Massachusetts Ave. N.W., Washington, D.C. 20005.

HONORS AND AWARDS

PONTIFICAL ORDERS

The Pontifical Orders of Knighthood are secular orders of merit whose membership depends directly on the pope. Details regarding the various orders are handled by a special agency in the Secretariat of Briefs, an office in the Papal Secretariat of State.

Supreme Order of Christ (Militia of Our Lord Jesus Christ): The highest of the five pontifical orders of knighthood, the Supreme Order of Christ was approved Mar. 14, 1319, by John XXII as a continuation in Portugal of the suppressed Order of Templars. Members were religious with vows and a rule of life until the order lost its religious character toward the end of the 15th century. Since that time it has existed as an order of merit. Paul VI, in 1966, restricted awards of the order to Christian heads of state.

Order of the Golden Spur (Golden Militia): Although the original founder is not certainly known, this order is one of the oldest knighthoods. Indiscriminate bestowal and inheritance diminished its prestige, however, and in 1841 Gregory XVI replaced it with the Order of St. Sylvester and gave it the title of Golden Militia. In 1905 St. Pius X restored the Order of the Golden Spur in its own right, separating it from the Order of St. Sylvester. Paul VI, in 1966, restricted awards of the order to Christian heads of state.

Order of Pius IX: Founded by Pius IX June 17, 1847, the order is awarded for outstanding services for the Church and society, and may be given to non-Catholics as well as Catholics. The title to nobility formerly attached to membership was abolished by Pius XII in 1939. In 1957 Pius XII instituted the Class of the Grand Collar as the highest category of the order; in 1966, Paul VI restricted this award to heads of state "in solemn circumstances." The other three classes are of Knights of the Grand Cross, Knight Commanders with and without emblem, and Knights. The new class was created to avoid difficulties in presenting papal honors to Christian or non-Christian leaders of high merit.

Order of St. Gregory the Great: First established by Gregory XVI in 1831 to honor citizens of the Papal States, the order is conferred on persons who are distinguished for personal character and reputation, and for notable accomplishment. The order has civil and military divisions, and three classes of knights.

Order of St. Sylvester: Instituted Oct. 31, 1841, by Gregory XVI to absorb the Order of the Golden Spur, this order was divided into two by St. Pius X in 1905, one retaining the name of St. Sylvester and the other assuming the title of Golden Militia. Membership consists of three degrees: Knights of the Grand Cross, Knight Commanders with and without emblem, and Knights.

ECCLESIASTICAL ORDER

Order of the Holy Sepulchre: Critical opinion is divided regarding various details of the history of the order. It is certain, however, that these knights first appeared in the Holy Land and were in existence at the end of the 11th century. Some assign earlier dates or origin, claiming as founders St. James the Apostle, first bishop of Jerusalem, and St. Helena, builder of the Basilica of the Holy Sepulchre. Others hold that Godfrey of Bouillon instituted the order in 1099 and that it took its name from the Holy Sepulchre where its members were knighted.

The order lost a great deal of prestige after the fall of the Latin Kingdom of Jerusalem and the consequent departure of the knights from the Holy Land. It was united with the Knights of St. John in 1489, came under the grand mastership of Alexander VI in 1496 and shortly thereafter was split into three national divisions, German, French and Spanish. Pius IX re-established the Latin patriarchate of Jerusalem in 1847 and gave the patriarch the faculty of conferring the order of knighthood. This right had been held by the Franciscan custos following the appointment of the Friars as guardians of the Holy Land in 1342. Three classes of membership were designated in 1868. Leo XIII later instituted the Cross of Honor (which does not confer knighthood) in three classes — gold, silver and bronze — and also the Dames of the Holy Sepulchre. From 1907 to 1928 the pope was grand master, an office now held by a cardinal. Revised statutes for the order went into effect in 1949, 1962 and 1967. The 1949 constitution enjoined the knights "to revive in modern form the spirit and ideal of the Crusades with the weapons of faith, the apostolate, and Christian charity."

The Order of the Holy Sepulchre now has five classes: 12 Knights of the Collar and four degrees, with separate divisions of each for men and women — Grand Cross, Commanders with Plaque, Commanders and Knights. Three honorary decorations are awarded, vis., Palm of the Order, Cross of Merit (which may be bestowed on non-Catholics), and the Pilgrim's Shell.

Investiture ceremonies combine a profession of faith with the ancient ritual of knighthood dubbing. Candidates do not take monastic vows but pledge an upright Christian life and loyalty to the pope.

The grand master of the order is Cardinal Maximilien de Furstenberg.

There are five lieutenancies of the order in the United States.

ORDER OF MALTA

The Sovereign Military Hospitaller Order of St. John of Jerusalem of Rhodes and of Malta traces its origin to a group of men who maintained a Christian hospital in the Holy Land in the 11th century. The group was approved as a religious order — the Hospitallers of St. John — by Paschal II in 1113.

The order, while continuing its service to the poor, principally in hospital work, assumed military duties in the twelfth century and included knights, chaplains and sergeants-at-arms among its members. All the knights were professed monks with the vows of poverty, chastity and obedience. Headquarters were located in the Holy Land until the last decade of the 13th century and on Rhodes after 1308 (whence the title, Knights of Rhodes).

After establishing itself on Rhodes, the order became a sovereign power like the sea republics of Italy and the Hanseatic cities of Germany, flying its own flag, coining its own money, floating its own navy, and maintaining diplomatic relations with many nations.

The order was forced to abandon Rhodes in 1522 after the third siege of the island by the Turks under Sultan Suliman I. Eight years later, the Knights were given the island of Malta, where they remained as a bastion of Christianity until near the end of the 18th century. Headquarters have been located in Rome since 1834.

The title of Grand Master of the Order, in abeyance for some time, was restored by Leo XIII in 1879. A more precise definition of both the religious and the sovereign status of the order was embodied in a new constitution of 1961 and a code issued in 1966.

Religious aspects of the order are subject to regulation by the Holy See. At the same time the sovereignty of the order, which is based on international law, is recognized by the Holy See and by 43 countries with which full diplomatic relations are maintained.

The four main classifications of members are: Knights of Justice, who are religious with the vows of poverty, chastity and obedience; Knights of Obedience, who make a solemn promise to strive for Christian perfection; Knights of Honor and Devotion and of Grace and Devotion — all of noble lineage; and Knights of Magistral Grace. There are also chaplains, Dames and Donats of the order.

The order, with five grand priories, three sub-priories and 38 national associations, is devoted to hospital and charitable work of all kinds in some 77 countries.

The Grand Master, who is the sovereign head of the order, has the title of Most Eminent Highness with the rank of Cardinal. He must be of noble lineage and under solemn vows for a minimum period of 10 years, if under 50.

The present Grand Master is Fra' Angelo de Mojana di Cologna, a lawyer of Milan, who was elected for life May 8, 1962, by the Council of State.

The address of headquarters of the order is Via Condotti, 68, Palazzo Malta, 00187 Roma, Italia.

PAPAL MEDALS

Pro Ecclesia et Pontifice: This decoration ("For the Church and the Pontiff") had its origin in 1888 as a token of the golden sacerdotal jubilee of Leo XIII; he bestowed it on those who had assisted in the observance of his jubilee and on persons responsible for the success of the Vatican Exposition. The medal bears the likeness of Leo XIII on one side; on the other, the tiara, the papal keys, and the words *Pro Ecclesia et Pontifice*. Originally, the medal was issued in gold, silver or bronze. It is awarded in recognition of service to the Church and the papacy.

Benemerenti: Several medals ("To a well-deserving person") have been conferred by popes for exceptional accomplishment and service. The medals, which are made of gold, silver or bronze, bear the likeness and name of the reigning pope on one side; on the other, a laurel crown and the letter "B."

These two medals may be given by the pope to both men and women. Their bestowal does not convey any title or honor of knighthood.

AMERICAN CATHOLIC AWARDS

Included are only those awards presented in 1983 as well as in previous years. Recipients of awards presented in previous years are listed in earlier editions of the Almanac.

Aquinas Medal, by the American Catholic Philosophical Association for outstanding outstanding contributions to the field of Catholic philosophy.

Jacques Maritain (1951), Etienne Gilson (1952), Gerald Smith, S.J. (1955), Gerald B. Phelan (1959), Rudolf Allers (1960), James A. McWilliams, S.J. (1961) Charles De Koninck (1964), James Collins (1965).

Martin C. D'Arcy (1967), Dr. Josef Pieper (1968), Leo R. Ward (1969), Bernard Lonergan, S.J. (1970), Henry B. Veatch (1971), Joseph Owens, C.SS.R. (1972), A. Hilary Armstrong (1973), Cornelio Fabro (1974), Anton Pegis (1975), Mortimer J. Adler (1976), Frederick C. Copleston (1977), Fernand Van Steenberghen (1978), John Paul II (1979), W. Norris Clarke, S.J. (1980), Ernan McMullin (1981), G.E.M. Anscombe (1982), William Wallace, O.P. (1983).

Berakah Award (1976), by the North American Academy of the Liturgy, to recognize distinguished contribution to the professional work of liturgy by a liturgist or person of an allied vocation.

Aidan Kavanagh, O.S.B. (1976), Godfrey Diekmann, O.S.B. (1977), Massey Hamilton Shepherd (1978), Rev. Frederick McManus, (1979), Horton Davies (1980), Frank Kacmarcik (1981), Robert W. Hovda (1982), James F. White (1983).

Brent Award (1976), by the Diocese of Arlington, Va., for distinguished service to fellowman.

Dr. Mildred F. Jefferson (1976), Most Rev. John J. Russell (1977), U.S. Rep. Henry J. Hyde and William B. Ball, Esq. (1978), Mrs. Hazel Hagarty (1979), Mother Mary Claudia, I.H.M. (1980), Dr. Josephina Magno (1981), Eduardo M. Azcarate (1982), U.S. Sen. Jeremiah A. Denton, Jr. (1983).

Christian Culture Award (1941), by Assumption University (Canada) to outstanding lay exponents of Christian ideals.

Sigrid Undset (1941), Jacques Maritain (1942), Philip Murray (1943), Frank J. Sheed (1944), Arnold M. Walter (1945), Henry Ford II (1946), George S. Sperti (1947), Richard Pattee (1948), Etienne Gilson (1949), Paul Doyon (1950), Christopher Dawson (1951), John C.H. Wu (1952);

Charles Malik (1953), Ivan Mestrovic (1954), F. W. Foerster (1955), Paul Martin (1956), Robert Speaight (1947), Allen Tate (1958), Barbara Ward (1959), John Cogley (1960), Peter Drucker (1961), Benjamin E. Mays (1962), John Quincy Adams (1963);

William Foxwell Albright (1964), Dr. Karl Stern (1965), John Howard Griffin (1966), Edith K. Peterkin (1967), Dr. Mircea Eliade (1968), Dr. James D. Collins (1969), Dorothy Day (1970), Dr. Marshall McLuhan (1971), James M. Cameron (1972), Jean Vanier (1973), Robert J. Kreyche (1974), John T. Noonan, Jr. (1975), Dorothy Donnelly (1976), William Kurelek (1977), Anthony Walsh (1978), Malcolm Muggeridge (1979), Conrad W.

Baars, M.D. (1980), Rosemary Haughton (1981), Roy Bonisteel (1982), The Hon. Jean Chretien, P.C., M.P. (1983).

Compostela Award, The (1982), by the Cathedral-Basilica of St. James (Diocese of Brooklyn) to men and women whose lives represent the noblest ideals of the cathedral tradition of fidelity to justice, truth, beauty and peace.

Most Rev. Carroll T. Dozier, Kitty Carlisle Hart, Mabel Mercer and Hon. Robert F. Wagner (1982), Hon. Mario M. Cuomo, Geraldine Fitzgerald, Jane Pickens Hoving and Isaac Bashevis Singer (1983).

The De La Salle Medal, by Manhattan College, for significant contribution to the moral, cultural or educational life of the nation.

John F. Brosnan (1951), Cardinal Francis Spellman (1952), Most Rev. Joseph P. Donahue (1953), Most Rev. Edwin V. O'Hara, posthumously (1956), Sr. Mary Emil, I.H.M. (1957), Msgr. Joseph E. Schieder (1958), Very Rev. Bro. Bertrand, O.S.F. (1959), Dr. Roy J. Deferrari (1960).

John Courtney Murray, S.J. (1961), Bro. Clair Stanislaus, F.S.C. (1962), Most Rev. Bryan J. McEntegart (1963), Sr. M. Rose Eileen, C.S.C. (1964), Mother Kathryn Sullivan, R.S.C.J. (1965), Bro. Bernard Peter, F.S.C. (1966), Dr. William Hughes Mulligan (1967), C. Alfred Koob, O. Praem. (1968), Theodore M. Hesburgh, C.S.C. (1970), Most Rev. Edwin B. Broder ick (1971), Very Rev. Bro. Charles Henry, F.S.C. (1972), Mary Shea Giordano (1973), Dorothy Day (1974), Henry Viscardi, Jr. (1975), Sister Elinor R. Ford, O.P. (1976), John D. de Butts (1977), Thomas A. Murphy (1978), Gabriel Hauge (1979), Irving S. Shapiro (1980), Maurice F. Granville (1981), Frank T. Cary (1982), Richard S. Shinn (1983).

Edith Stein Award (1955), by the Edith Stein Guild for service toward better understanding between Christians and Jews.

Sister Noemi de Sion (1956), Authur B. Klyber, C.SS.R. (1957), Rev. John M. Oesterreicher (1958), John J. O'Connor (1959), Victor J. Donovan, C.P. (1960), Jacques and Raissa Maritain (1961), Gerard E. Sherry (1962), Mother Kathryn Sullivan, R.S.C.J. (1963), Paulist Press (1964), Rev. Edward N. Flannery (1965), Mother Katherine Hargrove, R.S.C.J. (1966), Gregory Baum, O.S.A. (1967), Sr. Rose Albert Thering (1968), Msgr. Vincent O. Genova (1969), Dr. Joseph Lichten (1970), Philip Scharper (1971), Rabbi Marc Tanenbaum (1972), Leon Paul (1973), Msgr. James Rigney (1980), Most Rev. Francis J. Mugavero (1982), Dr. Eugene Fischer (1983).

Fidelitas Medal (1949), by Orchard Lake Schools (Sts. Cyril and Methodius Seminary, St. Mary's College, St. Mary's Preparatory), to an outstanding American Catholic of Polish descent for fidelity in serving God and country.

Msgr. Lucian Bojnowski (1949), Msgr. Adalbert Zadala (1950), Msgr. John Gulcz (1951), Joseph Kania (1952), Msgr. Francis Karabasz (1953), Rev. Valentine Biczysko (1954), Dr. Edwin Dobski

(1955), Very Rev. Justin Figas, O.F.M. Conv. (1956), Hon. Arthur Koscinski (1957), Miss Adela Lagodzinska (1958), Msgr. Casimir Piejda (1959), Msgr. Ladislaus Sikora (1960), Msgr. Vincent Borkowicz (1961), Msgr. Ladislaus Nowakowski (1962), Msgr. Peter Walkowiak (1963), Charles Rozmarek (1964), Rev. Simon Kilar (1965); Mother Mary Alexander (1966), Msgr. Francis Kowalczyk (1967), Cardinal John J. Krol (1968), Sen. Edmund S. Muskie (1969), Msgr. Peter Adamski (1970), Joseph Pranica (1971), Hon. Frank G. Schemanske (1972), Mrs. Dora Alska (1973), Benjamin Stefanski (1974), Robert Goralski (1975), Aloysius Mazewski (1976), Msgr. John Wodarski (1977), Dr. Zbigniew Brzezinski (1978), Msgr. Alexander Cendrowski (1979), Stanley (Bobby) Vinton, Jr. (1980), Rev. Anthony Iwuc (1981), Frank C. Padzieski (1982), Helen Zielinski (1983).

Franciscan International Award (1958), by the Conventual Franciscans (Prior Lake, Minn.) for outstanding contributions to the development of life.

Mr. and Mrs. Ignatius A. O'Shaughnessy (1959), Archbishop William O. Brady (1960), Lawrence Welk (1961), Charles Kellstad (1962), Dr. Finn J. Larsen (1963), Dr. Charles W. Mayo (1964), Ara Parseghian (1965), F. K. Weyerhaueser (1966); Aicoholics Anonymous (1967), James T. Griffin (1968), George S. Harris (1969), Baroness Catherine DeHueck Doherty (1970), Harry Reasoner (1971), Dr. Billy Graham (1972), Dr. and Mrs. John C. Willke (1973), Gov. Patrick J. Lucey (1974), Joe and Jan Rigert (1975), Dr. B. F. Pearson (1976), Francis S. MacNutt, O.P. (1977), Dr. Mildred F. Jefferson (1978), Bruce Ritter, O.F.M. Conv. (1979), John E. McCarthy (1980), William B. Wasson, O.F.M. (1981), Lorand and Anna Andahazy (1982), Urban Wagner, O.F.M. Conv. (1983).

John Courtney Murray Award (1972), by the Catholic Theological Society for distinguished achievement in theology. Originated in 1947 as the Cardinal Spellman Award.

Rev. Charles E. Curran (1972), Bernard Lonergan, S.J. (1973), George A. Tavard, A.A. (1974), Rev. Carl Peter (1975), Rev. Richard P. McBrien (1976), Frederick E. Crowe (1977), Edward J. Kilmartin, S.J. (1978), Bernard Cooke (1979), David Tracy (1980), Rev. Gerald Sloyan (1981), Rev. George J. Dyer (1982), William J. Hill, O.P. (1983).

John La Farge Memorial Award for Interracial Justice (1965), by the Catholic Interracial Council of New York. Presented annually to a leading citizen of the community regardless of race, color or creed for promoting social and interracial justice.

Cardinal Francis J. Spellman (1965), U.S. Sen. Jacob K. Javits (1966), Gov. Nelson Rockefeller (1967), George F. Meany (1968), Whitney M. Young, Jr. (1969), Harry Van Arsdale, Jr. (1970), John V. Lindsay (1971), Earl W. Brydges (1972), Louis K. Lefkowitz (1973), Arthur Levitt (1974), Robert F. Wagner (1975), Gustave L. Levy (1976), Cardinal Terence Cooke (1977), E. Howard Molisani (1978), Gov. Hugh L. Carey (1979), Sen. Daniel Patrick Moynihan, Hazel Dukes (1980), Hon. Edward Regan, Bayard Rustin (1981), Hon. William A. Shea, Frederick O'Neal (1982), Hon. Mario M. Cuomo (1983).

Laetare Medal (1883), by the University of Notre Dame for distinguished accomplishment for Church or nation by an American Catholic.

John Gilmary Shea (1883), Patrick J. Keeley (1884), Eliza Allen Starr (1885), Gen. John Newton (1886), Edward Preuss (1887), Patrick V. Hickey (1888), Anna Hansen Dorsey (1889), William J. Onahan (1890), Daniel Dougherty (1891), Henry F. Brownson (1892);

Patrick Donahoe (1893), Augustin Daly (1894), Mrs. Mary A. Sadlier (1895), Gen. William S. Rosecrans (1896), Dr. Thomas A. Emmet (1897), Timothy E. Howard (1898), Mary G. Caldwell (1899), John Creighton (1900), William B. Cockran (1901), Dr. John B. Murphy (1902);

Charles J. Bonaparte (1903), Richard C. Kerens (1904), Thomas B. Fitzpatrick (1905), Dr. Francis Quinlan (1906), Katherine E. Conway (1907), James C. Monaghan (1908), Frances Tiernan (Christian Reid) (1909), Maurice F. Egan (1910), Agnes Repplier (1911), Thomas M. Mulry (1912);

Charles G. Herbermann (1913), Edward Douglass White (1914), Mary V. Merrick (1915), Dr. James J. Walsh (1916), Admiral William S. Benson (1917), Joseph Scott (1918), George Duval (1919), Dr. Lawrence F. Flick (1920), Elizabeth Nourse (1921), Charles P. Neil (1922);

Walter G. Smith (1923), Charles D. Maginnis (1924), Dr. Edward F. Zahm (1925), Edward N. Hurley (1926), Margaret Anglin (1927), John J. Spalding (1928), Alfred E. Smith (1929), Frederick P. Kenkel (1930), James J. Phelan (1931), Dr. Stephen J. Maher (1932);

John McCormack (1933), Genevieve Garvan Brady (1934), Frank Spearman (1935), Richard Reid (1936), Jeremiah Ford (1937), Dr. Irvin Abell (1938), Josephine Brownson (1939), Gen. Hugh A. Drum (1940), William T. Walsh (1941), Helen C. White (1942);

Thomas F. Woodlock (1943), Anne O'Hare McCormick (1944), G. Howland Shaw (1945), Carlton J. H. Hayes (1946), William G. Bruce (1947), Frank C. Walker (1948), Irene Dunne (Mrs. Francis Griffin) (1949), Gen. Joseph L. Collins (1950), John H. Phelan (1951), Thomas E. Murray (1952);

I. A. O'Shaughnessy (1953), Jefferson Caffery (1954), George Meany (1955), Gen. Alfred M. Gruenther (1956), Clare Boothe Luce (1957), Frank M. Folsom (1958), Robert D. Murphy (1959), George N. Shuster (1960), Pres. John F. Kennedy (1961), Dr. Francis J. Braceland (1962);

Adm. George W. Anderson, Jr. (1963), Phyllis McGinley (1964), Frederick D. Rossini (1965), Mr. and Mrs. Patrick F. Crowley (1966), J. Peter Grace (1967), R. Sargent Shriver (1968), Justice William J. Brennan, Jr. (1969), Dr. William B. Walsh (1970), Walter and Jean Kerr (1971), Dorothy Day (1972), Rev. John A. O'Brien (1973), James A. Farley (1974), Sister Ann Ida Gannon, B.V.M. (1975), Paul Horgan (1976), Sen. Mike Mansfield (1977), Msgr. John Tracy Ellis (1978),

Helen Hayes (1979), Rep. Thomas P. O'Neill, Jr. (1980), Edmund S. Muskie (1981), Cardinal John Francis Dearden (1982), Edmund A. and Evelyn Stephan (1983).

Lumen Christi Award (1978) by the Catholic Church Extension Society to persons making an outstanding contribution in service to the American home missions.

Miss Florence Kaster (1978), Miss Joan Mulder and Isabel Dumont, M.D. (1979), Sr. Ida Brasseur, S.S.A. (1980), Msgr. Joseph G. Cassidy (1981), Bishop Sidney M. Metzger (1982), Joseph P. Hubbard (1983).

O'Reilly-Conway Medal (1979), by *The Pilot*, Boston archdiocesan newspaper, for distinctive contributions to journalism.

Anthony LaCamera (1979), Elliot Norton (1980), Frank Reynolds (1981), Ruth Mehrtens Galvin (1982), Gerard P. Rooney (1983).

Poverello Medal (1949), by The University of Steubenville (Ohio), "in recognition of great benefactions to humanity, exemplifying in our age the Christ-like spirit of charity which filled the life of St. Francis of Assisi."

Alcoholics Anonymous Fellowship (1949), Edward F. Hutton (1950), the Court of Last Resort, New York, N.Y. (1951), The Lions International (1952), Variety Clubs International (1953), Llewellyn J. Scott (1954), Dr. Jonas E. Salk and Associates (1955), Mother Anna Dengel (1956), Catherine de Hueck Doherty (1957), D. M. Hamill (1958);

Daniel W. Egan, T.O.R. (1959, posthumously), Mrs. Emma C. Zeis (1960), Donald H. McGannon (1961), Jane Wyatt (1962), Birgit Nilsson (1963), Arthur Joseph Rooney (1964), Joe E. Brown (1965), Project Hope (1966), Lena F. Edwards, M.D. (1967), VISTA (1968), Jack Twyman (1969), The Salvation Army (1970), Most Rev. John K. Mussio (1971). Bro. George J. Hungerman, F.M.S.I., M.D. (1972), The Dismas Committee of the St. Vincent de Paul Society (1973) U.S. Sen Mark O. Hatfield (1974), Sr. Mary Agatha, O.S.F., and Rev Kevin R. Keelan, T.O.R. (1975), Mother Teresa of Calcutta (1976), Dorothy Day (1977), Leon Jaworski (1978), Bishop Bernard J. Topel (1979), International Shrine Association (1980-81), Rev. Bruce Ritter, O.F.M. Conv. (1981-82), Rev. Richard Thomas, S.J. (1983).

Regina Medal (1959), by the Catholic Library Association for outstanding contributions to children's literature.

Eleanor Farjeon (1959), Anne Carroll Moore (1960), Padraic Colum (1961), Frederick G. Melcher (1962), Anne Nolan Clark (1963), May Hill Arbuthnot (1964), Ruth Sawyer Durand (1965), Leo Politi (1966), Bertha Mahony Miller (1967), Marguerite de Angeli (1968), Lois Lenski (1969), Ingri and Edgar Parin d'Aulaire (1970), Tasha Tudor (1971), Meindert DeJong (1972), Frances Clarke Sayers (1973), Robert McCloskey (1974), Lynd Ward and May McNeer (1975), Virginia Haviland (1976), Marcia Brown (1977), Scott O'Dell (1978), Morton Schindel (1979), Beverly Cleary (1980), Augusta Baker (1981), Theodore

Seuss Geisel (Dr. Seuss) (1982), Tomie De Paola (1983).

St. Bonaventure University Justice and Peace Medal (1981), by St. Bonaventure University (St. Bonaventure, N.Y.).

Bishop Thomas J. Gumbleton (1981), Eileen Egan (1982), Sister Joan Malone, O.S.F. (1983).

St. Francis de Sales Award (1959), by the Catholic Press Association for distinguished contribution to Catholic journalism.

Dale Francis (1959), Frank A. Hall (1960), John C. Murray, S.J. (1961), Albert J. Nevins, M.M. (1962), Floyd Anderson (1963), Rev. Patrick O'Connor (1964), John Cogley (1965), Joseph Breig (1966), John Reedy, C.S.C. (1967), Bishop James P. Shannon (1968), no award (1969), Msgr. Robert G. Peters (1970), Francis A. Fink (1971), Jeremy Harrington, O.F.M. (1972), Robert E. Burns (1973), Gerard E. Sherry (1974), John B. Sheerin, C.S.P. (1975), Lillian R. Block (1976), A.E.P. Wall (1977), Donald Thorman, posthumously (1978), Walter J. Burghardt, S.J. (1979), Thurston Davis, S.J. (1980), John F. Fink (1981), Allen C. Bradley, posthumously (1982), Ethel M. Gintoft (1983).

Signum Fidei Medal (1942), by the Alumni Association of La Salle College (Phila.) for noteworthy contributions to the advancement of humanitarian principles in keeping with Christian tradition.

Brother E. Anselm, F.S.C. (1942), Karl H. Rogers (1943), Very Rev. Edward V. Stanford, O.S.A. (1944), Mrs. Edward V. Morrell (1945), Cardinal Dennis Dougherty (1946), Max Jordan (1947), John J. Sullivan (1948), Dr. Louis H. Clerf (1949), Most Rev. Gerald P. O'Hara (1950), Most Rev. Fulton J. Sheen (1951);

John H. Harris (1952), James Keller, M.M. (1953), John M. Haffert (1954), Dr. Francis J. Braceland (1955), Matthew H. McCloskey (1956), Henry Viscardi, Jr. (1957), no award (1958), Dr. Joseph J. Toland, Jr. (1959), Luke E. Hart (1960), Joseph E. McCafferty (1961);

Martin H. Work (1962), R. Sargent Shriver (1963), Mother M. Benedict, M.D. (1964), Sen. Eugene McCarthy (1965), William B. Ball (1966), Frank Folsom (1967), Rev. Leon H. Sullivan (1968), Rev. William J. Finley (1969);

Dr. James W. Turpin (1970), Lisa A. Richette, Esq. (1971), Rev. Melvin Floyd (1972), Elwood E. Kieser, C.S.P. (1973), Msgr. Philip J. Dowling (1974), James C. Giuffre, M.D. (1975), Most Rev. Bernard J. Topel (1976), Mildred Jefferson, M.D. (1977), Judge Genevieve Blatt (1978), Rita Ungaro Schiavone (1979), Rev. Aloysius Schwartz (1980), Sister Mary Luke, O.P. (1981), William and Helene Sample (1982), Rev. Victor J. Eschbach (1983).

U.S. Catholic Award (1978), by editors of *U.S. Catholic* magazine for furthering the cause of women in the Church.

Sr. Agnes Cunningham, S.S.C.M. (1978), Sr. Marjorie Tuite, O.P. (1979), Sr. M. Theresa Kane, R.S.M. (1980), Most Revs. Raymond G. Hunthausen, Rembert G. Weakland, Charles A. Buswell, Michael F. McAuliffe, William E. McManus (1981), Mrs. Patricia C. Crowley (1982), Dr. Rosemary Radford Ruether (1983).